COMMENTARY ON HEBREWS

COMMENTARY ON
HEBREWS

Exegetical and Expository

Volume One

Chapters 1 – 7

William Gouge

Solid Ground Christian Books
Birmingham, Alabama, USA

Solid Ground Christian Books
2090 Columbiana Rd, Suite 2000
Birmingham, AL 35216
205-443-0311
sgcb@charter.net
http://solid-ground-books.com

A Commentary on the Epistle to the Hebrews
Exegetical and Expository – Volume One

William Gouge (1575-1653)

Taken from the 1980 edition by Kregel Publications, Grand Rapids, MI, which was based on the 1866 Nichols Edition

Solid Ground Classic Puritan Reprints

First printing of new edition April 2006

Cover work by Borgo Design, Tuscaloosa, AL
Contact them at nelbrown@comcast.net

Cover image is the Menorah, with Torah in background

ISBN: 1-59925-065-9 (hardcover)
ISBN: 1-59925-068-3 (paperback)

CONTENTS
OF VOLUME ONE

Foreword by *Dr. Peter Masters* vii
Biographical Sketch by *Dr. Joel Beeke* ix
Introductory Matters on the Epistle to the Hebrews 3
Chapter One 8
Chapter Two 89
Chapter Three 193
Chapter Four 289
Chapter Five 344
Chapter Six 383
Chapter Seven 466

FOREWORD

The Epistle to the Hebrews is in every possible sense a preacher's epistle: combining, in its chapters, the most sublime statements of the Saviour's Diety and power with the most moving exhortations to faith and service. Within its great body of doctrinal instruction are included all of the doctrines of grace and the fullest explanation of the "two covenants" to be found in any epistle.

It is a small wonder that such Christian giants as John Owen found material enough to fill volumes with solid exposition. But there can be no doubt whatsoever that the crowning commentary on this Epistle, as far as preachers are concerned, is the great classic, *Gouge on the Epistle to the Hebrews*, from the pen of Dr. William Gouge, here re-issued and entitled *Commentary on Hebrews*.

My first duty in the penning of this Foreword must be to extend, on behalf of all who will have this volume in their possession, the warmest thanks to the publishers for arranging its reprinting. The considerable size of this commentary, coupled with the need to introduce the name of Dr. Gouge to present-day preachers, has placed this work beyond courage of classical reprint houses until now.

That there should be any need to re-establish the name and reputation of Dr. Gouge among preachers is a sad reflection on our times. William Gouge attracted great crowds to hear his Gospel preaching and his heart-searching expository lectures delivered at Blackfriars, London during the early 17th century. His biographer tells us that his Wednesday evening lectures on Hebrews grew so famous that "when the godly Christians of those times came out of the country into London, they thought their business was unfinished until they had been at Blackfriar's lecture."

Dr. Gouge was renowned in those Puritan days for spirituality and scholarship, leaving a brilliant career at Cambridge University to preach the Word. Such was his learning that his appointment to the Westminster *Assembly of Divines* in 1643 was inevitable, and he was often called upon to deputize for the moderator.

A family man (with seven sons and six daughters), he was loved for his great humility and friendliness as well as the simple directness of his communicating ability, which makes his prose seem modern and vigorous even to this day.

This great *Commentary on Hebrews* is the substance of thirty years of weeknight lectures given at Blackfriar's; but, one must immediately emphasize that it is *not* the text of those lectures. The great expositor's method was to cull the essence of his lectures and compress the material into a form easily scanned and studied. His style is that of terse, clear notes profusely supplemented with numbered columns of homiletical and practical points. It bears no resemblance to those very long (however, excellent) spoken expositions so often issued under the names of Puritan divines.

The exegetical value of Dr. Gouge's commentary is enormous: every vital word in Hebrews being explained in a manner far superior to that which suffices for modern word studies.

The expository value of the commentary is equally rich: every doctrine, theme and argument which is found in the Epistle being given its own heading and section.

And finally, the suggestive value of the commentary is quite unsurpassed, and the user will find no other work of Hebrews in the same category. "We greatly prize Gouge" said C.H. Spurgeon, "upon any topic which he touches, he gives outlines which may supply sermons for months."

The re-issue of this unique work on this wonderful epistle can only stimulate and enrich the preaching of many pastors: opening doors of understanding and sounding the great rallying cry to faith and action, which is the climax of the Epistle to the Hebrews.

The original three large volume edition, now available in one binding, had been very difficult to secure for many years. So much so that most commentators, writing on this Epistle to the Hebrews in this century, do not list Gouge in their bibliographies (even Milligan could not lay hands on a set).

May the Lord greatly bless this magnificent help to many preachers of the Word in these needy times.

Dr. Peter Masters
"Spurgeon's" Metropolitan Tabernacle, London

BIOGRAPHICAL SKETCH

William Gouge (1575-1653) was born in Bow, near Stratford, in Middlesex County. He received a classical education at St. Paul's School in London and at Felstead in Essex. He was converted under the ministry of his uncle, Ezekiel Culverwell, a well-known Puritan. He then went to Eton College, where he gave himself to study, prayer, and searching God's Word. In his years at King's College, Cambridge, Gouge became known as an excellent logician and defender of Ramism. He was called an "arch-Puritan" by some students because of his strict godliness. He apparently never missed one of the chapel prayer services conducted every morning at 5:30. He read fifteen Bible chapters daily—five in the morning before chapel, five after dinner, and five before going to bed.

Gouge graduated from King's College with a bachelor's degree in 1598 and a master's degree in 1602. He became a fellow and a leading Hebrew scholar, and was appointed as a lecturer in logic and philosophy. In 1603, his father persuaded him to travel from Cambridge to London to meet Elizabeth Caulton, the God-fearing daughter of Henry Caulton, a former London merchant. The couple were soon married, and had thirteen children, eight of whom reached maturity. Gouge's biographer details the care Gouge took in conducting family worship.

In 1608, Gouge became a lecturer at the parish church of St. Anne Blackfriars, London, where he served for forty-five years until his death. He was appointed rector upon the death of Stephen Egerton in 1621. He preached regularly twice on the Lord's Day and once every Wednesday. After his sermons on Sunday morning, he invited poor people from the neighborhood to his house for dinner, after which they would discuss his sermon. His lectures on Wednesdays drew such large crowds that, according to his biographer, "When the godly Christians of those days came into London, they considered their business unfinished, unless they attended one of the Blackfriars lectures." Hundreds of people were converted and nurtured in the faith through his ministry. Brett Usher concludes, "Gouge's pulpit became the most celebrated in London" (*Oxford DNB*, 23:37).

Gouge was a hard worker, cheerful philanthropist, meek friend, great peacemaker, and an earnest wrestler with God. He wrote eleven treatises, some of which were extensive. He supported poor students at the university and contributed generously to the poor. He had such a meek disposition that his biographer wrote, "No one, his wife, nor children, nor servant with whom he lived and worked all those years ever observed an angry countenance, nor heard an angry word proceed from him toward any of them."

Gouge was "a sweet comforter of dejected souls, and distressed consciences," according to his biographer. He became a spiritual mentor to many ministers in London, helping many keep peace in their congregations. His confessions of sin were accompanied with "much brokenness of heart, self-abhorrency, and justifying of God." In prayer, he was "pertinent, judicious, spiritual, seasonable, accompanied with faith and fervor, like a true Son of Jacob wrestling with tears and supplications."

A contemporary wrote of Gouge: "He studied much to magnify Christ, and to debase himself." Gouge said of himself, "When I look upon myself, I see nothing but emptiness and weakness; but when I look upon Christ, I see nothing but fullness and sufficiency."

Throughout his pastoral years, Gouge continued his studies. He earned a Bachelor of Divinity degree at Cambridge in 1611, and eventually, a doctorate in divinity in 1628. His wife Elizabeth did not live to witness this occasion, however, as she died in 1625 while giving birth to their thirteenth child. Gouge never remarried.

For the most part, Gouge worked without interference from the government. However, he was harassed by authorities because of his Puritan sympathies in opposing new ceremonies ordered by Bishop Laud and for opposing Arminianism. Once he spent two months in prison for republishing Finch's *The Calling of the Jews*.

Gouge was a prolific writer. We are so grateful to Solid Ground Christian Books for reprinting his *magnum opus, A Commentary on the Epistle to the Hebrews*. This massive book, originally published in three volumes, contains the notes of more than a thousand sermons given over a thirty year period at Blackfriars. The first volume was published in 1655; Gouge was still working on the last half of the last chapter of Hebrews when he died. His son, Thomas, completed it, using his father's notes. It is a golden exposition of the fullness of Christ, second only to Owen on Hebrews.

Gouge's work abounds in helpful application. For example, in commenting on Hebrews 11:17, which describes Abraham offering up Isaac, Gouge, who buried several of his own children (including a murdered daughter), has a section on "yielding the dearest to God." He writes, "The grounds of our yielding to our dearest to God are such as these: 1. The supreme sovereignty of God, whereby he hath power to command us and all ours; and what he may command we must yield. 2. The right that God hath to all we have. 3. The might and power that God hath to take away all. Willingly to yield what he will have, is to make a virtue of necessity. 4. The due, which, in way of gratitude, we owe unto God. They that hold anything too dear for God are not worthy of God. 5. The bounty of God, who can and will beyond comparison recompense whatsoever is given to him. None shall lose by giving to God" (p. 806).

Buy and read Gouge on Hebrews. Use it as your daily Bible study. Its rich and varied practical and experiential applications sprinkled across every page will greatly enhance your spiritual life.

Gouge also wrote a classic on family living titled, *Of Domesticall Duties* (1622), last printed by Walter Johnson in facsimile in 1976. This 700-page penetrating analysis of the godly household for which Gouge became best known in his own day, is divided into eight sections dealing with the duties of family life. In the first part, Gouge explains the foundation of family duties, based on Ephesians 5:21–6:9. The second part deals with the husband-wife relationship. The third focuses on the duties of wives, and the fourth with the duties of husbands. The fifth examines the duties of children, and the sixth, the duties of parents. The final parts examine the relationships and duties of servants and their masters.

While some of Gouge's material is outdated, his emphasis and advice are timeless on the whole. Usher claims that Gouge is finally being "recognized as one of the subtlest of early modern writers to articulate the concept of 'companionable' marriage—his own was regarded as exemplary—and of considerate, rather than merely prescriptive, parenthood. His psychological insights into the nature of childhood and adolescence can be breathtaking in their modernity. He even touches on the question of child-abuse, a subject effectively taboo until the 1970s" (*Oxford DNB*, 23:38).

Gouge is a skilled expositor who draws practical applications from the Epistles in instructing families how to walk in a manner worthy of their Lord. As a father of seven sons and six daughters, Gouge knew whereof he spoke.

The Sabbath's Sanctification, recently reprinted by Presbyterian Armoury, is an 80-page treatise that Gouge originally wrote for his family's use. After briefly touching on the grounds for the morality of the Sabbath, he provides judicious directions for sanctifying it,

BIOGRAPHICAL SKETCH

carefully outlining the distinction between works of piety, mercy, and necessity. This is followed by some proofs that the Lord's Day is the Christian's Sabbath, with pertinent remarks on when the Sabbath begins. The subsequent section on aberrations of the Sabbath exposes the ungodly opinions and practices of those who desire to sanctify the Sabbath in name only. Gouge concludes his work with a number of motives which encourage Christians to keep this day holy to the Lord.

In addition to his two massive works and this small treatise on the Sabbath that have been reprinted, Gouge published a diversity of titles ranging from *The Whole Armour of God* (1616)—a major work on the Christian armor of Ephesians 6:10-20, overshadowed only by William Gurnall's even more massive masterpiece, to *A Short Catechism*, which was printed six times by 1636. Other titles by Gouge include an exposition of John's gospel (1630), *God's Three Arrows* (1631), and *The Saint's Sacrifice* (1632).

In 1643, Gouge was nominated to the Westminster Assembly. He took turns with Cornelius Burgess leading the sessions when the moderator or prolocutor, William Twisse, was not present. In 1644, Gouge was appointed to the committee that examined ministers; in 1645, he was assigned to the committee that drafted the Confession of Faith; and in 1647, he was elected as assessor after the death of Herbert Palmer. In 1648, he was on the committee that supported the Presbyterian system *de jure divino*, or divine right, which held that Presbyterian church government is commanded by God ("by divine law") in Scripture. Later that year, Gouge was asked to contribute notes on 1 Kings through Esther for what would become the second edition of the Westminster Assembly's *Annotations on the Bible*.

Gouge suffered from asthma and kidney stones in his later years. His faith held firm, however, through acute suffering until death. He would say, "[I am] a great sinner, but I comfort myself in a great Savior." Often he repeated Job's words: "Shall we receive good from the hand of God, and shall we not receive evil?" When a friend tried to comfort him by pointing to the grace he had received or the works he had done, his response was, "I dare not think of any such things for comfort. Jesus Christ, and what He hath done and endured, is the only ground of my sure comfort." As he approached death, he said, "Death, next to Jesus Christ, you are my best friend. When I die, I am sure to be with Jesus Christ. Jesus Christ is my rejoicing."

Gouge died December 12, 1653, aged seventy-eight. His funeral sermon was preached by William Jenkyn, his friend, pastoral assistant, and successor. According to William Haller, Gouge ranked with Sibbes and Preston among the influential Puritan ministers of London of the previous generation.

Dr. Joel R. Beeke
Puritan Reformed Theological Seminary
Grand Rapids, Michigan

COMMENTARY ON
HEBREWS

VOLUME ONE

CHAPTERS 1 – 7

COMMENTARY ON HEBREWS

SEC. 1. *Of the authority of this epistle.*

That we may with the better warrant collect articles of faith and rules for life out of this epistle, it is requisite that we be well informed in the divine authority thereof, and also well weigh the excellency of it.

These evidences following make clear the divine authority of this epistle.

1. The matter of it, which is beyond the reach of human invention. So profound mysteries are revealed therein, as could not be known but by divine revelation.

2. The manner of unfolding those mysteries, which is with such majesty and gravity as argueth a divine spirit.

3. The congruity of it with other canonical scriptures, so as, if all Scripture be given by inspiration of God, Πᾶσα γραφὴ θεόπνευστος, 2 Tim. iii. 16, then this also.

4. The direct refutation of pernicious heresies, which, since the writing of this epistle, have been forged, so as it must needs be inspired by a foreknowing Spirit.

5. The whole tenor of this epistle, and manner of expressing the legal ordinances therein, shew that this epistle was written while the temple stood, and Levitical rites were in use, which was in the apostles' time; so as, if it had not been canonical, it would questionless have been discovered by them.

6. The penman of it, whom we shall shew hereafter to be Paul the apostle.

7. The express approbation which St Peter gives of it, for he makes mention of an epistle which St Paul wrote to them, to whom he himself wrote his epistles, ἔγραψεν ὑμῖν, 2 Peter iii. 15, 16, who were Hebrews, 1 Peter i. 1; 2 Peter iii. 1.

These proofs of the divine authority of this epistle shew how justly it is accounted canonical, as it hath been in all ages of the church; for where catalogues of canonical scriptures have been made,[1] this epistle hath been put into the number, and they have been accounted heretics that have denied it to be canonical.[2]

Sec. 2. *Of the excellency of this epistle.*

Admirable is the excellency of every part of sacred Scripture, which savoureth of more than an human spirit. And this epistle hath sundry excellencies, which in a peculiar manner do commend it unto us; as,

1. The mysteries couched therein. The greatest and profoundest mysteries of our Christian religion are therein propounded: concerning God the Father, Son, and Holy Ghost; concerning the natures, person, and offices of Christ; concerning the sufficiency of Christ's sacrifice, and efficacy of his intercession; concerning the excellency of the new covenant; concerning the life of faith; and concerning the privilege of these latter times, &c.

2. The variety of histories therein recollected. We have in it a rehearsal of most of the memorable histories from the beginning of the world to the last age thereof; and not only of such as are registered in holy writ, but also of such as fell out since the prophets ceased to record any.

3. Explication of legal types, and application of them to their distinct truths. No other book is herein comparable to this epistle.

4. Confutation of heresies.[3] It may be termed the maul of popery, which is a mass of heresies. Popish heresies are most against the offices of Christ, espe-

---

[1] Athanas. in Synops. S. Scrip.; Aug. de Doctr. Christ., l. ii. c. viii.; Damasc. de fide, l. iv. c. xviii.

[2] Epiph. l. i. hær. xlii.; Philast. Catal. hæres. c. xlviii.

[3] Vide Whitak. Ἐρανιστὴν, in quo fragmenta veterum hæresium, indicantur, ad constituendum ecclesiæ pontificiæ ἀποστασίαν, collata.

cially against his priesthood. Those heresies are so fully met withal in this epistle, as if it had been written since popery began. God foreseeing what poisonous heresies would be broached, prepared this antidote against them.

5. The pithy persuasions unto all holiness and new obedience; the powerful encouragements to constancy and perseverance; the dreadful denunciations against apostasy and impenitency; the sweet consolations to such as for Christ's sake endure the cross, which are here and there throughout in this epistle mixed.

Thus much in general to commend this epistle unto us.

The title thereof is next to be considered.

Sec. 3. *Of the title.*

The Epistle of Paul the apostle to the Hebrews.

It is not probable that this title was set down by the first penman of this epistle; for he might as well have premised his usual inscription with his name and calling (which apostles do in all other their epistles) as have prefixed the foresaid title.

Titles before the apostles' epistles, and subscriptions after them, are not accounted canonical, as the epistles themselves, but supposed to be added by some that afterwards did transcribe the epistles. For there are gross mistakings and palpable errors in many of them.[1] And though some of them may hit the mark, and declare the truth, yet doth it not thereupon follow that they are canonical. Although everything that is canonical be most true, yet every truth is not canonical; for that only is accounted canonical which was given by inspiration of God, $\theta\epsilon\delta\pi\nu\epsilon\nu\sigma\tau\sigma\varsigma$.

Titles, therefore, and superscriptions added to the epistles of apostles, are no sufficient grounds of doctrine, nor may articles of faith or rules for life be founded on them; yet they give some light to the matter, and may be handled by way of preface.

As for the title of this epistle, no just exception can be taken against it. Every particle therein is undoubtedly most true.

It plainly demonstrates both the parties, and the means of the author's declaring his mind.

The parties are, 1, the penman or author; 2, the people to whom it was in special directed.

The author is described, 1, by his name, Paul; 2, by his calling, the apostle.

The people are described by their parentage, Hebrews.

The means is by way of writing a letter, the epistle.

Sec. 4. *Of the author of this epistle.*

The proofs before produced for the divine authority of this epistle give evidence that an apostle, or some other extraordinary minister, immediately inspired and infallibly insisted[1] by the divine Spirit, was the author of it.

Some have supposed it to be written by Luke the evangelist, or by Clemens;[2] some by Apollos, whose learning and eloquence, joined with great piety, is much commended,[3] who also, in special, is said to have mightily convinced the Jews, Acts xviii. 24, 25, 28.

But the evidences following do more than probably evince that Paul the apostle was the author of this epistle.

1. The ancient Greek churches accounted it to be St Paul's, and thereupon prefixed this title before it, The Epistle of Paul, &c.[4] And in the catalogue of St Paul's epistles this is reckoned up; whereupon there are said to be fourteen epistles of St Paul.

2. Both matter and manner of penning this epistle is agreeable to St Paul's other epistles.[5]

3. That which St Paul styleth his 'token in every epistle,' 2 Thes. iii. 17, is also in the close of this epistle thus set down: 'Grace be with you all, Amen.' Indeed, in most of his epistles he styles it 'the grace of Jesus Christ;' yet in both his epistles to Timothy and to Titus, it is as here.

4. The mention which is made of Timothy, who was St Paul's associate, of whom he oft makes mention in his other epistles, and gives the same epithet to him that is here, our brother Timothy. Compare with Heb. xiii. 23; 2 Cor. i. 1; Philem. 1.

To shew that that very Paul is here meant who was immediately called by Jesus Christ, and infallibly assisted by his Spirit, he is described by his extraordinary function, the apostle. Hereof see chap. iii. 1. Thus much of the author.

Objections made against this penman of this epistle are answered in their due places. See Chap. II. Sec. 27.

Sec. 5. *Of the Hebrews.*

The people to whom in special the apostle directed this epistle are styled Hebrews; whereby that nation which descended from Abraham is meant.

This title, *Hebrews*, is oft used in the Old and New Testament. It was first given to Abraham himself, Gen. xiv. 13; then to Joseph, when he was a servant in Egypt, Gen. xxxix. 14, 17; afterwards to all that stock, Gen. xl. 15; Exod. ii. 6; 1 Sam. iv. 6, 9; Acts vi. 1; Philip. iii. 5.

Abraham, the father of this people, was styled an Hebrew in two especial respects.[6]

---

[1] See Cudworth's Supplement to Perkins's Comment on the Epistle to Gal. in the conclusion.

[1] Qu. 'assisted'?—ED.
[2] Origines, ut refert Euseb. Hist. Eccl. l. vi. c. xxv.
[3] Beza in Annot. major.
[4] Παύλου τοῦ Ἀποστόλου, &c. Ita scriptum invenimus in omnibus nostris codicibus excepto uno.—*Beza loc citat.; Euseb. Hist. Eccl.* l. iii. c. iii. Plurima patrum testimonia, citantur a Whitakero.—*Controv.* i. *de S. Script.* q. i. c. xvi.
[5] Vide Piscat. Prolegom de authore hujus Epist.
[6] Vide August. de Civ. Dei. l. xvi. c. iii.; et Flor. Josep. Antiq. Jud. l. i. c. xiv.

1. Because he came from Heber, who was *pronepos*, the third from Shem, Gen. xi. 10, 14, 25. Shem, after the world was divided to the sons of Noah, was the first father of the blessed seed, Gen. ix. 26. After that the whole world began again to fall from God, and rebelliously conspired to build a tower that might keep them safe from another flood, so as God, to hinder that work, confounded their languages; but Heber separated himself from that impious society, and thereupon the name *Heber* was given him, which importeth a *passing over*, or *departing from*; which name was given by a prophetical prediction before the thing was done, as Noah's name was, Gen. v. 29, or for a memorial of his piety after he had given that proof thereof, as Israel's name was, Gen. xxxii. 28.

Heber, separating himself from those rebels, is further manifested by his retaining the primary, pure language, when among all the rebels it was confounded, Gen. xi. 9; for that primary language is called the Hebrew tongue, which, in the confusion of tongues, Heber retained and propagated to his posterity.[1]

Thus Heber became another father, and a preserver of the church. Hence is it that the first father, Shem, is said to be ' the father of all the children of Heber,' Gen. x. 21; that is, of the church which descended from Heber, which were the Hebrews.

As Heber withdrew himself from the wicked world in his time, so did Abraham in his time, being called of God, Gen. xii. 1, and so became another father of the church; whereupon, as he was called an Hebrew from Heber, so all his posterity were called Hebrews from him.

2. The other respect why Abraham was called an Hebrew was, because he *passed over* from his own country to Canaan; in which journey he passed over much land and sundry rivers, as Tigris, Euphrates, and Jordan: for the verb *Habar*, עָבַר, *transit*, signifieth to pass over; the noun *Heber*, עֵבֶר, *transitus*; and the word *Hebrew*, עִבְרִי, *transitor*, one that passeth over.

The ancient Greek interpreters of the Old Testament, commonly called the Septuagint, or Seventy, do thus interpret this title Hebrew, attributed to Abraham;[2] so do also sundry of the ancient fathers.[3]

By this name Hebrews, which was common to all the Jews,[4] the posterity of Heber and of Abraham were put in mind of their fathers separating themselves from profane persons and idolaters, and also were taught therein to imitate their fathers.

Sec. 6. *Of apostolical epistles.*

The means whereby the apostle declared his mind to these Hebrews was an epistle.

[1] לְשׁוֹן עֵבֶר, lingua Heber.; לָשׁוֹן עִבְרִית, Hebræa lingua, quam in confusione linguarum retinuit et propagavit Heber.
[2] ἀπήγγειλε τῷ Ἀβραμ τῷ περάτῃ, Gen. xiv. 13.
[3] Orig. in Mat. xiv.; Chrys. in Gen. xiv. Hom. 35.
[4] Judæos initio vocarunt Hebræos.—*Joseph. Antiq. Jud.* lib. i. cap. xiv.

An epistle is a writing sent to absent friends, wherein is declared that which concerns them to know.

The derivation of the Greek word shews it to be somewhat sent.[1] The common use of the word shews it to be a writing or a letter sent, and sent to such as are absent; because we cannot by word of mouth express our mind to them.

This is the benefit of an epistle, that thereby we may make known our minds one to another in absence as if we were present.[2] All sorts of things use to be made known to absent friends by epistles. They are ordinarily written in testimony of friends' mutual remembrance one of another, and of that love and good respect which they continue to bear one to another. Thus much did St Paul testify in his epistle to Timothy, chap. i. 3. Epistles are oft sent to commend one to another (hereunto the apostle alludeth, 2 Cor. iii. 1, in this phrase, ' Need we epistles of commendation?'), and to intercede for others, as Paul for Onesimus in his epistle to Philemon.

Epistles use to be more vulgar and loose than orations or pleadings at a bar of justice;[3] and among us, they use to be less accurate than sermons. Yet the apostles' epistles were no whit inferior to their sermons; but in the matter contained in them, and in the manner of penning them, they were as full, ponderous, and accurate, as any other parts of sacred Scripture. All the mysteries of godliness are in them distinctly, plainly, and fully laid down. It is observed,[4] that the very inscriptions which the apostles premise before their epistles do with such an admirable and inimitable succinctness comprise the sum of the whole evangelical mystery, as they being kept safe, the church hath enough to oppose against all heretics; what do then the whole bodies of those divine epistles?

The mysteries of the gospel are revealed by epistles, because that is the most familiar and friendly manner of making known a matter. Epistles use to be written to choice friends, as testimonies of singular affection to them.

Sec. 7. *Of St Paul's affection to the Hebrews.*

By the way, we may here take notice of St Paul's great and entire respect which he bare to his countrymen the Hebrews, in that he opens unto them the mysteries of salvation in the most friendly manner that could be, by writing an epistle unto them in particular; and sweetly persuading them to abide constant in the faith, that they might be the rather induced thereto. And this he doth not only by general instructions and exhortations in common to all of all sorts, but also by a familiar and friendly epistle in special directed to them.

[1] Ἐπιστολή of ἐπιστέλλω, *mitto ad.*
[2] Bono literarum eadem fere absentes, quæ si coram essemus consequemur.—*Cic. Epist. Famil.* lib. xv. epist. 14.
[3] Quid simile habet epistola aut judicio aut concioni?— *Cic. Epist. Famil.* lib. vii. epist. 21.
[4] Vide *Annot. major. in* Tit. i. 1.

St Paul planted not any church of the Hebrews alone, as he did of the Corinthians, Galatians, Ephesians, and other Grecians, for he was after an especial manner the apostle of the Gentiles, Rom. xi. 13, yet he took all occasions to gain and establish the Jews; thereupon he saith, 1 Cor. vi. 20, 'Unto the Jews I became as a Jew, that I might gain the Jews.' Hereby he giveth proof of that which he professeth: Rom. x. 1, 'My heart's desire and prayer to God for Israel is, that they might be saved;' and Rom. ix. 4, 'I could wish that myself were accursed from Christ for my brethren, my kinsmen after the flesh, who were Israelites.'

Oh that this mind were in all Christians towards their brethren, their kindred, their countrymen, and others to whom by any special bonds of relation they are knit! This is the best use that can be made of such bonds, and the most principal end that we ought therein to aim at, namely, a mutual, spiritual edification. Happy are those countries that have many such countrymen, who, though they have charges over other countries, yet cannot be unmindful of their own country; but being absent from them, will notwithstanding write to them of the common salvation; and that though the more abundantly they love them, the less they are loved of them; yea, though they persecuted them with all eagerness wheresoever they met them. Thus Paul manifested a true Christian spirit, by overcoming evil with goodness. Behold a pattern worthy of all imitation.

Sec. 8. *Of the general intendment of particular epistles.*

Quest. Was this epistle written for the Hebrews only?

Ans. Though it were in special manner directed to them, yet was it not written only for their use, but for the use also of the whole Christian church; and therefore it hath ever been read in all churches.[1] The apostle giveth a charge to particular churches, to whom in special he directed his epistles, to cause them to be read in other churches, Col. iv. 16; for the matter of apostolical epistles consisted of general doctrines and directions, fit for all Christians to know, believe, and obey. That which Christ saith of the word which he preached to his disciples in particular, Mark xiii. 37, 'What I say unto you, I say unto all,' may be applied to the epistles of the apostles; for in them they intended the good of all Christians. The particular inscription of their epistles to particular churches or persons, was as the ordinary dedication of books to particular persons, which are intended to the good of all.

St Luke dedicated his histories of the Gospel of Christ and the Acts of the Apostles to one man, and by name to Theophilus, Luke i. 3, Acts i. 1; yet he intended them to the good of all. St Paul, in that epistle which he directed only to Titus by name, concludes with this general benediction, 'Grace be with you all,' Titus iii. 15. The Epistle to Philemon was written upon a special occasion, yet so carried as sundry general instructions, meet for all Christians to know, are couched therein. All Christians therefore are to read and hear the epistles of the apostles, as heedfully as they were bound to do, unto whom in special they were directed.

As for this epistle to the Hebrews, it may seem, in sundry passages thereof, to be written in a prophetical spirit, to meet with sundry heresies that were in future times to be broached, rather than such as at that time were discovered. Such as these: a true, real, propitiatory sacrifice to be daily offered up, yea, such a sacrifice to be unbloody; sons of men to be sacrificing priests properly so called; many intercessors and mediators to be under the gospel; and sundry other which have been published by papists, long since this epistle was written. So as this epistle, in sundry respects, may be as useful to us who live in the time of popery, and are much infested with popish heresies, as to the Hebrews, if not more. Hitherto of the title.

Sec. 9. *Of the occasion of this epistle.*

The occasion of this epistle was twofold: 1, the immortal and insatiable malice of the unbelieving Jews against all that professed the name of Christ; 2, their inbred superstition about the Mosaical rites.

So implacable was their hatred of all that maintained the Christian faith, as in that cause they spared not their own countrymen, 1 Thes. ii. 14. St Paul, while he was of the Jewish religion, was highly esteemed of priests, rulers, and other Jews; but when he became a Christian, none was more fiercely and violently persecuted than he. So dealt they with all that were of that faith; and where they had not sufficient power of themselves, they stirred up the unbelieving Gentiles against all that professed the Christian faith, especially if they were Jews, Acts xiv. 2, 19. Hence it came to pass that these Hebrews, to whom in particular this epistle was directed, suffered much for their profession's sake, chap. x. 32, &c. Wherefore to encourage them unto all perseverance in the faith, and to keep them from apostasy and falling away from the truth received, the apostle wrote this epistle, which is filled with many forcible encouragements, and with terrible denunciations of sore vengeance against apostasy. St Paul's words were of old said to be thunders;[1] which is most true in this epistle, where he writes against apostasy, chap. vi. 4, 6, 8 and chap. x. 26–28, &c., and chap. xii. 25, 29. This was one occasion of this epistle, to uphold them in the Christian faith.

---

[1] Memento apostolicas epistolas non eis tantum scriptas, qui tempore illo quo scribebantur audiebant, sed etiam nobis; non enim ob aliud in ecclesia recitantur.—*Aug. contr. Crescon. gram* lib. i. cap 9.

[1] Paulum quotiescunque lego, videor mihi non verba audire, sed tonitrua.—*Hieron. Apol. advers. Jovinian.*

2. The Jews that lived after the truth of the Mosaical types was exhibited, were notwithstanding so superstitiously and pertinaciously addicted to those legal rites, as they would not endure to hear of the abrogation of them; but in maintenance of them, rejected the gospel. Yea, of those that believed in Christ, many thousands were too zealous of the law, Acts xv. 5 and xxi. 20. Wherefore, to root out that conceit, the apostle writes this epistle; whereby he proves, that by bringing in the new testament of the gospel, the old covenant of the law was abrogated; and that the law could not make perfect, chap. viii., ix., and x. And this was the other occasion of this epistle.

Sec. 10. *Of the scope and method of this epistle.*

That main point which is aimed at throughout the whole sacred Scripture, especially in the New Testament, is the principal scope of this epistle, and the main mark whereat the apostle aimeth therein, namely this, that Jesus Christ is the all-sufficient and only Saviour of man.

This was the sum of the first promise made to man after his fall, Gen. iii. 15.

This was the truth of all sorts of types, whether they were choice persons, sacrifices, sacraments, sacred places, sacred instruments, sacred actions, or any other sacred things.

This was the substance of the prophecies that were given by divine inspiration.

This was intended by the great deliverances which from time to time God gave to his church and people.

This was the end of writing the history of Christ by the evangelists.

This was the sum of the sermons of the apostles, recorded in the Acts, and the ground of all their sufferings.

This is also the sum of their several epistles.

That this may the more distinctly, clearly, and fully be demonstrated, the apostle doth to the life set out Christ's two natures, divine and human, in one person; his three offices, princely, prophetical, and priestly; together with the excellency and sufficiency of them. To this do tend all the divine instructions, refutations, exhortations, consolations, denunciations.

The several points of this epistle may all be comprised under two heads: 1, grounds of faith; 2, rules for life.

The grounds of faith are laid down from the beginning of the epistle to the 22d verse of the 10th chapter. Yet sometimes he falleth into pertinent digressions, by way of exhortation, consolation, and reprehension; to make them thereby to give the more diligent heed to those grounds of faith.

The rules for life are set out in the latter part of the 10th chapter, beginning at the 22d verse, and in the three last chapters.

The grounds of faith are all about Christ. These are,

1. Summarily propounded in the three first verses.
2. Largely amplified in the other parts of this epistle.

In the first general proposition, these grounds of faith are noted.

1. Christ's divine nature. This is manifested in this title, *Son;* and in this divine work, *making the world,* ver. 2.

2. Christ's human nature. This is intimated under this phrase, *purged our sins,* which presupposeth blood; for blood only purgeth sin, chap. ix. 22, and blood demonstrateth Christ's human nature.

3. The distinction of Christ's person from the person of the Father. This also is cleared by the title *Son* in this particle *by,* ἐν, διὰ, twice used in the second verse, and by those phrases, *brightness of his glory, image of his person.*

4. The union of Christ's two natures in one person. This phrase, *by himself purged our sins,* declares the sufferings of his human nature, and means it of his divine nature in one and the same person.

5. His princely or regal office. This is set out in these three phrases, *heir of all things; upholding all things by the might of his power; sat down on the right hand of the Majesty on high.*

6. His prophetical office. This is apparent in this phrase, *God spake unto us by his Son.*

7. His priestly office. For it appertains to a priest to *purge* away sins, and to be ever *at God's right hand* for us.

These points are further prosecuted in this epistle. For,

1. The divine nature, together with the princely office of Christ, are described in the 1st chapter.
2. His human nature in the 2d chapter.
3. His prophetical function in the 3d and 4th chapters.
4. His priestly office, from the 14th verse of the 4th chapter to the 22d of the 10th chapter.

The priestly office of Christ is simply and generally propounded in the three last verses of the 4th chapter, and also comparatively exemplified by two great types.

The first is of Melchisedec, to whom Christ is resembled, in the 5th, 6th, and former part of the 7th chapter.

The other is of Aaron, before whom Christ is preferred, from the 11th verse of the 7th chapter, to the 22d of the 10th chapter.

There are sundry digressions here and there inserted, which we shall observe as we meet with them.

The rules for life are, 1, persevering in the truth; 2, walking worthy thereof.

Persevering in the truth is much insisted upon, from the 22d verse of the 10th chapter to the 14th of the 12th chapter.

Walking worthy thereof, is set out in sundry divine admonitions, from the 14th verse to the end.

Hebrews 1

Sec. 11. *Of the meaning of the first verse.*

God, who at sundry times, and in divers manners, spake in time past, unto the fathers by the prophets, hath in these last days spoken unto us by his Son, whom he hath appointed heir of all things, by whom he also made the worlds; who, being the brightness of his glory, and the express image of his person, and upholding all things by the word of his power, when he had by himself purged our sins, sat down on the right hand of the Majesty on high.—Heb. i. 1–3.

These words, as they contain the sum of the doctrinal part of this epistle, so they serve for a preface thereto; which is here premised, to stir up all that should read it to a more diligent heeding thereof; for therein is set down the excellency of the New Testament above the Old.

True it is, that there is the same authority, even a divine authority, of both; and that they are both a manifestation of God's will. Therefore God is said to speak by the ministers of both. God being the author of the one and the other, they are both of the like authority; and God speaking in both, both declare the will of God. God spake in times past, and God spake in these last days: the same God by the prophets and by his Son.

The relation of this title *God*, ὁ Θεὸς, to the Son, sheweth, that the first person in sacred Trinity, the Father, is in particular meant; yet the other persons are not excluded. For the Son, Exod. iii. 2, 6, and the Holy Ghost also, Acts xxviii. 26, spake to the fathers. The same work may be done by the blessed Trinity, the order and manner of working being rightly applied to each person. For as the Son is from the Father, and the Holy Ghost from the Father and the Son; so the Father worketh by the Son, and the Son from the Father. Thus Jehovah the Son is said to rain fire from Jehovah the Father, Gen. xix. 24. Some of the ancient fathers, assembled in a council, were so confident of the truth of the application of that title *Jehovah*, twice used, once to the Father, and again to the Son, as they denounced anathema against such as should expound it otherwise.[1]

Thus though the Son spake to the fathers, yet may the Father, as here, be said to speak to the fathers by the Son; and 'by him to make the worlds,' as ver. 2.

How God of old manifested his will by parts, is thus further expressed, 'at sundry times.' This phrase is the exposition of one Greek word, but a compound word. According to the notation of it, it signifieth, by many parts or parcels, πολυμερῶς, *multifariam, multis vicibus*, which necessarily implieth a distinction of times; some at one time, some at another. Therefore it is not unfitly translated *at many times*.

God made known to Adam a Saviour of the seed of the woman, to overcome the devil, Gen. iii. 16. He confirmed the same by sacrifices, Gen. iv. 4. To Noah God by the ark declared, that few should be saved in comparison of the multitude that should perish; and that they who were to be saved, should be saved in the ark of Christ's church, 1 Peter iii. 20, 21. To Abraham God revealed his purpose of extending mercy to all nations, Gen. xxii. 18. To Jacob it was made known that the Messiah should come of the tribe of Judah, Gen. xlix. 10, Heb. vii. 14; to Moses, that he should be a prophet, Deut. xviii. 18; to David, that he should be a king, Ps. ii. 6, and a priest, Ps. cx. 4; to Isaiah, that he should be born of a virgin, Isa. vii. 14; to Micah, that he should be born in Bethlehem, Micah v. 2. Before the law, God gave to the fathers particular revelations fit for their times and their needs. Under the law, God delivered many ordinances, rites, types, ceremonies, and shadows, to foreshew evangelical truths, and to uphold their faith therein. For these ends also God sent divers prophets from time to time till the fulness of time.

This manifesting of God's will by parts, is here noted by way of distinction and difference from God's revealing of his will under the gospel; which was all at one time, namely, the time of his Son's being on earth; for then the whole counsel of God was made known, so far as was meet for the church to know it while this world continueth. In this respect Christ saith, John xv. 15, 'All things that I have heard of my Father, I have made known to you:' and John xiv. 26, 'The Comforter shall teach you all things, and bring all things to your remembrance, whatsoever I have said unto you.' The woman of Samaria understood thus much, John iv. 25, when she said, 'When the Messias is come, he will tell us all things.'

Obj. The apostles had many things revealed unto them, Gal. i. 12.

Ans. Those were no other things than what Christ had revealed before while he lived.

There is another difference in the word following, πολυτρόπως, *multimodis*, translated 'in divers manners;' for that God, who was pleased to reveal his will part by part, was also pleased to reveal it after divers ways. These were either extraordinary or ordinary. Extraordinarily God manifested his mind sometimes outwardly, sometimes inwardly; outwardly by voice or signs, but inwardly by revelation or inspiration. To give particular instances of all these:

1. God oft himself spake with his own voice, and that when men were awake or at sleep. God spake to Adam when he was awake, Gen. iii. 9, &c; and to

---

[1] Si quis illud, *pluit Dominus a Domino*, non de Patre ac Filio accipit, sed eundem a se ipso depluisse dicit, Anathema sit. Pluit enim Dominus Filius a Domino Patre. Sic Patres in concil. Sirm. *ut Socrat. Hist. Eccles.* l. ii. c. 30.

Solomon in a dream when he was asleep, 1 Kings iii. 5.

2. God spake by the voice of angels to Lot, Gen. xix. 1, &c. This phrase, chap. ii. ver. 2, 'the word spoken by angels,' sheweth that God oft revealed his will to men by angels.

3. God most frequently declared his mind by children of men, whom he oft endued with an extraordinary spirit. This much is intended in this phrase, 'God spake by the prophets.'

4. God's mind was sometimes made known by signs. In this respect a voice is attributed to signs; as when God thus said to Moses, 'If they will not hearken to the voice of the first sign, they will believe the voice of the latter sign,' Exod. iv. 8. Thus also God spake by his judgments; whereupon saith a prophet, 'Hear ye the rod, and who hath appointed it,' Micah vi. 9. Under this head sacrifices may be comprised; for God spake to Abel and to Cain by their sacrifices, Gen. iv. 4, 5; so to David by his, 1 Chron. xxi. 26; and to Solomon by his, 2 Chron. vii. 1; and to Elijah by his, 1 Kings xviii. 24, 38. By sundry other types did God also use to speak to his people: Exod. xxix. 42, and xxx. 6; 1 Sam. xxviii. 6; Judges vi. 37, &c. Visions also may be referred to this head; visions were visible representations of things presented to men's eyes, Isa. vi. 1, Ezek. i, 1.

5. God used to declare his mind inwardly by revelations, Isa. xxxviii. 4, 5, and by inspiration. Thus 'holy men of God spake as they were moved by the Holy Ghost,' 1 Peter i. 21. A difference betwixt revelation and inspiration was this, that revelations were of some particular matters, Dan. ii. 19; but inspiration implieth a more general assistance, 2 Tim. iii. 16.

6. The most usual and ordinary means of God's declaring his will to his people was by ordinary ministers (which were among the Jews, priests and Levites, Ezra viii. 4), and by the written word, Luke xvi. 31.

This variety of means whereby God spake to his people of old, is here intimated to shew that God doth now, under the gospel, more uniformly and constantly declare his mind; for the word whereby God speaking of old is set out is in the Greek a participle, λαλήσας, and hath reference to the verb ἐλάλησε, ver. 2; word for word it may thus be translated: 'At sundry times, and divers manners, God, speaking in time past,' &c., 'hath in these last days spoken,' &c. This relative expression of God speaking, implieth a difference betwixt God speaking then and now. Then variously, so many ways as we heard before; now uniformly, after one and the same manner, which is by preaching. So Christ made known the will of his Father, Mark i. 14, 38; so did his apostles, Mark vi. 12. Christ, after his resurrection, made them also so to do throughout the whole world, Mark xvi. 15. So they did, Acts viii. 4; for 'it pleased God by preaching to save them that believe,' 1 Cor. i. 21.

Obj. Paul and other apostles wrote sundry epistles, whereby they declared the will of God.

Ans. They wrote no other things than what they had preached. Such things they wrote, that they might remain upon perpetual record for the continual good of the church.

God is said to *speak*, both of old and now, by way of resemblance, after the manner of men. Men by speaking use to manifest their mind. This is the most frequent and accustomed manner of expressing a man's inward conceptions, even such things as they would have others to know and take notice of. In allusion hereunto, God's manifesting his mind is styled *speaking*. At the beginning, when God manifested his mind every day, this phrase is used, *God said*, Gen. i. 6, which is all one as this, *he spake*; and so it is translated, Ps. xxxiii. 9.

The time wherein God declared his mind, part by part, and sundry ways, is here styled 'the time past,' πάλαι, *olim, old times*, whereby he meaneth all that time that passed from the beginning of the world till the exhibition of the Son of God in the flesh. This is evident by the opposition of this phrase, *in time past*, to the *last days* mentioned in the next verse. The Greek word may thus be translated *of old;* whereby is hinted such a time as should be altered. What the apostle saith of the old covenant, may be applied to this old time, 'That which is old is ready to vanish away,' Heb. viii. 13; and we that live since that old time may say, 'Old things are passed away,' 2 Cor. v. 17. This sheweth that those were not times of perfection; if they had been perfect, no place should have been sought for other times. This style of those former times amplifieth the times whereunto we are reserved.

They who lived in those times are styled *fathers*, τοῖς πατράσιν; and by them are intended such as lived before the fulness of time, who may also be called ancestors. For it is usual in all sorts of authors to set out ancestors under this title fathers; because posterity by lineal degrees come from ancestors, as children from fathers. Thus is this title expressly expounded, Luke i. 55; for mention being made of God speaking to the fathers, by way of exposition it is added, to 'Abraham, and to his seed.' Now, because Abraham and his posterity were of old the only people of God, they are by a property styled fathers; and God is said in an especial manner to be the 'God of the fathers,' Acts v. 30. Thus is this title a title of honour, yet here it is used by way of diminution, intending such as lived out their course, and ended their days before the joyful and glorious times foretold by the prophets, and expected by those fathers, were come, Luke x. 24; John viii. 56; 1 Peter i. 11. The greatest that then lived was less than the least of the kingdom of God, which began with the manifestation of the gospel, Mat. xi. 11.

To these fathers God spake (as it is in the original)

ἐν τοῖς προφήταις, 'in the prophets,' and so in the next verse, ἐν υἱῷ, 'in the Son.' Both these phrases have an especial and distinct emphasis. The former importeth that God was after an especial manner in the prophets inspiring their minds, and ordering their tongues, so as they spake not their own words, but the very words of God.

As for the Son, all the fulness of the Godhead dwelleth in him bodily, σωματικῶς, Col. ii. 9. Not as in mere men, by assistance, efficacy, or power, but essentially and personally; that is, by union of the deity with the humanity in one person. Many interpreters, both ancient and modern,[1] do change this particle *in* to *by*, whom our English do follow. The transmutation of these two prepositions is usual in all sorts of authors, especially in sacred Scripture. Not unfitly may it so stand in this place; and because the prophets, who were indeed children of men, but sent of God, and by God instructed in his will, by speaking made known God's will, God is said to speak by the prophets.

Sec. 12. *Of prophets.*

The title *prophet* in English, and Latin *propheta*, is taken from the Greek, Προφήτης ἀ πρὸ et φημί, which, according to the notation thereof, signifieth one that foretelleth things to come; so doth also the Hebrew word.[2] Now, he that foretelleth things to come, must needs be instructed therein by God; for it is a divine property to foretell things future, Isa. xli. 22, and xlviii. 5. Hence is it that, in a large signification, he that was chosen of God to be his messenger, and to declare his will unto people, was called a prophet.

With this title *prophet*, sundry sorts of men were dignified and distinguished. As,

1. Heads of families; for it was their duty to instruct others in God's will, Gen. xviii. 19. Such an one was Abraham, Gen. xx. 7.

2. Such as gave themselves to be more than ordinarily instructed in God's will, that on all occasions they might declare it to others. Of these there were companies or societies, 1 Sam. x. 5, 10, and xix. 20. These had their colleges, 2 Kings xxii. 14. Among them some were masters or seniors, others juniors, called 'sons of the prophets,' 2 Kings ii. 3.

3. Such as God used to pen sacred Scriptures, 2 Peter i. 19.

4. Such as were endued with a special gift of interpreting Scripture,[3] 1 Cor. xii. 29. These were especially in the apostles' times.

5. All sorts of true preachers and ministers of God's words, Mat. x. 41, and xiii. 57.

[1] Chrysost. Theoph. Vatabl. Tr.
[2] נבא, *Vaticinatus est.* נבא, *propheta*, Jer. xxviii. 9. Propheta Dei est enunciator verborum Dei hominibus.—*Aug. quæst.* 17 *in Exo.*
[3] Prophetæ sunt quibus jam sub apostolis per gratiam donabatur interpretatio scripturarum.—*Aug. Ep.* 58.

6. Most strictly and properly such are styled prophets as were immediately stirred up of God, and extraordinarily assisted by his Spirit to such weighty matters as could not but by divine assistance be effected, John iii. 2. They are therefore set out by an ancient father under such a title as signifieth bearers of the Spirit.[1]

Some of these read such writings as by no learning or skill of man could be read, Dan. v. 17.

Others discovered secret counsels, 2 Kings vi. 12.

Others brought such things to men's minds as the men themselves had forgotten, Dan. ii. 24.

Others interpreted dreams, Gen. xl. 14, and xli. 38. Though the dreams which set out things to come were other men's dreams,[2] and in those dreams God shewed things to come to them that dreamed them (as to Pharaoh, Gen. xli. 25, and to Nebuchadnezzar, Dan. ii. 29), yet because they wanted understanding to conceive the meaning of those dreams, *they* cannot be said to have the spirit of prophecy, but they rather who expounded them; for prophecy appertaineth especially to the mind and the understanding.

Finally, Others did many extraordinary and miraculous works. Among these Moses excelled, and is in that respect said to be 'mighty in words and deeds,' Acts vii. 22.

There were also others said to prophecy, and called prophets, but improperly. As,

1. They who were used to foretell mysteries which they themselves understood not. Thus Caiaphas is said to prophesy, John xi. 51.

2. They who, if they understood what they foretold, yet had no good liking thereto.[3] They neither feared God, whose counsel they revealed, nor regarded God's people, for whose sake that gift was conferred upon them. Such an one was Balaam, who 'taught Balak to cast a stumbling-block before the children of Israel, and loved the wages of unrighteousness,' and yet is styled a prophet, 2 Peter ii. 15, 16.

3. They who pretended to know the counsel of the Lord, and to foretell what he had revealed to them, when there was no such matter. Such were Zedekiah, and the four hundred that conspired with him, all called prophets, 1 Kings xxii. 6, 10.

4. They who among the heathen noted such oracles and predictions of matters as were supposed in future times to fall out, as they were foretold. In such a sense Epimenides[4] is called a prophet, Titus i. 12.

But to leave those who are improperly called pro-

[1] Prophetæ sunt πνευματοφόροι, i. e. portantes spiritum, sive spirituales.—*Hieron. Com. in Saph.* c. 3.
[2] Lege Aug. de Gen. ad lit. l. xii. c. 9.
[3] Prophetarum nomen secundum regulam scripturarum bonis malisque commune est.—*Hieron. Comment.* lib. iv. *in Ezek.* xiii.
[4] Epimenidem prophetam vocavit, quia de oraculis scripsit atque responsis, quæ et ipsa futura prænuncient.—*Hieron. in Tit.* i. Vide Bezæ *Annot. in Tit.* i. 12.

phets, and to return to those who most strictly and properly were so called; God, for the clearer manifestation of his divine power in them, raised them up out of all sorts of people: many of them were of the priests, as Jer. i. 1, Ezek. i. 3; and Levites, as 2 Chron. xx. 14. Yea, also there were prophets of other tribes. Daniel was of Judah, Dan. i. 6; Elijah of Gad, 1 Kings xvii. 1; Elisha of Ephraim, 1 Kings xix. 16; Jonah of Zebulon, 2 Kings xiv. 25; others of other tribes. As respect in choosing prophets was not had to any one tribe, so nor to age, for children were chosen prophets, 1 Sam. ii. 18, and iii. 4, &c., Jer. i. 6; nor to education, for an herdsman was made a prophet, Amos vii. 14; nor to sex, for women were prophetesses, Judges iv. 4; Isa. viii. 3; 2 Kings xxii. 14; Luke ii. 33.

These extraordinary prophets were raised up, when the ordinary spiritual guides of the people, as priests and Levites, failed in a due performance of their duty; as in Eli's time, 1 Sam. ii. 12, and in Jeremiah's, Jer. xxvi. 8, or when such employments were to be performed as ordinary ministers could not or would not perform.

The employments were such as these:

1. To tell kings, priests, princes, yea, and a whole kingdom, of their sins and rebellions against God. Micaiah told Ahab the truth, when all besides flattered him, 1 Kings xxii. 13, 14. Elijah told Ahab of his bloody sin, and denounced God's judgment against him, 1 Kings xxi. 20, &c., when all the people conspired to shed innocent blood with him. Jeremiah told king, priests, princes, and all the people, of their apostasy, Jer. i. 18.

2. To restore religion, it being turned into idolatry. So did Samuel, 1 Sam. vii. 3, and Elijah, 1 Kings xviii. 21, &c.

3. To foretell God's judgments beforehand, that believers might be prepared the better to bear them: that impenitent might be made the more inexcusable; and that the severity of God's judgments might be the more justified, Jer. v. 13, Ezek. v. 8.

4. To make known God's mercies in the midst of judgments, and God's mind of doing good to them, after they have been scourged for their sins; thereby to provoke them to return to the Lord, Isa. iv. 2, Hosea vi. 1, 2.

5. To give evidences of the Messiah, thereby to establish the hope of such as should live and die before that fulness of time, and to direct them how to build their faith on him; and that by setting out his eternal deity, his true humanity, his conception, birth, growth, doctrine, miracles, passion, resurrection, ascension, intercession; his first and second coming; his spiritual and eternal kingdom, Acts x. 43: that such as should live when and after the Messiah was exhibited, might be assured that he was indeed the Christ.

6. To assure the Jews of a recalling after their rejection; and to reveal the calling of the Gentiles, Ezek. xxxvii. 19, Isa. ii. 2, 3, and liv. 1, 2, &c.

The chief of these extraordinary prophets was Moses, after whose time they were very rare till Samuel's time; but after kings were once anointed and set over the people, prophets were plentiful. There was never a king under whose reign there were not some prophets; and so continued till the captivity: yea, in and after the captivity, till the second temple was new built, God afforded extraordinary prophets to his church, Ezra v. 1.

Concerning the prophets here meant, all they whom God employed ordinarily or extraordinarily to declare his mind to his people, are to be understood in this place.

Of the evidences of the prophets' faith, see Chap. xi. 32, Sec. 225.

Sec. 13. *Of the last days.*

It was a great benefit that the fathers received from God speaking to them by his prophets. But behold a greater reserved to their children, even to all sorts of Christians, whether Jews or Gentiles, comprised under this particle *us;* for he meaneth all believers of the Christian faith, that have lived or shall live in these last days;[1] that is, from the beginning of Christ's executing his ministerial function, to the end of the world. These have now continued above sixteen hundred years; and how much longer they may continue, God knoweth.

It hath pleased God that these last days should be many, that the world might the longer enjoy the bright light of the gospel, and that all that are ordained to life might in their due time be called.

Quest. Why are they called the last days, as here, the last time, 1 John ii. 18; the ends of the world 1 Cor. x. 11; and why in the beginning of this time was the coming of the Lord said to draw nigh, James v. 8; and the end of all things to be at hand? 1 Peter iv. 7.

Ans. 1. By the exhibition of Christ, the prophecies and promises that in former times were made of Christ were accomplished; therefore, as the days wherein these promises and prophecies were first made known were counted the first days, so these wherein they were accomplished the last.

2. The new covenant of grace is in these last days fully revealed by the gospel, and ratified by the death of Christ, so as no clearer revelation nor former[2] ratification can be expected; and in this respect also they are fitly styled the last days.

3. No alteration of the state and order of God's church is to be expected after Christ exhibited; but a final end of all by Christ's second coming unto

---

[1] Ex hoc superiores existimus, quod nobis Dominus sit locutus, illis servi.—*Chrys. in loc.* Novissima hora dicitur tempus fidei Gentium.—*Hier. com. in* Micah iv.

[2] Qu. 'firmer?'—ED.

judgment; therefore these days may be accounted the ends of the world, and the end of all things to be at hand.

4. As God at first made all things in six days, and rested the seventh; so he continueth to govern the world in six distinct times,[1] which may be accounted as six days of the great week of the world; and eternity following an everlasting Sabbath.

The first of these days was from Adam to Noah; in it the covenant of grace was first made to man.

To second was from Noah to Abraham; in it that covenant was renewed.

The third was from Abraham to David; in it that covenant was appropriated to Abraham and his seed.

The fourth was from David to the captivity of Israel; in it that covenant was established in a royal line.

The fifth was from their captivity to Christ's coming in the flesh; in it, as the brightness of that covenant was eclipsed by the captivity, so it was revived by Israel's return out of the captivity, and re-edifying the temple.

The sixth was and still is, and shall be from Christ's first coming in the flesh, to his second coming in glory, even to the end of the world. In it that covenant, most clearly and fully laid open, was most firmly and inviolably ratified. Now, when the sixth day, which is the last day, is come, then the end of the week may well be said to be at hand, and the coming of the Lord, following thereupon, to draw nigh.

Sec. 14. *Of God's speaking by his Son.*

In these last days, that is, all the days of the gospel, it is said, *he hath spoken*. No limitation is here added, as before, in these phrases, 'at divers times and in sundry manners;' so as God's *speaking* is here to be taken simply for a full revelation of his whole will; not one part by one messenger, and another by another. These words, *at divers times and in sundry manners*, are extenuating words. God did once, fully, clearly, without such types, visions, and other obscure means, which were used in the time of the law, declare his whole counsel, so far as it is requisite to be known by man in this world.

Quest. Hath not God also spoken in these last days by men, as apostles and others?

Ans. 1. Till these last days, God spake not all by his Son incarnate.

2. This Son of God first made known to his apostles all things that he had heard of his Father, John xv. 15, Acts i. 7.

3. The Son sent his Spirit to instruct them, and that Spirit brought to their mind all things that Christ had said to them before, John xiv. 26.

[1] Sex ætatibus humanum genus hoc seculo per successiones temporum Dei opera insigniunt: quarum prima est ab Adamo usque ad Noen, &c.—*Aug. cont. Faust. Manic.* l. xii. c. viii.

4. Whereas St Paul had heard nothing of Christ on earth, he was rapt into heaven, and there was by Christ himself instructed in the counsel of God, Gal. i. 1, 12; Acts xxvi. 16; 2 Cor. xii. 2. Hence is it that St Paul and others prefix this title before their epistles, 'An Apostle of Jesus Christ.'

5. Other ministers declare that the apostles have revealed to them from Christ, 2 Tim ii. 2, Heb. ii. 3, so as now God hath made known all by his Son.

This is a very great commendation of the gospel; for never was there such a minister as the Son of God; never shall there be, nor can be the like. The description of the Son of God here following proveth as much. The use hereof is distinctly set down by this apostle, chap. ii. 1–3. See in particular Chap. ii. 22, Sec. 112.

Quest. Why doth he not say, *The Son spake;* but *God spake by the Son?*

Ans. 1. To add the more authority, for their sake who were not well instructed in the deity of the Son.[1]

2. Because he speaks of his Son incarnate.

This he did, ἡμῖν, to us, who have, do, and shall live in the last days; who are the children and successors of the fathers; being now in our time, as they were in their times, of the true church: so as the best things are reserved for us Christians, who are in that respect greater than they. The gospel is further commended to us by the immediate author thereof, the Son, even the Son of God, who became also a son of man, by assuming our nature; and so shewed himself to be the true Immanuel, God with us.[2] So is this name expounded, Mat. i. 23.

Sec. 15. *Of Christ's Sonship.*

The particle of relation *his*, inserted in our English, is not expressed in the Greek, yet necessarily understood, and therefore well supplied, for it hath relation to God before mentioned. Indeed, a simple expression of the phrase thus, ' by the Son,' wants not emphasis; for so it implieth a Son in a singular and peculiar excellency; such a Son as none like him. True it is, that this title *son* is attributed to sundry creatures, and that in relation to God; yet not properly, but only in regard of some special grace or dignity conferred upon them: and that, as God had given them their being, in which respect all creatures are God's sons; or as he has set his image on some of them above others, as on angels, on Adam, on governors, and such as are adopted sons and regenerated; but Christ is truly, ἀληθῶς, Mat. iv. 33, the one, εἷς, Mark xii. 6, own, ἑαυτοῦ, Rom. vi. 3, proper, ἴδιος, Rom. viii. 32, begotten, Ps. ii. 7,

[1] Non dixit, Christus locutus est, quoniam adhuc animæ eorum debiles erant, &c.—*Chrys. in loc.*

[2] עִמָּנוּ, *Nobiscum* אֵל *Deus.* See my explanation of the Lord's Prayer, entitled, A Guide to go to God, sec. 7. Dono gratiæ Spiritus S. filii Dei vocantur.—*Hier. Comment. in John,* cap. i.

only begotten, μονογενὴς, John i. 18, Son of God's love, ὑιος τῆς ἀγάπης, Col. i. 13. These and other like notes of distinction being expressly attributed to Christ as the Son of God, give evident proof that he is such an one, as none but he is or can be; whereas all others styled God's sons, have their title given them by favour, Christ hath it of due, even by nature.[1]

Christ is styled the Son of God in two especial respects:

1. As the second person in sacred Trinity, true God.

2. As God manifested in the flesh, God-man, Θεάνθρωπος.

In the former respect, he is the Son of God by eternal generation, as is evident in the first verse of this chapter, where we shall have a more fit occasion to speak of it.

In the latter respect, as God-man, he is the Son of God by the union of his human nature with the forementioned second person, who only is of all the persons the Son of God. For as neither the Father nor the Holy Ghost is the Son, so nor the Father nor the Holy Ghost did assume human nature, but the Son only. In regard of the nature, true it is, that God and man were united in one person: 'God was manifested in the flesh,' 1 Tim. iii. 16. But in regard of the person, the Son of God was also Son of man: 'The word was made flesh,' John i. 14. In this respect an angel saith of him that was born of the Virgin Mary, Luke i. 35, 'He shall be called the Son of God.'

So near is this union of God and man, as, though they be two distinct natures, and more different than any two other distinct things can be, yet they make but one person; as man's body and soul, which are different natures, make but one person. In this respect the union of Christ's natures is called an hypostatical union, that is, such an union as makes one subsistence or one person. Hence is it that the properties and effects of the one nature are attributed to the other: John iii. 13, 'The Son of man is in heaven.'

Son of man properly designs Christ's human nature, which was not in heaven while it was on earth, as then it was; but that person, in regard of his divine nature, was in heaven. So on the other side, God is said to purchase his church 'with his own blood,' Acts xx. 28. God, in regard of his divine nature, hath no blood; but he assumed an human nature, which had blood, and in that respect blood is attributed to God, by reason of the personal union of man with God. Thus is Christ God-man, the Son of God; and thus hath God in these days spoken to us in or by him. The Son, as God and second person, spake in times past by the prophets; yea, the Father also in that respect then spake by him.[1] For as God and second person he is ὁ λόγος, the word, and so was in the beginning, John i. 1. But in these last days he began to be God-man, and to be God's Son by union of his human nature with his divine. In this sense, therefore, the title Son is here used; so as in these last days God spake to us by his Son incarnate.

Of instructions and directions arising from this relation of Christ to God, see Chap. iii. ver. 6, Sec. 55.

Sec. 16. *Of Christ being appointed.*

To magnify the ministry of the gospel, and thereby the more to commend unto us the gospel itself, the apostle goeth on in describing the author thereof, the Son of God; and that both in a dignity conferred upon him, and also in his own divine worth.

The dignity is thus expressed, ὃν ἔθηκε, ' whom he hath appointed heir of all things.' This must needs be meant of Christ as mediator, even as the title Son before was meant; for as God he was not deputed or appointed to a thing.

God is said to appoint his Son,

1. By ordaining in his eternal counsel that his Son should be heir. As Christ was 'delivered by the determinate counsel of God to be slain,' Acts ii. 23, so was he appointed to be heir, 1 Peter i. 20.

2. By sending him into the world, or by giving him to be incarnate for that very end, Philip. ii. 7–9.

3. By raising him from the dead, and setting him at his right hand in heaven. On these grounds, St Peter thus saith, ' God hath made him both Lord and Christ,' Acts ii. 36.

This word *appointed* sheweth the right that Christ hath to his supreme dignity. That which is said of Christ's being priest, chap. v. 5, may be applied to this dignity: ' Christ glorified not himself' to be an heir; ' but he that said to him, Thou art my Son, to-day have I begotten thee;' appointed him heir.

Sec. 17. *Of Christ the heir,* κληρονόμον.

An heir,[2] saith the apostle, Gal. iv. 1, is Lord of all. On this ground the son of the bondwoman was cast out, that he might not be heir with the son of Sarah, nor part share with him, Gen. xxi. 10, 12. This title *heir* setteth out a dignity and dominion together, with the best right thereto that can be.

The dignity and dominion is the same that his Father hath. For an heir is a successor to his father in all that the father hath. In this metaphor caution must be put that it be not extended too far, by excluding the Father from any dignity or dominion.

---

[1] Ille quidem natura filius est, nos vero adoptione — *Hier. Comment. in* Eph. i.

[1] Si attendas distinctionem substantiarum, Filius Dei de cœlo descendit. Filius hominis crucifixus est. Si unitatem personæ, et Filius hominis descendit de cœlo, et Filius Dei est crucifixus.—*Aug. cont. Maxim.* l. iii. c. xx. 'See Chap. iv. ver. 12, Sec. 69.

[2] See ver. 4, Sec. 43, and ver. 14, Sec. 160.

Indeed, among men, the son hath not such dominion and possession of an inheritance till the father relinquish it (as Jehoshaphat gave the kingdom to Jehoram, his first-born, 2 Chron. xxi. 7; in which respect Jehoram is said to reign, 2 Kings viii. 16, even while Jehoshaphat was king), or till the father be through impotency excluded (as Uzziah when he became leprous, 2 Chron. xxvi. 21), or till he be forced from it (as Jehoahaz was, 2 Chron. xxxvi. 2, 4), or be dead, as David, though he were anointed and so made heir-apparent by God's appointment, yet would not take the kingdom upon him till Saul were dead, 1 Sam. xxvi. 10. But none of these can or may be imagined of God the Father : he neither will nor can give over his supreme jurisdiction, nor become impotent, nor be forced, nor die ; yet hath Christ an absolute jurisdiction, and a full possession of his inheritance together with the Father. The supreme sovereignty of the one, no whit at all hindereth the supreme sovereignty of the other : ' What things soever the Father doth, these also doth the Son likewise,' John v. 19. The difference is only in the manner. The Father doth all by the Son, and the Son doth all from the Father.

The apostle here sets out the dignity of Christ under this title *heir*[1] rather than *Lord*, as Acts ii. 36.

1. To give proof of that relation which he noted before, that Christ was truly and properly a Son; for he was the heir.

2. To shew the perpetuity thereof; for the heir ever abideth in the house, Gen. xxi. 10, John viii. 35.

3. To manifest the right that we have to be adopted sons and heirs : John viii. 36, ' If the Son shall make you free, ye shall be free indeed.' In this respect we are styled joint-heirs with Christ, συγκληρονόμοι Χριστοῦ, Rom. viii. 17.

This dignity of Christ to be heir, is further amplified by the extent thereof, in these words, *of all things*. The Greek πάντων may be restrained to persons, as being of the masculine gender; or extended to things, as of the neuter. This latter includeth the former; for if he be heir of all things, then also of all persons, for he that is heir and Lord of all things, must needs also be so of all persons: besides, it is more proper to say an heir of things than of persons. Well, therefore, hath our English taken away the ambiguity, by translating it, ' heir of all things ;' and thus it answers the prophetical promise, Ps. ii. 8, ' I shall give thee the heathen for thine inheritance, and the uttermost parts of the earth for thy possession.'

Sec. 18. *Of Christ the creator of the worlds.*

The apostle goeth on in setting out the dignity of Christ; and to that excellency which appertained to him as mediator betwixt God and man, he addeth a greater, being proper to him as he is God almighty, in these words, ' By whom also he made the worlds.'

Though this word ἐποίησεν, *made*, be a common work, attributed in other places to men's works as well as to God's, yet in this place it is taken for that divine work which is proper to God alone, *create*, as Acts xiv. 15, and xvii. 24, so as it pointeth at that first great work of God which is mentioned Gen. i. 1.

This is evident by the things made, comprised under this word *worlds*, τοὺς αἰῶνας.

The Greek word, according to the proper notation and most usual acceptation[1] thereof, signifieth *eternity*. It is oft put for an age.

The Hebrew hath a word עולם, which is every way taken in the same sense. The root or verb whence it cometh signifieth *to hide*. Thereupon time, the date whereof is hidden, is set out thereby, and that in these considerations following :

1. Eternity, Ps. xc. 2.
2. A long date, the end whereof was not known, Deut. xiii. 16.
3. Continuance of legal rites till they ended in their truth, Exod. xii. 24.
4. Continuance of rights till they determined in the jubilee, Exod. xxi. 6, Lev. xxv. 40.
5. The time of a man's life, 1 Sam. xii. 22.

By a metonymy, the same word setteth out the world, that was made in the beginning of time, and hath been continued throughout all times and ages.

And because the world (which compriseth under it all things that ever were made) is distinguished into three parts :

1. The invisible, glorious world of the blessed in heaven, called the highest world, עולם העיון, *superior mundus*.

2. The starry sky, wherein all that the Scripture styleth the host of heaven are contained ; and this is called the middle world, עולם התיכון, *medius mundus*.

3. The elements and all things compounded of them, or contained in them ; even all that space which is under the moon, and whatsoever is comprised therein. This is called the inferior world, עולם השפל, *inferior mundus*.

In regard of this distinction of parts, the plural number, *worlds*, is used. Answerably in Greek, a word of the same signification is used in the plural number, He made the worlds.[2]

These three words are distinguished into two, namely heaven and earth, Col. i. 16.

Thus we see how, under this word *worlds*, all things that ever were made, above and below, visible and invisible, are comprised, so as the making of the worlds setteth out the divine power of Christ.

Where it is said that God, *by him*, made the worlds, the Son is not set out as a mere instrument in this work, but as a primary and principal agent therein, together with the Father, for ' what thing soever the

---

[1] Hæredis utitur nomine, quod proprius sit filius, et quod dominationis illi nulla contingat amissio.—*Chrys. in loc.*

[1] αἰὼν quasi ἀεὶ ὤν.—*Arist* i. *de cœlo*. See my explanation of the Lord's prayer, entitled A Guide to go to God, sec. 224.
[2] τοὺς αἰῶνας. Of οἰκουμένη, see Chap. ii. Sec. 41.

Father doth, these doth also the Son likewise,' John v. 19. That particle, ὁμοίως, *likewise*, is not to be taken of doing different things like to another, for he there speaketh of the very same thing,[1] but of doing them by the same power, authority, dignity, with the same mind and will, after the same manner, to the same end, and that jointly together, the Father and the Son. Therefore, what the Father is said to do by the Son is in other places said to be done by the Son simply considered in and by himself, without relation to the Father, as John i. 3, ' All things were made by him,' πάντα δι᾽ αὐτοῦ ἐγένετο ; and Col. i. 16, ' All things were created by him,' τὰ πάντα δι᾽ αὐτοῦ ἔκτισται.

The Father is said to do this and that by the Son for these reasons :

1. To give proof of the distinction of persons.
2. To set out the order of the persons : the Father first, the Son second.
3. To declare their manner of working : the Father by the Son, and the Son from the Father, Gen. xix. 24.
4. To shew the consent of the distinct persons, Father and Son.
5. To demonstrate the identity of the essence of Father and Son, that both are one divine nature and essence, in that the same divine nature is attributed to both. This consequence is inferred upon a like ground, John v. 17, 18.

As the Father is here said to make the worlds by his Son, so of God in reference to the Son indefinitely it is said, ' By whom are all things,' chap. ii. 10.

The Son therefore is here declared to be true God.

Sec. 19. *Of Christ, the brightness of God's glory.*

Still doth the apostle proceed in setting out the divine glory of that Son by whom the Father hath made known his will to us under the gospel, in these words spoken of the Son in relation to the Father, ' who, being the brightness of his glory,' &c.

The word ἀπαύγασμα, translated brightness, is metaphorical, but very fit for the point in hand. The verb whence it is derived[2] signifieth *to send forth brightness*, or light, and the noun here used, such brightness as cometh from light, as the brightness, or light, or sunbeams issuing from the sun.

No resemblance taken from any other creature can more fully set out the mutual relation between the Father and the Son. For,

1. The brightness issuing from the sun is of the same nature that the sun is.
2. It is of as long continuance as the sun. Never was the sun without the brightness of it.[3]

3. This brightness cannot be separated from the sun. The sun may as well be made no sun, as have the brightness thereof severed from it.
4. This brightness is from the sun, not the sun from it.
5. This brightness cometh naturally and necessarily from the sun, not voluntarily and at pleasure.
6. The sun and the brightness are distinct each from other ; the one is not the other.
7. All the glory of the sun is in this brightness.
8. The light which the sun giveth to the world is by this brightness.

How distinctly and clearly doth this metaphor set out the great mysteries of our Christian faith concerning God the Father and Son ! For they are,

1. Of one and the same essence, John. x. 30.
2. Co-eternal, John. i. 1.
3. Inseparable, Prov. viii. 30.
4. The Son is from the Father : God of God, Light of light, very God of very God.[1]
5. The Son is begotten of the Father by nature, not by will, favour, or good pleasure,[2] Rom. viii. 7, 32,
6. The person of the one is distinct from the other. For the Father is not the Son, nor the Son the Father, John v. 17.
7. The incomprehensible glory of the Father most brightly shineth forth in the Son, John xvii. 5.
8. All that the Father doth in relation to creatures he doth by the Son. As in these respects Christ is fitly and justly styled brightness, so in regard of his surpassing excellency, he is said to be the brightness of glory. Of the Hebrew and Greek words translated *glory*, see chap ii. 7, sec. 60.

Glory attributed to a thing, in the Hebrew dialect, importeth the surpassing excellency thereof: as a crown of glory, Prov. xvi. 31 ; כסא כבוד, *gloriæ solium*, a throne of glory ; שם תפארת, *gloriæ nomen*, a name of glory, Isa. lxiii. 14 ; a most excellent and glorious crown, throne, and name. Thus to set out the surpassing excellency and most glorious majesty of God, he is styled ' the God of glory,' Acts vii. 2 ; ' the Father of glory,' Eph. i. 17. And his Son, ' the Lord of glory,' ' the King of glory,' 1 Cor. ii. 8, Ps. xxiv. 7. Never was any brightness like to the brightness here mentioned ; well therefore might it in regard of the excellency of it be styled ' brightness of glory.' Glory and excellency are set together, Isa. iv. 2, signifying the same thing. See more of glory, Chap. ii. Secs. 60, 93.

Our English doth here well insert this relative particle *his* in reference to the Father, thus, ' the brightness of his glory,' for the particle *his*, expressed by the original in the next clause, ' his person,' may have

---

[1] ταῦτα κατὰ τὴν ἐξουσίας ὁμοτιμίαν.—*Greg. Naz. Vid. Aug. cont. Serv. Adrian.*, cap. xiv. et xv.
[2] ἀπαυγάζειν, *splendorem reddere, seu lucem emittere*.
[3] Sicut flamma splendorem quem gignit tempore non præcedit ; ita Pater nunquam sine Filio fuit.—*Ambr. de Fide*, l. iv. c. iv.

[1] Θεὸς ἐκ Θεοῦ : καὶ φῶς ἐκ φωτὸς, Θεὸς ἀληθινὸς ἐκ Θεοῦ ἀληθινοῦ.—*Fidei Confes. Synod. Nicæn.*
[2] Generatio non in voluntatis possibilitate, sed in jure quodam et proprietate paterni videtur esse secreti.—*Ambr. de Fide*, lib. iv. cap. iv.

reference to both the branches, as 'his glory, his person.' This much amplifieth the point in hand, and sheweth that the Son was in his Father's greatest excellency no whit inferior to him, but every way equal.[1] He was brightness, the brightness of his Father, yea, also the brightness of his Father's glory. What excellency soever was in the Father, the same was likewise in the Son, and that in the most transplendent manner. Glory sets out excellency[2]; brightness of glory, the excellency of excellency.

Sec. 20. *Of Christ the excellency of his Father's person.*

To make the fore-named mystery the more clear, the apostle addeth another resemblance in these words, *and the express image of his person.*

This in the general importeth the same thing which the former did; so as the two metaphors are like the two visions which Pharaoh saw in a dream; they are doubled to shew that the point intended thereby is most certain and sure, Gen. xli. 32.

This phrase, *the express image,* is the exposition of one Greek word, χαρακτὴρ, which may thus fitly be translated *character.* The verb whence the word is derived, χαράττειν, *insculpere,* signifieth *to engrave;* and the word here used, the stamp or print of a thing engravened, as the stamp on money coined, the print on paper pressed by the printer, the mark made by a seal, or any like impression. There is another like word, χάραγμα, coming from the same root, oft used in the book of the Revelation, and translated 'a mark,' Rev. xiii. 16, 17, and xiv. 9, 11, and xv. 2; and in Acts xvii. 29 it is translated '*stone gravened.*' But the former significations of the word, *stamp, print, seal, or mark,* are most proper to this place. Nothing can be more like another than the picture or image on the thing stamped or printed, is to the picture or image on the tool, mould, seal, or instrument wherewith it is made; the one carrieth the very form of the other. Very fitly therefore is it by our English translated *the express image.*

Sec. 21. *Of the Son a distinct person.*

The next word is fitly translated person, τῆς ὑποστάσεως αὐτοῦ. According to the proper notation and derivation of the word, it signifieth a substance or subsistence,[3] which are in a manner Latin words, and set out the being of a thing; even a particular and distinct being, which is most properly called a person. The simple verb from whence this compound is derived[4] signifieth to set, to settle, to establish, Mat. xxv. 33, xii. 25.

[1] In hoc apparebit majestatis æqualitas, si nec inferiorem patre, nec posteriorem suspexeris.—*Bern. super Cant. Serm.* lxxvi.

[2] See the Guide to go to God; or my explanation of the Lord's Prayer, sec. 216, &c.

[3] ὑπόστασις ab ὑφίστασθαι, *subsistere* Substantia, subsistentia. [4] ἵστημι, statuo, stabilio.

Essence or *nature* importeth a common being, as Deity or Godhead, which is common to the Father, Son, Holy Ghost. For the Father is God, the Son is God, and the Holy Ghost is God. But subsistence or person implieth a different, distinct, individual, incommunicable, property; such are these three, Father, Son, Holy Ghost. For the Father is different from the Son and Holy Ghost, so the Son from the Father and the Holy Ghost, and so the Holy Ghost from the Father and the Son; and every of those distinct in himself, and so incommunicable, as neither of these persons is, or can be, the other.

Thus we see how these two words, *subsistence* and *person,* import one and the same thing; yet our English, for perspicuity's sake, hath rather used this title *person,* and that in imitation of the Latin fathers. For what in this mystery of the Trinity the Greek fathers called substances or subsistences, the Latin called persons.[1] They said that there were three substances and one essence, as we say there were three persons and one essence.

This relative particle *his,* added to the word person, hath relation to God mentioned in the first verse, as if he had more plainly thus said, 'the express image of the person of God.'

This Christ is in a double respect:

1. As he is the second person in the sacred and indivisible Trinity.

2. As he is Immanuel, God with us, God manifested in the flesh.

As he is the Son of God, the second person in Trinity, the whole divine essence, and all the divine properties are communicated to him. In this respect, the two fore-mentioned resemblances of *brightness* and *character,* and also all other resemblances which, by the wit of man, can be imagined, come short in setting out the relation betwixt the Father and the Son. They are not only like each other, but they are both the very same in nature. Resemblances may be some help to us, who are better acquainted with earthly and sensible things than with heavenly and divine; but they cannot possibly set out divine mysteries, especially such as are of all the deepest and profoundest, as the mysteries of the trinity of persons in the unity of essence, and the union of God and man, two distinct natures, in one person. Therefore, sundry resemblances are used: one to set out one point, another another; and yet all that can be used cannot, to the life and full, set out the mystery.

Again, As Christ's human nature is hypostatically united to the divine nature, Christ is visibly the character or express image of God. For in Christ incarnate the divine properties were made most con-

[1] Quod de personis secundum nostram, hoc de substantiis secundum Græcorum consuetudinem intelligitur. Sic enim illi dicunt tres substantias unam essentiam: quemadmodum nos dicimus tres personas unam essentiam.—*Aug. de Trin.* lib. vii. cap. iv.

spicuous, as almighty power, infinite wisdom, truth, justice, mercy, and the like. In Christ, as God man, 'dwelt all the fulness of the Godhead bodily,' Col. ii. 9. In this respect, the glory of Christ made flesh is said to be 'the glory as of the only begotten of the Father,' John i. 14; and in that flesh, saith Christ of himself, 'he that hath seen me hath seen the Father,' John xiv. 9. Thus the resemblance here used is very fit; for he that seeth the character or figure which is on the thing stamped or printed, sees therein the figure that is on the instrument wherewith it was stamped.

Sec. 22. *Of the benefits arising from the relation of the Son to the Father.*

By the resemblance of a character, we see what is to be sought in Christ, namely, whatsoever is in the Father. As the former metaphor implieth that the glory of the Father is invisible till it shine forth and shew itself in the Son, so this likewise declareth that the Father's excellency is, as it were, hid, and could not be known unless it were revealed and laid open in this character or express image. Again, as the former metaphor implieth that out of Christ, who is that brightness, there is no light at all, but mere palpable darkness (for God, who only is, as the sun, light in himself, and the fountain of all light to all creatures, doth by this brightness only shine out to us, John i. 9), so this metaphor importeth that in Christ the Father is truly and thoroughly to be known; for a character well made doth not only in part and obscurely, but fully and to the life, demonstrate the image that is on the stamp. It is truly and properly an 'express image.'

Sec. 23. *Of the fit resemblance of the Son to a character.*

To exemplify this latter resemblance of a *character*, as we have done the former of *brightness* in some particulars, take, for instance, the character or stamp that is on coin, and the engravement that is on the tool wherewith the character on the coin is made.
1. The character cometh from the engravement on the tool.
2. The character is most like to that engravement.
3. Whatsoever is on the engravement is also on the character.
4. The engravement and the character are distinct each from the other.

All these were before set down in the former metaphor of brightness, Sec. 19, but yet this of a character is not unnecessarily added; for by the vulgar sort it is better conceived, and it doth more sensibly set down the likeness and equality betwixt the Father and the Son than that of brightness doth, which is the principal end of using these resemblances.

To apply this resemblance: It doth, so far as an earthly resemblance can, set out these mysteries following concerning God the Father and God the Son.

1. The Son is begotten of the Father, Ps. ii. 7.
2. The Father is made manifest in the Son, Col. i. 15.
3. The Son is equal to the Father, Philip. ii. 6.
4. The Father and the Son are distinct each from other, John v. 32, and viii. 18.

These mysteries are expressly revealed in the sacred Scriptures, otherwise all the wits in the world could not have found them out by the fore-mentioned, or by any other resemblances. Resemblances are for some illustration of such things as may upon surer grounds be proved.

Sec. 24. *Of Christ upholding all things.*

As a further demonstration of Christ's dignity and dominion, the apostle attributes another divine effect to him. One was in these words, *made the worlds;* the other in these, *and upholding all things by the word of his power.*

The copulative particle *and* sheweth that, as the fore-mentioned resemblances of brightness and express image set out a divine dignity (for copulatives are used to join together things of like nature), so these words set out a divine dominion: they are all divine.

The word *upholding*, φέρων, is metaphorical, and by way of resemblance applied to Christ. It signifieth to bear, carry, or uphold a thing, as the friends who took up and brought to Christ a palsy man, φέροντες, Mark ii. 3; and also to move, carry, order, and dispose a thing, as the winds drive and carry ships hither and thither.[1] The LXX use this word to set out the Spirit's moving upon the waters at the first forming and creating things, Πνεῦμα Θεοῦ ἐπεφέρετο, Gen. i. 2. And the apostle useth it to set out the Spirit's guiding and disposing the prophets in penning the sacred Scriptures, φερόμενοι, 2 Peter i. 21. The word may fitly be here taken in all these significations; for neither do cross the other, but all well and truly stand together.

It is most clear that the divine providence is here described, being distinguished from the former work of creation. Now, God's providence is manifested in two things:
1. In sustaining all things that he made.
2. In governing them.

In that this divine work of providence is attributed to Christ, he is thereby declared to be true God.

To shew that that phrase which the apostle used before in a mutual relation between the Father and the Son about making the worlds thus, ' by whom he made,' derogateth nothing from Christ's supreme sovereignty or absolute power in that work, as if he had been used for a minister therein, here most simply, without any such relation, he attributeth the divine work to him, and extendeth it to all things that were made, excepting nothing at all, in this general phrase,

[1] Vide Erasmi Annotat. in Acta xxvii. 15, 17.

τὰ πάντα, 'all things,' whether visible or invisible, in heaven, on earth, or under the earth, Col. i. 16.

To give yet more evidence to Christ's true deity, he further adds this clause, ' by the word of his power.'

Sec. 25. *Of Christ's word of power.*

The particle translated *word* is not, in the Greek, that whereby Christ the Son of God is oft set out, λόγος, John i. 1; especially by St John both in his Gospel and Epistle, 1 John i. 1, but another, ῥῆμα, Mat. iv. 4, Heb. xi. 3, which importeth a command; in which sense it is used, Luke v. 5, for Christ is herein resembled to an absolute monarch, who at his word hath what he will [have] done. He needs no more but command. Thus it is said: Ps. xxxiii. 6, ' By the word of the Lord were the heavens made;' and in the way of exposition it is added (ver. 9), ' He spake and it was done: he commanded and it stood fast.'

Yet further, to amplify the sovereignty of Christ, the apostle addeth this epithet of power, τῆς δυνάμεως, which after the Hebrew manner is so expressed, to shew the prevalency of Christ's word; nothing can hinder it, it is a most mighty word. For the Hebrews use to set out a surpassing excellency, and an exceeding vileness of things by substantives. Thus the most mighty voice, arm, hand, and rod of the Lord is styled a voice, arm, hand, rod of power; and the mighty angels, angels of power. Yea, to amplify the almightiness of God's power, it is styled a power of might. On the other side, to set out the excessiveness of evil, the most wicked spirits are called spirits of wickedness, and most rebellious men, children of disobedience. Thus we see what the emphasis of this Hebrew phrase is, which sets out the irresistible power of Christ's word, whereby he supports and disposeth all things.

And that such is the power of Christ's own word, is evident by this reciprocal particle *his*, αὐτοῦ, *cum spiritu denso*; for it hath not relation to the Father, as it hath in this phrase, ' his person,' αὐτοῦ, *cum spiritu tenui*; but it reflecteth upon Christ's own person. The Greek makes an apparent distinction by a different spirit over the head of the first letter. Our English oft maketh a difference, by adding to the reciprocal word this particle *own*, as if here it had been thus translated, ' by the word of his own power,' or ' by his own word of power.'

Thus is the royal function of Christ set out to the life.

Sec. 26. *Of Christ's sufficiency for his priesthood.*

The manner of expressing the fore-mentioned excellencies of Christ is observable: they are set down in participles thus, ' who being, ὢν, the brightness,' &c., and ' upholding, φέρων, all things,' &c. This sheweth that they have relation to that which follows, and that as an especial cause thereof. Now that which follows, sets out Christ's priesthood, and that in both the parts thereof, which are, 1, expiation of our sins; 2, intercession at God's right hand.

For the full effecting of these, divine dignity and ability were requisite. Therefore to give evidence of Christ's sufficiency to that great function, he premiseth that excellent description of Christ's dignity and dominion, and that in such a manner, as shews him to be a most able and sufficient priest. For these phrases, ' being the brightness,' and ' upholding all things,' imply the ground of this sufficiency, as if he had more fully and plainly said, Seeing Christ is, or because he is, the brightness, &c. And because he upholdeth all things, &c. By himself he purgeth our sins; and having done that, he sat down on the right hand of the Majesty on high. Had he not been such a brightness, and had he not had such power as to uphold all things, he could not have purged away our sins (this work required a divine efficacy), nor could he have sat at God's right hand. This advancement required a divine dignity. Thus we see what respect the apostle had to the order of his words, and manner of framing his phrases.

Sec. 27. *Of Christ's purging.*

From the regal function of Christ, the apostle proceeds to his priesthood; the first part whereof is noted in these words, *When he had by himself purged our sins.*

The purging here mentioned, compriseth under it the expiation which Christ made by his death on the cross, which was an especial act of his priestly function, for it belonged to the priests under the law to offer up sacrifices, whereby expiation was made for people's sins.

The metaphor of *purging* is taken from the law, for ' almost all things are by the law purged with blood,' Heb. ix. 22. The word[1] here used is sometimes put for the *means* of purging, John ii. 6, and sometimes for the act itself of being purged, Mark i. 44. To *make purgation* (as the Greek phrase here soundeth), is to do that which is sufficient to purge, and by a metonymy of the cause, it also implieth the very act of purging. Now Christ, by shedding his blood, hath done that which is sufficient to purge away sin; yea, that which he hath done, doth indeed purge the soul, when it is rightly applied. In both these respects it is said, ' The blood of Christ cleanseth from all sin,' 1 John i. 7.

The purging therefore here meant, compriseth under it both the merit of Christ's sacrifice, whereby the guilt and punishment of sin is taken away, and also the efficacy thereof, whereby the power and dominion of sin is subdued.

This word *purged*, expounds two words of the original Greek, καθαρισμὸν ποιησάμενος, which the Rhemists, in imitation of the vulgar Latin, translating, as they suppose *verbatim*, word for word, do extenuate the

---

[1] καθαρισμὸς. See Chap. ix. 13, Sec. 75.

sense and come short of the mind of the apostle. They translate it thus, *purgationem peccatorum faciens*, making purgation of sins. Herein first they miss the emphasis of the tense, *aoristum prius medii*, which implieth a thing finished. The Latins wanting that tense, are forced to use the passive, and to change the case, thus, *purgatione facta*,[1] or a periphrasis, by premising a conjunction of the time past, thus, *postquam purgationem fecisset*. So our English, 'when he had purged;' very fitly according to the sense. But we have in our tongue a particle, which, joined to the verb, doth fully express the emphasis of the tense and voice, thus, *having purged*. Besides, they that translate it by the present tense, thus, 'making purgation,' imply that Christ is still tempering the medicine, as if the purgation were not absolutely finished while Christ was on earth. I deny not but that Christ still continueth to apply the merit and efficacy of this purgation; but there is difference betwixt making and applying a thing.

The verb καθαρίζω, whence the Greek word καθαρισμός is derived, is sometimes put for cleansing or purging the soul from the guilt of sin, and it importeth justification, and is distinguished from sanctification; as, where it is said, that Christ gave himself for the church, 'that he might sanctify it, having cleansed,' or purged it, ἵνα αὐτὴν ἁγιάσῃ, καθαρίσας, Eph. v. 26.[2] Sometimes it is put for purging the soul from the inherent filth of sin; as, where it is said, Christ gave himself for us, 'that he might redeem us from all iniquity' (this notes out our justification), 'and purify' or purge us, καὶ καθαρίσῃ, Titus ii. 14, this notes out our sanctification. And sometimes it compriseth under it both these benefits, as where mention is made of God's purifying or purging our hearts by faith, τῇ πίστει καθαρίσας τὰς καρδίας, Acts xv. 9. Faith applies the merit of Christ's sacrifice for our justification, and draws virtue from him for our sanctification. In this last and largest signification is this metaphor of purging here used, whereby it appears that Christ's purging is a perfect purging.

Sec. 28. *Of our sins purged by Christ.*

To discover the filth that by Christ is purged away, the purgation here mentioned is styled a purgation of sins,[3] ἁμαρτιῶν. Sin is the worst filth that ever besmeared a creature. It makes the creature loathsome and odious in God's sight. It makes it most wretched and cursed, for it pulleth upon the sinner God's wrath, which is an unsupportable burden, and presseth the soul down to hell. By sin angels of light became devils, and by reason of sin they are called foul and unclean spirits, Mark ix. 25, Rev. xviii. 2, Mat. x. 1. By purging away this kind of filth, Christ's sacrifice is distinguished from all the legal sacrifices and purifications. None of them can purge away sin. Sin makes too deep a stain even into the very soul of man to be purged away by an external and earthly thing. That which the apostle saith, Heb. x. 4, ' of the blood of bulls and goats,' which were the greatest and most efficacious sacrifices of the law, may be said of all external means of purifying. It is not possible that they should take away sins; therefore they are said to 'sanctify to the purifying of the flesh,' Heb. ix. 13, not to the purifying of the soul.

Quest. Was not legal uncleanness a sinful pollution?

Ans. Not simply as it was legal; that is, as by the ceremonial law it was judged uncleanness. For,

1. There were sundry personal diseases which by that law made those that were infected therewith unclean, as leprosy, Lev. xiii. 3, running of the reins, Lev. xxii. 4, issue from the flesh, Lev. xv. 2, and other the like.

2. There were also natural infirmities, which were counted uncleanness, yet not sins in themselves, as women's ordinary flowers, Lev. xv. 33, their lying in childhood, Lev. xii. 2.

3. Casual matters that fell out unawares, and could not be avoided, caused uncleanness, Lev. v. 2, Num. xix. 14.

4. So also did sundry bounden duties; for the priest who slew and burnt the red cow, and he who gathered up her ashes, were unclean; yea, and he who touched a dead corpse (which some were bound to do for a decent burial thereof), Num. xix. 7, 10, 11.

Quest. 2. Was it not a sin to remain in such uncleanness, and not to be cleansed from it?

Ans. It was; and thereupon he that purified not himself was to be cut off, Num. xix. 13, 26. But this sin was not simply in the legal uncleanness, but in the contempt of that order which God had prescribed, Lev. xxii. 9, or at least in neglect of God's ordinance.

The like may be said of an unclean person touching any holy thing, Lev. xxii. 3. It was sin if he came to knowledge of it, Lev. v. 3, because therein he wittingly transgressed God's ordinance.

Quest. 3. Were not sins also taken away by the oblation of legal sacrifices?

Ans. True it is, that by the offering up of those sacrifices, people were assured of the pardon of sin, but not as they were external things, but as they were types of the all-sufficient sacrifice of Christ. It was then people's faith in the mystical substance of those sacrifices (which was Christ) whereby they came to assurance of the pardon of sin.

It therefore remains a true conclusion, that sin is purged away by Christ's sacrifice alone; so as herein the sacrifice of Christ surpasseth all other sacrifices.

Whereas the apostle further addeth this relative par-

---

[1] Transferri poterat, *purgatione peccatorum facta*, ne sedendo videatur purgare. Prius enim purgavit morte sua, deinde consedit.—*Eras. Annot. in hunc loc.*

[2] See Domest. Dut. Treat. i., sec. 86.

[3] Of the notation of this word see Chap. viii. ver. 12, Sec. 76; see Chap. x. ver. 12, Sec. 35.

ticle ἡμῶν, *our*,—' our sins,'—he maketh a difference therein also betwixt the priests under the law, with their sacrifices, and Christ with his. For they offered for their own sins, Lev. xvi. 6, as well as for others; but Christ had no sin of his own to offer for. His sacrifice was to purge away *our* sins; *our* sins only, not his own. Thus is this phrase to be taken exclusively in relation to Christ himself; but in relation to others, inclusively: none, no, not the best, excepted. For the apostle, using the plural number indefinitely, includes all of all sorts, and, using the first person, puts in also himself, though an apostle, and so one of the most eminent Christians.

Sec. 29. *Of Christ's purging our sins by himself.*

A third difference betwixt Christ and the legal priest is in the sacrifice by which the one and the other purged people. The priest's sacrifice was of unreasonable beasts; Christ of himself: he ' by himself purged our sins.'

The first particle of this verse, ὅς, *who*, having reference to that excellent person who is described in the words before it and after it, noteth out the priest. This clause, δι' ἑαυτοῦ, *by himself*, sheweth the sacrifice or means of purging. The Son of God,[1] the creator of all things, the sustainer and governor of all, is the priest; and this priest offered himself, and so by himself purged our sins.

True it is that the human nature of Christ only was offered up, whereupon it is said that he was ' put to death in the flesh,' 1 Peter iii. 18, and ' suffered for us in the flesh,' 1 Peter iv. 1; yet by reason of the hypostatical union of his two natures in one person, he is said to ' give himself,' Eph. v. 2, and to ' offer up himself,' Heb. vii. 27; and thereupon it is said that ' he put away sin by the sacrifice of himself,' Heb. ix. 26; and, as here, purged our sins by himself. Forasmuch as it was impossible that the Word should die, being the immortal Son of the Father, he assumed a body that he might die for all, and yet remain the incorruptible Word.[2]

Great is the emphasis of that phrase; it sheweth that this work of purging our sins was above human strain, though an human act, or rather passion, were requisite thereto, as to suffer, to shed blood, to die; yet a divine value and virtue must needs accompany the same, to purge sin. It must be done even by him himself, who is God-man. He himself must be offered up. In which respect it is said that God ' hath purchased the church with his own blood,' Acts xx. 28.

This title *himself*, having reference to that person who

[1] See more hereof in Domest. Duties, treat. 1, sec. 31, on Eph. v. 25.
[2] Cum non esset possibile ipsum Verbum mori, quippe immortalem patris filium, corpus sibi quod mori possit accepit, ita corpus Verbi particeps factum, et moreretur pro omnibus, et inhabitans Verbum incorruptibile maneret.—*Athanas. lib. de Incarn.*

is both God and man, includes both the natures. This person, *himself*, offered up *himself* to purge our sins *by himself*. This is a great mystery; the like was never heard of. The priest that offereth, the sacrifice that is offered, one and the same. The same mystery is implied under this phrase, Christ 'sanctified the people with his own blood,' Heb. xiii. 12. But this of sanctifying or purging with or by himself hath the greater emphasis. More cannot be said to set out the invaluable price of our redemption, the indelible stain of sin, and available means of purging it. See Chap. ix. 12, Sec. 57.

Sec. 30. *Of Christ's glory after his suffering.*

A fourth difference betwixt Christ and the Levitical priesthood, is in these words, *He sat down at the right hand of the Majesty on high.*

Hereby is implied a continuance of Christ's priesthood after his death. This is denied of the priesthood under the law, chap. vii. 23. But Christ having by his death offered up a sufficient sacrifice for all our sins, and by his burial sanctified the grave, and that estate wherein the bodies of believers after death are detained till the day of consummating all things, rose from the dead, and ascended into heaven, there to continue an high priest for ever.

This then notes out another part of Christ's priesthood. The former was of subjection and suffering, this of dignity and reigning. By that was the work wrought, and price laid down; by this is the efficacy and virtue thereof applied, and the benefit conferred.

Fitly is this added to the former, to shew that Christ was so far from being vanquished and swallowed up by his sufferings for our sins, as thereby way was made for an entrance into the highest degree of glory that could be attained unto.

Sec. 31. *Of Christ's sitting and standing in heaven.*

The apostle, in setting down the high degree of Christ's exaltation, well poised his words, for every word hath its weight.

This, ἐκάθισεν, *he sat down*, importeth high honour, and a settled continuance therein. Sitting is a posture of dignity:[1] superiors sit when inferiors stand, Job xxix. 7, 8. Thus is 'the Ancient of days,' said to sit; and ten thousand thousands (ministering spirits) to stand before him, Dan. vii. 9, 10. In way of honour is the Highest thus set out, ' He that sitteth upon the throne,' Rev. v. 13. In this sense saith God to his Son, 'Sit at my right hand,' Ps. cx. 1. The authority also and power which Christ hath over all is hereby noted. For in this sense is this phrase oft used, as Ps. ix. 4, and xxix. 10, and xlvii. 8, Rev. xxi. 5.

Obj. Christ is said to stand on the right hand of God, Acts vii. 55.

[1] Sedere magistri demonstrat personam.—*Aug. lib. lxxx. Quæst.* q. 64. Sedere Dei est potentialiter super omnem creaturam rationalem præsidere.—*Aug. de essent. divin.*

Ans. Divers phrases may be used of the same thing in divers respects, and imply no contradiction; for, first, to speak according to the letter, a king may be said to sit on his throne, because that is his ordinary posture; and to stand at some special times; as Eglon arose out of his seat when Ehud said to him, I have a message from God to thee, Judges iii. 20.

There are three limitations wherein different acts cannot be attributed to the same thing.

1. In the same part, κατὰ τὸ αὐτὸ, *secundum idem.* In the very same part a man cannot be sore and sound.

2. In the same respect, πρὸς τὸ αὐτὸ, *ad idem*, a man cannot be alive and dead together in the same respect, but in different respects one may be so; for 'she that liveth in pleasure is dead while she liveth,' 1 Tim. v. 6.

3. At the same time, ἐν τῷ αὐτῷ χρόνῳ, *eodem tempore*, one cannot sit and stand together at the same time; at several times he may.

Again, to take this phrase metaphorically (as it is here to be taken), Christ may be said to sit, to shew his authority (as before); and to stand, to shew his readiness to hear and help.[1] In this respect did Christ most fitly present himself standing to Stephen, Acts vii. 55.

Sitting doth further set out continuance in a thing:[2] where Jacob saith of Joseph, 'His bow sat in strength,' ותשב, *et sedit*, we fitly, according to the true sense, translate it thus, 'his bow abode,' &c., Gen. xlix. 24. In like manner where Moses saith to Aaron and his sons, 'ye shall sit at the door of the tabernacle seven days,' we, according to the true meaning of the word in that place, thus turn it, 'ye shall abide,' Lev. viii. 35.

Standing also importeth as much, namely, continuance and perseverance in a thing.[3] To express this emphasis of the word, we do oft translate it thus, 'stand fast;' as 1 Cor. xvi. 13, 'Stand fast in the faith;' and Gal. v. 1, 'Stand fast in the liberty,' &c. Where the original Greek saith of the devil, John viii. 44, 'he stood not in the truth,' our English hath it thus, 'he abode not,' &c.

Wherefore by both these metaphors (sitting and standing) Christ's abode and continuance in heaven, as our high priest, prince, and prophet, and that for us, is plainly set out.

And to shew that this, his abode and continuance, hath no set date, this indefinite and everlasting phrase, *for ever*, is in other places added; as chap. vii. 25, and x. 12.

Finally, These metaphors note out Christ's rest and cessation from all his travails, labours, services, sufferings, and works of ministry, which on earth he underwent. Christ is now entered into rest, and so sitteth.

This implieth that nothing now remaineth more to be done or endured for purchase of man's redemption, his sacrifice was full and perfect; therefore going out of the world, he saith, 'It is finished,' John xix. 30.

Sec. 32. *Of the divine Majesty.*

To amplify the fore-mentioned dignity and sovereignty of Christ, the place where Christ sitteth is set out in two phrases:

1. 'On the right hand of the Majesty.'
2. 'On high.'

By the *Majesty* is meant God himself, as more plainly is expressed in other places, where Christ is said to be 'at the right hand of God,' Rom. viii. 34, and to be 'set down on the right hand of God,' Heb. x. 12.

Majesty, μεγαλωσύνη, importeth such greatness and excellency as makes one to be honoured of all, and preferred before all. It is a title proper to kings, who, in their dominions, are above all and over all. By way of excellency[1] a king is styled majesty itself;[2] as when we speak of a king, we say, *His Majesty*; when to him, *Your Majesty*. A word like to this coming from the same root, μεγαλειότης, Acts xix. 27, is translated 'magnificence,' which also is applied to God, and translated, as the word here, *Majesty*, 2 Peter i. 16.

To none can this title be so properly applied as to God himself, for all created greatness and excellency is derived from, and dependeth upon, God's greatness and excellency. Whereas majesty is attributed to created monarchs, it is because they bear God's image, and stand in God's stead. In this respect they are also styled *gods*, Ps. lxxxii. 6.

In this place this title is used,

1. To set out the high and supreme sovereignty of God, importing him to be 'King of kings, and Lord of lords;' for, to speak properly, God only hath majesty; and therefore by a property is styled the Majesty.

2. To magnify the exaltation of Christ, which is the highest degree that possibly can be, even to the right hand of him, or next to him, that only and justly is styled the Majesty.

3. To shew an especial end of Christ's high advancement, which was to reign and rule. This is the property of majesty; and for this end was Christ advanced next to the Majesty.

This is further evident by the addition of this word *throne*, as some do read it, thus, 'He sat down on the right hand of the throne of the Majesty on high.'[3]

---

[1] *Sedere judicantis est: stare adjuvantis.*—*Greg. Mag. Hom.* 29, *in. fest. ascen.* vide plura *ibid.* Stare Deus dicitur cum infirmos sustinet, &c. Stetit ad subveniendum.—*Aug. de Essent. Divin.*

[2] *Locutio Scripturarum sessionem pro commoratione posuit.*—*Aug. quæst. super Lev.* lib. iii. cap. xxiv. *Vide plura ibid. hac de re.*

[3] *Quid est, qui statis?* Qui perseveratis: quia dicitur de quodam qui archangelus fuit, et in veritate stetit.—*Aug. enarr.* n Ps cxxxiii.

---

[1] κατ' ἐξοχὴν. [2] *In abstracto.*

[3] ἐκάθισεν ἐν δεξιᾷ τοῦ θρόνου τῆς μεγαλωσύνης ἐν ὑψηλοῖς.—*Complut. codex.* Of Christ's throne, see Ver. 8, Sec. 106.

So is it read, chaps. viii. 1 and xii. 2, and that with an unanimous consent of all copies; so in Mat. xix. 28, and xxv. 31, and Acts ii. 30. So much also is here without question intended.

Now to sit on a throne of majesty, is to have power of reigning and ruling. This is yet further made clear by the end which the Holy Ghost setteth down hereof, Ps. cx. 1, which is to subdue his enemies; wherefore the apostle thus explaineth that phrase, 1 Cor. xv. 25, 'He must reign till he hath put all his enemies under his feet.' For *sitting on the right hand of Majesty*, the apostle puts *reigning*. So as to *sit on the right hand of Majesty*, and to *reign*, are equivalent terms.

Sec. 33. *Of Christ's advancement to God's right hand.*

This phrase *right hand*, attributed to God, must needs be metaphorically spoken; for God is not a body, nor hath any parts of a body properly appertaining unto him. He is a simple, pure, spiritual, indivisible essence. To imagine that God hath a body, or any parts of a body properly, is to make him no God.[1] Whosoever doth conceit any such thing of God, doth frame an idol for God in his heart. Such things are attributed to God in sacred Scripture for teaching's sake, to make us somewhat the better conceive divine things by such human resemblances as are familiar to us, and we well acquainted withal.

As for this particular metaphor of a *right hand*, it is very frequently attributed to God; and that in two respects:

1. To set out his power; 2. his glory.

There is no part of the body whereby men can better manifest their power than by their right hand. By their hands they lift, they strike, they do the things which require and declare strength. Of the two hands, the right useth to be the more ready, steady, and strong, in acting this or that. Therefore after the manner of men, ἀνθρωποπαθῶς, thus speaketh Moses of God, 'Thy right hand, O Lord, is become glorious in power: thy right hand, O Lord, hath dashed in pieces the enemy,' Exod. xv. 6. In like manner many admirable works are in other places attributed to God's right hand, that is, to his power.

Again, Because God's majesty is of all the most glorious, his right hand is accounted the greatest glory that can be.[2] In this latter respect is the metaphor here used. It is taken from monarchs, whose throne is the highest place for dignity in a kingdom.

To set one at the right hand of his majesty, is to advance him above all subjects, next to the king himself: as Pharaoh said to Joseph, Gen. xli. 40, 'Thou shalt be over my house, and according to thy word shall all my people be ruled: only in the throne will I be greater than thou.'

In places of state, the middle useth to be the highest; the right hand the next, the left the third.[1] In this respect the mother of Zebedee's children, leaving to Christ the highest place, desireth that one of her sons might be at his right hand, the other at his left, in his kingdom, Mat. xx. 21. Solomon, to shew he preferred his mother before all his subjects, set her on his right hand, 1 Kings ii. 16. So doth Christ manifest his respect to his spouse, Ps. xlv. 9. So doth God here in this place to his Son. For to sit on the right hand of the divine Majesty, is the highest honour that any can be advanced to.

Sec. 34. *Of Christ advanced as God-man.*

Christ's advancement is properly of his human nature.[2] For 'the Son of man' is said to sit at God's right hand, Mat. xxvi. 64, and Stephen with his bodily eyes saw him there, Acts vii. 56. That nature wherein Christ was crucified, was exalted;[3] for God, being the Most High, needs not be exalted.[4] Yet the human nature, in this exaltation, is not singly and simply considered in itself, but united to the Deity; so as it is the person, consisting of two natures, even God-man, which is thus dignified, next to God, far above all mere creatures. For as the human nature of Christ is inferior to God, and is capable of advancement, so also the person, consisting of a divine and human nature. Christ, as the Son of God, the second person in the sacred Trinity, is in regard of his deity no whit inferior to his Father, but every way equal; yet as he assumed our nature, and became a mediator betwixt God and man, he humbled himself, and made himself inferior to his Father. His Father therefore exalted him above all creatures, Philip. ii. 8, 9. The Scripture expressly testifieth that the Father advanced his Son; for he said to his Son, 'Sit at my right hand,' Ps. cx. 1. 'He set him at his right hand,' Eph. i. 20. 'God exalted him,' Acts v. 31. 'God hath given him a name which is above every name,' Philip. ii. 9. Now he that giveth is greater than he that receiveth.[5]

Sec. 35. *Of heaven the place of Christ's exaltation.*

The place where Christ is exalted is here indefinitely set down to be 'on high,' ἐν ὑψηλοῖς. Though

---

[1] Si quis in Deo humana membra, seu motus animæ more humano inesse credit, proculdubio in corde suo idola fabricat.—*Aug. de Essent. Divinit.*

[2] Dextra domini gloriam Patris significat.—*Aug. de Essent. Divinit.*

[1] Ad dextram locari magnus est honos habitus, in medio verò maximus.—*Alex.* l. ii. *Genial. dierum.*

[2] Beatitudinis Christi munera acquisita non possunt secundum quod natura Deus est, sed secundum quod natura homo factus est convenire.—*Vigil. cont. Eutych.* lib. v.

[3] In qua forma crucifixus est, ipsa exaltatus est.—*Aug. contr. Maxim.*

[4] Ὁ Θεὸς ὑψωθῆναι οὐ δεῖται, ὕψιστος ὤν.—*Greg. Nys. cont. Eunom.*

[5] In statu exaltationis Pater Filium ad dextram suam collocavit, eique nomen donavit, &c. Donans autem major est accipiente donum.—*Hilar. de Trin.* lib. ix.

the word be but of the positive degree, yet is it to be understood of the highest degree that can be; so high as none higher. Therefore the superlative degree is elsewhere used to set out the very same place that is here meant; as where the angels say, glory to God in the highest, ἐν ὑψίστοις, Luke ii. 14. The apostle, to shew that this place, and withal this dignity whereunto Christ was exalted, far surpasseth all other, useth a compound word, ὑπερύψωσε, which is not throughout all the New Testament used, but in this only case; and it implieth an exaltation above all other exaltations. The word is used Philip. ii. 9; it may be thus translated, ' super-exalted.' Our English, to express the emphasis of that compound word, useth these two words, ' highly exalted.' If ever any were highly exalted, much more Christ. Therefore other translators[1] thus express the foresaid emphasis, exalted into the highest height. The word is used to set out the highest exaltation that can be, even beyond all expression or comprehension.

To shew that Christ's exaltation is indeed a super-exaltation, the apostle advanceth it far above all other, even the highest and most excellent creatures that be, Eph. i. 21. Thus he is said to be ' higher than the heavens.' See Chap. vii. 26, Sec. 110.

More expressly this supereminent place is said to be the *heavens*, ἐν τοῖς οὐρανοῖς,[2] chap. viii. 1. The plural number is used to shew that he meaneth the highest heavens; that which in Canaan's dialect is styled the heaven of heavens, 2 Chron. ii. 6, and vi. 18, Neh. ix. 6, even that which compriseth in it all the other heavens, it being over all. In relation to two inferior heavens, it is styled ' the third heaven,' 2 Cor. xii. 2. For the Scripture maketh mention of three heavens. The first and lowest is the airy heaven, in which feathered fowls fly, Gen. i. 8; the second and middlemost is the starry heaven, in which the sun, the moon, and all the stars are contained, Gen. xv. 5; the third and highest is that where Christ now sitteth. This distinction giveth light to that phrase, ' far above all heavens,' Eph. iv. 10, whereby the supereminent height of Christ's exaltation is set forth. He there meaneth all the visible heavens, whether under or above the moon. For the human nature of Christ is contained within the third heaven, Acts iii. 21.

This place, as well as the other fore-mentioned points, amplifieth the exaltation of Christ.

Sum up the particulars, and we shall find verified what was said before, that every word hath its weight, and adds something to the excellency of Christ's exaltation.

1. He *sits:* namely as a Lord; and so continueth.
2. He sits by the *Majesty:* a great honour.

3. He sits on the *right hand* of the Majesty; next to him above all others.

4. He so sits *on high:* namely, as high as can be.

' When he had by himself purged our sins' (to do which, he humbled himself and became obedient unto death, even the death of the cross, Philip. ii. 8), ' he sat down on the right hand of the Majesty on high.'

Hitherto of the meaning of the words. The analysis or resolution of the three first verses followeth.

Sec. 36. *Of the resolution of the three first verses.*

Ver. 1. The three first verses of the first chapter contain the substance of all those mysteries which are more largely prosecuted in the body of the epistle.

The sum of all is, the excellency of the gospel.

The argument whereby the apostle doth demonstrate this point is comparative. The comparison is of unequals; which are the law and the gospel.

This kind of argument the apostle doth here the rather use, because of that high account which the Hebrews had of the law.

1. The comparison is first propounded in the first verse and former part of the second verse.

2. It is amplified in the latter part of the second verse.

In the proposition the apostle declares two points:
1. Wherein the law and the gospel agree.
2. Wherein they differ.

They agree in two things:
1. In the principal author, which is God: ' God spake in time past;' and ' God hath spoken in these last days.'
2. They agree in the general matter, which is, a declaration of God's will, implied under this word ' spake,' or ' hath spoken.'

The distinct points wherein they differ are five:
1. The *measure* of that which was revealed. Then God's will was revealed part by part; one part at one time and another at another; but under the gospel all at once.
2. The *manner* of revealing it: then after divers manners; under the gospel after one constant manner.
3. The *time:* that was the old time, which was to be translated into another, even a better time; this is styled ' the last days,' which shall have no better after them in this world.
4. The *subject*, or persons to whom the one and the other was delivered.

The former were ' the fathers,' so called by reason of their antiquity; but yet children who were in bondage under the elements of the world, Gal. iv. 3. The latter are comprised under this phrase ' unto us:' the least of whom is greater than the greatest of the fathers, Mat. xi. 11.

5. The *ministers* by whom the one and the other were delivered: the law by prophets; the gospel by the Son.

Ver. 2. The amplification of the comparison is by

---

[1] In summam'tulit sublimitatem.—*Beza.* ὑπερυψόω, Exalto supra quam dici possit.

[2] In regia cœlorum sedet Jesus ad dextram Patris.—*Tertul. de Resur. carn.*

a description of the Son, and that by his excellency and dignity. This is the main substance of the greatest part of this epistle; as it is in this and the next verse propounded, so it is prosecuted and further proved in the other verses of this chapter.

In these two verses Christ is set out,
1. By his relation to his Father.
2. By his divine works.

His relation is noted, 1, simply; 2, comparatively.

Simply under two titles:

The first title is *Son:* ' his Son;' this pointeth at the divine essence.

The second title, *heir:* this pointeth to his right of sovereignty; and it is amplified, 1, by the ground thereof, in this phrase, ' whom he hath appointed;' 2, by the extent thereof, in this, ' all things.'

Ver. 3. The comparative relation is in two resemblances:

1. *Brightness:* amplified by the surpassing excellency thereof, in this phrase, ' of his glory.'
2. *Character*, or *express image:* illustrated under this phrase, ' of his person.'

The works whereby Christ's excellency is described are of two sorts:
1. They are such as appertain to his divine nature.
2. Such as appertain to his mediatorship.

Of the former two sorts are mentioned: 1, creation; 2, providence.

Creation is set forth,
1. By the manner of working; in this phrase, *by whom.*
2. By the general matter, *the worlds.*

Providence is hinted in this word *upholding.* It is further illustrated by the extent, *all things;* and by the means, *the word:* amplified by the power thereof, *of his power.*

In Christ's work appertaining to his mediatorship, observe,
1. The order, in this phrase, *when he had.*
2. The kinds. These concern, 1, Christ's humiliation; 2, his exaltation.

A special work of Christ's humiliation was to *purge.*

This is amplified, 1, by the means, *by himself;* 2, by the matter, *our sins.*

In Christ's exaltation is set down,
1. His act, *sat down.*
2. The place. This is noted, 1, indefinitely, *on high;* 2, determinately, at the *right hand.*

This is amplified by the person at whose right hand he sat, thus expressed, *of the majesty.*

Sec. 37. *Of the heads of doctrines raised out of the 1st verse.*

I. *God is the author of the Old Testament.* That which the apostle here setteth down in this first verse is concerning such things as are registered in the Old Testament, of which he saith, ' God spake;' so as the Old Testament is of divine authority.

II. *God hath been pleased to make known his will.* This word *spake* intendeth as much. God's will is a secret kept close in himself, till he be pleased to make it known. In this respect it is said, that ' No man hath seen God at any time,' John i. 18; that is, no man hath known his mind, namely, till God make it known.

III. *Of old God made known his will by parts,* One time one part, another time another part, namely, as the church had need thereof, and as God in his wisdom saw it meet to be revealed.

IV. *God's will was of old made known divers ways.* Of the divers ways, see Sec. 11; for God ever accommodated himself to the capacity of his people.

V. *God's will was made known to men even from the beginning.* So far, even to the beginning, may this phrase, *in time past,* be extended. Thus the church was never without some means or other of knowing the will of God.

VI. *The Old Testament was for such as lived in ancienter times,* even before the fulness of time came, who are here called *fathers;* who, together with their seed, were but a little part of the world.

VII. *God made sons of men to be his ministers before Christ's time.* Thus much is intended under this word *prophets,* as here opposed to the Son of God. To them God first made known his mind, that they should declare it to his people.

VIII. *God endued his choice ministers with extraordinary gifts.* This word *prophets* intendeth as much.

All these points are more fully opened, Sect. 11.

Sec. 38. *Of the heads of doctrines raised out of the 2d verse.*

IX. *The best things are reserved for the last times.* The opposition which the apostle here maketh betwixt the time past and these last days, demonstrateth as much.

X. *The gospel also is of divine authority.* It is the gospel which the apostle intendeth under this phrase ' hath spoken;' and it hath reference to God, mentioned in the former verse.

XI. *The gospel was revealed to men by the Son of God.* God spake by his Son. The Son of God incarnate was the first publisher of the gospel, John i. 18.

XII. *Under the gospel, God's whole will is revealed.* Herein lieth the opposition betwixt that phrase, ' at sundry times,' ver. 1, being spoken of God's former dispensing of his will by parts, and his revealing of it under the gospel, John xiv. 26, Acts xx. 27. Hereupon a curse is denounced against such as shall teach any other gospel, Gal. i. 8, 9; and against such as shall take from or add to this gospel, Rev. xxii. 18, 19.

XIII. *Under the gospel, there is one only way of making known God's will.* This appears by the opposition of this phrase, ver. 1, 'in divers manners.' That only way is preaching, as hath been before shewed, Sec. 11.

XIV. *Christ was a prophet*, for God spake by him. He was (as he is styled, Luke vii. 16) a great prophet.

XV. *Christ hath an absolute jurisdiction.* He is an heir; an heir to the great King of heaven and earth. This sets forth Christ's kingly office.

XVI. *Christ as mediator received his dominion from his Father.* He 'appointed him heir.'

XVII. *Christ's dominion extendeth itself to all things.* This is expressly set down under this phrase, 'Heir of all things,' Ps. ii. 8.

XVIII. *Christ is the Creator*, John i. 2; Col. i. 16.

XIX. *The Father created by the Son.* This is expressly here set down, and it is to be taken in respect of the distinction that is betwixt their persons, and the order of their working. The Father worketh by the Son, and the Son from the Father.

XX. *All things in heaven and earth were created by the Son.* The word *worlds* implieth as much; for the plural number is used, to shew that the world above, and the world beneath,—even heaven, and all things therein, and earth, and all things therein,—were created by him.

Sec. 39. *Of the heads of doctrines raised out of the 3d verse.*

XXI. *Divine mysteries may be illustrated by sensible resemblances.* These two resemblances, *brightness, character*, are for that end here produced. There is in many visible and sensible creatures a kind of divine stamp. In that they are sensible, we that are best acquainted with visible and sensible matters are much helped in apprehending things mystical that are any ways like them.

XXII. *The Son is of the same essence with the Father.*

XXIII. *The Son is light of light, very God of very God.*

XXIV. *The Son is co-eternal with the Father.*

XXV. *The person of the Son is distinct from the person of the Father.*

XXVI. *The incomprehensible glory of the Father most brightly shineth forth in the Son*, so as the Father is made conspicuous in the Son.

These and other like mysteries are very pertinently set forth under these two resemblances, *brightness, character*; whereof see Sec. 19, &c.

XXVII. *Christ is the preserver and governor of all things.* This phrase, *upholding all things*, intendeth as much.

XXVIII. *Christ ordereth all things by his command.* The Greek word translated *word* importeth as much. See Sec. 25.

XXIX. *Christ's command is irresistible.* It is here styled 'the word of his power,' whereby he disposeth all things according to his own will, Ps. cxv. 3.

XXX. *Christ is a true priest.* The act of *purging*, applied to him, demonstrateth as much. For it is proper to a priest to purge, Lev. xiv. 14, &c., and xvi. 16.

XXXI. *Christ was a true man.* This phrase, *by himself*, sheweth that the sacrifice by which Christ purged was himself, namely, his body, or his human nature. For Christ 'hath given himself for us an offering and a sacrifice to God,' Eph. v. 2.

XXXII. *Christ was God and man in one person.* As man, he suffered and was made a sacrifice; as God, he added much merit to his sacrifice, as it purged away sin, chap. ix. 14.

XXXIII. *Christ's sacrifice was effectual to take away sin.* For it is directly said that 'he purged our sins,' chap. ix. 14.

XXXIV. *Christ was exalted after he had humbled himself.* His purging sin, implieth his humbling of himself unto death. When he had done this, then he sat, &c. This implieth his exaltation, Luke xxiv. 26, 46, Philip. ii. 8, 9.

XXXV. *Christ having finished his sufferings, ceased to suffer any more.* He sat down and rested, Rom. vi. 9, 10. As God, when he had finished all the works of creation, rested, Gen. ii. 2, Heb. iv. 10, so Christ after his sufferings.

XXXVI. *Christ as our priest ever presents himself before God for us*, namely, to make intercession for us. Christ's sitting implieth abode. This abode being at God's right hand, is before God, even in his sight. This is he that purged our sins, therefore he is there as our priest, and to make intercession for us. And because there is no limitation of his sitting or abode, it is to be taken for a perpetual act. All these are plainly expressed in other places, as chap. ix. 24, and x. 12, Rom. viii. 34.

XXXVII. *Christ as mediator is inferior to the Father.* The right hand is below him that sits on the throne, Mark x. 37.

XXXVIII. *Christ as mediator is advanced above all creatures.* The right hand is the next place to him that sits upon the throne, and above all that stand about the throne, as all creatures do, 1 Kings ii. 19, Gen. xli. 40, Eph. i. 20, 21, Philip. ii. 9.

XXXIX. *Christ is a king.* He sits on the right hand of the Majesty, or of the throne of the Majesty, chap. viii. 1. This is a royal kingly seat, Ps. cx. 1, 2, 1 Cor. xv. 25.

XL. *The highest heaven is the place of Christ's rest and glory.* This phrase, *on high*, intendeth as much. It is expressly said, that he is 'set on the right hand of the throne of the Majesty in the heavens,' chap. viii. 1. And it is also said, that 'the heaven must receive him until the time of restitution of all things,' Acts iii. 21.

Sec. 39 [*bis*]. *Of Christ's excellency.*

Ver. 4. *Being made so much better than the angels,*

as he hath by inheritance obtained a more excellent name than they.

Though the apostle premised the three former verses as a *proem,* and therein couched the sum of the doctrinal part of this epistle, yet he passeth from that general sum to the particulars, so as he maketh the one depend upon the other, as is evident by the participle γενόμενος, 'being made,' whereby that which followeth is knit to that which goeth before.

This verse, therefore, is a transition from the general to the particulars; for it followeth as a just consequence and necessary conclusion from the premises; and it is promised as the principal proposition of all that followeth in this chapter.

The excellency of Christ's person is the principal point proved from this verse to the end of this chapter, and that by an argument of unequals. The inequality is betwixt Christ and angels; he is infinitely preferred before them.

The apostle in the former verses proved Christ to be more excellent than the excellentest men; even such as God extraordinarily inspired with his holy Spirit, and to whom he immediately revealed his will, that they might make it known to others. Such were the patriarchs, prophets, and the heads of the people. But these, as all other men, notwithstanding their excellencies, were on earth mortal. Therefore he ascendeth higher, and culleth out the celestial and immortal spirits, which are called angels.

Angels are of all mere creatures the most excellent. If Christ then be more excellent than the most excellent, he must needs be the most excellent of all. This excellency of Christ is so set out, as thereby the glory and royalty of Christ's kingly office is magnified. For this is the first of Christ's offices which the apostle doth in particular exemplify: in which exemplification he giveth many proofs of Christ's divine nature, and sheweth him so to be man as he is God also; and in the next chapter, so to be God as he is man also: 'like to his brethren,' chap. ii. 17.

The comparison here made betwixt Christ and angels, is not a mere simple comparison, thus, Christ is more excellent than angels; but it is comparatively propounded as a comparison of a comparison, thus: Christ is 'so much better than angels, as he hath obtained a more excellent name.'[1] This comparative comparison much sets out the transcendency of the point, that he is beyond all comparisons, even infinitely better.

The word translated made, γενόμενος, is sometimes used declaratively, to shew that the thing spoken of is so and so, as where it is said, 'when Jesus was in Bethany,' Ιησοῦ γενομένου ἐν Βηθανίᾳ, Mat. xxvi. 6; and sometimes efficiently, as where it is said, Jesus was 'made an high priest,' ἀρχιερεὺς γενόμενος, Heb. vi. 20. Howsoever, this word, in relation to Christ's deity, cannot be taken but in the first sense only, declaratively; yet in regard of his human nature, and of his person, consisting of both natures, and of his offices, it may be taken in both senses; for in those three respects he was advanced, and made so and so excellent. Now the apostle speaks of him, not simply as God, but as God-man, king, priest, and prophet. Thus it is fitly and truly translated *being made,* namely, by his Father, who begat him, sent him into the world, and advanced him above all the world.

In this respect he is said to be *better,* that is, more excellent. For this comparison hath not so much relation to the goodness of Christ's person, as to the dignity thereof. In this sense is this word oft used in this epistle, and translated by some 'more excellent.' Yea, chap. vii. 7, it is opposed to less, and so signifieth greater: 'the less is blessed of the better,' that is, the greater in dignity or in office. So in our English, we style such as are more excellent to be better men.

The Greek comparative, κρείττων, is derived from a noun that signifieth *power,* κράτος; but it is frequently used for the comparative of the Greek positive, which signifieth *good,* ἀγαθός, and in that respect it is oft translated *better.* It is a general word, and applied to sundry kinds of excellencies: as to such things as are more commodious, 1 Cor. vii. 38; and more useful to others, 1 Cor. xii. 31; and more beneficial to one's self, Philip. i. 23; and more effectual, Heb. ix. 23; and more comfortable, 1 Peter iii. 17; and less damageable, 2 Peter ii. 21; and more excellent, Heb. x. 34; and more eminent or greater in dignity, Heb. vii. 7; and thus it is here to be taken.

Sec. 40. *Of angels' excellencies.*

The persons before whom Christ is here in excellency preferred, are styled angels: 'better than the angels.'

The signification of this name *angel,* the nature of angels, their special office and quality, is by this our apostle himself distinctly set down, ver. 7. Yet here it is meet that we consider some of the angels' excellencies, that so we may the better discern both the reason why the apostle doth give this instance of angels; and withal the surpassing excellency of Christ, who excels such excellent creatures.

Some of the angels' excellencies are such as follow:

1. *Angels are spirits.* The substance whereof they consist is spiritual. This is the most excellent substance that any creature can have, and that which cometh the nearest to the divine nature; for 'God is a spirit,' John iv. 24. A spirit is of substances the simplest, and freest from mixture and composition; the purest and finest, and every way in the kind of it the most excellent. A spirit is not subject to grossness, drowsiness, weariness, heaviness, faintness, sickness, diminution, alteration, putrefaction, consumption,

---

[1] τοσούτῳ—ὅσῳ. See Chap. vii. 22, Sec. 93.

or any like imperfections, which bodies, as bodies, are subject unto.

2. Angels, as at first created, and so remaining, are *after the image of God*; the purest, holiest, and readiest to all goodness of any mere creature. In regard of their likeness to God, they are styled 'sons of God,' Job i. 6. In regard of their promptness to goodness they are thus set out, 'Ye that do his commandments, hearkening to the voice of his words,' Ps. ciii. 20.

3. Angels are the *most glorious of all God's creatures*. In glory they surpass the brightness of the sun. To set out the glory of an angel, his countenance is said to be like lightning, and his raiment white as snow, and shining, Mat. xxviii. 3, Luke xxiv. 4. Upon an angel's approach into a dark prison, a light is said to shine in the prison, Acts xii. 7. The glory of the Lord (that is, surpassing, incomprehensible glory) is said to shine round about upon the apparition of an angel, Luke ii. 9. So resplendent is an angel's brightness, as it hath much affrighted worthy saints, Luke i. 12 and ii. 9. Yea, St John was so amazed at the apparition of an angel, as he fell at his feet to worship him, Rev. xix. 10 and xxii. 8.

4. Angels have the *highest habitations of all creatures*; far above the moon, sun, and all the glorious host of the highest visible heaven. They are in the invisible heavens, where the divine glory is most conspicuously manifested. In regard of the place of their residency, they are styled 'angels of heaven,' Mat. xxiv. 36.

5. Angels have the most *honourable function*; for 'they always behold the face of God in heaven,' Mat. xviii. 10. They are as the gentlemen of the bedchamber to a king; they minister to the Most High in an especial manner, Dan. vii. 10. Their principal attendance is upon the Son of God made man, John i. 51; and upon his mystical body, ver. 14.

Sec. 41. *Of Christ's excellencies above angels.*

In all the fore-mentioned excellencies is Christ more excellent than angels. For, 1, Christ's divine nature is infinitely more excellent than an angelical spirit; yea, his human nature, by the hypostatical union of it with the divine, hath likewise a dignity infinitely surpassingly an angel's nature.

2. Christ is the express image of the person of his Father, which is more than to be created, as angels were, after God's image.

3. Christ is the brightness of God's glory, therefore more glorious than the most glorious angels.

4. Christ is in heaven, at the right hand of the throne of the Majesty, therefore in place of residency higher than angels.

5. Christ's function, to be a mediator betwixt God and man, is greater than any of the functions of angels.

Therefore Christ is more excellent than angels in their greatest excellencies. Yet there is a greater excellency wherein Christ doth further excel angels, comprised under this phrase, *a more excellent name*. This doth the apostle largely insist upon and copiously prove, and that upon this ground. Superstitious persons, especially the Jews, among whom many extraordinary things were done by the ministry of angels, had in all ages too high an admiration of angels; so as they have deified them, and yielded divine worship unto them, whereby the glory of God hath been obscured, and Christ the less esteemed. It was therefore requisite to set out Christ's glory so as it might appear how, beyond comparison, Christ excelleth them; which in the general is thus expressed, 'He hath by inheritance obtained a more excellent name than they.'

Sec. 42. *Of Christ's name.*

A name is that whereby a thing is made known and distinguished from others, Gen. ii. 19, 20. It is sometimes taken for a mere titular distinction, as where the degenerate and apostate Jews are called the people of God, the children of Israel. God expressly saith, 'They are not my people,' Hosea i. 9; and Christ proveth that they are not Abraham's children, John viii. 39. Where it is said, Micah ii. 7, 'O thou that art named the house of Jacob,' a mere titular name is meant; and where Christ saith of Sardis, 'Thou hast a name that thou livest, and art dead,' Rev. iii. 1.

But the name here spoken of containeth a reality in it, Christ being indeed what he is named and said to be. It is not simply any of his titles, but that true relation which is betwixt God the Father and him; such a relation as no mere creature is capable of. What it is, is expressly set down in the next verse, namely, to be the 'Son of God.' True it is, that through grace and favour, God vouchsafed this name to sundry creatures, but not so properly as unto Christ. See Sec. 15.

This is that 'name which is above every name, at which every knee should bow,' Philip. ii. 9, 10. By virtue of this name, he became a fit mediator between God and man, a fit saviour and redeemer of man, a fit king, priest, and prophet of his church.; yea, and by virtue of this name, supreme sovereignty and absolute dominion over all creatures, infinite majesty, divine dignity, and all honour and glory is his; all worship, service, subjection, and duty is due unto him. This name, therefore, must needs be, beyond all comparison, a most excellent name; and in this respect, Christ may well be said to have 'a more excellent name' ($\delta\iota\alpha\varphi o\rho\dot{\omega}\tau\varepsilon\rho o\nu$) than angels, because there is no comparison between them. The comparative epithet, translated 'more excellent,' is derived from a compound verb, $\delta\iota\alpha\varphi\acute{\varepsilon}\rho\omega$, that signifieth to differ in excellency, or to excel, 1 Cor. xv. 41. It is translated to 'be better,' Mat. vi. 26, or to 'be of more value,' Mat. x. 31. The positive of this comparative, $\delta\iota\acute{\alpha}\varphi o\rho o\varsigma$, signifieth diverse or different, Rom. xii. 6. Of God's name, see Chap. ii. Sec. 112.

This word of comparison, *more excellent*, is not to be taken of an exceeding in the same nature and kind, as one man is more excellent than another; but in different natures and kinds (the notation of the word imports as much), for Christ, as the Son of God, is of a divine nature, even the creator of all, and preferred before all created spirits, which, though they be the most excellent of created substances, yet not to be compared with the Son of God. His name is infinitely more excellent than theirs; for, by reason of this name, he is the Lord of angels.

Sec. 43. *Of the right which Christ hath to his name.*

The right which Christ had to his foresaid name is thus set down: 'He hath by inheritance obtained.' All this is the interpretation of one Greek word, κεκληρονόμηκεν, which by this periphrasis is set out to the full. The right of inheritance which Sarah would not that the son of the bondwoman should have, is set out by this word,[1] and is thus expounded: 'shall not be heir,' or 'shall not by inheritance obtain,' or shall not inherit,' οὐ μὴ κληρονομήσῃ, Gal. iv. 30. This right Christ hath in a double respect:

1. As he is the true, proper, only begotten Son by eternal generation. For the Father, in communicating his essence to him, communicated also this excellent name here intended.

2. As his human nature was hypostatically united to his divine nature; for though, according to the flesh, he was not born of God the Father—in that respect he was without Father, ἀπάτωρ, Heb. vii. 3, born of a virgin—yet, that flesh being personally united to the only begotten Son of God, he was born the Son of God. In this respect an angel, speaking of his conception and birth, saith, 'That holy thing which shall be born of thee shall be called the Son of God,' Luke i. 35.

He was not then by grace and favour of no son made the Son of God, but as God, and as God man, he was the true begotten Son of God; and in both these respects the name here spoken of, by right of inheritance, belonged to him. Of Christ the heir, see Ver. 2, Sec. 17.

Sec. 44. *Of the resolution of the 4th verse.*

It was shewed before that the excellency of the gospel was much commended by the excellency of Christ, the author and matter thereof.[2] Thereupon the apostle did set out Christ's excellency to the life. This point he prosecuteth in this and the verses following, so as the sum of all is, a proof of Christ's excellency. This proof is by an argument of the greater compared with the less. The greater or more excellent is Christ, the less or inferior are angels. Now, angels are the most excellent of creatures. He, therefore, that is more excellent than they, must needs be most excellent. The argument may thus be framed:

He that is greater than angels is most excellent; but Christ is greater than angels; therefore he is most excellent.

This argument is first propounded in this verse; secondly, exemplified in the verses following.

In the general here propounded, two points are set down:

1. The degree of Christ's dignity.
2. Christ's right thereunto.

In the degree observe,

1. The creatures before whom Christ is preferred, *angels.*
2. The extent, how far Christ is preferred before them, in this phrase, *so much better.*

In Christ's right is set down,

1. The kind thereof, *he hath by inheritance obtained.*
2. The matter or thing obtained, *a more excellent name.*

Sec. 45. *Of the observations of the 4th verse.*

I. *Angels are the most excellent of creatures.* This is the reason why the apostle brings them into this comparison. If there had been any creatures more excellent than angels, Christ's excellency had not been so far set out as now it is; for it might have been objected that, though Christ were more excellent than angels, yet he was not the most excellent of all, there being other creatures more excellent than angels.

II. *Christ's excellency above angels is beyond all comparison.* This phrase, *so much better,* &c., implies as much.

III. *Christ's excellencies made him known to be what he is.* They gave him a name whereby he is so made known as he is distinguished from all others. Thus God's excellencies are styled his name, Exod. xxxiv. 5, 6.

IV. *Christ hath a just right to his excellency.* His right is a right of inheritance, which is the best right that can be.

V. *According to that excellency, which of right belongs to any, he is to be esteemed.* This is the end of setting out Christ's excellencies and his right to them, namely, to work in us an high esteem of him. Thus magistrates, ministers, masters, parents, and others, are to be esteemed according to that name which they have obtained.

Sec. 46. *Of the meaning of these words, 'For unto which of the angels said he at any time.'*

Ver. 5. *For unto which of the angels said he at any time, Thou art my Son, this day have I begotten thee? And again, I will be to him a Father, and he shall be to me a Son.*

In this verse the particular instance of the forementioned excellent name is given, which is Son, in reference to God.

---

[1] κληρονόμος, *hæres*; κληρονομεῖν, *jure hæreditario consequi.*
[2] Sec. 46.

This causal particle *for*, γὰρ, sheweth that that which followeth is a proof of that which went before. The proof is from an induction of a special name.

The proof is taken from testimonies of Scripture. A testimony of Scripture is a sound proof. This was it whereunto a prophet thus directed God's people: 'To the law and to the testimony,' Isa. viii. 20. Christ prefers it before the testimony of one risen from the dead, Luke xvi. 31; yea, before the testimony of John the Baptist, of his own works, and of his Father. For after he had produced those three testimonies, he advised to 'search the Scriptures,' and that because they testified of him, John v. 36–39.

Obj. 1. A testimony is but an artificial argument, which is counted the last and lightest of all arguments.

Ans. A testimony receiveth his force from the witness-bearer. An human testimony is not counted infallible, because men are subject to ignorance, error, and manifold corruptions. But a divine testimony is infallible, in that it resteth on the highest and soundest ground of truth, which is the word of God; for it is impossible for God to lie, Heb. vi. 18. See Chap. iii. 3, Sec. 26.

As for sacred Scripture, it is all 'given by inspiration of God,' 2 Tim. iii. 16, and 'holy men of God spake as they were moved by the Holy Ghost,' 2 Pet. i. 21.

The Scripture is as a long continued, approved record, it is as a law written, and hath continued many generations, and thereby gained the greater confirmation. Thus this proof is more sure and sound than any logical or mathematical demonstration can be. Nothing more convinceth a believer, or more prevaileth with him, than a Scripture proof.

Obj. 2. Heretics allege Scripture to prove their heresies.

Ans. This doth yet further confirm Scripture proofs, in that all of all sorts fly to it, as all fly to the law, and plead it. But did the Scripture ever make for any heresy? The devil himself alleged Scripture, Mat. iv. 6, but was confounded thereby, and so have all heretics been in all ages. Of heretics perverting Scripture, see *The Whole Armour of God*, treat. ii., part viii. Of God's word, on Eph. vi. 17, Sec. 16.

What cause have we in this respect to observe this direction, 'Search the Scriptures,' John v. 39, and in hearing the word preached, to 'Search the Scriptures, whether the things we hear be so,' as the men of Berea did, Acts xvii. 11.

We ought hereupon to have our judgments grounded on the Scriptures, our opinions ordered, and our doubts resolved thereby. Nothing ought to be taken as an article of faith, but that which may be proved thereby. The kind of argument here used is negative, it stands thus: the Scripture nowhere declareth angels to be sons of God. Therefore that name belongeth not to them.

In regard of an article of faith, a negative argument from Scripture is sound and good, because all articles of faith requisite to be believed are therein set down, so as if it be not to be found in the Scripture, we may well conclude that it is no article of faith.

The name which here is denied to belong to angels, is thus set down under an interrogation, 'Unto which of the angels said he?' &c. This interrogation importeth a strong negation, somewhat more than if he had in a plain negative thus said, 'Unto none of the angels said he,' &c. For hereby he putteth the matter to their consideration, and maketh them judges thereof, as if he had said, Think with yourselves, and call to mind what anywhere you have read in sacred Scripture; and tell me, if any such thing be spoken of an angel therein.

The distributive particle *which*, τίνι, *unto which*, implieth a number of angels; and by way of grant, a difference of degrees: as if he had said, Grant that there are different degrees of angels, and that some of them are more excellent than others; yet to none of them, no not to the most excellent, said he, Thou art my Son, &c.

The relative particle *he* hath reference to God the Father, as is evident by this, that he saith, 'Thou art my Son,' &c. Though David uttered the words, yet, as the assembly of apostles and disciples expound it, Acts iv. 25, 'God by the mouth of his servant David said.'

This manner of expression, *said he*, hath reference to the Old Testament, which, before Christ's time, was the only written word of God. And the extension of time in this phrase, at any time, ποτε, hath relation to the whole history of the Bible, from the beginning of Genesis to the end of Malachi. Not once in any part of any of these books is this name, *Son of God*, applied to angels.

Sec. 47. *Of the various acceptions of this title 'Son of God.'*

True it is, that where sons of God are said to present themselves before the Lord, Job i. 6 and ii. 1, angels are meant.[1] Angels also are meant, where it is said, 'All the sons of God shouted for joy,' Job xxxviii. 7. They are also styled, 'sons of the Mighty,' Ps. lxxxix. 6;[2] or, as many do translate it, 'sons of God.' It is manifest, then, that angels are called sons of God. Or if angels be not meant, then men are called sons of God.[3] If either angels or men be called sons of God, how can it be accounted a prerogative proper to Christ alone to be God's Son?

Ans. This title, *son of God*, is in sacred Scripture used two ways. See Sec. 15.

---

[1] Venerunt angeli Dei.—*Orig. in loc.* Qui Dei filii nisi electi angeli?—*Greg. Mag. in loc.*

[2] בני אלים. Sancti angeli qui sunt stabiles et deificati.—*Harm. in Ps.* lxxxviii.

[3] Filii Dei vel angeli vel sancti intelligendi sunt.—*Hier. comment. in Job* i.

1. Most properly, by nature and eternal generation.
2. By mere grace and favour, God accounting them to be his sons, and accepting them as sons. In this latter respect many mere creatures are styled God's sons;[1] but in the former respect, none but the second person in sacred trinity, who assumed our nature, and so became God-man in one person.

In this proper and peculiar respect angels are denied to be sons of God, and Christ alone affirmed to be the Son of God, as is evident by the words following, 'Thou art my Son,' &c. This was most properly applied to Christ, to whom God the Father, in a most proper and peculiar respect, so said. That apostrophe of the Father to his Son, and emphatical expression of the relative *thou*, אתה, σὺ, sheweth that an especial Son is meant; such a Son as none is or can be but he alone that is there meant. Of the difference betwixt Christ and other sons of God, see Sec. 15.

Sec. 48. *Of the scope of the second Psalm.*

This testimony, 'Thou art my Son, this day have I begotten thee,' is taken out of Ps. ii. 7. That psalm is wholly prophetical. There is never a clause therein but may most fitly be applied to Christ.[2]

The Jews, who make it altogether historical, and apply it only to David and his kingdom, shoot clean beside the mark, and mistake the sense of the psalm, and scope of the inditer thereof. Nor this text here alleged, nor the extent of the dominion promised (to the uttermost parts of the earth), nor the power promished of dashing all to pieces, nor the exhortation to all kings to fear him, nor the title Jehovah, ver. 11, nor the vengeance nor the blessedness mentioned in the last verse, can historically and properly be applied to David.

It is much more to the purpose of the Holy Ghost that if anything be there spoken of David, it be taken to be spoken of him as of a type of Christ, and so, not by way of allegory or allusion, but truly and principally, prophesied of Christ.

For this we have good proof, even from those that were immediately and infallibly assisted by the same Spirit that inspired the penman of the psalm, and knew his just and true meaning.[3] For the two first verses are by a joint consent of all the apostles applied to Christ, Acts iv. 25, 26. The 7th verse is also applied to him, as here, so Acts xiii. 33. The 8th verse is applied to him by an angel sent from heaven, who saith, Luke i. 33, that of Christ's kingdom there shall be no end,[4] no limit or bound, but extended to the uttermost part of the earth. He shall reign over the Gentiles, Rom. xv. 12. Yea, the 8th and 9th verses are by Christ himself applied to himself, Rev. ii. 26, 27, where he promiseth to him that keepeth his works unto the end power over the nations, and he shall rule them with a rod of iron; as the vessels of a potter, shall they be broken to shivers. The ground of this promise is thus expressed by Christ himself 'even as I received of my Father.' To this Son of God, therefore, did God the Father say, 'I will give thee the heathen,' &c., Ps. ii. 8, 9.

The eleventh verse, of serving the Lord with fear and trembling, is applied to Christ, Philip. ii. 12; yea, and the beginning of the 12th verse, Philip. ii. 10, 11. For to kiss the Son, and to bow the knee to him, and to confess him, are equivalent phrases, which in effect import one and the same thing.

The middle of the 12th verse, concerning their perishing, with whom the Son is angry, is applied to kings and great men, Rev. vi. 15, 16.

The last clause, of trusting in him, and of blessedness thence arising, is oft applied to Christ, as John xiv. 1, and vi. 47; Mat. xi. 6, Rev. xix. 9.

By all these particular applications it is most evident that the second Psalm is a proper prophecy of Christ. Hence it followeth that the proof here alleged truly and properly concerneth Christ, and is very pertinent to the purpose, as will further appear, by opening the meaning of these words, 'This day have I begotten thee.'

Sec. 49. *Of God's begetting his Son.*

This testimony, 'Thou art my Son, this day have I begotten thee,' is alleged to prove that Christ excelleth the most excellent creatures; and it sheweth that some high transcendent matter, which can no way be applied to any mere creature, is spoken of Christ, and that is to be a Son eternally begotten of God the Father.

To *beget*, in usual signification, is out of one's own essence to produce another like being. Thus Adam is said to beget a Son in his own likeness, Gen. v. 3. In allusion hereunto, these words *beget, begotten*, are applied to the first and second persons of the sacred Trinity in a mutual relation of one to the other, and that for teaching's sake, to make us by resemblances (such as we are well acquainted withal) somewhat according to our capacity, to understand of that mystery which is in itself unutterable, unconceivable, and incomprehensible.

No resemblances can to the life and full set out the profound mysteries of the Trinity of persons in the unity of nature, of the first person's begetting, of the second being begotten, of the third's proceeding.

Comparisons and resemblances are but dark shadows of those bright lights. We may not expect that earthly and human things should in every respect answer heavenly and divine mysteries. They are only to help our dull and weak understanding.

---

[1] Ille natus, nos adoptati, ille ab æterno filius unigenitus per naturam; nos a tempore facti per gratiam.—*Aug. Enar. in Ps.* lxxxviii.

[2] Aspice universas nationes, &c., et, si audes, nega prophetatum, &c.—*Tertul. adv. Marcion*, lib. iii.

[3] Audacis est hunc Psalmum interpretari velle post Petrum; imo de eo sentire aliud quam in Actibus Apostolicis dixerit Petrus.—*Hier. comment. in Ps.* 2.   [4] Syr. ףוס, *terminus*.

It is a great matter indeed to conceive a begetting which is not in time, but eternal,[1] as is God the Father's begetting God the Son, which implieth the Father's eternal communicating his whole essence to the Son. As this text, and Ps. ii. 7, so all the texts of Scripture, which style Christ the begotten Son of God, prove the point in general.

Sec. 50. *Of the special kind of God's begetting.*
In the divine generation, these distinct points following are observable:
1. God is a Father, even the first person in Trinity, begetteth. In this respect the Son of God is called the begotten of the Father, John i. 14.
2. God the Father[2] begat the Son of his very substance, 'very God of very God.' The title *God* properly taken and frequently applied to this Son, gives proof hereto, as John i. 1, Rom. ix. 5, and especially the title *Jehovah*, which is given to none but to the true God, Gen. xix. 24, John v. 14.
3. God the Father communicated his whole essence to the Son.[3] He begat another self of himself, even that which he himself is. In which respect this Son of God saith, 'I and my Father are one;' 'The Father is in me, and I in him,' John x. 30, 38.
4. God the Father's begetting his Son, is truly and properly eternal. It was before all time, it continueth throughout all times, it shall never have any date or end. In relation hereunto saith this Son of God, 'I was set up from everlasting, from the beginning, or ever the earth was. When there were no depths, I was brought forth; before the hills was I brought forth,' &c., Prov. viii. 23–25. In this sense he was called 'the first-born,' Col. i. 15 : first-born, because he was begotten before all things; and only-begotten, because he alone was properly begotten of God.[4]

Some of the ancient fathers and later divines do in this sense take this word *hodiè*, to-day; for it signifieth the present time; and in divine things there is a continual presence or presentness, as I may so speak; neither is there anything past, as if it ceased to be; or to come, as if it were not yet, or as if there had been a time when it was not.[5] The Greek word whereby eternity is set out (αἰὼν *quasi* ἀεὶ ὤν, Arist. lib. i. *de Cœlo*), signifieth a continual being of things.

5. God the Father's begetting his Son manifesteth an equality of Father and Son; for if the nature of both be inquired after, it will hereby be found to be God, and not one greater than another.[1] This also did the Son receive of the Father. He did not beget him equal,[2] and then add to him, when he was begotten, equality; but in begetting him he made him equal. For being in the form of God,[3] to be equal with God was no robbery, Philip. ii. 6, but nature; because he obtained it by being begotten, he did not usurp it by a proud advancing of himself. Where equality is, there is the same nature, and one substance.

Sec. 51. *Of the Father's and Son's one and the same essence.*
The Father's begetting of the Son giveth evidence to the two great mysteries of our Christian faith, which were implied under these two metaphors, brightness of his glory, and express image of his person.[4]
The two mysteries are these :
1. The Son is of the same essence with the Father.
2. The Son is a distinct person from the Father.

For the first: to beget doth in general imply a communicating of his essence that begetteth to him that is begotten. But the special begetting here intended declareth a communicating of the whole essence. Hence, by undeniable consequence, it followeth, that the begotten Son of God is of the same essence with the Father.

To make this mystery the more clear, the Greek church used a compound Greek word, which signifieth consubstantial, ὁμοούσιος, or of the same essence; a word which hath been used by the ancientest fathers,[5] and put into the Nicene creed[6] (which was ratified by the subscription of three hundred and eighteen bishops there assembled), and thus translated in our English Liturgy, 'Of one substance with the Father.' All

---

[1] ὁ Θεὸς ἀφ' ἑαυτοῦ ἐγέννησε τὸν μονογενῆ ἀῤῥήτως, καὶ ἀκαταλήπτως, καὶ ἀχράντως.—*Epiph. advers. Ar. Hær.*, 69, sec. 15. Generationem Filii enarrabilem existentem nemo novit, &c., nisi solus qui generavit Pater, et qui natus est Filius.—*Iren. advers. Hær.*, lib. ii., cap. xlviii. Revera magnum est mente concipere generationem, quæ non fit ex aliquo tempore, sed æterna est.—*Aug de Agon. Christian.*, c. xvi.
[2] Unigenitum Filium de sua substantia genuit Pater.—*Aug. Epist.* 66.
[3] Gignit hypostasis.—*Athan. Dialog.* ii. *de Trin.* Ex ipsa essentia Patris est genitus—*Chrysost. Hom.* ii. *in Heb.* i. Genuit de se alterum se. Genuit id quod ipse est.—*Aug. Epist.* lxvi. Sic genuit ex se Filium, ut totum quod in se erat, esset et maneret in filio.—*Chrysol. Serm.* lx.
[4] Primogenitus, ut ante omnia genitus; unigenitus, ut solus ex Deo genitus.—*Tertul. advers. Prax.*
[5] Quod dicit, *ego hodiè*, Deus heri et cras non habet, sed semper hodie habet.—*Arnob. in Ps.* ii.; *Aug. Enar. in Ps.* ii. Quo sempiternam generationem ut catholica fides prædicat.—*Hier. in Ps.* ii.; *Haymo in Ps.* ii. Per *hodiè* æternitatem intelligi voluit.—*Zanch. de tribus Eloh.* lib. ii. cap. iv.; *Mollerus prælect. in Ps.* ii. 8, *aliique*. Of this day, see Sec. 58, &c.

[1] In Deo Patre et Deo Filio, si utriusque natura quæratur, uterque Deus; nec magis magnus alter altero Deus.—*Aug. Epist.* lxvi.; Lege plura ibid.
[2] Qu. 'unequal'?—Ed.
[3] In forma Dei æqualem esse Deo non ei rapina fuit, sed natura; quoniam id nascendo sumpsit, non superbiendo præsumpsit.—*Aug. ibid.* Ubi æqualitas est, ibi eadem natura, unaque substantia.—*Hier.* lib. ix. *Comment. in Quest.* 28.
[4] Quem constat de Patre naturaliter genitum, constat non aliud esse quam Deum. Hic itaque de Patre sempiternus existens, unam tenuit cum Deo Patre naturam, &c.—*Fulgent. ad Trasim. Reg.* lib. iii. cap. iii. [5] Justin Mart.
[6] υἱὸν τοῦ Θεοῦ τὸν μονογενῆ ὁμοούσιον τῷ Πατρί.—*Ruffin. Eccl. Hist.* lib. i. cap. 1, 9; *Epiph. advers. Hær. Art. Hær.* lxix. sec. 11.

the places that set out the unity of the Father and the Son,[1] such as these, 'I came forth from the Father,' John xvi. 28; 'I and my Father are one,' John x. 30; and all the places that style the Son God, give proof hereunto. So do the divine incommunicable properties attributed to the Son; as eternity, Isa. ix. 6, Col. i. 17; ubiquity, Mat. xviii. 20, and xxviii. 20; omnipotency, Philip. iii. 21; immutability, Heb. i. 12; omniscience, John i. 48, and xxi. 17. The like may be said of divine effects done by the Son; as creation, John i. 3; sustentation, Col. i. 17; miracles, John xv. 24; remitting sin, Mat. ix. 6; quickening the dead in sin, John v. 21; raising himself, Rom. i. 4; raising others, John v. 28, 29.

Sec. 52. *Of the Father and the Son distinct persons.*
The other mystery is this, the Son is a distinct person from the Father.

These two relative considerations, *beget, begotten,* necessarily imply a distinction.[2] It hath been before shewed that the distinction is not in nature, essence, or substance; therefore the fathers have of old used this word *person* to shew wherein the distinction consisteth. Of this word *person,* see Sec. 21.

That the Son is a person or subsistence, is evident by these phrases in Scripture which give him a particular and proper subsistence; as this title, *I am,* which Christ applieth to himself, John viii. 58; and this, 'The Son hath life in himself,' John v. 26; and this, 'What thing soever the Father doth, these also doth the Son likewise,' John v. 19; and many the like.

That the person of the Son is distinct from the person of the Father, is manifest by these correlative titles,[3] *Father, Son,* and correlative actions, *beget, begotten;* and such phrases as these: 'The Word was with God,' John i. 1; 'The Son is in the bosom of the Father,' John i. 18; 'I came forth from the Father,' John xvi. 28. And such as set out their distinct order and manner of working: as, 'God made the worlds by the Son,' ver. 2; 'He hath chosen us in him,' Eph. i. 4; 'The Lord rained from the Lord,' Gen. xviii. 24; 'The Lord said unto my Lord,' Ps. cx. 1.

For further clearing this great mystery of the generation of the Son of God, let us consider the difference betwixt it and other generations and operations.

Sec. 53. *Of the difference betwixt the generation of the same person as Son of God and Son of man.*
1. The generation of the Son of God was eternal

[1] Aliud non est homoousion, quam quod dicit, ego Deo Patre exivi; et ego et Pater unum sumus.—*Ambr. de Fide contra Arr.* cap. v.

[2] Pater alius a Filio, dum alius qui generat, alius qui generatur.—*Tertul. advers. Prax*; *Justin Mart. loc. cit.*; *Tertul. advers. Prax.*; *Lact. de vera Sap.* lib. iv. cap. xxxix., *aliique.*

[3] Pater et Filius personarum sunt ab invicem proprietate distincti.—*Aug. de Fide ad P. Diac.* cap. i.; *Lege Fulg. ad Transim. Reg.* lib. iii. cap. iii.

before the world, but of the Son of man in the last days of the world, 1 Peter i. 20. This was that fulness of time which the apostle mentioneth, Gal. iv. 4.

2. The former was without mother, the latter without father. Thus may we reconcile these different terms, 'without father, without mother,' Heb. vii. 3.

3. By the former, Christ did really and fully partake of the divine nature; he was true God, very God of very God; yet being a distinct person, he became fit to assume man's nature. By the latter, he so really assumed man's nature as he became a true man,—man of the substance of his mother; and that after such a manner as he was declared thereby to be true God, and in that respect 'called the Son of God,' Luke i. 35; yea, he was 'God manifested in the flesh,' 1 Tim. iii. 16.

4. By the former he became fit to be a mediator in all things which required divine dignity, authority, power, worth, merit, and efficacy; by the latter he became fit to be a mediator in all such things as required infirmity, ministry, service, or any kind of suffering.

Sec. 54. *Of the difference betwixt divine regeneration*[1] *and predestination.*

There are among other divine operations three, which are in themselves very remarkable, yet not to be compared to the divine generation of the Son of God. Those three are these, predestination, creation, regeneration. A due consideration of the difference betwixt them and this, will much illustrate this.

1. The generation of the Son of God doth differ from predestination, which is an internal and eternal work of God, in that it is a personal act, proper to the Father alone,[2] and that only in relation to the Son. But predestination is an essential act, if I may so use this word, common to all the persons, Father, Son, Holy Ghost; and that in relation to angels and men.

Besides, predestination, as all other works of God towards creatures, is an act of God's will, merely voluntary; God might if he would have forborne to do it: 'He wrought all things after the counsel of his own will,' Eph. i. 11. But the divine generation, though it be a free act, without any constraint, yet is it not a work of counsel and will, but of nature and necessity.[3] The Father cannot but beget the Son.

Sec. 55. *Of the difference betwixt divine generation and creation.*

Besides the fore-mentioned differences, there are others also betwixt divine generation and creation. For,

1. Creation was a work out of God, in and upon

[1] Qu. 'generation'?—ED.

[2] Generatio solius patris propria est.—*Fulgent. Res.* 2. *ad Ferrand.*

[3] Generatio non est voluntatis opus, sed naturæ proprietas.—*Cyril. Thesau.* lib. i. cap. iii.

creatures. But divine generation is an internal work,[1] in God himself, upon the very Creator, if I may so speak.

2. Creation is a making of that which was not, and that out of nothing; but divine generation is of that which ever was, and that of the very substance of God.

3. Creation was a work in the beginning, Gen. i. 1. Divine generation was before that beginning, even eternal, Prov. viii. 22, 23. Not as 'In the beginning God created the heaven and the earth,' so In the beginning *he made* the Word,[2] but 'In the beginning *was* the Word,' John i. 1.

4. Creation had an end, Gen. ii. 1, 2. The divine generation continueth ever, without all end.

5. Creation was of many things diverse from the Creator, not like to him; the divine generation is of that which is most like, yea, of the very same essence.

Sec. 56. *Of the difference betwixt divine generation and regeneration.*

There are other differences than those mentioned before, betwixt the divine generation of the Son of God, and the spiritual regeneration of sons of men.

1. There is a time for regeneration; for the time was when they that are regenerate were no children of God, Eph. ii. 12; and many that yet are not born again shall be regenerate, John x. 16 and xvii. 20. But in divine generation, there never was a time wherein the Son of God was no Son.[3]

2. Regeneration presupposeth a former birth and being. The very word, which signifieth to be born again, John iii. 3, importeth as much; but no such matter may be imagined of the divine, eternal generation.

3. Regeneration respecteth not the substance of the party regenerate, for the body and soul, and all the parts of the one, and powers or faculties of the other, are the very same before and after generation.[4] But divine generation is in regard of the very essence of the Son of God.

4. Regeneration is an alteration of the person regenerate, and that in his condition and in his disposition. In regard of his condition, of a child of wrath, Eph. ii. 3, he is made an heir of the grace of life, 1 Peter iii. 7; in regard of his disposition, of darkness he is made light, Eph. v. 8. But in divine generation there is no alteration at all; the Son is ever the same, ver. 12.

5. In regeneration there is a growth and increase, 1 Peter. ii. 2. But divine generation is ever most absolutely and infinitely perfect.

6. Regeneration is of God's mere will and free grace, James i. 18. No mere man is by nature the son of God;[1] but it hath been shewed that divine generation is of nature. See Sec. 50.

Sec. 57. *Of the difference betwixt divine and human generation.*

Many of the differences betwixt the divine generation of the Son of God, and human generations of sons of men, are such as were noted before. I will therefore give but a touch of them, as being pertinent to the present point, and add some others thereunto.

1. The generation of the Son of God is eternal, but of sons of men temporal.

2. That is an internal work of the Father, this external.

3. That is a perpetual permanent act, this transient.

4. That importeth a necessary mutual subsistence of him that begetteth, and him that is begotten, in and with one another: 'Thou in me, and I in thee,' saith the Son unto his Father, John xvii. 21. But in human generation, he that begetteth subsisteth without him that is begotten.

5. That setteth out an equality of persons; in this, children as children are inferior to their parents.

6. That doth not presuppose no-being, as if the Son of God had of no son been begotten a son; this is a begetting of him to be a son, which was no son before. In human generation that is which was not before.

7. In divine generation none is before or after the other.

In human generation, he that begetteth is before the begotten, and that not only in order of cause, but also in time.

8. That is without all passion: this cannot be so; for as there is an action in that which begetteth, so a passion in that which is begotten.

9. In that which begetteth and he which is begotten is the very same in substance, ὁμοούσιος. In this, father and son may be and are of the like nature or essence, ὁμοιούσιος, but not the very same. The one is both *alius* and *aliud*, another person, and another substance distinct from the other. They are two.

10. In that, the whole substance is communicated; in this, but a part.

11. In that, there is no diminution at all; in this, there is.

12. In that, all is divine and supernatural, both the substance and also the manner of working; in this, all is natural and sensible.

Sec. 58. *Of the particle 'this day,' applied to Christ's incarnation.*

Hitherto of this great mystery of divine generation set down in this phrase, 'I have begotten thee;' we

---

[1] υἱὸν ἐγέννησεν οὐκ ἔξωθεν ἑαυτοῦ.—*Epiph. advers. hæres. Arrian. hæres.* 69, sec. 26.

[2] Non sicut in principio fecit Deus cœlum et terram, ita in principio fecit Verbum, sed in principio erat Verbum.—*Aug. Ep.* 69.

[3] Ille nunquam filius non fuit. Nos tunc Spiritum adoptionis accepimus quando credidimus in filium Dei.—*Hier. Commen. in Eph.* i.   [4] Qu. 'regeneration'?—ED.

[1] Non est naturæ filius sed arbitrio Dei.—*Hier. Comment. Mat.* v. lib. x.

will further consider the just sense of the particle *this day*, annexed thereunto.

It was shewed before, Sec. 50, how that might set out eternity, in that it importeth a continual present time, without respect to the time past or future.[1] In this sense it would best agree with this mystery of the divine generation, simply considered in itself. But here the apostle setteth out the Son of God, as 'God manifest in the flesh,' Immanuel, God with us, God-man, God-man in one person.

Thus (as the Word was made flesh, and dwelt among us) 'God hath spoken unto us in these last days by his Son;' thus hath God 'appointed him heir of all things;' thus hath he purged our sins; thus sits he down at the right hand of the Majesty on high; yea, thus in the second Psalm, this Son of God (as God-man) is styled the Lord's Anointed; thus God saith of him, 'I have set my King upon my holy hill of Sion;' thus also he saith to him, 'Ask of me, and I will give thee the heathen for thine inheritance.'

Seeing therefore that both the psalmist and the apostle speak of the Son of God incarnate, and made a Son of man, the particle *this day* may not unfitly be applied to such times as the Son of man was on earth manifested to be the Son of God, especially at the time of his incarnation. For then was the Word first made flesh; so as then might the Father say of a Son of man, 'This day have I begotten thee;' that is, even now it is manifest that a son of man is the begotten Son of God.

Besides, Christ's incarnation was so strange, his mother being a pure virgin, as she herself said, 'How shall this be?' At that time therefore said the angel to the Virgin Mary, 'That holy thing which shall be born of thee, shall be called the Son of God,' Luke i. 34, 35.

After his conception, before his birth, his name was set down *Jesus*, and that upon this ground, 'He shall save his people from their sins,' Mat. i. 21, which none could do but the begotten Son of God.

Answerably at the day of his birth an angel said, 'To-day is born a Saviour, which is Christ the Lord,' Luke ii. 11. Could so much be said of any but of the begotten Son of God? Here by an angel's voice the *hodiè, to-day*, is expressly set down of the day of Christ's birth. Hereupon on that day a multitude of the heavenly host sang, 'Glory be to God in the highest,' Luke ii. 14.

Where a prophet of old prophesied of the birth of this God-man, thus he sets it out, Isa. ix. 6, 'Unto us a child is born, unto us a son is given; and the government shall be upon his shoulder: and his name shall be called Wonderful, Counsellor, The mighty God, The everlasting Father, The Prince of peace.'

[1] Quod dictum est, *hodie*, præsentis est temporis: potest tamen et secundum carnem hoc accipi dictum—.*Chrys. Hom.* ii. *in Heb.* i.

Can this possibly be meant of any but the begotten Son of God?

Thus we see how fitly this particle, *this day*, may be applied to the time of Christ's incarnation, which was first wrought in and by his conception, and then manifested to the world in and by his birth.

Sec. 59. *Of the particle 'this day' applied to Christ's resurrection.*

There was another time wherein Christ was on earth manifested to be truly and properly begotten of God, and that was at his resurrection; for when he had so far subjected himself to the power of his enemies, as to suffer them to do to the very uttermost what possibly they could—for men, 'after they have killed the body, have no more than they can do,' Luke xii. 5—to shew that by his divine nature he could undo all, and make all void, he rose again from the dead. Thus was he 'declared to be the Son of God with power,' namely, 'by the resurrection from the dead, Rom. i. 4; 'for it was not possible' that the Son of God 'should be holden of death,' Acts ii. 24.

Sundry both ancient and later divines[1] do apply these words, 'This day have I begotten thee,' to the resurrection of Christ; for by that power which Christ had to raise himself from the dead, it evidently appeared that he was indeed the begotten Son of God; of such power as the Father had; and therefore of the very substance of the Father: true God in power, true God in essence. This they do the rather thus apply, because St Paul himself seemeth so to do, Acts xiii. 33.

Concerning St Paul's particular application of this text to Christ's resurrection, much is disputed *pro et con*, for it and against it.

There are two principal points which the apostle laboureth to prove in that sermon, Acts xiii. 17: one, that God 'according to his promise raised unto Israel a Saviour,' verse 23; the other, that this Saviour being put to death, God raised him from the dead, verse 30. Now, in verse 33, the former of these two points seemeth to be proved by this testimony, 'Thou art my Son, this day have I begotten thee;' and the latter by two other testimonies, verse 34, 35. But to which of those two points soever that text be applied, either to God's raising unto Israel a Saviour Jesus, or to God's raising this Jesus from the dead, it is most clear that the apostle produceth this text, 'Thou art my Son, this day have I begotten thee,' unto the Son of God manifested in the flesh; and that he applieth *this day* to that distinct time wherein God manifested his Son, or shewed him forth to the world.[2]

[1] Ad resurrectionem spectare videtur.—*Amb. de Sacram.* lib. iii. cap. i. *Ita Hilarius et Theodorus Antioch. Flaminius in Explan. Ps.* ii., *Vatab. Annot.* in Ps. ii. 7. *Calvin Comm.* in Acts xiii. 33, *aliique plurimi.*

[2] Solenne et legitimum manifestationis tempus Spiritus S. hic designat.—*Calv. Comment. in Ps.* ii. 7.

Sec. 60. *Of the many evidences of Christ's divine generation.*

Quest. 1. Were there not other times wherein Christ was manifested to be the Son of God, besides his conception, birth, and resurrection?

Ans. Yes, very many. He was manifested to be the Son of God, and that after his wonderful birth:

1. By Simeon's and Anna's testimonies when he was presented in the temple, Luke ii. 29, 38.
2. By the star that conducted the three wise men out of the east to him, and by their worshipping him, and offering gifts to him, Mat. ii. 2, 11.
3. By his disputing with the doctors in the temple at twelve years old; and telling his mother that he must be about his Father's business, Luke ii. 42, 46, 49.
4. By John the Baptist's testimony of him, Luke iii. 16, 17, John i. 29, and iii. 29, &c.
5. By the Father's testimony of him at his baptism; and by the Holy Ghost's lighting upon him, Mat. iii. 16, 17. The like testimony was given at his transfiguration, Mat. xvii. 5, and a little before his passion, John xii. 28.
6. By his manner of resisting and commanding the devil away, Mat. iv. 3, &c.
7. By discovering men's inward disposition, John i. 47, and ii. 25, and vi. 70; and thoughts, Mat. ix. 4, and xvi. 7, 8.
8. By his divine doctrine, John vii. 46.
9. By his many mighty miracles, John xv. 24.
10. By his manner of forgiving sin, Mat. ix. 2, 6.
11. By the power which he gave to his disciples, Mat. x. 1, Mark xvi. 17, Mat. xvi. 19; yea, and by breathing the Holy Ghost into them, John xx. 22.
12. By overthrowing them that were sent to apprehend him, John xviii. 6.
13. By his manner of giving up the ghost, and the wonders thereat, Mat. xxvii. 54, Mark xv. 39.
14. By his ascension, Acts i. 9.
15. By the gifts he gave after his ascension, Eph. iv. 8.
16. By the functions of King, Prophet, and Priest, conferred on him, Heb. v. 5.

By these and other notable evidences the eternal Son of God (who from the beginning did, as it were, lie hid in the bosom of the Father, and under the law was shadowed over), was manifested to be the begotten Son of God.[1]

Sec. 61. *Of the extent of 'this day.'*

Quest. 2. If there be so many days wherein Christ was manifested to be the Son of God, how is it said, σήμερον, 'this day,' as if there were but one only day?

Ans. This day is not always strictly referred to one set day, consisting of twelve or twenty-four hours, but to a determined present time, which may consist of many hours, days, and years.

Moses oft setteth down the time of Israel's abode in the wilderness under 'this day,' as Deut. x. 15, and xxvi. 16–18, and xxvii. 19.

It is usually put for that time wherein they live; concerning whom it is spoken; as 1 Chron. xxviii. 7, Jer. xliv. 2, Dan. ix. 7, Luke iv. 21. And it is used to distinguish present times from former times; as 1 Sam. ix. 9, 'He that is this day[1] called a prophet, was before that time called a seer.' In like sense, yesterday is put for former times, as where the Lord saith, 'yesterday my people;'[2] that is, 'of late my people,' or heretofore. Thus yesterday is opposed to this day; as where Christ is said to be the same yesterday (in former times before he was exhibited in the flesh), and to-day (now since his incarnation), and for ever, Heb. xiii. 8.

That *this day* may have a long date, is evident by the apostle's own explication thereof; for where the psalmist had said, Ps. xcv. 7, 'To-day if you will hear his voice,' the apostle, who lived above a thousand years after him, applieth *this day* to his own times, and saith, Heb. iii. 13, 'Exhort one another daily, while it is called to-day.'

Thus we see how this day may, according to the use of it in sacred Scripture, be applied to a long date; and particularly to the whole time of Christ's manifesting himself in the flesh, to be the begotten Son of God, from the beginning of his incarnation to his ascension into heaven; yea, and to future times also, by reason of the evidences which he giveth of his true deity. For he promised to send the Holy Ghost to his disciples, John xvi. 7, and to be with his church alway even unto the end of the world,[3] Mat. xxviii. 20. The accomplishment hereof is an undeniable evidence of Christ's true deity.

How 'this day' may be extended to eternity, was shewed before in Sec. 50.

Sec. 62. *Of manifesting Christ's divine generation.*

Quest. 3. How can the limitation of *this day* to the time of Christ's incarnation, stand with Christ's eternal generation, set out under this phrase, 'I have begotten thee.'

Ans. In Scripture, matters are then said to be done, when they are manifested to be done. Whereas, Heb. viii. 13, by bringing in a new covenant, the former is said to be made old; the meaning is, that it is manifested to be old. But more pertinently to our present purpose, Christ, at the moment of his concep-

---

[1] Significat eum qui fuerat ab initio absconditus in arcano Patris sinu, et obscurè deinde sub lege adumbratus, ex quo prodiit cum claris insignibus, cognitum fuisse Dei filium.—*Vat. Annot. in Psalm* ii. 7.

[1] היום, *hodie.*
[2] אתמול עמי, *Heri populus meus*—Micah ii. 8.
[3] Pulchre Pater dicit ad Filium, *Ego hodie genui te*, hoc est, quando redemisti populum, quando ad coeli regnum vocasti, quando implesti voluntatem meam, probasti meum te esse Filium.—*Amb. de Sacr.* lib. iii. cap. i.

tion, is said to be 'called the Son of God,' Luke i. 35, because then he began to be manifested so to be. In this sense, this high transcendent prophecy, 'Unto us a child is born, unto us a Son is given, and the government shall be upon his shoulder; and his name shall be called Wonderful,' &c., Isa. ix. 6, 7, is to be taken.

This manifestation of Christ's divine generation in set and certain times, by visible and conspicuous evidences, doth no whit cross or impeach the eternity and incomprehensibleness thereof. For to declare and manifest a thing to be, presupposeth that it was before it was manifested; neither doth it necessarily imply any beginning of that before; no more than those phrases, 'Before the mountains were brought forth, thou art God,' Ps. xc. 2; 'Before the hills I was brought forth,' Prov. viii. 25.

The full meaning therefore of the apostle in alleging this testimony, 'Thou art my Son, this day have I begotten thee,' may, for perspicuity's sake, be thus paraphrased, as if God the Father had thus said to God the Son: Thou, and thou alone, art my true proper Son, not by grace or adoption, but by nature and eternal generation; and now I do in this last age of the world declare thee so to be by thine incarnation, doctrine, works, resurrection from the dead, and ascension into heaven, whereby it manifestly appeareth that thou infinitely dost surpass all the angels in heaven.

Sec. 63. *Of Solomon a type of Christ.*

To the fore-named testimony, which proveth Christ to be the begotten Son of God, another is added to the very same purpose, as these copulative particles καί, *and,* πάλιν, *again,* import. Hereby it is evident that sundry testimonies may be produced to prove the same point, Rom. v. 10, &c.

1. This sheweth consent of Scripture.
2. It more works, as many blows knock a nail up to the head.
3. Many testimonies may better clear the point, and one place be a commentary to another.

Though this be lawful, yet a mean must be kept therein, and care be taken wisely to observe when there is need of adding testimony to testimony. See Sec. 77.

This latter testimony is taken out of a promise made to David; it is twice recorded, as 2 Sam. vii. 14, 1 Chron. xvii. 13, and it is repeated by David the third time, 1 Chron. xxii. 10.

The apostle faithfully quoteth the very words of the promise, which are these, 'I will be to him a Father, and he shall be to me a Son.'

Our English makes a little difference in translating the Hebrew and the Greek. For that they turn the Hebrew, 'I will be his Father, and he shall be my Son,' which is in effect the same, *his Father,* and *a Father to him, his Son,* and *a Son to him,* are all one in sense. The two original languages do directly answer one another.[1]

In the repetition of this promise, 1 Chron. ii. 10, the order is inverted, for it is thus set down, 'He shall be my Son, and I will be his Father.' This inversion of words no whit at all altereth the sense, but affordeth unto us this observable instruction, that the Father was not before the Son, nor the Son before the Father, nor in time, nor in order, both co-eternal, both equal: the glory equal, the majesty co-eternal, as it is in Athanasius his creed.[2] Therefore in one place the Father is first set down, in another the Son; for the Son was always with the Father, and always in the Father:[3] with the Father, by an inseparable distinction of the eternal Trinity; in the Father, by a divine unity of nature. This is further manifest by a distinct expression of both the relatives; for he contents not himself to say, 'I will be a Father to him,' but he adds, 'he shall be a Son to me,' to shew that the Father never was without the Son.

The fore-mentioned promise, as it is a promise, hath immediate relation to the Son of David, even to Solomon by name, 1 Chron. xxii. 9, and thereupon this threatening ('if he commit iniquity I will chasten him') is added, 2 Sam. vii. 14, for Christ was not subject to sin.

There be that say that Solomon in his sins might be a type of Christ, as Christ is an head of a body, and considered with the body, as Mat. xxv. 40; Acts ix. 4; 1 Cor. xii. 12; and so this threatening, 'If he commit iniquity I will chasten him,' applied to Christ; or else as Christ was our surety, and took our sins upon him, and was chastened for them.[4]

But it is not necessary that all things which were in such persons as were types of Christ should be applied to Christ. Not Solomon, nor David, nor Aaron, as sinners in regard of their sins, were types of Christ; though he was 'in all points tempted like as we are, yet without sin,' chap. iv. 14. No kind of persons were more proper types of Christ than the high-priests, yet were they not types in all things that pertained to them; they were of the tribe of Levi; they offered sacrifices for their own sins; they oft renewed their sacrifices; they had successors when they died. In none of these were they types of Christ. See Chap. I. 5, Sec. 12.

[1] אני אהיה לו לאב והוא יהיה לי לבן: Ἐγὼ ἔσομαι αὐτῷ εἰς πατέρα, καὶ αὐτὸς ἔσται μοι εἰς υἱόν.

[2] ἴση ἡ δόξα: συναΐδιος μεγαλειότης.

[3] Cum Patre semper, et in Patre semper est Filius; cum Patre per distinctionem indissociabilem Trinitatis æternæ: in Patre per divinam unitatem naturæ.—*Amb. de fide*, lib. iv. cap. iv.

[4] Christus dupliciter potest intelligi habere peccatum: vel quia suscepit in se, et luit peccata nostra in suo corpore; vel quia peccata quæ hærent in corpore et in membris videri possunt aliquo modo pertinere ad caput.—*P. Mart. Comment. in 2 Sam.* vii. 14. Sic fere Osiander et Lava. Comment. in 2 Paralip. xvii. 13, aliique.

But the excellent prerogatives heaped up together have not relation to Solomon alone. The prerogatives as they are propounded to David in the name of the Lord, are these in order.

1. I will set up thy seed after thee, which shall succeed out of thy bowels, 2 Sam. vii. 12.
2. I will establish his kingdom, *ibid.*
3. He shall build a house for my name, 2 Sam. vii. 13.
4. I will establish the throne of his kingdom for ever, *ibid.*
5. I will be his Father, and he shall be my Son, 2 Sam. vii. 14.
6. I will settle him in my house, and in my kingdom for ever, 1 Chron. xvii. 14.
7. He shall be a man of rest, and I will give him rest from all his enemies, &c., 1 Chron. xxii. 9.

These, at least most of them, were literally meant of him, who by name is expressed, Solomon; yet not singly and simply considered in himself alone, but as a type of Christ.[1] For David and his posterity had their royal dignity conferred upon them, not so much for their own sakes, as that they might be a foregoing type and a visible representation of Christ's royal dignity, and of that redemption and salvation which he should bring to the people of God. So as those excellencies which in the letter are spoken of David, Solomon, and others, are mystically, truly, and principally foretold of Christ, whereby the benefit of those promises was infinitely increased, and the comfort of true believers above measure enlarged. This the apostles, who were inspired with a divine Spirit, well knew; and thereupon on all occasions applied those types to their intended truth, as here in this place.

True it is that David's son by Bathsheba was named Solomon;[2] but the mystical truth of his name (as of the name of Melchisedec, chap. vii. ver. 7) was manifested in Christ Jesus. Read the 72d Psalm, which carrieth this title, 'for Solomon,' and it will be found that Christ is the true Prince of peace, which Solomon's name importeth, and that all things there set down are fulfilled in Christ.

But to compare the type and truth together in such particulars as are mentioned in the promise made to David, 2 Sam. vii. 12, these instances following are to be observed.

1. Solomon was a man of rest; and Christ was the Prince of peace, Isa. ix. 6. God 'gave Solomon rest from all his enemies,' such as were the Philistines, Aramites, Moabites, Ammonites, and others like them; but Christ so judgeth among the nations as they 'beat their swords into ploughshares,' &c., Isa. ii. 4, and 'the wolf shall dwell with the lamb,' &c., Isa. xi. 6-9; yea, God in giving Christ 'hath raised up an horn of salvation for us in the house of his servant David, that we should be saved from our enemies, and from the hand of all that hate us,' Luke i. 69, 71; not only from men but from devils also, for he hath 'spoiled principalities and powers,' Col. ii. 15.

2. God gave peace and quietness to Israel in Solomon's days; but Christ is our peace, Eph. ii. 14; and it pleased the Father to reconcile all things to himself by Christ, Col. i. 20.

3. Solomon was the seed that proceeded out of David's bowels, whom God set up after David; but Christ was that promised seed that by an excellency and property was called the son of David, Mat. i. 1, who also by lineal descent proceeded out of David's bowels. An ancient father expounding this phrase, Out of thy bowels, thus, Out of thy belly (as the LXX and vulgar Latin do), hath this comment upon it:— If you simply take this of Solomon it is ridiculous, for then might David be thought to have brought forth Solomon as a mother. Hereupon he applieth this to the Virgin Mary, out of whose womb Christ came.[1] But that father mistook the mark, for the Hebrew word properly signifieth the bowels (as our English turns it); and it is elsewhere applied to men, as Gen. xv. 4, 2 Sam. xvi. 11. And in 1 Chron. xvii. 11 it is thus expressed, 'which shall be one of thy sons;' therefore Solomon must not be clean excluded, but be immediately intended, yet as a type, and Christ most principally, as the truth and substance.

4. God established Solomon's kingdom, but much more Christ's, 'whose kingdom cannot be moved,' Heb. xii. 28, as Solomon's was; for first ten tribes fell away from his son, 1 Kings xii. 20, and afterwards the whole kingdom was translated from Solomon's race to Nathan's. Compare Mat. i. 12 with Luke iii. 27, where therefore it is further said, 'I will establish the throne of his kingdom for ever.' If this be applied to Solomon, it must be taken improperly for long date, but applied to Christ it is most truly and properly spoken: 'For he shall reign over the house of Jacob for ever, and of his kingdom there shall be no end,' Luke i. 33; so as this extent of the promise to everlastingness evidently proves that Christ is here principally intended.[2]

5. Where it is further said that the promised son of David should build an house for the name of the Lord, this is true of the earthly temple built of stone and timber, and garnished with gold, silver, silk, and

---

[1] Promissi series Christum spopondit.—*Amb.* lib. iii. Comment. in Luc.

[2] Totum psalmum, qui figuratè tanquam in Salomonem dicitur, si legere vellet, inveniret Christum verè regem Pacificum : hoc enim Salomonis nomen interpretatur : in quo cognosceret completa omnia quæ ibi dicuntur, &c.—*Aug.* contra Faust. Manich. lib. xiii. cap. vii. Lege Aug. Enar. in Ps. lxxi. and in Ps. cxxvi.

---

[1] ממעיך; LXX, ἐκ τῆς κοιλίας σου; Vet. Lat. *ex ventre tuo*. Si in Salomone simpliciter edisseres, risum mihi incuties. Videbitur enim David peperisse Salomonem. At et hic Christus significatur, ex eo ventre semen David, qui est ex David, id est Mariæ.—*Tertul. adver. Marcion*, lib. iii.

[2] Thronus in ævum et regnum in ævum magis Christo competit, quam Salomoni temporali scil. regi.—*Tert. loc. citat.*

other like ornaments, which was a typical house for God's name, 1 Kings v. 5; but Christ built the mystical, spiritual, true house of God, which is the church of the living God,[1] Heb. iii. 3, 6, 1 Tim. iii. 15.

Well, therefore, and that most fitly and properly, may this part of the promise, 'I will be a Father to him, and he shall be a son to me,' be applied to Christ. To Solomon it was spoken in a type; to him indeed God was a father in favour and love, and he was a son to God, as he bare God's image, being a king, and through the grace of adoption and regeneration. But God is a father to Christ by begetting him, and communicating his whole essence to him; and Christ is a son to God by being properly begotten of God, of the same essence with him.[2]

Thus is this testimony as pertinent to the apostle's purpose as the former, *Father* and *Son* being here properly taken in a like mutual relation of one to another.

Quest. How then is this set down in the future tense, as of a thing to come, *I will be, He shall be,* seeing the divine generation is eternal?

Ans. As in the former testimonies, so in this, the apostle setteth out the Son of God incarnate, whereby he was visibly manifested to be the true, proper, only begotten Son of God, so as this promise is of a future, conspicuous declaration of an eternal relation; as if the promise had been thus made, I will manifest that I am the Father of that Son which I will raise up to thee, and that he is my Son. In like manner saith the angel to the Virgin Mary, 'That holy thing which shall be born of thee shall be called the Son of God,' Luke i. 35.

Sec. 64. *Of the resolution of the fifth verse.*

The exemplification of the former comparison (ver. 4) here begins, and continueth to the end of this chapter.

In this exemplification there are sundry proofs given, both of Christ's excellency above angels, and also of angels' inferiority to Christ.

Christ's excellency is exemplified in eight particulars, which are these:

1, That relation which is betwixt God the Father and the Son, in this verse; 2, that worship which is due unto Christ, ver. 6; 3, Christ's divine nature, ver. 8; 4, Christ's royal function, ver. 8; 5, the eminency of Christ's gifts above others, ver. 9; 6, Christ's great work of creation, ver. 10; 7, Christ's immutability, vers. 11, 12; 8, Christ's glory and dignity, ver. 13.

[1] Quia ædem Dei magis Christus ædificaturus esset, hominem scil. sanctum, in quo potiore templo inhabitaret Dei Spiritus, in Dei Filium magis Christus habendus esset, quam Salomon filius David.—*Tert. loc. citat.* Salomon ædificavit templum Domino in typo quidem et in figura futuræ ecclesiæ, &c.—*Aug. Enar. in Ps.* cxxvi.

[2] Quis est iste proprius Dei Filius, nisi cui dictum est, Filius meus es tu, Ego hodie genui te?—*Ambr. lib. iii. Comment. in Luke.*

The inferiority of angels is exemplified in three particulars:

1, That duty which they owe to Christ, namely, to worship him, ver. 6; 2, their created nature, ver. 7; 3, their office to attend upon saints, ver. 14.

In this verse the first branch of the exemplification of Christ's excellency above angels is set down.

The sum of it is, the relation betwixt God the Father and Christ.

In setting down hereof we are to observe, 1, the proof; 2, the point.

The proof is taken from testimonies of Scripture, which are two.

The first is taken out of Ps. ii. 7, wherein observe,

1, The manner of producing the testimony; 2, the matter whereof it consisted.

The manner is noted two ways:

1, Negatively. Because no mention is made in Scripture of any angel to be God's son, the apostle concludes that no angel is God's son.

2. Interrogatively, whereby he propounds the case to them to judge of it: 'Unto which of the angels said he,' &c.

The matter of the testimony consisteth of a relation, whereof observe:

1, The circumstances; 2, the substance.

The circumstances are two:

1. An apostrophe of the Father to the Son, *Thou art.*
2. The time, *This day.*

The substance of the testimony sets out:

1. The kind of relation, *my Son.*
2. The ground of it, *I have begotten thee.*

The other testimony of Scripture is taken out of 2 Sam. vii. 14.

In producing this testimony observe:

1, The connection of it with the former in this phrase, *And again.*

2. The substance thereof. Wherein again observe,

(1.) The manner of expressing it, by way of promise, *I will be,* &c.

(2.) The matter thereof. Which expresseth,

[1.] The relative, *a Father.*

[2.] The co-relative, *a Son.*

Sec. 65. *Of the doctrines arising out of the fifth verse.*

I. *A testimony of Scripture is a sound proof.* See Sec. 46.

II. *A negative argument from Scripture is a good argument.* This is to be taken of articles of faith, and such things as are necessary to be known by Christians; for in such things the whole counsel and will of God is made known unto us by the Scriptures. Hereupon a curse is denounced against such as take from or add to the Scriptures, Rev. xxii. 18, 19.

III. *Christians ought to be so expert in the Scriptures as to know what is therein set down, or what not.* This I gather from the apostle's interrogation, 'Unto which of the angels,' &c. Hereby he would have them judge of the truth of what he said, which they could not do unless they had been well exercised in the Scriptures.

IV. *No angel is properly God's Son.* For they are angels concerning whom the apostle propounded this question, and that by way of negation.

V. *Christ is the true and proper and only Son of God.* This is the main scope of this testimony. See Sec. 15.

VI. *The Father acknowledgeth Christ to be his Son.* This apostrophe, 'thou art,' &c., expressly sets down the Father's acknowledgment. This is to strengthen our faith the more in this great article, as Mat. iii. 17, and xvii. 5.

VII. *The true Son of God is begotten of God.* The inference of the latter part of this testimony upon the former plainly proveth the doctrine of this great mystery. See Sec. 49, &c.

VIII. *The generation of the Son of God is an eternal generation.* This is gathered from one signification of the particle, *this day*. See Sec. 50.

IX. *God gave visible evidences of his Son's eternal generation.* This also ariseth from this word, *this day*. See Sec. 58, &c.

X. *Sundry testimonies may be alleged for one and the same point.* Here the apostle joineth several testimonies by these conjunctives, *and again*.

XI. *God continueth to be the same to his Son.* This word of promise, 'I will be to him a Father,' intends as much. As he is ever the same in his essence, so also in his will and affection towards his Son.

XII. *The Son of God is such to his Father as his Father is to him.* The addition of this co-relative, 'He shall be to me a Son,' upon the former part, 'I will be his Father,' imports so much.

XIII. *The truth of what was promised to Solomon as a type was accomplished in Christ.* This application unto Christ of that which was first spoken unto Solomon proves as much.

Sec. 66. *Of bringing Christ into the world.*

Ver. 6. *And again, when he bringeth in the first-begotten into the world, he saith, And let all the angels of God worship him.*

Here the apostle produceth another argument to prove the excellency of Christ above angels. The first clause, καὶ πάλιν, *and again*, importeth as much. Such a phrase was used before (Sec. 63) to note a connection of two confirmations of one and the same argument. Here it is used to distinguish two arguments produced for proof of the main point.

The point is, that Christ is more excellent than angels. The argument is, because he is the only true Son of God. This argument was confirmed, first by one testimony out of Ps. ii. 7 ; and then by another argument out of 2 Sam. vii. 14. Before this latter, to shew that it tendeth to the same purpose that the former did, he premiseth this clause, *and again*.

Here to that argument taken from Christ's dignity, he added another, taken from the subjection of angels to Christ. And because it proveth as much as the former did, he saith, *And again*.

In the Greek a particle of opposition (δὲ, *but*) is used, which is here well turned into a copulative, *and*; for all the testimonies tend to the same scope.

In the Greek also the words are somewhat otherwise placed than in our English, word for word thus, ὅταν δὲ πάλιν, &c., 'but when again he bringeth in,' &c. This may seem to imply that Christ was twice brought into the world. And there be that apply this to Christ's second coming in his glory, and all the holy angels with him, Mat. xxv. 31, and say that then again God brought him into the world.[1] But that second coming of Christ is not agreeable to the scope of that psalm out of which this testimony is taken, nor yet to the scope of the apostle in this chapter, which is to set out the dignity and excellency of the Son of God made flesh, and so sent into the world.

Wherefore, to avoid that mistake, most translators[2] and expositors turn it as our English hath done, and so place this particle *again* as it may have reference to this verb, λέγει, he saith ; as if it had been thus expressed : 'And again he saith, when he bringeth in,' &c.

The notation of the Greek word here translated *world*, οἰκουμένην, sheweth that he understandeth the habitable part of the earth,[3] where men abide ; so as the Son of God was unto sons of men to be as one among them.

By *bringing into the world* is meant a manifestation in the world. Then was Christ first manifested when he was incarnate, or born ;[4] as we say of a child new born, it is brought into the world. Yet is not this phrase to be restrained only to that time, or to that act ; but also to be extended to all those evidences whereby, in the world, he was manifested to be the Son of God, especially to that dignity and dominion which the Father gave him over the whole world, in that he made him 'heir of all things,' ver. 2 ; 'gave him the uttermost parts of the earth for his possession,' Ps. ii. 8 ; yea, and 'all power in heaven and earth,' Mat. xxviii. 18, so as the bringing him into the world may imply a setting of him a king in the world, and over all the world, even over all things that be under God.[5]

By virtue of this high dignity and supreme sovereignty, the Father subjected all creatures to his Son, as he was God manifested in the flesh. The angels themselves were not exempted ; for he hath set him

---

[1] Loquitur de secundo Christi adventu, cum ad judicandum veniet, quæ est secunda introductio in hunc mundum inferiorem.—*Ribera, Comment. in* Heb. i. 6.
[2] Syr. Heb. Lat. aliique.
[3] Ea mundi pars quæ est habitabilis.—*See* Chap. ii. Sec. 41.
[4] Introitum assumptionem carnis appellat.—*Chrys.*
[5] Introducit in orbem, cum ei committit orbem terrarum. —*Chrys.*

'far above all principality and power, and might, and dominion, and every name that is named, not only in this world, but also in that which is to come,' Eph. i. 21.

If the 97th Psalm, whereunto the apostle hath relation, be observantly read, that which I have said will be found to be especially there intended; for it is a prophecy of Christ's royalty, the magnificence whereof being set out in the six first verses, in the seventh he denounceth confusion on such as worship false gods, and chargeth all that, by reason of any divine excellency conferred on them, have this glorious title *gods* attributed unto them, to worship this true God, the Lord Christ, so exalted.

Sec. 67. *Of Christ the first-begotten.*

Him whom before the apostle styled the Son, the Son whom the Father begat, he here calleth the 'first-begotten,' πρωτότοκος.

How Christ is begotten of the Father, hath been before shewed, Sec. 49, &c. Here we are to declare how he is the first-begotten; for by way of excellency and property is this title here given unto him.

The word translated *first-begotten* is a compound of a verb that signifieth to bring forth, or to beget, τίκτω, *pario*; and of an adjective that signifieth first, πρῶτος, *primus*. It is translated also *first-born*. It is in sacred Scripture applied to sons of men, as well as to the Son of God.

When it is spoken of mere men, it is translated first-born. They are so called for order or honour's sake.

In regard of order, sons of men are styled first-born, simply and relatively.

1. Simply, for such as first open the womb, though no other come out of the same womb.[1] Thus is it expounded Exod. xiii. 2. In this sense Israel, who at that time was God's only son, is styled his first-born, Exod. iv. 22; and Jesus, as born of the virgin Mary, is thus styled her first-born, Mat. i. 25.

2. Relatively, in relation to others that follow after out of the same womb; as 1 Sam. xvii. 13, 'Eliab the first-born, and next unto him Abinadab,' &c. In regard of this relative consideration, some translate it thus, 'Eliab the eldest.'

For honour's sake, they are styled first-born to whom the pre-eminence and privileges of the first-born do belong.

The pre-eminency was, to be as a lord and ruler over the family.

In this respect Cain is said to have the excellency, and to rule over his brother, Gen. iv. 7.

The priviledge of the first-born was to have the inheritance, or at least a double portion, Deut. xxiii. 15–17.

Both these, namely, the pre-eminency and the inheritance, upon just ground might be transferred from the eldest to the better deserving son. Thus were both translated from Esau to Jacob, Gen. xxvii. 28, 29; and the former was translated from Reuben to Judah; and the latter from Reuben to Joseph,[1] 1 Chron. v. 1, 2.

In relation to the honour of first-born saints, as having reference to God, and mystically and spiritually styled first-born, Heb. xii. 23.

This title is attributed to the Son of God in regard of his natures and person.

1. In relation to his divine nature, he is the first-begotten of God, in regard of the eternity of his Sonship. Thus is he styled 'the first-born of every creature,' Col. i. 15; that is, begotten before any creature was made, even eternally. He is said to be born or begotten, to set out his divine nature (being the very same with the Father, whereas all creatures are made); and first-born or first-begotten, to shew that he was before all, even eternal. And thus is he also the only begotten Son of God, John iii. 16.

2. In relation to his human nature, he is said to be the first-born of his mother, the virgin Mary, Mat. i. 25, for he first opened her womb; yea, he was the first that ever was conceived of the Holy Ghost, and born of a virgin.

3. In regard of his person, consisting of two natures, God and man hypostatically united together, he is said to be 'the first-born from the dead,' Col. i. 18; or the 'first-begotten of the dead,' Rev. i. 5; for as man he died, as God he raised himself from the dead, Rom. i. 4. He is said to be the first-begotten of the dead in respect of honour and order.

(1.) In honour. In that he rose as a priest and Lord to ascend up into heaven, and to sit at his Father's right hand, there to make intercession for his church, Rom. viii. 34; and to rule and govern the same, Acts ii. 32, 33, &c. These are the privileges of the first-born.

(2.) In order. In that none rose to glory, never to die again, before him.[2] Many were raised from the dead before he rose again; but they were raised to such a life as they had before, a mortal life subject to death; and, answerably, they died again. But Christ 'being raised from the dead, dieth no more,' Rom. vi. 9. Very probable it is that they who were raised out of their graves at Christ's resurrection went after him into heaven, and returned not to death again. In

---

[1] *Mos est divinarum Scripturarum ut primogenitum non eum vocent quem fratres sequuntur, sed eum qui primus natus sit.*—*Hier. Comment. in* Mat. i.

[1] *Primogenitus Esau, sed benedictionem patris Jacob præripuit; primogenitus Reubin, sed tamen benedictio seminis Christi transfertur ad Judam.*—*Hier. Comment. in* Isa. i. *Primogenitus, inquit, non primo creatus, ut et genitus pro natura, et primus pro perpetuitate, credatur.*—*Amb. de Fide ad Grat.* lib. i. cap. iv.

[2] *Primogenitum a mortuis dicit, resurrectio enim mortuorum ut jam non moriatur, ante illum nulla.*—*Aug. Expos. quæst. ex Epist. ad Rom.* 56.

this respect Christ is such a first-born as many will follow after him, so as he may well be said to be 'the first-born among many brethren,' Rom. viii. 29.

Though Christ, in regard of his divine nature, and by virtue of his eternal generation, be the only begotten Son of his Father; and in regard of his human nature, by reason of the perpetual virginity of his mother, her only begotten Son; yet may he well be said to have brethren, and that in two especial respects:

1. Because the Son of God and sons of men are of one, even of one and the same nature; therefore 'he is not ashamed to call them brethren,' Heb. ii. 11.

2. Because he hath adopted them to be the sons of his Father; for we children of men are said to have the 'adoption of children by Jesus Christ,'[1] Eph. i. 5.

In this respect Christ styles his disciples whom he had adopted 'brethren,' Mat. xxviii. 20. For he himself renders this reason for calling them brethren, my Father is their Father, John xx. 17.

That which the apostle here intendeth under this title *first-begotten*, is to set forth the excellency of the person of Christ as God-man, and that,

1. In his priority, which is eternity as he is God, Prov. viii. 24, 25.

2. In his dignity, being the most excellent of all, Gen. xlix. 3.

3. In regard of his dominion over all, Ps. ii. 6, 7.

4. In regard of the largeness of his inheritance, Ps. ii. 8.

In these respects it might well be said to the most excellent of creatures, 'Let all the angels of God worship him;' for the eternal, the most excellent, the Lord of all, and the heir of all, is to be worshipped by all creatures, not the angels excepted.

Sec. 68. *Of saints being first-born.*

Obj. Sons of men, even mere men, are also styled first-born, Exod. iv. 21, Jer. xxxi. 9, Heb. xii. 23.

Ans. They are not so styled *absolutely*, as considered in themselves, but *relatively*, as they are mystically united to Christ, and are his members. By virtue of that union, the privilege and prerogative of the Head is attributed to the members. In this respect they are said to be 'heirs of God, joint heirs with Christ,' Rom. viii. 17. Thus also hath he made them 'kings and priests unto God,' Rev. i. 6.

2. Men are not styled first-born *properly*, as Christ is the first-born; but *metaphorically*, by way of resemblance. Saints are to God as first-born in regard of God's respect to them. God esteemeth them all his first-born; he loveth them, he honours them, he gives an inheritance to them as to his first-born. Thus is the phrase expounded Jer. xxxi. 9, where God saith, 'I am a Father to Israel, and Ephraim is my first-born.'

[1] Jus filiorum adoptionemque cæteris conciliavit.—*Atha. serm.* 4, *contra Arian.*

3. Men are not styled first-born *simply*, as so born from the womb, but *comparatively*, in regard of those that are without Christ, 'children of disobedience,' and 'heirs of wrath,' Eph. ii. 2, 3. Thus Israel was God's first-born, Exod. iv. 22, in comparison of the Egyptians and other people, that were aliens from the commonwealth of Israel, and strangers from the covenant of promise.

4. No son of man is God's first-born *eternally*, before all times, but *respectively*, in reference to future times. Thus the whole stock of Israel (who were the first general assembly of saints, among whom God continued his church till the Gentiles were called) are, in reference to the Gentiles, who were grafted in the stock for the Jews that were broken off, styled 'first-fruits,' Rom. xi. 16; and 'first-born,' Exodus iv. 22, 23.

Sec. 69. *Of David God's first-born.*

Obj. 2. David, by a kind of property and excellency, is called God's first-born, Ps. lxxxix. 27; where God thus saith of him, 'I will make him my first-born, higher than the kings of the earth.'

Ans. Howsoever that may in some respects be applied to David, who was a true adopted child of God, the first of God's faithful ones that as king reigned over that ancient people of God, who was also the head of those kings on whom the kingdom over Israel was established, and more excellent than all the kings of the earth in his time; yet those excellent prerogatives which are mentioned in that psalm, were but poor and slender in comparison of what they are, if they should be no other than what rested in David's person.

We are therefore to know that David was an especial type of Christ, and that many super-excellent prerogatives, which are proper to the only begotten Son of God, are there applied to David, merely as a type of that Son of God, and as a dark shadow of his incomparable and incomprehensible excellencies; that so God's people, who lived before Christ was exhibited, might have some representations (so far forth as in mortal men they could be set out) of Christ's surpassing glory, and infinite blessings that in him were brought to men. That therefore which is promised, Ps. lxxxix. 27, is properly meant of Christ, and typically applied to David.

Thus we see that (albeit sons of men in some improper respects are styled God's first-born) properly Christ Jesus is only his first-born; even that first-born who only is worthy to have the honour intended in these words, 'Let all the angels of God worship him.'

Thus it may appear that the honour of being first-born is due unto him. It is confirmed by divine testimony in this phrase, λέγει, 'he saith;' *he,* that is, God the Father. For it is the Father that taketh such and such care of the Son, and commandeth all to honour him.

Sec. 70. *Of God's title given to angels.*

Before the testimony alleged, this copulative particle καί, *and*, is prefixed thus, 'and worship him,' &c., to shew that this is not the only argument whereby Christ's divine excellency is proved; but it is as one added to others, with which it may be coupled, and it implieth, that as all sorts of men, so *and* all angels also are to worship Christ.

The testimony itself is taken out of Ps. xcvii. 7, the last clause of which verse is, as our English and sundry other translators turn it, 'Worship him, all ye gods.'

The original Hebrew word אלהים, which the LXX Greek translators turn *angels*, is one of God's titles. The first title that in sacred Scripture is attributed to God is this, ברא אלהים, Gen. i. 1, 'God created.'

Among the ten titles that in the Old Testament are given as names to God,[1] two of them are common to creatures, which are אדון, Adon, and אלהים, Elohim. The former of these is attributed to a governor of a family, or of a polity, and ordinarily translated Lord, as Gen. xviii. 12 and xl. 1. Governors bear God's image, are in his place, and therefore have his style given to them.

The latter, being of the plural number, is attributed to God, to set out the plurality of persons, but oft joined with a verb of the singular number to note the unity of nature; ויאמר אלהים, Gen. i. 3.

2. It is applied to idols, Judges xvii. 5. For worshippers of idols do account them gods; and to set out their superstitious conceit of them, they are styled gods.

3. It is given to men of eminent place and excellent parts, Exod. xxii. 28, vii. 1, Ps. lxxxii. 6; for these after an especial manner bear the image of God.

4. It is ascribed to angels, Ps. viii. 5, because they are of all creatures the most excellent, and the fairest representation of God's excellency. See Sec. 107.

Therefore, not without cause is the word by the ancient Greek translators turned *angels*; and the apostle, who was guided by the same Spirit that the psalmist was, quoting it so, gives evident proof that angels are there meant.

So again is the very same Hebrew word by the same Greek interpreters translated *angel*, Ps. viii. 5, and justified by the apostle, Heb. ii. 7.

The Chaldee paraphrase doth in sundry other places so expound it.[2]

So much also will follow by just and necessary consequence; for if all gods, that is, all creatures that in any respect may be called gods, are to worship Christ, then angels also.

[1] Vide Hieron epist. ad Marcel, de decem Dei nominibus.
[2] Ps. lxxxvi. 8, באלהים; *Targum.*, באנגלג; Job i. 6, בני אלהים; *Targum*, ביתי מלאכיא; 1 Sam. xxviii. 13, אלהים; *Targum*, מלאכא.

Sec. 71. *Of angels' relation to God.*

The angels here spoken of are called angels of God in sundry respects.

1. They are of God, as created by him, the work of his hands, Col. i. 16.

They bear God's image, and of all creatures are most like unto God in the kind of their substance, which is spiritual, and in the glory thereof. In this respect they are styled sons of God, Job i. 6.

3. They are God's special and principal servants, continually attending upon him, Ps. lxviii. 17 and ciii. 20, 21, Dan. vii. 10, Mal. xviii. 10.

4. They have ever remained stedfast with God, notwithstanding other angels 'left their own habitation,' Jude 6. Therefore, for distinction's sake, the good angels are called 'angels of God,' but evil angels, 'angels of the devil,' Mat. xxv. 41, 2 Cor. xii. 7.

Sec. 72. *Of varying from the letter of the text.*

Obj. This correlative *of God*, is not in the original Hebrew text, Ps. xcvii. 7.

Ans. It is not against the text, but rather implied therein. For,

1. They that are styled *gods*, may justly be said to be *of God*.

2. Christ would not accept worship done to him by angels of the devil, Mark iii. 11, 12. Can we then think that the Father would command such angels to worship his Son? And if angels of the devil be not there meant, then they must needs be angels of God which are intended in the place quoted.

3. To take away all ambiguity, the LXX adds this relative particle *his* thus, 'Worship him, all ye *his* angels,' ἄγγελοι αὐτοῦ; and the apostle, to make the point appear more clear, expresseth the correlative thus, 'angels of God.' See Chap. xiii. ver. 6, Sec. 78.

Because I shall oft have occasion to make mention of the seventy interpreters of the Old Testament into Greek, who are oft expressed by these letters LXX, I think it meet, at this first mention of them, distinctly to set down their history, as an ancient father[1] hath left it upon record, thus: Ptolemy, the son of Lagus, desirous that the library which he had made in Alexandria might be replenished with worthy books of all sorts, prayed the Jews at Jerusalem to have their Scriptures interpreted into the Greek tongue; thereupon, they who were then under the Macedonians sent to Ptolemy seventy elders, such as perfectly understood the Scriptures, and the Hebrew and Greek tongue, according to his desire. He, willing to make proof of them, and fearing lest they should conceal by their interpretation that truth which was in the Scriptures, by a mutual consent severed them one from another, and commanded every one of them to interpret the same scripture; and this they did in all the books. But when they met together in one before

[1] Irenæus advers. hæres. lib. iii. cap. xxv.

Ptolemy, and compared their interpretations, God was glorified, and the Scriptures believed to be truly divine; all of them rehearsing the same scripture, both in the same words, and in the same names, from the beginning to the end, that even the present Gentiles might know, that by the inspiration of God, the Scriptures were interpreted.

Such additions of words or alterations of phrases, as make to a more perspicuous expression of the author's mind, may well be done by such as quote his sayings;[1] for such as only cite testimonies for proof of a point are not so strictly tied to the words as translators are. It is enough for the former to retain and express the true meaning of the text which they cite, though it be in other words.

Thus, change of phrase doth oft better express the mind and meaning of the author than a translation word for word; therefore, a faithful interpreter stands not over strictly upon the letter. That which the apostles aimed at, was not to hunt after letters and syllables, but to prove doctrines. See Chap. III. ver. 9, Sec. 100. and Chap. IX. ver. 20, Sec. 106.

This may serve in general to answer the alteration of the person in expressing worship: for the psalmist useth the second person, as speaking to the angels, thus, 'worship him, all ye angels,' השתחוו, προσκυνήσατε, adorate. And the apostle useth the third person as speaking of the angels thus, 'let all the angels worship him,' προσκυνησάτωσαν, adorent. Both phrases set forth one and the same sense.

As for the difference, this reason may be given.

The psalmist, endeavouring to set out the magnificence of Christ in the best manner that he could, amongst other very elegant expressions, useth this rhetorical apostrophe to the angels, 'Worship him, all ye gods.' But the scope of the apostle is only to give a proof of Christ's excellency above angels. For this purpose, it was the fittest expression to set it down positively thus, 'Let all the angels of God worship him.'

Sec. 73. *Of all angels alike subject to Christ.*

This general particle *all* is expressed because there are many angels; for Michael had an army of angels to fight against the dragon and his angels, Rev. xii. 7, and Christ could have had 'more than twelve legions,' that is, 79,992, to have guarded him, Mat. xxvi. 53. Daniel makes mention of 'thousand thousands,' yea, of 'ten thousand thousands,' Dan. vii. 10. And to shew that their number exceeds all number, the apostle styles them 'an innumerable company of angels,' Heb. xii. 22. But be they never so many, they are comprised under this particle *all*, so as all and every one of them must worship Christ.

Yea, if there be distinct and different degrees among them, and several orders, all those degrees and orders, whether more or less eminent, superior or inferior, are comprehended under this universal particle *all*; for, as the apostle noteth in the last verse of this chapter, they are 'all ministering spirits.' If they be 'all ministering spirits for them who shall be heirs of salvation,' much more are they all to worship Christ; for he is the creator of all, even of thrones and dominions, and principalities and powers, Col. i. 16. He is the head of all, Col. ii. 10, and he is advanced far above them all, Eph. i. 21.

If, therefore, these titles of distinction, principalities, powers, &c., give any pre-eminence to some of the angels above others, yet that pre-eminence doth not exempt them from this duty of worshipping Christ Jesus, at whose name 'every knee must bow, of things in heaven or earth,' Philip. ii. 10.

Not without cause therefore this general particle *all* is here used: 'Let all the angels of God worship him.' He that saith *all*, excepteth none at all.

Sec. 74. *Of worship.*

The evidence here noted whereby Christ is declared to be more excellent than all the angels is in this act, *worship*, enjoined to angels; for he that is worshipped is thereby manifested to be far more excellent than they who worship him. Worshipping one is much different from blessing one. That is an act of the inferior, this of the superior: 'Without all contradiction, the less is blessed of the better,' Heb. vii. 7. And without all contradiction the better is worshipped of the less, especially if worship be taken as here in this place.

The Hebrew word used by the psalmist, שחה, *procubuit, incurvatus est*, and translated *worship*, cometh from a root that signifieth to bow down; as Isa. li. 23, 'Bow down, that we may go over thee.' It is most frequently used in the last conjugation,[1] which addeth much emphasis, and importeth both a reciprocal action, reflecting upon one's self, thus, 'He bowed himself,' 1 Sam. xx. 41, and also a thorough, serious performance thereof, even to the ground; and therefore the word *earth* is oft added thereto, to shew a bowing as low as can be, even to the earth or ground, Gen. xxxiii. 3. It is most frequently used for an expression of honour and reverence to another, namely, to him unto whom or before whom this gesture is performed, which some translators set out by this paraphrase,[2] 'They bowed themselves, presenting honour,' and others express it by this one word,[3] *adore* or *worship*.

---

[1] Nec verbum de verbo curabit reddere fidus interpres.—*Hor. de Art. Poet.* Curæ fuit non verba et syllabas aucupari, sed sententias dogmatum ponere.—*Hier. ad Pan. de opt. Gen. Interpret.* See the Whole Armour of God on Eph. vi. 17, treat. ii. par. 2, sec. 8.

[1] Hithpael. In hac conjugatione actio ferè est recriproca.—*Martin. Gram.*, Heb. cap. xvi., et vehementia significatur.—*Pagn. Instit.* Heb. cap. xxxvii.
[2] Incurvarunt se, honorem exhibentes.—*Tremel. et Jun. in Gen.* xxxiii. 6.
[3] Adoravit. *Vet. Lat.* in Gen. xviii. 2, et xix. 1, et xxiii. 7.

The Greek word here used by the apostle is somewhat answerable to the Hebrew, for it is compounded of a word[1] that signifieth *to kiss;* for they that do honour or reverence to others, use to kiss their mouth,[2] as of old they were wont; yea (as now), their[3] hands, knees, and (as it is done to the pope) feet and shoes; yea, the very earth where they stand.

The frequent mention of kissing, to set out reverent and humble subjection in sacred Scripture, sheweth that this was an accustomed gesture of testifying reverence and honour.

When Pharaoh advanced Joseph next to himself, and would that all his people should yield reverent subjection to him, thus he expressed it: 'On thy mouth shall all my people kiss, Gen. xli. 40; that is, as the last English translators have turned it, shall be ruled, or as others,[4] shall obey, or shall be subject.

Thus when Samuel had anointed Saul to be king, he kissed him, 1 Sam. x. 1, in testimony of reverence and subjection. In this respect Moses kissed his father-in-law, Exod. xviii. 7. And idolaters in this respect are said[5] to 'kiss the calves,' Hosea xiii. 2; and they who would not yield honour and subjection to Baal are thus set out, 'Their mouth hath not kissed him,' 1 Kings xix. 18; yea, the reverence and obedience which is required of sons of men to the Son of God is thus expressed, 'Kiss the Son,' Ps. ii. 12.

But to let pass the metaphor, the word used by the apostle doth usually signify, as here it is translated, *worship.*

Worship is a reverent manifestation of that high esteem which we have of another, and it is divine or civil.

Sec. 75. *Of the difference between divine and civil worship.*

Divine worship is that which is performed in acknowledgment of Deity, or any divine excellency in that to whom it is performed. This is due to God alone,[6] for it is written, 'Thou shalt worship the Lord thy God, and him only shalt thou serve,' Mat. iv. 10. That exclusive particle *only* must be referred to *worship* as well as to *serve,* or else it gives not a full answer to the devil's temptation; for where the devil tempted Christ to worship him, Christ repels it with this answer, 'Thou shalt worship the Lord.' Now the sense of the answer lieth in this, that God *only* is to be worshipped; therefore none else. Nor apostle, Acts x. 26, nor angel, Rev. xix. 10, would accept such worship tendered to them, because it was proper to God alone. Yea, Mordecai would rather hazard his own and all the Jews' lives than yield such worship to a mere man, Esther iii. 2. The fiery furnace could not move Daniel's three companions to yield worship to an image, Dan. iii. 18.

Civil worship is that which is performed in acknowledgment of some eminency or excellency in them to whom it is performed.[1] Thus it hath been performed to angels in regard of their eminency in glory, Gen. xix. 1; to kings for their eminency in dignity and authority, 2 Sam. xxiv. 20. So also in like respect to other governors, Gen. xlii. 6; and to parents, Exod. xviii. 7, 1 Kings ii. 19; and to masters, 2 Sam. xviii. 21. Such worship hath also been performed to men for the excellency of parts and gifts wherewith God hath endowed them, 2 Kings ii. 15.

In all these and other places, where reverence is shewed to men, the very word which the psalmist useth, Ps. xcvii. 7, and is translated *worship,* is used; so as of necessity we must distinguish betwixt the kinds of worship, when it is done to the Creator and when to creatures.

In the psalm quoted, and in this text, it is most manifest that divine worship is meant, which angels are commanded to yield to Christ, whereupon by an undeniable consequence it followeth that Christ is infinitely more excellent than angels.

It is further observable that this duty of worshipping Christ is not left as an arbitrary matter to the angels, to do it, or not to do it, but it is put as a duty upon them, and that by way of command: 'Let all the angels of God worship him.' If angels, much more men must worship Christ. See Sec. 128.

Sec. 76. *Of the resolution of the sixth verse.*

Ver 6. *And again, when he bringeth in the first begotten into the world, he saith, And let all the angels of God worship him.*

The second argument to prove Christ's excellency above angels is in this verse. It is taken from that worship which is due to Christ; and it is so set down as withal the inferiority of angels to Christ is proved thereby.

Two arguments, proving two distinct points, are here couched together.

The first is to prove Christ's superiority. It may be thus framed: he who is to be worshipped is greater than they who are to worship him. But Christ is to be worshipped by angels; therefore Christ is greater than angels.

---

[1] Κύω et κυνίω, *osculor.* Gestus eorum qui venerantur aliquem. Olim solebant, os et oculos oculari; nunc manus, genua, pedes. Populi orientales demittunt se pronos in terram, eamque ubi ore attigerint, rursus se erigunt, et semel iterumque venerabundi saluntantesque incurvant corpora. Hinc προσκυνέω, adoro, veneror.

[2] עַל־פִּיךָ יִשַּׁק כָּל־עַמִּי *super os tuum osculabitur omnis populus meus.* [Gen. xli. 40.—Ed.]

[3] Qui adorant deosculari solent manum.—*Hier. Comment. in Hosea* xiii.

[4] LXX, ὑπακούσεται. Vet. Lat., Obediet.

[5] Adorantes vitulos.—*Hier.*

[6] Adorari non creaturæ, sed Domini est.—*Chrys. Hom.* xxxii. *in John* iv.

[1] Adoratio hominibus honorificentiæ causa exhiberi solet a patribus, sicut de Abraham scriptum est, adoravit filios Heth.—*Aug. Quæst. super Exo.* lib. ii. sec 99.

The second is to prove angels' inferiority. It may be thus framed: They who are to worship, are inferior to him that is to [be] worshipped by them. But angels are to worship Christ; therefore angels are inferior to Christ.

In setting down these arguments, such a connection is used as was before, ver. 5, in producing two testimonies, thus, *and again*. The main argument is set down in a charge, about which two points are noted:
1. The time when the charge was given.
2. The duty charged.

The time is set out by an act of God, 'when he bringeth.' This is amplified, 1, by the object, 'the first begotten; 2, by the place, 'into the world.'

In the duty is expressed, 1, the kind, worship; 2, the persons. These are of two sorts:

(1.) They who are to perform the duty, *angels*. Angels are here described,
[1.] By their generality, *all*.
[2.] By their excellency, *of God*.

(2.) The person to whom the duty is to be performed, is expressed in this relative *him*, namely, the first begotten.

Sec. 77. *Of the doctrines arising out of the sixth verse.*

I. *Argument must be added to argument to prove the same point.* For here is another argument than that which was produced, ver. 5, to prove the excellency of Christ. This is evident by this transition, *and again*. In the former verse, testimony was added to testimony, to confirm the same argument; here argument is added to argument, to prove the same point. That which God saith to Moses concerning two signs, Exod iv. 8, 'It shall come to pass, if they will not believe thee, neither hearken to the voice of the first sign, that they will believe the voice of the latter sign,' may be applied to two arguments. See Sec. 63.

II. *The Son of God is begotten of the Father.* See the 7th Doctrine on ver. 5, Sec. 65.

III. *Christ is the first-begotten of the Father.* In what respects this is to be taken, is distinctly shewed, Sec. 67.

IV. *God visibly manifested his Son to men on earth.* The word of *bringing in* implieth a manifestation. Under *world* men on earth are comprised. Read John i. 14; 1 Tim. iii. 16; 1 John i. 1.

V. *God speaketh in the word.* Ver. 1, Chap. iii. 7, Acts iv. 25.

VI. *Divine worship is due to Christ.* Ps. ii. 11; Mat. ii. 11 and v. 2; Luke xxiv. 52. For Christ is the Son of God, true God; and the Father wills 'that all men should honour the Son, even as they should honour the Father,' John v. 23.

VII. *Creatures are bound to worship Christ.* The charge here set down importeth as much.

VIII. *The most excellent creatures must worship Christ.* For angels are of all creatures the most excellent, and they are here enjoined to do it.

IX. *No degree among angels exempteth any of them from subjection to Christ.* For this duty is enjoined to them all, none exempted.

X. *Angels are God's special attendants.* In this respect they are here styled angels of God.

Sec. 78. *Of the coherence of the seventh verse.*

Ver. 7. *And of the angels he saith, Who maketh his angels spirits, and his ministers a flame of fire.*

To amplify the former argument, whereby the apostle proved the excellency of Christ above angels, taken from the inferiority of angels, manifested by their worshipping him, he addeth another evidence of their inferiority, manifested by their manner of serving him. And to shew that there is as good ground and reason for this as for the former, and that angels are as much bound to this as to that, he premiseth in this verse the like preface as in the former, thus, 'And of the angels he saith,' even he that said, 'Let all the angels worship him,' saith also, 'He maketh them spirits.'

Thus may this verse have relation to that which goeth before, as a fit dependence thereon, and so this copulative *and* join two evidences of the inferiority of angels together.

It may also have a fit reference to that which followeth in the 8th verse; and that as an evidence of the infinite disparity betwixt angels and Christ, which the apostle proveth by a third argument, taken from the high sovereignty of Christ, in the verses following. In this verse there is one part of the dissimilitude or disparity betwixt Christ and angels; the other parts are in the 8th and 9th verses. The disparity is this, angels are ministers, but Christ a Lord and King. The adversative particle *but*, in the beginning of the 8th verse, which is a note of an assumption or of opposition, importeth this latter reference.

In this preface, 'of the angels he saith,' there is some ambiguity in the particle translated *of*, πρός, for properly and usually it signifieth *to*; but it [is] apparent in the text quoted that he speaketh not to angels, for he useth not the second but the third person. The apostle therefore imitateth the Hebrew, who put the particle which signifieth *to*, for that which signifieth *of* or *concerning* (אל pro על), Gen. xx. 2, 2 Sam. xxi. 2.

He expresseth the title *angels*, to shew distinctly what kind of spirits and ministers the psalmist meaneth, and also how pertinent the text which he quoteth is to the point in hand.

There is in the Greek an ordinary note of asseveration, μὲν, as is oft translated *verily*. See Chap. iii. 5, Sec. 50.

Sec. 79. *Of the various acception of angels, spirits, ministers, flame of fire.*

This text is taken out of Ps. civ. 4, and word for

word translated by the apostle, as it was long before by the Greek LXX. But because many of the words are of diverse significations, sundry expositors do otherwise take them. For,

1. The word translated angels, מלאך, *missus, nuncius, legatus, angelus*, is oft put indefinitely for messengers; even such as are sent of man, Gen. xxxii. 3, or of God, and these both corporal substances, Isa. xlii. 19, Mal. iii. 1, and also spiritual, Gen. xxxii. 1.

2. The word translated spirits, רוחות, *spiritus*, is put for winds, Ezek. xxxvii. 9; for souls of men, Num. xxvii. 16; for angels, ver. 14; and for the Holy Ghost, Gen. i. 2, Mat. iv. 1.

3. The Hebrew word translated ministers, משרתים, *ministri*, is applied to such as do service to God, whether in the invisible heaven, as angels, or in the visible heavens, as stars, winds, clouds, and other meteors, Ps. ciii. 21, or on earth, as children of men, Isa. lxi. 6.

The Greek word, λειτουργούς, according to the notation of it,[1] setteth out such as are deputed to public services, in which respect their ministry is the more honourable. I find it five times used in the New Testament, in every of which places it importeth a public employment. Epaphroditus, who was publicly employed by the church, is so styled, Philip. ii. 25, and governors of commonwealths, Rom. xiii. 6, and an apostle of Jesus Christ, Rom. xv. 15, and Christ himself, Heb. viii. 2, and the angels here in this place. The more honourable their function was, the more is Christ's dignity amplified thereby, in that such honourable ministers were inferior to him. See Chap. viii. 2, Sec. 3.

4. This phrase, a flame of fire, אשׁ להט, *ignis flammans*, or, flaming fire, as it is literally taken for flaming fire on earth, Ps. lxxxiii. 14, and for the lightning falling down from heaven, Ps. xxix. 7, so it is mystically used to set out the glory of God, Dan. vii. 9, and the fierceness of his wrath, Isa. xxix. 6, 2 Thes. i. 8, and for fervour and zeal, Ps. xxxix. 3.

Sec. 80. *Of the meaning of the 4th verse of the 104th Psalm.*

In regard of the diverse acceptations of these words, some apply them to airy and fiery meteors, as to winds and lightning. Thus most of the Jewish, and many of our modern expositors[2] take these words, as if we should translate them according to their sense, 'Who maketh the winds his messengers, and the lightning his ministers.' Thus they invert the plain order of the words,[3] putting that in the first place, namely, spirits or winds, which in the text is in the latter place, and angels or messengers in the latter, which are in the first. The like inverting of order is in the second clause, and in both places without any need.

Obj. In the former verse the psalmist speaks of the winds.

Ans. It followeth not thereupon that he must needs speak of the winds in this verse, for the scope of the psalmist is not to treat only of the winds, but to set out the magnificence of God in the variety of creatures.

The scope of that psalm is in the first clause of the first verse noted in these words, 'Bless the Lord.'

The sum thereof is in these, 'My God, thou art great,' &c.

In the sequel of the psalm he exemplifieth that sum, in sundry particular great and glorious works of God.

He beginneth with that visible glorious work which God first made, the light; to which he addeth the highest visible heaven, ver. 2; then he mentioneth the waters, clouds, and winds, under the foresaid heavens, ver. 3; and before he descendeth lower, to the earth, and the things thereon, he bringeth in the angels, whom God useth to do his works, in heaven and on earth, ver. 4. In the verses following he sets out God's great works on the earth and waters below.

Thus we see how fitly the testimony quoted may, according to the most plain, proper, literal, and grammatical sense, be applied to angels. To make this the clearer, the Greek interpreters set such an article before these two words, *angels, ministers*, as declare those other words, spirits, flame of fire, to be attributed to them, τοὺς ἀγγέλους, τοὺς λειτουργούς.

Many of the ancient fathers[1] acknowledge that which the Greek and the last English translators have set down to be the true literal meaning of the psalmist; and thereupon infer, that both the nature and office of those celestial creatures is noted. For the word angel points at their office; spirit, at their nature. In that they are or have a being, they are spirits; in that they do this or that, they are angels.[2]

Thus the testimony taken from the psalmist being applied to angels, is most pertinent to the proof of the point for which the apostle doth produce it. But applied to winds and lightnings, it is little to the purpose.

It is said that the apostle applieth that which is spoken of winds and lightnings, to angels, by way of analogy and resemblance, comparing angels to winds and lightnings; and in similitude referreth that to the invisible creatures, which the psalmist attributeth to visible.[3]

---

[1] Quasi, λειτουργούς, qui publicum munus obierunt.
[2] Vide Vatabl. Annot. in Ps. civ. 4. Calvinus, Musculus, Beza, Flaminius. Aliique in eundem Psa.
[3] Prædicatum loco subjecti, et subjectum loco prædicati.

[1] Hieron. August. Arnob. Prosp. Theod. aliique.
[2] Quæris nomen ejus naturæ? Spiritus est. Quæris officium? Angelus est. Ex eo quod est, spiritus est: Ex eo quod agit, angelus est.—*Aug. Enar. in Ps.* ciii.
[3] Sic fere Prosp. Argumentum a simili esse videtur, cum ad angelos transfert apostolus quod proprie de ventis dictum est.—*Calvin in Heb.* i. 7. Chaldæus item exponit Ps. civ. 4, per similitudinem.

angel, and may be well reckoned among the titles given to angels.

4. *Sons of God*, Job i. 6. Thus they are called, not only because they received their being from God, and are sustained by him, but also, being once made after the image of God, they still retain that image.

5. *Gods*.[1] So doth that word signify which we translate angels, Ps. viii. 5. It is attributed to angels to set out their excellency; for excellent things are in Canaan's dialect styled gods, Ps. lxxxii. 1, 6. The same title is given them Ps. xcvii. 7, and translated gods.

6. *Cherubim*, Gen. iii. 24, Ezek. x. 1. *Cherub* taken indefinitely importeth a figure or image; most usually a resemblance of a young man. So were angels set out when a resemblance or picture was made of them, and when they appeared in a visible shape. They appeared in the shape of a man, to shew they were creatures of knowledge and understanding[2] (as men endued with reasonable souls are); and of a young man, to set out their beauty, vigour, strength, and other like excellencies appertaining to youth.

7. *Seraphims*. This title is twice, and only twice, attributed to angels, Isa. vi. 2, 6. The title cometh from an Hebrew root,[3] that signifieth to burn. It is attributed to those fiery serpents which in the wilderness bit and stung the people to death, Num. xxi. 6. Angels are called seraphim,[4] either from the particular act of theirs in touching the prophet's lips with a burning coal, Isa. vi. 6, or else more indefinitely from their fervent zeal in executing the will of their Lord. In allusion hereunto, it is thus written: 'He maketh his angels spirits; his ministers a flame of fire,' Ps. civ. 4.

8. *Watchers*.[5] He that is styled a watcher, Dan. iv. 13, was an angel, and by the ancient Greek translators of the Old Testament is so called. The plural number, watchers,[6] is used Dan. iv. 17. This title is given to angels,

(1.) In regard of their nature; for they being spirits are not subject to heaviness, drowsiness, and sleepiness, but wake and watch continually day and night.

(2.) In regard of their function, which is 'always to behold the face of God,' Mat. xviii. 10, and to be ever ready at hand to do his will, Ps. ciii. 20. This they cannot do without continual watching.

(3.) In regard of that constant continual care which they have to keep saints from the manifold dangers whereunto they are subject. Saints have enemies which continually watch night and day to do them some mischief: 'Your adversary the devil,' saith an apostle, 1 Peter v. 8, 'as a roaring lion, walketh about, seeking whom he may devour.' The good angels therefore continually watch to keep them safe from his clutches. In relation to their continual watchfulness, angels are said to be 'full of eyes round about,' Ezek. i. 18.

9. *Holy ones*. So they are called Dan. iv. 13, 17. There these two titles, *watcher* and *holy one*, are applied to one and the same person. This title is given unto them in regard of that holiness wherein they were at first created, and in which they still abide; which maketh them to delight in holiness, and to practise holiness. Therefore they are justly styled holy angels, Mark viii. 38, Mat. xxv. 31.

10. *God's host*. Angels are so called,[1] Gen. xxxii. ii.; Ps. ciii. 21; Luke ii. 13; and that because God useth them as an host to protect his saints, 2 Kings vi. 17; and to destroy his enemies, 2 Chron. xxxii. 21; Rev. xii. 7.

11. *Thrones*; θρόνοι, Col. i. 16. This word must needs be expounded metonymically (if it be applied as many ancient and later divines apply it,[2] to angels); for thrones, properly taken, are royal seats, made for kings to sit upon, and then especially when they shew forth their magnificence. In this proper signification many judicious divines[3] take this word *thrones* to be used, Col. i. 16, and apply it to the invisible heavens, where God especially setteth out the glory of his majesty. Therefore heaven is said to be God's throne, Mat. v. 34; and for excellency's sake the plural number may be used. But applied to angels, they are so called in regard of their dignity and excellency; being fit to sit on thrones, at least in comparison to other creatures. Thus, tropically, thrones are put for such as sit, or are worthy to sit, on thrones.

12. *Dominions*; Κυριότητες, Col. i. 16. This title is fitly added to the former, to shew that God, who hath conferred such excellency and dignity on angels, as the fore-mentioned title *thrones* implieth, hath also given them dominion and rule; whereby, as lords under God, they order and govern matters and persons in the world. The devils have a dominion and government over wicked ones; in which respect they are styled 'rulers of the darkness of the world,' Eph. vi. 12, and that for executing greater vengeance on

---

[1] אלהים. In Hebræo pro eo quod est ab angelis, qui dicuntur, מלאכים, Deum habet, hoc est, אלהים.*

[2] Cherubim interpretantur *scientiæ multitudo*.—*Hier. Comment. in Ezek.* xxviii. Ita ferè Chrys. de incompr. Dei Nat. Hom. iii. See Chap. ix. ver. 4, Sec. 32.

[3] שרף, *seraphim*. Præter hunc locum in Scripturis canonicis alibi legisse me nescio.—*Hier. in Isa.* vi.

[4] Seraphim interpretantur ἐμπρηστὰς, quod nos dicere possumus *incendentes*, sive *comburentes*; juxta illud quod alibi legimus, 'qui facit angelos suos spiritus, et ministros suos ignem urentem.'—*Hier. Comment. in Isa.* vi. Sic Chrys. loc. citat. [5] עִיר, ἄγγελος.

[6] עִירִין. עִיר, significat *angelos*, quod semper vigilent, et ad Dei imperium sint parati.—*Hier. Comment. in Dan.* iv.

* This note we give as it stands in the original, though we do not understand it.—*Ed.*

[1] Castra Dei quæ vidit Jacob in itinere, nulla dubitatio est, quin angelorum fuerit multitudo: ea quippe in Scripturis militia cœli nominatur.—*Aug. quæst. super Gen.* cap. 101.

[2] Chrys. Hier. Theoph. Aug. Erasm. Zanch., aliique.

[3] Calv. Comment. in Col. i. 16. Dan. Isagog. Chr Par. ii. cap. 14.

them. In like manner may good angels have dominion for procuring and effecting greater good.

13. *Principalities;* ἀρχαί, Col. i. 16. This title is somewhat more special than the former. *Dominions* indefinitely and generally note such as have authority, without respect to any particular jurisdiction; but *principalities* are such as have a special and peculiar jurisdiction. In this sense the apostle admonisheth Christians to be 'subject to principalities,' Titus iii. 1, that is, to such as have authority over them in particular; for every one is not bound to be subject to every dominion. This title is attributed to good angels, Eph. iii. 10, Col. i. 16, because God doth oft set some of them over particular polities, and kingdoms, and persons. It is also applied to evil angels, Eph. vi. 12, Col. i. 15, because for their greater advantage they take to themselves special jurisdiction over particular places and persons.

14. *Powers;* ἐξουσίαι, Col. i. 16. The Greek word properly signifieth that right which governors have to exercise their authority:[1] so is our English word *power* oft used; as John x. 18, where Christ thus saith, 'I have power,' ἐξουσίαν ἔχω, 'to lay down my life, and I have power to take it again;' and where Peter saith to Ananias, of the price which he had for his land, 'Was it not in thy power?' ἐν τῇ σῇ ἐξουσίᾳ, Acts v. 4. This title then sheweth that angels have a good right to that government which they take upon them.

Obj. These titles, *principalities and powers*, are attributed to devils, Eph. vi. 12, Col. ii. 15.

Ans. The same titles may be applied to different persons in different respects. This great title *God* is attributed to the Creator, to angels and men; yea, and to the devil too, 2 Cor. iv. 4. The different respects wherein the foresaid titles are given to good and evil angels are these:

(1.) Good angels are principalities and powers by God's special appointment. God hath given them the dominion which they have, and a right thereunto. Devils have theirs by a divine permission; yet they are but usurpers thereof.

(2.) Good angels are principalities and powers over saints especially, and most properly for their good; but devils are over the wicked, in which respect they are said to be 'rulers of the darkness of this world,' Eph. vi. 12; and that in judgment, to execute vengeance on them; and in this respect God may be said to make them principalities and powers, to be his executioners to inflict the sorer vengeance.

15. *Mights;* δυνάμεις, Rom. viii. 38. This title imports strength and ability to accomplish what they undertake. In this respect they are said to be 'mighty in strength;' גברי כח, or, as our English translate it, to 'excel in strength,' Ps. ciii. 20. Many instances are throughout the Scriptures given of their might and strength.

[1] ἐξεῖναι, licere. Inde, ἐξουσία, licentia, jus, potestas.

Sec. 61. *Of the like excellencies of every angel.*

Concerning the fore-mentioned titles, two things are to be observed:

1. That many of them are not simply and properly to be taken (as if angels were indeed flames of fire, or fair youths, or sat on thrones), but by way of similitude, the more conspicuously to set out sundry excellencies in them.

2. That the distinct titles do not so much set out distinct persons, or orders, or degrees among the angels, as distinct properties, gifts, and excellencies in them; as is evident by this phrase applied to angels in four several apparitions: 'they four had the face of a man and the face of a lion on the right side; and they four had the face of an ox on the left side; they four also had the face of an eagle,' Ezek. i. 10. So as one was not as a man alone, and another as a lion, and a third as an ox, and a fourth as an eagle; but all four had one likeness. Hereby it was implied, that every angel was prudent as a man, courageous as a lion, laborious as an ox, swift as an eagle. In like respects the same person was called a prophet, a man of God, and a seer, 1 Sam. iii. 20 and ix. 6, 11. And the same thing a dream, a vision, a revelation, Dan. ii. 28; see chap. ii.

Thus much of the titles attributed to angels.

Sec. 86. *Of the nature of angels.*

Angels are created spirits subsisting in themselves. Every word in this brief description so makes to the nature of angels, as it distinguisheth them from all others.

1. They are *spirits;* so they are expressly called in this verse and verse 14. This importeth both their being, and also the kind of their being. Spirits are substances, and have a true real being, as the souls of men have, which are styled spirits, Eccles. xii. 7, Heb. xii. 9, 23.

The offices deputed by God to angels, the great works done by them, the excellent gifts wherewith they are endued (as knowledge, wisdom, holiness, strength, &c.), do plainly demonstrate that they are true real substances.

Hereby they are distinguished from all mere imaginations and phantasies, which are conceptions in men's minds of such things as never were, nor ever had any true being at all; as those *intelligentiæ* which, philosophers conceit, do turn the celestial orbs.

They are also hereby distinguished from physical qualities, philosophical accidents, and from mere motions, affections, inspirations, and such other things as have no true real being at all.

The title *spirit* doth further import their kind of being to be spiritual, which is the most excellent being that can be. Herein it is like to the divine being; for 'God is a spirit,' John iv. 24.

Hereby the being of angels is distinguished from all kind of corporeal substances, which are sensible, visible, subject to drowsiness, weariness, heaviness, fainting, diminutions, decay, destruction, and sundry other infirmities, to which spirits are not subject.

2. They are *created*. This was proved before, Sec. 81.

Hereby angels are distinguished from their Creator, who is a spirit, but uncreated. Angels are styled gods, and sons of God (as was shewed Sec. 70), and endued with sundry excellencies above other creatures; yet, being created, neither are they to be accounted truly and properly gods, nor anything proper to the Deity is to be attributed or done to them.

3. They *subsist in themselves*. Though they have their being from God, and are preserved, sustained, and every way upheld by God, so as they have their subsistence from God, yet God hath so ordered it as it is in themselves. Angelical spirits have neither bodies nor any other like thing to subsist in.

Hereby they are distinguished from the souls of men, which are spirits, Luke xxiii. 46, Heb. xii. 23, but have their subsistence properly in their bodies. This phrase, Gen. ii. 7, 'God breathed into man's nostrils the breath of life, and he became a living soul,' imports as much. So doth this philosophical principle, The soul in infusing it into the body is created, and in the creation of it is infused.[1]

True it is that the soul may be separated from the body, and retain the spiritual being which it hath; but so as it longeth after the body, and is restless till it be reunited to the body: 'We would not be unclothed,' that is, we do not simply desire a putting off the body from the soul, 'but clothed upon,' that is, have immortality put upon our bodies, without separating their souls from them, 2 Cor. v. 4. As for the souls which are separated from their bodies, they cry, 'How long, O Lord, holy and true,' Rev. vi. 10. This shews a desire of union with their bodies again.

Angels being God's special messengers, they were thus constituted spirits subsisting in themselves, that they might be the more fit messengers and ministers to execute God's will more readily, more speedily, and every way more thoroughly. For, being spirits, they are not hindered by such incumbrances and infirmities as bodies are; and, subsisting in themselves, they need not such *organa*, such instruments and parts of a body, as the souls of men do.

This of the nature of angels.

Sec. 87. *Of the knowledge of angels*.

The properties of angels are many, and those very excellent ones. Some of the principal are these which follow:

1. Great knowledge. For they are intellectual or understanding creatures, able to conceive any mysteries that are or shall be revealed. They understand according to the spiritual power of an angelical mind, comprehending all things that they will together most easily.[1] Angels, being in heaven, know all the counsel of God that is there made known. That which Christ saith of them, Mat. xviii. 10, 'In heaven they do always behold the face of my Father,' implieth that they are privy to the whole counsel of God revealed in heaven; yea, on earth also they frequent the assembly of saints. Thereby they come to know the whole counsel of God on earth made known to the church. In this respect the apostle saith, that 'Unto the principalities and powers in heavenly places is made known by the church the manifold wisdom of God,' Eph. iii. 10. They are very inquisitive after all divine mysteries; for of those things which prophets foretold, and apostles preached, it is thus said, 'which things the angels desire to look into,' 1 Peter i. 12. This restrictive phrase, 'no, not the angels,' Mark xiii. 32, importeth the great measure of knowledge which angels have; for it followeth, 'nor the Son:' 'Of that day and that hour knoweth no man, no, not the angels which are in heaven, neither the Son.' By the two last phrases it is implied that if any creatures knew that secret, surely the Son and the angels would know it.

Obj. It is an impeachment of their knowledge not to know all things.

Ans. It is no impeachment of a creature's knowledge not to know such things as belong not to him to know; which are such as 'the Father hath put into his own power,' Acts i. 7; and many things to come, Isa. xli. 23; and the thoughts of men's hearts, 1 Kings viii. 39; and any secret which belongs to the Lord, Deut. xxix. 29.

Satan deluded our first parents by suggesting to them a conceit of knowledge of more than was meet to be known.

The gift of knowledge which angels have is the rather necessary, because their main function is to be God's messengers, to declare and execute his will; which they cannot well do without knowledge thereof.

Sec. 88. *Of the prudence of angels*.

A second property of angels is prudence. This is usually joined with knowledge; for knowledge works prudence, and prudence directeth knowledge. An apostle, therefore, thus coupleth them together, 'Who is a wise man, and endued with knowledge?' James iii. 13. Wisdom presupposeth knowledge, yea, also it 'findeth out knowledge of witty inventions,' Prov. viii. 12. It maketh men find out more and more knowledge, and that of more than ordinary and vulgar things. In regard of that excellent wisdom which angels have, Tyrus, which was counted very wise, is styled a cherub, that is, an angel, Ezek. xxviii. 3, 4,

---

[1] Creando infunditur, et infundendo creatur.

[1] Secundum potentiam spiritalem mentis angelicæ, cuncta quæ voluerit, simul notitia facillima comprehendentem—*Aug. de Gen. ad lit.* lib. iv. cap. xxxii.

16, 17. The ancient Grecians styled all sorts of angels Δαίμονες, by reason of their wit and wisdom.[1]

That prudence which good angels have, is the more necessary, because the evil angels, against whom good angels have a charge to defend saints, are exceeding crafty and subtle. The devil hath his wiles, his manifold windings and turnings; he is as crafty as a fox. There is need, therefore, of a prudent Hushai to bring to nought the plots of such a crafty Ahithophel.

Sec. 89. *Of the purity of angels.*

A third property of angels is purity. Their purity is a perfect purity, without mixture of any impurity or sin. This is set out by that pure and white linen wherewith they are said to be clothed, Rev. xv. 6. In this respect they are styled 'holy angels,' Mark viii. 38.

Under this head is comprised their sincerity; for 'in their mouth is found no guile: they are without fault before the throne of God,' Rev. xiv. 5. Whatsoever those heavenly spirits make show of, they indeed intend and do it from the heart.

Hereunto may be added their integrity, which is an universal subjection to every part of God's will. In all places they attend upon their Lord, and always behold his face, Mat. xviii. 10, to know what his will is that [they] may do it. They are therefore said, Ps. ciii. 20, to 'do his commandments, hearkening to his word.' Hereby they shew that they are yet still ready further to do whatsoever he shall require.

These properties are necessary to make angels fit to appear in the presence of the pure and holy God in heaven. But 'there shall in no wise enter into heaven any thing that defileth,' Rev. xxi. 17. God is 'of purer eyes than to behold evil; he cannot look on iniquity,' Hab. i. 13; 'Neither shall evil dwell with him,' Ps. v. 4.

Sec. 90. *Of the glory of angels.*

A fourth property of angels is, glory. They are very glorious. Such is the brightness of their glory as it is resembled to lightning, Mat. xxviii. 3. Just men are said to shine as the sun in the kingdom of their Father, Mat. xiii. 43; much more angels.

Children of men on earth cannot endure the brightness of an angel's presence when he appeareth in his glory. When Balaam saw an angel stand in the way before him, 'he fell flat on his face;' and his ass did what it could to shun the angel, Num. xxii. 31-33. The keepers of Christ's sepulchre, at the sight of an angel, did 'shake and become as dead men,' Mat. xxviii. 4. Not only wicked men have been dazzled, amazed, and affrighted with the appearance of an angel, but also pious men, men of great faith and courage. The shepherds that durst tarry all night with their sheep in the field, at the sight of an angel were 'sore afraid,' Luke ii. 9. Zechariah, a good priest, at the like sight, 'was troubled, and fear fell on him,' Luke i. 12. John the divine was so amazed at the sight of an angel as he 'fell at his feet to worship him,' Rev. xix. 10, and xxii. 8; yea, Daniel, 'a man greatly beloved,' at the sight of an angel, 'was afraid, and fell upon his face,' Dan. viii. 17. The glory, therefore, of angels must needs be surpassing great.

Angels are the chiefest servants and most principal attendants on God. Now, courtiers, who are the king's special attendants, as gentlemen of his bed-chamber and privy-chamber, use to be, for the honour of their sovereign, most gorgeously attired. In allusion to that ancient custom, thus saith the Lord, 'Behold, they that wear soft clothing are in kings' houses,' Mat. xi. 8. Answerably, it is requisite that angels, even for the glory of their Lord, be of all creatures the most glorious.

Sec. 91. *Of the power of angels.*

A fifth property of angels is, power. They are mighty in power. Hereupon there are attributed to them these and such like titles: 'mighty,' 2 Thes. i. 7; 'strong,' Rev. v. 2. And they are said to 'excel in strength,' Ps. ciii. 20. They are resembled to horses and chariots of fire, 2 Kings vi. 17. Horses and chariots are powerful; horses and chariots of fire are invincible.

Angels protected Elisha against an army of enemies; yea, one angel destroyed in one night 185,000 soldiers in their one camp, 2 Kings xvii. 35. Do not these evidences demonstrate that angels are mighty in power, and that both to offend and defend?

It is necessary that they should be so, because the church and children of God, over whom the angels have a charge, have in this world against them not only mighty, malicious, fierce, cruel children of men, but principalities, powers, rulers of the darkness of this world, spiritual wickedness in high places,[1] Eph. vi. 12.

Sec. 92. *Of the speed of angels.*

A sixth property of angels is speed, or quickness in motion;[2] by reason of their extraordinary speed, they are said to have wings to fly, Isa. vi. 2. In the time of Daniel's making a prayer, an angel came from the highest heaven to him on earth; for in the beginning of Daniel's supplication the angel was sent forth, and while he was praying the angel was come to him; in which respect the angel is said to fly swiftly, Daniel ix. 21, 23.

They must needs be exceeding swift, swifter than any corporal substances in these especial respects.

1. They cannot be hindered by any bodily impedi-

---

[1] Δαίμων, *quasi δαήμων, doctus, peritus, prudens. Illæ virtutes nomina sortiuntur, quæ sapientiam, &c., consignatissime indicent.*—Chrys. de incomp. Dei Nat. Hom. iii.

[1] Of the power of the devil, see the Whole Armour of God, on Eph. vi. 12, sec. 12, 14, 20.

[2] *Angeli terram circumeunt adinstar avium*, Hier. in Ecc. 8.

ments; no corporal substance can any whit stay their course, or slacken their enterprise; they can pass through and pass over all such things as would stop and hinder any bodies; as castles, cities, stone walls, iron gates, rivers of waters, seas, woods, or any other like things.

2. They have no corporal gravity, nor any other like quality to slacken their motion.

3. They need not such space of time to pass from place to place, as bodies need; even on a sudden they can be in divers places which are millions of miles asunder; as the highest heaven and earth is.

4. They have a greater propensity and forwardness to do any task enjoined by their Lord, than other creatures: this is a great means of putting them on to do what they are enjoined with all celerity.

On these grounds we may well think that the sun in his course cannot be swifter than they, nor the sight of the eye, nor the lightning from heaven more quick than they.

It is necessary that angels be so quick.

1. Because the extremes of heaven, and betwixt heaven and earth, are far remote, one from another: and oft occasions are offered for angels to go suddenly from one extreme to another.

2. Because many saints in the world (whose distress requires present succour) are very far distant one from another.

3. Because devils are swift unto mischief; and it is meet the good angels be as quick to protect, as evil ones to annoy.

Sec. 93. *Of the zeal of angels.*

A seventh property of angels is zeal. Their zeal is most fervent; in this respect they are called *seraphim*, Isa. vi. 2, 6.[1] *Saraph* signifieth *to burn;* thence *seraphim*, such as burn with zeal. Hereunto the Holy Ghost alludeth in this phrase, a flame of fire; for zeal is a fervour:[2] it is attributed to fire, to set out the burning heat of it; and it is ordinarily used to set out the ardour or fervency of the affections. Now, because angels are forward and fervent in accomplishing what they undertake; zeal may well be reckoned up among their properties.

Zeal puts life and heat into them, and that in every thing that they do; it makes earnest in whatsoever is good; it makes them (to use the word as it is oft used in a good sense) impatient at every dishonour done to God, and wrong to any of his saints.

This zeal is necessary for them, by reason of the fiery fury and malicious madness of devils and their instruments, in plotting and practising against God and his glory, and against saints and their good. It is requisite that angels, being messengers of God and ministers for saints, be, in maintaining the cause of God and his saints, as zealous as devils and wicked ones are furious against that cause.

Sec. 94. *Of angels' constancy.*

The eighth property of angels is constancy. They are unalterably constant in good; their constancy hath respect both to their condition, and also unto their disposition.

In regard of their condition, they are immortal, everlasting, and never decay. In this respect (as well as in other repects) men and women after the resurrection, when there shall be no more death or any alteration, are said to be equal unto the angels, Luke xx. 36. Their nature giveth proof hereof. For spirits are not subject to decay.

In regard of their disposition, as it hath hitherto, so it will for ever remain good, and very forward thereunto; they never yet yielded to any evil, nor ever waxed weary of any good, nor ever repented them of doing the good which they had done. They have hitherto constantly persisted, and will for ever hereafter with like constancy persist, in doing the will of their Lord; and that without any interruption or intromission for a time, or without revolt and apostasy for ever. In regard of their constancy, they are said to serve God day and night, Rev. vii. 15, and always to behold his face, Mat. xviii. 10.

Their unalterable constancy is requisite, because their Lord whom they serve is Jehovah, that changeth not, Mal. iii. 6, even 'the Father of lights, with whom is no variableness neither shadow of turning,' James i. 17. Should the good angels decay or fall away, where should the immortal and immutable God have constant servants? Man proved a rebel against his Lord: so did many of the angels, which are turned into devils. By reason of their fall, God established the good angels that stand, and this is the true cause of their unalterable constancy.

Sec. 95. *Of divine expressions of the excellency of angels.*

The excellency of angels is further set out by sundry divine expressions, whereby excellent things are illustrated by applying them to angels, as 'the tongue of angels,' 1 Cor. xiii. 1; 'angels' food,' Ps. lxxviii. 25. Thereby is meant the most excellent tongue and the most excellent food that can be; as if angels did speak with a tongue, they would speak with such a tongue; or if they did eat any food they would eat such food.

The excellency of God is set out by such like phrases as, 'a prince of God,' Gen. xxiii. 6; 'an host of God,' 1 Chron. xii. 22; 'a city of God,' Jonah. iii. 3; 'a mountain of God,' Ps. xxxvi. 6; 'cedars of God,' Ps. lxxx. 10. By these phrases it is declared, that the more excellent anything is, the more it appertaineth to God; and the more anything appertains to God, the more excellent it is. If God's

---

[1] שרף, *ussit;* שרפים, *urentes.*
[2] Heb. x. 27. πυρὸς ζῆλος, *ignis fervor.* ζέιν *fervere, inde* ζῆλος *zelus.*

excellency be thus set forth, surely the excellency of angels must needs be very much amplified by the fore-mentioned phrases.

Sec. 96. *Of the functions of angels in relation to God.*

The functions of angels are comprised under the signification of this word *angels*, which signifieth *messengers:* and under that other word *ministers*.

Their functions are many; they may all be brought to three heads, for they are such as are performed,

1. To God their supreme Lord.
2. To the Son of God, their head.
3. To sons of men, Christ's members.

First, The functions which angels perform to God are these:

1. They attend God's presence. This they do for the honour of his majesty, and to set out his magnificence; this, their attendance, is thus set out, 1 Kings xxii. 19, 'I saw the Lord sitting on his throne, and all the host of heaven standing by him on his right hand and on his left.' By *the host of heaven*, angels are meant.

2. They follow the Lord whithersoever he goeth. In this respect they are styled the 'chariots of God;' that is, such as follow him for his service. That angels are thereby meant, is evident by the psalmist's own expression of himself, Ps. lxviii. 17, 'The chariots of God are twenty thousand, even thousands of angels;' and the Lord is there said to be 'among them,' because they are ever about him whithersoever he goeth.

3. They are God's messengers, to be sent up and down on God's errands. Their usual title *angel* importeth as much; and so much is expressly set down, Ps. civ. 4. In this respect they are said to 'minister to him,' Daniel vii. 10.

4. They are much employed about declaring the will of God. By angels God delivered his law on mount Sinai, Acts vii. 53, Gal. iii. 19. To this hath the apostle relation, Heb. ii. 2.

Obj. God himself 'spake all these words,' Exod. xx. 1.

Ans. God was indeed the true, primary, principal author of the law. Angels were his ministers in delivering it; they were as heralds, who in the presence of the king publish his proclamation. The word spoken by prophets is styled 'the word of the Lord,' Isa. i. 10. Of that which prophets uttered it is said, 'Thus saith the Lord,' Exod. xi. 4. Angels were God's ministers in delivering his law sundry ways. See more of this in Chap. ii. Sec. 9.

(1.) They were attendants on God when it was delivered. They earnestly desire to be where God's counsel is made known; they were therefore in the assemblies of God's people where the mysteries of the gospel were published, Eph. iii. 10.

(2.) They were witnesses and approvers of the law. In this respect saints are said to judge the world, 1 Cor. vi. 2, in that they are witnesses and approvers of Christ's judgment. So Mat. xix. 28.

(3.) They were as the mouth and voice of God in delivering the law. In this respect, saith the apostle, 'As though God did beseech you in us, we pray you in Christ's stead to be reconciled unto God,' 2 Cor. v. 20. In this sense, saith the apostle, the word spoken by angels was stedfast, Heb. ii. 2.

It is also manifest that in sundry other particulars God used to make known his will by angels, as Gen. xvi. 7, 9, and xix. 1; 1 Kings xix. 5; 2 Kings i. 3; Daniel vii. 16; Luke i. 13, 26, and ii. 10; Acts i. 11, and v. 19, 20, and viii. 26, and x. 3; Rev. i. 1.

5. They are God's ministers, to execute and perform what God will have done. In this respect angels are said to 'ascend and descend on the ladder that reached from earth to heaven,' Gen. xxviii. 12, and to 'do his commandments, hearkening to the voice of his word,' Ps. ciii. 20. This is further evident by the many particular employments mentioned in sacred Scripture whereunto God put them: as to bring Lot out of Sodom, Gen. xix. 1, &c.; Israel out of Egypt, Num. xx. 16; to stop Balaam's course, Num. xxii. 22; to stop lions' mouths, Daniel vi. 22.

6. They are executioners of God's judgments; witness the angel that slew seventy thousand with the pestilence in three days, 2 Sam. xxiv. 15, 16; and the angel that slew an hundred and eighty-five thousand in one night, 2 Kings xix. 35. In this respect angels are said to have the vials full of the wrath of God, Rev. xv. 7. They are mighty and terrible, and one angel is able to do more than millions of men; therefore God useth them for the greater terror to men.

7. They are special instruments of praising God. Excellently are they set forth in performing this duty, Rev. vii. 11, 12. And they are said, Rev. iv. 8, in extolling the name of the Lord, not to rest day or night, that is, never to cease in performing that duty. Because this is an especial work of theirs, the psalmist oft calls upon them to perform it, as Ps. ciii. 20, and cxlii. 2. Not as if they were negligent therein;[1] but thereby he sheweth how ready they are to perform it, and so commends them for it, and therein makes them examples to others.

Sec. 97. *Of the functions of angels in relation to Jesus Christ.*

The functions which angels perform to the Son of God distinctly are especially such as they perform to him being incarnate, even as he is also Son of man.

In general it is said, that the angels ascend and descend upon the Son of man, John i. 51; relation is therein had to Gen. xxviii. 12. By that ladder Christ is meant, who by his human nature touched the earth, and by his divine nature reached up to

---

[1] Qui monet ut facias quod jam facis, ille monendo
 Laudat, et hortatu comprobat acta suo.—*Ovid de Trist.*

heaven. The angels ascending and descending imports the continual service they do to him; and that they are deputed of the Father thereunto the apostle proveth, Heb. i. 6, and the psalmist also, Ps. xci. 11.

Particular functions expressed to be done by angels to Christ are these.

1. To foretell his conception, Luke i. 30, 31.
2. To declare his birth, Luke ii. 9–11.
3. To prevent his danger, Mat. ii. 13, 14.
4. To minister unto him in his need, Mark i. 13.
5. To protect him from enemies, Mat. xxvi. 53.
6. To confirm and comfort him in his agony, Luke xxii. 43.
7. To open his grave at the time of his resurrection, Mat. xxviii. 2.
8. To witness his resurrection to them that looked for him, Luke xxiv. 5, 6, 23.
9. To confirm his ascension into heaven, Acts i. 10, 11.
10. To accompany him into heaven, Ps. lxviii. 17, 18; Eph. iv. 8.
11. To attend and magnify him in heaven, Rev. v. 11, 12.
12. To reveal what he will have done, Rev. i. 1, and xxii. 16.
13. To fight with him against his enemies, Rev. xii. 7.
14. To gather out of his kingdom all things that offend, Mat. xiii. 49, 50.
15. To accompany him at his last coming, Mark viii. 38; Mat. xxv. 31.
16. To execute his last judgment, Mat. xiii. 49, 50.

Sec. 98. Of the function of angels in relation to the bodies of men in this life.

The functions which angels perform to men are performed to them especially as they are adopted of God, and members of Christ; for all saints have angels attending on them.[1]

Functions of angels to such have respect to them in this world, or in the world to come. In this life they tend to the good of their bodies or of their souls, and that either by procuring positive good things, or preventing and redressing of evils.

In general, it is the function of angels to attend on saints, and to minister unto them,[2] ver. 14. In this respect they are styled 'their angels,' Mat. xviii. 10. They are as those servants who are appointed by a king to attend his children, and thereupon are called the prince's servants.

Particular functions of angels which concern the good of saints' bodies in this life, are these that follow:

1. Angels are as stewards, to provide for men in time of need. Hereof we have a memorable history, 1 Kings xix. 5–7.
2. They are as physicians, to cure their maladies, John v. 4.
3. They are as nurses, to bear them, as it were, in their arms, and to keep them from hurt, Ps. xci. 11, 12.
4. They are as guides, to direct them in the right course, and to keep them from wandering, Gen. xxiv. 7, and xxxii. 1.
5. They are as soldiers, to guard them, and to keep them safe from danger, Ps. xxxiv. 7. Hereof we have a great instance, 2 Kings vi. 17. They are also as soldiers, to destroy the enemies of the church, 2 Kings xix. 35.
6. They are as rescuers, saviours, and deliverers, to pull saints out of danger, and to set them free, Acts v. 19, and xii. 7, 8, &c.

To these may be referred their restraining of things hurtful by nature from doing hurt, Dan. vi. 22.

Obj. How may these extraordinary instances be ordinarily applied?

Ans. 1. Extraordinary instances do shew what angels are able and ready to do at the pleasure of the Lord.

2. They shew what God will put them to as he seeth cause; so as on these grounds we may expect the like, if God see it good.

3. These extraordinary instances are as pertinent to our purpose as that reason which the apostle useth, Heb. xiii. 2, to press the duty of hospitality, namely, their receiving of angels unawares.

4. These are visible and sensible demonstrations of their invisible and sensible care over us.

5. The argument follows from the greater to the less; for if angels did such extraordinary matters for saints, much more may we expect ordinary matters. Such an argument is pressed, James v. 17, to quicken us up to pray.

Sec. 99. Of angels' functions over men's souls in this life.

In regard of men's souls in this life, angels are,

1. As prophets or teachers, to instruct them,[1] Dan. viii. 16, 17, and ix. 22; Luke i. 14, 15, 34, 35; Acts i. 11.
2. As consolators, to comfort them in their fears and perplexities, Gen. xxi. 17; Isa. vi. 6, 7.
3. As coadjutors, to stand with them against Satan, Jude 9; Zech. iii. 1.
4. As fellow-members, to rejoice at the conversion of sinners, Luke xv. 10.
5. As tutors, to punish them for their offences, that so they might be roused out of their sins, and brought to repentance, 2 Sam. xxiv. 16.

---

[1] *Omnes sancti angelos habent.*—*Chrys. in Mat.* xviiii. Hom. 60.

[2] *Ipsi angeli nobis servire dicuntur, dum propter nos in ministerium mittuntur.*—*Aug. medit.* lib. ii. cap. iii.

[1] *Sancti angeli hominum saluti ministrant.*—*Chrys. de Patien. Job,* Hom. iii.

Sec. 100. *Of angels' functions to saints in the life to come.*

In regard of saints after this life, angels are,

1. As watchers, to attend the separation of body and soul, and instantly to take their souls and carry them to heaven,[1] Luke xvi. 22.

2. As keepers,[2] at the last day to gather all the elect together, Mat. xxiv. 31.

3. As fanners or fishers, to separate the evil from the good, Mat. xiii. 49.

4. As companions in heaven, to join with saints in praising God, Rev. vii. 9–11.

The fore-mentioned distinct functions of angels do lead us on further to consider the benefits which we reap by them.

Sec. 101. *Of the benefits which saints receive by the ministry of angels.*

The benefits which we receive by the ministry of angels concern the good of our bodies or of our souls, and that in this life and in the life to come. They may all be reduced to these heads:

1. An exceeding high honour to have such attendants; for they are 'ministering spirits for us,' ver. 14. It was counted the highest honour that could be done to him whom the king delighted to honour, that one of his noble princes should wait upon him; but all the noble princes of God attend on saints. Well, weigh their fore-mentioned properties (Sec. 87), and this honour will conspicuously appear to be the greater. Surely this is an undoubted evidence that saints are the spouse of Christ, members of his body, and adopted to be God's children, and heirs of his kingdom. These are the true and proper grounds of this high honour. Mortal kings use so to honour their spouses and children. Adam in his innocency had not such honour.

2. Protection from dangers; for 'the angel of the Lord encampeth round about them that fear him, and delivereth them,' Ps. xxxiv. 7. And God hath given them a charge to keep his saints in all their ways, &c., Ps. xci. 11, 12. There are many, many dangers from which we are, time after time, protected by angels, though we do not visibly see it. That which the Scripture revealeth, we may as safely, and ought as confidently, believe as if visibly we saw it. The benefit of this protection is the greater, in that it is against spiritual enemies and spiritual assaults, Eph. vi. 12. This is a great amplification of the benefit; for good angels are more in number than devils, and stronger in power. They are more prudent than devils are subtle; they are more speedy in coming to our succour than devils are, or can be, in coming to annoy us; they are more fervent and zealous for our good than devils are, or can be, fierce and malicious to our hurt; they do more carefully and constantly watch for our safety than devils do, or can do, for our destruction, though, like roaring lions, they walk about seeking whom they may devour. In regard of these angelical protectors, we may say, as Elisha did, 2 Kings vi. 16, 'They that be with us are more than they that are against us;' yea, though all the wicked of the world and all the fiends of hell be against us.

3. Supply of all our wants. They can do it; they are willing and ready to do it; yea, they do indeed actually do it, though we do not sensibly discern it. Abraham's servant saw not the angel which went before him and prospered his journey, yet an angel did so, Gen. xxiv. 7. Angels invisibly do many good offices for us. As devils do oft work in us doubting and despair, so the good angels do oft put life and spirit into us, whereby we are comforted and established. An angel strengthened Christ in the extremity of his agony, Luke xxii. 43. The like they do to the members of Christ: they are sent forth to minister for them, ver. 4. Surely their ministry extendeth to such things as are needful for saints and useful unto them.

Sec. 102. *Of the resolution of the seventh verse.*

Ver. 7. *And of the angels he saith, Who maketh his angels spirits, and his ministers a flame of fire.*

In this verse is laid down the second argument,[1] whereby the apostle proveth angels to be inferior to Christ, and thereupon Christ to be more excellent than angels. The argument may be thus framed: They who are made spirits and ministers are inferior to him that made him so;

But angels are made spirits and ministers by Christ;

Therefore angels are inferior to Christ.

That angels are so made, is in express terms set down.

That Christ made them so is implied in this phrase, *who maketh,* for it hath reference to the last clause of the second verse.

The sum of this verse is, a description of angels.

Two points are observable therein:

1. The connection of this verse with the former in this phrase, 'And of the angels he saith.'

2. The description itself. This consists of two parts:

The first sets down the nature of angels, *spirits.*

The second, their office, *ministers.*

Both those are amplified,

1. By their principal efficient, the Son of God, *who made them.*

2. By their quality, in this metaphor, *a flame of fire.*

Sec. 103. *Of the observations arising out of the seventh verse.*

I. *God hath made known what is to be known of angels.* This he hath made known in his word; for thereunto the apostle refers us in this phrase, 'And

---

[1] Angeli nunc hic, nunc ibi esse potuerunt, qui hinc illinc quem Deus voluit abstulerunt.—*Aug. de cura pro mor. gerend.* cap. xv. [2] Qu. 'reapers'?—ED.

[1] Of the first argument, see Sec. 76.

of the angels he saith;' even he that made known in his word what is to be known of his Son, made known also what is to be known of angels. Angels are invisible, spiritual, and celestial substances, so as we could not know anything to the purpose concerning them, except God had revealed it. Search therefore the Scriptures, thereby to learn what thou wouldst know of them, and content thyself with that which is revealed in the Scriptures concerning them.

II. *Christ is the Creator of angels.* This relative *who* hath reference to Christ. This doctrine is expressly set down, Col. i. 16.

III. *Christ is the Lord of angels.* He ordereth and disposeth them to such offices and services as he pleaseth. The particle of the present tense, *who maketh,* implieth a continual act of providence. In this respect Christ is said to be 'the head of all principality and power,' Col. ii. 10.

IV. *Angels are spirits.* They are here expressly so called. See Sec. 86.

V. *Angels are ministers.* See Sec. 96, &c.

VI. *Angels are very fervent in their enterprises.* This metaphor, *a flame of fire,* imports as much. See Sec. 93.

Sec. 104. *Of the connection of the eighth verse with the former.*

But unto the Son he saith, Thy throne, O God, is for ever and ever; a sceptre of righteousness is the sceptre of thy kingdom.—Heb. i. 8.

The inferiority of angels to Christ being sufficiently proved in the former verses, the superiority and dignity of Christ is further prosecuted in the six verses following.

The first particle *but,* importeth an opposition betwixt this that is here set down, and that which went before, for the dominion of Christ is here opposed to the subjection of angels.

The *Son* here meant is that very Son of God, of whom mention was made before, vers. 2, 5, 6. See Secs. 15, 49, 51.

This phrase *he saith* is not in the original, yet of necessity to be understood, to make the sentence perfect. The learned languages, when they have occasion in divers sentences together to use the same verb, account it an elegancy to leave it out in the latter clauses. It is here to be taken in the same sense wherein it was taken vers. 6, 7, and it implieth that there is as good proof of the dignity of Christ as there was of the inferiority of angels, even divine testimony; God that testifieth the one testifieth the other, he saith of the one as well as he saith of the other.

Sec. 105. *Of the main scope of the 45th Psalm.*

The testimony intended under this phrase, *he saith,* is taken out of Ps. xlv. 6, 7. That psalm is an express prophecy of Christ.

Many take that psalm to be a congratulatory hymn upon the marriage of Solomon, and so expound it historically. Most of the Jewish rabbins apply it wholly that way. But there are many points therein, which cannot with any probability be applied to Solomon. To let pass sundry other passages in other parts of the psalm, few of the points noted in the two verses which the apostle hath quoted out of that psalm can fully come up to Solomon. Nay, some of them cannot well and truly be applied to him, as this apostrophe, *O God,* as here (see Sec. 107), simply set down; nor that continuance of time comprised under this phrase (see Sec. 108), *for ever and ever;* for Solomon's throne did not properly for ever continue. Besides, his sceptre was not in all things a sceptre of righteousness; witness the many wives and concubines that he had, many of them being strangers, which was directly against the law; witness also the idolatry that he yielded to, 1 Kings xi. 1, &c.; and witness the heavy burdens which he laid upon the people, intimated 1 Kings xii. 4. Finally, the extent of that anointing above all others, mentioned in the psalm, cannot properly be applied to Solomon, though he had many endowments above sundry other men. Such transcendent excellencies are applied to the person intended in this psalm, as some of the Jews themselves do apply them to the Messiah, and two or three times use this phrase, O King Messiah, in applying sundry passages to him.

It is sufficient for us Christians to persuade us, that the Son of God and his excellency is set out in this psalm, because an apostle guided by the same Spirit that the psalmist was, doth so directly and expressly apply it to Christ, as here it is applied.

Sec. 106. *Of Christ's throne.*

The manner of setting out Christ's dignity is very elegant and emphatical. It is by a rhetorical apostrophe: 'Thy throne, O God.' It imports a joyful congratulation of Christ's glory and dignity, for this relative *thy* hath reference to the Son, mentioned in the beginning of the verse. An apostrophe, when it is used in commendation of a person, addeth much emphasis, and putteth life into the speech. It doth in a manner single out the person to whom it is declared, to be observed of all. As here it is applied to Christ, it further shews, that Christ's excellencies may be spoken of to himself even face to face, for they are his due, and there is no fear of vain-glory in him, Rev. iv. 10, 11. See 125 in the end.

A throne is a royal seat, a seat proper to a king. So much is intended by this phrase, 'Only in the throne will I be greater than thou,' Gen. xli. 40. That was spoken by a king upon advancing one above all his subjects; only he excepts his own royal dignity, which he setteth out under this word *throne.* These two words, *throne, kingdom,* are oft joined together; thus, 'the throne of his kingdom,' 2 Sam. vii. 13, Deut, xvii. 18; and it is called a 'royal throne,' Esther v. 1;

a 'kingly throne,' Daniel v. 20. A throne is metonymically put for a kingdom, 2 Sam. vii. 16, 1 Kings i. 37. Kings used to sit on their throne when they would set out their royalty, 1 Kings xxii. 10, 19, Acts xii. 21; and when they executed public judgment, 1 Kings vii. 7. In this respect it is styled a 'throne of judgment,' Prov. xx. 8; and thrones are said to be prepared for judgment, Ps. ix. 7 and cxxii. 5; and God is said to 'sit on a throne judging,' Ps. ix. 4. In allusion to this right, Christ thus saith to his disciples, 'Ye shall sit upon twelve thrones judging,' Mat. xix. 28.

This metaphor is here applied to Christ, to set out his kingly office, together with his dignity, royalty, and majesty; for the throne whereon Christ is said to sit is styled a 'throne of majesty,' Heb. viii. 1; yea, also, Christ's supreme function of judging is hereby intimated, for God ordained him to be judge, Acts x. 42.

Now, Christ is truly and properly a king, the most high, supreme sovereign over all. And this he is,

1. As he is true God; for the Lord is king, Ps. x. 16; God is king, Ps. xlvii. 7, 8.
2. As he is the Son of God, the second person in sacred Trinity, Ps. xcviii. 6, Isa. xxxiii. 22.
3. As he is God-man, the Messiah, Zech. ix. 9.

This last respect is here especially intended; for it is the main scope of the apostle to set out the excellency of Christ as God manifested in the flesh, preached unto the Gentiles, and believed on in the world.

Sec. 107. *Of the title* GOD *applied to Christ.*

The title God, Θεός, is here properly to be taken. It setteth out the divine nature of Christ. It is thus oft attributed to Christ in the New Testament; as John i. 1, Rom. ix. 5, 1 Tim. iii. 16, Heb. iii. 4.

The word used Ps. xlv. 6 (whence this testimony is taken) is of the plural number, אלהים (as was shewed on ver. 6, Sec. 70), and attributed to creatures; see Sec. 118. When it is applied to creatures, it is spoken of many together; as to idols, Exod. xxii. 20; or angels, Ps. viii. 5; or men, Ps. lxxxii. 1, 6. If at any time it be applied to one single creature, some circumstance or other is added thereto, to demonstrate that a creature is intended thereby; as where it is applied to one calf, it is styled a 'god of gold,' Exod. xxxii. 31; and the name of the idol is expressed, Judges xvi. 23, thus, 'Dagon their god.' So where Moses is styled god, his name is expressed; and the person to whom he was a god, namely, Pharaoh, Exodus vii. 1. But in this place there is no circumstance that restrains it to a creature; therefore it is to be applied to him that is truly, properly, and essentially God.

This apostrophe, *O God,* may be used by the psalmist, inspired and guided by the holy God, as by himself spoken to the Messiah, as Ps. lxviii. 7, or the first person in Trinity may be brought in speaking to the second, even the Father to his Son, as Ps. cx. 1. All tends to the same end, namely, to declare Christ to be true God.

This is further manifest by the title *Jehovah,* which is a name so proper to the true God, as it is not in any part of Scripture attributed to any but to the true God;[1] and it is attributed to the Son of God, and that as a distinct person from the Father, Gen. xix. 24. So as the Son is most true God, most properly so called in this and sundry other places. So he is called *Lord,* ver. 10, Sec. 128.

Sec. 108. *Of the everlastingness of Christ's kingdom.*

These words, 'for ever and ever,' εἰς τὸν αἰῶνα τοῦ αἰῶνος, have reference to the throne of Christ, whereby his kingdom is set out; so as it declares the everlastingness of Christ's kingdom.

The Greek word here translated *ever* is the same that was translated *worlds,* ver. 2. According to the notation of the Greek word, αἰεὶ ὤν, it signifieth ever-being, namely, one and the same; see Sec. 18. Sometimes the singular number is singly used, as Mark iii. 29, εἰς τὸν αἰῶνα; and sometimes doubled, as here. Ofttimes the plural number is singly used, as Luke i. 32, εἰς τοὺς αἰῶνας; but most frequently doubled, εἰς τοὺς αἰῶνας τῶν αἰώνων, especially in the book of the Revelations, where it is fifteen times doubled.

The doubling of the word addeth emphasis, and ratifieth the certainty of the point, as the doubling of Pharaoh's dreams did, Gen. xli. 32.

This word hath reference sometimes to former times, and intendeth eternity without beginning, as Eph. iii. 11, κατὰ πρόθεσιν τῶν αἰώνων, and is translated *eternal.* It hath also reference to future times, and intendeth everlastingness; as John vi. 51, 'He shall live for ever,' ζήσεται εἰς τὸν αἰῶνα. Sometimes it implieth a continuance to the end of the world, as Luke i. 55; or the end of a man's life, as John viii. 35.

Though the word *ever,* singly used, may synecdochically be put for a time that hath a date or period, yet whenever it is doubled it signifieth an everlasting continuance, without any date or end at all.

In the Hebrew text, which is here quoted, there is a particle[2] added to the word *ever,* which in that use always intendeth a proper everlastingness, without any period or end at all, and thereupon translated 'for ever and ever.'

Christ, in regard of his divine nature, as the Son of God, is a king for ever in the largest sense, having respect to former and future continuance, before and after all times, even 'from everlasting to everlasting,' Ps. xc. 2.

[1] Of the title *Jehovah,* see the Church's Conquest, on Exodus xvii. 15, sec. 72.

[2] עולם ועד. In seculum et usque, notat tempus longius quam seculum: æternum. In immensum auget orationis pondus.

But in regard of his office, as God-man, and mediator betwixt God and man, this continuance hath respect to the future, and implieth an everlasting continuance. And that,

1. From his ascension, when he was actually set upon his throne in heaven. This exaltation of Christ is frequently noted to be after his humiliation and subjection unto death, Acts ii. 36, and v. 30, 31; Rom. viii. 34; Philip. ii. 8, 9.

2. From his incarnation. For so soon as his human nature was united to his divine (which was at his first conception) he had right to his royal dignity. Thereupon it is said, ver. 6, 'when he bringeth in the first-begotten into the world,' &c. So soon as he was born he was acknowledged a king, and answerably he was worshipped, and presents brought to him, Mat. ii. 2, 11.

3. From the beginning of the world, even so soon as man fell, as Mediator he was also King. That which was said of Christ in regard of his sacrifice, he was a 'Lamb slain from the foundation of the world,' Rev. xiii. 8, may be applied to his royalty, he was a King from the foundation of the world. For in every point of his Mediatorship he was the 'same yesterday, and to-day, and for ever,' Heb. xv. 8; that is, in all former times, in the present time, and for all future times. This was Christ in four especial respects.

(1.) In regard of God's decree, which was before all times.

(2.) In regard of God's promise, Gen. iii. 15.

(3.) In regard of the efficacy of Christ's mediatorship, for it was effectual to all purposes so soon as God had promised him.

(4.) In regard of the virtue of faith, which is 'the substance of things hoped for,' Heb. xi. 1.

From what time soever we take the rise or beginning of Christ's kingdom, as he is Mediator, the continuance of it is everlasting; it hath no date at all, Ps. cxlv. 13; Daniel vii. 4; Luke i. 33.

Sec. 109. *Of Christ's giving up his kingdom to his Father.*

Against the eternity of Christ's kingdom may be objected, that Christ shall deliver up the kingdom to God the Father, and that the Son himself shall be subject unto him that put all things under him, 1 Cor. xv. 24, 28.

Ans. 1. That which is spoken of Christ's delivering up the kingdom to the Father, is meant of that full victory and conquest which Christ shall get, and thereby, as it were, bring unto his Father a settled and an established kingdom. In this respect he may be said to settle his Father in his kingdom, in reference to such as rebelled against him or fell from him.

2. That phrase of delivering up the kingdom to the Father may be understood of the manner of Christ's regiment by his ministers, ordinances, and other like means; all things being accomplished by these for which they were ordained, they shall cease, and in this respect be said to be delivered up to God.

3. All enemies being subdued, Christ hath no occasion of using authority over them. There is no fear of their rising against him.

4. As for this phrase, 'The Son also himself shall be subject,' it is to be taken in regard of his human nature and office of mediation, in which respect he is subject to the Father.

If hereupon it be objected that in these respects Christ was always subject to the Father, I answer,

That the excellency of his deity being till then as it were clouded under the veil of his flesh and of his office, it did not so conspicuously, fully, and perfectly appear, as at the end of the world it shall. This subjection then is to be taken comparatively, in reference to that infinite difference which then shall be manifested betwixt the divine and human nature of Christ.

When the Son of God assumed human nature to the unity of his divine nature, 'the Word was made flesh,' John i. 14, and 'God was manifested in the flesh,' 1 Tim. iv. 16. Now though it pleased the Deity to make itself in a manner visible in that flesh, John xiv. 9, yet was the flesh as a veil obscuring the surpassing brightness of the deity. And although by divine words and works uttered and done in this flesh, by enduring that heavy burden which was laid on it for our sins, by the resurrection of it from the dead, by the ascension of it into heaven, and by the high exaltation of it at the right hand of God, the deity did by degrees more and more brightly and clearly shew itself forth, yet still the flesh remained as a veil and a cloud. But when the enemies of all sorts shall be subdued, then will the deity of the Son so brightly and conspicuously shew itself, as the humanity shall be no veil unto it, but rather it shall appear to be infinitely inferior to it, and in this respect subject unto it; so as the human nature of Christ shall not lose any dignity which it had before, but the divine nature shall more clearly manifest itself in itself, and (as we speak) in its own likeness. The subjection therefore of the Son is to be taken of the clear manifestation of the excellency of the deity, not of any diminution of the dignity of the humanity.

5. The subjection before mentioned may be understood of the body of Christ; and Christ, because he is the head of that body, be said to be subject; for this subjection to the Father is set down as a high degree of honour and happiness. To what higher degree can any creature attain unto than to be God's subject? Now because the whole body of Christ shall not be fully brought into the protection and tuition of the Father before that day, therefore by a kind of excellency the Son, in regard of his mystical body, is said then to be subject.

6. All may be taken of Christ's kingdom of intercession and grace, whereof the church, so long as it

was militant, had need, but not of his kingdom of glory, in which his church shall triumph.

Sec. 110. *Of the necessity of Christ's continual sitting upon his throne.*

There is an absolute necessity that Christ's throne should be 'for ever and ever,' because there never was nor can be any worthy, meet, or able to succeed Christ in the throne, and to go forward with that work which he had begun; wherefore, that his good beginning might not prove vain, it was necessary that he should have an everlasting kingdom. Among men a good supply may be made, and one man may go on with that good work which another hath begun, and perfect the same. David made great preparation for the temple, 1 Chron. xxii. 2, &c., and xxviii. 11, &c., but his son Solomon perfected the temple after the death of his father, 2 Chron. v. 1. But there is one only true natural Son of God, one Mediator between God and man, so as there can be none like to him to succeed him on the throne. Besides, Christ ever liveth, and therefore needeth no successor; but all men are mortal, and are not suffered to continue by reason of death. This reason the apostle rendereth of the difference betwixt the priesthood of men, which was changeable, and the unchangeable[1] priesthood of Christ, Heb. vii. 23, 24.

This everlastingness of Christ's kingdom doth much commend the same, and sheweth it to be far more excellent than all the kingdoms of men, and that it shall stand when all others are brought to nought. Christ shall be the conqueror over all.

In this respect he is to be feared above all, and to be trusted unto more than all, Daniel vi. 26, and vii. 14; 1 Tim. iv. 10.

Sec. 111. *Of Christ's Sceptre.*

There is another sign here used to set out Christ's kingdom, that is, a 'sceptre:' indeed the Greek word (ἡ ῥάβδος. See Chap. ix. 4, Sec. 28) used by the apostle, signifieth a wand, or stick, or staff; it is by the Septuagint oft used, as here, for a sceptre. So the Hebrew word שבט, is indefinitely put for a staff or a stick, but more especially for a sceptre, as Gen. xlix. 10; Num. xxiv. 17.

In the book of Esther there is oft used a compound Hebrew word,[2] which signifieth such instrument as kings used to sway, which is properly a sceptre; this is so proper to a king as he is called a sceptre-holder or sceptre-bearer,[3] Amos i. 5-8. As a throne and a crown, so a sceptre are all ensigns proper to a king, and that to set out his majesty and authority. Therefore, when a king was chosen, and inaugurated, and anointed, they were wont to put a sceptre into his hand.

A king, by swaying his sceptre this way or that way, manifesteth his mind. When he inviteth any to come to him, or would have silence made, or vouchsafe grace and favour to any, or declare his dislike of a thing and displeasure, he doth it by the motion of his sceptre, so as his mind may be discerned thereby. When Ahasuerus would give an evidence of his favour to Esther, he held out his sceptre to her, Esther v. 2, and viii. 4. Because a sceptre is proper to a king, by a metonymy it is oft put for a kingdom or royal dignity, as Gen. xlix. 10, Num. xxiv. 17. And the destruction of a king and kingdom is set out by breaking a sceptre, Isa. xiv. 5, Zech. x. 11.

That a royal sceptre is here meant, is evident by the word *kingdom* annexed to it, 'the sceptre of thy kingdom.' And that by this sceptre the government of a kingdom is here meant, is manifest by the epithet of righteousness added thereto, a 'sceptre of righteousness,' that is, a righteous government of a kingdom. In this respect a king is said to have a sceptre to rule, Ezek. xix. 14.

There are two things whereby the apostle commendeth the foresaid sceptre: one is, the dignity of it; the other is, the equity of it.

The *dignity* is the greatest that can be implied in this word *kingdom*. A sceptre of a kingdom is a royal sceptre, such as kings only sway. Other commanders may have sceptres (though not so properly as a king), for mention is made of 'sceptres of rulers' in the plural number, as Isa. xiv. 5, Ezek. xix. 11. Such a sceptre may be a sceptre of a city, of a tribe, of a province, or of such a jurisdiction as he possesseth who holdeth the sceptre.

The *equity* of the former sceptre is thus set out, 'a sceptre of righteousness,' which implieth that the king who swayeth the sceptre, ordereth all things in his kingdom most justly and righteously.

Order of matter requireth that the latter clause should be in the former place, thus, 'the sceptre of thy kingdom is a sceptre of righteousness;' but the learned languages place an elegancy in transposing the parts of a sentence.

According to the order of matter, we will first speak of the kingdom of Christ, and then of the equity thereof.

Sec. 112. *Of Christ's kingdom.*

Christ's kingdom is expressly mentioned in this phrase, 'the sceptre of thy kingdom.' The relative particle *thy* hath reference to Christ, as was before shewed on this phrase, 'thy throne,' Sec. 106.

ita etiam virga tam regiæ quam judiciariæ potestatis est indicium.—*Basil magn. explic. Ps.* xliv.

---

[1] ἀπαράβατον. *Quod præterire non potest*, i.e. *perpetuum*. Perpetuum autem sacerdotium dicitur sacerdotis perpetui respectu.—*Beza Annot. in Heb.* vii. 24.

[2] שרביט componitur ex שר *et* שבט *virga et principe;* significatque virgam qualem princeps solet tenere, nimirum σκῆπτρον, *sceptrum.*

[3] תומך שבט σκηπτροῦχος, *sceptritenens*, σκηπτροφόρος, *sceptrum ferens.* Sicut Thronus regni est symbolum et tessera,

Frequent mention is made of Christ's kingdom, and that before he was exhibited in the flesh, and since.

Before it was typified, as by the kingdom of other kings of Judah, so in particular by the kingdom of David, 2 Sam. vii. 12–16; Isa. ix. 7, and xvi. 5; Jer. xxiii. 5, 6, and xxxiii. 17.

This kingdom of Christ was also prophesied of before his incarnation, Gen. xlix. 11–13; Num. xxiv. 17; Daniel ii. 44; Micah iv. 8. After his exhibition in the flesh, this kingdom of Christ was published by his forerunner, Mat. iii. 2; by Christ himself, Luke iv. 43, and viii. 1; and by his apostles, Luke ix. 2. This kingdom did the apostles most set forth after Christ's ascension, Acts viii. 12, and xx. 23, and xxviii. 31. Christ's kingdom is that estate where Christ ruleth.[1]

As God, by his absolute power he reigneth over all creatures everywhere, Ps. ciii. 19.

As Christ is God-man, God manifested in the flesh, 'all power is given unto him in heaven and earth,' Mat. xxviii. 18; yet hath Christ a peculiar kingdom, wherein he reigneth over a select people called out of the world, who are a willing people, Ps. cx. 5.

This kingdom is sometimes called 'the kingdom of God,' Mark i. 14, 15; and that in five especial respects:

1. By a kind of excellency; for excellent and eminent things are said to be of God, as Gen. xxiii. 6; Ps. lxxxvii. 3; 1 Chron. xii. 22; Ps. lxxx. 10, and xxxvi. 6; Gen. xxx. 8.

2. In relation to the king thereof, Christ Jesus, who is true God, John i. 49, Rom. ix. 5.

3. In opposition to kingdoms of men, Dan. v. 21, John xviii. 36.

4. In regard of the laws, privileges, and immunities thereof, which are all divine and of God, Deut. iv. 8, Rom. xiv. 17.

5. In reference to the end thereof, which is God's glory, Philip ii. 9–11.

It is also called 'the kingdom of heaven,' Mat. iii. 2, and iv. 17; and that in five other respects:

1. To distinguish it from the kingdoms of the world, which the devil shewed to Christ, Mat. iv. 8.

2. To shew the kind of laws, ordinances, and appurtenances thereof, which are all heavenly, Heb. ix. 23.

3. To demonstrate the qualification of the subjects thereof, whose inward disposition and outward conversation is heavenly, Heb iii. 1, Ps. iii. 20.

4. To set out the extent thereof. It doth not only reach from Euphrates to Sihor, as Solomon's kingdom did, 1 Kings iv. 21, or from India to Ethiopia, over an hundred and twenty-seven provinces, as Ahasuerus his kingdom did, Esther i. 1, but to heaven itself, yea, and that throughout the whole earth and the whole heaven, Ps. cxxxv. 6, Mat. xxviii. 18.

[1] Of Christ's kingdom, see my Guide to go to God, or Explan. of the Lord's Prayer, 2 Petit., sec. 35.

5. To manifest the end of calling men into the church, which is Christ's kingdom of grace on earth, that they might be fitted for heaven, which is the kingdom of glory, Col. i. 12, 13, 1 Peter i. 3, 4.

Well may the estate where Christ ruleth be accounted and called a kingdom, because all things which constitute a kingdom appertain thereto; such as these:

1. An high supreme sovereign, who is a true, proper king, an absolute monarch, which Christ is, Isa. ix. 6; Ps. ii. 6; 1 Tim. vi. 15.

2. There be subjects that take him for their king, and willingly subject themselves to him, Ps. xviii. 44, and cx. 3.

3. There is a distinct particular dominion or state, in which that king reigneth and ruleth, Ps. ii. 6.

4. There be laws and statutes whereby this kingdom is governed, the most righteous, equal, and prudent laws that ever were. These are registered in God's word, the holy Bible: read what is said of them, Deut. iv. 8; Ps. xix. 7; 2 Tim. iii. 15–17.

5. There [be] privileges and immunities appertaining to this kingdom, such as never any kingdom had the like. Some of the privileges are these:

(1.) A right to the things of this world, 1 Cor. iii. 22, 23.

(2.) A free access to the throne of grace at all times, Eph. ii. 18, and iii. 12, Heb. iv. 16. This privilege will appear to be a great one, if we well weigh the readiness of him that sits on the throne to accept us; the abundance of blessings that are there treasured up, and the assurance that the subjects of this kingdom have to attain their desires.

(3.) A right to Christ himself, and in him to all things that are his. And what is not his? Rom. viii. 32.

(4.) A right to heaven itself, 1 Peter i. 4; Luke xii. 32; Mat. xxv. 34.

The immunities of Christ's kingdom are such as these:

1. Freedom from all inconvenient and burdensome laws, whether ceremonial, judicial, or moral, Rom. vii. 4, Gal. iv. 5.

2. From sin, Rom. vi. 18, 22. We are freed from sin,—

(1.) In regard of the guilt of it, Rom. viii. 33.

(2.) In regard of the dominion and power of it, Rom. vi. 14.

(3.) In regard of the punishment of it, Rom. viii. 1.

3. From the sting of death, 1 Cor. xv. 53.

4. From the power of Satan, Heb. ii. 14.

Who would not be of this kingdom? What care should they have that are of it to abide in it, and to say, 'The lines are fallen unto me in pleasant places; yea, I have a goodly heritage,' Ps. xvi. 6. How sedulous should they be to bring others thereinto, Cant. viii. 8. How conscionable ought the subjects of this kingdom to be in walking worthy thereof, Eph. iv. 1, Col. i. 10.

Sec. 113. *Of the righteousness of Christ's kingdom.*

The Greek word[1] joined by the apostle to the sceptre here mentioned, signifieth rectitude, straightness, evenness; it is opposed to crookedness, roughness, unevenness. So doth the Hebrew word[2] also signify; it is fitly applied to a sceptre, which useth to be straight and upright, not crooked, nor inclining this way or that way; so as that which is set out by a sceptre, namely, government, is hereby implied to be right and upright, just and equal, not partially inclining to any side. The government of a good king is frequently set out by this phrase, 'He did that which was right,' הישר, 1 Kings xv. 5, 11, and xxii. 43; and it is opposed to declining to the right hand or to the left, 2 Kings xxii. 2. According to the true meaning of the word in this place, it is not unfitly translated 'righteousness;' and so it is expounded in the next verse. These two words in Hebrew, which signify righteousness, צדק, and rectitude or equity, ומישרים, are oft joined together, as importing the same thing, Prov. ii. 9, Ps. lviii. 1.

This phrase, a 'sceptre of righteousness,'[3] is a rhetorical phrase, very elegant and emphatical. It implieth a most just and equal ordering all things in the kingdom, so as nothing but that which is right, without all appearance of any unrighteousness, is to be found in Christ's administration of his kingdom. The substantive *righteousness*,[4] is oft put for the adjective *righteous;* and that to declare the superlative degree thereof, as Deut. xxiv. 13; Ps. cxix. 172; Isa. i. 26; Jer. xxxiii. 15; 2 Tim. iv. 8; Heb. vii. 1.

Hereby it appeareth that Christ doth most righteously order the affairs of his kingdom. In this respect he is styled a 'righteous judge,' 2 Tim. iv. 3, and a 'righteous branch;' and 'this is his name whereby he shall be called, The Lord our righteousness,' Jer. xxiii. 5, 6; 'Justice and judgment are the habitation of his throne,' Ps. lxxxix. 14. His laws and statutes are all righteous, Ps. xix. 7, &c. His word, which in special is counted to be his sceptre, teacheth all righteousness, maketh his subjects righteous, and leadeth them in that only right way which bringeth them to the crown of righteousness. There is no true righteousness but that which is found in this kingdom. The members of this kingdom are the only true righteous men, all others are but righteous in show. The rewards which Christ giveth, and the judgments which he executeth, are all righteous.

Thus he brings most glory to himself, and doth most good to others, which are two main ends whereat Christ aimeth.

Happy are those men, happy are those subjects which are of this kingdom, and governed by the laws thereof.

Blessed be the Lord which delighted in his church to set his Son on the throne thereof; and to put this sceptre of righteouness into his hand; because the Lord loved his church for ever, therefore made he his Son king, to do judgment and justice.

How should this allure us to come to this kingdom, to abide therein, to [be] subject to the laws and ordinances thereof.

Oh the folly of those who will not have this man to rule over them, Luke xix. 14, 27, but will break his bands, Ps. ii. 3. They are like to the trees, Judges ix. 14, 15.

Sec. 114. *Of the extent of righteousness.*

Thou hast loved righteousness, and hated iniquity; therefore God, even thy God, hath anointed thee with the oil of gladness above thy fellows.—Heb. i. 9.

In the beginning of this verse, the apostle further amplifieth the righteousness of Christ's kingdom. It might be thought that the mention of the everlasting throne of Christ had been sufficient to the apostle's purpose, which was to demonstrate Christ's excellency above angels. But to move the Hebrews the rather to submit themselves to Christ's government, he doth not only give an hint of Christ's righteous sceptre, but also produceth all that the prophet had foretold of Christ's righteous government; and that both in regard of the cause thereof, which was his love of righteousness, and also in regard of the parts thereof, which are to love righteousness and hate iniquity, that so they whom he instructed herein might themselves follow after righteousness, and avoid and fly from all iniquity. It was a great matter that he had spoken of, the government of Christ's kingdom, therefore he returns to it again.[1]

The manner of laying down this exemplification is the same that he used in propounding the point itself, namely, by way of apostrophe, speaking unto Christ himself, 'Thou hast loved,' &c. This adds much emphasis.

Though our English use one and the same word in the former verse, and in this verse too, namely, *righteousness;* yet both by the psalmist in Hebrew, and by the apostle in Greek, two several words are used.

In the three learned languages, Hebrew, Greek, and Latin, one and the same word is put for justice and righteousness.[2]

The notation of the Greek word used by the apostle will be a good help to find out the nature of the thing.

A learned philosopher makes the notation of the word translated *righteous*, to be from dividing into two equal parts,[3] because by justice or righteousness

---

[1] εὐθύτης, *rectitudo*, εὐθύς *rectus*, ab εὖ et τίθημι.
[2] מישור.   [3] See Sec. 25, on this phrase, *word of power*.
[4] Abstractum pro concreto. In regno Christi est pura ustitia.—*Basil. Mag. Explic. Ps.* xliv.

[1] Quod jam magnum quiddam locutus est, iterum illud se curare festinat.—*Chrys. Hom.* 3, *in* cap. i. *ad Heb.*
[2] צדק, δικαιοσύνη, *justitia.*
[3] ὀνομάζεται δίκαιον ὅτι δίχα ἐστίν, ὥσπερ ἄν εἴτις ἴσοι δίκαιον.—*Arist. Ethic.* lib. v. cap. vii. Justitia est virtus, qua sua cuique tribuuntur.—*Aug. de lib. arbit.* lib. i. Sic *Arist. loc. citat.* Sic *Cic. de Finib.* lib. v. Aliique plurimi.

matters are so equally poised and distributed, as every one hath that which belongs to him, or is meet for him. Thus it compriseth both reward and revenge; the one and the other being by righteousness so ordered as it is meet to be ordered. The notation of our English word *righteousness* is agreeable to the meaning and sense of that notation; for righteousness is to do right to every one. Thus both philosophers and divines, ancient and modern, have defined it: righteousness is a virtue whereby to every one his due is given. On the contrary, wrong done to any is called unrighteousness or injustice, $ἀδικία$.

Thus is that righteousness whereby Christ ordereth the affairs of his kingdom, as was shewed before, Sec. 113.

Of righteousness put for God's faithfulness, see Chap. vi. 10, Sec. 61.

Sec. 115. *Of Christ's love of righteousness.*

That which puts on Christ to sway his sceptre righteously, and righteously to govern his people, is not so much any advantage which himself expects from his subjects, as an inward inclination in himself thereunto, and a delight therein. So much doth this word *love,* 'Thou hast loved righteousness,' intend. In this did the man after God's own heart manifest his love of God's commandments, in that he delighted in them : 'I will delight myself,' saith he, 'in thy commandments, which I have loved,' Ps. cxix. 47 ; yea, they who love a thing will also earnestly and zealously put themselves on to practise and exercise the same. So much is intended in this phrase, 'My hands will I lift unto thy commandments, which I have loved,' Ps. cxix. 48. When the soul of a man is duly affected with righteousness, and his heart set upon it to love it, he will take all occasions to practise it ; nothing more puts on one to do a thing than love : 'My soul hath kept thy testimonies, and I love them exceedingly, saith the psalmist,' Ps. cxix. 167.

This love of righteousness rested not only in that which was in Christ, and practised by him, but also it extended itself to the righteousness of his subjects; even to their righteous disposition and righteous conversation : so as the righteous government of this King is manifested both in his own righteous ordering the affairs of his kingdom, and also in his subjects ordering their affairs, when they have to do with their sovereign and their fellow-subjects. Christ loveth and delighteth in the righteous, and will thereupon reward their righteousness : thus saith the psalmist to this purpose, 'The righteous Lord loveth righteousness; his countenance doth behold the upright,' Ps. xi. 7. And again, 'The Lord loveth the righteous,' Ps. cxlvi. 8.

Sec. 116. *Of Christ's hatred of iniquity.*

To Christ's love of righteousness is added his hatred of iniquity, because these two are contrary one to another. Men use to be contrarily affected to contrary objects ; vain intentions and God's law are directly contrary one to another ; thereupon saith the psalmist, 'I hate vain thoughts, but thy law do I love,' Ps. cxix. 113. We are commanded to 'hate the evil and love the good,' Amos v. 5.

The word translated *iniquity* is a general word, which signifieth a transgression of the law, $ἀνομία$,[1] and it is so translated, 1 John iii. 4 ; it is also translated *unrighteousness,* and directly opposed to *righteousness,* 2 Cor. vi. 14 ; for righteousness is a conformity to the law, which is the rule of righteousness, so as transgression must needs be contrary thereunto.

The word *iniquity* is of as large an extent as unrighteousness, and implieth an unequal dealing, which is contrary to the rule or law of God.

This sheweth that Christ was so far from dealing unjustly and doing any unrighteousness, as he hated it even in others.

Hatred is directly contrary to love; and as love importeth a delight in a thing, so hatred a loathing and detesting of it. A prophet giveth this advice, 'Hate the evil,' Amos v. 15 ; an apostle thus expresseth it, 'Abhor that which is evil,' Rom. xii. 9. Therefore that which God hateth is said to be an abomination unto him, Isa. i. 13, 14 ; Prov. vi. 16.

By this hatred of iniquity an evident proof both of the truth of Christ's love and also of the greatness thereof is given ; it was so great as it made him hate the contrary. This is a great amplification of love, and it shews that they which hate not iniquity do not in truth and fervency love righteousness : it is therefore set down as a note of an unrighteous man, that he abhors not evil, Ps. xxxvi. 4.

Hereby may righteous magistrates, righteous ministers, righteous masters, and all righteous persons be proved.

That which is said of righteousness itself may be applied to persons qualified therewith. Christ loveth the righteous, and hateth the unrighteous : 'The way of the wicked is an abomination to the Lord ; but he loveth him that followeth after righteousness,' Prov. xv. 9. So may we do, so must we do ; we may, we must love the righteous, 2 John 1, and hate the unrighteous, Ps. cxxxix. 21, 22 ; not simply their persons, but their evil qualities. In regard of men's persons, we are commanded to love our enemies, yea, though they be wicked ; even such as curse us and persecute us, Mat. v. 44. But in regard of their quality, we must hate even the garment spotted with the flesh, Jude 23.

Christ's love of righteous and hatred of unrighteous persons, manifesteth the righteous government of his kingdom, in that he dealeth with every one according to his works, rewarding the righteous (which is a fruit of his love) and punishing the unrighteous, which is an effect of his hatred, and both according

---

[1] $ἄνομος$ componitur ab *a privativo et* $νόμος$.—*Lex.*

to their works, which is the evidence of his justice and righteousness.

Thus is Christ set forth as righteous in himself, and righteous in the administration of his kingdom. He is a righteous person and a righteous king, who also maketh his kingdom and the subjects thereof all righteous.

Sec. 117. *Of the meaning of this relative particle 'therefore.'*

Upon the former description of Christ's righteousness this inference is made, 'Therefore God hath anointed thee.' This may be taken as the cause of Christ's righteousness, or as a consequence following from thence.

The Hebrew phrase, על כן, is oft used to set out the cause of a thing, as Gen. xviii. 5, על־כן עברתם, 'Therefore are ye come,' that is, for this cause. The same phrase is translated with a causal particle, Gen. xxxviii. 26, על־כן לא־נתתיה, 'Because I gave her not,' &c. It is also used to declare a consequence or an effect, as Ps. i. 5, על־כן לא־יקמו, 'Therefore the ungodly,' &c. So Gen. ii. 24, על־כן יעזב, 'Therefore shall a man leave,' &c. The Greek phrase, διὰ τοῦτο, also used by the apostle, is sometimes put for a cause, as Mat. xiii. 13, 'Therefore spake I to them in parables;' and it is thus translated, 'for this cause,' John xii. 27, 1 Tim. i. 16. It is also put for an effect or consequence, as Mat. xiv. 2.

It may in the one or the other sense be here taken. As a cause, it implieth that God's anointing Christ, that is, pouring his Spirit upon him, made him to be so fit and able a king as he was. As an effect, it intendeth that Christ, being most righteous, and every way able and fit to govern the kingdom, God therefore anointed, that is, deputed, him thereto.

In this respect it must have reference to Christ's human nature, or to his person as mediator, God-man: thus, 'God gave the Spirit unto him, not by measure,' John iii. 34 ; and 'the Spirit of the Lord was upon him,' Luke iv. 18.

This word of inference, *therefore*, may also be taken as a manifestation of God's anointing him : thus, Christ loved righteousness, therefore it was manifest that God anointed him ; as where Christ saith, '*therefore* the kingdom of heaven is like unto a certain king,' Mat. xviii. 23 ; it is manifest that the kingdom of heaven is like, &c.

This relative *therefore*, as it noteth a cause, hath reference to the former part; thus, God hath anointed thee, therefore thou lovest righteousness. As it declareth a consequence, it hath reference to the latter part; thus, 'Thou lovest righteousness, therefore God hath anointed thee,' that is, saw it meet to anoint thee.

None of these senses cross the other, but they may well stand together ; for God may anoint Christ, and depute him to his function, because he loveth righteousness ; and Christ may manifest his love of righteousness because God hath anointed him.

Finally, both the Hebrew and Greek phrase, translated *therefore*, is sometimes used for ornament's sake, or to begin a sentence, as in English we use this phrase, *Now then*. It is also used to couple sentences together, Gen. xxxiii. 10, John vii. 22.

Sec. 118. *Of the meaning of this phrase, 'God, thy God.'*

The author of the anointing here mentioned, is set out very emphatically (at least as our English and some other translators express it) by a rhetorical figure, doubling the same word in the same sense, thus, 'God, even thy God.' Hereby it is intimated that the matter here set down is true, faithful, and worthy of all observation and acceptation. In like manner doth the Lord set out himself in relation to his church, saying, Ps. l. 7, 'I am God, even thy God.' This he doth that his people might take the more thorough notice thereof, and that their faith might be the more strengthened thereupon.

The notation of the Hebrew title thus translated *God*, implieth God to be of might and power,[1] and is by some translated *the strong God*.[2]

The Hebrew noun is of the plural number, אלהים, but the verb *anointed*, to which the Hebrew title hath reference, is of the singular number, משחך, which intimateth a plurality of persons, and unity of essence.

The title *God*, as here used, in the first place, may be of the vocative case, as it is in the former verse, and translated *O God;* and by an apostrophe applied to Christ ; for this particle *even* (which is a note of apposition, joining two words together, which have reference to one and the same thing) is neither in the Hebrew nor Greek text, but inserted by our English translators. In Hebrew, אלהים, Greek, Θεός, and Latin, *Deus*, this title is both in the nominative and vocative case, the very same for syllables and letters. In the nominative case it is spoken of the Father, as our English sets it down ; in the vocative case it is spoken to the Son. Many of the ancient fathers[3] and *pater*-expositors[4] take it in the vocative as spoken to the Son.

It may be objected that thence it will follow that God is of God.

Ans. I deny not, but that it will so follow, and therein is nothing against the orthodox faith ; for the Son of God is very God of very God ; see Sec. 19. In regard of his divine essence he is very God, Rev. iv. 8. In regard of his distinct persons, as the Son in relation to his Father, he is of God ; in this re-

[1] אל ab איל *potens, fortis.*
[2] Aquila, ἰσχυρόν, Tremel. et Jun. *Deum fortem*, Gen. xiv. 22. [3] August. Chrys. Theoph. Harm. aliique.
[4] Bucer, Moller. Scultet. aliique. O Deus, unxit te Deus tuus. Deus ungitur a Deo. Sic accipite, sic intelligite, sic a Græcis evidentissimum est.—*Aug. Enarr. in Ps.* xliv.

spect, as we may say, O Son, thy Father, so O God, thy God.

Besides, the Son of God assumed man's nature; hereby God and man became one person. Thus he is God, and God is his God. He is God in regard of his divine nature, and God is his God in regard of his human nature, yea, and in regard of both natures united in one person.

In this latter respect, as Christ is God-man, God may be said to be his God three ways:

1. As Christ's human nature was created of God, and preserved by him like other creatures.

2. As Christ is mediator, he is deputed and sent of God, John iii. 34, and he subjected himself to God, and set himself to do the will of God, and such works as God appointed him to do, John iv. 34 and ix. 4. In these respects also God is his God.

3. As Christ God-man was given by God to be an head to a mystical body, which is the church, Eph. v. 22. God thereupon entered into covenant with him in the behalf of that body, Isa. xlii. 6 and xlix. 8. Thus he is called the messenger, Mal. iii. 1, and mediator of the covenant, Heb. viii. 6. Now God is in an especial manner their God, with whom he doth enter into covenant; as he said unto Abraham, 'I will establish my covenant between me and thee,' &c., 'to be a God unto thee,' &c., Gen. xvii. 7. As God made a covenant with Abraham and his seed, so also with Christ and his seed, which are all the elect of God, even the whole catholic church. This is the seed mentioned, Isa. liii. 10. So as by special relation betwixt God and Christ, God is his God in covenant with him. God also is, in especial manner, the God of the elect through Christ.

This special relation, *thy God*, having reference to Christ, is under the gospel, God's memorial; as under the law his title was, 'the God of Abraham, the God of Isaac, and the God of Jacob.' For with them God made his covenant, and in them with their seed, Gen. xvii. 7, and xxvi 3, 4, and xxviii. 13, 14.

This title, 'the God of Abraham, Isaac, and Jacob,' God assumed to himself, Exod. iii. 15, 16; and the seed of those patriarchs oft called on God by that title, and pleaded it before him, to enlarge their desires, and to strengthen their faith. This they did by calling to mind that relation which was betwixt God and their fathers, with whom God had made an everlasting covenant, to extend to them and their seed, Exod. xxxii. 11, 1 Kings xviii. 36, 1 Chron. xxix. 18.

How much more may we have our desires enlarged, and faith strengthened, in that relation which is betwixt God and Christ, and how may we plead it, and say, O God of thy Son Jesus Christ, remember thy covenant made with him and in him. Hereupon it is that Christ saith, 'Verily, verily, I say unto you, Whatsoever ye shall ask the Father in my name, he will give it you,' John xvi. 23. When the children of Israel were in great distress, 'the Lord was gracious unto them, and had compassion on them, and respect unto them, because of his covenant with Abraham, Isaac, and Jacob,' &c., 2 Kings xiii. 23. How much more will God be gracious to us because of his covenant with his Son Christ! This is the truest and surest ground of Christian confidence and boldness in approaching to the throne of grace.

The psalmist, who lived many hundred years before the apostles, having by the Spirit of truth registered this relation betwixt God and the promised Messiah, giveth evidence thereby, that the understanding and believing Jews conceived that Messiah to be true God, the Son of God; and that God was the God of that Messiah in special, and by virtue thereof, 'the God of Abraham, Isaac, and Jacob,' Exod. iv. 5; 'the Lord God of Israel,' Exod. v. 1; 'the Lord God of the Hebrews,' Exod. ix. 1; 'the God of the Jews,' Rom. iii. 29; 'the God of Jeshurun,' Deut. xxxiii. 26; 'the Lord of Elijah,' 2 Kings ii. 14; 'the God of Daniel,' Dan. vi. 26; 'the God of Shadrach, Meshach, and Abed-nego,' Dan. iii. 28; 'Gentiles,' Rom. iii. 29; 'my God,' Exod. xv. 2; 'our God,' Exod. v. 8; 'thy God,' Deut. x. 14; 'your God,' Gen. xliii. 23; 'his God,' Exod. xxxii. 11; 'their God,' Gen. xvii. 8. All these, and other special relations to God, do give evidence of God's singular respect to those who are in covenant with him, and whose God he is.

In reference hereunto they are called God's *peculium*,[1] a peculiar treasure unto him, his proper stock or flock, Exod. ix. 15, Mal. iii. 17. They are also called a peculiar people, 1 Peter ii. 9. All this ariseth from that special relation which Christ hath to God, that God is his God: 'Ye are Christ's, and Christ is God's,' saith the apostle, 1 Cor. iii. 21. Hereupon it was that Christ said, 'I ascend to my Father and your Father, and to my God and your God,' John xx. 17.

Sec. 119. *Of God's anointing his Son.*

God, who was in special the God of his Son, is here said to have anointed him, ἔχρισέ. See Chap. iii. 6, Sec. 54. This is metaphorically spoken in reference to an ancient, continued inaugurating and settling of kings in their kingdom, which was by anointing them, or pouring oil upon their heads: as Saul, 1 Sam. x. 1; David three times, first by Samuel, 1 Sam. xvi. 13; secondly, by the men of Judah, 2 Sam. ii. 4; thirdly, by the elders of Israel, 2 Sam. v. 3; Solomon twice, 1 Kings i. 39, 1 Chron. xxix. 22; Jehu, 2 Kings ix. 6; Joash, 2 Kings xi. 12; Jehoahaz, 2 Kings xxiii. 30; yea, they who chose Absalom to be king anointed him, 2 Sam. xix. 10. In allusion hereunto kings are styled 'anointed,' even the Lord's anointed, 2 Sam. xix. 21, Lam. iv. 20.

Anointing being performed by God's appointment, implieth two things,

---

[1] סגלה, *Id quod proprium et singulariter charum est.*

1. A deputation to the kingdom.[1]
2. An ability to execute the royal function.

Both these are evident in the first king that was set over Israel. By Samuel's anointing Saul, Saul was deputed to the kingdom; and being anointed, 'the Spirit of the Lord came upon him, and God gave him another heart,' 1 Sam. vi. 9.

That wherewith kings were anointed was oil. Samuel took a vial of oil and poured it on Saul's head, 1 Sam. x. 1. He also took an horn of oil and anointed David, 1 Sam. xvi. 13. So did Zadok anoint Solomon, 1 Kings i. 39 ; so did he that anointed Jehu, 2 Kings ix. 6 ; and others that anointed other kings. All these were anointed with external material oil ; but to shew that anointing had a mystical signification, they who had not such oil poured on them are called the Lord's anointed, Ps. cv. 15.

Oil, and anointing therewith, being mystically taken, as here they are, setteth out the Spirit, and the gifts and graces thereof. In this respect Christ saith of himself, ' The Spirit of the Lord is upon me, because he hath anointed me to preach,' &c., Luke iv. 18. And the apostle Peter saith of him, 'God anointed Jesus of Nazareth with the Holy Ghost, and with power,' Acts x. 38.

This is in special to be applied to the human nature of Christ, yet so as united to the divine nature, both making one person ; for God, singly and simply considered in himself, never was nor can be anointed, no, not metaphorically, as here the word is taken. God cannot be deputed to any function. God needs not the Spirit to be poured on him, nor needs he any gift of the Spirit to be enabled to anything that he doth. He is of himself all-sufficient.

But Christ, as man, and as mediator between God and man, was by God his Father deputed unto his royal function, Ps. ii. 6, as he was to his priestly office, Heb. v. 5 ; yea, and in that respect also, God gave him the Spirit, though not by measure, John iii. 34.

Both the Hebrew name *Messiah*, and the Greek name *Christ*, do signify *anointed*. They remain memorials of the anointing here specified. See Chap. iii. ver. 6, Sec. 64.

Sec. 120. *Of the fit resemblance of anointing with oil.*

Very fitly is this metaphor of anointing with oil used to set out the mystery of the Spirit and the gifts thereof, especially if it be extended to the mystical body of Christ, in reference both to the head thereof and also to the members ; for the oil wherewith Christ was anointed was like the oil poured on Aaron's head, 'It ran down upon the beard, and went to the skirts of his garment,' Ps. cxxxiii. 2, 3. So the Spirit poured on Christ, as head of the church, ran down upon his body, and upon the several members thereof.

[1] Of God's deputing Christ to his function, see Chap. ii. 3, Sec. 2.

This is to be observed, because many of the particular resemblances here following cannot be applied to the anointing of the head alone, but may be applied to the anointing of the body and members.

The resemblances betwixt oil and the Spirit shall be set forth in ten distinct particulars.

1. Oil is a nourishing kind of food, as honey and butter. Hereupon it is often joined with them, Job xxix. 6, Ezek. xvi. 13. It is also joined with meat and drink, Ezra iii. 7 ; with meal, 1 Kings xvii. 12 ; with bread, Hosea ii. 5 ; fine flour, Lev. ii. 4 ; and with wine, 2 Chron. xi. 11. All these are nourishing food. Oil is very wholesome to be eaten : it much helpeth digestion ; it is therefore eaten with raw herbs and other cold things. It is also a means to expel such things as annoy the stomach ; and it is an antidote against poison.

Nothing is more nourishing and wholesome to the soul than the Spirit and the graces thereof. It maketh God's word to give a good relish ; it helps the soul well to digest the word ; yea, it makes it sweet and pleasant, Ps. cxix. 103. The Spirit expels carnal lusts of all sorts, and it is a most sovereign antidote against all poisonous corruptions.

2. Oil is of singular use to supple hard, swelling tumours, to ease pains in the flesh or bones, to keep sores from rankling, and to heal wounds, Luke x. 34, Isa. i. 6.

The Spirit mollifieth hard hearts, assuageth perplexed spirits, easeth troubled consciences, and healeth the wounds of the soul made by Satan's assault, Isa. lxi. 1–3.

3. Oil is useful to strengthen weak joints, to make them quick and nimble. They, therefore, that strive for the mastery in wrestling, running, and other like exercises, use to anoint their joints.

The Spirit helpeth our infirmities, Rom. viii. 26. It putteth life and spirit into us ; for it is a spirit of life, Rom. viii. 2.

4. Oil makes the countenance fresh and comely ; it makes the face to shine, Ps. iv. 15 ; Mat. vi. 17. It revives the spirit within, and makes it cheerful.

It is the Spirit and the graces thereof that makes men comely and amiable before God, angels, and saints. Of the inward joy of the Spirit we shall speak in the next Section.

5. Oil hath not only a sweet smell in itself, but also it sendeth forth a fragrant and pleasing savour. The house was filled with the sweet savour of the ointment that was poured on Christ's head, John xii. 3.

The Spirit, both in Christ, Cant. i. 2, and also in his members, causeth a sweet savour. Ministers are a sweet savour of Christ, 2 Cor. ii. 15. The prayers of saints are sweet as incense, Ps. cxli. 2, Rev. viii. 3 ; their beneficence is as an odour of a sweet smell, Philip. iv. 18.

6. Oil maintains the light of lamps. It causeth them to give light, and, by a continual supply of oil,

lamps continue to burn, and to send forth their light. Under the law, oil was prepared for the light of the tabernacle, Exod. xxv. 6; and this preparation was continued day after day, Lev. xxiv. 2, 3.

It is by the Spirit whereby our minds are enlightened, and by the continual operation thereof the light of understanding increaseth more and more. It is therefore called ' the spirit of revelation in the knowledge of Christ;' and it is given ' that the eyes of our understanding might be enlightened,' Eph. i. 17, 18. Believers also are said to ' have an unction from the Holy One to know all things; the same anointing teacheth them of all things,' &c., 1 John ii. 20, 27.

7. Oil is of a searching and piercing nature; it will pierce even into the bones, Ps. cix. 18.

But the Spirit is of all things the most searching; for ' the Spirit searcheth all things, yea, the deep things of God,' 1 Cor. ii. 10.

8. Oil was one of the things which of old were offered unto God for sacrifices. When Jacob set up a pillar as an altar, he poured oil upon the top of it, Gen. xxviii. 18, and xxxv. 14. Under the law, it was offered up with their meat-offerings, Lev. ii. 1, 16. Hence is it that Jotham bringeth in the olive-tree thus speaking, ' Should I leave my fatness wherewith, by me, they honour God and man,' &c. The fatness of that tree is oil. God was honoured thereby in that it was offered up to him for sacrifice; man was honoured thereby in that he was consecrated by it to an high office, as of a king, or priest, or prophet.

Christ was a ' sacrifice to God for a sweet-smelling savour,' Eph. v. 1; and the very bodies of his members are a living sacrifice to God, Rom. xii. 1, Philip. ii. 17. So are their works of charity, Philip. iv. 18; and their praising of God, Heb. xiii. 15.

9. Oil, and anointing dead corpses therewith, preserveth them from putrefaction. Of old, therefore, they were wont to anoint dead corpses therewith, Mark xvi. 1, Luke xxiii. 56. The Spirit subdues corruption and keeps men from sending forth ill savours, as filthy communication, and a filthy conversation.

10. Oil is a most precious thing. This epithet *precious* is oft attributed to ointment, as 2 Kings xx. 13; Ps. cxxxiii. 1; Eccles. vii. 1; Mat. xxvi. 7. Kings were wont to treasure it up among other precious things, Isa. xxxix. 2; and among things useful and necessary for man, 2 Chron. xxxii. 28, Hosea ii. 8.

What more precious than the Spirit of God, than the gifts and graces thereof! What more needful, and what more useful!

Sec. 121. *Of oil of gladness.*

The oil wherewith Christ was anointed is here called the *oil of gladness.* We heard before that this oil setteth out the Spirit of God, and the gifts and graces thereof. Now, joy is in Scripture said to be ' joy of the Holy Ghost,' 1 Thes. i. 6; ' joy in the Holy Ghost,' Rom. xiv. 17; and joy is reckoned up among the fruits of the Spirit, Gal. v. 22. So as it is that Spirit that is in Christ and his members which maketh this to be oil of gladness.

This phrase *oil of gladness* is an Hebraism, like to that which is before set down, ver. 8, *sceptre of righteousness.* See Sec. 113.

This Hebraism here intendeth two things:

1. The excellency of this gladness. No external joy is to be compared to it.

2. The quantity of that joy, it is exceeding great; it far surpasseth all the joy that ever was or can be, which is further manifested in this phrase following, ' above thy fellows.'

This epithet *gladness* is here attributed to this oil in relation to Christ the head, and to all believers his members.

It hath relation to Christ in two respects:

1. As it quickened him up and made him joyful in all his undertakings for our redemption. Christ being by his Father deputed to his function, most willingly and joyfully undertook it and managed it: ' As a bridegroom coming out of his chamber, he rejoiced as a strong man to run his race,' Ps. xix. 5. When he cometh into the world, he saith, ' I delight to do thy will, O my God,' Ps. xl. 8. When he was in the world, he said, ' My meat is to do the will of him that sent me, and to finish his work,' John iv. 34.

2. Gladness hath relation to Christ, by reason of the fruit that sprouted out from thence. His coming into the world, and doing, and enduring what he did, was matter of rejoicing to others; in which respect, the prophet exhorteth ' the daughter of Zion to shout, and to be glad and rejoice with all the heart,' Zeph. iii. 14, Zech. ix. 9. And the angels that brought the first news of Christ's birth, do thus proclaim it: ' Behold, I bring you good tidings of great joy, which shall be to all people,' Luke ii. 10.

2. This epithet *gladness* hath relation to the members of Christ in two respects:

(1.) As the things whereof in Christ they are made partakers are matters of great joy; for so many and so great are the benefits which believers receive from Christ, by virtue of that anointing, as they very much rejoice their hearts. Many of these benefits are expressly set down, Isa. lxi. 1–3. Other benefits are in other places distinctly noted, as redemption from sin, reconciliation with God, justification in his sight, adoption, regeneration, sanctification, and the end of all, eternal salvation. If any things in the world cause true joy and gladness, surely these effects which flow from the anointing of Christ will do it.

(2.) As the members of Christ are quickened up by that Spirit which cometh from him, do and endure readily, willingly, cheerfully, joyfully, what the Lord calls them unto, as Ps. cxxii. 1, 1 Chron. xxix. 9, 17. It is said of those on whom the Spirit rested, that ' they received the word gladly,' and mutually communicated together with gladness. On a like ground, the eunuch whom Philip baptized, and Paul's jailor, are said to rejoice, Acts viii. 39, and xvi. 34.

This fruit of joy gives evidence of a believer's union with Christ, and of the abode of Christ's Spirit in him, for the Spirit is as oil, of a diffusing nature. Hereby we may gain assurance to our own souls, and give evidence to others of the spirit that is in us. So did the Jews of old, 1 Chron. xxix. 9, and Christ's disciples, Luke x. 17, and Christians in the primitive church, Heb. x. 34, Philip. ii. 17, 18.

To shew ourselves true members of Christ, we ought further so to carry ourselves in our several functions, as we may cause others to rejoice. So did Solomon, 1 Kings v. 7, and Hezekiah, 2 Chron. xxix. 36, and the apostles, Acts xv. 31. This we shall do by diligence, faithfulness, justice, equity, uprightness, mercifulness, and by disposing of our affairs to the good of others; so did Christ.

Sec. 122. *Of the fellowship betwixt Christ and saints.*

The abundant measure of the Spirit in Christ is further amplified by comparing it with that measure which is in others. It far exceeds all others.

The persons with whom the comparison is made, are styled Christ's fellows. Both the Hebrew[1] and and Greek[2] word imply such as partake of one and the same condition. See Chap. iii. 1, Sec. 17.

Hereby in special professors of the true faith are meant:

In general, this word *fellows* may be extended to all, men and angels. All are styled his fellows, in regard of that low degree whereunto the Son of God, Creator of all things, humbled himself by assuming a created substance, so that as he was a creature, angels were his fellows; yea, it is said, chap. ii. 9, that he was 'made a little lower than angels, for the suffering of death,' yet all the gifts and endowments of all the angels are not comparable to those which Christ had: 'He was crowned with honour and glory above them,' chap. ii. 7.

But to let the angels pass, we will insist upon the comparison, as it hath relation to the church, and to the several members thereof. These may be said to be Christ's fellows in eight distinct respects:

1. As fellow-creatures, Job i. 12, Heb. ii. 14.
2. As joint-members of the same mystical body. Christ is indeed the head, Eph. i. 22, 23, but the head is a part of the body, and the body is said to be the fulness of Christ, Eph. i. 23.
3. As made under the law, Gal. iv. 4.
4. As a Son of one and the same Father, John xx. 17. Hereupon he and they are fellow-brethren, chap. ii. 11, 12.

[1] חבר *a* מחבריך *conjunctus est.* Usurpatur de iis qui sunt ejusdem conditionis. Eccl. iv. 10.

[2] μετόχους, *participes consortes, a* μετέχειν, *habere cum aliis, partem habere, participem esse.* See Chap. ii. 14, Sec. 139.

5. As co-heirs or joint-heirs, Rom. viii. 17.
6. As subject to the same infirmities, chap. iv. 15.
7. As liable to death, chap. ii. 14, 15, ix. 27, 28.
8. As honouring his members to reign with him, 2 Tim. ii. 12, 1 Cor. vi. 2.

As this fellowship betwixt Christ and his members setteth out the low degree of Christ's humiliation, so the high degree of the exaltation of saints.

For the Son of God to be a fellow with sons of men is a great debasement, and for sons of men to be fellows with the Son of God, is as great an advancement.

What love hath Christ shewed to us herein!

How are we bound to Christ hereby!

Should not we imitate Christ, and condescend to men of low estate! Rom. xii. 16.

Sec. 123. *Of the pre-eminency of Christ's gifts above others.*

This phrase, *above thy fellows*, sets down a fifth proof of Christ's excellency above angels.

Though it pleased Christ to condescend so low as to become a fellow with us, yet even in that low estate did his Father so dignify him, as he poured his Spirit on him more abundantly than on all others whatsoever. 'Thou art fairer than the children of men,' saith the psalmist of him, Ps. xlv. 2. The phrase may be extended to all manner of excellencies: 'He is mightier than I,' saith he, that was greater than any born of women before him, Mat. iii. 11. None of the angels ever had such gifts as Christ. They learned of the church what Christ revealed to the church, Eph. iii. 10. Both men and angels had their stint and measure, but 'God gives not the Spirit by measure unto Christ,' John iii. 34. 'It pleased the Father that in him should all fulness dwell,' Col. i. 19. 'In him are hid all the treasures of wisdom and knowledge,' Col. ii. 3.

Christ is an head from whom the members must be supplied, so as he receives not for himself alone, but for his whole body: 'Of his fulness have we all received, and grace for grace,' John i. 16.

Particular members of the mystical body may have the fulness of vessels, but this is the fulness of a fountain.

Here lieth a main difference between the Mediator and mere men. The most that can be said of the best of them is, that they have but enough for themselves, as the wise virgins said, Mat. xxv. 9. Christ alone is that overflowing spring who hath enough for all others, John i. 16.

This is the true treasure of the church, which was typified by the ark. The ark was as a little chest or cabinet, in which jewels and other precious things and treasures are kept. In this respect it set out Christ to be as a treasure, in which all the precious things tending to salvation are hid.

This is matter of great comfort in regard of our own emptiness or scantiness. This is enough to embolden us to go to Christ. He is not like to those pits where they who are sent unto them can find no water, Jer. xiv. 3.

Oh the folly of papists, who 'forsake the fountain of living waters, and hew them out cisterns, broken cisterns, that can hold no water,' Jer. ii. 13.

Had we sense of our own spiritual need, and faith in the all-sufficiency of Christ, we should ourselves readily go to him, and bring unto him all such as are in any spiritual need; even as they did who flocked to Christ in regard of their spiritual[1] maladies.

Sec. 124. *Of sundry heresies confuted by that which is noted of Christ.*

An ancient father[2] hath out of the testimony taken from Ps. xlv., and applied by the apostle to Christ, confuted sundry ancient heresies, after this manner following.

The apostle hath here smitten the Jews, and Paulus Samosatenus, and Arians, and Marcellus, and Sabellius, and Marcion, and Photinus also. How so? The Jews, by shewing them that there are two persons and one God; other Jews, I say the disciples of Paulus Samosatenus, while he here sheweth that testimony that speaketh of an eternal and uncreated substance. For that he might shew that a thing made differeth from the eternity of the Creator, he saith, 'Thy throne, O God, is for ever.' He smiteth the Arians, in shewing that he was neither a servant nor creature; and Marcellus and others, because the two persons, according to their subsistencies, are distinct one from another. He smiteth the Marcionites, while he sheweth, that not the deity but the humanity was anointed.

Sec. 125. *Of the resolution of verses 8, 9.*

Ver. 8. *But unto the Son he saith, Thy throne, O God, is for ever and ever; a sceptre of righteousness is the sceptre of thy kingdom.*

Ver. 9. *Thou hast loved righteousness, and hated iniquity; therefore God, even thy God, hath anointed thee with the oil of gladness above thy fellows.*

Two proofs are here couched together of Christ's excellency above angels. See Sec. 64, ver. 8.

One is taken from his divine nature.

The other from his royal dignity.

The sum of this verse is a testimony of Christ's excellency. Therein observe two points:
1. The proof produced.
2. The points proved.

In the proof is observable,
1. The manner of producing it.
2. The kind of proof.

The manner of producing it is by way of opposition, implied in the particle *but;* the opposition is to that which he had said before of angels, that they are ministers, *but* to the Son, he is a King.

[1] Qu. 'bodily'?—ED.
[2] *Chrys. Hom. 3 in cap* i. *ad Heb.* Istos etiam hæreticos eodem testimonio refellit.—*Theophylactus Enar. in Heb.*

The kind of proof is a testimony; hereof see Secs. 46 and 65.

In the testimony are to be considered both the persons and the point.

The persons are of two sorts:
1. The author that giveth the testimony.
2. The object to whom the testimony is given.

The author is not expressed in the original, but yet necessarily implied; and our English hath made a good supply in this phrase, *He saith.*

The object to whom the testimony is given, is expressed under this word of relation, Son, *unto the Son.*

The points proved are,
1. Christ's divine nature, *O God.*
2. His royal dignity. This is first propounded, then amplified.

(1.) It is propounded, implicitly, under two signs, a throne, a sceptre; and expressly under this word kingdom.

(2.) It is amplified by two properties:
[1.] Eternity, *for ever and ever.*
[2.] Equity, *righteousness.*

In the ninth verse is an illustration of the foresaid righteousness.

In this illustration are two branches:
1. The cause of Christ's righteous dealing.
2. A consequence following thereupon.

The cause is double; each cause is set out by a distinct affection, and a distinct object.

The former affection is *love*, the latter *hatred*.

The object of the former is *righteousness*, of the latter *iniquity*. As the affections love and hatred are contrary, so the the objects, righteousness and iniquity. In this respect they may well stand together, and that as two causes. For love of righteousness moves a man to deal righteously, so also doth hatred of iniquity.

In the consequence we are to observe,
1. The manner of expressing it.
2. The matter whereof it consisteth.

The manner is by an apostrophe to Christ, *O God.*

The matter consists of an honour done to Christ. This is set out,
1. By the author that doth him that honour.
2. By the kind of honour done to him.

The author is God, amplified by a special relation to Christ, *his God.*

The kind of honour consisteth of two parts:
1. Deputing Christ to a royal function.
2. Enabling him well to manage it.

Both these are implied under this metaphor, *anointed with oil.*

They are also both amplified by the quality and quantity of them.

The quality is *gladness.*

The quantity is beyond all others, *above thy fellows.*

All these points are amplified by an apostrophe

which runneth through the whole testimony, and is seven times expressed in these notes, *O, thy, thou, thee; thy* is four times expressed.

Sec. 126. *Of the doctrines arising out of the 8th and 9th verses.*

I. *More excellent things are spoken of the Son of God than of angels.* This particle *but*, being here used in opposition to that which was before said of angels, declares as much. See Sec. 104.

II. *God would have the excellencies of his Son to be known.* 'For to the Son he saith,' namely, that others might hear it and know it. So Ps. ii. 6, 7; John v. 20, 23.

III. *Christ is true God.* The title God is here properly applied to him. See Sec. 107.

IV. *Christ is a king.* The ensigns of a king, throne and sceptre, are attributed to him; yea, an express mention is made of his kingdom, see Sec. 112. Christ, therefore, is every way to be esteemed as a king.

V. *Christ as king judgeth.* A throne is a place of judgment, 1 Kings vii. 7. Christ now judgeth the world, John v. 22, 23. But his full and final judgment will be at the end of the world, Acts xvii. 31.

VI. *Christ is an everlasting king*, see Secs. 108, 110. His throne is for ever and ever.

VII. *Christ hath a peculiar kingdom.* This relative *thy* is discriminative and appropriative. It putteth a difference between his and others' kingdom; it sheweth that this kingdom is proper to Christ. See Sec. 112.

VIII. *Christ orders the matters of his kingdom as he will.* The sceptre attributed to Christ intendeth, that as a king by moving his sceptre he manifesteth his mind, and that answerably obedience is yielded to him. See Sec. 111.

IX. *Christ ordereth the affairs of his kingdom most uprightly.* His sceptre is in that respect styled a sceptre of rectitude. See Sec. 113.

X. *Righteousness is to be loved.*

XI. *Iniquity is to be hated.* Both these are here commended in Christ's example.

XII. *Love of righteousness put Christ on to deal uprightly.* The inference of this verse upon the former, demonstrateth as much; see Sec. 115. Love of righteousness will put us on to do the like.

XIII. *Love of righteousness and hatred of iniquity go together.* They are here joined together in Christ; and wheresoever the one is, there will be the other. Righteousness and iniquity are so directly opposed, and contrary each to another, as they do in a manner force from men contrary affections. See Sec. 116.

XIV. *God is in an especial manner the God of Christ.* See Sec. 118.

XV. *God hath the power of deputing and enabling men to their function.* Anointing, which is here attributed to God, implieth both these. See Sec. 119.

XVI. *Christ was deputed by God to his function.*

XVII. *Christ was enabled by God well to execute his function.* God, that anointed him, did both these. They are both grounds of faith to trust in Christ, and of obedience to submit to him.

XVIII. *The Spirit was in Christ.* This may be gathered from the metaphor of oil. To give a visible evidence hereof, the Spirit from heaven descended like a dove, and lighted upon Christ, Mat. iii. 16. Hence is it that the Spirit is also communicated to believers, for they are members of his body.

XIX. *The Holy Ghost causeth gladness.* He is this 'oil of gladness.' See Sec. 121.

XX. *Christ with much alacrity did and endured whatsoever he undertook.* See Sec. 121.

XXI. *The Son of God made himself equal to sons of men.* They are 'his fellows,' Ps. xli. 9 and lv. 13. See Sec. 122.

XXII. *The gifts of Christ far surpassed the gifts o all others.* See Sec. 123.

XXIII. *Christ's glory may, and must, be declared even to himself.* This I gather from the apostrophe, whereof see Sec. 106, and 125 in the end of it.

Sec. 127. *Of the fit application of* Ps. cii. 25 *to Christ.*

And, Thou, Lord, in the beginning hast laid the foundation of the earth; and the heavens are the works of thine hands.—Heb. I. 10.

The first particle, *and*, being copulative, sheweth that the apostle goeth on in proving the point in hand, so as

A sixth proof of Christ's excellency is here produced. It is taken from a divine work proper to God, which is creation. The kind of argument is, as the former, a divine testimony; it is taken out of Ps. cii. 25. The argument may be thus framed:

The Creator is more excellent than creatures;
But Christ is the Creator, and angels creatures;
Therefore Christ is more excellent than angels.

That Christ was the creator is here proved; that angels are creatures was proved, ver. 7. See Secs. 81, 86.

Against this proof concerning Christ, two things are excepted:

1. That the title *Lord* is not in the Hebrew text.
2. That the psalm out of which the proof is taken makes no mention of Christ.

To the first, I answer, that though it be not expressed, yet it is necessarily understood. For this relative *thou* must have an antecedent. The antecedent in the verse immediately before is *God*, to whom the prophet by an apostrophe turneth his speech, 'O God;' and in two verses before, this title *Lord* is twice expressed. Neither is there any other antecedent to which this relative *thou* can have any show of reference. Now, because the psalmist had in the verse immediately before named God, he needed not name him again. He was sufficiently understood under this relative *thou*; but the apostle, quoting this verse alone, must, to make the sense full, and to shew whom he meant, insert this title *Lord*. This he did the rather because the LXX (those ancient Greek interpreters of the Old Testament, which the Greek churches then used, as we do now the English translations) had inserted it.

To the second exception, that the psalmist maketh no mention of Christ in that psalm, I answer three things:

1. That the three persons in sacred Trinity are one in essence, mind, will, and work, John v. 17–20. What the one doth, the other also doth, so as the same act may be applied to any one of them.

2. Wheresoever mention is made of any act of God in reference to a creature, it is most properly the act of the Son, for the Father doth all by the Son. In particular, ' by him he made the worlds,' ver. 2.

3. The kingdom of Christ is expressly described in the latter part of the psalm, ver. 12, &c. And that for the comfort of the church, to support her in her great distress, being much overwhelmed with sore affliction by reason of the Babylonish captivity. To exemplify this in a few particulars: Who had mercy on Zion? Who built up Zion? Was it not the Lord Christ? Whose name do the converted Gentiles fear? Whom do the kingdoms serve? Is it not the Lord Christ? Ps. cii. 13, 15, 16, 22.

It is therefore evident that this text (as the former were) is most fitly applied to Christ.

The apostle had before, ver. 2, said, that God by the Son made the worlds. Here, to shew that the Son was not (as Arius taught) an instrument or minister in that great work, but the principal author, he doth in special thus apply it to the Son: ' Thou, Lord, in the beginning hast laid,' &c.

The first particle, *and*, hath reference to the first clause of the 8th verse, namely, to these words, ' Unto the Son he saith;' which words are here understood as if he repeated them again, ' And unto the Son he saith, Thou, Lord,' &c.; ' Unto the Son' there ' he saith, Thy throne,' &c.; ' And unto the Son' here 'he saith, Thou, Lord,' &c. There is the same author of that and this testimony.

The Greek word *Lord*, Κύριε, is apparently of the vocative case, and further declared to be by an apostrophe directed to the Lord, by this particle of the second person, *thou*. See Sec. 106.

Sec. 128. *Of the title ' Lord' applied to Christ.*

The Greek word translated *Lord*, Κύριος, being applied to God, is ordinarily put for *Jehovah*, which is the most proper name of God,[1] and never attributed to any but to the true God. True it is, that in the Hebrew there is another name of God, אדון, Exod. xxiii. 17, Joshua. iii. 11, which is translated *Lord*, and ofttimes attributed to man, as Gen. xviii 12, and

[1] See the Church's Conquest on Exod. xvii. 15, sec. 72.

xlv. 8 ; yet usually this name, when it is put for God, is pointed with such pricks or vowels as Jehovah is, אֲדֹנָי and with these points it is never attributed to any but to God.

In this text the title *Lord* is, without question, the interpretation of *Jehovah* ; for the title *Jehovah* is in that psalm seven times used, as ver. 1, 12, 15, 16, 19, 21, 23, and once *Jah*, יָהּ, ver. 18, which is an abbreviation of *Jehovah*.

Wherefore the title *Lord* doth here intend *Jehovah*, and being applied to Christ, setteth out his divine nature, and declareth him to be true God, even that God who hath his being of himself, and ever continueth of and by himself, the eternal and immutable God, even ' he which is, which was, and which is to come,'[1] Rev. i. 4; ' the Lord that changeth not,' Mal. iii. 6, who, in regard of his self-existency, giveth to himself this title, אהיה אשר אהיה, ' I am that I am;' and also this, אהיה, ' I am,' Exod. iii. 14. Thus this title *Lord* in relation to *Jehovah* giveth further proof of the true and proper divinity of Christ.

To Christ, by an excellency and property, is this title *Lord* frequently attributed. David, long before Christ's incarnation, in the Spirit called him Lord, Mat. xxii. 43. The angel that brought the first news of his birth, styles him ' Christ the Lord,' Luke ii. 11. Both his disciples and others in his life so called him. After his resurrection, when he was discerned by John, John said to Peter of him, ' It is the Lord,' John xxi. 7. Christ himself thus saith, ' Ye call me Lord, and ye say well, for so I am,' John xiii. 13. It was usual with the apostles in their epistles thus to style him ' the Lord Jesus,' Rom. i. 8; and he is said to be ' the one Lord Jesus Christ,' 1 Cor. viii. 6. A prophetess called him *Lord*, anon after he was conceived, even while he was in his mother's womb, Luke i. 43.

Christ is Lord in sundry respects.

1. As God, in regard of his divine nature. God said, ' I am the Lord,' Exod. vi. 2.

2. As the Son of God, in regard of his person ; for of the Son in relation to the Father it is said, ' The Lord rained fire from the Lord,' Gen. xix. 24.

3. As God-man, in regard of the hypostatical union of Christ's two natures in one person. Thus saith Thomas to Christ on earth, ' My Lord and my God,' John xx. 28.

4. As king of the church, in regard of that authority and dignity whereunto God hath advanced him : ' I have set my King upon my holy hill of Sion,' saith the Father to the Son, Ps. ii. 6 ; ' God hath made him both Lord and Christ,' Acts ii. 36.

On these grounds divine worship hath been yielded unto him on earth as unto the Lord. In his infancy, Mat. ii. 11 ; in his man-age, Mat. viii. 2 ; after his resurrection, Mat. xxviii. 9 ; in the time of his ascension, Luke xxiv. 52 ; and now also, Christ being in heaven, and sitting as Lord on his throne, is worshipped, Rev.

[1] ὁ ὤν, καὶ ὁ ἦν, καὶ ὁ ἐρχόμενος.

iv. 10, and v. 14. Thus he is still, and ever shall be, worshipped as the true Lord by his church.

Answerably all other divine respect is to be yielded to him. He is to [be] loved with all the soul, with all the heart, with all the mind, and with all the strength. Accordingly is he to be feared, admired, adored, called upon, believed in, served, obeyed, subjected unto, praised for all things, in all things glorified, preferred before all, advanced above all, and every way esteemed as a Lord, even our Lord, the most high supreme Sovereign over all.

Sec. 129. *Of Christ's eternity.*

The eternity of this Lord is further set out in this phrase κατ' ἀρχάς, ' in the beginning,' namely, in the beginning of time, so as that which was before that beginning, was without beginning, properly eternal. Thus is the eternity of God manifested in the very first word of the holy Bible, Gen. i. 1, and the eternity also of the Son of God, John i. 1. He that in the beginning laid the foundation of the earth, was before that foundation was laid, and before that beginning. In that respect saith the Son of God of himself: 'The Lord possessed me in the beginning of his way, before his works of old : I was set up from everlasting, from the beginning, or ever the earth was,' &c., Prov. viii. 22, 23, &c.

As the eternity of the Creator is by this phrase, *in the beginning,* intended, so the plain contrary concerning creatures is expressed. Creatures being made in the beginning, then first began to be ; they were not before, therefore not eternal. But the Creator then being, and making the world, was before the beginning, and had no beginning ; therefore eternal. Here, then, is manifested the difference betwixt the Creator and creatures in reference to the beginning. The Creator then was even as he was before. He did not then begin to be, but manifested himself to be what he was before ; but creatures then began to be what they were not before.

As the former reference of this phrase, *in the beginning,* to the Son refutes Samosatenus, Macedonius, Arius, and other heretics, that denied the eternity of the Son of God, so the latter reference thereof to creatures refutes Aristotle[1] and other philosophers, who held the world to be eternal, which is a point not only improbable, but also impossible,[2] for then should there be no creatures. A creature cannot be but created. If no creature, then all a creator, even one and the same with God himself. Eternity and unity are convertible terms. There can be but one eternal, as there is but one almighty, one infinite ; yet from that position of the world's eternity, there would be more than one infinite ; for there must be an infinite number of souls of men and other things if the world were eternal in Adam's time, and all that have been since added to the world would make up more than infinite.

[1] Arist. de Cœlo, lib. iii. cap. ix. x.
[2] Mundum ab æterno constare improbabile et impossibile est.—*Aug. Quæst. ex Vet. Test.,* q. 28.

That gross error of the world's eternity is so express against the light of nature, as by many solid arguments, drawn from natural principles, other heathen philosophers have refuted it.

There were other heretics who had this conceit, that the matter of the elements of which the world was made, was not made of God, but was co-eternal with God.[1] This conceit of the eternity of *prima materia,* the first matter out of which they say all things were at first created, is as much against the light of God's word and the light of nature, and as derogatory to the eternity of God, as the former of the world's eternity. Eternity is one of God's incommunicable properties. Whatsoever is made eternal beside God is made equal to God, yea, a very God.

Sec. 130. *Of the extent of heaven and earth.*

In setting down the creation, two words are used, which comprise in them all things that were made, namely *heaven* and *earth,* and that by two tropes : one is a metonymy, whereby the continent is put for all things contained therein ; the other is a synecdoche, whereby a part is put for the whole. The earth is the middle centre of the whole world, and the heaven is the uttermost circumference that compasseth all about, so as all between them are comprised under them. In this large sense these two words are oft used, as Gen. i. 1, 2 Kings xix. 15, 2 Chron. ii. 12, Ps. cxxi. 2, Jer. xxxii. 17.

Under this word *earth,* the sea and all waters below are comprised ; for the earth and sea make but one globe, Gen. i. 9, 10. They were divided at first, and so continue, for the better use of man, and of other creatures living on earth. Thus not only all things that move upon the earth, or grow out of the earth, or are within the earth, but also whatsoever is in the sea, or swims thereupon, is to be understood under this word *earth.*

There is mention made in Scripture of three heavens.

1. The air, wherein birds and fowls do fly, wherein are the clouds also, so as all the space betwixt the earth and the moon is called the first heaven.

2. The firmament, wherein are all sorts which are called the host of heaven, Deut. iv. 19, is the second heaven.

3. That invisible place where are the angels and glorified saints, and the human nature of Christ, and where God doth most manifest his glory, is the third heaven, 2 Cor. xii. 2. Beyond this is nothing at all. In regard of this distinction of heaven, the plural number *heavens* is used.

Thus we see how these two words, *earth, heavens,* may be put for all creatures.

As for the order of the words, in setting earth before heaven, the Holy Ghost is not over strict or curious in

[1] Seleuciani, vel Hermiani elementorum materiam de qua factus est mundus, non a Deo factam dicunt, sed Deo coëternam.—*Aug. Hæres. Hær.* 59.

his method. Though for the most part the heaven for excellency's sake be set before the earth, yet many times, as here, earth is put before heaven, Judges v. 4, Ps. lxviii. 8, Isa. xlv. 12, Jer. li. 15.

Some probable reasons may be given of putting earth before heaven, as,

1. The earth was made before the visible heavens, Gen. i. 10, 14.

2. The earth is set down as a foundation of the world, and foundations use to be first mentioned, 1 Kings vi. 37, 38, Ezra iii. 11, Zech. iv. 9.

3. The earth is the centre of the world, the heavens the circumference thereabout. He beginneth therefore with the centre, and proceeds to the circumference.

4. The earth is man's habitation, Acts xvii. 26. From thence he beholdeth the heavens. Speaking, therefore, to men, he first sets out the place of their habitation.

Sec. 131. *Of the earth being a foundation.*

The creation of the earth is thus set out: 'Thou hast laid the foundation thereof.' This is the interpretation of one Greek word, $ἐθεμελίωσας$. A foundation,[1] from whence the verb is derived, signifieth that which is put under other things to support and bear them up. It useth, therefore, to be sound, solid, strong, and laid on firm and sure ground, Luke vi. 48. It is most frequently put for the foundation of an house, which beareth up all the rest of the building, 1 Cor. iii. 10–12. A foundation remaineth firm, stable, unmoveable. The word here used is also translated thus: 'grounded,' $τεθεμελιωμένοι$, Eph. iii. 18, and 'settled,' 1 Peter v. 10. It is there joined with two other words which signify a fast fixing of a thing, 'stablish, strengthen, and settle,' $στηρίξαι$, $σθενῶσαι$, $θεμελιῶσαι$.

This phrase, *laid the foundation*, applied to the earth, implieth two things:

1. That the earth is the lowest part of the world. It being the centre, whatsoever is about it is over it. Hereupon this word *beareth* is oft attributed to the earth, as Deut. iv. 39; Joshua ii. 11; 1 Kings viii. 23; Isa. li. 6; Jer. xxxi. 37; Acts ii. 19.

2. That the earth is immoveable. This inference is thus made upon this very phrase, 'Who laid the foundations of the earth, that it should not be removed,' Ps. civ. 5.

In these and other like respects is this metaphor *foundation* oft attributed to the earth, as Job xxxviii. 4, Ps. lxxxii. 5. And the earth is said to be established, and thereupon to abide, Ps. cxix. 90, and lxxviii. 69. By the stability of the earth sundry benefits accrue to the inhabitants thereof.

1. The constancy of the motions of the heavens, and of the host thereof, is better observed, and the admirable effects arising from thence, are the better discerned.

2. The stability of the earth is very useful to plants, beasts, and men, that abide thereon. The damages and mischiefs that fall out upon earthquakes give further proof hereof.

It is a gross error of Aristarchus, Samius, Copernicus, and other philosophers,[1] who imagine that the earth continually moveth, and that the heaven and the host thereof do but seem to our sight to move, as the banks and trees thereon do to such as are in a boat rowed with oars, or in a ship under sail. This conceit cannot stand with the metaphor of a foundation, here and in other places applied to the earth.

Sec. 132. *Of heaven the work of God's hand.*

That which is here spoken of the heavens in relation to God, 'the heavens are the works of thy hands,' is to be taken metaphorically, by way of resemblance to men, who use with their hands to make what they make. Of the second temple it is thus said, 'Zerubbabel hath laid the foundation of this house, his hand shall finish it,' Zech. iv. 9; and wonders are said to be done 'by the hands of the apostles,' Acts xiv. 3. Men work with their hands, Eph. iv. 27; and they do other things with their hands. Hereupon idolaters are said to make idols with their hands, Isa. xxxi. 17, and idols are styled 'the work of men's hands,' Isa. xxxvii. 19, Jer. x. 3, 9; yea, the benefit that ariseth from the thing men do, is called 'the fruit of their hands,' Prov. xxxi. 31, and 'the labour of their hands,' Ps. cxxviii. 2.

In allusion hereunto, the things which God doth or maketh are said to be the work of his hands, and his hands are said to make them, Job x. 38. Because men know not how any should see without eyes, hear without ears, speak without a mouth, tread without feet, do this or that without hands; eyes, ears, mouth, feet, hands, and other parts of man are attributed to God, 1 Pet. iii. 12; Num. xii. 8; Lam. iii. 34; Ps. cxix. 73.

But to shew that properly God hath no hands, his works are oft said to be without hands, Dan. ii. 34, 45, and viii. 25, Job xxxiv. 20. Yea, herein lieth a difference betwixt the things of God and men, that they are without hands, but these with hands, Col. ii. 11; Eph. ii. 11; Heb. ix. 11, 24. Yea, in proper speech the heaven itself, that here metaphorically is said to be the work of God's hand, is elsewhere said to be made without hands, 2 Cor. v. 1, Acts xvii. 24.

Sec. 133. *Of anthropomorphites.*

The anthropomorphites[2] do hereupon err, not know-

---

[1] $θεμέλιον$ of $τιθέναι$, *ponere*; $θεμέλια solent structuræ ὑποτίθεσθαι, supponi, seu imo loco poni, ut cætera strues possit eis superstrui.*

[1] $ἔνιοι κειμένην ἐπὶ τοῦ κέντρου φάσιν αὐτὴν εἰλεῖσθαι περὶ τὸν διὰ παντὸς τεταμένον πόλον.$—*Arist de Cœlo*, lib. ii. cap. xiii.

[2] *Anthropomorphitas vocant, quoniam Deum sibi fingunt cogitatione carnali in similitudinem imaginis corruptibilis hominis.*—*Aug. de Hæres. Hom.* 1. *Deum ipsum omninò*

ing the Scriptures nor the power of God, in that they literally and properly apply to God such parts of men as are metaphorically, and only by way of resemblance, for teaching's sake, attributed to him. They feign God to themselves by a carnal cogitation to be after the image of a corruptible man, and that God is altogether a body, imagining that whatsoever is not a body is no substance at all. But they are much deceived, for spirits are not only true substances, but every way the most excellent substances; bodiliness doth but add grossness, heaviness, drowsiness, and sundry other weaknesses to a substance.

Concerning the members of God which the Scripture frequently mentioneth, that no man should believe that we, according to the form and figure of flesh, are like to God, the same scripture saith, that God hath wings, which we have not. Therefore when we hear of wings, we understand protection, Ps. ix. 4. So when we hear of hands, we must understand operation; and if the Scripture mentions any other like thing, I suppose it to be spiritually understood.

Sec. 134. *Of the reasons why the heavens are said to be the works of God's hands.*

The heavens are here, and in other scriptures, expressly said to be the works of God's hands. In that,

1. They were made as well as the earth. There be that grant that the earth and the things here below had a beginning; but imagine that the heavens and the things therein were eternal, without beginning. The very first verse of the Bible expressly disproves this error, for there it is expressly said, that the heaven was created; so also in sundry other places.

2. God himself made the heavens. They were the work of his own hands, made by his own power, not by angels, as the Menandrians, Saturninians, Cerinthians, Merinthians, and other heretics thought.[1] Nor were they made by the casual concurrence of certain motes, which they call *atomi*, as Democritus, Leucippus, and other Epicurean philosophers dreamed. They imagined their *atomi* to be small, indivisible bodies, such as appear in the sun-beams when the sun shineth through an hole. They say, that by the conjunction of these all things at first were made, and that into these all things at last shall be dissolved.

3. The heavens were made without instruments, even with God's hands, and nothing else. It is one of the Epicurean philosopher's arguments against the making of the heavens, that there could not be sufficient instruments for effecting so great a work: 'What iron tools,' saith he, 'what levers, or crows, what ministers could be had to help on so vast a fabric?'[1] O blind and stupid philosopher, that can no better discern between divine and human works, betwixt the first creating of things by God, and the after-making of things by man! God had no need of any help at all.

4. The heavens are as a canopy to cover all the earth. For the use of hands, especially when both hands are used, is to stretch a thing and to spread it abroad. The Lord in express terms saith, 'My hands have stretched out the heavens,' Isa. xlv. 12. These phrases of *stretching forth* and *spreading out* the heavens art oft attributed unto God, as Isa. xl. 22; Jer. xli. 15; Ps. civ. 2; Job ix. 8, and xxxvii. 18.

5. Great diligence was used in making the heavens. Mention of *hands* in the plural number implieth thus much, for careful and diligent persons will put both their hands to what they do; slothful and careless persons will use but one hand, and put the other into their bosom or pocket, Prov. ix. 24, and xxvi. 15.

6. The heavens being said to be the work of God's hand, imply the great power of God, who with his hands, that is, by himself, can make so fair and great a work as the heavens are. Therefore the heaven is called 'the firmament of his power,' Ps. cl. 1. And God is said to have 'made the heaven by his great power and stretched out arm;' and thereupon it is inferred, that 'there is nothing too hard for him,' Jer. xxxii. 17.

7. The heavens bear the clearest evidence of God's excellencies, Ps. viii. 3, and xix. 1. Of a picture made by Apelles, which was admirable in all men's eyes, they said, This is the work of Apelles's hands.

Sec. 135. *Of the resolution of the tenth verse.*

Ver. 10. *And, Thou, Lord, in the beginning hast laid the foundation of the earth; and the heavens are the works of thine hands.*

The connection of this verse with the former, set out by this copulative particle *and*, manifesteth an addition of another argument to prove the same point. Hereof see Sec. 77.

The sum of this text is, the creation of things.

Two special points thereabout are here noted:
1. The Creator that made all.
2. The creatures that were made.

In setting out the Creator, observe,
1. The manner of attributing this work unto him, by an apostrophe, *thou*. See 106, and 125, and 127 in the end.
2. The title given unto him, *Lord*.

In the creatures note,
1. What is common to all.

---

pus esse præsumunt, putantes quicquid corpus non est, prorsus nullam esse substantiam.—*Aug. Ep.* 112. De membris Dei quæ assiduè Scriptura commemorat, ne quisquam secundum carnis hujus formam et figuram nos esse crederet similes Deo, propterea et eadem Scriptura et alas Deum habere dixit, quas nos utique non habemus, &c.—*Aug. Ep.* 111.

[1] Menander mundum asserebat ab angelis factum. Saturninus angelos septem fecisse mundum dicebat. Sic Cerinthiani, Merinthiani, aliique.—*Aug. de Hæres. Arist. de Cœlo.* lib. iii. cap. iv. *Cic. de Nat. deor.* lib. i., *Idem de fin. bon. et mal.* lib. i.

[1] Quæ ferramenta? qui vectes? quæ machinæ? qui ministri tanti operis fuerunt?—*Cic. de Nat. deor.*

2. Wherein they are distinguished one from another. Two things are common to all:
1. The same Lord that made all, implied in this copulative *and*.
2. The same time wherein all were made, *in the beginning*.

There are also two things wherein the creatures differ:
1. Their distinct kinds, *earth, heaven*.
2. Their distinct ends.

One to be as a foundation, *laid the foundation*.

The other to be as a cover over all, and conspicuously to manifest the glory of God, in this phrase, *the work of thine hands*.

Sec. 136. *Of the observations arising of the tenth verse.*

I. *Christ is Jehovah.* The title Lord importeth as much. See Sec. 128

II. *Christ is the Creator of all*, John i. 2, Col. i. 16.

III. *The beginning of time was at the creation ;* for this phrase *in the beginning* hath reference to the creation. Before that there was no time. See Sec. 129.

IV. *Christ was eternal.* He made the things that were made in the beginning. So as he was before them, and before the beginning, therefore without beginning, and eternal. See 119.

V. *The earth was made.* For when the foundation of it was laid, it was made. See 131.

VI. *The earth is immoveable.* See 131.

VII. *The heavens were made as well as the earth.* See 132.

VIII. *The same Lord that made earth made also the heavens.* The copulative particle *and*, which here knits heaven and earth together, demonstrates the truth of these two doctrines.

IX. *All creatures are within the compass of heaven and earth.* These two kinds are here put for all creatures whatsoever. See 130.

X. *Christ can establish and turn about what he will.* The earth is a massy and ponderous piece, and hath nothing to rest upon but the air ; yet it is there laid as a foundation, and remains unmoveable. The heavens are of an incomprehensible bigness, yet he maketh them continually to run about.

Of other observations arising from this phrase, *the work of thine hands*, see Sec. 131.

Sec. 137. *Of the difference betwixt Christ's and creatures' immutability.*

They shall perish, but thou remainest ; and they all shall wax old as doth a garment ; and as a vesture shalt thou fold them up, and they shall be changed : but thou art the same, and thy years shall not fail.—Heb. I. 11, 12.

Out of Ps. cii. ver. 26, 27, the apostle produceth another proof of Christ's excellency, taken from his immutability and unchangeableness ; and to shew that even herein Christ surpasseth all creatures, the point is set down by way of opposition : the creatures are mutable, but Christ is immutable ; therefore more excellent.

This relative *they* being in Greek of the masculine gender, αὐτοί, hath particular reference to the heavens, οὐρανοί, in the latter end of the former verse ; which word is also of the same gender. Yet withal it includeth the earth before-mentioned, and all things in heaven and earth, not the angels themselves excepted ; for it is the most principal scope of the apostle to advance Christ above angels, as ver. 4–7.

Obj. There are many creatures that shall never perish :[1] ' The earth abideth for ever,' Eccles. i. 4. That which is said of the sun's and moon's continuance for ever, Ps. lxxii. 5, 17, and lxxxix. 37, may be applied to heaven and all the host thereof : ' The sun and moon endure throughout all generations ;' ' It shall be established for ever as the moon,' &c. The angels, also, even the good angels, are still, and ever will continue, as they were at first created. They were the evil angels that ' kept not their first estate, but left their own habitation,' Jude 6.

Ans. 1. This phrase *for ever* is sometimes put for the world's continuance, Mat. xi. 14. Thus, though the fore-mentioned creatures continue firm and stable all the time of this world, yet at the end of the world they may be altered, as the earth, and heaven, and hosts thereof. See Secs. 137, 139.

2. As for angels, they have indeed from the beginning continued, and shall everlastingly continue in the same estate and condition ; yet there is a great difference betwixt Christ's immutability and theirs ; for,

(1.) Christ was as he is from all eternity, Ps. xc. 2, Prov. viii. 22, &c. But angels had a beginning, Col. i. 16, before which they were not what now they are.

(2.) Christ was originally of and by himself as he is ; angels not so. Christ made them angels. He might have made them mortal and mutable creatures.

(3.) Christ, by his own power and wisdom, continueth the same as he is. Angels are confirmed and established by Christ, Eph. i. 10.

(4.) Comparatively it is said of Christ, ' Who only hath immortality,' 1 Tim. vi. 16. The creatures' excellencies, compared with the excellencies of Christ, are as the light of the moon and stars ; and as artificial lights compared to the light of the sun, none of them are seen in the bright shining of the sun, so the immutability of the creatures is as no immutability compared to Christ's.

Sec. 137. *Of the different manner of creatures perishing.*

The Hebrew word translated *perish*, אבדו, is put for any kind of perishing, whether by degrees or at once. Things that rot, consume by little and little. In this sense this word is applied to the memorial or name of wicked men, which is said to perish, אבד, Ps. ix. 6,

---
[1] See the Guide to go to God, or an explanation of the Lord's Prayer, sec. 226.

in that by little and little they are clean forgotten, and thus said to rot, ירקב, Prov. x. 17. Things that rot by degrees come to nought.

At once; things are said to perish when they are suddenly destroyed. Thus a righteous man is said to perish, Isa. vii. 1; that is, suddenly to be taken away, as Ezekiel's wife was with a stroke, Ezek. xxiv. 16.

So the Greek word used by the apostle ἀπολοῦνται, is sometimes put for a sudden destruction, as Luke xvii. 27–29, where it is applied to those that perished by the flood, and by fire and brimstone from heaven.

It is also put for withering by degrees, as the grace of a flower perisheth, James i. 11.

There are some who conceive that earth and heaven do waste by degrees, and through continuance of ages do wax old and fail. They say that there is not now that clearness of light nor vigour of stars that was in former times, and that the strength of the earth doth every year decay.[1]

Others are of opinion that the heaven and all the host thereof still retain that virtue, vigour, and strength which they had when they were first made; and that the earth, though in the superficies of it, whereon men and beasts tread, and which is daily digged and ploughed up, may have some of the strength thereof exhausted, yet in the main body and innermost part of it, it still remaineth the same, and so shall do to the end of the world. See Sec. 139.

Yet in that at length they shall be *changed*, they may be said to *perish*; in this sense it is said, that 'heaven and earth shall pass away,' Mark xiii. 31.

Thus one way or other all creatures perish.

Lifeless and senseless creatures in the earth and water; vegetable plants; fish, fowls, beasts, and other creatures that have sense, together with the bodies of men, perish by little and little; the heavens, with their hosts, and the substance of the earth, shall on a sudden be changed; devils are in their quality altered from that they were at first made, so also souls of men. God's angels are in their nature alterable; there is a possibility for the third, which is the invisible and highest heaven, to be destroyed, if it seemed good to the supreme Sovereign so to deal with it. In these respects all creatures may be said to perish.

Sec. 138. *Of the manner of setting out Christ's immutability.*

Both the psalmist and the apostle turn from the creatures to the Creator, the Lord Christ; and by continuing the apostrophe (whereof see Secs. 106, 127), direct their speech to him, saying, 'Thou remainest.' This they do by way of opposition, as this particle *but*, δὲ, sheweth; intimating thereby that Christ, in that which is here truly spoken of him, excelleth all creatures. See Sec. 141. This is further manifest by the express mention of the pronoun *thou*, אתה, σύ.

The verb whereby the constancy and immutability of Christ is set down, in Hebrew, signifieth an unmoveable standing or abiding, עמד, *stetit immotus*. It is applied to idols fast fixed, so as they cannot be removed, Isa. xlvi. 7; to a mountain, Ps. xxx. 7; and to the word and counsel of God, Ps. xxxiii. 9, 11. Fitly, therefore, is it here used to set out Christ's stability.

The Greek word, διαμένεις, is a compound word, and the composition adds much emphasis. The simple verb implieth a steady standing or abiding, but the compound a permanent or unalterable remaining to be so or so. They who observed a constant abiding of creatures in that frame wherein at first God made them, thus express it: they continue, or remain as they were, 2 Peter iii. 4.

Though the Hebrew and Greek words in their signification do fitly answer each other, yet there is some difference in their tenses. The Hebrew is of the future tense, 'shalt remain,' תעמד; the Greek is of the present tense, or 'remainest,' διαμένεις. But this difference may easily be reconciled. For,

1. It is usual with the Hebrews to change tenses,[1] especially the perfect, present, and future tenses; as, Exod. xv. 1, 'Then sang Moses;' Hebrew, ישיר משה, *Moses canit*, 'Moses shall sing.' So Isa. iii. 16.

2. The difference betwixt the present and future tenses of the fifth conjugation in Greek is only in the accent, so as the accent being altered, the Greek may be of the same tense that the Hebrew is.[2]

3. Either tense makes to the point in hand. The present tense, 'thou remainest,' implieth a continuance in that which Christ was before; the future, 'thou shalt remain,' implieth also as much. Either of them being taken (as in this testimony they are) in opposition to things that perish, do demonstrate an unchangeable constancy in Christ. Hereof see more, Sec. 112.

Sec. 139. *Of creatures waxing old.*

To make that point of the mutability of creatures more clear, two resemblances are used: one taken from the waxing old of a garment, the other from the folding up of a vesture.

This particle *all* is added, to shew the extent of that relative *they* in the beginning of this verse. Of this extent, see Sec. 136.

The resemblance of waxing old is taken from such things as by continuance do use to waste. The Hebrew, יבלו, is attributed to an old person, Gen. xviii. 12; to bones, Ps. xxxii. 3; to flesh and skin wasted, Lam. iii. 4; to man's form or beauty, Ps. xlix. 14;

---

[1] Mundum videmus passioni subjectum, et per secula senectute deficere credimus et finiri.—*Aug. quæst. ex Vet. Test.* q. 28. Non est nunc illa claritas luminis, nec sunt illæ stellarum vires quæ fuerunt, terræ etiam vires deficiunt quotannis.—*Moll. prælect. in Ps.* cii. 27.

[1] Enallage temporis.
[2] διαμένεις, præsent; διαμενεῖς, futu.

to garments, shoes, sacks, and bottles, Josh. ix. 4, 5, 13 ; to a vintage, Isa. xxxii. 10.

The Greek word παλαιωθήσονται is applied to money bags, Luke xii. 33 ; and to the covenant veiled over with legal rites, Heb. viii. 13. A noun, παλαιός, coming from the same root, is attributed to garments and bottles, Mat. ix. 16, 17 ; and to leaven, 1 Cor. v. 8.

All the fore-mentioned instances by experience are known to consume by degrees ; so do all things here below. As for the heavens, they may be said to wax old as doth a garment, in that they are appointed to an end,—to an end, I say, of what they are now, 2 Peter iii. 10. The longer, therefore, they have continued, the nearer they approach to that end ; as a garment, the longer it is worn, the nearer it is to its end.

The comparison betwixt heavens and garments is to be taken not simply of the manner of their coming to an end, by decaying and wasting more and more ; but indefinitely, in regard of the end itself, namely, that they shall have an end.

The other comparison, ver. 12, is added to give further light to the point in hand. It is joined with a copulative and, καὶ, ' And as a vesture,' &c.

These two words, garment, vesture, in general intend one and the same thing. The former, garment, both in Hebrew[1] and Greek,[2] signifieth anything that one useth to put upon his body ; so doth also the latter,[3] vesture. It is put for a covering over a woman's head, 1 Cor. xi. 15.

In reference to this latter, it is said, Thou shalt fold them up, ἑλίξεις, volves. The Greek word here used is not elsewhere in the New Testament.

1. Some take it for such a folding up of a large broad vesture as bringeth it into a very small compass, and maketh it appear very little in comparison of that which it seemed to be before. So the heavens, which are now spread over the whole world, shall be brought to little or nothing. It is said, that ' The heavens shall be rolled together as a scroll,' Isa. xxxiv. 4. A scroll was a fair piece of paper or parchment, or rather many pieces stitched and pasted one to another, wherein such things as use now to be printed were written, and then rolled up, as inventories of wills are ; and being rolled up, they were compacted in a small volume, and nothing therein written could be discerned. Mention is made of such scrolls or rolls, Ezra vi. 1, 2, Isa. viii. 1, Jer. xxxvi. 2, Ezek. ii. 9.

2. Others take the word for turning a thing ; as when a garment is some while worn on the one side, the other side is turned. To this they apply these words, ' We look for new heavens and a new earth,' 2 Peter iii. 13 : new, not in the substance, but in the quality thereof more glorious than before.

Thus the phrase of rolling up, or turning the heavens, doth not intend an utter abolition, but a clear renovation of them.

The Hebrew word gives proof hereunto ;[1] for it properly signifies, as by our English it is translated, to change. Hereupon sundry expositors suppose another Greek word,[2] somewhat like this, to be used by the apostle, a word that signifieth to change. But seeing the former word, translated fold up, may include that sense, why should any think of altering the text from the agreement of all the Greek copies therein, and of the Seventy whom the apostle follows, and of sundry Greek fathers ?

This that hath been distinctly and largely set down by the Holy Ghost, of the alteration of creatures, and that both simply thus, ' They shall perish,' and also symbolically, under the resemblances of a garment waxing old, and a vesture folded up, doth much amplify the unchangeable constancy of Christ ; for contraries laid together do illustrate each other,[3] as black and white, coarse and fine, pain and ease, heaven and hell ; so also vanity and stability, mutability and immutability.

Sec. 140. *Of Christ's power about altering creatures.*

The author of the mutability of creatures is the Lord Jesus, to whom it is here said, ' Thou shalt fold them up.' He that createth all, hath an absolute power to preserve, alter, and destroy all, as it pleaseth him. It was this Lord Jesus that said, ' Every living substance that I have made will I destroy,' Gen. vii. 4. And again, ' I will shake the heaven, and the earth shall remove out of its place ;' I will clothe the heaven with blackness ;' ' I create new heavens,' &c., Isa. xiii. 13, and l. 3, and lxv. 17.

This Lord Jesus, being true God, is the most high supreme sovereign of all ; he doth all, ' that men may know, that he whose name alone is Jehovah, is the most high over all,' Ps. lxxxiii. 18.

As he hath supreme authority, so he hath also almighty power ; he is able to bring to pass what he will : ' By the word of the Lord were the heavens made,' Ps. xxxiii. 6, and by the same word they may be changed.

Therefore it is here added, ' and they shall be changed.' Because the Lord Jesus hath a mind to change them, they shall be changed ; for who hath resisted his will ? All things are alike to him. Whether is it easier to say to that that was not, ' Let there be light ' in the heaven, Gen. i. 14, or to say, ' Let the heavens be folded up and changed ' ? Upon the same ground that the former was effected, the latter also shall be accomplished.

As the power of the Lord Jesus in creating and

---

[1] בגד. [2] ἱμάτιον ab ἕννυμι induo.
[3] לבוש a לבש, induit. περιβόλαιον a περιβάλλειν, circumjicere.

[1] חלף, mutatus est. Inde החליף mutavit.—*Erasmus, Beza, Ribera.* [2] ἀλάξεις.—*Chrysost. Theophylact.*
[3] Παραλληλα τῷ ἐναντίῳ μάλιστα φαίνεσθαι, dixit Arist. Rhet., lib. iii. cap. ii.

preserving all things tendeth much to the strengthening of our faith in the accomplishment of all his promises, and in obtaining our lawful desires of such things as are needful and useful, and in protecting us from matters hurtful and dangerous; so his power in altering and abolishing what he pleaseth, is of use to make us stand in awe of him, and to be afraid of offending his majesty, and provoking his wrath.

The Lord's power in creating and preserving things for strengthening our faith is pressed, Ps. cxlvi. 5, 6, Isa. xxxvii. 16, &c., Jer. xxxvii. 17, Acts iv. 24.

His power in altering and abolishing the heaven and other things, for working fear and awe in us, is pressed, Isa. xiii. 13, and xxxiv. 1, 4, Luke xxi. 26, 2 Peter iii. 10, 11.

The former sheweth that he is the Lord of life, and hath power to save and defend, therefore trust on him, Ps. cxxiv. 8.

The latter, that he is the Lord of death, and can destroy, therefore fear him, Luke xii. 5.

Sec. 141. *Of Christ's immutability.*

The immutability of creatures being distinctly set out, the apostle returneth to the main point intended, which is Christ's immutability. It was before generally set down in this phrase, 'Thou remainest,' Secs. 136-138. Here it is illustrated in these two other branches, 'thou art the same, thy years shall not fail.'

Though all these three phrases in general intend one and the same thing, namely, immutability, yet, to shew that there is no tautology, no vain repetition of one and the same thing therein, they may be distinguished one from another.

1. The first, *thou remainest*, pointeth at Christ's eternity before all times; for it implieth his being before, in which he still abides.

2. The second, *thou art the same*, declares Christ's constancy. There is no variableness with him; thus, therefore, he saith of himself, 'I am the Lord, I change not,' Mal. iii. 6.

3. The third, *thy years shall not fail*, intendeth Christ's everlastingness; that he who was before all times, and continueth in all ages, will beyond all times so continue.

Thus these three phrases do distinctly prove the three branches of this description of Christ, 'which is, and which was, and which is to come,' Rev. i. 4.

This name that Christ assumeth to himself, I AM, and this, I AM THAT I AM, Exod. iii. 14, and this also, JEHOVAH, Exod. vi. 3, do demonstrate a perpetual continuing to be the same. In this respect he thus saith, 'I the Lord, the first, and with the last, I am he,' Isa. xli. 4, or, as some translate it, I am the same; for it is the very same word both in Hebrew and in Greek that is here translated *the same*.[1] This immutable constancy of the Lord is confirmed by this testimony, 'with whom is no variableness nor shadow of turning,' James iii. 17, no show or appearance of alteration.

This may be exemplified in all the things that are Christ's.

1. His essence and being. This is especially here intended. So also Exod. iii. 14.

2. His counsel. Immutability is expressly attributed thereunto, Heb. vi. 17. 'It shall stand,' Ps. xxxiii. 11, Prov. xix. 21, Isa. xlviii. 10. It shall stand immutably, inviolably.

3. His attributes. Sundry attributes for teaching's sake,[1] by way of resemblance, are ascribed to the Lord. In this respect it is said, 'his compassions fail not,' Lam. iii. 22; 'his mercy endureth for ever,' Ps. cxviii. 1; 'his love is everlasting,' Jer. xxxi. 3; 'his righteousness endureth for ever,' cxi. 3. So his truth, Ps. cxvii. 2; so his judgments, Ps. cxix. 160.

4. His word endureth for ever, 1 Peter i. 25. This is manifested in the law, whereof not one tittle shall fail, Luke xvi. 17, and in the gospel, which is an everlasting gospel.

5. His bonds whereby he binds himself to us are unalterable, as promises and oaths. These are the two immutable things intended, Heb. vi. 18, and his covenant also, Jer. xxxiii. 20, 21.

See more hereof, Chap. xiii. 8, Sec. 112.

Sec. 142. *Of objections against the Lord's immutability answered.*

Obj. Christ was made man in the fulness of time, and died, Gal. iv. 4, 1 Cor. xv. 3; yea, 'being in the form of God, he made himself of no reputation,' Philip. ii. 6, 7, or he brought himself to nothing.[2] From hence it is inferred that he was changed in his very essence.

Ans. Immutability attributed to Christ is properly meant of his divine nature, which was no way altered by assuming his human nature; for he became man, not by conversion of the Godhead into flesh, but by taking of the manhood into God,[3] so as he remained in his divine nature, when he was incarnate, the very same that he was before, without any addition, diminution, or alteration.

Of other objections answered, see Chap. vi. 17, Sec. 136.

Sec. 143. *Of Christ's everlastingness.*

The last phrase whereby Christ's immutability is set out, is this, 'thy years shall not fail.' Years are not properly applied to the Lord; for eternity admits no distinction of times, as things temporary do, 2 Pet. iii. 8. The Holy Ghost doth herein speak of the Lord as we mortal creatures use to speak one of another;

---

[1] נוּה, ὁ αὐτός.

[1] ἀνθρωποπαθῶς.
[2] ἐκένωσε exinanivit, a κενὸς vacuus, inanis.
[3] οὐ τροπῆ τῆς θεότητος εἰς σάρκα, ἀλλὰ προσλήψει τῆς ἀνθρωπότητος εἰς Θεόν.—*Sym. Athan.*

for the continuance of temporary things which have a beginning, and shall have an end, are distinguished by hours, days, weeks, months, and years. The longest ordinary distinction of times is a year. That continuance which exceedeth that date useth to be set forth by multiplying years, as two years, ten years, an hundred years, a thousand years, and so forward. The fewer of these distinctions that any pass over, the shorter their continuance is; the more they pass over, the longer is their continuance. If still they continue year after year, and that without date or end, so as still their years continue and cease not, they are counted everlasting, their years fail not, οὐκ ἐκλείψουσι.

In this respect, that we might the better discern the continuance of the Lord, years are attributed to him, as Job x. 5, 'Are thy years as the days of man?' Are they so short, or have they an end as man's days? 'Can the number of his years be searched out? Job xxxvi. 26. They are without number, and cannot be found out. His years are throughout all generations, Ps. cii. 24. They ever continue. In this respect the psalmist saith to the Lord, 'From everlasting to everlasting thou art God,' Ps. xc. 2. Fitly, therefore, is this phrase, *shall not fail*, added to the years which are spoken of the Lord.

The Hebrew word,[1] Ps. cii. 27, is diversely taken.

1. It signifies the perfecting of a thing, as when the bud of a flower is grown to the maturity thereof, it is said to be perfect,[2] Isa. xviii. 5. The perfection of God's law is set out by an adjective derived from this root, Ps. xix. 7.

2. The finishing of a thing, and that in a fair manner, is expressed by this word, thus the work of Solomon's pillars are said to be finished,[3] 1 Kings vii. 22.

3. Consuming and destroying a thing is declared by the same word, thus the rebellious people in the wilderness are said to be consumed,[4] in that they were destroyed, Deut. ii. 16.

It is in this testimony used in the middle sense for ending and finishing a thing, and being negatively used, it implieth that the years of the Lord shall never be finished nor have any end. Thus they shew him to be everlasting. He shall for ever continue as he is.

The Greek word here used by the apostle, ἐκλείψουσι, intendeth as much as the Hebrew doth. It is applied to the expiring of a man's life, Luke xvi. 9, 'when you fail,' ἐκλίπητε; that is, when you cease to be in this world, when you depart or die. Christ expresseth the perseverance of faith by such a negative phrase, as is in this text, thus, 'that thy faith fail not,' μὴ ἐκλείπῃ, Luke xxii. 32.

Sec. 144. *Of Christ's everlasting continuance as he is mediator.*

As by way of resemblance this description of everlastingness, 'Thy years shall not fail,' may be applied to the deity of Christ, so most properly to his human nature, to his mediatorship, as he was God-man; to all his offices, to the merit, virtue, and efficacy of all that he did and endured for man's redemption, to his mystical body, and to the gifts and graces which he bestoweth on his members.

1. In regard of his human nature, his years shall not fail, in that ' being raised from the dead he dieth no more,' Rom. vi. 9. He continueth ever, he ever liveth, Heb. vii. 24, 25.

2. As mediator he is said to ' live ever to make intercession for us,' Heb. vii. 25.

3. As king he shall reign for ever, and there shall be no end of his kingdom, Luke i. 33.

4. He is ' a priest for ever,' Ps. cx. 4.

5. In respect to his prophetical office, he is styled an ' everlasting light,' to instruct and direct his people, Isa. lx. 19, 20.

6. In regard of the merit and virtue of what he did and suffered, he is the same for ever, Heb. xiii. 8.

7. His gifts are without repentance, Rom. xi. 29. They are such as he never repenteth the giving of them; and thereupon he never takes them away. As for such apostates as have clean put them away, they never had any true, sound, sanctifying, saving grace, 1 John ii. 19.

8. That body whereof he is the head must also continue for ever. If the years of the head shall not fail, can the years of the body fail? On this ground it is that the gates of hell shall not prevail against the church, Mat. xvi. 18.

Sec. 145. *Of the uses of Christ's immutability.*

The eternal and everlasting immutability of Christ our Redeemer and Saviour is many ways of singular use.

1. It demonstrateth Christ to be true God, Mal. iii. 6.

2. It distinguisheth him from all creatures (as here in this text), from idols especially, Isa. xli. 4 and xliv. 6.

3. It strengtheneth our faith in all his divine properties, promises, and former works, Ps. xliv. 1, 2, and xc. 1, 2; Gen. xxxii. 10–12; Heb. xiii. 5, 6.

4. It instructeth us in an especial use of God's former dealings with men, which is in like good courses to expect like blessings, and in like evil courses to expect like judgments: for the Lord is ever the same, and ever of the same mind; what in former times was right in his eyes and acceptable unto him, is so still, Rom. iv. 23, 24. What formerly offended him and provoked his wrath, still so doth, 1 Cor. x. 5, 6, &c.

5. It assureth us of his continual and perpetual care of his church, Mat. xxviii. 20, yea, and of the church's perpetual continuance, Mat. xvi. 18.

6. It encourageth us against all attempts of enemies, present and to come, Ps. cx. 1, Rev. ii. 10.

---

[1] יתמו à תמם [2] תם פרח [3] תתם [4] תמו.

7. It teacheth us to do what in us lieth for perpetuating his praise; and for this end both to set forth his praise ourselves all our days, Ps. civ. 33, and also to teach our posterity so to do, Ps. lxxviii. 5, 6.

8. It directeth us how to be like to Christ, namely, in constancy and unchangeableness in our lawful promises, oaths, vows, and covenants, Neh. v. 12, 13; Ps. xv. 4; Eccles. v. 4; Jer. xxxiv. 10, 18, and in our warrantable enterprises, 1 Cor. xv. 58.

9. It admonisheth us to submit ourselves to the Lord's ordering providence; all our strivings against the same cannot alter this purpose, 1 Sam. iii. 18.

10. It establisheth such as have evidence of their election and calling, against all Satan's assaults and fears arising from our weak flesh, 2 Peter i. 10.

Sec. 146. *Of the resolution of* Heb. i. 11, 12.
Ver. 11. *They shall perish, but thou remainest; and they all shall wax old as doth a garment;*
Ver. 12. *And as a vesture shalt thou fold them up, and they shall be changed: but thou art the same, and thy years shall not fail.*

Christ's excellency is further set out in these two verses. See Sec. 64. The proof thereof is taken from Christ's immutability. The sum of this text is in these two words, Christ's immutability. The argument to prove Christ's excellency herein, is drawn from a comparison. The comparison is betwixt Christ and creatures. The argument may be thus framed;—

He who is immutable is more excellent than the things that are mutable;
But Christ is immutable, and all creatures mutable;
Therefore Christ is more excellent than all creatures.
There are parts of text.
1. The mutability of creatures.
2. The immutability of Christ.
The mutability of creatures is declared two ways:
1. Simply, 'They shall perish.'
2. Symbolically, by two resemblances.
One resemblance is taken from a garment, 'as a garment.'
The other from a vesture, 'as a vesture.'
The former importeth a corruption by degrees, 'waxeth old.'
The latter implieth a renovation, 'fold them up.'
This latter is amplified,
1. By the efficient, which is Christ, 'Thou shalt.'
2. By the effect, 'They shall be changed.'
The immutability of Christ is set out in three branches:
1. His eternity, 'Thou remainest.'
2. His stability, 'Thou art the same.'
3. His perpetuity, 'Thy years shall not fail.'

Sec. 147. *Of the doctrines arising out of* Heb. i. 11, 12.
I. *Creatures decay.* This is to be applied most properly to things sublunary, which are in the air, earth, and waters. See Sec. 137.

II. *The longer creatures continue, the nearer they are to their end.* They wax old. See Sec. 139.

III. *Such creatures as decay not shall be renewed.* This phrase *folded up* intends as much. See Sec. 139.

IV. *All creatures are subject to alteration.* This general particle *all* demonstrates as much; either they shall decay or be renewed.

V. *Comparisons make points more clear.* For this end these two comparisons, of a vesture and garment, are here produced.

VI. *It is Christ that altereth creatures.* This phrase, 'Thou shalt fold them up,' is directed to Christ. See Sec. 140.

VII. *Creatures are at Christ's dispose.* What Christ will alter 'shall be changed.' See Sec. 140.

VIII. *Christ is whatever he was.* This phrase *thou remainest* implieth as much. See Secs. 138, 141.

IX. *There is no alteration in Christ.* He is the same. See Sec. 141.

X. *Christ will for ever continue the same.* 'His years shall not fail.' See Sec. 143.

Sec. 148. *Of the 110th Psalm applied to Christ.*
But unto which of the angels said he at any time, Sit on my right hand, until I make thine enemies thy footstool? Are they not all ministering spirits, sent forth to minister for them who shall be heirs of salvation?—Heb. I. 13, 14.

The apostle further proceedeth in setting out Christ's excellency above angels. This here he doth by declaring the dignity whereunto his Father advanced him above angels.

This he here bringeth in by way of opposition, as the first particle *but*[1] implieth. This opposition may have reference to that meanness which he had before said of the creatures about their perishing. But here a far greater matter is said of Christ; or it may have reference to that which follows after, as if it had been thus expressed, He said to Christ, 'Sit on my right hand.' But to which of the angels did he say any such thing? Or this particle of opposition, *but*, may be here put for the copulative *and*, and so have reference to the former proofs of Christ's excellency above angels; for it is a seventh proof of that point. See Sec. 64.

The apostle bringeth in this proof after the same manner that he did a former, ver. 5. 'To which of the angels said he at any time?' Hereof see Sec. 46.

The proof is taken from a different degree betwixt Christ and angels. The argument may be thus framed:

He that sitteth at God's right hand is far more excellent than ministers;
But Christ sitteth at God's right hand, and angels are ministers;

[1] δὲ. See Chap. ii. 6, Sec. 50.

Therefore Christ is far more excellent than angels. The former part of the assumption is in ver. 13. The latter part in ver. 14.

This proof is set out by a divine testimony, taken out of Ps. cx. 1. That psalm is wholly prophetical. The prophecy therein contained is of Christ, especially of his kingly and priestly functions; for proof of them, it is oft quoted in the New Testament, as Mat. xxii. 44; Heb. v. 6, 10, and vii. 17, 21.

There is also in this psalm an express prophecy of the calling of the Gentiles, ver. 6, which manifesteth the enlargement of Christ's kingdom.

Concerning the point in hand, the psalmist expressly sheweth the persons by whom and to whom that which in the text is set down was first spoken, in these words, 'The Lord said unto my Lord.'

The former title, Lord, which is in the Hebrew יהוה, *Jehovah*, is spoken of the Father; the latter, לארני, of the Son, who was that Messiah whom the Jews expected. It was God the Father that said to God the Son, 'Sit at my right hand.' Indeed, the latter word, translated *Lord*, is sometimes applied to men, as Gen. xxxii. 4. But it is in this place uttered by a king, who was under no man as to his Lord; therefore it must be meant of him that was God.

Christ, by this argument, proveth himself to be the Son of God, in that David, who was his father after the flesh, giveth him this title, *my Lord*, Mat. xxii. 43.

It appears that the teachers of the Jews held this psalm to be a prophecy of Christ, in that they denied not this testimony to be meant of Christ, when Christ produced it to prove the Messiah to be more than a son of man. Otherwise they would readily have denied the proof, and said that David did not there speak of his Son, rather than be put to silence as they were, Mat. xxii. 46.

Sec. 149. *Of God's setting Christ on his right hand.*

The main substance of the proof is in this phrase, 'Sit on my right hand.' This is to be taken of Christ as mediator, God-man; for in that respect hath God exalted him. Him whom God raised from the dead, he set on his right hand, Eph. i. 20, Rom. viii. 34. But he was true man that was raised from the dead; therefore he was true man that was so exalted next unto God, 'far above all principality, and power, and might, and dominion, and every name that is named, not only in this world, but in that which is to come,' Eph. i. 21.

Of this phrase, *sit at God's right hand*, and of the dignity thereby intended, see Secs. 31–34.

The ground of this high dignity was of God. Jehovah, the only true God, said to him, 'Sit on my right hand.' Christ set not himself there; he glorified not himself to sit at God's right hand, but Jehovah, that said to him, 'Sit on my right hand,' glorified him herein: 'God hath highly exalted him, and given him a name which is above every name.'

God was pleased thus highly to exalt his Son in sundry respects:

1. In regard of that entire love which, as a Father, he did bear to a Son, John iii. 35, and v. 20.

2. In regard of the low degree of Christ's humiliation, Philip. ii. 8, 9; Eph. iv. 9, 10.

3. In regard of that charge which Christ undertook, to provide for his church, and to protect it. Hereunto is he the better enabled by that high advancement, Mat. xxviii. 18–20; John xvii. 2.

4. In regard of the saints, who are Christ's members, that they might with stronger confidence depend on him, Ps. lxxx. 17, 18; 2 Tim. i. 12.

5. In regard of his enemies, that he might be the greater terror unto them, and be more able to subdue them, Ps. cx. 2.

Sec. 150. *Of Christ's continuance at God's right hand.*

To the greatness of Christ's dignity is added his continuance therein, which is until one principal end of his high advancement shall be accomplished, which is the subduing of all his enemies.

This word *until*, ἕως ἄν, though it point at a time how long Christ shall retain his dignity, yet it setteth not down a date thereof or a period thereto; for it hath not always reference to the future time as excluding it, but to that whole space of time that is to pass to the accomplishing of the thing mentioned, including in it all that space of time; and that because the question is concerning it alone; as where Christ saith, 'Till heaven and earth pass, one jot, or one tittle, shall in no wise pass from the law,' Mat. v. 18, his meaning is not that the law shall pass when heaven and earth pass away, but that so long as the world continueth, the law shall remain to be the rule of righteousness.

This word *until* oft implieth rather a denial of a determination than an affirmation thereof, as 2 Sam. vi. 23, where it is said that 'Michal had no child until the day of her death.' None will imagine that after her death she had any, but because the question of having a child must be about the time of her life, this phrase, 'until the day of her death,' is used. In the same sense a like phrase of the virgin Mary's bringing forth the Lord Jesus is used, Mat. i. 25. Joseph 'knew her not till she had brought forth her first-born son;' that is, he never knew her.

Thus is this word *until* here to be taken: 'Sit on my right hand until I make thine enemies my footstool.' Sit till then, and ever after that; so as here is implied an everlasting continuance of Christ's dignity. If until all his enemies be subdued, then for ever; for what shall hinder it when there be no enemies? Will his subjects hinder it? Will his members that are advanced with him hinder it? Will good angels, whose ministry is made the more glorious thereby, hinder it? Will his Father, whose love and respect to him is unchangeable and everlasting, hinder it?

Obj. Subduing of enemies is here set down as the end of Christ's sitting at God's right hand. When that end is accomplished, there will be no need of his sitting there.

Ans. Though subduing of enemies be one end, yet it is not the only end. Sundry other ends have been noted before, Sec. 149.

It will be requisite that Christ, having to the full accomplished all things that were to be done or endured for man's full redemption and eternal salvation, should for ever retain that dignity whereunto he was advanced after he had accomplished all. To depart from any part of his dignity at any time would be some impeachment of his glory.

Obj. 2. It is expressly said that when the end cometh, 'the Son shall deliver up the kingdom to God the Father.' And 'when all things shall be subdued unto him, then shall the Son also himself be subject,' &c., 1 Cor. xv. 24, 28.

The answer to these words is set down before, Sec. 109.

Sec. 151. *Of Christ's enemies.*

The time of Christ's sitting at God's right hand being thus expressed, 'until I make thine enemies thy footstool,' plainly declareth that Christ hath enemies, and shall have enemies so long as this world continueth. These enemies are not only such as directly oppose Christ himself, as the scribes and pharisees, priests and rulers among the Jews, who at length brought him to that shameful death upon the cross, Acts ii. 23; or as Saul, who afore his taking up into heaven, 'thought with himself that he ought to do many things contrary to the name of Jesus,' Acts xxvi. 9; and Julian, who with his breath breathed out this scornful title against Christ,[1] *Vicisti Galilæe, O Galilean, thou hast overcome;* but also such as revile, wrong, oppress, or any way persecute the church of Christ, or any of the members of his body. It was in relation unto them that Christ said to Saul, when he 'breathed out threatening and slaughter against the disciples of the Lord,' 'Saul, Saul, why persecutest thou me?' Acts ix. 1, 4; for believers are so united unto Christ, as members unto an head, Eph. i. 22, 23; and thereupon it is, that 'he that toucheth them toucheth the apple of his eye,' Zech. ii. 8.

That we may the better discern who and what these enemies are, I will endeavour to rank them out, as it were, in battle array.

In a well set army there is a general, and under him colonels, captains, lieutenants, majors, corporals, ancients, trumpeters, drummers, scouts; and of soldiers there useth to be a vanguard, main battalion, rear, right and left wings, and ambushments.

[1] Theodoret. Eccl. Hist. lib. iv. cap. xxv.

The general is 'that great dragon and old serpent, which is called the devil and Satan,' Rev. xii. 9. Colonels, captains, and other commanders and officers, who whet on and embolden all such as take part with Satan, are all sorts of infernal spirits and fiends of hell. The van is made up of atheists, idolaters, persecutors, and other like open and impudent enemies of the church. The battalia consists of all manner of profane and licentious persons. In the right wing are all the lusts of the flesh, in the left all the honours and pleasures of the world. In the rear follow sin, death, grave, and hell itself, with such like mortal enemies, and their deadly instruments. In ambushment lie hypocrites, false brethren, corrupt teachers, and treacherous politicians.

There being such enemies, it much concerns us to be very watchful against them, and to take heed of security; and we ought to be 'strong in the Lord, and in the power of his might,' Eph. vi. 10. Yea, we ought always to be prepared, and stand armed with the whole armour of God, Eph. vi. 13, &c.

Obj. Christ on his cross 'having spoiled principalities and powers, made a show of them openly, triumphing over them in it,' Col. ii. 14, 15. 'And when he ascended up on high, he led captivity captive,' Eph. iv. 8. By captivity are meant such spiritual enemies as held men in captivity. By leading captive is meant a conquest and triumph over them. If Christ did this on his cross, and at his ascension, how do they still remain enemies?

Ans. 1. Though they be made captives, yet still they retain the mind and disposition of enemies, and so are indeed enemies.

2. Though they be overcome and triumphed over, yet the Lord voluntarily suffers them, to try what they can do. He suffers them to fight and to assault his members, but so as he himself remains the moderator of the fight, to pull them back, to beat them down as he pleaseth; as bear-herds that have their bears at command, will suffer them to fight with their dogs. But when the church is fully perfected, then shall they be so destroyed as they shall not so much as assault any of the members of Christ.

Sec. 152. *Of the church's encouragement against her enemies.*

It is a ground of great comfort and encouragement to the church, that her enemies are Christ's enemies; she may be sure of sufficient protection. To Christ all the fiends of hell, and all the wicked in the world, are nothing.

He that in the days of his flesh, with a word of his mouth, caused a multitude that came to apprehend him, to 'go backward, and fall to the ground,' John xviii. 6, can, with a blast of his nostrils, now that he is at the right hand of his Father, drive all his enemies into hell, how many and how mighty soever they be.

Besides, the Lord Christ hath an absolute command over all in heaven and earth, to use them as his instruments to annoy his enemies. 'They fought from heaven, the stars in their courses fought against Sisera,' Judges i. 20. The waters above and below met together to drown the old world, Gen. vii. 11. Fire and brimstone fell from heaven and destroyed sundry cities, Gen. xix. 24. The earth opened and swallowed up sundry rebels, Num. xvi. 32. Frogs, lice, flies, grasshoppers, and sundry other creatures, destroyed the Egyptians, Exod. viii. 6, &c. The sea overwhelmed Pharaoh with his whole host, Exod. xiv. 28. The Lord can make his enemies destroy one another, 2 Chron. xx. 23, 24. Thus there wants no means for the Lord when he pleaseth to destroy his church's enemies.

But yet, if by reason of the foresaid army of enemies, they seem terrible unto us, it will be useful to take notice of an army more mighty and better prepared and furnished for our defence; for Michael hath his army, as well as the dragon hath his, Rev. xii. 7.

This latter army, in opposition to the former, may be thus set forth: the general is the Lord Christ; his colonels, captains, and other officers, which direct and encourage Christ's soldiers, are all sorts of angels. In the van are martyrs, confessors, and such as manifest more might and courage in suffering, than the stoutest enemies in persecuting. In the battalia stand all zealous professors of the truth: in the one wing, against the flesh and the lusts thereof stands the Spirit, and the gifts and graces of it; in the other wing, against the world and the vanities thereof, stands faith, hope, and the powers of the world to come, with all manner of blessings accompanying the same. In the rear, against sin, death, and the other mortal enemies, stands Christ's obedience, passion, burial, resurrection, ascension, intercession, with the merit, virtue, efficacy, and power of them all. To prevent all ambushments, are such as are made wise by the word of God, as David was, Ps. cxix. 98, and Neh. vi. 7, &c.

Now set army to army, squadron to squadron, foot to foot, weapon to weapon, and judge on which side there is greatest assurance of victory. On the forementioned grounds we have cause to say, 'Fear not, they that be with us are more than they that be with them,' 2 Kings vi. 16.

Sec. 153. *Of God's putting down Christ's enemies.*

Concerning the foresaid enemies, the Father saith to his Son, 'I make, θῶ, thine enemies thy footstool;' or as it is Ps. cx. 1, 'I will make,' אשית, &c. The present and future tenses are oft put one for the other. Both being used by the same Spirit, one by the prophet, the other by the apostle, implieth that God doth now, and ever will continue, to subdue the enemies of Christ.

Obj. It is said, 1 Cor. xv. 25, that 'Christ must reign until he hath put all enemies under his feet.'

Ans. 1. Though the Father and the Son be distinct persons, yet they are of one and the same nature, and in that respect the same action is attributed to the one and the other; 'My Father worketh hitherto, and I work;' and 'what things soever the Father doth, these also doth the Son likewise,' John v. 17, 19; for as they are one in essence, so in mind, and will, and works.

2. Matters are spoken of Christ, sometimes in relation to his divine nature, sometimes to his human nature, and sometimes to his office or mediatorship, which he performeth in his person as God-man.

In relation to his divine nature, he himself putteth all enemies under his feet, 1 Cor. xv. 25.

In relation to his human nature, which retains the essential properties of a man, the Father makes Christ's enemies his footstool; for the human nature is finite, only in one place at once. All the excellencies thereof, though far surpassing the excellencies of other creatures, are in measure with a certain proportion. That which is said of God's giving the Spirit to Christ not by measure, John iii. 39, is to be understood comparatively in reference to all other creatures; they have the measure of vessels, Christ hath the measure of a fountain, which may be accounted without measure. Notwithstanding this fulness of Christ, in relation to his human nature, God is said to advance him, to assist him, to do this and that for him; so here God is said to make his enemies his footstool. This act of God may also have relation to the office of Christ as he is mediator; for in that respect he is under the Father, and depends upon the Father, and is assisted by the Father. Because, sometimes, in relation to Christ's human nature, this act of subduing Christ's enemies is attributed to the Father; and sometimes in relation to his divine nature, it is attributed to himself, this apostle useth an indefinite word of the passive voice, *be made*, 'till his enemies be made his footstool,' Heb. x. 13.

For the phrase here used and applied to the Father, it declareth this act of subduing all manner of enemies to be a divine act, done by a divine power; so as all the power of all enemies, if it could be united together, could not stand against this power. 'Who would set the briars and thorns against God in battle? He would go through them, he would burn them together,' Isa. xxvii. 4. This is it that makes the devils to tremble, James ii. 19, Luke viii. 28.

Did wicked men, persecutors, profane persons, and all that oppose Christ, his church, his gospel, or ordinances, know and believe as much as the devils do in this case, they could not but tremble. A great encouragement this is to the members of Christ, that the church is assisted with a divine power, able to subdue all the enemies; so as they need not fear what any of them or all of them can do.

Sec. 154. *Of making enemies a footstool.*

The manner of expressing the destruction of Christ's enemies is in this phrase, *thy footstool*, 'I will make thine enemies thy footstool.'

Both the Hebrew[1] and the Greek[2] double the word foot, and thus express it, 'the footstool of thy feet;' the Latin[3] also doth herein imitate them.

The Hebrew word translated *footstool*, is six times used in the Old Testament, and hath always the word *feet* added to it, as 1 Chron. xxviii. 2; Ps. xcix. 5, and cxxxii. 7, and cx. 1; Isa. lxvi. 1; Lam. ii. 1.

The LXX, who translated the Hebrew into Greek, do herein follow the Hebrew; so do the penmen of New Testament, who wrote in Greek; and that in eight several places, as Mat. v. 35, and xxii. 44; Mark xii. 36; Luke xx. 43; Acts ii. 35, and vii. 49; Heb. i. 13, and x. 13. Once the word footstool is singly, used without the addition of that other phrase of feet, James ii. 3, ὑπὸ τὸ ὑποπόδιον σου.

The addition of the word *feet*, 'under the footstool of thy feet,' importeth emphasis, and implieth the lowest dejection that can be. But because this addition soundeth not well in our English, our translators leave it out.

A footstool is that which one puts under his feet, and sets his feet upon. It is in Scripture used two ways.

1. In reference to a place.
2. In reference to persons.

1. To set out a place where one delights to set his feet, or to abide.

2. To set out such persons as in indignation one trampleth under his feet.

When this metaphor of a footstool in relation to God is applied to a place, it intendeth his gracious presence. Thus the earth in general is styled his footstool, Isa. lxvi. 1. From thence Christ maketh this inference, that men swear not by the earth, because it is God's footstool, Mat. v. 34, 35.

In particular the temple is styled God's footstool, 1 Chron. xxviii. 2. In this respect the church is advised to 'worship at his footstool,' Ps. xcix. 5. And the church complaineth, Lam. ii. 1, that God 'remembered not his footstool.'

2. When in relation to God this metaphor of a footstool is applied to persons, it intendeth such enemies as God utterly subdueth, and on whom he executeth just and severe revenge, as Ps. cx. 1; which text is oft quoted in the New Testament, namely, by Christ, Mat. xxii. 44, by Peter, Acts ii. 35, and by Paul in this place. This apostle doth plainly express the meaning of it in this phrase, 'he hath put them under his feet,' 1 Cor. xv. 25.

The metaphor is taken from the practice of men, who, when they have utterly vanquished their deadly enemies, in testimony of that full conquest and absolute power they have over them, yea also of their indignation against them, and revenge of them, will set their feet upon them, and trample on them; so did Joshua make the captains of his army put their feet upon the necks of the kings of those cursed Canaanites whom they subdued, Joshua x. 24. Thus Jehu also trod Jezebel under foot, 2 Kings ix. 33. Thus also it is said of Christ, 'I will tread them in mine anger, and trample them in my fury, Isa. lxiii. 3.

By this it appears that Christ's enemies shall be utterly subdued. In allusion hereunto, David, as a type of Christ, thus saith, 'Thou hast given me the necks of mine enemies, that I might destroy them that hate me; I did beat them small as the dust before the wind, I did cast them out as the dirt in the streets,' Ps. xviii. 40, 42; and again, 'he it is that shall tread down our enemies.'

This is so done that the whole mystical body of Christ might have rest and quiet, which were not possible unless such malicious and mischievous enemies were totally and finally subdued.

This is a strong inducement for us to stand and fight against these enemies, and to expect and wait for this day of conquest; for this gives us assurance of a full and final conquest. The phrase importeth as much.

Sec. 155. *Of the apostle's manner of proving his point, ver.* 14.

The second part of the assumption (mentioned Sec. 148) is here proved. It was this: angels are *ministers*; that it may be the better discerned what kind of ministers they are, their nature, that they are *spirits*, and their office *ministering*, and their warrant *sent forth*, and their charge for whom they minister, *such as shall be heirs of salvation*, are expressly set down, ver. 14.

The manner of setting down these points is emphatical, it is by way of interrogation. An interrogation about things affirmed implies a strong affirmation; as if it were a matter unquestionable, undeniable, and so clear, as whosoever duly considereth it, cannot but acknowledge it to be most true. Where God saith to Cain, 'If thou do well, shalt thou not be accepted?' Gen. iv. 7, he declares it to be so manifestly true, that Cain himself could not deny the truth of it. By such a manner of declaring a matter, he that propounds the point leaves it to the judgment of him to whom the question is propounded to judge of the truth thereof.

Sec. 156. *Of the excellency of the ministers here mentioned, and of their warrant.*

In setting down the ministry of angels, the apostle mentioneth their nature, that they are *spirits*, to

---

[1] הדם לרגליך.   [2] ὑποπόδιον τῶν ποδῶν σου.
[3] Scabellum pedum tuorum.

amplify their ministry. This epithet, *ministering*, in Greek, λειτουργικὰ, is derived from that word which is translated *ministers*, λειτουργοὶ, ver. 7. It sheweth that their ministry is a special and public function, and that an honourable one also, and yet they are inferior to Christ. See Sec. 79.

Spirits, πνεύματα, are the most excellent substances, of all creatures the most glorious, of best understanding, and greatest prudence; the purest, the strongest, freest from all bodily infirmities, such as cannot be hindered by any incumbrances. Of all these excellencies, see Sec. 86, &c.

The act attributed to them in this word *to minister*, is in Greek from another root, and so expressed as it also implieth an office, thus, εἰς διακονίαν,[1] 'for the ministry;' so is this phrase translated, 1 Cor. xvi. 15, 2 Tim. iv. 11. A public officer of the church is set out by a title that is derived from διάκονος, the same root, and translated deacon, Philip. i. 1, 1 Tim. iii. 8. Thus it intendeth as much as the former did. Both of them are joined together, ἡ διακονία λειτουργίας, and thus translated 'administration of service,' 2 Cor. ix. 12. This word then declareth that angels do not only some services for saints, but that they have an office to minister for them, as deacons had for the poor, Acts vi. 1, 3. That angels have a charge is evident, Ps. xci. 11, 12.

The ground of their function or warrant to execute the same, is in this phrase *sent forth*, ἀποστελλόμενα, namely, from God. The composition of the Greek word, ἀπὸ and στέλλειν, implieth that they were sent from one. Now who can that be but their Lord in heaven? For they have no other Lord that hath power to send them. They are therefore sent of God; so are they oft said to be, as Gen. xxiv. 7, 40; Num. xx. 16; Dan. iii. 28, and vi. 22. In this respect they are styled 'angels of God,' ver. 6. See Sec. 71.

This shews that they assume not this office to themselves.

It also shews that upon God's pleasure they undertook it, Ps. ciii. 20.

All the fore-mentioned points are applied to all the angels, as is evident by this general particle *all*, 'Are they not all?' Thus much is implied in the seventh verse, where the creation and ministry of angels are joined together, 'He maketh his angels and his ministers,' &c. If *angels*, then *ministers*; if *made*, then *ministers*. What was said of the subjection of all angels to Christ, Sec. 73, may be applied to the ministry of them all unto the members of Christ.

Sec. 157. *Of particular angels attending particular persons.*

Concerning the ministry of angels, a question may be moved, Whether every heir of salvation have a proper and peculiar angel attending upon him? Some of the ancient fathers,[1] schoolmen,[2] and papists,[3] hold the affirmative, for which they produce these arguments.

Arg. 1. Jacob thus saith of his angel: 'The angel which redeemed me from all evil, bless the lads,' Gen. xlviii. 16.

Ans. 1. How could this angel be Jacob's proper angel, when Jacob prays that he would bless his grandchildren? By this he should be their angel as well as his.

2. That angel was Christ. Christ is the common protector of us all; besides, it is Christ that redeemeth his from all evil, which no angel can do.

3. Finally, Jacob hath in speech reference to Gen. xxxi. 11, 13, where the angel that appeared to him styled himself 'the God of Bethel,' which was Christ Jesus, and also to the angel that wrestled with him, of whom he saith, 'I have seen God face to face,' Gen. xxxii. 24, 30. This likewise was Christ.

Arg. 2. Christ styled the particular angels of little ones *their angels*, Mat. xviii. 10. Therefore every one hath a particular angel for his patronage.[4]

Ans. 1. It followeth not, for Christ useth the plural number, *their angels*, which may imply many angels for every one, as one for one.

2. They are called *theirs*, because they are appointed by their Father, among other functions, to take care of his little ones; not only of one by one, but also of one by many, as an host did of Jacob, Gen. xxxii. 1, and also of many by one, as Acts v. 19.

Arg. 3. The Christians said in reference to Peter, 'It is his angel,' Acts xii. 15.[5]

Ans. 1. That might be a sudden speech of men astonished, and then no sufficient ground for a sound argument.

2. They might be misled by a common error of the times, as Christ's disciples were, Mat. xvii. 10, Acts i. 6.

3. They might use that phrase to put off the maid's persisting to affirm that Peter was there, with that vulgar opinion; as if one should importunately say of my friend whom I knew to be dead and buried, that he saw him alive, I to put him off should say it was his ghost then.

4. They might think it to be an angel sent from God to comfort and encourage Peter, and by Peter desired to carry them word thereof, and yet not one that continually waited on him as his peculiar protector.

5. The word *angel* signifieth a messenger (as is before shewn, Sec. 82). Thus it may be taken for a man sent as a messenger from him.

---

[1] Of this Greek word, see Chap. ii. 12, Sec. 70.

[1] Magna dignitas animarum, ut unaquæque habeat ab ortu nativitatis in custodiam sui angelum delegatum.—*Hier. in Mat.* xviii.
[2] Thom. par. i. q. 113, art. 2.
[3] Douay Annot. on Gen. xxviii. 16.
[4] Rhem. Annot. on Mat. xviii. 10.
[5] Rhem. Annot. on Acts xii. 15.

This conceit of every one's having a proper, peculiar angel to attend upon him for his patronage, is not to be harboured in our breast. For,

1. It hath no ground or warrant in God's word. I may in this case say, 'To which of the angels said God at any time,' Wait on such an one, and never leave him, night nor day?

2. One and the same angel hath attended upon divers persons, and brought several messages to the one and the other, as Gen. xviii. 21, Luke i. 19, 26.

3. One and the same angel hath delivered sundry persons at once, Acts v. 18, 19.

4. Many angels have jointly together protected the same person, 2 Kings vi. 17, Ps. xci. 11.

5. It lessens the comfort which Christians may receive from the guard of an host of angels, as Gen. xxxii. 1, or from legions of angels, as Mat. xxvi. 53, or from the innumerable company of angels, as Heb. xii. 22. It impaireth that comfort by appropriating single angel to a single person.

6. It cometh too near to the heathenish conceit of a good and evil genius,[1] to attend each particular person. For there is as great probability for one devil as a tempter, continually to assault every one, as for one good angel to protect him.

7. The difference about the time of particular angels first undertaking this particular function,[2] is against them that hold it an argument of the uncertain truth thereof. Some[3] hold it to be at the time of one's nativity. Others at the time of one's baptism. Others at the time of one's conversion.[4] Some at one time, some at another. I find none of them to make mention of any angels guarding an infant in the mother's womb. An infant even in his mother's womb is subject to many dangers, and then needs such a guardian as well as after. But to let this conceit pass, it is enough to know and believe what the word of God hath revealed about this point, that the holy angels of God have a charge over us, and take an especial care of us, not one only but many.

Sec. 158. *Of the persons for whom angels minister.*

The foresaid ministry of angels is in special for saints, the members of Christ, who believe in him; these are here styled 'heirs of salvation.' In this respect angels are by a property called 'their angels,' Mat. xviii. 10. And they are said to 'encamp about them that fear the Lord,' Ps. xxxiv. 7. This is further evident by the many services which angels do to them and for them. Whereof, see Sec. 98, &c.

Saints are God's children, and joint-heirs with Christ, Rom. viii. 16, 17. God therefore appoints those his servants to attend them. They are all members of the mystical body of Christ, in which respect that charge which extendeth itself to Christ and all his members is set down in the singular number as spoken of one; thus, *over thee:* 'He shall give his angels charge over thee,' Ps. xci. 11.

Of the benefits which redound to saints by angels' attendance on them, see Sec. 101.

The persons to whom angels minister are thus described, 'who shall be heirs of salvation,' or as it is in the Greek, τοὺς μέλλοντας κληρονομεῖν σωτηρίαν, 'who shall inherit salvation;' so as they are set out by that estate whereunto they were ordained, and by the right which they have thereunto. Salvation is that whereunto they are ordained, and their right is a right of inheritance.

Sec. 159. *Of salvation.*

The word here translated *salvation* is frequently used in the New Testament. I find it three times put for temporal preservation or deliverance; as Acts vii. 25, where this phrase, δίδωσι σωτηρίαν, *give salvation*, is thus translated (according to the true meaning) 'deliver;' and Acts xxvii. 34, where the same word is turned 'health;' and Heb. xi. 7, where this phrase, εἰς σωτηρίαν, 'to the salvation,' is thus expounded, 'to the saving.'

The Hebrew word, ישועה *vel* תשועה, which the LXX use to interpret by the word in this text translated *salvation*, sets out for the most part some temporary preservation and deliverance. But in the New Testament it sets out (except the three fore-mentioned places) the eternal salvation of the soul; and that as it is begun and helped on in this world, Luke xix. 9, 2 Cor. xvi. 2; or perfected in the world to come, 1 Peter i. 5, 9.

There is another Greek word, σωτήριον, derived from the same root, and translated *salvation*, four times used in the New Testament,—namely, Luke ii. 30 and iii. 6, Acts xxviii. 28, Eph. vi. 17,—but for the most part put metonymically for the author and procurer of salvation, the Lord Jesus Christ.

The primary root, σῶς, from whence all the Greek words are derived which[1] signify not only safe, exempt, and free from all evil, danger, and fear, but also entire and perfect; so as it setteth out both the privative part of blessedness, full freedom from sin, Satan, death, hell, and all fears; and also the positive part thereof, integrity, and perfection of soul and body, and of all gifts and graces appertaining to them; and withal immortality, agility, beauty, and other excellencies even of the body, Philip. iii. 21.

By the salvation here mentioned is meant that blessed and glorious estate which is in heaven reserved for the whole mystical body of Christ.

Well may that estate be called salvation, in that all that have attained, or shall attain, thereunto, are delivered out of all dangers, freed from all enemies, and set safe and secure from all manner of evil.

---

[1] Plato in Politic.
[2] Lege Origen. in Mat. Tract. 5.
[3] Rhem. Annot. on Mat. xviii. 10.
[4] Cum quis susceperit fidem, tunc Christus tradit eum angelo.—*Origen in Mat. Tract.* 5.

[1] Qu. 'doth'?—Ed.

Into heaven, where that rest, safety, security, and salvation is enjoyed, no devil, no evil instrument, can enter to disturb the same: 'There shall God wipe away all tears from their eyes; and there shall be no more death, neither sorrow, nor crying, neither shall there be any more pain,' Rev. xxi. 4. All contentment, agreement, tranquillity, unanimity, joy, pleasure, and what can be desired, shall be there everlastingly enjoyed.[1] There shall be a continual communion with glorious angels, glorified saints; yea, with Christ, the head and husband of his church, and with God himself, whom we shall in his glory so far behold as our nature is capable of beholding such glory. This beautiful vision will not only fill our heads with admiration, but our hearts with joy and delight. These are the things 'which eye hath not seen, nor ear heard, neither have entered into the heart of man,' 1 Cor. ii. 9.

Sec. 160. *Of our right to salvation by inheritance.*

The right which saints have to salvation is thus expressed, τοὺς μέλλοντας κληρονομεῖν, 'who shall inherit,' so as the right is by inheritance.

The Greek word that signifieth to inherit, κληρονομέω, is compounded of a noun, κλῆρος, that signifieth a lot or portion, and a verb, νέμω, to give, distribute, or set apart. For an inheritance is a lot or portion given and set apart for one; most properly, such a portion as a father sets apart for his sons to possess and enjoy, Joshua xvii. 14, 1 Kings xxi. 3. Of all titles an inheritance useth to be the surest, that which hath no date. See ver. 2, Sec. 17.

In this respect this metaphor of inheriting is applied to eternal life, Mat. xix. 29; to a kingdom, Mat. xxv. 34; to the promises, namely, to those blessed things in heaven which are promised, Heb. vi. 12; and to all things, namely, all the joys of heaven, Rev. xxi. 7.

Salvation is also called an inheritance, Acts xx. 32, Eph. i. 14, 18, Col. iii. 24, 1 Peter i. 4; and they to whom salvation belongs are called heirs, Gal. iii. 29, Titus iii. 7, James ii. 5.

This right of inheritance is the best thing that any can have. The ground of it is the good will, grace, and favour of a Father, Luke xii. 32; and that from all eternity, Mat. xxv. 34. The persons to whom it belongs are children of God, Rom. viii. 17; such as are begotten again, 1 Peter i. 3, 4; and adopted, Rom. viii. 15, 17; and united to Christ, John xvii. 21.

The time of enjoying that inheritance is everlasting, Heb. ix. 15, 1 Peter i. 4. Herein lieth a difference between leases, which have a date, and inheritances, which have no date.

The quality of this inheritance is incorruptible and undefiled.

[1] Of eternal salvation, see Chap. v. 9, Sec. 50, 51; of the glory of it, see Chap. ii. 10, Sec. 93; that it is a reward, Chap. vi. 9, Sec. 57.

Sec. 161. *Of the time and certainty of inheriting salvation.*

The fruition of the aforesaid privileges is expressed is the future tense, μέλλοντας, 'shall inherit.' Saints are, while here they live, *heirs*. They have a right to salvation as soon as they are regenerate. The firstborn is an heir while he is a child, before he come to possess the inheritance, Gal. iv. 1, 5, 7. We are therefore said to be 'begotten again to this inheritance,' 1 Peter i. 3, 4. And it is said to saints, 'Ye shall receive,' ἀπολήψεσθε, the reward of the inheritance, Col. iii. 24, namely, when this life is ended; for the soul, when it leaves the body, presently enjoys the inheritance. The apostle intendeth the spirits of saints where in the time present he saith, 'they inherit the promises,' Heb. vi. 12. And at the resurrection, both body and soul shall enjoy the same; for to such as are raised, and have their bodies and souls united, will the great God say, 'Inherit the kingdom,' Mat. xxv. 34.

Though the possession of this inheritance be to come, while the heirs thereof here live, yet it is sure and certain. What title so sure among men as inheritance? Much more sure is this inheritance of salvation than any earthly inheritance can be. For,

1. It is prepared for us from the foundation of the world, Mat. xxv. 34.

2. It is purchased by the greatest price that can be: 'The precious blood of the Son of God,' Eph. i. 14, 1 Peter i. 19.

3. It is ratified by the greatest assurance that can be, the death of him that gives it, Heb. ix. 14.

4. It is sealed up unto us by that Holy Spirit of promise, which is 'the earnest of our inheritance,' Eph. i. 13, 14.

5. God's promise is engaged for it, therefore they who possess it are said to 'inherit the promises,' Heb. vi. 12.

6. The faith of believers addeth another seal thereto, John iii. 33.

7. It is reserved in heaven for us, 1 Peter i. 4. In heaven 'neither moth nor rust doth corrupt, nor thieves do break through, nor steal,' Mat. vi. 20.

Sec. 162. *Of instructions and directions arising from the inheritance of salvation.*

Such an inheritance as salvation made sure to us, affords sundry instructions and directions. Instructions are such as these:

1. It commends God's philanthropy, his peculiar love to men, who by nature are children of wrath and heirs of hell, yet made to be partakers of the inheritance of salvation, Eph. ii. 2, 3; Col. i. 12; Titus iii. 3–5.

2. It takes away all conceit of merit by man's works; for an inheritance is the free gift of a father.

3. It is enough to uphold our spirits against penury,

ignominy, and all manner of misery in this world. An heir that, as long as he is a child, differeth nothing [from] a servant, but is under tutors and governors, yet, because he is lord of all, will not be dejected, but will support himself with this, that he hath a fair inheritance belonging to him.

4. It is a great encouragement against all things that may threaten death, yea, and against death itself, in that death brings us to the possession of this excellent inheritance.

Directions are such as these:

1. Subject thyself to thy Father's will, and to that government under which he sets thee, because thou art his heir, Gal. iv. 2.

2. Raise up thy affections to the place of thine inheritance, and set thy heart thereon, Col. iii. 1; Mat. vi. 21.

3. 'Love not the world, neither the things that are in the world,' 1 John ii. 15. Salvation is not there to be had.

4. Moderate thy care about earthly things; thou hast a heavenly inheritance to care for.

5. Suffer with joy all things for thy profession's sake, knowing that thou hast an heavenly inheritance, Heb. x. 34.

6. Search thine evidences about this inheritance. There is great reason that in a matter of so great consequence, thou shouldst be sure of thy evidence for thy right hereto, 2 Peter i. 10.

7. Expect with patience the time appointed for the enjoying this inheritance. Through faith and patience the promises are inherited, Heb. vi. 12.

8. Walk worthy of this high calling, Eph. iv. 1, and of God who hath called thee to his kingdom and glory, 2 Thes. ii. 12.

9. Be ever thankful for this privilege especially, Col. i. 12; 1 Peter i. 3, 4.

10. Despise not any of these heirs because they are here poor and mean, James ii. 5. Ishmael was cast out because he mocked the heir, Gen. xxi. 9, 10.

Sec. 163. *Of the resolution of the 13th and 14th verses.*

In these two last verses, the eighth and last proof of Christ's excellency is set down. See Sec. 64.

The sum of them is a difference betwixt Christ and angels.

The parts are two:

The first is the dignity of Christ, ver. 13.

The second is the inferiority of angels, ver. 14.

In setting down Christ's dignity, both the manner and matter is observable.

The manner is in this phrase, ' Unto which of the angels said he at any time ?' Hereof see Sec. 64.

The matter declares two things:

1. The kind of dignity.
2. The continuance thereof.

In the kind, we may observe, 1, the ground of it, God's will, God *said* Sit; 2, the greatness of it. This is set down,

1. By an act, *sit*; 2, by the place.

The place is set out under a metaphor, ' on my right hand.'

This shews, 1, Christ's inferiority to God.

2. His superiority above all creatures.

The continuance noteth out a double end:

1. The time how long: *until.*
2. The reason why: to *make thine enemies*, &c.

In expressing this latter end, observe,

1. A *concessum*, or thing taken for granted, *enemies.*
2. A consequence, which is their utter destruction, in this phrase, *make thy footstool.*

In describing the inferiority of angels, two things are remarkable:

1. The manner, by an interrogation, *Are they not?* &c.
2. The matter. Wherein is declared,

1. The nature of angels, *spirits.*
2. Their function.

Both these are amplified by this particle of universality, *all.*

The function of angels is set out,

1. By the kind thereof, *ministering*; 2, by the end.

In the end is expressed, 1, an act, to *minister.*

2. The persons, for whom. These are described,

1. By their privilege, *salvation.*
2. By their right thereunto, *inherit.* This is illustrated,

1. By the time of enjoying their inheritance, which is to come.

2. By the certainty thereof. Both these are implied under a note of the future tense, $\mu\acute{\epsilon}\lambda\lambda o\nu\tau\alpha\varsigma$, *shall.*

Sec. 164. *Of the doctrines arising out of the 13th and 14th verses.*

Of the doctrines arising out of these words, ' To which of the angels said he at any time,' see Sec. 65.

I. *God the Father is the author of Christ's exaltation.* He said *Sit.* See Sec. 149.

II. *Christ as mediator is inferior to the Father.*

III. *Christ as mediator is advanced above all creatures.* These two doctrines are gathered out of this phrase, ' On my right hand.' See Doct. 37, 38, on ver. 4, Sec. 38.

IV. *Christ hath enemies.* The mention of *enemies* shews as much. See Sec. 151.

V. *Christ's enemies shall be subdued.* God undertakes as much: *I put.* See Sec. 153.

VI. *Christ's enemies shall be utterly subdued.* The metaphor of making them his *footstool* proves this. See Sec. 154.

Ver. 14. VII. *Emphasis is to be added to weighty matters.* This is manifest by the manner of expressing this point, by an interrogation, *Are they not?*

VIII. *Angels are spirits.*

IX. *Angels are ministers.* These two are expressed in this phrase, *ministering spirits.* See Sec. 156.

X. *Angels' ministry is especially for saints.* Saints are here intended under this phrase, which shall be *heirs.* See Sec. 158.

XI. *Every angel, of what degree soever, is a minister to saints.* The general particle *all* implies as much. See Sec. 156.

XII. *Salvation belongs to saints.* See Sec. 159.

XIII. *Salvation belongs to saints by right of inheritance.* See Sec. 160.

XIV. *The fruition of saints' inheritance is to come.* See Sec. 161.

XV. *Saints are sure of salvation.* These two last doctrines arise out of the note of the future tense, *shall be.* See Sec. 162.

Hebrews 2

Sec. 1. *Of the resolution of the second chapter.*

The apostle having distinctly and largely set out the excellency of Christ's divine nature and royal function in the former chapter, in this he sets out his human nature, and the excellency of it.

Elegantly he passeth from the one to the other by a transition, wherein he sheweth an especial use to be made of the former point.

This is indeed a digression, in regard of the matter of doctrine; but a most pertinent and profitable digression, and that in the five first verses of this chapter. In the rest of the chapter, the other article concerning Christ's human nature is distinctly demonstrated.

The sum of the transition is an exhortation to give good heed to the gospel.

This exhortation is first propounded, verse 1, and then enforced in the four next verses.

Two points are noted to enforce the duty. One is the damage; the other, the vengeance which may follow upon the neglect of the gospel.

The damage is intimated in this phrase, ' Lest we should let them slip.'

The vengeance is first propounded in this phrase, ' How shall we escape;' and then aggravated.

The aggravation is demonstrated, 1, by an argument from the less; 2, by the excellency of the gospel.

The argument from the less is concerning the word of angels, who are in the former chapter proved to be far inferior to Christ; which point is illustrated, ver. 5.

The excellency of the gospel is set out,

1. By the matter which it holdeth out, *salvation,* ver. 3.

2. By the means of making it known. These means are, 1, the publishers; 2, the evidences thereof.

The publishers were of two sorts : 1, the principal author ; 2, ear-witnesses thereof, ver. 3.

The evidences were signs, &c., ver. 4.

About Christ's human nature two things are demonstrated :

1. The low degree of Christ's humiliation in assuming our nature: 'Thou madest him lower than angels,' ver. 7.

2. The high exaltation thereof through Christ's assuming it: 'Thou crownedst him with glory,' ver. 7.

For the better manifestation of these principles, the apostle proves the main point, that Christ was man, by sundry arguments.

The first argument is a divine testimony; that is, 1, propounded, ver. 6–8 ; 2, applied to the person here spoken of, ver. 9.

The second argument is taken from the end of Christ's incarnation, which was ' to taste death for every man.' This could he not have done if he had not been man, ver. 9.

A third argument is raised from the equity and meetness of the matter, ' It became him,' ver. 10. God would bring his children to glory by suffering. It was therefore ' meet to make the Captain of their salvation perfect through sufferings ;' which could not be unless he had been man.

A fourth argument is taken from a special function which Christ undertook, namely, to sanctify the elect: ' He that sanctifieth, and they who are sanctified, must be all of one,' ver. 11. Hence the apostle maketh this inference, ' He is not ashamed to call them brethren,' ver. 11. This may also be taken as a proof of the point, Christ's own witness thereof, confirmed in the next verse.

The fifth argument is taken from that opportunity which Christ, being man, had to exercise his three great offices of prophet, prince, and priest.

1. His prophetical office is set out in a divine prediction, ' I will declare thy name,' ver. 12. It is further amplified by the ground of his encouragement to hold out therein (which is expressed in a divine testimony, ' I will put my trust in him,' ver. 13); and by the fruit or effect thereof, expressed in another like testimony, ' Behold I, and the children,' &c., ver. 13. These testimonies are further proofs of Christ's human nature.

2. Christ's kingly office is set out in two especial effects thereof ; one to ' destroy the devil,' which he did by death, and therefore was man, ver. 14. The other to ' deliver them who were in bondage,' ver. 15, which deliverance also he wrought by death. The two effects of Christ's kingly office are proved by the main point in hand, and set down by an opposition of two different natures, of angels and of Abraham. Christ destroyed not the devil for angels, but for men: he delivered not angels, but men; there-

fore he 'too knot the nature of angels, but men,' ver. 16.

3. Christ's priestly office is set out in this phrase, an high priest; and it is amplified,

(1.) By two needful qualities, *merciful, faithful*.

(2.) By two useful effects: *to make reconciliation*, ver. 17; *to be able to succour*, ver. 18. It was requisite in these respects that he should be man.

Sec. 2. *Of the inference made upon Christ's excellency.*

Therefore we ought to give the more earnest heed to the things which we have heard, lest at any time we should let them slip.—Heb. ii. 1.

In the five first verses of this chapter, the apostle declares a duty to be performed in regard of that excellent teacher which God sent (namely, his Son, more excellent than the excellentest mere creature) to reveal his gospel to men. This duty is to give more than ordinary heed unto that gospel. Thus much is intended under this particle of inference, *therefore;* or as it is in the Greek, διὰ τοῦτο, for this, even for this cause. Because God had vouchsafed so excellent a teacher, he must be the more carefully attended unto. Of this particle of inference, see Chap. i. Sec. 117.

This here hath reference to all the branches of Christ's excellency mentioned in the former chapter. Because he is *God's Son*, therefore give heed. Because he is *the heir of all*, therefore give heed. Because he *made the worlds*, therefore give heed. The like may be inferred upon all the other special excellencies of Christ. They are so many grounds of the apostle's exhortation; and the inference may be added as a conclusion of every one of them severally, as here it is of all of them jointly.

The eminency of an author in dignity and authority, and the excellency of his parts in knowledge, wisdom, and other gifts, do much commend that which is spoken by him. If a king, prudent and learned, take upon him to instruct others, due attention and diligent heed will be given thereunto. 'The queen of the south came from the uttermost parts of the earth to hear the wisdom of Solomon,' Mat. xii. 42. She counted Solomon's servants, who stood continually before him and heard his wisdom, to be happy, 1 Kings x. 8. Job was the 'greatest of all the men of the east, and he was a perfect and upright man: thereupon 'when the ear heard him it blessed him,' Job i. 1, 3, and xxix. 11. But behold a greater than Solomon, a greater than Job, is here intended by the apostle: 'Therefore we ought to give the more earnest heed,' Heb. xii. 25. It was usual with the prophets to premise before their prophecies such phrases as these, 'The word of the Lord;' 'Thus saith the Lord,' Hosea i. 1, 2, and iv. 1, Exod. iv. 22, and v. 1, and that purposely to work the more heed and attention in people to that which was spoken. This may be a forcible motive diligently to exercise ourselves in all the holy Scriptures; because 'all Scripture is given by inspiration of God.

Sec. 3. *Of the necessity of performing duty.*

The foresaid inference is by the apostle made a matter of necessity, as the phrase, *we ought*, importeth.

The Greek verb is impersonal, δεῖ, and may be thus translated, *it behoveth;* and so it is translated Luke xxiv. 46. In regard of the necessity which it intendeth, it is oft translated *must*, and that in a double relation: one to God's decree, the other to God's charge. The former respecteth God's determinate counsel, his secret and absolute will; the latter his revealed word and approving will.

In the former relation it is said, 'Thus it must be,' Mat. xxvi. 54.

In the latter thus, 'A bishop must be blameless,' 1 Tim. iii. 2; that is, it is his duty to be so.

Here it is used in this latter relation to duty, and in that respect well translated *we ought;* that is, it is our duty, yet so as a necessity lieth upon us. It is not an arbitrary matter, left to our own will to do or not to do; but by reason of the sovereignty and power which God hath over us, and charge which he hath laid upon us, we are bound to observe it. It may be said of hearing the gospel what Paul said of preaching it, ' Necessity is laid upon me; yea, woe is unto me, if I preach not the gospel,' 1 Cor. ix. 16. It may be said in this case what Christ said to every of the seven churches of Asia, 'He that hath an ear, let him hear,' Rev. ii. 7, 11, 17, 29, and iii. 6, 13, 22.

As God's ordinance and charge requireth as much, so our own good, our best good, the spiritual edification and eternal salvation of our souls. As it is our duty in regard of God's commandment, we ought to obey God, so it will be our wisdom so to do. We ought to do the things which make to our own happiness.

Sec. 4. *Of inciting ourselves to that whereunto we stir up others.*

It is observable how the apostle ranks himself in the number of those on whom he layeth this necessity. He speaketh not to them in the second person, *ye ought*, but in the first person and plural number, *we ought;* I and you, you and I, even all of us. It is noted as a property of a good husband, who would have that to be well effected whereupon he puts others, to go along himself, and to put to his own hand, that by his own practice and pattern he might the more quicken them whom he employeth.[1] This difference useth to be put betwixt a man careful about his undertakings, and a man careless therein. This latter may in a morning say to others, *Go, sirs*, to such a task, and he himself lie in his bed, or pursue his

[1] Of practising ourselves, that whereunto we incite others, see *The Saints' Sacrifice*, on *Ps.* cxvi. 19, Sec. 121.

pastime; but the other saith, *Gaw, sirs*, that is, go we, let us go together, I will go with you. This ought to be the care of such as incite others to duty; they must also speak to themselves, and quicken up their own spirits thereto. Hereby they shall much more effectually work upon their hearers; for when hearers observe that their teachers lay no more on them than upon themselves, they willingly put their shoulder under the burden. A teacher's example prevails much with hearers, John xiii. 15. Joshua's pattern is pertinent to this purpose; for thus he saith of himself, and of such as were under his charge, 'We will serve the Lord,' Joshua xxiv. 18.

Sec. 5. *Of giving heed to the gospel.*

The duty which the apostle presseth upon himself and others, as a matter of necessity, is to 'give earnest heed to the things which they had heard.' Hereby he means the gospel, which he styles *salvation*, and of which he saith, 'It was first spoken by the Lord, and afterwards by his apostles,' ver. 3, 4. Of these excellencies of the gospel, we shall speak in their due place.

By expressing the matter in the time past, 'things which we have heard,'[1] he giveth us to understand that the gospel had been formerly preached unto them, even before he wrote this epistle; so as he wrote no new doctrine, but rather endeavoured to establish them in that which they had received. He counts it safe to write the same things to them, Philip. iii. 1; even the same which they had heard before. Hereby he watered what had been sown amongst them. Whether the seed of the gospel had been cast among these Hebrews by himself or some other, he doth not declare; but certain it is, that that precious seed had been cast among them. They had heard the gospel; he doth here water it, that the crop may be the more plentiful.

For this end, he calls upon them to give heed thereto, προσέχειν, *adhibere sc. animum*. This is the interpretation of one Greek word, but a compound one, which signifieth to set a man's mind on a thing.

I find it used in the New Testament in a double relation : 1, to things hurtful ; 2, to things useful.

In the former respect it signifieth to beware, or to take heed of a thing; as προσέχετε, 'Beware of false prophets,' Mat. vii. 15; προσέχετε ἑαυτοῖς, 'Take heed to yourselves,' Luke xxi. 34.

In the latter respect it signifieth to give heed, or to attend; as, 'They gave heed to those things which Philip spake,' Acts viii. 6; and 'Lydia attended to the things which were spoken of Paul,' Acts xvi. 14. It is also of attending to the duties of one's calling, Heb. vii. 13; 1 Tim. iv. 13. It is here taken in the latter sense, and intendeth more than a bare hearing of a matter.

This being applied to God's word, is opposed to all manner of slighting it, whether by contempt or neglect of it. He that despiseth the word of the Lord, Num. xv. 31, and they that speak against it, Acts xiii. 45, and they that turn away their ears from the truth, 2 Tim. iv. 4, and they that make light of the offer of grace, Mat. xxii. 4, 5, and they whose hearts are to the word as the wayside, or the stony or thorny ground to the seed, Mat. xiii. 19, &c., do all of them that which is contrary to this duty; they do not give such heed to the word as is here required. The duty here intended is a serious, firm, and fixed setting of the mind upon that which we hear; a bowing and bending of the will to yield unto it; an applying of the heart to it, a placing of the affections upon it, and bringing the whole man into a holy conformity thereunto. Thus it compriseth knowledge of the word, faith therein, obedience thereto, and all other due respect that may any way concern it, 2 Tim. ii. 7; Mat. xv. 10, and xiii. 23; Acts iv. 4, and xvi. 14.

The comparative particle, περισσοτέρως, 'more earnest,' further sheweth that a diligent attention is here intended. The positive in Greek, περισσόν, signifieth that which is more than usual or ordinary; that which excelleth or exceedeth. It is translated 'advantage,' Rom. iii. 1, and 'above measure,' Mark x. 26. It hath reference both to that which is good, and also to that which is evil, and signifieth an exceeding in the one and in the other. In setting out Christ's gift, it is translated 'abundantly,' περισσὸν ἔχωσιν, John x. 10; and in aggravating Paul's rage, it is translated 'exceedingly,' περισσῶς, Acts xxvi. 11; and in Peter's over-confident profession, 'vehemently,' ἐκ περισσοῦ, Mark xiv. 31.

The comparative degree addeth much emphasis, and intendeth a greater care and endeavour about the matter in hand than in any other thing; as if he had said, More heed is to be given to the gospel than to the law; more to the Son than to any servant; for he speaks of the gospel preached by Christ.

It may be here put for the superlative degree, and imply the greatest heed that may possibly be given, and the best care and diligence and utmost endeavour that can be used. Thus it is said of the Scriptures, 'We have a more sure word,' βεβαιότερον, that is, a most sure word, 2 Peter ii. 19. Thus this very word in my text is oft put for the superlative degree; as where Paul saith of himself, 'In labours more abundant (περισσοτέρως), in prisons more frequent,' that is, most abundant, most frequent, 2 Cor. xi. 23.

Hereby, as he doth incite them for the future to make the best use that possibly they can of the gospel that had been preached unto them, so he gives a secret and mild check to their former negligence, implying that they had not given formerly such heed as they should have done to so precious a word as had been preached unto them, but had been too careless thereabouts, which he would have them redress for the future.

---

[1] τοῖς ἀκουσθεῖσι, aorist. participl. past.

Sec. 6. *Of the damage of neglecting the gospel.*

To enforce that diligence in giving heed to the gospel, the apostle addeth the damage which may follow upon neglect thereof, in these words, 'lest at any time we should let them slip.'

The Greek word παραρρυῶμεν, translated *let slip*, is not elsewhere to be found in the New Testament. It signifieth *to flow besides*,[1] as waters that flow besides a place. The word preached, if it be not well heeded, will pass clean besides us, and do us no good at all.

The word also may signify to flow through a thing, as water put into a colander or riven dish, it slips through or runs out; thus it is quickly lost and doth no good. The Greek word here used is used by the Greek LXX, Υἱὲ μὴ παραρρυῇς, Prov. iii. 21, and opposed to keeping sound or safe.

A forgetful memory may fitly be resembled to a colander; a colander lets out water as fast as it receiveth it.

An apostle resembles a forgetful hearer to 'one that beholdeth his natural face in a glass, and goeth away, and straightway forgetteth what manner of man he was,' James i. 23, 24. Both resemblances tend to the same purpose, which is, to demonstrate the unprofitableness of negligent and careless hearers.

The fault here intimated is contrary to that duty which is enjoined, in these words, 'settle it in your hearts,' Luke xxi. 14.

Because this act of slipping out, or sliding by, is here spoken of persons, not of things, as if it had been thus translated, 'lest we slip out,' thus some expound it, lest we perish, as waters that slip out of the channel are soon dried up. This interpretation is confirmed by these kind of speeches : 'We must needs die, and are as water spilt on the ground, and cannot be gathered up again,' 2 Sam. xiv. 14 ; 'I am poured out like water,' Ps. xxii. 14 ; 'The waters fail from the sea, and the flood decayeth and drieth up,' Job. xiv. 11 ; 'They are dried up, they are gone away from men,' Job. xxviii. 4.

In the general both senses tend to the same purpose, namely, to demonstrate the damage that followeth upon neglect of the gospel.

The preaching of the gospel is by God's institution 'the power of God unto salvation,' Rom. i. 16. The damage, that it proves altogether fruitless.

In the former sense the gospel is to them that hear it as lost. In the latter sense they themselves that hear it are lost, and miss of the salvation which the gospel bringeth unto them. Such hearers were they of whom these and other like complaints have been made : 'Oh that my people had hearkened unto me !' Ps. lxxxi. 13 ; 'Forty years long was I grieved with this generation,' Ps. xcv. 10 ; 'I have laboured in vain, I have spent my strength for nought,' Isa. xlix. 4 ; 'O Jerusalem, Jerusalem, how oft would I have gathered thee together, even as a hen gathereth her chickens under her wings, and ye would not !' Mat. xxiii. 37.

This phrase, *lest at any time*, is the interpretation of one Greek word, which though sometimes it imports a doubtfulness, or a peradventure, as we speak, and is translated *lest haply*, Luke xiv. 29, *if peradventure*, 2 Tim. ii. 25, yet it doth not so always. Where it is said, 'lest at any time thou dash thy foot against a stone,' Mat. iv. 6, it is most certain that if the angels kept us not, we should dash our feet against stones. And where it is said, 'lest at any time they should see with their eyes,' Mat. xiii. 15, it is certain that they whose eyes are closed shall not see with their eyes. And also where it is said, 'Take heed lest there be an evil heart,' ver. 12, assuredly there will be an evil heart in them that do not take heed. So assuredly they who are negligent hearers of the gospel will lose the profit thereof. And though for a while they may retain it in their minds and memories, yet it will some time or other be lost, unless they give the more diligent heed thereto. Fitly, therefore, is this circumstance of time expressed, 'lest at any time.' Of this phrase see more Chap. iii. 12, Sec. 125.

Sec. 7. *Of the resolutions and instructions of* Heb. ii. 1.

Therefore we ought to give the more earnest heed to the things which we have heard, lest at any time we should let them slip.

This text doth in part set out the use to be made of the gospel. There are two observable things therein to be considered :

1. The inference of it upon that which goes before, διὰ τοῦτο, *therefore.*

2. The substance thereof in the rest of the verse.

Concerning the substance there is observable :

1. A duty prescribed.

2. A motive used to enforce the same.

About the duty we may distinctly note,

1. The matter whereof it consisteth.

2. The manner of expressing it.

In the matter is distinctly noted,

1. An act enjoined, προσέχειν, *to give heed.*

2. The object thereof, ἀκουσθεῖσι, *the things which we have heard.*

Both these are amplified by the persons who exhort and are exhorted, ἡμᾶς, *we.*

The manner declares,

1. The necessity of the point, δεῖ, *ought.*

2. The diligence to be used, περισσοτέρως, *more earnest.*

The motive is taken from the damage that is like to follow upon neglect of the duty prescribed, μήποτε, *lest.*

That damage, as it is propounded, admits a double consideration :

1. The loss of the word that is heard.

---

[1] παρὰ, *præter*, ῥύω, *fluo*.

2. The loss of the parties that negligently hear it, *lest, παραρρυῶμεν, we should let them slip.*
This is amplified by the time, *at any time.*

Doctrines arising out of verse 1.

I. *Use is to be added to doctrine.* The five first verses of this chapter do expressly lay down a main use of the doctrine of Christ's excellency set out in the former chapter.

II. *The more excellent the teacher is, the more is his word to be regarded.* This ariseth out of this inference *therefore.* Because God spake to us Christians by his Son, *therefore* we must the more heed him. See Sec. 2.

III. *Due attention is to be given to God's word.* The act whereby the duty here required is expressed in this phrase, 'give heed,' proves as much. See Sec. 5.

IV. *Greater attention is to be given to the gospel.* It is the gospel whereunto this word of comparison, *more earnest*, hath reference. See Sec. 5.

V. *Matters of weight again and again delivered are to be attended unto.* This is intended under the expressing of the object here set down in the time past, *have heard.* 'The things which we have heard.' See Sec. 5.

VI. *We are bound to perform duty answerable to the means afforded.* There is a necessity intimated in this word *ought.* It is no arbitrary matter; a necessity lieth upon us so to do.

VII. *In provoking others to duty, we ought to incite ourselves.* See Sec. 3. The apostle includeth himself together with others, by using the first person of the plural number, *we.* See Sec. 4.

VIII. *The benefit of the gospel, if it be slightly heeded, may be lost.* See Sec. 6.

IX. *Men that hear the gospel may be lost.* These two last doctrines I gather from the various acceptions of the word translated *let slip*. See Sec. 6.

X. *The fault of losing the benefit of the gospel is in those that hear it.* The manner of inferring the motive upon the duty thus, *lest we should,* declares as much. See Sec. 6.

XI. *What is not at once lost, may be lost at another time.* This is intended under this phrase, *lest at any time.* See Sec. 6.

Sec. 8. *Of the apostle's manner of enforcing his matter.*

Ver. 2. *For if the word spoken by angels was stedfast, and every transgression and disobedience received a just recompence of reward;*

Ver. 3. *How shall we escape, if we neglect so great salvation; which at the first began to be spoken by the Lord, and was confirmed unto us by them that heard him;*

Ver. 4. *God also bearing them witness, both with signs and wonders, and with divers miracles, and gifts of the Holy Ghost, according to his own will.*

The first particle of this text, as our English sets it down, being a causal conjunction γὰρ, *for*, sheweth that it follows as a reason of that which went before; a reason to persuade the Hebrews to attend diligently to the gospel. The apostle useth one motive before, Sec. 6. He addeth this to enforce them the further to observe his instruction, and that not only by adding one reason to another, as two blows strike a nail deeper in than one, but by producing another more forcible motive than the former.

The former motive was taken from a damage, namely, loss of a benefit which might have been received by well heeding the gospel; but this is vengeance, sore vengeance, even sorer than the vengeance which was wont to be executed under the law, as the interrogation in the third verse doth plainly demonstrate.

The next particle εἰ, *if*, though it be a conditional conjunction, yet doth it not always leave a matter in suspense and doubt, as if there were question thereof whether it should be so or no. It is oft used to lay down a sure, certain, infallible, undeniable ground to infer another truth thereupon. Where Christ saith, 'If I say the truth, why do ye not believe me?' John viii. 46. He maketh no question of what he spake, whether it were true or no, but layeth it down as an unquestionable point that he spake truth, and thereupon he aggravated their unbelief.

If this manner of arguing be put into a syllogistical form, this will appear most clearly thus:

If I speak truth, you ought to believe me;

But I speak truth; therefore ye ought to believe me.

So here, if slighting the word of angels were sorely punished, much more shall the slighting of Christ's word be punished.

This manner of arguing shews that the apostle's argument is taken *a minori ad majus*, from the less to the greater; for it was a less sin to slight the word of angels than the word of Christ.

Of this kind of conditional expression, see Chap. iii. 5, 6, Sec. 60: see also *The Saints' Sacrifice* on Ps. cxvi. 14, sec. 90.

Sec. 9. *Of the word spoken by angels.*

By *the word spoken by angels,* ὁ δι' ἀγγέλων λαληθεὶς λόγος, is in general meant that message or errand, as we speak, which angels brought from God to men, even so much of God's will as he was pleased to reveal to men by the ministry of angels.

Of angels and their several functions, see chap. i. Secs. 70, 71, 82, &c.

Some restrain the word here intended to the law delivered on mount Sinai, and for that purpose allege Acts vii. 53, and Gal. iii. 19.

Again, some say that the law is not here meant, and that upon these grounds:

1. That God himself delivered it; for it is expressly said in relation to the moral law, 'God spake all these words,' Exod. xx. 1; and in the preface of

that law, he that gave it saith, 'I am the Lord thy God,' &c., Exod. xx. 2.

2. That Christ the Son of God delivered it, for of him speaketh this apostle in these words: 'Whose voice then shook the earth,' Heb. xii. 26. He there hath reference to the law.

3. That Moses delivered it; for it is expressly said, 'The law was given by Moses,' John i. 17.

The seeming differences about the giving of the law may easily be reconciled by a due observing of the different respect wherein the one and the other is said to deliver the law.

1. The Son of God is true God, even Jehovah, as hath been shewed out of the former chapter, Secs. 107, 128, so as what is done or said by the Son, is done or said by the true God. Besides, the Father doth what he doth, and speaketh what he speaketh, by the Son; and the Son doth and speaketh all from the Father. So as the law may well be said to be delivered by God, and by the Son of God, without any seeming contradiction at all.

2. As for that which is spoken of Moses, that the law was given by him, it is to be taken ministerially and secondarily. God having published the law on mount Sinai, afterwards wrote it in two tables, which he gave to Moses, and Moses in his name gave it to the people. In like manner God made known all the other laws, both ceremonial and judicial, to Moses first, and then Moses from the Lord declared them to the people.

3. Whatsoever can be said of angels delivering the law, it must needs be taken ministerially. This phrase, 'They received the law by the disposition of angels,' may be thus taken, 'in the troops of angels,' or 'among the hosts of angels.' The Greek word translated *disposition* is of the plural number, εἰς διαταγὰς, and sometimes signifieth companies disposed together, or set in order.[1] It is said that in the delivering of the law, 'the Lord came with ten thousands of saints,' Deut. xxxiii. 2. These saints were holy angels, even those 'twenty thousand thousands of angels,' mentioned on the like occasion, Ps. lxviii. 17. This phrase also, 'the law was ordained by angels,' Gal. iii. 19, may be taken to be *among angels*, who attended the Lord in delivering the law, as they will attend him in his coming to judgment, Mat. xxv. 31. Hereof see more on the first Chap. sec. 96. The apostle, therefore, may here have reference to the law, and that may be one 'word of angels' here meant. But this must not be restrained only to the giving of the law, but rather extended to other particulars also, which at other times angels delivered from God to men; for before the gospel was established in the Christian church, God frequently delivered his will to men by the ministry of angels, as we shewed in the first chapter, Sec. 96. And wheresoever any judgment was executed upon any person for any light esteem of that message which was brought by an angel, the same may be here understood and applied to the point in hand.

Sec. 10. *Of the respect due to God's word by any minister delivered.*

Some[1] take the word *angels* in the larger sense, for any manner of messengers from God that brought his word to his people.

Of this large extent of *angels*, see on the first chapter, Secs. 79, 82.

If angels be here thus largely taken, under the word of angels may be comprised every declaration of God's will by any minister, whether ordinary, as prophets[2] and Levites, or extraordinary, as prophets, or celestial, as the heavenly spirits. For the word or message of any messenger sent of God is to be received as spoken by God himself, Isa. xiii. 20, Gal. iv. 14, 1 Thes. ii. 13.

In this sense the comparison will lie betwixt the ministry of God's word before the exhibition of Christ and after it, and proves the ministry of the word since Christ was exhibited to be the more excellent.

This comparison will well stand with the main scope of the apostle, which is to incite Christians to have the gospel and the ministry thereof in high esteem.

But that which the apostle hath delivered in the former chapter, and further delivereth in this chapter, ver. 5, 7, 16, of celestial angels, clearly manifesteth that such heavenly spirits are here principally intended.

By just and necessary consequence it may be inferred that the word of all God's ministers before the time of the gospel was such as the word of angels is here said to be, 'stedfast,' &c.

Sec. 11. *Of the stedfastness of God's word.*

Of the foresaid word of angels, it is said that it was 'stedfast,'[3] βέβαιος, that is, firm, stable, inviolable, that which could not be altered, that which might not be opposed, gainsaid, or neglected. It is attributed to God's promise, which never failed, Rom. iv. 16, to an anchor that fast holdeth a ship, Heb. vi. 19, and to a testament ratified by the testator's death, which no man altereth, Heb. ix. 17, Gal. iii. 15.

The reason hereof resteth not simply on the authority or infallibility of angels who delivered the word, but rather on the authority and infallibility of the Lord their master who sent them. For the word of an angel was the word of God, as the word of the Lord's prophet was the word of the Lord, 1 Sam. xv. 10, and as the word of an ambassador or of a herald is the word of the king or of him that appointed him; for if they be faithful, as good angels are, they will deliver nothing but that which is given them in charge; and that they will also deliver in the name of their master that sent them.

---

[1] Heinsius Exerc. Sacr. in loc.   [2] Qu. 'Priests'?—ED.
[3] See Chap. iii. ver. 6, Sec. 68. Of the word βεβαιόω, see Sec. 25; and of the noun βεβαίωσις, see Chap. vi. 16, Sec. 121.

---

[1] διατάττειν, in ordines disponere; διατάττειν στρατὸν —Herod

The word of angels therefore being the word of the Lord, it must needs be stedfast. For with the Lord 'there is no variableness, neither shadow of turning,' James i. 17. 'I am the Lord,' saith God of himself, 'I change not,' Mal. iii. 6.

Sec. 12. *Of the stedfastness of the several kinds of God's laws.*

Some object the abrogation of the law, which is said to be delivered by angels, against the stedfastness thereof.

For a fuller answer hereunto, I will endeavour to shew in what respect the several kinds of God's law may be said to be stedfast, notwithstanding any abrogation of any of them.

God's law is distinguished into three kinds; judicial, ceremonial, and moral.

1. The judicial law was stedfast so long as the policy to which the Lord gave it continued.

2. The ceremonial law was stedfast till it was fully accomplished in the truth and substance thereof, and in that accomplishment it remains everlastingly stedfast.

3. The moral law, which is here taken to be especially intended, was ever, and ever shall be, a stedfast and inviolable law. It 'endureth for ever,' Ps. xix. 9. This is it of which Christ thus saith, 'It is easier for heaven and earth to pass, than one tittle of the law to fail,' Luke xvi. 17.

Indeed, Christ hath purchased for such as believe in him, a freedom from the law, in regard of sundry circumstances, such as these:

1. In regard of an end for which it was at first instituted, namely, to justify such as should in themselves perfectly fulfil it. The end is thus expressed, 'The man which doth those things shall live by them,' Rom. x. 5. *The man,* namely, he himself, in his own person; not by another, nor a surety for him. *Which doth,* namely, perfectly, without failing in any particular. *Those things,* namely, all the things in their substance and circumstances, that are comprised in the law. Our freedom from the law is thus expressed: 'We have believed in Jesus Christ, that we might be justified by the faith of Christ, and not by the works of the law,' Gal. ii. 16.

2. In regard of the penalty of the law, which is a curse for every transgression; according to this tenor thereof, ' Cursed is every one that continueth not in all things which are written in the book of the law to do them,' Gal. iii. 10. Our freedom from this curse is thus set down: 'Christ hath redeemed us from the curse of the law, being made a curse for us,' Gal. iii. 13; and thus: 'There is no condemnation to them which are in Christ Jesus,' Rom. viii. 1.

3. In regard of the rigour of the law, which accepts no endeavours without absolute perfection. The tenor of the curse imports as much; for it pronounceth every one cursed that continueth not in all things, Gal. iii. 10. Our freedom from this rigour is thus exemplified: 'If there be first a willing mind, it is accepted according to that a man hath, and not according to that he hath not,' 2 Cor. viii. 12.

4. In regard of an aggravating power which the law hath over a natural man. For a natural man committeth sin, even because the law forbids it; and in despite of the law; and thus the law makes 'sin exceeding sinful,' Rom. vii. 13. From this we are freed by the grace of regeneration, whereby we are brought to 'delight in the law of God, after the inward man;' and 'with the mind to serve the law of God,' Rom. vii. 22, 25. But notwithstanding our freedom from the moral law in such circumstances as have been mentioned, that law remaineth most stedfast and inviolable in the substance of it; which is an exact form and declaration of that which is good and evil, just and unjust, meet and unmeet; and of what is due to God or man; and of what is a sin against the one, and a wrong unto the other.

Herein lieth a main difference betwixt the divine law, and all human laws. These are subject to alterations and corrections, or amendments; for which end parliaments and councils are oft convocated

Sec. 13. *Of the respects wherein the word of angels was stedfast.*

The word of angels may be said to be stedfast in three especial respects.

1. In the *event;* in that whatsoever they declared by prediction, promise, or threatening, was answerably accomplished.

Of predictions, take these instances, Gen. xvi. 11, 12, and xxxi. 11, 12; Zech. i. 9, &c.; Mat. xxviii. 5, 7; Acts x. 3, &c.; Rev. i. 1.

Of promises, take these, Gen. xviii. 10; Judges xiii. 3; Mat. i. 20; Acts xxvii. 23.

Of threatenings, take these, Gen. xix. 13; 2 Kings i. 3, 4.

These particulars are sufficient to prove the point in hand. As for the general, I dare boldly say, that never was any matter of history, or promise of good, or threatening of judgment, declared by an angel, but answerably it was accomplished; and in that respect an angel's word was stedfast.

2. The word of angels was stedfast in regard of the *bond* which bound them to whom any duty was enjoined, or direction given, to observe the same. For they were extraordinarily sent from God; yea, they were the chiefest of God's messengers. Saints thereupon believed their word, and obeyed their charge. As Manoah, Judges xiii. 8, 12; Elijah, 1 Kings xix. 8; 2 Kings i. 15; the Virgin Mary, Luke i. 38; Joseph, Mat. i. 24, and sundry others.

3. Their word was stedfast in regard of the *penalty* which was inflicted on such as believed not, or obeyed not their word. Hereof see Secs. 16, 17.

Sec. 14. *Of the difference between transgression and disobedience.*

Upon the stedfastness of God's word, though spoken by angels, it is inferred that 'every transgression and disobedience received a just recompence of reward.' This inference is joined to the stedfastness of their word by a copulative particle, Καὶ, *and;* which sheweth that this penalty is a motive to give good heed to their word, as well as the stedfastness thereof, and that it is an effect that will assuredly follow thereupon. For because the word of angels was stedfast, therefore every transgression was punished.

There are two words in this inference, namely, παράβασις, *transgression,* and παρακοὴ, *disobedience,* which in the general may intend one and the same thing; and yet here be also distinguished by their degrees, yea, and by their kinds. The verb παραβαίνειν, from whence the first word in Greek is derived, properly signifieth *to pass over a thing;* metaphorically having reference to a law, or any other rule, it signifieth to swerve from that rule, or to violate and break that law, παραβαίνειν τὴν ἐντολὴν, Mat. xv. 3. In this metaphorical sense this word is oft used in relation to the law of God, and put for any breach thereof, as Rom. iv. 15, Gal. iii. 19. It is put for the first sin of Adam, Rom. v. 14, and for Eve's special sin, 1 Tim. ii. 14.

The other word, according to the notation of it in Greek, intimateth a turning of the ear from that which is spoken; and that with a kind of obstinacy and contumacy; as where Christ saith of an obstinate brother, 'if he neglect to hear,' παρακούσῃ, Mat. xviii. 17, or obstinately refuse to hear.

I find the word παρακοὴ, here translated *disobedience,* twice opposed to a willing and *ready obedience,* ὑπακοὴ, namely, of true saints, 2 Cor. x. 6, and of Christ, Rom. v. 19. This opposition importeth a wilful disobedience; or a contumacy, as some[1] here translate the word.

Others[2] under the former word *transgression,* comprise sins of commission; and under the latter word, *disobedience,* sins of omission. For the verb from whence the latter word is derived, signifieth to neglect or refuse to hear, Mat. xviii. 17.

There is questionless a difference betwixt these two words, either in the degrees, or in the kinds of disobedience; in which respect the universal, or (as here it is used) distributive particle, πᾶσα, *every,* is premised; to shew that no transgression, great or mean, in one or other kind, passed unpunished.

Let not any think, by mincing his sin, to escape punishment. A prophet having reckoned up a catalogue of sins, some greater, some lighter, maketh this inference, 'If a man do the like to any one of these things, he shall surely die,' Ezek. xviii. 10, 13. Every particular branch of God's law is as a distinct link of a chain; if any one link fail, the whole chain is broken. The will of the law-maker is disobeyed in every transgression, James ii. 10, 11. Herein lieth a main difference betwixt a faithful servant of God, and a formal possessor; the former makes conscience of every sin, the latter of such only as are less agreeable to his own corrupt humour, or such as he conceiveth most damageable to himself.

Sec. 15. *Of punishments on transgressors.*

The memorable judgments executed on the Israelites after the law was given unto them on mount Sinai, do give evident proof of the divine vengeance which was executed on the transgressors thereof. Many of those judgments are reckoned up together, 1 Cor. x. 5, &c.

I will endeavour further to exemplify the same in particular judgments executed on the transgressors of every one of the particular precepts, or of denunciations of judgments against them.

1. Moses and Aaron, for their transgressions against the first commandment, because they believed not, but rebelled against God's word, died in the wilderness, and entered not into Canaan, Num. xx. 12, 34.

2. The Israelites that worshipped the golden calf, Exod. xxxii. 6, 28, and joined themselves unto Baal-Peor, Num. xxv. 3-5, and the sons of Aaron, that offered strange fire, Lev. x. 1, 2, were all destroyed for their idolatry against the second commandment.

3. The blasphemer against the third commandment was stoned, Lev. xxiv. 11, 23.

4. He that gathered sticks upon the Sabbath day was also stoned for violating the fourth commandment, Num. xv. 32, 36.

5. Korah, Dathan, and Abiram, with such as took part with them, perished for breaking the fifth commandment in rising up against Moses and Aaron, their governors in state and church, Num. xvi. 3, 32, 35.

6. A murderer was to be put to death, and not spared, Num. xxxv. 31.

7. Zimri and Cosbi were suddenly slain together for their impudent filthiness, and the people that committed whoredom with the daughters of Moab, Num. xxv. 1, 8, 9.

8. Achan, for coveting and stealing what God had forbidden, was destroyed, with all that belonged to him, Joshua vii. 21, 24, 25.

9. A false witness was to be dealt withal, as he had thought to have done to his brother, Deut. xix. 19. His doom is this, 'He shall not be unpunished; he shall perish,' Prov. xix. 5, and xxi. 28.

Not to insist on any more particulars, these and all other transgressions, together with their punishment, are comprised under these words, 'Cursed be he that confirmeth not all the words of this law to do them,' Deut. xxvii. 26.

Instances of particular judgments on such as be-

---

[1] Beza.

[2] παράβασις, *transgressio prohibitionum;* παρακοή, *omissio præceptorum.*—Paræus in loc.

lieved not, or disobeyed the message that was brought unto them by angels, are old Zacharias, who was struck dumb, Luke i. 20, and Lot's wife, who was turned into a pillar of salt, Gen. xix. 17, 26.

'Now all these things were our examples, and are written for our admonition, upon whom the ends of the world are come, 1 Cor. x. 6, 11.

Angels are not now sent to us; yet are the ministers of God's word sent unto us of God. The Lord that sends is rather to be respected than the messengers that are sent. That, therefore, which is here said of recompensing disobedience to the word of angels, may be applied to all disobedience against any minister sent of God, John xiii. 20, Luke x. 16.

Sec. 16. *Of the reward of transgressors.*

The judgment on transgressors is thus expressed, 'received a just recompence of reward.'

This phrase, *recompence of reward*, is the interpretation of one Greek word, μισθαποδοσίαν, but a compound word, and so compriseth under it two words, whereof the one, ἀποδιδόναι, signifieth a rendering; the other, μισθός, a reward. The verb whence it is derived, μισθοδοτεῖν, signifieth to give a reward.

These two words, *render, reward*, are sometimes distinctly set down without composition, as ἀπόδος τὸν μισθόν, δοῦναι τὸν μισθόν, Mat. xx. 8, Rev. xi. 18.

He that hath the office or power to give or render a reward is styled μισθαποδότης, a rewarder, Heb. xi. 6. Sec. 23.

The word used in this text, I find three several times in this epistle, as here, and chap. x. 35, Sec. 132; and xi. 26, Sec. 125; in all which it implieth a reward whereby somewhat is recompensed.

The word μισθός, translated reward, is diversely taken, according to the persons to whom, and work for which, it is given. If to a person accepted of God, for a work approved by him, it importeth such a reward as compriseth under it grace, mercy, blessing. If to a wicked person, for an evil work, it intendeth a fearful revenge, and compriseth under it anger, terror, curse. Christ useth this word in an indefinite sense, which in one case may be applied one way, in another case another way. 'My reward is with me,' saith Christ, 'to give every man according to his work,' Rev. xii. 12. As men and their works are different, some good, some evil, so is Christ's reward different. The reward of the good is eternal life; and of the evil, indignation and wrath, Rom. ii. 6-8.

In regard of this difference, we read of μισθὸν δικαίου, 'the reward of a righteous man,' Mat. x. 41, and of μισθοῦ τῆς ἀδικίας, 'the reward of iniquity,' Acts i. 18, or 'the reward of unrighteousness,' which is also called 'the wages of unrighteousness,' 2 Peter ii. 13, 15. In this latter sense the word is here used, and importeth revenge.

Judgment executed on the wicked for their wickedness, is called a reward, because it is as due unto him, as the reward which useth to be given to a diligent and a faithful labourer is due to him.

This word in Greek is used to set out that which the labourers in the vineyard received for their labour, and is translated *hire*, τὸν μισθόν, Mat. xx. 8.

There is another Greek word, ὀψώνιον, translated wages ('the wages of sin is death,' Rom. vi. 23), which doth somewhat more fully set out the reason of this word *reward*, applied to workers of evil. It is taken from the allowance or pay which is given to soldiers. *Annona quæ militibus in singulos menses dabatur.* In this proper signification it is used, Luke iii. 14, and translated wages or allowance.[1] It is also used, 1 Cor. ix. 7, and translated *charges*. That word is likewise used for allowance due to a minister of the word, 2 Cor. xi. 8.

Both this word turned *wages*, and also the other, *reward*, intend that which is due to the thing for which it is given. Reward is due to the evil works of unbelievers upon desert; but to the good works of believers upon God's gracious promise and faithfulness in making his word good.

Sec. 17. *Of the just punishment of transgressors.*

To shew that punishment on transgressors is most due, this epithet, ἔνδικον, *just*, is premised, thus, 'a just recompence of reward.' Therefore, the damnation of such is also said to be just, δίκαιον, Rom. iii. 8, and that 'it is a righteous thing with God to recompense tribulation to them,' 2 Thes. i. 6. And in this respect the judgment of God is said to be righteous, Rom. ii. 5. It is but one word in Greek, δικαιοκρισία, that setteth out 'a righteous judgment.' It is compounded of these two words, *righteous, judgment;* and shews that righteousness is inseparable from God's judgment: his judgment is always righteous.

It must needs be so, because God, that rendereth the recompence, is a most just judge, Gen. xviii. 25, Ps. ix. 8, Rom. iii. 6.

Why, then, may some say, are not all transgressors punished? for experience of all ages giveth proof that many transgressions and transgressors have from time to time been passed over.

To remove this scruple, we must distinguish betwixt believers and others.

Christ, as a surety, hath received a just recompence of reward for all the transgressions of all such as have believed in him, or shall believe in him. Besides, the Lord, in wisdom and love to such, oft taketh occasion from their transgressions, to inflict temporary punishments on them, not in revenge, nor for satisfaction, but for their spiritual profit, Heb. xii. 10.

Unbelievers that receive not a recompence of reward for their evil deeds in this life, have their recompence treasured up to the full against that day which is styled 'the day of the righteous judgment of God,' Rom. ii. 5.

[1] τὰ ὀψώνια, *salaria, stipendia merita militiæ.*

Thus sooner or later, in one kind or other, 'every transgression and disobedience receiveth a just recompence of reward.'

Transgression is said to *receive* a reward, because the transgressor receiveth it, and that for his transgression.

Transgression, therefore, by a metonymy of the effect, is put for a transgressor. A transgressor is said to receive the reward here intended, not as a willing act on his part, but as it is a due debt, and so to be received; for punishment is as justly due to a transgressor, as any good reward to him that doth that which is required of him. Punishment is a satisfaction for a transgression, even as for a debt that is due; in which respect sins and transgressions are styled *debts*, Mat. vi. 12; and they on whom the punishment is inflicted, are in the Greek[1] and Latin[2] dialect said to *pay* the punishment; because, by enduring punishment, a kind of satisfaction is made; and they who make the satisfaction, pay the debt. This payment doth not necessarily imply a voluntary act, but an act that is most due and just. The sense, the grief, the smart, the pain of a punishment or judgment, lieth on him that is punished or judged. These, therefore, may well be said to receive the recompence that is or shall be inflicted. 'They that resist shall receive to themselves damnation,' Rom. xiii. 3. They cannot avoid it; will they, nill they, they shall have it. He that is just in giving to every one their due, inflicts it.

Thus every word in this clause setteth out the equity of the judgment here denounced. 1, it is *a reward;* 2, it is *a rendering* of that which is due; 3, it is *just;* 4, it is *received* as that which is due and just.

Sec. 18. *Of the certainty of judgment.*

Ver. 3. From the just punishment which was inflicted on such as transgressed the word of angels under the pedagogy of the law, the apostle makes this inference, 'How shall we escape if we neglect,' &c.

The manner of expressing this inference (by an interrogation $\pi\tilde{\omega}\varsigma$, *how*) addeth much emphasis; and sheweth that the consequence inferred is a just consequence, and without all question most true; even so as they themselves cannot deny it. It is somewhat like to this expression, 'Thinkest thou this, O man, that judgest them which do such things, and doest the same, that thou shalt escape the judgment of God?' Rom. ii. 3. See on Chap. i. Sec. 46 and 145.

The word translated *escape*, $\dot{\epsilon}\kappa\varphi\epsilon\nu\xi\dot{o}\mu\epsilon\theta\alpha$, useth to have reference to some evil of punishment, or to some danger or damage; and implieth a flying from it, or an avoiding of it.

[1] Δίκας διδόναι, τίνειν, ἐκτελεῖν, ἀποδιδόναι, ἀποτίνειν, ἐκτίνειν, τινύειν.
[2] Poenas pendere, expendere, dependere, dare, persolvere, luere, vapulare.

I find the Greek word seven times used in the New Testament; twice for escaping out of the danger wherein men were. And it is translated, according to the notation, of the word *fled;* as where the jailor thought that his prisoners had been *fled,* Acts xvi. 27; and where the exorcists *fled* out of the house where a demoniac set upon them, Acts xix. 16. Once it sets out a preventing of danger intended by man; as, where the apostle saith, 'I escaped his hands,' 2 Cor. xi. 33. Once also it sets out a preventing of divine judgment, Luke xxi. 36. Three times it is negatively used, to shew, that in such and such cases, judgment cannot be avoided, but shall assuredly be inflicted, as Rom. ii. 3, 1 Thes. v. 3, and in this place.

This manner of expressing the sure and sore vengeance here intended, is like to that commination which is denounced against the transgression of the third commandment, in these words, 'the Lord will not hold him guiltless,' Exod. xx. 7. He shall assuredly be found guilty, and answerably judged. It is also like to Heb. x. 29, and xii. 25. To shew that he himself as well as others, and others as well as himself, are all, without exception of any, liable to the judgment, he expresseth the first person and plural number, *we,* $\dot{\eta}\mu\epsilon\tilde{\iota}\varsigma$.

This shews that there are degrees both of sin and judgment; for, according to the heinousness of sin, will be the heaviness of judgment. 'Jerusalem was in all her ways corrupted more than Samaria or Sodom: therefore she did bear her own shame, for the sins which she committed more abominable than they,' Ezek. xvi. 47, 52. 'It shall be more tolerable for Tyre and Sidon than for Chorazin and Bethsaida, and for Sodom than for Capernaum, at the day of judgment,' Mat. xi. 22, 24.

Hereby is the wisdom of God manifested, in putting difference betwixt the kinds of sin; and his justice, in proportioning punishment according to the kinds of sin.

It will be therefore our wisdom, as to take heed of every transgression, so to take due notice of the aggravation of a transgression, to make us the more watchful and circumspect thereabout.

Sec. 19. *Of neglecting salvation.*

Neglecting, $\dot{\alpha}\mu\epsilon\lambda\dot{\eta}\sigma\alpha\nu\tau\epsilon\varsigma$, is the act under which the thing here taxed is expressed. *Neglect* may seem to intend a small degree of sin, especially as it is opposed to contempt, and when it is distinguished from diligent care; for we say of him that is not so diligent in his duty as he ought to be, that he is negligent.

In this extenuating sense, saith the apostle, οὐκ ἀμελήσω, 'I will not be negligent to put you in remembrance,' 2 Peter i. 12; I will let slip no opportunity. St Paul in this sense adviseth Timothy, μὴ ἀμέλει, not to 'neglect the gift that was in him,' 1 Tim. iv. 14.

Thus may the word be here pertinently used, and that in regard of the worth of salvation here mentioned; for in the least degree or in the meanest manner to disrespect so precious, so needful, so useful a thing as salvation, is a great point of folly, of ingratitude, yea, and of rebellion. And it sheweth, that they to whom this salvation is brought, ought not any way to disesteem it; they ought not to neglect it.

The word *neglect* may further, according to the notation of the Greek, imply a despising or despiting of a thing. For the simple verb μέλει, of which this is compounded, signifieth to have an especial care of a thing. It sets out that care which God hath of his children, for 'he careth for you,' αὐτῷ μέλει περὶ ὑμῶν, 1 Peter v. 7. What greater care can there be, than that which God taketh of his?

The compound with a privative particle, ἀμελεῖν, as the word in my text is, letteth out a disposition so far from tender care and great respect, as it implieth the clean contrary; namely, an utter rejecting (as where God saith of the Jews whom he cast off), κἀγὼ ἠμέλησα αὐτῶν, 'I regarded them not;' or I cared not for them, Heb. viii. 9; yea, and a plain despising of a thing, and a scorning of it; as where it is said of them that were invited to the wedding of the king's son, ἀμελήσαντες, 'they made light of it,' or they cared not for it. That this intended a despising of it, is evident by the effects that are noted to follow thereupon; which were, preferring their farm and merchandise before the king's son's marriage; the entreating of the king's servants that were sent to them despitefully, and slaying them,' Mat. xxii. 5, 6. Doth not the hog, that prefers garbage, offal, or any filthy refuse, before silver, gold, and pearl, contemn these precious things? Do not dogs, that fly in the faces of such as bring things of great worth unto them, despise them? This word then of *neglecting*, here used and applied by the apostle to so precious a thing as *salvation*, can intend no less than a despising thereof. This therefore is a great aggravation of their sin, who live under the gospel, and any way slight the same. And it nearly concerns us to whom this salvation is tendered, to take heed of neglecting the same.

Sec. 20. *Of the word of salvation.*

That precious thing which is here said to be neglected, is σωτηρία, salvation. Hereof see Chap. i. Sec. 159.

The eternal salvation of the soul is the salvation here aimed at. But by a metonymy, the gospel that revealeth that salvation is here meant.

As here, κατ' ἐξοχήν, by an excellency, it is called *salvation*; so more especially it is styled 'the gospel of salvation,' Eph. i. 13; the 'word of salvation,' Acts xiii. 26; the 'power of God unto salvation,' Rom. i. 16; 'The grace of God which bringeth salvation,' Titus ii. 11. The time of the gospel is also called 'The day of salvation,' 2 Cor. vi. 2. Ministers of the gospel are 'they which shew unto us the way of salvation,' Acts xvi. 17.

That under this word *salvation*, the gospel is here meant, is evident, by the opposition thereof to 'the word spoken by angels,' ver. 2. That word was before the time of the gospel, and it is comprised under this title, *law*. Now, here he preferreth the gospel before the law; therefore the gospel must needs be here meant.

Fitly may the gospel be styled salvation in sundry respects, as,

1. In opposition to the law, which was a 'ministration of condemnation,' 2 Cor. iii. 9. But this of salvation, Eph. i. 13.

2. In regard of the author of the gospel, Jesus Christ, who is *salvation* itself, Luke ii. 30.

3. In regard of the matter of the gospel, Acts xxviii. 28. Whatsoever is needful to salvation is contained in the gospel, and whatsoever is contained in the gospel maketh to salvation.

4. In regard of God's appointing the gospel to be the means of salvation: 'For it pleased God by preaching the gospel to save those that believe,' 1 Cor. i. 21.

5. In regard of the end of the gospel, which is to 'give knowledge of salvation,' Luke i. 77, 1 Peter i. 9.

6. In regard of the powerful effects of the gospel: It is 'the power of God to salvation,' Rom. i. 16.

Quest. If salvation be appropriated to the gospel, how were any of the Jews that lived before the time of the gospel saved?

Ans. They had the gospel, Heb. iv. 2, Gal. iii. 6. In this respect Christ is said to be 'slain from the foundation of the world,' Rev. xiii. 8; to be 'ever the same,' Heb. xiii. 8.

The first promise made to man, in the judgment denounced against the devil immediately after man's fall, Gen. iii. 15, contained the sum of the gospel. Abel's sacrifice, Gen. iv. 4, and Noah's, Gen. viii. 20, 21, and others, and the sundry types of the ceremonial law, and sundry prophecies and promises in the prophets, set out Christ, the substance of the gospel; but not so clearly, so fully, so powerfully as the ministry of the gospel.

In this respect, not simply, but comparatively, salvation is appropriated to the ministry of the gospel; and a main difference made betwixt it and the ministry of the law, 2 Cor. iii. 6, 7.

Oh how blind are they who trust to any other means of salvation than the gospel! Such blind beetles were Jews, who would be justified and saved by the law; and papists, by their works; and enthusiasts, by the inspiration of their own brains; and the vulgar sort, by their good meaning.

It will be our wisdom to give good entertainment to the gospel, to be well instructed therein, to believe in it, to subject ourselves thereto, and to be conformable to it in the whole man.

Our labour herein is not lost. Salvation is a sufficient recompence. I suppose there is none so desperate, but, like Balaam, he could wish to die the death of the righteous, and that his last end might be like his, Num. xxiii. 10. Let our care be to use the means, as well as to desire the end. To us is the word of this salvation sent, Acts xiii. 26. If we neglect the gospel, we put away salvation, and 'judge ourselves unworthy of eternal life,' Acts xiii. 46.

Sec. 21. *Of the great salvation of the gospel.*

The excellency of the aforesaid salvation is set out in this word, τηλικαύτης, 'so great.' The relative ἡλίκος, whence this is derived, is sometimes joined with a word of wonder, thus ; θαυμαστός ἡλίκος, *Mirus quantus*, how wondrous great. In like manner this word here, so wondrous great.

It is a relative, and withal a note of comparates ; yet hath it here no correlative nor reddition to shew how great it is.

I find in other places a reddition joined with it ; as where mention is made of a very great earthquake, it is thus expressed, τηλικοῦτος ὅιος, so mighty an earthquake ; such an one as was not since men were upon the earth, Rev. xvi. 18.

This manner of setting down the word without a co-relative wants not emphasis, for it implieth it to be wonderful great ; so great as cannot be expressed.

Where the apostle maketh mention of a very great danger, wherein he despaired even of life, he thus sets it out, ' God delivered us from so great a death,' 2 Cor. i. 10, so great, as one would have thought none could have been delivered from it. In like manner, this phrase here intimateth, that this salvation is so great, as never the like was brought unto men before, nor can a greater be expected hereafter.

Well may the salvation brought unto us by the gospel be styled, *so great*, in three especial respects :

1. In regard of the clear manifestation thereof. The types, prophecies, and promises under the law were very dark and obscure, in regard of the clear preaching of the gospel. Now salvation is so clearly revealed, as a clearer manifestation thereof is not to be expected in this world. The veil which was upon the heart of the Jews is taken away under the gospel ; and now we all with open face behold as in a glass the glory of the Lord, 2 Cor. iii. 15, 16, 18.

2. In regard of the large spreading forth of this gospel. Thus said the Lord to his Son of old concerning this point ; ' It is a light thing that thou shouldest be my servant, to raise up the tribes of Jacob, and to restore the preserved of Israel ; I will also give thee for a light to the Gentiles, that thou mayest be my salvation unto the ends of the earth,' Isa. xlix. 6.

3. In regard of the efficacy and the power of God. Prophets complained of the little fruit that they reaped of their labours, thus : ' I have laboured in vain, I have spent my strength for nought,' Isa. xlix. 4 ; ' Who hath believed our report ?' Isa. liii. 1 ; ' The word of the Lord was made a reproach unto me, and a derision daily,' Jer. xx. 8. But the apostles in most of their epistles give thanks for the efficacy of the gospel in those churches to whom it was preached ; as Rom. i. 8 ; 1 Cor. iv. 1, 4, 5 ; Philip. i. 3, 5 ; Col. i. 3, 4 ; 1 Thes. i. 2, 3 ; 2 Thes. i. 3 ; 1 Peter i. 3 ; 2 John 4.

This on the one side doth much amplify the blessing of the gospel ; and it ratifieth the promise which God of old thus made to his church, ' I will do better unto you than at the beginning,' Ezek. xxxvi. 11. For under the gospel, ' God hath provided a better thing for us,' Heb. xi. 40, namely, 'a better covenant,' Heb. viii. 6 ; 'a better testament,' Heb. vii. 22 ; ' better promises,' Heb. viii. 6 ; ' better sacrifices,' Heb. ix. 23 ; ' a better hope,' Heb. vii. 19.

So great are the things by the gospel revealed unto the church, as in former ages were not made known, Eph. iii. 5. 'Many prophets, and kings, and righteous men desired to see these things, but saw them not,' Mat. xiii. 17, Luke x. 24. After this salvation, not only the prophets have inquired, but also 'the angels desire to look into it,' 1 Peter i. 10, 12.

On the other side, this great salvation is a great aggravation of all neglect thereof. On this ground Christ aggravateth the Jews' contempt of the gospel in his time ; and plainly telleth them, that ' the men of Nineveh, and the queen of the south, shall rise up in judgment against them, because a greater than Jonas and a greater than Solomon was among them,' Mat. xii. 41, 42. ' This is the condemnation, that light is come into the world, and men loved darkness rather than light,' John iii. 19.

This nearly concerns us, who live in this last age of the world, wherein this great salvation hath broken through the thick cloud of antichristianism, and brightly shined forth to us ; and who live in that place of the world where able ministers and powerful preachers abound.

As God in this his goodness hath abounded to us, so should we abound in knowledge, in faith, in hope, in charity, in new obedience, and in all other gospel-graces. St Paul upon the apprehension of the abounding of God's grace towards him over and above others, maketh this inference, ' I laboured more abundantly than they all,' 1 Cor. xv. 10. Greater blessings require greater thankfulness. God had abounded to Judah in blessings more than to Israel ; thereupon a prophet maketh this inference, ' Though thou Israel play the harlot, yet let not Judah offend,' Hosea iv. 15.

Sec. 22. *Of Christ the preacher of the gospel.*

The excellency of the fore-mentioned salvation is set out by the first publisher thereof, who is here styled the Lord, διὰ τοῦ Κυρίου. Of this title Lord, given to Christ, see Chap. i. ver 10, Sec. 128. It is here used to set out the dignity of the author of the gospel; thereby to commend it the more unto us.

Obj. God was the author of the word which angels spake unto his people, and in that respect that word was divine. Can there be any greater authority of a word than to be divine?

Ans. Though there be no greater authority than a divine authority, yet there may be sundry differences between the things that are divine. For,

1. Of divine truths there may be degrees: some may be of greater moment, or of greater consequence than others. To pay tithes under the law was a divine injunction; but 'judgment, mercy, and faith,' were 'weightier matters of the law,' Mat. xxiii. 23.

2. There were different kinds of revealing divers truths, some more obscurely, some more clearly, 2 Cor. iv. 14, 18.

3. Some divine truths were more strongly confirmed than others. Priests under the law were 'made without an oath, but Christ with an oath;' so as Christ's priesthood was more strongly confirmed, Heb. vii. 20, 21.

4. More excellent ministers may be used in dispensing some divine truths than in others. 'Behold a greater than Jonas is here,' 'Behold a greater than Solomon is here,' saith Christ of his own ministry, Mat. xii. 41, 42.

In all these doth the latter word, here spoken of, excel the former.

1. In the very *matter* thereof. Such mysteries are revealed by the gospel, as 'in other ages were not made known,' Eph. iii. 5. 'The law made nothing perfect, but the bringing in of a better hope did,' Eph. vii. 19. In this respect the gospel is here styled *salvation*, rather than the law.

2. In the *manner* of revealing. The gospel is far more clear and effectual, 2 Cor. iii. 18. See Secs. 20, 21.

3. In the *ratification*. The gospel is much more firm than the law. See Sec. 36.

4. In the *minister*. None comparable to the Son of God, the first preacher of the gospel. See Chap. i. Sec. 14.

If Christ the Lord vouchsafed to be a minister of the gospel, who shall scorn this function? The pope, cardinals, sundry bishops, and others that pretend to be Christ's vicars, are far from performing that which Christ did in this kind; and many that lay claim to Peter's keys, are far from observing the advice which he, for the right use of them, thus gave: 'Feed the flock of God which is among you, taking the oversight thereof, not by constraint, but willingly; not for filthy lucre, but of a ready mind; neither as being lords over God's heritage, but being ensamples to the flock,' 1 Peter v. 2, 3. Many took more lordship upon them over God's flock, than Christ the true Lord did while he was on earth; yet it was he that brought this great salvation.

Of Christ's being a prophet, see verse 12, Sec. 112. Of his being a minister, see Chap. viii., Sec. 3.

Sec. 23. *Of preaching the gospel.*

The relation of the foresaid salvation is expressed in this word λαλεῖσθαι, *spoken:* namely, by voice or word of mouth. 'The mouth speaketh,' saith Christ, τὸ στόμα λαλεῖ, Mat. xii. 34. And of God it is said, ἐλάλησε διὰ στόματος; 'He spake by the mouth of his holy prophets,' Luke i. 70. So men are said to speak with the tongue, γλώσσαις λαλῶ, 1 Cor. xiii. 1. And words are said to be spoken, τὰ ῥήματα τοῦ Θεοῦ λαλεῖ, John iii. 34, and xiv. 10.

The correlative to *speaking* is *hearing;* 'We do *hear* them *speak*,' Acts ii. 11. For by hearing that which is spoken by one is best understood by another; and by a right understanding of the truth and good of that which is spoken, it comes to be believed. Hence is it that God hath appointed speaking of his word to be the ordinary means of salvation, 1 Cor. i. 21.

Speaking the word is oft put for preaching it, and so translated, as Acts. viii. 25, 'When they had preached the word of God,' λαλήσαντες. And Acts xiii. 42, the Gentiles 'besought that these words might be preached,' λαληθῆναι.

Thus, by our former English and others, it is translated in this text 'which at the first began to be preached,' &c. Without all question, so much is here intended by the apostle. For he must needs mean such a speaking of the word as might make it powerful to that great salvation which he mentioned before. For that purpose, no speaking is comparable to preaching.

Preaching is a clear revelation of the mystery of salvation by a lawful minister.

No man can attain salvation except he know the way thereto. 'People are destroyed for lack of knowledge,' Hosea iv. 6. But what good doth any reap by knowledge, unless he believe what he knoweth? 'The word preached did not profit them, not being mixed with faith in them that heard it,' Heb. iv. 2. 'But how shall any believe in him of whom they have not heard? and how shall they hear without a preacher? and how shall they preach except they be sent?' Rom. x. 14, 15.

He who is sent of God, that is, set apart, according to the rule of God's word, to be a minister of the gospel, doth himself understand the mysteries thereof, and is enabled to make them known to others; he also standeth in God's room, and in God's name makes offer of salvation, 2 Cor. v. 20. This moves men to believe and to be saved. This is the ordinary way appointed of God for attaining salvation. This course Christ, who was sent of God, took; 'He went throughout every city and village preaching, and shewing the glad tidings of the kingdom of God,' Luke viii. 1. He commanded those whom he sent so to do, Luke ix. 2, Mark xvi. 15.

So did they whom he immediately sent, Acts v. 42; so have done others after them; and so will do all true and faithful ministers of Christ to the world's end.

Preaching being a means sanctified of God unto salvation, how diligent and faithful ought ministers of the gospel to be in preaching the same! Thereby they may save themselves and them that hear them, 1 Tim. iv. 16. But idol and idle ministers, such as cannot or care not to preach the word, do much hinder men from this great salvation. How beautiful ought the feet of them to be that preach the gospel of peace, and bring glad tidings of good things! Rom. x. 15. If this great salvation, the effect of preaching, were duly weighed, ministers would be diligent in preaching, and people patient in hearing the same. For this is a strong motive to enforce the one and the other. Both preaching and hearing have need to be pressed upon men's consciences.

See more of preaching God's word, Chap. xiii. Sec. 97.

Sec. 24. *Of Christ's first publishing the gospel.*

The first that clearly and fully preached the gospel of salvation, was the Lord Christ. It took beginning to be spoken by him; according to the Greek phrase, ἥτις ἀρχὴν λαβοῦσα λαλεῖσθαι. Till he came and preached, people sat in darkness, and in the shadow and region of death; but when he began to preach, they saw great light, Mat. iv. 16.

It cannot be denied but that the substance of the gospel, and therein salvation, was preached from the beginning of the world (as hath been shewed before, Secs. 20, 21), but so dark was that kind of light, as, like the light of the moon when the sun shineth, is accounted no light. The day taketh his beginning from the rising of the sun, and the light that cometh from thence. So salvation, here spoken of, taketh beginning from Christ's preaching the gospel.

Besides, Christ is the substance and truth of all the shadows, figures, types, prophecies, and promises of that salvation which was set out by them. When Christ the Lord came, and declared himself to be the substance and truth of the law, he might well be accounted the first publisher of salvation.

Obj. It is said of the ministry of John the Baptist, 'The beginning of the gospel of Jesus Christ,' Mark i. 1.

Ans. John's ministry, in reference to the ministry of the law and the prophets, may be said comparatively to be 'the beginning of the gospel;' because it was in the very time wherein Christ, the substance of the gospel, was exhibited. John was Christ's messenger, sent before his face, to prepare the way before him, Mark i. 2. Thus it is said, that all the prophets and the law prophesied until John, Mat. xi. 13.

In John's time was Christ actually exhibited. He was baptized by John, Mat. iii. 13, &c. And John declared him, pointing him out, as it were, with the finger, saying, 'Behold the Lamb of God,' John i. 29. John also heard of the works of Christ, Mat. xi. 2. In this respect it is said, that, 'Among them that are born of women, there hath not risen a greater than John the Baptist,' Mat. xi. 11.

John's ministry was a middle ministry between the law and the gospel, between the prophets and Christ. He took part of both kinds. He preached that the kingdom of heaven was at hand, Mat. iii. 2. But Christ, that 'the kingdom of God is come unto you,' Mat. xii. 22.

Thus in regard of the fulness of the gospel, and of a distinct and clear manifestation of all things that appertained to this great salvation, Christ most truly and properly is said to be the first that preached it.

Behold here the benefit of Christ's being sent into the world. Then first came that true, full, and bright light of the world: 'He that followeth this light, shall not walk in darkness, but shall have the light of life,' John viii. 12. Fitly to the point in hand may I apply that which is said, John i. 18, 'No man hath seen God at any time: the only begotten Son, which is in the bosom of the Father, he hath revealed him.'

Sec. 25. *Of confirming the word.*

Though Christ's own publishing of the gospel were sufficient to make it 'worthy of all acception,' yet is it said to be 'confirmed,' ἐβεβαιώθη. That is confirmed which is further proved or fulfilled, or made more sure and certain. Thus Christ is said to confirm the word of his apostles with signs, βεβαιοῦντος, Mark xvi. 20; and God, by sending his Son, to 'confirm the promises made to the fathers,' βεβαιῶσαι, Rom. xv. 8. That also which is kept from failing or from being altered, is said to be confirmed. So God doth confirm his unto the end, βεβαιώσει, 1 Cor. i. 8; and establish them, βεβαιῶν, 1 Cor. i. 21; and we are called upon to be established with grace, βεβαιοῦσθαι, Heb. xiii. 3.

But that which Christ spake needeth not in any such respect to be confirmed. He is a 'faithful and true witness,' Rev. iii. 14. He is 'the way, the truth, and the life,' John xiv. 6; that only true way that leadeth unto life. So as there was no fear of any uncertainty, or of any failing in his word.

Christ's word therefore was confirmed for these and other like reasons.

1. Because he was not at all times, in all places, present with his church, to urge and press his word upon them. For this end he sent forth in his lifetime disciples to preach, Luke ix. 2 and x. 1. And after his ascension he gave apostles and others, 'for the perfecting of the saints,' Eph. iv. 11, 12.

2. Because of our weakness, Christ confirmed his word, to support us, 'that we might have strong consolations.' For this end God confirmed his promise by an oath, Heb. vi. 17, 18.

3. Because of the commendable custom of men,

who use to confirm their own words by the consent and testimony of others. Thus St Paul, in his incriptions of his epistles, joins with himself Sosthenes, 1 Cor. i. 1; Timothy, 2 Cor. i. 1; Silvanus and Timothy, 1 Thes. i. 1; Timothy with the bishops and deacons, Philip. i. 1; all the brethren which were with him, Gal. i. 2.

4. Because by God's law and man's, 'at the mouth of two or three witnesses, every word shall be established,' Deut. xix. 15.

Thus Christ's word was confirmed,

1. In that there were many witnesses of the same truth wherein they all agreed, Luke xxiv. 48, Acts ii. 32.

2. In that such as despised him in his lifetime, after his resurrection and ascension were wrought upon, Acts ii. 37.

3. In that by reason of the power of the Spirit in them, they who preached the gospel of Christ after him were 'received as an angel of God, even as Christ Jesus,' Gal. iv. 14.

4. In that many who never heard Christ themselves, believed that word that Christ had preached, but was made known to them by others, 1 Peter i. 8.

Thus it appears that this confirming of Christ's word addeth nothing to the authority thereof. The church may confirm the sacred Scriptures to be the word of God, yet confer nothing to their authority. Divine mysteries may be confirmed by human testimonies, yet no authority brought thereby to those mysteries.

God being pleased thus to confirm the gospel to us, it ought to be a stedfast word to us (see Sec. 11); we ought with all stedfastness of faith to receive it, and to continue stedfastly therein, as the Christians of the primitive church did in the apostles' doctrine, Acts ii. 42.

Sec. 26. *Of apostles.*

They by whom Christ's word was confirmed, were they that heard him, ὑπὸ τῶν ἀκουσάντων. Hereby are meant such as Christ chose to be his disciples, who continually followed him, who heard his sermons and saw his works; whom he made apostles, Luke vi. 13.

An apostle, ἀπόστολος, according to the notation of the Greek word,[1] signifieth one that is sent from another. Thus an apostle saith, 'Christ sent me,' ἀπέστειλε, 'to preach the gospel,' 1 Cor. i. 17.

The Greek word is used for a messenger, and so translated, Philip. ii. 25.

Most frequently in the New Testament an apostle is put for such an one as was sent and deputed to a peculiar function; which was an extraordinary function, endowed with many privileges.

Apostles therefore were distinguished from other ministers, both by the manner of calling them, and also by the privileges confirmed[1] on them.

Their calling was immediate from Christ himself. That may be applied to all the apostles which St Paul saith of his own particular calling: 'An apostle, not of men, neither by man, but by Jesus Christ,' Gal. i. 1.

Their special privileges were these:

1. To plant churches, and to lay the foundation. In this respect saith the apostle, 'I have laid the foundation,' 1 Cor. iii. 10.

2. To be immediately inspired, John xiv. 26, Gal. i. 12.

3. To be infallibly assisted by the Holy Ghost, John xvi. 13 and xxi. 24.

4. To be limited to no place, but sent out into the whole world, Mat. xxviii. 19.

5. To have a power to give the Holy Ghost, Acts viii. 17.

6. To confirm their doctrines by miracles, Mat. x. 1, Acts ii. 43 and v. 12.

7. To understand and speak all manner of tongues, Acts ii. 11.

8. To execute visible judgments on notorious sinners, Acts v. 5 and xiii. 11.

These privileges evidently demonstrate that the apostles were extraordinary ministers, of extraordinary abilities, whereby they were the better fitted to their extraordinary work.

This gives evidence of the wisdom of Christ in ordering the affairs of his church, and of his care thereabouts, in that he enableth, provideth, and prepareth for his church such ministers as may be fittest for the present estate and condition thereof. It is an especial part of wisdom to take due notice of the present particular charge which is under one, and answerably to provide for it. It is noted as a point of prudence in Saul, that 'when he saw any strong man, or any valiant man, he took him unto him,' 1 Sam. xiv. 52, namely, to be a leader, and to have a command in his army. Christ in his wisdom doth not only find such, but also he makes such as the present state and need of his church requireth.

Sec. 27. *Of confirming the gospel to them that then lived.*

About confirming the gospel, this clause is added, εἰς ἡμᾶς, 'to us.' Hereby the penman of this epistle includes himself in the number of those to whom the gospel is here said to be confirmed, as he did before in the number of those whom he exhorted to give diligent heed to the gospel, and to beware that they let not slip what they had heard; and whom he told, that they should not escape if they neglected so great salvation.

From this expression, 'confirmed to us by them that heard him,' we may well infer that this epistle was written in the apostle's days; yea, and by one of the apostles.

---

[1] στιλλειν, *mittere*, ἀποστιλλειν, *cum mandatis mittere. Mittere legatum.* Ἀπόστολος, *legatus, qui mittitur cum mandatis.*

[1] Qu. 'conferred'?—Ed.

Of the author of this epistle, see the title, Sec. 4.

But, on the contrary, it is by many[1] hence inferred that neither Paul nor any other of the apostles was the author thereof, because he saith that it was confirmed to them by the apostles. Whence they gather, that the penman hereof received not the gospel from Christ, which Paul did, Gal. i. 12; and all the other apostles, Mat. xxviii. 20, Acts i. 3.

Many answers may be given to this objection.

1. The two Greek pronouns of the first and second persons plural, ἡμεῖς, ὑμεῖς, have so small a difference, and that in one only letter, as one may soon be put for the other. Judicious Beza[2] saith that he hath oft noted this mistake. If, therefore, the second person plural were here put, thus, 'was confirmed *to you*,' εἰς ὑμᾶς, that scruple is clean taken away.

2. This phrase, *unto us*, may be referred to the time as well as to the persons; as if it had been thus translated, *until us*, or *to our days*, ἕως εἰς ἡμᾶς; implying that the gospel, from Christ's own preaching thereof, was confirmed by the apostles to their very days.

3. The apostle may use the first person, as he was a member of that mystical body, whereof they, to whom he wrote, were also members, and by virtue of that communion, included himself; though it did not in particular concern himself. Thus he puts himself in the number of those who shall be living at Christ's last coming, where he saith, 'we shall not all sleep,' 1 Cor. xv. 51, yet he himself slept many hundred years ago. So 1 Thess. iv. 17.

4. The gospel might be confirmed to Paul by other apostles, though it was immediately revealed unto him by Jesus Christ. Not that that confirmation wrought in him any greater assurance of the truth thereof, but that it established the church more therein, by the mutual consent of other apostles with him; to this purpose, saith the apostle, 'I communicated unto them the gospel, &c., lest by any means I should run, or had run in vain,' Gal. ii. 2.

5. The confirmation here intended may have reference to the miracles which were wrought by the apostles. Thus might the gospel be confirmed, not only to other believers, but also to the apostles themselves; even by the miracles which they themselves and others also did. To this purpose tends the prayer of the apostles, Acts iv. 29, 30.

6. The words do not necessarily imply that the penman of this epistle, or any other person, was confirmed, but rather that the gospel itself was confirmed. Hereof see Sec. 25.

Sec. 28. *Of God working miracles.*

The apostle yet further proceeds in setting down another confirmation of the gospel. It was first preached by Christ, then confirmed by the apostles, and now again by God himself, τοῦ Θεοῦ; namely, by

[1] Cajetan, Calvin, Hosman. [2] Beza Annotat. major. in loc.

such divine works as could not be performed, but by a divine power, the very power of God. For God hath restrained the power of all creatures within a compass. They cannot do anything above or beyond the course of nature, much less against it. This prerogative the Lord of nature hath reserved to himself; 'that men may see and know and consider, and understand together that the hand of the Lord hath done this,' Isa. xli. 20. 'The things which are impossible with men, are possible with God,' Luke xviii. 27. 'For with God all things are possible, Mark x. 27. 'Nothing shall be impossible with him,' Luke i. 37.

As God can and doth daily work by means, so, when it pleaseth him, he can work without means, by extraordinary means, and by contrary means.

1. Without means, God made the world, Gen. i. 3, Ps. xxxiii. 9. Moses remained alive forty days and forty nights, and neither ate bread nor drank water, Deut. ix. 9. So Elijah, 1 Kings xix. 8. And Christ, Mat. iv. 2.

2. The extraordinary means which God hath used have been manifold; as,

(1.) In the very thing itself or kind of means. Manna, wherewith the Lord fed the Israelites forty years together, was a grain that fell from heaven, Exod. xvi. 4, &c. The like was never heard of before, or since.

(2.) In the quantity of the means. The meal and oil wherewith the prophet Elijah and the widow of Zarephath and her household were nourished for three years together, was in the kind of it ordinary, 1 Kings xvii. 12, &c.; but that so little meal as could make but one little cake, and so little oil as was but sufficient for that cake, should feed so many, so long, was extraordinary and miraculous. The like may be said of the five loaves and two fishes wherewith Christ fed five thousand men, besides women and children, Mat. xiv. 17, &c.

(3.) In the quality of the means. That Daniel and his three companions, should for three years, feed on pulse only, and drink water only, and yet their countenances appear fairer and fatter than they who did eat of the choicest meat and drink that could be provided for that end, was also miraculous, and appeared to be an especial work of God, Daniel i. 5, &c.

(4.) In the manner of providing means. That ravens should be Elijah's caterers, constantly to provide him bread and flesh in the morning, and bread and flesh in the evening, was extraordinary, 1 Kings xvii. 6. So also that water, upon striking of a rock with Moses his rod, should flow forth and run like a river, Exod. xvii. 6, Ps. cv. 41.

3. That the three servants of God should be preserved safe in the midst of an hot fiery furnace, was against means, or by contrary means; for fire is an ordinary means to consume things cast thereinto, Daniel iii. 27. The like may be said of Daniel's preservation in the den of lions, Daniel vi. 22.

All these, and other like works, that are beyond the course of nature, are done by God himself. Of them all it may be said, 'This is the finger of God,' Exod. viii. 19.

Sec. 29. *Of creatures' disability about miracles.*
Sundry objections are made against the foresaid truth, but they may all easily and readily be answered.

Obj. 1. Christ, in the days of his flesh, wrought miracles.

Ans. Christ, in the lowest degree of his humiliation, retained his divine dignity, and ever remained to be true God, 'one with the Father,' John x. 30. 'He being in the form of God, thought it not robbery to be equal with God, but made himself of no reputation,' Philip. ii. 6, 7. 'What thing soever the Father doth, these also doth the Son likewise,' John v. 19. Christ, by his miracles, proved himself to be true God, Mat. ix. 6. This, therefore, confirmeth the point, that Christ the true God wrought miracles.

Obj. 2. Prophets, apostles, and others, who were mere men, wrought miracles, as Moses, Exod. iv. 8; Elijah, 1 Kings xvii. 21, 22; Elisha, 2 Kings iv. 25; all the apostles, Mat. x. 1.

Ans. God wrought those miracles by them. They were but God's ministers and instruments therein. Peter acknowledges as much, Acts iii. 12, 16. Thereupon, Peter, when he miraculously cured Æneas, thus saith unto him, 'Æneas, Jesus Christ maketh thee whole,' Acts ix. 34.

Obj. 3. Wicked men have wrought miracles, as Judas, Mat. x. 1, 4; and such as followed not Christ, Luke ix. 49; and they of whom Christ saith, 'Depart from me, ye that work iniquity,' Mat. vii. 22, 23.

Ans. God may and oft doth use wicked men to confirm his truth by miracles, as well as to preach it.

Obj. 4. Miracles may be wrought against the truth; for in the law it is said, 'If there arise among you a prophet, or a dreamer of dreams, and giveth thee a sign or a wonder; and the sign or the wonder come to pass, whereof he spake unto thee, saying, Let us go after other gods; thou shalt not hearken,' Deut. xiii. 1–3.

Ans. 1. In the text there is only a supposition made, *if there be;* which doth not necessarily imply that such a thing may be.

2. There may be *signs* and *wonders* done, which are not true *miracles.*

3. Their foretelling of a thing may be upon mere conjecture, as fortune-tellers guess at things to come. But herein is nothing extraordinary.

4. God may work by such evil instruments, in such an evil cause, to try whether his people will be drawn by any means from a known truth. This may seem to be implied in these words, 'For the Lord your God proveth you, to know whether you love the Lord your God, with all your heart, and with all your soul,' Deut. xiii. 3.

Obj. 5. The sorcerers in Egypt wrought miracles. For it is said that 'they also did in like manner with their enchantments,' Exod. vii. 11, 12, 22, and viii. 7; they did as Moses had done before; they turned the rods into serpents, and water into blood; and they brought abundance of frogs.

Ans. In outward appearance, there was some likeness betwixt the things which Moses did, and which the sorcerers did; but in the truth and substance of the things, there was a very great difference.

The things which Moses did were true and proper miracles; but the things which the sorcerers did, they did only appear unto man's eye to be so;[1] for the devil can present to the eye of man shows and shapes of such things as indeed are not. But suppose that the things which the sorcerers pretended were real; that there were true serpents, true blood, true frogs; the devil might secretly bring from other places such things, and present them before Pharaoh, and before them that were present with him: and this not above, much less against, the course of nature.

Obj. 6. A woman that had a familiar spirit raised Samuel after he was dead, 1 Sam. xxviii. 11, 12.

Ans. That which appeared to be like unto Samuel, was not Samuel himself, but the devil presented unto Saul a shape like unto Samuel; in which the devil himself spake unto Saul. Though he pretended to foretell things future, yet he did it but by guess. He saw the Philistines very well prepared, and he observed that God had utterly forsaken Saul; and thereupon took the boldness to foretell, that the Lord would deliver Israel into the hand of the Philistines, and that Saul and his sons should be with Samuel, who was then dead; that is, they should be dead also, 1 Sam. xxviii. 19.

Obj. 7. St Paul saith, that the coming of antichrist is 'after the working of Satan, with all power and signs,' 2 Thes. ii. 9.

Ans. In the next clause it is added, 'and lying wonders.' This last clause shews that the signs before mentioned were but counterfeit, not true miracles.

Papists, who are the antichristians, do exceed above all others in counterfeiting miracles, which are but plain deceits and illusions.

It remains, notwithstanding all that hath been or can be objected, that God alone doth true miracles. 'Whatsoever the Lord pleased, that did he in heaven, and in the earth, in the seas and all deep places,' Ps. cxxxv. 6, and so can he still do.

While we have God for our God, we need not fear, nor faint by reason of any danger or want for means; but when we know not what we do, to 'lift up our eyes upon him,' 2 Chron. xx. 12, and in faith to say,

[1] Magorum serpentes, qui per Moysis serpentem devorantur, imaginarii fuerunt.—*Aug. de Mirab. S. Scrip.* lib. i. cap. xvii.

'God will provide,' Gen. xxii. 8. We ought on this ground to be of the mind of those three faithful servants of God, who by a king were threatened with a burning fiery furnace, and say, 'Our God whom we serve is able to deliver us from the burning fiery furnace, and he will deliver us.' Ps. xlvi. is worthy our serious and frequent meditation for this purpose. It is by many styled *Luther's Psalm*; because Luther oft said it and sung it, especially in the time of any trouble. So trust to the power of God in all straits, as ye subject to his will, and prescribe no means to him; but refer the manner of working to his wisdom. For he hath said, 'I will never leave thee nor forsake thee,' Heb. xiii. 5.

Sec. 30. *Of God's bearing witness to his word by his works.*

Of those works, which could not be done but by God himself, it is said, that God 'did bear witness' thereby. For such works do evidently demonstrate that such a word is divine, God's word sent from God himself. The greater the works are, the more excellent and more sure is the word that is ratified thereby.

To bear witness to a thing is to confirm the truth of it.

The word which the apostle here useth is a double compound, συνεπιμαρτυροῦντος. The simple verb, μαρτυρεῖν, signifieth to witness a thing, John i. 7. The compound, ἐπιμαρτυρεῖν, to add testimony to testimony; or to add a testimony to some other confirmation, as 1 Peter i. 12. The double compound, συνεπιμαρτυρεῖν, to give a joint testimony; or to give witness together with one another. So much signifies another like Greek compound, συμμαρτυρεῖν, used by the apostle, Rom. viii. 16, and translated 'bear witness with.'

Thus God by his works did witness with his Son, and with his apostles, to that gospel which they preached. God's works give a most clear and sure evidence to that for which they are wrought or produced. When the people saw how God had led them through the depths, and how the waters had covered their enemies, 'then they believed his words,' Ps. cvi. 9–12. When others saw the fire that upon Elijah's prayer fell from heaven, they fell on their faces, and said, 'The Lord he is God, the Lord he is God,' 1 Kings xviii. 39. When the widow of Zarephath saw her son that was dead restored to life by Elijah, she said, 'Now by this I know that thou art a man of God, and that the word of the Lord in thy mouth is truth,' 1 Kings xvii. 24. On such a ground said Nicodemus to Christ, 'We know that thou art a teacher come from God; for no man can do these miracles that thou doest, except God be with him,' John iii. 2. When the Jews had seen the miracle that Jesus did, they said, 'This is of a truth that prophet that should come into the world,' John vi. 14. On this ground doth Christ oft produce his works to witness who and what he was: 'The works which the Father hath given me to finish, the same works that I do, bear witness of me that the Father hath sent me,' saith Christ, John v. 36. And again, 'The works that I do in my Father's name, they bear witness of me;' thereupon he addeth, 'Though ye believe not me, believe the works,' John x. 25, 38.

This witness that God hath given, gives good evidence of his special care over his church, in that he laboureth so much to establish her in the word of salvation. For he thought it not enough to have the gospel once published, though it were by his Son; or to have it further confirmed by other witnesses, and those many; but he further addeth other witnesses, even his own divine works; which may well be accounted witnesses, for they have a kind of voice; according to that which the Lord himself saith, 'It shall come to pass, if they will not believe thee, neither hearken to the voice of the first sign, that they will believe the voice of the latter sign.'

Papists, upon this kind of witness by miracles, do exceedingly insult against protestants, and that in two especial respects.

1. In regard of a pretence of many miracles wrought for confirmation of their church and their doctrines.
2. In regard of the want of miracles among protestants; whence they infer, that we have neither true church nor true ministry.

To the first ground of their insultation, I answer, that they prove themselves thereby, if at least the kind of their miracles be thoroughly examined, to be plain antichristians. For whosoever shall judiciously read their legends and authors,[1] that have written of their miracles, shall find them so ridiculous, as they plainly appear to be lying wonders; and the apostle saith, that the coming of antichrist is after such a manner, 2 Thes. ii. 9.

As for the other part of their insultation, I answer, that we have all the miracles that Christ and his apostles did to confirm our church, our ministry, and doctrine. For our church is built upon Christ the chief corner-stone, and upon that foundation which his apostles laid. And our ministry is according to the order which Christ and his apostles have ascribed[2] unto us; and our doctrine is the same which Christ and his apostles preached. What need we, then, any other confirmation than that which is here set down by our apostle? Indeed, if we joined new articles of faith, or preached another gospel than they did, or had another way of ordaining ministers than they have warranted unto us, miracles would be necessary for confirming such new things.

Sec. 31. *Of signs, wonders, and miracles.*

The means whereby God did bear witness to the gospel, are set out in four words: *signs, wonders,*

---

[1] Brist. in Motiv. Coster. Enchir. cap. ii. Boz. de Sign. cap. i.   [2] Qu. 'prescribed'?—ED.

miracles, gifts. The three former set out the same things.

1. *Signs*, according to the notation of the word, imply such external visible things, as signify and declare some memorable matter which otherwise could not be so well discerned, nor would be believed. 'We would see a sign from thee,' say the pharisees to Christ, Mat. xii. 38. And they desired him that he would 'shew them a sign,' Mat. xvi. 1.

These two words, *see, shew*, imply that a sign is of some external visible thing that may be shewed and seen. And extraordinary it must be, because it useth to be for confirmation of some secret and divine matter. Thus the pharisees would have a sign 'from heaven,' Mat. xvi. 1, which must needs be extraordinary. Thereupon *signs* and *wonders* are oft joined together, as John iv. 48, Acts ii. 43, and iv. 30, and vii. 36. Our last translators do oft translate this Greek word, which properly signifieth *signs*, they translate it *miracles*, as Luke xxiii. 8, John ii. 11 and John iii. 2.

2. The Greek word translated *wonders*, is used by all sorts of authors for some strange thing, that may seem to foretell some other thing to come. 'I will shew wonders in heaven,' saith the Lord, Acts ii. 19. Those strange things which by the ministry of Moses were done in Egypt, in the Red Sea, and in the wilderness, are set out under this word *wonders*, Acts vii. 36. Our English doth fitly translate the Greek word *wonders*. By reason of the effect, they cause wonder; and by reason of the strangeness of them, they are wonderful, Mat. xv. 31; Mark vi. 51; Acts iii. 10. Our English word *miracle*, according to the notation of the Latin word whence it is taken, signifieth a matter of wonder.

3. The Greek word here translated *miracles*, properly signifieth *powers*. It is derived from a verb that signifieth *to be able*. This word in the singular number is put for a man's ability, Mat. xxv. 15, for his strength, 2 Cor. i. 8; and also for strength in the sun, Rev. i. 16; and in sin, 1 Cor. xv. 56. It is also put for virtue in one, Mark v. 30; and for the power of man, 1 Cor. iv. 19; of a prophet, Luke i. 17; of the spirit, Eph. iii. 16; of Christ, 2 Cor. xii. 9; and of God, Mat. xxii. 29. In the plural number it is put for angels, Rom. viii. 38, 1 Peter iii. 22, which excel in strength, Ps. ciii. 20; and for the firm and stable things in heaven, Mat. xxiv. 29; and for extraordinary works. Hereupon they are styled in our English mighty deeds, 2 Cor. xii. 12; mighty works, Mat. xi. 20–23; wonderful works, Mat. vii. 21; and frequently, as here in this text, miracles, Acts ii. 22, and xix. 11, 1 Cor. xii. 10, 28, 29. For miracles (as hath been shewed, Sec. 28) cannot be wrought but by an extraordinary power, even the power of God himself. Fitly therefore is this word *powers* used to set out miracles; and fitly is it here, and in other places, translated *miracles*.

Sec. 32. *Of the distinction betwixt signs, wonders, miracles.*

Some distinguish these three words into three sorts of miracles, each exceeding others in greatness or degrees; as

1. *Signs*, the least kind of miracles, as healing diseases.

2. *Wonders*, a greater kind, as opening the eyes of the blind, ears of the deaf, giving speech to the dumb, and other like, which cause wonder.

3. *Powers*, or miracles, the greatest kind of them; as giving sight to the born blind, raising the dead, even one four days dead, and dispossessing the devil.

This distinction is too curious. For every true miracle requires a divine and almighty power; and to the Lord it is as easy to give sight to him that was born blind, as to restore it to him that had it before: 'There is no restraint to the Lord to save by many or by few,' 1 Sam. xiv. 6.

Besides, the penmen of the New Testament do promiscuously use these words for the same things. Sometime all sorts of miracles are comprised under *signs*, John xx. 30; sometimes under *powers*, and translated *mighty works*, Mat. xi. 20; sometimes under *signs and wonders*, as Acts ii. 43; and sometimes under all the three words that are here mentioned, as Acts ii. 22, 2 Cor. xii. 12.

I suppose that all these three words may have reference to the same mighty works.

This variety of words setteth out the diverse properties of the same things.

Signs shew that they must be external and visible, that they may the better signify and manifest some other thing, not so visible.

Wonders shew that by reason of the strangeness of them, being above or against the course of nature, they cause wonder.

Powers (here translated *miracles*) shew that they are done by an extraordinary and almighty power.

Thus the same extraordinary things were in the Old Testament set out by divers words, *dreams, visions, revelations*. Dreams, because men in their sleep dream of them. Visions, because some visible objects were represented to them. Revelations, because God thereby revealed some unknown matter to come. Thus 'God, that revealeth secrets, made known to Nebuchadnezzar what should be in the latter days in a dream by vision,' Dan. ii. 22. Thus are divers names given to angels, which do set out distinct properties in the same angels, rather than several persons, as hath been shewed, Chap. i. Sec. 85.

Sec. 33. *Of a miracle.*

A miracle, according to the notation of the Latin word *miraculum*, from whence this English word is taken, signifieth such a thing as causeth wonder, or is in itself wonderful. In the common use of it, it signifieth a wonder in the highest degree, which ariseth from something that is supernatural.

From the fore-mentioned three words, and the end of setting them down here, this description of a miracle may be raised.

A miracle is a visible, wonderful work, done by the almighty power of God, above, or against the course of nature, to confirm some divine truth.

1. A miracle is a work or a true act, not a mere show or appearance of that which is not. Herein it differs from such an appearance as was represented to Saul, 1 Sam. xxviii. 12 : and from all juggling delusions; such as the sorcerers of Egypt used, Exod. vii. 11, 12, and viii. 7.

2. It is a visible work, such an one as men may see, and thereupon be moved therewith, as the Israelites were, 1 Kings xviii. 39. The pretence of transubstantiation, wherein no visible alteration of the creature is to be seen, is against the nature of a miracle, which is a sign.

3. It is above the course of nature, or against it. Herein lieth the very form of a miracle; whereby it is distinguished from other wonders, which may be extraordinary, though not simply supernatural; such as the second beast did, Rev. xiii. 13.

4. It is done by the almighty power of God. No man, no angel, whether good or evil, can alter the course which the Creator hath set to his creature. That power God hath reserved to himself. Pretended miracles wrought by the power of the devil, are but pretended.

5. The proper end of a true miracle is to confirm a divine truth; this was proved before, Sec. 30. All the miracles boasted of by papists, for proof of any of their heretical and idolatrous positions, or practices, are counterfeit.

Sec. 34. *Of the diversity of miracles.*

The miracles whereby the gospel was confirmed are here said to be *divers*, ποικίλαις. This may be referred to the multitude of them. For though very many of them be registered in the New Testament, yet it is said that Christ did many other signs, John xxi. 30.

To the multitude of Christ's miracles may this also be applied, 'There are many other things which Jesus did, the which, if they should be written every one, I suppose that even the world itself could not contain the books that should be written,' John xx. 25.

But this word *divers* hath reference most properly to the different kind of miracles; as, curing diseases, restoring senses and limbs, raising the dead, dispossessing devils, &c.

This word is attributed to such things as are many in their number, and various in their kinds: as to pleasures, Titus iii. 3; to lusts, 2 Tim. iii. 6; to doctrines, Heb. xiii. 9; to temptations, James i. 2 ; yea, and to such diseases as Christ cured, Mat. iv. 24. All these are said to be divers; and they are every way so diverse, as neither the number nor the several kinds of them can be reckoned up.

Concerning the diversity of miracles, whereby the gospel was confirmed, God had therein respect to men's backwardness in believing, and to the manifold oppositions against the gospel. If a few miracles would not serve the turn, there were many ; if this or that kind of miracles wrought not on men, yet other kinds might, according to that which is recorded of the diverse signs which God commanded Moses to shew: 'It shall come to pass, if they will not believe thee, neither hearken to the voice of the first sign, that they will believe the voice of the latter sign. And it shall come to pass, if they will not believe also these two signs, that thou shalt take of the water of the river, and pour it upon the dry land, and it shall become blood,' Exod. iv. 8, 9.

Though Pharaoh's heart were out of measure hard, and by nine several plagues was not moved to let Israel go, yet by another, which was diverse from all the rest, he was moved, Exod. xii. 30, 31. Many blows, especially with divers hammers, one heavier than another, will drive a great spike up to the head into such a rough piece of timber as a few blows with one light hammer could not make entrance thereunto.

It appears that it was the multitude and diversity of miracles that wrought upon the Jews in that they said, ' When Christ cometh, will he do more miracles than these which this man hath done ?' John vii. 31.

This is one end why God in all ages hath furnished his church with variety of ministers, endued with divers gifts, that the church might be more edified thereby. When Barnabas, a son of consolation, Acts iv. 36, little moves people, Boanerges, sons of thunder, may work upon them, Mark iii. 17. Sometimes an Apollos, an eloquent man, and mighty in the Scriptures, and fervent in the spirit, may much help such as believe through grace, and may convince the gainsayers, Acts xxiv. 25, 27, 28.

Sec. 35. *Of the gifts of the Holy Ghost.*

The fourth means whereby God confirmed the gospel were *gifts of the Holy Ghost ;* that is, such gifts as the Spirit of God wrought in men.

The Greek word μερισμοῖς, here translated gifts, properly signifieth *divisions* or distributions. This very word in the singular number is translated *dividing asunder,* ἄχρι μερισμοῦ, Heb. iv. 12.

Another word, μεριστής, derived from the same root that this is, is translated *a divider,* Luke xii. 14.

The verb μερίζειν signifieth to divide (as where it is said of Christ, 'He divided, ἐμέρισε, the two fishes among them,' Mark vi. 41) or to distribute, as where it is said, ' God hath distributed (ἐμέρισε) to every man,' 1 Cor. vii. 17 ; so 2 Cor. x. 13.

Now, the church being as a body consisting of many members, the Holy Ghost doth divide and distribute gifts needful for the whole body to and among the several members thereof, to one one gift, to another another, 1 Cor. xii. 8, &c. Hence in Greek they are called divisions, μερισμοὶ, or distributions; and because they arise not from ourselves, but are given by another, and that most freely, they are not unfitly translated *gifts*.

In other places another word (χαρίσματα) is used to set out the very same things that are here intended, and it properly signifieth *free gifts*, Rom. xii. 6.

The word that signifieth distributions is here translated gifts, because they confirm the gospel (which is the main end why mention is here made of them), as they are gifts extraordinarily given by the Holy Ghost.

Ghost is an ancient English word, that signifieth the same thing that *spirit* doth. The word that in Greek signifieth *spirit*, Πνεῦμα, is oft translated *ghost*, especially when it is spoken of the departing of a man's soul or spirit from his body. Of Christ it is said, 'He gave up the ghost,' Mat. xxvii. 50, John xix. 30.

He that here and in many other places is called Holy Ghost, is also called Holy Spirit, Πνεῦμα ἅγιον, Luke xi. 13, Eph. i. 13, and iv. 30. Here the third person in sacred Trinity is meant.

This epithet *holy*[1] is attributed to the Spirit,

1. In regard of his divine property, in which respect the Father, John xvii. 11, and Son also is styled holy, Acts iv. 27, 30.

2. In regard of his special function or operation, which is to make holy. In this respect he is called 'the Spirit of holiness,' Rom. i. 4, and sanctification is appropriated unto him, 2 Thes. ii. 13, 1 Peter i. 2.

Of the Holy Ghost, see more, Chap. iii. 7, Sec. 74.

Though every good gift be of the Holy Ghost, Gal. v. 22, yet here such extraordinary gifts as in the apostles' times were conferred on any are especially meant, such as were before Christ's exhibition foretold, Joel ii. 28, 29, and after Christ's ascension were abundantly poured out, Acts ii. 3.

That extraordinary gifts are here intended is evident, in that they are here joined with signs, wonders, and miracles, and because they are brought in for the very same end, namely, for confirmation of the gospel.

Those miracles were extraordinary, and gave evident proof of the divine calling of them who are endued therewith, and of the divine truth of that doctrine for which they were given.

By the gifts of the Holy Ghost poured on them, who on the day of pentecost were assembled together, an apostle proves to the Jews that that Jesus whom they had crucified was both 'Lord and Christ,' Acts ii. 33, 36. By like gifts did he confirm the calling of the Gentiles, Acts xi. 15–17.

Those gifts were diverse, as well as the miracles before mentioned. This is particularly exemplified, 1 Cor. xii. 4, &c. They are distributed into three general heads: 1, gifts; 2, administrations; 3, operations.

1. Under *gifts*, χαρίσματα, are comprised such abili-

[1] Of this epithet *holy*, see Chap. iii. 1, Sec. 5.

ties as the Spirit freely giveth unto men to perform the duties of their functions. Of these gifts the apostle reckoneth up sundry particulars, as wisdom, knowledge, faith, &c.

2. Under *administrations*, διακονίαι, are comprised such callings and functions as God hath ordained for the good of his church. Of these sundry kinds are reckoned up, 1 Cor. xii. 28.

3. Under *operations*, ἐνεργήματα, such fruits and effects as issue from the forenamed gifts, well employed in men's several functions. The notation of the word[1] intimates as much.

Sec. 36. *Of the difference betwixt the wonders under the law and under the gospel.*

There were indeed at the delivery of the law thunder and lightning, and other great signs, distinctly set set down, Exod. xix. 16, &c., and Heb. xii. 18, &c. Moses also did very great wonders, Deut. xxxiv. 11, 12, Ps. lxxviii. 12, &c., Acts vii. 36. So did other prophets, especially Elijah and Elisha; but the gospel was confirmed with more and greater miracles, John vii. 31, and ix. 32, and xv. 24.

The miracles which Christ did excelled all the miracles done before him, in five especial respects:

1. In the *ground* or *power* of doing them; for Christ did what he did by his own power, in his own name, Mark i. 27, and ii. 5, 6, &c.; but others did their great works by power received from God, and in the name of the Lord. The Lord sent Moses to do all the signs and wonders which he did, Deut. xxxiv. 11.

2. In the very *matter* and *kind* of works which Christ did. Never any restored sight to one that was born blind but Christ, John ix. 32. This very work was greater than all the works that Moses did in Egypt, the Red Sea, and wilderness; and than the standing still of the sun and moon upon Joshua's prayer, Joshua x. 12, 13; or than the sun's going back at Isaiah's prayer, 2 Kings xx. 11; or than the miracles done by the ministry of Elijah and Elisha; for in these and other miracles recorded before Christ's time there was but an alteration of the ordinary course of nature; but in giving sight to a man that never had sight before, was a new creation. Besides, we never read of any devils dispossessed before Christ's time. This is most certain, that never any raised himself from the dead by his own power before Christ; but herein Christ ' declared himself to be the Son of God with power,' Rom. i. 4.

3. In the *manner* of working his great works. Christ did what he did with authority and command, Mark i. 27, and ii. 11, and v. 41; others did what they did with prayer and submission to God's will, 1 Kings xvii. 20, 2 Kings iv. 33, and v. 11.

4. In the *end*. Christ's end in working miracles was to set out his glory together with his Father's, to shew that he was the Son of God, true God, Mark ii.

[1] ἐνεργεῖν, *efficaciter agere*.

10, and that men might be brought to believe in him. This is evident by the question which Christ propounded to the man that was born blind, and had sight given him by Christ. The question was this: 'Dost thou believe on the Son of God?' John ix. 35. The prophets did what they did with respect to God alone, and to shew that what they did or spake was by commission from the Lord, 1 Kings xviii. 36, 37.

5. In the *extent*. Christ's cures of many men's bodies extended also to the cure of their souls. This is evident by the pardon of sin which he gave to the man whom he cured of his palsy, Mat. ix. 2; and also by this exhortation to another man whom he cured, 'Behold, thou art made whole; sin no more,' John v. 14.

But the gifts of the Holy Ghost which are here mentioned, do beyond all exception demonstrate that the gospel had a greater confirmation than the law, because never were such gifts given before Christ's time. Of these gifts, see Sec. 35.

Sec. 37. *Of God's will in ordering works and gifts.*

The fore-mentioned diversity of miracles and distribution of gifts, were ordered and disposed, κατὰ τὴν αὐτοῦ θέλησιν, 'according to the will' of God. This act of distributing is attributed to God, 1 Cor. vii. 17; to his Son, Eph. iv. 7; and to his Spirit, 1 Cor. xii. 11. And for kind, number, and measure of gifts, all are ordered by the will of this one God, 'according to *his own* will,' αὐτοῦ, not another's. The Greek word intends as much.

The will of God is that rule whereby all things are ordered that he himself doth, and whereby all things ought to be ordered that creatures do.

Hereupon God's will is distinguished into his secret and revealed will. This distinction is grounded on these words, 'The secret things belong unto the Lord our God, but those things that are revealed belong unto us,' Deut. xxix. 29.

The secret will of God is called his 'counsel,' Isa. xlvi. 10; 'the counsel of his will,' Eph. i. 11; 'his purpose,' Rom. viii. 28; 'his pleasure,' Isa. xlvi. 10; 'his good pleasure,' Eph. i. 9; 'the good pleasure of his will,' Eph. i. 5.

The other is commonly called God's word, and that after the manner of men, because the ordinary means whereby men make known their minds is the word of their mouth; therefore the revelation of God's will is called God's word, whether it be by an audible voice from God himself, as Mat. iii. 17; or by the ministry of angels, ver. 2; or by the ministry of men, Hosea i. 2.

This is also called 'the good, and acceptable, and perfect will of God,' Rom. xii. 2.

This revealed will of God is that which is principally intended in the second petition of the Lord's prayer.

Here God's secret will is meant; this is that supreme and absolute will of God, by which all things are, and without which nothing can be, Ps. cxv. 3, Eph. i. 11, Rom. xi. 34.

This is God's only rule; he hath nothing else to regulate any purpose or act of his but his own will. As therefore he disposeth all things, so in special the gifts of the Holy Ghost, 'according to his will.' See verse 9, Sec. 78; and Chap. vi. 17, Sec. 130.

The grounds following do demonstrate the equity hereof.

1. God is the fountain whence all gifts flow: 'Every good gift, and every perfect gift, is from above, and cometh down from the Father of lights,' James i. 17. All are his. Hereupon he thus presseth his right against such as were not contented with that portion which he gave them: 'Is it not lawful for me to do what I will with mine own?' Mat. xx. 15.

2. God is the most supreme sovereign over all, he is the Lord and Master of all; he therefore hath power to order the places, and duties, and parts of all, as he pleaseth, according to his own will. In reference hereunto thus saith David, 'The Lord God of Israel chose me before all the house of my father, to be king over Israel for ever. For he hath chosen Judah to be the ruler: and of the house of Judah, the house of my father: and among the sons of my father, he liked me to make me king over all Israel: and of all my sons, he hath chosen Solomon my son to sit upon his throne,' &c., 1 Chron. xxviii. 4, 5.

3. God is the wisest of all. He is wise in heart, Job ix. 4; yea, mighty in wisdom, Job xxxvi. 5; 'his understanding is infinite,' Ps. cxlvii. 5; he is 'only wise,' Rom. xvi. 27. He therefore best knoweth what is fittest for every one; and he is fittest to order it according to his will.

4. God's will is the rule of righteousness. Whatsoever is ordered thereby, and agreeable thereto, is righteous; and whatsoever cometh from it is altogether righteous: 'The Lord is righteous in all his ways.' His ordering therefore of matters must needs be according to right and equity.

5. The Lord fitteth gifts and functions one to another; such gifts as are needful for such a function, and such a function as is fittest for such gifts. The Lord gave talents to every of his servants, 'according to his several ability,' Mat. xxv. 15; and having called Bezaleel to the work of the tabernacle, he 'filled him with the Spirit of God in wisdom, and in understanding, and in knowledge, and in all manner of workmanship, to devise cunning works,' Exodus xxxi. 2, 3, &c.

This teacheth us every one to be content with our own measure which God hath proportioned to us, for we may be assured thereupon that it is the fittest and best for us. Hast thou a small measure? Bear it patiently, that measure is fittest for thee. Hast thou a great measure? Use it conscionably, that is fittest for thee. If thou grudgest, thou grudgest against the most high, wise, righteous God, the fountain of all blessings. Remember Aaron's and Miriam's fault, and God's answer thereto, Num. xii. 2, 8. Let the consideration hereof suppress in thee all murmuring and repining against that measure which others have received.

Obj. We are exhorted 'earnestly to covet the best gifts,' 1 Cor. xii. 31; and to 'seek to excel,' 1 Cor. xiv. 12; and to 'grow up in all things,' Eph. iv. 15.

Ans. None of these, nor any such like exhortations, are contrary to Christian contentedness. For,

1. Though a man covet a more excellent gift than God hath ordained for him, yet when he seeth that God hath bestowed such and such a gift upon him, less than his desire, he may quietly subject himself to God's wise disposition, and rest contented therewith; for the will of God being now made known to him, he may persuade himself, that the gift he hath is best for him.

2. Seeking to excel, is not ambitiously to strive for the highest places and greatest offices in the church, as Diotrephes did, 3 John 9; but every one to strive in his own place to do most good in God's church. This therefore is the full exhortation, 'Seek that you may excel to the edifying of the church,' 1 Cor. xiv. 12. So as this teacheth us how to make the best use of the place wherein God hath set us, and of the parts which he hath given us.

3. A continual growth in grace is no more opposite to Christian contentedness, than the growth of the little finger is to the place wherein it is set. Growth and contentedness may well stand together; yea, they always go together. Growth in grace received, sheweth our good liking thereof, and that we think it the fittest for us, and are thereupon stirred up to nourish and cherish it, to keep it from decay, and to increase it more and more.

Sec. 38. *Of the resolution of the 2d, 3d, and 4th verses of the second chapter.*

The sum of these verses is, a motive to enforce a diligent heeding of the gospel. Two general points are to be observed:
1. The inference.
2. The substance.

Ver. 2. The inference is in this causal particle, γὰρ, *for.*

The substance setteth out an argument, *a minore ad majus,* from the less to the greater.

In laying down that argument we are to observe,
1. The manner of propounding it.
2. The matter whereof it consisteth.

The manner is by way of supposition; in this conditional particle, εἰ, *if.*

The matter declares the two parts of the argument. The argument is comparative.

The first part thereof setteth out just vengeance on transgressors of the word of angels. This is the less, ver. 2.

The second part setteth out greater vengeance on transgressors of the gospel, ver. 3, 4.

In the former we have,
1. A description of that whereupon vengeance was executed.
2. A declaration of the kind of vengeance.

The thing described is set out,
1. By the means of making it known, λαληθεὶς λόγος, *the word spoken.*
2. By the ministry thereof, δι' ἀγγέλων, *by angels.*
3. By the stedfastness of it, ἐγένετο βέβαιος, *was stedfast.*

In the declaration of the vengeance is set down,
1. The fault.
2. The punishment.

The fault is expressed in two kinds:
1. *Transgression,* παράβασις.
2. *Disobedience,* παρακοή.

Both these are manifested by their extent, in this particle *every,* πᾶσα.

The punishment is set out,
1. By the kind of it, μισθαποδοσίαν, *recompence of reward.*
2. By the equity, in these two words, ἔνδικον, *just,* ἔλαβεν, *received.*

Ver. 3. In the second part of the comparison we are likewise to observe:
1. The manner of setting it down, by an interrogation, Πῶς, *how?*
2. The manner. Herein is declared,
1. The judgment.
2. The cause thereof.

In the judgment are noted,
1. The persons liable thereunto, in this pronoun of the first person plural, ἡμεῖς, *we.*
2. The kind of judgment is expressed in this word, ἐκφευξόμεθα, *escape.*

The cause is, 1, propounded; 2, aggravated.

In the proposition there is noted,
1. The act wherein the sin consisteth, ἀμελήσαντες, *neglect.*
2. The object. Which manifesteth,
1. The benefit neglected, σωτηρίας, *salvation.*
2. The excellency of that benefit, τηλικαύτης, *so great.*

The aggravation thereof is manifested,
1. By the publication of that salvation.
2. By the ratification thereof.

The publication of salvation is here commended by the principal author thereof; who is set out,
1. By his dignity, διὰ τοῦ Κυρίου, *the Lord.*
2. By his ministry. Herein is expressed,
1. The kind of it, in this word *spoken,* λαλεῖσθαι.
2. The pre-eminence of it, *at first began,* ἀρχὴν λαβοῦσα.

The ratification is there expressed, ἐβεβαιώθη, *was confirmed.* About which is further set down,
1. The persons that confirm it.
2. The means whereby it was confirmed.

The persons admit a double consideration :
1. Who confirmed it.
2. To whom it was confirmed.

The persons confirming it were,' 1, men ; 2, God. The men were such as heard Christ, ὑπὸ τῶν ἀκουσάντων.

The persons to whom they confirmed it are expressed in this pronoun of the plural number and first person, *us*, εἰς ἡμᾶς, *to us*.

Ver. 4. The other person confirming is set out,
1. By his title God, τοῦ Θεοῦ.
2. By the kind of ratification, bearing them witness, συνεπιμαρτυροῦντος.

In setting down the means of ratification are noted,
1. The kind of them.
2. The rule whereby they are ordered.

The kind of means are of two sorts : 1, works ; 2, gifts.

Works are here set out,

By their distinct sorts, which are three : 1, signs, σημείοις ; 2, wonders, τέρασι ; 3, miracles, δυνάμεσι.

2. By their variety, in this word divers, ποικίλαις.

Gifts are described, 1, by their author, the Holy Ghost, Πνεύματος ἁγίου.

2. By their distribution, μερισμοῖς. This is implied in the Greek word used by the apostle.

The rule is thus manifested, according to his own will, κατὰ τὴν θέλησιν.

Here observe,
1. The kind of rule, will.
2. The property of it, his own, αὐτοῦ.

Sec. 39. *Of the doctrines arising out of the 2d, 3d, and 4th verses of the second chapter.*

1. *Motive may be added to motive.* To that motive in the former verse, taken from the damage of not heeding the gospel, in these verses another motive is added, taken from the vengeance that will follow thereupon. For men are hardly brought to believe divine truths.

II. *Suppositions may imply unquestionable truths.* The manner of the apostle's arguing by way of supposition, *if*, proveth as much. See Sec. 8.

III. *Angels were of old God's ministers to his church.* They 'spake his word.' See Sec. 10.

IV. *God's word is stedfast.* So is it here expressly said to be. See Secs. 11, 12.

V. *Divine vengeance may be a motive to forbear sin.* The inference of the vengeance upon the word spoken proves as much ; for it is here to that very end alleged.

VI. *There are different kinds of sin.* The distinction betwixt transgression and disobedience imports thus much. See Sec. 14.

VII. *No sin shall pass unrevenged.* This general particle, *every*, intends this.

VIII. *Punishment is due to transgression.* It is therefore styled 'a recompence of reward.' See Sec. 16.

IX. *Divine vengeance is most just.* So it is here expressly said to be. See Sec. 17.

X. *Transgressors shall receive vengeance, will they nill they.* This verb *received* intimates this point. See Sec. 17.

XI. *Revenge of sin is most sure.* This interrogative *how* intimates as much. See Sec. 18.

XII. *There are degrees of sin and judgment.* The inference of the latter part of the comparison upon the former, declares the truth of this point. For neglect of the gospel is made a greater sin than neglect of the law ; and a greater judgment is thereupon inferred. See Sec. 18.

XIII. *It is very dangerous to neglect the gospel.* There is no way of escaping for such. See Sec. 19.

XIV. *The greatest as well as the meanest, falling into the same sin, are liable to the same judgment.* This pronoun *we* includes the apostle himself and all to whom he wrote. See Sec. 18.

XV. *The gospel brings salvation.* It is thereupon styled *salvation*. See Sec. 20.

XVI. *The salvation wrought by the gospel is very great.* This word *so great* intends as much. It is far greater than that which by the ministry under the law was brought to people. See Sec. 21.

XVII. *Christ was a preacher.* He is here said to preach. See Sec. 22.

XVIII. *The word is made profitable by preaching.* For this end Christ preached it. See Sec. 23.

XIX. *Christ was the first preacher of the gospel.* This is here expressly asserted. See Sec. 24.

XX. *God would have his word confirmed.* See Sec. 25.

XXI. *Many preachers of the same truth confirm it the more.* Thus, by other preachers, the gospel which Christ first preached was confirmed. See Sec. 25.

XXII. *Apostles succeeded Christ.* These were they who heard him. See Sec. 26.

XXIII. *Preachers confirm the gospel to others.* It was confirmed unto us, saith the text. See Sec. 27.

XXIV. *God addeth his witness to the ministry of his servants.* This is here expressly set down. See Sec. 28.

XXV. *God only can work miracles.* This is here set down as God's proper act. See Sec. 28.

XXVI. *Miracles are above the power of creatures.* This followeth from the former by just consequence. See Sec. 29.

XXVII. *Works are witnesses to God's word.* God, by his works, bare witness to his apostles. See Sec. 30.

XXVIII. *Signs, by visible objects, confirm divine matters.*

XXIX. *Wonders, by the strangeness of them, do the like.*

XXX. *Miracles also do so by a divine power manifested in them.* These three last doctrines arise out of the notation of those words, *signs, wonders, miracles.* See Secs. 31, 32.

XXXI. *Divers miracles were wrought to confirm the gospel.* See Sec. 34.

XXXII. *Men's gifts are of the Holy Ghost.* He gives them, 1 Cor. xii. 11. Therefore they are here styled 'gifts of the Holy Ghost.' See Sec. 35.

XXXIII. *Extraordinary gifts were abundantly given at the first preaching of the gospel.* The church had need of them. See Sec. 35.

XXXIV. *Gifts of the Holy Ghost were confirmations of the gospel.* They are in this respect joined with miracles. See Sec. 35.

XXXV. *Men's functions and abilities are of God.* Ibid.

XXXVI. *The gospel had greater confirmation than the law.* See Sec. 36.

XXXVII. *God hath no other rule than his own will.* This relative, *his own,* implies as much.

XXXVIII. *God orders men's parts and places according to his will.* See Sec. 37.

Sec. 40. *Of the inference of the fifth verse upon that which goeth before.*

Ver. 5. *For unto the angels hath he not put in subjection the world to come, whereof we speak.*

In this verse the apostle hath an eye to that main point which he insisted upon in the former chapter; (which was, that Christ is more excellent than angels), and also to the argument in the verse immediately going before, whereby he proved that more heed is to be given to the word of Christ, than to the word of angels.

In reference to the former chapter, a ninth argument is in this verse added to those eight which were produced in the former chapter, to prove the foresaid excellency of Christ above angels. See Chap. i., Sec. 64.

In reference to the former part of this chapter, this verse containeth a reason why Christ's word is to be preferred before the word of angels : namely, because God hath given a greater authority to Christ, than ever he did to angels. The first particle of this verse, *for,* sheweth that a reason is contained therein.

This reason is here set down as a double transition.

The first is from Christ's excellency in reference to his divine nature, unto his excellency in reference to his human nature.

The other is, from the apostle's exhortatory digression, unto his doctrinal point about Christ's excellency.

In the former chapter the apostle sets out the excellency of Christ being God, yet so as he considered him also to be man, even God-man.

In this chapter he sets out the excellency of Christ being man, yet so as he considereth him also to be God, even God-man.

The reason here produced is comparative. The comparison is of unequals: for it is betwixt Christ and angels.

1. The inferiority of angels is declared in this verse.

2. The superiority of Christ is proved. Verses 6–9.

The manner of expressing the inferiority of angels is like that which was used Chap. i. Sec. 46. It is expressed negatively, ' Unto the angels hath he not put,' &c.

In this place the kind of argument is the stronger, in that it is denied to them by him who only hath the supreme and absolute power to confer jurisdiction upon any, or to withhold it from any, and that is God. For this relative *he* hath reference to him that is mentioned in the verse immediately going before, thus, ' God bearing witness.'

The argument may be thus framed.

He to whom God hath put in subjection the world to come, is more excellent than they to whom he hath not put it in subjection; but God hath put the world to come in subjection to Christ, and not to angels; therefore Christ is more excellent than angels.

The latter part of the assumption is in this verse.

The former part in the verses following.

Sec. 41. *Of the world to come.*

The word translated *world,* οἰκουμένην, properly signifieth a place inhabited. For it is derived from a noun that signifieth a house or habitation, οἶκος, and from a verb that signifieth to dwell or inhabit, οἰκέω. It is another word than that which was used, Chap. i. verse 2, and translated *worlds,* αἰῶνας. For that word hath reference to the time wherein all things were made and continue (see Chap. i. Sec. 18). But this hath reference to the place wherein men dwell. It is the same word that is used Chap. i. Sec. 66. But it is here used in another sense. There it was put for the earth, but here it is metonymically put for inhabitants, not in earth only, but in heaven also. And in reference to earth, by a synecdoche, the better part of inhabitants thereon are meant, namely, saints, Ps. xxxvii. 11, Mat. v. 5. In this sense another word translated *world* is also used, κόσμος, 2 Cor. v. 19.

The *world,* then, in this place, is put for the *church,* which compriseth under it the whole number of God's elect, called or to be called. In this sense it is also called 'the kingdom of God,' Mat. vi. 33; 'the kingdom of his Son,' Col. i. 13; 'the kingdom of heaven,' Mat. iii. 3.

That this word *world* is in this place so used, is evident by this epithet *to come,* added thereto. For this world is to be considered, either in the inchoation and progress thereof, or in the consummation and perfection of it.

In the former respect it is styled ' the world to come,' μέλλουσαν, in reference to the saints that lived before Christ was exhibited in the flesh, and longed to see this world, Mat. xiii. 17; John viii. 56; 1 Pet. i. 10, 11. Thus John the Baptist, after he was born and exercised his ministry, is said to be ' Elias to come,' Mat. xi. 14, in reference to a former prophecy, Mal. iv. 5.

In the latter respect, this world is said *to come,* in reference to such saints as have grace begun in them, but cannot have it perfected till this life be ended. So as in regard of the perfection, both of particular members, and also of the whole mystical body, this world, even now since Christ exhibited, is truly said to come. Thus is this title, *to come,* oft used, as Mat. xii. 32; Eph. i. 21.

In like respects all things under the gospel are said to 'become new,'[1] 2 Cor. v. 17.

Sec. 42. *Of appropriating the 'world to come' to the latter times.*

Considering that the saints who lived before Christ was exhibited, were members of the true church and mystical body of Christ, this question may be moved, How, in reference to them, the world is said to come?

Ans. Many things, in case of difference betwixt the time of the law and gospel, are to be taken comparatively, and that, as in other cases, so in this particular.

1. Christ, under the law, was in so many types and shadows typified out unto saints then living, as they could not so fully and clearly discern him, as now we do.

2. Their faith in the Messiah was grounded on promises of his to come; but our faith is settled on Christ actually exhibited. He is now in his human nature really settled on his throne; and in that respect this *world,* that was then *to come,* is more fully made subject to him.

3. In regard of the number of those that under the gospel are made subject to Christ, the Christian church may be counted a world, and that in comparison of the number of those that were under the law. For they made but a small nation.

Sec. 43. *Of being put in subjection.*

This phrase, *put in subjection,* is the interpretation of one Greek word, ὑπέταξε, but a compound one, which signifieth, to put under.

The simple verb, τάττειν, signifieth to *appoint, place,* or *set in order.* It is used to set out God's ordaining persons to life,—'As many as were ordained (τεταγμένοι) to eternal life, believed,' Acts xiii. 48,—and men's determining matters, Acts xv. 2, ἔταξαν; and appointing place and times, ἐτάξατο, Mat. xxviii. 16, Acts xxviii. 23.

The preposition ὑπό, with which the word is compound, signifieth *under.* Answerably it is translated, 'put under.' We see not yet all things put under him, ὑποτεταγμένα, verse 8. Now they who are by him that hath authority put under another, are brought to be in subjection to him. It is therefore in this sense applied to subjects and servants, 1 Pet. ii. 13, 18; to wives, 1 Pet. iii. 1; to children, Luke ii. 51; to the church, Eph. v. 24.

It here importeth two things;—

1. Sovereignty and authority on God's part, who is here said to put under. This is exemplified, verse 8. Thus may such as are most unwilling to be brought under, be put in subjection, as the devils themselves, Luke x. 17, 20.

2. Duty on the church's part, in a willing submitting of itself to Christ. In this respect wives are charged to submit themselves to their own husbands, 'as the church is subject unto Christ,' Eph. v. 22, 24.

In both these respects are the good angels subject unto Christ, 1 Pet. iii. 23.

Sec. 44. *Of the subjection denied to angels.*

This honour, to have the church put into subjection to them, is expressly denied to angels; so saith this text, 'he hath not put in subjection unto angels the world to come.' That honour, which God, the most high, supreme sovereign over all, vouchsafeth not to a creature, is denied to him; he hath no right to it. Were it meet that he should have it, the wise God would bestow it on him.

Angels are of creatures the most excellent; (Of the excellency of angels, see Chap. i. Sec. 40, 85); yet this world to come, consisting of such inhabitants as are mystically so united to Christ, as they make one body with him (which body is called Christ, 1 Cor. xii. 12), are too excellent to be put in subjection to any but Christ, who is the true and only head of the church. Though angels be more excellent than any children of men, singly and simply considered in themselves, yet children of men, as they are united to Christ, and make one body with him, are far more excellent than all the angels. It is therefore very incongruous that they who are the more excellent should be put in subjection to those who are less excellent, yea, to those who are appointed to be ministers and, as I may so speak, servants unto him.[1]

Sec. 45. *Of arguments for angels' authority over the church answered.*

The fore-mentioned point will appear more clear by answering such arguments as are alleged to prove the authority of angels over Christ's church.

Arg. 1. Angels are styled 'thrones, dominions, principalities, and powers,' Col. i. 16, all which titles imply superiority and authority over others.

Ans. 1. Those titles are used to set out the excellency and dignity of angels, rather than their authority and command over others. They who have dominion, principality, and power, and who sit on thrones, are among men the most excellent. These titles, then, shew that angels are the most excellent among all creatures.

Ans. 2. If authority be yielded unto them, yet that

---

[1] Of the things under the gospel called *new,* see my sermon on Ezek. xxxvi. 11, entitled, *The Progress of God's Providence.*

[1] Qu. 'them'?—ED.

authority is only deputative in reference to that message or work which is enjoined on them; such an authority as kings' ambassadors and messengers have.

Arg. 2. They are called princes of particular countries, as of Persia and Græcia, Dan. x. 13, 20. Now princes have subjects put into subjection unto them.

Ans. 1. Persia and Græcia were then of this world; but we speak of the world to come, which is the church.

Ans. 2. It cannot be proved that those princes there meant were angels; they were the monarchs of those nations; as Cambyses or Darius of Persia, and Alexander of Greece.

Arg. 3. Michael the angel was prince of the Jews, Dan. x. 12, 21.

Ans. Indeed Michael is styled an archangel; but thereby is meant the head of angels, the Lord Jesus Christ. See Chap. i. Sec. 83.

Arg. 4. Evil angels are 'rulers of the darkness of this world,' Eph. vi. 12; why may not then good angels be rulers of the world to come?

Ans. 1. Evil angels usurp power and authority above that which is meet, which the good angels will never do.

Ans. 2. The children of this world put themselves in subjection to evil angels, and so become their slaves, but the children of the world to come will subject themselves to none but to Christ, no, not to the good angels.

Arg. 5. The men of this world are put in subjection to Christ; therefore the subjection of the world to come is no good proof of Christ's excellency.

Ans. 1. Though the men of this world are put into subjection to Christ, yet not after such a manner as the world to come, who are put in subjection to Christ as members to their head, so as from their head they receive such a spirit as makes them willingly and cheerfully submit themselves to him; but the men of this world are *per* force made subject to Christ, as to an absolute, supreme, almighty Lord over them, who can and will keep them under.

Ans. 2. The question here being principally about the church, the apostle thought it sufficient to exemplify the point in the world to come.

Sec. 46. *Of the unlawfulness of worshipping angels or any other creatures.*

God having reserved this as a privilege to his church, not to be put in subjection to angels, how basely and unworthily do they carry themselves, who, pretending to be of this world to come, do notwithstanding put themselves into subjection to angels! So do such as worship angels. It appears that men were too much addicted to this kind of superstition in the apostles' time, for it is condemned by an apostle, and the vain pretence for it is discovered, Col. ii. 18. That pretence is styled 'voluntary humility,' which is, as of old it was called, will-humility and hypocritical humility. Indeed it is an high presumption against God, who only is to be worshipped, and against his Son Christ, who only is advanced to the right hand of God (see Chap. i. Sec. 13), and against the saints, who are of this world to come, and in that respect not put in subjection unto angels. To make pretence of worship for which there is no warrant in the word of God, favoureth too rankly of intolerable insolency. Angels themselves, who well understand what is due or not due unto them, have utterly refused to be worshipped by men, Rev. xix. 10, and xxii. 9.

In this it is manifest that papists are not of this world to come, because in their doctrine they maintain that angels are to be worshipped, and in their daily practice do worship angels.

The pope of Rome doth also herein shew himself to be plain antichrist, in that he putteth all that adhere to him in subjection to himself, as to Christ's vicar, and as to the head of the church, which is Christ's prerogative, given unto him by the Father, Eph. i. 22. To what bishop said God at any time, Be thou the head of my church? or, Let my church be put in subjection to thee? Is not this to 'oppose and exalt himself above all that is called God, or that is worshipped'? 2 Thes. ii. 4.

Let us, brethren, 'stand fast in the liberty wherewith Christ hath made us free,' Gal. v. 1. Let us not slavishly put ourselves in subjection to any to whom God hath not put us in subjection, but let us reserve ourselves free for him alone to whom God hath put us in subjection. He is the only Lord of our conscience, to him only let us be in subjection.

Sec. 47. *Of adding this clause, 'whereof we speak.'*

This correlative *whereof* hath reference to the word *world* going before, for they are both of the same gender, namely, the feminine. The word here translated *world*, is the very same that is used, chap. i. ver. 6, in this phrase, 'When he bringeth in the first begotten into the world.' The *world* may there be taken in a larger extent than here, by reason of that restrictive epithet, *to come.*

Though world in the former place may comprise under it the whole earth and all the inhabitants thereon, yet doth it most especially intend the militant church. For as Christ gave himself for the church, Eph. v. 25, so God in special gave Christ to his church; and he brought his first-begotten into the world for his church's sake. Had not the church been in the world, God would not have brought his first-begotten into the world.

Besides, the world there spoken of may well be accounted the same that is here meant, even the 'world to come;' because God's first-begotten was then brought into the world, when it began to be actually that world to come which was before prophesied of. It was the exhibition of Christ that made it another world, a new world, a world to come; in that Christ, by being brought into the world, accomplished all the types, shadows, prophecies, and promises concerning himself. The world then was accounted the world to come.

In regard of the sense and intent of the apostle, this phrase, 'whereof we speak,' may also have reference to the last days, mentioned in chap. i. ver. 2. For this world to come is in those last days, in which God speaks unto us by his Son.

It may further have reference to the last clause of the last verse of the first chapter. For the 'heirs of salvation' are the most special and principal inhabitants in this world to come: yea, they are the only true members thereof; so as in speaking of the world to come he speaks of the heirs of salvation.

Finally, All that in the former part of this chapter is spoken of the gospel, and of the duty that belongs to those that enjoy the privilege thereof, and of the manifold means whereby God confirmed it unto us, all these things concern this world to come. So as in all these also he speaketh of the world to come.

The apostle here useth a verb of the present tense (thus, 'whereof we speak'), not of the preter tense, or time past (whereof we have spoken), to shew that all his discourse appertains to this world to come.

Sec. 48. *Of the resolution of the fifth verse of the second chapter.*

The sum of this verse is, a restraint of angels' authority.

Two points are herein to be observed,
1. The inference set out in this causal particle *for.*
2. The substance, wherein is noted,
1. The kind of authority here intimated.
2. The restraint thereof.

In setting down the kind of authority he sheweth,
1. The persons whom it concerns.
2. The act wherein it consisteth.

The persons are,
1. Propounded in this phrase, *world to come.*
2. Amplified in this, *whereof we speak.*

The authority is thus expressed, *put in subjection.*

In the restraint we are to observe,
1. The persons, both who restrains, *he,* and also who are restrained, *angels.*
2. The form of restraint in these words, *hath not put,* &c.

Sec. 49. *Of the instruction arising out of* Heb. ii. 5.
1. *The more excellent the persons are, the greater heed is to be given to their word.* This ariseth from the causal particle *for.* Therefore more diligent heed is to be given to Christ's word than to the word of angels, because he is more excellent than they.

II. *God gives authority and dignity.* This relative *he* hath reference to God, who putteth in subjection whom he will and to whom he will.

III. *None have right to any authority that have it not of God.* Because God hath not put the world to come in subjection to angels, therefore angels have no authority over the world to come.

IV. *There was a church to come after the expiration of the Jewish synagogue.* In this respect the Christian church is here called *the world to come.*

V. *The full perfection of the church is yet expected.* For this phrase *world to come* hath also reference to a time yet to come; and that after the last day.

VI. *Angels have not authority over Christ's church.* It is Christ's church of whom the apostle here saith, that it is not put in subjection to angels.

VII. *The prerogative of the Christian church is a very great one.* For it is much spoken of by the apostle. This is it that is mainly intended in this phrase, *whereof we speak.* He is here and there, even everywhere, speaking of it.

Sec. 50. *Of the apostle's manner of producing a divine testimony.*

Ver. 6-8. *But one in a certain place testified, saying, What is man, that thou art mindful of him? or the Son of man, that thou visitest him? Thou madest him a little lower than the angels; thou crownedst him with glory and honour, and didst set him over the works of thy hands: Thou hast put all things in subjection under his feet, &c.*

The apostle here begins to set out the excellency of Christ's human nature; in amplifying whereof, he continueth to the end of this chapter.

In the four verses following, he proveth Christ to be more excellent than angels. Now, angels are of all mere creatures the most excellent. Christ therefore must needs be the most excellent of all.

This argument of unequals the apostle began in the former verse, where he gave proof of the inferiority of angels. Here he sheweth that that which was denied to angels is granted to Christ. Therefore he bringeth in that which is spoken of Christ, with this particle of opposition, *but,* δέ;[1] which is here made the note of an assumption, thus, God put not the world to come in subjection to angels, *but* to Christ he did. Though that assumption be not in express terms set down, yet to make it the more clear and evident, the apostle sets it down in a divine testimony, which in general terms he thus produceth, 'One in a certain place testifieth.' If upon that which was asserted in the former verse, it should be demanded, seeing God hath not put in subjection to angels the world to come, to whom hath he put it? The answer is this, 'One (τίς) in a certain place testifieth,' &c. He expresseth not the author, but indefinitely saith, one (or a certain man, as the Greek particle here used is translated in other places, Luke ix. 57, and xiii. 6); nor the book, but saith, πού, 'in a certain place.' This is the interpretation of one Greek particle, which being accented (ποῦ), signifieth, *where?* Mat. ii. 2, or *whither?*

[1] See ver. 8, Sec. 63, and Chap. i. 13, Sec. 140, and Chap. xi. 1, Sec. 2.

1 John ii. 11; but without an accent it signifieth *a certain place*, as here, and chap. iv. 4, and xi. 8.

This was usual with the penmen of sacred Scripture. Sometimes they only set down a text of Scripture, giving no note of author, or place, as Rom. x. 18. Sometimes this indefinite phrase is used, '*He saith*,' Heb. xiii. 5. Sometimes this, 'The Holy Ghost saith,' Heb. iii. 7. Sometimes this phrase, 'It is written,' Mat. xxi. 13. Sometimes this, 'In the law it is written,' John viii. 17. Sometimes 'a prophet' is indefinitely set down, Mat. i. 22. Sometimes the name of the prophet is expressed, Mat. ii. 17. Sometimes the 'book of Moses,' Mark xii. 26; and the 'book of Psalms,' Acts i. 20. Once 'the second Psalm' is mentioned, Acts xiii. 33.

Scriptures might be thus indefinitely quoted, because the churches to whom the evangelists and apostles wrote, were so well acquainted with the Scriptures, as the naming of a scripture might be sufficient for them readily to find it out, because they well knew where it was written; or it may be that the apostles did it purposely, to move them more diligently to search the Scriptures, that so they might the better acquaint themselves therewithal.

It is said of the Jews, that they were so versed in the Hebrew text (which was their mother language), as they could readily tell how many times such and such a word was used in the Hebrew Bible; and that they trained up their children to be as expert therein. To them there needed no more but the very naming of a text of Scripture.

Were our people as expert in the Scriptures, which we have translated in our mother tongue, a great deal of pains might be spared by our ministers in quoting the book, chapter and verse, wherein the text that we quote is set down.

Let us be stirred up so diligently to exercise ourselves in the holy Scriptures, and to be so well acquainted therewith, as it may be sufficient to hear a testimony or a phrase of Scripture, though the particular place be not expressed.

Sec. 51. *Of the Scriptures testifying.*

This word translated *testified*, διεμαρτύρατο, is a compound word. The simple verb, μαρτυρεῖν, signifieth to *testify*, John iii. 11; or to bear witness, John i. 7.

The compound, διαμαρτύρεσθαι, addeth emphasis, and implieth more than a bare affirming or witnessing a thing. It also signifieth a confirming and adding further witness to a truth.[1] It is therefore added to preaching. He commanded us to preach and to testify, Acts x. 42. After that Peter had preached to the Jews, it is added, that, 'with many other words he did testify,' Acts ii. 40.

I find this compound word fourteen times used in the New Testament. In every of those places it carrieth an especial emphasis, as where Dives desires

[1] See verse 4, Sec. 30.

that Lazarus, who was then dead, might be sent to his brethren, 'to testify unto them,' Luke xvi. 28, that is, by an unquestionable evidence to convince them of hell's torment.

Here it implieth a confirmation of the point in question, namely, that the world to come was put in subjection to Jesus. It is one special end of sacred Scripture to testify the truth, such truths especially as concern Jesus Christ, John v. 39; Luke xxiv. 27; Acts x. 43.

The psalm out of which this testimony is taken, is the eighth psalm. That it testifieth of Jesus, is evident by the many passages that are therein applied to Christ in the New Testament: as this, 'Out of the mouth of babes and sucklings thou hast ordained strength;'[1] or as the LXX (whom the Evangelist followeth) κατηρτίσω αἶνον, 'hast perfected praise,' Mat. xxi. 16. And this, 'Thou hast put all things under his feet,' is three times applied to Jesus, as 1 Cor. xv. 27, Eph. i. 22; and here, in this text, where the apostle proves that this can be meant of no other, verses 8, 9. Thus he first produceth the testimony itself, verses 6–8, and then applieth it to Jesus, the person intended therein, verses 8, 9.

Take we a brief view of the whole psalm, and it will evidently appear that Christ is set out therein.

The main scope of the psalm is, to magnify the glory of God; this is evident by the first and last verses thereof. That main point is proved by the works of God, which in general he declares to be so conspicuous, as very babes can magnify God in them to the astonishment of his enemies, verse 2.

In particular, he first produceth those visible glorious works that are above; which manifest God's eternal power and Godhead, verse 3. Then he amplifieth God's goodness to man (who had made himself a mortal miserable creature, verse 4), by setting forth the high advancement of man above all other creatures, not the angels excepted, verses 5–8. This cannot be found verified in any but in the man Christ Jesus.

This evidence of God's goodness to man so ravished the prophet's spirit, as with an high admiration he thus expresseth it, 'What is man,' &c. Hereupon he concludeth that psalm as he began it, with extolling the glorious excellency of the Lord.

Sec. 52. *Of the Scripture's sufficient authority in itself.*

Though, in setting down this testimony, the apostle nameth not the author or penman of the psalm, yet in the title it is expressly said to be, 'A Psalm of David.' The apostle concealeth his name, not upon any doubt that he had of David's penning it, or in any disrespect (for he expressly nameth him, chap. iv. 7; and putteth him into the catalogue of God's worthies, chap. xi. 32) but to shew that the sacred Scripture hath sufficient authority in itself, and needs not any further authority

[1] יסדת עז

from any man. Many books are compiled in the Bible, whose penman or publisher is not named, as the book of Judges, and Ruth, the two books of Kings and Chronicles, Esther, and this epistle.

The apostle hath quoted this testimony word for word, not varying from the psalmist in sense or syllables, especially as the LXX have translated it (see Chap. i. 6, Sec. 72.)

By this expressing of his mind in the very words of Scripture, he maketh the point to be more heeded and regarded.

Sec. 53. *Of Christ's meanness amplifying his greatness.*

The main intent of the apostle in quoting the foresaid testimony, is, to set out the excellency and dignity of Christ; yet he beginneth with his low degree, *man, son of man.*

This he doth in three especial respects.

1. That he might set out Christ's excellency, as he was man; for in the former chapter, he had set forth his excellency as he was God.

2. That his excellency might be the more magnified. For the low degree whereunto Christ subjected himself, doth much amplify his glorious exaltation, as Philip ii. 8, 9. To this very end the Holy Ghost doth oft set down the low degree of those whom God hath highly advanced. Israel was advanced above all nations; to magnify God's goodness therein they are oft put in mind of their former low condition; yea, they are enjoined to make an annual commemoration thereof, Deut. xxvi. 1, 2, &c. David doth this way amplify God's goodness to himself, Ps. lxxviii. 70, 71; so doth the Virgin Mary, Luke i. 48.

3. That the exception made against Christ's meanness might appear to be but a frivolous exception. For the apostle here grants that Christ in his human estate was as mean as the meanest; yet withal inferreth that it was no hindrance to the height of his exaltation.

Some suppose that that which is here spoken of as *man*, is meant of the first man in his pure and innocent estate; because God then gave him 'dominion over the fish of the sea, and over the fowl of the air, and over the cattle, and over all the earth,' &c., Gen. i. 26.

Ans. 1. I deny not, but that such a dominion in regard of sundry of those particulars which are mentioned, Ps. viii. 6–8, was given to the man here described. But it doth not hence follow that the first Adam should be here meant; for he forfeited that dominion by his transgression.

2. The first title which is given to the man here meant, cannot be applied to the first Adam in his pure estate: for then he was not a mortal miserable man.

3. Adam was not a son of man, as this man is here said to be; Adam was not born of man, but created of God, Gen. ii. 7.

4. Adam being made immortal, he was not then in that respect lower than angels, as the man here meant is said to be, verse 9.

5. The glory and honour with which this man is here said to be crowned, far exceeded all that glory and honour which was then conferred upon Adam.

6. *All things,* simply taken without any restraint (as here they are taken) were not put in subjection to Adam. Angels were never put in subjection to Adam, but they are to this man, verse 8.

In the two latter respects no mere man since the fall, nor the whole stock of mankind, simply considered in itself, can be here meant. It remains, therefore, that the man here spoken of is more than man, even the man Jesus Christ, who is God-man.

Yet I will not deny but that the whole mystical body of Jesus Christ may be here included; namely, all that by faith are united unto Christ; for all they, together with their head, have this title *Christ* given unto them, 1 Cor. xii. 12. In this respect the dignities belonging unto Christ, as the head of that body, appertain also to the body of Christ. Hence it is that all things are said to be theirs, because they are Christ's, 1 Cor. iii. 22, 23, and they are said to be 'quickened together with Christ, and raised up together, and made to sit together in heavenly places in Christ Jesus,' Eph. ii. 5, 6; they are also 'heirs of God, and joint heirs with Christ,' Rom. viii. 17.

Sec. 54. *Of these titles, man, son of man.*

The person here spoken of is set forth by two titles, man, son of man. The first of these titles, אנוש, in Hebrew signifieth a mortal, miserable man. It cometh from a verb, אנש, *ægrotavit desperate,* that importeth a desperate case. It is oft translated *desperate,* as 'desperate sorrow,' Isa. xvii. 11, and 'incurable sorrow,' Jer. xxx. 15. This word is used where the psalmist saith, 'Put them in fear, O Lord, that the nations may know themselves to be but men,' Ps. ix. 20, that is, weak, mortal, miserable. Of this title *man*, in another sense, see my sermon on 2 Chron. viii. 9, *Of the dignity of Chivalry,* Sec. 3.

The other title, *son of man*, is added as a diminution, for *man* in the second place is Adam. Adam was the proper name given to the first man, the father of us all, and that by reason of the red earth,[1] out of which he was made, Gen. ii. 7. After man's fall, it became a common name to all his posterity, by reason of that mortality which seized on them all, whereby they came to return to that out of which they were made, according to this doom, 'Dust thou art, and to dust shalt thou return,' Gen. iii. 19. Thus this title *Adam* sets out the common frail condition of mankind; so doth the Greek word here used, according to the notation of it. It signifieth one that looks upward.[2] Being succourless in himself, he looks up for help elsewhere, as 2 Chron. xx. 12. In this respect

---

[1] אדם, *rubruit*; אדמה, *terra subrufa*; אדם, *homo.*
[2] ἄνθρωπος *dicitur παρὰ τὸ ἄνω ἀθρεῖν, a suspiciendo sursum.*

Bildad styleth him a worm, Job xxv. 6. This word *son*, annexed unto man, *son of man*, adds a further diminution, and implieth somewhat less than a mean man.

This particle *son* prefixed, בן אדם, son of man, doth further shew that he was born of man, and that he did not, as some heretics[1] have imagined, bring his body from heaven. See more of this title in my treatise *Of the Sin against the Holy Ghost*, sec. 11.

The meanness of Christ's estate here in this world is thus further described by a prophet: 'His visage was marred more than any man, and his form more than the sons of men,' Isa. lii. 14. Yea, Christ himself is brought in, thus speaking of himself, 'I am a worm, and no man,' Ps. xxii. 6.

To add more emphasis to his low degree, those titles are interrogatively thus expressed, 'What is man, the son of man?' Hereby two things are intended:

1. The nothingness of that man in himself to deserve anything at God's hand. This must be taken of the human nature of Christ, and that abstracted from the divine nature; not of his person, in which the two natures were united. Or else it must be taken of the mystical body of Christ here warfaring on earth, consisting of weak, unworthy children of men.

2. The freeness of God's grace and riches of his mercy, that was extended to such a mean, weak, unworthy one.

This cannot but cause much admiration, and that admiration is couched under the interrogation, 'What is man?'

If the effects of God's kindness to man, which follow in the testimony, be duly observed, we shall find it to be a matter of more than ordinary admiration. It was a matter far less than this which made Job, with a like expostulatory admiration, to say unto God, 'What is man, that thou shouldst magnify him, and that thou shouldst set thine heart upon him?' Job vii. 17.

Sec. 55. *Of God's being mindful of man.*

That wherein God manifested his free grace and rich mercy to man is expressed under these two words, *mindful, visit*.

Both these words have reference to God, as is evident by this apostrophe, 'Thou art mindful.' The psalmist begins the psalm with an apostrophe to God thus, 'O Lord our Lord,' and continueth the same to the end of the psalm, so as he must needs here be taken in this verse to direct his speech unto God. This apostrophe doth also amplify the grace here intended, namely, that so great an one as the Lord should be so gracious unto so mean a man as is here described.

Both the Hebrew תזכרנו, and the Greek word, μιμνήσκη, translated *mindful*, do signify *to remember*. The Hebrew word is so translated, Ps. ix. 12, 'He remembereth them;' and the Greek word, Luke i. 72, 'to remember his holy covenant.'

To *remember* importeth two things.
1. To hold fast what is once known.
2. To call to mind what is forgotten. Of these two acts of memory, see Chap. xiii. Sec. 12, 24.

This act of remembering is applied not to man only, but to God also.

To God it is most properly applied in the former signification; for God ever fast holds in memory, and never forgets what he once knows: 'Known unto God are all his works from the beginning of the world,' Acts xv. 18.

Yea, also in the latter signification, that act of remembering is attributed unto God; as where it is said, 'Did not the Lord remember them? and came it not into his mind?' Jer. xliv. 21. The latter phrase sheweth that the act of remembering attributed to God in the former clause, is meant of calling to mind what was formerly known. Job oft calleth on God to remember him, זכר, in this sense, chap. vi. 7, and x. 9, and xiv. 13. In this respect God is said to have remembrancers, המזכרים, *rememorantes*, Isa. lxii. 6, to whom he thus saith, 'Put me in remembrance,' Isa. xliii. 26; and to this end he is said to have 'a book of remembrance,' ספר זכרון, *memoriæ liber*, Mal. iii. 17. But surely these things cannot properly be spoken of God; they are to be taken tropically, by way of resemblance, after the manner of man.

There is also a third act that is comprised under this word *to remember*, which is, seriously to think on, and consider such and such a person or case. Thus is the foresaid Hebrew word, translated, Neh. v. 19, 'Think upon me, my God.' So Gen. xl. 14, 'Think on me.'

To apply all to the point in hand: God never forgat the man here spoken of, but still held him in mind and memory. And though by extremity of misery and long lying therein God might seem to have forgotten him (as the church complaineth, Lam. v. 20), yet by affording seasonable succour, God shewed that he ever held him in memory, oft thought on him, and in his greatest need in special manner called him to mind; thus was God every way mindful of him. Behold how this mindfulness of God is set out to the life, Isa. xlix. 15, 16. It is not man's low estate that makes God unmindful of him, Ps. cxxxvi. 23, and cxvi. 6. This is a ground of comfort and confidence in our mean estate, Ps. lxxix. 8.

Sec. 56. *Of God's visiting man.*

This other word, תפקדנו, ἐπισκέπτῃ, *visitest*, doth intend a further care of God. To visit one, signifieth to go to the place where he is, to see him; and that not once only, but often. Thus the Hebrew word פקד is used, Ps. lxxx. 14; and the Greek word too, ἐπεσκέψασθε, Mat. xxv. 36.

Now, because sight of misery works compassion, and

---
[1] Marcianitæ, Origenistæ, Docetæ.

compassion moves to succour such as are in distress, to visit signifieth to succour one, as Jer. xv. 15, James i. 27.

Both these words, *mindful, visit*, are also applied to punishment and judgment.

We shewed before that to be mindful of, and to remember, are interpretations of one and the same original word. Now, God is said to 'remember iniquity' in judgment, and so to 'visit sins,' Jer. xiv. 10, Hosea viii. 13 and ix. 9.

But the persons visited, or the cause of visiting, or some circumstance or other, will apparently demonstrate what kind of visiting is meant, whether in mercy or judgment.

It is most evident that the former kind of visiting is here intended.

This latter word of *visiting*, added to the former of being *mindful*, sheweth that, as God had this man in mind, so he was careful to afford him all needful succour, and to testify all good respect to him, as is manifested in the words following. We are to be mindful of, and oft to go unto, and look upon such things as are dear unto us, and which we have in high account, so as God's special love of this man is herein set out.

Sec. 57. *Of Christ's being made low.*

In the seventh verse there is an exemplification both of Christ's low estate, and also of God's mindfulness of him, and gracious visiting of him.

He still continues his apostrophe to God, to whom he saith, ' Thou madest him a little lower,' &c.; so as both the low degree, and also the high advancement of Christ and his mystical body, is ordered by God. God maketh low; God setteth up on high, 1 Sam. ii. 7, Ezek. xvii. 24; should not this make us content, that God ordereth our estate ? Job i. 21.

Both the Hebrew, תחסרהו *à* חסר, *deficit*, and Greek word, ἠλάττωσας, *ab* ἐλαττόω, *minuo*, translated 'made lower,' impleth the failing of a thing from that which it was before. The Hebrew word is used to set out the failing of the waters when Noah's flood decreased, Gen. viii. 4; and, negatively, it is applied to the widow's oil that did not fail, 1 Kings xvii. 14, 16. The Greek word is used of the Baptist, who said, ' I must decrease,' ἐλαττοῦσθαι, John iii. 30. Thus may this most fitly be applied to Christ, who, by reason of his incarnation and passion, is said to 'descend,' Eph. iv. 9; to 'come down,' John vi. 38; and to 'make himself of no reputation,' Philip. ii. 7. This he did by the appointment and will of his Father, who is here said to 'make him lower.' And this he did to accomplish all works of service and suffering that were requisite for our redemption and salvation.

Sec. 58. *Of Christ's being made lower than angels.*

That the humiliation of Christ might not be stretched far, two limitations are here annexed :

One, of the persons; the other, of the time or degree.

The persons below whom Christ was put are here styled *angels*.

The Hebrew word, אלהים, is one of God's titles; and by many thus translated, ' Thou madest him lower than God ;' but that title is also frequently attributed to men, and to angels, as hath been shewed before, Chap. i. Sec. 70.

The main scope of the apostle, and his particular application of these persons to angels, ver. 9, plainly sheweth that that Hebrew title here belongeth to angels. Much hath been spoken in the former chapter, and in the beginning of this chapter, about the excellency of Christ above angels; wherefore, to prevent what might be objected against that excellency, by reason of Christ's human nature, of the infirmities thereof, and of his sufferings therein, it is granted, that indeed he was 'made lower than angels,' yet so as that mean condition which he underwent might be a means of his advancement, even in his human nature, above angels; to demonstrate thereby, that that means was so far from impeaching his greatness, as it made way thereto, and amplified the same.

Besides, in mentioning angels, who are spiritual substances, he impleith that his human nature only was so humbled and made low; so as he was not made lower than any other creatures besides angels. This is one limitation of Christ's humiliation.

Yet if we consider that he who is ' the head of all principality and power,' Col. ii. 10, infinitely better than angels (as hath been shewed, Chap. i. Sec. 41), was made lower than angels, and became such a man, such a Son of man, as is intended in the former verse, we shall find that this degree of Christ's humiliation is a matter of the greatest admiration that ever was given. Never was the like, never shall, never can, there be the like pattern given. Angels and men may stand amazed hereat.

Who now should not be content to be abased to any low degree whereunto the Lord shall subject him ? It is required that ' this mind be in us that was also in Christ Jesus,' Philip. ii. 5. He that hath made Christ low, hath power to make us low also. If we willingly submit ourselves to his pleasure in abasing us, he will also exalt us in due time.

Sec. 59. *Of Christ 'but little' lower than the angels.*

Another limitation is of the *time* or *degree* of Christ's humiliation. I use this disjunction of time *or* degree, because the Greek word used by the apostle, βραχύ τι, hath reference to both; to the *time*, and is translated 'a little while,' Luke xxii. 58, and ' a little space,' Acts v. 34. To the *quantity*, Job vi. 7, Heb. xiii. 22. The Hebrew word, מעט, used by the psalmist, hath, for the most part, reference to the degree or measure, and is translated *little*, as Ps. xxxviii. 16, ' A little that a righteous man hath,' &c. Yet is this Hebrew word sometimes also used to set out the time, as Deut. vii. 32, 'The Lord will put out those nations by little and little,' that is, some at one time, and some at another.

On the other side the Greek word also is put for measure, as John vi. 7, 'Take a little.' Our English translators have observed that the Greek word may signify either time or measure, in that they put one in the text, and the other in the margin, thus, 'a little lower,' or 'a little while inferior.'

Both these acceptions may well stand, and be applied to the point in hand. For Christ's humiliation may well be said to be a little in measure and in time, and both these simply and comparatively.

1. Simply, because for measure it was no other than is 'common to man,' ἀνθρώπινος, and for continuance it was, at the furthest, but from his conception to his ascension.

2. Comparatively, it was but light in measure, having reference to his almighty power; and but short in time, having reference to his eternity.

Christ verily, as a surety for sinners, underwent the wrath of God and curse of the law, Gal. iii. 13, which was so heavy a burden as it troubled his soul, John xii. 27, made him 'exceeding sorrowful to the death,' Mark xiii. 34, and it cast him into such an agony as 'his sweat was as it were great drops of blood falling down to the ground,' Luke xxii. 44. It made him once and twice and again thus to pray, 'O my Father, if it be possible, let this cup pass from me,' Mat. xxvi. 39, and to cry out and say, 'My God, my God, why hast thou forsaken me?' Mat. xxvi. 46. In these respects, if ever any on earth were such an one as the fore-mentioned Hebrew word signifieth, a miserable man in a desperate and incurable case, Christ, as a mere man, according to human strength, was in that his bitter agony. Yet in regard of the union of his divine nature with the human, that agony was neither desperate nor incurable, but tolerable and momentary. He well endured it, and freed himself from it. Thus was it but little in regard of measure and time.

Christ' humiliation was thus moderated, because it it was not for his own destruction, but for the salvation of others. In relation to his bitter agony, it is said that 'in the days of his flesh he offered up prayer and supplication with strong crying and tears : and that he was heard in that he feared,' Heb. v. 7.

By God's ordering his Son's estate in his sufferings, we may rest upon this, that he will answerably order the sufferings of the members of Christ, so as they shall neither be too heavy nor too long, they shall be but little in measure and time. This the apostle thus expresseth : 'Our light affliction, which is but for a moment,' &c., 2 Cor. iv. 17 ; and again : 'There hath no temptation taken you, but such as is common to man ; and, 'God will not suffer you to be tempted above that you are able; but will, with the temptation also make a way to escape,' 1 Cor. x. 13.

Their sufferings are by God inflicted, not in hatred, but in love; not for their destruction, but for their instruction. This is a forcible motive to patience.

Herein lies a main difference betwixt the afflictions of Christ's members and others. Though God correct the former, yet his mercy shall not depart away from them; but from others it may clean depart, 2 Sam. vii. 15.

Sec. 60. *Of God's crowning Christ with glory and honour.*

The point which the apostle principally aimeth at, is the excellency of Christ, which he doth here set out two ways :

1. Singly in this phrase, 'crowned with glory and honour.'

2. Relatively in this, 'set him over the works, &c.

To shew the ground of this exaltation of Christ, the apostrophe to God is still continued thus : Thou crownest him, תעטרהו, ἐστεφάνωσας αὐτὸν. See Sec. 55.

This metaphor of crowning hath reference to a royal dignity. To crown is properly to set a crown upon one's head ; and that act declareth one to be a king. Thus it is said of Solomon, 'Behold king Solomon with the crown wherewith his mother crowned him,' Cant. iii. 12. Of Christ's royal dignity, see Chap. i. Sec. 106, 111, 112.

Of God's conferring upon Christ that royalty whereunto he was advanced, see Chap i. Secs. 119, 149.

This metaphor of crowning may also have reference to Christ's labours and travails in his lifetime ; and to the reward which God gave him after he had fully accomplished all, and gotten an absolute conquest over all his enemies. In public undertakings, the champion that hath well finished his task, and overcome, was, in way of recompence, crowned. Hereunto alludeth the apostle in this phrase, 'They which run in a race run all ; but one receiveth the prize. They do it to obtain a corruptible crown,' 1 Cor. ix. 24, 25. Thus Christ, after he had run his race, and overcome, was crowned by his Father. To this tendeth that which is said of Christ, Philip. ii. 8, 9, 'He humbled himself, and became obedient unto death, even the death of the cross. Wherefore God also hath highly exalted him.'

Thus may all the members of Christ expect, after they have finished their course, and overcome, to be crowned. The apostle, with strong confidence, expected as much, for thus he saith, 'I have fought a good fight, I have finished my course, I have kept the faith ; henceforth there is laid up for me a crown of righteousness,' 2 Tim. iv. 7, 8. With the expectation hereof do the apostles incite Christians to hold out in doing the work of the Lord, 1 Peter v. 4, and in enduring temptations, James i. 12 ; for he that can and will perform what he hath promised, hath made this promise, 'Be thou faithful unto death, and I will give you a crown of life,' Rev. ii. 10.

To amplify that royal dignity, these two words, *glory, honour,* are added.

Glory is oft put for the excellency of a thing (see Chap. i. ver. 3, Sec. 19), so as this dignity was the most excellent that any could be advanced unto. The Hebrew word, כבוד, *gloria*, according to the notation thereof, כבד, *gravis fuit*, importeth a ponderous or substantial thing, opposed to that which is light and vain.

The Greek word, δόξα (δοκέω, ἔδοξα, *statui*), sets out that which is well spoken of, or is of good report, and a glory to one.

The other word, *honour*, הדר, *ornavit* (הדר, *ornatus*, *decor*, *honor*), in Hebrew implieth that which is comley or bright. It is translated beauty, Ps. cx. 3.

The Greek word τιμή (α τίειν, *in honore seu in pretio habere*), intendeth that a due respect be given to such as we have in high account. Where the apostle exhorteth to render unto others their due, he thus exemplifieth it, 'honour to whom honour is due,' Rom. xiii. 7. The duties, therefore, which inferiors owe to their superiors are comprised under this word *honour*; as the duty of servants, 1 Tim. vi. 1; of children, Eph. ix. 2; and of subjects, 1 Peter ii. 17. This, then, sheweth that as Christ is most excellent in himself, so he is highly to be esteemed by others. Honour is due unto him, therefore honour is to be yielded to him, Ps. xlv. 2, 3, 11, 17. We honour kings crowned with gold; shall we not honour Christ crowned with glory? These are fit epithets to set out the royal dignity of Christ. They shew him to be most excellent in himself, and to be highly esteemed by others. When the apostle saith of Christ, 'God hath exalted him, and given him a name which is above every name,' he sets out his *glory*; and where he addeth, 'that at the name of Jesus every knee should bow,' he sets out his *honour*. By this the ignominy of the cross is taken away.

Sec. 61. *Of dominion given to Christ.*

God contented not himself that he had advanced the foresaid man to a royal dignity, and that to the most excellent that could be, but also added dominion and jurisdiction unto him. For it is further said, in the apostrophe to God, 'and didst set him over the works of thine hands.'

This copulative *and* here joineth together the distinct parts of Christ's advancement.

In this phrase, 'thou didst set,' which is the interpretation of one Greek word, κατέστησας, there is some difference from the Hebrew, תמשילהו, *dominari fecisti eum*, which is thus translated, 'thou madest him to have dominion.'

The Greek word is somewhat more general than the Hebrew. It signifieth to appoint, or to set, or place, as Heb. v. 1. Every high priest is *ordained*,' καθίσταται, *constituitur*, or appointed. And James iii. 6, 'The tongue is *set* in our members,' or 'among our members.'

But the Hebrew word more especially signifieth to rule, as Gen. iv. 7, 'Thou shalt rule over him,' תמשל־בו. And in the third conjugation, 'to make to rule,' or to give power to rule,' as Dan. xi. 39, 'He shall cause them to rule,' המשילם, *dominari faciet eos*. This conjugation is in the text in hand used by the psalmist. When the preposition which signifieth *over*, ἐπί, is added to the verb that signifieth *to set*, as in this text it is, it intendeth as much as the Hebrew word doth, namely, to be set over others to rule them, or to be appointed to rule, or to be made to rule. So it is oft translated: Mat. xxv. 21, 23, 'I will make thee ruler over many,' ἐπὶ πολλῶν σε καταστήσω. This, then, implieth an higher degree of advancement, which is authority and rule.

This point is further amplified by the extent thereof, in this phrase, 'over the works of thy hands.'

Of the meaning of this phrase, see Chap. i. Secs. 132, 134.

The difference betwixt this phrase, 'works of thy hands,' in this place, and the former, is this, that here it is taken in a larger extent than there. There it comprehended only the heavens; but here all manner of creatures, both above and below, not any at all excepted. The indefinite expression of 'the works of God's hands' intends as much.

This is further confirmed in the next verse by this general particle *all*, 'all things,' πάντα, whereof see Secs. 67, 68.

Sec. 62. *Of the subjection of all things to Christ.*

Ver. 8. To make Christ's rule the more absolute, this is further added, 'Thou hast put all things in subjection under his feet.' This is the rather added to make up that part of the assumption which seemed to be wanting, ver. 5. The whole assumption was to have been this, 'To Christ he hath put in subjection the world to come, but to angels he hath not put it in subjection.' The latter part is there set down, the former here; at least in the full sense, though not in the very words: for instead of *the world to come*, he here saith *all things*, which is more than that. It is a logical and true principle, that under the greater, the less is comprised. Now, *all things* may well be accounted the greater in reference to *the world to come*.

Again, where he there said, *unto them*, he here saith, *under his feet*, which implieth a greater degree of subjection on their part who are put under, and of dominion on his part under whose feet they are put.

This phrase, *under his feet*, implieth that they are brought as much under him as any can be brought. They are not *beside* him, as the princes stood beside the king of Judah, Jer. xxxvi. 21, but under him; not *under his hand*, as soldiers under the hand of their captain, 2 Sam. xviii. 2, but *under his feet*; not *at his feet*, as the ten thousand that went at Barak's feet, Judges iv. 10, but *under* his feet. Lower than under one's feet cannot any be put. Thus, therefore, do the people of God express the subjection of Gentiles under them: Ps. xlvii. 3, 'He shall subdue the people under us, and the nations under our feet.' It doth withal imply that there is no fear of any creatures freeing themselves from subjection under Christ. They who are under one's feet are kept down from rising up against him.

The phrase applied to Christ's enemies, implieth an utter subduing of them, and his just indignation against them, as hath been shewed, Chap. i. Sec. 154.

Not enemies only, but all of all sorts are thus put in subjection under Christ, which intimateth that all yield obedience unto him; some as his enemies, perforce, others willingly, Ps. cx. 2, 3; so as Christ's dominion is not a mere titular matter. As he hath power to command, so subjection is yielded to his command.

It is therefore a point of egregious folly to be like unto those who sent this message after this Lord, 'We will not have this man to rule over us,' Luke xix. 14. All are put under his feet; will they, nill they, they shall be subject unto him. 'Who hath resisted his will?' Rom. ix. 19.

In the days of his flesh, fishes, Luke v. 6, winds, sea, Mat. viii. 27, diseases, Luke iv. 39, the worst of men, John ii. 15, and xviii. 6, and devils themselves, Mark i. 28, were all subject unto him. Mark what a gentile said of the commanding and overruling power of Christ, Luke vii. 7, 8.

As it is our duty, so it will be our wisdom, voluntarily to submit to Christ, and to yield willing obedience to him.

This is the property of his people, Ps. cx. 3. Thus shall we make a virtue of necessity. We are put under Christ's feet. There is therefore a necessity of submitting. But free and willing subjection is a virtue.

Sec. 63. *Of humiliation the way to exaltation.*

All the fore-mentioned branches of Christ's advancement, which are here, and Isa. liii. 12; Eph. iv. 10; Philip. ii. 10, and in sundry other places inferred upon his humiliation, afford unto us sundry considerable observations, as,

1. That working and suffering are the ways to glory and honour.
2. That works of service and suffering were requisite for man's redemption and salvation, ver. 10.
3. That God was mindful of his Son in his meanest and lowest estate (Sec. 55), according to that which is written of the Son in relation to his Father, 'Thou will not leave my soul in hell; neither wilt thou suffer thy Holy One to see corruption. Thou wilt shew me the path of life,' &c., Ps. xvi. 10, 11.
4. That all the members of Christ's body have good ground to be confident, that after they have done and endured what God shall call them unto, they shall be recompensed with a crown of glory, 1 Peter v. 4.

Christ therefore is to be looked on, as well advanced as debased; in his exaltation and in his humiliation; in heaven at his Father's right hand, as well as on the cross, or in the grave; crowned with glory, as well as with thorns, Heb. xii. 1.

Thus will our faith be better settled and more strengthened, as Stephen's was, when he 'saw the Son of man standing at the right hand of God,' Acts vii. 56.

Thus shall we with much patience, contentedness, and cheerfulness, do and endure what God by his providence calleth us unto; knowing that, 'If we suffer with Christ, we shall also reign with him,' 2 Tim. ii. 12.

Sec. 64. *Of the resolution of* Heb. ii. 6, 7, *and first part* 8th.

Ver. 6–8. *But one in a certain place testified, saying, What is man, that thou art mindful of him? or the son of man, that thou visitest him? Thou madest him a little lower than the angels; thou crownedst him with glory and honour, and didst set him over the works of thy hands: thou hast put all things in subjection under his feet.*

This text is a testimony taken out of Ps. viii. 4–6.
The sum of it is, Christ's exaltation.
About it two points are observable:
1. The manner of bringing in the testimony.
2. The matter contained therein.

The manner is manifested two ways:
1. By an indefinite pointing at, 1, the penman, *one;* 2, the place, *in a certain place.*

In the matter two points are distinctly demonstrated:
1. The low degree *from* which Christ was exalted;
2, the high degree *to* which Christ was exalted.

That low degree is set down, 1, simply, ver. 6; 2, comparatively, ver. 7.

In the simple consideration of Christ's low degree, observe,
1. The titles under which it is couched.
2. The manifestation of God's tender respect to him therein.

The titles are two: 1, man; 2, son of man.
The manifestation of God's respect is in two phrases: 1, mindful; 2, visit.

In the comparative expression of Christ's low degree are noted,
1. The persons.
2. The point.

The persons are of two sorts:
1. The efficient or author who put him under, *God,* implied in this apostrophe, and under this relative *thou.*
2. The object or persons under whom he was put, *angels.*

The point or comparison itself declares,
1. The degree of humiliation, *lower.*
2. A restraint or limitation thereof, *little.* This

hath reference both to the measure, and also to the continuance of his humiliation, little in measure, little, or short in time.

In the high degree whereunto Christ was advanced, two things are noted:

1. The person that exalted him. Even the same that humbled him, *thou*.
2. The kind of advancement. This consisteth of two parts:
    1. Dignity; 2, authority.

His dignity is,
1. Propounded in this metaphor, *crowned*; so as it was royal.
2. Amplified, and that two ways:
    1. By the excellency of that crown; *crown of glory*.
    2. By the esteem of others; *honour*.
3. His authority is manifested two ways:
    1. By his jurisdiction over others.
    2. By others' subjection to him.

His jurisdiction is set out,
1. By the kind of it, *set over*.
2. By the subjects over whom he is set, *the works of thine hands*.

Others' subjection is set down,
1. By the persons or things subjected to him, *all things*.
2. By the low degree of his subjection, *under his feet*.

Sec. 65. *Of the instructions raised out of* Heb. ii. 6, 7, *and former part of the* 8*th*,

I. *To allege a proof of a point, is as much as to allege the point itself.* This I gather from the note of an assumption, δὲ, *but*. For in ordinary course this should have followed, 'But unto Jesus he hath put in subjection the world to come.' Instead thereof, the apostle produceth a testimony of Scripture that proves as much.

II. *Sacred Scripture receives no authority from the penman thereof.* This is one reason why the apostle nameth not the psalmist, but saith, τίς, 'one.' See Sec. 52.

III. *It is sufficient to quote the words of Scripture.* This is sufficient, though no book, nor chapter, nor verse be quoted. See Sec. 50.

IV. *The Old Testament testifieth of Christ,* διεμαρτύρατο. See Sec. 51.

V. *Man of himself is a mean, mortal, and miserable creature.* The Hebrew word translated man, intends thus much. See Sec. 54.

VI. *Man comes of man.* Every one is a 'son of man,' υἱὸς ἀνθρώπου, and descends from Adam. See Sec. 54.

VII. *Christ was a mean man.* This title *man* is here especially meant of Christ. See Secs. 54, 59.

VIII. *Christ was born of man.* Even he also was a son of man. See Sec. 54.

IX. *Nor Christ, nor any of his members are ever out of God's mind.* He is mindful of man, μιμνήσκῃ. Christ, the head, is here to be considered with all his members. See Sec. 55.

X. *God had an especial care of Christ and of his members.* He visited them, ἐπισκέπτῃ. See Sec. 56.

XI. *It is God that maketh low.* This apostrophe, 'Thou hast made him lower,' ἠλάττωσας, is directed to God. See Sec. 57.

XII. *Christ was made low.* This positive is comprised under the comparative, *lower*.

XIII. *The Lord of angels was made lower than angels.* This relative *him*, αὐτὸν, hath reference to him which is the head of all principality and power, Col. ii. 10.

XIV. *Christ's abasement was but a small abasement.*

XV. *Christ was humbled but for a short time,* βραχύ τι. These two last doctrines arise out of this particle of diminution, *little*. See Sec. 59.

XVI. *Christ's exaltation followed upon his humiliation.* The order of setting the one after the other intimateth as much.

XVII. *The same God that made Christ low, highly advanced him.* The apostrophe made to God about Christ's humiliation, is continued to God about Christ's exaltation.

XVIII. *Christ is advanced to a royal estate.* God crowned him, ἐστεφάνωσεν.

XIX. *Christ is advanced to glory,* δόξα. See Sec. 60.

XX. *Honour,* τίμη, *accompanieth glory*. See Sec. 60.

XXI. *Christ hath authority added to his dignity.* See Sec. 61.

XXII. *Christ's authority is over God's creatures,* even the works of his hands, κατέστησας ἐπὶ τὰ ἔργα. See Sec. 61.

XXIII. *Every creature is put under Christ.* This general, *all things,* πάντα, intends as much.

XXIV. *Creatures are under Christ as low as can be.* This metaphor, *under his feet,* demonstrates as much. See Sec. 62.

Sec. 66. *Of the extent of this word* '*all things*.'

Ver. 8. *For in that he put all in subjection under him, he left nothing that is not put under him. But now we see not yet all things put under him.*

The apostle having largely and faithfully cited the very words of a divine testimony to confirm the excellency of Christ, he proceedeth to declare the meaning thereof in such particulars as most concerned the party intended.

The first particle, *for,* γὰρ, implieth an explanation of that which goeth before; as if he had said, David there speaketh of Christ, *for* this is the meaning of his words.

Herein lieth the force of the apostle's argument:

David saith, All things are put under the feet of the man of whom he speaketh;

But all things are put under the feet of none but of Jesus:

Therefore none but Jesus can be the man of whom David speaketh.

If any creature at all be exempted from that general *all things*, Christ is not absolutely supreme.

To shew that the force of the argument lieth in this general, *all things*, the apostle resumes the word of the psalmist thus: 'In that he put all in subjection under him.'

In this repetition, instead of *under his feet*, this indefinite phrase is used, *under him*, which is in effect as much as the former; for they who are absolutely put under one, are put under his feet. A man's feet are part of himself. The former is the more emphatical, but it was sufficient once to express that emphasis.

It cannot be denied but that this general, *all*, hath in sundry places restraints or limitations.

1. It restrains to all kinds and sorts of things, as in this phrase, 'All things continue as they were from the beginning of the creation,' 2 Peter iii. 4. Many millions of particulars have perished, as of men, beasts, fowls, fishes, plants, minerals, &c., but yet the kinds of them remain.

2. It is used synecdochically, as where the woman of Samaria saith, 'He told me all things that ever I did,' John iv. 29; she means many secret things.

Where the word is taken in these or in any other respects improperly, it may be discerned either by some circumstance of the text, as where God saith he 'will destroy all flesh,' Gen. vi. 17, and that 'all flesh died,' Gen. vii. 21, the context sheweth that such as were in the ark must be excepted; or by some other scripture, as this general, 'The blood of Christ cleanseth from all sin,' 1 John i. 7; hath an exception of total apostasy, Heb. vi. 6; of the sin against the Holy Ghost, Mat. xii. 32; and of final impenitency, Luke xiii. 3. But where there is nothing in the text, nor in any other part of Scripture, nor in common reason and understanding, to limit this general, it is to be taken in the largest extent, as John i. 3, Mat. xi. 27, and in this place.

Obj. The psalmist seems to restrain this general to things living on the earth and in the waters; for he doth give instance in these particulars: 'All sheep and oxen, yea, and the beasts of the field, the fowl of the air, and the fish of the sea,' Ps. viii. 7, 8.

Ans. He doth not restrain it to those creatures, but only exemplifieth it in them. Now, for an exemplification, it is sufficient to reckon up some particular instances, though all be not mentioned. Where the apostle reckoneth up seventeen fruits of the flesh, he addeth this clause, *and such like*, to shew that there were many other besides those seventeen, Gal. v. 19–21.

Particular instances of some generals are so many as we may say of them what the evangelist did of Christ's works, 'There are also many other, the which, if they should be written every one, I suppose that even the world itself could not contain the books that should be written,' John xxi. 25.

2. The psalmist, alluding to Gen. i. 26, and ix. 2, resteth in those particulars which are there mentioned.

3. As Moses, so the psalmist thought it sufficient to exemplify the dominion of man over such sensible creatures as were visible, and might be seen and experimentally known to be put under man.

4. The psalmist doth implicitly intend Christ, but the apostle plainly, directly, and explicitly speaketh of him: and his main scope was to advance Christ above all invisible creatures, even angels themselves. Therefore it concerned him to shew the uttermost extent of those *all things*, which he doth in this phrase, 'He left nothing that is not put under him,' that is, he includeth and compriseth every creature, invisible or visible, above or below, celestial or super-celestial, terrestrial or sub-terrestrial, not angels, not devils excepted.

Sec. 67. *Of all things put under Christ.*

This phrase, 'not put under,' is the interpretation of one Greek word, ἀνυπότακτον, *decompositum*, which I find in three other places of the New Testament, and translated 'disobedient,' 1 Tim. i. 9; 'unruly,' Titus i. 6, 10.[1]

The Greek word, as here taken, is most properly used of oxen, horses, and other beasts which will not be brought under the yoke. In other authors, the word is used to set out such as are *sui juris*, of themselves, subject to none, or under the command of none. In this sense it may fitly be here taken; for in reference to Christ there is not any creature so of itself as it is not under his power, government, and command.

If it be taken in the former sense, it implieth thus much: there is none, be he never so refractory and stubborn, but is under the command of Christ, Mat. viii. 8, 9. And if otherwise they will not, they shall be forced to obey, as Mark i. 27. See more hereof Sec. 62.

Because the point most questioned was about the persons or things put under Christ; therefore the apostle yet further insisteth on that general *all*, and sheweth that it must be taken without limitation or exception of any. For this cause, by way of explanation, he addeth this clause, 'He left nothing that is not put under him,' that is, no creature is exempted from subjection under Christ.

Sec. 68. *Of subjection of all things denied to any man.*

Against the extent of the foresaid subjection of all

[1] τάττειν. See Sec. 43.

things, the apostle produceth an objection in these words, 'But now we see not yet all things put under him.'

There are seven words in that objection which carry an especial emphasis.

1. *But*, δέ, see ver. 6, Sec. 50. This is an adversative conjunction, which oft implieth an objection, as Rom. iii. 5, 'But if our unrighteousness,' &c. So here it intendeth an objection; and such an one as in the matter of it cannot be denied to be true.

2. *Now.* This conjunction is ordinarily used to set out the time present; yet it is sometimes used as a mere supplement, or complement; as Now then, Go to now, What now: so 1 Cor. xii. 1, 2. Thus in Hebrew, עתה, Ps. ii. 10 and xxxix. 7. The Grecians use to put a note of difference on this particle: when it signifieth the time present, they use to put an accent over it, νῦν, as John iv. 23; but when they use it for a supplement, they set it down without any accent, νυν. Here it is accented with a circumflex; and it setteth out the time present; namely, the time of our pilgrimage, while here we live on earth, even those days of our flesh, as the apostle styles this time, Heb. v. 7.

3. *Not yet.* These two words are but one in Greek, οὔπω; and it useth to have reference to some remarkable matter or time; as to Christ's suffering, John vii. 6, 8, 30; to professors' martyrdom, Heb. xii. 4; to the full consummation of all things, 1 John iii. 2. To that time, namely, to the continuance of the world unto the last day, it hath reference in this place.

4. *We see*, ὁρῶμεν. This is here to be taken of seeing with the eyes of the body; as where an angel saith of Christ, 'There shall ye see him,' ὄψεσθε, Mat. xxviii. 7. In the passive it implieth a clear manifestation, as Heb. ix. 28, Sec. 142, ὀφθήσεται. Of different kinds of seeing, see Sec. 72.

It here intendeth a visible experience or proof of a thing; and it implieth that men are hard to believe things which they see not; because they did not visibly see all things under Christ, they deny it so to be.

5. *All things*, τὰ πάντα. This is to be taken in the largest extent; no creature exempted; as was before shewed, Sec. 66.

6. *Put under*, ὑποτεταγμένα, see Sec. 43. This is to be taken of the lowest degree of subjection; even under one's feet; as hath been before shewed, Sec. 67.

7. *Him*, αὐτῷ. This relative hath an indefinite reference to him that was styled *man*, ver. 6, even as if he had said, *to any man*.

No natural man out of Christ was ever so advanced. As for believers, who are true members of Christ, though in Christ, as they are united to him, they have a right to all things: 'All things are theirs,' 1 Cor. iii. 21–23, yet 'now we see not all things put under' any of them. 'It doth not yet appear what we shall be,' 1 John iii. 2. We here, as heirs, are under tutors. This world is a place of probation. It becomes us to wait for the glory that is to come.

Thus the apostle hath laid down the objection to the full; as if somewhat more largely he had thus expressed it: It hath not in this time of life, nor will be while this world continueth visibly seen, that all things, without any exception, have been put in subjection to any one man.

The apostle denieth not the truth of anything in this objection, in regard of the matter thereof, but granteth every clause therein. Only he denieth the consequence inferred thereupon, which is this, that therefore all things are not put under Jesus. The falsehood of this inference is manifested in the next verse.

It was not without cause that the apostle here produced this objection; for an objection against a truth gives an occasion to him that loveth, and desireth to maintain that truth, to answer it; and a pertinent and a proper answer doth more clear and prove the truth, so as truth many times receives advantage from objections made against it. It is therefore usual with the penmen of sacred Scripture to propound and answer objections. Ezek. xii. 22, &c.; and xviii. 2, &c.; Rom. vi. 1, &c.; 2 Peter iii. 4, &c.

Sec. 69. *Of Christ's dominion far exceeding all others.*

The foresaid objection being in the matter and substance of it true, doth much amplify the dominion of Christ. For thereby it plainly appeareth, that Christ's dominion is such an one, as never any had the like. Experience giveth proof to the truth hereof.

'Solomon reigneth over all kingdoms from the river Euphrates unto the border of Egypt,' 1 Kings iv. 21; and 'Ahasuerus, from India even to Ethiopia, over one hundred and twenty-seven provinces,' Esther i. 1. But Christ's dominion hath no limits nor bounds.

Nebuchadnezzar was a 'king of kings;' his dominion was 'to the end of the earth,' Dan. ii. 37 and iv. 22. The Lord gave to Cyrus all the kingdoms of the earth, Ezra i. 1. All the world was taxed by Cæsar Augustus, Luke i. 1. But these phrases, 'the end of the earth,' 'all kingdoms of the earth,' 'all the world,' are synecdochically used, the whole being put for a part. Besides, no part of their dominions ever reached unto heaven, as Christ's doth. That which is said of Nebuchadnezzar's greatness reaching unto heaven, Dan. iv. 22, is hyperbolical.

Sec. 70. *Of the pope's usurped power over earth, purgatory, hell, and heaven.*

We may here take notice of the intolerable arrogancy of the pope of Rome, who challengeth an universal jurisdiction in earth, purgatory, hell, and heaven.

1. On earth he takes him to be, not only a monarch over the catholic church throughout the whole

world, but also to have power over all kingdoms, to set up and put down kings. The pope gave the West Indians to the Spaniards. Not only those flatterers and deifiers of the pope,[1] who lived before the Jesuits (who as cunning refiners undertook to allay the gross and palpable blasphemies of former papists, the substance whereof they themselves maintained), but also Bellarmine himself,[2] one of the most subtle refiners, avoucheth, that the pope hath power to change kingdoms; and to take them from one, and confer them upon another, as the chiefest spiritual prince.

2. Concerning purgatory, it is said,[3] that the pope if he would might empty all purgatory.

3. Concerning hell, it is said,[4] that though the pope should thrust an innumerable company of souls into hell, none may judge him for it.

4. Concerning heaven, they comprise a supreme power of putting into, or casting out of heaven under the keys, which, papists say, Christ gave to Peter alone, and in Peter to his successor the pope. Thereupon the pope takes upon him to canonize, and make glorious saints in heaven whom he pleaseth.

The 8th Psalm (out of which the foresaid testimony is taken) is by sundry papists applied to the pope; and also the first verse of the 24th Psalm. Doth not he who assumeth to himself these, and other things higher than these, exalt himself above all that is called God; and therein shew himself to be plain antichrist? 2 Thes. ii. 4.

Sec. 71. *Of the resolution and observations of part of the eighth verse.*

8. *For in that he put all in subjection under him, he left nothing that is not put under him. But now we see not yet all things put under him.*

In this text is laid down the difference betwixt Christ's dominion and others'.

Hereof are two parts:
1. The extent of Christ's dominion.
2. The restraint of others' dominion.

The former is set out by an explanation of that divine testimony which he had produced. Here then we may observe,
1. A citation of the text itself.
2. The explanation thereof.

In the citation there is observable,
1. The maner of quoting it, thus, *For in that.*
2. The matter. Wherein four distinct persons are to be noted:
1. The agent, *he put.*
2. The patients, *all.*

[1] Johan. Capist. Panormit. Alban. Jacobat. Gratian. Joan. de Pacif.
[2] *Bellarm. de Rom. Pont.* lib. v. cap. vi.—Papa potest mutare regna, et uni auferre, et alteri conferre, tanquam summus princeps spiritualis.
[3] Papa, si vellet, posset totum Purgatorium evacuare, *Johan. Angel.*
[4] Gratian. 440; Bellarm. de Sanct. Beat. lib. i. cap. ix.

3. The low degree, *in subjection under.*
4. The person under whom they were put, *him,* that is, Christ.

The explanation is in these words, ' He left nothing that is not put under him.' This shews the full extent of *all.*

The restraint of others' dominion is here set down by way of objection, yet so as the matter contained therein is not denied. Hereof see Sec. 68.

In this objection observe, 1, the substance; 2, the circumstance thereof.

The substance is, 1, generally intimated in this adversative conjunction, *but,* δὲ.

2. It is particularly expressed, *now we see not,* &c.

In that expression is set down,
1. The main point objected, *all things not put under him,* αὐτῷ τὰ πάντα ὑποτεταγμένα.
2. The proof thereof, *we see not,* ἐρῶμεν.

The circumstance concerns the time in two English words, *now, yet,* οὔπω.

The observations hence arising are these:

I. *There is a great difference betwixt Christ's dominion and others'.* This ariseth from the general scope of this text. See Sec. 69.

II. *Points questioned must be clearly propounded.* This ariseth from the inference of this explanation upon the former testimony, implied in this causal particle, *for.* See Sec. 66.

III. *It is God that puts one under another.* This relative *he* hath reference to God. See Sec. 57.

IV. *Creatures are under Christ.* They are put in subjection under him. See Sec. 67.

V. *Creatures are as low as can be under Christ.* This phrase, *under him,* is as much as *under his feet.* See Sec. 62.

VI. *No creature at all is exempted from subjection under Christ.* ' He left nothing that is not put under him.' See Sec. 67.

VII. *Objections against a point may be produced.* This particle *but* intendeth as much. See Sec. 68.

VIII. *Experience of all ages is a good proof.* This phrase, *we see not,* intends as much. Withal it implies another point, viz.,

IX. *Men hardly believe that which they see not.*

X. *In this world no man ever had an absolute monarchy.* These particles, *now, yet,* set out the time of this world. This phrase, *not all things under him,* denies an absolute monarchy. See Sec. 69.

XI. *The fulness of saints' glory is not here discerned.* See Sec. 68.

Sec. 72. *Of seeing Jesus.*

Ver. 9. *But we see Jesus, who was made a little lower than the angels for the suffering of death, crowned with glory and honour; that he by the grace of God should taste death for every man.*

The answer to the former objection is here so plainly and fully set down, as thereby it evidently appears what *man* was meant in the fore-quoted testimony, namely, Jesus, who is expressly named, and proved to be the only man that was there intended. This answer is brought in by way of assumption, as this assuming note *but* declareth, see Sec. 50; or, to explain the passage more clearly, it may be brought in with discretive notes, thus: *though* we see no other man, *yet* we may discern *Jesus* so and so exalted.

The word here translated, we *see*, βλέπομεν, is sometimes put for bodily sight, sometimes for spiritual.

If the sight here in this verse mentioned be taken for bodily sight, it must be applied to the witnesses of Christ's resurrection, whereof mention is made, 1 Cor. xv. 5-7, and of his ascension, Acts i. 9, 10, and to the visible evidences which he gave of his supreme power in heaven, Acts ii. 33, and iv. 10, and ix. 5, &c.

But all these visible evidences were accomplished before the time of the apostle's writing this epistle. And the apostle here speaking in the present tense of a present and continued sight, must needs be understood to speak of a spiritual sight. Though our English use one and the same word, namely, *see*, in the objection and in the answer; yet in the Greek there are two words differing in sense and syllables.

The former is taken of the sight of the body. See Sec. 68.

This latter, of the sight of the mind, Heb. iii. 19, Rev. iii. 18.

Both the Greek words are oft used in the one and the other sense. The former word, ὁράω, sets out the sight of the mind, Heb. xi. 27, James ii. 24; and this latter, βλέπω, sets out the sight of the body, Mat. xi. 4, and xii. 22.

But here it must be taken for the sight of the mind; for Jesus is crowned with glory in heaven, where men on earth see him not.

That we may the better discern how men are said to see Christ in glory, it will not be unseasonable to set out the different kinds of sight expressed in Scripture.

There is a sight of the body, and of the mind: both these are exercised on earth and in heaven; on earth, ordinarily and extraordinarily. To exemplify these.

1. All among whom Christ conversed in the days of his flesh on earth, saw him with their bodily eyes after an ordinary manner, Mat. viii. 34.

2. Stephen and Paul saw him with their bodily eyes after an extraordinary manner, Acts vii. 56, 1 Cor. xv. 8. We do not read of any other that saw Christ after his ascension.

3. All of all sorts shall see Christ with their bodily eyes at the day of judgment, Mat. xxiv. 30, and xxvi. 64.

4. Glorified saints shall see him with a beatifical vision in heaven, Rev. xxii. 4.

The sight of the mind consisteth in two things:

1. In understanding things to be as they are, though they be invisible to the bodily eye, John ix. 39.

2. In believing what they conceive to be true, Heb. xi. 27.

Thus, as the body, so the soul hath two eyes, which are knowledge and faith. The former is here especially intended, yet the latter is not to be excluded; for true Christians believe what they know of Christ. As in Greek, to express the two fore-mentioned kinds of sight, there are two distinct words; so also there are the like in sundry Latin translations, and might also in our English be distinguished, by translating the former thus, 'We see not;' the latter thus, 'We perceive.' This latter word is so translated, 2 Cor. vii. 8.

This metaphor of seeing, is used in spiritual matters, because we are as much assured of them, as if we beheld them with our bodily eyes: 'We believe, and are sure,' saith Peter, John vi. 69. Believers are as sure that Christ is now in heaven, at God's right hand, crowned with glory and honour, as Thomas was that Christ was risen from the dead, when he saw Jesus before him, and put his hand into Christ's side, John xx. 27, 28.

Nothing can be more sure than that which God's word affirmeth. Believers, who lived before Christ was exhibited, were in their souls certain and sure of everything that God had foretold concerning the Messiah. In this respect Christ saith, 'Abraham rejoiced to see my day; and he saw it, and was glad,' John viii. 56. How much more may believers be sure of those things which in God's word are revealed of the glory of Christ. Of such, saith Christ, 'Blessed are they that have not seen, and yet have believed,' John xx. 29.

As for this particular of Christ's being crowned with glory, it is testified by four evangelists, and by all the apostles whose writings are come to our hands; and by the gifts that Christ conferred on sons of men, whether extraordinary, Acts ii. 33, and iii. 16, or ordinary, Eph. iv. 8, &c. Well, therefore, might the apostle say of himself and other believers, 'We see Jesus.' They did as well know that Christ in heaven was crowned with glory, as they, who on earth saw it, knew that he was crowned with thorns.

What may be thought of them that live under the light of the gospel, whereby the great mysteries of Jesus Christ are fully and clearly revealed, and yet, if they be demanded, whether ever they saw Jesus crowned with glory, and sitting at God's right hand, and making intercession for us, will be ready to answer, after such a manner as the Ephesians did, Acts xix. 1, 2, we have not so much as heard of any such thing? What may be thought of such, but that 'the god of this world hath blinded the minds of them which believe not, lest the light of the glorious gospel of Christ, who is the image of God, should shine unto them'? 2 Cor. iv. 4. If they be blessed, who have not seen, and yet have believed, John xx. 29, surely the case of those who do not now see Jesus crowned with glory and honour, must needs be a most wretched case.

As for us, who can say, with this blessed apostle, 'We see Jesus crowned,' what cause have we to bless God for this evidence of his good providence, that our Saviour, after all his sufferings, being entered into glory, that glory should be so clearly revealed, and we to see him crowned with glory? Christ, who is in heaven, is to us on earth invisible, in regard of bodily sight; yet by faith we see him, which is enough to work in us such a spirit as Moses, Heb. xi. 27, and Stephen had, Acts vii. 56.

Let us therefore make use of this spiritual sight, till we come to the beatifical sight of Jesus.

Sec. 73. *Of this title Jesus.*

The person of whom the apostle here speaketh is here styled by his proper name Jesus, Ἰησοῦς, which is the Greek expression of Jeshua, and signifieth a saviour. *Jesus*,[1] in Hebrew, is the same that *Saviour* is in English; so as these two phrases, 'Jesus, which is called Christ,' Mat. i. 16, and 'a Saviour, which is Christ,' Luke ii. 11, intend one and the same thing.

This name *Jesus* was by God himself given to his Son; for before the conception of Christ, an angel from God thus saith to her that was to be his mother, 'Thou shalt call his name Jesus,' Luke i. 31; and again, after he was conceived, but before his birth, it was said to his reputed father, 'Thou shalt call his name Jesus,' Mat. i. 21. Actually it was given to him at his circumcision, Luke ii. 21, as our name useth to be given to us at our baptism.

By this name he was called in his infancy, Mat. ii. 1, Luke ii. 27; in his childhood, Luke ii. 43; in his youth, Luke ii. 52; in his man-age, Mat. iii. 13; so all his lifetime: by friends, John i. 45; foes, John xviii. 5, 7; countrymen, John vi. 42; aliens, John xii. 21; at his death, Mat. xxvii. 37; after his death, and that by angels, Mat. xxviii. 5, Acts i. 11; by evangelists, Luke xxiv. 15; apostles, Rom. viii. 11; yea, and by devils, Acts xix. 15.

This title *Jesus* is a most honourable title, intimating that full salvation which he bringeth to his people. The angel that brought the message of his birth and name rendereth this reason thereof, 'He shall save his people from their sins,' Mat. i. 21. In this respect he is styled ' A Saviour,' Luke ii. 11; ' Our Saviour,' 2 Tim. i. 10; ' The Saviour of the body,' Eph. v. 23; ' The Saviour of the world,' John iv. 42; ' The Saviour of all men,' 1 Tim. iv. 10; yea, ' salvation ' itself, Luke ii. 30.

By the name *Jesus* people were put in mind of that great end of his coming into the world, namely, to save them.

Yet the envious Jews under this name scorned and

[1] יהושע *ab* ישע, *salvavit*.

derided him, by adding his country thereunto; thus, ' Jesus of Galilee,' ' Jesus of Nazareth,' Mat. xxvi. 69, 71; and in scorn this title was set over his head, ' This is Jesus,' &c., Mat. xxvii. 37.

The apostle, therefore, in setting forth the excellency of Christ, oft useth this name *Jesus*. It is oftener used alone, without any addition, in this epistle than in any other one epistle, that these Hebrews might be kept from that base conceit which their countrymen had of Jesus, and move them to have him in high esteem.

There are two whom the Seventy in the Old Testament style Jesus; namely, Joshua the son of Nun, Josh. i. 1, and Joshua the son of Josedech, Haggai i. 14. Both these were accounted saviours of Israel, in regard of temporal deliverances, and therein were types of Christ.

In the New Testament, where mention is made of Joshua, he is styled Jesus, as Acts vii. 45, Heb. iv. 8. There is mention of another also called Jesus, Col. iv. 11, who, being a Jew, was, as is probable, in Hebrew called Joshua.

The apostle had before called Christ the ' Son of God,' ' the first begotten,' ' God,' ' Lord,' which are titles proper to his divine nature. But here he speaketh of his excellency as *man;* and thereupon giveth him that title which setteth out the distinct reason why, being God, he assumed man's nature; namely, that he might be a fit and able Saviour of man: fit, as he was man; able, as he was God.

Well may this title *Jesus*, in regard of the signification of it, be given unto Christ. For,

1. He was a *true* Saviour, Heb. viii. 2, not a typical Saviour, as Joshua and other like saviours, Neh. ix. 27.

2. He was a most *free* Saviour: ' According to his mercy he saved us,' Tit. iii. 5; ' not for price,' 1 Pet. i. 18.

3. He was an *all-sufficient* Saviour. He satisfied divine justice, assuaged divine wrath, endured the infinite curse of the law, overcame death, hell, and him that had the power of them, ver. 14, Rev. i. 18.

4. He was an *universal* Saviour; the Saviour of all that are or shall be saved, 1 Tim. iv. 10.

5. He was a *total* Saviour. He saveth soul and body, 1 Cor. vi. 20.

6. He was an *everlasting* Saviour. He brings all that believe in him to everlasting life. As he is, so he was from the beginning, and ever will continue so, Heb. xiii. 8, Rev. xiii. 8, Heb. vii. 24.

7. He was a *perfect* Saviour, Heb. vii. 25. He leaves nothing simply in the case of salvation for any other to do.

8. He is the *only* Saviour, Acts iv. 12, Isa. lxiii. 5. On these grounds it becomes us,

1. To consider the need that we have of a Saviour. This will make us inquire how we may be saved, Acts xvi. 30.

2. To fly to Christ for salvation. He invites all so to do, John vii. 37. He casts away none that come unto him, John vi. 37.
3. To trust on him, Acts xvi. 31, 1 Tim. iv. 10.
4. To rejoice in him, Luke i. 47.
5. To bless God for him, Luke i. 68.
6. To serve him who saveth us, Luke i. 74, 75.
7. To do all in his name, Col. iii. 17.

Of this title *Jesus*, joined with the other, *Christ*, see Chap. iii. 1, Sec. 29.

Sec. 74. *Of applying the testimony.*

That it may the more evidently appear that Jesus was especially intended in the foresaid testimony, the apostle applieth to him both that low estate to which the man mentioned by the psalmist was humbled, and also that high estate whereunto he was advanced; and both these in the very words of the testimony: the former thus, 'Who was made a little lower than the angels;' the latter thus, 'crowned with glory and honour.' The meaning of both these hath been before declared. See Sec. 57.

This high exaltation of Christ is here again brought in, to prove that 'all things were put under him;' for the first particle of this verse, *but*, hath reference to the exaltation of Christ, as if they had been thus joined together: 'But we see Jesus crowned with glory and honour.' The thing questioned in the former verse was this, 'We see not yet all things put under him.' To that, in way of opposition, the apostle addeth this, 'But we see Jesus crowned.' This crowning of Jesus is a clear demonstration that all things are put under his feet, for it sheweth that he hath dignity and authority over them all. And it is here again, upon the mention of Christ's suffering, set down, to take away the scandal of Christ's cross; for Christ crucified was 'unto the Jews a stumblingblock, and unto the Greeks foolishness,' 1 Cor. i. 23. But the glory of Christ after his suffering made his suffering to be accounted no despicable matter, but rather most glorious, it being the way to a crown of glory and honour.

To shew wherein Jesus was made lower than angels, this phrase is inserted, 'For the suffering of death.'

The preposition translated *for*, διὰ, is diversely used in the New Testament. It is sometimes set before the genitive case, and then it signifieth the efficient cause, and that principal, as Rom. i. 5; or instrumental, as Mat. i. 22; or the means whereby a thing is effected, as Acts v. 12. In all these senses it is translated *by*. See Chap. iii. 16, Sec. 164.

Sometimes it is set before the accusative case, and is translated *for;* then it signifieth the final cause, as Mat. xiv. 8, 9; and in this sense it is sometimes translated *because*, as Mat. xiii. 21. In the next verse both cases are joined to it, so as it signifieth both the final and the efficient cause. Here it is joined with the accusative case; but the sentence is so placed between the humiliation and exaltation of Christ, as it may refer to either. Some refer it to the one, some to the other.

It being referred to Christ's humiliation, implieth the end of his being made less than angels, namely, 'for death,' that he might suffer death, or that he might die. For Jesus, as God, was eternal, immortal, and could not die; but as man he was mortal, he could, he did die.

Some place Christ's humiliation below angels in his death, and thus translate it, 'lower than the angels by the suffering of death.' Our English giveth an hint of this, by putting this diverse reading in the margin, thus, 'or, *by*.' But the accusative case, with which the preposition is here joined, will hardly bear that interpretation.

Again, others refer this clause, concerning Christ's death, to his exaltation, thus: 'We see Jesus, for the suffering of death, crowned;' which is as if he had said, Because he suffered death he was crowned, &c.

If this be taken of the order or way of Christ's entering into glory (namely, that after he had suffered death, he was crowned with glory), it well agreeth with other scriptures, which thus speak: 'Ought not Christ to have suffered these things, and enter into glory?' Luke xxiv. 26; 'He became obedient to death, wherefore God also hath highly exalted him,' Philip ii. 8, 9. But thereupon to infer what papists[1] do, that Christ, by his passion, merited his own glorification, is no just consequence, nor an orthodox position. For,

1. The Greek phrase noteth the final rather than the meritorious cause.

2. The glory whereunto Christ was advanced, was due to him by virtue of the union of his human nature with his divine.[2]

3. The glory whereunto he was advanced was too great to be merited.

4. It impaireth the glory of Christ's passion, to say that hereby he merited for himself, implying that he aimed therein more at his own glory than our good.

5. It lesseneth God's love to man, as if God should give his Son to suffer, that thereby he might attain unto another glory than he had before.

6. Christ going out of the world thus prayeth: 'O Father, glorify thou me with thine own self, with the glory which I had with thee before the world was,' John xvii. 5. How was that merited in the world which he had before the world was?

7. The Rhemists themselves,[3] and other papists, acknowledge that Christ was, straight upon his descending from Heaven, to be adored by angels, and all other creatures.

I suppose that the main scope of the apostle is, to set out the end of Christ's being made lower than angels, namely, that he might be a sacrifice to expiate

[1] Rhem. Annot. on this place.
[2] See Domest. Dut., Treat. i. on Eph. v. 25, sec. 32.
[3] Rhem. Annot. on Heb. i. 16.

man's sin; and thereby to make reconciliation betwixt God and man.

In this respect the first interpretation is the fittest, namely, that Christ was made man for this very end, that he might die. This is most agreeable to the proper meaning of the phrase and mind of the apostle.

Thus do many ancient and later divines[1] take it. This is a second proof of Christ's true manhood, namely, his death. See Sec. 1.

Sec. 75. *Of Christ's being man to die.*

Had not Christ assumed a human nature, which (in the substance, and sundry infirmities thereof) is inferior to the angelical nature (which is spiritual and incorruptible), he could not have died. To imagine that as God ('who only hath immortality,' 1 Tim. vi. 16) he should die, would imply the greatest contradiction that could be. God is a spirit of spirits, more free from any corporal infirmity and from death than any created spirits can be. Yet to effect what Christ did by his death, he that died must be God. For Christ died not as a private person to pay his debt, but as a surety for man, and a redeemer of man. For man therefore he was to satisfy infinite justice; to remove the insupportable curse of the law; to break the bonds of death; to overcome the devil, that had the power of death. No single creature could do all these. Immanuel, God with us, God made man, died, and by death effected whatsoever was requisite for man's full redemption. As by being man he was made fit to suffer, so that manhood being united to the Deity, was made able to endure whatsoever should be laid upon it, and thereby also an infinite value, worth, and merit was added to his obedience, for it was the obedience of him that was God, but in the frail nature of man.

Behold here the wonder of wonders. Christ undertakes a task above the power of all the angels, and to effect it he is made lower than angels. If ever power were made perfect in weakness, it was in this.

Sec. 76. *Of Christ's sufferings.*[2]

The apostle here addeth suffering to death (for the suffering of death),[3] to shew that it was not an easy, gentle, light departure out of this world, but a death accompanied with much inward agony and outward torture.

This word in the plural number, *sufferings*, is frequently used in the New Testament, both to set out the manifold sufferings of Christ, as 1 Pet. i. 11, and also the sufferings of Christians for Christ's sake, as Rom. viii. 18. The singular number, *suffering*, is used in this only place, but collectively it compriseth under it all that Christ endured, either in body or soul. To demonstrate the truth hereof, the apostle with an emphasis thus expresseth the kind of his death, 'even the death of the cross,' Philip ii. 8, which was a cursed death, Gal iii. 13.

This will yet more evidently appear, if to Christ's external sufferings be added the sufferings of his soul, see Chap. v. 7, Sec. 38. A prophet saith, that 'his soul was made an offering for sinners,' Isa. liii. 10. This was manifested by an inward agony, concerning which he himself thus saith, 'My soul is exceeding sorrowful unto death;' with strong crying and tears, he thus prayeth, 'O my father, if it be possible, let this cup pass,' yea, again and the third time he fell on his face, and prayed in the same manner. Such was his agony, as 'his sweat was as it were great drops of blood falling to the ground.' So great was his agony, as an angel is said to appear unto him from heaven strengthening him. When he was upon the cross, he cried with a loud voice, saying, 'My God, my God, why hast thou forsaken me?' Do not these effects further prove that the apostle had cause to add *suffering* to Christ's death, and to style it, 'suffering of death.'

All this was to keep us from suffering what by our sins we had deserved. For 'Christ hath redeemed us from the curse of the law, being made a curse for us,' Gal. iii. 13. Who is able to 'comprehend the breadth, and length, and depth, and height of Christ's love to us, which passeth knowledge'? Eph. iii. 18, 19.

What now should not we do and endure for Christ's sake, thereby to testify our love to him?

Sec. 77. *Of this reading 'without God.'*

The proper end of Christ's suffering is thus expressed, 'that he by the grace of God should taste death for every man.'

This conjunction, *that*, is a note of the final cause, as Mat. v. 16. What in special that end was, is shewn in this phrase, 'for every man.' Hereof see Sec. 83.

The chief procuring cause is here said to be, 'the grace of God.' It appears that some of the ancients[1] read the clause otherwise than now we read it, though it be confirmed by a constant consent of all Greek copies as we now have it.

That other reading is thus, 'that, χωρὶς Θεοῦ, *sine Deo, without God* he might taste death.' The Greek words, χάρις Θεοῦ, *gratia Dei*, translated *grace*, in the nominative case, and *without*, are somewhat like. They differ but in one letter. Thence might the mistake arise. For some have here taken grace in the nominative case, for Christ who died; as if he had said, 'that the grace of God might taste death for every man.' He called him grace who tasted death for the salvation of all, saith one;[2] and the Son is called the

---

[1] Chrys. in Heb. ii., Hom. iv.; Theod. in. loc.; Aug. contr. Maxim. lib. iii. cap. xviii.; Ambr. Bullin. Bez. Sun. Pareus.
[2] See Sec. 96.
[3] Διὰ τὸ πάθημα ἃ πάσχω, patior.

[1] Ambr. de fide ad Grat. lib. ii. cap. iv.; Fulgent. and Trasimund. Reg. lib. iii. cap. xx.; Vigil. contr. Eutych.
[2] Jesum gratiam nominat qui pro omnium salute gustavit mortem.—*Ambr. de fide ad Grat.*, lib. ii. cap. iv.

grace of God the Father, saith another.¹ But the word used by the apostle is of the dative case, so as hereby the likeness of the Greek words is taken away, and the mistake appears to be greater.

The sense wherein the fathers used this phrase, *without God*, was this, that though Christ consisted of two natures, divine and human, yet he suffered only in his human nature, his deity did not suffer.

But Nestorius, a notorious heretic, and his followers, inferred from those words, *without God*, that Christ's human nature was a distinct person of itself, and so suffered without God, not united to God; for they held that God and man in Christ were two distinct persons.

Thus we see what advantage is given to heretics by altering the words of Scripture.

Sec. 78. *Of God's grace the cause of Christ's death.*

To come to the true reading of this text, which is this, 'by the grace of God.' Grace is here put for the free favour of God. Thus it is oft taken in the holy Scriptures. See Chap. iv. 16, Secs. 96, 97.

All blessings tending to salvation, yea, and salvation itself, are ascribed thereunto: as election, Rom. xi. 5; redemption, Eph. i. 7; vocation, 2 Tim. i. 9; justification, Rom. iii. 24; salvation, Eph. ii. 8.

It was therefore of God's grace that Christ was given to man, and that he did what he did, and endured what he endured for man, John iii. 16, Eph. ii. 4, 7.

There is nothing out of God to move him to do anything: 'He worketh all things after the counsel of his own will,' Eph. i. 1. See more hereof, Sec. 37, and Chap. iv. 16, Sec. 97.

As for man, there can be nothing in him to procure so great a matter as is here spoken of, at God's hand.

By this it is manifest, that God's free grace, and the satisfaction that Christ hath made for our sins, may stand together.² Christ's satisfaction is so far from being opposite to the freeness of God's grace, as it is the clearest and greatest evidence that ever was, or can be given thereof. More grace is manifested in God's not sparing his Son, but giving him to death for us, than if by his supreme authority and absolute prerogative he had forgiven our sins, and saved our souls. We that partake of the benefit of Christ's death, nor do, nor can make any satisfaction at all. For God to impute another's satisfaction to us, and to accept it for us, is mere grace; and that the rather, because he that is true God, even the proper Son of God, made that satisfaction.

Thus we see how, in working out our redemption, divine grace and justice meet together, and sweetly kiss each other: justice, in reference to the Son of God, who hath satisfied God's justice to the full; grace, in reference to us, who neither have made, nor can make, any satisfaction at all.

Learn hereby to ascribe what thou hast or hopest for to grace, and wholly rely thereupon. It is the surest ground of comfort, and safest rock of confidence that poor sinners can have.

Paul ascribes all in all to it, 1 Cor. xv. 10, 1 Tim. i. 14. He taketh all occasions of setting it forth, yet never satisfieth himself therein. He styleth it 'abundance of grace,' Rom. v. 17; 'Exceeding abundant grace,' 1 Tim. i. 14; 'Riches of grace,' Eph. i. 7; 'Exceeding riches of grace,' Eph. ii. 7.

Let us be like minded. Let us acknowledge the grace of God to us, and ascribe all the good we have thereunto. Let us so deeply meditate thereon, as we may be ravished therewith. Let us so apply it to ourselves, as we may render all the praise of what we have, or are able to do, to this grace of God.

Had it not been by the grace and good pleasure of God, no violence, or force of man or devils, could have brought Christ to die. Did he not with a word of his mouth drive back those that came to apprehend him? John xviii. 6. He could have had more than twelve legions of angels to defend him, Mat. xxvi. 53; he was 'delivered by the determinate counsel of God,' Acts ii. 23. And this God did upon his free grace and good will towards man. This moved Christ to 'lay down his life,' John x. 18; and to 'give himself,' Eph. v. 25.

Sec. 79. *Of tasting.*

The evidence of the grace of God here specified is thus expressed, 'That he should taste death,' &c. Of tasting, see Chap. vi. 4, Sec. 33.

To taste is the proper act of that sense which is called *taste*. Thereby is discerned the savour of things, and men distinguish betwixt sweet and sour, fresh and salt, and other like different tastes, Job xii. 11; 2 Sam. xix. 35. In sacred Scripture it is taken two ways.

1. Indefinitely, for the participation of a thing, and that affirmatively, ('The ruler of the feast tasted of the water that was made wine;' that is, he drank it, John ii. 9); and negatively, 'None of them shall taste of my supper;' that is, shall eat thereof, Luke xiv. 24.

2. Exclusively, by way of diminution, implying a small quantity. This also affirmatively ('I did but taste a little honey;' that is, I took but a little quantity, 1 Sam. xiv. 29): and negatively 'Taste not,' Col. ii. 21; that is, take not the least quantity.

In the former sense it is taken for eating, and so translated, Acts x. 10, and xx. 11.

In the latter sense it is opposed thereunto: 'When he had tasted thereof, he would not drink,' Mat. xxvii. 34. Eating and drinking in this case intendeth the same thing.

It is oft, in the New Testament especially, meta-

---

¹ Gratia Dei Patris appellatur Filius, eo quod nobis a Deo Patre gratià sit datus, et quod gratis pro nobis mortem sustinuit.—*Primas.*

² See Chap. ix. 7, Sec. 43.

phorically used, and applied both to things comfortable, (as to 'the heavenly gift,' 'good word of God,' Heb. vi. 4, 5; and 'graciousness of God,' 1 Pet. ii. 3), and also to such things as are grievous, as to that which of all things is most bitter unto natural men, namely, death: 'They shall not taste of death,' Mat. xvi. 28; so John viii. 52, and here.

The ground of this phrase may arise from the ancient custom of the Grecians in putting men to death, which was by giving them a cup of poison to drink.[1] In allusion hereunto death is styled a *cup* (especially death inflicted by men, accompanied with some horror), and suffering death a drinking of that cup, John xviii. 11; Mat. xx. 22, 23.

It was usual with the prophets so to set out God's judgments under this metaphor of a cup, a cup being metonymically put for the liquor in the cup, which in this case is taken to be bitter and deadly, Isa. li. 17–22; Jer. xxv. 15, 17, 28; Ezek. xxiii. 31, &c. To drink, or taste of such a cup, is to partake of the grievous and bitter thing that is intended thereby, whether it be death, or any other affliction or judgment.

The liquor in the cup, whereof Christ is here said to taste, is plainly expressed to be death. How bitter his death was, hath been shewed before. Sec. 76.

Sec. 80. *Of Christ's tasting death.*

Christ suffering death is here set out under this metaphor of tasting, in three respects.

1. In that he did truly and really partake thereof. The history of his passion, punctually set forth by four evangelists, which are four authentic witnesses, gives abundant proof hereunto. He was our surety, and took our sins on him, and undertook to make full satisfaction for them. To do this he must of necessity partake of death, even such a death as he did suffer. This real suffering of Christ is to be held as an undeniable ground of faith.

2. In that Christ was not swallowed up of death. For he was but three days under the power of death, and in none of those days did he 'see corruption,' Acts ii. 31. In both these was Jonah a type of Christ, Jonah i. 17 and ii. 10; Mat. xii. 40. This doth much strengthen our faith, in that our surety, who did really partake of death, did yet but taste thereof. He was not utterly destroyed thereby.

3. In that he began to us in that cup. A physician will himself taste of the potion that he hath prepared for his patient, to encourage his patient more contentedly and readily to drink it up. For by the physician's first tasting of it, the patient is assured that there is no hurtful thing therein, but that which is good and wholesome. Even so Christ tasting death, encourageth believers to submit unto it. It is said of the unicorn, that he putting his horn into the water, draws out all the poison thereof, and then other beasts drink of it after him. Thus from Christ's death it is that the

[1] Plato in Phædone.

sting of death is pulled out (1 Cor. xv. 55, 56). His tasting of death hath seasoned and sweetened death unto us, so as that which was sharp vinegar and bitter gall to him, is sweet wine to us. Thus it is set out in the Lord's supper, Luke xxii. 20. It is a cup of consolation, Jer. xvi. 7; of benediction, 1 Cor. x. 16; of salvation, Ps. cxvi. 13.

Sec. 81. *Of Christ's dying for every man.*

The persons for whom Jesus tasted that bitter cup of death, are set forth in this indefinite phrase, *for every man*. This collective phrase in the singular number, is answerable to the general in the plural number, *for all*, 2 Cor. v. 15. It was before noted (Sec. 66) that this general or indefinite particle, *all*, or *every one*, admits limitations. In this case of Christ's death, it must needs be limited. For in another place Christ saith, 'I lay down my life for the sheep,' John x. 15; but every man is not of Christ's fold, nor one of those sheep. It is said again, 'He shall save his people,' Mat. i. 21; of this number every man is not. He 'gave himself for the church,' Eph. v. 25; of which society none are but the elect. Christ made intercession for those for whom he died, Rom. viii. 34. But he prays not for the world, John xvii. 9. They for whom he died are redeemed, Rev. v. 9; but Christ hath redeemed men *out of* every kindred, and tongue, and people, and nation; not every one in each of these. From redemption follows remission of sins, Col. i. 14; but all have not their sins pardoned. The Father gave some *out of* the world to Christ, John xvii. 6.

This universal particle, *all*, or *every one*, must therefore have here some limitation; as on all hands it is granted to have in these words of Christ, 'I, if I be lifted up from the earth, will draw all men unto me,' John xii. 32.

Limitations are such as these:

1. In regard of distinct sorts and kinds of persons. So is the general particle limited, Gen. vii. 14; Mat. iv. 23; Luke xi. 42.

2. In regard of the universality of the elect. These are they of whom Christ thus saith, 'All that the Father giveth me, shall come unto me: and him that cometh unto me I will in no wise cast out,' John vi. 37. God's people have their fulness, and in the elect there is a kind of special universality; so as the whole world may seem to be redeemed out of the whole world.[1]

3. In regard of the indefinite offer of the benefit of Christ's death to every one, none excepted, Isa. lv. 1, Rev. xxii. 17.

4. In regard of the sufficiency of the price. Christ's death was sufficient to redeem every one. In this re-

[1] Habet populus Dei plentitudinem suam. In electis specialis quædam censetur universitas: ut de toto mundo totus mundus liberatus videatur.—*Ambros. de vocat. Gent.* lib. i. cap. iii.

spect it is said, 'The blood of Christ cleanseth from all sin,' 1 John ii. 7.

5. In regard of the impotency of all other means. There is no other means to redeem man but the death of Christ; so as every one that is redeemed is redeemed by his death. In this respect saith the Lord, 'I am the Lord, and beside me there is no Saviour,' Isa. xliii. 11. Where in a city there is but one physician, we use to say, all that are sick are cured by him, meaning all the sick that are cured.

Sec. 82. *Of God's impartiality.*

This in general verifieth that which was of old affirmed by Moses, Deut. x. 17; by Elihu, Job xxxiv. 19; by Jehoshaphat, 2 Chron. xix. 7; by Peter, Acts x. 35; by Paul, Rom. ii. 11, and sundry others; namely, that 'with God is no respect of persons.' All sorts, in all nations, whether male or female, great or mean, free or bond, learned or unlearned, rich or poor, or what other outward difference may be betwixt them, all are alike to God.

By this may every one be bold to apply Christ's death to himself. Hereof see more in *The Whole Armour of God*, on Eph. vi. 16, treat. 2, *of faith*, secs. 29, 30, &c.

Sec. 83. *Of Christ's dying for us.*

The end of Christ's death being thus set down, *for every one*, sheweth that it was man, even man's good for whom and for which Christ died, Rom. v. 8. His birth, his life, his death, were all for us children of men. A prophet, who was a son of man, thus setteth out Christ's birth: 'Unto us a child is born, unto us a son is given,' Isa. ix. 6. And an angel speaking to sons of men, thus: 'Unto you is born a Saviour,' Luke ii. 11. The obedience of Christ's life was also for us, Rom. v. 19; so he died for us,[1] 1 Thes. v. 10. The like is said of his burial; for in regard of the benefit which we receive from Christ's burial, we are said to be buried with him, Rom. vi. 4, Col. ii. 12; yea, he was 'made sin for us,' 2 Cor. v. 21, and 'a curse for us,' Gal. iii. 12. For us he vanquished the devil, Heb. ii. 14. The like also of his resurrection, Rom. iv. 25; of his ascension, John xiv. 2; of his intercession, Rom. viii. 34; and of his abode in heaven, John xvii. 24. All is for us.

Good ground we have hereupon to apply, as other things of Christ, so especially that which is here in particular expressed, his death; and to rest thereon, as on a satisfaction for our sins, and as the means of pulling out the sting of death, 1 Cor. xv. 55, and making it a sweet sleep to us, 1 Thes. iv. 14, 15.

Sec. 84. *Of the resolution of* Heb. ii. 9.

But we see Jesus, who was made a little lower than the angels for the suffering of death, crowned with glory and honour; that he by the grace of God should taste death for every man.

The sum of this verse is, the end of Christ's humiliation.

This is set down by way of answer to the objection propounded in the former verse. The objection was against the supreme authority of Christ over all creatures. Of the objection, see Sec. 68.

The answer hath reference unto two branches of the objection:

One concerns the person intended; which was man, meaning a mere man. This the apostle so yields unto, as notwithstanding he affirmeth Jesus, who was more than man, to be so highly exalted as is mentioned in the testimony.

The other concerns the evidence alleged against the foresaid supreme authority, which is thus set down, 'we see not yet,' &c.

This he answereth, by a distinction of sights, to this purpose: Though with bodily eyes we can see no such matter, yet we may with the eyes of our soul. See Sec. 72.

In setting down the foresaid end, two points are distinctly expressed:

1. A description of Christ's humiliation.
2. A declaration of the end thereof.

Christ's humiliation is set down by the low degree thereof; and that comparatively in reference to angels, thus, 'lower than angels.' Hereof see Sec. 64.

The end is, 1, generally propounded; 2, particularly exemplified.

In the general is declared,

1. The end itself.
2. The consequence that followeth thereupon.

The end itself is,

1. Propounded in this word, *death*.
2. Aggravated by this epithet, *suffering*.

The consequence following was exaltation.

This is, 1, propounded in the metaphor of a crown; which implieth a royal dignity.

2. It is amplified two ways:

(1.) By the excellency of that crown, in this word *glory*.

(2.) By the esteem that others have of it, in this word *honour*. Of these two words, see Sec. 60.

In the particular exemplification of the end are set out,

1. The manner of Christ's partaking of death, in this metaphor *taste*.
2. The causes thereof; which are two:
1. The procuring cause, 'the grace of God.'
2. The final cause, 'for every man.'

Sec. 85. *Of doctrines raised out of* Heb. ii. 9.

I. *Objections against truth are to be answered.* Thus such clouds as obscure truth will be removed. Thus may men be kept from forsaking the truth. This particle *but* intendeth the doctrine. See Sec. 68.

---

[1] See ver. 15, Sec. 148.

II. *Christ is the Saviour of man;* for he is *Jesus.* See Sec. 73.

III. *Things super-celestial may be seen.* Super-celestials are such as are above the stars, even in the highest heaven, where Jesus hath abode ever since his ascension. There may we now see him, namely, with the eyes of the soul. See Sec. 72.

IV. *Truths invisible are most sure to believers.* They are believers of whom the apostle thus saith, 'we see.' See Sec. 72.

Of doctrines raised out of these words, 'made a little lower than the angels,' and out of these, 'crowned with glory and honour,' see Sec. 65.

V. *Christ was incarnate, that he might be a fit sacrifice.* See Secs. 74, 75.

VI. *Christ suffered unto death.* His death is here expressly mentioned.

VII. *Christ's death was with great suffering.* It is here styled the suffering of death. See Sec. 76.

VIII. *Great glory followed upon Christ's great suffering.* This phrase, the 'suffering of death,' imports great suffering; and this, 'crowned with glory,' great glory; and the order of setting down these two shews that the latter followed upon the former. See Sec. 74.

IX. *Christ's high dignity giveth proof of the subjection of all things under him.* The apostle here proveth that subjection by Christ's dignity. See Sec. 74.

X. *God's free grace was the procuring cause of Christ's suffering for man.* This is here directly set down. See Sec. 78.

XI. *God's grace and Christ's merit may stand together.* See Sec. 78.

XII. *Christ was not swallowed up of death.*

XIII. *Christ actually and really died.*

XIV. *Christ began the cup of death to us.* These three last doctrines arise from this metaphor *taste.* See Sec. 80.

XV. *Christ died for all, of all sorts.* See Sec. 81.

XVI. *Christ died not for himself.* See Sec. 74.

XVII. *God is no respecter of persons,* for he gave his Son for all men. See Sec. 81.

XVIII. *Man's good was the end of Christ's sufferings.* See Sec. 81.

Sec. 86. *Of the respect wherein 'it became God' that his Son should be man, and suffer for man.*

Ver. 10. *For it became him, for whom are all things, and by whom are all things, in bringing many sons unto glory, to make the Captain of their salvation perfect through sufferings.*

The first particle of this verse, γὰρ, *for,* shews that it is added as a reason of that which goes before. In general, it is a third reason to prove that Christ was man. See Sec. 1. In particular, it declareth the reason of the last clause of the former verse, which is this, ' By the grace of God Christ tasted death for every one.' If the question be asked, Why God's grace chose that way to redeem man? here is a ready answer: ' It became him' so to do.

The Greek word ἔπρεπε, translated *became,* is diversely used.

1. It implies a *necessity* of doing this or that, as in this phrase, ' Such an high priest became us, who is holy,' &c. Heb. vii. 29. It was necessary that we should have such an one; no other could serve the turn.

2. It implies a *duty,* as in this phrase, ' It becometh us to fulfil all righteousness,' Mat. iii. 15. It is our duty so to do.

3. It implies an *answerableness* or agreement of one thing to another, as in this phrase, ' Speak thou the things which become sound doctrine,' Tit. ii. 1; that is, as are agreeable thereto.

4. It implies a *decency,* comeliness, and glory of a thing, as in this phrase, ' Which becometh women professing godliness,' 1 Tim. ii. 10. He there speaketh of women adorning themselves with good works; and this is a decent and comely thing, the beauty and glory of professors. Thus it is here taken; for never did anything more make to the glory of God than his making of his Son lower than angels, that he might taste death for every one.

We read, that upon the first news of Christ coming into the world, a multitude of angels thus praised God, ' Glory to God in the highest,' &c., Luke ii. 14; and Christ himself, when he was going out of the world, thus saith to his Father, ' I have glorified thee on earth,' John xvii. 4. And upon his suffering, Christ said, ' Father, glorify thy name;' and the Father thus answered, ' I have both glorified it, and will glorify it again,' John xii. 28. All this was in relation to Christ's humiliation, even unto death.

Sec. 87. *Of God's glory in giving his Son to die.*

If we take a view of God's special properties, we shall find the glory of them so set forth in Christ's incarnation and passion, and the redemption of man thereby, as in nothing more. I will exemplify this in five of them.

1. The *power* of God hath been often manifested by many wonderful works of his since the beginning of the world. The book of Job and book of Psalms do reckon up catalogues of God's powerful and mighty works; but they are all inferior to those works which were done by the Son of God becoming man and dying; for hereby was the curse of the law removed, the bonds of death broken, the devil and his whole host vanquished, infinite wrath appeased. The Son of God did all this, and much more, not by arraying himself with majesty and power, but by putting on him weak and frail flesh, and by subjecting himself to death. Herein was strength made perfect in weakness, 2 Cor. xii. 9.

2. The *wisdom* of God was greatly set forth in the first creation of all things in their excellent order and

beauty, and in the wise government of them; but after that by sin they were put out of order, to bring them into a comely frame again was an argument of much more wisdom; especially if we duly weigh how, by the creature's transgression, the just Creator was provoked to wrath. To find out a means, in this case, of atonement betwixt God and man, must needs imply much more wisdom. For who should make this atonement? Not man, because he was the transgressor; not God, because he was offended and incensed. Yet God, by taking man's nature upon him, God-man, by suffering, did this deed; he made the atonement. God having revealed this mystery unto his church, every one that is instructed in the Christian faith can say, Thus and thus it is done. But had not God, by his infinite wisdom, found out and made known this means of reconciliation, though all the heads of all creatures had consulted thereabout, their counsels would have been altogether in vain. We have therefore just cause, with an holy admiration, to break out and say, 'Oh the depth of the riches both of the wisdom and knowledge of God,' Rom. xi. 33.

3. The *justice* of God hath been made known in all ages by judgments executed on wicked sinners; as the punishment of our first parents, the drowning of the old world, the destroying of Sodom and Gomorrah with fire and brimstone, the casting off the Jews, the casting of wicked angels and reprobate men into hell fire; but to exact the uttermost of the Son of God, who became a surety for man, and so to exact it as in our nature, he must bear the infinite wrath of his Father, and satisfy his justice to the full, is an instance of more exact justice than ever was manifested.

4. The *truth* of God is exceedingly cleared by God's giving his Son to die, and that in accomplishment of his threatening and promises.

For threatening, God had said to man, 'In the day thou eatest of the tree of the knowledge of good and evil, thou shalt surely die,' Gen. ii. 17. How could God's truth have been accomplished in this threatening, and man not utterly destroyed, if Christ had not died in our nature?

For promise, the first that ever was made after man's fall was this, 'The seed of the woman shall bruise the serpent's head,' Gen. iii. 15. As this was the first promise, so was it the ground of all other promises made to God's elect in Christ. Now God having accomplished this promise by giving his Son to death, how can we doubt of his truth in any other promise whatsoever. The accomplishment of no other promise could so set out God's truth as of this; for other promises do depend upon this, and not this on any of them. Besides, this is the greatest of all other promises. We may therefore on this ground say, 'He that spared not his own Son, but delivered him up for us all, how shall he not with him also freely give us all things?' Rom. viii. 32.

5. God's *mercy* is most magnified by sending his Son into the world to die for man. 'The mercies of God are over all his works,' Ps. cxlv. 9; but the glass wherein they are most perspicuously seen is Jesus Christ made man, and made a sacrifice for man's sin. This is set out to the life: 'God so loved the world, that he gave his only begotten Son, that whosoever believeth in him should not perish, but have everlasting life,' John iii. 16.

Sec. 88. *Of the necessity of Christ's being man to die.*

On the fore-mentioned grounds, there was a necessity of Christ's suffering. In this respect a *must* is attributed to that which is here said, *it became*. So saith Christ of himself, he 'must suffer,' Mat. xvi. 21; and 'thus it must be,' Mat. xxvi. 54; 'The Son of man must be lift up,' John iii. 14; 'Ought not Christ to have suffered these things?' Luke xxiv. 56.

This may serve to stop the mouths of such conceited persons as are over-busy in inquiring after God's supreme high prerogative, namely, whether he could not by virtue of it have forgiven man's sin, without any such satisfaction, and by this grace received him to glory?

Since 'it became God' to take this course, and that the Holy Ghost saith, 'It must be so;' O man, 'who art thou that repliest against God?' When God's will is manifested, it is over-much curiosity to dispute about his prerogative. Moses hath set down a singular rule for us to order our reasonings by, which is this, 'Those things which are revealed belong unto us,' Deut. xxix. 29. It may be that these grounds, *it became him, it must be*, are expressed to prevent all further disputes about this point.

It much becomes us who look to partake of the benefit of that which became God so to order, to be very circumspect over ourselves, and to take heed that we pervert not that to God's dishonour which so much became him. They pervert it who take occasion from God's grace in giving his Son, and from the satisfaction which his Son hath given for our sins, to continue in sin. This is it concerning which the apostle, with great indignation and detestation, saith, 'God forbid,' Rom. vi. 2. This is to 'turn the glory of God into lasciviousness,' Jude 4. This is to tread under foot the Son of God,' &c., Heb. x. 29. What greater aggravation can there be of a sin than this?

Sec. 89. *Of these phrases, 'for whom, by whom, are all things.'*

These phrases, 'for whom,' δι' ὅν, 'are all things,' and 'by whom,' δι' οὗ, 'are all things,' have reference to God, who gave his Son to death; and by them he is described.

These two prepositions, *for, by*, are the interpretation of one Greek word, διά, which is the same that in the former verse is translated *for* ('for the suffering,' διὰ τὸ πάθημα). The variation of the cases joined to the preposition varieth the interpretation.[1] Hereof see Sec. 74; of the Greek noun, see Sec. 76.

The former, δι' ὅν, sets out God as the final cause, for whose glory all things are. In this sense it is said, 'The Lord hath made all things for himself,' Prov. xvi. 4; namely, for his own glory. To this very purpose saith the apostle, 'All things are to him,' εἰς αὐτὸν, Rom. xi. 36. These prepositions, διὰ, *for*, and εἰς, *to*, intimate one and the same thing, which is the end. Thus the woman is said to be made, διὰ τὸν ἄνδρα, 'for the man,' 1 Cor. xi. 9; which is, for the man's sake, for his good, Gen. ii. 18. The Greek phrase, εἰς αὐτὸν, which signifieth *to him*, is translated *for him*, chap. i. 16. To make this more clear, our English often addeth this particle, *sake*, which is a note of the final cause; as, διὰ τὴν βασιλείαν, 'For the kingdom of heaven's sake,' Mat. xix. 12; διὰ τὸ ὄνομά μου, 'For my name's sake,' saith Christ, Luke xxi. 17; διὰ τὸ εὐαγγέλιον, 'For the gospel's sake,' 1 Cor. ix. 23.

The latter phrase, δι' οὗ, *by whom*, sets out God as the efficient, and creator of all. In this sense this phrase is applied to Christ: 'By him were all things created,' Col. i. 16.

It is also applied to his blood, as to the procuring cause of redemption: 'He hath purchased the church with his own blood,' Acts xx. 28.

This general, τὰ πάντα, 'all things,' is to be taken in the largest extent that can be, nothing at all excepted. So it is taken John i. 3, Col. i. 16, Heb. i. 3, and in other places where mention is made of creation and providence. (See more of this general, Sec. 66.) Here it is expressly mentioned, to shew the ground of God's putting all things in subjection under Christ's feet; even because 'all things were for him, and by him.' God had power to dispose all things as he would, because all things were 'by him.' He made all. And he had a right so to do, because all were made 'for him;' even for him to dispose of them as he would. See Sec. 37.

These phrases, *for him* and *by him*, have reference both to creation and also to providence. For 'God worketh hitherto,' John v. 17, namely, by his providence; and thereby all things are preserved, Ps. cxlvii. 8, 9; and ordered, Ps. xxxiii. 13, &c.

In the foresaid description of God, the final cause, *for whom*, is set before the efficient, *by whom*, to shew what it was that God put on to make, preserve, and govern all things. Surely he put himself on; he aimed at himself, even at his own glory. That all things might be *for him*, all things were *by him*.

All things being for God, we also, all we have, and all we can do, ought to be for him: 'Glorify God in your body, and in your spirit, which are God's,' 1 Cor. vi. 20. 'Whether ye eat or drink, or whatsoever ye do, do all to the glory of God,' 1 Cor. vi. 31. See more hereof in my *Explanation of the Lord's Prayer*, entitled *A Guide to go to God*, petit. i. sec. 30, 31.

All things being by God, it is our duty to acknowledge that 'in him we live, move, and have our being,' Acts xvii. 28; and that as all things were created, so they are preserved and governed by him, Job xxxviii. 4, &c., Ps. civ. 2, &c.; and thereupon to fly to him in all our needs, distresses, and dangers. To call upon him, and depend on him for every good thing; to commit our souls, bodies, states, endeavours, even all that we have, to him; to be content with every event; to submit all our purposes to his will; and for all things to bless him, Job i. 21

We ought the rather to be thus minded, because God doth nothing but what becometh him. This description of God, 'for whom are all things, and by whom are all things,' is added to this motive, 'it became him,' to shew that there is a comeliness in all things done by him: 'He hath made everything beautiful in his time,' Eccles. iii. 11. Wherefore, though we can see no reason of God's doings, yet we may see good reason to account them the best.

This title, *by whom*, having reference to God (as also Rom. xi. 36), giveth a full answer to the Arians, who from this phrase, 'All things were made by him,' John i. 3, infer that the Son is inferior to the Father, and his instrument in making the world.

Sec. 90. *Of sons in relation to Christ.*

This clause, *in bringing many sons unto glory*, seemeth by our English translators to have reference to him who is described in the former words, namely, to God. Surely the thing itself may well be applied to God, and imply a reason why it became God to make his Son perfect through sufferings, even because his purpose was to bring many other sons to glory; and the best way to bring them thereunto was by his Son's suffering.

This is a good and congruous sense, but the construction of the Greek words will not bear it; for the antecedent, αὐτῷ, to which this relative in that sense should have reference, is of the dative case; but the relative, ἀγαγόντα, is of the accusative, of which case the word translated *captain*, τὸν ἀρχηγὸν, is. Now, it is without all question that Christ is meant under that word *captain;* therefore, in grammatical construction, this act of bringing many sons to glory is to be applied to Christ.

Thus it sheweth a reason why Christ himself passed by suffering unto glory, namely, that thereby he might bring many sons to glory. Both references tend to the same scope. The latter attributes that act to the Son which the former doth to the Father. In this there is no great incongruity; for the Father and Son are one in essence, mind, will, and work: 'What thing soever the Father doth, these also doth the Son likewise,' John v. 19.

Against the reference, of 'bringing sons unto glory,'

---

[1] Accusative, δι' ὅν; genitive, δι' οὗ.

made to Christ, it is objected that the persons here said to be brought to glory are called Christ's *brethren*, ver. 11. If they be his brethren, how can they be his sons?

Ans. 1. They are not called *his sons* in relation to Christ, but indefinitely *sons;* so as it may be thus explained, Christ brought many sons of God to glory.

Ans. 2. The same persons that in one respect are called Christ's brethren, may in another respect be called his sons. How saints are called Christ's brethren, see Sec. 106; they are called his sons in these respects.

(1.) As Christ is 'the everlasting Father,' Isa. ix. 6, thus he hath given them their being, and adopted them into his family.

(2.) As the Father hath given all his elect unto Christ, to be nourished and nurtured by him; thus they who were nurtured and instructed by ancient prophets are called 'sons of the prophets,' 2 Kings ii. 3. In like manner, and on the same ground, the elect of God are called Christ's sons. They whom ministers beget unto the Lord are called their sons, Philem. 10, much more they who are saved by Christ may be called his sons.

(3.) As Christ bears a fatherly affection to them; loving them as sons, taking an especial care of them as of his sons, purchasing an inheritance for them, and doing all the good he can for them.

The sons of God and the sons of Christ are all one, even such as are adopted and regenerate; for by the grace of adoption, and by the work of regeneration, we are made the sons of God, and heirs of glory, Rom. viii. 15-17, 1 Pet. i. 3, 4; these are 'sanctified and cleansed with the washing of water by the word,' Eph. vi. 25; these 'have washed their robes, and made them white in the blood of the Lamb,' Rev. vii. 14; and thus are they fitted for glory.

Boast not of any title to glory till thou hast evidence of thy sonship, that thou art adopted and born again: 'The son of the bond woman shall not be heir with the son of the free woman,' Gal. iv. 30.

How may we have evidence that we are sons?

Ans. By the Spirit, Rom. viii. 14. The Spirit worketh two things.

1. An earnest desire of God's fatherly favour, Gal. iv. 6.

2. A careful endeavour to please and honour God, Col. i. 10, Mal. i. 6. The former is a fruit of faith, the latter of love. Hence arise grief for the provocations of God's wrath, and indignation at the dishonour done to God.

By these evidences we may know that we are the sons here meant, and having that assurance, no doubt can be made of obtaining glory; for Christ undertaketh to bring such to glory. In this respect salvation, by a kind of property, is said to be theirs, for Christ is styled 'the captain of *their* salvation.' All sons, and none but sons, shall be saved: Jesus 'shall save his people,' Mat. i. 21; he is 'the Saviour of the body,' Eph. v. 23. 'If children, then heirs,' Rom. viii. 17, not otherwise.

With much confidence may sons rest upon such a father as Christ is, to be much pitied and succoured in all their distresses, to have all their wants supplied, to be tenderly dealt with in all their weaknesses, to be sufficiently provided for with all needful good things, to be safely protected against all dangers, to have whatsoever may be expected from such a father. Consider, on the one side, the love and care of natural fathers to and for their children, yea, and of apostles too for those whom they begat by the gospel; and, on the other side, well weigh how far Christ exalteth all those fathers in power, wisdom, and goodness, and you shall find just cause with confidence to rest on him at all times, on all occasions.

By virtue of this relation, it becomes us all, who account ourselves to be in the number of God's elect, and to be given by him as sons to Christ, it becomes us every way to shew ourselves to be Christ's sons, even in our inward disposition, and also in our outward conversation, and thereupon to love him and fear him, to reverence and obey him, in all things to please him and honour him, to depend on him for all needful good things, and to be content with that condition wherein he sets us, and with those gifts of soul, body, or state that he is pleased to bestow upon us. In a word, what duties soever in God's word are required of sons as sons, we must conscionably perform to Christ, whose sons we are.

That these duties may be performed according to the extent of the persons whom they concern, we must take notice that as all sorts and conditions of men, great and mean, rich and poor, young and old, so also both sexes, male and female, are comprised under this relative *sons;* for that is the nature of relatives, to comprise both under one, as under this title *men*, indefinitely used, women also are comprised, and under *brethren* sisters also. To manifest this, the other relative daughters are oft expressed, as, 'Ye shall be my sons and daughters,' 2 Cor. vi. 18.

Sec. 91. *Of the multitude of them that shall be saved.*

The sons before mentioned are said to be πολλοί, 'many;' though this include not all the sons of Adam; for 'they that have done evil shall come forth unto the resurrection of damnation,' John v. 29, and this Captain of salvation will say to multitudes at the last day, 'Depart from me, ye cursed, into everlasting fire,' Mat. xxv. 41, yet this includeth a very great multitude. For it was in relation to these sons, who are the spiritual seed of Abraham, that God said to Abraham, Isaac, and Jacob, 'Thy seed shall be as the stars of heaven, and as the dust of the earth,' Gen. xv. 5, xxvi. 4, xxviii. 14. And the prophecies of multitudes to come in are meant of these sons, such as these: 'Many people shall say, Let us go up to the house of God,' Isa. ii. 3, Mic. iv. 2; 'Many shall come from the east and west,' &c. Mat. viii. 11; and, 'My righteous servant shall justify many,' Isa. liii. 11; 'The Son of man came to give his life a ransom for many,' Mat. xx. 28; 'His blood is shed for many,' Mat. xxvi. 28; 'By the obedience of one shall many be made righteous,' Rom. v. 19. In particular, John saith, 'I beheld, and lo, a great multitude, which no man could number, of all nations, and kindreds, and people, and tongues, stood before the throne,' &c. Rev. vii. 9. All these were the sons here mentioned. See Chap. vi. 14, Sec. 107, and Chap. ix. 22, Sec. 140.

Obj. It is oft said that few are chosen, few enter in at the strait gate, Mat. vii. 14, xx. 16. Hereupon the flock of Christ is styled 'a little flock,' Luke xii. 32, and they are styled 'a remnant,' Isa. i. 9; 'a tenth,' Isa. vi. 13; 'a vintage,' Micah vii. 1, and they are resembled to those few that were in the ark when the whole world was drowned, and in Sodom when the four cities were destroyed with fire and brimstone. See Chap. xi. 7, Sec. 32.

Ans. Comparatively they are indeed but few, in regard of the multitudes of evil ones that ever have been, and ever will be in the world. But simply considered in themselves, they are very, very many. When Elijah thought that he alone had been left, the Lord gave him this answer, 'I have reserved to myself seven thousand,' Rom. xi. 3, 4.

This is a matter of great comfort, in regard of the multitudes that perish, that there are also many that shall be saved.

It is also a great encouragement to inquire after the way to salvation, and to use the means sanctified for attaining thereunto. There is 'a fountain opened' to cleanse us from sin, Zech. xiii. 1. Let us not fear that it will be dried up because many go to partake thereof. Be rather encouraged to go with those many thereunto. Fear not that heaven will be filled up, for there are 'many mansions,' John xiv. 2. A poor man long waited at the pool of Bethesda, though the time of cure was but at a certain season, and only one could be cured at that season, John v. 4, 5, &c.; but the pool for salvation cureth at all times all that go into it. We read of three thousand converted by one sermon, Acts ii. 41, and five thousand by another, Acts iv. 4, and it is after this registered that 'multitudes of believers were added to the Lord,' Acts v. 14; and that 'the number of disciples was multiplied,' Acts vi. 1; and that 'the churches were established in the faith, and increased in number daily,' Acts xvi. 5; and that many thousands[1] of Jews believed, Acts xxi. 20, besides the Gentiles that embraced the faith.

After those days, yea, and in these our days, have the churches of Christ wonderfully increased.

A strong inducement this is, both to ministers to preach the gospel, and also to people to attend thereupon, in that there are many sons: and they must all be brought to glory.

Sec. 92. *Of 'bringing' sons to glory.*

It is said of those many sons, that by Christ they are brought to glory.

The verb $\dot{\alpha}\gamma\alpha\gamma\acute{o}\nu\tau\alpha$, translated *brought*, is diversely used, as,

1. To go of one's self, even upon his own voluntary motion; as where Christ saith, $\ddot{\alpha}\gamma\omega\mu\varepsilon\nu$, 'Let us be going,' Mat. xxvi. 46.

2. To be led by another, but willingly: thus Andrew brought, $\ddot{\eta}\gamma\alpha\gamma\varepsilon\nu$, Simon to Jesus, John i. 42.

3. To be brought forcibly, as men use to bring malefactors to execution. 'There were also two other malefactors led, $\ddot{\eta}\gamma o \nu \tau o$, with Jesus to be put to death,' Luke xxiii. 32.

4. To bring such as are no way able to go of themselves: thus the good Samaritan brought, $\ddot{\eta}\gamma\alpha\gamma\varepsilon\nu$, the man that was wounded and left half dead, to an inn, Luke x. 34.

That we may the better discern how this word *bringing* is here used, we are to take notice that the sons here said to be brought, are neither able nor willing of themselves to go to glory. Christ therefore bringeth them thither by certain degrees.

1. He quickeneth them that are dead in sins, Eph. ii. 1, 5.

2. He sheweth them the way wherein they may come to glory. For 'he is the true light which lighteneth every man that cometh into the world,' John i. 9. Thereupon he thus saith of himself, 'I am the light of the world: he that followeth me shall not fall into darkness, but shall have the light of life,' John viii. 12.

3. He goeth as a guide before them; for he is that good shepherd that 'goeth before his sheep, and the sheep follow him: for they know his voice,' John x. 4.

4. He communicates his Spirit unto them, whereby they are so enlightened, as they discern the way wherein they should walk, Eph. i. 8, 9, and enabled and persuaded to walk therein, 'For the law of the Spirit of life in Christ Jesus hath made us free:' and 'As many as are led by the Spirit of God, they are the sons of God,' Rom. viii. 2, 14.

Christ's bringing sons to glory, informs us in these two principles:

1. Man cannot of himself go to glory.

2. Christ can and will bring all the elect to glory. 'We have no sufficiency of ourselves, but our sufficiency is of God,' 2 Cor. iii. 5. 'As the branch cannot bear fruit of itself, except it abide in the vine: no more can ye, except ye abide in me,' saith Christ to his sons, John xv. 4.

Sec. 93. *Of the glory of heaven.*

That whereunto Christ bringeth his sons is here

---

[1] πολλαι μυριαδες, μυριας, *decem millia.*

styled *glory*. Hereby is meant that happy estate which is purchased by Christ in heaven. This estate is oft set out by this epithet; as Rom. viii. 18, 2 Cor. iv. 17, 1 Peter v. 1, 10.

Glory is a transcendent word, and compriseth under it all manner of excellencies. The infinite excellency of God himself, and of his divine attributes, is termed glory; as, 'the glory of God,' Acts vii. 55; 'the glory of his majesty,' Isa. ii. 10, 21; 'the glory of his power,' 2 Thes. i. 9; 'the glory of his grace,' Eph. i. 6. In this respect, where the apostle would to the uttermost that he could, commend, and set forth the excellency of the Son, he doth it thus, 'who is the brightness of his Father's glory;' see Chap. i. Sec. 19.

There is an especial emphasis in this word *glory*, as it is here used. It goeth beyond the superlative degree, and implieth more than most glorious. It compriseth under it whatsoever may be counted glorious; and that in the most eminent kind and degree that can be.

In heaven is the God of glory, Father, Son, and Holy Ghost. In heaven is that Son of God incarnate, advanced to the highest glory that can be; there he is crowned with glory.

Heaven itself is the most bright and beautiful place that ever God made. The sun itself is not so bright, nor so full of light. There is that 'light which no man can approach unto,' $\dot{\alpha}\pi\rho\dot{o}\sigma\iota\tau\sigma\nu$, 1 Tim. vi. 16.

There shineth forth the brightness of God's glory in the fulness of it. There the brightness of angels (a little part whereof amazed men on earth, as Dan. viii. 17, Luke i. 12 and ii. 9) is most conspicuously manifested. There Christ's glorified body (whose face on earth did shine at his transfiguration, as the sun, Mat. xvii. 2), continually shineth out. There also are the glorified saints, whose bodies shall be fashioned like unto the glorious body of Christ, Philip. iii. 21. They shall there shine as the firmament, as the stars, Dan. xii. 3; as the sun, Mat. xiii. 43.

If joy and delight, if honour and dignity, if full satisfaction of all good things, may add anything to glory, full satisfaction is to be found in heaven.

The glory of heaven is set out by all signs of glory: as 'an inheritance in light,' Col. i. 12; 'the riches of the glory of that inheritance,' Eph. i. 18; 'an inheritance, incorruptible, undefiled, and that fadeth not away,' 1 Peter i. 4; 'a crown of life,' James i. 12; 'a crown of righteousness,' 2 Tim. iv. 8; 'a crown of glory,' 1 Peter v. 4; 'God's throne,' Mat. v. 34; the 'thrones of his glory,' Mat. xix. 28; 'a throne of the majesty,' Heb. viii. 9; 'the kingdom of God,' 1 Cor. vi. 9; 'the kingdom of heaven,' Mat. viii. 11; and 'an everlasting kingdom,' 2 Peter i. 11.

The estate, then, which is in heaven reserved for saints, must needs be a most excellent and glorious estate. The apostle, in setting out the glory of it, useth an high and transcendent expression, 2 Cor. iv. 17, for he styleth it 'a weight of glory.' It is not like the glory of this world, light, frothy, vain, like hail or ice, which in the handling melt; but sound, solid, substantial, and ponderous, and that not for a short time, but for ever. It is an 'eternal weight,' without date, without end; and to shew that this glory exceeds all degrees of comparison, he uses an emphatical Grecism, which addeth hyperbole to hyperbole; which, because other tongues cannot word for word express to the full, they are forced to use words and phrases which exceed all comparison: as 'wonderfully above measure;'[1] 'above measure exceedingly;'[2] 'exceedingly exceeding;'[3] or, as our English, 'a far more exceeding weight of glory.' Of this glory it may well be said, 'eye hath not seen, nor ear heard, neither hath it entered into the heart of man,' 1 Cor ii. 9. It is not therefore without cause that the apostle prayeth, 'That the eyes of our understanding may be enlightened, that we may know what the riches of the glory of his inheritance in the saints is,' Eph. i. 18. 'For it doth not yet appear what we shall be.' When Paul was caught up into this glory, he heard unspeakable words, $\ddot{\alpha}\rho\rho\eta\tau\alpha$ $\dot{\rho}\dot{\eta}\mu\alpha\tau\alpha$, which it is not lawful for a man to utter, 2 Cor. xii. 4.

To this glory doth the only begotten Son of God bring his adopted sons, to shew both the magnificence of his Father, and also the value of his own merit.

The magnificence of a great monarch is manifested by the greatness of the gifts or honours that he conferreth. When Pharaoh would honour Joseph, 'he set him over all the land of Egypt,' Gen. xli. 41. So did Nebuchadnezzar to Daniel, Dan. ii. 48; and Darius also, Dan. vi. 2, 3; and Ahasuerus to Haman, Esther iii. 1, and to Mordecai, Esther viii. 15.

As for the price whereby such an inheritance, as is comprised under this word *glory*, it must needs be more worth than all the kingdoms of the world, and the glory of them, because the glory here intended far surpasseth them all. I reckon that this present world is not worthy to be compared with that glory.

One reason of setting out the future estate of saints under this title *glory*, may be to shew that all things below are but base, vile, and contemptible in comparison of it.

Who would not, who should not, long after this glory, even more than an heir after his inheritance?

Did we seriously set before us an idea or representation of this glory, we should undoubtedly say, 'Blessed is he that shall eat bread in the kingdom of God,' Luke xiv. 15; or as Peter, at the transfiguration of his Master, 'It is good to be here,' Mat. xvii. 4. Is it good to be there? Then inquire after the way that may bring us thither, and walk in it. 'Strive to enter in at the strait gate,' Luke xiii. 24. Do as our Captain did, 'endure the cross, and de-

---

[1] Mirè supra modum.—*Erasm.*
[2] Supra modum in sublimitate.—*Vulg. Lat.*
[3] Excellenter excellens.—*Beza.*

spise the shame, for the glory that is set before us,' Heb. xii. 2. 'The sufferings of this present time are not worthy to be compared with this glory,' Rom. viii. 18. No labour, no pains, no sufferings, can in this case be too much, and his glory will abundantly recompense all. In saying glory, I say enough.

Sec. 94. *Of Christ's continuing to bring us to glory.*

The participle *bringing* (ἀγαγόντα, ab ἄγω, duco), implies a leading one willingly, not by force, Acts v. 26. Thus Christ bringeth his sheep into his fold, John x. 16, for it is thus added, 'They shall hear my voice.'

It implieth also a kind of tender and gentle leading. It is applied to them that brought sick and weak ones to Christ, Luke iv. 40, and to him that brought one half dead to his inn, Luke x. 34,

The joining of this act of *bringing*, with the end, *to glory*, εἰς δόξαν ἀγαγόντα, setteth out a continuance of Christ's act till he have accomplished his intended end. He ceaseth not to lead and carry us on till he have set us in glory.

This phrase of *bringing to*, is oft used to set out the continuance of an act. It is said of the pitiful Samaritan, who had compassion on a succourless man, that 'he brought him to an inn,' Luke x. 34, and that a centurion took order that Paul should be brought to a castle, Acts xxiii. 10. He feared lest Paul should have [been] pulled in pieces of the multitude; therefore he would not have him left till he were safe in the castle.

Thus Christ will not leave us in this world unto our spiritual enemies till he have brought us to glory. It is his promise, never to 'leave us nor forsake us,' Heb. xiii. 5, but to 'confirm us unto the end,' 1 Cor. i. 8.

On this ground saith the apostle, 'I am confident of this very thing, that he which hath begun a good work in you, will confirm it unto the day of Jesus Christ,' Philip. i. 6. And Christ saith of himself, 'Him that cometh to me I will in no wise cast out,' John vi. 37. In this respect, Jesus is styled 'the author and finisher of our faith,' Heb. xii. 2. For,

1. 'This is the will of the Father, that of all which he hath given unto Christ he should lose nothing, but should raise it up again at the last day,' John vi. 39.

2. His love is unchangeable, John xiii. 1.

3. He is faithful, and will do what he hath promised, 1 Thes. v. 24.

Admirable is the comfort and encouragement which hence ariseth, in regard of our own weakness and proneness to come short of this glory; and also in regard of the many stumbling-blocks which lie in the way, and of the many enemies that oppose us and seek to hinder us in our endeavour after glory. Our comfort and encouragement is, that Christ hath undertaken to bring us to glory, and none can hinder what he undertakes; so as we may and ought to 'hope to the end for the grace that is brought unto us in the revelation of Jesus Christ,' 1 Peter i. 13. This we may do the more confidently, because the ground of our confidence is not in ourselves, who are mere sons of men, but in the Son of God.

In regard of ourselves, we may 'not be high-minded, but fear,' Rom. xi. 20, but in regard of Christ, we may be persuaded, 'that neither death, nor life, nor any other thing shall be able to separate us from the love of God which is in Christ Jesus our Lord,' Rom. viii. 38, 39.

Sec. 95. *Of Christ the Captain of our salvation.*

To encourage us to our course to glory, he that undertakes to bring his sons thereunto, is styled 'the captain of their salvation.'

By *salvation* is meant the very same thing that was comprised under *glory*, even our future happiness. Why it is called *glory*, was shewed Sec. 93; why *salvation*, Chap. i. Sec. 159.

The root ἀρχή, from whence the Greek word, ἀρχηγός, translated *captain*, is derived, signifieth both a beginning, *principium*, and also a principality, *imperium*. Answerably the word here used signifieth both a *captain*, that goeth before and leads on his soldiers; and also an *author* and first worker (*architectus*), of a thing. It is translated 'author,' Heb. xiii. 2, and 'prince;' as, 'prince of life,' Acts iii. 15. The author of life, who hath purchased and procured it; and the guide, who leadeth us thereto, going in the way before us.

To shew that Christ is the author and worker out of our salvation, these two words *prince* and *saviour* are joined together, Acts v. 31. Thus this word here translated captain, is four times, and only four times, used in the New Testament; in all which, both significations, namely, *captain* and *author*, may be implied, and both may well stand together. The author of a thing may be a guide and leader of others thereto. So is Jesus in reference to salvation.

To shew that Christ is the author of our salvation, another word, which properly signifieth a cause, even the efficient cause, is attributed to him, and translated 'author of salvation,' αἴτιος, Heb. v. 9. Yea, he is styled salvation itself, τὸ σωτήριον, Luke ii. 29. On this ground was the name Jesus given him. See Sec. 73. See Chap. v. ver. 9, Sec. 50.

That Christ also is our captain and guide to salvation, is evident by other metaphors attributed to him in reference to salvation; as a *shepherd* that goeth before his sheep, John x. 2, 4, 14; a *mediator* that presents men to God, 1 Tim. ii. 5; an *high priest*, who is for men in things appertaining to God, Heb. v. 1; a *way* in which one goeth to a place, John xiv. 6; yea, *a new and living way*, Heb. x. 20: *new*, in that there never was the like before; *living*, in that it puts life into them that walk therein, and brings them to eternal life.

Christ is our captain, both to direct us, and also to encourage us. We of ourselves are blind in reference to spiritual and heavenly things; we know not the way; we cannot see it, we cannot walk in it without a guide. The eunuch who was asked, if he understood what he read, answered, 'How can I, except some man should guide me?' Acts viii. 31.

Christ is a *light*, to shew us the way, John viii. 12, and a *guide*, to lead us along therein, Luke i. 79.

We are also full of fears and doubts; but Christ going before us puts spirit, life, and resolution into us. The speech of Abimelech, 'What ye have seen me do, make haste and do as I have done,' Judges ix. 48, put life into his soldiers, and made them readily do the like. So did a like speech and practice of Gideon, Judges vii. 17. For this end, therefore, thus said Christ to his disciples, 'I have given you an example, that ye should do as I have done to you,' John xiii. 15.

Let us therefore take courage, and being instructed in the right way, and led on by so skilful a guide, so valiant a captain, so tender a shepherd, so merciful an high priest and a mediator, so gracious with the Father, let us 'look unto Jesus, the author and finisher of our faith,' Heb. xii. 22; 'let us go boldly unto the throne of grace, that we may obtain mercy, and find grace to help in time of need,' Heb. iv. 16. Doubt not of entering into glory, having such a captain.

Sec. 96. *Of Christ's sufferings.*[1]

Concerning this captain, it is further said, that he was 'made perfect through sufferings.'

In the former verse, the apostle used this word in a singular number, πάθημα, because he restrained it to Christ's death, and added it as an epithet thereunto, τὸ πάθημα τοῦ θανάτου, to shew that Christ's death was a suffering death, accompanied with much inward anguish and outward torment. But here the plural number is used, διὰ παθημάτων, to intimate all Christ's sufferings, from his entering into the world to his going out of the same. For they were all ordered by God, and all tended to the very same end that is here intended, namely, the bringing of sons to glory.

I suppose it hereupon meet to take a brief view of the many kinds of Christ's sufferings.

General heads of Christ's sufferings are such as these: Christ's sufferings were either co-natural, such as appertained to his human nature; or accidental, such as arose from external causes. Of such endurances as were co-natural, see Sec. 169.

Accidental crosses were either such as was assaulted withal, or were inflicted upon him.

Many were the temptations wherewith he was assaulted, both by Satan and also by men; yea, and by God himself.

Satan tempted him to most horrible sins, as, diffidence, presumption, and idolatry, Mat. iv. 3, 6, 9. But nothing did cleave to him thereby. The purity of his nature was as a sea to a fire-brand, which soon quencheth it. Christ's purity was as clear water in a glass,

[1] See Sec. 76.

which hath no dregs, no filth at all in it; though it be shaken never so much, yet it remaineth clear. Christ saith of himself, 'The Prince of this world cometh, and hath nothing in me,' John xiv. 30. It is evident that Satan tempted Christ, after those fierce assaults in the wilderness. For at the end of them it is said, 'When the devil had ended all his temptations, he departed from him for a season,' Luke iv. 13. This phrase *for a season*, implieth that Satan afterwards set upon him again. And this phrase, 'The prince of the world cometh,' John xiv. 30, being spoken a little before the time of Christ's death, further sheweth that the devil set upon him again. These temptations of Satan were no small sufferings.

Christ was also tempted by men, and those both adversaries and friends. The Pharisees and Sadducees, and others like them among the Jews, oft tempted him, as Mat. xvi. 1, and xix. 3, and xxii. 18; John xviii. 6.

His disciples also tempted him, as Peter, Mat. xvi. 22; and James and John, Mark x. 35; and Thomas, John xx. 25–27. These temptations, from his disciples especially, could not but much trouble him. Witness the sharp rebuke that he gave to Peter, Mat. xvi. 23. Yea, the temptations of his adversaries the Jews, stirred up anger in him, and grieved him much, Mark iii. 5, and viii. 12.

Finally, Christ was tried and proved, and in that respect tempted by God himself, as by the Spirit of God, when he was 'led up of the Spirit into the wilderness to be tempted of the devil,' Mat. iv. 1. And by the Father, who so withdrew his assistance and comfort from him, as forced him to cry out and say, 'My God, my God, why hast thou forsaken me?' Mat. xxvii. 46.

Afflictions inflicted on him were very many. For order and distinction's sake, they may be considered in his non-age, man-age, and time of death.

In his non-age these may be accounted sufferings.

1. His mean birth, in the stable of an inn, where he was laid in a manger, Luke ii. 7.

2. His flight in the night time into Egypt, upon Herod's prosecution. This was aggravated by the slaughter of all the infants in Bethlehem, and in all the coasts thereof, Mat. ii. 14–16.

3. His parents' offence at his abode in Jerusalem, Luke ii. 49.

What afflictions he endured all the time of his private life, who knoweth?

In his man-age his afflictions were greater, as manifold prosecutions, and that with a purpose to have destroyed him. Thus was he prosecuted by his own countrymen, Luke iv. 29; and by the common sort, John viii. 59; the rulers, priests, pharisees, sent officers to take him, John vii. 32; Herod threatened his life, Luke xiii. 31. By reason of these prosecutions, he was forced sometimes to pass through the middle of them, so as they could not discern him, Luke iv. 30, John viii. 59; sometimes he hid himself,

John xii. 36; sometimes he fled from country to country, and from town to town, as, John iv. 3, 4, from Judea to Samaria, and through it to Galilee, from Nazareth to Capernaum, Luke iii. 31, from Jerusalem to the place beyond Jordan, John x. 40.

His greatest afflictions were about the time of his death, when the hour of his adversaries and power of darkness was come; Luke xxii. 13. These may be drawn to two heads. Outward in body; inward in soul. Of these see Sec. 76.

Sec. 97. *Of Christ made perfect by suffering.*

Christ by his suffering is said to be made perfect. The Greek word τελειῶσαι, according to the notation of it, signifieth to finish or accomplish a thing,[1] to put an end unto it; or to perfect it. The Greek noun τέλος, *finis*, whence this verb is derived, signifieth an *end*, chap. iii. 6. For that which is brought to an end, so as there is no further proceeding therein, is said to be perfected, and that is accounted to be made perfect which is fully and absolutely done, so as nothing needeth to be added thereto. Hence the adjective translated *perfect*, τέλειος, Mat. v. 48, and the substantive translated *perfection*, τελειότης, Heb. vi. 1, Luke i. 45.

This word is variously translated. As,
1. To finish a thing, John iv. 34, Acts xx. 24.
2. To fulfil what was foretold, John xix. 28.
3. To make perfect, Heb. x. 1-14, and xii. 23.
4. To consecrate, Heb. ii. 28, that is, to set apart to an holy use, and that with special solemnity. The Greek Septuagint do use this word in this sense, Exod. xxix. 9, 22, 26, 29, 33. The Greek fathers[2] do apply this term to initiating persons by baptism, whereby they were solemnly consecrated and brought into the church.
5. To die; and that as a sacrifice offered up to God, Luke xiii. 32. In this sense Greek fathers apply this word to martyrdom.

Not unfitly in every of those senses may it here be taken, at least every of those acceptions give great light to that which is here spoken of Christ. For,
1. Christ by his sufferings finished that work and satisfaction which was on earth to be done. Therefore on the cross he said, 'It is finished,' John xix. 30.
2. By his sufferings were sundry prophecies fulfilled, Luke xxiv. 25-27, 45, 46.
3. By his sufferings Christ was made a full and perfect redeemer, Heb. vii. 26. Nothing needed more to be added thereunto.
4. By his sufferings Christ was solemnly consecrated to be our everlasting high priest, Heb. vii. 28.
5. By his sufferings to death Christ was made an offering for all sins, even a true, real, propitiatory sacrifice, Heb. x. 10.

The scope of the apostle in this place is to remove that scandal of Christ's sufferings, whereat both Jews and Gentiles stumbled. For this end he here sheweth that Christ's sufferings turned more to his glory and ignominy.[1] They were honourable ensigns and solemn rites of advancing him to glory.

For by his sufferings he vanquished all his and our enemies; he gloriously triumphed over them all; he satisfied the justice of God, and pacified his wrath; he reconciled God and man, and merited remission of sins and eternal salvation; yea, by his suffering he became a pattern and guide to us, and made the way of suffering passable for us to follow him therein, so as we may thereupon pass it through more easily.

Though Christ were ever perfect in himself, yet for bringing us to glory much was wanting till he had finished his sufferings, but thereby all that wanted was supplied, and he made perfect. Wherefore, glorious things are spoken of the cross of Christ, as 1 Cor. i. 18, Gal. vi. 14, Eph. ii. 16, Col. i. 20, and ii. 14, 15.

Who now that duly considereth the end of God in suffering his Son to suffer what he did, will be ashamed of the cross of Christ? It becomes us rather to glory therein, as the apostle did, Gal. vi. 14.

Great reason there is that we should so do, for in Christ's humiliation consisteth our exaltation; in his cross, our crown; in his ignominy, our glory; in his death, our life.

That we may thus do, we must behold Christ's sufferings, not with the eye of flesh, but of faith. Jews and Gentiles beholding Christ with no other eye than the eye of flesh, despised him by reason of his sufferings; for flesh can see nothing therein but folly, baseness, ignominy, contempt. But faith beholds wisdom, victory, triumph, glory, and all happiness.

As this affords matter of glorifying in Christ's sufferings, so also of contentment, patience, comfort, rejoicing, and glorying in our own sufferings for Christ's sake.

God hath appointed sufferings the highway and common road for all his to enter into glory thereby, Acts xiv. 22.

As thereby he maketh the head conformable to the members, ver. 14, so the members also conformable to the head, Philip. iii. 10.

Christ's blood was that holy oil wherewith he was anointed to be a triumphant king over all his enemies, and this oil is like that which was poured on Aaron's head and descended down upon his body, Ps. cxxxiii. 2. It pleased the Lord that the holy consecrating oil of suffering, which was poured on Christ our head, should descend upon us his members, that we should thus also be consecrated and made heirs of salvation. We ought therefore even to rejoice therein, as kings' sons when they are consecrated and made princes or dukes. Thus have the prophets and apostles done: they rejoiced in their sufferings, Mat. v. 12, Acts v. 41.

---

[1] See Chap. v. 9, Sec. 94.

[2] Dionys. Areopag. Greg. in Macab. Lucan. Euseb. Hist. Eccl. lib. v.

[1] Qu. 'Christ's sufferings and ignominy turned more to his glory'?—ED.

This Christ requireth, Mat. v. 12. Oft do we read of Paul's glorying in his chains, bonds, and imprisonment, Eph. vi. 20, Acts xxviii. 20, 2 Cor. xi. 23.

Thus have martyrs embraced the stake whereat they have been burnt with joy, and kissed the chains wherewith they were bound.

Among other arguments to move us both patiently to bear, and also joyfully to embrace the cross, let this be thought on, that it is the oil to anoint us for a kingdom, and an honourable rise to settle us on a throne.

Sec. 95. *Of the resolution of the tenth verse of the second chapter.*

The sum of this text is a reason of Christ's sufferings. This is, 1, generally propounded; 2, particularly exemplified.

In the general, 1, the ground; 2, the equity of the point is declared.

The ground is in this phrase, 'It became him.' Here is implied,

1. The principal author in this relative *him.*
2. The procuring cause whereby that author was moved. This was the decency of the thing, *it became.*

The equity of the reason is hinted in a description of the author. He is described by his relation to creatures, and that two ways:

1. As the supreme end, *for whom.*
2. As the efficient, *by whom.*

Both these are amplified by the extent of the correlative, *all things.*

In the particular exemplification is set down the main point, that Christ suffered. About it is declared,

1. A description of him that suffereth.
2. A declaration of the end of his sufferings.

He is described by two undertakings:

1. By bringing others to glory.
2. By being a Captain of their salvation.

In the former three points are expressed:

1. Christ's act, *bringing.*
2. The subjects or persons, *sons.*

These are amplified by their multitude, *many.*

3. The end to which they are brought, *glory.*

The latter hath reference to the main reason, *it became God,* and shews what it was that became him. In setting down whereof is noted,

1. God's act, *to make perfect.*
2. The person made perfect, *Captain of their salvation.* Here consider,

First, Christ's office, *Captain.*

Secondly, The end whereunto, *salvation.* This is amplified by the persons to whom salvation belongeth, *their.*

Thirdly, The means whereby he was made perfect, *through suffering.*

Sec. 99. *Of the observations gathered out of* Heb. ii. 10.

I. *God was the principal author of Christ's sufferings.* This relative *him* hath reference to God. See Secs. 37, 78.

II. *It was most meet by the sufferings of the Son of God to save sons of men.* This phrase, 'It became him,' proves this point. See Sec. 86.

III. *All things are for God's glory.* This phrase *for whom* intends so much. See Sec. 89.

IV. *All things are ordered by God.* This phrase *by whom* intends so much. See Sec. 89.

V. *God aimed at himself in making and governing all.* The order of these two phrases, *for whom* and *by whom,* implies thus much. See Sec. 89.

VI. *Saints are sons.* So they are here called, and that in relation to Christ and to his Father. See Sec. 90.

VII. *Saints' future estate is a most glorious estate.* They shall be brought to glory. See Sec. 93.

VIII. *Christ brings saints to glory.* This act is here expressly applied to him. See Sec. 92.

IX. *Christ leaves not his till they be settled in heaven,* for he undertakes to bring them to glory. See Sec. 94.

X. *Many shall be saved.* This is here set down almost in the same words. See Sec. 91.

XI. *Christ is our Captain.* This is here taken for granted. See Sec. 95.

XII. *It is salvation that Christ leadeth his unto.* In this respect he is here styled the Captain of our salvation. See Sec. 95.

XIII. *Salvation is proper to sons.* It is here styled *their* salvation. Sec. 90.

XIV. *Christ's sufferings were many.* See Sec. 96.

XV. *Christ by suffering was solemnly advanced to glory.* See Sec. 97.

XVI. *Christ by his sufferings made up whatsoever was requisite to bring man to glory.* See Sec. 97.

Sec. 100. *Of the conformity of the Son of God and saints in suffering.*

Ver. 11. *For both he that sanctifieth and they who are sanctified are all of one: for which cause he is not ashamed to call them brethren.*

This verse is here inferred as a confirmation of that which goeth before. This causal particle, γὰρ, *for,* implieth as much. It confirms the main point in hand, namely, that Christ was true man; and it is added as a fourth proof thereof. See Sec. 1.

It hath also an immediate reference to the last clause of the former verse; and sheweth a reason, why it became God to make perfect the Captain of our salvation through sufferings; even because he and we are ' all of one.'

Herein lieth the equity of Christ's sufferings, that therein and hereby he might be like to us. For ' in all things it behoved him to be made like unto his brethren,' ver. 17. Christ was herein of Moses his mind; he would suffer affliction with his people, Heb. xi. 25. He would not go another way to glory than they did, with whom he was of one. Thus much doth the inference of Christ being one with us, upon his sufferings import.

This doth exceedingly commend unto us the love of Christ, and it demonstrateth an equity of our suffering with him and for him; for we also are of one with him. Hereby shall we gain assurance to our own souls, and give evidence to others, that we are of one with him, namely, by our willingness to be conformable to him, and to drink of that cup whereof he hath drunk, as he said to his disciples, Mat. xx. 23.

Sec. 101. *Of sanctifying, and the divers kinds thereof.*

This first clause, *he that sanctifieth*, is a description of Christ, and that in relation to the members of his mystical body, who are said to be sanctified.

To sanctify, according to the Latin notation, *sanctificare* (from whence our English is translated), is to make holy. So doth the Hebrew in the third conjugation signify, הקדיש, *sanctificavit*. The Greek word also ἁγιάζων, which the apostle here useth, intendeth as much. It is derived from a root that signifieth a sacred thing,[1] worthy of good account, a thing honoured, and highly esteemed, being freed from such blemish as might dishonour it. The Greek word translated *holy*[2] is from the same root.

To sanctify, is an act attributed to the Creator and to creatures.

1. To the Creator, in reference to himself and others.
1. To himself, two ways.

(1.) In manifesting the excellency of his power, justice, and other attributes, Ezek. xxviii. 22, and xxxviii. 23.

(2.) In vindicating his righteousness from unjust imputations, Ezek. xxxvi. 23.

2. To others.

(1.) In a real conferring of holiness upon them, 1 Thes. v. 23. Thus each person in the sacred Trinity is said to sanctify, as the Father, Jude 1; the Son, Eph. v. 26; the Holy Ghost, Rom. xv. 16.

(2.) In setting apart to sacred employments. Thus God sanctified his Son, John x. 36; and the Son sanctified himself, John xvii. 19. Thus God sanctified men, Jer. i. 5, beasts, Num. viii. 17, and other things, Exod. xxix. 44, yea, and times too, Gen. ii. 3.

2. To creatures this act of sanctifying is attributed, as to men and others.

Men are said to sanctify God, themselves, other men, and other things.

1. Men sanctify God two ways.

(1.) By acknowledging his excellencies, Mat. vi. 9.

(2.) By an undaunted profession of his truth, 1 Pet. iii. 15.

2. Men sanctify themselves, by preparing themselves to perform holy services holily, 1 Chron. xv. 14.

3. Men sanctify other men.

[1] ἄζω seu ἄζομαι, *venero.* Inde ἅγιος, *res sacra, res veneratione digna.*

[2] *Hinc* ἅγιος *sanctus*, holy. See Chap. iii. Sec. 5.

(1.) By being God's ministers, in setting them apart to sacred functions, Lev. viii. 30.

(2.) By preparing them to holy services, Exod. xix. 10, 1 Sam. xvi. 5.

(3.) By using means of reconciliation between God and them, Job i. 5.

4. Men sanctify other things.

(1.) By employing holily such times and things as are holy, Exod. xx. 8.

(2.) By using means that others may observe holy duties aright, Joel i. 14.

(3.) By dedicating and consecrating them to the Lord for his service. Thus under the law men sanctified houses and lands, Lev. xxvii. 14–16.

Other things, besides men, are said to be sanctified two ways.

1. Typically, as sundry rites under the law, Heb. ix. 13, Mat. xxiii. 17–19.

2. Ministerially, as the word and prayer under the gospel, 1 Tim. iv. 5. The word, by giving us a warrant for what we use or do; prayer, for obtaining a blessing thereupon.

Sec. 102. *Of Christ sanctifying.*

This act of sanctifying, here mentioned, properly belongeth to Christ, and that as he is God-man, the mediator betwixt God and man. He is by an excellency and property styled a sanctifier, 'He that sanctifieth,' because in most of the fore-named respects he may be said to sanctify.

1. Christ, in reference to himself, sanctifieth. 'I sanctify myself,' saith he, John xvii. 19. As the Father set him apart, and deputed him to be a priest and sacrifice for men, so he voluntarily undertook what his Father deputed him unto: 'He offered up himself,' Heb. vii. 27; 'He gave himself,' Eph. v. 2; 'By this will are we sanctified,' Heb. x. 10.

2. He sanctified the Lord God (as we are enjoined, 1 Pet. iii. 15), in that 'he made a good confession before Pontius Pilate,' 1 Tim. vi. 13; I have glorified thee on earth,' saith he to his Father, as he was going out of the world, John xvii. 4.

3. He sanctifieth others, and that sundry ways.

(1.) In setting men apart to sacred functions, he gave some apostles, and some prophets, &c., Eph. iv. 11.

(2.) In furnishing men with gifts; when he ascended up on high, he gave gifts unto men, Eph. iv. 8.

(3.) In purging men from their pollutions. Hereof see Chap. i. 3, Secs. 27–29.

(4.) In enduing them with sanctifying graces: 'Of his fulness have all we received, and grace for grace,' John i. 16. Thus is he made sanctification to us, 1 Cor. i. 30.

(5.) In being a means of reconciliation betwixt God and us, verse 17. What Job did to his children after their feastings, Job i. 5, Christ doth continually by his intercession, Heb. vii. 27.

(6.) By taking us into a conjugal society with himself, Eph. v. 31, 32, we are sanctified to him, as the unbeliever is sanctified to the believer, 1 Cor. vii. 14.

(7.) In dedicating and consecrating his church to God as first fruits, James i. 18.

The apostle, by ascribing this act of sanctifying to Christ, gives us to understand that he is the author of his church's sanctification, 1 Cor. i. 30, for Christ is the only all sufficient head of the church. As all life, sense, motion and vigour, descends from the head to all the members, so all manner of spiritual life and grace from Christ. 'God gave not the Spirit by measure to him,' John iii. 34, for 'it pleased the Father that in him should all fulness dwell,' Col. i. 19. There is in Christ's death a mortifying power, whereby 'our old man is crucified with him,' Rom. vi. 6; and there is in his resurrection a quickening virtue, that like as Christ was raised up from the dead, so we also should walk in newness of life, Rom. vi. 4.

How this act of sanctifying is attributed to the Father also, and the Holy Ghost, and to the word and ministers thereof, see *Domest. Dut.* on Eph. v. 30, treat. i., sec. 76.

We are the rather to take notice of this, that Christ undertakes to be a sanctifier, that in all our needs we may have recourse to him for grace. Thus we are invited to do, Isa. lv. 1, Mat. xi. 28, John vii. 37.

That we may receive grace from Christ, we must be well informed in the means which he hath sanctified to sanctify us. These are his holy ordinances: in special, his word, and prayer, 1 Tim. iv. 5. As we find any sanctifying grace wrought in us, we ought, with thankfulness (as the tenth leper did, Luke xvii. 16), to acknowledge from whence it cometh; and withal, we ought to use what we receive to the glory of him that hath sanctified us, 1 Pet. ii. 9.

Sec. 103. *Of those who are sanctified.*

The co-relative which answereth to the fore-mentioned sanctifier, is comprised in this phrase, 'they who are sanctified.' This passive *sanctified* sheweth that this is a privilege conferred on them. They were not so by nature, they were not so of themselves; even they were of the common stock, of the polluted mass, no better than the worst. Of such saith the apostle, 'We were by nature the children of wrath, even as others,' Eph. ii. 3; 'We ourselves also were sometimes foolish, disobedient,' &c., Tit. iii. 3; in regard of natural condition, 'there is none righteous, no not one,' Rom. iii. 10; such were they of whom the apostle saith, 'But ye are sanctified,' 1 Cor. vi. 11.

This giveth evidence of the free grace of God, and it doth much commend his love. It is a means to strip us of all self-boasting, and to humble us deeply. It is an especial ground of giving all praise to God.

The same word in the passive, ἁγιαζόμενοι, is here used that was before in the active, ἁγιάζων, so as in the same respect wherein Christ sanctifieth any, they are sanctified. Particular instances are such as follow:

1. They are by Christ set apart and deputed to be kings and priests, Rev. i. 6.

2. They are by Christ enabled to those functions and services whereunto they are set apart, Eph. iv. 7.

3. They are by Christ purged from their pollutions, Heb. i. 3.

4. They are endued with all needful sanctifying graces, 1 Cor. i. 7, John i. 16.

5. By Christ they are reconciled unto God, Col. i. 21.

6. They are espoused to Christ, 2 Cor. xi. 2.

7. They are as first-fruits to God, Rev. xiv. 4.

They who are thus sanctified are the elect of God, called by the gospel, and so true members of the mystical body of Christ.

Under this act of sanctifying and being sanctified, all the graces whereof here in Christ we are made partakers are comprised, so as to be sanctified, is to be perfected, Heb. x. 14.

These relatives, *sanctifier, sanctified*, joined together, give evidence of a conformity betwixt the head and members of the mystical body in holiness. As the head is, so will he make his members to be. As he is holy, so shall they be.

This is a great inducement unto us, to use the means sanctified of God for effecting this work of sanctification. For Christ performeth what he undertaketh, in that way, and by those means, which are sanctified thereto. Wherefore, as Christ is the sanctifier, so use the means wherein he useth to sanctify; 'and as he which hath called you is holy, so be ye holy in all manner of conversation,' 1 Pet. i. 15.

Sec. 104. *Of the Son of God and sons of men being one.*

The two fore-mentioned relates, *sanctifier* and *sanctified*, are said to be 'all of one.' The Greek word in the case here used, ἐξ ἑνὸς, and translated *of one*, is common to all genders. Some, therefore, take it in the masculine, and refer it to God, as if this were the meaning. The Son of God and saints are all of God. This, in the general matter, is a truth, but not a truth pertinent to the point in hand; for the apostle allegeth here this union as a reason why Christ was man, and suffered for such and such, namely, because he and they were 'of one.' But it cannot be truly said that he was man, and died for all that were of God, in that they had their being of God. In this sense, not only men, but angels also, and all other creatures (for whom Christ neither took upon him man's nature, nor undertook to suffer), are of God.

Others apply this *one* to Adam, of whom, as concerning the flesh, Christ came, Luke iii. 23, 38. This also is a truth; but I suppose it to be more agreeable to the apostle's scope to take this particle *of one* in the neuter gender, as if it were thus expressed, 'of one stock,' and that for these two reasons:

1. The Greek particle ἐκ, translated *of*, is properly a note of the material cause.

2. This must have reference to the sanctified as well as to the sanctifier; for 'all are of one.' As the sanctifier is of the same stock whereof the sanctified are, so the sanctified of the same whereof the sanctifier.

In the former respect, that human nature whereof the sanctified are is the stock whereof Christ also is; and the spiritual nature whereof Christ is (called the divine nature, 2 Peter i. 4), is the stock whereof the sanctified are. In this respect such are said to be ' of Christ's flesh and of his bone,' Eph. v. 26, which phrase is mystically and spiritually to be taken. In relation to this spiritual being, sanctified ones are styled *spirit*, John iii. 6; and they are said to be ' in the Spirit,' to be ' after the Spirit,' to ' mind the things of the Spirit,' and to ' walk after the Spirit;' and the Spirit is said to ' dwell in them,' Rom. viii. 4, 5, 9.

Of this mystical union betwixt Christ the sanctifier, and saints the sanctified, see more in *Domest. Dut. on Eph.* v. 30, treat i. sec. 70, &c.

This general particle *all*, πάντες, as it includes the head and the body, so it compriseth under it all the members of that body. If it had reference to the head and body only as to two distinct parts, he would have said *both* are of one, rather than *all*, for *all* compriseth more than two. But because the body consisteth of many members, and all the members are sanctified, he fitly and properly useth this general *all*, and thereby gives us to understand that all that are Christ's are partakers of the same spiritual being.

This is evidenced by Christ's prayer, ' that they all may be one,' &c., John xvii. 21. The metaphors whereby the union betwixt Christ and saints is set out, give further proof hereof, as head and members, 1 Cor. xii. 12, vine and branches, John xv. 5, shepherd and sheep, John x. 14. Now, members, branches, and sheep are all of one; so are brethren also, which title is used in this verse.

This union of all should work unity, unanimity, amity, charity, sympathy, and condescension to them that are of low estate, and a willingness to be conformable to them that suffer for Christ and his gospel's sake. Of this mind was Moses, Heb. xi. 25.

Sec. 105. *Christ's doing things upon just cause.*

From the fore-mentioned union of Christ and saints, the apostle maketh this inference: 'For which cause he is not ashamed to call them brethren.' Because he and saints were of one, he called them brethren.

This note of inference, *for which cause*, sheweth that Christ would do what he had cause and reason to do. Christ being sent to save that which was lost, Mat. xviii. 11, and to give his life a ransom for many, Mat. xx. 28, for this cause he would not desire to be freed from that hour, John xii. 28.

For this cause he acknowledged before Pontius Pilate that he was a king, John xviii. 37. For this cause Christ confessed to God among the Gentiles, Rom. xv. 9; for this cause is he the mediator of the New Testament, Heb. ix. 15.

Were we of this mind, how many excellent works, much tending to God's glory, our own and others' good, would be willingly performed, which are now wholly omitted! Most are so far from being of Christ's mind herein, as they do the things that are evidently without cause: 'They transgress without cause,' Ps. xxv. 3. David much complaineth of wrongs done to him without cause, Ps. xxxv. 7, and lxix. 4, and cix. 3, and cxix. 78, 161. Christ maketh such a complaint, John xv. 25.

Let us advisedly and seriously consider what cause there is for us to do such and such things, and as there is cause, do them.

Sec. 106. *Of Christ and saints being brethren.*

In that which is here inferred one thing is taken for grant, another is expressed as a consequence following thereupon.

The thing taken for grant is a relation betwixt Christ and saints; namely, that they are brethren.

Of the divers acceptions of this word *brother*, see Chap. xiii. Sec. 3.

The relation betwixt the Son of God and sons of men is a mixed relation, partly natural, partly spiritual.

Natural is, that the Son of God became a son of man, descending, according to the flesh, from the same stock that we do, even from Adam, Luke iii. 23, 38.

Spiritual is, that sons of men are made partakers of the divine nature; for in that very respect wherein ' he that sanctifieth and they who are sanctified are of one,' they are also brethren.

Thus this relation is properly betwixt Christ and saints; for though Christ assumed the common nature of man, yet all men are not made partakers of the divine nature. This is proper to the regenerate, who are born again, and that of God, John i. 13, and adopted as children into God's family, which is the church.

Of such as these saith Christ, 'Behold my brethren,' Mat. xii. 49; 'Tell my brethren,' Mat. xxviii. 10; ' Go to my brethren,' John xx. 17; and more generally at the last day Christ giveth this title *brethren* to all his elect, whom he setteth at his right hand, Mat. xxv. 40.

As this gives evidence of the low condescension of the Son of God, so also of the high exaltation of sons of men; for the Son of God to be a brother to sons of men is a great degree of humiliation, and for sons of men to be made brethren with the Son of God is an high degree of exaltation; for Christ's brethren are in that respect sons of God, heirs of heaven, or kings, not earthly, but heavenly; not temporary, but everlasting kings.

Behold the honour of saints. Men count it an

honourable privilege to be allied to honourable personages. Such matches are much affected. But all alliance with men are but baseness to this. Who can sufficiently declare the excellency of the Son of God. Besides, this is no titular, but a real privilege. By virtue hereof God is our Father, John xx. 17; we have a right to all that is Christ's, 1 Cor. iii. 22; and we are co-heirs with Christ, of the heavenly inheritance, Rom. viii. 17.

Herewith we may uphold ourselves against all the scoffs and scorns of the world, and against all outward meanness.

Quest. May we, by virtue of this relation, call the Son of God our brother?

Ans. We have no example of any of the saints that ever did so. They usually give titles of dignity to him, as *Lord, Saviour, Redeemer,* &c. Howsoever the Son of God vouchsafe this honour unto us, yet we must retain in our hearts an high and reverent esteem of him, and on that ground give such titles to him as may manifest as much. Inferiors do not use to give like titles of equality to their superiors, as superiors do to their inferiors. It is a token of love in superiors to speak to their inferiors as equals; but for inferiors to do the like, would be a note of arrogancy.

Sec. 107. *Of 'calling' brethren.*

Christ is said to call them brethren. To call, in this place, καλεῖν, is not a mere nominal, titular, or complimental word, but very emphatical. It implieth an open acknowledgment of a thing, and a free possession thereof. Thus God said of the Gentiles, 'I will call them my people,' Rom. ix. 25, that is, I will before all the world declare and profess that they are my people, and acknowledge them for my own. Thus is this word taken, Mat. v. 9, 19; and in the negative, saith the prodigal to his father, 'I am no more worthy to be called thy son,' Luke xv. 21; and Paul, 'I am not meet to be called an apostle,' 1 Cor. xv. 9. The prodigal was his father's son, and Paul was an apostle; but both the one and the other thought himself unworthy to be acknowledged such as they were.

Christ, where he vouchsafeth a dignity and privilege, will openly acknowledge it. 'Behold my brethren,' saith he to his disciples, Mat. xii. 49. Such will he confess before his Father which is in heaven, Mat. x. 32, and before the angels of God, Luke xii. 8, Rev. iii. 5. He giveth a good proof hereof, sitting on his throne of glory, where he saith to all his brethren, 'Come, ye blessed of my Father, inherit the kingdom,' &c., Mat. xxv. 34.

Thus ought we to call and acknowledge one another according to those relations wherewith God hath knit us one to another.

Sec. 108. *Of Christ's 'not being ashamed' of his brethren.*

To shew that the meanness and manifold imperfections of children of men shall be no impediment to Christ's gracious and glorious acknowledgment of them to be his brethren, it is here further said, that 'he is not ashamed to call them brethren.'

The root, τὸ αἰσχος, *fœditas*, from whence the Greek verb, translated *ashamed*, is derived, signifieth filthiness. Thence a noun, αἰσχύνη, *pudor ob turpia*, signifying shame at some unbeseeming thing, is drawn; as where Christ saith to him that affected the highest room, 'Thou begin with shame, μετ' αἰσχύνης, to take the lowest room,' Luke xiv. 9; and again, 'that the shame of thy nakedness do not appear,' Rev. iii. 18. Now shame is a disturbed passion upon conceit of disgrace. From that noun the simple verb, αἰσχύνομαι, *pudefio*, which signifieth 'to be ashamed,' ariseth.

The word here used, ἐπαισχύνομαι, *valde pudefio*, is a compound, and the composition addeth emphasis. When it is affirmatively used, it signifieth to be much ashamed. 'What fruit had you then in those things whereof you are now ashamed,' ἐπαισχύνεσθε? Rom. vi. 21. True converts are much ashamed of their sins past. When it is negatively used, it signifieth to be nothing at all ashamed; as where the apostle saith, 'I am not ashamed, ἐπαισχύνομαι, of the gospel of of Christ,' Rom. i. 16. So it is also used in reference to sufferings for Christ, 2 Tim. i. 8, 12, 16. This very word is applied to God in reference to such as believed on him, 'God is not ashamed to be called their God,' Heb. xi. 16. God was not at all ashamed of that relation which was between him and them; nor is Christ at all ashamed at this title *brethren*, in reference to himself and saints, notwithstanding his own infinite excellencies and men's meanness, baseness, and filthiness in themselves.

This is one special point wherein Christ manifesteth himself to be 'meek and lowly in heart.'

We ought to learn of him so to be, Mat. xi. 29. All ages cannot afford such a parallel. Abraham's example in calling Lot *brother*, Gen. xiii. 8; and Joseph's, when he was advanced to be next unto the king, in acknowledging his brethren, Gen xlv. 4; and Moses, when he was accounted Pharaoh's daughter's son, acknowledging the Hebrews to be his brethren, Exod. ii. 11, and iv. 18, were very rare; but no more comparable to this of Christ, than the light of a dim candle to the bright shining of the sun.

This pattern of Christ is the rather to be noted, because it stripped such as are ashamed of their relations to others of all excuse. Some husbands are ashamed of their wives when they are raised to high dignities; some children in like cases are ashamed of their parents; some servants of their masters, and so in other relations. Can any be more highly advanced than Christ? Some are ashamed of the meanness and disparity of those to whom by some bond of relation they are knit; might not Christ have been in this respect much more ashamed of us?

But what shall we say of those that are ashamed of

Christ's brethren, even in this respect, because they are his brethren, and make a sincere profession of the true faith? Oh more than monstrous impudency! Yet thus are husbands, wives, parents, children, and others ashamed of their wives, husbands, children, parents, and others, even because they profess the faith, and are called Christ's brethren.

This respect of Christ to his brethren is a great encouragement and comfort to such as are despised and scorned by men of this world for Christ's professing of them.

The greatest impotency[1] and arrogancy in this kind is to be ashamed of Christ himself. Yet it was foretold that some should hide their faces from him, Isa. liii. 3. Fearful is the doom that Christ doth thus denounce against such: 'Whosoever shall be ashamed of me, and of my words, in this adulterous and sinful generation, of him also shall the Son of man be ashamed when he cometh in the glory of his Father, with the holy angels,' Mark viii. 38.

Sec. 109. *Of the resolutions and observations of* Heb. ii. 11.

The sum of this verse is a reason of Christ's suffering in man's nature, which was a conformableness to other men.

Two points are herein observable: 1, the substance of the text; 2, a consequence.

In the substance two things are expressed: 1, a difference betwixt Christ and saints; 2, an union.

The difference is, that one is an agent, 'he that sanctifieth;' the other a patient, 'they who are sanctified.'

In this union is noted, 1, the kind of it, *of one*; 2, the extent, *all*.

The kind of union is a common stock. This admits a double consideration.

1. The stock whereof Christ is one with us; that is, the human nature.

2. The stock whereof we are one with Christ; that is, the divine nature.

The consequence is, 1, generally intimated in this phrase, 'for which cause;' 2, particularly expressed.

In the particular is noted, 1, a relation, *brethren*; 2, a manifestation thereof.

In the manifestation is set down, 1, the means whereby it was manifested, *called*; 2, the grounds of manifesting it, *not ashamed*.

Observations hence arising are these:

I. *Union is a cause of conformity*. The causal particle *for*, whereby the union of Christ with saints is inferred as a reason of his suffering in man's nature, intends that which is here observed. See Sec. 100.

II. *Christ sanctifieth men*. In this respect this style is given him, 'He that sanctifieth.' See Sec. 102.

III. *Saints were as others*. The word *sanctified* presupposeth as much. See Sec. 103.

[1] Qu. 'Impudency'?—ED.

IV. *Such as are Christ's are sanctified*. This is here clearly expressed. See Sec. 103.

V. *Christ is of the same stock whereof others are*. In this respect he is 'of one.' See Sec. 104.

VI. *Saints are of the same stock whereof Christ is*. In this respect they are 'of one.' See Sec. 104.

VII. *All saints have the same spiritual being*. All are of one with Christ. See Sec. 104.

VIII. *That for which there is cause must be done*. See Sec. 105.

IX. *Christ and saints are brethren*. See Sec. 106.

X. *Christ acknowledgeth such as are his*. To call is to acknowledge. See Sec. 107.

XI. *Christ accounts relations betwixt him and saints to be no disgrace unto him*. He is not ashamed thereof. See Sec. 108.

Sec. 110. *Of the apostle's testimony from* Ps. xxii. 22.

Ver. 12. *Saying, I will declare thy name unto my brethren, in the midst of the church will I sing praise unto thee.*

This text is here alleged as a proof of that respect which Christ manifested to his sanctified ones, in acknowledging them to be his brethren. The proof is taken from a divine testimony. Of this kind of proof, see Chap. i. Secs. 46, 65.

The first word being a participle, λέγων, *saying*, sheweth a dependence of this verse on that which went immediately before, and such a dependence as gives an evidence of the truth thereof; and in that respect it is an apparent proof of it. It hath reference to Christ calling men brethren; for in this testimony he doth expressly call them so.

This testimony is taken out of Ps. xxii. 22. That psalm is a most clear prophecy of Christ. Many passages therein are directly applied to Christ in the New Testament; as,

1. This clause in the very beginning of the psalm, 'My God, my God, why hast thou forsaken me?' Mat. xxvii. 46.

2. This in the seventh verse, 'All they that see me laugh me to scorn;' they 'shake the head,' Mat. xxvii. 39.

3. This in the eighth verse, 'He trusted in the Lord, let him deliver him,' Mat. xxvii. 43.

4. This in the sixteenth verse, 'They pierced mine hands and my feet,' John xix. 37, and xx. 25.

5. This in the eighteenth verse, 'They part my garments among them, and cast lots upon my vesture,' Mat. xxvii. 35.

6. This in the two-and-twentieth verse, 'I will declare thy name,' &c., is here in my text.

This psalm, as it sets out the sufferings of Christ to the full, so also his three great offices. His sufferings are copiously described from the beginning of the psalm to ver. 22.

The prophetical office of Christ, from ver. 22 to ver. 25.

That which is foretold about his vows (ver. 25,) hath respect to his priestly function. In the rest of the psalm the kingly office of Christ is set forth.

All the distinct points of that psalm were accomplished in Christ. It is gathered from the title, that this psalm was to be sung every morning in the temple, to support the hope of God's people in the promised Messiah.

This testimony therefore is most pertinently produced to prove the point in hand, and Christ himself is here brought in to be the utterer and publisher thereof, as an evidence that he called men his brethren.

As this testimony proves that point in particular, so in general it proves the main point, that Christ was man; and it points at Christ's prophetical office, for which it was requisite that he should be man, as it was foretold, Deut. xviii. 18. Thus it is a fifth argument to demonstrate that point. See Sec. 1.

It doth withal render a reason why it was requisite that the Son of God should be a son of man, namely, that he might 'declare God's name unto his brethren,' who were sons of men.

In quoting this testimony, the apostle holds close to the words of the prophet. A little difference there is in our English translation, but that little is more than needed. For 'congregation,' here is 'church;' both these words intend one and the same thing. For 'praise,' here is 'sing praises.' The Hebrew word signifieth both. The psalms which used to be sung have their name from this root.[1]

There is in one word a difference betwixt the LXX and the apostle, but the word in the one, διηγήσομαι, and the other, ἀπαγγελῶ, signifieth one and the same thing.

Sec. 111. *Of Christ's declaring God.*

The word ἀπαγγελῶ, which the apostle here useth, translated *declare*, is more emphatical than διηγήσομαι, that which the LXX useth. This is a compound word. The simple verb ἀγγέλλω signifieth to make known or declare. From it is derived the word *angel*, ἄγγελος, which in the general signifieth a messenger sent to declare his mind who sent him.

The verb admits sundry compositions, every of which adds much emphasis. As,

1. To explain, or clearly and fully to declare a thing. 'When the Messiah cometh, he will tell, ἀναγγελεῖ, us all things,' John iv. 25, namely, fully and clearly.

2. To divulge and spread abroad. 'That my name might be declared, διαγγελῇ, throughout all the earth,' Rom. ix. 17.

3. To celebrate or shew forth. 'Ye do shew, καταγγέλλετε, the Lord's death,' 1 Cor. xi. 26.

4. To shew forth or make evident. 'Shew forth, ἐξαγγείλητε, the praises of God,' 1 Pet. ii. 9.

5. To profess: openly and freely to declare. 'Professing, ἐπαγγελλομέναις, godliness,' 1 Tim. ii. 10; and to promise. 'God promised,' Tit. i. 2.

[1] תהלים *ab* הלל in Hiphil. *Laudavit sancte.*

6. To command or enjoin. 'I command,' παραγγέλλω, saith the apostle, 1 Cor. vii. 10.

7. To shew beforehand, or foretell, προκατήγγειλε, Acts iii. 13–24.

8. Among other compounds, that which is here used by the apostle wants not his emphasis, for it imports a declaring of that which is for that end received. This is the word which Christ useth to John's disciples. 'Shew, ἀπαγγείλατε, John again those things which ye do hear and see,' Mat. xi. 4. This also is the word which the apostle twice useth in this manner: 'We have seen it, and shew it unto you. That which we have seen and heard declare we unto you,' 1 John i. 2, 3.

Two points are here intended under the full sense of this phrase, 'I will declare.'

1. Christ had from another that which he delivered to others. The preposition ἀπὸ, with which the Greek verb is compounded, implieth as much, and other places of Scripture do expressly shew who that other was, namely, he that sent him, even his Father. For thus saith Christ: 'My doctrine is not mine, but it is his that sent me,' John vii. 16; and 'I speak to the world those things which I have heard of him that sent me; as the Father hath taught me, I speak these things,' John viii. 26–28. This is to be taken of Christ as God's minister and messenger, and that in our nature.

2. Christ concealed not that which his Father appointed him to make known; he declared it. The psalmist by way of prophecy bringeth in Christ affirming as much of himself, thus, 'I have preached righteousness,' &c. I have not hid thy righteousness within my heart; I have declared thy faithfulness and thy salvation: I have not concealed thy lovingkindness and thy truth,' Ps. xl. 9, 10. Yea, Christ himself pleadeth this as an evidence of his faithfulness to his Father, while he was on earth, thus, 'I have manifested thy name unto the men which thou gavest me,' &c., 'for I have given unto them the words which thou gavest me,' John xvii. 6–8. For indeed this is an especial point of faithfulness, and 'Christ was faithful to him that appointed him,' Heb. iii. 2.

In both these is Christ a precedent and pattern to us, and we ought in both these to be faithful to him that hath appointed us. See *The Whole Armour of God*, on Eph. vi. 19, treat. iii. part vii. sec. 180, &c.

Sec. 112. *Of Christ's declaring God's name in man's nature.*

That which Christ declared, is here said to be the name of God, for it is God, even his Father, to whom Christ here saith, 'I will declare thy name.'[1]

Under the name of God is comprised everything whereby God hath made himself known unto us. See more of God's name in my *Explanation of the Lord's Prayer*, entitled, *A Guide to go to God*, secs. 20, 21.

[1] Of name of God, see Chap. xiii. 15, Sec. 144.

This phrase, *I will declare thy name*, implieth that Christ maketh known whatsoever is meet to be known of God, so much of God's excellencies, and so much of his counsel as is to be known. Thus is this title *name* used, John xvii. 6, 26. That which the apostle saith of himself, might Christ say most properly, and in the largest extent, 'I have not shunned to declare all the counsel of God,' Acts xx. 27. For this end did Christ take upon him to be the prophet of his church, and that in our nature. He was that prophet in two respects.

1. Because none else knew the name of God; none else knew God's excellencies and God's counsels. Thus much is intended under this phrase, 'No man hath seen God at any time,' John i. 18; and under this, 'No man in heaven, nor in earth, neither under the earth, was able to open the book, neither to look thereon,' Rev. v. 3.

2. Because Christ to the full knew all; 'for in him are hid all the treasures of wisdom and knowledge,' Col. ii. 3; thereupon it is said, 'The only begotten Son which is in the bosom of the Father, he hath declared him,' John i. 18; and, 'He hath prevailed to open the book and to loose the seven seals thereof,' Rev. v. 5-9.

This Christ did in our nature, because we were not able to endure the brightness of the divine Majesty to speak unto us: witness the affrightment of the Israelites at hearing God's voice in delivering the law, Exod. xx. 19. This reason is rendered of God's making his Son a prophet in our nature, Deut. xviii. 15, 16.

Of the difference betwixt Christ and others declaring God's will, see Chap. i. Sec. 14.

The duty hence arising is expressly laid down by Moses, thus: 'Unto him ye shall hearken,' Deut. xviii. 15; and by God himself thus, 'Hear ye him,' Mat. xvii. 5. See more hereof Sec. 5; and Chap. iii. 1, Sec. 25; and ver. 7, Secs. 77, 78.

How can we now hear Christ?

Ans. 1. Many of Christ's sermons and instructions are recorded by the evangelist, so as in well heeding them we hear Christ.

2. Christ instructed his apostles in all things needful for his church to know. For thus saith he to them, 'All things that I have heard of my Father, I have made known unto you,' John xv. 15; and Christ commanded his apostles 'to teach people to observe all things whatsoever he had commanded them,' Mat. xxviii. 20; and so they did, ver. 3, 1 John i. 3. Yea, Christ gave pastors and teachers after them, and endowed them with gifts sufficient for the building up of his church, Eph. iv. 11, 12; and these stand in Christ's stead, 2 Cor. v. 21; and Christ speaks in them, 2 Cor. xiii. 3. Hereupon saith Christ, 'He that receiveth whomsoever I send, receiveth me,' John xiii. 20. Thus we see how Christ may be hearkened unto in all ages, even to the end of the world.

Of Christ's being a preacher, see ver. 3, Secs. 22-24.

Sec. 113. *Of appropriating Christ's prophetical office to his brethren.*

The special persons for whom Christ was a prophet are styled brethren, and that in relation to Christ himself; for thus he himself calls them. Of this relation, see Secs. 106, 107.

Express mention is here made of this relation, to shew who they be for whom in special Christ took upon him to be a prophet, namely, for his spiritual kindred. These are the babes to whom the mysteries of the gospel are revealed, Mat. xi. 25; these are they to whom it is 'given to know the mysteries of the kingdom of heaven,' Mat. xiii. 11; these are they of whom Christ in his preaching said, 'Behold my mother and my brethren,' Mat. xii. 49. For these and these alone are given to Christ. Of these thus saith Christ, 'I have manifested thy name unto the men which thou gavest me out of the world'; 'I have given unto them the words which thou gavest me.' 'I have declared unto them thy name, and will declare it,' John xvii. 6, 8, 26.

Quest. Why did Christ himself preach to all of all sorts? and why commanded he his disciples 'to teach all nations, and to go into all the world, and preach the gospel to every creature?' Mat. xxviii. 19, 20, Mark xvi. 15.

Ans. For his elect's sake, which were here and there in every place mixed with reprobates, as good corn is mixed with tares, and solid grain with chaff. The elect only receive the benefit of Christ's prophetical office; others are more hardened thereby, Mat. xiii. 13-15.

Hereby such as are kindly and effectually wrought upon by the ministry of the gospel, wherein Christ's prophetical office is executed, may know that they are Christ's brethren, chosen of God, given to the Son of God, heirs of eternal life.

Sec. 114. *Of Christ's prophetical office setting forth God's praise.*

Another branch of Christ's prophetical office is thus set down: 'In the midst of the church will I sing praise unto thee.'

The addition of this clause to the former, gives us to understand that Christ's prophetical office tended to the setting forth of the praise of God, as well as to the instructing of men in God's will. Hereupon saith Christ to his Father, when he was going out of the world, 'I have glorified thee on earth,' John xvii. 4.

As his love to man moved him to undertake the former, so his zeal of God's glory put him on to the latter.

Those two duties, of instructing man, and praising God, belong to all faithful prophets of the Lord, and they ought to aim at both. Yea, they are both so linked together, as they can hardly, if at all, be severed. For he that declareth God's name aright unto men, doth therein set forth God's praise; and he whose heart is set upon setting forth God's praise, will declare his name to men, because thereby God's praise is set forth.

Sec. 115. *Of singing praise.*

This phrase, *I will sing praise*, is the interpretation of one Greek word. The root, ὑμνεῖν, *celebrare*, signifieth to celebrate one's praises. Thence proceedeth a noun, ὕμνος, which signifieth an hymn or song in in one's praise. The heathen used to set out an accurate form of praises, especially of the praises of their gods, under this word *hymn.* It is twice used in the New Testament, Eph. v. 19, Col. iii. 16. And in both places it is joined with psalms and spiritual songs. Psalms, ψαλμοί, were such as found in the book of Psalms; hymns, ὕμνοι, such as were composed in special for the praise of God; songs, ὠδαί, such as were metrically and artificially penned. Because such songs for the most part were light and lascivious, he addeth this epithet, 'spiritual,' to teach Christians to take heed of wanton songs.

From that noun *hymn*, the verb here used by the apostle, ὑμνεῖν, is raised. It implieth two things:

1. The matter of duty, which is the setting forth of God's praise.
2. The manner of praising him, cheerfully, melodiously, with singing.

Of praising God, namely, what it is to praise him, for what he is to be praised, and why this duty is to be performed, see my *Explanation of the Lord's Prayer*, entitled, *A Guide to go to God*, secs. 238-240.

Of solemn praise and manifestation thereof, and unsatisfiedness therein, see *The Saints' Sacrifice*, on Ps. cxvi. 12, secs. 1, 85, 86, 108.

The prime, principal, and proper object of praise, whom Christ would praise, was God. It was God to whom he thus directed his speech, 'I will praise *thee*.' See *The Saints' Sacrifice*, on Ps. cxvi. 12, sec. 79.

St. Paul in another place thus bringeth in Christ performing this duty: 'For this cause I will confess to thee among the Gentiles, and sing unto thy name.'

Christ in his lifetime accomplished that which was by the psalmist foretold of him, and that according to the literal sense of the word, 'He sang praises to God.' The very word of the text is used, where it is said of Christ and his disciples, 'They sang an hymn,' Mat. xxviii. 30.

This practice of Christ doth not only justify and warrant this manner of setting forth God's praises by singing, but also commends it much unto us. For Christ's practice of an imitable duty is a great commendation of that duty. We are oft exhorted to be followers of him.

As this duty is here commended, so it is also expressly commanded, Eph. v. 19, Col. iii. 16.

Good warrant there is for performing this duty privately, alone, or in a family, and publicly in a congregation.

This direction, 'Is any man merry? let him sing psalms,' James v. 13, warrants singing by one alone.

Paul and Silas their singing of psalms, Acts xvi. 25, warrants singing by two or three together.

The fore-mentioned practice of Christ and his disciples singing after supper, Mark xiv. 26, warrants singing in a family.

And this phrase, 'When you come together, every one of you hath a psalm,' 1 Cor. xiv. 26, implieth the Christian's course in singing psalms publicly in churches. Hereunto tendeth the mention of a church in this text.

This manner of setting forth God's praises, even by singing, is frequently mentioned in the last book of the New Testament, which foretelleth the then future estate of the Christian church, Rev. v. 9, and xiv. 3, and xv. 3.

They therefore straiten this duty too narrowly who restrain it to the pedagogy of the Jews. Then indeed it was more frequently used, especially with all manner of musical instruments. For then even the external man needed more outward and sensible means of quickening it.

Singing was under the law so highly accounted of, as he that was said to be a man after God's heart, 1 Sam. xiii. 14, hath this title, as an high commendation given unto him, 'The sweet psalmist of Israel,' 2 Sam. xxiii. 1.

Though singing be not now altogether so needful in regard of the external rite and manner of quickening, as it was under the law, yet is it not under the gospel needless or useless. For though Christians be men, in reference to the non-age of the Jews, yet are they not made perfect while here they live. This is the privilege of those saints that are taken out of this world. They are 'spirits of just men made perfect,' Heb. xii. 23.

Where the apostle exhorteth to be 'filled with the Spirit,' he addeth thereupon, 'speaking to yourselves in psalms and hymns,' &c., Eph. v. 18, 19. Hereby he gives us to understand that it comes from the fulness of the Spirit, that men are enabled to sing and make melody in their hearts to the Lord.

Many benefits accrue from this evidence of the fulness of the Spirit in us.

1. The spirits of men are thereby more quickened and cheered; and so they are made more cheerful and ready to praise the Lord. This makes our praising of God to be more acceptable to him. Hereupon David exhorteth to 'make a joyful noise unto God,' Ps. lxxxi. 1.

2. Others are hereby exceedingly affected, and their hearts and spirits stirred up to give assent unto our praises, and together with us to sing and praise the Lord. Hereupon saith the apostle, 'Speak unto yourselves in psalms,' Eph. v. 19.

3. An holy zeal of God's glory is manifested hereby,

and hereby men testify that they are not ashamed to profess and set out the holy name of God, so as many may take notice thereof. In singing, our tongue doth sound out aloud the praises of God. This holy zeal did he express, who said, 'I will give thanks unto thee, O Lord, among the heathen : and sing praises unto thy name,' Ps. xviii. 49.

This being a lawful and useful duty, we ought not to be ashamed of performing it. In churches men will sing, because all or the most so do ; but in families how few do it ! They fear I know not what brand of preciseness in performing family duties. They are rare Christians that make conscience of making their house a church. They who are negligent herein, keep away much blessing from their house, but by performing household duties of piety, God's blessing is brought to a family, as it was to the house of Obed-Edom while the ark was there. The practice of Christ in singing psalms with his family, is sufficient to move us to do so.

Sec. 116. *Of cheerfulness in praising God.*

By singing praise, cheerfulness in performing the duty is intended. This the psalmist thus expresseth, 'My mouth shall praise thee with joyful lips,' Ps. lxiii. 5. Thereupon he exhorteth to 'make a joyful noise unto God,' Ps. lxvi. 1.

As God loves a cheerful giver, 2 Cor. ix. 7, so a cheerful setter forth of his praise. A cheerful performance of duty argueth a ready and willing mind, and this doth God highly accept : 'Take,' saith the Lord, 'of every man that giveth willingly with his heart,' Exod. xxv. ; 'Whosoever is of a willing heart, let him bring an offering to the Lord,' Exod. xxxv. 5 ; 'The people of Israel rejoiced, for that they offered willingly : because with perfect heart they offered willingly to the Lord ;' 'As for me,' saith David, 'I have willingly offered all these things : and now have I seen with joy, thy people to offer willingly unto thee,' 1 Chron. xxix. 9-17. Now praise is an especial offering to be given to God, Ps. cxvi. 17, Heb. xiii. 15 ; we ought therefore in performing this duty to quicken up our spirits, as the psalmist did, Ps. lvii. 7, 8.

Sec. 117. *Of Christ's praising God in the midst of the church.*

To manifest yet further the holy zeal of Christ in praising God, the place of his doing it is thus set out, 'in the midst of the church.'

The Hebrew and the Greek word translated in the psalm *congregation*, and here *church*, signify one and the same thing, and admit a like notation.

The Hebrew root קהל, *congregare*, signifieth to gather together; thence a noun, קהל, *congregatio*, which signifieth a congregation, or a company of people assembled together. Both verb and noun are thus joined, 'They gather the congregation together,' ויקהלו הקהל Num. xx. 10.

The Greek root καλεῖν, *vocare*, signifieth to call; the compound ἐκκαλεῖν, *evocare*, to call out. Thence the word here translated church, ἐκκλησία, *cœtus evocatus*, and congregation, Acts xiii. 43, in general signifieth an assembly of people. The assembly of those heathen that cried up their Diana, in Greek is set out by the same name that is here translated *church*, Acts xix. 32, 41. Assemblies used to be called out of their houses or habitations to assemble or meet together. Hereupon when an assembly is dissolved, every man is said to return to his house, 1 Kings xii. 24.

For the most part the Greek word is by the penmen of the New Testament appropriated to an assembly of saints, namely, such as profess the gospel. Such assemblies are our churches, not only by reason of their calling and coming out of their private houses to one assembly, but also by reason of their calling out of the world, or out of that natural, corrupt, and miserable condition wherein they were conceived and born. In this respect they are oft styled, 'The called,' as Rom. i. 7, 1 Cor. i. 2, 9, Mat. ix. 13. For then are we made actual members of the church, when we are effectually called.

In common use this word *church* is metonymically put for the place where such assemblies meet. Thus the word *synagogue* (which signifieth the same that church doth) is put for an assembly, and so translated, James ii. 2 ; and for a congregation, Acts xiii. 43. It is also put for the place where people assemble, as this phrase implieth, 'He hath built us a synagogue,' Luke vii. 5.

Here in this text, *church* is put for an assembly of saints.

That which is principally here intended is, that Christ would set forth God's praise publicly, among the people of God, not in a private corner, or among a few of them, but in the midst of them, so as all might hear. It was Christ's usual course to make choice of those places where most of God's people were assembled, that he might spread his Father's name the further. When he was but twelve years old, he sat in the temple among the doctors, Luke ii. 46 ; at every feast, when all the people of God assembled together, he went to the temple, and there preached among them ; he went also to their synagogues on the Sabbath days, Luke iv. 16, because there many people used to assemble ; the like he did at other times, and in other places where there were presses of people, he used to preach unto them, Luke v. 1, Mat. v. 1, Mark ii. 2. But not to insist on more particulars, Christ thus saith of himself, 'I spake openly to the world : I ever taught in the synagogue and in the temple, whither the Jews always resort : and in secret have I said nothing,' John xviii. 20.

This he did upon very weighty causes. As,

1. To shew that he was not ashamed of his calling, or of his doctrine. He was not like those that 'creep into houses, and lead captive silly persons,' 2 Tim. iii.

16, who labour to sow tares of schism and heresy secretly, when and where the Lord's seedsmen are absent, as the enemy did, Mat. xiii. 25.

2. To shew his desire of doing the most good he could. The greater the number of people that heard him were, the more might reap the fruit of his labours.

3. To shew his zeal for the glory of his Father. The sounding forth of God's praise in assemblies among much people greatly maketh to God's glory, in that many may thus be brought to know God, to acknowledge him, and to join in praising him, 1 Cor. xiv. 25.

The apostles, after Christ's time, imitated their master herein: 'Peter and John went up together into the temple at the hour of prayer,' Acts iii. 1; then did the people assemble themselves in the temple: 'Paul and Barnabas went into the synagogue on the Sabbath day,' Acts xiii. 14. By this means the churches increased exceedingly. In this regard the apostle professeth that he was 'not ashamed of the gospel,' but that he was ready to preach it at Rome also, Rom. i. 15, 16. As he had preached it in other populous places, so would he also in that city, which was the most populous place of all the world at that time. We ought to be followers of them, even as they also were of Christ, 1 Cor. xi. 1.

The foresaid practice of Christ is of use to stir up people to frequent public assemblies where God's praise is sounded forth, that so they may join with such as sing praises to God, and reap the benefit of the mysteries that are there revealed concerning God's name. Christ hath promised his presence in such places, Mat. xviii. 20. See Chap. iii. 1, Sec. 27.

Sec. 118. *Of the apostle's fit application of a divine testimony to Christ.*

Ver. 13. *And again, I will put my trust in him. And again, Behold I, and the children which God hath given me.*

In this verse two other evidences of Christ's prophetical office and of his human nature are set down. The former is the ground of that encouragement which Christ had to hold out in executing his office, which was his confidence in God, declared in a divine testimony; the latter is an effect of that his office.

Because the manner of bringing in this proof is like the former; both of them being taken out of the Old Testament, he thus joineth them together, 'and again.' Of this transition see Chap. i. Sec. 77.

In opening the former scripture, four questions are to be resolved.

1. Whence the testimony is taken.
2. How fitly it is applied to Christ.
3. How truly it proveth Christ's human nature.
4. How pertinently it is inferred on the execution of Christ's prophetical office.

For the first, this phrase, 'I will put my trust in him,' is in many places of the Old Testament, especially the book of Psalms.

But there are two places, at either of which, or at both which, the apostle may have an eye.

One is Psalm xviii. 2, where the words of this text are according to the Hebrew.

Obj. The Seventy have not in their translation of that place the very words which the apostle here useth.

Ans. 1. Penmen of the New Testament do not always tie themselves to the words of the Seventy; instance Mat. ii. 6, 15, 18; no, nor this apostle, instance chap. iii. 9. Evangelists and apostles were not translators of the Old Testament; they only took proofs out of the same; for which purpose it was enough to hold the true sense and meaning of the Holy Ghost, though they expressed it in other words.

Ans. 2. The very words which the apostle useth are also used by the Seventy in the said psalm, as it is registered 2 Sam. xxii. 3.

The other place whereunto the apostle may have an eye is Isa. viii. 17. There the Seventy use the very same words which the apostle here doth, though our English thus translate them, 'And I will look for him.'

Quest. Can one proof be taken out of two places?

Ans. Yea, if they set down one and the same thing, and that in the very same words. The evangelists, in quoting a testimony, oft name *prophets* in the plural number, as Mat. ii. 5, 23, John vi. 45, Acts xiii. 40.

This, duly weighed, taketh away the ground of that dispute which is betwixt expositors about the place out of which this testimony should be taken. Some affirm that it is taken out of Ps. xviii. 2, others out of Isa. viii. 17. Arguments *pro* and *con* are brought on both sides. But I suppose that this dispute might have been spared; for, to come to the second point,

2. Both the psalmist and the prophet Isaiah may be fitly applied to Christ.

In that psalm there are sundry points that can be applied to none properly but to Christ; as this, 'Thou hast made me the head of the heathen,' ver. 43; and this, 'As soon as they hear of me, they shall obey me: the strangers shall submit themselves to me,' ver. 44; and this, 'He sheweth mercy to his anointed, to David and to his seed for evermore,' ver. 50.

Besides, these words, 'Therefore will I give thanks to thee among the heathen, and sing praises unto thy name,' ver. 49, are expressly applied to Christ, Rom. xv. 9.

Obj. The title of Psalm xviii. sheweth that in special manner it concerned David, being his 'song when the Lord had delivered him from the hand of all his enemies, and from the hand of Saul;' and it is set in the history of David's life (2 Sam. xxii. 1, &c.), to shew that it concerned him.

Ans. It cannot be denied but that this psalm concerned David, and is fitly put among his acts, for he was the author and editor thereof. In this respect it might justly have been registered in the history of his life, though it had been wholly prophetical, even a mere prophecy of Christ. Neither can it be denied but that the title intendeth it to be meant of David; for the psalm is in part historical, and concerneth David himself; yet to us he was a type of Christ. That which in the history concerned David as a type, may in a mystery concern Christ as the truth. Besides, that scripture which in some parts of it is only historical (as Ps. xl. 12), may in other parts be only prophetical, and appliable to Christ, as Ps. xl. 6, 7. The like is observed in 2 Sam. vii. 12-14. As for the other place, namely, Isa. viii. 17, that chapter also may be typical, and concern the prophet who wrote it, and Christ also the truth of the type. Sundry passages of that chapter are in the New Testament applied to Christ, as that in ver. 13, 'Sanctify the Lord,' 1 Pet. iii. 15; and that in ver. 14, 'He shall be for a sanctuary,' 1 Pet. ii. 4; and that in vers. 14, 15, 'He shall be for a stone of stumbling,' &c., Mat. xxi. 44, Luke ii. 44, Rom. ix. 32, 1 Pet. ii. 8; and that in ver. 18, 'are for signs and wonders in Israel,' Luke ii. 34, Heb. x. 33; and that in ver. 18, 'Behold I, and the children whom the Lord hath given me,' here in this text. Seeing so many points of that chapter are applied to Christ, why may not this also—'I will put my trust in him'—which is in the midst of them, be applied to him? Thus we see how fit a reference this testimony hath unto Christ, as it is taken both out of Ps. xviii. 2, and also out of Isa. xviii. 18.

3. It proves Christ to be a true man, in that, as other men, he stood in need of God's aid, and thereupon, as other sons of men, his brethren, he puts his trust in God.

4. It is also pertinently inferred upon the execution of Christ's prophetical function, in that it shews the reason why he declared God's name to his brethren, and why he would sing praises to God in the midst of the church, and be neither ashamed nor afraid so to do, namely, because he put his trust in God.

Sec. 119. *Of Christ's putting his trust in God.*

The Hebrew word which the Psalmist useth, חסה, signifieth to *rest upon one*, to be preserved and kept safe by him. The bramble, therefore, in the parable thus useth this word, 'Put your trust in my shadow,' חסו, Judges ix. 15; a noun thence derived, מחסה, is translated refuge, Ps. xlvi. 1, and in sundry other places.

In Isa. viii. 17, another Hebrew word is used, וקויתי; but that which signifieth the same thing, and by the Septuagint, is translated as here in this text, and in 2 Sam. xxii. 3.

The noun derived from this verb, תקוה, *spes*, signifieth hope or trust, and so it is oft translated by our English, as Ps. lxxi. 5, Job iv. 6.

The Greek phrase used by the apostle carrieth emphasis, ἔσομαι πεποιθὼν ἐπί αὐτῷ: it implieth trust on a good persuasion that he shall not be disappointed. It is translated *confidence*, Philip. vi. 6. Word for word it may here be thus translated, 'I will be confident in him.'

The relative *him* hath apparent reference to God, Ps. xviii. 2, Isa. viii. 18, so as Christ himself, being man, rested on God to be supported in all his weaknesses, and to be enabled to go through all his undertakings, and well accomplish them.

He had many enemies, and was brought to very great straits, Ps. xviii. 3-5; yea, he and his were 'for signs and wonders,' even 'in Israel,' Isa. viii. 18; yet he fainted not, but put his trust in the Lord. His greatest enemies gave testimony hereunto, saying, 'He trusted in God,' Mat. xxvii. 43. Though they said it in derision and scorn, yet it was a truth.

This was further manifested by the many prayers which time after time he made to his Father, Heb. ix. 7.

He did the rather put his trust in God, and manifest as much, that he might, in his own example, teach us what to do in our manifold straits. Thus, when he was assaulted by the devil, he repelled his temptations by the word of God, Mat. iv. 4, vii. 10, that he might thereby teach us how to resist the devil.

Christ, as man, well knew his own insufficiency, and the all-sufficiency of God. Were we thoroughly acquainted with our own impotency, and well instructed in God's omnipotency, we should herein imitate Christ; and in testimony thereof, in all straits fly unto God, and in all straits pray and say, as Jehoshaphat did, 'We know not what to do; but our eyes are upon thee,' 2 Chron. xx. 12.

The description of him in whom Christ putteth his trust, Ps. xviii. 2, and that before and after the manifestation of his confidence, declareth the sure ground that he had to put his trust in God. The description is set down in sundry metaphors, as 'rock,' 'fortress,' 'strength,' 'buckler,' 'horn of salvation,' 'high power,'[1] and 'deliverer,' set out the impregnable power of God, and shew how sure and safe a refuge he is to those that fly to him, and put their trust in him. See more hereof in *The Whole Armour of God*, on Eph. vi. 10, secs. 4-6.

The inference of Christ's confidence upon his boldness in singing praise unto God in the midst of the church, sheweth the reason of that his boldness; even because he put his trust in God.

Confidence in God drives out all fear of man, and shame by reason of man. So much doth he testify who said, 'My soul trusteth in thee;' and thereupon added, 'I will sing and give praise,' Ps. lvii. 1, 7; and again, 'In God I will praise his word, in God I have put my trust; I will not fear what flesh can do unto me,' Ps. lvi. 4. This was it that made prophets,

[1] Qu. 'tower'?—ED.

apostles, and other faithful ministers so bold as they were in sounding forth God's praises. They trusted in God.

Surely we may try and prove ourselves, and give evidence to others of our confidence in God. If fear, shame, or any by or base respect to man, keep us from an open setting forth of God's praise, we do not put our trust in God.

Sec. 120. *Of the apostle's fit application of* Isa. viii. 18 *to Christ.*

The apostle addeth a third testimony to prove the same point, as is manifest by repeating the second time this phrase, 'and again.' See Chap. i. Sec. 77.

The testimony is this, 'Behold, I, and the children which God hath given me.' This, without all question, is taken out of Isa. viii. 18. In words there is a full agreement between the Hebrew original, and the Greek translation thereof, and the apostle's quotation; so also in the sense, for the prophet bringeth in this sentence as a prophecy of Christ. Many things which were historically true of the prophet in that chapter, may typically be applied to Christ. This was before in part declared, Sec. 118, and may more fully be cleared by taking a view of the particular passages of the prophet in that chapter.

In that chapter, two main points are set down.

1. A denunciation of judgment against the wicked.
2. A promise of mercy and safety to the righteous.

The former is set down from the beginning of the chapter to the 10th verse.

The latter from thence to the end of the chapter.

In laying down the promise, the prophet taketh his rise from the highest, safest, and surest ground of all comfort, namely, the proposed Messiah, ver. 14, concerning whom, he declareth what should be the events that would fall out at his coming, and that both in regard of the wicked and of the righteous. The wicked should stumble and fall to their utter destruction; the righteous should be established for ever, ver. 14, 15.

For a further confirmation of these things thus foretold, the prophet is commanded to bind up the word of God among the disciples, that so it might be kept close from the incredulous and remain among the faithful, ver. 16. Hereupon the prophet professeth, that notwithstanding God's just indignation, conceived against the house of Jacob, he will continue to look for help from the Lord, and trust in him, ver. 17: so did Christ.

To shew the ground of his confidence, Christ is brought in offering himself, and all those who believed on him, unto his Father, notwithstanding that they were in the world accounted wonders and monsters.

Thus these words being properly intended of Christ, are fitly by the apostle applied to him.

Others take them properly meant of the prophet himself, and that in regard of his function, in which respect they may be applied to all the ministers of God; and if to all, then most especially to Christ, the chiefest and head of all. Thus the apostle's application of this testimony to Christ, may by just consequence be sound and good.

I rather incline to the former application of the words, by way of prophecy, for three especial reasons.

1. Because sundry other passages of this chapter are so applied in other places of the New Testament, as was before shewed, Sec. 118.
2. Because the latter phrase of this testimony—'whom the Lord hath given me'—is oft, and that very properly, in other places applied to Christ, as John vi. 39, 65, and xvii. 6, 8, 9; but we never read it in a spiritual sense spoken of any other prophet or minister.
3. The apostle's allegation and application is without all question much more pertinent, if the words be taken as a prophecy.

Sec. 121. *Of Christ's being one with saints.*

The foresaid testimony being applied to Christ, giveth proof of his human nature, and shews him to be one with us, and that in three respects.

1. In that he ranketh himself in the number of saints, saying, 'Behold, I, and the children;' and so presenteth himself with the rest of God's children unto God, as to a common Father of them all; according to that which elsewhere he saith, 'I ascend unto my Father and your Father,' &c., John xx. 17.
2. In that he presenteth himself unto God as his minister, who had faithfully fulfilled the task which was committed to his charge. Hereupon it followeth that he was inferior to his Father, who appointed him a prophet.
3. In that the nature of relation, intimated in this word *children*, implieth that he is of the same nature with them; for father and children, properly taken, are all of the same nature.

Sec. 122. *Of the efficacy of Christ's prophetical office.*

Obj. This relative *children* may have reference to God the Father who gave them, as well as to Christ who bought them.

Ans. It may not be denied but that saints are God's children as they are regenerate, John i. 13, 1 Peter i. 3; and as they are adopted, Rom. viii. 15, 16. But the prophet and apostle do both speak of Christ's prophetical office; and, to shew the power thereof, these children are brought in, as begotten by Christ's word and ministry: and in this respect they are styled children in reference to Christ.

The prophet Isaiah maketh mention hereof, to shew, that notwithstanding the infidelity, obstinacy, and apostasy of the greater part of them which professed themselves the people of God, Christ, by his gospel should so work upon all those that were given unto him by his Father, as they would all hearken unto his voice and follow him, till, all being gathered together, both he and they should be presented unto God his Father.

To this very purpose is it here also applied by the apostle, to shew the power and efficacy of Christ's prophetical office; that notwithstanding he took upon him man's weak nature, and met with many obstacles, yet through the help of God, in whom he trusted, he should bring many children with him to glory.

Sec. 123. *Of the manner of quoting a text.*

Concerning the expression of this testimony, it may seem to be an imperfect sentence, because the latter part set down by the prophet, is left out in this quotation.

Ans. So much is quoted as served to the apostle's purpose, and in the quotation of a text so much is sufficient. Compare Mat. iv. 15, 16, with Isa. ix. 1, 2, and you may observe the like. The apostle quoteth only these words, 'and to thy seed,' Gal. iii. 16, which make not a full sentence, yet they were enough to his purpose.

2. This sentence, as quoted by the apostle, is a full proposition; for this note of attention, *behold*, compriseth under it that which maketh the words joined with it a full proposition, as Mat. xii. 18.

3. The verb substantive, which would make up this sentence, useth to be understood, and so it is, Isa. viii. 18.

Sec. 124. *Of this particle* behold.

This title, *behold,* ἰδού, useth to be prefixed before remarkable matters.

It is a note of demonstration, of attention, of admiration.

1. Where a matter worthy to be seen, or earnestly desired, is to be seen, this particle is premised, as if it were said, Behold it is here before you; or, Behold it is here to be seen. Thus it declareth the evidence of a thing, as where it is said, 'Behold there came wise men from the east,' Mat. ii. 1. And so it is a note of demonstration.

2. When a matter that deserves more than ordinary attention is delivered, men used to premise this particle *behold,* as when Christ uttered that excellent parable, that setteth down the different kinds of hearers, he thus begins ' Hearken, behold,' Mat. iv. 3.

3. When a strange and wonderful matter, that will hardly be credited, is delivered, we thus express it, *behold*; as, 'Behold I shew you a mystery,' 1 Cor. xv. 51. That mystery was a great wonder indeed; namely, that ' we shall not all sleep.'

Here the word *behold* may be taken in all those three respects. For,

1. It doth point out and plainly demonstrate, who they be that may with confidence present themselves to God, namely, Christ and his children.

2. It shews that it is a point well worthy to be marked, that Christ should take of sons of men to be his children, and present them to his Father.

3. It is that which causeth wonder to all the world.

In a word, this note *behold* implieth that the point here noted is a very remarkable point, worthy of all acceptation, 1 Tim. i. 15. Of all mysteries, the mysteries that concern Jesus Christ are the most remarkable. This note therefore, *behold*, is frequently set before them, both in the Old and New Testament, as Isa. vii. 14, and xxviii. 16, and xxxii. 1, and xlii. 1; Zech. iii. 8, and ix. 9; Mat. xii. 41; Luke ii. 34; Jude ver. 14; Rev. i. 7, 18. They are therefore with the more diligence to be attended unto, and with the greater care to be heeded. See Sec. 5.

Here in particular this particle, *behold*, setteth out a matter of admiration, which was done to the astonishment of the world. This is further manifest by the prophet's adding this clause, ' are as signs and wonders.' For the greater part, even of those among whom Christ exercised his prophetical office, rejected his ministry. ' He came unto his own, and his own received him not,' John i. 11. Yet, notwithstanding the obstinacy of the greater part, Christ himself persisted in exercising his function, and they that were given him of his Father, hearkened to his word, believed and obeyed the same, and so followed him, as he presented them with himself to his Father. This was the wonder, and thereupon it might well be said *behold*.

Oh that ministers and people would so carry themselves, as in this respect to be as signs and wonders; and all to say of them, *behold*. When all flesh was corrupt before God, Noah remained upright, Gen. vi. 9, &c. Joshua professeth, that though all Israel should serve other gods, he and his house would serve the Lord, Joshua xxiv. 15. Though Elijah knew none to remain faithful with the Lord but himself, yet he remained very zealous for the Lord, 1 Kings xix. 10. When many that followed Christ departed from him, the twelve disciples abode with him, John vi. 68. These, and others like to them, have been willing to make themselves signs and wonders in all ages by cleaving close to Christ.

This is a point of trial, whereby our faithfulness may be proved. If we shrink from Christ for the world, as Demas did, 2 Tim. iv. 10, or for persecution, as they who are resembled to the stony ground, Mat. xiii. 21, or because the doctrine of the gospel seemeth hard and harsh, as the Capernaitans did, John vi. 66, or for any other by-respect, we have not that courage and confidence, as may cause others to say of us, *Behold*.

Sec. 125. *Of Christ's going with those whom he led to God.*

This pronoun of the first person, *I*, hath respect to the Son of God, who very elegantly, by a double rhetorical figure, is here brought in speaking to his

Father, and that by way of rejoicing for the good success of his ministry, 'Behold I and the children,' &c. As if he had said, Here am I, O Father, whom thou didst send out of thine own bosom from heaven to earth, to gather thine elect out of the world. I have done that for which thou sendest me, 'Behold, here am I and they.'

This is a speech of much confidence, arising from his faithfulness, crowned with good success. This made him with much cheerfulness present himself to God. Thus did the two faithful servants cheerfully appear before their Lord, to give up their account. Faithful servants may be assured of the Lord's gracious approbation and bountiful remuneration. But on the other side, slothfulness and unprofitableness makes servants afraid to appear before their Lord. See all these exemplified, Mat. xxv. 20, &c.

What an encouragement is this for ministers of God's word and other servants of the Lord, to improve to the best advantage they can, the talent which the Lord hath committed to them, that with confidence they may say to God, 'Behold I.'

Of Christ's faithfulness, see more on chap. iii. 2.

This express mention of himself, 'Behold I,' sheweth that he would not send others to God without himself: herein he shews himself to be that good shepherd that 'goeth before his sheep,' John x. 4. In this respect he is styled the 'Captain of their salvation,' ver. 10. See Sec. 95.

He would not leave them till he had presented them to his Father, to be settled in that inheritance which he had purchased for them.

This is a worthy pattern for all that have a charge committed to them, to abide with them, to be an example unto them, not to leave them, or send them away to the work of God themselves alone; but to go with them, and hold out with them, so as every one that hath such a charge may say, as our head here doth, 'Behold I.' In doing this we shall save ourselves as well as others, 1 Tim. iv. 16. The apostle had an especial care hereof, as appeareth by this his profession, 'I keep under my body, and bring it into subjection, lest that by any means, when I have preached to others, I myself should be a cast-away,' 1 Cor. ix. 27.

What a miserable thing is it for ministers to be like them who built the ark wherein Noah and his family were preserved, but they themselves perished.

To prevent this, in preaching to others we must preach to ourselves; from our own hearts to our own hearts. For in exercising our ministry we sustain a double person; one of a preacher, another of a hearer. They who so do in their approaching to God will say, 'Behold, I.' Of inciting ourselves to that whereunto we stir up others, see Sec. 4.

Sec. 126. *Of Christ's bringing others to God.*

The Lord Christ thought it not enough to present himself to his Father, but he brings others also, whom he joins with himself by this copulative *and*. Thus in that powerful prayer which at his going out of the world he made to his Father for himself, he joins those whom his Father had given unto him, and saith, 'I pray for them which thou hast given me, for they are thine.' 'Neither pray I for these alone (meaning his disciples), but for them also which shall believe on me through their word,' John xvii. 9, 20.

For their sake Christ came into the world. For their sake he sanctified himself, John xvii. 19. For their sakes he became poor, 2 Cor. viii. 9. For their sakes he did and endured what he did and endured. See Sec. 83.

Herein Christ manifested his zeal of God's glory (for the more were brought to God, the more glory redounded to God), and also his good respect to others, for it was a singular benefit, an high honour, to be, by and with Christ, presented to God. He thus makes them partakers of his own glory, John xiv. 3, and xvii. 21, &c.

They whose hearts are inflamed with a zeal of God's glory, and filled with love of their brethren, will be like-minded; they will endeavour to lead on others with them in such courses as may bring them to God. Such a magistrate will say, Behold I and my subjects; such a minister, Behold I and my people; such a father, Behold I and my children; such a master, Behold I and my servants; such a tutor, Behold I and my pupils. So others that have charge.

Such, as they honour God and do good unto others, so they do much promote their own glory. For 'They that be wise shall shine as the brightness of the firmament; and they that turn many to righteousness as the stars for ever and ever,' Daniel xii. 3.

Of inciting others to go along with us in duty, see *The Saints' Sacrifice* on Ps. cxvi. 19, sec. 120.

Sec. 127. *Of the efficacy of preaching the gospel.*

This bringing of others to God is here brought in as an effect of Christ's prophetical office, and manifesteth the efficacy of the gospel, whereby all that belong to God are brought in to him. Though by nature they are dead in sin, yet the sound of Christ's mighty voice pierceth into their ears and heart. Hereupon saith Christ, 'The dead shall hear the voice of the Son of God; and they that hear shall live,' John v. 25.

We have an evidence hereof in Christ's ministry while he lived on earth; for saith he to his Father of his disciples, 'While I was with them in the world, I kept them in thy name,' John xvii. 12.

The efficacy also of Christ's prophetical office hath been manifested since his ascension, by the ministry of his apostles and of their successors in all ages.

This is a forcible motive to incite us ministers to be diligent in declaring God's name and preaching the gospel. We may rest upon it, that our labour shall not be in vain. The efficacy of Christ's prophetical function since his ascension, hath been very great. All that belong to God shall by the preaching of the gospel be brought to God. Though there be many incredulous and obstinate, yet Christ hath his children, and they will receive our word. If it were duly weighed, what an honour it is to be spiritual fathers, and what recompence follows thereon, it would certainly put on ministers to preach the gospel with all diligence.

This also may be a motive to people, to give good heed to the preaching of the gospel. As this is to be done, in regard of the excellency of the teacher (as was shewed before, Sec. 2), so also in regard of the efficacy of the gospel. 'Hear, and your soul shall live,' Isa. lv. 3. For 'the word of God, which liveth and abideth for ever,' is an 'incorruptible seed,' out of which men are 'born again,' 1 Peter i. 23.

Sec. 128. *Of Christ's children*.

They who are brought in to God by the gospel, are styled children, παιδία, and that in relation to Christ, as he was a prophet, and begat them by the gospel, as was shewed Sec. 122.

This very title is given by Christ to his disciples, John xxi. 5. According to the Greek notation, it signifieth such as are instructed. A Greek word, παιδεύω, that signifieth to instruct, is thence derived. The Greek word here used is a diminutive,[1] and translated 'little children,' Mat. xviii. 3, and xix. 13, 14, for little children are specially to be instructed, 'train up' (or instruct, חנך, *instrue*.) 'a child,' Prov. xxii. 6. The LXX use the same word, παιδίον, there in the singular number, which the apostle doth here in the plural.

Other ministers, who are means of converting men, which is a spiritual begetting of them, are styled 'fathers,' 1 Cor. iv. 15, and they who are begotten 'sons,' 1 Cor. iv. 14, or children. The Greek word, τέκνα, there used by the apostle, signifieth such as are begotten, for it is derived from a verb, τίκτω, *pario*, *gigno*, that signifieth to bring forth or beget.

The very word used in this text, παιδία, is also put for such as are begotten by the ministry of men, and translated 'little children,' 1 John ii. 13, 18.

If they who are instructed by men (who are but 'ambassadors for Christ,' and instruct in Christ's stead, in whom Christ speaketh, 2 Cor. v. 20, and xiii. 3), are called and accounted their children, much more justly are they to be called and accounted children of Christ, who is the highest and chiefest doctor; and by whose word and Spirit they are most properly begotten.

Of this relation betwixt Christ and saints, his children, see more on Sec. 90.

Sec. 129. *Of God's power to exact an account*.

The reason of Christ's bringing the foresaid children

[1] παῖς, inde παιδίον.

to God is thus expressed: 'Which God hath given me.' The reason is taken from God's commending them to Christ's care. The argument may be thus framed:

They who are commended by the supreme Lord to be fitted for and presented to himself, must be so presented to him;

But God, the supreme Lord, hath committed such and such to Christ to be so presented to himself;

Therefore Christ so presents them.

There are four words in this reason, every of which carry emphasis. 1. This title, *God*. 2. His act, *hath given*. 3. This relative, *which*. 4. This other relative, *me*.

1. The express mention of God in this reason, intendeth a high supreme sovereignty which he hath over all, and a power which he hath to impose a task, and exact an account of well employing the same; hereupon Christ putteth a *must* upon himself about doing the work that he which sent him appointed him to do, John ix. 4.

This made him so willing and forward therein as he made his meat to do the same, John iv. 34. And he pleaded as much before his Father, John xvii. 4.

Concerning others, even all of all sorts, evidence is given of God's committing a charge to them, and exacting an account of them, in the parable of the talents, for therein the Lord appointed to every servant his task, and taketh a particular account of each one, rewarding the faithful and punishing the unfaithful, Mat. xxv. 14, &c.

The parable of the steward gives further evidence of God's sovereignty in calling men to an account, Luke xvi. 2, and the apostle's frequent mention of the account which we must all give to God, Rom. xiv. 12; 2 Cor. v. 10; Heb. xiii. 17; 1 Peter iv. 5,

This is a strong motive to provoke us unto all diligence and faithfulness in improving, to the best advantage that we can, the talents that we have. They are given to us by him that hath a sovereignty and absolute power over us; that can and will call us to an account; that can and will abundantly reward the faithful, and take sore revenge of the unfaithful, Mat. xxv. 23, 24, &c. See Chap. iv. 13, Sec. 39.

Sec. 130. *Of God's free giving*.

2. The *act* here attributed to God in this word *given*, ἔδωκεν, manifesteth God's free grace. For to give is an act of favour and grace; it is opposed to meriting, purchasing, exchanging, or returning a valuable consideration. That which is bestowed upon merit, purchase, exchange, or any like consideration, cannot properly be said to be given.

This word is oft used to set out the free grace and favour of God to man; and that in bestowing his Son upon him. 'God so loved the world, that he gave his only begotten Son, &c.,' John iii. 16; Christ expressly declareth this to be the ground of any one's coming to him: 'All that the Father giveth me shall come to me,' John vi. 37, 39. All things that saints have, or can hope for, are freely conferred upon them; 'the Lord will give grace and glory,' Ps. lxxxiv. 11; 'The Lord will give a crown of righteousness,' 2 Tim. iv. 8; 'It is your Father's good pleasure to give you the kingdom,' Luke xii. 32.

To make this the more clear, the apostles oft use a verb, χαριζεσθαι, gratis donare, which is derived from a noun, χάρις, gratia, that signifieth free grace, and is translated 'freely to give,' Rom. viii. 32, 1 Cor. ii. 12; and frankly to forgive, Luke vii. 42.

Though Christ, being given, meriteth for us remission of sins by his blood, and purchased the heavenly inheritance, Acts xx. 28; Eph. i. 7–14; yet to effect those things for us, Christ was freely given to us, and we to him. See more hereof, Sec. 78.

Sec. 131. *Of God's power in choosing or refusing whom he will.*

3. The parties given to Christ are comprised under this relative *which*. This relative hath reference to the children before mentioned. Those children are a peculiar people: 'All are not children,' Rom. ix. 7, 8. Nor are all given by God to Christ. That there is a set and certain number given to Christ, is evident by sundry passages in the prayer which Christ made to his Father at his going out of the world. Eight several times is this word *given* there used, and that to set out God's free grace therein, John xvii. 2, 4, 6, 7, 9, 11, 12, 24.

God being the supreme sovereign over all, hath power to choose or refuse, to take or leave whom he will. This the apostle exemplifieth by a comparison taken from a potter, Rom. ix. 21. Surely there is infinitely a far greater difference between the Creator and creatures, than between a potter and clay. This power of God over creatures doth the apostle in that chapter plentifully prove, both by divine testimonies taken out of the Old Testament, and also by other solid arguments.

Let not, therefore, any dare to open his mouth and plead against God, because he useth this his prerogative in choosing some and leaving others. This use of this great mystery doth the apostle thus press: 'O man, who art thou that repliest against God? Shall the thing formed say to him that formed it, Why hast thou made me thus?' Rom. ix. 20. If we cannot fathom the depth of this mystery, nor discern the equity thereof, let us impute it to the shallowness of our apprehension, and cry out with the apostle, 'Oh the depth of the riches both of the wisdom and knowledge of God,' Rom. xi. 33. Far be it from us to impute any unrighteousness to God; it should seem that in the apostle's time some in this case did so. For the apostle in reference to such thus saith, 'What shall we say then? Is there any unrighteousness with God?' With much indignation doth the apostle thus reject that conceit: 'God forbid,' Rom. ix. 14.

Sec. 132. *Christ the means of bringing all good to man.*

4. The relative *me* hath reference to Christ; for it is Christ that saith, Behold I, &c. God being to make choice of a peculiar people, that they might be vessels of mercy and glory, commended them to his Son, to be fitted and so brought thereunto. Where it is said God loved the world, it is added, he gave his only begotten Son, &c., John iii. 16. All the blessings whereof we are made partakers, are conferred upon us in and with Christ. We are chosen in Christ, made accepted in him, we have redemption in him, Eph. i. 4, 6, 7; we are reconciled to God by him, Col. i. 20, 21; justified by his blood, Rom. v. 9; called by him, 1 Peter v. 10; sanctified in him, 1 Cor. i. 2; saved through him, Rom. v. 9, 10. This course of bringing men to glory by Christ, doth very much amplify divine mercy, and sundry other divine properties, as hath been shewed, Secs. 87, 88.

Behold here the difference betwixt the execution of that part of God's decree which respecteth man's salvation, and of that whereupon followeth man's condemnation. The benefit of the former is wholly out of man, and only in Christ. Christ doth whatsoever is meritorious to bring the elect unto salvation. The issue of the other is altogether in man himself, who meriteth by sin his own damnation.

The former is to be observed to strip man of all boasting, and to make him give all the glory to God.

The latter to clear and justify God, and to lay all the blame on man.

Sec. 133. *Of restraining the benefit of Christ's offices to the elect.*

The whole reason thus set down, *which God hath given me*, implieth a restraint of the efficacy of Christ's prophetical office to them alone whom God hath given him. It intendeth that all they shall partake of the benefit of Christ's prophetical office, and thereby be brought to God, and none but they. To the like purpose saith Christ, 'All that the Father giveth me shall come to me,' John vi. 37. This phrase is both extensive and exclusive, it extendeth itself to every one of God's elect, who are given by God to Christ, and it excludeth all but them. So much is intended by this phrase, 'As many as were ordained to eternal life believed,' Acts xiii. 48. All they, and none but they. This exclusive restraint Christ doth somewhat more expressly set down, where he saith to his disciples, 'Unto you it is given to know the mysteries of the kingdom of heaven, but to them it is not given,' Mat. xiii. 11. See more hereof, Sec. 113.

The special reason hereof is thus rendered by Christ himself: 'Even so, Father, for so it seemed good in thy sight,' Mat. xi. 26. And again, 'It is your Father's good pleasure to give you the kingdom,' Luke xii. 32. See more hereof, Sec. 37.

That which is here intended of the restraint of the

efficacy of Christ's prophetical office, may be applied to the restraint of the benefit of his other offices; yea, and of all that he did and endured for man. All is restrained to the elect whom God hath given to his Son; see Sec. 81. Yea, it may also be applied to the efficacy of the gospel preached by Christ's ministers. Their ministry is effectual only to the elect, Acts xiii. 48.

Quest. Why then is the gospel preached to all, even to reprobates as well as to the elect?

Ans. 1. Because these cannot be discerned one from the other here in this world.

2. Because these are here in this world mixed together, as wheat and chaff in the barn.

3. To make the reprobate the more inexcusable.

By the efficacy of the gospel, men may know that they are the elect of God given to Christ, and shall be eternally saved.

They who reap any benefit by the ministry of the gospel ought not to attribute it to any wit, wisdom, conceit, memory, or other parts of their own, but only to the good pleasure and gift of God. The praise which Christ gave to his Father in the behalf of babes, Mat. xi. 25, must, such as are effectually wrought upon, much more give unto God in behalf of themselves, and say, 'Not unto us, O Lord, not unto us, but unto thy name give glory,' Ps. cxv. 1.

A due consideration of this point will keep us from spiritual pride and arrogancy, and make us humble before God, and thankful unto him. See more hereof Sec. 162.

Sec. 134. *Of the resolution of* Heb. ii. 12, 13.

Ver. 12. *Saying, I will declare thy name unto my brethren, in the midst of the church will I sing praise untò thee.*

Ver. 13. *And again, I will put my trust in him. And again, Behold I and the children which God hath given me.*

The sum of these two verses is a description of Christ's prophetical office. This is here brought in as a confirmation of Christ's human nature, wherein he executed that function. See Sec. 1.

In this description two points are considerable:

1, The inference; 2, the substance.

The inference in this word *saying*, in particular verifieth that which was asserted in the words immediately preceding, namely, that Christ was 'not ashamed to call men brethren.'

The argument may be thus framed:

He that saith of men, 'I will declare thy name unto my brethren,' is not ashamed to call them brethren;

But Christ saith of men, I will declare thy name unto my brethren;

Therefore Christ is not ashamed to call men brethren.

The substance containeth a proof of Christ's prophetical office, about which we may observe,

1. The kind of proof; 2, the point proved.

The kind of proof is a divine testimony. Of this kind there be three particulars:

1. The execution thereof, ver. 12. This is taken out of Ps. xxii. 22.

2. The ground of Christ's courage in executing it, ver. 13. This is taken out of Ps. xviii. 2.

3. The efficacy thereof, ver. 13. This is taken out of Isa. viii. 18.

1. The execution of Christ's prophetical office consists of two parts:

1. To declare God's name.

2. To sing praise to him.

In the former, four particulars are expressed:

1. The prophet, *I*. 2. The act, *will declare*. 3. The subject matter, *thy name.* 4. The object to whom, *my brethren.*

In the latter, four other particulars are expressed:

1. The same person or prophet, *I*. 2. Another act, which is to *sing praise*. These two words are the translation of one Greek word. 3. The person whose praise he would set forth, *unto thee.* 4. The place where he would do it, *in the midst of the church.*

2. The ground of Christ's courage was his confidence. Here is expressed,

1. The connection of this with the former, in this phrase, *and again.*

2. The main proposition. Herein are three particulars:

1. The kind of confidence, *put trust.* 2. The person who doth put his trust, *I will*, saith Christ. 3. The person on whom, *in him*, namely, God.

3. The efficacy of Christ's prophetical office was in fitting those for God who were given to him. Here also are expressed as before,

1. A connection of this with the former, *and again.*

2. A proposition. Wherein observe,

1. An evidence of the power of Christ's ministry; 2, the reason thereof.

In the evidence are set down,

(1.) An act, which demonstrateth the evidence intimated in this particle, *behold.* This intendeth a presenting unto God such as were fitted for him.

(2.) The persons presenting, in this pronoun, *I*; and presented, in this relative, *children.*

The reason is taken from a trust committed unto Christ in these words, 'which God hath given me.' Here observe,

1. The kind of trust, *given.*

2. The truster, or person that committeth the trust, *God.*

3. The trusted, or persons that are given, in this relative *which.* That hath reference to *children.*

4. The trustee, or person who is entrusted, in this pronoun *me*, which hath reference to Christ.

Sec. 135. *Of observations raised out of* Heb. ii. 12, 13.

I. *A divine testimony is a sound proof.* See Chap. i., Secs. 46, 61.

II. *Christ was a prophet.* He himself here saith, 'I will declare,' which is an act of a prophet or preacher. See Secs. 111, 112, and 23, 24.

III. *Christ received what he delivered.* He delivered nothing of his own head. See Sec. 111.

IV. *Christ delivered what he received.* He concealed nothing. The word *declare* includeth both these. See Sec. 112.

V. *Christ made known what was to be known of God.* The name of God intends as much. See Sec. 112.

VI. *Christ executed his prophetical office in man's nature.* The main scope of the apostle in this place is to set forth Christ's human nature, and what he did therein. See Sec. 112.

VII. *Saints are Christ's brethren.* See Sec. 106.

VIII. *Christ's brethren do especially partake of the benefit of Christ's prophetical office.* To them in special he saith, 'I will declare God's name.' See Sec. 113.

IX. *Christ was careful to set forth his Father's praise.* This phrase, *unto thee*, hath reference to God the Father. See Sec. 114.

X. *God is praised by singing.* Therefore Christ professeth to sing praise. See Sec. 115.

XI. *God is to be praised with cheerfulness.* Singing implieth a cheerfulness of spirit. See Sec. 116.

XII. *God is to be praised in great assemblies.* 'The midst of the church' implies a great assembly. See Sec. 117.

XIII. *Divers testimonies may be produced to prove the same point.* Here the apostle useth this phrase, 'and again,' in reference to a former testimony. See Chap. i.

XIV. *Christ himself trusted on God.* He here expressly professeth as much. See Sec. 119.

XV. *Christ is one with us.* See Sec. 121.

XVI. *Christ's ministry was powerful.* See Sec. 122.

XVII. *Mysteries of Christ are remarkable.* This particle *behold* intends so much. See Sec. 124.

XVIII. *Christ brought others to God.* Sec. 126.

XIX. *Christ accompanied those whom he brought to God.* See Sec. 125. The connection of these two words, *I, children*—I and my children,—intends the two last points.

XX. *The ministry of the gospel is effectual.* The presenting of children to God is here brought in as a demonstration of the efficacy of the gospel. See Sec. 127.

XXI. *Saints are Christ's children.* So they are here called. See Sec. 128.

XXII. *God hath power to exact an account.* Because God gave these children to Christ, Christ, to make up his account, brought his children to God. See Sec. 129.

XXIII. *God freely bestowed men on Christ.* This word *given* includes freeness under it. See Sec. 130.

XXIV. *God hath power to choose and refuse whom he will.* This act of giving is here restrained to children. See Sec. 131.

XXV. *Christ is the means of all good to men.* To him are they given who are brought to God for good. See Sec. 132.

XXVI. *The elect alone partake of the benefits of Christ's offices.* These are they who are given to Christ, and by Christ brought to God. See Sec. 133.

Sec. 136. *Of the transition betwixt verses* 13 *and* 14.

Ver. 14, 15. *Forasmuch then as the children are partakers of flesh and blood, he also himself likewise took part of the same; that through death he might destroy him that had the power of death, that is, the devil; and deliver them who through fear of death were all their lifetime subject to bondage.*

From the prophetical office of Christ, which he exercised in his human nature, the apostle proceedeth to set down special acts of his kingly office, which he also performed in the same nature.

Very elegantly doth the apostle pass from the one point to the other. For upon the mention of children belonging to Christ, the apostle taketh occasion to shew that Christ would be of the same nature whereof they were, though it were a frail and infirm nature; even 'flesh and blood.'

The inference of this latter upon the former point, is set down in two particles, 'forasmuch then,' both which intend a reason. The former word ἐπεί, translated 'forasmuch,' is also translated with this causal particle, 'for that,' chap. v. 2, and 'so then,' chap. ix. 26, and x. 2; and also with this, 'because,' chap. vi. 13, and xi. 11.

The other particle, οὖν, properly signifieth *therefore;* and so it is translated, even joined with the same particle that here it is, thus, ἐπεί οὖν, 'seeing therefore,' chap. iv. 6.

It is evident hereby that the Son of God became a son of man for their sake whom God had given to him.

Of the Son of God being one with sons of men, see Sec. 104.

To declare that in the conformity of Christ to others, the apostle intends the same persons whom he mentioned before, he useth the very same words, παιδία, children, in both places. Of this title *children*, see Sec. 128.

Sec. 137. *Of this phrase, 'flesh and blood.'*

That wherein Christ is here said to be conformable to these children is styled 'flesh and blood.'

Flesh in Scripture is used properly or tropically.

1. *Properly*, for that part of the man which covereth

the bones, and is covered with skin;[1] through which the veins, nerves, sinews, arteries, and other ligaments of the body do pass.

Thus doth Job distinguish flesh from skin, bones, and sinews, John x. 11. Thus distinguished, it is a soft substance made of blood coagulated.

2. *Tropically*, flesh is used sundry ways; as,

(1.) By a synecdoche; as when it is put,

[1.] For the whole body, distinguished from a man's soul: 'The dead bodies of thy servants have they given to be meat unto the fowls,' &c., 'the flesh of thy saints unto the beasts of the earth,' Ps. lxxix. 2.

[2.] For the person of man, consisting of body and soul: 'All flesh shall see the salvation of God,' Luke iii. 6.

In these two respects flesh is attributed to Christ; namely, in reference to his body, 1 Peter iii. 18, and to his whole human nature, John i. 14, 1 Tim. iii. 16.

[3.] To a man's wife, who is styled his flesh, Gen. ii. 23, and by rule of relation to a woman's husband. For man and wife are said to be one flesh, Mat. xix. 5.

[4.] For such as are of kin. St Paul thus styles those that were of the stock from whence he came, 'Them which are of my flesh,' Rom. xi. 14.

[5.] For a neighbour: 'Hide not thyself from thine own flesh,' Isa. lviii. 7.

Kinsmen and neighbours are of the same flesh; the former more near, the latter more remote; therefore both are called flesh.

[6.] For all creatures clothed with flesh: 'God giveth food to all flesh,' Ps. cxxxvi. 25.

(2.) By a metonymy, as when flesh is put,

[1.] For corruption: 'That that is born of the flesh is flesh,' John iii. 6. Flesh in the latter place is put for corruption of nature.

[2.] For infirmity. Thus horses are said to be flesh, Isa. xxxi. 3, in regard of their weakness; and in this respect are opposed to spirit.

[3.] For outward appearance: 'Ye judge after the flesh,' John viii. 15; that is, as things outwardly appear.

Corruption, weakness, outward show, are but adjuncts or accidents, which belong to men's bodies, which are flesh.

(3.) By a metaphor, as when flesh is put,

[1.] For abrogated ceremonies. This the apostle intends, where he saith, 'Are you now made perfect by the flesh?' Gal. iii. 3.

[2.] For human excellencies: 'We have no confidence in the flesh,' Philip. iii. 3. He means thereby such prerogatives as men esteemed excellencies, and used to boast in them.

These and other like things are as flesh alone, without spirit; which consume, putrefy, and vanish to nothing, as mere flesh doth.

[1] Σὰρξ μεταξὺ τοῦ δέρματος καὶ τοῦ ὀστοῦ.—Arist. de Hist. Animal, lib. iii. cap. xvi.

Flesh is here put for the human nature; and that as it is accompanied with manifold frailties.

By way of diminution, *blood* is added thereunto, 'flesh and blood.'

Blood is a liquor consisting of the four humours; in it life and spirit is conveyed through the whole body. The philosopher saith that blood is the matter of the whole body.[1]

By a metonymy, blood is put for life and for death: for life, because it is the means of life, Gen. ix. 4; for death, because upon shedding of blood death followeth, Gen. xxxvii. 26. Compare Ps. lxxii. 14 with Ps. cxvi. 13. In this respect Christ's blood is put for his death, Rom. v. 9, Eph. ii. 13.

By a metaphor, blood is put for the corruption of nature, John i. 13, Ezek. xvi. 6.

Blood is here joined with flesh, to shew that quick flesh is here meant; flesh that hath blood in it, and by reason thereof is subject to many infirmities, yea, and sensible of them.

As good blood is the nourishment of the flesh, and makes it quick and fresh, so the distemper of blood causeth many maladies in the flesh. By the wasting of the blood the flesh consumeth.

Fitly are these two, 'flesh and blood,' joined together. I find them thus joined five times in the New Testament: here; Mat. xvi. 17; 1 Cor. xv. 50; Gal. i. 16; Eph. vi. 12.

Flesh and blood thus joined, set out in general man's external substance, which is visible and sensible, and in that respect opposed to spirit, Luke xxiv. 39.

In particular, 'flesh and blood' is put,

1. For man's earthly disposition, and incapacity of heavenly mysteries; so as of himself he can neither know them, nor make them known. Thus 'flesh and blood' is opposed to God, who is omniscient, and revealeth what mysteries he pleaseth to whom he will, Mat. xvi. 17, Gal. i. 16.

2. For man's weakness. Thus it is opposed to principalities and powers, Eph. vi. 12.

3. For mortality, whereunto our sins brought us. Thus it is opposed to glorified bodies, 1 Cor. xv. 50.

Here it is used in the general acception of the phrase, as *flesh* was noted before to be used, namely, for human nature, subject to manifold infirmities.

Flesh and blood, as it is a visible substance, so it is gross, heavy, drowsy, subject to hunger, thirst, cold, heat, pain, wearisomeness, sickness, fainting, yea, and death itself.

In regard of the outward visible part, a man is little better than a brute beast, which is also flesh and blood, Eccles. iii. 19. Sundry beasts, in sundry excellencies, appertaining to flesh and blood, go beyond men; as in bigness, swiftness, strength, vigour of several senses, as of sight, hearing, smelling, tasting, touching, and other like endowments.

[1] αἷμα ὕλη ἐστὶ παντὸς τοῦ σώματος.—Arist. de part. Animal., lib. ii. cap. iv.

That flesh and blood is such as hath been shewed, it came first from sin; for sin brought death, and all manner of infirmities are concomitants to death.

This is a point most worthy their due and serious consideration, who are or may be puffed up by reason of their reasonable soul, or any abilities thereof; or by reason of the comely feature, beauty, strength, or other excellencies of the body; or by reason of victories over enemies, successes in their endeavours, honours, dignities, revenues, stately palaces, sumptuous houses, or any other like things. Notwithstanding these or any other like excellencies, they who lay claim to those excellencies are but flesh and blood. Flesh and blood are in this case like the peacock's black feet: when her gay feathers are in her eye, she struts up herself in beholding them; but when her eye is cast on her black feet, down falls her gay feathers. A due consideration of flesh and blood would take away all proud conceits of any outward excellencies. Considering all others are as we are, flesh and blood, what folly is it to trust in man, Isa. xxxi. 3, or to fear man? Isa. li. 7, 8.

Sec. 138. *Of saints being flesh and blood.*

Of the foresaid flesh and blood, Christ's children, that is, such as being elected and given by God to Christ, and thereupon redeemed, called, justified, and sanctified, are here said to be partakers, κεκοινώνηκε. The Greek verb is derived from a root, κοινὸς, that signifieth *common*, and it implieth to have a thing in common with others. Thus, as the children are here said to be 'partakers of flesh and blood,' so the Gentiles are said to be 'partakers of the Jews' spiritual things,' ἐκοινώνησαν, Rom. xv. 27; that is, all to have them in common, one as well as another.

Concerning this common condition of children, apostles, who were eminent among these children, thus say of themselves, 'We also are men of like passions (ὁμοιοπαθεῖς) with you,' Acts xiv. 15.

Regeneration altereth not the outward constitution or condition of men. Sin did not alter man's substance, for Adam, after his fall, retained that body and soul, with the several powers and parts of each, which he had before. So regeneration took not away flesh and blood in the substance thereof, nor the common infirmities of it.

Indeed, transgression altered the good quality that was in man's body and soul, namely, the integrity, the holiness and righteousness in which he was created after God's image. So regeneration altereth man's evil disposition and corruption wherein he was conceived and born, but not his outward condition or constitution. Whether he were tall or low, fat or lean, healthy or sickly, strong or weak, straight or crooked, fair or foul, rich or poor before his regeneration, he remains the same afterward for aught that regeneration doth to the contrary.

The Lord will have his children to retain, as others, flesh and blood, and remain subject to all manner of infirmities, for sundry weighty reasons.

1. That they might not, by reason of any spiritual privileges, be too much puffed up; for the children, while here they live, are too prone thereunto, 2 Chron. xxxii. 25, 2 Cor. xii. 7.

2. That in God's presence they might the more abase, yea, and abhor themselves, Job xl. 4, and xlii. 6.

3. That they might learn to lay forth their misery, and plead their weakness before God, Job. vi. 12.

4. That they might take heed of provoking God's wrath against themselves, who are but flesh and blood, Acts ix. 5.

5. That they might have the more compassion on others, Heb. v. 2, Gal. vi. 1.

6. That they might be the more circumspect over themselves, 1 Tim. iv. 16.

7. That they might be more careful in using all means needful and useful for flesh and blood, Eph. vi. 10–12.

8. That they might the better discern what cause they have to exercise the duty of invocation, Ps. cxvi. 2, yea, and of gratulation too, for God's supporting, as he doth, such as are flesh and blood.

9. That they may more confidently depend on God, 2 Chron. xx. 12.

10. That they might not rest on man for revelation of divine truth, Mat. xvi. 17.

These, and other like ends, instruct us in so many duties arising from this our condition, that we are flesh and blood.

Sec. 139. *Of Christ's being flesh and blood.*

The conformity of Christ to his children is thus expressed: καὶ αὐτὸς παραπλησίως μετέσχε τῶν αὐτῶν, 'he also himself likewise took part of the same.' Every of these words have their emphasis.

1. This copulative, καὶ, *also*, hath reference to the children before mentioned: 'he also;' he, as well as they. Though there were an infinite disparity betwixt Christ and his children, yet he refused not conformity with them, or otherwise this copulative *also*, or *and*, may be translated *even*, 'even he,' which is a note of special emphasis.

2. This reciprocal pronoun, αὐτὸς, *himself*, hath reference to Christ's eminency, and it implieth that he that was true God, the Creator, Preserver, Redeemer, and Father of those children, suffered not his infinite excellency to be any hindrance to this his low condescension. 'He himself.'

3. The Greek word παραπλησίως, translated *likewise*, implieth a nearness to one. The root whence it sprouteth, πέλας, signifieth near. A word of the same stem is used in this phrase, 'nigh unto death' (παραπλήσιον), Philip. ii. 27. The adverb here used is not elsewhere found in the New Testament, but in other Greek authors it is frequent; by them it is oft joined

with another word (ὁμοίως) which more expressly setteth out the same thing that this doth. That other word is oft used in the New Testament, and joined with this copulative καί, also; as where Christ saith, ταῦτα καὶ ὁ υἱὸς ὁμοίως ποιεῖ, 'These also doth the Son likewise,' John v. 19. By comparing that place with this text, we may observe, that he who himself also was likewise equal with God, did also himself likewise take part of the same nature with man.

4. The word, μετέσχε, here translated 'took part,' is another than the former, κεκοινώνηκε, translated 'are partakers.' The former implieth that all of all sorts were by nature subject to the same common condition; but this other intendeth a voluntary act of Christ, whereby willingly he took upon himself to be like his brethren. He *was* before; he was true God, eternal, all-sufficient, and needed not in regard of himself to be as the children were. A like word to this is used, ver. 16, 'he took on him,' ἐπιλαμβάνεται. See Sec. 159.

The Greek word in the latter place, μετέσχε, according to the notation of it, signifieth *to have with*, or to have of that which another hath. Christians are said to be partakers of the Lord's table, one with another to receive the benefit thereof, 1 Cor. x. 21. They who mutually partake of the same commodity are called partners, μέτοχοι, from the same original, Luke v. 7. See Chap. iii. Sec. 17.

5. This relative, τῶν αὐτῶν, 'the same,' hath reference to 'flesh and blood.' The relative is of the plural number, to shew that it includeth both; for the one and the other is of the singular number, but both joined include the plural.

This doth emphatically set forth Christ, not only to be true man, but also subject to all manner of frailties, so far as they are freed from sin, even such as accompany flesh and blood, as was before shewed, Sec. 137.

Behold how low the Son of God descended for us sons of men! Herein appeared love.

How ought this conformity of Christ, to take part of flesh and blood, quicken us up to take part of that divine nature, whereof an apostle speaketh, 2 Peter i. 4, that so we may be like him in those excellent graces wherein he made himself a pattern to us while he was on earth: as in meekness and humility, Mat. xi. 29; in love, Eph. v. 2; in forgiving others, Col. iii. 13, in compassion, Luke x. 37; in patience under sufferings, and contempt of the world, Heb. xii. 2. Christ's conformity to us was in much meanness, ours to him is in much glory. Upon this ground doth the apostle press a like exhortation, Philip. ii. 5. What if we be called to conformity with Christ in suffering, in bearing reproach, or undergoing ignomiony for righteousness' sake? 'The servant is not greater than his master,' Mat. x. 24, 25. The head, who was himself full of glory, vouchsafed to take part of flesh and blood, that he might suffer for flesh and blood; shall then the members think much to be conformable to their head in anything that he shall call them to?

Sec. 140. *Of heresies against the apostle's description of Christ's human nature.*

This description of Christ's human nature, 'he also himself likewise took part of the same,' meets with sundry heresies that have been broached against the human nature of Christ.

The Proclianites[1] held that Christ came not in the flesh at all. How then did he take part of the same flesh and blood that we have?

The Manichees[2] maintained that Christ was not in true flesh, but that he shewed forth a feigned species of flesh to deceive men's senses. If so, then did he not likewise take part of the same with us.

The Cerdonians[3] denied that Christ had flesh at all. This is like the first heresy.

The Valentinians[4] taught that Christ brought a spiritual and celestial body from above. Then did he not likewise take part of the same flesh and blood that we do.

The Apollinarists[5] say that Christ took flesh without a soul. Among other arguments, they produce this and other like texts, where mention is made only of flesh and blood. But the apostle here speaketh of the visible part of man; comprising the invisible part, which is his soul, by a synecdoche, under the visible, which is flesh and blood. But this phrase, 'he also himself likewise took part of the same,' sheweth, that as our flesh and blood is animated with a reasonable soul, so also Christ was. By the like reason they might say that Christ's body had no bones, because it is said, 'The word was made flesh,' John i. 14; yea, by the like reason they might say, that the Israelites which went down into Egypt had no bodies, because it is said of them, 'all the souls,' Gen. xlvi. 15.

An ancient father[6] attributed this heresy to the Arians also, and for refutation thereof produceth all those texts of Scripture which make mention of the soul of Christ, whereby he proveth that Christ had a soul as well as a body.

The Ubiquitarians[7] hold that the divine properties,

---

[1] Proclianitæ Christum non in carne venisse dicunt.—*August. de Hæres. ad Quodvult Deum. Hære.* 60.

[2] Manichæi, Christum non fuisse in carne vera, sed simulatam speciem carnis ludificandis humanis sensibus præbuisse.—*Ibid. Hær.* 46.

[3] Cerdoniani negant Christum habuisse carnem.—*Ibid. Hær.* 21.

[4] Valentiniani asserunt Christum a profundo spiritale vel cœleste corpus secum attulisse.—*Ibid. Hær.* 11.

[5] Apollinaristæ dicunt Christum carnem sine anima suscepisse.—*Ibid. Hær.* 55.

[6] Aug. contr. Serm. Arian. cap. ix.

[7] Ubiquitarii affirmant Christum secundum humanam naturam potentiæ divinæ, id est, omnipotentiæ, participem factum esse; et scientiæ infinitæ, id est, omniscientiæ: et Christi corpus esse ubique præsens.—*Eckhard. fascic. controv. Theol.* cap. vi. q. x.

as omnipotency, omnisciency, omnipresence, &c., are in the human nature of Christ; which, if so, Christ took not likewise part of the same flesh and blood that we do. The like may be said of popish transubstantiation.[1]

There are other sorts of heretics, namely, the Samosatenians,[2] who broached this heresy, that Christ then only began to be, when he came endued with flesh; whereby they imply that he was not before. But this phrase, 'he took part of the same,' sheweth, that he was before he took part of flesh and blood.

Our divines form a like phrase to infer the eternity of the word. The phrase is this, 'In the beginning was the Word,' John i. 1. Because the Word *was* in the beginning, it is necessarily implied, that he did not then first take his beginning, but was before.

Sec. 141. *Of Christ's destroying the devil.*

The end of Christ's assuming his human nature is thus set down: 'that through death he might destroy him that had the power of death.'

The general end is implied. That which is expressed is an end of that end, or a mighty effect that followed thereupon: which was to destroy the devil.

The general end was to die. For if he had not been flesh and blood, he could not have died.

This general end is implied under this phrase, 'through death;' as if he had said, that he might die, and by death destroy the devil. Of Christ's being man, that he might die, see Sec. 75.

The powerful effect which was accomplished by Christ's death (which was also a special end why he died), was the destruction of him that had the power of death.

The primary root whence the word translated *destroy* is derived, is a noun, ἔργον, that signifieth a *work*; as where it is said that the Son of God was manifested, 'that he might destroy the works, τὰ ἔργα, of the devil,' 1 John iii. 8. Thence is derived a verb, which signifieth to work. 'He worketh, ἐργάζεται, the work of the Lord,' 1 Cor. xvi. 10. But a privative particle being added, the noun signifieth not working,[3] or idle, Mat. xx. 3. And another compound added thereunto signifieth to make void: Rom. iii. 31, 'Do we make void, καταργοῦμεν, the law?' or to make of non-effect: Rom. iv. 14, 'the promise made of non-effect,' κατήργηται. And thereupon to bring to nought: 1 Cor. i. 28, 'to bring to nought, καταργήσῃ, things that are.' And to destroy: 1 Cor. vi. 13, 'God shall destroy,' καταργήσει, &c.

By the aforesaid derivation and various signification of the word, it appeareth that it doth not always signify to annihilate a thing, and bring it utterly to nought; for the devil that is here spoken of still retains his being and substance, and ever shall retain it, both for the greater terror of the wicked, and also for his own greater misery. But it implieth that he is so vanquished, as he shall never prevail against the members of Christ. In this sense is this very word used, where the apostle saith, that the body of sin is destroyed, καταργηθῇ, Rom. vi. 6. It cannot be denied but that 'the devil, like a roaring lion, walketh about, seeking whom he may devour,' 1 Peter v. 8; and that many of God's children are so buffeted and ensnared by him, as they may seem to be overcome of him; which cometh to pass partly by their own fault, in that they do not manfully stand against him, but too slavishly yield unto him; and partly, by God's wise ordering the matter, for the better proof of the graces which he bestowed on his children; but yet this ever hath been, and ever shall be, the issue, that he never prevaileth against God's children; but that they in all assaults remain conquerors. This was foretold of old, where, speaking to the devil of Christ, the seed of the woman, the Lord saith, 'it shall bruise thy head,' Gen. iii. 15. The devil assaulted Christ himself, but prevailed not. For after Christ had said, 'Get thee hence, Satan,' the devil left him, Mat. iv. 10, 11. It appears afterwards, about the time of Christ's last sufferings, that the prince of this world came again to assault Christ, but, saith Christ, 'He hath nothing in me,' John xiv. 30. That phrase sheweth, that the devil could not prevail against Christ. Neither could he prevail against Job, though he had liberty to do what he could do against Job himself, and against all that Job had (Job's life only excepted), Job i. 12 and ii. 6. He desired to sift Peter as wheat; but yet he could not make Peter's faith to fail, Luke xxii. 31, 32. To this tends this phrase, 'The prince of this world is judged,' John xvi. 11; and this, 'the prince of this world shall be cast out,' John xii. 31; and this, Christ 'led captivity captive,' Eph. iv. 8; and this, 'He hath spoiled principalities and powers,' &c., Col. ii. 15. For such is Satan's might, compared unto men, such his malice, as if he were not thus destroyed, no flesh would be saved.

Hereby we have evidence of the provident care of our Captain, who, knowing what flesh and blood is, and what our enemies are, hath first himself vanquished them, and then provided sufficient armour for his children to stand safe against them, Eph. vi. 12, &c.

This is a great comfort against the terror of the devil. Many fearful and terrible things are written of him in the Scripture. Observe, in particular, how he is described, Eph. vi. 12. But this, that he is destroyed by our Captain, who did take part of flesh and blood, is a great comfort to us, who are flesh and blood.

This also is an encouragement to stand against him,

---

[1] Papistæ asserunt per consecrationem panis et vini conversionem fieri totius substantiæ panis, in substantiam corporis Christi domini nostri: et totius substantiæ vini, in substantiam sanguinis ejus.—*Concil. Trident.* 3 *Sess.* cap. iv.

[2] Samosateni docent, ab eo duntaxat tempore quo Christus carne præditus advenit, esse cœpisse.—*Epip. adv. hær.* tom. ii. lib. ii.

[3] ἀργοὺς quasi ἀεργούς.

and to resist. He is an enemy spoiled. Hereupon an apostle thus encourageth us: 'Resist the devil, and he will fly from you,' James iv. 5. There is assurance of victory to such as believe. If Satan get the upper hand, it is by reason of our timorousness and want of faith. As the ancients by faith 'were made strong, waxed valiant in fight, turned to flight the armies of the aliens,' Heb. xi. 34, so may we in this spiritual combat with the devil. The phrase of Christ's 'leading captivity captive,' Eph. iv. 8, is spoken of our spiritual enemies, and implieth that they are as captives chained, so as Christ lets them out and pulls them in as it pleaseth him. If he suffer any of them to assault any of his children, he himself will order the combat as seemeth good to himself. He will suffer them to fight so long as he seeth cause; if he espy an enemy ready to get an advantage, he will quickly pull him back. This is a great encouragement.

Sec. 142. *Of that death whereof the devil hath power.*
He that Christ so destroyed is here said to 'have the power of death.'

Death here is to be taken in the uttermost extent, and to be applied to all kinds of death, temporal, spiritual, and eternal; for he was the original cause and first author of sin, by which all these kinds of death came upon man, Rom. v. 12.

By sin mortality seized on man, for God at first made man's body immortal.

By sin man forfeited that image of God wherein consisted his spiritual life, Eph. ii. 1.

By sin man made himself guilty of eternal damnation, Rom. vi. 23.

This extent of death giveth evidence of the malicious and mischievous mind of Satan. As in general he aimed at man's destruction—he was a murderer from the beginning—for death is the destruction of a thing, so he extended his malice as far as he could, even to body and soul, and that in this world and the world to come. He contents not himself to annoy the body, and that unto death, but also vexeth and perplexeth the soul. Instance his dealing with Saul, 1 Sam. xvi. 14; yea, he seeketh the eternal damnation of man's soul and body. Thus much is comprised under this phrase, 'he seeketh whom to devour,' 1 Pet. v. 8.

Sec. 143. *Of that kind of power which the devil hath over death.*

The Greek word τὸ κράτος, whereby Satan's power is set forth, is somewhat emphatical. It is twelve times used in the New Testament, and in every of those places, except this, attributed to God, so as for the most part it sets out a divine and almighty power, even the power of him that saith, 'See now that I, even I, am he, and there is no God with me: I kill, and I make alive,' Deut. xxxii. 39, 1 Sam. ii. 6. He it is of whom it is said, 'after he hath killed, he hath power to cast into hell,' Luke xii. 5. He that said, 'I have the keys of hell and of death,' Rev. i. 18, was true God; therefore here it sets out a subordinate power given by God to him that hath it, 'Power was given to him that sat on the pale horse,' Rev. vi. 8; for as Christ said to Pilate, 'Thou couldst have no power at all against me, except it were given thee from above,' John xix. 11, so the devil could have no power at all, except it were given him from above. But the power that is given him is a great power, for *power of death* must needs be a great power. What is stronger than death, which overcometh all living creatures? Who can stand against death?

In regard of the greatness of the power of the devil, a *woe* was denounced 'to the inhabitants of the earth and of the sea;' and this reason is rendered thereof, 'for the devil is come down unto you, having great wrath,' Rev. xii. 12.

Sundry are the respects wherein the devil may be said to have the power of death.

1. As he is the executioner of God's just judgment. He is in this regard as an hangman, who may be said to have the power of the gallows, because he hangeth men thereon.

2. As he is like an hunter, fisher, fowler, or falconer. He hunteth, fisheth, and fowleth for the life, not of unreasonable creatures only, but also of reasonable men.

3. As he is a thief, and continually layeth wait for blood, and seeks the precious life of man's body and soul.

4. As a continual tempter, to allure or drive men into sin, and thereby to death. Herein he spared not Christ himself, Mat. iv. 1, &c. As at first he dealt with the first man, so ever since hath he dealt with his whole posterity. This moved the apostle to say, 'I fear lest by any means, as the serpent beguiled Eve through his subtilty, so your mind should be corrupted,' 2 Cor. xi. 3.

5. As he is an accuser of men (hereof see more, Sec. 145), and as an adversary to press God's just law against men, and to call for judgment against them.

6. As he is a tormentor; for when he hath drawn men to sin, he affrighteth them with the terror of death and damnation.

In general, nothing is more terrible than death. In this respect death is called the king of terrors, Job xviii. 14.

This kind of power, namely, of death, attributed to the devil,

1. Sheweth wherein his strength especially lieth, even in doing mischief and bringing men to destruction. 'His power is to hurt men.' In this respect he hath names of destruction given unto him, as 'in Hebrew Abaddon, and in Greek Apollyon,' Rev. ix. 11, and he is styled a murderer, John viii. 44.

2. It manifesteth the vile slavery and woful bondage

of the devil's vassals. They serve him who hath the power of death, and doth what he can to bring all to death. What can any expect from him but death? The task that he puts on them is sin, the wages which he gives is death, Rom. vi. 23. Herein such as, having been rescued out of his power, retain a lingering mind after it again, are worse than the Israelites, who, having tasted of manna, lusted after the fish, cucumbers, melons, leeks, onions, and garlic that they had in Egypt, and said, 'Let us return into Egypt,' Num. xi. 5, and xiv. 4. Such are all they as are not truly regenerate, but remain in their natural estate, though they profess the faith.

3. It is an incitation unto those to whom this kind of power is made known, to be more watchful against Satan, more manful in resisting him, and the better prepared against his assaults. Hereof see more in *The Whole Armour of God*, on Eph. vi. 12, treat. i. part iii. sec. 2, &c.

4. It warneth all of all sorts to renounce the devil and all his works, to come out of his Babel, to come into and abide in the glorious liberty of the sons of God, which Christ hath purchased for us, and to renounce Satan's service. As the devil hath the power of death, so Christ hath the power of life, John vi. 39, 40.

5. It amplifieth both the glory and also the benefit of that conquest which Christ hath gotten over him that hath the power of death. The glory of that victory appeareth herein, that he hath overcome so potent an enemy as had the power of death; the benefit thereof herein appears, that he hath overcome so malicious and mischievous an enemy as exercised his power by all manner of death. Hence ariseth the ground of this holy insultation, 'O death, where is thy sting?' 1 Cor. xv. 55. He who had the power of death being destroyed, death now can have no more power over them that are redeemed by Christ. Hereof see more, Sec. 148.

Sec. 144. *Of Christ overcoming the devil by death.*

The means whereby Christ overcame him that had the power of death, is expressly said to be death. To achieve this great and glorious victory against so mighty and mischievous an enemy, Christ did not assemble troops of angels, as he could have done, Mat. xxvi. 53, and as he did, Rev. xii. 7, in another case, nor did he array himself with majesty and terror, as Exod. xix. 16, &c.; but he did it by taking part of weak flesh and blood, and therein humbling himself to death. In this respect the apostle saith, that Christ 'having spoiled principalities and powers, made a show of them openly, triumphing over them in the cross,' meaning thereby his death. The apostle there resembleth the cross of Christ to a trophy whereon the spoils of enemies were hanged. Of old conquerors were wont to hang the armour and weapons of enemies vanquished on the walls of forts and towers.

To this purpose may be applied that which Christ thus saith of himself, 'If I be lifted up from the earth, I will draw all men unto me,' John xii. 32. Hereby he signifieth both the kind of his death and also the power thereof: the kind under this phrase *lifted up*, namely, upon the cross; the power under this, *I will draw all men unto me*, shewing thereby that he would rescue them from Satan to himself.

Christ, by his death, offered himself up a sacrifice, whereby such a price was paid for our sins, as satisfied God's justice, pacified his wrath, removed the curse of the law, and so spoiled Satan of all his power, wrested his weapons out of his hands, set free those whom he held captive, and brought himself into captivity. Thus was he as a bee that had lost her sting, which might buz and make a noise, but could not sting.

Christ also by his death hath clean altered the original nature of our death, which was a passage from this world into Satan's prison, even into hell itself, where his vassals are tormented; but now it is made a passage into heaven, where he hath nothing at all to do, so as thereby believers are clean out of his clutches, so as he cannot so much as assault them. This being done by Christ's death, thereby is the devil spoiled of his power. This God thus ordered:

1. To accomplish that ancient promise to the seed of the woman, which was Christ, and threatening against the serpent, which was the devil: Gen. iii. 15, 'It shall bruise thy head,' that is, Christ should utterly vanquish the devil. The means whereby that should be accomplished was this, 'Thou shalt bruise his heel,' Gen. iii. 15. By the heel is meant Christ's mortal body, which was bruised by death.

2. To deliver man by satisfying justice. Had the devil been by an almighty power vanquished, justice had not thereby been satisfied.

3. To magnify the power of the conquest the more; for divine power is made perfect in weakness, 1 Cor. xii. 9.

4. To bring the greater ignominy and shame upon the devil; for what greater ignominy than for an enemy to be vanquished in his own kingdom, and that with his own weapon. The strongest and sharpest weapon that Satan had was death, and by it he did most hurt. Christ dealt in this case as Benaiah did with an Egyptian, he plucked the spear out of his hand, and slew him with his own spear, 2 Sam. xxiii. 21.

5. To take away the ignominy of the cross of Christ. Jews, pagans, and all infidels scoff at our crucified God; but this glorious victory which Christ by his death obtained on the cross, sheweth, that it is a matter of much glory and much rejoicing. The apostle apprehended so much hereof as comparatively he would glory in nothing, saving the cross of our Lord Jesus Christ,' Gal. vi. 14.

6. To put a difference betwixt Christ's death and the death of all others, even of the best of men. The

death of others is only a freedom from troubles of soul and body, and an attaining unto rest and glory, which is by virtue of Christ's death. Christ's death is a conquering death, a death that tends to the advantage of all that believe in Christ.

7. To take the old wily serpent in his own craft. Satan laboured at nothing more than to bring Christ to death; he used scribes, pharisees, priests, rulers and people of the Jews, yea, Judas, Pilate, and his soldiers, as his instruments herein. They thought all sure if Christ might be put to death; but Christ's death proved Satan's destruction. Thus God 'taketh the wise in their own craftiness,' Job v. 13.

On these and other like grounds, may we look upon the cross of Christ as the Israelites, when they were stung with fiery serpents, looked on the brazen serpent, Num. xxi. 9; Christ himself teacheth us to make this application, John iii. 14, 15.

Sec. 145. *Of exemplifying of an indefinite point.*

That none might mistake the apostle about the person that is said to be destroyed, he explains himself, as this phrase τουτέστι, *that is*, sheweth. That phrase is used in interpreting a strange word. Where the apostle had used this Hebrew word *Aceldama*, he addeth, ' *that is*, the field of blood,' Acts i. 19; and in clearing an ambiguous word, where the apostle had used this phrase *in me*, he addeth, ' *that is*, in my flesh,' Rom. vii. 18; and in opening the sense of a mystery, or an obscure sentence, this mystery, ' In Isaac shall thy seed be called,' is thus opened, '*that is*, they which are the children,' &c., Rom. ix. 8; and in exemplifying such things and persons as are indefinitely propounded, as here in this phrase, '*that is*, the devil.'

Power of death may be thought to appertain to God, to whom belong the issues of death, Ps. lxviii. 20, and so indeed it doth, as he is the high supreme Lord over all, and judge of all. Lest, therefore, any should overmuch spend their thoughts about him who is here said to be destroyed, the apostle plainly expresseth whom he meaneth. Herein he doth as Esther; after she had indefinitely complained to the king of one that had sold her and her nation unto death, upon the king's inquiry who it was, she plainly and directly answered, 'The adversary and enemy is this wicked Haman,' Esth. vii. 6.

Sec. 146. *Of the devil an accuser.*

This title διάβολος, *devil*, in the Greek signifieth an *accuser*. It is derived from a root, βάλλειν, that signifieth *to cast*, as John viii. 7; thence a compound, διαβάλλειν, which signifieth *to strike through*, metaphorically to *accuse*, Luke xvi. 1. An accusation falsely and maliciously made striketh a man, as it were a dart, through the heart. The noun διάβολος is oft translated ' a false accuser,' as 2 Tim. iii. 3, Tit. ii. 3. Thus this title *devil* setteth out this disposition, which is to be a false and malicious accuser. To prove as much, another word, κατήγορος, which more properly signifieth an accuser, is attributed to him, Rev. xii. 10. That word in Greek is derived from a root ἀγορά, *forum*, which signifieth a place of judicature, and a noun compounded and derived from thence signifieth such an one as in such places useth to accuse others, and plead against them, Acts xxiv. 8, John viii. 10.

The title ἀντίδικος, *adversary*, attributed to the devil, 1 Pet. v. 8, intendeth as much; the root δίκη, *lis*, from whence the Greek word is derived, signifieth *strife*, contention or suit of law; thence a compound verb ἀντιδικεῖν, which signifieth *to stand against one in suit of law*. He who doth so is properly termed an adversary, who pleads against one in a court of justice, or in any other public assembly, and to prejudice the cause, raiseth false accusations and forgeth unjust crimes against him. Such an one was Doeg, 1 Sam. xxii. 9, against whom David penned the fifty-second psalm.

Never was there, nor ever can there be, such an accuser as the devil: ' as his name is, so is he.' He spareth none, nor ever ceaseth to accuse. He accused God to man, Gen. iii. 5; and man to God, Job i. 9, 10; and man to man, 1 Sam. xxii. 9; and man to himself, as Mat. xxvii. 4, 5. These two latter instances, of Saul and Judas, are the rather applied to the devil, because that the Holy Ghost doth expressly note that an evil spirit, even the devil, came upon the one, 1 Sam. xvi. 14, and upon the other, Luke xxii. 3.

Behold here by what spirit false accusers and forgers of unjust crimes against the children of God are guided: I may say of all them as Christ did of the Jews, ' Ye are of your father the devil, and the lusts of your father ye will do,' John viii. 44.

Sec. 147. *Of all the devils combined in one.*

That which is here said of the devil in the singular number, is to be extended to all the infernal spirits. They are indeed many, for so they say of themselves, ' We are many,' Mark v. 9; and we read that the devils made an host to fight against Michael and his angels, Rev. xii. 7. All that host consisted of devils. If at once there were a whole legion in one man (which is computed to contain about 6666) how many are there in all the world besides? for we may suppose that no man is free at any time, but hath devils about him to solicit him to sin. The innumerable number of good angels hath been noted before, Chap. i. Sec. 73. It is indeed probable that there are not so many angels that fell as stood, yet they that fell might be also an innumerable company; but they are here and in sundry other places set down as one devil. The reasons hereof may be these.

1. *Devil* is a collective word, and compriseth under it all the evil spirits; as Jew, Gentile, Turk, &c.

2. They are all under one head; for we read of a 'prince of devils,' Mark iii. 22, and the name *devil* is given to this one head, as is clear by this phrase,

'The devil and his angels,' Mat. xxv. 41. Under the head all the members are comprised, as under *Israel* all that descended from Israel.

3. All the evil spirits concur in one mind, and aim at the same end; and thereupon are all counted as one devil.

4. Their forces are so united and combined, as if they were all but one. Thus it is said, 'That all the children of Israel went out, and the congregation was gathered together as one man,' Judges xx. 1.

This word *devil*, being here thus comprehensively taken, doth much amplify the power of Christ in subduing all the power of hell. And it giveth evidence of our freedom from all our spiritual enemies. And it is a strong ground of confidence to rest on Christ, and not to fear any fiend of hell.

Sec. 148. *Of Christ's vanquishing the devil for our deliverance.*

Ver. 15. *And deliver them who through fear of death were all their lifetime subject to bondage.*

Both the copulative particle, καὶ, and also the setting down of this verb *deliver*, ἀπαλλάξῃ, in the same mood and tense that the other verb destroy, καταργήσῃ, in the former verse was, sheweth, that that act of destroying the devil, and this of delivering us, do both tend in general to the same purpose; namely, to declare the ends of Christ's assuming our nature, and subjecting himself therein to death. One was to destroy the devil; the other to deliver us.

This latter is set down in the latter place, because it is also an end of the former. For this end did Christ destroy the devil, that he might rescue and free us from the power of the devil:[1] as Abraham destroyed those enemies that had taken Lot captive with the rest that dwelt in Sodom, that he might deliver Lot and the rest of the people from those enemies, Gen. xiv. 14; and as David destroyed the Amalekites, that he might deliver his wives and children, and others that were taken by them, out of their hands, 1 Sam. xxx. 9, &c. Man, by yielding to the devil's temptations, Gen. iii. 6, became his slave, and was in bondage under him, as the apostle sheweth in the words following. It was therefore for our liberty that Christ vanquished the devil in the manner that he did, rather than for his own glory.

So implacable and unsatiable an enemy was the devil, as he would not let us go but perforce. Christ therefore thought it not enough to satisfy God's justice, and pacify his wrath; but he would also vanquish that implacable enemy, and so deliver us out of his hands. This therefore was an end of the former end. Our deliverance was the end of destroying the devil. Christ's death was for us and our good; see Sec. 83. Thanks, therefore, to thee, O Saviour, that hast destroyed so mighty an adversary of ours by thine own death.

Sec. 149. *Of natural men's fear of death.*

The miserable condition here intended, is said to be 'fear of death.' Death here is taken in as large an extent as it was, Sec. 142, namely, for temporal, spiritual, and eternal death. Death, even death of the body,[1] which is a separation of the soul from the body,[2] is by the heathen counted the most terrible of all things,[3] and the greatest of all evils; every living thing shunneth death;[4] this they do naturally, upon a desire of preserving their being, and love of life. On this ground it was that Satan said to the Lord, 'Skin for skin, and all that a man hath will he give for his life,' Job ii. 4. This works in men a fear of death.

Fear is a disturbed passion, arising from the expectation of some evil which he would shun. For the Greek word cometh from a verb[5] that signifieth to flee from; and this word here used by the apostle, is sometimes put for flight. Men use to flee from such things as they fear; and if men could, they would flee from and avoid death. Death, therefore, being taken to be the greatest of evils, and man continually expecting it, must needs fill man's heart with fear, even fear of a bodily death. Of fear of man, see Chap. 13, Sec. 84. But to such as are instructed in the nature of sin, which addeth a sting to death, and in the resurrection of the body, and the intolerable and everlasting torment of body and soul in hell, death must needs be a far greater fear, till they have some assurance of their deliverance from it. For death, as it was first inflicted for sin, is the very entrance into eternal damnation; how then can the thought and remembrance of death be but very dreadful? It was fear of death that made Adam and Eve to hide themselves from God's presence when they heard his voice in the garden, Gen. iii. 8. This was it that made Cain say, 'My punishment is greater than I can bear,' Gen. iv. 13. This made Nabal's heart to die within him, 1 Sam. xxv. 37. And it made Saul to fall along on the earth as a man in a swoon, 1 Sam. xxviii. 20. This made Felix to tremble when he heard Paul preach of the judgment to come, Acts xxiv. 25. Fear of the second death makes kings and great men, yea, and bondmen too, cry to the mountains to fall on them, and to hide them from the face of him that sitteth on the throne, and from the wrath of the Lamb, Rev. vi. 15, 16. Surely there is nothing more difficult than not to fear death.[6] The conscience

---

[1] *Gratias tibi Christe Salvator, quod tam potentem adversarium nostrum dum occideris occidisti.*—*Hier. ad Heliod. Epitaph. Nepot.*

[1] θάνατος ὀνομάζεται λύσις καὶ χωρισμὸς ψυχῆς ἀπὸ σώματος. Plat. in Phædo. [2] θάνατος φοβερώτατον.

[3] θάνατον ἡγοῦνται τῶν μεγίστων κακῶν εἶναι.

[4] *Omnis res vivens fugit mortem.*—*Aug. de lib. arbit.*, lib. ii. cap. iv.

[5] φέβομαι, *fugio;* præter Med. πέφοβα. Inde φόβος, *fuga,* *timor.* φοβερός, *terribilis* Heb. x. 27, 31.

[6] *Nihil difficilius est quam non metuere mortem.*—*Aug. de Quan. animæ,* c. 33.

of men unregenerate doth bring in a bill of indictment against them and convince them of rebellion against the great Lord; they are in that respect as a malefactor who is arraigned and condemned, and liveth in fear of the gallows, and is much disquieted therewith, taking no joy or comfort in his food, sleep, or any way else. An evil conscience to the soul is as the gout or stone in the body, which tortureth it in the midst of feasts, pastimes, and greatest merriments; yea, it is like the handwriting that appeared to Belshazzar, Dan. v. 5, 6.

Obj. It is said that 'the houses of the wicked are safe from fear,' and that 'they die in full strength, being wholly at ease and quiet.' Job xxi. 9, 23.

Ans. 1. All other joy only is from the teeth outward (as we speak) they have no true, sound, inward joy; they have not the ground of true joy, which is an assurance of God's favour in Christ.

2. Their joy is but short: 'As the cracking of thorns under a pot, so is the laughter of fools,' Eccles. vii. 6.

3. Many times it falleth out, that when they seem to be very jocund, there is some inward terror in the soul: 'Even in laughter the heart is sorrowful,' Prov. xxiv. 13.

4. Their joy is inconstant, they have their fits of anguish and vexation, Lam. v. 15.

5. All their joy is but as in a dream; like him 'that dreameth he eateth, but when he is awake his soul is empty,' Isa. xxix. 8. His rejoicing ariseth from the slumbering of his conscience, which for the time ceaseth to terrify him.

6. A man may be so intoxicated, and as it were made drunk with earthly conceits, as he may end his days in a foolish pleasing conceit; as a thief made drunk may die in a desperate merriment, and that under the gallows. Heretics may be so intoxicated with their errors as to suffer death for them with much seeming joy; ambitious persons may, with an outward glory, cast themselves into the jaws of death, as Marcus Curtius;[1] but albeit no effects of fear appear in such, yet because the cause of fear is not taken away, they cannot be truly said to be freed from fear; if not before, yet at the great day of judgment shall their fear break forth and their trembling appear. In which respect saith Christ, 'Woe unto you that laugh now, for ye shall lament and weep,' Luke vi. 25; 'Go to now, ye rich men, weep and howl for your miseries which shall come upon you,' James v. 1.

Woful, woful in this respect, must needs be the state of unregenerate men, for nothing can seem blessed to him over whose head terror doth always hang. Damocles, a flatterer of Dionysius the tyrant, said to his face, that he was the happiest man in the world, and made mention of his wealth, and power, and majesty, and abundance of all things. Hereupon the tyrant set that flatterer in a royal estate, at a table furnished with all dainties, and attended upon as a king, but with a heavy sharp sword hanging by a horsehair over his head; this made him quake and tremble, and desire to be freed from that estate. Thereby was declared how miserable a thing it is to live in continual fear. Some see it, and are in that respect the more terrified, others are the more senseless but not the less miserable.

There is no cause to envy a natural man's condition, though he abound never so much in wealth, honour, pleasure, or any other thing that the natural heart of man desireth. Who would envy Dives his condition, that duly weigheth his end? Luke xvi. 19, &c. This is it which the psalmist forewarneth us of, Ps. xxxvii. 1. David, in his own example, sheweth how prone we are hereunto, Ps. lxxiii. 3, &c.; and therefore we had need to be the more watchful against it.

Sec. 150. *Of a natural man's bondage.*

It is here further said that φόβῳ θανάτου, *metu mortis*, 'through or by fear of death, they are subject to bondage.' The terror with which unregenerate persons are afflicted is aggravated by a kind of bondage whereinto it brings them; for the fear of death is like a scourge, which keeps them that are under it in bondage, so as they dare not speak, nor stir, nor attempt anything for their freedom. They who are in such a manner under the lash, as we speak, are in a miserable bondage.

The word δουλεία, translated *bondage*, is a relative; it hath reference to a superior power which keeps one in awe. The noun δοῦλος, whence it ariseth, signifieth a servant. Servant,[1] according to the master to whom he hath relation, implieth a dignity or a slavery. 'A servant of God,' Titus i. 1; 'of the Lord,' Luke i. 38; 'of Jesus Christ,' Rom. i. 1, are honourable titles: but 'a servant of sin,' Rom. vi. 20; 'a servant of corruption,' 2 Peter ii. 19; and 'of the devil,' Eph. ii. 3, are base and servile titles. So the verb *to serve* is taken in a good and in a bad sense, as to serve the law of God and the law of sin, Rom. vii. 25.

But the word here translated *bondage*, being five times used in the New Testament, is always taken in a bad or base respect, as here, and Rom. viii. 15, 21; Gal. iv. 24, and v. 1.

The bondage here meant is spiritual, under sin and Satan; it compriseth under it a miserable anxiety and perplexity of mind, upon a continual expectation of death and damnation.

The word ἔνοχος, translated *subject*, intendeth such an one as is bound or fast tied to a thing. The verb whence it is derived, ἐνέχεσθε, is translated 'entangled,'

---

[1] M. Curtius equo quam poterat maximè exornato insidens armatum se in specum immisit.—*T. Liv.*, Dec. i. lib. vii. Nihil ei beatum est cui semper aliquis terror impendeat.—*Cic. Tusc. Q.* lib. v.

[1] Of the notation of *Servus*, see *Domestic. Dut.* on Eph. vi 5, treat. i. sec. 124.

Gal. v. 1. Here is implied such a subjection as a man cannot free himself from it. It is translated 'guilt,' Mark xiv. 64, 1 Cor. xi. 27, James ii. 10. He that is guilty of a penalty is bound to undergo it.

To the same purpose this very word is five times translated 'in danger of,' as Mat. v. 21, 22; Mark iii. 29. Such danger is intended as he that is in it cannot free himself from it; like that wherein Joseph was, being cast into a pit, Gen. xxxvii. 24; and wherein Jeremiah was in the dungeon, Jer. xxxviii. 6.

Sec. 151. *Of the continuance of a man's bondage all his life.*

The aforesaid thraldom is aggravated by the continuance thereof, expressed in this phrase, 'all their lifetime.' There is a special græcism which intendeth a continuance of the aforesaid fear and bondage even so long as a man liveth, and that without intermision.

Quest. How can any be said to be delivered from that to which they are subject or fast tied unto all their lifetime?

Ans. This continuance all their lifetime is to be taken,

1. Of the time wherein men lived before they were delivered, even all the time of their life wherein they were in bondage.
2. Of such as never were, nor ever shall be, delivered.
3. Of the time of the bondage here intended. It is not for a set determined time, as an apprenticeship, but of a time without date, as of a bondslave.

This continued subjection to bondage doth further set out the miserable condition of natural men, who are in perpetual bondage. The apostle setteth it forth under a fit type, which was Agar, who, under a type, representeth the mother of all born after the flesh. Of her it is said, 'She gendereth unto bondage;' and again, 'She and her children are in bondage,' Gal. iv. 24, 25.

Well weigh the masters under which such are in bondage, and it will evidently appear how woful a plight they are in.

1. They are servants of sin, whose wages is death, Rom. vi. 17, 23.
2. They are 'of their father the devil, and the lusts of their father they do. He was a murderer from the beginning,' John viii. 44.
3. They are in bondage under the law, Gal. iv. 3; and that in regard of the rigour thereof, James ii. 10, and of the curse thereof, Gal. iii. 10.
4. They are children of wrath, Eph. ii. 3, even of God's wrath, which is an insupportable burden.
5. They shall come forth to the resurrection of condemnation, John v. 29. This is it that will make them put themselves in the dens and in the rocks of the mountains, &c., Rev. vi. 15, 16.

A due consideration of a natural man's bondage is of great force to beat down all high conceits that he may have of himself. What if he be as great a conqueror as Alexander was, as highly promoted as Haman, as deep a politician as Ahithophel, as rich as Dives, as mighty as Goliath, as comely as Absalom, yet so long as he remains in his natural condition he is a very base slave; God, as a just and severe judge, will exact the uttermost of him, which, because he performeth not, his wrath will lie heavy upon him. The law will be as a bond or obligation against him, the devil ready to arrest him and cast him into the prison of hell. Everything that the natural man enjoyeth makes his bondage the worse: the ambitious man is made the greater slave by his honours, the rich man by his wealth, the voluptuous man by his pleasure, the politician by his wit; so others by other things.

Sec. 152. *Of deliverance from spiritual bondage.*

From the foresaid evils, fear of death and bondage, deliverance is procured by the Lord Jesus.

The verb ἀπαλλάξῃ, translated *deliver*, is a compound. The simple verb ἀλλάττειν signifieth *to change*, 1 Cor. xv. 51, Gal. iv. 20. The compound ἀπαλλάττειν signifieth *to change from*, namely, from one state or condition to another. They who, having been in bondage, are delivered, are changed from one state to another, from a miserable condition to a happy.

Three times is this compound word used in the New Testament, and in every of them it intendeth such a change or deliverance, as here, and Luke xii. 58, and Acts xix. 1, 2.

This deliverance pre-supposeth a former miserable condition. Men are not said to be delivered from a good and happy condition: they are willing to continue and abide therein; but from a bad and miserable condition to be delivered is acceptable to any one. As when the Israelites were delivered from the Egyptians, Exod. xviii. 10; and men from their spiritual enemies, Luke i. 74. Such a deliverance is that which the apostle here speaketh of, a deliverance from the worst bondage that any can fall into. Where the apostle, in reference to this bondage, thus complaineth, 'O wretched man that I am, who shall deliver me from the body of this death?' he himself gives this satisfaction, 'I thank God through Jesus Christ our Lord,' Rom. vii. 24, 25. That for which he thanks God is, that Christ had delivered him from the foresaid bondage; which he further confirmeth in these words, 'There is now no condemnation to them that are in Christ Jesus,' Rom. viii. 1. That redemption which is frequently attributed to Christ intendeth this deliverance.

The word λύτρωσις, which most usually setteth out that redemption, is derived from a verb, λύω, *solvo*, which signifieth to *loose or unbind* one. Now, there is a double bond whereby men may be said to be bound. One is the bond of law, as an obligation whereby a man stands bound to pay a debt. See Chap. iii. 12, Sec. 62. The other is a bond of violence, as when a man is bound by cords, chains, or other like means, Acts xxii. 30.

In the former sense men are redeemed by payment of the debt, which is a point of justice. Thus Christ is said to 'redeem us by a price,' which was his own 'precious blood,' 1 Peter i. 18, 19. In this respect another word, ἀγοράζειν, is used, which signifieth *to buy;* and we are said to be bought, ἠγοράσθητε, 1 Cor. vi. 20 and vii. 23. Thus Christ bought us of his Father; and by giving his blood for our redemption, satisfied the justice of his Father.

In the latter sense men are redeemed by might and force. This is an act of power. Thus Christ overcame that tyrant that held us in bondage, and so delivered us. Hereof see Sec. 141.

This deliverance is here amplified by the extent of it, for the benefit thereof extended to all of all sorts. This is implied under these indefinite relatives, 'them, who,' τούτους, ὅσοι. The correlative in Greek, ὅσοι, implieth a generality. It is translated sometimes 'as many as,' Mat. xiv. 36; sometimes 'all they that,' Luke iv. 40; sometimes 'whosoever,' Luke ix. 5.

This indefinite particle doth not intend that every one that was subject to the foresaid bondage was delivered; but that there were none so deeply implunged therein, and so fast held thereby, but might be delivered by Christ. Of Christ's dying for every man, see Secs. 81, 82.

Of all deliverances, this here spoken of is the most admirable in the kind, and most beneficial to us that partake of the benefit thereof. Was the Israelites' deliverance from the Egyptian bondage, or from the Babylonish captivity, a benefit worthy to be kept in perpetual memory? Surely then much more this. There is as great a difference betwixt them and this, as betwixt a tyrant that is but flesh and blood, and principalities and powers, as betwixt earth and hell, as betwixt temporary and everlasting. The difference is greater than can be expressed, whether we consider the bondage from which, or the means by which, we are delivered. This deliverance was it which made that good old priest which had been dumb, when his mouth was opened, thus to praise God: 'Blessed be the Lord God of Israel: for he hath visited and redeemed his people,' Luke i. 68, &c.

How ill doth it become those who think and profess that they are delivered, to walk as slaves who are not delivered. With great vehemency thus doth the apostle protest to such: 'This I say, and testify in the Lord, that ye henceforth walk not as other Gentiles,' &c., Eph. iv. 17. Having changed our master, it is most meet that we should change our service; the law of nature and of nations requireth as much. 'Ye were sometime darkness, but now are ye light in the Lord; walk as children of light,' Eph. v. 8. This was the principal end for which Christ 'delivered us out of the hand of our enemies,' namely, 'that we might serve him without fear, in holiness and righteousness before him, all the days of our life,' Luke i. 74, 75. We may not therefore any longer be servants of sin, Rom. vi. 12; nor of Satan, 1 Peter v. 9; nor of men, 1 Cor. vii. 23. They who do so make void that for which Christ hath taken flesh and blood, and therein by death destroyed the devil.

Sec. 153. *Of the resolution of* Heb. ii. 14, 15.

Ver. 14. *Forasmuch then as the children are partakers of flesh and blood, he also himself likewise took part of the same, that through death he might destroy him that had the power of death, that is, the devil.*

Ver. 15. *And deliver them who through fear of death were all their lifetime subject to bondage.*

In these two verses is a description of Christ's kingly office.

This is set out by two effects accomplished by his death, so as a further proof is herein given of Christ's human nature united to his divine.

Two points are hereabouts observable:

1. A connection of Christ's regal function with his prophetical, in this phrase, 'Forasmuch then as the children are partakers of flesh and blood.'

2. The demonstration of this royal power.

The connection sheweth a reason why Christ exercised his kingly office in man's nature, namely, because the children which God had given him were so.

In setting down this reason observe,

1. The relation of the persons at whose good he aimed, *the children.*

2. Their constitution, *flesh and blood.*

3. Their participation therein, *are partakers.*

In the demonstration of Christ's royal power is set down,

1. The nature wherein he exercised it.

2. The acts whereby he manifested it.

About the foresaid nature is set down,

1. The person that assumed it, *he himself.*

2. The kind of nature, *the same.*

3. The manner of assuming it, *he took part.*

4. His resemblance therein to others, *also, likewise.*

The acts of his royal function are two:

1. A conquest, ver. 14.

2. A deliverance, ver. 15.

In setting down the conquest we may discern,

1. The manner of expressing it; by way of a final cause, *that he might.*

2. The matter whereof it consisteth. This setteth out,

(1.) The kind of conquest, *destroy.*

(2.) The means whereby he accomplished it, *by death.*

(3.) The enemy conquered. He is set out,

[1.] By his power; *him that had the power of death.*

[2.] By his name, *devil.*

The second act of Christ's royal function is set out as the former.

1. By the manner of expressing it, which is by way of a final cause, implied in this copulative, *and,* as if he had said, 'And that he might.'
2. By the matter whereof it consisteth. Herein is set down,
(1.) The kind of act, *deliver.*
(2.) The extent thereof, *them who,* or *whosoever.*
(3.) The parties delivered. These are described by that miserable condition wherein they were before they were delivered. This condition is set out two ways :
[1.] By that fear wherein they are, aggravated by the object thereof, *death.*
[2.] By that bondage wherein they were. This is aggravated.
First, By the straitness of the bond, *subject,* or fast held.
Secondly, By their continuance therein all their lifetime.

Sec. 154. *Of the observations collected out of* Heb. ii. 14, 15.

I. *Man's nature is of a frail constitution.* It is flesh and blood, visible, sensible, mutable, mortal, corruptible. See Sec. 137.

II. *Saints are of the same constitution with others.* By the children are meant saints, and these are said to be partakers of flesh and blood. See Sec. 138.

III. *The Son of God became man.* This relative, *he himself,* hath reference to Christ's eminency, even as he was God. See Sec. 58.

IV. *Christ voluntarily became man.* This word, *took part,* implieth as much. See Sec. 139.

V. *Christ would partake of the very same nature that others had.* So much is expressed under this phrase, *the same.* See Sec. 139.

VI. *Because the rest of God's children were flesh and blood, Christ would therefore be so.* This is gathered from these words, *forasmuch, also, likewise.* See Sec. 136.

VII. *Christ hath vanquished Satan.* This word, *destroy,* is a word of conquest. See Sec. 141.

VIII. *Satan hath the power over death.* The very words of the text declare thus much. See Sec. 143.

IX. *Doubtful points are to be explained.* This phrase, *that is,* is a phrase of explanation. See Sec. 145.

X. *Satan is an accuser.* This is gathered from the notation of the Greek name translated *devil.* See Sec. 146.

XI. *Christ by death vanquished him that had the power of death.* So much is expressed in the very words of the text. See Sec. 144.

XII. *Christ assumed man's nature to destroy man's enemy.* He was flesh and blood that he might destroy the devil. See Sec. 139.

XIII. *Christ conquered Satan to deliver man.* The copulative particle *and* intends as much. See Sec. 148.

XIV. *Men naturally dread death.* This is here taken for grant. See Sec. 149.

XV. *Man's natural estate is a bondage.* This also is here taken for grant. See Sec. 150.

XVI. *Man is fast held in his bondage.* The Greek word translated *subject* intendeth as much. See Sec. 150.

XVII. *Man is a slave all his life long.* How this holds true is shewed, Sec. 151.

XVIII. *Christ hath delivered his from their natural bondage.* This is here necessarily implied. See Sec. 152.

XIX. *There are none so fast held in bondage but may be delivered by Christ.* See Sec. 152.

XX. *Fear of death is a very bondage.* They that fear death are here said to be subject to bondage. See Sec. 150.

Sec. 155. *Of the transition betwixt Christ's princely and priestly function.*

Ver. 16. *For verily he took not on him the nature of angels ; but he took on him the seed of Abraham.*

This verse is here inserted as a fit transition betwixt the princely and priestly office of Christ. It hath reference to them both, as an especial reason of the one and of the other. In reference to the former, it sheweth a reason of the two fore-mentioned acts of Christ's kingly office. Why he destroyed the devil, and why he delivered man that was in bondage ; even because he took not on him the nature of angels, but the seed of Abraham. The first particle, γὰρ, *for,* intendeth as much. In reference to the latter, which is Christ's priestly function, this verse layeth down the ground of all the particulars following, ver. 17, 18. He was made like to his brethren ; he was a merciful and faithful high priest, &c. Even because ' he took on him the seed of Abraham.'

The Greek conjunction δὴ, translated *verily,* is a compound. The simple is a note of asseveration or ratification ; it is translated *doubtless,* 2 Cor. xii. 1, which is all one as this word *verily.* The particle ποῦ δήπου, with which it is here compounded, pointeth at some place. In that respect it may be thus translated, he *nowhere* took on him : So the vulgar Latin,[1] and our ancient notes. Thus it may have reference to the Old Testament ; whereunto the apostle hath oft reference, as chap. i. 5, &c., and in this chapter, ver 6, 12, 13. In this sense it may imply that the Scripture nowhere testifieth of Christ that he took on him the nature of angels, &c., and therefore it may be inferred that he did not take the nature of angels on him.

Whether we take this word as a note of asseveration, or as pointing to the Old Testament, the same sense

---

[1] Nunquam, *Vulg. Lat.* In no place, *Ancient Eng. Translat.*

remaineth; for both ways it addeth emphasis to the negative, 'he took not.'

Sec. 156. *Of the meaning of this word, 'he took him.'*

The Greek word ἐπιλαμβάνεται, thus translated, 'he took on him,' is compounded of a verb, λαμβάνειν, that signifieth to *take*, Mat. xiv. 19, or to *receive*, Mat. vii. 8; and a preposition ἐπί, which hath various significations: as *at*, Luke xxiii. 40, *to*, John xxi. 11, *in*, Mat. xxii. 2, *upon*, John xix. 19, and sundry others. Answerably words compounded with that preposition have divers significations. Thus this word in my text signifieth,

1. To catch one being ready to perish, Mat. xiv. 31.
2. To take one that cannot see, to lead and direct him, Mark viii. 23.
3. To take one to him for his good, Luke xiv. 4.
4. To lay hold upon one against his mind, Luke xxiii. 26.
5. To lay fast hold on a thing which he would not lose, 1 Tim. vi. 12.
6. To take one kindly by the hand, to testify a desire of confederacy with him, Heb. viii. 9.

In all these significations may this word here be applied to Christ in reference to man. For,

1. Christ catched man being ready utterly to perish.
2. He took man stark blind, to open his eyes.
3. He took man full of sores, to cure him.
4. When man was unwilling to come, Gen. iii. 8, Christ took him.
5. He laid fast hold on man, and would not let him go.
6. Most kindly he took man by the hand, and entered into covenant with him.

Yea, further, he took man's nature upon him. Thus do most interpreters, both ancient and modern,[1] here expound this word. So do our English translators. This phrase, *the nature of*, is not in the Greek original; but implied under that word, *took on him*, and it is in our English, as in other translations, inserted, more fully to express the meaning of the Greek word.

Indeed, many expositors, both of former and later times, do take this word in this text properly to signify Christ's apprehending or laying hold on man, when man would have run away from him; but withal they do infer that for that end Christ assumed man's nature. So as herein all agree, that Christ assuming our nature is here intended; only some would have it properly intended in the meaning of the word, others would have it implied by just and necessary consequence.

The Greek word ἐπιλαμβάνεται is of the present tense, 'he taketh,' yet for perspicuity's sake it is translated in the preterperfect tense, 'he took,' for it is usual in the Hebrew dialect to put one tense for another: as the present for the future, Zech. ix. 9, to shew that divine promises of future good things, are as sure and certain as things present. So here the present tense is put in for the preterperfect, which signifieth the time past, to represent a thing past as ever in doing. This, therefore, is an elegant and emphatical Hebraism.

Sec. 157. *Of Christ not assuming the nature of angels.*
Of angels we have largely spoken on Chap. i. Sec. 81, &c.

This phrase, 'he took not angels,' is here set down in opposition to that kind of nature which Christ assumed to him. This particle of opposition, ἀλλά, *but*, intends as much.

It shews that what Christ did not for angels, he did for man; and what he did for man, he did not for angels.

This negative, 'he took not on him the nature of angels,' is here premised for weighty reasons.

1. In reference to the fifth verse, where it is said that 'God put not in subjection unto the angels the world to come.' Here a reason thereof is shewed; namely, because Christ was not one with angels, he took not upon him their nature.

2. It giveth an instance of God's sovereignty and justice. For God hath power to leave sinners in that miserable estate, whereunto they have implunged themselves, and justly may he so do, for thus in justice hath he dealt with the angels that sinned. 'The angels which kept not their first estate, but left their own habitation, he hath reserved in everlasting chains, under darkness, unto the judgment of the great day,' Jude 6, 2 Peter ii. 4.

3. To amplify God's mercy to man. It is a very great amplification of mercy, that it is such a mercy as is not extended to others, though those others stood in as much need thereof, Ps. cxlvii. 20.

4. It demonstrateth more fully the kind of nature which Christ assumed; that it was not an angelical, a spiritual, a celestial nature, as some heretics have imagined. See Sec. 140.

This word *angels* is indefinitely to be taken with reference to all sorts of angels, good or bad. It sheweth that the good angels had not so much honour conferred upon them as man had, namely, to be one with Christ. In this respect even the good angels are inferior to saints, for they are sent forth to minister for them, Heb. i. 14.

It sheweth also that evil angels have not that mercy shewed unto them which men have, namely, to have the Son of God in their nature, a Saviour, to save them.

This negative, that 'Christ took not on him the nature of angels,' refutes the opinion of the Chiliasts or Millennaries, who hold that the very devils shall be released out of hell after a thousand years. None can be freed but by Christ; but with Christ they have nothing to do. See more hereof in my *Treatise of the Sin against the Holy Ghost*, secs. 29–31.

---

[1] Ambros., Chrysost., Calvin, Beza, Pareus, aliique.

Sec. 158. *Of objections against this truth,* 'Christ took not on him the nature of angels,' answered.

Obj. 1. Christ appeared unto men in the shape of an angel, Exodus. iii. 2, 6 ; Judges xiii. 3, 17, 18.

Ans. Though it were the Son of God that appeared unto men, and he be called an angel, yet that shape wherein he appeared was not the shape of an angel, but rather of a man; neither was that the true human nature of Christ which he afterwards assumed, but only a visible human nature which he assumed for that present time and use.

Obj. 2. Christ is expressly called *angel*, Isa. lxiii. 9 ; Mal. iii. 1.

Ans. He is so called, not in regard of his nature, but of his office. So men are called angels, Rev. i. 20.

Obj. 3. Christ is called 'the head of all principality and power.' Under these words angels are comprised.

Ans. Christ is indeed the head of angels, but not by virtue of any mystical union, but by reason of that pre-eminency which he hath over them. Thus is he said to be 'far above all principality,' &c., Eph. i. 21. And also by reason of that authority he hath over them, Heb. i. 6, 7, 14.

Obj. 4. Christ is said to 'gather together in one all things which are in heaven and on earth,' Eph. i. 10. By 'things in heaven' are meant angels.

Ans. 1. It is not necessary that angels should be there meant, but rather glorified saints.

2. If angels be there meant, the gathering of them together is not to be taken of an union with Christ, but rather of a reconciliation betwixt angels and men, or of the establishing of the good angels that fell not.

Sec. 159. *Of the privilege of believers above angels.*

To shew that that very mercy which was not vouchsafed to angels was vouchsafed to men, the apostle doth not only use this particle of opposition, ἀλλὰ, *but* (which Solomon in like cases frequently useth, as Prov. x. 2), but also he repeateth the same word again, wherein the grace not granted to angels is comprised, which is this, ἐπιλαμβάνεται, 'he took on him.' So as to man was granted that which was not vouchsafed to angels. Of that grace see Sec. 157.

This is such an evidence of God's peculiar respect to man, as it made the angels themselves desire to behold the riches of God's mercy herein, 1 Pet. i. 12.

If to this general we add other peculiar exemplifications of God's mercy to man, over and above that which he shewed to angels, we shall more clearly discern the exceeding greatness of God's favour to man. Some particulars are these.

1. Christ is given a Saviour to lost man, Luke ii. 11. No Saviour is afforded to angels.

2. Men are as members of one body, mystically united to Christ their head, so as they altogether, with the Son of God, are one Christ, 1 Cor. xii. 12. No such honour is vouchsafed to angels.

3. All things are put in subjection to man, not so to angels, vers. 5, 6, &c.

4. Men shall judge the angels, 1 Cor. vi. 3; angels shall not judge men.

5. Angels are 'ministering spirits sent forth to minister for them that shall be heirs of salvation,' Heb. i. 14; men are not sent forth to minister for angels.

Some make the reason of that difference which God put between men and angels to be this, that all the angels fell not, and thereupon they infer that Christ need not take on him the nature of angels for the good angels' sake, because they were but a part; for he will take the nature for all, or none. This reason cannot hold, in that he took man's nature for the good and benefit only of 'the seed of Abraham.' See Sec. 162.

Others put the reason of the foresaid difference between men and angels in the heinousness of the sin of angels, and thereupon they aggravate the sin of angels by sundry circumstances: as, that they were the more excellent creatures; that they had more light of understanding; that they first sinned; that they were not tempted to sin as man was; and that they tempted man, and so were murderers of man, John viii. 44.

I will not essay to extenuate any of these aggravations; but this I may boldly say, that these and other like reasons, taken from difference in creatures, much derogate from the supreme sovereignty of God, who thus saith, 'I will be gracious to whom I will be gracious: and I will shew mercy on whom I will shew mercy,' Exod. xxxiii. 19. That which about God's sovereignty exercised on man and man, in reference to the elect and reprobate, is distinctly set down by the apostle, Rom. ix. 21, &c., may not unfitly be applied to his sovereignty exercised on men and angels: 'Hath not the potter power over the clay, of the same lump to make one vessel unto honour, and another unto dishonour?' &c.; 'Is it not lawful for me,' saith the Lord, 'to do what I will with mine own?' This, then, is the reason that we must rest upon, 'So was God's good pleasure.' He would not shew that mercy to angels which he did to men.

Of God's peculiar love to man, see my treatise entitled, *A Plaster for the Plague*, on Num. xvi. 46, sec. 34, 35.

The privileges which God hath given to men more than to angels aggravateth their dotage who adore angels. Therein they dishonour God, in giving to creatures that honour which is due only to the Creator, and they do too much debase themselves, in dejecting themselves below those above whom God hath advanced them. A good angel would not accept of such adoration, Rev. xix. 10, and xxii. 8, 9.

The foresaid privilege doth further aggravate man's backwardness about the things that make to the honour of God. God having honoured men above angels, equity and gratitude require that men should endeavour to honour God more than the angels do; but they fail so much herein, as they come very short of other creatures in glorifying God. Behold the heavens, they 'declare the glory of God,' Ps. xix. 1. The whole host of heaven constantly keepeth that course wherein God at first set them. Those stars that are called wandering, wander according to their appointed course, and are constant therein. Look down upon the earth, and you shall find all manner of trees and plants bringing forth their fruit in their season, according to the first appointment, Gen. i. 12. Yet men exceedingly fail in those courses which God hath appointed unto them. We may justly take up the prophet's complaint in this respect, and say, 'Hear, O heavens, and give ear, O earth,' &c. Isa. i. 2, &c. Let the consideration of God's respect to man above angels quicken us up to outstrip, if it were possible, the very angels in glorifying God. At least let our endeavour be to come as near them therein as possibly we can. This is a point intended in the third petition, where Christ directeth us to pray that God's 'will be done on earth, as it is in heaven,' Mat. vi. 10.

Consider, therefore, what is said of angels, 'They excel in strength, they do his commandments, hearkening unto the voice of his word,' Ps. ciii. 20; they minister unto God, Dan. vii. 10; 'They do always behold the face of God,' Mat. xviii. 10; namely, to know his will what they should do. They suddenly, upon all occasions, assemble in multitudes to praise God, Luke ii. 13, 14: 'There is joy in the presence of the angels of God over a sinner that repenteth,' Luke xv. 10. In these and other like duties that concern us we ought to be followers of them.

Sec. 160. *Of Christ's eternal Deity.*

This word ἐπιλαμβάνεται, 'he took on him,' as it setteth out the human nature of Christ, so it giveth a hint of his divine nature, for it presupposeth that Christ was before he took on him the seed of Abraham, John viii. 58. He that taketh anything on him must needs be before he do so. Is it possible for him that is not to take anything on him? Now Christ in regard of his human nature was not before he assumed that nature, therefore that former being must needs be in regard of his divine nature; in that respect he ever was, even the eternal God. Being God, he took on him a human nature, so much was before implied under this word μετέσχε, *took part,* 'He also took part of the same,' ver. 14, Sec. 139.

Sec. 161. *Of Christ taking on him seed.*

That which Christ took on him is here said to be σπέρμα, *seed.*

Seed in relation unto man is by a metonymy put for children: for seed is the matter out of which children arise, Luke i. 55, John viii. 33, Acts, vii. 5, 6. Rom. iv. 16, 18.

The apostle doth here purposely use this word *seed,* to shew,

1. That Christ came out of the loins of man, as Jacob's children, and their children are said to come out of his loins, Gen. xlvi. 26, Exod. i. 5; and all the Jews are said to 'come out of the loins of Abraham,' Heb. vii. 5; and Solomon is said to 'come out of the loins of David,' 1 Kings viii. 19. In a man's loins his seed is, and it is a part of his substance: thus it sheweth that Christ's human nature was of the very substance of man.

2. That Christ was the very same that was promised to be the Redeemer of man, for of old he was foretold under this word *seed,* as, 'The seed of the woman,' Gen. iii. 15; 'The seed of Abraham, Gen. xii. 18; 'The seed of Isaac,' Rom. ix. 7, Heb. xi. 18; 'The seed of David,' 2 Sam. vii. 12, and xxii. 51.

Sec. 162. *Of Christ's taking on him the seed of Abraham.*

Christ was indeed the seed of the first woman, Gen. iii. 15, which was the mother of all mankind; his genealogy therefore reacheth even unto Adam, Luke iii. 38, for Christ assumed the common nature of man, and not of any particular person. Yet here the apostle ascendeth no higher than to Abraham, who was the twentieth generation from Adam, not excluding all who lived before Abraham, but restraining the benefit to such as are of the faith of Abraham, and in that respect children of Abraham, Gal. iii. 7, 9.

When almost all the world was addicted to idolatry, it pleased God to call Abraham out of his own native country, and to enter into covenant with him and his seed, to be their God, and to take them for his people, Gen. xvii. 17, Exod. xix. 3, 6. Therein he made Abraham a kind of head and stock of his church, and that not only of such as should descend from him after the flesh, but also of all that should believe, Rom. iv. 11. In reference hereunto is Christ said to 'take on him the seed of Abraham.' Fitly in this case doth the apostle make mention of Abraham.

1. Because the promise of the Messiah to come of his seed was oft made to Abraham, as Gen. xii. 3, and xiii. 15, 16, and xv. 5, 6, and xvii. 7, 17, and xviii. 18, and xxi. 12, and xxii. 18. So as the faith of believers was the more settled in this, that Christ took on him the seed of Abraham.

2. Because Christ assumed man's nature in special for the sake of Abraham's seed, which properly are they who were chosen of God to eternal life. To this purpose tendeth that distinction which the apostle maketh between the children of the flesh and children of promise, Rom. ix. 7, 8.

Thus, 'if we be Christ's, then are we Abraham's seed, and heirs according to the promise,' Gal. iii. 29. To this very purpose is it that the evangelist Matthew begins the genealogy of Christ with Abraham, Mat. i. 2.

No reason can be fetched from Abraham as a man, a son of Adam, why God should prefer him before any other son of Adam. We must rest in that which Christ affirmeth in another case, 'Even so, Father, for so it seemeth good in thy sight,' Mat. xi. 25, 26. This the apostle largely proves, Rom. ix. 15, &c.

As it was in the case betwixt men and angels, Sec. 159, so is it in this case between men and men.

If that respect which God manifested to man more than to angels afforded matter of high admiration and much gratulation, much more doth this difference between men and men.

Though Christ assumed the common nature of men, yet he took on him the seed of Abraham. To this seed in peculiar was he given to save them. This is his people whom he shall save from their sins, Mat. i. 21.

Bless the Lord, 'ye seed of Abraham his servant, ye children of Jacob his chosen,' 'He is the Lord our God,' &c., 'He hath remembered his covenant for ever, which covenant he made with Abraham,' Ps. cv. 6, &c.; 'Thou Israel art my servant, Jacob whom I have chosen, the seed of Abraham my friend,' &c., Isa. xli. 8, 9. Ye are they with whom the covenant of God is most firm and sure. 'Thus saith the Lord, If my covenant be not with day and night, and if I have not appointed the ordinances of heaven and earth, then will I cast away the seed of Jacob, and David my servant, so that I will not take any of his seed to be rulers over the seed of Abraham,' Jer. xxxiii. 25, 26; 'Now to Abraham and his seed were the promises made,' Gal. iii. 16.

Of restraining the benefit of Christ to the elect, see Sec. 133.

Sec. 163. *Of sundry principles of faith confirmed, and errors refuted, by these words, 'He took on him the seed of Abraham.'*

That which hath been before noted, Secs. 104, 106, 139, concerning Christ and other men, being of one and the same flesh and blood, and in that respect brethren, is confirmed by this phrase, 'He took on him the seed of Abraham.'

Both the ancient fathers and also later divines have much insisted on this text, to prove sundry principles of our Christian faith, concerning,

1. Christ's eternal deity. Hereof see Sec. 160.

2. His true humanity. In that he took upon him the seed of man, it is evident that he was a true man. Seed is the matter of man's nature, and the very substance thereof.

3. The root out of which Christ assumed his human nature, even the seed of man. It was not created of nothing, nor was it brought from heaven, but assumed out of the seed of man. This was thus foretold: 'There shall come forth a rod out of the stem of Jesse, and a branch shall grow out of his root,' Isa. xi. 1; and an angel thus saith of Christ to the Virgin Mary: 'That holy thing which shall be born of thee,' Luke xi. 35.

4. The subsistence of Christ's human nature in his divine nature. The human nature of Christ never had a subsistence in itself. At or in the very first framing or making it, it was united to the divine nature, and at or in the first uniting it, it was framed or made. Philosophers say of the uniting of the soul to the body, in creating it it is infused, and infusing it it is created.[1] Much more is this true concerning the human nature of Christ united to his divine; fitly, therefore, is it here said, that he took on him the seed, not a son, of Abraham.

5. His two distinct natures. He took on him man's nature, being God before; so as they were two, and those two distinct natures.

6. The union of the two natures. He assumed or took on him the one to the other, and so made of those two natures one person. This union is evidenced in these phrases, 'The word was made flesh,' John i. 14; 'God was manifested in the flesh,' 1 Tim. iii. 16; 'Christ came of the Father, as concerning the flesh, who is over all, God blessed for ever,' Rom. ix. 5. This true real union, the Greek fathers,[2] to free it from mistakings, have set out negatively and affirmatively with sundry emphatical words. As,

1. Without alteration or change, $\dot{\alpha}\tau\rho\acute{\epsilon}\pi\tau\omega\varsigma$, whereby is intended that the divine nature still remained the same; and in assuming the humanity, was no whit at all changed, as wine is changed by putting water into it; nor was the human altered into the divine, as water was turned into wine, John ii. 9.

2. Without division, $\dot{\alpha}\delta\iota\alpha\iota\rho\acute{\epsilon}\tau\omega\varsigma$, so as they both make but one and the same person. They are indeed two distinct natures, but so united as both make one only person, both have one and the same subsistence. As the Son of God hath a peculiar subsistence in himself, so the human nature which he assumed subsisteth therein.

3. Without confusion, $\dot{\alpha}\sigma\upsilon\gamma\chi\acute{\upsilon}\tau\omega\varsigma$. Those two natures are united in one person, yet not by confusion of substance, as if the human nature were transfused into the divine, and both made but one nature. They remain two distinct natures, each having distinct properties, distinct wills, distinct operations and actions.

Without separation, $\dot{\alpha}\chi\epsilon\rho\acute{\upsilon}\tau\omega\varsigma$, never to be disunited or severed one from the other. On earth they were first united, in heaven they will ever so abide. As the infirmities of the flesh caused no separation, so neither will the glory of the Deity. In this respect we may say, 'Jesus Christ, the same yesterday, and to-day, and for ever,' Heb. xiii. 8.

The affirmative word which they use to set out this union, $o\dot{\upsilon}\sigma\iota\omega\delta\tilde{\omega}\varsigma$, signifieth *essentially* or *substantially*, not as in the mystery of the Trinity, where the distinct persons are all of one nature or essence, but be-

---

[1] Creando infunditur, et infundendo creatur.
[2] Concil. Calced.

cause the distinct natures of Christ make but one person, and thus the union may be said to be essential, not accidental. The apostle useth a like emphatical word where he saith, that 'in Christ dwelleth all the fulness of the Godhead bodily,' σωματικῶς, Col. ii. 9. This word *bodily* intendeth as much as the former word *essentially* or *substantially*, or as some translate it, *personally*. By this word the union of God with Christ is distinguished from all other unions. God of old manifested himself in the cloud, in the rock, in the ark, in the tabernacle, in the temple; but figuratively God also manifested himself in his prophets, but virtually by the operation of his Spirit; but never was he in any person or in any thing as in Christ.

This text hath also been used as a maul to knock down sundry heresies, whereof see Sec. 140.

Sec. 164. *Of the resolution of* Heb. ii. 16.

In this verse is set down a difference of Christ's respect to angels and men. Hereabout observe,

1. The inference upon that which went before. It is brought in as a reason why Christ destroyed the devil and delivered man. See Sec. 155.

2. The substance. In it there is,

1. A proof of the point, verily, δήπου.

2. The point itself. Herein are two parts, one negative, the other affirmative.

In the negative is declared what Christ did not for angels. Therein is set down,

1. An act of grace not vouchsafed, οὐκ ἐπιλαμβάνεται, *he took not on him*.

2. The object or persons to whom that act was not vouchsafed, ἀγγέλων, *angels*.

In the affirmative is declared what he did.

Betwixt the two parts is placed a particle of opposition, ἀλλὰ, *but*.

In the latter part is set down,

1. An act of grace vouchsafed, ἐπιλαμβάνεται, *he took on him*.

2. The object or persons to whom he vouchsafed it. That object is,

1. Generally implied, σπέρματος, *the seed*.

2. Particularly exemplified, Ἀβραάμ, *of Abraham*.

Sec. 165. *Of the observations arising out of* Heb. ii. 16.

I. *Christ destroyed such sinners as he did not undertake for.*

II. *Christ delivered such as he undertook for.* These two observations I gather out of this causal particle *for*. See Sec. 155.

III. *Weighty matters are more than ordinarily to be pressed.* Christ's different respect to angels and men is a weighty matter, and such a word as this *verily* is a more than ordinary affirmation. See Sec. 155.

IV. *Means of grace is not afforded to those to whom grace is not vouchsafed.* Grace was not vouchsafed to the angels; therefore Christ, the means of grace, is not afforded to them. See Sec. 157.

V. *Angels had not that grace afforded to them which was vouchsafed to man.* This very phrase, *he took not on him*, whereby the grace vouchsafed unto man is expressed, is denied in reference to angels. See Sec. 157.

VI. *Christ preferred men before angels.* The particle of opposition intendeth as much. See Sec. 159.

VII. *God's goodness is ever working.* This I gather from the apostle's expressing an act past in the present tense. See Sec. 156.

VIII. *Christ was before he assumed man's nature.* See Sec. 160.

IX. *Christ assumed to his divine nature our nature.*

X. *Christ's human nature subsisted in his divine nature.*

XI. *Christ was man of man.*

XII. *Christ had two distinct natures.*

XIII. *Christ's two natures were united in one person.* Of these five latter observations, see Sec. 163.

XIV. *Christ was exhibited as he was promised.* He was promised under the seed of Abraham, and he took on him the seed of Abraham.

XV. *Christ became man for the elect's sake.* The elect are comprised under the seed of Abraham. Of these two last observations, see Sec. 162.

Sec. 166. *Of the necessity of Christ being man.*

Ver. 17. *Wherefore in all things it behoved him to be made like unto his brethren, that he might be a merciful and faithful high priest in things pertaining to God, to make reconciliation for the sins of the people.*

To Christ's prophetical and kingly offices the apostle addeth his third, which is his priestly office, and that to prove the main point in hand, namely that Christ was man, otherwise he could not have been a priest; for 'every high priest is taken from among men,' &c., Heb. v. 1.

As the last two verses of this chapter have a general reference to Christ's human nature, set out ver. 10, 11, &c., so they have also a special reference to the last clause of the verse going before, and that as a necessary consequence following thereupon. Because Christ took on him the seed of Abraham, therefore it behoved him to be made like unto him.

The particle of inference, ὅθεν, translated *wherefore*, properly signifieth a place whence one cometh, Acts xiv. 26, or where one doth a thing, Mat. xxv. 24, 26, or a condition or danger from whence one is brought, Heb. xi. 19.

It is also frequently used to set out a consequence following from another thing, as, because the Lord Jesus had most evidently made himself known to Paul, *thereupon* he was 'not disobedient unto the heavenly vision,' Acts xxvi. 19.

In this sense is this word five several times used in this epistle, as here, chap. iii. 1, and vii. 25, and viii. 3, and ix. 18.

The necessity of the consequence is implied in this word ὤφειλε, *it behoved*. See Chap. iii. 5, Sec 14.

This word hath reference,

1. To a debt that one ought to pay, Mat. xviii. 28, Luke vii. 41.
2. To a duty that one ought to perform, 2 Thes. i. 3.
3. To a punishment which ought to be inflicted, John xix. 7.

In all these senses it is here fitly used.

1. Christ, as a surety for man, Heb. vii. 27, ought to pay man's debt, Prov. vi. 1, 2.
2. As he was sent of the Father, he ought to do that for which he was sent, John ix. 4.
3. As he took upon him the sins of the elect, the punishment of them ought to be inflicted upon him, 2 Cor. v. 21.

Such a word as this was used before, ver. 10, Sec. 86. But the two words there and here do differ in syllables and sense. Answerably our translators do differently translate them: there, ἔπρεπε, 'it became;' here, ὤφειλε, 'it behoved.' The former is attributed to God the Father; this is referred to God the Son, and that in regard of his human nature. That signified a comeliness or a meekness; this a necessity, yet no absolute necessity, but a necessity on supposition, in regard of that order which God had set down to redeem man by a ransom, and by satisfaction to his justice. Now, Christ hereunto voluntarily subjected himself, and in that respect it behoved him to do what he undertook to do. He bound himself to partake of our infirmities. See Sec. 88.

This he did in respect to his Father's purpose, which was foretold by the prophets; and therefore Christ would accomplish it. Hereupon Christ himself saith, 'Thus it is written, and thus it behoved Christ to suffer,' Luke xxiv. 46.

This he did also in regard of our weakness, that he might the rather encourage and embolden us to go to him, and to trust unto him. If Christ had not had experience of our infirmities, we could not with such boldness go unto him as now we do, Heb. iv. 15, 16.

This doth highly amplify Christ's love to us, who, being most free and bound to nothing, for our sakes bound himself to do and endure what he did. A servant's love to his master, wife, and children, was tried by a voluntary binding of himself to his master, and suffering his ear to be bored through, Exod. xxi. 5, 6. Christ did more; he suffered his side, hands, and feet to be bored through, and his side to be pierced, yea, and his very soul too, Isa. liii. 10.

How are we bound to bind ourselves to Christ! Bounden duty, gratefulness, our own good and benefit, require thus much. Let us therefore bind ourselves by voluntary covenant and vows, that so we may be kept from starting from Christ.

Sec. 167. *Of Christ's brethren.*

That whereunto Christ was bound is thus expressed, 'To be made like unto his brethren.'

This is the third time that this relative *brethren*, in reference to Christ, is here in this chapter used, and that still in the very same sense; see Secs. 106, 113. It setteth out the same persons that were intended under these titles, 'sons,' Sec. 90; 'sanctified ones,' Sec. 103; 'children,' Sec. 128; and 'seed of Abraham,' Sec. 162. All these point at the elect of God, for whose sake in special Christ took on him the common nature of man; for he was made like unto man for the elect's sake, who are given unto him of his Father, Sec. 132. Christ principally intended their good by being made like to man, and they reaped the benefit thereof, yea, to them that benefit is restrained; see Sec. 133.

Sec. 168. *Of Christ being made like to man.*

The word ὁμοιωθῆναι, translated *made like*, doth for the most part set forth a mere resemblance or likeness of a thing, as Mat. vii. 26, and xiii. 24. But here it is taken for more than a bare resemblance, even for a participation of essence.

In the former respect, we may say of a picture, It is made like such a man; but in the latter respect, we may say of a child, who partakes of his father's nature in the substance, constitution, disposition, and manifold affections and passions, He is made like unto his father.

A word, ὁμοίωμα, sprouting out of the same root, is used by the apostle to set out Christ's participation of our nature; as thus, 'God sent his Son in the likeness of sinful flesh,' Rom. viii. 3; and thus, 'Christ was made in the likeness of man,' Philip. ii. 7. A like word, ὡς, is used to set out the identity of the glory of the Son with the glory of the Father: 'We beheld his glory, the glory as of the only begotten of the Father,' John i. 14. Thus this word here answereth to that *likewise*, ver. 14. See Sec. 139.

These words of likeness are used to set out both the reality of a thing, and also an apparent manifestation thereof.

The apostle here intends the very same thing that he did before under these phrases, 'all of one,' Sec. 104; 'he also himself likewise took part,' Sec. 139; 'he took on him the seed of Abraham,' Secs. 159, 162. All these phrases, and this here in the text, with emphasis demonstrate the truth and reality of Christ's human nature, that he was a man, such a man as we are.

Sec. 169. *Of this general 'all things,' wherein Christ was made like to man.*

Though every particular be comprised under this general *all things*, yet they may be ranked under such heads as will shew that they were very many. Those heads are these:

1. The essential parts of man's nature, which were soul and body.
2. The powers of his soul; as understanding and will, together with his affections; both liking, as hope,

desire, love, and joy; and disliking, as fear, anger, hatred, grief; and all manner of senses; both internal, as the common sense, phantasy, and memory; and external, as sight, hearing, smelling, tasting, feeling.

3. The several and distinct parts of the body, whether inward or outward, which are very many, and well known, the outward especially.

4. The growth of the parts of Christ's body, and endowments of soul. As other men, so Christ at first was little. He was nine months in his mother's womb; being born, he was wrapped in swaddling clothes, and carried in arms, Luke ii. 7, 28. He also 'increased in wisdom and knowledge,' Luke ii. 52. Hereby is proved a growth in powers of soul and parts of body.

5. Sundry infirmities of soul; besides the affections before mentioned, ' he groaned in the Spirit, and was troubled,' John xi. 33, and was afflicted with other soul-sufferings; whereof see Sec. 76.

Sundry infirmities of body; as hunger, thirst, cold, wearisomeness, sleepiness, fainting, mortality.

7. Manifold temptations.
8. Manifold afflictions.

Of Christ's temptations and other afflictions, see Sec. 96.

Sec. 170. *Of sin and sicknesses wherein Christ was not like man.*

True it is that Christ was not subject to sin; he was holy, harmless, undefiled, separate from sinners, Heb. vii. 26; he was pure in his conception, Luke i. 35; he 'knew no sin,' 2 Cor. v. 21; 'he did no sin, neither was guile found in his mouth,' 1 Peter ii. 22. We read not that any sickness ever seized upon him, nor defect of nature, as blindness, lameness, deafness, dumbness, or any other the like. Hereupon a question is moved, How it can be true that Christ was made like man in this general extent, *all things?*

Ans. 1. Generals admit some particular exceptions. The apostle himself thus expresseth the exception of sin: ' He was in all points tempted like as we are, yet without sin,' Heb. iv. 15.

2. Though sin in our nature be an inseparable adjunct, yet is it not essential thereunto. A man may be a true man though he have no sin in him; instance Adam in his innocency, and glorified saints after the resurrection.

3. Christ, as surety for sinners, was like to sinful men, in that our sins were imputed to him, and he bare the burden of them. Thus it is said, that ' he was made sin for us,' 2 Cor. v. 21; but to be himself tainted with sin was not possible, by reason of the union of his human nature with his divine. If such a thing could have been, it would have crossed the main end of his being like unto man, namely, to be a mediator betwixt God and man, to make satisfaction for the sins of others, &c.

As for sicknesses, and other like infirmities, they were personal, and not inseparable from man's nature; for there are many particular men that were never blind, deaf, dumb, lame, sick of the palsy, pleurisy, and other particular diseases.

Besides, sicknesses and other personal infirmities would have been an hindrance to those works which he was to accomplish for our redemption. They would have kept him from going up and down to preach the gospel, and to do sundry other good things, Acts x. 38. Sight wrought compassion in him, Mark vi. 34. Hearing others' cries moved him to help them, Mark x. 48, 49. By his speech he comforted such as were in distress, Mat. ix. 2. Had he wanted those parts, he had been much hindered.

Obj. It is said, that ' himself took our infirmities, and bare our sicknesses,' Mat. viii. 17.

Ans. Those phrases are used of Christ's removing and taking away from sundry men sundry infirmities and sicknesses, which he did with such compassion, as he might seem to bear them himself, in regard of a fellow-feeling.

Sec. 171. *Of the ends why Christ was made like to man in all things.*

The ends why Christ might be made like to man in the foresaid universal likeness, were such as these:

1. To give a surer evidence of the truth of his human nature. Thus this is a confirmation of this great article of our Christian faith, that Christ was a true man.

2. To give assurance of his compassions towards us in regard of our infirmities, Heb. iv. 15.

3. That no gifts or parts of learning, wisdom, purity, or any other excellency, exempts men from infirmities, for who more excellent than Christ? Thus this is a ground of contentation.

4. To demonstrate that infirmities and afflictions, simply considered in themselves, are no arguments of God's displeasure or indignation. Thus this is a ground of patience.

5. To be an example, that we might have a pattern for well-carrying ourselves in such cases. Thus this is a direction.

6. To make them more easy to us; for Christ, by putting his shoulder under the burdens that lie upon us, hath taken away the greatest heaviness of them, and made them to us portable. This is a ground of encouragement.

7. To sanctify them unto us, for whatsoever Christ underwent, he sanctified: he sanctified divine ordinances, by observing them himself; he sanctified the creatures that are useful for man, by using them himself.

Other ends follow more distinctly to be handled in the words following in this chapter.

All the fore-mentioned ends, and others also like to them, demonstrate that Christ was in all things like to us for our good. The benefit thereof redounds to us.

How just and equal is it that we should endeavour in all things wherein we may be like to him, to endeavour to be so. It will be our wisdom, our honour and glory so to be, yea, though it be in suffering. The apostles 'rejoiced that they were counted worthy to suffer shame for Christ's name,' Acts v. 41. If we be like him here in afflictions and sufferings, we shall be like him hereafter in glory, 2 Tim. ii. 12.

Sec. 172. *Of Christ a true priest.*

The most useful and behoveful office that Christ undertook for man, is comprised under this compound, ἀρχιερεύς, *high priest.*

The Hebrew word translated priest, is derived from a verb that signifieth in general to minister, כהן, *ministravit.* The noun also in general signifieth a minister; it is sometimes used for a minister in civil affairs, and is translated prince or ruler,[1] Gen. xli. 45, 2 Sam. viii. 18, xx. 26. Most frequently it is put for a minister in sacred matters, and translated *priest.*[2]

The Greek word is derived from an adjective, ἱερός, *sacer,* ἱερεύς, *sacerdos,* that signifieth holy. The function of a priest is sacred, and thereupon his name, that carrieth holiness in it, is given unto him. Aaron, by reason of his function, is styled 'God's holy one,' Deut. xxxiii. 8, and 'the saint of the Lord,' Ps. cvi. 16.

The notation of the Latin word[3] is most proper to the title, which signifieth priest; for it is from giving or offering sacred things.

Our English word *priest* is supposed to be a contract of a Greek word that signifieth a president,[4] or one that is set over others, or put before them. For priests are over God's people in spiritual matters concerning their souls.

According to the several notations in every language was Christ a priest; for,

1. He was a prince, Isa. ix. 6; and a minister for God's church, Rom. xv. 8.

2. He was an holy one, Luke i. 35; Acts ii. 27, and iii. 14.

3. He offered himself a sacrifice to God, Eph. v. 2.

4. He is set over the house of God, Heb. iii. 6.

All those things whereby this apostle describeth a priest, chap. v. 1, do most properly belong to Christ; for,

1. A priest is *taken from among men.* Christ also himself likewise took part of the same flesh and blood whereof other men are partakers. See Sec. 139.

2. A true priest is *ordained.* Christ also 'glorified not himself to be made an high priest;' but his Father glorified him in that respect, Heb. v. 5, he ordained him.

3. A priest is *for men.* What Christ undertook he undertook for us. See Sec. 83.

4. A priest is *in things pertaining to God.* Thus much is expressly affirmed of Christ in this verse: He is 'a priest in things pertaining to God.' He is the one mediator between God and men, 1 Tim. ii. 5.

5. A priest *offereth up sacrifices.* 'Wherefore, it is of necessity that Christ have somewhat also to offer,' Heb. viii. 3. 'He hath given himself for us an offering, and a sacrifice to God for a sweet-smelling savour,' Eph. v. 2. A priest offereth for sins. Christ 'by himself purged our sins.' See Chap. i. Sec. 28.

By all these it appeareth that Christ is a true priest. Thus was he foretold to be, Ps. cx. 4, Zech. vi. 13. Thus is he very oft testified to be in this epistle.

In that he is said to be a true priest, this epithet *true* is not here opposed to false and deceitful, but to typical and metaphorical priests. He is a priest indeed; such an one as really, in truth and deed, effecteth all that is to be done by a priest.

All the priests under the law were typical, even types of Christ: that is, such as could not themselves perform indeed what was typified by them, as to make atonement, to take away sin, to satisfy justice, to pacify wrath, to reconcile to God, to make persons and services acceptable to God, &c.; yet they shew that there was a priest to come that could and would indeed perform all that belonged to a priest. This was Jesus Christ.

All called priests in the New Testament are but metaphorical, priests by way of resemblance, because they do such like offices as priests did, and offer such things to God as were like to sacrifices. Their offices are to approach to the throne of grace, to pray for themselves and others, to offer gifts and services to God.

Of Christians' particular sacrifices, see Sec. 175.

In this respect it was thus foretold concerning Christians, 'Ye shall be named the priests of the Lord,' Isa. lxi. 6; 'I will take of them for priests and for Levites, saith the Lord,' Isa. lxvi. 21. And in the New Testament it is said, Christ 'hath made us priests unto God,' Rev. i. 6, and v. 10; yea, Christians are said to be 'an holy priesthood,' 'a royal priesthood,' 1 Peter ii. 5, 9.

Christ and Christ alone was a true priest, in that all things requisite for a true priest were found to be in him, and in him alone; for he was both God and man, and, as God-man in one person, he was our priest.

All those things which concern a priest may be drawn to two heads: 1, matters of ministry; 2, matters of dignity.

1. In regard of ministry, a true priest must,

(1.) Obey and fulfil the law. Christ thus saith of himself, 'It becometh us to fulfil all righteousness,' Mat. iii. 15.

(2.) Be subject to infirmities, Heb. iv. 15.

(3.) Suffer, Heb. v. 8.

(4.) Die, ver. 9, 10.

(5.) Be made a curse, Gal. iii. 13.

These and other things like to them, Christ could not have done and endured except he had been a creature, even a man.

---

[1] כהן, *Minister, in politicis princeps.*
[2] *Minister in sacris, Sacerdos.*
[3] *Sacerdos,* a sacris dandis seu offerendis.
[4] προϊστώς, *seu,* προστάτης, *priest.*

2. In regard of dignity, a true priest must be,
(1.) Of divine dignity, to be worthy to appear before God.
(2.) Of almighty power, to bear the infinite burden of sin, to endure the curse of the law, to overcome death, devil, and hell.
(3.) Of infinite merit, to purchase, by what he did and endured, divine favour and heavenly glory.

No mere creature was capable of these requisites.

3. Finally, a true priest must be a mediator betwixt God and man. He must be fit and able to appear before God, Heb. viii. 1; and such an one as men may appear before him, Heb. iv. 15, 16. In this respect an hypostatical union of the divine and human nature in one person was requisite for a true priest. This could none be but Jesus Christ, God-man, Immanuel, God manifested in the flesh, 1 Tim. iii. 16. By virtue of this union, Christ himself was all in all. As man, he was a fit sacrifice: 'He gave himself an offering and a sacrifice,' Eph. v. 2. As God, he was the altar that sanctified that sacrifice; for 'the altar sanctifieth the gift,' Mat. xxiii. 19. As God-man in one person, he was the priest that offered that sacrifice upon that altar: 'Through the eternal Spirit he offered himself,' Heb. ix. 14.

Herein the sufficiency of Christ's priesthood is evidenced, in that each nature did what was proper to it.[1] By the human nature, all matters of service and suffering were done and endured; by the divine nature, all matters that required divine authority and dignity were performed. From the union of those two natures in one person, the accomplishment (ἀποτέλεσμα), consummation, and perfection of all arose.

See more hereof Chap. ix. 14, Sec. 78.

Sec. 173. *Of Christ an high and great priest.*

As Christ was a true priest, so he is here styled by the apostle 'an high priest.' In Greek these two words are compounded in one, ἀρχιερεὺς, which, word for word, we may translate *arch-priest*, as archangel, ἀρχάγγελος, 1 Thes. iv. 16, Jude 9; arch-shepherd, or chief shepherd, ἀρχιποίμην, 1 Peter v. 4; arch-builder, ἀρχιτέκτων, or master-builder, 1 Cor. iii. 10; arch-publican, or chief publican, ἀρχιτελώνης, Luke xix. 2. In the Hebrew, the phrase translated *high priest* is great priest, הכהן הגדול, Lev. xxi. 10. And the same person translated in English *chief priest*, is in Hebrew head priest, כהן הראש, 2 Kings xxv. 18.

Aaron was the first that had this title given unto him, Lev. xvi. 3; and the eldest son of the family of Aaron was successively to be high priest, after the death of the former high priest, Exod. xxix. 29, 30.

There were sundry duties and dignities proper to the high priest for the time being; as,

[1] Agit utraque forma in Christo cum communione alterius, quod utriusque proprium est; Verbo operante quod Verbi est, et carno exequente quod carnis est.—*Leo. Epist.* x. *ad Flavian.*

1. To enter into the most holy place, Lev. xvi. 3.
2. To appear before God for the people, Exod. xxviii. 29.
3. To bear the sins of the people, Exod. xxviii. 38.
4. To offer incense, Lev. xvi. 12, 13.
5. To make atonement, Lev. xvi. 32.
6. To judge of uncleanness, Lev. xiii. 2.
7. To determine controversies, Deut. xvii. 8, 12.
8. To bless the people, Num. vi. 23.

Christ is styled high priest,

1. For excellency's sake, to shew that he was the chiefest and most excellent of all.
2. To demonstrate that he was the truth, whom Aaron and other high priests typified.
3. To assure us that all those things which were enjoined to Aaron as high priest, were really in their truth performed by Christ. For,
1. Christ entered into the true holy place, which is heaven, Heb. ix. 24.
2. Christ truly appeareth before God for us, Heb. ix. 24.
3. Christ hath borne all the sins of all the elect, 2 Cor. v. 21.
4. Christ's intercession is the true incense which makes things that are pleasing and acceptable to God to be so accepted for us, Eph. i. 6.
5. By Christ we have received the atonement, Rom. v. 11.
6. Christ purgeth our sins, Heb. i. 3.
7. Christ is the supreme judge and determiner of all controversies.

Christ is also called 'a great high priest,' Heb. iv. 14, to add emphasis unto this excellency. Never was there, never can there be, any like to him in dignity and excellency. Nor Aaron, nor any other, had both these titles, *great*, *high*, given unto them. Though an *high priest* under the law were in Hebrew styled a *great priest*, Num. xxxv. 24, 28, yet never was any called *great high priest* but Christ only. He indeed was great in his person, being God-man; great in his sacrifice, being an human nature united to the divine; great in the works that he did, and continueth to do, all of them carrying a divine value and efficacy.

By the way, note the intolerable arrogancy of antichrist, that man of sin, who takes to himself this style, *pontifex maximus, the greatest high priest!* two degrees higher than that which is attributed to Christ.

Sec. 174. *Of the excellency and benefits of Christ's priesthood.*

These two titles, *high*, *great*, applied to Christ as priest, do imply that he was a most excellent priest. Those titles simply taken, import an excellency. In reference to others, comparatively taken, they import a super-excellency above all others. Never was there, nor never can there be, such an excellent priesthood as Christ's was, which the apostle in this epistle proveth by sundry evidences.

1. The dignity of his person. Christ was not only a son of man, but also the Son of God. Other priests were mere sons of men, Heb. vii. 28.

2. The purity of his nature. Christ was 'holy, harmless, undefiled, separate from sinners;' all other priests were sinners, Heb. vii. 26, 27.

3. The eminency of his order. Christ was 'a priest after the order of Melchisedec,' Heb. v. 6. None so but he.

4. The solemnity of his ordination. Christ was made priest with a sacred oath; others without an oath, Heb. vii. 20, 21.

5. The kind of his priesthood. Christ was a true, real priest; others only typical, or metaphorical. See Sec. 172.

6. The unchangeableness of his office. Christ's priesthood was unchangeable; others' office passed from one to another, Heb. vii. 23, 24.

7. The everlastingness of his priesthood. Christ 'abideth a priest continually;' others were 'not suffered to continue by reason of death,' Heb. vii. 3, 23, 24.

8. The perfection of Christ's priesthood. Christ by his priesthood effected to the uttermost what was to be effected by a priest. But the priesthood under the law made nothing perfect, Heb. vii. 11, 25.

These excellencies are every one expressly noted by this apostle, and shall be more distinctly and largely handled in their several places.

So excellent a priesthood as Christ's is cannot but bring many benefits to Christ's church. For,

1. It is necessary that the church have a priest to be for it in things appertaining unto God; and that by reason of the infinite disparity and disproportion that is betwixt God and man. Hereof see *The Whole Armour of God*, on Eph. vi. 18, treat. iii. part ii. sec. 62.

2. It is also necessary that Christ be the priest of the church; and that by reason of that infinite dignity, authority, power, and worth which belongs to that priest. Hereof see Sec. 172.

All the benefits that flow from Christ's office and passive obedience, from his death and sacrifice, from his burial and resurrection, from his ascension and intercession, are fruits and effects of his priesthood. For as our priest he subjected himself to the service and curse of the law: he offered up himself a sacrifice; he was buried, and rose from the dead; he entered into heaven, and there maketh continual intercession for us.

Particular benefits of Christ's priesthood are these that follow.

1. Satisfaction of divine justice. For Christ as our priest and surety, standing in our room, in our stead, and for us, satisfied divine justice. Without this satisfaction no mercy could be obtained, but through this satisfaction way is made for all needful mercy. In this respect, it is said, that 'God is just, and a justifier of him which believeth in Jesus,' Rom. iii. 28.

To justify a sinner is a work of great mercy, yet therein is God just, because he doth it upon satisfaction.

2. Pacification of God's wrath. Offence of justice incensed God's wrath; satisfaction of justice pacifieth the same. When Phinehas had executed justice on Zimri and Cozbi, God said, 'Phinehas hath turned my wrath away,' Num. xxv. 11. If upon man's execution of just judgment upon delinquents, which is but one part of satisfaction, God's wrath was turned away, much more will it be pacified by that full satisfaction which the Son of God hath made. In this respect Christ is said to be 'the propitiation for our sins,' 1 John ii. 2, that is, the means of pacifying God's wrath; and we are said to be 'saved from wrath through Christ,' Rom. v. 9, and to be 'delivered from wrath,' 1 Thess. i. 10. This did Christ as priest, as is evident by the types under the law. For by legal priests God's wrath is said to be pacified, Num. xvi. 46-48.

3. Pronouncing[1] God's favour. This follows necessarily upon pacifying wrath, as upon removing of darkness light followeth. God 'reserveth not wrath, because mercy pleaseth him,' Micah vii. 18. So as the brightness of mercy dispelleth the cloud of wrath. That Christ procureth mercy and favour for man, is evident by this style which God giveth him, 'This is my beloved Son, in whom I am well pleased,' Mat. iii. 17. God hereby setteth forth Christ to be such an object of his good pleasure, as he is well pleased with every one whom he beholds in Christ. That Christ procureth favour, as he is a priest, is evident by this inference upon Christ's priesthood : 'Let us therefore come boldly unto the throne of grace, that we may obtain mercy,' Heb. iv. 16. Christ as a priest is God's favourite and our advocate, 1 John ii. 1.

4. Redemption out of that miserable estate whereunto man by sin had plunged himself. This followeth upon the former points: for divine justice being satisfied, wrath pacified, and favour procured, Christ once vanquished the devil. Satan could not stand against Christ, nor could the power of hell hold such as Christ redeemed. Though this be a private benefit, yet if we well weigh the malicious and mischievous disposition of the devil, that held us in bondage, and the miserable condition in which we lay, we may soon discern how great a benefit it is. That redemption is wrought by Christ, is expressly set down, Eph. i. 7; and that it is a fruit of his priesthood is evident by this phrase, 'Christ by his own blood entered in once into the holy place, having obtained eternal redemption for us,' Heb. ix. 12.

5. Access to the throne of grace. The infinite disparity betwixt God and man manifesteth this to be a great prerogative, and the rich treasure of all good

---

[1] Qu. 'Procuring?'—ED.

things tending to life and happiness, which is to be found at the throne of grace, manifesteth this to be an unspeakable benefit. That we have access to the throne of grace by Christ, is evident by this phrase, 'Through Christ we have access unto the Father,' Eph. iii. 18. That this is by virtue of Christ's priesthood, is evident by this phrase, 'Seeing we have a great high priest, let us come boldly unto the throne of grace,' Heb. iv. 14, 16.

6. Reconciliation with God. This the apostle sets down as a fruit of Christ's priesthood in this very verse. Whereof see more, Sec. 180.

7. Justification. This also is a very great benefit, that wretched vile sinners should be justified in his sight, who is of perfect and infinite purity. This cannot be by any righteousness of our own. For 'in God's sight no man living can be justified,' Ps. cxlvii. 2. It must needs, therefore, be by the righteousness of another, and that other can be none but Jesus Christ; by the faith of Jesus Christ we are justified, Gal. ii. 16. This was done by Christ's undertaking to be *for us*, which is the office of a priest. Under this head, reconciliation, adoption, and other like Christian prerogatives are comprised.

8. Sanctification. This must needs be a great benefit, because it is a renovation of God's image in us, Eph. iv. 24. That this is by Christ is evident, in that Christ is made unto us sanctification, 1 Cor. i. 30. That this is by virtue of Christ's priesthood is evident, in that it ariseth from the death and resurrection of Christ, Rom. vi. 5, 6, which are the effects of Christ's priesthood.

9. Eternal salvation. This is the end of all the rest, without which they are of no use. This, therefore, must needs be a great benefit. That this cometh by Christ is evident by his name *Jesus*, Mat. i. 21. That this is an effect of Christ's priesthood, is evident by this inference, Christ 'hath an unchangeable priesthood,' wherefore 'he is able also to save them to the uttermost,' &c., Heb. vii. 24, 25.

Sec. 175. *Of duties arising from Christ's priesthood.*

Such an office, so excellent, so needful, so useful to us, as Christ's priesthood is, cannot but require much duty from us. By virtue thereof, Christ gave himself for us. Do not we then owe ourselves, and all that we have, and all that we can do, to Christ? But in special we ought so to account of Christ, and so to use him, as the Jews did their high priests.

1. Negatively, they might not 'curse the ruler of their people,' Exod. xxii. 28. Thereby was meant their high priest, for so it is applied, Acts xxiii. 4, 5. Under this negative is comprised an high esteem and honourable mention of their priest. Much more must we so respect Christ.

2. In matters of controversy, they were to go unto the priests, and do according to the sentence which the priest should give, Deut. xvii. 8, 9. Christ declareth his sentence by his written word; to that therefore must we stand.

2. In case of uncleanness the Jews went to the priest to judge thereof, and to be cleansed therefrom, Lev. xiii. 2, &c. It is the blood of Christ. that cleanseth from all spiritual uncleanness, 1 John i. 7. Go to Christ therefore to be cleansed.

4. The Jews brought all their oblations and sacrifices unto their priests, Lev. v. 8, 12, 16, 18. We must do all in the name of Christ, Col. iii. 17. That general is exemplified in the particulars following:

(1.) Miracles were done in the name of Christ, Mark xvi. 17.

(2.) Baptism was administered in his name, Acts ii. 38. So the Lord's supper.

(3.) Christians assembled together in the name of Christ, 1 Cor. v. 4.

(4.) They executed ecclesiastical censures in the name of Christ, 2 Thess. iii. 6, 12.

(5.) They prayed in the name of Christ, John xiv. 13, and xvi. 23.

(6.) They gave thanks in his name, Eph. v. 20, Heb. xiii. 15.

(7.) All things wherein we have to do with God are to be done in the name of Christ, Heb. v. 1.

(8.) All other lawful things, as eating, drinking, doing the works of our calling, exercising works of justice, works of mercy, and all lawful works, are to be in the name of Christ, Col. iii. 17.

5. Christ by his priesthood hath made us priests, Rev. i. 6. We therefore must offer such sacrifices unto God as are warranted in God's word. Particulars are these:

(1.) Our bodies, Rom. xii. 1.

(2.) Our hearts, Prov. xxiii. 26, especially broken hearts, Ps. li. 17.

(3.) Prayers, Ps. l. 13, 15, and cxli. 2.

(4.) Praises, Hosea xiv. 2, Heb. xiii. 15.

(5.) Fruits of righteousness, Ps. iv. 5, Micah vi. 8.

(6.) Our riches, Prov. iii. 9. These are made sacrifices,

[1.] By benevolence to the poor, Heb. xiii. 16.

[2.] By relieving ministers, Philip. iv. 18.

(7.) Our lives, Philip. ii. 17.

(8.) Such as are under our charge, Josh. xxiv. 15.

Sec. 176. *Of Christ's mercifulness.*

There are two properties attributed to Christ as high priest.

1. Merciful.
2. Faithful.

The former of those properties is so set down as it may be referred either to the person or to the office of Christ. As referred to his person, it may be thus translated: 'That he might be merciful, and a faithful high priest.' Thus these two adjuncts are referred unto two subjects, *merciful* to the person of Christ, *faithful* to his office. As referred to his office, it may be thus translated : 'That he might be a merciful and faithful high priest.' Thus the two adjuncts are referred to one subject, which is the office of Christ. Both references do in general tend to the same scope, yet I suppose the latter to be more pertinent, because it is the main scope of the apostle in this verse to shew how fit a high priest Christ was. Now mercifulness tendeth much to the fitness of a high priest. Of the high priest under the law it is said, ' He can have compassion,' Heb. v. 2.

The word ἐλεήμων, translated *merciful*, is derived from a root ἔλεος, that signifieth *mercy* or *pity*. Now the proper object of mercy is misery; thereupon a word derived from the same root, ἐλεεινὸς, signifieth *miserable*, Rev. iii. 17. The verb derived from the same word is oft used by such as were in misery and sought mercy of Christ; as the blind men who said unto him ἐλέησον ἡμᾶς, ' Have mercy on us,' Mat. ix. 27. The Hebrew word רחם, which is oft translated *mercy*, signifieth also *bowels*, for mercy ariseth from the moving of the bowels at the sight of misery. To have compassion, or mercy, is frequently set out by a word, σπλαγχνίζεσθαι, that signifieth to have the bowels moved, as Mat. ix. 36, Luke x. 33, and xv. 20. Yea, these two words, bowels and mercy, are oft joined together, as thus, εἴ τινα σπλάγχνα καὶ οἰκτιρμοί, ' If any bowels and mercies,' Philip ii. 1; and thus, σπλάγχνα οἰκτιρμοῦ, ' bowels and mercies,' Col. iii. 12. A like phrase, σπλάγχνα ἐλέους, is translated ' tender mercy,' Luke i. 78.

This I have noted about the word, to shew that Christ was much moved at man's misery, and thereupon greatly pitied him, and took all occasions to afford him all needful succour. The history of his life registered by the evangelist gives abundant proof hereof : he was moved with compassion at their bodily diseases, Mat. xv. 32 ; and at their spiritual distresses, Mat. ix. 36.

That he might be thus moved, he subjected himself to the infirmities and distresses whereunto other children of men were subject. This is evident by the apostle's manner of bringing in this property, thus, ' that he might be merciful.'

Upon this inference two doubts arise :

1. Whether Christ as God were not merciful.
2. Whether Christ as man had not been merciful, though he had not been subject to human infirmities and distresses.

To the first I answer, that neither mercy nor any other like property is attributed to God properly as a passion, but tropically, and that to demonstrate that the effects of such affections do come from him. Men that have bowels of compassion in them, and are truly and thoroughly affected with the miseries of others, will be ready to afford them what help they can. Even so, because the Lord is ready to succour such as are in misery, he is said to be merciful, full of compassion, and to have bowels of mercy. See more hereof in *The Saints' Sacrifice*, on Ps. cxvi. 5, Sec. 29.

To the second I answer, that Christ as man would questionless have been merciful, though he had not been subject to human frailties and miseries. The very union of the human nature with the divine would have moved him to have shewed mercy to such as were in misery; yet it cannot be denied but that the experience which he had of man's miseries moved him as he was man to be the more pitiful. They who have been pained with the gout, stone, or other tormenting maladies, use to pity others that are so pained, and that more, for the most part, than they who never felt any such pain.

Besides, this inference may be made in reference to our apprehension and persuasion of his mercifulness, as if it had been said, we could not have been persuaded that he would have been sensible of our miseries, and thereupon merciful to us, if he had not been made like unto us in all things.

That which is noted of Christ's mercifulness in reference to his priesthood, is a ground of much encouragement for us in all our needs to have recourse unto him. This property is oft applied unto God for this very end, Joel ii. 13, Ps. lxxxvi. 15, and cxvi. 5. This was a motive which the servants of an earthly king pressed upon their master, to seek favour and grace of another king : ' We have heard,' say they, ' that the kings of the house of Israel are merciful kings,' 1 Kings xx. 31. This assuredly was the cause that moved all of all sorts who were any way afflicted and distressed with diseases and other maladies, to come to Christ, and to bring their friends to him while he lived on earth. They observed him to be merciful and full of compassion ; and this is often noted to be the ground of his succouring those that were afflicted. When he saw a widow following her only son to the grave and weeping, he had compassion on her, and thereupon raised her son to life, Luke vii. 13, 14. We need not be discouraged from going unto Christ, by reason of our apprehension of our own unworthiness and wretchedness. The more deeply we are affected therewith, the more will our merciful high priest pity us, and be ready to afford all reasonable succour unto us. Such he invites to come unto him, and to such he promiseth aid. Consider what persons he entertained in the days of his flesh, even such as the proud priests and pharisees scorned and loathed, as Mary, ' out of whom went seven devils,' Luke viii. 2 ; and her that was counted and called a sinner, Luke vii. 39, &c. ; and Levi and Zaccheus, and other publicans, Mat. ix. 10, Luke xix. 5.

This inference, ' He was made like unto his brethren, that he might be merciful,' sheweth that Christ every way endeavoured even to persuade us of his mercifulness. He would have been as merciful as he was, though he had had no experience of our frailties in himself ; but we should not have been so well persuaded thereof, and thereupon not so readily have gone to him.

Where the mind is not persuaded of one's goodness, hardly will he seek help of him.

This doth much amplify Christ's indulgency and tender respect to us; he hath an eye not only upon our wretchedness, which makes us stand in need of mercy, but also upon our weakness, which makes us backward in seeking help of him. Christ, therefore, having provided help for us, is desirous that we should partake of the benefit thereof. For this end he caused the holes that were made in his side, hands, and feet when he was crucified, to be open in his glorified body, to persuade his disciples of the truth of his resurrection, whereupon 'he shewed his disciples his hands and his feet,' Luke xxiv. 40; and to Thomas, who at first believed not that he was risen, he said, 'Reach hither thy finger, and behold my hands, and reach hither thy hand, and thrust it into my side, and be not faithless but believing,' John xx. 27. For this end he did also eat and drink with his disciples after his resurrection, Luke xxiv. 43, Acts x. 41. For this end he hath added unto his word, sacraments; all these are to move us readily to fly to him and perfectly to rest upon him.

Sec. 177. *Of Christ's faithfulness.*

This epithet is here expressly applied to Christ's priesthood, thus, 'a faithful high priest.'

The Greek word πίστις, from whence this epithet πιστὸς is derived, signifieth *faith*. According to this notation, the word here translated *faithful* signifieth a believer, or one that professeth the true faith, as Eph. i. 1, 1 Tim. i. 12; in this sense it is opposed to an unbeliever or an infidel, 2 Cor. vi. 15.

As this word *faithful* is put for a special property, it is taken two ways.

1. Passively; so it setteth forth a thing or a person to be believed or trusted. In this sense it is attributed to the word, or to a sentence and saying which is most certain and sure, and thereupon to be believed: 'This is a faithful saying,' saith the apostle, 1 Tim. i. 15, 'and worthy of all acceptation.' This latter clause sheweth in what respect the word *faithful* is used. So also God is called faithful, because he is to be trusted in for the accomplishment of what he undertaketh, 1 Cor. i. 9, 2 Thes. iii. 3.

2. Actively, and that in reference to words or deeds.

To words, when one performeth what he hath promised.

To deeds, when one accomplisheth what he undertaketh.

In both these respects it is attributed to God, Heb. x. 23, 1 Thes. v. 24. Most usually it is attributed to such as well discharge that trust which is committed to them. In this respect, they who well employed and improved their talents are styled faithful, Mat. xxv. 21, 23.

Thus it is attributed to wives, 1 Tim. iii. 11; to children, Titus i. 6; to servants, Mat. xxiv. 4, 5; to a steward, Luke xii. 42; to a minister, Col. iv. 7; to a witness, Rev. i. 5; to a martyr, Rev. iv. 9; Silvanus, 1 Peter v. 12; Antipas, Rev. ii. 13.

In all the fore-mentioned respects, this epithet *faithful* may be applied to Christ. For,

1. He was the head of the church, and the chief professor of the faith, Eph. v. 23, 1 Tim. vi. 13, and in that respect may be accounted a believer, πιστὸς.

2. He was most worthy to be believed, for he was the 'faithful and true witness, Rev. iii. 14.

3. He might safely be trusted to, for he was a sure rock: 'He that believeth on him shall not be confounded,' 1 Peter ii. 6.

4. He performed whatsoever he promised: 'There was no guile found in his mouth,' 1 Peter ii. 22. 'He is faithful that promiseth,' Heb. x. 23.

5. He accomplished whatever he undertook, Heb. iii. 2, John xix. 28, 30.

6. He subjected himself to be a Son of man, John i. 51; to be a servant, Philip. ii. 7; to be a steward, Heb. iii. 2; to be a minister, Rom. xv. 8; to be a witness, Rev. iii. 14; to be a martyr, for he sealed up the truth of God with his blood, 1 Tim. iii. 16. In all these relations was Christ faithful, and in particular in that which is here noted in the text, 'he was a faithful high priest.'

In the function of his priesthood he was faithful,

1. To God, who appointed him to be a priest.
2. To his brethren, for whose sake he was a priest.

He was faithful to God and man,

(1.) In the matter or thing enjoined to him, which he accomplished to the full in all points.

(2.) In the manner of doing it, according to the mind of him that appointed him, and for the best advantage to them for whom he was appointed.

(3.) In the continuance, he finished all that was appointed to him, John xvii. 4.

His faithfulness to God was manifested in these particulars:

[1.] He did by himself what he was entrusted withal: 'He offered himself,' Heb. ix. 14. He himself was the priest and sacrifice; he entrusted no other. He himself declared his Father, John ii. 18.

[2.] He held close to the will of him that appointed him, Heb. iii. 2. He did nothing of himself, John v. 30. He so ordered all as he might best please and honour his Father, John vii. 16–18, and xvii. 4.

[3.] He neither withheld nor concealed anything that by his Father's appointment he was to do or believe, Ps. xl. 9, 10.

[4.] He ceased not to do his work till all was finished; for thus he professeth of himself, 'I have finished the work which thou gavest me to do,' John xvii. 4.

His faithfulness to man was manifested in these particulars.

[1.] In his word he was a 'faithful witness,' Rev. i. 5. All the promises of God in him are 'yea, and in him amen,' 2 Cor. i. 20. They are all propounded, ratified, and performed in him.

[2.] In deed, and that in these respects.

First, In performing what he did for their good: 'I will lay down my life for the sheep,' saith he, John x. 15.

Secondly, In doing all that was needful for them, he 'saves them to the uttermost,' Heb. vii. 25.

Thirdly, In continuing his intercession till he bring them into the holy places, Heb. ix. 28, and x. 12, &c.

As the former attribute applied to Christ, *merciful*, was a ground of encouragement to fly to Christ; so this, *faithful*, to rely upon him, and perfectly to trust on him. We safely commit our souls to him as unto 'a faithful high priest.' They who refuse to rely on him, much dishonour him, as if he were not faithful, and they deprive themselves of many great benefits that otherwise they might receive from him. Let us, therefore, duly weigh and often meditate on this excellent property of Christ, that he is a faithful high priest, that so our faith may be more strengthened and established on him.

Sec. 178. *Of Christ's mercifulness and faithfulness meeting together.*

These two attributes, *merciful, faithful*, are joined together by this copulative *and*, which sheweth that he who was merciful in regard of his inward disposition, and thereupon had compassion on those who were in misery, was also faithful in succouring such as he pitied. He did not love in word, neither in tongue only, but in deed and truth, 1 John iii. 18. He did not say to such as he pitied, 'Depart in peace, be you warmed and filled,' but he *gave* them those things that are needful for them; he was merciful and faithful; his mercifulness was the ground of his faithfulness, and his faithfulness was an evidence of his mercifulness. As there was a readiness in him to will by reason of his mercifulness, so there was a performance also out of that which he had, according to the advice of the apostle, 2 Cor. viii. 11, by reason of his faithfulness. This is plainly set forth in the parable of the Samaritan, who doth lively set forth Christ himself: that Samaritan saw a man stripped of his raiment, wounded, and left half dead, thereupon he had compassion on him; this shewed him to be merciful. Upon this he went to him, and bound up his wounds, pouring in oil and wine, and took further care of him; this shewed him to be faithful, Luke x. 30, &c. What Christ said to the lawyer, to whom he spake his parable, may be said to every of us, 'Go, and do likewise,' Luke x. 37.

Sec. 179. *Of things pertaining unto God.*

The object whereabout Christ's priesthood was exercised is said to be 'things pertaining to God,' that is, wherein he had to do with God for man. In all the services of his office and calling as a priest he had to do with God, and that for man, Heb. v. 1. In which respect he is reputed a mediator between God and man.

Those things may be drawn to two heads:

1. The things wherein God had to do with his people, namely, in making known God's mind and will to them. This he did in God's name, so as he stood in God's room therein. So he pronounced pardon of sin unto them in God's name, and blessed them in God's name, Num. vi. 23.

2. The things wherein the people had to do with God. All their services which they performed to God, and sacrifices which they offered up unto God, were to be tendered to God by a priest, Lev. v. 8, &c. Of those particular services and sacrifices, see Sec. 175.

There was an absolute necessity of a priest to be for man in things appertaining unto God, upon these reasons:

1. The infinite disparity which is between God and man. God is of infinite glory and majesty, and dwells in that light that no man can approach unto, 1 Tim. vi. 16. Man is but dust and ashes, Gen. xviii. 27.

2. The direct enmity and disposition that is between God and man, Rom. v. 10, Col. i. 21.

3. The plain contrariety in condition between God and man, God being most pure and holy, man most polluted and unholy.

Obj. How was it, then, that mere men were priests in things pertaining unto God?

Ans. The priests under the law were not *properly*, but only *typically*, in things pertaining unto God.

They entered not into the glorious presence of God, but only into the holy place made with hands, which was a representation thereof. They did not properly present the prayers of people to God, but only were a type of him that did it. The sacrifices which they offered up did not properly take away sin, but were types of that sacrifice which did it. The truth of all the things wherein those priests had to do with God were accomplished in Christ, who, though he were a true man, yet was he not a mere man, but God also, and so became a man fit to be in things pertaining to God. Christ, therefore, alone, is that true high priest that is for man in things pertaining to God.

Hence we may observe,

1. That there is no immediate access for man to God without a priest.

2. That there is no priest that can be properly for man in things pertaining unto God but Jesus Christ, God-man. None could pacify God's wrath, none could satisfy his justice, none could procure his favour, none could purge away sin, none could bring sinners into God's presence, but Christ.

Oh how miserable are they who are without a priest; they can have nothing to do with God; they still remain enemies to him, as contrary as light and darkness, life and death, and God still remains a consuming fire to them. Such also are they who have not a true priest, for that is all one as to have no priest at all.

Learn we hereby how to come to God, not barely and simply in ourselves (so we go to a consuming fire), but through Jesus Christ.

Of doing all wherein we have to do with God, in the name of Christ, see Sec. 175.

Sec. 180. *Of reconciliation made by Christ.*

The most principal end of Christ's priesthood is thus expressed : ' To make reconciliation for the sins of the people.' The Greek word ἱλάσκεσθαι, translated ' to make reconciliation for,' hath reference sometimes to the party offended, and signifieth to be propitious or merciful in pardoning the offence, as where the penitent publican thus said to God, ἱλάσθητι, ' Be merciful unto me a sinner,' Luke xviii. 13 ; sometimes to the thing which giveth the offence. Then it signifieth to expiate, or to make satisfaction for, and that so as the party offended be pacified thereby. Thus it is here taken, and it importeth as much as this phrase, ' He purged our sins,' Heb. i. 3. To this purpose also tendeth our English translation of this word in this text, ' to make reconciliation for sins ;' that is, to use such means as may pacify God, against whom sins are committed, and thereby reconcile God and sinners.

From the Greek verb used in this text two nouns are derived, both which are translated propitiation, and applied to Christ. One, ἱλασμός, 1 John ii. 2, and iv. 10 ; the other, ἱλαστήριον, Rom iii. 25.

Propitiation is a pacification and appeasing of one offended.

The latter of those two words is attributed to the cover of the ark, and translated ' mercy-seat,' Heb. iv. 5 ; for God did use there to appear in mercy, grace, and favour, as a God pacified, and pardoning sin. A like word is attributed by the Greek LXX to that ram which was offered up for reconciliation, and styled κριός ἱλασμοῦ, the ram of atonement, Num. v. 8. There is also an adjective, ἴλεως (*attica inflexio*), derived from the foresaid verb, and translated *merciful*, Heb. viii. 12.

Of the Hebrew word which importeth as much as this Greek word doth, see *The Plaster for a Plague*, on Num. xvi. 46, sec. 25 ; and of Atonement with God, see ibid., sec. 33.

Under this act of reconciliation, which is here made an end of Christ's priesthood, are comprised all the benefits thereof, for all tended to this. This act, end, and benefit of Christ's priesthood was typified under the law by that legal reconciliation which was made by the priest, whereof mention is made Lev. vi. 30, and viii. 15, 2 Chron. ix. 24. All the places that make mention of atonement made by the priest for any give further proof hereof. Reconciliation and atonement do signify one and the same thing. If priests under the law did make a legal reconciliation and atonement, much more doth Christ, the true priest, make a true and real reconciliation betwixt God and man. It is therefore said that ' when we were enemies, we were reconciled to God by the death of his Son,' Rom. v. 10. And again, ' You that were alienated now hath he reconciled,' Col. i. 21.

This reconciliation is a re-uniting of persons at odds. It hath relation to a double estate, one precedent, the other subsequent.

The precedent importeth two things.

1. A primary mutual amity ; 2. A breach of that amity.

The subsequent estate is a making up of that breach, and uniting again of those who were disunited. All these may be exemplified in the case betwixt David and Absalom. David entirely loved Absalom ; but Absalom, by the murder which he committed on his brother, provoked his father against himself, and thereupon fled from him ; yet, by the mediation of Joab, Absalom was again brought into favour with his father, 2 Sam. xiv. 33 ; even thus stands the case between God and man.

For effecting reconciliation under the law, priests did two things.

1. They offered a sacrifice, Lev. xvi. 11, 2 Chron. xxix. 23, 24.

2. They offered incense, Lev. xvi. 12, 13, Num. xvi. 46. In both these they were types of Christ.

1. Their sacrifices typified the sacrifice of Christ, Heb. x. 5, &c.

2. Their incense typified the intercession of Christ; for as the priests offered incense after their sacrifice, so Christ, after he had offered himself a sacrifice for our sins, maketh continual intercession for us, Heb. x. 12.

Of Christ's intercession typified by incense, see *The Plaster for the Plague*, on Num. xvi. 46, Sec. 38.

Christ offered up but one sacrifice, and that but once, Heb. vii. 27, and x. 10 ; for it was every way so perfect, as there needed no other to be added to it, nor that to be reiterated.

Christ's intercession is continual and perpetual, Heb. vii. 25, and x. 12 ; for thereby the merit and virtue of Christ's sacrifice is from time to time continually applied to God's people, who stand in continual need thereof.

The fore-mentioned reconciliation is amplified by that which is taken away thereby, even *sins*. In that it is said that Christ maketh reconciliation for sins, the meaning is, that, by appeasing God's wrath, he hath freed us from the guilt and punishment of sin. Hereby is intended as much as was comprised under this phrase, ' purged our sins.' See Chap. i. Sec. 28.

Sec. 181. *Of the people for whom reconciliation is made.*

The persons for whom Christ is here said to make

reconciliation are thus expressed, 'The people,' τοῦ λαοῦ.[1]

By *people* are here meant the whole number of God's elect, for whom God hath entered into a new covenant in and with Christ, of whom God saith, 'Thou art my people,' Hos. ii. 23; these are styled 'the people;'—

1. In allusion to the custom of priests under the law, who made an atonement for the people, Num. xvi. 47.

2. By way of exclusion, to shew that the reconciliation was not for his own sins, but for the sins of others, which are styled the people. Herein Christ, the true high priest, differed from the high priest under the law, 'who made atonement for himself and for the people,' Lev. xvi. 24; but Christ for the people alone.

3. For limitation's sake, to shew that Christ made not reconciliation for all and every man, but only for such as may be comprised under this word 'the people,' which is restrained by this relative *his*, 'his people,' Mat. i. 21.

Some here restrain this title *the people* to the nation of the Jews, but that is directly contrary to the end of Christ's coming, which was to reconcile both Jews and Gentiles unto God: 'For he is our peace, who hath made both one, and hath broken down the middle wall of partition between us,' Eph. ii. 14.

I will not deny but that the Jews may typically be put for the number of the elect, and so they comprised under this word. They only who are chosen out of the world and given to Christ, are the people here intended. Thus this phrase setteth forth the same persons that were set forth by these phrases, 'the seed of Abraham,' ver. 16; 'children,' ver. 14; 'brethren,' ver. 12. Of restraining the benefit of what Christ did and suffered to the elect, see Secs. 81, 113, 133, 162.

Sec. 182. *Of Christ's suffering being tempted.*

Ver. 18. *For in that he himself hath suffered, being tempted, he is able to succour them that are tempted.*

This causal particle, γὰρ, *for*, sheweth that this verse is added as a reason of that which went before. It hath reference to the qualification which made Christ a fit high priest. That was a conformity to his brethren. For he is said to be 'in all things made like to his brethren,' not only in nature, but also in infirmities and sufferings, and in all manner of trials and temptations.

Now if a reason be demanded why Christ should this way be qualified to his priesthood, a direct answer is given in this verse; namely, because thereby he might better succour such as are tempted.

The proposition is set down in this verse, thus: He that suffered being tempted, is able to succour them that are tempted.

[1] Of the notation of this word, see Chap. iv. 9, Sec. 157.

The assumption may be raised out of the former verse, thus: But Christ being in all things made like unto his brethren, suffered, being tempted.

Therefore, Christ, in all things being like his brethren, was able to succour them that are tempted.

This phrase, ἐν ᾧ, 'in that,' hath especial reference to this word 'suffered.' It was not simply this that he was tempted, that made him able to succour; for God himself may be tempted, Num. xiv. 22. And man may be so tempted as to be very little or nothing at all moved therewith. But such temptations as make one suffer, do so work on him, as he is thereby put on to pity others that are so tempted, and to succour them in what he can.

Here then is set out the extent and extremity of Christ's temptations. They were such as made him suffer.

This leadeth us to consider both the kinds and also the degrees of Christ's temptations.

Of tempting in general, and of persons tempting and tempted, see *The Guide to go to God*, or *The Explanation of the Lord's Prayer*, on Petit. vi., sec. 170.

The verb here used, πειρασθείς, is of the passive voice, and setteth out such temptations as Christ was assaulted withal. Of the distinct kinds of those temptations, see Sec. 96.

Here we will further consider how, πέπονθεν, he suffered under them.

1. Being led by the Spirit into the wilderness, he there continued forty days fasting, and was thereupon an hungered, Mat. iv. 1, 2. Hunger is a suffering, so also is wearisomeness, and other like infirmities, under which Christ suffered.

2. Satan, in tempting him, hurried him from the wilderness to a pinnacle of the temple, from thence into an exceeding high mountain, Mat. iv. 5, 8. This must also needs be a suffering; besides, Satan's temptations so troubled him, as they forced him to say, 'Get thee hence, Satan,' Mat. iv. 10.

3. The temptations of the pharisees, and others like to them, made him angry; and they grieved him, Mark iii. 5.

4. Peter's tempting him made him say unto him, 'Get thee behind me, Satan; thou art an offence unto me,' Mat. xvi. 23.

5. All his sufferings in his body were effects of his adversaries tempting him. Of those sufferings, see Sec. 96.

6. His greatest sufferings were upon his Father's tempting, proving, and trying him. These made him complain and say, 'Now is my soul troubled,' &c., John xii. 27. And again, 'My soul is exceeding sorrowful, even unto death:' and thus to pray, 'O my Father, if it be possible, let this cup pass from me,' Mat. xxvi. 38, 39. These cast him into an agony, and made his sweat as it were great drops of blood fall down to the ground, Luke xxii. 44. These made

him cry out upon the cross, 'My God, my God, why hast thou forsaken me?' Mat. xxvii. 46. These made him 'offer up prayers and supplications with strong crying and tears,' Heb. v. 7.

On these grounds might the apostle well say that 'he suffered being tempted.' Never any upon any temptation suffered more.

It is observable that the apostle addeth this reciprocal relative, αὐτὸς, *himself;* which sheweth that that which he suffered was not by a sympathy in reference to others' sufferings, but he suffered all those things in his own person. He 'his *own self* bare our sins in his *own* body,' &c., 1 Peter ii. 24; and this was it which made him the more to sympathise with the sufferings of others, and to be the more ready to succour them in their sufferings.

The ends of Christ being made like unto his brethren, set down, Sec. 171, may in particular be applied to the point in hand, of his sufferings being tempted.

By Christ's sufferings being tempted,

1. He comes to have experience of our sufferings in like cases, in that he hath felt the weight of them himself.

2. In his own experience he knows the danger whereunto we are subject by such temptations.

3. By his suffering he hath pulled out the sting of those temptations; so as we, though we be assaulted, shall not be vanquished thereby.

4. He hath made himself a pattern to direct us how to stand against such temptations. For he did not withstand them by his divine power, but answered them with scriptures and reasons, and such like weapons as he hath put into our hands to resist temptations withal.

Sec. 183. *Of Christ's being able by suffering to succour.*

One especial end or effect of Christ's temptations, and sufferings thereby, is thus expressed: 'He is able to succour them that are tempted.' This, in general, shews that his temptations and sufferings were for our good. Our good was one special end of all that Christ, as Mediator, did and endured. See Sec. 83.

The word δύναται, translated, 'he is able,' in this place implieth a fitness and readiness to do a thing. Where it is said of the unjust steward, 'Thou mayest, (δυνήσῃ), be no longer steward,' Luke xvi. 2, it is intended, that he was not fit to continue in that office. The same Greek verb is used in that place and this.

1. Christ, by suffering being tempted, experimentally discerned unto what sufferings others being tempted might be brought.

2. The bowels of his compassion were thereby the more moved towards others in like cases.

3. He better observed how comfortable succour would be in such cases.

4. He perceived thereby what kind of succour was most seasonable in such and such temptations.

In these and other like respects is Christ said to be 'able to succour them that are tempted.'

Sec. 184. *Of Christ's readiness to succour.*

The word, βοηθῆσαι, translated 'to succour,' is in the Greek very emphatical, and pertinent to the point in hand. According to the notation[1] of it, it signifieth, to run to the cry of one. It is used by such as being in great distress cried for succour, as Mat. xv. 25, Mark ix. 22, yea, by such as were in spiritual distress, Acts xvi. 9. The Jews which thought their temple to be profaned by such as Paul brought, 'cried out and said, Men of Israel, help,' Acts xxi. 28. The word translated *help*, is the same that here in this text is used, and it implieth that they should run and speedily come to succour. The name of God in Greek[2] is said to have the notation from this, that he useth to run, that is, speedily to afford succour to such as are in distress. The Greek word applied to God, and translated *helper*, βοηθός, is derived from the word in my text, Heb. xiii. 6.

This notation of the word sheweth, that that sense and experience which Christ had of suffering being tempted, makes him exceeding forward to succour those that suffer in a like case. If he hear any complain and cry out of their sufferings, he presently runs and makes haste to succour them. That help which God affordeth to such as come to the throne of grace, is expressed under a word, βοήθεια, derived from the same root, Heb. iv. 16.

So violent are many temptations, so weak is man of himself, and so unable to resist them, or to stand under them, as Christ is moved to run to succour him, as tender parents will run to succour their helpless child in distress or danger. When Peter was ready to sink, and cried, 'Lord, save me,' immediately Jesus stretched forth his hand and caught him, Mat. xiv. 30, 31.

Sec. 185. *Of the temptations whereunto men are subject.*

The persons whom Christ is so ready to succour, are thus set down, πειραζομένοις, 'them that are tempted.' The same verb, though in a different form, is here used, that was before in this verse applied to Christ, and intended especially to those who are styled his brethren, ver. 17.

These are tempted as Christ himself was,

1. By God, to prove them, as Abraham was, Gen. xxii. 1; or to manifest that grace which God hath bestowed on them, as Job was, Job i. 7; or to discover corruptions in them, as Hezekiah was, 2 Chron. xxxii. 31.

2. By Satan, and that always, to sin, 2 Cor. xi. 3.

---

[1] βοηθεῖν, πρὸς βοὴν θεῖν.   [2] Θεὸς, i. e. ἐπὶ βοὴν θέων.

3. By good men, upon a mistake of doing good, Acts xxi. 12.

4. By evil ones, as Joseph was tempted by his mistress, Gen. xxxix. 7.

5. By a man's own self, James i. 14. A man tempts himself sometimes by overmuch confidence and boldness, Mat. xiv. 28, 29; and sometimes by too much diffidence, Gal. ii. 12.

By this kind of tempting a man's self, Christ was never tempted.

Christ's succour here spoken of is to be extended to all manner of temptations, even to such as bring men to sin. For Christ succoured them in pardoning their sin, and in pulling them out of the snares of sin, wherewith they are entangled.

Sec. 186. *Of experience of suffering causing succour to others that suffer.*

This effect following upon Christ's suffering being tempted, namely, that he is fit and ready to succour others that are tempted, giveth evidence of an especial benefit of God's providence in suffering both his only begotten Son, and also his adopted children, to be so far tempted as to suffer thereby. By this means they are brought to afford mutual succour one to another in like case. Thus saith the apostle, 'God comforteth us in all our tribulations, that we may be able to comfort them which are in any trouble, by the comfort wherewith we ourselves are comforted of God,' 2 Cor. i. 4. The Lord, to stir up the Israelites to succour strangers, rendereth this reason, 'Ye know the heart of a stranger: seeing ye were strangers in the land of Egypt,' Exod. xxiii. 9; a like reason is rendered of shewing mercy to servants, Deut. v. 15. It is found by experience that child-bearing women are more pitiful to others in their travails than such women as are barren. The like may be said of such as are afflicted with any painful malady. Much more humanity useth to be shewed in the city to such as are visited with the plague than in the country, because in the city more use to be infected therewith. They who are themselves afflicted better know that others who, being so afflicted, complain and seek succour, have cause so to do. But they who are never afflicted, think that they who complain, complain more than is need. This was the case of Job's friends. In a natural body, when one member hath been wounded or bruised, though it be healed, yet the smart of a wound or bruise will soonest come to it.

1. From hence it appears that it is expedient that ministers of God's word be men of like passions with others, as the apostles say of themselves, Acts xiv. 15, that so they may more commiserate others. If ministers themselves had never been in a natural estate, but always entire, they could not so pity others, as now they do. The like may be said of magistrates, and of all that have power and authority over others.

2. God's wisdom is herein manifested, in that he suffers flesh to remain in the best, that thereby they may be moved the more to bear with others. David having fallen, pressed this as a motive to be restored: 'Then,' saith he, 'will I teach transgressors thy ways,' Ps. li. 13. Christ suffered Satan to sift Peter, that when he was converted he might 'strengthen his brethren, Luke xxii. 31, 32. This is a good use which saints may make of their slips.

3. Oh how great is the inhumanity of such as having tasted of misery, and being delivered from the same, are hard-hearted to those that fall into the like misery and refuse to succour them; yea, rather deal hardly with them, and add to their affliction. This was it which Nehemiah upbraided to the Jews after their return from captivity, Neh. v. 7, &c. The like doth Jeremiah while the Jews were besieged, Jer. xxxiv. 13, &c. The like may be upbraided to such as have power among us, in commonwealth, church, or family.

4. For our parts, as God by his providence hath made us able and fit to succour others, let us herein shew ourselves like unto Christ; let us open our bowels to such as are in distresses. Note Gal. vi. 1, Titus iii. 3. Let all of all sorts, magistrates, ministers, masters, rich men, old men, men in health, and such as have been tempted or afflicted, learn to succour others.

See more hereof, Chap. v. 2, Sec. 9.

Sec. 187. *Of the resolution of* Heb. ii. 17, 18.

Ver. 17. *Wherefore in all things it behoved him to be made like to his brethren, that he might be a merciful and faithful high priest, in things pertaining to God, to make reconciliation for the sins of the people.*

Ver. 18. *For in that he himself hath suffered, being tempted, he is able to succour them that are tempted.*

The sum of these two verses is a description of Christ's priesthood.

Herein observe, 1, the inference, 2, the substance.

The inference intends a reason of Christ's taking upon him man's nature, which is, that he might be a fit priest. This is,

1. Generally propounded in this particle of inference, *wherefore*.

2. Particularly exemplified.

In the exemplification is a declaration of Christ's human nature. About which are noted,

1. The evidence thereof, 'made like to his brethren.' Here observe,

1. A resemblance, *made like*.

2. The parties resembled.

(1.) Christ himself.

(2.) His brethren.

2. The extent of that evidence, *in all things*.

3. The ground of it, *it behoved*.

About the substance of the description of Christ's priesthood, observe,

1. An expression of the kind of office, *high priest*.

2. An amplification thereof by two properties, *merciful, faithful*.

3. An addition of the ends, which are two.
One hath a reference to God, ver. 17.
The other to man, ver. 18.
That which hath reference to God is, 1, generally propounded, *in things pertaining to God*; 2, particularly exemplified.

In that particular there is set down,
1. The principal work of an high priest, *to make reconciliation*.
2. The subject matter for which reconciliation is made, *for sins*.
3. The persons who reap the benefit of that reconciliation, *the people*.

Ver. 18. The other end of Christ's priesthood, which hath reference to man, is added as a reason of the extent of Christ's conformity to man. See Sec. 182.

Here is set down, 1, the ground of that reason; 2, the kind of it.

The ground was suffering. This is set out,
1. By the patient that suffered, *himself*.
2. By the cause of his suffering, *being tempted*.

The kind of that end was *to succour*.
This is amplified,
1. By the motive, *he is able*.
2. By the persons succoured, *them that are tempted*.

Sec. 188. *Of the doctrines raised out of* Heb. ii. 17, 18.

I. *Christ conformed himself to what he undertook.* He 'took on him the seed of Abraham,' wherefore he was made like his brethren.

II. *There was a necessity of Christ's being man.* 'It behoved him.' See Sec. 166.

III. *Christ was such a man as others.* 'He was made like.' See Sec. 168.

IV. *Christ assumed the common nature of man for the elect's sake.* These are the 'brethren' to whom Christ is made like. See Sec. 167.

V. *Christ in all things was like man.* Not only in man's nature, but in infirmities, in temptations and afflictions. See Sec. 169.

VI. *Christ is a true priest.* VII. *Christ is an high priest.* These two doctrines are expressly set down. See Secs. 172, 173.

VIII. *Christ is merciful.* See Sec. 176.

IX. *Christ was faithful in what he undertook.* He was a faithful high priest. See Sec. 177.

X. *Christ was man that he might be a fit priest.* This end is expressly set down. See Sec. 172.

XI. *Christ is for man in the things wherein man hath to do with God.* See Sec. 179.

XII. *Christ our high priest hath made reconciliation with God.* See Sec. 180.

XIII. *By the reconciliation which Christ hath wrought, sin is taken away.* See Sec. 180.

XIV. *Reconciliation made by Christ is for a peculiar people.* See Sec. 181.

XV. *Christ was subject to temptations.* See Sec. 182.

XVI. *Christ himself suffered under his temptations.* See Sec. 182.

XVII. *Men are subject to be tempted.* See Sec. 185.

XVIII. *Christ is ready to succour such as are tempted.* See Sec. 184.

XIX. *Christ's suffering made him more ready to succour others in their sufferings.* See Sec. 186.

XX. *Temptations make men stand in need of succour.* See Sec. 184.

Hebrews 3

Sec. 1. *Of the resolution of the third chapter.*

The apostle having distinctly set out the divine nature of Christ, and with it his royal function, in the first chapter, and his human nature in the second chapter, in which he exercised his three great offices of king, priest, and prophet, whereof he gave a touch in the seven last verses of the former chapter; he further setteth forth Christ's prophetical function in this third chapter, and in thirteen verses of the fourth chapter.

In this chapter is, 1, laid down the main point, that Christ was an apostle and a priest.

2. An exemplification of Christ's prophetical office. Of the exemplification there are two parts:

1. A declaration of Christ's faithfulness in executing his office, verses 2–6.

2. A dissuasion from disrespecting that office of Christ, verse 7, &c., to the end of this chapter.

Christ's faithfulness is illustrated by a comparison, and that two ways:
1. By way of similitude.
2. By way of dissimilitude.

Both the similitude and dissimilitude are betwixt the same persons, namely, Christ and Moses.

1. In regard of similitude, Christ was 'faithful as Moses,' verse 2.

2. In regard of dissimilitude, Christ was 'more excellent than Moses.'

The dissimilitude is exemplified in two pair of relations:

One is betwixt a *builder* and a *house built*,
The argument thus lieth:

A builder of a house is more excellent than any part of the house built;

But Christ is the builder, and Moses a part of the house;

Therefore Christ is more excellent than Moses.

The proposition is in the 3d verse; the assumption in the 4th.

The other pair of relations is betwixt a *son* (who is the Lord) and a *servant*.

This argument thus lieth:

The son, who is lord, is more excellent than any servant;

But Christ is the Son and Lord, and Moses a servant;

Therefore Christ is more excellent than Moses.

The proposition is in the 6th verse; the assumption in the 5th.

By way of prevention, that the Jews might not be puffed up with this conceit, that they are the only house of God, the apostle gave a general description of Christ's house, which he extendeth to all believers, verse 6.

The dissuasion from disrespecting Christ is,

1. Generally propounded in a divine testimony, from the beginning of the 7th to the 12th verse.

2. Particularly applied, from the beginning of verse 12 to the end of the chapter.

In the divine testimony is expressed,

1. The author thereof, *The Holy Ghost*, ver. 7.
2. The matter, which containeth two branches:
(1.) A duty implied, *If you will hear his voice*, ver. 7.
(2.) A vice forbidden; that is,
[1.] Expressed, *harden not your hearts*, ver. 8.
[2.] Exemplified.

In the exemplification are declared,

1. The persons who committed the vice, *your fathers*, ver. 9; and the place where it is committed, *in the wilderness*; and the time, how long, *forty years*, ver. 9.

2. The consequence that followed thereupon. This is twofold:

1. A grieving of God: *I was grieved*, saith the Lord.
2. Incensing his wrath: *I sware in my wrath*, ver. 11. This latter is aggravated by a fearful effect, *They shall not enter into my rest*, ver. 11.

In the application of the said divine testimony, there is,

1. A direction for the right use thereof.
2. An exposition of sundry passages in it.

Of the direction there are two parts:

1. An admonition to take heed of that vice whereby the foresaid Jews provoked God, ver. 12.
2. An incitation to use an especial means that may keep them from it, which is mutual exhortation, amplified by their continuance therein, daily, &c., ver. 13.

Both the parts of the direction are enforced by the benefit of observing them, ver. 14.

The exposition of the foresaid divine testimony is continued from the beginning of the 15th verse of this chapter to the 14th verse of the 4th chapter.

The passages of that testimony expounded are three: two in this chapter, as,

1. The time expressed under this word, *to-day*, ver. 15.
2. The persons therein intended. These are set down,

1. Negatively, by way of exemption, *some, not all*, ver. 16.
2. Affirmatively, by way of determination, who they were.

That more distinct notice might be taken of them, the apostle sets them down by a dialogism, wherein two questions are propounded, and direct answers made unto them.

Quest. 1. *With whom was God grieved?* To this such an answer is made, as specifieth both the cause of grieving God, *they that sinned;* and the effect that followed thereon, whereby it was manifest they had grieved God, *Their carcases fell in the wilderness*, ver. 17.

Quest. 2. *To whom sware he*, &c. This is answered, by declaring the particular sin that incensed God's wrath, *They believed not*, &c., ver. 18.

On this last resolution the apostle maketh an express conclusion, *So we see*, &c., ver. 19.

The third point propounded is *rest*, in the next chapter.

Sec. 2. *Of regarding what Christ hath done for us.*

Ver. 1. *Wherefore, holy brethren, partakers of the heavenly calling, consider the Apostle and High Priest of our profession, Christ Jesus.*

The apostle having set forth the two natures of Christ, his divine and human, and withal his excellency above all creatures by virtue of his divine nature; and the benefits that redound to us by his exercising of his three great offices in his human nature, here he teacheth to make an especial use of all; which use is intended in these two words, *wherefore, consider.*

This use he doth so artificially frame, as he maketh the setting down of it a fit transition betwixt the second and third chapter.

The transition is a perfect transition; for it looketh both ways, to that which went before (so it sheweth the use that we must make thereof), and to that which followeth. So it layeth down the groundwork of those exhortations which follow: that groundwork is this, 'Christ Jesus is the Apostle and High Priest of our profession.'

The Greek particle ὅθεν, translated 'wherefore,' is the very same that was used chap. ii. ver. 17. Thereof see more, Chap. ii. Sec. 166. It was shewed, Chap. ii. Sec. 2, that the excellency of the teacher requires the greater heed in hearers; but this inference further sheweth, that the lower any condescendeth for our good, and the greater the benefits be that redound to us thereby, the more we ought to observe those things that are made known concerning him. Who could descend lower than the Son of God, by subjecting himself to death for us? All that Christ did and endured was for us, even for our good, see Chap. ii. Sec. 83, *wherefore* we ought to consider him. This argument Moses useth to stir up the Israelites to attend to God and his law: 'The Lord shall open unto thee his good treasure,' Deut. xxviii. 12. So doth the wise man, Prov. iv. 1, 2. Nature itself putteth on everything to seek its own good.[1]

In regard of us Christians, as prudence on our own behalf in helping on our own good requires as much, so gratefulness towards Christ. Shall the Son of God descend so low as he did, and endure so much as he did, and all for our sake, and we not regard it? 'Do ye thus requite the Lord, O foolish people?' Deut. xxxii. 6.

This is a great aggravation of Christians' neglect of the duty, implied under this note of reference, *wherefore*. The Levites herewith aggravated the sins of the Jews, and justified God's heavy judgments against them, in that God 'gave them right judgments, true laws, and good statutes;' yea, also his 'good Spirit to instruct them,' and yet they regarded him not.

Let us for our part take due notice of all that Christ hath done and suffered for us, to be thoroughly affected therewith, and to make a right use of all.

Sec. 3. *Of brethren in reference to saints.*

The apostle, to work the more upon these Hebrews, manifesteth both his entire affection to them (by styling them *brethren*), and also his good opinion of them, by calling them *holy*, and *partakers of the heavenly calling.*

Of the divers acceptation of this title *brethren*, see Chap. iii. 1, Sec. 3.

Some[2] take the word *brethren* in this place to be used in relation to saints of Christ, as it is used, chap. ii. ver. 11, 12. But that reference cannot well here stand. The word useth to be some note of restriction, when this reference is used in relation to Christ, as 'the brethren of the Lord,' 1 Cor. ix. 5, or 'his brethren,' Acts i. 14, or Christ himself is brought in so calling them, as chap. ii. ver. 11, 12.

When a mere man speaks to others, and calls them brethren, this relation is to be taken betwixt him that speaketh, and them to whom he speaketh. Thus this title here hath relation betwixt the apostle and those to whom he wrote.

Because they were Hebrews, to whom in special this epistle was directed, it may be supposed that the apostle useth this title in reference to that common stock whence he and the Hebrews came, as where he saith, 'Brethren, children of the stock of Abraham,' Acts xiii. 26; and ' my brethren, my kinsmen according to the flesh,' Rom. ix. 3. But this attribute *holy* will not well admit that restriction; for most of the Jews were, through their unbelief, cut off from the holy root.

All the Jews are not to be wholly exempted; such as remained not in unbelief are here intended, as well as Gentiles.

This title *brethren*, in this place, is to be taken in a spiritual sense, and that in reference to a mutual profession of the same faith. Thus it is taken ver. 12, and chap. x. ver. 19, and chap. xiii. ver. 22, and in other epistles of the apostles for the most part.

In this sense all Christians, of what stock or degree soever they be, whether Jews or Gentiles, great or mean, male or female, free or bond, magistrate or subject, minister or people; all sorts of Christians are knit together by a common mutual bond.

They 'all have one Father,' Mal. ii. 10, Eph. iv. 4.

One mother, the church; for they are 'born again by the word of God,' which is proper to the church, 1 Peter i. 23.

One elder brother, who is 'the first-born amongst many brethren,' Rom. viii. 29.

One and the same privileges, Eph. iv. 4–6.

They are all one in Christ, Gal. iii. 28.

One and the same inheritance belongeth to them all, 1 Peter i. 4, and iii. 7.

In these and other like respects they are also styled members of the same body, 1 Cor. xii. 12. And branches of the same vine, John xv. 5. See more hereof, Sec. 17.

1. God hath thus nearly linked them together, to shew that he is no respecter of persons; therefore that title which the Grecians use to give to an only Son ($\dot{\alpha}\gamma\alpha\pi\eta\tau\acute{o}\varsigma$), is given to them all in reference to God, Eph. v. 1. Hereof see Sec. 17.

2. Hereby is shewed that Christians should live in love amongst themselves, 1 Peter iii. 8; and maintain peace, Gen. xiii. 8; and be of the same mind and affection, 1 Cor. i. 10; and ready to help and succour one another, Exod. xvii. 11; and carry themselves as equals one to another, Rom. xii. 16. Not swelling one against another, 2 Cor. xii. 20. In a word, all kind of Christian duties are much enforced by the relation of *brethren*.

Sec. 4. *Of this title of insinuation, brethren.*

The apostle here inserteth this title *brethren*, to manifest his own mind and affection to them; for hereby he professeth himself to be a brother to them, of the same father and mother, of the same household, a co-heir with them, and withal affectioned as a brother toward them, yea, and to be as one of their equals. See Chap. x. 19, Sec. 52.

This he doth to insinuate his own soul more kindly into theirs, to sweeten his exhortations and admonitions, to enforce them the more, to shew that what he doth he doth in love for their good. To other churches he doth somewhat more enlarge his heart

---

[1] Omnia bonum appetunt. —*Ethic.* lib. i. cap. i.
[2] Junius in sacris Paral. lib. iii. in Heb. iii. 1.

even in this kind, as Rom. xii. 1, 1 Cor. i. 10, Gal. iv. 12, 19, Philip. iv. 1.

Herein the apostle makes himself a pattern to ministers, masters, tutors, and all others that are in place to instruct, direct, incite, or restrain others; they may by this pattern learn how to work upon those with whom they have to do; affection is rather to be shewed than authority: 'Though I might be much bold in Christ to enjoin thee that which is convenient, yet for love's sake I rather beseech thee,' saith the apostle to Philemon, vers. 9, 10.

I deny not but that authority and severity at some times, in some cases, to some persons, is to be used: 'Rebuke with all authority,' Titus ii. 15; 'I will not spare,' 2 Cor. xiii. 2. But if mildness, gentleness, and kindness may prevail, use these rather.

Of that modesty and humility which is couched under this title *brethren*, see *The Whole Armour of God* on Eph. vi. 10, sec. 30.

Of Christ not ashamed to call men *brethren*, see Chap. ii. Secs. 107, 108. Of sweetening jealousies and other bitter pills herewith, see Sec. 121 of this chapter; see also Chap. vi. 9, Sec. 54.

Sec. 5. *Of this epithet 'holy;' to whom and to what it is attributed.*

The epithet, ἅγιος,[1] which the apostle here gives to the brethren, *holy*, is an high and honourable title. It is elsewhere in like manner given to others, as 1 Thes. v. 27, 'All the holy brethren.'

The most excellent that are have this title *holy* attributed unto them, as God himself, Rev. vi. 10; Father, John xxvii. 11; Son and Spirit, Luke i. 35; and the excellentest of his creatures, both persons, and things, and those above and below.[2]

1. Above; the heavens, Heb. ix. 12; the angels, Mark viii. 38; and glorified men, 1 Thes. iii. 13, are called holy.

2. Below; professors of the true faith, Col. iii. 12; whether single persons, male, Mark vi. 20; and female, 1 Peter iii. 5; and children born of such, 1 Cor. vii. 14, or the whole society and communion of them. These are called 'an holy priesthood,' 'an holy nation,' 1 Peter ii. 5, 9, 'an holy temple.' More eminently they who are of extraordinary functions in the church, as apostles and prophets, are called holy, Rev. xviii. 20.

3. The privileges and gifts that God bestoweth on his church are also called holy: as 'holy Scriptures,' Rom. i. 2; 'holy law,' holy commandments,' Rom. vii. 12; 'holy covenant,' Luke i. 72; 'holy calling,' 2 Tim. i. 9; 'holy faith,' Jude ver. 20; 'holy conversation,' 2 Peter iii. 11. And the parts of men's bodies used in devotion, as 'holy hands,' 1 Tim. ii. 8; and Christians' mutual salutations, as 'an holy kiss,' Rom. xvi. 16.

4. Sundry places were so called, as Jerusalem, Mat. iv. 5, 'the holy city,' because it was a type of the church, and of the kingdom of heaven, and because the temple wherein God was worshipped was there; and 'the holy mount,' 2 Peter i. 18, where Christ was transfigured; and the place where God in special manifested his presence was called holy ground, Acts vii. 33.

The Hebrew word קדוש, *sanctus*, which is translated *holy* in the Old Testament, is applied to the temple and to the several parts and courts thereof, and to all the persons and things appertaining thereto, as priests, Levites, altars, sacrifices, incense, oil, water, vestments, all manner of utensils, ordinances, and other things which were for sacred uses.

When the Greek word used in the text is set alone as a substantive, and not as an adjective joined with another, it is translated *saint*, 'salute every saint,' ταυτα ἅγιων; thus, for the most part, it is translated in the plural number, ἅγιοι, 'saints,' which is all one as 'holy ones.'

Sec. 6. *Of the causes of men's being holy, and of calling them so.*

This excellent prerogative of being holy cannot arise from men's selves. 'Who can bring a clean thing out of an unclean? Not one,' Job xiv. 4. The stock whence all men sprout was most impure and unholy; but 'every good and every perfect gift is from above, and cometh down from the Father of lights,' James i. 17. This Father of lights communicateth holiness to sons of men two ways.

1. By imputing unto them the righteousness of his Son. Thus we are said to be 'made the righteousness of God in Christ,' 2 Cor. v. 21, and Christ is said to be 'made of God righteousness unto us, 1 Cor. i. 30.

2. By conveying his Spirit into us, who altereth our nature and disposition, and enableth us to perform the works of righteousness. In this respect he is not only called 'the Holy Ghost,' of which phrase see more, ver. 7, but also 'the Spirit of holiness,' Rom. i. 4, because he worketh holiness in us; and sanctification is said to be 'of the Spirit,' 2 Thes. ii. 13, because it is wrought in us by the Spirit of God.

Thus, this excellent title *holy* gives no matter of boasting unto man; for 'What hast thou that thou didst not receive? Now, if thou didst receive it, why dost thou glory as if thou hadst not received it?' 2 Cor. iv. 7. But it giveth just and great cause of glorying in God, of giving all praise to God for it, and of using this divine property to the glory of his name.

The apostle here giveth these Hebrews this title, not so much in regard of their parentage, because the

---

[1] Of the derivation and notation of this Greek word, see Chap. ii. Sec. 100.

[2] The heathen, in regard of that esteem which they had of their gods, styled them 'the holy gods,' Dan. iv. 8, 9.

root from whence they sprouted was holy, Rom xi. 16. For the partition wall betwixt Jew and Gentile was now broken down, and all that were of the faith of Abraham were counted to be of Abraham's seed, Gal. iii. 7. In this respect, all that were born of parents professing the faith were counted holy, 1 Cor. vii. 14.

The apostle therefore here gives them this title,

1. In regard of their profession, whereby they were distinguished from profane persons.

2. In regard of his opinion of them; for he judged them to be true members of the holy church, as he did of those to whom he said, 'Ye are washed, ye are sanctified, ye are justified, in the name of the Lord Jesus, and by the Spirit of our God,' 1 Cor. vi. 11. Thus he usually styleth all to whom he wrote, ἅγιοι, 'saints,' that is, holy ones.

Ques. How did the apostle know that they were holy?

Ans. By their holy profession; for the ground of judging others is not certainty of knowledge, but the rule of love, which 'believeth all things and hopeth all things,' 1 Cor. xiii. 7, that is, the best that may be believed, or hoped of them. Thus, another apostle termeth those to whom he wrote, *elect*, 1 Peter i. 2, yet election is one of God's secrets.

Besides, he giveth this title indefinitely, so as they that are truly holy might apply it to themselves. For a sermon may be preached, or a letter written to a whole assembly, without manifesting any difference betwixt person and person, when that which is preached or written is specially intended to those who in truth are such as they profess themselves to be.

This is not to 'justify the wicked,' for that is 'an abomination,' Prov. xvii. 15. And a woe is denounced against them that 'call evil good,' Isa. v. 20. When matters are apparent, judgment must answerably be given. Love makes not men blind. When men are plainly discerned to be unholy, to call them holy is not to think or speak the best, but the worst. But when we see nothing to the contrary, then are we to judge the best of professors. It is better to judge an hypocrite upright (if we know him not to be an hypocrite) than an upright man an hypocrite. For we may well judge otherwise than the truth is, so we judge not otherwise than love requireth.

How contrary to this apostolical practice is the censure of many in this age; who, on this ground, that men are careful to keep a good conscience, and fearful to commit the least sin, judge them to be dissembling hypocrites. Profession of sincerity makes many to be more vilely thought of.

More diametrically opposite to the rule of love is their censure, who, on every occasion, are ready to call such as are not of their mind damned reprobates. Christ saith, 'With what judgment ye judge, ye shall be judged,' Mat. vii. 2. What judgment then can such look for?

Sec. 7. *Of the excellency, utility, and necessity of being holy.*

The apostle could not have given unto them a more excellent attribute than this, *holy*. For,

1. There is nothing wherein a creature can be more like to his Creator, than in being holy. It is said that God at first 'created man in his own image,' Gen. i. 27. This image of God the apostle expoundeth to be holiness, Eph. iv. 24. It is the greatest excellency that can be conferred on a creature, to be after the image of his Creator; that is, like unto him.

2. Nothing so fits us for glory as holiness. Not riches, for they profit not in the day of wrath, Prov. xi. 4. The rich man when he died went to hell, Luke xvi. 23. Not dignity, nor power, for 'the kings of the earth, and the great men, and the chief captains' desired to be 'hid from the wrath of the Lamb,' Rev. vi. 15, 16. Not worldly policy. Ahithophel was so eminent in policy, as 'his counsel was as if a man had inquired at the oracle of God,' 2 Sam. vi. 23, yet he hanged himself, 2 Sam. xvii. 23. Not immunity from death; for many wicked men shall be living at the moment of Christ's coming to judgment, and thereupon shall not die, 1 Cor. xv. 51. Not the resurrection of the body; for there is a 'resurrection of damnation,' John v. 29. Not immortality; for the devils are immortal. Not anything at all without holiness; 'without which no man shall see the Lord,' Heb. xii. 14.

3. Nothing makes such a difference betwixt persons as holiness and unholiness. Herein lay the difference betwixt man in his entire estate, and corrupt estate. Adam, before his fall, and after his fall, had the same soul and body in substance, and the same faculties of one, and parts of the other; but his holiness in soul and body was lost, that made the difference. This makes the difference betwixt the regenerate and unregenerate. Holiness is it which makes the greatest difference betwixt good angels and devils. Devils retain a spiritual and angelical substance. Take holiness from good angels, they will be devils. Add holiness to devils, they will be good angels.

4. Holiness is the greatest glory in heaven. One were better be holy in hell, than unholy in heaven. Holiness would make hell to be no hell; as the fire in which God's three faithful servants were, was to them no fire, Dan. iii. 27; and unholinesss would make heaven to be no heaven.

5. Holiness is the excellency of God's excellencies. They who best know what is God's chiefest excellency, thus double and treble this attribute, 'Holy, holy, holy is the Lord of hosts,' Isa. vi. 3, Rev. iv. 8. Holiness is the excellency of God's eternity, omnipotency, immutability, wisdom, and other divine attributes. Were it possible that holiness could be severed from them, it might be said of them, אי כבד *ubi gloria?* 'Where is the glory?' 1 Sam. iv. 21. Eternity without holiness would be so much the worse; the longer the

worse. So omnipotency, the more mighty, if unholy, the more dangerous; so wisdom without holiness, the more crafty to hurt; so immutability without holiness, the more resolute in mischief. Therefore God is said to be glorious in holiness, Exod. xv. 11. This adds a glory to all his excellencies. That life of God from which the Gentiles are said to be alienated, Eph. iv. 18, is holiness; so as holiness is not only the life of angels, and of others in heaven, but even of God himself. It makes us live as God lives, and work as God works.

As the excellency of holiness is very great, so also is the utility thereof. If it be demanded, What is the profit thereof? we may answer (as the apostle did of circumcision, Rom. iii. 2), 'Much every way.' For this is that godliness which is profitable unto all things, having promise of the life that now is, and of that which is to come, 1 Tim. iv. 8. Promises of temporal and spiritual blessings in this life, promises of freedom from damnation, and of fruition of salvation in the life to come, are appropriated to saints, who are the holy ones here spoken of. These are they of whom the apostle saith, 'Whether the world, or life, or death, or things present, or things to come, all are yours,' 1 Cor. iii. 22.

From the foresaid excellency and utility of holiness, followeth an absolute necessity thereof. It is better for us not to be, than not to be holy. It is as necessary as happiness itself: 'Without holiness no man shall see God,' Heb. xii. 14. They shall neither have any spiritual communion with God here in this world, nor partake of that celestial communion which is called a beatifical vision, which surpasseth all human expression and apprehension. It is such as 'eye hath not seen, nor ear heard, nor ever entered into the heart of man,' 1 Cor. ii. 9.

Sec. 8. *Of God's respect to saints in making them holy.*

That which hath been shewed of the excellency, utility, and necessity of being holy, affordeth an instruction about that good respect which God beareth to his saints. For he makes them partakers thereby of his greatest excellency; yea, even of the excellency of his excellencies. The apostle to this purpose saith, that we are 'partakers of his holiness,' Heb. xii. 10. In this respect they are styled, 'The people of his holiness,' Isa. lxiii. 18. This is more than if he had endued us with his power, or with his wisdom, or with any other like divine attribute. When a king inquired, 'What shall be done unto the man whom the king delighteth to honour?' answer was made, 'Let the royal apparel which the king useth to wear be put on him, and the crown royal be set upon his head,' Esther vi. 7, 8. Holiness is God's royal robe, it is his royal crown. Well therefore may it be said of saints decked with this holiness, Behold the men whom the King of heaven delighteth to honour!

'This honour have all the saints. Praise ye the Lord,' Ps. cxlix. 9.

Sec. 9. *Of the world's perverse esteem of holiness.*

The corrupt and perverse judgment of the men of this world is hereby also manifested, in that they do meanly esteem so excellent a thing as holiness is. They esteem nothing less worth, nothing more base, nothing more vile. Herein they shew themselves like swine, which trample precious pearls under their feet, Mat. vii. 6. The apostle speaking of himself, and other holy brethren, thus sets out the world's account of them: 'We are made a spectacle' (θέατρον, *spectaculum,* a gazing stock) 'unto the world, and to angels, and to men. We are made as the filth of the world, and are the offscourings of all things to this day,' 1 Cor. iv. 9, 13. We need not search after former ages of old time for proof hereof; the very times wherein we live give too evident demonstration hereof. This may seem strange, that so precious a thing as holiness should be so vilified. But if we well weigh the persons that so basely esteem it, we cannot think it strange; in their disposition they are as hogs and dogs. Christ therefore would not have that which is holy given to them. That grave, just, severe censure which the Lord giveth of them, Mat. vii. 6, is enough against this corrupt opinion of the world.

Sec. 10. *Of men's backwardness in seeking after holiness.*

Many that profess the true faith, and have the word of God to be their instructor, may be thought to be better instructed in the worth of spiritual matters than the aforesaid men of the world; yet too many of these are too too backward in seeking after holiness. It is the Lord's charge to 'seek first the kingdom of God and his righteousness,' Mat. vi. 33, to seek holiness before and above all other things; but commonly it is the last thing which men seek after, and with least care and diligence. It is said of manna, that it was ' angels' food,' Ps. lxxviii. 25, so delightsome it was, so wholesome, every way so excellent, that if angels had taken any food, they would have eaten that food; yet the Israelites, after they had some while enjoyed it, accounted it 'light bread,' and 'loathed it,' Num. xxi. 5. Difficulty in obtaining holiness cannot justly be pretended; for an especial means tending thereunto is that word which is 'very nigh unto thee, in thy mouth, and in thy heart, that thou mayest do it,' Deut. xxx. 14. This is the gospel, even 'the word of faith which we preach,' Rom. x. 8, yet how little is this word regarded? I may in this case say, 'Wherefore is there a price in the hand of a fool to get' holiness, ' seeing he hath no heart to use it?' Prov. xvii. 16. Were [men] careful to get holiness, more would be holy than are; and they that are in some measure holy, would be more holy. Many in this case shew what kind of spirit they have, even a fleshly, carnal, sluggish spirit; a spirit that savoureth not the things of God.

Sec. 11. *Of following after holiness.*
We that are well instructed in this excellent property, ought to stir up our spirits, and put forth our strength in following holiness. This doth the apostle intend in this phrase, 'follow holiness,' Heb. xii. 14. The Greek word διώκετε, translated *follow*, signifieth a pursuing of such as fly from one, as hunters and hounds follow the game, if it be possible they will get it. Set such before you, and thus reason with yourselves: Shall instinct of nature stir up unreasonable creatures to put forth their utmost power to get what they have a mind to, and shall not reason much more put us on to get so fair a game as holiness is? Or further, set hunters or runners in a race before you, and thus say to your souls: Shall reason put on natural men to strive in worldly things for the mastery, and shall not religion, grace, spiritual understanding, and a good conscience, put us on to give all diligence for attaining this prize of holiness? 'They do it to obtain a corruptible crown, but we an incorruptible,' 1 Cor. ix. 25.

Sec. 12. *Of directions to be holy.*
That we may be such 'holy brethren' as are here set down.
1. Be well informed in the nature of holiness; for superstition, hypocrisy, yea, and idolatry itself, make pretence of holiness. If the mark be mistaken, the more pains we take and diligence we use, the further we shall be off from it. The faster a traveller goes in a wrong way, the farther he may be from the place to which he desires to go. The Jews, 'being ignorant of God's righteousness, and going about to establish their own righteousness, were farthest off from true holiness. See Sec. 6, of the holiness here meant.
2. 'Cleanse yourselves from all filthiness of the flesh and spirit.' Thus may you 'perfect holiness in the fear of God,' 2 Cor. vii. 1. It is a course which all of all sorts observe for perfecting of a thing, namely, first to remove the impediments: thus physicians purge out peccant humours; chirurgeons draw out festering matter; husbandmen stock up broom, briars, thorns, and all noisome weeds; 'Every man that striveth for the mastery, is temperate in all things,' 1 Cor. ix. 25. In this respect, that which philosophers hold of privation, may prove true, that there must be a privation of one form before there can be an induction of another. This is the constant doctrine of the Scripture: 'Break up your fallow ground, and sow not among thorns,' Jer. iv. 3. 'Wash ye, make you clean, put away the evil of your doings,' Isa. i. 16. 'Put off the old man, which is corrupt, according to the deceitful lusts,' Eph. iv. 22. Except we take this course, all our labour after holiness will be in vain.

3. Have special care of your company. Avoid the society of unholy ones. Associate thyself with holy ones, that in you may be accomplished this proverb, Birds of a feather will fly together. 'Depart from me, you evil doers; for I will keep the commandments of my God,' Ps. cxix. 115. He implies thereby, that while he kept company with them, he could not keep God's commandments: 'All his delight was in the saints,' Ps. xvi. 3. That this means is very powerful, is evident by these proverbs: 'He that walketh with wise men shall be wise,' Prov. xiii. 20; 'With an evil man thou shalt not go, lest thou learn his ways,' Prov. xxii. 24, 25.

4. Be conscionable and constant in using such means as God has sanctified for obtaining holiness; for God will be found in his own way. He communicated grace in and by the means which himself hath ordained for that end. He hath in much wisdom ordered them, and he will not suffer his wisdom to be crossed by man's foolish conceit.

The means are, 1, public; 2, private; 3, secret.
(1.) Public means are the word and sacraments.
By the word, faith and repentance are wrought and increased. In these the two kinds of holiness, justification and sanctification, consist.

By the sacraments, the same graces are ratified and sealed. Circumcision was 'a seal of the righteousness of the faith which Abraham had,' Rom. iv. 11; baptism was also a seal of repentance, Acts ii 38.
(2.) Private means are, reading God's word, Deut. xvii. 19, Acts viii. 28, and xvii. 11; and holy conference, Deut. vi. 7, 1 Thes. v. 11, Luke xxiv. 32.
(3.) Secret means are,
[1.] Examination of one's self, Ps. iv. 4, 1 Cor. xi. 28. By this one may know his spiritual estate.
[2.] Meditation, Ps. i. 2, and cxix. 15, 97. This must be on God's word and works of mercy and judgment, on ourselves and others. This will keep out evil thoughts, and fill our mind with good thoughts.
5. Be instant and constant in prayer, and that for the Holy Spirit, which is promised to those that ask him, Luke xi. 13. This Spirit it is which makes us holy.
6. Be patient under crosses; for God doth chasten his that they might be partakers of his holiness, Heb. xii. 10. See more hereof in that place.

Sec. 13. *Of saints' calling.*
The apostle's good opinion of these Hebrews is further manifested under this phrase, 'partakers of the heavenly calling.'
The original verb, καλεῖν, signifieth to call on by voice. When Christ said to his disciples, 'Follow me,' he called them, ἐκάλεσεν αὐτούς, Mat. iv. 19, 21.
This word *call* is in Scripture used diversely: as,
1. To give a real being to a thing, Rom. iv. 17.
2. To manifest a thing to be as it is, Luke i. 32, 35.

3. To acknowledge one. See Chap. ii. Sec. 107.

4. To give a name to one, whereby he is distinguished from others, Mat. i. 25.

5. To depute to a function; and that both extraordinary, Rom. i. 1, and ordinary, Heb. v. 4: Rom. x. 15, 'How shall they preach except they be sent?' that is, called.

6. To set in a condition or state of life, 1 Cor. vii. 17, 20.

7. To turn one to the true religion, 1 Cor. i. 24. This is the calling here intended.

The Greek word κλῆσις, here translated *calling*, is eleven times used in the New Testament, and only once put for a civil condition of life, 1 Cor. vii. 20. In all the other places it is used in a spiritual sense, and setteth out the alteration of a man's natural condition, which is a translation, or bringing him out of Satan's dominion, unto God's kingdom, 1 Thes. ii. 12.

This an apostle doth thus express: God 'hath called you out of darkness into his marvellous light,' 1 Peter ii. 9. By *darkness* he meaneth that woful and miserable estate wherein by nature men lie under the prince of darkness, in the darkness of error and iniquity, subject to utter darkness. By *light* he meaneth the sweet and comfortable light of grace, and the eternal light of glory.

This is styled a calling, because it is effected by the call of God.

The call of God is twofold:

1. Outward, by the ministry of the word; and that in a double respect:

One on God's part only, in offering the means; as when 'he sent forth his servants to call them that were bidden to the wedding, and they would not come,' Mat. xxii. 3.

The other on man's part also, by an outward yielding to the call; as he that came to the wedding and had not on a wedding garment, Mat. xxii. 11.

In the former respect, all that hear the sound of the gospel are called.

In the latter respect, all hypocrites that live in the church, and profess the faith, are called; as Cain, Ham, Saul, Judas, Demas, Ananias, Sapphira, and sundry others.

2. Inward, by the operation of the Spirit, who inwardly stirs up men's spirits heartily to accept God's gracious invitation, and so to attend to God's word as they do truly and savingly believe. Thus was Lydia called, Acts xvi. 14.

Of this calling, therefore, there are two parts:

1, God's invitation; 2, man's acceptation. 'I call unto them,' saith the Lord; 'they stand up together,' Isa. xlviii. 13.

This is that calling which makes a link of the golden chain that reacheth from predestination to glorification, Rom. viii. 30. These are they who are said to be 'with Christ, being called, and chosen, and faithful,' Rev. xvii. 14.

The outward calling may make men members of a visible church, yet it is an aggravation of their just damnation, Mat. xi. 22, 24.

The inward calling wrought by God's Spirit makes men members of the invisible church, and is the means of their eternal salvation; for 'all things work together for their good,' Rom. viii. 28, &c.

This is the calling here intended, and it is proper and peculiar to such as are indeed 'holy brethren, called to be saints,' Rom. i. 7, 1 Cor. i. 2.

Such were they to whom the apostle said, 'Ye see *your* calling,' 1 Cor. i. 26; 'Make *your* calling sure,' 2 Peter i. 10. These by an excellency are styled κλητοί, 'the called.'

Sec. 14. *Of the causes and effects of saints' calling.*

1. The principal author of the foresaid calling is God, 1 Thes. ii. 12. The Father, in reference to whom this calling is styled 'his calling,' αὐτοῦ, Eph. i. 17, 18; the Son, who came to call sinners, Mat. ix. 13; and the Holy Ghost, who worketh in us the graces whereby we yield to the call, 1 Cor. xii. 2, &c.

2. The procuring cause is God's free grace and rich mercy; for 'he hath called us with an holy calling, not according to our works, but according to his own purpose and grace,' 2 Tim. i. 9. Men before their calling are 'dead in sin,' Eph. ii. 1; and were 'alienated from the life of God,' Eph. iv. 18. If God, of his mere mercy and free grace, did not call them, they would not, they could not, turn to him. Men at their first calling are mere patients.[1] They have not such ears as can hear God's call, nor such eyes as can see the excellency of that calling, nor such feet as can carry them to him that calls, nor such hands as can receive the good things that are offered by that calling. It is God that openeth ears, enlighteneth eyes, and enableth other parts to employ aright their distinct functions toward the effecting of this great work: 'It is God which worketh in you both to will and to do,' Philip. ii. 13. God first puts life into them that are dead, and then affords continual assisting grace for persisting and persevering in that Christian course whereunto they are called.

3. The instrumental causes which God useth for the effecting this great work are ministers of his word. These are those servants whom he sends forth to call men, Mat. xxii. 3. By their preaching of the word both that woful estate wherein men lie by nature is discovered, and also that excellent and blessed estate whereunto they are called is made known. The former is ordinarily done by preaching law, 'whereby is the knowledge of sin,' Rom. iii. 20, and vii. 7. Hence ariseth sight and sense of sin, grief, horror, and despair for the same.

The latter by preaching the gospel, which is 'the

---

[1] The Greek words κλητοί, κεκλημένοι, whereby the called are set out, are passive, and imply that the called are at first patients.

power of God unto salvation to every one that believeth,' Rom. i. 16; yea, 'faith cometh by hearing' the gospel, Rom. x. 17.

4. The highest and chiefest end of saints' calling is the glory of God's grace and mercy: 'God would make known the riches of his glory on the vessels of mercy, even us whom he hath called,' Rom. ix. 23, 24.

The subordinate end is in reference to man, and that to make him partaker of grace here, Gal. i. 6, and of glory hereafter, 1 Peter v. 10.

5. The effects of this calling are faith and repentance, the understanding being enlightened by God's word about the misery of man's natural condition, and happiness of his renewed estate; and the will being, by God's Spirit, made inclinable and ready to receive that good that is made known in the gospel, by faith resteth on Christ for pardon of sin and reconciliation with God, and then sets himself to change his former course of life, by breaking off his former iniquities, and by conforming himself to the image of him that hath called him in holiness and righteousness.

Sec. 15. *Of the heavenly calling.*

The calling of saints is here commended unto us by this attribute ἐπουράνιου, *heavenly*. The Greek word is a compound, and hath reference to the highest heaven, where the throne of God is, and where Christ now is in his human nature.[1] This compound is in the New Testament used eighteen times: six times in this epistle, and everywhere to set forth such things as belong to the highest heavens, or tend thereunto. It is here in this place attributed to saints' calling.

1. To distinguish it from earthly callings. Thus our heavenly Father is distinguished from earthly fathers, Mat. xviii. 35, and heavenly bodies from earthly, 1 Cor. xv. 40.

2. To shew the excellency thereof. For excellent things are called heavenly; great, deep, excellent mysteries are called heavenly, John iii. 12.

3. To declare the end of this calling, which is to bring us to an heavenly kingdom, 1 Thes. ii. 12, namely, an inheritance incorruptible, reserved in heaven, 1 Peter i. 4.

In regard of this excellency, the calling of saints is also called an *high* calling, Philip. iii. 14, and an *holy* calling, 2 Tim. i. 9.

This particular excellency here mentioned by the apostle is of force to enamour our souls the more therewith, and to raise up our hearts unto heaven, seeking the things that are above.

It doth also instruct us how to walk worthy of this calling, namely, by an inward heavenly disposition, and an outward heavenly conversation.

Sec. 16. *Of the privileges of saints' calling.*

This epithet *heavenly* implieth a great privilege of the calling of saints; for it implieth one special end thereof, which is to fit us for heaven. There are also sundry ends noted in other places, which are as so many other privileges, such as these that follow;—

1. Spiritual life. This the apostle intendeth where he joineth these two together, God 'quickeneth the dead, and calleth,' &c., Rom. iv. 17. Before men are called, they are 'dead in sins,' Eph. ii. 1; but when Christ effectually calleth any, his voice pierceth into their soul as powerfully as it did into the body of the damsel which was new dead, Mark v. 41, 42; or of the young man that was carrying out on a bier to be buried, Luke vii. 13–15; or of Lazarus that had been dead four days, John xi. 43, 44. This is evident by this promise of Christ, 'The dead shall hear the voice of the Son of God, and they that hear shall live,' John v. 25; this is such a privilege as scarce a greater can be desired. 'All that a man hath will be given for his (temporal) life,' Job ii. 4; what then for spiritual life?

2. Light and sight. These I join together; because one without the other is of no use. Of what use is light to a blind man? And of what use is sight to him that hath no light to see by? Besides, by these two an effectual calling is distinguished from a mere formal calling. They who are only outwardly called have light shining upon them, in that they have the word preached unto them. In this respect it is said, 'The light shineth in darkness, and the darkness comprehendeth it not,' John i. 5; but they who are inwardly called have also sight given unto them, the eyes of their understanding are opened:' 'I have called thee,' saith the Lord to his Son, 'to open the blind eyes,' Isa. xlii. 6, 7; and the apostle saith that he was sent 'to open men's eyes, and to turn them from darkness to light,' Acts xxvi. 19. That this is a privilege of saints' calling is evident by this phrase, 'God hath called you out of darkness into his marvellous light,' 1 Pet. ii. 9. Though this privilege be not greater than the former, yet it adds much thereunto, for what is life to them that live in darkness, but a kind of death? It is very uncomfortable; therefore darkness and death are oft joined together, Isa. ix. 2, Job x. 21, 22; so, on the contrary, life and light are joined together, John i. 4, to shew that life is no life without light. Eternal death is in Scripture set out by darkness, Mat. viii. 12.

3. Holiness. God hath called us unto holiness, 1 Thes. iv. 7. How great a privilege this is hath been before shewed, Sec. 7.

4. Liberty. The apostle expressly saith, that we are 'called unto liberty,' Gal. v. 13. Before we are called, we are in bondage under Satan, sin, and death, Eph. ii. 2, Rom. vi. 17, Heb. ii. 5; yea, under the rigour and curse of the law, Gal. iii. 10, and under the infinite wrath of God, Eph. ii. 3. Now according to the lords under whom we are in bondage is our bondage the more grievous. From all the aforesaid bondage we are called and set at liberty. This privi-

---

[1] ἐπουράνια dicuntur quæ supra cœlos sunt, ut ἐπιχθόνια quæ super terram.

lege much amplifieth the benefit of both the former. To bondslaves what is life? even worse than death. And light and sight are of little use to such as have no liberty to use them, but rather an aggravation of their misery.

5. Communion or 'fellowship of Jesus Christ,' 1 Cor. i. 9. By virtue of their effectual calling, saints are engrafted or incorporated into Christ Jesus, and made members of his mystical body, 1 Cor. xii. 12. Hereby we come to be his, and he to be ours, and we to have a right to all that is his, as our mediator, 1 Cor. iii. 22, 23. This is a greater privilege than all the other; without this the other are no privileges at all. Without Christ life is but a death, light but darkness, sight but blindness, liberty but bondage. By virtue of this fellowship God is our Father, John xx. 17; Christ our head and husband, Eph. v. 23, 32; yea, our brother, Heb. ii. 11, 12; the Holy Ghost is our comforter and instructor, John xiv. 26; angels our attendants, Heb. i. 14; heaven our inheritance, 1 Pet. i. 4; all things are ours, 1 Cor. iii. 22, 23.

6. Eternal life and salvation. 'Lay hold,' saith the apostle, 'on eternal life, whereunto thou art called,' 1 Tim. vi. 12; God hath called you to salvation, 2 Thes. ii. 13, 14. This is styled God's kingdom and glory, 1 Thes. ii. 12. This in reference to our good is the main end of all that Christ did and suffered for us; it must needs therefore be a very great privilege. The first privilege was spiritual life, the last is eternal life.

Sec. 17. *Of the sense of this word 'partakers.'*

The good opinion of the apostle about their calling, to whom he wrote, is especially manifested in this word *partakers*. For hereby he sheweth that he was persuaded that they had a part therein.

Of the notation of the Greek word μέτοχοι, translated 'partakers,' see Chap. i. Sec. 122, and Chap. ii. Sec. 139.

Here two things are especially intended under this word 'partakers.'

1. All saints have a like share in the heavenly calling; they being partakers thereof, have every one part therein as well as a right thereto. All the Israelites were in this sense partakers of the same privileges: 'They were all under the cloud, and all passed through the Red Sea, and were all baptized, &c., and did all eat the same spiritual meat, and did all drink the same spiritual drink,' 1 Cor. x. 2–4; 'Ye are all one in Christ Jesus,' Gal. iii. 28. The eight unities mentioned by the apostle, Eph. iv. 4–6, intended thus much, for all believers make *one body;* they have all *one spirit;* they are all called *in one hope;* they are all servants *of one Lord;* there is *one faith* belonging to them all, and *one baptism;* they have all *one God,* and *one Father.* In reference to that one Father all believers are styled τέκνα ἀγαπητά, 'dear children,' Eph. v. 1. Great is the emphasis of the Greek word translated *dear;* it signifieth a beloved one, one that is so loved as all love is cast on him. It is most properly attributed to an only child. Where God saith to Abraham, 'Take thine only son,' אֶת־בִּנְךָ אֶת־יְחִידְךָ, Gen. xxii. 2, the LXX thus translate it, take 'thy beloved son,' τὸν υἱόν σου τὸν ἀγαπητόν. He who in Hebrew is called an only son, בֶּן־יָחִיד, is in Greek called a beloved son, υἱὸς ἀγαπητός. So also do other authors use that Greek word both of male and female, as παῖς ἀγαπητός, an only son, παρθένος ἀγαπητή (Xenoph. in Cyrop.), an only daughter. So when one hath but one only eye, that eye in Greek is called ὀφθαλμος ἀγαπητός, a beloved eye. This title, ἀγαπητός, beloved one, is oft attributed to Christ, Mat. iii. 17, and xvii. 5, and xviii. 12, and that most properly, for he is the only begotten of God, μονογενής, John iii. 16. This title *beloved one* is indeed oft used in the plural number, including many, ἀγαπητοῖς Θεοῦ, as Eph. v. 1, Rom. i. 7, and xi. 28; but they are all in God's account as an one only child. Thus they are all as one spouse to Chrift, Cant. iv. 8, 2 Cor. xi. 2. They are also all heirs, Rom. viii. 17; and kings, Rev. i. 6; and that of the same inheritance, and of the same kingdom. Now there useth to be but one heir of the same inheritance, and one king of the same kingdom. These therefore are as one; for they have all one spirit, Eph. iv. 4; and they all make one mystical body, which body is styled Christ, 1 Cor. xii. 12. In this respect the duties which are required of us as brethren, Sec. 3, are by this unity further pressed upon us.

2. They to whom the apostle wrote, were internally and effectually called. To be partakers of a thing, is not only to have a right thereto by reason of our profession, but also to have a part and a share therein, and that really, actually. Thus we are said to be 'partakers of Christ,' v. 14; and to be partakers of God's chastisements, Heb. xii. 8; the husbandman is said to be 'partaker of his hope,' in that he doth in very deed partake of the benefits thereof, 1 Cor. ix. 10.

The apostle doth use this emphatical word *partakers*, and applies it to them all, as he did that former excellent style, 'holy brethren.'

Of giving such titles to all members of the church, see Sec. 6.

Sec. 18. *Of signs of saints' calling.*

The excellency, utility, and necessity of the heavenly calling, gives us all just cause thoroughly to search and examine ourselves thereabout, that we be not deceived in a matter of so great consequence, and think we are internally and effectually called, when our calling is only external and formal.

This use is the rather to be made of this point, because the evidences of an effectual calling are especially inward, in the soul and spirit of a man; and 'what man knoweth the things of a man,' namely, such as are within him, 'save the spirit of man which is in him?' It will be therefore not unseasonable to give some signs of this calling. They are such as follow:

1. Illumination. Hereby I mean in special a distinct understanding of the mysteries of godliness, particularly of the work of the law and the gospel on us. Our calling is 'from darkness to light,' 1 Pet. ii. 9. They therefore who still remain in darkness, the darkness of ignorance, and cannot find themselves to be enlightened with true knowledge, are not called. Of those who are called the Lord saith, 'They shall all know me,' Jer. xxxi. 34. Though this be not sufficient, yet it is necessary.

2. Sense and feeling of that woful estate wherein by nature men are. Such they are whom Christ thus invites and calls: 'Come unto me, all ye that labour and are heavy laden,' Mat. xi. 28. As for such as think themselves righteous, and that their estate is good enough, such as never were brought to feel the heavy burden of sin, Christ saith, 'I am not come to call the righteous,' Mat. ix. 13.

3. Detestation and loathing of one's former estate, and wicked course of life, together with a true and sound turning from the same, which is repentance; for Christ came to call sinners to repentance, Mat. ix. 13. They therefore that are not brought to repentance, but continue to live, lie, and delight in sin, are not called.

4. Sanctification and renovation of the whole man, and a delight in holiness: for 'God hath called us to holiness,' 1 Thes. iv. 7.

5. Contempt of this world, of the promotions, profits and pleasures thereof: for 'Christ gave himself, that he might deliver us from this present evil world,' Gal. i. 4. To this purpose tends the call of the Lord; 'Come out from among them, and be ye separate, saith the Lord, and touch not the unclean thing; and I will receive you,' 2 Cor. vi. 17.

6. Peace and unity. This the apostle intends in these words: 'Let the peace of God rule in your hearts, to the which also ye are called,' Col. iii. 15. He calls it the 'peace of God,' because God hath settled and established it among his people: 'God hath called us to peace,' 1 Cor. vii. 15.

7. Readiness to bear all manner of afflictions which by God shall be laid on us, or persecutions which by man shall be inflicted for the gospel's sake: 'For even hereunto are we called,' 1 Peter ii. 21.

8. Love of God. Hereby they who are called are described. These two are joined together, 'them that love God,' 'and 'them that are called,' Rom. viii. 28.

9. Love of the brethren. The apostle presseth this point by this argument, 'As ye are called in one hope of your calling,' Eph. iv. 4.

10. A cheerful expectation of eternal happiness. For 'God hath called us to eternal glory,' 1 Peter v. 10.

Sec. 19. *Of sundry uses of saints' calling.*

This point of the heavenly calling of saints, affords matter of confutation, humiliation, reprehension, admiration, gratulation, consolation, direction, exhortation.

1. The error of attributing such free will to man in his corrupt estate, as to be able thereupon to turn from darkness to light, is confuted, in that unless God both outwardly by his word, and inwardly by his Spirit, call him, he cannot come. 'No man can come to me,' saith Christ, 'except the Father draw him,' John vi. 44.

The word *calling* refutes another error about the universality of it, for we are called out from others.

2. That woful plight wherein ourselves were before our calling, and wherein others still lie which are not yet called, gives great matter of humiliation; for it is an estate of darkness and death, under the power of sin and Satan.

3. Sundry sorts are upon this call of God to be taxed. As,

(1.) Such as turn their ears, or harden their heart against the means God affordeth to call them. Such were those of whom Wisdom complaineth, Prov. i. 24, &c., and of whom the Lord thus saith, 'I have spread out my hands all the day unto a rebellious people,' Isaiah lxv. 2.

(2.) Such as, after they are called of God, so open their ears to others, as they are 'soon removed from him that called them,' Gal. i. 6.

(3.) Such as abide in their profession, yet live as if they were not called. These are ungodly men, 'turning the grace of our God into lasciviousness,' Jude 4. 'Through these the name of God is blasphemed,' Rom. ii. 24.

4. All things in this calling afford great matter of admiration. As,

(1.) The author thereof, God himself.

(2.) The only procuring cause, his free grace.

(3.) The persons called, who were enemies to God, dead in sins, vassals of Satan.

(4.) The many and great privileges of their calling, whereof see Sec. 16.

(5.) The ends whereunto they were called, particularly their glorious inheritance in heaven.

5. As other evidences of God's grace afford much matter of gratulation, so our calling in special. For it is the first of our actual enjoying those things which God hath before the world prepared, and Christ in the fulness of time purchased for us. This is comprised under that, for which the apostle 'blesseth God the Father of our Lord Jesus Christ,' 1 Peter i. 3.

6. This call of God is a point of exceeding great comfort to us weak children of men, who are not able of ourselves to stand steadily. 'The calling of God is without repentance,' Rom. xi. 29. God never repenteth him of calling his elect. For 'faithful is he that calleth you, who also will do it,' 1 Thes. v. 24, He will establish them, and bring them to that end whereunto he hath called them. On this ground the apostle prayeth, that they who are called may be made perfect, stablished, strengthened, settled, 1 Peter v. 10.

7. By the excellency of this calling we are directed to rest contented therewith, whatsoever our outward con-

dition be; and to say, 'The lines are fallen to me in pleasant places; yea, I have a goodly heritage,' Ps. xvi. 6. We need not envy the richest citizens, nor noblest courtiers, nor greatest officers. This calling far exceeds all. Of being content, see Chap. xiii. Sec. 62, &c.

8. This calling gives just occasion of earnest exhortation unto two points especially.

1. To ' make this calling sure.' An apostle adviseth to ' give diligence' hereunto, 2 Peter i. 10. This may be done by giving good heed to the signs mentioned Sec. 18.

2. To walk worthy of the vocation wherewith ye are called,' Eph. iv. 1.

Sec. 20. *Of walking worthy our calling.*

Of this general phrase, *walk worthy*, see my *Sermon on Ezek.* xxxvi. 11, entitled *The Progress of Divine Providence*, in the latter end thereof.

Concerning particular rules for walking worthy of our Christian calling, respect must be had, 1, to the author; 2, to the means; 3, to the ends thereof.

I. For the author. It is God that hath called us; our eyes, therefore, must be fixed on him, that we may conform ourselves to him, and shew ourselves children answerable to such a Father. Thus shall we ' walk worthy of the Lord,' Col. i. 10, and ' worthy of God who hath called us,' 1 Thes. ii. 12. For this end we must observe those particulars wherein God hath set himself a pattern before us, and therein shew ourselves like unto him. Thus shall we shew ourselves ' partakers of the divine nature,' 2 Peter i. 4; yea, thus shall we ' shew forth the praises (or virtues, τὰς ἀρετὰς,) of him that hath called us,' 1 Peter ii. 9.

Particulars registered in God's word to this end are these:

1. Holiness in all manner of conversation, 1 Peter i. 15.
2. Goodness. They that do good for goodness' sake, even to them that hate them, are ' the children of their Father which is in heaven, Mat. v. 44, 45.
3. Kindness, for God is kind to the unthankful, Luke vi. 35.
4. Mercy. ' Be ye merciful,' saith Christ, ' as your Father also is merciful,' Luke vi. 30.
5. Love. The apostle gives this instance of following God, Eph. v. 1, 2. Much doth the beloved disciple press this upon this very ground, 1 John iv. 11.
6. Forgiving one another. ' Forgive one another, as God for Christ's sake forgave you,' Eph. iv. 32.
7. Longsuffering, Eph. iv. 2.

II. For the means, which is the word of God. That sets forth the very image of God, and that which is pleasing and acceptable unto him. This therefore must be set before us as a rule to conform ourselves thereunto. Thus shall we ' walk worthy of the Lord unto all pleasing,' Col. i. 10. The apostle commends the Romans for ' obeying from the heart that form of doctrine which was delivered to them,' Rom. vi. 17, or that form whereunto they were delivered, εἰς ὃν παρεδόθητε τύπον. This phrase is metaphorical, taken from a mould whereinto metal is cast; the metal is thereby formed into that very form or shape which the form itself hath. If the form be square or round, so will the metal be; if there be any engravement upon the form, the metal will bear the same. Thus they who obey the word will be such as the word requireth them to be; and because the word hath God's image engraven upon it, they who obey the word will shew forth that very image.

III. The ends of our Christian calling are great and glorious, which require that Christians do answerably carry themselves. Human and common wisdom teacheth all men to carry themselves answerable to that place whereunto they are called, and dignity whereunto they are advanced. If a mean man be advanced to an honourable condition, or a poor man to a place of much profit, or a servant made a master, and a subject a magistrate, they will not carry themselves as mean and poor persons, or as servants and subjects, but according to their present advanced condition. Should not they who are called to the high and honourable calling of saints, much more carry themselves worthy of that calling, and answerable thereunto?

The particular ends of saints' calling set down in God's word are these that follow:

1. Light. God ' hath called you out of darkness into his marvellous light,' 1 Peter ii. 9. By darkness he meaneth that natural state of ignorance and sinfulness wherein all men before their calling lie. By light he meaneth a contrary state, which is illumination and regeneration, wrought in us by the light of of the gospel, and by the work of God's Spirit.
2. Holiness. ' God hath called us to holiness,' Col. iv. 7.
3. Liberty. ' Ye are called unto liberty,' Gal. i. 13.
4. Fellowship of the Son of God. By God ' you were called unto the fellowship of his Son,' 1 Cor. i. 9.
5. Peace. God hath ' called us to peace,' 1 Cor. vii. 15.
6. Suffering wrongs. ' For even hereunto were ye called,' 1 Peter ii. 21.
7. Blessing such as revile us. ' Knowing that ye are thereunto called,' 1 Peter iii. 9.
8. The kingdom of God. ' God hath called you unto his kingdom,' 1 Thes. ii. 12.
9. Glory. ' God hath called you unto his glory,' 1 Thes. ii. 12. By God's glory is here meant that spiritual glory whereby saints are made far more eminent than the most glorious natural men.
10. Salvation, eternal life, and eternal glory, 2 Thes. ii. 13, 14; 1 Tim. vi. 12; 1 Peter v. 10.

They who carry themselves answerably to those fore-named ends walk worthy of their calling. As,

1. They who order their affairs with good understanding as children of light.

2. They who are holy in all manner of conversation.
3. They who behave themselves as free men, and live not as slaves to sin and Satan.
4. They who are acted by the Spirit of Christ.
5. They who follow after peace, and, as much as lieth in them, live peaceably with all men.
6. They who can bear with wrongs, and not seek after revenge.
7. They who can bless and pray for those that curse them.
8. They who as kings can rule over their passions, and keep under their corruptions.
9. They who manifest a spiritual and divine glory in their holy conversation.
10. They who set salvation before their eyes, and shew that that is the mark whereat they aim; that lay hold of eternal life, and with patience wait for eternal glory.

All these, and other like unto them, do walk worthy of their holy calling, in that they aim at the ends whereunto God hath called them.

I might hereunto add, a conscionable practice of those particular graces wherein the apostle himself doth exemplify this worthy walking, as lowliness, meekness, &c., Eph. iv. 2.

In a word, the practice of all manner of Christian graces doth shew forth the praises or virtues of him who hath called us, and in that respect is a walking worthy of a Christian's calling.

Sec. 21. *Of considering.*

The apostle having endeavoured to insinuate himself into the hearts of those to whom he wrote by these fair and friendly, high and honourable titles, 'holy brethren, partakers of the heavenly calling,' he presseth them well and thoroughly to weigh what he is further to declare unto them, and that under this word *consider*.

I find eleven several Greek words used in the New Testament, which our English do express by this word *consider*, and I observe some special emphasis in every of them.

There are four simple verbs in Greek used, and seven compounds.

1. A word that properly signifieth to see or behold, ἰδεῖν, and that with bodily eyes, is oft referred to the mind, and intendeth a serious observing of a matter. It is said that the apostles, in a matter of great moment, came together to consider of that matter, Acts xv. 8.
2. Another word, θεωρεῖν, which useth to be applied to the bodily sight, is also transferred to the mind, and signifieth a serious observance. 'Consider how great this man was,' Heb. vii. 4.
3. Another word which properly signifieth to view as a watchman, σκοπεῖν, *speculari*, or a spy doth, even as narrowly and diligently as may be. Thus we must 'consider ourselves,' Gal. vi. 1, that is, take due and thorough notice of ourselves, and of our manifold infirmities, and temptations whereunto we are subject.
4. The last simple verb, νοεῖν, properly respecteth the soul, and according to the notation of it, it signifieth to turn a matter up and down in one's mind, that he may to the full observe it. To this purpose saith the apostle, 'Consider what I say,' 2 Tim. ii. 7.
5. The first simple verb hath a compound, συνιδεῖν, which addeth further emphasis, and implieth a serious consulting with one's self of such and such a matter. Thus is Peter said to consider that strange providence that befell him, Acts xii. 12.
6. The second simple verb hath also his compound, ἀναθεωρεῖν, which signifieth a reviewing of a thing, and a diligent pondering upon it. Hereof see more, Chap. xiii. 7, Sec. 109.
7. The fourth simple verb hath in like manner his compound, κατανοεῖν, which signifies thoroughly to think of a matter, so as he may come to a more full knowledge thereof. This word is used to set out Peter's considering the strange vision that was shewed him, Acts xi. 6. This is the word that is used here in this text.
8. There is another compound, συνιέναι, which intendeth a casting as in a man's mind, or consulting with one's self about a matter. The disciples of Christ are checked for failing herein. They considered not (οὐ συνῆκαν), the miracle of the loaves.
9. There is likewise a compound, ἀναλογίζεσθαι, which signifieth to recount with one's self, and to review a thing again and again. 'Consider, ἀναλογίσασθε, him that endured,' &c.
10. Another compound like this, διαλογίζεσθαι, is used, which signifieth to reason with one's self about a matter that seemeth strange, that they may the better discern it. For failing herein, Caiaphas checked the rest of the council that they did not consider, οὐδὲ διαλογίζεσθε, such a thing, John xi. 50.
11. There is another compound, καταμανθάνειν, which signifieth so to observe a thing as one may be well informed and instructed thereabout. 'Consider (καταμάθετε) the lilies,' saith Christ.

These eleven several Greek words doth our English translate with this one word *consider*. Our English word hath an emphasis in it, and implieth a very special observing of a thing.

Sec. 22. *Of considering weighty matters.*

The matter which the apostle would have them so to observe is as great and weighty a matter as can be, as will appear in opening the words following.

In general, it hence appeareth, that matters of weight are to be well weighed. The several texts before quoted, about the different Greek words, give so many proofs of the point.

If matters be not at first duly considered, and thoroughly weighed, they may slip out; see hereof Chap. ii. 1, Sec. 6.

But by well weighing of them, the understanding will better conceive them, the memory retain them, the heart relish them, and so a man may be brought to make the better use of them.

Ministers may here learn so to press matters of moment upon their people as they may consider them, and thereupon to call upon them to consider such and such a point; as the apostle did, 'Consider what I say; and the Lord give thee understanding,' 2 Tim. ii. 7. Thus they shall shew that they can distinguish betwixt matters that differ, and can discern what points are of most and best use; that they desire the profit of their people, and are loath that weighty matters should be lost.

That people may make the better use of this point, two prudent practices are especially to be observed: one with themselves, another with others.

1. That with themselves is *meditation*. This is an especial part of consideration. Hereby we call to mind what we have heard or read, and so conceive it the better. That which is not thoroughly conceived at first, by meditation may be better understood. Meditation to man is as chewing the cud to sundry beasts, whereby that which they eat is better digested. Sundry beasts which chewed the cud were under the law counted clean, which in a figure commendeth meditation. Surely this brings much profit, which they find who carefully use it.

2. The practice with others is *conference*. This may be more useful than meditation, because thereby we have not only our help, but also the help of others. Hereby we may also bring help to others.

Sec. 23. *Of Christ above all to be considered.*

That weighty point which the apostle would have them to consider is Christ himself. If anything in the world be to be seriously considered, surely Christ above all, and that in his excellencies: 'Consider how great this man was,' Heb. vii. 4; and in his meanness, 'Consider him that endured such contradiction,' &c., Heb. xii. 3; yea, in his humanity, and in the exaltation thereof, 'Remember that Jesus Christ, of the seed of David, was raised from the dead,' 2 Tim. ii. 8. It is very observable, that this remarkable note of consideration, *behold*, is in Scripture oftener prefixed before the mysteries of Christ, and that both in the Old and New Testament, than before any other one mystery whatsoever.

The dignity of Christ's person, the admirable union of his two natures, the excellency of his offices, his low descent for our sakes, the extent of his sufferings, his full conquest over all our enemies, his glorious exaltation, and the incomparable benefits that we reap by Christ, are all very forcible motives to stir us up to consider him.

The apostle was so far ravished with the apprehension of Christ Jesus, as he saith, 'I determined not to know anything among you, save Jesus Christ, and him crucified,' 1 Cor. ii. 2. And again, 'I count all things but loss for the excellency of the knowledge of Christ Jesus my Lord,' Philip. iii. 8.

This sets an high commendation on the sacred Scripture, that it setteth out Christ so much as it doth, and that both in the Old and New Testament: in the Old, by promises, prophecies, types, figures, and other like means; in the New, plainly, perspicuously, and that in his conception, birth, private life, public ministry, great works, great sufferings, death, burial, resurrection, ascension, sitting at the right hand of his Father, continual intercession for us, his power of judging all, and eternal glory.

It will therefore be an especial point of prudence in us diligently to read the Scriptures, and that for this end especially, that we may know and consider Christ.

In reading the Scriptures, mark such places especially as set out Jesus Christ; meditate on them, and thus consider him.

Sec. 24. *Of Christ an apostle.*

That which the apostle would have us especially to consider in Christ concerneth two of his offices, namely, his prophetical office, in this word *apostle;* and his priestly function, in this, *high priest.*

Though it be the prophetical office of Christ which is set out under this word *apostle,* yet that word is used because an apostle was the chiefest minister that ever was instituted under the New Testament, Eph. iv. 11; and an apostleship had more privileges conferred upon it than ever any other function in the church, before or since the apostles' times, had. This amplifieth the excellency of Christ's prophetical office, and sheweth that it is of the most excellent kind.

Of the meaning of this word *apostle,* see Chap. ii. 3, Sec. 26. There was shewed how apostles, properly so called, were distinguished from other ministers, both in the manner of their calling, and also in the special privileges that belonged thereunto. That which is further to be declared concerning Christ's apostleship is to prove that Christ was an apostle,

1. In his general function.
2. In his special calling thereunto.
3. In the privileges that appertained to that function.

I. The general function of Christ, as a prophet, an apostle, and minister of the word of God, was to make known the will of the Father unto his people. That Christ did this, hath been before shewed, Chap. i. 2, Sec. 14, and Chap. ii. 3, Secs. 22, 24, and 12, Secs. 111, 112.

II. His special call to that function was immediate from the Father. Christ thus saith of himself, 'As my Father hath sent me, even so send I you,' John xx. 21. Oft doth Christ make mention of this, that his Father sent him. Where Christ saith to the Jews, 'Ye have neither heard the Father's voice at any time, nor seen his shape,' John v. 37, he speaketh it in an opposition betwixt the Jews and himself, and giveth them to understand that what they had not done he had done. He had both heard his Father's voice and seen his shape. Therefore he thus saith, 'Not that any man hath seen the Father, save he which is of God, he hath seen the Father,' John vi. 46. To the same purpose tends this, 'No man hath seen God at any time; the only begotten Son, which is in the bosom of the Father, he hath declared him,' John i. 18.

III. The privileges which belonged to an apostolical function, and in a most eminent manner appertained unto Christ, were these eight that follow:

1. Christ laid the foundation; for he first preached the gospel in paradise, Gen. iii. 15. Of Christ's first publishing the gospel, see Chap. ii. 3, Sec. 24; yea, Christ himself was the very foundation, 1 Cor. iii. 11. He is also the chief corner-stone, Eph. ii. 20. There is mention made of 'the foundation of the apostles and prophets;' but that is tropically spoken, in that they were ministers to lay the proper foundation, which is Jesus Christ.

2. The whole world was Christ's jurisdiction. No limits were set to his function: 'The uttermost parts of the earth were for his possession,' Ps. ii. 8. He 'preached peace to them that were nigh, and to them that were afar off,' Eph. ii. 17.

3. He had his gifts immediately by the Spirit, Isa. xi. 2, Luke ii. 20. Not by any means of man.

4. He received the Spirit more abundantly than any other. He received it 'not by measure,' John iii. 34; 'All the treasures of wisdom and knowledge were hid in him,' Col. ii. 3; yea, 'the fulness of the Godhead' dwelt in him,' Col. ii. 9; he was so full, as 'out of his fulness we all receive,' John i. 16.

5. He could not but have infallible assistance, in that he was the very truth itself, John xiv. 16; and the Spirit of God was upon him, Luke iv. 18.

6. He also must needs have power of giving gifts, in that he was the prime author of all gifts: 'He gave gifts unto men,' Eph. iv. 7; 'He, 'breathing on his disciples, said, Receive ye the Holy Ghost,' John xx. 22.

7. About miracles he had more power than ever any other. Never any wrought miracles more in number, and more strange in their kind, than any prophets or apostles, John ix. 32, and xv. 24; but that which most distinguisheth Christ's power in this respect from others, is, that Christ wrought them in his own name, but others in the name of Christ, Mark i. 27, Acts iii. 12, 16, and iv. 10.

8. Vengeance especially belongeth unto Christ, Rom. xii. 19. When the apostle delivered the incestuous person over to Satan, he did it in the name, and with the power, of our Lord Jesus Christ, 1 Cor. v. 4.

Thus it appears that all things belonging to an apostleship did truly, properly, and pertinently belong to Christ; so as this title *apostle* is here most fitly applied to him, and in so eminent and excellent a manner can be attributed to no other.

Sec. 25. *Of duties arising from Christ's apostleship.*

An especial duty hence arising, from heaven enjoined to us by the Father himself, is this, ' Hear ye him,' Mat. xvii. 5. Every particular about Christ's apostleship doth much press this point.

1. The general, that he was a minister of the gospel, requireth that he be hearkened to, Deut. xviii. 19.

2. He had seen the Father, and was in his bosom, and knew his whole counsel: whom, then, should we hear, if not him?

3. He was immediately sent of the Father, as the most extraordinary ambassador of God, even his own Son. If a king send his son an ambassador, shall not he have audience? Mat. xxi. 37.

4. He is the only sure foundation; on whom can we more securely rest than on him? Therefore hear him.

5. By reason of the extent of Christ's jurisdiction, he brake down the partition wall betwixt Jew and Gentile, and 'hath made both one,' so as now 'we are no more strangers,' Eph. ii. 19. We being of Christ's sheepfold, ought in that respect to hear him, John x. 16.

6. That immediate understanding which Christ had of God's whole counsel, without any means on man's part, should make us give the more heed to him.

7. That abundance of Spirit which was in him gives us just occasion the rather to hearken unto him.

8. He having power to give gifts, by hearkening to him we may be enlightened, and made partakers of all needful graces.

9. Should we not hear him, who confirmed his doctrine with such miracles as he did?

10. The vengeance which he can pour upon the rebellious, should move us to turn an obedient ear to his word; for our God is a consuming fire.

How Christ may now be heard, is shewed Chap. ii. 12, Sec. 112.

Other special duties do arise from the distinct branches of Christ's apostleship, such as these that follow.

1. Obey Christ, as he is in general a minister, and hath the rule over his church, and watcheth for our souls, Heb. xiii. 17.

2. Believe his word, because he was in the bosom of his Father, and knew his whole counsel, John i. 17, 18. The Jews are reproved because they believed not him who had seen the Father, John v. 37, 38. Upon this, that Christ had seen the Father, he maketh this reference, 'He that believeth on me, hath everlasting life,' John vi. 46, 47.

3. Receive, and that with all reverence, him whom the Father immediately sent. For this end the father so sent his son, saying, 'They will reverence my son,' Mat. xxi. 37.

4. So settle thy faith on Christ the only foundation, as it may never be removed from him. When Christ said to the twelve, 'Will ye also go away?' Peter answered, 'Lord, to whom shall we go? Thou hast the words of eternal life,' John vi. 67, 68.

5. Do what may be done for bringing all of all sorts into the sheepfold of Christ. By virtue of the extent of Christ's apostleship, the gospel is everywhere to be preached, Mat. xxviii. 19.

6. If any preach any other gospel than that which Christ preached, who had the Spirit of truth in him, let it be detested. For Christ's gospel was 'not of man,' Gal. i. 9, 11.

7. Open your mouth wide, and crave abundantly of Christ what is needful, for he hath the Spirit in abundance, and 'out of his fulness we may all receive grace for grace,' John i. 16.

8. Depend on him for such gifts as thou hast not, and give him the praise of such as thou hast, for he 'giveth gifts,' Eph. iv. 8.

9. Adhere to that truth which Christ hath ratified with his miracles.

10. Fear to provoke him who hath a power to take vengeance.

Sec. 26. *Of Christ's being both an apostle, and also an high priest.*

The second point which the apostle would have them to consider was, that Christ is an high priest.

Of Christ's being a priest, and an high priest, see Chap. ii. 17, Secs. 172, 173, &c.

The excellencies of Christ's offices, and the benefits which we reap thereby, do give just occasion to consider this apostle and this high priest.

Of the excellency and benefits of Christ's prophetical office, see Chap. i. 2, Sec. 14, and Chap. ii. 3, Sec. 22, and verse 12, Secs. 111, 112.

Of the excellency and benefits of Christ's priesthood, see Chap. ii. 17, Sec. 174.

The function of an apostle and an high priest were the greatest functions that ever God instituted in his church. None greater than an high priest under the law; none greater than an apostle under the gospel. Fitly, therefore, doth the apostle here apply them to Christ, who is the most excellent of all, and undertook for his church those things which were of greatest concernment for her.

These two offices, *apostle* and *high priest*, were never joined in one man; but here they are by this copulative particle, καὶ, *and*. The same Jesus that was an apostle, was also an high priest; he therefore is all in all. Several persons among men are to be deputed to several functions; but Christ alone is sufficient for all functions. As for continuance of the same function, there needs many men, because they are mortal, and they must supply it one after another; but Christ continueth ever, Heb. vii. 23, 24. So for performing several and distinct duties, there needs several distinct men, because all abilities are not in any one man; yet Christ is able to manage all, for 'it pleased the Father that in him should all fulness dwell,' Col. i. 19.

Thus have we no need to go to any for the furthering of that which Christ undertakes. He performs the parts of an high priest, he also performs the parts of an apostle. This also he doth in all things that are absolutely necessary for the eternal happiness of his church.

Sec. 27. *Of profession.*

The Greek word, ὁμολογία,[1] here used by the apostle, is a compound, and properly signifieth a consent. In the New Testament it is used for a confession or profession of a thing, 1 Tim. vi. 12, 13. It is also used to set out the faith or religion which Christians profess, Heb. iv. 14.

Here it may be taken either for an act on our part, and thus translated, the apostle and high priest whom we confess and profess so to be, or for the subject matter, namely, the faith or religion which we profess. Neither of these cross the other, but may both well stand together. For Christians do on all occasions actually profess that which is the object of their profession.

The former acception of the word sheweth that true Christians do profess Christ to be their apostle and high priest, that is, their instructor and intercessor. They are not ashamed of him, for he is not ashamed of them. See Chap. ii. 11, Sec. 108.

The latter, that Christ, as an apostle and high priest, is the principal subject of the Christian religion. He is that foundation whereupon other articles of the Christian faith are erected, 1 Cor. iii. 10–12, Acts iv. 12.

The very word *profession*, as here used, implieth that Christians openly professed their faith. Thus the apostle himself openly professeth his faith, saying, 'This I confess, that after the way which they call heresy, so worship I God,' &c., Acts xxiv. 14. This is that 'good profession' which is commended, and which is testified of Christ himself,[2] 1 Tim. vi. 12, 13. An apostle prescribeth this as a duty under another like word, namely, ἀπολογία, *apology*, translated to 'give an answer,' 1 Peter iii. 15.

This is set down as an especial fruit of faith, for 'with the heart man believeth, and with the mouth confession is made,' Rom. x. 10. 'I believed, therefore have I spoken,' Ps. cxvi. 10. 'We also believe, and therefore speak,' 2 Cor. iv. 13.

This also is set down as the way to salvation. 'With the mouth confession is made unto salvation,' Rom. x. 10. How unworthy of their holy profession do they carry themselves, who being in the number of those that profess the true faith, through fear or shame forbear to make open profession of that faith. Some count it a point of wisdom to conceal their faith,

---

[1] Of the verb ὁμολογεῖν, see Chap. iii. 15, Sec. 144.
[2] See Chap. iii. ver. 12, Sec. 117.

and to shew themselves close men, so as none shall know what they are resolved to stand to. Surely this wisdom was never learned in Christ's school. He that was made wise by God's word, professeth to 'speak of God's testimonies even before kings, and not to be ashamed,' Ps. cxix. 46. These are like the Laodiceans, which were neither cold nor hot. But of all, they were most grievous to Christ, who thereupon threatens to spue them out of his mouth, Rev. iii. 16. At the great day will Christ shew himself to be ashamed of such, Mark viii. 38.

Sec. 28. *Of Hebrews being Christians.*

This relative ἡμῶν, *our*, annexed to *profession*, being of the first person and plural number, includeth both the author of this epistle, and those also to whom it was written; and sheweth that they were all of the same profession, which was the Christian religion. For howsoever the greatest part of the Jews, by reason of their obstinacy in rejecting Christ, were cast off, yet, 'at that present time also there was a remnant according to the election of grace,' Rom. xi. 5; and by this relative *our*, he giveth them to understand, that as he himself, so they also were of that remnant.

A great encouragement this was for them to hold fast their profession, and though the greatest part of the Hebrews had rejected that profession, yet they to live and die therein; and therefore to 'consider the apostle and high priest of their profession,' that they might the better know him, believe on him, and submit themselves to him.

Such Jews as are now of the Christian profession, for God hath in all ages reserved a remnant to himself, may apply this to themselves.

Sec. 29. *Of Jesus Christ joined together.*

That the Hebrews might the more distinctly know who that apostle and high priest was whom they ought to consider, the apostle sets him down by name under these two titles, *Christ Jesus*. These two titles are applied to him, as our proper and surname to us.

Jesus was his proper name, and by this was he most usually called while he lived on earth, as appears by the history of the Evangelists: 'A man that is called Jesus made clay,' &c., saith the man that, being born blind, received sight, John ix. 11. And in the Acts, where the apostles' dealing with the Jews is most insisted on, *Jesus* is oftenest mentioned. In the epistles which were sent to the Gentiles, the title Christ is most frequently used. In this epistle, *Jesus* is used as oft as *Christ*. Both in and since the apostles' time, the title *Christ* hath been more frequent in Christians' tongues and pens than *Jesus*.

Christ is a common name of the whole stock or family that cometh from God, even of all God's children. Therefore, they are called 'Christians,' Acts xi. 26. Yea, this very title *Christ*, is applied to them all, 1 Cor. xii. 12, Gal. iii. 16. In the Hebrew dialect, this title was of old given to all saints, as where the Lord saith, 'Touch not mine anointed,' Ps. cv. 15, or 'my Christs,' משיחי, χριστῶν μου, LXX, *Christos meos*. *Jesus Christ* are titles of different languages. The former is Hebrew, the latter Greek; yet all other languages retain these two names, according to their proper dialect.

Among other reasons of giving two titles of these two languages, Hebrew and Greek, to the same person, by both which, and by either of which, he is distinguished from all others, this may be a principal one, that 'There is neither Jew nor Greek, but all are one in Jesus Christ,' Gal. iii. 28.

The whole world was then distinguished into these two sorts, Jew and Greek, Rom. i. 16, and x. 12. For by Christ the partition wall betwixt Jew and Greek, or Gentile, was broken down, Eph. ii. 14. Had not thus much been intended, he might have been called *Jesus Messiah*, which implieth as much as *Jesus Christ*.

This affords matter of gratulation to us Gentiles. The Jews' *Jesus* is our *Christ*; *Jesus Christ*, one and the same person. He is not only *Jesus* for the Jews, but *Christ* for the Gentiles, Mat. i. 16, Luke ii. 11. On this ground, forms of gratulation were prescribed to the Gentiles, whereof the apostle gathereth a catalogue together, Rom. xv. 9, &c. We are of these Gentiles; it therefore becomes us well to meditate on that advice which the apostle gives, Eph. ii. 11–13. This may also be an incitation to us to do what lieth in our power, by prayer or otherwise, for recalling the Jews. The name *Jesus* is still due to our *Christ*. He retaining that name will be ready to receive the Jews coming unto him. 'I am Jesus,' saith he to persecuting Saul, a Jew, implying thereby that he was ready to be a Saviour unto him.

Of this title *Jesus*, see more on Chap. ii. ver. 9, Sec. 73.

Of this title *Christ*, see more on ver. 6 of this chapter, Sec. 54.

Sec. 30. *Of the resolution of* Heb. iii. 1.

Wherefore, holy brethren, partakers of the heavenly calling, consider the Apostle and High Priest of our profession, Christ Jesus.

The sum of this verse is, an especial use of Christ undertaking for us.

Two points are here distinctly to be weighed:

1. The inference of this text upon that which went before, *therefore.*

2. The substance of the whole text. Herein is set down,

1. A description of the parties to whom the duty is prescribed.

2. A declaration of the distinct duty.

The parties are described,

1. By their relation.
2. By their vocation.

In setting down their relation we may observe,
1. The kind of it, in this word *brethren*.
2. The quality of it, in this epithet *holy*.

Their vocation is illustrated,
1. By the reality of it, in this word *partakers*.
2. By the excellency of it, *heavenly*.

About the duty is expressed,
1. An act, *consider*.
2. The object thereof.

The object consisteth of two parts of mysteries :
1. Two offices of Christ, *apostle* and *high priest*.
2. Two names, *Christ, Jesus*.

Sec. 31. *Of the observations arising from* Heb. iii. 1.

I. *The good done for us is duly to be regarded by us.* This particle of inference, *wherefore*, intends as much. See Sec. 2.

II. *All sorts of saints are brethren.* Both ministers and people, yea, all sorts among them are here styled *brethren*. See Sec. 3.

III. *It is a great honour to be holy.* For honour's sake doth the apostle style them *holy*. See Sec. 5, &c.

IV. *Saints have a peculiar calling.* It is a peculiar calling that is here intended. See Secs. 13, 14.

V. *The peculiar calling of saints is celestial.* It is here styled heavenly. See Sec. 15.

VI. *Saints are really called.*

VII. *All saints have the like privileges.*

These two latter doctrines are gathered out of the word *partakers*. See Sec. 17.

VIII. *Saints must be judged according to their profession.* So doth the apostle here judge them. See Sec. 6.

IX. *Instructors must insinuate themselves into the hearts of their hearers.* This is the reason why the apostle doth attribute the fore-mentioned dignities to them. See Sec. 4.

X. *Matters of moment must be advisedly pondered.* This is the intendment of this word *consider*. See Sec. 22.

XI. *Christ ought most of all to be considered.* He is that weighty matter whom the apostle would have them to consider. See Sec. 23.

XII. *Christ is an apostle.* He is here so expressly styled. See Sec. 24.

XIII. *Christ is the true high priest.* He is here by an excellency so called. See Sec. 26.

XIV. *Christ was a minister both of the law and the gospel.* An high priest was the chiefest minister of the law, and an apostle of the gospel. See Sec. 26.

XV. *The faith is openly to be professed.* The word *profession* importeth as much. See Sec. 27.

XVI. *Sundry Jews have been Christians.* Jews are included under this relative *our*, ' our profession.' See Sec. 28.

XVII. *Our Saviour had his distinct names.* They are here expressed, *Jesus, Christ*.

XVIII. *One of our Saviour's names was an Hebrew name.* This was *Jesus*.

XIX. *The other of our Saviour's names was Greek.* This was *Christ*.

XX. *All nations have a right to the same Saviour.* The meeting of these two names in the one only Saviour implies as much.

Of the four last doctrines, see Sec. 29.

Sec. 32. *Of faithfulness, and that to him that appointed us.*

Ver. 2. *Who was faithful to him that appointed him, as also Moses was faithful in all his house.*

The apostle having declared Christ to be a prophet, he further proceedeth to set forth Christ's manner of executing his prophetical office, which was with all faithfulness.

This the apostle doth both by a simple expressing of the point, and also by a comparative illustration thereof.

The simple proposition is thus expressed, ' Who was faithful to him that appointed him.'

This relative *who* is not in the Greek, where, word for word, it is thus set down, ' being faithful,' πιστὸν ὄντα. This kind of connection makes this a part of the former sentence, as if it had been thus rendered, ' Consider Christ Jesus, being faithful,' and it implieth an especial reason why we should the more seriously consider Christ, even because he was faithful ; for his faithfulness made him every way fulfil what was meet to be done for us. Thereupon we may more confidently rest upon him, and in that respect ought the more seriously to consider him.

What it is to be *faithful*, and how Christ shewed himself faithful, both to God and man, in all things that he undertook, hath in general been manifested, Chap. ii. 17, Sec. 177. We shall have occasion to speak more distinctly of Christ's faithfulness in his prophetical office, when we come to the comparison betwixt him and Moses. Sec. 39.

The general point of Christ's faithfulness is amplified by that respect he had therein to ' him that appointed him,' which was his Father, Heb. v. 5.

They that appoint a task to any, do therein trust them. Now, faithfulness much consisteth in a due fulfilling of that trust which is committed to any. The servants that improved their talents, according to that which their master who appointed them expected of them, are accounted and called faithful, Mat. xxv. 21, 23.

Faithfulness is opposed to deceitfulness ; a faithful man will not deceive him that trusts him. If he do, he is not counted faithful.

Christ, in manifesting his faithfulness, had his eye especially upon ' him that appointed him.' He was faithful to him. His care was to approve himself to him. This was his care in his very youth: 'I must be about my Father's business,' saith he, Luke ii. 49. So the like in his man-age: 'I must work the work of him that sent me while it is day,' John ix. 4; yea, in the last act of his life, while he was drinking his bitter cup, he thus saith to his Father, 'Not as I will, but as thou wilt,' Mat. xxvi. 39.

1. He did bear such respect to his Father as in all things he sought to please him: 'For I came down from heaven,' saith he, 'not to do mine own will, but the will of him that sent me,' John vi. 38.

2. He knew that he was to give an account to his Father, which he did in the latter end of his life, John xvii. 4, &c.

3. He had a great desire to approve himself unto his Father. His Father said to him, 'Behold my servant whom I uphold, mine elect in whom my soul delighteth,' Isa. xlii. 1. His desire, therefore, was to be in the number of those to whom his Father saith, 'Well done, thou good and faithful servant,' &c., Mat. xxv. 21.

This is a strong prop to our faith; for hereby we may be assured that what Christ doth will be accepted of his Father, in that he did it according to his Father's will, to whom he was faithful. Now, what Christ did as mediator, he did for us, and we reap the benefit thereof.

Herein is Christ a pattern, as to all others who desire to approve themselves to God, so to ministers especially, whom Christ as a prophet hath left in his stead. We therefore must be faithful to him that hath appointed us. Herein shall we walk worthy of the Lord unto all well-pleasing, Col. i. 10. For this end observe these few rules:

1. Be careful thyself to do what the Lord hath appointed thee to do, and put it not off to others. We must every one give an account of such as are committed to our charge, Ezek. iii. 17, &c; Heb. xiii. 17; 1 Peter v. 2, 4. The good shepherd knoweth his own sheep, and goeth before them, John x. 4.

2. Deliver nothing but what thou hast received from the Lord.

3. Conceal nothing that thou hast received, but declare the whole counsel of God.

4. Declare God's word as the word of God.

Of the three last points, see *The Whole Armour of God* on Eph. vi. 19, secs. 181-183.

5. Seek not to please men. 'If I yet pleased men, I should not be the servant of Christ,' Gal. i. 10. So contrary is man's humour to God's will, as both cannot well be pleased.

6. So order all as God may be glorified. This must be preferred before thine own profit and praise.

Sec. 33. *Of Christ's deputation to his prophetical office.*

The Greek word translated *appointed*, properly signifieth made, ποιήσαντι. Hereupon the Arians produce this text to prove that Christ as God was made, and that he was not God eternal.

Sundry answers may be given to this cavil.

1. The apostle doth not here speak of Christ's divine nature, but of his prophetical office.

2. The word here used ποιεῖν, doth not always signify to give a being to a thing, but sometimes to depute and advance to a place or office. The word which in Hebrew answereth to this, עשׂה, *fecit*, and which the LXX do translate with this word, is thus fitly expressed in our English, 'The Lord that advanced, עשׂה, ὁ ποιήσας, Moses and Aaron,' 1 Sam. xii. 6. Where the apostle saith, that God 'made, ἐποίησε, Jesus Lord,' Acts ii. 36, he meaneth that he appointed him to be a Lord; therefore he thus expresseth the same point in another place: 'Him hath God exalted, ὕψωσε, to be a Prince,' Acts v. 31. It is in common speech of him that advanceth another to a dignity usually said, he made him such and such a man.

3. This that is here said of God's *making* Christ, hath reference to the former verse, and in special to these two offices, *apostle, high priest*. These being here understood or again repeated, will make the sense clear, thus, 'who was faithful to him that made him an apostle and high priest.'

It is God the Father that is here said to make or appoint Christ, as it is more fully expressed, Heb. v. 5. This being applied unto God the Father, puts it out of all doubt and question, that Christ himself was deputed to the offices which he did undertake. He did not of himself thrust himself into them. This was expressly proved to have relation to Christ's royal function out of the mentioned phrase, 'Thy God hath anointed thee,' Chap. i. 9, Sec. 119. It is also as expressly proved of his priestly function, Heb. v. 5.

Here this is in particular applied to his prophetical office.

Of his immediate calling thereto, see Sec. 24.

These phrases, 'God gave his Son,' John iii. 16; 'sent him,' John iii. 34; anointed him,' Luke iv. 18, and such like, give evident proof of the point.

Hereof, that all might take more distinct notice, Christ himself oft maketh mention of doing his will that sent him, John iv. 34, and v. 30, and vi. 38, and ix. 4.

1. This was an encouragement unto Christ himself to go on in his work, because God appointed him thereto, John iii. 34.

2. It was a great inducement to others to attend upon his ministry, and well to heed it, John xi. 42, and xii. 44, 45, and xiii. 20.

3. It was a warrant and defence to Christ against his adversaries' oppositions, John v. 23, and vii. 16.

Obj. The person here said to be appointed is true God; how then could he be deputed to this or that?

Ans. 1. One person may send another, as the first person may send the second, and the first and second the third. Indeed, they are all equal, Philip. ii. 6;

but by a mutual consent one equal may be sent of another, John xvi. 26.

2. The Son, by assuming man's nature and sundry offices, made himself in those respects inferior to his Father, John, xiv. 28. And in this especial respect was Christ appointed by God.

This gives us just cause to accept Christ for our prophet, and every way to esteem him as a prophet, because the Father appointed him, 'He that receiveth me,' saith Christ, 'receiveth him that sent me,' John xiii. 20. Of particular duties concerning this point, see Sec. 26.

Sec. 34. *Of God's appointing ministers.*

That which is here said of the warrant that Christ had for his function, may be extended to all others' functions, specially in the church of God; and therein most of all to ministers of the word, for it is such a function that is here intended whereunto God appointed Christ. It is God's appointment that makes a true minister: 'No man taketh this honour unto himself, but he that is called of God,' Heb. v. 4. Ordinary and extraordinary ministers under the law and gospel were thus proved to be true ministers. The apostle exemplifieth this in Aaron, Heb. v. 4. Abijah herein made a difference betwixt the true priests and Levites, which served in the temple, and those false priests which Jeroboam made, 2 Chron. xiii. 9, 10. They were appointed by God, but not these. Hereby also extraordinary prophets justified their ministry, Jer. xvii. 16, Amos vii. 15; so likewise did the apostles, Rom. i. 1, 1 Pet. i. 1; the ministry of Timothy is so justified, 1 Tim. iv. 14. This warrant have the ordinary ministers of the New Testament, Eph. iv. 11.

The Lord is the high supreme Sovereign and chief Governor, as in the world, so especially in the church. He thereupon hath power to order and dispose places and functions as he pleaseth. Among men, they who are appointed by their sovereign to such or such an office, have a right unto it; so in a family, they who are appointed by the chief governor thereof. Much more they who are appointed by the Lord, for none have such an absolute sovereignty as he.

What may we now think of the manifold functions that are usurped in the church of Rome? Did God ever appoint a pope to be an universal bishop and head over the whole church? Did God ever appoint cardinals in his church? or abbots, or priors, or friars, or monks, or Jesuits, or sacrificing priests, or any other ministerial functions besides pastors and teachers?

What may we think of such women as presume to preach in public? Did that God (who by the mouth of his apostle said once and again, 'It is not permitted unto women to speak or to teach,' 1 Cor. xiv. 34, 1 Tim. ii. 12), did he appoint such?

Did God appoint boys, serving men, tradesmen, soldiers, or other like persons, who never understood tongues, arts, no, nor the body of divinity, upon a mere pretence of 'gifted brethren,' to be ministers of Christ, and stewards of the mysteries of God?

Sec. 35. *Of such ordinary ministers as under the gospel are appointed by God.*

There are three especial points that do demonstrate a ministerial function to be appointed of God.

1. The kind of ministry.
2. Ability to perform it.
3. A due setting apart thereto.

The kind of an ordinary ministerial function in the New Testament is expressed under these two words 'pastors, teachers,' Eph. iv. 11; both these are sometimes comprised under the word *teachers*, 1 Cor. xii. 28, 29. Answerably they are both exercised by one man, who is both the pastor and teacher of one congregation.

Their duties are thus distinguished: 'He that teacheth let him wait on teaching, he that exhorteth on exhortation,' Rom. xii. 7, 8.

Though these be the principal acts of pastors and teachers, yet the Lord seeing it meet to add seals, which are the sacraments, to his word, hath committed to these ministers the administration of those sacraments, Mat. xxviii. 19, 1 Cor. xi. 27. God hath also committed to them the keys, that is, the censures of the church, Mat. xvi. 19.

2. A gift and ability for performing those functions is given by God to those whom he appoints; so as that which the apostle saith of himself may be applied to all true ministers appointed of God, 'God hath made us able ministers of the New Testament,' 2 Cor. iii. 6.

The ability which God in this kind giveth, is,

(1.) To open the true and plain meaning of the Scripture.

(2.) To declare the fundamental points of true religion.

(3.) To refute errors and heresies contrary thereunto.

(4.) To make fit application, by exhortation, persuasion, consolation, reprehension, &c.

(5.) The gift of prayer may be added hereunto.

3. For a right setting apart to a ministerial function, these particulars are warranted by God's word.

(1.) That a testimony be given of their godly and sober life; 'He must have a good report of them which are without,' 1 Tim. iii. 7.

(2.) That examination be made of his gifts. This the apostle implieth under this phrase, 'Lay hands suddenly on no man,' 1 Tim. v. 22. The church of Ephesus is commended for trying ministers, Rev. xii. 2. In this case they must be examined about their ability in tongues, arts, grounds of divinity, yea, and about the true grace of God in them.

(3.) That exhortation be given them faithfully to discharge their function. Christ gave exhortation and direction to his disciples when he sent them out to preach, Mat. x. 5.

(4.) That invocation be made for God's blessings on them. Prayer was made for Barnabas and Saul when they were sent forth 'to the work whereunto the Holy Ghost called them,' Acts xiii. 2, 3.

(5.) That they be publicly set apart by other ministers, and that with imposition of hands, 1 Tim. iv. 14, and v. 22.

(6.) That all these be done in a solemn assembly, where there may be many witnesses, and many may join in craving a blessing. The apostles 'ordained elders in every church,' Acts xiv. 23.

(7.) That the day of ordination be a day of humiliation and of fasting, to sharpen our prayers the more thereby, Acts xiii. 3, and xiv. 23.

If to these there be added on the ministers' part a faithful execution of their function (which God testifieth concerning Moses, Num. xii. 7); and if withal the efficacy of God's power accompany their ministry, then is a farther stamp and seal for confirmation thereof added. The apostle much presseth this for confirmation of his own ministry, Eph. iii. 7, 2 Cor. iii. 8, 1 Cor. ix. 1. It cannot be avouched that this efficacy is always alike; in some it is more powerful, in some less; but where there is an apparent efficacy and blessing, there is a confirmation of that ministry.

If all the fore-mentioned points be applied to the ministers of reformed churches, and in special to the ministers of the church in England, we shall find them to be appointed of God; answerably they ought to be esteemed; in testimony of a good esteem of them we must,

1. Bless God for the ministry we have, Rom. x. 15.
2. Attend on their ministry, Acts xvi. 14.
3. Forsake them not, Heb. x. 25.
4. Pray for them, Eph. vi. 19.
5. Be subject to them, Heb. xiii. 17.
6. Respect them as God's ministers, 1 Cor. iv. 1.
7. Grudge not their maintenance, 1 Cor. ix. 7, 14.

Sec. 36. *Of comparing Moses and Christ.*

The apostle proceedeth to amplify the faithfulness of Christ by resembling it to the faithfulness of Moses, yet so as he doth also much prefer Christ before Moses, ver. 3, &c.

Herein we may observe the wisdom of the apostle, who maketh choice of such a pattern as was among the Hebrews, to whom he wrote, in highest account. 'Ye trust in Moses,' saith Christ to the Jews, John v. 45; 'We are Moses' disciples,' say the Jews of themselves, and 'we know that God spake unto Moses,' John ix. 28, 29. Moses his faithfulness was expressly commended by God, Num. xii. 7; and it was much celebrated, and held to be the best pattern. Now, when they should hear that Christ was no whit inferior to Moses, but in sundry respects more excellent, they could not but have their hearts raised to an high esteem of Christ.

The apostle gives Moses his due, and resembles Christ to him to avoid envy and to gain credence; yet also he extols Christ above Moses, to draw them from Moses to Christ, from the law to the gospel. See Sec. 45.

We may learn hereby, as we have occasion to compare things, not to withdraw true praise from any, but to give to every one their right. This is to be done in comparing persons, callings, or anything else. Many offend in the contrary; they will dispraise some persons and callings to extol others the more.

Sec. 37. *Of the meaning of these words, 'Moses in all his house.'*

The name *Moses* was given to the man here spoken of by Pharaoh's daughter, because (saith she) 'I drew him out of the water,' Exod. ii. 10. For that name is derived from a verb that signifieth to draw out, משה, *extraxit*,[1] and that out of waters, Ps. xviii. 16.

God appointed Moses to be the chief governor over his people, Acts vii. 35, who are comprised under this word *house*; for it is metonymically here taken, an house for the inhabitants in a house, which are ordinarily called a family. Therefore, by way of exposition, it is said, 'whose house we are,' ver. 6. Thus also Christ is said to be 'over the house of God,' Heb. x. 21; and the church is said to be 'the house of God,' 1 Tim. iii. 15; and judgment is said to 'begin at the house of God,' 1 Peter iv. 17, that is, the people of God.

This relative, αὐτοῦ, *his*, hath reference to God, comprised under this phrase, 'that appointed him;' for Moses was but a servant in the house, ver. 5. Therefore the house was not his.

I will not deny but that this relative may also have reference to Christ, who is resembled to Moses, and intended under this phrase, 'who was faithful.' Besides, it is afterwards said, that 'Christ as a Son was over his own house, whose house we are,' ver. 6. But betwixt these there is no discrepancy, for the Father and Son are one God, and the same things are oft attributed to both, John v. 17.

This reference declareth the reason that moved Moses to be so faithful, namely, because the house in which he was appointed a steward was God's house; the people over whom he was set were God's people. In this respect he wished that they were all prophets, because they were the Lord's people, Num. xi. 29. He earnestly desired that a good governor might succeed him, 'that the congregation of the Lord be not as sheep which have no shepherd,' Num. xxvii. 17.

To amplify his care in this respect, this general particle *all*, ἐν ὅλῳ, is added; for Moses was both a civil and an ecclesiastical governor; he was a prince and a prophet, Acts vii. 35, 37. He directed the people both concerning their dealing one with another, and also concerning their worshipping of God. His faithfulness was manifested in both; in the things

---

[1] See the *Church's Conquest*, on Exod. xvii. 9, sec. 5.

concerning God and his service, and in the things concerning the people and their welfare. This is a great amplification of his faithfulness.

Faithfulness in Moses was the more commendable, because he was entrusted with the dispensation of all God's counsel to that people. What Moses spake not, was taken to be not of God. See Chap. vii. 14, Sec. 76.

Sec. 38. *Of resemblance betwixt unequals.*

Concerning the resemblance here made betwixt Christ and Moses, a doubt arises how the less can illustrate the greater; how Christ's faithfulness can be amplified by Moses his faithfulness.

Ans. 1. Unequals may be compared in quality and likeness, though not in equality. Thus there are many resemblances betwixt the Creator and creatures.

2. To such as are better acquainted with the less than with the greater, the less may illustrate the greater. If a man have all his life been enclosed in a dark dungeon, where he never saw the light of sun or day, but only used candle-light, by that candle-light one may set out the excellency of the light of the sun. Thus the faithfulness of Moses being better known to the Jews than Christ's faithfulness to them, it may be amplified by resembling it to Moses his faithfulness; therefore he prefixeth this emphatical particle, $\varkappa\alpha i$, *also,* or *even.*

3. That which the apostle addeth of Christ's excellency above Moses, ver. 3, doth further clear the doubt, for it sheweth that Christ was not only like to Moses, even in Moses his chiefest excellency, but also infinitely surpassed him. See Sec. 45.

That we may the better discern how fitly the apostle hath brought in this resemblance, we will set down particular instances of Moses his faithfulness, and that throughout the whole course of his life, and withal shew how in every particular Christ was as faithful as Moses.

Sec. 39. *Of Moses's and Christ's faithfulness compared together.*

1. Moses would not be corrupted nor detained from God's house (I mean from God's people) by the greatest enticements that the world afforded, namely, the promotions, profits, and pleasures of Egypt, Heb. xi. 24-26.

2. Nor the pride, nor the stout heart, nor the threats of Pharaoh, could keep Moses from declaring the Lord's message unto him, Exod. v. 1, &c.

3. The murmuring of the people over whom Moses was set, kept not him from seeking their good, Exod. xiv. 12, 13, and xvi. 6, 7.

4. Moses had his warrant for all that he did from God, that appointed him, both in regard of the things which he did, and also of the manner of doing them. For proof hereof, compare Exod. xxv. 26, &c., where the charge is given, with Exod. xxxv. 36, &c., where the execution of the charge is set down.

5. Moses faithfully delivered all things that were given him in charge, whether they were great or small, pleasing or displeasing, to the people, Exod. xxxiii. 3.

6. When Moses had no express direction in a particular case from the Lord, he inquired of the Lord, and waited for an answer, Num. ix. 8, and xv. 34, Lev. xxiv. 12.

7. When Moses heard better advice than himself had first conceived, and perceived it to be agreeable to God's will, he followed it, Exod. xviii. 19, &c.

8. Moses envied not at any on whom the Lord bestowed the same gift that he had, Num. xi. 29.

9. Moses strained himself to the uttermost, yea, and beyond his strength, to do good to the people that were under his charge, Exod. xviii. 18.

10. Moses had respect to every one in the house or

1. Christ left the glory of heaven to redeem his church: 'Ye know the grace of our Lord Jesus Christ, that though he was rich, yet for your sakes he became poor,' 2 Cor. viii. 9.

2. Christ was not terrified by the threats, plots, and practices of priests, scribes, pharisees, rulers of the Jews, Herod, or any others, Luke xiii. 32, John vii. 28, &c.

3. Christ endured the contradiction of sinners against him, Heb. xii. 3.

4. Christ thus saith of himself, 'The Son can do nothing of himself, but what he seeth the Father do,' John v. 19; and again, 'I came down from heaven not to do mine own will, but the will of him that sent me,' John vi. 38.

5. Christ thus saith of himself to the Father, 'I have given unto them the words which thou gavest unto me;' 'I have declared unto them thy name, and will declare it,' John xvii. 8, 26.

6. Christ needed not this, for 'in him were hid all the treasures of wisdom and knowledge,' Col. ii. 3. If he had needed, he would have inquired.

7. So wise was Christ, as he ordered all things to the best, so as he needed no better advice than his own. He was wisdom itself.

8. Christ gave such gifts to others as himself had, Mat. x. 1, John xvi. 15, and xx. 21, 22.

9. Christ's agony sheweth that he put forth his utmost for his church's good, Luke xxii. 42-44.

10. In Christ all are one, free or bond, Gal. iii. 28.

congregation of Israel, whether princes or people, great or mean; he was no respecter of persons. He gave this charge to others, as he practised it himself, Deut. i. 16, 17.

11. Moses was careful for his posterity, and for the welfare of God's people that should live after him. Witness the many prayers he made, and directions which he gave for this end, and in particular his care for a good governor to succeed him, Num. xxvii. 16.

11. The commandments which Christ gave to the apostles, and the things pertaining to [the] kingdom of God, of which he spake after his resurrection, Acts i. 2, 3, demonstrate his care for future times.

Sec. 40. *Of being faithful like Christ and Moses.*

The fore-mentioned branches of the faithfulness of Moses and of Christ are not only for our instruction in those things that belonged to them, but also for our direction, that we also may be like unto them both, as they were like one another. This that we may be,

1. We must take heed that we be not entangled with the world, with the profits, honours, and delights thereof. These are sore temptations. They were the last wherewith Satan assaulted Christ, Mat. iv. 8, 9; that old disciple Demas was beguiled herewith, 2 Tim. iv. 10.

2. We may not fear the face of man, Luke ii. 4; if we do, we shall hardly do any good thing.

3. We may not regard people's murmurings; they are for the most part so blind, as they see not their own good. We must more respect this good than their displeasure.

4. We must have our warrant from God for what we teach others, lest for doctrines we teach the commandments of men.

5. We may not conceal any truth of God upon by and undue respects; when we are not fully resolved of a case, we must consult with God's word, Isa. viii. 20, Ps. cxix. 24.

6. We must follow better advice when it is given, and not to be too stiff and peremptory in our own opinion, Job xxxi. 13, 2 Kings v. 14, 1 Sam. xxv. 32, &c.

7. We may not envy at the gifts which God bestoweth on others, but rather rejoice thereat.

8. We must not be slothful, but put forth our strength to the utmost.

9. We may not be respecters of persons, James ii. 1; we must impartially do good to all of all sorts.

10. We must be careful of our posterity, and for the future estate of the church, and that by prayer, by well instructing the younger sort, and by providing successors.

Sec. 41. *Of the dependence of the third verse on the former.*

Ver. 3. *For this man was counted worthy of more glory than Moses, inasmuch as he who hath builded the house hath more glory than the house.*

Here the apostle begins to prefer Christ before Moses. This he doth under two metaphors; the first is taken from a builder and a house, in this and the next verse.

The first particle whereby this dissimilitude is brought in, sheweth that it dependeth upon something that went before as a cause or reason thereof; for it is a causal particle, *for.* It cannot with any good congruity have reference to the words immediately going before. What consequence can there be in this, Christ was like to Moses, for he was worthy of more honour; but if it have reference to all that went before, especially to the exhortation in the first verse, ' Consider the apostle and high priest,' &c., the consequence will be very clear; even thus, Consider the apostle and high priest that was faithful as Moses, for he is more excellent than Moses.

Hence it will follow, that Christ's excellency is of force to draw our minds and hearts after him. This argument is oft used by the prophets, who use to set out God's excellency above idols, above men, above all creatures, for this very end, to withdraw the hearts of people from doating upon idols, and placing confidence in man, or in any other creature, unto God himself. This may be a general use of all that hath or may be spoken of Christ's excellency. See Chap. ii. 1, Sec. 2. See also Sec. 23 of this chapter.

Sec. 42. *Of the meaning of these words,* 'counted worthy.'

This noun is the interpretation of one Greek particle, οὗτος, which is a relative pronoun, and properly signifieth no more than *this* or *he;* but it being [1] of the masculine gender, the word *man* is frequently joined with it to shew the meaning of it. Sometimes even in Greek, the word man is expressed, as Mark xv. 39, ὁ ἄνθρωπος οὗτος; John ix. 16, οὗτος ὁ ἄνθρωπος. It is used sometimes by way of excellency, as Heb. vii. 4, Luke xxiii. 41, and sometimes by way of derision and scorn, as Mat. xxvii. 47. In this sense it is oft thus translated; 'This fellow,' Mat. xii. 24, Acts xviii. 13. Here it is taken in the better sense by way of excellency and eminency.

The word, ἠξίωται, translated 'counted worthy,' sometimes intends a grace and favour, as when it is applied to God in reference to men. Thus mention is made of God's counting us 'worthy of his calling,' 2 Thes. i. 11. Sometimes it signifieth a due, a desert,

[1] See Chap. vii. 4, Sec. 31.

a worth in the thing or person accounted worthy. Thus it is here used. Christ was indeed worthy of all glory, for he was 'the brightness of the glory of his Father,' Heb. i. 3.

This word is here fitly used to shew, that the worth in him was so evident and conspicuous as he could not but be accounted a worthy one.

The word *accounted worthy* may have reference to God or man.

To God, who thoroughly knew the difference betwixt Jesus his Son and Moses his servant.

To man, namely, to such men as are of the church, who are well instructed and informed in the excellency of Christ and meanness of the best men, and thereupon will account him worthy of more glory than Moses, though Moses among mere men was a most excellent one.

The verb being set down in the passive voice—'was counted worthy,'—and no distinct mention of any in particular that so accounted him, it may be referred either to God or man, or rather to both, yea, and to angels too; for by God, angels, and men, even by all that have understanding and a right knowledge of Christ, is Christ accounted worthy of more glory than any mere creature whatsoever.

Sec. 43. *Of counting Christ worthy of glory.*

That which Christ is here said to be worthy of, is *glory*. Of the derivation and notation of the Greek word translated *glory*, and of the difference of it from the other word following, translated *honour*, see Chap. ii. 7, Sec. 60.

Here it intendeth that Christ is worthy to be well spoken of, to be praised, and to have his name every way celebrated. The apostle saith of 'elders that rule well, especially they that labour in the word and doctrine,' that they are to be 'counted worthy of double honour,' 1 Tim. v. 17. Never did any elder rule so well, nor so labour in the word and doctrine as Christ; he therefore, above all, is to be counted worthy of glory. If servants must 'count their own masters worthy of all honour, that the name of God and his doctrine be not blasphemed,' 1 Tim. vi. 1, how much more ought every one of us that are servants to this high supreme Lord, who is in special manner our own Master, count him worthy of all honour. Assuredly the name of God and his doctrine will exceedingly be blasphemed if we do it not. This is that Lord who is worthy to be praised, Ps. xviii. 3. The celestial spirits, who best know what is most due to this Lord, do so account of him.

Two especial reasons are rendered by those heavenly spirits why they account the Lord Jesus worthy of all glory; one is his high supreme sovereignty, manifested by his creating all things, and that for his own pleasure, which they thus express: 'Thou art worthy, O Lord, to receive glory, and honour, and power, for thou hast created all things, and for thy pleasure they are and were created,' Rev. iv. 11. The other is taken from his redeeming of the church, and the benefits that follow thereupon, which they thus express: 'Thou art worthy to take the book, and to open the seals thereof.' And again, 'Worthy is the Lamb to receive power, and honour, and glory, and blessing, &c.; for thou wast slain, and hast redeemed us to God by thy blood; and hast made us unto our God kings and priests,' &c., Rev. v. 9, 12.

'Give therefore unto the Lord glory and strength; give unto the Lord the glory due unto his name,' Ps. xxix. 1, 2.

For this end learn to know what is his due, what he is worthy of. Be well instructed in his excellencies as he is the Son of God, Chap. i. 3, and as he is the Mediator betwixt God and man; thereby thou shalt understand that he is infinitely above all thy praises. This is it that will enlarge thy heart, and open thy mouth to praise him with the utmost of thy power.

Hereunto we shall much more be incited, if we duly weigh his low condescension, his great undertakings, his bitter sufferings, his glorious conquest over sin, Satan, death, and hell, the high exaltation even of his human nature, the many and great benefits that we reap by all these.

Were our souls thoroughly affected with the aforesaid considerations, we should count him most worthy of all glory, and never be satisfied with setting out his praises. Hereof see more in *The Saints' Sacrifice* on Ps. cxvi. 17, sec. 108.

Sec. 44. *Of Christ's surpassing glory.*

The apostle doth not content himself with a simple expression of Christ's worth, but comparatively amplifieth it by this particle of comparison, πλείονος, *more*.

The Greek word is used to set forth sundry kinds of degrees, as,

1. Of number: 'More than (πλείους), twelve legions of angels,' Mat. xxvi. 53.

2. Of distance of place: 'That it spread no further' (ἐπὶ πλεῖον), Acts iv. 17.

3. Of time: 'To tarry longer' (ἐπὶ πλείονα χρόνον), Acts xviii. 20.

4. Of measure or quantity: 'Lovest thou me more (πλεῖον) than these?' John xxi. 15.

5. Of weight: 'No greater (πλέον) burden, or no heavier,' Acts xv. 28.

6. Of worth: 'Behold a greater (πλεῖον) than Jonas, a greater than Solomon,' Mat. xii. 41, 42.

7. Of excellency: 'A more excellent (πλείονα) sacrifice,' Heb. xi. 4.

All those fore-mentioned degrees may fitly be applied unto Christ, who in all these respects, and what other may be thought of, is to be accounted more worthy of glory than Moses or any other.

1. There were in number more excellencies in Christ than in any other: 'God anointed him with the oil of gladness above his fellows,' Ps. xlv. 7. 'God

giveth not the Spirit by measure unto him,' John iii. 34.

2. Christ is celebrated throughout the whole world; no man's name for distance of place is further made known; all people are to laud him, Rom. xv. 21. 'A great multitude which no man could number, of all nations and kindreds, and people, and tongues, stood before the throne, and before the Lamb, and cried, saying, Salvation to our God, which sitteth upon the throne, and unto the Lamb,' Rev. vii. 9, 10.

3. Christ from everlasting to everlasting is God, Ps. xc. 2; and glory is ascribed unto this our God for ever and ever, Rev. vii. 12.

4. For measure of glory, Christ is advanced above all: 'Thou art fairer than the children of men,' Ps. xlv. 2. 'As the apple trees among the trees of the wood, so is my Beloved among the sons,' Cant. ii. 3. And again, 'He is the chiefest among ten thousand,' Cant. v. 10.

5. Such a weighty crown of glory was set on Christ's head as never on any other's, Heb. ii. 7, Cant. iii. 11.

6. Christ's worth far exceeded all others. When John wept because no man was found worthy to open and read the book, he was thus comforted: 'Weep not: behold the Lion of the tribe of Judah, the root of David, hath prevailed to open the book.' Hereupon they sung this new song, 'Thou art worthy to take the book,' &c., Rev. v. 4, 5, 9.

7. Christ must needs be more excellent in glory than any other, for he is the brightness of his Father's glory,' Heb. i. 3.

Sec. 45. *Of the prerogatives of Moses, wherein Christ excels him.*

The person before whom Christ is here preferred is Moses.

That we may the better discern the excellency of Christ set out in this comparison of unequals betwixt Christ and Moses, it is meet to take distinct notice of the prerogatives of Moses, and withal to observe how Christ excelled Moses in all of them.

I will exemplify this in ten particular branches:

1. Moses was a prophet; yea, 'there arose not a prophet since in Israel like unto Moses,' Deut. xxxiv. 10.

2. God made Moses a governor over his people. He was a ruler, Acts. vii. 35.

3. Moses was a saviour and deliverer of the people, Acts. vii. 35. 'I will send thee unto Pharaoh,' saith the Lord unto Moses, 'that thou mayest bring forth my people, the children of Israel, out of Egypt,' Exod. iii. 10.

4. Moses was God's special ambassador, to whom God revealed all the commandments, and the statutes, and the judgments, which he should teach the people, Deut. v. 31.

5. Moses was as God's special friend: 'With him he spake mouth to mouth,' Deut. xii. 8.

6. Moses saw the back parts of God himself, Exod. xxxiii. 23.

7. Moses was mighty in words and in deeds, Acts vii. 22.

8. Moses his face shone so as the people were afraid to come nigh him, Exod. xxxiv. 36.

9. Moses was learned in all the wisdom of the Egyptians, Acts vii. 22.

10. When Moses died, God buried him, Deut. xxxiv. 6.

Notwithstanding all the prerogatives of Moses, he remained a mere man and mortal, yea, subject to sin, whereby he so provoked God as he was not suffered to lead Israel into Canaan, and there to settle them, Deut. xxxii. 51, 52.

1. God saith of his Son to Moses, 'I will raise them up a Prophet from among their brethren like unto you,' Deut. xviii. 18; 'This was a Prophet mighty in deed and word before God and all the people,' Luke xxiv. 19; yea, he was greater than Moses.

2. Christ is Lord over all: 'All power is given to him in heaven and in earth,' Mat. xxviii. 18.

3. Christ was a greater Saviour from a more cruel tyrant, and from a greater bondage, Heb. ii. 14, 15.

4. Christ needed not any revelation: 'For it pleased the Father that in him should all fullness dwell,' Col. i. 19.

5. Christ was more: 'He is the only begotten Son, which is in the bosom of the Father,' John i. 18.

6. Christ is in the Father, and the Father in him: 'He that hath seen him hath seen the Father,' John xiv. 9, 10.

7. Christ was more mighty: 'Never man spake like him,' John vii. 46; Christ 'did the works which none other man did,' John xv. 24.

8. Christ 'his face did shine as the sun, and his raiment was white as the light,' Mat. xvii. 2; Christ is 'the brightness of the glory of his Father,' Heb. i. 3.

9. In Christ 'was hid all the treasures of wisdom and knowledge,' Col. ii. 3.

10. Christ being dead, was raised again and taken into heaven, Acts. i. 9.

Christ, notwithstanding his abasement, was true God and eternal: 'He did no sin,' 1 Peter ii. 22. He leads his people into the heavenly Canaan. Herein was Joshua a type of Jesus.

Had the Jews that lived in Christ's time known and believed the great difference betwixt Christ and Moses, they would not have so lightly esteemed him as they did, much less have rejected him. Christ's excellencies were evidently made known to them by his doctrine and works, concerning which some of them said, 'When Christ cometh, will he do more miracles than those which this man hath done?' And again: 'Never man spake as this man,' John vii. 31, 46; 'But the god of this world hath blinded their minds, lest the light of the glorious gospel of Christ, who is the image of God, should shine unto them,' 2 Cor. iv. 4.

The like may be said of their posterity, the Jews that have lived since their days, and of whom there are many yet living.

Did Turks, Saracens, and others which account Moses to be a great prophet, and receive his books as canonical, understand the difference betwixt Christ and Moses, they would certainly entertain the gospel, and believe in Jesus, and prefer him before Moses.

As for us that know and believe the difference betwixt Christ and Moses, let us know and believe that there is an answerable difference between the law and the gospel, and thereupon be moved to have the gospel in as high an account as ever any of the Jews had the law. For this end let us set the pattern of David before us, who could not satisfy himself in setting out his high esteem thereof, and great delight therein. Read for this purpose Ps. xix. 7, &c., and Ps. cxix. throughout. This moved him to lay that charge upon his son, to 'keep the statutes of God as they are written in the law of Moses,' 1 Kings ii. 3. Behold also the pattern of Josiah, who 'turned to the Lord with all his heart, and with all his soul, and with all his might, according to all the law of Moses,' 1 Kings xxiii. 25. Of the Jews that returned from the captivity, it is said that 'they entered into a curse, and into an oath, to walk in God's law, which was given by Moses.'

We ought not only so to esteem of the gospel, but also to give more earnest heed thereto. See Chap. xxi. Sec. 25. As Moses, the lawgiver, could not bring Israel into Canaan, so the law can bring none to heaven. But Joshua settled them there; so Jesus by the gospel settleth believers in heaven.

Sec. 46. *Of honour due to a builder.*

The apostle further proceeds to amplify the disparity betwixt Christ and Moses by a particular exemplification of the excellency of Christ above Moses. This he doth under the metaphor of a builder, and an house built. The argument may be thus framed:

The builder of an house is worthy of more glory than the house.

But Christ is the builder, and Moses a part of the house built.

Therefore Christ is worthy of more glory than Moses.

The proposition is in the latter part of the third verse.

The assumption in the verses following.

The conclusion in the former part of this third verse.

The participle ὁ κατασκευάσας, whereby the builder is here set out, is in Greek a compound. The simple verb σκευάζειν signifieth to prepare or to put on, or to adorn. I find it not in the New Testament, but it is frequent in other authors.

This compound is oft used in the New Testament, and that to set out John's preparing a way, Mat. xi. 10; and the making of the tabernacle, Heb. ix. 2; and ordaining the things thereof, Heb. ix. 6; and preparing or building the ark, Heb. xi. 7, 1 Peter iii. 20.

Here it is fitly translated, 'he who doth build,' or a builder, in that it hath reference to an house built. A builder is the efficient cause of that which he buildeth, and in that respect worthy of more honour than the effect or the work done; for if there be any excellency in a thing built, that excellency cometh from the builder. When men behold an edifice substantially, artificially, and curiously built, they use to commend the builder. Moses blessed Bezaleel and Aholiab, and the other workmen that built the tabernacle, when he looked upon all the work, and beheld that they had done it as the Lord had commanded, Exod. xxxix. 43. An honourable mention is made of Solomon, even after the captivity, for the temple which he built, Ezra v. 11. Though Nebuchadnezzar offended through the pride of his heart in boasting of his great palace, yet this his speech,—'Is not this great Babylon that I have built for the house of my kingdom?' Dan. iv. 30, —sheweth that the honour of a fair building appertaineth to the builder. On the contrary, he that beginneth a building, and is not able to finish it, makes himself a laughing-stock, Luke xiv. 29.

It is a senseless thing to attribute the glory of that which is received from another, to the subject matter in which it is.

What praise is it to the timber or stones, or other materials, that they make up a fair and glorious edifice? Can the timber cut down, hew, square, fit, and lay itself in order to make up the edifice? Can stones, or clay, or iron, or any other material, do the like? Can silver, or gold, or precious stones, polish or put themselves in those places and ranks, where they may beautify a building?

The workman that sits, prepares, lays all sorts of materials in their due places, who fastens them together, who erects the edifice, and perfects it, deserves the glory of his workmanship, and by due hath the praise thereof.

To apply this to the most famous and glorious building that ever was, which is the church of God: 'We as lively stones are built up a spiritual house,' 1 Pet. ii. 5. 'We are built upon the foundation of the apostles and prophets, Jesus Christ himself being the chief corner-stone,' Eph. ii. 20, &c. Should we hereupon think to have the glory hereof? Not unto us, not unto us, but unto our builder, the Lord Jesus Christ, the glory be given.

We are by nature rough, untoward, unfit to make a temple for God; we are dead in sin. Unless by the axe of God's word, the operation of God's Spirit accompanying the same, we be hewed and squared; unless the hard knobs of obstinacy be chopped off; unless the bark of civility and formal profession be pulled away; unless the sprouts of pride be paired off; unless the hollow dots of hypocrisy be made plain and even; unless the rotten holes of lusts be cut out; unless we be quickened and made living stones, fit for a spiritual building; unless we be gathered together, and united to Christ the foundation, and one to another, as mutual parts of the same building, we can never make up a temple for God to dwell in. In that therefore we are 'an habitation of God through the Spirit,' the praise is due to Christ the builder of this house.

Sec. 47. *Of the meaning of these words, 'For every house is builded of some man.'*

Verse 4. '*For every house is builded by some man, but he that built all things is God.*

The apostle here proveth that assumption which was set down in the former section, namely, that Christ is the builder, and Moses a part of the house built. This causal particle, γὰρ, *for*, whereby this verse is knit to the former, implieth that this is a proof of that which went before.

Of this assumption there are two parts.

One, that Christ is the builder.

The other, that Moses is part of the house built.

Both these parts are proved by two general undeniable principles.

The latter part, concerning him that was built, is first proved in these words, 'Every house is builded of some man.'

The Greek pronoun translated *some man*, τίς (ὑπό τινος), is an indefinite particle, as that οὗτος, which in the former verse was translated *this man*. See Sec. 42. As there, so here, the word *man* is added by our English. It may have reference to any one of the masculine gender, not God himself excepted.

Mention being here made of 'every house,' πᾶς οἶκός, I will endeavour distinctly to set forth what kinds of houses are mentioned in Scripture.

An house hath reference to God or man.

To man properly or tropically.

An house is properly put for a building made by man, and fitted for man's habitation; as the house where Job's children feasted together, and with a violent wind fell upon them,' Job i. 18, 19.

Tropically it is taken three ways.

1. By the metonymy, for the inhabitants thereof, Acts x. 2; or for the goods and commodities therein, Mat. xxiii. 14.

2. By a metaphor.

(1.) For a nation, as 'The house of Israel,' Josh. xxi. 45. And 'the house of bondage,' that is, the land of Egypt, Exod. xx. 2.

(2.) For a tribe, as 'the house of Levi,' Ps. cxxxv. 20.

(3.) For the grave, which as an house holdeth our body, Job xxx. 23.

(4.) For our body, which as an house holdeth our soul, 2 Cor. v. 1.

3. By a synecdoche, an house is put for kindred, who though they be not in a man's family, yet appertain thereunto. Abraham chargeth his servant to take a wife for his son, 'of his father's house,' Gen. xxiv. 40. Thus an house is put sometimes for predecessors, as Joseph is said to be 'of the house of David,' Luke i. 27. And sometimes for posterity; thus God promiseth to 'build Jeroboam a sure house,' 1 Kings xi. 38.

To God an house hath reference, either above or below.

1. Above; heaven is said to be his house, John xiv. 2.

2. Below; God's house hath reference to places or to persons.

(1.) For place, under the law the tabernacle was called God's house, Judges xviii. 31. And the temple, 1 Kings viii. 10, and the synagogues, Ps. lxxxiii. 12, and any place where God manifested his presence; as an open field, Gen. xxviii. 17.

Finally, Every place where God's people assemble to worship him, is called and counted the house of God, Isa. lvi. 7.

(2.) For persons, God's house compriseth under it,

[1.] The whole number of such as are called, even the universal church throughout the world, Heb. x. 21.

[2.] Particular assemblies or congregations, 1 Tim. iii. 15.

[3.] Individual persons, 1 Cor. vi. 19, 2 Cor. vi. 16.

Here, in this text, *house* may be taken either for an earthly material house built by man, or for a spiritual house built by God.

If this phrase, *every house*, be properly taken for an earthly house, it intends a resemblance and an experimental proof; as if he had said, We see by experience that all houses wherein men dwell, are built by some man or other; so Moses, being of the spiritual house of God, must needs be built.

If it be taken for a spiritual house, then it implieth that not only earthly houses wherein men dwell, but also spiritual houses and temples of the Holy Ghost, are built by some.

Thus this general particle πᾶς, *every*, may have reference to both kinds of houses, earthly and spiritual.

Both acceptions of the word *house*, in the proper and metaphorical sense, tend to the same scope, namely, to prove that Moses was brought to be of the house of God, which is the church, not by himself, but by another. Who that other was, is expressed in these words, 'He that hath built all things is God.'

The word *builded*, κατασκευάζεται, in Greek is the verb of that participle which was used in the former verse, ὁ κατασκευάσας, and thus translated, 'who hath builded.' This and that signify the same thing.

Sec. 48. *Of ministers receiving from Christ what they are or have.*

That which the apostle intendeth under this general, 'Every house is builded of some man,' concerneth Moses in special, who in his time was for place and parts the most eminent and excellent in God's church; yet was he built. What is said of him may be extended to all that ever were, are, or shall be, in the church of God. All are built; all are brought into the church; all have their gifts and graces, their places and functions, their privileges and prerogatives, bestowed and conferred upon them. This apostle includeth himself among the other members of God's church, where he saith, 'Whose house are we,' ver. 6. He saith indefinitely of all Christians, without excepting any, 'In Christ you also are builded together,' Eph. ii. 22. Another apostle in such an extent saith the like: 'Ye also, as lively stones, are built up a spiritual house,' 1 Peter ii. 5. More expressly to the point in hand saith the apostle of himself, 'By the grace of God I am what I am,' 1 Cor. xv. 10; and again, 'I thank Christ Jesus our Lord, who hath enabled me,' 1 Tim. i. 12.

Obj. The apostle maketh himself a master builder, who laid the foundation: and he maketh other ministers 'builders upon that foundation,' 1 Cor. iii. 10. By the same reason Moses and the prophets may be counted builders, yea, and chief builders.

Ans. We must distinguish betwixt the person and function of a prophet, apostle, and other minister.

In regard of other persons, they are born in the same condition, and subject to the same passions and infirmities that others are, Acts xiv. 15, as insufficient of themselves to do anything as of themselves, as any other. 'We are not sufficient of ourselves,' &c., saith an apostle, 2 Cor. iii. 5. Ministers, even the best ministers, stand in as much need of means both for preservation of their body, and also for the salvation of their souls, as others do.

In regard of their functions, Christ doth indeed communicate his dignity and work with them. The apostle saith of himself and other ministers, 'We are workers together, συνεργοί Θεοῦ, with God,' 1 Cor. iii. 9. In the same respect also he saith, 'We are ambassadors for Christ, we pray you in Christ's stead,' 2 Cor. v. 20.

But Christ doth so communicate his work and office to them, as he retaineth all the power in his own hands. Ministers are only instruments, and their ministry is of power, so much and so long as it pleaseth God to add his blessing thereto, without which blessing they are nothing. 'Neither is he that planteth anything, neither he that watereth, but God that giveth the increase,' 1 Cor. iii. 7. 'Without me,' saith Christ to his disciples, 'ye can do nothing,' John xv. 5.

Thus though ministers in regard of their office be sowers, planters, waterers, fathers, builders, &c., yet in regard of their persons, they are God's corn, plants, gardens, children, houses. So was Moses, so were all other prophets, so were the apostles and all other ministers.

The Jews, therefore, had too high a conceit of Moses. They accounted him their lord and master, and professed themselves to be his disciples, and that in opposition to Christ, John ix. 28; yea, they 'trusted in Moses,' John v. 28.

Men may also have ministers of the gospel in too high an esteem. Indeed, it is the most usual fault to despise ministers; yet some are prone to fall into the other extreme. People ought to take heed thereof, for it is a kind of secret idolatry, and it may draw our mind too much from Christ himself.

Let ministers also take heed of thinking too highly of themselves. They are but parts of that house whereof other Christians also are parts. Let them, therefore, make themselves equal to them of the lower sort, and account all of this spiritual house as brethren. Christ himself was 'not ashamed to call them brethren,' Heb ii. 11, Sec. 108. See Secs. 3, 4, of this chapter.

Ministers being of this house that is built by another, they must be diligent in using the same means for their spiritual edification, that they teach others. They pray for themselves, and preach to themselves, and partake themselves of the sacraments, lest they prove like the builders of Noah's ark, who perished with the wicked world.

Finally, Moses being, as others, of that house that was built, people must not expect too great matters from their ministers, as if they were the builders of the house. They must use them as ministers of God, depending on God for his blessing, yet must they pray for them, and bear with them, and succour them, and do all meet kindnesses for them.

Sec. 49. *Of the church having what it hath by Christ.*

The second part of the assumption, set down Sec. 46, is here proved. It is this: Christ is the builder. It is proved by a general thus: 'God hath built all things,' therefore God hath built that house whereof Moses is a part.

This title Θεός, God, must here in particular be applied to Christ,[1] or else there is no consequence in the argument.

The apostle doth purposely express Christ under this title *God*, for these reasons:

1. The work he speaks of is a divine work, proper to God.

2. It sheweth, that without question and beyond comparison, Christ was greater than Moses.

[1] Christ true God. See Chap. i. 8, Sec. 107.

3. This ratifieth what he had before declared in the first chapter concerning Christ, that he was true God.

Some restrain this general $τὰ\ πάντα$, 'all things,' to the church: as if he had said, God hath built up all members of the church, and all things appertaining thereunto. Thus they restrain this phrase, 'Who worketh all things after the counsel of his own will,' Eph. i. 11, to the things of the church.

If the phrase be taken in the most general extent that may be, even for all creatures, it will tend to the same scope; for then the argument will be this, from the general to the special, he that hath built all things hath assuredly built the church and the several members thereof, and all things appertaining thereto.

To shew that this general tendeth to the same end that the point proved doth, which is thus laid down: verse 3, 'He who hath builded ($κατασκευάσας$) the house, hath more honour than the house.' The apostle useth the very same word both here and there.

This manner of expressing the builder before mentioned by this title *God*, and by the extent of his work, *all things*, much amplifieth the excellency of Christ above Moses; and it confirmeth two great articles of our Christian faith, which are these:

1. Christ is true God. Hereof see more Chap. i. 8, Sec. 107, where this title *God* is applied to him; and Chap. i. 10, Sec. 128, where this title *Lord*, as the interpretation of *Jehovah*, is applied to him.

2. Christ is the creator of all things, for so much this word *built*, in reference to this extent *all things*, importeth. Hereof see more Chap. i. 2, Sec. 18, and Chap. i. 10, Sec. 127.

Two arguments are here set down against Arius.

1. The title *God*, which is properly taken.

2. The work of *creating all things*, which is proper to the true eternal God.

The special point here intended by the apostle is, that the church is made an house of God, and the several members of the church so ordered and qualified as they make up that church, and all this by Christ. By Christ, children of men, who are by nature dead in sin, are quickened and made lively stones; by him they are gathered together, and endued with all needful graces, whereby they come to be an holy house, and a fit temple for God to dwell in. 'The Son quickeneth whom he will,' John v. 21; 'In Christ all things are gathered together in one,' Eph. i. 10; 'Of his fulness have all we received, and grace for grace,' John i. 16. In this respect Christ is styled 'The Head of the church, and the Saviour of his body,' Eph. i. 22, and v. 23.

1. The members of the church, before they were members, were dead and scattered, and destitute of all grace. Therefore there must be some to quicken them, to gather them, and to furnish them with grace.

2. Christ of all is the fittest to do this. He is the very wisdom and the power of the Father. By him all things were made, and all things are preserved, sustained, and ordered. Most meet, therefore, it is that the church should receive her spiritual being and preservation, and every good thing, from and by Christ.

3. For working the great work of man's redemption, which is proper to the church, Christ humbled himself even to death, the death of the cross. Most meet it is, therefore, that he should have the honour of building up his church. Thus he seeth of the travail of his soul, and is satisfied, according to the promise, Isa. liii. 11; read Philip. ii. 8–11.

This honour is given to the Son of God, 'that all men should honour the Son, even as they honour the Father,' John v. 23.

Let us therefore, that are of this house, that find ourselves quickened, gathered, and built up in this holy house, and freed from our former miseries, acknowledge as much, as Naaman did, 2 Kings v. 15; or rather, as the tenth leper did, turn back, and glorify God, Luke xvii. 15. Let us return all the praise and glory of all the beauty we have to Christ, and not arrogate anything to ourselves, but with humble thankfulness say, 'By the grace of God I am what I am,' 1 Cor. xv. 10; and thus, 'I live; yet not I, but Christ liveth in me,' Gal. ii. 20.

Sec. 50. *Of a faithful servant.*

Ver. 5. *And Moses verily was faithful in all his house, as a servant, for a testimony of those things which were to be spoken after.*

Ver. 6. *But Christ as a Son over his own house; whose house are we, if we hold fast the confidence and the rejoicing of the hope firm unto the end.*

The second metaphor[1] or comparison, whereby the excellency of Christ above Moses is set forth, is in these two verses. It is taken from the difference betwixt a son, who is heir and lord of an house, and a servant, who is only a minister therein.

The argument may be thus framed:

A son ruling over his own house is more excellent than a servant therein;

But Christ is such a son, and Moses was such a servant;

Therefore Christ is more excellent than Moses.

The proposition is taken for grant as a truth most evident and clear.

Both the parts of the assumption are largely exemplified.

The latter part first in the 5th verse, then the former part in the 6th verse.

I will follow the apostle's order, and begin with the exemplification of Moses's inferiority, which is set down in three particulars:

1. Moses was a *servant*, but Christ the *Son*.

2. The house where Moses was was *another's*, but the house was Christ's *own*.

3. Moses was only *in* the house, but Christ was *over* the house.

[1] Of the two metaphors, see Sec. 41.

That this point might be the better heeded, the apostle sets it down with this note of asseveration, μέν, verily.

The conjunction is that which is ordinarily used to confirm a point, and it implieth that the matter here set down is a matter of moment, and in that respect the more to be regarded.

That which before he had said, of Moses being 'faithful in all his house,' is here again repeated; because it is a matter very observable, and because it addeth much to the commendation of Moses. For that condition of Moses, that he was a servant, may seem to be a matter of abasement; but this, that he was a faithful servant, much honoureth him. And the joining of his faithfulness with his condition of being a servant sheweth one reason of his faithfulness, even because he was a servant; and withal it sheweth a special duty of a servant, which is to be faithful, Mat. xxiv. 41, and xxv. 21.

1. That trust that is reposed in servants requires that they be faithful. It is a matter of great consequence to be faithful in the trust that is reposed in one, and it deserveth much commendation, and procures also remuneration, Mat. xxv. 21, 23; but, on the contrary, it is a great crime, yea, and a great aggravation of one's fault, to fail trust.

2. Servants are to give an account of that with which they are trusted. Do ye not remember what the lord said to his steward, who was his servant? 'Give an account of thy stewardship,' Luke xvi. 2. Were not all the servants to whom talents were committed called to an account? It is expressly said, that 'the lord reckoned with them;' he reckoned both with the faithful and unfaithful, Mat. xxv. 17, &c. Well, mark the issue that followed upon that reckoning, both in relation to the faithful and also to the unfaithful servants.

Oh consider this, all ye that are God's servants! Whether magistrates in the commonwealth, or ministers in the church, or appointed to any other function by God, be faithful as a servant.

Sec. 51. *Of this particle 'as,' and this epithet 'servant.'*

The first difference here expressed betwixt Moses and Christ is, that Moses was a *servant*.

The manner of expressing this point, by this note of similitude, ὡς, *as*, doth not here intend a mere likeness; as if he had not been indeed a true, proper servant, but a servant only in some resemblance and properties appertaining to a servant; but it rather importeth a clear manifestation of what he was. As he was indeed a servant, and knew himself to be a servant, so he manifested himself to be one by his faithful service, and other properties of a good servant. He carried himself in his place as a servant, not as a lord. Thus this very particle *as* is used for the manifestation and demonstration of the reality of a thing in this phrase, 'We beheld his glory, the glory as of the only begotten (δόξαν ὡς μονογενοῦς) of the Father,' John i. 14. Moses was truly and properly a servant in relation to God, whose servants all are, Ps. cxix. 91; especially saints, of what rank or degree soever they be. See more hereof in *The Saints' Sacrifice*, on Ps. cxvi. 16, sec. 99.

The original word, θεράπων, here translated *servant*, carrieth an especial emphasis. Throughout the whole New Testament I find it nowhere else, but here only used; but in other authors frequently. It setteth out such an one as is officious, desirous to please his master; ready to do his duty, and that willingly. There is a verb of the same kind that signifieth to seek to please.

Sec. 52 *Of Moses being a servant.*

Moses was the chief governor over the people, yet in reference to God a servant. So God calleth him, Num. xii. 7, 8; so he styleth himself, Exod. iv. 10; so do others call him, Deut. xxxiv. 5; Joshua i. 1. This title in sacred Scripture is given to no one man more frequently than to Moses.

The authority and dignity which he had was not from himself, for there is no power but of God, Rom. xiii. 1. It was the Lord that said unto him, Thou shalt be instead of God, Exod. iv. 16.

All the power that men have is subordinate. They who are over others are themselves under authority, Mat. viii. 9; and they have a Lord to whom they are to give an account, Luke xvi. 2.

Moses made a twofold use hereof: one in reference to God, another in reference to the people.

1. In reference to God:

(1.) Upon all occasions he testified a reverent respect to his divine majesty. When God made known himself unto him, 'He hid his face; for he was afraid to look upon God,' Exod. iii. 6.

(2.) He earnestly desired an evidence of God's favour: 'If now I have found grace in thy sight, O Lord, let my Lord, I pray thee, go amongst us,' Exod. xxxiv. 9.

(3.) He was ready to obey cheerfully, sincerely, as one who was to give an account, Heb. xi. 26, 27.

(4.) He preferred the glory of his Lord, even to his own glory and salvation, Exod. xxxii. 10, 32.

2. In reference to the people he was as a servant, in that he was,

(1.) Meek and humble. He was not like that servant who smote his fellow-servants, Mat. iv. 29. It is testified that 'Moses was very meek, above all the men that were upon the face of the earth,' Num. xii. 3.

(2.) He did willingly partake of that portion which God allotted out unto his people, and put his shoulders under their burden: 'He chose rather to suffer affliction with the people of God, than to enjoy the pleasures of sin,' Heb. xi. 25.

(3.) He much pitied and commiserated the people, and that when they murmured against him, Exod. xiv. 11–13.

(4.) He oft prayed and earnestly cried unto God for them, Exod. xxxii. 11, 31, Num. xii. 13.

Then who are in Moses his place (as princes of state and ministers of the word are) must be of Moses's mind. They must know that they are God's servants, and answerably carry themselves both to God and his people. It will therefore be very useful for them oft to meditate on this pattern. Of Moses's faithfulness, see Sec. 39.

Of this phrase, 'in all his house,' see Sec. 37.

Sec. 53. *Of Moses and other ministers for a testimony.*
An especial end why Moses was made a servant in God's house, is thus set down : ' For a testimony of those things which were to be spoken after.' The word, μαρτύριον, *testimony*, signifieth a witness-bearing ; it comes from the same root that that word did which is used Chap. iii. 4, Sec. 30, and spoken of God's bearing witness, συνεπιμαρτυροῦντος.

It here intendeth two things :
1. A confirmation of the truth of a thing.
2. An evidence against such as believed not.

In both these senses Christ thus useth this word : ' Shew thyself to the priest, for a testimony unto them,' Mat. viii. 4. This he speaks to a leper whom he hath cleansed, that he should go to the priest, that by the priest the truth of the miracle might be confirmed (for the priest could judge of a leprosy whether it were thoroughly cleansed or no), and that the unbelieving Jews might be convinced about the power of Christ.

The manner of expressing this clause thus, εἰς μαρτύριον, '*for a testimony,*' pointeth at the end of Moses' ministry, which was to bear witness unto and to confirm God's truth.

Of confirming the truth of God, see Chap. ii. 3, Sec. 25.

That whereof Moses was to be for a testimony is thus expressed: ' Of those things which were to be spoken after.' All this is the interpretation of one Greek word, λαληθησομένων, which is of the future tense. To express the emphasis thereof more fully, this particle *after* is added.

The future things whereof Moses was to be for a testimony were,

1. Such as Moses himself was to deliver to the people ; for Moses bare record of, and gave witness to, such things as God would have the people take notice of. Thus it is said of John, ' He bare record of the word of God,' Rev. i. 2, 3.

2. Such things as Christ and his apostles in their time preached ; for thus saith Christ, ' These are the words which I spake unto you, that all things must be fulfilled which were written in the law of Moses concerning me,' Luke xxiv. 44. To the like purpose St. Paul ' persuaded the Jews concerning Jesus out of the law of Moses,' Acts xxviii. 23. Hence it is that Christ said to the Jews, ' Had ye believed Moses, you would also have believed me, for he wrote of me,' John v. 46.

3. Such things as this apostle hereafter sets down in this epistle, which are types that prefigured Christ, of which he saith, ' This is the sum, we have such an high priest,' &c. Heb. viii. 1. Thus the word may be translated, ' which shall be spoken after.'

Neither of the foresaid interpretations do cross the other ; but all in substance agree, for the things which were in the types which Moses delivered to the people were by Christ and the apostles revealed in their truth, and in this epistle the types and truth are both declared.

That which is here said of the end of Moses his ministry, that it was for a testimony of God's truth, is in the general true of all ministers. ' All the prophets gave witness' of such things, Acts iv. 43 ; John the Baptist came ' for a witness to bear witness of the light,' John i. 7 ; Jesus Christ himself was ' a faithful witness,' Rev. i. 5 ; the apostles were to be witnesses unto Christ, Acts i. 8.

God had these witnesses both to make known his will to his church, and also to confirm and ratify the same by evidence out of God's word ; yea, also by their answerable practice, and by their suffering for what they preached.

Herein we have an evidence of God's good providence to his church, who never left it without witness. Moses was for a testimony in his time ; prophets succeeded him, John them, apostles him, and ordinary ministers in all ages since the apostles' days succeeded them.

Happy are they who give such heed thereunto, as they reap the benefit thereof; but their judgment is the greater who, having witness given to the light, walk in darkness, and remain ignorant and obstinate. But whether men regard this witness or no, it shall not be in vain ; the truth of God is more justified thereby, and unbelievers made more inexcusable.

As Moses and the prophets gave witness to the things which were to be done at Christ's first coming, so ministers, who live in these latter days, give witness to the things which shall be done at his last coming.

Sec. 54. *Of this title ' Christ.'*
Ver. 6. *But Christ as a Son over his own house ; whose house are we, if we hold fast the confidence, and the rejoicing of the hope firm unto the end.*

This particle δὲ, *but*, implieth a difference betwixt that which went before, and that which followeth. The difference, or rather dissimilitude, is betwixt Moses and Christ, who is far the more excellent. The inferiority of Moses being distinctly set down in the former verse, the excellency of Christ above Moses is as distinctly exemplified in this verse, and that in the three particular branches mentioned, Sec. 50.

Because in setting out his excellency he had mentioned God, verse 4, and applied it to him, to shew whom he meant under that title *God*, he here expressly nameth Christ.

Christ in Greek[1] signifieth the same that Messiah in Hebrew[2] doth, namely, anointed. An evangelist cleareth this point where, upon mention of Messiah, he saith, 'which is, being interpreted, the Christ,' John i. 41. And he who by the psalmist is in reference to God called 'his Messiah,' or 'his Anointed,' Ps. ii. 1, is by the apostles called 'his Christ,' Acts iv. 26. The word *Messiah* in Hebrew is oft by our English translated *anointed*, as 1 Sam. ii. 10, 2 Chron. vi. 26. Ps. lxxxiv. 9, and by the Greek LXX translated Christ.

To shew that this name *Christ*, is by an excellency and property attributed to Jesus our Saviour, it is many times expressed with an emphasis thus: 'the Christ,' John xx. 31; 'that Christ,' John vi. 69. 'very Christ,' Acts ix. 22; 'the Lord's Christ,' Luke ii. 26; 'The Christ of God,' Luke ix. 20. The priests and scribes which rejected that Christ knew that the promised Messiah was 'that Christ,' whereupon they said to John, 'Why baptizest thou, if thou be not that Christ?' John i. 25. And they thus adjure Jesus himself, 'Tell us whether thou be the Christ,' Mat. xxvi. 63; yea, the common people knew as much, for 'all men mused in their hearts of John, whether he were the Christ or no,' Luke iii. 15; and of Jesus himself they said, 'Do the rulers know indeed that this is the very Christ?' John vii. 26; and the woman of Samaria said of him, 'Is not this the Christ?' and again, 'I know that Messias cometh which is called Christ,' John iv. 25, 29.

This title Christ or Anointed importeth three things.

1. The functions which Jesus undertook for man's salvation, even the functions of such as were anointed under the law. These are of three sorts.

(1.) Kings. Of anointing these, see Chap. i. 9, Sec. 119. Now Christ was that promised King, of whom the other were types.

(2.) Priests were anointed, Lev. viii. 12, 30. Hereunto the psalmist alludeth, where he maketh mention of precious ointment upon the head of Aaron, Ps. cxxxiii. 2. Of Christ's priesthood see Chap. ii. 17, Sec. 172.

(3.) Prophets. There is one instance of anointing a prophet. For God giveth this charge to Elijah, 'Thou shalt anoint Elisha to be prophet in thy room.' Prophets are in special manner called God's anointed. For where God saith, 'Touch not mine anointed,' by way of exemplification he addeth, 'and do my prophets no harm,' Ps. cv. 15. Prophets were types of Christ, Deut. xviii. 15, &c. That text is expressly applied to Christ, Acts. iii. 22, &c. Jonas also was a type of Christ, Luke xi. 30. The Jews that lived in Christ's time knew that the promised Messiah should be a prophet, John vi. 14, and vii. 40, Mat. xxi. 11. In all these places there is an emphatical expression, *the* prophet, *that* prophet. Of Christ's prophetical function, see

2. The title *Christ*, or *anointed*, implieth the right that Christ had to undertake those functions. He that anointed Christ, which was his Father, Heb. v. 5, he appointed him, and thereby gave him a right to his office. See more hereof, verse 2, Sec. 33.

3. It implieth an ability that Christ had to perform those functions whereunto he was anointed; hereupon Christ saith, 'The Spirit of the Lord is upon me, because he hath anointed me,' Luke iv. 18. This phrase, 'The Spirit of the Lord is upon me,' implieth the abilities that were conferred upon him by the Spirit of God, and that in a more than ordinary manner; for he was 'anointed above his fellows,' see Chap. i. 9, Sec. 123.

Of the difference betwixt this name *Christ* and the other name *Jesus*, see Sec. 29.

Sec. 55. *Of Christ a Son in reference to God.*

The first branch of Christ's excellency wherein he is preferred before Moses, is his dignity, arising from his birthright. This is here set down in the same manner that the inferiority of Moses was, by a particle of resemblance, ὡς υἱὸς, *as*. Hereof see Sec. 51.

Here this phrase, *as a Son*, may be taken two ways.

1. By way of resemblance, thus: As in men's families the son and heir is counted more excellent than any servant, so the Son of God in the house of God. In this sense it is thus fitly translated, 'as a Son.'

2. By way of eminency, thus, as the true, proper Son of God, more excellent than all mere creatures. In this sense it was thus fitly translated, 'as the Son.' Thus it implieth, that it is no usurpation for Christ to be over the house of God; it is his right, as he is the Son of God.

The former sense cometh up to this latter, and infers the same conclusion, that Christ, being the true proper Son of God, must needs be more excellent than Moses, that was but a servant.

By this argument the apostle proved Christ to be more excellent than angels, Chap. i. Secs. 42, 47.

This title *Son*, in reference to God, attributed to Christ, affords matter of instruction and direction.

I. Instructions are these,

1. *Christ is true God.* As a son of man is true man, so the Son of God is true God.

2. *Christ is God eternal.* Divine generation is an eternal act.

3. *Christ is equal with God.* The Son is equal with the Father.

4. *In Christ God is well-pleased*, Mat. iii. 17.

5. *In Christ we are adopted God's sons and made heirs*, Gal. iv. 4–6.

6. *In Christ we are made free*, John viii. 36.

---

[1] χρίειν, *ungere*, Heb. i. 9; χρίσμα, *unctio*, 1 John ii. 20, 27; Χριστός. *unctus.*

[2] משׁח, *unxit*; משׁיח *Messiah, unctus.*

II. Directions are these,
1. *Honour Christ as God*, John v. 23.
2. *Hear him*, Mat. xvii. 5.
3. *Believe on Christ*, John iii. 16.
4. *Submit to Christ*, Ps. ii. 12.
5. *Confess Christ*, 1 John iv. 15.
6. *Depart not from Christ*, John vi. 68, 69.
7. *Tread not Christ under foot*, Heb. x. 29.
8. *Wait for Christ from heaven*, 1 Thes. i. 10.

Sec. 56. *Of Christ the governor of his church.*

The second branch of Christ's excellency, wherein he is preferred before Moses, is his authority, implied under this preposition, ἐπὶ, *over;* he was over his house as a Lord and a governor, who had a supreme power to order all things therein as it pleased him. In reference hereunto these titles, κυριος, *Lord*, Mat. xiii. 51, ἐπιστάτης, *magister;* καθηγήτης, *doctor;* διδάσκαλος, *præceptor;* ῥαββὶ, *rabbi;* Master, Luke viii. 24, Mat. xxiii. 8, Mat. xxvi. 18, Mark ix. 5, were frequently given to him in his lifetime, yea, and this title also, οἰκοδεσπότης, *pater-familias*, master of the house, Mat. xix. 25. As there were none who excelled him in dignity, so nor in knowledge, prudence, or any other gift that made one fit to be over the church, the Lord and Master therein, and head thereof.

Intolerable in this respect is the arrogant presumption of him who is styled the head of the catholic church, and universal bishop. Hereof see more.

The aforesaid authority of Christ teacheth us to reverence Christ, according to that which is said, 'At the name of Jesus every knee shall bow,' Philip. ii. 10, and to obey him, and to subject ourselves to his ordinances, and to be subject to his word.

Sec. 57. *Of the propriety which Christ hath to his church.*

The third branch of Christ's excellency is that propriety which he had to the house over which he was. It is said to be, αὐτοῦ, *his own*.

Of the house wherein Moses was, it is said to be in reference to God his house, αὐτοῦ; the same house is here meant; but in reference to Christ it is called his own, αὐτοῦ. In the Greek, only one tittle makes the difference between the words.

This propriety which Christ hath in the church is proper and peculiar to him, no creature may lay claim to it. The apostle hath reference to Christ in this phrase, 'The house of God, which is the church of the living God,' Eph. iii. 15. To him also he hath reference in this phrase, 'Of whom the whole family of heaven and earth is named,' Eph. iii. 15. And in this, 'Ye are the temple of the living God,' 2 Cor. vi. 16.

The Scripture noteth many grounds of this propriety, as,

1. Christ purchased his church, Acts xx. 28.

2. He built it, verse 4. In this respect it is said, 'To whom coming as unto a living stone, ye also as lively stones are built up a spiritual house,' 1 Peter ii. 4, 5. And again, 'In whom you also are builded together,' Eph. ii. 22.

3. God hath given the church to his Son, Ps. ii. 8.

The church being Christ's own house, how can we doubt but that his eye will be continually thereupon, and his presence therein, and that he will take especial care thereof to provide all needful things for all? The apostle saith, 'If any provide not for his own, and especially for those of his own house, he is worse than an infidel,' 1 Tim. v. 8. Can any now imagine that Christ will not provide for them of his own house? It is said of Joseph, 'That he nourished his father, and his brethren, and all his father's household with bread, according to their families,' Gen. xlvii. 12. Much more will Christ nourish those of his own family. He will in this respect do more for his church, than for all the world besides. Men use to bestow more cost on their own houses, than others'. Of comforts and duties hence arising, see the next section.

That right which Christ hath over his church, giveth him an absolute power to order it as he will. He may establish or alter ordinances as he will. He changed the legal ordinances into evangelical. He hath established evangelical ordinances to be perpetual to the end of the world. No man, which is but a servant, hath such a power.

Sec. 58. *Of those who are the house of Christ.*

The apostle, to explain that metaphor of an house more fully, addeth this phrase, 'whose house are we.'

This pronoun *we* may be taken two ways:

1. Jointly for the whole catholic church, which is the society and communion of all that ever did or shall believe in Jesus Christ.

2. Distinctly, for every particular believer. For the body of a particular professor is said to be 'the temple of the Holy Ghost,' 1 Cor. vi. 19. In this sense they may be taken for the house of Christ synecdochically, as particular stones of that building; for they are called 'lively stones,' 1 Peter ii. 5.

Thus the privileges of Christ's house may belong to every of them.

Fitly are saints in the former joint consideration styled an house; for,

1. As stones and timber, they are brought together and fitly laid, and that for God to dwell among them, 2 Cor. vi. 16.

2. As an house is set upon a foundation, Luke vi. 48, so are saints 'built upon the foundation of the apostles and prophets, Jesus Christ himself being the chief corner-stone,' Eph. ii. 20.

3. As Solomon's temple was beautified and adorned with silver, gold, variety of pictures, and other ornaments, 2 Chron. iii. 4, 1 Kings vi. 29; so saints are

decked and adorned with the various graces of God's Spirit, Gal. v. 22, 23.

4. As an house inhabited hath a governor over them, so the society of saints have one over them who is called οἰκοδεσπότης, the 'master of the house,' Mat. x. 25.

5. As in a house there is θεραπεία, *famulitium*, Luke xii. 42, an household, which consisteth of children, servants, and others ; so in the church of God, Mat. xv. 26, Luke xi. 7.

6. As in a great house there are variety of officers, so in the church there are stewards, ministers, and others, 2 Cor. xii. 28.

7. As in a well-governed house there are good orders for the good government of it, so in the church of Christ, 1 Tim. iii. 15.

8. As in a house all needful provision useth to be stored up, so in this house of Christ there is bread of life, water of life, and needful food and refreshing.

Singular comforts must needs hence arise to those that are parts and members of this house; and that by reason of,

1. The sure foundation whereon it is settled, 1 Cor. iii. 11.

2. The fast knitting of the parts of the house together, Eph. ii. 21.

3. The excellent ornaments thereof, which are the glorious graces of God's Spirit.

4. The good laws and constitutions for better governing the same, being all contained in the word of God.

5. The wise governor thereof.

6. The excellent household.

7. The useful offices in it.

8. The variety and sufficiency of provisions appertaining thereto.

That which is expected of such as are of this house is,

1. That they 'cleanse themselves from all filthiness of the flesh and spirit,' 2 Cor. vii. 1, and vi. 16–18. Otherwise this house of Christ may prove the devil's stye.

2. That they deck and adorn themselves with the graces of God's Spirit, Col. iii. 12.

3. That they be subject to their governor, and to the good orders that he establisheth among them.

4. That they be content with the place and portion which the master of the household allots unto them.

5. That they maintain unity amongst themselves ; for 'an house divided against itself shall not stand,' Mat. xii. 25.

6. That they improve to the best advantage they can the talent which their Lord committeth unto them, Mat. xxv. 20.

Sec. 59. *Of the excellency and extent of Christ's house.*

These two relatives, *whose, we*, being joined together in reference to an house thus, 'whose house are we,' do exceedingly commend the church of God, which is intended hereby. All the world admired Solomon's temple, but behold here a more glorious edifice. The stones hereof are living stones ; the ornaments thereof, the graces of God's Spirit ; the provision thereof, such as endureth to everlasting life ; all things appertaining thereunto, spiritual, celestial.

It was before implied (Sec. 48) that Moses was of this house ; here it is said of Christians, 'We are the house,' whereby it is manifest that the church of the Old and New Testament was one and the same. The apostle speaking unto Christians, who were Gentiles, in reference unto the Jews, saith, 'Ye are fellow-citizens with the saints, and of the household of God,' Eph. ii. 19. And in reference to the ancient church of the Jews, it is said to the society of Christian Gentiles, 'Thou being a wild olive tree, wert graffed in amongst them, and with them partakest of the root and fatness of the olive tree,' Rom. xi. 17. Both they and we have one God, one Saviour, and the same means of salvation in regard of the substance. 'They did eat the same spiritual meat, and drink the same spiritual drink,' that we do, 1 Cor. x. 3, 4.

On this ground the apostle exhorteth us to be followers of them, Heb. vi. 12, and xii. 1.

On this ground they prayed for our calling, Ps. lxvii. 3, &c.

We therefore ought also to pray for their re-calling, and to use all the means we can to help on the same.

Sec. 60. *Of the meaning of this conjunction,* '*if.*'

The evidence whereby we may know whether we be of the house of Christ or no, is thus set down, 'If (ἐὰν) we hold fast the confidence,' &c.

This manner of setting down the evidence by a conditional particle, *if*, doth not necessarily imply that the foresaid graces, confidence and hope, may totally and finally be lost ; for,

1. The particle *if* doth not always leave a matter in doubt, but rather layeth down a ground of confirming another truth ; as if this argument of the apostle were thus framed :

They who hold fast their confidence unto the end, are the house of Christ ;

But we that have confidence shall hold it fast to the end :

Therefore we are the house of Christ.

Will an angel preach another gospel than Paul did? yet such a supposition is made, Gal. i. 8, 9.

See more of this kind of arguing, Chap. ii. ver. 2, Sec. 8.

2. The apostle wrote to a mixed company, whereof some had sound saving grace in them ; others had but a show of grace, making a profession of what they had not. These might totally and finally lose what they seemed to have, as Demas did, 2 Tim. iv. 10. In regard of them, this conjunction *if* might be conditionally used.

3. Means must be used, by those which are sound, for growing and persevering in that grace which they have. To stir up such to be careful and diligent in using those means, the apostle thus expresseth this evidence, 'If we hold fast;' yea, he includeth himself by expressing the point in the first person, *we*, implying that he himself had need to look to his own standing. See Chap. ii. Sec. 4.

There is in the Greek a little particle, περ, ἐάνπερ, added to this conjunction, which carrieth some emphasis with it, and it may be thus translated, *si modo, if at least*, or *siquidem, if truly*. Thus is this conjunction with that particle used, ver. 14, and Chap. vi. 3.

Sec. 61. *Of confidence.*

The graces whereby the evidence of being Christ's house is manifested are, as they are here expressed, confidence and hope.

The Greek word, παῤῥησία, translated *confidence*, is compounded of two words, whereof one signifieth speech,[1] the other everything or anything.[2] It is translated sometimes boldness, Acts iv. 13; sometimes plainness, 2 Cor. iii. 12; it is oft used in the dative case adverbially, and translated boldly, John vii. 26; openly, Mat. viii. 32; plainly, thus it is opposed to an obscure proverb, John xvi. 25, 29. It is also used with a preposition, and translated *freely*, Acts ii. 29.

The word is opposed to fearfulness or shamefulness, which makes men loath to utter many things which they ought to make known.

I find it six times by our translators interpreted *confidence*; as here in this text, and chap. x. 35, and Acts xxviii. 31, and 1 John ii. 28, and iii. 21, and v. 14.

Confidence will make a man utter his whole mind, and not be afraid nor ashamed to publish that which he thinks meet to be made known.

The word here used hath sometimes reference to God, as Heb. iv. 16; and sometimes to man, as where it is said of the rulers of the Jews, that 'They saw the boldness of Peter and John,' or their confidence, Acts iv. 13.

In this later sense it implieth a free and resolute profession of the faith. Thus do some here take it, and so make a constant standing to the truth, and an undaunted maintaining thereof, even unto blood, to be an evidence that we are the house of Christ, and animated by his Spirit. This is a congruous sense, well expressing the emphasis of the Greek word. To this purpose doth this apostle more expressly exhort, to 'Hold fast the profession (ὁμολογίαν), of our faith without wavering,' Heb. x. 23.

But most expositors take the word here, as having reference to God, and to intend such a resting on God, and placing our trust in him, which is the nature of confidence, as it makes us boldly to go to God, and freely to pour out our own whole souls before him, as we are required, chap. iv. 16.

In this respect they make it an effect of faith, and metonymically put it for faith itself. Thus doth this text fitly answer another like text, where the apostle saith, 'You hath he reconciled, if ye continue in the faith, grounded and settled, and be not moved away from the hope of the gospel,' Col. i. 23.

Faith may here be the more fitly intended, because it is that grace whereby we are united to Christ, whereby we receive spiritual life from him, and are made lively stones, whereby we grow up unto an holy temple, yea, whereby Christ dwelleth in our hearts, and so we come to be his house.

This faith, where it is well rooted, will sprout forth. A believer will not be tongue-tied. Faith works boldness of speech. See more hereof in *The Saints' Sacrifice*, on Ps. cxvi. 10, sec. 67. In this respect, confidence, as it is here used, may comprise under it both the cause and the effect, both faith and profession. Faith is the cause of confidence, profession is an effect thereof. By faith, we gain assurance to ourselves that we are Christ's house; by profession of faith, we give evidence to others that we are that house. Fitly, therefore, hath the apostle used a word that compriseth both under it.

They who through fear or shame refuse to profess Christ and his gospel, and they to whom the thought and presence of God is terrible, who dare not approach unto him, nor call him Father, but behold him as a severe judge, have cause to suspect they are not of the house of Christ, in that they want that confidence which is here set down.

That we therefore may attain it and retain it, let us acquaint ourselves with all the evidence of God's favour that we can, and meditate on his promises, and duly weigh his properties, as his free grace, rich mercy, almighty power, infallible truth, everywhere present, with the like. Let us go out of ourselves, and behold him inviting all to come to him, and accepting all that come; thus may, thus will the soul be established, and confidence bred and preserved in it.

Of saints' confidence in professing that relation which is betwixt God and them, see *The Saints' Sacrifice* on Ps. cxvi. 16, sec. 100.

Sec. 62. *Of hope, an evidence that we are Christ's.*

The other evidence, that we are the house of Christ, is *hope*. Hope necessarily followeth upon faith. 'Faith is the substance of things hoped for,' Heb. xi. 1. And hope is an expectation of that which is believed. Hope makes one wait for the fruition thereof. Hereby is faith sustained. Where there is no hope, there is no faith; where hope faileth, faith fainteth.

---

[1] ῥῆσις, *oratio*.

[2] πᾶν, *omne*; παῤῥησία, quasi πανρησία. *Libertas quidvis loquendi, cum libere dicimus omnia quæ dicenda sunt.*

Where there is no faith, there can be no spiritual life, no communion with Christ, no right to him. These two graces, faith, hope, are in all that are the house of Christ.

Of the nature of hope, what it is; of the properties of it; of the agreement and difference betwixt faith and it; of the need and use of it; of getting, preserving, and well-managing of it, see *The whole Armour of God*, on Eph. vi. 17, treat. ii. part 7, sec. 3, &c.

Hope gives evidence that we are the house of Christ, in that it keepeth from falling away from Christ. It is as 'an anchor of the soul, sure and stedfast,' Heb. vi. 19. This world is as a sea; Christ's church, which is the house here spoken of, as a ship therein; Satan's assaults, persecutions in the world, all manner of troubles, are as violent winds, which blow against that ship, but it hath such an anchor as holds it fast; no other ship hath the like; all other ships are tossed up and down, and at length overwhelmed in the sea. If, therefore, we have this anchor of hope, which holds us fast, there is a good evidence that we are the house of Christ.

Sec. 63. *Of true rejoicing, what it is, and whence it ariseth.*

That hope which giveth evidence that we are the house of Christ, is here set out by an especial effect, which is *rejoicing*.

The Greek word, καύχημα, imports an high degree of rejoicing, such an one as causeth a glorying or boasting in a thing; and so in other places it is translated, 'It were better for me to die, than that any man should make my glorying (τὸ καύχημα) void,' saith the apostle, 1 Cor. ix. 15. And again, 'Lest our boasting (τὸ καύχημα) of you should be in vain,' 2 Cor. ix. 3. There is another like word, καύχησις, which signifieth the same thing, frequently used. The root[1] whence the Greek words are derived, signifieth a *neck*. For they who will glory in a thing will stretch forth their neck, Isa. iii. 16.

The word here used and applied to hope, sheweth that true Christian hope produceth a great degree of rejoicing; even such a degree as cannot be abated by affliction, Rom. v. 2, 3.

This rejoicing is an expression of that joy which is in a man, and a manifestation of one's liking of it, and delighting in the good which he hath.

Joy is a liking, dilating affection. Or more fully to express the nature of it, joy is a liking affection, which enlargeth the heart upon the apprehension of some good thing.

Of the general nature of an affection, and of the difference betwixt liking and disliking affections, see *The Saints' Sacrifice*, on Ps. cxvi. 1, sec. 4.

That whereby joy is differenced is in this word *dilating*, or in this phrase, 'which enlargeth.' For

[1] αὐχὴν, *cervix*; inde, αὐχεῖν, *gloriari*. αὐχη et αὔχημα *gloriatio*; per prothesin, καύχημα.

desire lifts up the heart after the thing desired. *Love* unites the heart to the thing loved. *Joy* enlargeth the heart with a pleasing content in that which it apprehendeth to be good. Thus it is said of the church, that in regard of the confluence of people, her 'heart should be enlarged,' Isa. lx. 5, that is, she should rejoice. Joy is contrary to grief. Now grief contracteth and straiteneth the heart, and consumeth it, Ps. xxxi. 9, 10. But joy enlargeth and reviveth it, Gen. xlv. 27.

The proper object of true Christian rejoicing, is that which concerns our true happiness. The disciples who rejoiced in the power of their ministry, in that the devils were made subject to them, were somewhat checked by Christ, who said, 'In this rejoice not, that the spirits are subject unto you; but rather rejoice, because your names are written in heaven,' Luke x. 17, 20. Common gifts are not the proper ground of rejoicing. Now casting out of devils was but a common gift, which hypocrites had, but the writing of their names in heaven tended to their eternal happiness; therefore, in this latter they were to rejoice.

Hope is a saving grace, so as it properly produceth rejoicing; so doth faith, Acts. xvi. 34, so do other like graces.

As for other things which do not make thereunto, they may be enjoyed by him on whom the guilt of sin lieth, and who is himself under the dominion of sin; who is a slave to Satan; over whom the wrath of God hangeth; who shall be excluded out of heaven, and eternally damned. What matter of true rejoicing then can there be in such things?

Here, by the way, we may be informed in the deceitful rejoicing of most men. Take a view of the ordinary matters of rejoicing, and you shall find cause to say, as the wise man doth, 'Vanity of vanities, all is vanity, yea, vexation of spirit,' Eccles. i. 2, and ii. 11. This we may find from the cradle to the grave. The child rejoiceth in baubles; the young maid in her beauty; the young man in his properness; the strong man in his strength; the scholar in his learning; the honourable man in his dignities; the rich man in his wealth; the counsellor in his great practice; so others in other like things. Are any of these like that power of the disciples' ministry, concerning which Christ said, 'In this rejoice not,' Luke x. 20. In pangs of gout and stone, in sickness, in death, in the day of judgment, what joy and rejoicing can those produce? Have they not a sting in their tail? Note the issue of Nebuchadnezzar's rejoicing in his great Babel, and Belshazzar's rejoicing in his cups, Dan. iv. 27, 28, and v. 5. I may therefore well say to him that spends his time in pleasure, 'In this rejoice not;' to him that, Dives-like, is daily arrayed in glorious apparel, and fareth delicately, 'In this rejoice not;' and of such as have great success in their undertakings, either in war or merchandising, or any other like, 'In this rejoice not.'

Sec. 64. *Of the rejoicing of hope in troubles.*

Well might the apostle attribute rejoicing to hope, because hope maketh us cast our eyes on the end of our faith, which is hoped for, 'the salvation of our souls,' 1 Peter i. 9. Hereby it cometh to pass, that as an husbandman beholding his ground that is sowed with corn fairly to grow up, rejoiceth in the expectation of a great harvest; so we, that have sown here to the Spirit, rejoice in hope and expectation of reaping life everlasting, Gal. vi. 8.

Though believers, before they come to the fruition of that end, are oft in sore troubles, outward and inward, in body and soul, in goods or good name; sometimes immediately from God, and sometimes through the malice of men, yea, sometimes from the apprehension of their own sins; yet there is no estate, whereunto in this world they can be brought, but his hope of the issue thereof, and glory following thereon, may produce a rejoicing. The Hebrews 'took joyfully the spoiling of their goods, knowing in themselves that they had in heaven a better and an enduring substance,' Heb. x. 34.

I. Believers are subject to persecution: but the cause, their present assistance, and future recompence, do all give matter of rejoicing.

1. Their cause is the most glorious that can be; Christ's name, Acts v. 41.

2. Their assistance is more than ordinary,[1] 2 Tim. iv. 16–18. Such hath been their assistance, as they have sung for joy in the midst of their greatest trials, Acts xvi. 25.

3. The end is such, as no suffering is worthy thereof, Rom. viii., 2 Cor. iv. 17. Therefore Christ exhorteth his, when they are persecuted, to 'rejoice, and be exceeding glad; because great is their reward in heaven,' Mat. v. 11, 12.

II. Believers are also subject to wrongs and oppressions of worldlings; and though not simply for the gospel, yet for their sheep-like and dove-like disposition, in that they are not forward to revenge wrong. 'He that departeth from evil maketh himself a prey,' Isa. lix. 15. But the apostle Peter saith, that 'this is thankworthy, if a man for conscience toward God endure grief, suffering wrongfully.' And again, 'If, when he doth well, and suffereth for it, he take patiently, this is acceptable with God,' 1 Peter ii. 19, 20. That which is thankworthy and acceptable with God, is matter of rejoicing.

III. Believers likewise are, as others, subject to torturing and tormenting diseases, yea, and to the uncomfortable disease of the plague. But,

1. They know that these things are ordered by God in wisdom, in love, for their need, and for their good; and in that respect rejoice. A wise man is glad, when a skilful and faithful physician or chirurgeon undertakes to cure him, though he be forced to drink

[1] See a *Recovery from Apostasy*, on Luke xv. 32, sec. 25, 26.

fulsome potions, to drink bitter pills, to endure cupping, lancing, cutting, splinting, searing, yea, sawing off a limb. Much more believers are glad at God's chastisements, though they be grievous.

2. Believers, in all their pains and anguishes, use to call to mind the pains of hell which their sins deserve, in comparison whereof all that can be endured in this world is but as a flea-biting. Now, that faith which they have in their freedom from God's wrath, from the power of sin and Satan, from the curse of death and damnation, makes them rejoice in all bodily pains.

3. God useth in all the distresses of his saints, whether public or private, for maintenance of the gospel, or trial of their graces, to give them such a spirit of consolation, as makes them rejoice under their crosses. It is God's usual dealing to increase the consolations of his Spirit, according to the need of his servants, 2 Cor. i. 5.

IV. Believers are subject to spiritual desertions. But though these may seem to be as water that quencheth all the fire of spiritual joy, yet the Lord reserveth some sparks of comfort and confidence in the souls of true believers, as he did in his Son, who in his bitterest agony, thus cried to his Father, 'My God, my God, why hast thou forsaken me?' Mat. xxvii. 46. On this ground said Job, 'Though he slay me, yet will I trust in him,' Job xiii. 15. Besides, that inward grief will turn into greater joy. After sundry dismal, showery, cloudy, dark days, when the clouds are dispelled, the sun seemeth to shine more brightly and more comfortably; so the Spirit of joy, after such desertions. Many of David's psalms which begin with sighs and groans, and expressions of much grief, do end in praisings and rejoicings.

Sec. 65. *Of rejoicing of hope standing with mourning, weeping, and brokenness of heart.*

Obj. We are commanded to weep, Joel ii. 17. And Christ pronounceth them blessed who mourn, Mat. v. 4, and weep, Luke vi. 31; and a broken spirit, and a contrite heart, are said to be the sacrifices of God, Ps. ii. 17. How then can rejoicing of hope stand with these?

Ans. 1. Those and other like charges to weep and mourn were given on special occasions, and that for sin or judgment. The end thereof was to bring comfort and joy to the soul.

2. The blessing pronounced to mourning and weeping, is in regard of the consequence and event that should follow thereupon; which are comfort and laughter, Mat. v. 4, Luke vi. 21.

3. There may be a mixture of joy and grief in the same person, at the same time, but in different respects. In respect of sin, and apprehension of God's displeasure, there may be grief; but in respect of God's mercy, Christ's sacrifice, and faith therein, there will be rejoicing. A saint while he is confessing his sin, useth to be much dejected and broken in spirit, but in the apprehen-

sion of the atonement made by Christ, his spirit reviveth, rejoiceth, and praiseth God. As 'in laughter the heart is sorrowful,' Prov. xiv. 13; so in weeping the heart may be joyful.

4. There is a time to weep, and a time to laugh, Eccles. iii. 4. In this respect directions to weep and directions to rejoice, having respect to their distinct and due seasons, do not thwart each other.

Sec. 66. *Of errors contrary to the rejoicing of hope.*

This property of rejoicing, attributed to hope, discovereth sundry errors; some in opinion, some in practice. One error in opinion is of papists especially, who make uncertainty a property of hope, and teach, that it is against the nature of hope to be sure and stedfast.

Ans. 1. Herein they expressly thwart the Scripture, which attributeth full assurance to hope, and termeth hope 'an anchor of the soul, both sure and stedfast,' Heb. vi. 11, 19. In this respect it is said, that 'hope maketh not ashamed,' Rom. v. 5, because it disappointeth him not of that which he hopeth for.

2. They strip hope of that property which the apostle here attributeth to it; for rejoicing cannot arise from that which is uncertain, or from a doubting of that which we hope for, but rather from an assurance of receiving it.

3. They take away the difference betwixt the hope of saints in reference to eternal life, and of worldlings in reference to the things of this life. The hope of worldlings is mixed with doubtings, fears, and griefs, because the event of the things they hoped for is uncertain; but so is not the glory which true believers hope for.

A second error in opinion is their conceit, that think a Christian's life is a life full of fear, grief, and perplexity.

Ans. I will not deny but that believers, by reason of the mixture of the flesh with the spirit in them, have many times occasions of fear, grief, and perplexity; yet not such as depriveth them of the rejoicing here intended. The believers' sorrow is not like the sorrow of worldlings: theirs is 'a godly sorrow, which worketh repentance to salvation, not to be repented of; but the sorrow of the world worketh death,' 2 Cor. ii. 10. Many times when worldlings seem jocund, they have heaviness within them; but when Christians seem outwardly pensive, they have much comfort within. The seeming outward joy of worldings, take it at the best, is fading: 'As the crackling of thorns under a pot, so is the laughter of a fool,' Eccles. vii. 6, Prov. xi. 7. But to those that were of Christ's house, saith he, 'Your heart shall rejoice, and your joy no man taketh from you,' John xv. 22.

A third error in opinion is, that expressions of joy, in special by laughter, are unlawful; and thereupon advise Christians to go always as mourning, and to be ever dejected; and for proof, allege that Christ never laughed.

Ans. The many exhortations in Scripture to rejoice, and approved patterns of saints that have rejoiced, yea, and laughed, Gen. xvii. 17, and xxi. 6, Ps. cxxvi. 2, are sufficient to disprove the foresaid error. As for Christ himself, it is expressly said, that 'he rejoiced in spirit,' Luke x. 21, which is the ground of true laughter. This third error is an uncomfortable error, which is enough to keep men from professing the Christian religion.

An error in practice is of them who profess faith and hope in Christ, and yet are always dejected in spirit, walking heavily; they will not be comforted, nor made cheerful.

They are in sundry respects to be blamed. For,

1. They give too great cause of justifying the error last mentioned, that rejoicing is unlawful.

2. They wrong themselves, in making their life more miserable than otherwise it might be, and putting away such comforts as God hath provided for them.

3. They prejudice other weak ones in disheartening them. They discourage such as have entered into the Christian list, and deter such as have not entered from entering.

4. They disgrace the holy profession, as if it were the most uncomfortable profession in the world.

5. They dishonour God, as if he were an hard master; so as no profit, joy, or comfort were to be found in serving him.

Sec. 67. *Of believers' rejoicing.*

Just cause is here given to exhort and incite such as profess to have hope in Christ, to testify the truth of their hope by rejoicing: 'Rejoice in the Lord alway; and again I say, rejoice,' Philip. iv. 4; 'Rejoice evermore,' 1 Thes. v. 16. None have such just and true cause of rejoicing. The dignities, honours, pleasures, profits, and other like things wherein the men of this world rejoice, are vain, like ice, hail, and snow, which waste in the handling. They may be taken from us, Job i. 21, or we from them, Luke xii. 20; but Christians have matter of true rejoicing, that which is solid, unutterable, everlasting.

Among other Christian duties this is much pressed in Scripture. Moses doth at least ten times inculcate it in that last book which he uttered in the last month of his age, and that either by advice, Deut. xxxiii. 18, or by promise, Deut xii. 12. The sweet singer of Israel hath ten times ten times in like manner pressed the same in his book of Psalms. So other prophets also call upon the people of God to rejoice, Isa. lxvi. 10, Zeph. iii. 14, Zech. ix. 9; so Christ, Mat. v. 12; and his apostles, Philip. iv. 4, 1 Peter iv. 13, James i. 9; yea, and the angels from heaven, Rev. xix. 7.

None have greater cause of rejoicing than believers,

for their names are written in the book of life, Luke x. 20. Christ, the greatest matter of rejoicing, is theirs; they have a right to all that Christ did and endured for man; yea, to the things of this world, and to heaven itself.

As they have in these respects just cause of rejoicing, so the blessed effects that follow upon their rejoicing, are forcible inducements to perform the same. For,

1. By their rejoicing, the author and giver of joy is much glorified. It shews that he is so kind and good a master every way, as his servants much rejoice in him.

2. It is a great inducement to draw on others who are without, to like that profession which causeth such rejoicing, and themselves to take upon them that profession.

3. It sweetens our whole life; it sweetens all that we do for preservation of nature, as eating, drinking, sleeping, and other refreshings; it sweetens the works of our calling; it sweetens the duties of piety which we perform to God, and the duties of justice and charity which we do to man; it sweetens all manner of sufferings; it sweetens our very deathbed.

Sec. 68. *Of perseverance without intermission or revolt.*

That which maketh confidence and rejoicing a true, sure, and infallible evidence of being Christ's house, is perseverance therein.

Therefore the apostle addeth this caution, 'If we hold fast firm unto the end.'

The apostle's expression is very emphatical. There are three words used, every of which imply the point intended.

1. The verb $\kappa\alpha\tau\acute{\alpha}\sigma\chi\omega\mu\epsilon\nu$, 'hold fast,' is in Greek a compound. The simple verb, $\check{\epsilon}\chi\epsilon\iota\nu$, signifieth *to have*; but this compound, so to have it as never to let it go, and this is to hold fast. So is this word, Heb. x. 23, 1 Thes. v. 21.

2. The adjective $\beta\epsilon\beta\alpha\acute{\iota}\alpha\nu$, translated *firm*, importeth such a stedfastness as can never be taken away. See more hereof, Chap. ii. 2, Sec. 11. It implieth an holding fast without intermission.

3. This last clause, $\mu\acute{\epsilon}\chi\rho\iota\ \tau\acute{\epsilon}\lambda\text{ous}$, *unto the end*, shews that such a perseverance is here intended, as will neither be interrupted nor clean broken off; for the end here meant is the last period of one's life. So is the word taken, ver. 14, Mat. x. 22, Rev. ii. 26.

To shew that it implieth a perpetual continuing in a thing, it is translated *continual*, Luke xviii. 5, and it is applied to such a perpetuity as is eternal, John xiii. 1, 1 Cor. ii. 8.

The perseverance here set down is opposed to a double kind of hypocrisy.

One, of such as make show of confidence and rejoicing by fits. Sometimes they are exceeding bold and jocund; other times they are full of fear and anguish. They are like men sick of an ague, sometimes well, sometimes ill. It falls out with such many times, as, notwithstanding their well days, they die in a fit. They deal with the graces of God's Spirit as children do with a bird that they hold by a string: sometimes they will hold it in, and sometimes let it fly out, so as the bird on a sudden, they letting go their hold, flies clean away. This intermission argueth unsoundness, and is contrary to the caution here prescribed.

The other is of such as repent their good beginnings, and prove plain apostates. They are like such as, having left their colours, will be hanged rather than return to them again.

These are in a most woful plight. The last state of such a man is worse than the first, Luke xi. 26, 2 Peter ii. 20. These are like Nebuchadnezzar's image, whose head was of fine gold; his feet, part of iron, and part of clay, whereby it came to be broken to pieces, Dan. ii. 32–34. Such were Saul, Joash, Judas, and others, whose end was memorable and miserable. In this case I may use Christ's memento, 'Remember Lot's wife,' Luke xvii. 32.

Sec. 69. *Of motives to perseverance.*

If divine exhortations to a grace, and earnest dissuasions from the contrary; if earnest supplications for obtaining a grace, and hearty gratulations for enjoying it; if gracious promises made to a grace, and fearful denunciations against the want of it; if a blessed recompence of those who have attained it, and woful revenge on those that have failed therein, be motives of force to enforce a point, forcible motives are not wanting to press this point of perseverance.

Many instances might be given out of God's word to exemplify every of these. Of each take one instance:

1. For exhortation, 1 Cor. xv. 58.
2. For dissuasion, Heb. iii. 12.
3. For supplication, 1 Thes. v. 23.
4. For gratulation, 1 Thes. iii. 8, 9.
5. For promise, Mat. x. 22.
6. For threatening, Heb. x. 38.
7. For recompence, Rev. xii. 11.
8. For revenge, Acts i. 17, 18.

Just and great reason there is thus to press this point of perseverance; for,

1. All the benefits that we can expect from any grace dependeth upon persevering therein. Thereby the prize is obtained. It is constancy that sets the crown upon all good endeavours, 2 Tim. iv. 7, 8.

2. All Christian privileges and divine promises are limited therewith, as here in this text, 'If we hold fast.' 'If ye abide in me,' saith Christ, John xv. 7; 'if ye continue in the faith,' Col. i. 23.

3. All the benefit of what hath formerly been done is lost if he hold not out to the end, Ezek. xviii. 24.

As a man in a race, who runs swiftly at first, if he hold not out, gets nothing by his former swiftness.

4. Not the benefit only is lost, but great damage ensueth thereupon: 'the last state of that man is worse than the first,' Luke xi. 26. As a man in ascending a ladder, if, after he have got up many steps, he let go his hold and fall down, he doth not only lose the benefit of his former pains, but also gets a bruised body, and, it may be, broken bones, whereby he is made less able to climb up again than he was before. Hereupon it is said, 'It had been better for them not to have known the way of righteousness, than, after they have known it, to turn from the holy commandment.'

How requisite it is for saints to proceed and persist in grace, see *The Saints' Sacrifice*, on Ps. cxvi. 9, sec. 60.

Sec. 70. *Of means for perseverance.*

To help us on in holding out, these graces following, among others, are very useful:

1. Humility. This is the basis and foundation whereon the fore-mentioned house is settled. If an house want a foundation, how can it stand, especially against storms and tempests? Luke vi. 49. Christ saith that a man which builds a sure house digs deep, Luke vi. 48. Digging deep is in an humble soul. Many promises are made to the humble, Micah vi. 8: 'God giveth grace to the humble,' Prov. iii. 34. For this very end we are forbidden to be high-minded, lest we fall, Rom. xi. 20. Self-conceitedness and pride make men careless, Rev. iii. 17, and God is provoked against such, 'for he resisteth the proud,' James iv. 6.

2. Sincerity. This is an inward soundness. If the foundation be not sound, the edifice cannot be well settled on it. Soundness is that which maketh last and endure. Sappy, rotten timber will quickly fail. Counterfeit grace will not last.

3. A settled resolution to hold out to the end. 'I have sworn, and I will perform it, that I will keep thy righteous judgments,' saith a constant servant of the Lord, Ps cxix. 106. Nothing will daunt or turn back such an one. See more hereof in the *Recovery from Apostasy*, on Luke xv. 31, sec. 44.

4. Jealousy. Jealousy, I say, in regard of the temptations whereunto we are subject, and of our own weakness. Satan is subtle, 1 Peter v. 8; sin is deceitful, Heb. iii. 13, and we of ourselves are foolish, and prone to yield to sin and Satan. If we be secure or careless, we may be soon taken as birds in a net. This is a great cause of backsliding; therefore we are oft admonished to fear, Heb. iv. 1, Rom. xi. 20, Philip. ii. 12.

These two, *resolution* and *jealousy*, may well stand together, if the former be placed on God's promises and the Spirit's assistance, and the latter on temptations whereunto we are subject, and our own weakness.

5. Prudence. For the manifestation hereof,

(1.) Avoid occasions which may draw thee out of thy Christian course. This the apostle intendeth under this phrase, 'Cast away every weight,' Heb. xii. 1. To avoid uncleanness, the wise man gives this advice, 'Remove thy way far from a strange woman, and come not nigh the door of her house,' Prov. v. 8. To press this the further, he useth these metaphors: 'Can a man take fire in his bosom, and his clothes not be burnt? can one go upon hot coals, and his feet not be burnt?' Prov. vi. 27, 28. Peter's thrusting himself among the servants and officers in the high priests' hall was an occasion of the temptation which brought him to deny his master, John xviii. 16–18.

(2.) If occasions cannot be avoided, but that thou beest forced to 'sojourn in Meshech, and to dwell in the tents of Kedar,' Ps. cxxvi. 5, then take heed of yielding to temptations. Stand out against them as Joseph did, Gen. xxxix. 9. Remain righteous as Lot did in Sodom, 2 Peter ii. 8. 'Give no place to the devil,' Eph. iv. 27; but withstand sin in the beginning. It is not safe to dally with temptations. If Satan get in a claw, he will soon put in his whole paw, and then head, body, and all. If waters make a little breach, floods will soon follow.

(3.) If thou be overtaken with a temptation, lie not in it; but as soon as thou canst recover thyself, do as in this case Peter did. So soon as he observed his Lord's beck, and heard the cock crow, whereby he was put in mind of his sin, presently 'he went out and wept bitterly,' Luke xxii. 60–62.

(4.) Being recovered, take heed of falling back again. A relapse is dangerous in bodily diseases, much more in spiritual. The Spirit is much grieved thereby. Christ gave this advice to a woman taken in adultery, and forgiven, 'Go and sin no more,' John viii. 11. This advice he backed with a strong reason thus, 'Sin no more, lest a worse thing come unto thee,' John v. 14.

6. Growth in grace. By this we shall be the more strengthened, and the better enabled to hold out. Use what means are prescribed to this purpose: 'As newborn babes, desire the sincere milk of the word, that ye may grow thereby,' 1 Peter ii. 2; 'Stir up the gift of God which is in thee,' 2 Tim. i. 6. Standing at a stay may occasion falling away. In endeavours to grow in grace, never think thou hast done enough, but follow the apostle's advice, Philip. iii. 13, 14.

7. Walking with God. By this, he that never saw death, pleased God all the days of his life. Compare Gen. v. 24 with Heb. xi. 5. Of the emphasis of this phrase, *walked with God*, see *The Saints' Sacrifice*, on Ps. cxvi. 9, sec. 58.

Walking with God implieth a setting of God before our eyes. This will make us to endeavour in all things to please him, which the apostle expresseth under this phrase, 'Walk worthy of the Lord unto all pleasing,'

Col. i. 10. This will make us in all things to hold close to God, and it will be an especial means to pull us in when we are about to start from God.

8. Stedfast expectation of the prize or reward that is set before thee. It is said of Moses, that he 'had respect unto the recompence of the reward,' Heb. xi. 26. This made these Hebrews to hold out: 'They knew that they had in heaven an enduring substance,' Heb. x. 34. Of Christ himself it is said, 'For the joy that was set before him, he endured the cross,' Heb. xii. 2. This must needs uphold those that believe it, and keep them stedfast unto the end, because all that we can do or endure here is 'not worthy to be compared with the glory that is promised,' Rom. viii. 18; 'For our light affliction, which is but for a moment, worketh for us a far more exceeding and eternal weight of glory,' 2 Cor. iv. 17. Of the emphasis of this phrase, see *A Recovery from Apostasy* on Luke xv. 31, sec. 27. Hereupon the apostle gives this admonition, 'Let us not be weary in well doing: for in due season we shall reap if we faint not,' Gal. vi. 9. And again: 'Be ye stedfast, unmoveable, always abounding in the work of the Lord, forasmuch as you know that your labour is not in vain in the Lord,' 1 Cor. xv. 58.

9. Prayer, faithful, fervent, constant prayer. Christ used this means for himself, Heb. v. 7. This means he also used, that Peter's faith might not fail. Experience sheweth that the more we fail herein, the more we decay; but the more fervent and constant we are herein, the more stedfast we remain. This is to be added to all other means, because by faithful prayer the Holy Spirit is obtained, Luke xi. 13, without which we cannot hold out; but by it we shall persevere.

By the foresaid means we may continue to enjoy our spiritual strength, as Caleb did his bodily strength, Joshua xiv. 11, and as Moses, whose natural force abated not, Deut. xxxiv. 7; 'We shall still bring forth fruit in old age,' Ps. xcii. 14.

Of circumspection in preventing apostasy, see Sec. 122.

Sec. 71. *Of the resolution of* Heb. iii. 2–6.

2. *Who was faithful to him that appointed him, as also Moses was faithful in all his house.*

3. *For this man was counted worthy of more glory than Moses, inasmuch as he who hath builded the house hath more honour than the house.*

4. *For every house is builded by some man; but he that built all things is God.*

5. *And Moses verily was faithful in all his house as a servant, for a testimony of those things which were to be spoken after;*

6. *But Christ as a Son over his own house; whose house are we, if we hold fast the confidence, and the rejoicing of the hope firm unto the end.*

The sum of all these verses is, a description of Christ's faithfulness in the execution of his prophetical office.

This is set down,
1. Simply.
2. Comparatively.

In the simple expression there is,
1. An affirmation of the point, *who was faithful.*
2. A declaration of the person to whom he was faithful, *to him that appointed him.*

The comparison whereby the point is amplified is betwixt Christ and Moses.

This is set out two ways:
1. By similitude, in the latter part of the second verse.

Of the similitude, the proposition, or former part, is thus expressed, *Moses was faithful in all his house.*

The reddition or latter part is intimated by the inference of that proposition on that which went before, and that by this note of similitude, *as.*

In the proposition three distinct points are set down,
1. The person with whom Christ is compared, *Moses.*
2. The point wherein they are compared, *faithful.*
3. The place in which that faithfulness was shewed. This is set forth,
1. By the kind of place, *house.*
2. By the Lord thereof, *his.*
3. By the extent, *all.*

2. Christ and Moses are compared by dissimilitude.

This is, 1, generally propounded; 2, particularly exemplified.

In the general is noted,
1. The persons between whom this dissimilitude is, *this man* (who is Christ) and *Moses.*
2. The matter of the dissimilitude. Here observe,
1. What that matter was, *glory.*
2. The grounds thereof, *counted worthy.*

The particular exemplification is by two pair of relatives, one a *builder*, and an *house*, ver. 3, 4.

The other, a *son*, and a *servant*, ver. 5, 9.

The former, concerning the builder and an house, is,
1. Propounded, ver. 3; 2, proved, ver. 4.

In the proposition are expressed,
1. Both parts of the dissimilitude, *he that built*, and *the house.*
2. The matter wherein they are unlike, *honour.* In this phrase, 'hath more honour.'

In the proof two things are confirmed:
1. That Moses was an house built.
2. That Christ was the builder.

Each of these are confirmed by a general case taken for grant.

The first case granted is this: 'Every house is builded by some man.' Hence it followeth that Moses (who was at least a part of an house) was builded.

The other case granted is this: 'He that built all things is God.' Hence it followeth that Christ (who is God) built Moses.

The other pair of relatives (which is of a *son* and a *servant*) is largely set down, ver. 5, 6.

The latter relative is first described, ver. 5. Herein is,

1. A repetition of what was before asserted.
2. An addition.

Three things are repeated:

1. The person, *Moses*.
2. The point wherein he was commended, *faithful*.
3. The place, *with the Lord*, and the extent hereof, *in all his house*.

Two things are added:

1. The correlative, wherein consists another dissimilitude, *servant*.
2. The end why he was a servant. Here are noted,
   1. The kind of end, *for a testimony*.
   2. The matter thereof, *of those things which were to be spoken after*.

The former relative concerning the Son is, **1**, propounded; 2, expounded.

In the proposition, 1, the Son here meant is named Christ.

2. The house over which he ruleth is thus limited, *his own*.

In the exposition there is,

1. A declaration of the point, *whose house are we*.
2. A limitation thereof.

The limitation is, 1, in this conditional particle *if*; 2, exemplified.

In the exemplification there is,

1. An act required; 2. The subject matter of that act.

The act is set forth,

1. By the kind of it, *hold fast*.
2. By the manner of performing it, *firm*.
3. By continuance therein, *unto the end*.

The subject matter consists of two branches: 1, confidence; 2, hope.

The latter is amplified by an effect thereof, *rejoicing*.

Sec. 72. *Of observations collected out of* Heb. iii. 2-6.

I. *Christ was deputed to his prophetical office.* This is here taken for grant, in that it is said, 'He was faithful to him that appointed him.' See Sec. 33.

II. *Christ was faithful in that which he was trusted withal.* See Secs. 32, 38.

III. *God's deputation makes a true minister.* This is gathered out of this word *appointed*, as here used. See Sec. 34.

IV. *There may be a resemblance betwixt unequals.* There is here a resemblance made betwixt Christ and Moses. See Sec. 38.

V. *Moses was a faithful minister.* This is here plainly expressed. See Sec. 38.

VI. *God's ministers must be faithful;* for this end the faithfulness of Christ and Moses is here set down. See Sec. 39.

VII. *Christ of all was most worthy of glory;* this is the main point proved in these verses. See Secs. 42-44.

VIII. *Moses was an eminent minister.* Moses, among others, is here called out to be compared with Christ; his prerogatives are distinctly set down, Sec. 45.

IX. *Christ was more excellent than Moses.* This is expressly set down. See Sec. 45.

X. *A builder is more excellent than the thing built.* This metaphor is used to set out Christ's excellency above others. See Sec. 46.

XI. *Ministers have received what they are or have.* This is implied under this phrase, 'Every house is builded.' See Sec. 48.

XII. *Christ is true God.* He is here so called. See Sec. 49.

XIII. *Christ is the creator of all.* This is intended under this metaphor, 'He that built all things.' See Sec. 49.

XIV. *The church is built up by Christ.* This is the special thing intended under this phrase, 'He that built all things is God.' See Sec. 49.

XV. *A servant must be faithful.* This is here intended in the pattern of Moses. See Sec. 50.

XVI. *Governors are servants;* so was Moses. See Secs. 51, 52.

XVII. *Ministers are God's witnesses.* As Moses, so all other ministers are for a testimony. See Sec. 55.

XVIII. *God beforehand makes known his pleasure;* so much is intended under this phrase, 'Those things which were to be spoken after.' See Sec. 55.

XIX. *Christ is the anointed;* this title *Christ* importeth as much. See Sec. 54.

XX. *Christ is God's Son.* This is intended under this relative *Son*. See Sec. 55.

XXI. *Christ is the governor of the church.* This preposition *over* importeth a government. See Sec. 59.

XXII. *The church is Christ's own.* It is his own house. See Sec. 57.

XXIII. *Saints are Christ's house.* This pronoun *we* means saints. See Sec. 58.

XXIV. *Believers under the law and gospel make one house.* Moses was under the law, and we are under the gospel. See Sec. 59.

XXV. *They who stand must take heed lest they fall.* So much is hinted under this conjunction *if*. See Sec. 60.

XXVI. *The best have need to look to their standing.* The apostle puts himself under this caution by using a verb of the first person, 'If we hold fast.'

XXVII. *Confidence is one evidence of our right to Christ.* Mention is made of confidence to that end. See Sec. 61.

XXVIII. *Hope also is an evidence of our right to Christ.* To this end it is added unto confidence. See Sec. 62.

XXIX. *Rejoicing ariseth from hope;* it is therefore here added as an epithet to hope. See Sec. 63.

XXX. *Perseverance is an evidence of soundness;* it is here set down for that end by way of supposition, 'If we hold fast.' See Sec. 68.

XXXI. *Perseverance must be without intermission;* for this end this epithet *firm* is added. See Sec. 68.

XXXII. *True perseverance holds out till death;* so much is intended under this phrase, *to the end.* See Sec. 68.

Sec. 73. *Of the inference of that which follows upon that which went before.*

Ver. 7. *Wherefore, as the Holy Ghost saith, To-day, if ye will hear his voice.*

From the beginning of the second verse to this, the apostle hath largely set down Christ's faithfulness in executing his prophetical office; and that toward us, who are his house. Hereupon he inferreth a dissuasion from disrespecting Christ, which is continued to the end of this chapter.

This first particle, διό, *wherefore*, is a note of inference.

This is the first place in this epistle where the Greek word is used, yet other Greek words to the same sense have been used, as chap. ii. vers. 1, 17.

This inference may have reference either to all that hath been spoken before of Christ's excellency and faithfulness, thus: Because Christ was so excellent and faithful a prophet, as never any the like; we must therefore take heed that we harden not our hearts against him, nor depart from him; or more immediately to the last clause of the former verse, thus: Because if we hold fast the confidence, &c., we give evidence thereby that we are the house of Christ; we ought *therefore* to take heed that we harden not our hearts, and depart from Christ.

The former reference sheweth that Christ's care in executing his function for our good, ought to make us careful in attending to him, and cleaving close to him.

The latter reference sheweth that we ought in this respect to take heed that we fall not from Christ, because holding fast our confidence is an evidence of our communion with him, namely, that we are his house, and he our Lord. Hence it followeth that means must be used for holding fast confidence.

I take the former reference to be the more proper to this place, and so it intends the same point that was before noted, Sec. 2.

This note of inference, *wherefore*, looking backward, may intend either the point that immediately followeth in the divine testimony, or that which is set down, ver. 12, &c. If thus, then the testimony must be included in a parenthesis, and this particle *wherefore* be taken as joined with the 12th verse, thus, 'Wherefore, take heed,' &c.

Sec. 74. *Of expressing one's mind in the words of the Holy Ghost.*

The apostle expresseth his mind concerning the use which we are to make of Christ's faithfulness in his office under the very words of sacred Scripture, which questionless he doth to make it the more regarded; for to express God's mind in his own words addeth great weight to the point. The apostle doth the like chap. ii. vers. 6, 7, and in sundry other places of this epistle. A very great part thereof is penned in Scripture words and phrases; for he wrote to the Hebrews, who were well exercised in the Old Testament, and had it in high account.

In quoting the testimony, he expresseth neither book, nor psalm, nor verse. Of this manner of quoting Scripture, see more, Chap. ii. Sec. 50; but the words of Scripture are so expressly set down, as it may be found out where they are, especially by such as are so exercised in the Scriptures as these Hebrews were.

The apostle faithfully declareth the mind of God therein, though there be some little difference in words, especially in their order or joining together, which we shall note in due place.

The testimony continueth from this verse to the 12th, and it is taken out of Ps. xcv. 7–9, and xix. 11.

David was the penman of this as of the other Psalms; therefore David's name is sometimes expressed before texts quoted out of the book of Psalms, as chap. iv. 7, Mat. xxii. 43, Luke xx. 42, Acts ii. 25, Rom. iv. 6 and xi. 9.

To shew that the Holy Ghost spake what David uttered in the Psalms, Peter useth this phrase, 'The Holy Ghost by the mouth of David spake,' Acts i. 16; and again, speaking to God, thus saith, 'Who by the mouth of thy servant David hast said,' Acts iv. 25.

The apostle's manner of quoting this testimony thus, 'The Holy Ghost saith,' doth demonstrate sundry principles of our Christian faith; as,

1. The Holy Ghost is true God; for 'God spake by the mouth of David,' Acts iv. 25. Where David said, 'The Spirit of the Lord spake by me,' he addeth, 'The God of Israel said,' 2 Sam. xxiii. 2, 3. 'All Scripture is given by inspiration of God,' 2 Tim. iii. 16. And 'God spake by the prophets,' Heb. i. 1; and they 'spake as they were moved by the Holy Ghost,' 2 Peter i. 21.

2. The Holy Ghost is a distinct person. This phrase, *the Holy Ghost saith*, intendeth as much,

3. The Holy Ghost was before Christ was exhibited in the flesh, for he spake by David, whose son Christ was many generations after David; yea, mention is made of this Spirit of God to be before any creatures were, Gen. i. 2. So as the Holy Ghost is God eternal.

4. The Scriptures of the Old Testament are of divine authority; 'Holy men of God spake as they were moved by the Holy Ghost,' 2 Peter i. 21.

Of this title *Holy Ghost*, see Chap. ii. ver. 4, Sec. 35.

The apostle useth this particle of resemblance, καθὼς, *as*, to shew what he delivereth afterwards is agreeable to the mind and words of the Holy Ghost. This particle may have reference to ver. 12, and to express the mind of the apostle more fully, the other particle of resemblance, *so*, may be there inserted, thus, 'As the Holy Ghost saith, so take heed,' &c.

Though the testimony quoted were written, yet it is expressed under this word λέγει, *saith*, to shew that the word is as a sermon preached, that so we should give the more heed thereto.

Here it is not expressed to whom he saith, because it is intended to every one, and every one should attend unto it as spoken to him in particular.

Sec. 75. *Of the apostle's fit applying a divine testimony.*

The main scope of this testimony (as it was first uttered by the psalmist), is to admonish such as from time to time should live in the church, to take heed of rebelling against Christ, as the Israelites in the wilderness had done.

Many interpreters, both ancient[1] and modern,[2] apply that psalm to Christ; for this title, צור ישענו, 'the Rock of our salvation,' or, as the LXX render it, τῷ σωτῆρι ἡμῶν, 'our Saviour,' ver. 2, doth most properly belong to Christ, and Christ is that Shepherd whose sheep we are, Luke xiii. 20. And it is expressly said of the Israelites in the wilderness, that they tempted Christ, 1 Cor. x. 9. Hereupon this adverb of time, σήμερον, *to-day*, is applied to the time of grace wherein God speaks to us by his own Son,[3] chap. i. 2.

In this respect this testimony is most pertinently quoted for the point in hand; for David, foreknowing that God would send his Son to be a Saviour and Shepherd of his church, exhorteth all the members thereof to rejoice in him, with all reverence to worship him, and to take heed of being like to the rebellious Israelites in the wilderness.

Now, because the apostle had set forth the faithfulness of the Son of God in his prophetical office, he fitly putteth the Hebrews in mind of that seasonable admonition of the psalmist, to keep them from being like their forefathers, and to quicken them up to a more diligent heeding of Christ's word, which is the gospel.

Sec. 76. *Of taking the first opportunity of grace.*

The first word of the foresaid divine testimony, σήμερον, *to-day*, is diversely taken, as was shewed, Chap. i. 5, Sec. 61.

Here it signifieth the time present, yet so as it includes a continuance of a time present. As that present time wherein David lived was to him, and to those that then lived, *to-day;* so that present time wherein the apostle and other Christians with him lived, was to them *to-day*, and the time wherein we now live, is to us *to-day*.

This word, then, *to-day*, intends that instant wherein God affords an opportunity of getting grace or obtaining any blessing. It may here have reference to that which immediately followeth, of hearing Christ's voice; as if he had said, If ye will now hear his voice while he speaketh unto you.

Or it may have reference to the inhibition of not hardening their heart; as if he had said, If ye will hear Christ's voice, then harden not your heart in this time that he is speaking unto you.

In the Greek there is a comma put after this word *to-day*, whereby is intended the latter reference.

In the general, both references tend to the same scope, which is, that the present opportunity of God's offering grace must be taken; we must hearken to him while he speaketh, and we may not harden our hearts against him when he speaketh. When Samuel, though he were but a child, understood that the Lord called him, he presently answered, 'Speak, for thy servant heareth,' 1 Sam. iii. 10. Ruth was but a young woman, yet she, understanding that the God of Naomi was the only true Lord, saith to her mother-in-law, 'Thy God shall be my God,' and thereupon would needs go with her to be among the people of that God, Ruth i. 16, &c. Zaccheus, in his man-age, coming to know Jesus to be the promised Messiah, readily entertained him, Luke xix. 5, 6. The penitent thief, at the time of his death, knowing Christ to be the promised King, believed on him, and confessed him, Luke xxiii. 41, 42. Thus in what estate of our age soever, means of calling us to Christ are afforded, we must even then without delay, to-day, take that opportunity. 'I made haste, and delayed not,' saith the psalmist, Ps. cxix. 60. When Christ called Zaccheus, 'he made haste and came down,' Luke xix. 6. When Christ called Simon and Andrew, 'they straightway left their nets, and followed him,' Mat. iv. 20. 'When it pleased God to reveal his Son' in Paul, immediately he preached him, Gal. i. 16.

1. It is God which 'worketh in us both to will and to do,' Philip. ii. 13; and 'no man can come to Christ except the Father draw him,' John vi. 44. Is it not then a point of wisdom to yield when God draws? The church promiseth as much, saying, 'Draw me, I will run after thee,' Cant. i. 3. If we harden our hearts, and hear not Christ speaking to us to-day, how can we expect that he should hear us to-morrow? 'They shall call upon me, but I will not answer,' saith Wisdom, Prov. i. 28.

---

[1] August. Hiero. Arnob. Haimo.
[2] Tremel. et Jun. Moller.
[3] *Hodie*, id est, in hoc tempore gratiæ, quum nobis loquitur per proprium filium.—*Haimo in hunc Psal.* In Christo prophetia loquitur et populo Judæorum, et populo Gentium.—*Aug. Enar. in hunc Psal.*

2. Thou 'knowest not what a day may bring forth.' Therefore put not off the grace that is offered thee to-day. 'Boast not thyself of to-morrow,' Prov. xxvii. 1. The rich fool that thought to enjoy his goods many years was taken from them that night, Luke xii. 19, 20.

3. By putting off an opportunity, men make themselves more unfit for another opportunity; for sin, the longer it groweth, the stronger it groweth, and the heart useth to be more hardened by putting off means of softening.

As they who had received grace were exhorted to persevere therein, Sec. 69; so they who have not yet attained grace are to be exhorted to accept the means of grace tendered to-day. Even now, while the word soundeth in your ears, hear, and harden not your hearts; 'Behold, now is the accepted time; Behold, now is the day of salvation,' 2 Cor. vi. 2. Put not off to-day, much less let childhood put off to youth, or youth to man-age, or man-age to old age, or old age to deathbed.

Of the common allegation of the thief's repentance on the cross, see *The Whole Armour of God*, on Eph. vi. 14, treat. ii. part ii. sec. 12.

Sec. 77. *Of hearing aright.*

This phrase, 'if ye will hear his voice, containeth in the substance of it the most principal and proper duty that is required of Christians in relation to Christ's prophetical office. In the manner of setting it down, it implies a forcible motive against hardening our hearts; for they who harden their hearts cannot hear Christ's voice as they should.

Some expound this conditional conjunction *if* with a conjunction of the time; thus, *when* ye will hear his voice, harden not your heart.

Which way soever we take it, it intendeth a duty; and such a duty as compriseth much more than the bare hearing the sound of a voice with the outward ear, for he whose heart is hardened may so hear. Pharaoh himself, whose heart was exceedingly hardened, so heard the voice of God. Where Christ saith, 'He that hath an ear, let him hear what the Spirit saith,' Rev. ii. 7, implieth that a man may hear the Spirit inwardly speaking to the soul, as well as an outward audible voice.

Of that inward spiritual hearing there are three acts:

1. To understand what is outwardly heard by the ears of the body. Where the prophet rebukes the people for being without understanding, he saith, 'They have ears, and hear not,' that is, understand not; and thereupon adviseth them to hear, Jer. v. 21.

2. To believe what they understand. Where Christ reproveth the Jews for not believing, he addeth, 'He that is of God heareth God's words; ye therefore hear them not' (that is, ye believe them not), 'because ye are not of God,' John viii. 46, 47. And where he said, 'Ye believe not, because ye are not of my sheep,' he addeth, 'My sheep hear my voice,' that is, believe it, John x. 26, 27.

3. To obey it. Where the Israelites, upon hearing the law in great terror delivered, thus said to Moses, 'Speak thou with us, and we will hear,' Exodus xx. 19, in another place it is thus expressed, 'We will hear it, and do it,' Deut. v. 27.

In all these senses is this word *hear* to be taken in this text, and Isa. lv. 3, and Mat. xvii. 5.

To hear only with the ears of the body, and not to understand, believe, or obey, is so far from a full duty, and true virtue, as it makes us liable to judgment.

To hear and not to understand, is to be like the pathway upon which the corn is cast; but because it is not covered with earth, the fowls pick it up, and it doth not fructify, Mat. xiii. 19.

To hear and not believe, makes us like to them whom 'the word preached did not profit, not being mixed with faith,' Heb. iv. 2.

To hear and not to do, is to be 'like a foolish man, which built his house upon the sand,' Mat. vii. 26, 27.

It is therefore our duty, when the word of God is preached,

1. To open the ears of our head, for they are the doors to let in God's word. This is one main end why ears are given to us, and they cannot be better used.

2. So to heed the word heard and meditate thereon, so as we may understand the mind of God therein. This is it which Christ requireth, Mat. xv. 10; for this end the apostle prayeth for 'the spirit of wisdom and revelation,' Eph. i. 17; this grace is promised to the wise, but denied to the wicked, Daniel xii. 10.

3. Mix faith with hearing, else the word will lose its power; for it is 'the power of God unto salvation to every one that believeth,' Rom. i. 16. God gives preachers, that men should hear the word and believe, Acts xv. 7.

4. Add obedience. All blessing is annexed to this, Luke xi. 28; this giveth evidence of our right understanding the word and believing the same.

They who thus hear have hearing ears; such ears to hear as Christ requireth, Mat. xiii. 9, Rev. ii. 7; and they who thus hear will be kept from hardness of heart. This supposition, ἐὰν ἀκούσητε, 'if ye will hear,' and the consequence inferred thereupon, 'harden not your hearts,' doth evidently demonstrate that a right hearing will prevent hardness of heart; especially hearing of Christ's voice, that is, the gospel. It is the gospel that maketh and keepeth a soft heart. See Chap. ii. 3, Secs. 20, 21; see also *The Whole Armour of God*, treat. ii. part. v. on Eph. vi. 15, secs. 4–6; *ibid.*, part. vi. on Eph. vi. 16, sec. 21.

Sec. 78. *Of Christ's voice.*

The particular object of hearing, as aforesaid, is

Christ's voice. For this relative, αὐτοῦ, *his*, hath reference to Christ.

We shewed before, Sec. 75, that the psalmist spake of Christ. More evident it is that the apostle speaketh of Christ in all the precedent verses; so as without all question Christ's voice is here meant, namely, his word, which in the days of his flesh he uttered by his own lively voice, and afterward by the voice of his apostles. The substance of all being written and registered, is further made known by the voice of his ministers age after age. Thus may we still hear Christ's voice. See Chap. ii. 12, Sec. 112.

In general, by *Christ's voice* is meant the word of God, which is the only proper object of a saving hearing, of hearing to life, John v. 25.

In particular, the gospel is intended under *Christ's voice*. See Chap. ii. 3, Secs. 20–24.

We may not, in regard of this particular reference to Christ, put difference betwixt the word of God, of Christ, and of the Spirit; for they are all one. Therefore Christ blameth them who hear not God, John viii. 47; and God commandeth to hear his Son, Mat. xvii. 5; and Christ commandeth to hear the Spirit, Rev. ii. 7.

But there is a direct difference betwixt the word of God and the word of man, as man. To 'teach for doctrines the commandments of men,' is blameable, Mat. xv. 9.

Only God's word is the ground of faith and rule for obedience; and that both in regard of God's high supreme sovereignty (who hath power to promise and command what he will), and also in regard of the perfection and purity of his nature.

The Turk's Alcoran, the Jew's Cabala, the papist's traditions, the dictates of philosophers or poets, or any other inventions of men, which are by ignorant and foolish persons made the grounds for their faith and rules for their obedience, are with indignation to be detested, especially when they are obtruded instead of Christ's voice. Let us learn to 'try the spirits, whether they are of God,' 1 John iv. 1. It is the note of Christ's sheep to know the voice of their shepherd, John x. 4. For this end be well exercised in Christ's word: 'Search the Scriptures,' John v. 39; and pray for 'the Spirit of wisdom and revelation in the knowledge of Christ,' Eph. i. 17.

Sec. 79. *Of the heart.*

Ver. 8. *Harden not your hearts.*

To prevent an hindrance of aright hearing Christ's voice, the apostle thus adviseth those to whom he wrote, 'Harden not your hearts.'

Here just occasion is given to consider what *the heart* is, and what it is to *harden*.

The *heart*, properly taken, is a little fleshy piece within the breast of the body, under the left pap, triangular, broad at the top and sharp at the bottom. It is the fountain of life, the root whence all the spirits sprout forth, that which first liveth and last dieth in man.

Heart metaphorically is attributed to the Creator, and to sundry creatures.

1. To the Creator, to set out the greatness of his liking or disliking a thing. David is said to be 'a man after God's own heart,' 1 Sam. xiii. 14, Acts xiii. 22. He was one whom God well liked and approved. On the other side, concerning the men of the old world, it is said, 'It grieved the Lord at his heart' that he had made man, Gen. vi. 6. He much disliked and disapproved the men that then lived.

2. Heart is attributed to senseless creatures, to set out the innermost part or midst of them, because the heart is within a man's body, even almost in the midst thereof. Thus it is said, 'The depths were congealed in the heart of the sea,' Exod. xv. 8. And Christ was 'three days and three nights in the heart of the earth,' Mat. xii. 40.

3. Heart is ascribed to reasonable creatures, to signify sometimes the whole soul, and sometimes the several faculties appertaining to the soul.

(1.) It is frequently put for the whole soul, and that for the most part when it is set alone; as where it is said, 'Serve the Lord with all your heart,' 1 Sam. xii. 20.

(2.) For that principal part of the soul which is called the mind or understanding. 'I gave my heart to know wisdom,' Eccles. i. 17. In this respect, darkness and blindness are attributed to the heart, Eph. iv. 18, Rom. i. 21.

(3.) For the will: as when heart and soul are joined together, the two essential faculties of the soul are meant, namely, the mind and will: *soul* put for the mind, *heart* for the will. 'Serve the Lord with all your heart, and with all your soul,' Deut. xi. 13.

(4.) For the memory. 'I have hid thy word in my heart,' saith the prophet, Ps. cxix. 11. The memory is that faculty wherein matters are laid up and hid.

(5.) For the conscience. It is said that 'David's heart smote him,' that is, his conscience, 1 Sam. xxiv. 5, 2 Sam. xxiv. 10. Thus is heart taken, 1 John iii. 20, 21.

(6.) For the affections: as where it is said, 'Thou shalt love the Lord thy God with all thy heart, and with all thy soul, and with all thy mind,' Mat. xxii. 37. By the *mind* is meant the understanding faculty; by the *soul*, the will; by the *heart*, the affections.

Here in this text the heart is put for the whole soul, even for mind, will, and affections. For blindness of mind, stubbornness of will, and stupidity of affections go together.

Sec. 80. *Of hardening the heart.*

There are two words used in the New Testament to set out the act of hardening, as it hath reference to the heart.

One is taken from a Greek root, πῶρος, that signifieth an hard brawny skin, which fasteneth together broken bones, or that flesh and skin on the hand or feet which is made hard and insensible by much labour and travel. It signifieth also *blind*. See Sec. 87.

Hence is derived a word oft used in the New Testament, πώρωσις, *obduratio*, and translated *hardness*, Mark iii. 5; and a verb, πωρόω, *durum reddo*, which signifieth to harden, John xii. 40, Mark vi. 52.

The foresaid Greek root, πῶρος, *porus*, *lapis Pario similis*, doth also signify a stone somewhat like white marble; and the verb thence derived, πωρόω, *in lapidosum duritiem commuto*, signifieth to turn into a stony hardness.

This is a fit metaphor to express the sense of the point in hand. For an hard heart is like to brawny flesh and skin, which is not sensible of any smart, though it be pricked or cut. Nor threats nor judgments move an hard heart: witness Pharaoh's disposition. Yea, further, an hard heart is resembled to a stone, Ezek. xi. 19. A stone will sooner be broken all to pieces than softened by blows; so a man of an hard heart will sooner be utterly confounded by God's judgments than brought to yield to them.

The other word used in Scripture to set out an hard heart is taken from another Greek root, σκέλλω, *exsicco*, *arefacio*, which signifieth to dry up, or draw out the juice or moisture of a thing, whereby it comes to be hard; for moisture makes things soft, dryness makes them hard. Hence is derived an adjective, σκληρός, *durus ex ariditate*, which signifieth hard through dryness.

Metaphorically, this epithet is in Scripture added to sundry things, as 'an hard speech,' John vi. 60, Jude 15; 'an hard master,' Mat. xxv. 24; hard or fierce winds, James iii. 4; an hard or difficult matter, Acts ix. 5. A substantive also, σκληρότης, *durities*, is thence derived, which signifieth hardness, Rom. ii. 5; and a verb, σκληρύνω, *induro*, which signifieth to harden, Rom. ix. 18, Acts xix. 9. From the foresaid root there is a compound, σκληροκαρδία, *duritia cordis*, which signifieth hardness of heart, Mat. xix. 8, Mark xvi. 14; and another compound, σκληροτράχηλος, *durus cervice*, which signifieth hard or stiff-necked, Acts vii. 51. Physicians use a word, derived from the foresaid verb, to set out such drugs or medicines as have a force of hardening, σκληροντικὰ φάρμακα, *indurantia medicamenta*.

This latter metaphor is here used by the apostle, and again vers. 13, 15, and Chap. iv. 7. It is as fit a metaphor as the former, and implieth that an hard heart is dry and destitute of all grace, of all spiritual moisture, sense, and life.

The apostle here sets down this act of hardening as a man's own act, and that upon himself, thus speaking unto them, 'Harden not your heart. I think it meet hereupon to declare,

1. What hardness of heart is.
2. What are the ordinary causes thereof.
3. How man hardeneth his own heart.
4. What is the danger and damage of a hard heart.
5. How hardness of heart may be discerned.
6. How hardness of heart may be prevented or redressed.

Sec. 81. *Of hardness of heart, what it is.*

I. Hardness of heart is an insensibleness of such means as are afforded to draw one from wickedness, or rather a wilful obstinacy against them; for without man's will the heart cannot be hardened. Therefore here, and in sundry other places, as Exod. ix. 34, 1 Sam. vi. 6, 2 Chron. xxxvi. 13, this act is applied to man himself; for the will is free, and cannot be compelled or forced. Take away freedom from the will, and you take away the nature of the will. Therefore God himself, when he converteth a sinner, worketh in him both, θέλειν, 'to will and to do:' first to will, then to do, Philip. ii. 13.

That we may the better discern how wilfulness causeth the hardness of heart here spoken of, we are to consider hardness of heart in a double respect: as it is natural, and as it is habitual.

1. Natural hardness of heart is in all men. As other corruptions seized on man's nature by Adam's fall, so hardness of heart. Man by nature is given to withstand and oppose against all means afforded to keep him from sin, and in this opposition to remain obstinate, so as to be confounded rather than yield. This is that stony heart that is in man by nature, Ezek. xi. 19.

2. Habitual hardness of heart is an increase of the former, and that by man's further wilfulness. All mankind in Adam's loins, as he was a public person, wilfully opposed against God; and every one, in his own person, is given by nature more and more to oppose, but some more obstinately and impenitently than others. In such the apostle joineth 'hardness' and 'an impenitent heart' together, and sheweth that such treasure up to themselves wrath, Rom. ii. 5. Adam's first sin had wilfulness in it, so as there is wilfulness in man's natural hardness, much more is there wilfulness in his habitual hardness.

Obj. Against this it is objected that God, and Satan, and other men do harden a man's heart.

Ans. In general, I answer that none of those do free a man from wilfulness in that hardness of heart which seizeth on him; so as in this respect we may say to him that is of an hard heart, O man, 'thou hast destroyed thyself,' Hosea xiii. 9.

To clear this point more fully, I will distinctly shew how God, how Satan, how other men are said to harden a man's heart.

God doth it in justice, Satan in malice, other men in wilfulness.

Sec. 82. *Of God's hardening man's heart.*

God is said to harden as a judge, inflicting hardness of heart as a punishment, Rom. i. 24. Now, because man wittingly did that which deserves that punishment, he hardens his own heart; even as a thief, who is condemned by the judge, may be said to hang himself.

That God's justice may in this point be more clearly manifested, observe the particular respects wherein God is said to harden man's heart. They are these:

1. In that all actions and motions, as they are actions and motions, come from God, as our very being doth: for 'in him we live, and move, and have our being,' Acts xvii. 28. But the pravity of the action or motion cometh from man, therefore man properly hardeneth himself.

2. In that God hinders not men from doing that which hardeneth; but God is the most high supreme sovereign; there is none above him to bind him to do anything. He being not bound to hinder men from doing what they do, who can, who shall blame him? Mat. xx. 15. Man himself doth the very deed.

3. In that he withholdeth or withdraweth his softening Spirit; for man's own spirit is a resisting spirit, Acts vii. 51. It must be a higher and stronger spirit which keepeth man's spirit in compass; but God's withholding or withdrawing his Spirit, is in justice for some sin of man.

4. In that God offereth the occasions whereby man's heart is hardened, as his word, sacraments, mercies, judgments, miracles, and such like. But these occasions are in themselves good; their proper end is to soften. It is by man's perverting them that they harden; man in this case is like the spider that sucketh poison out of sweet flowers.

5. In that God giveth over to Satan, who hardeneth man's heart; but God doth this as a just judge, Satan being his executioner. Man himself brings this judgment upon himself.

Sec. 83. *Of Satan's and other men's hardening one's heart.*

As for Satan, though he may enter into a man as he entered into Judas, John xiii. 27; and provoke men to sin, as he did David, 1 Chron. xxi. 1; and beguiled them through his subtilty, as he beguiled Eve, 2 Cor. xi. 3; and sift them, as he sifted Peter, Luke xxii. 31; yet he cannot force man's will to sin. See *The Whole Armour of God*, on Eph. vi. 12, treat. i. part iii. sec. 17.

As for other men, they can less force man's will than Satan. What they do is either by counsel, as the sorcerers hardened Pharaoh's heart, Exod. vii. 11; or by expostulation, as Jezebel hardened Ahab's heart, 1 Kings xxi. 7; or by persuasion, as the princes hardened Zedekiah's heart, Jer. xxxviii. 4, 5, 25; or by example, as the four hundred prophets hardened one another, or were all hardened by Zedekiah's example, 1 Kings xxii. 11, 12. If a man himself yield not, all that other men can do will not harden him; therefore, man properly hardeneth himself.

It will stand a man in no stead to put off the blame of this sin from himself to any other. This is it that keeps men from being duly humbled, and from true repentance, whereby the heart comes to be more hardened; yet too prone are men so to do. Some impute their hardness to God, as Adam; some to Satan, as Eve, Gen. iii. 12, 13; others to other men, as Saul, 1 Sam. xv. 21.

Would we lay the blame on ourselves, as we ought, we might be brought to such a sense of the burden that lieth on us, as Christ would be moved to ease us, Mat. xi. 28.

Sec. 84. *Of the causes of hardness of heart.*

II. The ordinary causes of hardness of heart are such as these:

1. Natural hardness. This is the original cause of habitual hardness. If that be not taken away, this will accompany it; both will be mixed together. In this respect it is said of the unconverted Gentiles, that they were 'past feeling.' This is set down as an effect of natural hardness, Eph. iv. 18, 19; for the word, πώρωσις, going before, translated *blindness*, doth also signify *hardness*, as is shewed, Sec. 87.

2. Unbelief. This makes men disrespect promises, threatenings, mercies, judgments, and all other means which are of use to soften or break men's hearts. This was the great sin of the Israelites, who hardened their hearts in the wilderness, Deut. i. 32, and ix. 25, Ps. lxxviii. 22, 32. Therefore the apostle, to prevent hardness of heart, admonisheth those to whom he wrote, to take heed of unbelief, ver. 12, 13. See Sec. 120.

3. Hypocrisy. By this men cover and hide their sin, whereby they wax bold in sinning. It is said of obdurate sinners, that they 'lurk privily,' Prov. i. 18; and say, 'No eye shall see us,' Job. xxiv. 15.

4. Pride. For this is ordinarily joined with scorn, disdain, and such like vices as make men refuse and reject the means which might mollify their hearts. Thus was Pharaoh's heart hardened, Exod. v. 2; and the heart of the Jews, Jer. xliv. 16.

5. Presumption. When sins are committed against knowledge, conscience, light of nature, and motions of the spirit, they are as heavy weights that press out all spiritual sense and life. As a great blow so stuns one, as it makes him senseless, so a presumptuous sin will make a man's spirit senseless. After that Zedekiah had broken his oath with the king of Babel, Ezek. xvii. 16, his heart was hardened against all the good counsel that the prophet Jeremiah gave him, Jer. xxxviii. 17, &c.

6. Oft committing, or long lying in the same sin. Many small knocks or blows, long continued, do in time as much as a great blow at once. Men's hands and heels use to be hardened by much work and long travel.

7. *Relapse.* To return to sin after a man hath manifested solemn repentance, as the swine after it is washed returneth to the mire, especially if it be to the same sin, as the dog licketh up the vomit he had formerly cast out, is to make way for the devil's re-entry, whereby a man's heart will be so hardened, as his latter end will be worse than his beginning, 2 Peter ii. 20, &c., Mat. xii. 43, &c. Against this doth Christ give prudent caveats, John v. 14, and viii. 11.

8. *Lewd company.* Lewd companions will by evil counsel, bad example, bold encouragement, make men impudent and obstinate in sinning. The wise man therefore much dissuadeth from such company, Prov. i. 10, &c.

9. *Superfluity of the things of this world*, as of wealth, honour, ease, pleasure, applause, and other such things as men by nature delight in. These are like weeds, thorns, and briers, which draw out the moisture of the earth, and make it dry and hard, or as weights that press out the juice of fruits, and make them hard. These make the things of the Spirit of life to be nothing at all regarded. This cause of hardening is then most prevalent, when men are raised from a mean estate to a great one, or from a troublesome estate, to a quiet and pleasing estate. If iron be taken out of the fire, and put into cold water, it waxeth hard.

10. *Multitude of crosses not sanctified.* These are as many blows upon the smith's anvil. King Ahaz, ' in the time of his distress, did trespass yet more against the Lord,' 2 Chron. xxviii. 22. 'The wrath of God came upon Israel, and slew the fattest of them. For all that they sinned still,' Ps. lxxviii. 31, 32.

Sec. 85. *Of man's hardening himself.*
III. Man hardeneth himself two ways : 1, privatively; 2, positively.

1. Privatively, by refusing or rejecting means whereby his heart might be softened.

Means of softening a man's heart are public, private, and secret.

1. Public means are public ordinances of God, as the word read and preached, the sacraments, praying, and praising God; yea, also God's works, and those both of mercy and judgment, whether ordinary or extraordinary.

2. Private means are, reading and expounding God's word in private places, private praying and praising God, repeating sermons, private instruction, mutual holy conference, and such like.

3. Secret means, reading the word and other good books alone, praying and praising God alone, meditation and examination of one's self.

The Jews in the apostles' time hardened their hearts by putting away from them the word of God, Acts xiii. 46 ; and in John Baptist's time, they 're-jected the counsel of God against themselves, being not baptised of John,' Luke vii. 30. They refused to subject themselves to that ordinance. In Christ's time they hardened their hearts by opposing against his miraculous works, Mat. xii. 24, John xv. 24.

About means which are to soften men's hearts, men diverse ways beguile themselves, so as they harden their hearts thereby. As,

(1.) By putting off for the present such means as might soften them to another time; as he that said to Paul, ' Go thy way for this time; when I have a convenient season, I will call for thee,' Acts xxiv. 25. But that season never came.

(2.) By thinking they have done enough, when it is but little that they have done, yet can say, ' Behold, what a weariness is it !' Mal. i. 13.

(3.) By resting in the outward work, as they who said, ' Wherefore have we fasted, and thou seest not ?' Isa. lviii. 3.

(4.) By doating upon human ordinances, as they who ' in vain worshipped God, teaching for doctrines the commandments of men,' Mat. xv. 9.

2. Positively. Men harden themselves by a slavish yielding to the causes of hardening men's hearts, mentioned Sec. 84. This they do by nourishing their natural hardness : by opposing against God's truth in his promises and threatenings, by hiding their sin, by pride, by presumption, by long lying in sin, by returning to sin after repentance, by setting their hearts too much on the things of this world, by perverting God's chastisements.

In that hardness of heart ariseth from one's self, even from his own wilfulness, it nearly concerns us to be the more watchful over ourselves, and to withstand the very beginning of hardness. For Satan is very subtle, and seeks to beguile a man by degrees; and sin is deceitful and of a bewitching nature. It soaks into a man insensibly, and we of ourselves are very foolish, like the silly fish that with a fair bait is soon taken. Hence it is that from small beginnings many come to this high pitch, even to be hardened in heart.

When men are tempted to sin,
1. There is a thought of committing it, Gen. xxxviii. 15.
2. A plain consent to yield to it, Ps. l. 18.
3. An actual committing of it, 2 Sam. xi. 4.
4. An iteration of it, Judges xvi. 1, 4.
5. A custom therein, 1 Sam. ii. 13.
6. An excusing of it, 1 Sam. xv. 15.
7. A justifying it, Isa. v. 23, Luke xvi. 15.
8. A glorying in it, Ps. lii. 1.
9. An habit that they can scarce do otherwise, Jer. xiii. 23.
10. Hardness of heart, Rom. ii. 5.

By these degrees it cometh to pass that sin, which upon the first temptation seemed horrible, and upon the first committing thereof much perplexed the soul, and seemed to be an insupportable burden, making the sinner thus to complain : ' Mine iniquities are gone over my head ; as an heavy burden, they are too heavy for me,' Ps. xxxviii. 4 ; appears in time not to be so burdensome, but rather light and easy, yea, so unsensible as they can scarce perceive it, like him that saith, 'They have stricken me, and I was not sick: they have beaten me, and I felt it not: I will seek it yet again,' Prov. xxiii. 35. Yea, further, it comes by degrees to be pleasing and delightful; so sweet in his mouth as he hides it under his tongue, Job xx. 12.

Sec. 86. *Of the danger and damage of hardness of heart.*

IV. The danger whereinto men fall by hardness of heart, and the damage which they receive, is greater than can be expressed. It brings a man into the most desperate case, that in this world a man can be brought into by any other thing, except it be by the sin against the Holy Ghost, whereunto hardness of heart makes a great way. Shame, grief, fear, may be means to keep men that are not hardened from running on in their desperate courses; but hardness of heart is a spiritual senselessness, and keeps from such passions as shame, grief, and fear. It makes men audacious in sinning. A troubled conscience casts a man into a most woful plight, but a hardened heart is far worse than a perplexed soul. The troubled conscience may for the present seem more bitter, but if the issue of the one and the other be duly considered, we shall find that there is no comparison betwixt them, but that the hard heart is far the worst. The troubled conscience, by accusing, galling, perplexing, and not suffering a man to be quiet, may so deject him as to restrain him from sin, and bring him to repentance. But an hard heart puts on a man more and more to sin, and that with greediness, Eph. iv. 18, whereby his condemnation is increased. In this respect it were better for a man to die with a troubled conscience and despairing heart, than with a seared conscience and a hard heart.

Sec. 87. *Of the signs whereby a hard heart may be discerned.*

V. Hardness of heart is accompanied with blindness of mind. Therefore, there is one Greek noun, πώρωσις, that is put for both; answerably it is sometimes translated *hardness*, Mark iii. 5, and sometimes *blindness*, Rom. xi. 25, Eph. iv. 18.

There is also a verb, πωρόω, *obcæco*, coming from the same root, that is translated sometimes to harden, as καρδία πεπωρωμένη, *cor obduratum*, Mark vi. 52, and viii. 17; sometimes to blind, as Rom. xi. 7, ἐπωρώθη νοήματα, *occæcatæ sunt mentes*, 2 Cor. iii. 14. In that hardness of heart and blindness of mind go together, he that hath an hard heart cannot well discern it, but yet by others it may be observed, and that by the effects thereof.

There are two especial effects that do discover an hard heart:

1. Careless security. When men are senseless, and as senseless persons lie in sin, where there is no sense commonly there is no life. A living man that hath a stone in his kidney or bladder will certainly feel it and complain of it. Now a hard heart is an heart of stone; had he spiritual life in him, he would certainly feel it and complain of it. Senselessness, therefore, shews that a man's heart is so hardened as he hath no spiritual life in him.

From this careless security proceedeth both a dissolute negligence, and also a blockish stupidity.

(1.) Dissolute negligence makes men consider nothing, nor lay anything to heart: 'The righteous perisheth, and no man layeth it to heart; and merciful men are taken away, none considering that the righteous is taken away from the evil to come,' Isa. lvii. 1. This is spoken of men of hard hearts. Such men let all things pass, whether matters of rejoicing or matters of mourning, without any inquiring after the cause, end, and use thereof, Mat. xi. 17.

(2.) Blockish stupidity makes men lie under those judgments which fall even upon their pates, like beasts. When Nabal heard of the danger wherein he had been by refusing to relieve David and his soldiers, 'his heart died within him, and he became as a stone,' 1 Sam. xxv. 37. Though they be overpressed, even out of measure, above their strength, yet have they no heart to pray for release or ease.

2. Wilful obstinacy is another effect which discovers an hard heart. This makes men,

(1.) To oppose against all the means which God affordeth to reclaim them, as his word, works, &c.

(2.) To resist the very motions of God's Spirit, as the hard-hearted Jews had always done, Acts vii. 51. From hence proceedeth malice against those that bear the image of God, as the Scribes and Pharisees hated the Son of God, and all that believed in him, John ix. 22, and the apostles, and them that believed through their word, Acts iv. 5, &c.; yea, such as be hard-hearted come to be haters of God himself, and endeavour to put out the very light of nature, Rom. i. 28, 30.

Sec. 88. *Of remedies for preventing or redressing hardness of heart.*

VI. Hardness of heart being such as hath been set out, it is very requisite that remedies be prescribed for preventing or redressing it. They are such as these:

I. Take heed of all and every of those causes whence hardness of heart ariseth. These are distinctly set down, Sec. 84. Take away the cause, and the effect will follow; where the cause remaineth, the effect also will remain. Withal, endeavour to get such virtues and graces as are contrary to the fore-mentioned causes of hardness, for one contrary will expel another.

As light, being contrary to darkness, keepeth out or expelleth darkness, so virtues contrary to the causes of hardness, will prevent or redress the same. Those graces are these that follow :

1. Regeneration. Hereby natural hardness is removed.
2. Faith. Hereby unbelief is redressed.
3. Sincerity. This keeps out hypocrisy.
4. Humility. Hereby pride and other like vices are kept down.
5. A fear of God. This will withhold us from gross sins.
6. Christian prudence. This will make men wary of multiplying sins, and long lying therein.
7. Spiritual watchfulness. This will uphold in such a course as will preserve us from relapse.
8. Holy jealousies, lest we should by company be drawn aside.
9. Contempt of this world, and of the things thereof, that we be not ensnared and overcome thereby.
10. Patience under all crosses, as laid on us by our heavenly Father for our good.

II. Labour to feel the heavy burden of sin, as he did that said, ' My sins are too heavy for me,' Ps. xxxviii. 4. For this end consider,

1. That sin destroyed all mankind; it poisoned Adam and all his posterity, Rom. v. 12.
2. That it made paradise too hot for Adam to abide in it, Gen. iii. 23, 24.
3. That it caused all the fearful judgments that have been executed from the beginning of the world.
4. That when saints apprehend it unpardoned, their conscience is a very rack unto them.
5. That when impenitents feel the burden of it, it makes their very life a burden unto them. Instance Judas, Mat. xxvii. 4, 5.
6. That it makes the damned in hell weep and gnash their teeth, Mat. xxv. 30. For their torment is endless, easeless, merciless, remediless.
7. That it holds the angels that fell in everlasting chains under darkness, Jude 6.
8. That albeit Christ had no sin in himself, yet when the burden of our sin as a surety lay upon him, it cast him into a bitter agony, and made ' his sweat as it were great drops of blood falling down to the ground,' Luke xxii. 44. There is no looking-glass that can so to the life set out the horror of sin as this of Christ.

III. When thou art overtaken with a sin, speedily return from it and repent. So did Peter: so soon as, by hearing the cock crow, and discerning his Lord's beck, he was put in mind of his sin, he presently repented, ' he went out and wept bitterly,' Luke xxii. 60–62. The longer sin continues, the stronger it groweth. It will fret like a canker, and eat up the life of the soul; therefore put not off repentance.

IV. After thou hast repented, be more watchful over thyself, that thou fall not into a relapse. If after the hand be blistered and healed a man use the hammer again, it will wax the harder.

V. Be constant in using means sanctified for softening the heart. Among other means, hearing the gospel is an especial one to keep or drive off hardness of heart; see 77, in the end of it. Therefore suffer the word to work on thee as it did on Josiah, 2 Kings xxii. 19. Neither put it off as Felix did, Acts xxiv. 26 ; nor mock at it as the Jews did, Acts ii. 13 ; nor blaspheme it as other Jews did, Acts xiii. 45. To public means add private, yea, and secret too.

VI. Walk continually before God, as Enoch did, Gen. v. 24. This will keep thee from yielding to temptations even in secret, Gen. xxxix. 9.

VII. Apply judgments on others to thyself, and by judgments on thyself be moved to examine thyself, and so humble thyself before God. Joseph's brethren by this means were brought to sight of their sin, Gen. xlii. 21.

VIII. Learn to number thy days aright. This will make thee account every day thy last, and make thee live as if it were the last day thou shouldst live on earth, and it will make thee think more frequently of that account thou art to give to God.

IX. At the end of every day examine thyself, and consider what sins have passed from thee. This may be a means of renewing repentance, and keeping thee from a hard heart.

X. While thy heart is soft, pray against hardness of heart, and desire others to pray for thee.

Sec. 89. *Of forbearing such sins as have been judged in others.*

Ver. 8. *As in the provocation, in the day of temptation in the wilderness.*

The former point, of hardening one's heart, is exemplified both by the prophet, and also by the apostle in the pattern of those Israelites, whom God brought out of Egypt, and in an especial manner tutored forty years together in the wilderness.

This first particle ὡς, *as*, is a note of comparison. It being added to a prohibition, thus, ' Harden not your hearts, *as* such and such did,' intendeth, that we should take heed of being like unto them, who have sinned in former times, against whose sins God hath manifested his indignation: for as the sin of those ancient Israelites is distinctly set down, verses 8, 9, so also God's just indignation against them, verses 10, 11.

This may be a good caveat to us, in reading the sins of others in former times, especially those that are registered in sacred Scripture, and in observing such evidences as are recorded of God's displeasure against them, to take heed that we fall not into the same, or the like sins. See Secs. 95, 158. See more of this point on Chap. xiii. 5, Sec. 68.

Sec. 90. *Of registering predecessors' sins.*

The sin against which God's people are here forewarned, is generally set down in these two words :

παραπικρασμος, provocation; πειρασμος, temptation. The latter shews the reason of the former. For if the question be asked, how they provoked God ? the answer is, They tempted him. Of tempting God, see Sec. 96.

The former word, παραπικρασμος, is a compound. It is compounded of a simple noun πικρός, that signifigth *bitter*, James iii. 11, 14. Thence a verb, πικραίνειν, *acerbare, amaritudinem afferre*, which signifieth to embitter, or to make bitter, Rev. viii. 11, and x. 9, 10. The preposition παρα adds an aggravation, and the verb παραπικραίνειν, *acerbare, exasperare, ad amaritudinem, seu amaram iram, concitare*, compounded therewith, signifieth to provoke to bitter anger; greatly to provoke, much to embitter. It is used verse 16; thence is this word παραπικρασμος, provocation, derived. It is twice used in this chapter, here and ver. 15.

The Hebrew word מריבה, which is used by the psalmist, signifieth strife or contention, or contradiction. It is translated strife, Num. xxvii. 14, and chiding,[1] Exod. xvii. 2. For chiding is a striving or contending by words, or a contradicting. The Israelites did chide with Moses, Exod. xvii. 7, and thereby provoked the Lord, whose servant Moses was.

These two words, *provocation* and *temptation*, are used in the abstract, to aggravate the heinousness of their sin.

Many learned expositors of the 95th Psalm retain the Hebrew words מריבה, *Meribath*, and מסה, *Massah*, as names of that place where the Israelites provoked God. For upon that occasion those names were given to that particular place where the Israelites in a high degree provoked and tempted God, Exod. xvii. 8. But the words used by the apostle in this place are taken appellatively, and fitly translated *provocation* and *temptation*.

In these two words, whether they be taken as particular names, *Meribah* and *Massah*, or as two expressions of their sin, *provocation* and *temptation*, do plainly express the heinousness of the sin; in that, as it was a tempting of God, so it was a provoking him to great wrath; and the manner of expressing them, giveth us to understand that it is behoveful for succeeding generations, that notorious sins of predecessors be kept on record.

These very titles, *provocation, temptation*, are a kind of record, whereby the sins comprised under them are brought to mind and kept in memory.

The many names given to places occasioned by a sin, gives further proof hereunto, as *Esek*, strife, Gen. xxvi. 20; *Sitnah*, hatred, Gen. xxvi. 21; *Kibrothhattaavah*, graves of lust, Num. xi. 34; *Bethaven*, the house of iniquity, Hosea iv. 15. Yea, the registering of all those notorious sins which are recorded in Scripture do further confirm the point.

When sin is beheld in others, specially as provoking God's wrath and pulling judgment upon the sinner, it appears in its own colours, horrible and detestable, and so is an occasion for them who so behold it, more carefully to avoid it. This is the main drift of the apostle in this place.

It is therefore an especial point of wisdom, to take due and thorough notice of the sins of former ages; of the kinds of them, of the causes of them, and of the effects that have followed thereupon, especially if God have executed any remarkable judgment and vengeance thereupon: as here, the kind of sin, 'temptation;' the cause thereof, 'hardness of heart;' the effect that followed thereupon, 'provocation' of God's wrath; and the judgment, which was, excluding from rest, verse 11, are distinctly set down.

This is to be done, not for approbation, or imitation of the sin recorded; in that respect no sin ought to be once named amongst us, Eph. v. 3, but for greater detestation thereof, to make us more abhor it. Indeed, if there were not in us a proneness of nature to rush into sin of our own accord without example, the memory of sin were better be clean blotted out. But there is no sin whereinto others before us have fallen, whereof the seed is not in us. Therefore for suppressing of sin, the infamy that hath followed such as have fallen thereinto, and God's judgments thereupon, may be, and ought to be, oft called to mind.

Sec. 91. *Of the extent of this word 'day.'*

To this latter word *temptation*, the time of committing that sin is thus annexed, κατὰ τὴν ἡμέραν, 'in the day of temptation.' This also includes their provocation; for when they tempted God, and as long as they tempted him, they provoked him.

This phrase, *in the day*, is not that Greek word[1] which was translated *to-day*, verse 7. That was an adverb, this a substantive, yet both of them come from the same Greek root.

The word here used is properly put for that time wherein the sun is up, from the rising to the setting thereof, Mat. xx. 2, 6, 12, Luke xxiv. 29. The Greek word signifieth light as well as day.[2] Of this day there are commonly accounted twelve hours, John xi. 9.

It is also put for a natural day, consisting of four and twenty hours, and so compriseth the night under it. Where Luke, speaking of Christ's fasting, mentioneth 'forty days,' Luke iv. 2, Matthew, speaking of the same point, saith, 'He fasted forty days and forty nights,' Mat. iv. 2. Luke, therefore, compriseth the nights under the word days. The Grecians, to express the space of four and twenty hours more distinctly, use a word compounded of night and day,[3] which is thus translated 'a night and a day,' 2 Cor. xi. 25.

---

[1] ריב lis, jurgium. וירב et jurgavit.

[1] σήμερον. Atticè τήμερον, quasi τῇδε ἡμέρᾳ, hac ipsa die.
[2] ἅμα ἡμέρᾳ, cum luce vel prima luce, Thucyd. προς ἡμέραν, sub lucem, Lysias.
[3] νυχθήμερον, ἡμερονύκτιον, diei et noctis spatium.

This word *day*, here used, is oft indefinitely put for *time*, as where it is said, 'The day shall declare it,' 1 Cor. iii. 13, that is, time will manifest it. And again, 'Now is the day of salvation,' 2 Cor. vi. 2, that is, the time wherein God offereth means of salvation; that is also put for a set determinate time, as Heb. viii. 9.

The former word, *to-day*, is sometimes addded to this indefinite word, *day*, τῇ σήμερον ἡμέρᾳ, *hodierno die*, when it is restrained to a set day, and thus translated, 'this day,' Acts xx. 26.

Here *the day* may be extended to all the time that the Israelites abode in the wilderness. For all that time they tempted and provoked God, as is evident by the express mention of forty years, verse 9, which was the time of their abode there.

This circumstance of time may thus word for word be translated, *according to the day*. Thus our former English translators of the Bible have rendered this phrase.

This translation confirmeth the extent of their provocation to their continuance in the wilderness.

Their continuance so long is a great aggravation thereof, as we shall shew on this phrase, *forty years*, in the next verse, Sec. 100.

Sec. 92. *Of the wilderness as a place of extraordinary provision.*

The place where their sin was committed, is here said to be the wilderness.

The wilderness here intended was a large vast place betwixt the Red Sea and Jordan. Through the Red Sea they came into it, Exod. xv. 22, and through Jordan they went out of it, Joshua iii. 1, &c.

This was a very barren place, it had no springs nor rivers of water in it. It had no woods nor orchards for shelter, or fruit. It was not fit to sow corn or other seed, or to set trees or other plants therein. It afforded no manner of ordinary commodities for man's use; neither were there any cities, towns, or houses therein for their habitation.

God purposely brought his people into that place to prove them, Exod. xx. 20, Deut. ii. 16. For he made that his school; where he gave them all his ordinances, and did more and greater wonders than ever he did, from their first being a people to the coming of the Messiah.

That place, and the time of the Israelites' abiding therein, was an especial type of the abode of the church militant here on earth. Very frequent mention is made of the particular acts of God's providence in that place and time, both by succeeding prophets, and also by Christ and his apostles.

Here the apostle expressly mentioneth the wilderness,

1. To point out the distinct history which he aims at, that thereby they might the more distinctly know the sin that he would have them to take heed of.

2. To prevent an objection. For they who tempt will be ready to say, Is there not cause? Am I not in such and such straits? Am I not brought to such and such wants? To answer that, the apostle shews how they provoked God, who tempted him in the wilderness, where they were brought to very great wants and straits.

3. To aggravate the sin, and that by the many evidences of that care God took of them, and of that provision which he made for them according to their needs.

When they were in a place where they had no ordinary means to guide them, and were to travel sometimes in the day, sometimes in the night, 'the Lord went before them by day in a pillar of a cloud, to lead them the way, and by night in a pillar of fire to give them light,' Exod. xiii. 21. When Pharaoh pursued them with a mighty host so close, as they knew not where to escape, God opened a way for them through the Red Sea, Exod. xiv. 22. Where they could find no water but that which was bitter, God made those waters sweet, Exod. xv. 25. When they had no bread to eat, God gave them manna from heaven. So also he gave them quails, when they had no flesh, Exod. xvi. 13, 15. Where at another time they had no water at all, God caused water to flow out of a rock for them, Exod. xvii. 6. When their implacable enemies, the Amalekites, set upon them, the Lord delivered those enemies into their hands, Exod. xvii. 13. The Lord so ordered matters while they were in the wilderness, that their clothes for forty years waxed not old upon them, nor their shoes, neither did their feet swell, Deut. viii. 4, and xxix. 5. In all that time they lacked nothing, Deut. ii. 7, Neh. ix. 21.

Notwithstanding these, and other like seasonable fruits of God's providence over them, they continued to tempt and provoke God, even in the wilderness, the place of his extraordinary providence.

Hereby we see that no evidences of God's care, power, goodness, and other divine excellencies, will work upon incredulous persons. All the miracles that Christ wrought, wrought nothing upon the Jews among whom he lived.

We shewed before, Sec. 84, that unbelief was an especial cause of hardness of heart. Nothing works upon an hard heart. See Sec. 128.

What cause have we in this respect to judge ourselves to be much hardened in our hearts, who have long lived in Christ's school, where we have had his word, and all his sacred ordinances, to build us up in our most holy faith; who also have long lived, not in a barren and dry wilderness, but in a fertile place, flowing with milk and honey, as Canaan did; where we need no manna to fall from heaven, because the earth brings forth store of corn; where we need not that rocks should be smitten to send forth water, because springs of sweet water are in every corner, and rivers of water run through all the parts of the land;

and other like blessings so abound, as we need not such extraordinary provisions as were made for the Israelites in the wilderness. If the wilderness, in regard of God's extraordinary provision for them, did aggravate their sins, how much more doth England, and God's gracious dealing with us therein, aggravate our sins! Oh, let us consider this, that we may endeavour to walk more worthy of God's favours to us than formerly we have done.

Sec. 93. *Of the wilderness as a place wherein the Israelites were brought to great straits.*

As the wilderness was considered in the former section a place of God's extraordinary providence and goodness, so it may be also considered as a place wherein the Israelites were oft brought to great straits; and yet that did not excuse their sin in tempting God. For by their tempting God in the wilderness, they provoked him ; so as straits and distresses are not sufficient excuses of tempting God. We ought not to doubt of God's providence, or of his power, or of his goodness, or of any of his divine attributes, because we are in want, or in any other strait. The devil took an occasion from Christ's being forty days in the wilderness, to solicit him to use an indirect course for providing sustenance to himself; but Christ refused so to do, Mat. iv. 3, 4 : 'If thou faint in the day of adversity, thy strength is small,' Prov. xxiv. 10. The day of adversity is the time for a man to manifest his courage; to faint then, when he should shew most courage, argues little or no courage.

God's power and providence is not straitened by men's straits. He can work as it pleaseth him, without means, as in creating all things; or with means, and those ordinary, which are comprised under daily bread, Mat. vi. 11, or extraordinary ; and that,

1. In the kind, Exod. xvi. 17.
2. In the quantity; as the little meal in the barrel and oil in the cruse nourished Elijah, a widow, and her family a long time, 1 Kings xvii. 16.
3. In the quality; as coarse pulse nourished Daniel and his companions, as well as the daintiest meat that a king could afford, Dan. i. 12, &c.
4. In the manner of getting; as a raven was Elijah's cater to provide him bread and meat morning and evening, 1 Kings xvii. 6.

Yea, God can preserve by contrary means; for Jonah was preserved from being drowned in the belly of a whale, Jonah i. 17.

We ought in this respect to arm ourselves against trial; and beforehand to meditate on God's power, wisdom, goodness, providence, presence, truth, and faithfulness; and to be of his mind, who said, 'Though I walk through the valley of the shadow of death, I will fear no evil,' Ps. xxiii. 4.

How doth this aggravate their incredulity, who in time of peace, plenty, and all needful prosperity, through distrustfulness tempt God. How many covetous rich men, upon fear of future want, treasure up all that they can any way get! How many timorous persons, living where the gospel is maintained, upon fear of a change, yield to superstition and idolatry ! If being in the straits of a wilderness excuse not a man from tempting God, can such as tempt God in a plentiful and secure Canaan think to be excused ?

Sec. 94. *Of the adverb οὗ, when or where.*
Ver. 9. *When your fathers tempted me, proved me, and saw my works forty years.*

In this verse the apostle doth more particularly exemplify the sin here forbidden.

The first particle, οὗ, *ubi*, being an adverb, and set alone, as here it is, is put for the place, and translated *where*, as Mat. xviii. 20; Luke iv. 16, 17; Acts iii. 13; Rom. iv. 15; Rev. xvii. 15. When it is joined with a preposition that limiteth it to the time, ἕως οὗ, *donec*, it signifieth time, and is translated *till*, Mat. i. 25 ; Mark xiii. 30, μεχρις οὗ *usquedam, until* ; Mat. xvii. 9, ἕως οὗ, *usque quo, while*, Mat. xiv. 22. Thus there is a proposition joined with this adverb, ἄχρις οὗ, *quoad*, ver. 13, and translated *while*.

I find not this adverb set alone, as here it is, in the New Testament, put for the time, but everywhere for the place. By most expositors it is here so taken.

The Hebrew word אֲשֶׁר, *quo, ubi*, used Ps. xcv. 9, is also put for the place, and translated *where* in our former English; and so do most expositors there translate it, and in other places also, as Gen. ii. 11, and xxviii. 13.

Whether this adverb be taken for the time when, or for the place where, both tend to the same end, namely, to declare that particular sin against which the apostle forewarns the Hebrews, even that which the Israelites committed in the wilderness, and that while they were there; so as this adverb, whether it be taken for time or place, hath reference to the last word of the former verse, which is, the wilderness.

Sec. 95. *Of avoiding the sinful courses of forefathers.*

The person whose ill example is to be shunned, are here set down under this relative, οἱ πατέρες, *fathers.*

The Hebrews came from Abraham, Isaac, and Jacob, and by a lineal descent from those Israelites that were in the wilderness. Hereupon this correlative ὑμῶν, *your*, is here used.

In relation to the Jews, both Abraham, and also all others descending from him and living under the law, are called *fathers* in the New Testament. See Chap. i. 1. Sec. 11. But here it is restrained to such Israelites as lived in the wilderness; so in sundry other places, as John vi. 31, 49, 58; Acts iii. 22, and vii. 38, 39; 1 Cor. x. 1. These fathers therefore were they whom the Lord delivered out of the Egyptian bondage, and brought with a mighty hand by great wonders into a place of freedom, where after an especial manner he nurtured them, as was shewed in Sec. 92.

The apostle sets them out under this title *fathers*, because people use to be much opinionated with an high conceit of their fathers; so were the Jews especially, and in that respect prone to imitate them in every thing, even in their evil courses. Therefore, to root out that conceit, the Holy Ghost in the 95th Psalm, and in this place, expresseth their fathers, and sets them out to be notorious rebels, and as rebels severely punished by God.

Can we now think that the practice of ancestors, who are called fathers, is in itself a sufficient warrant for their posterity, who come after them, to do as they did, and to tread in their paths? It is expressly said that God gave laws which should be made known to the generation to come, that they 'might not be as their fathers, a stubborn and rebellious generation,' &c., Ps. lxxvi. 5, 6, 8. This charge is expressly given by the Lord, 'Be ye not as your fathers,' Zech. i. 4. Stephen doth thus aggravate the sins of the Israelites: 'As your fathers did, so do ye,' Acts vii. 51.

Our fathers were of the same mould as we are, all sprouting out of the same cursed stock. They ignorant of God's will as well as we; they of a rebellious disposition as well as we; they prone to all manner of sin as well as we. What sin might not be justified if the practice of ancients were a sufficient warrant?

This is a point to be the rather observed in these days, because the pattern of fathers and ancestors is much stood upon; it is a common plea, when an evil practice is spoken against, to say, Our fathers did so. Many superstitious and idolatrous courses are hereby patronized. The Lord in his law makes this an aggravation of sin, that children walk in the evil courses of their fathers: 'I am a jealous God,' saith the Lord, 'visiting the iniquities of the fathers upon the children,' Exod. xx. 5, namely, such children as tread in their fathers' steps.

Sec. 96. *Of tempting God.*

The sin of the fore-mentioned fathers is set down in these two words, ἐπείρασαν, *tempted*, ἐδοκίμασαν, *proved;* the latter being added as an explanation of the former; for to tempt one is to try or prove whether he be such an one as he is taken to be, or can and will do such and such a thing.

This latter word *proved*, may be added as an effect or consequence following upon the former; as if it had been said, By tempting God they proved and found by experience that God was indeed such a God as he had made himself known to be. The Greek word δοκιμάζειν, here translated *proved*, signifieth to *discern*, and is so used and translated twice in one verse, 'Ye can discern the face of the sky, and of the earth, but how is it that ye do not discern this time?' The Hebrew word בחן, also so used, Gen. xlii. 15, 16. Hereupon God is said to be a trier, בחן, of the heart, Ps. vii. 9, Jer. xvii. 10; that is, one who findeth out and discerneth what is in man's heart.

If it be here taken as an explanation of the former word, and so set forth in general the same sin that the former doth, then two words are here used for the greater aggravation of the sin.

Of the meaning both of the Hebrew word נסו, used by the psalmist, and also of the Greek word ἐπείρασαν, here used by the apostle, and translated *tempted*, and of the divers kinds of temptations, see the *Guide to go to God, on the Lord's Prayer*, Pet. vi. sec. 170.

Tempting of God in this place is set down as a sin which provoked God, and so is taken in the worst sense. In general, every transgression is a tempting of God; in which respect it is said of those who tempted God, that they hearkened not to his voice, Num. xiv. 22. Thus their idolatry, Exod. xxxii. 4; their rebellion, Num. xvi. 2; their adultery, Num. xxv. 1, and other notorious sins, are so many particular instances of their tempting God; for by such sins men make a trial of God's justice, whether he will execute vengeance upon them or no.

In particular, men tempt God by two extremes: one is presumption, the other is distrustfulness. Both these arise from unbelief. That distrustfulness ariseth from unbelief is without all question. And howsoever presumption may seem to arise from overmuch confidence, yet if it be narrowly searched into, we shall find that men presume upon unwarrantable courses, because they do not believe that God will do what is meet to be done, in his own way. Had the Israelites believed that God in his time and in his own way would have destroyed the Cananites, they would not have presumed, against an express charge, to have gone against them without the ark of the Lord, and without Moses, as they did, Num. xiv. 40, &c.

Men do presumptuously tempt God, when, without warrant, they presume on God's extraordinary power and providence; that whereunto the devil persuaded Christ when he had carried him up to a pinnacle of the temple, namely, to cast himself down, was to tempt God; therefore, Christ gives him this answer, 'Thou shalt not tempt the Lord thy God,' Mat. iv. 5-7.

Men distrustfully tempt God when in distress they imagine that God cannot or will not afford sufficient succour. Thus did the king of Israel tempt God when he said, 'The Lord hath called these three kings together, to deliver them into the hand of Moab,' 2 Kings iii. 13. So that prince who said, 'Behold, if the Lord would make windows in heaven, might this thing be?' 2 Kings vii. 2.

As the Israelites in the wilderness tempted God through presumption, Num. xiv. 44, so most frequently through distrustfulness; as at the Red Sea, when Pharaoh pursued them, Exod. xiv. 11, 12; and at Marah, where the waters were bitter, Exod. xv. 23,

24; and in Sinai, where they wanted bread, Exod. xvi. 2, 3; and in Rephidim, where they wanted water, Exod. xvii. 3; and in Kadesh, upon the like occasion, Num. xx. 2; and in Kibroth-hattaavah, where they lusted after flesh, Num. xi. 4; and when the spies were returned from searching the land, Num. xiv. 2; and when the Lord had executed just judgment on rebels, Num. xvi. 41; and when they compassed the land of Edom, Num. xxi. 4, 5, and at sundry other times.

The heinousness of this sin is manifest by the causes and effects thereof, and also by the severe judgments inflicted thereupon,

I. The causes of tempting God are these,

1. Want of understanding. This doth Moses thus set out: 'The Lord hath not given you an heart to perceive, and eyes to see, and ears to hear unto this day,' Deut. xxix. 4.

2. Forgetfulness. This the psalmist thus expresseth, 'They forgat his works, and his wonders that he had shewed them,' Ps. lxxviii. 11; 'They soon forgat his works,' &c., Ps. cvi. 13.

3. Unbelief. 'Ye did not believe the Lord your God,' saith Moses to the Israelites, Deut. i. 32, and ix. 23. This cause of the Israelites tempting God doth the psalmist oft mention, Ps. lxxviii. 22, 32, and cvi. 24. Yea, Moses and Aaron were hereby brought to tempt the Lord, Num. xx. 12.

4. Too light esteem of God. 'Who is the Lord, that I should obey his voice?' saith Pharaoh, who exceedingly tempted God, Exod. v. 2.

II. The effects arising from that sin of tempting God, or concomitants which go along with it, are

1. Murmuring against God, Num. xiv. 29, and against his ministers, Num. xiv. 2.

2. Impatience in straits. 'They waited not for his counsel,' Ps. cvi. 13.

3. Rebellion. The psalmist styleth these tempters of God, 'a stubborn and rebellious generation,' Ps. lxxviii. 8.

4. Blasphemy. What a blasphemous speech was this, 'Is the Lord amongst us or no?' Exod. xvii. 7.

5. Apostasy. 'They said one to another, Let us make a captain, let us return into Egypt,' Num. xiv. 4. 'They turned back and dealt unfaithfully,' &c., Ps. lxxviii. 57.

III. The judgments inflicted on the Israelites who tempted God in the wilderness, were very terrible, as plague, Num. xvi. 46; fire, Num. xi. 1; fiery serpents, Num. xxi. 6; the earth swallowing them up, Num. xvi. 32; their enemies destroying them, Num. xiv. 45; multitudes destroyed together, as two hundred and fifty, Num. xvi. 35; three thousand, Exod. xxxii. 28; fourteen thousand seven hundred, Num. xvi. 49; four and twenty thousand, Num. xxv. 9; yea, by times all above twenty year old that came out of Egypt, save two only, Num. xiv. 29, 30, and xxvi. 65.

How watchful ought we to be against a sin so heinous, so terrible! We are exceeding prone hereunto. By open notorious sins men tempt God, and prove whether he be a God of vengeance; by secret sins, whether he be an all-seeing God; by covetous practices, whether he is a provident God; by despair, whether he be a merciful God. Thus in other sins we tempt him in other his divine excellencies.

For preventing and redressing this sin, it will be good frequently and seriously to meditate on God, on his glorious majesty, on his supreme sovereignty, on his almighty power, on his absolute jurisdiction, on his unsearchable wisdom, on his free grace, rich mercy, abundant kindness, great forbearance, and other divine excellencies; yea, and on his great and glorious works in all ages performed.

As we acquaint ourselves with these, so it will be our wisdom to submit ourselves wholly to his guiding providence, and make his will the rule of ours, taking heed how we bring his actions to the bar of our reason.

Sec. 97 *Of God's providing for ungrateful ones.*

It was shewed in the beginning of the former section that the Greek word ἐδοκίμασάν, translated *proved*, signifieth also to *discern*, and by experience to find a thing to be so and so. A noun derived from thence, δοκιμή, signifieth *experience*, Rom. v. 4, and *experiment*, 2 Cor. ix. 13, and *proof* of a thing, 2 Cor. ii. 9, xiii. 3. Here it may intend that by their tempting of God, they came to have a real and experimental proof of God's power, providence, and other divine excellencies.

Observe the particular instances noted in the former section of their tempting God, and you shall find extraordinary proofs and experiments of God's extraordinary providence. Thereupon a path was made in the sea, Exod. xiv. 22; bitter waters were made sweet, Exod. xv. 25; manna and quails were given, Exod. xvi. 12; waters flowed out of the rock, Exod. xvii. 6; the brazen serpent was erected, Num. xxi. 8; and sundry other great works done.

God doth this in reference to himself, to the upright, and to the ungrateful.

1. God doth hereby commend unto us his free grace, his abundant kindness, and his great patience and much forbearance. Herein is verified that which Christ said of his Father, that 'he is kind unto the unthankful, and unto the evil,' Luke vi. 35.

2. There were some upright and faithful mixed with the multitude of incredulous and rebellious Israelites, as Moses, Aaron, Hur, Caleb, Joshua, and others, whereof, though many of them for some particular sins entered not into Canaan, yet were they accepted and approved by God. For their sakes God gave common proofs of his providence promiscuously to all of all sorts. Had there been ten righteous ones found in Sodom, both that and the other cities about it might have been preserved from the fire and brimstone that destroyed them, Gen. xviii. 32. For Jehoshaphat's sake, God extra-

ordinarily provided water to preserve the armies of three kings, 2 Kings iii. 14. The whole world receiveth much good for the sake of the elect and upright that are therein.

3. God, in bestowing blessing upon the incredulous and rebellious, affordeth thereby external means to reclaim them; but they by their obstinacy against those means make themselves the more inexcusable, and increase their just condemnation the more, Rom. ii. 1, 4, 5.

This kindness of God so far manifested to those rebellious Israelites is a sure ground of encouragement to God's faithful and upright servants to seek and expect all needful blessing from him in all their needs and straits. Are not the faithful much better than the faithless? If God so fed, clothed, preserved, protected, and directed incredulous and unbelieving persons, what will he not do for his elect, effectually called, who in faith call upon him? Mat. vi. 26, 30, Luke xviii. 7.

Sec. 98. *Of outward blessings no sure evidences of God's fatherly love.*

These two words, *tempted, proved*, being joined together, and referred to the same persons, shew that they who did the one did also the other. They who tempted God, by experience found that God was a God of power, able to help in the greatest distress; a God of truth, faithful in keeping promise; a God of wisdom, ordering matters in the fittest season; a provident God, affording all things needful for people; yet were these no sure tokens of his fatherly love to them, for they so tempted him as they grieved him, and he was displeased with them.

God bestows outward blessings on such as have no assurance of his fatherly favour: 'The Lord set a mark upon Cain, lest any finding him should kill him,' Gen. iv. 15. It doth not follow that Hagar in truth feared God, because God heard her child's voice, and provided water for her and him, Gen. xxi. 19. God gave to Esau 'the fatness of the earth, and the dew of heaven,' and yet loved him not, Gen. xxvii. 39, Mal. i. 2.

Outward worldly blessings concerning this life and our temporal estate, are common to all of all sorts; yea, many of them to brute beasts. God 'giveth to the beast his food,' Ps. cxlvii. 9; 'He preserveth man and beast,' Ps. xxxvi. 6.

Yea, God oft giveth outward blessings in wrath: 'He gave Israel a king in anger,' Hosea xiii. 11. When he gave quails to the Israelites, 'while the flesh was yet between their teeth, ere it was chewed, the wrath of God was kindled against them,' Num. xi. 33.

We are not therefore to judge of God's favour by outward blessings, nor think that he loves us because he provides supply for our needs, or recovers us out of sickness, or easeth us in our pains, or freeth us from our enemies, or bestoweth other like blessings upon us. Tempters of God may prove and find God in this kind to be good unto them. See the reasons hereof in the former section. There are better and surer evidences of God's fatherly love, namely, the inward testimony of God's Spirit, and the effectual operation thereof in regenerating us, and working many sanctifying graces in us, and keeping us from tempting God.

Sec. 99. *Of men's tempting God though they see his works.*

For further aggravation of their sin there is added a third act: 'They saw my' works, saith God.

In Hebrew, a word of the singular number is used thus, פָּעֳלִי, *opus meum, my work*. But that word is there collectively taken, and the singular number synecdochically put for the plural. So Ps. xliv. 1, and lxiv. 9. But the apostle, expressly to clear the mind of the Holy Ghost, useth the plural number thus, τὰ ἔργα μου, 'my works.'

Though both the Hebrew and Greek words translated *works* are used to set out common and ordinary works, yet also, especially when they have reference unto God, they are oft put for extraordinary works, works of wonder, even miraculous works, as Ps. xliv. 1, John v. 36.

The works here intended are those many and great wonders which the Lord did, from Israel's passing through the Red Sea into the wilderness, to their going through Jordan into Canaan.

Some of them were works of mercy, in providing for them things needful, and delivering them from dangers, whereof see Sec. 92.

Others were works of judgment, in punishing them for their sins, whereof see Sec. 96.

These were not works done in former ages, or in far remote parts of the world, to the notice whereof they could not come but by hearsay only; but they were works done among them, done upon them, so as they saw them.

Both the Hebrew word רָאָה, used by the psalmist, and also the Greek word εἶδον used by the apostle, signify a *seeing* of a thing present with the bodily eyes, Deut. vii. 19, Mark xi. 20.

Here is mention made of mighty works, and of their express seeing of them. What clearer evidence could they have of God's power and providence? Yet they tempted him. The clearest evidences which God can give of himself and of his divine excellencies, work not upon incredulous and obdurate hearts. Such wonders did God in Egypt, as the Egyptians themselves could say to Pharaoh, 'Knowest thou not yet that Egypt is destroyed?' Exod. x. 7; yet did not Pharaoh yield. Undeniable demonstrations were given by Christ's birth, life, works, doctrine, death, resurrection, ascension, and gifts that followed thereupon, that Jesus was the promised Messiah; yet to this day will not the Jews believe him so to be. Blindness of mind and hardness of heart possessed them. Besides their own natural blindness and hardness, 'the god of this world hath further blinded their minds and hardened their hearts, lest the light of the glorious gospel of Christ should shine unto them,' 2 Cor. iv. 4. By experience we find that the clearest and brightest light doth no good to blind eyes.

We have in this respect great and just cause to take heed how we provoke God to give us over either to our own corruptions, or to the malice of Satan. For preventing this, let us not close our eyes against any light shewed unto us, lest we prove like these Israelites, who, though they saw with their own eyes God's wonderful works, yet continued to tempt him.

Sec. 100. *Of God's continuing to shew his power among such as oppose it.*

There is yet a further aggravation of their sin by the time, here set down under this phrase, *forty years.*

In Ps. xcv. 10, this circumstance of time, 'forty years,' is referred to God, and to his grieving for their obstinacy. For God is there thus brought in complaining, 'Forty years long was I grieved,' &c.

The reason why God continued so long to be grieved, was because they continued so long to tempt him.

The apostle therefore doth not alter the sense of the prophet's words by referring them to another clause, but makes it the more clear. So long as they tempted God they grieved him. Therefore, in that they tempted him forty years, they grieved him forty years. This the apostle himself asserts under this question, ver. 17, 'With whom was he grieved forty years?'

Thus, whether we refer the forty years to their sin, or to God's displeasure thereat, the sense remains the same.

To satisfy all doubts about this and other like alterations, we must remember, that the penmen of the New Testament were not translators of the Old, but such as quoted here and there some places for proof of the point in hand; to which purpose it was sufficient for them to give the sense of the place, though they altered the words. See Chap. i. 6, Sec. 72. and Chap. ix. 20, Sec. 106.

As this time, *forty years,* hath reference to that which goeth immediately before, thus, 'they saw God's works forty years,' it gives evidence of God's doing wondrous works all that time, notwithstanding their tempting of him. For man's incredulity cannot hinder the working of God's power. 'What if some did not believe? shall their unbelief make the faith of God without effect?' Rom. iii. 3. An incredulous prince would not believe that God could give such plenty as was promised by the prophet, when Samaria by a long siege was almost famished, yet 'it came to pass as the man of God had spoken,' 2 Kings vii. 18. Nor the Jews, nor the disciples of Christ, could be brought to believe that Christ should rise again from the dead, yet he did rise again the third day.

Obj. It is said that Christ 'did not many mighty works in his own country, because of their unbelief,' Mat. xiii. 58.

Ans. That is not to be taken of weakening Christ's power, as if man's unbelief would hinder it, but of withholding the benefit of Christ's power from unbelievers. Unbelief is as a strong and high dam against a flowing river, which doth not dry up the spring, nor the flowing of the waters, but only keeps the waters from running into that channel where the dam is set. The waters still flow up, and rise higher and higher against the dam, and because they are kept from running through the dam, they make another passage and therein flow on. Thus Christ left his own country, and went into other places, and there manifested his power. 'The word preached did not profit the Israelites, not being mixed with faith in them that heard it,' yet in itself, 'the word of God is quick and powerful,' &c., Heb. iv. 2, 12.

This mighty power of God still working, even when men oppose against it, may be some stay to troubled consciences, and to such as are inclined to despair.

Sec. 101. *Of God's long sufferance.*

The time of forty years hath reference to God's continuing to do wonders, not only by works of judgment, but also of mercy, grieving so long at the obstinacy of his people; and thus it giveth us to understand, that the Lord is a God of longsuffering and great forbearance. Thus is he frequently set forth in sacred Scripture, as Exod. xxxiv. 6, John iv. 2, Ps ciii. 8.

Here is mention made of forty years' forbearance. He did forbear the old world one hundred and twenty years, Gen. vi. 3, and the Amorites four hundred years, Gen. xv. 13, and the polity of the Jews eight hundred years, and the Christian state above sixteen hundred, and the world about six thousand. Every of us have good evidence of God's longsuffering in ourselves. Our people had been no people, our sun had been darkness, our souls had been in hell ere this, if the Lord had not been a God of much patience.

This God doth manifest himself to be,

1. To set forth his own glory; for when he proclaimed his name, among other excellencies he sets down this, 'longsuffering,' Exod. xxxiv. 6.

2. To bring men to repentance. 'Despisest thou the riches of God's goodness, and forbearance, and longsuffering; not knowing that the goodness of God leadeth thee to repentance? Rom. ii. 4.

3. To keep us from destruction. 'The Lord is longsuffering to us-ward, not willing that any should perish,' 2 Peter iii. 9.

4. To bring us to salvation. 'Account that the longsuffering of the Lord is salvation,' 2 Peter iii. 15.

These being the ends which God aimeth at in his longsuffering, we that have experience of this divine property (as who hath not?) ought to have an eye at those ends. And,

1. To magnify the name of God, even in and for this excellent property.

2. To endeavour after repentance, and so long as God beareth us to renew our repentance.

3. To come out of all those courses that lead to destruction.

4. To lay hold on eternal life while we have time so to do.

In these respects let us oft cast our eye back upon our former courses. We may, many of us, say, If God had not long borne with me, I had now been in a most woful plight. If God had cut me off, and taken me out of this world at such a time, in such a course, as I then eagerly pursued, I could have had little or no hope. But now, blessed be God, I have better hope that my desperate course is made known to me, I loathe it, God hath given me some measure of repentance, and assurance of his favour; I dare cast my soul on Jesus Christ for remission of sins, and reconciliation with God. I am persuaded that when I die, I shall be saved.

These, these are they that have cause to magnify the patience of God.

We ought further in forbearance, and longsuffering, to set God before us, and to endeavour, as in other graces, so in this, to be like unto God, Col. iii. 13, Eph. iv. 32.

We may not be hasty to take revenge upon every offence, but rather try if, by forbearing, the wrong-doer may be bettered. 'Be not overcome of evil, but overcome evil with good,' Rom. xii. 21.

Sec. 102. *Of the heinousness of sin continued in.*

Verse 10. *Wherefore I was grieved with that generation, and said, They do alway err in their hearts; and they have not known my ways.*

The fearful effect of their sin is here propounded in this verse, and aggravated in the next.

This first particle, διὸ, (see Chap. vi. ver. 1, Sec. 2). *Wherefore*, is not in the psalm, but here fitly added by the apostle, to set out more distinctly, both the cause of God's grief, and also the effect or consequence of the people's sin. It is the very same that was used before, ver. 7, Sec. 73. It giveth to understand, that long continuing in sin, grieveth God's Spirit. Because they tempted God forty years, *therefore* God was grieved.

To this purpose is this time of Israel's continuing forty years to sin against God oft pressed, as Num. xxxii. 13; Amos v. 25; Acts vii. 42, and xiii. 18. This their long continuing in sin is also upbraided as a great aggravation thereof, Exod. xvi. 28; Neh. ix. 30; Ps. lxxviii. 40; Luke xiii. 34. For,

1. Sin, the longer it continueth, the stronger it groweth, and proves to be the more daring and outfacing, and in that respect the more provoking, Jer. xliv. 17.

2. Continuance in sin is a multiplication of sin, and in that respect an addition of more fuel, which maketh the flame of the fire greater. Thus God's Spirit is more grieved, and his wrath more incensed, whether by the same man lying in one sin, or adding sin to sin, or by other men, children, or other successors, treading in the footsteps of their fathers and predecessors.

This may be a forcible motive to such as have sinned to repent, and not to continue in sin. As continuing in sin causeth grief and wrath, so 'there is joy in the presence of the angels of God over a sinner that repenteth,' Luke xv. 10.

This also may be a warning to such as observe the sins of others, to take heed that they hold not on in the same course, lest they cause more grief and wrath.

Sec. 103. *Of God's grieving at sinners.*

The Greek word προσώχθισα, translated *grieved*, is emphatical.

Some derive it from a noun, ὄχθη, *ripa*, that signifieth a bank of a river, or a bunch in a man's body. Thence cometh a simple verb, ὀχθεῖν, *gravate ferre*, which signifieth to take a thing grievously. For the heart of him who is grieved or offended, doth, as it were, swell and rise up.

The compound here used, προσώχθισα, signifieth to be much grieved and exceedingly offended.

There is another Greek noun, ἄχθος, *pondus, dolor*, like to that before mentioned, differing only in one small letter, and signifieth a *weight* or *grief*; and a verb thence derived, ἄχθομαι, *pondere premor, molestè fero*, which signifieth to be pressed with a burden, or to be offended.

Both notations or derivations of the word here used tend to the same purpose, namely, to set out the greatness of God's displeasure, which he took at their manifold kinds of tempting him, and at their long continuing so to do.

The compound here used, προσώχθισα, doth add aggravation to the offence which God took at his people. It is nowhere else used in the New Testament, but here and ver. 17. Yet by the Greek interpreters of the Old Testament it is frequently used.

It is used to set out the great grief and offence which Rebekah conceived at Esau's hatred of his brother, and thus translated, 'I am weary, προσώχθικα, of my life,' Gen. xxvii. 46; and penitents loathing themselves for their former sins, Ezek. xxxvi. 31; and a land's vomiting out her inhabitants for their monstrous abominations, Lev. xviii. 25.

The same Hebrew word[1] that is used Ps. xcv. 10, and translated *grieved*, is also used Ezek. xxxvi. 31, (the place before mentioned, and translated *loathe*).

These significations of this word shew that it carrieth much emphasis, and imports an high degree of God's displeasure.

Herein such passion, by way of resemblance for teaching's sake, is attributed to God, as is incident to parents and other governors, who, earnestly desiring

[1] נקטתה a קוט, *nauseabitis vosmetipsos.*

the good of those that are under them, are exceedingly grieved and offended when they see them stubbornly run on in destructive courses, notwithstanding all the means that have been used to reclaim them.

Under the law, a parent that had a stubborn and rebellious child, that regarded no admonition, but despised private correction, brought him forth to the judges to stone him to death, Deut. xxi. 18, &c. This is a manifestation of very great displeasure, and much aggravates the child's stubborn disposition. In this respect saith God to his people, 'O Ephraim, what shall I do unto thee? O Judah, what shall I do unto thee?' Hosea vi. 4. And our Lord Christ, 'O Jerusalem, Jerusalem, how often would I have gathered thy children together, even as a hen gathereth her chickens under her wings, and ye would not!' Mat. xxiii. 37.

This great displeasure of God against his people's obstinacy is set out to the life in the parable of the vineyard, Isa. v. 4, 5; and of the fig-tree, Luke xiii. 7. The more the good of any is sought, the more are they grieved and offended who in love seek their good, if their love and the effects thereof be neglected and despised.

This should warn us to take due notice of all the evidences of the kindness of God our Father, and of his care about our good, that we may make the right use of all, and to fear lest by stubbornness and obstinacy we provoke him to turn his favour into displeasure, his love into grief and offence.

Sec. 104. *Of the meaning of this word 'generation.'*

The word דור, translated *generation*, doth in the Hebrew signify the continuance of time, and it is put for the space of a hundred years; as where God saith 'in the fourth generation,' Gen. xv. 16. The Lord before had made mention of four hundred years; this fourth generation was the last hundred of those four hundred.

The Greek word, $\gamma\varepsilon\nu\varepsilon\tilde{\alpha}$, here used, is derived from a verb, $\gamma\varepsilon\nu\nu\alpha\omega$, *gigno*, that signifieth *to beget*; and it signifieth sometimes a multitude of people, and so is translated a *nation*, in which there useth to be multitudes of people: as where a multitude of impious ones are called 'a perverse nation,' Philip. ii. 15; and sometimes for a continuance of people, or a succession of one after another, as where mention is made of fourteen generations, Mat. i. 17; and where it is said, 'This generation shall not pass,' Mat. xxiv. 34.

The word, as here used, may include both these significations, which do aggravate the wretched disposition of that people in these two respects:

1. In that they all conspired together in their sins except a few. Thus doth Christ aggravate the sin of the people in his time, in that they all rejected him and his ministry, and thereupon saith that 'the men of Nineveh, and the queen of the south, shall rise up in judgment with this generation,' Mat. xii. 41, 42, that is, with the whole nation. Plagues that infect a whole city are counted great judgments; a leprosy that spreadeth itself over a man's whole body is counted a grievous malady; so a poison that infecteth all the blood in a man's body. In like manner, contagious sins that infect a whole nation are detestable sins. By this did Daniel aggravate the sins of the Israelites that were carried captive into Babylon, and justify God's severe judgment upon them; for, saith he, 'All Israel have transgressed, therefore the curse is poured upon us,' Dan. ix. 11.

Consent of multitudes in sin is so far from extenuating it, as it doth the more aggravate it. Wherefore, 'if sinners entice thee, consent thou not,' Prov. i. 10.

2. This word *generation* doth aggravate their sin, in that it implieth a continuance therein, as was shewed ver. 9, Sec. 95, even from parents to children.

The apostle doth fitly add a relative, $\dot{\varepsilon}\kappa\varepsilon\dot{\iota}\nu\eta$, *this*, which is not in the Hebrew, to demonstrate what kind of people he speaks of, even those which lived in the wilderness, and saw the mighty works of God. With them therefore, in particular, is God grieved who do provoke God.

Sec. 105. *Of God's complaining of people.*

This phrase, $\kappa\alpha\grave{\iota}\;\varepsilon\tilde{\iota}\pi o\nu$, *and said*, being applied to God, implieth a complaint, and that on God's part; for he was so much and so long provoked by his people, as he was forced to complain of them.

God's complaints of his people are in other places more expressly and emphatically set out, as Num. xiv. 11, 27; Deut. xxxii. 29; Ps. lxxxi. 11, 13; Isa. xlviii. 18; Mat. xxiii. 37.

His fatherly affection towards his people forceth him thus to do. When a father seeth his son run headlong into desperate courses, from which he will by no means be restrained, he useth to complain of his foolish and perverse disposition.

That which is noted to accompany God's complaint, namely, great wrath and sore vengeance, ver. 11, and in the places before quoted, is a forcible inducement to move us carefully to avoid all such courses as may give occasion to God to complain of us.

Is not he the God of our being, life, preservation, comfort, confidence, and eternal salvation? Shall we then make him to complain of our ungraciousness?

Oh remember what he is, what he hath done for thee, what thou mayest further expect from him, and thereupon set thyself so to please him in all things, that he may never repent of what he hath done for thee, but rather delight in doing more, and continuing to be ever kind unto thee.

Sec. 106. *Of the meaning of these words, 'they do alway err in their heart.'*

The matter of God's complaint is set out in two particulars: 1, their stubbornness; 2, their ignorance.

The former is thus expressed, ἀεὶ πλανῶνται τῇ καρδίᾳ, 'they do alway err in their hearts.' The Hebrew thus, עם תעי לבב הם, 'it is a people that do err in their heart.'

Though there be some difference in words betwixt the Hebrew and Greek, yet the sense is the same in both; for this Hebraism, עם תעי, 'a people erring,' signifieth a continuance in a thing. It is a participle of the present tense,[1] and intendeth a present being to be so and so, as it hath been before.

The Greek translators, to express the emphasis of that Hebraism in their own dialect, add this adverb, ἀεὶ, always.

The word עם, translated *people*, is of the singular number; but it is a collective word, and compriseth many under it. It signifieth a multitude of persons; therefore the Greek translators use the plural number, πλανῶνται, 'they do err.'

The apostle, in both these diversities, followeth the Septuagint. Of the LXX, see Chap i. 6, Sec. 72.

The verb translated *err* is of the passive voice.

The active, πλανάω, *seduco*, signifieth to *seduce* or *deceive*, as Mat. xxiv. 4, 5, 11.

The passive, πλανάομαι, signifieth *to err*, Mat. xxii. 29, πλανᾶσθε, *erratis*; for they that err are deceived by themselves or others.

Both the Hebrew, תעה, and Greek words, πλανᾶσθαι, are applied to silly sheep, which go astray from the rest of the flock, and from their shepherd, and so fall into many dangers, Isa. liii. 6, Mat. xviii. 12, 13.

The folly of those who go astray out of the ways of God, and wander in the ways of wickedness, is set out to the life.

To aggravate their sin the more, the ground thereof is thus declared, τῇ καρδίᾳ, *in heart*. This relative *their* is not unfitly added by our English, to shew that their own evil disposition caused them to go astray.

Of the heart, and of the diverse significations thereof, see ver. 8, Sec. 79.

Heart is here put for the *will*.

Men may be said to err three ways:

1. In the mind or understanding. So did they of whom the prophet saith, 'They that erred in spirit shall come to understanding,' Isa. xxix. 24. The latter clause declares the meaning of the former, and shews, that by erring in spirit, he means erring in understanding. And Christ, where he saith, 'Ye do err, not knowing the Scriptures,' Mat xxii. 29, sheweth that he meaneth erring in knowledge.

2. In will or heart; for the Scripture doth oft put these one for another. This is here especially meant, and of it we shall speak more in the next section.

3. In the life and actions of men. To this purpose saith the wise man, 'He is in the way of life that keepeth instruction; but he that refuseth reproof, erreth,' Prov. x. 17.

[1] בנוני. *Benoni. Participium præsens, medium inter perfectum et futurum.*

The former clause sheweth, that the erring which he speaketh of, is in the way and course of a man's life. To this purpose, saith the apostle, 'they have forsaken the right way, and are gone astray,' 2 Peter ii. 15, or erred, viz. out of the right way.

The first kind of error, is ignorance.

The second, wilfulness.

The third, rebellion.

Sec. 107. *Of wilfulness, aggravating sin.*

The erring in heart here intended, is such perverseness of will as made them depart from the ways of the Lord, and stubbornly oppose against him. See Chap. x. 26, Sec. 88.

This is it that much grieved the Lord, and forced him to complain against them. Of God's complaining, see Sec. 105.

Of sinners' wilfulness and stubborness, Wisdom complains, Prov. i. 24, 25; and God himself, Isa. i. 4, 5. And he tells his prophet, 'that they are impudent and hard-hearted,' Ezek. iii. 7.

This wilfulness makes men refuse and reject the means which God affords for their good, and brings them into an incurable condition, Prov. i. 24-26.

How earnest should we be in beating down our stout stomachs and proud hearts. Such hearts are in us all by nature, but much increased by our own perverseness. Think how little thou gainest thereby. It is the almighty God against whom thou standest out: 'He with the froward will shew himself froward, Ps. xviii. 26. Observe how parents deal with stubborn children; they will make them feel the smart of their wilfulness. Is it safe for the earthen pot to dash itself against the iron pot?

Pray to God to give thee a heart of flesh, which may be affected with his mercies, tremble at his judgments, and melt at his word. Pray that thy will may be made pliable to God's will. To this we ought to give the more diligence, because it is very hardly rooted out, as the phrase next to be spoken of sheweth.

Sec. 108. *Of the danger of wilfulness.*

The Hebrew phrase, whereby the wilfulness of the aforesaid persons is set out word for word, is this, עם תעי, *a people erring*. They are so given to err as they will not be drawn from it; they will still remain such as they are, and never reclaim it. Witness Pharaoh and his servants, Exod. ix. 34. Witness, as these Israelites in the wilderness, so others after them: 'God set watchmen over them, saying, Hearken to the sound of the trumpet; but they said, We will not hearken,' Jer. vi. 17. Witness especially the Jews in Christ's time, of whom it is said, 'Though Jesus had done many miracles before them, yet they believed not on him,' John xii. 37. And of the Jews in the apostles' time it is said, that 'They were filled with envy, and spake against those things which were spoken by Paul, contradicting and blaspheming,' Acts xiii. 45.

Wilfulness takes away all spiritual sense, and exceedingly hardeneth men's hearts, so as no sufficient means can be used to mollify them, and to alter this their evil disposition.

How should this move us to take heed of giving any way to this wilful and stubborn disposition. It is a bitter root. We ought not to suffer ' any root of bitterness to spring up and trouble us,' Heb. xii. 15.

Sec. 109. *Of sin aggravated by continuing therein.*

This adverb, ἀεί, *alway*, intendeth a long continuance in sin; and it is here brought in as a further aggravation of the sin of the Israelites in the wilderness. By this circumstance doth Stephen aggravate both their sin, and also the sin of their successors, saying, ' Ye do always resist the Holy Ghost,' Acts vii. 51. And the lying disposition of the Cretians is thus aggravated, ' The Cretians are always liars,' Titus i. 12. This kind of aggravation is frequently set out under this expostulatory phrase, ' how long,' as Num. xiv. 11, 22, 27; 1 Kings xviii. 21; Ps. iv. 2; Jer. iv. 14. See Sec. 102.

Sin is of an increasing nature. Though at first it may seem to be but as a grain of mustard-seed, yet by long growing it may come to be as the greatest of trees, that cannot be bowed nor rooted up.

A strong incitation this is to such as have long run on in sin, at length to repent, and return to their Father, as the prodigal did. By repentance mercy may be obtained, but obstinacy and impenitency implungeth into utter destruction. Well observe God's pithy expostulation with Israel, ' As I live, saith the Lord God, I have no pleasure in the death of the wicked; but that the wicked turn from his way and live: turn ye, turn ye from your evil ways; for why will ye die, O house of Israel ?' Ezek. xxxiii. 11. On the other side, Christ hath with a strong asseveration averred twice together this doom, ' Except ye repent, ye shall all perish,' Luke xiii. 3, 5. A man, by an ' impenitent heart, treasureth up unto himself wrath against the day of wrath,' Rom. ii. 5.

Sec. 110. *Of God's ways.*

Hitherto, of the first part of God's complaint, which was of their stubbornness, see Sec. 106. The other part is their ignorance, thus set down, ' And they have not known my ways.'

This ignorance, as it is a distinct sin in itself, so it was the cause of the former sin; whereupon some turn this copulative *and* (as it is in the Hebrew, ו), and adversative *but* (as it is in Greek, δὲ), into a causal *for*.

Here we are to consider two points:
1. What are the ways of God.
2. How their not knowing of them was an aggravation of their sin.

A *way*, ὁδός, is that course wherein one walketh.

The Hebrew verb דרך, *calcavit*, whence this word *way* is derived, signifieth to tread upon; as, ' Thou shalt tread the olives,' Micah vi. 15; ' And I will tread them in mine anger,' Isa. lxiii. 3.

The Greek word translated *way*, is derived from a verb which signifieth to go.[1] According to both these derivations, a way is that whereon one treads, or wherein he goeth.

It is attributed unto God metaphorically, and that in two respects:
1. Actively; setting out that way wherein God himself walks.
2. Relatively; intending that way wherein he would have us to walk.
1. Of the former kind there are two sorts:
(1.) God's secret way. This is his unsearchable counsel. Hereof saith the apostle, ' How unsearchable are his judgments, and his ways past finding out !' Rom. xi. 33. And God himself by his prophet thus, ' My ways are higher than your ways, and my thoughts than your thoughts,' Isa. lv. 9.
(2.) His manifest way. Under this in special are contained his works, whereby he declares himself and his divine properties unto us, as power, wisdom, truth, mercy, justice, wrath, &c. In reference hereunto, thus saith Moses of God, ' He is the rock, his work is perfect; for all his ways are judgment: a God of truth, and without iniquity; just and right is he,' Deut. xxxii. 4. In reference also hereunto, the psalmist thus saith, ' The Lord is righteous in all his ways, and holy in all his works,' Ps. cxlv. 17.
2. The ways wherein God would have us to walk are his precepts, whereof thus saith the psalmist: ' Shew me thy ways, O Lord; teach me thy path.' ' The Lord will teach sinners in the way; and the meek he will teach his way,' Ps. xxv. 4, 8, 9; Isa. ii. 3. And God himself thus saith, ' Oh that my people had hearkened unto me, and Israel had walked in my ways !' Ps. lxxxi. 13.

The two latter kinds of ways are here especially meant, namely, his works and his precepts.

The works of God are styled his ways, because we may see him, as it were, walking therein; for by his works we may discern the footsteps of his properties and providence: ' They have seen thy goings, O God, even the goings of my God,' Ps. lxviii. 24. By the goings of God, are meant the distinct acts of the divine providence. Where it is said to God, ' Thy way is in the sea, and thy path in the great waters,' reference is had to God's manifestation of his power, wisdom, mercy, and justice, in dividing the Red Sea for the Israelites to pass through it, and overwhelming their enemies thereby, Ps. lxxvii. 19.

In this respect, that God's works are ways wherein he may be seen walking, it is our duty,
1. To understand the ways of God, so far as he is

---

[1] ὁδός derivatus ab ἴω vado.

pleased to walk in them, and to make them known to us. Thereby he shews himself to be such a God as none can be imagined to be like unto him ; so as we may say unto him, 'How terrible art thou in thy works !' Ps. lxvi. 3 ; 'Among the gods there is none like unto thee, O Lord ; neither are there any works like unto thy works,' Ps. lxxxvi. 8.

2. To acknowledge the equity and righteousness of God's ways : 'The Lord is righteous in all his ways, and holy in all his works,' Ps. cxlv. 17. This is it whereabout God makes with the Israelites this vehement expostulation, and that again and again : 'Hear now, O house of Israel, Is not my way equal ? are not your ways unequal ?' Ezek. xviii. 25, 29, and xxxiii. 17, 20. To impeach God's ways of iniquity is an high degree of blasphemy.

3. To admire and magnify the Lord in his ways : 'All the kings of the earth shall praise thee, O Lord. Yea, they shall sing in the ways of the Lord,' Ps. cxxxviii. 4, 5. Much is this duty pressed in and under the title of God's works : 'I will praise thee, O Lord, with my whole heart: I will shew forth all thy marvellous works,' Ps. ix. 1 ; 'Many, O Lord my God, are thy wonderful works which thou hast done,' Ps. xl. 5.

God's precepts are frequently styled his ways. To demonstrate this more clearly, this epithet *way* is oft joined with God's precepts and commandments. Thus prayeth David : 'Make me to understand the *way* of thy precepts ;' 'Teach me, O Lord, the *way* of thy statutes ;' 'Make me to go in the *path* of thy commandments.' And thus he professeth, 'I will run the *way* of thy commandments,' Ps. cxix. 27, 32, 33, 35.

God by his precepts doth declare unto men how they should carry themselves towards him and towards one another ; so as they are as a way for them to walk in, to observe and to do them.

God's precepts are not for mere speculation, but for practice. It is the proper use of a way to walk in it.

Of practising God's commandments, see *The Saints' Sacrifice*, on Ps. cxvi. 9, sec. 59.

Sec. 111. *Of ignorance aggravating a sin.*

That which is here set down of the Israelites' not knowing God's ways, is set down by way of aggravation. We must therefore here consider in what respect ignorance may be an aggravation ; for Christ makes it a matter of extenuation, saying, 'He that knew not, and did commit things worthy of stripes, shall be beaten with few stripes,' Luke xii. 48. Upon this ground Christ thus prayed for sundry of the Jews, 'Father, forgive them ; for they know not what they do,' Luke xxiii. 34. An apostle also doth herein extenuate the sin of the Jews, in that they did it through ignorance, Acts iii. 17 ; and Paul sets it down as an occasion of the mercy which he found, 1 Tim. i. 13.

To clear the point in hand more fully, it is meet distinctly to set down the kinds of not knowing.

Men may be said not to know simply or relatively.

1. Simply, when there is in them a mere want of knowing such and such a thing.[1] This is called *nescience ;* and it is blameless and without sin in three cases :

(1.) When it is of things which cannot be known ; as the perfection of God's excellencies : 'Canst thou by searching find out God ? canst thou find out the Almighty unto perfection ?' Job xi. 7 ; 'God dwelleth in the light which no man can approach unto ; whom no man hath seen nor can see,' 1 Tim. vi. 16 ; 'There shall no man see God and live,' Exod. xxxiii. 20.

(2.) When it is of things that are not to be known ; as God's secret counsels : 'The secret things belong unto the Lord our God ; but those things which are revealed belong unto us,' Deut. xxix. 29. Thus it is said of the day of judgment, 'Of that day, and that hour, knoweth no man, no, not the angels which are in heaven, neither the Son,' Mark xiii. 32.

(3.) Of such things as are not meet or fit to be known. In this respect Christ saith to his disciples, 'It is not for you to know the times or the seasons, which the Father hath put in his own power,' Acts i. 7.

2. Relatively, men are said not to know, in reference to such knowledge as they might or should have. This is properly called *ignorance.*

Ignorance is a privation of knowledge.

Now a privation presupposeth a contrary habit of that which one hath had, or is capable of having ; as blindness presupposeth sight in him that is blind, or at least such a subject as was capable of sight. A man that never had sight may be said to be blind, John ix. 1, because he was capable of sight.

Ignorance thus properly taken is simple or wilful.

Simple ignorance is in two cases.

1. When means are not afforded to know what we ought to know. In this respect the apostle saith of the times wherein the Gentiles wanted means of knowledge, 'The times of this ignorance God winked at,' Acts xvii. 30. This kind of ignorance is sinful; and that because God at first gave man ability to know whatsoever was meet for him to know. That men after Adam's fall knew not their duty, it was their own fault.

2. When means afforded are too slightly used to find out the true case of a thing. The ignorance which Abimelech had about Sarah to be the wife of Abraham was a simple ignorance, because he was deceived by Abraham's speech, Gen. xx. 5, yet was it sinful, in that it was possible for him to have found out the truth of that case, if he had used his utmost endeavour.

Simple ignorance in both the fore-mentioned cases may be either of the law, or of a fact.[2]

[1] Ignorantia* dicit simplicem scientiæ negationem. Ignorantia importat scientiæ privationem.—*Th. Aquin. sum. Theol. pri. 2d Quest.* 76, *Art.* 2. [* Qu. 'nescientia'?—ED.]

[2] Ignorantia juris vel facti.

The former is the more general, and the more blameable. We say of the laws of a land, that every one should know the law; and that ignorance thereof excuseth no subject that liveth under that law. Much more are all bound to know the law of God; because that law was first written in man's heart, Rom. ii. 15. Christ saith of the servant that knew not his master's will, and did commit things contrary thereunto, that he shall be beaten. A master's will made known, is a law to his servant; though one particular servant know it not, yet is he not excused thereby from blame and punishment, Luke xii. 48.

The latter, which is ignorance of a fact, is more special respecting some particular branches of the law. As Paul's persecuting Christians. He knew that blasphemy, persecution, and oppression in general were sins against the law; so that there was not ignorance of the law in him. But to blaspheme the name of Christ, to persecute and oppress Christians, which were particular facts, he knew not to be sin; for he saith, 'I verily thought with myself, that I ought to do many things contrary to the name of Jesus,' Acts xxvi. 9. So as this was ignorance of such and such facts. Christ saith in the like case, 'They which kill you will think they do God service,' John xvi. 2.

Simple ignorance in the several kinds thereof may extenuate sin, Luke xii. 48.

Wilful ignorance is in two other cases:

1. When means afforded for knowledge are neglected;[1] as the Israelites, who inquired not at the ark which they had among them, in the days of Saul, 1 Chron. xiii. 3, too much neglected the means which God afforded, of knowing his will. In this respect, the sins which they committed upon ignorance of God's will, were sins of wilful ignorance.

2. When means afforded are rejected. This is it which Christ thus layeth to the charge of the Jews, 'How often would I have gathered thy children together, and ye would not!' Mat. xxiii. 37.

In these respects ignorance may be said to be voluntary.

1. Indirectly: when one, by reason of pains, or other employments, neglecteth to learn that which might restrain him from sin. To this tends that reason which Jeroboam rendered to keep the Israelites from going up to the temple, to be instructed there in the will of God. 'It is too much for you to go up unto Jerusalem,' 1 Kings xii. 28. To the same purpose tend the excuses which they made that refused to go to the king's supper. One pretended his ground which he had bought; the other his yoke of oxen, Luke xiv. 18, 19.

[1] Ignorantia est voluntaria: vel directè, sicut cum aliquis studiosè vult nescire aliqua ut liberius peccet: vel indirectè, sicut cum aliquis propter laborem, vel propter alias occupationes, negligit addiscere id per quod à peccato retraheretur. *T. Aquin. Sum. Theol. prim. 2d quæst. 76. Art. 3.*

2. Directly: when one will purposely be ignorant of his duty, for this very end, that he may more freely go on in his sin; as the Jews, which gave this answer to the prophet of the Lord, 'As for the words that thou hast spoken to us in the name of the Lord, we will not hearken unto thee: but we will certainly do whatsoever goeth forth out of our own mouth,' &c., Jer. xliv. 16, 17.

The former of these is so far from extenuating of sin, as it causeth some aggravation thereof.

The latter doth out of measure aggravate the sin.

Ignorance properly taken is a sin. See Chap. v. 2, Sec. 10.

The ignorance comprised in these words, 'They have not known my ways,' is wilful ignorance, and that not only in the indirect kind, but also in the direct. It was an affected ignorance, most wilful, and therefore it is here well set down as a great aggravation. Of their wilfulness in sinning against God, see Sec. 107.

Sec. 112. *Of the danger and damage of ignorance.*

That which hath been noted of ignorance aggravating sin, shews, that the position of papists concerning ignorance to be the mother of devotion, is a most absurd position. I would demand, Whether devotion be a good thing or no? If good, How can it be the child of such an evil as ignorance is? Can sweet water come from a salt spring? James iii. 12. Who can bring a clean thing out of an unclean thing? Not one, Job xiv. 4. Surely the devotion which is pretended to come from ignorance is mere superstition, or, which is worse, idolatry. 'When you knew not God, you did service unto them which by nature are no gods,' Gal. iv. 8.

It is also made by the Holy Ghost the mother of self-conceit, Rom. x. 3; of contempt of holy things, Jude 10; of lust, 1 Thes. iv. 11; of murder, Luke xxiii. 24; of all manner of sin, 1 Tim. i. 13. Experience sheweth, that where there is no knowledge, there is little conscience. Of the heinousness of ignorance, see *The Whole Armour of God* on Eph. vi. 17, sec. 24.

They savour too rank of that popish error, who think that much knowledge is not fit for common people; and thereupon do what they can to suppress frequent and powerful preaching.

Hereby it further appears, that it is a most woful plight wherein most people lie; and those not only savages, pagans, Turks, Jews, papists, but also the common sort of protestants. For ignorance blindeth the minds of most; which makes them so provoke God as they do. The devils are said to be the 'governors of the darkness of this world,' Eph. vi. 12. Who can be meant by *darkness*, but blind and ignorant persons? such as 'the god of this world' is said to have 'blinded,' 2 Cor. iv. 4. No marvel that Satan ruleth over such, for they cannot discern his power, malice, subtlety, sedulity, and mischievous enterprises. When the troops of Syria were smitten with blindness, they were easily led into the midst of their enemies, 2 Kings vi. 18, 19, &c. So ignorant persons are easily drawn into Satan's power. Consider the case of a blind man, how ready he is to wander out of his way, to stumble at this stone, to rush against that post, to fall into any pit or pond : such is the case of an ignorant man.

The sin of ignorance, therefore, is a sin for which ignorant persons ought to be deeply humbled, as for a disgraceful and dangerous sin, and withal earnestly to crave pardon for this sin. The sacrifices that were offered under the law for ignorance, Lev. xv. 27, &c., afford good ground for performing this duty.

It is a vain conceit that many have, that their ignorance will be a sufficient plea against divine judgment. Where Christ aggravateth sins against knowledge, he concludeth, that they also who sin in ignorance shall be beaten, Luke xii. 48. Though some kind of ignorance may somewhat extenuate a sin, yet no ignorance of that which a man may and should know, can make him blameless.

It concerns all that have power over others to do what they can to bring men to knowledge of God's ways, lest, for not knowing them, they provoke God's wrath. No man ought to suffer his brother to lie under such a burden, much less they that have a charge, and in that respect ought to have the greater care over him.

Magistrates, therefore, must take order to set up the light of God's word in all places where they have any command. Ministers must be diligent and conscionable in preaching the same. Parents and ministers must instruct their family; catechising is of special use hereunto.

As for ignorant persons themselves, they must use all means that God affordeth to bring them to knowledge of his truth. To neglect or to reject means, is to turn simple ignorance into wilful ignorance, and thereby to make a man's case the more woful.

Sec. 113. *Of turning God's patience into vengeance.*
Ver. 11. *So I sware in my wrath, They shall not enter into my rest.*

The effect of the fore-mentioned wilfulness of the Israelites in the wilderness was a fearful effect, in that it grieved God, as is shewed before in Sec. 102, &c. But here it is much aggravated, in that it provokes him to swear vengeance.

The particle of reference is in the Hebrew a relative, אשר, *quibus*, and translated 'unto whom;' namely, unto those Israelites that sinned.

In the Greek it is a conjunction, ὡς, *ita*, which implieth an inference of an effect following upon that which goeth before: they sinned, so God swore punishment. Some translate it *therefore*, ὥστε, *itaque*. All tends to the same purpose; namely, that man's obstinacy so incenseth God, as he cannot forbear revenge, and thereupon swears it.

Sec. 114. *Of God's swearing, and that in wrath.*

For abuse of God's fatherly affection makes him take unto himself the passion of a judge, and to turn grief into wrath; yea, to lay down his rod, and take up a sword; and to withdraw all blessings, and think of utter destruction. The curses that are inferred upon God's blessings, Levit. xxvi., Deut. xxviii., do give proof hereunto. This made God to turn *Ammi* into *Lo-ammi*, Hos. i. 9. This is by woful experience verified in the rejection of the Jews, and casting off the seven churches of Asia, and most of the other churches which were planted by the apostles.

This God doth to manifest his power in beating down the stoutest and stubbornest, Lev. xxvi. 19, and to make others fear.

This may be a warning to us to take heed of walking stubbornly against God, lest we provoke him to deal thus with us. Note Lev. xxvi. 18, &c., Ps. xviii. 26.

We ought the rather to lay this to heart, because God's swearing vengeance, after forty years' forbearance, gives evidence that there may be an end of God's patience. The general deluge that swept away the whole world, the fire and brimstone that destroyed the Sodomites, and other judgments that God hath executed upon his people, give evident proof hereof. Well note Isa. v. 5, Luke xiii. 9.

An oath, or swearing, is a solemn confirmation of a matter to gain credence thereunto. An oath is used, that that which is so attested should not be slighted, but stedfastly believed. This phrase, 'an oath for confirmation,' Heb. vi. 16, implieth that confirmation of a thing is the end of an oath.

The root שבע, *septem, septies*, from whence the Hebrew verb נשבע (*in niphal*), *juravit*, translated *swear*, is derived, signifieth seven, or seven times. Seven is counted a number of perfection. Such a confirmation is an oath, as if the thing were confirmed as much as might be, even seven times over.

Of the five kinds of bonds whereby a matter in an oath is confirmed, applied to God, and of God's swearing, see *The Church's Conquest*, on Exod. xvii. 16, sec. 80.

The Scripture expresseth two cases wherein God useth to swear.

One was in making promises, as Gen. xxii. 16, Ps. cxxxii. 11.

The other in denouncing threatenings, as here, and Deut. i. 34.

Both of them are for confirmation of his word.

In the former case, he swears in mercy and tender respect to his children, and that to strengthen their faith in his promise, and to move them to give all credence thereunto, and with patience to wait for the accomplishment thereof. Thus God swore to Abraham, as this apostle testifieth. See Chap. vi. 13, Sec. 97.

In the latter case he swears in wrath, the more to affright and terrify those against whom he swears, that they may know that the doom denounced against them shall surely be executed. Thus the Lord swore to the Israelites here, and thereupon the apostle thus brings it in, 'I sware in my wrath.'

Here just occasion is given to speak of God's wrath, namely, how wrath or anger may be attributed unto him. But hereof see *A Plaster for the Plague*, on Num. xvi. 46, secs. 41, 42.

Sec. 115. *Of the form of God's oath.*

The form of God's oath is not here expressed; yet, by the manner of setting down the words, it may well be understood to be some kind of imprecation in case he did not perform what he had threatened.

Both the Hebrew, אִם־יְבֹאוּן, and the Greek, εἰ εἰσελεύσονται, *si introibunt*, do thus express the oath of God, *If they shall enter.* Our English doth set down the sense of the oath thus, *They shall not enter;* but they do not fully express the emphasis of the phrase. There is an elegant figure,[1] which in English we may style *silence*, whereby men conceal and utter not something which may well be understood, but they are not willing to express.

This is frequent in oaths, as where Elijah saith to Ahab, 'As the Lord God of Israel liveth, if there be dew,' 1 Kings xvii. 1; and where Zedekiah saith to Jeremiah, 'As the Lord liveth, if I put thee to death, if I give thee into the hand of these men,' Jer. xxxviii. 16. To make up the full sense, such a phrase as this may be understood, 'Let me not be accounted true,' or, 'Repute me a liar.' To like purpose saith David, 'If I come into the tabernacle of my house, if I go up into my bed, if I give sleep to my eyes,' Ps. cxxxii. 3, 4. So Christ, 'Verily I say unto you, if a sign be given unto this generation,' Mark viii. 12; and God himself, 'Once have I sworn by my holiness, if I lie unto David,' Ps. lxxxix. 35; and here, 'I sware in my wrath, if they shall enter.' Here may be understood, Let me not be accounted a God, or let me not be accounted true. As in other things, so in this, God speaketh to men after the manner of man;[2] he submitteth his truth to man's judgment. This, then, implies a very strong negation. A stronger cannot be expressed.

This is to root infidelity out of men's hearts.

That which is concealed in the foresaid oaths being some imprecations against one's self, sheweth that men should be very tender of making imprecations. Hereof see *The Whole Armour of God*, on Eph. vi. 18, Sec. 55.

Sec. 116. *Of the rest denied to the incredulous Israelites.*

The particular punishment or revenge which God sweareth to inflict upon them is deprivation of his promised rest, thus set down in our English, 'They shall not enter into my rest.'

The rest here meant, as it hath reference to those Israelites who provoked God to swear, is the land of Canaan.

This is called rest, in reference to their many travels and troubles that they had in the wilderness and in the land of Egypt.

The Hebrew word מְנוּחָתִי, *requies mea*, used by the psalmist, is derived from a root, נוּחַ, *quievit*, that signifieth to rest from trouble or labour. This is evident by the reason which Lamech renders of the name which he gave to his son Noah. Noah, נֹחַ, *Noah*, see Chap. iv. 4, Sec. 31, cometh from the same root, and signifieth rest. The reason which his father gave thereof is thus expressed: 'He shall comfort us concerning our work and toil of our hands,' Gen. v. 29. Lamech, by divine inspiration, foresaw that God in Noah's time would ease the earth of that intolerable burden of wickedness wherewith the multitude of giants, who were cruel, tyrannical persons, overloaded it, so as, by the ceasing of that violence, there should be rest.

He had therefore a name of rest given him, because rest should be in his days, as Solomon, which signifieth *peace*, had that name given him, because peace was in his days, 2 Chron. xxii. 9, שְׁלֹמֹה *à* שָׁלוֹם *pax*.

The Greek noun κατάπαυσις, here used, is a compound. The simple verb παύειν, signifieth in general to cease or leave off, Luke v. 4, and xi. 1. It is in particular applied to the allaying or ceasing of storms, as Luke viii. 24; and to mischievous opposition against truth, Acts xiii. 10; and to appeasing uproars, Acts xx. 1; and to leaving off violent beating, Acts xxi. 32; and to leaving off sin, 1 Pet. iv. 1.

The verb καταπαύειν, compounded with the preposition κατά, here used, signifieth to restrain, Acts xiv. 18. It is used sometimes intransitively, without governing any case, as in this phrase, 'God did rest,' Chap. iv. 4; so ver. 18; sometimes transitively, as in this phrase, 'Jesus gave them rest,' or 'Joshua made them rest'; that is, he procured rest for them, Chap. iv. 8.

A noun, κατάπαυσις, that cometh from this compound verb is here used, and signifieth rest; even such a rest as freeth from travels and troubles.

Fitly is this word used in this place; for the rest here spoken of, whether it be taken literally for Canaan, or mystically for heaven, is a freedom from travails and troubles.

Eight several times is this noun used in this and the next chapter, and translated *rest*. There is another word σαββατισμος, once only used in the New Testament, and translated *rest*, which, according to the notation of it, signifieth the keeping of a Sabbath, Chap. iv. 9, Sec. 31.

The children of Israel were under sore bondage, and subject to much labour, toil, and oppression in

---

[1] ἀποσιώπησις, *reticentia*.   [2] ἀνθρωποπαθῶς.

the land of Egypt; and in the wilderness they had no settled place of abode, but were forced to remove from station to station. In Canaan they were a free people under no bondage, and according to their several tribes and families they had a set and settled habitation: which as an inheritance was given to them and their posterity. In this respect Canaan had this title given unto it, *rest*.

This title, *rest*, doth both amplify God's great care over his church, and also aggravate the judgment here denounced.

1. It amplifieth God's providence in this, that howsoever in wisdom he may suffer his church for some time to be under sore pressures, and to be brought to sundry straits, yet rest shall be the end of all. This he prepareth, this he will give to his. After that the Israelites had been settled in Canaan, they were for their sins molested by their enemies; yet God gave them rest again, Judges iii. 11, 32, and v. 31. So after David's wars and troubles God gave Israel rest on every side, 1 Chron. xxii. 18; yea, after they had been seventy years in captivity, he brought them to this land of rest again, Ezra ii. 1. In the apostles' time, after some persecution, 'the churches had rest,' Acts ix. 31; and in Constantine's time, after the ten persecutions; and in Queen Elizabeth's time, after the Marian persecution. This the Lord thus ordereth here in this world, to uphold the spirits of his servants, that they should not faint under their troubles and trials; but hold out upon an expectation of rest. Men labour and travel all the day in hope of rest in the night.

But heaven especially is that rest which God hath prepared for all his. This is that 'rest which remains to the people of God,' Heb. iv. 8. Herein the Israelites were a type of the church of God in this world. This world is as an Egypt and a wilderness to the church of God; but heaven is their Canaan. As Christ, 'for the joy that was set before him, endured the cross, despising the shame,' Heb. xii. 2, so let us for this rest that is set before us. Of the true rest, see Chap. iv. 1, Sec. 8.

2. This title *rest* doth aggravate the judgment inflicted upon the Israelites, in that it was a deprivation of that which might most of all uphold and support their spirits in their troubles and travels: which was, that they should have rest. Rest was prepared for them; but they through their incredulity and manifold rebellions deprived themselves thereof. See Sec. 118.

They so far deprived themselves of that rest, as God sware, they shall not enter (εἰσελεύσονται) into it. They should be so far from having any possession therein, and long living, dying, and being buried therein, as they should not so much as set a foot therein, or have their bones carried thereinto, as Joseph's were, Exod. xiii. 19, Josh. xxiv. 32.

Our English doth interpret the Greek word in the full latitude thereof, thus, *enter into*; for it is a compound. The simple verb ἔρχομαι, *eo, venio*, signifieth to *go*, or to *come*; and the the preposition εἰς, *into*. This compound is used to set out the utter exclusion of hypocrites, other wicked, and all unregenerate persons out of heaven, Mat. v. 20, and vii. 21, John iii. 5, Rev. xxi. 27.

In this the type, which is Canaan, fitly answereth the truth, which is heaven.

This emphasis of the word, which setteth forth their utter exclusion out of Canaan, doth aggravate their judgment.

Sec. 117. *Of rest styled God's rest.*

The fore-mentioned rest is further amplified by appropriating it to God, who calls it κατάπαυσίν μου, *my rest*.

By an excellency is that rest called *God's rest*, and that in sundry respects.

1. It was a rest which God had promised to their fathers.

2. By God they were conducted, and brought out of Egypt through the wilderness unto it.

3. By God, they who entered in were settled therein.

4. God had his habitation there among them.

There was his tabernacle, and ark, and afterward his temple set. In what respect heaven is called God's rest, see Chap. iv. 1, Sec. 9.

God doth here purposely appropriate this rest unto himself, to make them who enjoyed it, and found the benefit of it, more thankful and obedient; and to aggravate the sin of those who, by their incredulity, deprived themselves thereof. For they deprived themselves of an especial pledge of God's favour.

Learn hereby to acknowledge that rest and quiet, which any way you have, to be God's. The rest which we have had in this land since Queen Mary's days, is God's; the rest that this city hath had in special, or any other cities or towns. The rest that we have in our houses, or in our beds, when we quietly sleep therein, is God's. God gives, God continues it. To God praise and thanks is to be given for the same: and the good and benefit we reap thereby is to be turned to the glory of his name.

Sec. 118. *Of man's forfeiting the benefit of God's promise.*

Quest. How can God's oath for depriving the Israelites of this rest stand with the promise which he sware to their fathers of giving it them?

Ans. By distinguishing the persons who entered into that rest, and who were deprived thereof, the two oaths of God may easily be reconciled, and stand together without any contradiction.

His oath of promise was made to such as should believe the word of God, and walk in the way of God.

His oath of threatening was made against the incredulous, who would not follow that course which God had prescribed for entering into that rest.

God's oath of promise was accomplished in those that entered. His oath of threatening was accomplished in those who were destroyed in the wilderness. This resolution may be gathered out of God's own words, Deut. i. 34, 35, &c.

By this we see that incredulous and rebellious persons deprive themselves of the benefit of those promises which are made to the faithful. Thus the old world deprived themselves of the benefit of the ark, 1 Pet. iii. 20.

Thus Lot's sons-in-law deprived themselves of that preservation which they might have had, Gen. xix. 14. Memorable in this case is the example of the incredulous prince, who, upon the relieving of Samaria, was trod to death, 2 Kings vii. 17, &c. The pharisees rejected the counsel of God against themselves, Luke vii. 30; so did the wicked guests, Luke xiv. 18, &c.

Faith and obedience are two conditions which God requireth of those to whom he maketh his good and gracious promises. Though it be most true that God doth all the good which he doth, and bestoweth all the blessings which he bestoweth, upon his free grace and mere mercy, and that man's faith and obedience doth not simply move God to make promise of good unto him or to do good unto him, yet he requires these, as means, wherein and whereby man should be partakers of his grace, and whereby man may gain assurance to himself, and give evidence to others, that God intendeth such and such good things to him. In this respect they who believe not are said to put away from them that which God hath promised, Acts xvii. 46.

For unbelief is as a thick mist before the eyes of our understanding, Luke xix. 42; and brings obstinacy upon the will, Exodus v. 2, Num. xiv. 41.

Wherefore, as we desire to partake of the benefit of God's promise and covenant, let us take heed of forfeiting the same by not observing the course which God hath prescribed. God hath promised to give to them that ask, Mat. vii. 7; but 'if we regard iniquity in our heart, the Lord will not hear,' Ps. lxvi. 18. God hath promised not to fail nor forsake his, Heb. xiii. 5; yet will he forsake them that forsake him, Deut. xxxi. 16, 17.

Of forsaking the promise of celestial rest, see Chap. iv. 1, Sec. 7.

Sec. 119. *Of the resolution of* Chap. iii. 7–11.

Ver. 7. *Wherefore (as the Holy Ghost saith, To-day if you will hear his voice,*

Ver. 8. *Harden not your hearts, as in the provocation, in the day of temptation in the wilderness:*

Ver. 9. *When your fathers tempted me, proved me, and saw my works forty years.*

Ver. 10. *Wherefore I was grieved with that generation, and said, They do always err in their hearts, and they have not known my ways.*

Ver. 11. *So I sware in my wrath, They shall not enter into my rest.)*

In these five verses God's dealings with the Israelites in the wilderness is set down. The end hereof is to deter Christians from disrespecting Christ; this is done by way of dissuasion.

The dissuasion is,
1. Generally propounded in the foresaid verses,
2. Particularly exemplified in the rest of the chapter.

In the general observe,
1. The manner of propounding it.
2. The matter whereof it consisteth.

The manner is in these words, ' Wherefore, as the Holy Ghost saith.'

Herein are four distinct points observable:
1. The inference, in this word *wherefore*.
2. The resemblance, in this particle *as*.
3. The principal author, *the Holy Ghost*.
4. The kind of expressing his mind, in this word *saith*.

The matter sets out, 1, a virtue; 2, a vice.

The virtue is premised as a means to prevent the vice, as is evident by this conditional conjunction *if*.

The virtue is set out by an act, *hear;* and the object, *voice;* limited by a double restriction: 1, of the person, *his;* 2, of the time, *to-day*.

The vice prohibited is set out,
1. By the kind of it, vers. 8, 9.
2. By the consequence following upon it, vers. 10, 11.

The kind of vice is, 1, propounded; 2, aggravated.

It is propounded,
1. Under an act forbidden, *harden not*.
2. Under the object thereof, *your heart*.

The aggravation is taken,
1. From the place where this sin was committed.

The place is described,
1. By two titles (taken from their sins, *provocation, temptation*, amplified by the time, *to-day*).
2. By the barrenness of it, *wilderness*.

2. An aggravation is taken from the persons who committed the sin.

The persons are described,
1. By a note of relation, *fathers*.
2. By a distinct expression of their acts, which were two, *tempted, proved;* and enforced, 1, by the means of restraining them, *they saw my works;* 2, by continuance thereof, *forty years*.

Herein two points are intended,
1. God's patience, in continuing to do wonders forty years.
2. Their obstinacy, in continuing to sin all that time, though they saw his works so long.

2. The consequence following upon their sin hath reference to God, and that in two respects:
1. To his fatherly affection, ver. 10.
2. To his just indignation, ver. 11.

His fatherly affection is, 1, implied; 2, manifested. God's fatherly affection is implied,
1. By the kind of it, in this phrase, *I was grieved*.

2. By the persons at whom he was grieved, *this generation*.

Generation intendeth two points: 1, a multitude; 2, a succession of people.

The manifestation of God's affection is,

1. Generally hinted by his complaint, in this word *said*.

2. It is particularly expressed in the substance of the complaint, which consisteth of two vices, whereof he complaineth.

The former is set out, 1, by an act, *they erred*; 2, by the subject thereof, *in heart*; 3, by the continuance therein, *always*.

The latter is set out, 1, by a deficiency, *they know not*; 2, by the object thereof, *my ways*.

2. God's righteous indignation is manifested in his oath, which is, 1, generally expressed, *I sware*; 2, particularly described.

God's oath is described,

1. By the provoking cause, *wrath*.
2. By the form of it, implied in this particle *if*.
3. By the matter, which is deprivation of what otherwise they might have had.

This deprivation is aggravated,

1. By their utter exclusion, *shall not enter*.
2. By the place from whence they were excluded.

The place is illustrated,

1. By the commodity of it, *rest*.
2. By the excellency of that commodity, in reference thereof to God, *my rest*.

Sec. 120. *Of observations collected out of* Heb. iii. 7–11.

I. *Christ's faithfulness must make Christians heedful in attending to him.* The particle of inference, *wherefore*, intends thus much. See Sec. 73.

II. *The apostle delivered what was agreeable to the mind of the Spirit.* He wrote as the Holy Ghost spake. This particle *as* sheweth the agreeableness. See Sec. 74.

III. *The Holy Ghost is the author of the Old Testament.* He therein spake. See Sec. 74.

IV. *The word written is as a sermon spoken.* The testimony here alleged is taken out of the word written, yet of it this verb *saith* is used. See Sec. 74.

V. *The first opportunity for grace is to be taken.* This is intended under this word, *to-day*. See Sec. 76.

VI. *God's word is man's rule.* God's word is implied under this phrase, his voice, which is here set down as our rule. See Sec. 78.

VII. *God's word is to be heeded.* We must *hear* it. See Sec. 77.

VIII. *Hearing God's word is a means to prevent hardness of heart.* The manner of premising this duty with this conditional particle, *if*, intends thus much. See Sec. 77.

IX. *Man's heart may be hardened.* This is here taken for grant in that he admonisheth them not to harden their hearts. See Sec. 80, &c.

X. *Man may harden his own heart.* This relative, *your*, hath reference to those that are admonished not to harden their hearts. See Sec. 85.

XI. *Hardness of heart is an hindrance to profitable hearing.* In that he infers this admonition, not to harden their heart, upon the duty of hearing, he sheweth that they whose hearts are hardened cannot well hear God's word. See Sec. 77.

XII. *Sins of predecessors are to be avoided.* This note of resemblance, *as*, hath reference to their predecessors, to whom they must not be like. See Sec. 89.

XIII. *Notice is to be taken of the sins of former ages.* These two titles, *provocation, temptation*, are records of former sins, that so succeeding persons may take notice thereof. See Sec. 90.

XIV. *Man's continuing in sin is a day of sinning.* For this end is the Israelites continuing to tempt God, called 'the day of temptation.' See Sec. 91.

XV. *Kindness works not on incredulous.* Many and great were the kindnesses which God shewed to the Israelites in the wilderness, yet in the wilderness they remained obstinate. See Sec. 92.

XVI. *Straits are no just cause of distrust.* The Israelites are blamed for their unbelief in the wilderness, though therein they were brought to many straits. See Sec. 93.

XVII. *Sins of forefathers are no warrant to successors.* The children that came from the Israelites in the wilderness are here warned to take heed of their fathers' sins. See Sec. 95.

XVIII. *It is a great sin to tempt God.* Tempting of God is here set down as an high provocation of God. See Sec. 96.

XIX. *God is kind to the ungrateful.* This word *proved*, being added to *tempted*, sheweth that they who tempted God had sundry proofs of his goodness. See Secs. 97, 98.

XX. *Extraordinary works work not on incredulous.* Who ever saw greater works of God than the Israelites in the wilderness? They saw these works, and yet believed not. See Sec. 99.

XXI. *Man's unbelief straiteneth not God's power.* Though the Israelites in the wilderness believed not, yet God all that time, even forty years, continued to do wonders; they saw his works. See Sec. 100.

XXII. *God is of long-suffering.* He continued to be grieved forty years together. See Sec. 101.

XXIII. *Continuance in sin much aggravates sin.* This particle of inference, *wherefore*, having reference to God's swearing vengeance upon their forty years' provocation, proveth as much. See Secs. 102, 109.

XXIV. *Man's obstinacy grieves God.* It was Israel's obstinacy that provoked God to say, 'I was grieved.' See Sec. 103.

XXV. *Conspiracy of many in sin is one aggravation.*

XXVI. *Continuance after others in the like sin is another aggravation.* These two observations arise from the meaning of this word *generation*. See Sec. 104.

XXVII. *God is oft forced to complain of his people.* This word *said*, as here used, is a word of complaint. See Sec. 105.

XXVIII. *Wilfulness aggravateth sin.* Erring in heart is a kind of wilfulness. This is here set down as an aggravation. See Secs. 106, 107.

XXIX. *God's works are his ways.* Therein he makes himself to be seen as it were walking before us. Therefore they are here called his ways. See Sec. 110.

XXX. *Some ignorance aggravateth sin.* Their *not knowing* is here set down as an aggravation. See Sec. 111.

XXXI. *God's patience may be turned into just vengeance.* This particle *so*, sheweth that by abuse of patience God was brought to swear judgment. See Sec. 113.

XXXII. *God may be brought to swear vengeance.* This is here plainly expressed. See Sec. 114.

XXXIII. *God may be incensed to wrath.* For here he saith of himself, 'I sware in my wrath.' See Sec. 114.

XXXIV. *Men must be tender of imprecations.* The manner of God's oath, whereby the imprecation is left to be understood, intendeth as much. See Sec. 115.

XXXV. *There is a rest prepared for God's people.* This is implied under this word *rest*. See Sec. 116.

XXXVI. *The rest of God's people is in special manner God's rest.* For thus God styleth it, *my rest.* See Sec. 117.

XXXVII. *Men may deprive themselves of the benefit of God's promises.* God had promised this rest to the children of Israel, yet these Israelites deprived themselves thereof. See Sec. 118.

Sec. 121. *Of this title 'brethren,' used in admonitions and reprehensions, &c.*

Ver. 12. *Take heed, brethren, lest there be in any of you an evil heart of unbelief, in departing from the living God.*

Here the apostle beginneth distinctly to lay down the use which we are to make of Christ's prophetical office.

The use in general is, that we cleave close to Christ, and never start from him.

In laying down this use, the apostle hath an eye to the fore-named divine testimony, as to the groundwork of this use. Hereupon he maketh a fit application thereof to those in particular to whom he wrote, vers. 12–14, and addeth thereunto a clear exposition of many passages in that testimony in the other verses of that chapter.

In his application he useth a pithy dissuasion from backsliding, ver. 12, and giveth a good direction to prevent the same, ver. 13, &c.

The dissuasion may have an immediate reference to that which in the six first verses of this chapter is set down, concerning Christ's prophetical office. Thus the whole divine testimony being included in a parenthesis, this verse may be referred to the first particle of the seventh verse, thus, 'Wherefore take heed,' &c., see Sec. 73. Or else it may have reference to this note of comparison, *as*, ver. 7, and then for perspicuity's sake, the other particle of comparison, *so*, be here prefixed in this manner : 'As the Holy Ghost saith,' &c. 'So take heed,' &c. Both references tend to the same end.

The apostle inforceth this admonition by this mild, sweet, insinuating title, ἀδελφοί, brethren. Here he seems to be jealous of them, and to fear that they might prove apostates. Wherefore, to make this bitter pill of jealousy and fear to be the better taken, he sweetens it with this title, which is an especial evidence of his entire love to them, and tender care over them. This is yet more fully evidenced, Gal. iv. 11, 12, Heb. vi. 9.

Of this title *brethren*, see Secs. 3, 4. There it was shewed that exhortations are thus to be sweetened. So are admonitions, 2 Thess. iii. 15, commands, 2 Thess. iii. 6, prohibitions, James ii. 1, reprehensions, James iii. 10, and other like kinds of dealing. For these are as fulsome potions and bitter pills, they have need of sweetening that they may the better relish. Thus it is manifested that commands, admonitions, prohibitions, reprehensions, fears, and jealousies, do not proceed from anger or hatred, but from love and good will, and tend not to the disgrace but to the good of those to whom they are applied.

That therefore which the apostle in this kind practised himself, he gave in charge to his successor, 1 Tim. v. 1, 2 Tim. ii. 25, and is to be observed of all that have power and occasion to command, exhort, dissuade, forbid, and reprove others.

Sec. 122. *Of circumspection in preventing apostasy.*

The word βλέπετε, whereby the apostle setteth out his admonition, properly signifieth to see. It is applied in the New Testament both to corporal and also to spiritual sight. See Chap. ii. 9, Sec. 72.

Seeing is an especial means to avoid danger. Blind men, that cannot see, if they walk abroad without a guide, are ready to rush upon every wall, to knock themselves by every post, to stumble at every block, to fall into every ditch that is in the way where they pass, and to implunge themselves into many other dangers.

Now, because seeing is a means to prevent such mischiefs, prudent care in avoiding danger is set out under this word *see*, and it is thus translated in a spiritual sense, Heb. xii. 25. It is also thus translated, *look to*, 2 John 8., *beware*, Mark xii. 38, *take heed*, Luke xxi. 18 ; so here in this text.

It being here premised as a means to avoid backsliding and falling away, sheweth that great circumspection must be used for preventing apostasy, yea, and other sins also. To this purpose is this *caveat* in this very word frequently used in the New Testament, and in other like words and phrases both in the Old and New Testament, as Deut. iv. 9, 15, and xxix. 18; Prov. iv. 23, 26; Mat. xvi. 6; Rom. xi. 20; Heb. iv. 1, and xii. 15.

Great need there is of much circumspection, in regard, 1, of sin, whereby men are brought to fall away; 2, of Satan, who continually tempts men thereto; 3, of ourselves, who are too prone to decay; 4, of God, who may be provoked to leave us to sin, Satan, and ourselves.

1. For sin, it is exceeding deceitful. Therefore this apostle attributeth unto it this epithet *deceitfulness*, ver. 13. Sin never presents itself in its own colours, but takes upon it the shape of some virtue or other, as superstition the dress of religion, licentiousness of Christian liberty, covetousness of thriftiness, prodigality of liberality; and it ever makes some pretence of delight, profit, advancement, or other like thing that gives content to man, as Gen. iii. 6, and xxxiv. 23, Mark xii. 7, Prov. vii. 18. Herein it shews itself to be a brat of the devil, and like to its sire, for Satan can translate himself into an angel of light, 2 Cor. xi. 14.

Sin is also of a bewitching nature. It insensibly soaks into a man, as lust did into David, 2 Sam. xi. 2, &c.; and when once it hath possessed a man, that man's heart cannot be withdrawn from it, as appears by David's prosecuting his lust, not only by committing adultery with Uriah's wife, but also by making him drunk, and working his destruction, 2 Sam. xi. 13, 14. Yea, it so bewitched Samson, as though he knew that Delilah had consented to the Philistines to betray him into their hands, yet he could not leave her, Judges xvi. 5, &c. Even so, many are so bewitched with sin as though they know it will cost them both their temporal and eternal life, yet they cannot give it over. See more of sin's deceitfulness, Sec. 148.

2. For Satan, he is a mortal enemy, unplacable, sedulous, restless, and very terrible. All these are set forth to the life in these words: 'Your adversary the devil, as a roaring lion, walketh about, seeking whom he may devour,' 1 Peter v. 8.

1. His name, διάβολος, *devil*, declares him to be an accuser, and therein one that seeketh all the advantages that he can against us.

1. He is an adversary,[1] who will do us all the spite he can, as an adversary in law.

3. He is a lion, strong, ravenous, fierce, and cruel.

4. He is as a roaring lion, doing what he can to affright us, and make us yield to him.

5. He walketh up and down. Herein he shews himself to be sedulous, yea, and restless, Mat. xii. 43.

6. He seeks whom he may devour. This declares im to be a deadly enemy. He aims at our death, ven the damnation of our souls.

Is there not just cause to be very watchful against such an enemy?

[1] ἀντίδικος, *contra-litigator*. Est verbum forense.

3. For ourselves. We are exceeding foolish, like the silly fish that by a bait is soon taken with the hook. By reason of the flesh that is in us, we are prone and forward to yield to every temptation. As dry tinder soon takes the least spark of fire, and as gunpowder, taking the least spark, is soon all on a flame, so we by nature are soon taken with the least temptation, and soon set all on fire. Besides, there is in us a natural proneness of ourselves to decay in grace, and to fall from it, as in a stone, weight of lead, or any other earthly and heavy thing, to fall downward, if continually by some means or other it be not held up, or as water to wax cold, if fire be not continually kept under it.

4. For God. He is oft provoked by men's security and carelessness to leave them to the temptations whereunto they are subject, which if he do, how can we stand? Take instance in this case of Peter, Mat. xxvi. 33, 70.

Hereby we may take information of one special reason of men's failing and falling away from God, namely, their want of circumspection; they do not take that heed which they should. If men that are circumspect be notwithstanding oft overtaken, how is it possible that they who are secure and careless should stand firm and stable? It is noted of the men of Laish that they dwelt careless, quiet, and secure, whereupon they were soon surprised by their enemies, Judges xviii. 7, &c. Even so in regard of men's spiritual estate; they who are careless are a prey for the devil, Mat. xii. 44, and for such as he sets on work.

In this respect there is just cause earnestly to incite men to use all diligence about the Christian care in preventing sin. They who use the greatest diligence that they can hereabout, find all too little. Let me therefore again and again inculcate this apostolica caveat, 'Let him that thinketh he standeth, take heed lest he fall,' 1 Cor. x. 12. Be not secure, but fear. Be not over bold, but fear: 'Be not high-minded, but fear,' Rom. xi. 20. Ever maintain an holy jealousy over thyself, which is comprised under this word *fear*, chap iv. 1.

Of means to prevent falling away, and to remain stedfast, see Sec. 70.

Sec. 123. *Of circumspection over a man's self.*

This phrase, *in any of you*, intends an extent of the foresaid duty of circumspection. This word *in any*, ἔν τινι, extends the duty to others, as well as this word ὑμῶν, *of you*, applies it to men themselves.

Indeed, this *caveat* is oft restrained to men themselves, as Mark xiii. 9, Luke xvii. 3, Philip. ii. 12, Col. iii. 16, 1 John v. 21. For,

1. Every one is nearest to himself; according to this proverb, Near is my shirt, but nearer is my skin. Now our greatest care must be of the nearest to us.

2. Every one hath an especial charge of himself, even they who have charge over others: 'Take heed

unto yourselves, and to all the flock,' saith the apostle to the elders of Ephesus, Acts xx. 28. The reason hereof may be this: in doing this, they 'shall both save themselves and them that hear them,' 1 Tim. iv. 16.

3. Every one best knows himself, and can best discern when he begins to decay: 'What man knoweth the things of a man, save the spirit of a man which is in him?' 1 Cor. ii. 11. On this ground the apostle thus exhorteth, 'Examine yourselves, prove your own selves: know ye not your own selves,' &c., 2 Cor. xiii. 5.

4. Every one is especially to give an account of himself, Rom. xiv. 12, 2 Cor. v. 10.

They therefore who put off this duty from themselves are most blameworthy. Of this sort are,

1. They who seem to take care of others, but have no care of themselves. Soundly and sharply doth the apostle upbraid the Jews in this respect, Rom. ii. 21, &c. There are many magistrates that will be careful to keep others in compass of law, yet much transgress themselves. Many ministers will cry out against other men's committing those sins whereunto they greedily give themselves. The like may be said of husbands, parents, masters, tutors, and such as have otherwise charge over others. These, and others like them, are like the builders of Noah's ark, who built that which was a means to preserve Noah and his family, but entered not themselves thereinto. He was not of this mind who said, 'I keep under my body, and bring it into subjection; lest that by any means, when I have preached to others, I myself should be a castaway,' 1 Cor. ix. 27.

2. They who clean put off this duty from themselves to others, as the younger to the elder, subjects to magistrates, hearers to teachers, poor to rich, females to males. I suppose none will so do in the case of their body and temporal estate. Doth not this argue a fleshy and earthy disposition? See ver. 13, Sec. 147.

All that was delivered in the former section, may in special be applied to a man's care of himself.

Sec. 124. *Of circumspection over others.*

Though this be a necessary and bounden duty for every one to be circumspect over himself; yet must not the duty of circumspection be bounded, limited, and restrained only to men's selves; it must also be extended to others. Where the apostle saith, 'Take heed unto yourselves,' he addeth, 'and to all the flock,' Acts xx. 28. And where another apostle saith, 'Keep yourselves,' &c., he addeth, 'and others save,' &c., Jude 21, 23. This duty is more expressly extended to others, Deut. xiii. 12, &c.; Heb. xii. 15; Gal. vi. 1, 2; 1 Thes. v. 11, 14.

Weighty reasons there are to press this extent of this duty of circumspection. As,

1. The near union of all Christians. They are children of the same Father. 'Have we not all one Father?' Mal. ii. 10. Of this union, see more, Sec. 17.

2. The like common condition of all. Others as ourselves are subject to manifold infirmities, and to all sorts of temptations; they have also the same enemies that we have, and they are as prone to fall away as we are. Thus in these and sundry other like respects, there is as great need of being careful over others, as over ourselves.

3. The extent of brotherly love. This is thus set down, 'Thou shalt love thy neighbour as thyself,' Mat. xxii. 39. This is the law and the gospel, the prophets and apostles. This is the sum of that doctrine which in the law and gospel, by the prophets and apostles, is taught concerning one another. If you do this, you do well, James ii. 8. Such an affection do men bear to themselves, as they will not stick at any pains or cost to do themselves good, or to prevent any hurt or damage that might befall themselves. Were the extent of brotherly love observed, we should be, we would be, like-minded to others.

4. The zeal that we ought to bear to the glory of God; for to keep men from falling from God, so as they may ever remain faithful to him, adds much to his glory. Constant and continual faithfulness in servants, is an evidence of his goodness whom they serve. It gives proof that they serve a good master, which makes much to his glory.

Hereby we see the scantiness of their duty, who wholly cast off all care of keeping others from falling from God, supposing it enough that they take care of themselves. This latter, of caring for themselves, is commendable; but the other, concerning their brother, ought not to be neglected.

Some will be ready to say, 'Am I my brother's keeper,' Gen. iv. 9.

To these I answer, that that was the speech of a murdering Cain. The truth is, that we are every one our brother's keeper, and ought to take care of our brother. They therefore who are careful over themselves, are to be exhorted to extend their care in this kind to their brother also. This especially concerns them who have charge over others. See Chap. ii. 13, Sec. 126.

The pronoun τίνι, *any*, excludeth not any, of what sex, age, degree, condition, or distinction soever they be; if at least they may in charity come under th title of a brother. For this, as other Christian duties, is to be performed without partiality, 1 Tim. v. 21, James iii. 17. Herein we shall shew ourselves like unto God, 2 Chron. xix. 7. See Chap. vi. 11, Sec. 78.

Sec. 125. *Of perpetual circumspection.*

The aforesaid duty of circumspection over ourselves, with the extent thereof over others, is amplified by continuance therein, in this phrase, *lest at any time*. This is the interpretation of one Greek word, μήποτε, whereof see Chap. ii. 1, Sec. 6.

The first particle μή, *lest*, is a note of prevention, and hath reference to the first word, *take heed*. The other particle, ποτε, translated *at any time*, is a note of constancy or perpetuity.

It here implieth an holy jealousy in the apostle, as 2 Cor. xi. 2, 3, lest hereafter sometime or other they might fall away, though they now stood; and it intendeth a perpetual watchfulness. This is more fully expressed in these words, ' It is good to be zealously affected always in a good thing,' Gal. iv. 18. Hereupon he is pronounced happy that feareth alway, Prov. xxviii. 14.

Man by his natural disposition is very prone to decay in grace, if care be not taken to nourish grace, and to make it increase more and more; as water, though seething hot, is prone to wax cold, if fire be not kept under it. Besides, the devil is restless, 1 Peter v. 8, Mat. xii. 43, &c. The apostle, that well knew this, thus saith to those over whom he had a charge, ' I will not be negligent to put you always in remembrance,' 2 Peter i. 12.

It well becomes us therefore to persevere in all our good beginnings. Hereof see more, Sec. 68.

Sec. 126. *Of looking to the heart.*

The object whereabout men ought to take most heed, is here set down to be the heart: and that in general, that it be not evil; and in special, that unbelief seize not upon it.

Of the *heart*, and of the divers acceptions thereof, see Sec. 79.

The heart is here taken in the largest extent, for the whole soul of man, consisting of two especial faculties, understanding and will. For as faith exerciseth itself in both these, so unbelief depraveth both. Such virtues and vices as are directly contrary one to the other, have the same object.

The apostle, in mentioning the heart, striketh at the very root, and gives us to understand, that the heart is especially to be looked unto: ' Keep thy heart with all diligence,' Prov. iv. 23, or word for word, ' above all keeping ;' above thy coin or jewels, ' For a man's life consisteth not in the abundance of the things which he possesseth,' Luke xii. 15. But ' out of the heart are the issue of life,' Prov. iv. 23 Yea, keep thine heart above thine eyes, ears, tongue, hands, feet, or any parts of thy body.

1. The heart is as a queen, and hath an absolute command over all the parts of the body. As Josiah the king caused all his subjects to stand to the covenant which he had made with God, 2 Chron. xxxiv. 32, so will the heart cause the whole body. Barnabas therefore exhorteth such as were turned to the Lord, 'that with purpose of heart they would cleave unto the Lord,' Acts xi. 23. God himself wished that there were in his people ' an heart to fear him, and to keep all his commandments always,' Deut. v. 29.

2. The heart is a spring, whence all manner of affections and actions do flow; and they are so qualified as the heart is. ' A good man, out of the good treasure of his heart, bringeth forth that which is good ; and an evil man, out of the evil treasure of his heart, bringeth forth that which is evil,' Luke vi. 45. Philosophers say, that the heart of the body is the fountain of natural life. The heart first lives in him, and last dies in him. So the heart of the soul is the fountain of spiritual life. It is like leaven, Mat. xiii. 33. It is first seasoned itself with grace; then it seasoneth the whole man. If grace be clean out of the heart, there is no hope of recovering it.

3. The heart is as God's throne, whereon he alone will sit. It is his secret closet, whereinto he alone will come. It is thereupon noted, that to search the heart is one of God's incommunicable properties, Jer. xvii. 9, Acts i. 24. This therefore the Lord most desireth, Prov. xxiii. 26, Deut. v. 9.

4. The integrity of the heart is so acceptable to God, as a man of an upright heart is said to be ' a man after his own heart,' 1 Sam. xiii. 14, Acts xiii. 22. This therefore Hezekiah is bold thus to plead before God : ' I beseech thee, O Lord, remember now how I have walked before thee in truth, and with a perfect heart,' 2 Kings xx. 3.

Though there may be many failings in that which men do, yet, if they prepare their heart to seek the Lord, the Lord will pass by those failings, Gen. xx. 6, 2 Chron. xxx. 19, 20. But, on the contrary, though never so great and glorious things be done, and not with an upright and pure heart, they are an abomination to the Lord, Isa. lxvi. 3, Mat. xv. 8.

On these and other like grounds, there is great and just cause to take heed of the heart, and to keep it with all diligence. A queen useth to have a strong guard to watch for her safety. Springs also use to be charily kept. What care can be sufficient to keep that wherein God doth most delight ? God hath placed the heart in the midst of a man, and compassed it about with ribs for the greater safety. If a man's heart be ready to faint, the blood in the body will quickly come about it to refresh it. Thus nature itself teacheth us to have an especial care of the heart, as it is spiritually taken.

Sec. 127. *Of an evil heart.*

The greater heed must be taken to the heart, because otherwise it may soon prove to be *an evil heart*, which the apostle implieth by adding this epithet, *evil*, to the heart here in this place.

The Greek word πονηρός signifieth a troublesome evil, or evil that troubleth a man. It is derived from a noun[1] that signifieth labour or trouble. In this sense, as here, the heart is called evil; so the conscience, Heb. x. 22. For an evil conscience is troublesome. So some men are in this respect called *evil men*,

[1] πόνος, *labor, molestia;* πονηρός, *malus, qui molestiam facessit.*

2 Thes. iii. 2; yea, Satan, who is most troublesome, is styled ὁ πονηρὸς, *the evil one*, Mat. xiii. 19, 1 John v. 18; and troublesome times are said to be αἱ ἡμέραι πονηραί, *evil days*. This Greek word is translated *grievous*, Rev. xvi. 2.

This *caveat* against an evil heart the apostle giveth to those whom he called 'brethren,' and 'partakers of the heavenly calling,' ver. 1, whereby he sheweth that he had a holy jealousy over them, and this in two respects:

1. In that there might be many hypocrites among them. For visible churches are mixed societies, Mat. xxii. 14. Hypocrites have evil hearts. They have לב ולב, 'a heart and a heart,' Ps. xii. 2: one is an outward, seeming, fair heart, whereby they beguile men; the other an inward evil heart, after which they themselves do walk, Jer. vii. 24, and xi. 8.

2. In them that are effectually called there is a remainder of an evil heart; for they are but in part regenerate while here they live. Some evil doth still cleave to their heart, so as, without taking good heed, more evil will increase upon them. It is said of some, that 'they proceed from evil to evil,' Jer. ix. 3; and that they 'wax worse and worse,' 2 Tim. iii. 13.

This may in part befall such as are regenerate, if they be not watchful over themselves.

True it is that there is in every one by nature an evil heart; yea, 'every imagination of the thoughts of man's heart is only evil continually,' Gen. vi. 5. Every word in this description of a natural man's heart hath its emphasis; as,

1. The *heart*, which is a spring from whence all words and actions flow.
2. The *thoughts*, which are the innermost motions of the heart.
3. The *imagination*, that is, the first rise or groundwork of those thoughts.
4. *Every* imagination; not only some few, but all of them.
5. Is *evil*: it is not only somewhat tainted, but plainly evil.
6. *Only*. Evil not in part only, as if there were some good mixed, but wholly, altogether evil.
7. *Continually* evil, not for a time, or at fits, as if sometimes it might be good, but at all times, without intermission, evil.

This is the disposition of every natural man's heart. There is further an acquired evil, more evil added to that natural evil, an increase of evil. There may be an increase of evil in his heart who is regenerate.

In this respect it will be a part of prudence to avoid all occasions whereby men may be brought to wax worse than they are. Of avoiding occasions, and observing other rules for preventing all backsliding, see Sec. 70.

Sec. 128. *Of unbelief the cause of an evil heart.*

The cause of the foresaid evil heart is here hinted to be unbelief. Our English doth fitly and fully answer the Greek, ἀπιστία, which is a privative compound, and directly contrary to belief, or faith. Unbelief and faith are set in opposition one to the other, as Rom. iv. 20, and xi. 20. So the adjective believing and unbelieving, or not believing, John xx. 27; and believers and unbelievers, or such as believe not, as 1 Cor. xiv. 22, 2 Cor. vi. 15. So also the verb to believe, and not to believe, Mark xvi. 6, Acts xxviii. 24. Answerably these contraries have their contrary operations: 'By faith the heart is purified,' Acts xv. 9. By unbelief the heart is made evil, as here, and the mind and conscience is defiled, Titus i. 15.

Unbelief was the door by which sin first entered into man's heart. For when the devil had said, contrary to God's express word about eating of the tree of knowledge, Gen. ii. 17, 'Ye shall not surely die,' God's word was not believed, and thereupon the first sin was committed, Gen. iii. 4-6.

Unbelief makes void all the means which God affordeth to keep evil out of the heart, as are directions, instructions, persuasions, dissuasions, promises, threatenings, blessings, judgments. None of these, nor any other means like these, will any whit at all prevail with an unbelieving heart: 'The word preached did not profit them, not being mixed with faith in them that heard it,' Heb. iv. 2. There is no grace for which the word doth not afford sufficient encouragement to labour after it. There is no sin against which the word doth not afford sufficient ground to forsake it. Yet neither the one nor the other are any whit at all available with an unbeliever.

Of the heinousness of unbelief, see *The Whole Armour of God*, treat. ii. part vi., on Eph. vi. 16. Of faith, *ibid.* secs. 133, 134.

We are advised to 'look diligently, lest any root of bitterness, springing up, trouble us,' Heb. xii. 15. Among other roots, we are especially to take heed lest unbelief sprout up. This is a root of much bitterness, therefore carefully to be rooted out. Of inward corruptions it is one of the greatest breeders.

Faith is the mother of all graces: see *The Whole Armour of God*, treat. ii. part vi.; of faith, sec. 8; and unbelief is the mother of all vices. The unbeliever regards neither promises nor threatenings, nor any other part of God's word, so as the fear of God cannot possess his heart; and if no fear of God, then no conscience of any sin. Abraham said, 'Because I thought, Surely the fear of God is not in this place, they will slay me,' &c., Gen. xx. 11. When the apostle reckons up a catalogue of gross sins, he concludes all with this, 'There is no fear of God before their eyes,' Rom. iii. 18. Hereupon Christ, having said that 'the Spirit will reprove, or convince the world of sin,' addeth, 'because they believe not on me,' John xvi. 9; whereby he giveth us to understand that unbelief is the cause of all sin. For the unbeliever hath no right to Christ; and in him that is out of Christ, nothing but sin can be found.

Of the heinousness of unbelief, see ver. 18, Sec. 171.

Sec. 129. *Of the damages of unbelief.*

It is a dangerous thing not to believe men when they declare such truths as are for our good. Instance the case of Gedaliah, wherein his incredulity cost him his own life, and the lives of all his friends with him, Jer. xl. 14, 16, and xli. 2, 3. Much more dangerous must it needs be not to believe God, all whose words are truth, and for our good if we rightly use them.

Many and great are the damages which in Scripture are set down to ensue upon unbelief; such as these:

1. Unbelief hardens men's hearts against means afforded for their good, 2 Kings xvii. 14; Exod. ix. 19, 21.
2. It keeps them from being established in the way of God, Isa. vii. 9.
3. It makes them reject those whom God sends, John v. 38; Mat. xxi. 32.
4. It takes away the profit of God's word, Heb. iv. 2.
5. It perverts the plainest manner of teaching, John iii. 12, and x. 25.
6. It makes miracles not to be regarded, John xii. 37.
7. It enrageth men's minds against the truth, Acts xvii. 5.
8. It moved the apostles to depart from people, Acts xix. 9.
9. It makes men unfit to call on God, Rom. x. 4.
10. Unbelievers can in nothing please God, Heb. xi. 6.
11. They are no sheep of Christ, John x. 26.
12. They are under Satan's power, 2 Cor. iv. 4.
13. To unbelievers nothing is pure, Titus i. 15.
14. The gifts which Christ bestows upon them are fruitless and without power, Mat. xvii. 20.
15. Christ's own power is stinted to them, Mat. xiii. 58.
16. Unbelief makes men do detestable acts, 1 Tim. i. 13.
17. It was an especial cause of the rejection of the Jews, Rom. xi. 20.
18. It was the cause of many external judgments, ver. 19, Heb. xi. 31; for it makes men run headlong into danger, Exod. xiv. 23.
19. It excludes from heaven, Heb. iv. 11.
20. It thrusts down to hell, Luke xii. 46; Mark xvi. 16; John iii. 18; 2 Thes. ii. 12; Rev. xxi. 8.

Can that which is in itself so heinous a sin, and which hath so many fearful effects following upon it, be accounted an infirmity? Many do so account unbelief to be, and thereupon give too much way unto it, and nourish it too much. If we would judge it as indeed it is, a true, proper sin, an heinous sin, a cause of many other gross sins, a sin most dishonourable to God, and damageable to our own souls, we should take more heed of it, and be more watchful against it.

Sec. 130. *Of preventing and redressing unbelief.*

For keeping out or casting out unbelief, these directions following will be useful:

1. Use all means to get, prove, preserve, and exercise faith (hereof see *The Whole Armour of God*, treat. ii. part vi. on Eph. vi. 16; of Faith, sec. 17, &c.). As life keepeth out or driveth out death, and light darkness, and heat cold, and other like contraries one another, so faith unbelief; if not wholly (for faith and unbelief may stand together in remiss degrees; see *The Whole Armour of God*, of Faith, sec. 39), yet so as unbelief shall not bear sway in the heart.
2. Set God always before thee, and frequently and seriously meditate on God's presence, providence, power, truth, mercy, and other like excellences. Due meditation on these is a singular antidote against unbelief.
3. Give good entertainment to the Holy Spirit of God; stir up and cherish the good motions thereof. Hereby thy spirit will be quickened and revived, as Jacob's was, Gen. xlv. 27, and it will not continue under the dumpishness of unbelief.
4. Do not wilfully and obstinately stand against any good counsel given, or duty required, or direction prescribed, as the Egyptians did, Exod. ix. 21. Unbelief useth to be joined with obstinacy, as in Pharaoh, who said, 'Who is the Lord, that I should obey his voice?' Exod. v. 2; and in the Israelites, who one while through diffidence return to Egypt, and another while presume to go against the enemy without, yea, against the mind of the Lord, Num. xiv. 4, 40, &c.; and in that prince who said, 'Behold, if the Lord would make windows in heaven, might this thing be?' 2 Kings vii. 2; yea, and in Thomas too, who said, 'I will not believe, except I shall see,' &c., John xx. 25. As wilfulness and obstinacy are joined with unbelief, so they do increase and aggravate it.
5. When thou findest thy heart dull, heavy, doubting, distrustful, use thy judgment and understanding. Thereby reason and discourse with thy stubborn will, and say (as David did, Ps. xlii. 5, 11), 'Why art thou cast down, O my soul?' &c. Why art thou so stubborn, O my will? Why dost thou not believe? Hath God said this and that? Is he not true and faithful? Is he not able to make good his word?

Of a man's reasoning with himself, see *The Saints' Sacrifice*, on Ps. cxvi. 7, secs. 47, 48.

Sec. 131. *Of professors falling away.*

Unbelief is here aggravated by a fearful effect, which is apostasy, thus expressed, 'In departing from the living God.'

The Greek word ἀποστῆναι, translated *departing*, is a compound.

The simple verb ἵστημι signifieth *to stand*, Mat. xx. 3, 6, 32; and *to establish*, Rom. iii. 31, and x. 3.

The compound, ἀφίστημι, signifieth to *depart*, Luke xiii. 27; to *fall away*, Luke viii. 13; to *refrain*, Acts v. 38; to *withdraw*, 1 Tim. vi. 5; and to *draw away*, Acts v. 37. The noun, ἀποστασία, that signifieth *apostasy*, is derived from this verb, 2 Thes. ii. 3.

This word here used implieth, that they to whom the apostle gave this *caveat* professed the true faith, and that they had given up their names to God. Why else should they be warned to take heed of departing from God?

It is therefore possible that professors may fall from their holy profession; even they who profess that they believe in God may depart from him. The many *caveats* given in sacred Scripture to take heed hereof do prove as much (see hereof Sec. 122); so do the threatenings denounced against backsliders, Deut. xxix. 20; Joshua xxiv. 20; 2 Chron. vii. 19, 20; Isa. i. 28; Ezek. xviii. 24; Heb. x. 38. So also do sundry predictions of such as fell away, as Deut. xxxi. 16, &c.; 2 Thes. ii. 3; 1 Tim. iv. 1; 2 Peter ii. 1, 2. But especially instances of such as have departed from their profession; as Saul, 1 Sam. xv. 23; Joash, 2 Chron. xxiv. 17, &c.; Judas, Acts i. 17, &c.; Demas, and such as forsook Paul, 2 Tim. iv. 10, 16; and they of whom the beloved disciple complaineth, 1 John ii. 19; and this our apostle also, Heb. x. 25, in these words, 'as the manner of some is,' whereby he gives us to understand that it was then usual for professors to revolt. The Greek word, ἔθος, *mos, consuetudo*, there translated *manner*, signifieth also *custom* and *wont*; and is so translated, Luke ii. 42, and xxii. 39. It was too usual with the Jews, time after time, to apostatise, and depart from the Lord; as Exod. xxxii. 1; Judges ii. 12; 1 Kings xii. 30. So among Christians, Acts xx. 30. The ages after the apostles, and that from time to time, even to these our days, give too evident proof hereof. Are not all the churches planted by the apostles departed from the Lord? Who were those stars whom the tail of the dragon drew from heaven, and threw to the earth? Rev. xii. 4. Were they not professors of the faith? How did this whole land revolt in Queen Mary's days? And it is like so to do again upon a like change.

Many make profession on by-respects, to serve the time, and to serve their own turns; so as their profession is not seasoned with sincerity and soundness, which are necessary to make a good foundation. Where they are wanting, no stability can be expected. Such a foundation is like the sand, whereupon, if an house be built, it cannot stand, Mat. vii. 26, 27.

By this we see that profession doth not simply argue a true insition into Christ. Indeed, we may judge of such as Christ did of him that discreetly answered him, to whom Christ thus replied, 'Thou art not far from the kingdom of God,' Mat. xii. 34; for 'charity believeth all things, and hopeth all things,' 1 Cor. xiii. 7, that is, the best of every one. Yet can we not absolutely conclude, simply from profession, that such an one is a member of Christ. If a professor revolt, we may say, as 1 John ii. 19.

This that hath been shewed of professors revolting giveth evidence of the necessity of men's trying and examining themselves, according to the apostle's earnest exhortation, 2 Cor. xiii. 5. Examination in this kind must be about the soundness of men's heart, and the right ends of their profession. Surely the disciples had well tried themselves in this case, who said to Christ, 'We believe, and are sure, that thou art that Christ,' John vi. 69, and thereupon professed that they would never depart from him. Of objections against this trial of a man's self, see *The Whole Armour of God*, treat. ii. part vi. on Eph. vi. 16; of Faith, secs. 36, 37, &c.

Sec. 132. *Of the persons and grace that cannot utterly be lost.*

For further clearing this point of departing from God, or falling from grace, it will be requisite distinctly to consider,

1. What persons may fall.
2. From what grace they may fall.
3. How far they may fall.

1. The persons about whom the question is, are professors of the true faith: saints by calling, or called to be saints, Rom. i. 7, 1 Cor. i. 2. These are of two sorts:

1. Chosen and called, Rev. xvii. 14. Their calling is an inward and effectual calling.

2. Called, but not chosen, Mat. xxii. 14. Thei calling is only external and formal.

These latter may fall from that which the former cannot fall from, and also fall much further. See Sec. 131, and Sec. 134.

2. The grace, from which men's falling in departing from God is questioned, is either remaining in God himself, or inherent in man. Election is an a of God residing in himself, and altogether dependin on his good pleasure. Justification also consists in God's accepting our persons, not imputing our sin unto us. But faith whereby we are justified, and the several fruits of sanctification, are inherent in man wrought in him by the Spirit of God. These graces inherent in man are of two sorts. They are either in truth, and in the judgment of certainty; or in appearance only, and in the judgment of charity.

3. Concerning the degree or measure of falling from grace, that may be either in truth, in whole, or for ever; or only in sense, in part, or for a time.

To apply these distinctions:

1. The elect being effectually called, cannot in truth totally and finally fall away. This proviso, *if it were possible*, Mat. xxiv. 24, being interposed in the case of falling away, and that in reference to the elect, sheweth,

that it is not possible that the elect should utterly be drawn from Christ.

2. No true sanctifying, saving grace can be totally lost. In this respect the beloved disciple saith, that, 'Whosoever is born of God, doth not commit sin; for his seed remaineth in him: and he cannot sin, because he is born of God,' 1 John iii. 9. They who are born of God are endued with true, saving, sanctifying grace. To commit sin is wholly to give himself over to sin; and so utterly to fall from grace. This the regenerate cannot do. This reason is there rendered, because 'the seed of God,' that is the Spirit of God, by virtue whereof we are, as it were, out of a certain seed, born again, and made new men, 'abideth in us.'

3. They who are effectually called, and endued with such grace, cannot finally fall away. For these are given to Christ, and for this end, that he should 'not lose them, but raise them up again at the last day,' John vi. 39. In this respect they are resembled to a 'tree planted by the rivers of water, that bringeth forth his fruit in his season, whose leaf also shall not wither,' Ps. i. 3; and to mount Zion, 'which cannot be removed, but abideth for ever, Ps. cxxv. 2; and to 'an house built upon a rock, which, though the rain descended, and the floods came, and the winds blew, and beat upon that house, yet it fell not,' Mat. vii. 24, 25.

How far hypocrites and reprobates may fall, see Chap. vi. 6, Sec. 37.

Sec. 134. *Of the grounds of saints' stability.*

The grounds whereupon the elect, effectually called, and endued with saving grace, are so established, as they can never totally fall, are these, and such like.

1. The stability of God's decree: 'Whom God did predestinate, them he also called; and whom he called, them he also justified; and whom he justified, them he also glorified,' Rom. viii. 30. So as God will bring his elect to glory. Therefore, they cannot finally fall. Election is that 'foundation of God which standeth sure, having this seal, The Lord knoweth them that are his,' 2 Tim. ii. 19. Therefore, the Lord will keep them safe.

2. The faithfulness of God's promises, 1 Cor. i. 8, 9, 1 Thes. v. 24. Now God hath made many promises for keeping his saints, so as utterly they shall never depart from him, as Isa. liv. 10, Jer. xxxii. 40, Mat. xvi. 18, John vi. 39.

3. God's constant care over them: 'Though they fall, they shall not be utterly cast down, for the Lord upholdeth them with his hand,' Ps. xxxvii. 24, 1 Cor. x. 13.

4. Their insition into Christ, and union with him, being members of his body, Eph. i. 22, 23, and v. 23, 1 Cor. xii. 12. If a member of Christ's body should be clean cut off, that body would be imperfect. See *Domest. Dut.* on Eph. v. 30, treat. i. secs. 71, 78.

5. Christ's continual and effectual intercession, Rom. viii. 34. A particular instance hereof we have in Peter's case, to whom Christ thus saith, 'I have prayed for thee, that thy faith fail not,' Luke xxii. 32. A more general instance we have in that effectual prayer which Christ made to his Father, a little before his departure out of the world, John xvii. 11, &c.

6. The abode of the Spirit in them. Concerning that Spirit, Christ thus saith, 'I will pray the Father, and he shall give you another Comforter, that he may abide with you for ever,' John xiv. 16. That Spirit is called, 'the anointing which abideth in saints,' 1 John ii. 27. And 'the Spirit that dwelleth in them,' Rom. viii. 11. See Chap. i. 14, Sec. 161.

These grounds, as they are evident proofs of the stability of saints, so they shew that this doctrine giveth no matter of boasting to man, but returneth all the glory to the blessed Trinity. See Chap. vi. 11, Sec. 75.

Sec. 135. *Of objections against the certainty of saints' perseverance.*

1. Some object against the immutability of election, as if the very elect might fall. Their objections are of four sorts.

Obj. 1. Christ threateneth to take away one's part out of the book of life.

Ans. In Scripture, a man is said to be written in the book of life, either in the judgment of certainty, as Rev. xxi. 27, or in the judgment of charity, and that by reason of their profession. To take away the part of such out of the book of life, is to manifest, that he never had any part therein.

Obj. 2. David maketh this imprecation, 'Let them be blotted out of the book of the living,' Ps. lxix. 28.

Ans. This imprecation was by divine inspiration made againt Judas, and others like him, whose names are said to be written in the book of life by reason of their profession, only in the judgment of charity.

Obj. 3. Christ promiseth not to blot out of the book of life the name of him that overcometh, Rev. iii. 5.

Ans. His name was indeed written in the book of life, and Christ here promiseth to manifest as much.

Obj. 4. Moses thus prayeth concerning himself, 'If thou wilt not forgive their sin, blot me out of thy book,' Exod. xxxii. 32.

Ans. That was a matter which, in a rapture of zeal for God's glory, and of love to his people, he could have wished.[1] It is not to be taken for a simple and absolute prayer. It was like Paul's wish, Rom. ix. 3. Where God saith to Moses, 'Whosoever hath sinned against me, him will I blot out of my book,' it is to be taken of God's manifesting him never to be written therein.

Obj. Others object sundry suppositions, as this,

[1] Votum affectûs non effectûs.

'When the righteous man turneth away from his righteousness, &c., he shall not live,' Ezek. xviii. 24.

Ans. 1. A supposition doth not infer a necessity or certainty of a thing, only it declareth a necessity of the consequence; as if we should say, When God fails of his promise, he is not faithful. See Sec. 60.

Ans. 2. By *righteous man* there may be meant one that is righteous only in profession, and in the judgment of charity.

Obj. Exhortations to hold out, admonitions to take heed of falling away, Heb. xii. 15, and threatenings against such as fall away, Heb. x. 38, are also objected.

Ans. These and such-like are used as means to make men look to their standing, and to make them watchful against falling away; but do not necessarily imply that they may fall, especially totally and finally.

Obj. Sundry instances of such as have fallen are alleged; as,

(1.) The angels that fell, and Adam.

Ans. These are nothing to the purpose; for the question is of believers in Christ, who are established by him. Angels and Adam stood by their own strength.

(2.) Saul, Judas, and such others as clean fell away. See Sec. 131.

Ans. These were hypocrites, and never had any true sanctifying grace. Such were they who are said to 'have no root in them,' Luke viii. 13, and the branch that is said to be 'taken from the vine,' John xv. 2, and they whose love is said to wax cold, Mat. xxiv. 12, and they who are said to be 'fallen from grace,' Gal. v. 4, and to have 'made shipwreck of faith,' 1 Tim. i. 19, and to 'depart from the faith,' 1 Tim. iv. 1, and to 'err from the faith,' 1 Tim. vi. 14, and to 'turn like a dog to his vomit, and like a swine that was washed to her wallowing in the mire,' 2 Pet. ii. 22, and to 'fall away,' Heb. vi. 6, and to 'sin wilfully after they have received the knowledge of the truth,' Heb. x. 26. None of these, nor any like to them, had true saving grace in them. Of them all it may be said, 'If they had been of us, they would no doubt have continued with us,' 1 John ii. 19.

(3.) Paul,[1] Peter, and such others as were elect, and effectually called.

Ans. Though these fell into very great sins, yet they did not sin in such a manner as to be accounted totally to depart from God, or to lose all grace. The arguments alleged in the former section do prove as much. How far such may fall shall be shewed in the next section.

Sec. 136. *Of the degrees of the falls of such as are effectually called.*

They who are effectually called, through security, pride, inward and outward temptations, may so far fall as to lose,

[1] Qu. 'David'?—ED.

1. All that joy and comfort wherewith they were before upheld.

2. All assurance and sense of the Spirit's abode in them, so as they may, in their opinion, think him clean departed.

3. The fruits of the Spirit, and the power and efficacy of his grace, so as they shall find no growth of grace, but rather a decay in faith, love, zeal, gift of prayer, and other like fruits. They shall be as trees in winter; they shall wax cold and remiss in the duties that formerly they performed.

4. They may be given over to their own lusts, and to such gross and grievous sins as natural men would be ashamed of.

5. They may have a troubled tormenting conscience, and thereby be put, as it were, upon a rack, so as that which brought them much quiet and peace before will be a terror and torture unto them; yea, they may be brought to the very pit of despair.

6. They may be brought not only inwardly, but also outwardly, to feel the shame and smart of their foul fall, and to have sore judgments executed on themselves, children, and others belonging unto them.

7. They may be long under the inward and outward effects of their folly, and not easily recover themselves, but sigh, groan, weep, cry, roar, before they receive sound comfort.

8. They may utterly lose the measure and degree of that grace they had before, at least of their former joy and comfort, and carry the grief of their fall even to their grave.

Most of these, if not all of them, may be exemplified in David, and that out of Psalm li.; for it is manifest that he lost,

(1.) The joy and comfort that formerly he had, in that he thus prayeth, 'Restore unto me the joy of thy salvation,' ver. 12.

(2.) The sense that he had of God's presence with him, and of the abode of the Spirit in him, which made him thus to pray, 'Cast me not away from thy presence, and take not thy Holy Spirit from me,' ver. 11.

(3.) The power and efficacy of God's grace; manifested in this clause, 'Uphold me with thy free Spirit,' ver. 12, which is as if he had said, I feel myself very weak, and unable to perform any good duty; my former strength is wasted; uphold, strengthen, enable me again by thy Spirit to perform the duties which thou requirest.

(4.) That he was given over to his own lusts, and to other temptations, is evident by his adultery, by seeking to make Uriah drunk, by contriving his death, with the destruction of many other of his soldiers. As the title of the psalm, so this part of his prayer, 'Deliver me from blood-guiltiness,' is a sufficient proof, besides the express history of all these, 2 Sam. xi. 4, &c.

(5.) That he had much trouble of conscience, is

evident by these phrases, 'My bones waxed old through my roaring all the day long: for day and night thy hand was heavy on me,' &c., Ps. xxxii. 3, 4.

(6.) The outward judgments that were executed on him are evident in the history recorded after his fall. Heavy judgments were denounced against him, 2 Sam. xii. 10, &c., and answerably were they executed.

(7.) With how much ado he recovered himself, is evident by his many grievous complaints, such as these, 'Have mercy upon me, O Lord, for I am in trouble: mine eye is consumed with grief, yea, my soul and my belly,' &c., Ps. xxxi. 9, 10.

(8.) Whether he ever recovered his former joy and comfort again is uncertain. Surely Samson, Solomon, Asa, and others did not.

Sec. 137. *Of the occasions and consequences of saints' folly.*

The foresaid degrees of the fall of such as are effectually called and regenerate, do happen partly by reason of outward temptations (as Lot was tempted by his daughters, Gen. xix. 31, &c., and Peter by those that saw him at the high priest's hall, Mat. xxvi. 69), and partly by those inward corruptions that remain in them; for though they be truly regenerate, yet they are but in part regenerate. The flesh remaineth in the best so long as they remain in this flesh, Rom. vii. 18, &c.

Particular corruptions which occasion saints' falls are these:

1. High-mindedness. Thus much the apostle implies by this admonition, 'Be not high-minded, but fear,' Rom. xi. 20.

2. Self-conceitedness. This was it that made Laodicea lukewarm; she thought she had need of nothing, Rev. iii. 16, 17.

3. Overmuch confidence. This was the occasion of Peter's fall, Mat. xxvi. 33.

4. Too much boldness. Solomon was too bold in suffering his wives to worship each of them their own gods; thereupon he himself went after other gods, 1 Kings xi. 5, &c.

5. Too great security. David was overtaken hereby, 2 Sam. xi. 2.

6. Too little fear and jealousy over one's self. By this means was Lot seduced, Gen. xix. 33.

In that true saints have such occasions of falling so far and so foully as the foresaid instances do demonstrate, the apostle's *caveat* of taking heed is duly to be observed by the best of us, the rather because of the evil consequences that follow upon saints' falls. For,

1. God is exceedingly dishonoured thereby.
2. The holy profession is disgraced.
3. The church and communion of saints is scandalised.
4. The gospel is blasphemed,
5. The weak are made to stumble, Gal. ii. 13.

6. Enemies take occasion of insulting, Lam. i. 7–9.

Sec. 138. *Of Christ the living God.*

The apostle, to add the more force to his admonition, setteth out him from whom such as fall away depart, in these words, Θεοῦ ζῶντος, *the living God*, whereby he declares his divine nature, *God*, and his excellent property, *living*,

Under this description, Christ is comprised. For the apostle's main scope is to stir up the Hebrews to keep close to Christ, whom they had professed. He gave to Christ this title, *God*, before, ver. 4. Sec. 49. That Christ is true God, is proved, Chap. i. 8. Sec. 107. In what respect Christ is God our Lord, and what duties thereupon are expected of us, in reference to Christ, hath been declared, Chap. i. 10. Sec. 128.

This epithet *living*, applied to God, the living God, is used two ways:

1. Essentially; as God, he is the living God, Ps. lxxxiv. 2, 1 Thess. i. 9.

2. Personally, and distinctly to each person; to the Father, Mat. xvi. 16; to the Son, 1 Tim. iv. 10; and to the Holy Ghost, 2 Cor. vi. 16. Here it is personally used, and that in reference to the Son.

The Son is the living God two ways:

1. Originally; in which respect it is said, 'In him was life,' John i. 4; and again, 'As the Father hath life in himself, so hath he given to the Son to have life in himself,' John v. 26.

2. Operatively; in this respect it is said, that 'the dead shall hear the voice of the Son of God; and they that hear shall live,' John v. 25; and Christ thus saith of himself, 'I am the resurrection and the life: he that believeth in me, though he were dead, yet shall he live,' John xi. 25. Thus is he called 'the prince of life,' Acts iii. 15, and life itself, John xiv. 6. It is Christ that gives life to all. He gives the natural life, John i. 4, and spiritual life, Gal. ii. 20, and eternal life, 1 John v. 20. In this respect Christ is the fountain of life, an open fountain, an over-flowing, ever-flowing fountain.

Indeed, God as God is a fountain of life, and a full fountain; but so deep, as all the means in the world out of Christ cannot draw out water of life from thence. I may, in this respect, say hereof, as the woman of Samaria said of Jacob's well, 'Thou hast nothing to draw with, and the well is deep,' John iv. 11. Yea, it is a closed well, and herein like to Laban's well, a great stone is upon the well's mouth, Gen. xxix. 2. All the men in the world are not able to roll away that stone. But Christ, God-man, is that true Israel who is able to roll away the stone, to open the well, and to draw water out of it. He is 'a fountain opened to the house of David,' that is, to the church of God, Zech. xiii. 1.

Herein is our God, the Lord Jesus Christ, distinguished from all the gods of the Gentiles, who are not living gods, Ps. cxv. 5, &c., and from angels and saints, whom papists trust unto, and yet they can give no life; yea, and from all creatures whatsoever, for none of them have life in themselves, nor can give life to others.

Sec. 139. *Of duties due to Christ as he is the living God.*

Sundry duties are to be performed unto Christ in this respect, that he is the living God.
1. Acknowledge him to be the true God, Joshua iii. 10, Jer. x. 10.
2. Be zealous of his honour, 1 Sam. xvii. 26, 2 Kings xix. 4, 16.
3. Fear him that hath the absolute power of life, Luke xii. 5, Heb. x. 31.
4. Tremble before him, Dan. vi. 26, Deut. v. 26.
5. Adore him, Rom. xiv. 11.
6. Serve him, 1 Thes. i. 9, Heb. ix. 14.
7. Turn to him, Acts xiv. 15.
8. Long after him, Ps. xlii. 2, and lxxxiv. 2.
9. Hold close to him, John vi. 68, 69.
10. Seek life of him, John vi. 33, and v. 40.
11. Trust in him, 1 Tim. iv. 10, and vi. 17.
12. Account it a great privilege to be his son, Hosea i. 10, Rom. ix. 26, Heb. xii. 22.
13. Pervert not his word, Jer. xxiii. 36.
14. Never depart from him, Heb. iii. 12.

Sec. 140. *Of the resolution of Heb. iii. 12.*

Ver. 12. *Take heed, brethren, lest there be in any of you an evil heart of unbelief, in departing from the living God.*

The sum of this verse is, a *caveat* against apostasy. Hereof are two parts,
1. An expression of the *caveat*.
2. A description of apostasy.

In the expression of the *caveat*, observe,
1. A mild insinuation, in this word *brethren*.
2. A prudent admonition: whereof are four branches.
1. The kind of admonition, by a caveat, *take heed*.
2. The end of the admonition, to prevent an evil, *lest*.
3. The extent, to ourselves and others, *any of you*.
4. The continuance therein, *at any time*.

In the description of apostasy two points are noted:
1. The ground of it, whence it ariseth.
2. The nature of it, wherein it consisteth.
The ground is,
1. Generally propounded.
2. Particularly exemplified.
The general is set out,
1. By the subject, *an heart*.
2. By the quality of it, *evil*.
The nature of it is set out,
1. By the proper act, to *depart*.
2. By the subject from which they depart. Here is expressed,
1. The person, *God*.
2. His property, *living*.

Sec. 141. *Of observations arising out of Heb. iii. 12.*

I. *Admonitions are needful for Christians.* This phrase, *take heed*, is an admonition. See Sec. 122.
II. *Admonitions must be seasoned with mild insinuations.* Such an one is this title *brethren*. See Sec. 121.
III. *Every one must be circumspect over himself.* This relative *you* hath reference to one's self. See Sec. 123.
IV. *Our circumspection must extend to others.* This word *any* hath reference to others. See Sec. 124.
V. *Our circumspection must be perpetual.* This phrase, *at any time*, intends a perpetuity. See Sec. 125.
VI. *Means must be used to prevent sin.* This particle *lest*, is a note of prevention. See Sec. 125.
VII. *The heart must especially be looked unto.* This is the end why mention is here made of the heart. See Sec. 126.
VIII. *There is an evil heart.* The epithet *evil*, here annexed to the heart, demonstrates thus much. See Sec. 127.
IX. *Unbelief is the cause of an evil heart.* This phrase, 'an evil heart of unbelief,' intends as much. See Sec. 128.
X. *Unbelief is the cause of apostasy.* So it is here made to be. See Sec. 129.
XI. *Professors of the gospel may fall away.* This admonition to such implies so much. See Sec. 131.
XII. *Christ is true God.* He is here so called. See Sec. 138.
XIII. *The true God is the living God.* He is here so styled. See Sec. 128.

Sec. 142. *Of adding directions to admonitions and exhortations.*

Ver. 13. *But exhort one another daily, while it is called To-day, lest any of you be hardened through the deceitfulness of sin.*

Here begins the apostle's direction for preventing apostasy. See Sec. 121.

In it is prescribed a sovereign remedy to make it the more useful, ver. 13, with a strong reason added thereto, ver. 14.

The remedy prescribed is a continual, mutual exhortation of one another.

The first particle, ἀλλὰ, *but*, being a conjunction of opposition to an odious vice, implieth, that by the means here prescribed, the vice whereof they were before forewarned, may be avoided. To this purpose is this particle of opposition frequently used in Solomon's Proverbs. So Rom. xiii. 14, 1 Peter i. 14, 15. But most pertinent to the point in hand is a like direction of this apostle, thus set down, 'Not forsaking the assembling of yourselves together, but exhorting one another,' Heb. x. 25.

By this it is manifest that it is behoveful to add directions for avoiding such sins as we dissuade men from. Christ, the best of teachers, taught much after this manner: as 'Lay not up for yourselves treasures upon earth: but lay up for yourselves treasures in heaven,' Mat. vi. 19, 20; so John vi. 27, Mat. x. 28. See Chap. vi. 3, Sec. 26.

By this means prohibitions, admonitions, reprehensions, and other like endeavours to keep from sin, are more useful and effectual. So also are exhortations and incitations to duty. Many that see an equity of forbearing that which is forbidden, and doing that which is required, fail of putting the one and the other in execution, for want of directions to do the same.

Commendable, therefore, is that course which many prudent teachers do use, to add to other uses of their doctrines, rules and means for the avoiding that which their doctrine disproves, and performing that which their doctrines require.

Sec. 143. *Of the benefit of exhortation.*

The Greek word παρακαλεῖτε, translated *exhort*, is a compound. The simple verb καλεῖν, *vocare*, signifieth to *call*. It is used in this verse and phrase, καλεῖται, 'called to-day:' thereupon this compound signifieth to *call for*, Acts xxviii. 20, παρεκάλεσα. We use to call for those to whom we intend some good, either by direction, admonition, exhortation, or consolation. In this respect it signifieth also to *beseech*, Rom. xv. 30; and to *comfort*, 2 Cor. vii. 6. Most frequently it is translated, as here, to *exhort*.

To exhort one to a duty, is to call upon him, and to stir him up to do it. In reference to spiritual duties, we are very dull and heavy, and need exhortation and incitation. Witness the disciples both at Christ's transfiguration, and also at his passion. One would have thought that the glory of the one, and their compassion at the other, might have so roused up their spirits, as to have kept them waking; but neither the one nor the other did it. At both times Christ withdrew himself with them to pray (this is a spiritual and heavenly duty), yet at both times they were heavy with sleep, Luke ix. 28, 32, and xxii. 45. These were men regenerate, endued with true sanctifying grace; and that so far as the spirit of them was willing; but Christ renders the reason of their heaviness and drowsiness, 'The flesh is weak,' Mat. xxvi. 41. Now the flesh is in the best. The best therefore have need to be exhorted.

Yea, further, exhortations are needful for those that are ready and forward, to put them on the more. As in striving for the mastery, they who are forward to put out their best ability for the prize, by acclamations and shoutings, are the more put on; so Christians, in their Christian course, by exhortations. Exhortation, therefore, is needful for all, and useful to all.

Sec. 144. *Of private inciting one another.*

This phrase, *one another*, is the interpretation of one Greek word, ἑαυτούς, which properly signifieth *yourselves*; and so for the most part is translated, as where it is said, 'ye justify yourselves,' Luke xvi. 15; and 'yield yourselves,' Rom. vi. 13; and 'examine yourselves,' 2 Cor. xiii. 5.

Here, indeed, it is fitly translated *one another*; for it is improper to say, 'Exhort yourselves.' But here he speaks to a multitude who are one body, 1 Cor. xii. 12, one house, ver. 6, yet many members of that body and house. In reference to the multitude of members, he saith, 'Exhort one another;' yet because they are all of one body and one house, he expresseth his mind under a word that signifieth themselves. By reason of this union, the word ἀλλήλους, that properly signifieth *one another*, is translated *yourselves*, 1 Thes. v. 11. What is said to be done to them as members, is done one to another; and what is done to them, as united in a body, is said to be done to themselves.

Two points may here be observed:

1. That in exhortations and incitations to others, we do the like ourselves.

2. That we endeavour to bring others to such common duties as we judge to be useful for ourselves.

Of both these, see *The Saints' Sacrifice*, on Ps. xvi. 19, sec. 120, 121.

This mutual admonishing one another is especially meant of private Christians, and their seeking to edify one another. This is exemplified in sundry particulars: as to 'care one for another,' 1 Cor. xii. 25; 'to pray one for another,' James v. 16; 'to love one another,' John xiii. 34; 'to admonish one another,' Rom. xv. 14; 'to comfort one another,' 1 Thes. iv. 18; 'to edify one another,' 1 Thes. v. 11; 'to be kind one to another,' Eph. iv. 32; 'to have compassion one of another,' 1 Peter iii. 8; to 'have peace one with another,' Mark ix. 50.

By private, mutual exhortations, and performing other like duties one to another, private Christians come to be as ministers of God, yea, as gods one to another. For God is good, and doth good, Ps. cxix. 68. Thus shall Christians shew that goodness is in them, by these fruits of goodness that proceed from them.

By mutual exhortations, and other like duties, private Christians shall much help on the public ministry of the word. In that by this means Christians are better fitted to profit by the public ministry.

This is the rather to be done by private Christians, because they have frequent opportunites of doing it.

Sec. 145. *Of edifying others daily.*

The foresaid duty of mutual exhortation is to be performed daily, or every day, as the Greek phrase soundeth, καθ' ἑκάστην ἡμέραν. The very same words of that Greek phrase are not elsewhere in the New Testament used; but like phrases, as καθ' ἡμέραν, Acts ii. 46, 47; τὸ καθ' ἡμέραν, Luke xi. 3; and some, as emphatical as the phrase in this verse, namely, πασαν τε ἡμέραν, Acts v. 42, and κατα πᾶσαν ἡμέραν, xvii. 17. These are all translated *daily*, which here implieth a constant performing of a duty; that we think it not enough that we have sometimes performed it, but we must still be doing it day after day. We may not be 'weary in well-doing,' 2 Thes. iii. 13; but, as we have any opportunity, still be doing more and more good in this kind, Gal. vi. 9, 10.

Exhortations, admonitions, and other like means of edification, are spiritual food, whereby the soul is nourished unto spiritual and eternal life. Wherefore, as bodily food is daily ministered (in which respect it is called 'daily bread,' Luke xi. 3), so ought the spiritual food to be daily given: thus more fruit and comfort may be thence expected.

Of continually doing good, see Sec. 125.

Sec. 146. *Of taking the opportunity of edifying others.*

This phrase, *while it is called To-day*, seems to imply a restraint; for the Greek words, ἄχρις οὗ, *donec, usque, quo, quoad*, translated *while*, do signify a limitation, and are ordinarily translated *till*, as Acts vii. 18, 1 Cor. xi. 26 and xv. 25, Rev. ii. 25; or *until*, as Gal. iv. 19; but here it is such a restraint as intendeth a very large extent.

The day is properly that time wherein light appeareth. Thus it is opposed to the night, which is a time of darkness; see Sec. 91. In the day time, while it is light, men use to work and travel, Ps. civ. 23, which they cannot so well do in the night. Hereunto Christ alludes, saying, 'I must work while it is day: the night cometh when no man can work,' John ix. 4.

To day (τὸ σήμερον¹) is indefinitely put for the time wherein a thing may be done.

The apostle's meaning is, that they should exhort one another while there is time and opportunity to do that duty. Thus this phrase may be taken three ways:

1. In reference to the means which God affordeth for working grace in men. In this respect *to-day* is put for that time which is called 'the day of salvation,' 'the accepted time,' 2 Cor. vi. 2.

2. In reference to particular men's lives; and that,

(1.) To the life of him that exhorteth; in which sense an apostle saith, 'I think it meet, as long as I am in this tabernacle, to stir you up,' 2 Peter i. 13.

(2.) To the life of him to whom the exhortation is given; for while a man lives, there may be hope of doing him good in the judgment of charity.

3. In reference to the church, which shall continue so long as this world lasteth. Thus *to-day* may extend to the end of the world; for so long as there are professors of the faith on earth, they ought to exhort one another. An apostle hath care of those that should survive after his decease, 2 Peter i. 15.

In the first reference, which is to the means of grace,

¹ See Sec. 76, and Chap. iv. 7, Sec. 43.

this limitation, 'while it is called To-day,' is used as a motive to stir them up to perform this duty of mutual exhortation, in that there is a special time, called *to-day*, wherein we may do good thereby; which time will not always last, for it hath a date and period. Therefore he addeth this verb, καλεῖται, *called*, which implieth a manifestation of a thing, as Luke i. 35, so as we ought to take that season which God is pleased to offer unto us of doing what good we can for the mutual establishing of one another.

It was before shewed that opportunity must be taken for our own spiritual good (Sec. 76); here the apostle adviseth to take the season of doing good to others.

This phrase, 'the fields are white already to harvest,' John iv. 35, implieth a season and opportunity of reaping. And it is used by Christ to shew the reason why he then would not suffer himself to be hindered from preaching the gospel, no, not by taking his ordinary food. He layeth a necessity upon taking the season of doing good: 'I must work,' saith he, 'while it is day,' John ix. 4.

A forcible reason hereof is rendered in these words, 'the night cometh, when no man can work.' When the season is gone, all hope of doing good is taken away. Christ hereupon wisheth that Jerusalem had in her day known the things which belonged to her peace; but, saith he unto her, 'now they are hid from thine eyes,' Luke xix. 42. Experience verifies that which the wise man hath thus testified, 'There is no work, nor device, nor knowledge, nor wisdom in the grave,' Eccles. ix. 10. So there may be while we live a time wherein no means will do any good, namely, when the 'candlestick shall be removed out of his place,' Rev. ii. 5; and the kingdom of God shall be taken away, Mat. xxi. 43; then, though men cry, they shall not be heard, Prov. i. 28.

This nearly concerns us, for yet it may be said, 'Behold, now is the accepted time; behold, now is the day of salvation,' 2 Cor. vi. 2. Now, therefore, ministers, magistrates, parents, other governors, yea, and private friends, must be all careful to put the apostle's advice in practice 'while it is called to-day.'

Sec. 147. *Of the damage of neglecting means for softening the heart.*

To enforce the foresaid duty of mutual exhorting one another, and that from time to time, so long as the season continueth, the apostle declareth the danger of neglecting the same, in these words, 'lest any of you be hardened.' He had before shewed, ver. 8, the great damage of hardness of heart, he doth therefore here inculcate that damage, to make them the more watchful against it.

The manner of bringing in this damage is by way of caution and prevention, in this particle *lest*. In the Greek it is thus, ἵνα μή, *that not*; as if he had said, that not any of you, or that none of you, be hardened. Hereby it appeareth, that where means of softening are omitted or neglected, the heart will be hardened. As the heart of man is of its own nature hard, so after it is by public or private means softened, f those means be not still used, the heart will fall to its native hardness. As wax, and clay, and other like things, which are naturally hard, will upon withholding means of softening, after they have been once softened, fall to their native hardness, so the heart of man. Or as water, though it be made scalding hot, if fire be taken from it, will soon wax cold of itself; and as all manner of heavy things, being by some means or other drawn upwards, will of themselves fall down again if those means be taken away; so the heart, there is a natural proneness and inclination in it to hardness.

The indefinite expression, 'lest any of you,' τίς ἐξ ὑμῶν, implieth that all of all sorts, even the best, were subject to this decay and to this hardening of their heart. In this respect they ought all of them to be careful in practising the fore-mentioned duty mutually one to another among all sorts of them. See verse 12, Sec. 123.

Of hardness of heart, and of the great damage thereof, see Sec. 80, &c.

Sec. 148. *Of the deceitfulness of sin.*

The apostle doth further declare the ground of that proneness to wax hard in this phrase, ' through the deceitfulness,' ἀπάτῃ, or ' with the deceitfulness of sin.' So as it is by the manifold deceits of sin that it prevails so much as it doth upon men. The particular deceits hereafter specified give evident proof hereunto.

By sin is here in special meant the corruption of nature, that corruption in which all are conceived and born, which they carry about them so long as they retain their mortal body. It is that which in Scripture is called the *flesh,* opposed to the *spirit.* It continually lusts against the spirit, Gal. v. 17, and is ever soliciting a man to evil, and hindering him in every good thing that he enterpriseth, Rom. vii. 18, &c. It containeth in it all manner of evil lusts, Eph. iv. 22, which are called τας ἐπιθυμίας τῆς ἀπατης, ' lusts of deceitfulness,' or ' deceitful lusts,' because a man is exceedingly deceived therewith. By reason hereof, deceitfulness is attributed to riches, ἀπατη τοῦ πλούτου, Mat. xiii. 22. For this inbred corruption maketh men so to doat on riches, as they prefer them before true godliness and heavenly happiness.

Though in some special respects the inward corruption may justly be styled deceitful, yet is not this evil quality to be restrained only to it. As the dam or mother is, so are her imps and brats. Both innate corruption, and also outward sins sprouting from thence, are all deceitful. The apostle attributeth this very epithet, *deceiveableness,* to unrighteousness, ἀπάτη της ἀδικίας, 2 Thes. ii. 10. He also calls philosophy, that is, men's conceits, grounded upon their own corrupt reason and sense, 'vain deceit,' κένη ἀπάτη, Col. ii. 8. And another apostle calls the lascivious practices and unseemly carriages of some formal professors ἀπάταις ἀυτῶν, ' their own deceivings,' wherein they sported themselves, 2 Peter ii. 13.

In all these places the word of the text is used, even six times, whereof some speak of our natural corruption, others of the fruits thereof. In this text, sin may indefinitely be taken for any kind of sin, inward or outward, for every sin is deceitful.

The verb ἁμαρτάνειν, from whence the Greek noun translated *sin* is derived, hath a notation from an Hebrew root, המרה, *amarum reddidit, exacerbavit, provocavit,* Ps. lxxviii. 17, that signifieth to embitter and provoke; for every sin exasperates and provokes God. See Secs. 90, 103. In that respect it hath many deceitful devices.

All the devices of sin are as fair baits whereby dangerous hooks are covered over to entice silly fish to snap at them, so as they are taken and made a prey to the fisher.

There is a Greek word, δελεάζειν, *inescare,* thrice used in the New Testament, which is taken from that practice of a fisher.

Our English translate it *enticed,* δελεαζόμενος, James i. 14; *beguiling,* δελεάζοντες, 2 Peter ii. 14; *allure,* δελεάζουσι, ver. 18. The primitive root δόλος, *dolus,* from whence the Greek word is derived, signifieth deceit. Thence a noun δέλεαρ, *quasi* δόλεαρ, *esca qua animalia capiuntur,* which signifieth meat, or a bait, whereby fish, fowl, or other living creatures are taken; and the foresaid verb, δελεάζω, which signifieth to lay a bait, or to catch with a bait, and, metaphorically, to entice, allure, and beguile.

This deceitfulness of sin is a strong inducement to make us watchful against it, and that the rather because of our foolish disposition and proneness of nature to snap at every bait, and to yield to every temptation. Hereof see Sec. 122.

No man is willing to be beguiled. Though most men love to be flattered, and delight therein, yet when they discern that their flatterers mock them, they are offended.

That we may the better discern the mockings and cozenages of sin, I will set some of them before you.

The deceits which sin useth are such as these:

1. Sin presents itself in another dress than its own.
2. It pretends fair advantages.
3. It insensibly soaketh into men's hearts.
4. It so bewitcheth those that give entertainment to it as it cannot be cast off.

Of these four particulars, see Sec. 122.

5. It accommodates itself to particular men's humours, as Zedekiah and the four hundred false prophets, observing that Ahab was set to go against Ramoth-Gilead, answerably ordered their prophecies, even so as best befitted his humour, 1 Kings xxii. 6. Thus lust

sets upon the phlegmatic humour, pride on the sanguine, anger on the choleric, revenge on the melancholy, passion of the female sex, lasciviousness, on youth, stoutness on the strong man, covetousness on the old man, so the like on others.

6. When once it begins to tempt a man, it will hardly cease till it hath prevailed against him. Though the Spirit resist it, yet will it continue to resist the Spirit, Rom. vii. 21, 23. 'When lust hath conceived, it bringeth forth sin; and sin, when it is finished, bringeth forth death,' James i. 15.

7. It works itself into a man by degrees. At first it saith, as Lot did of Zoar, Gen. xix. 20, 'Is it not a little one?' But that little one is like a 'little leaven' which 'leaveneth the whole lump,' 1 Cor. v. 6. At first it saith, Taste a little; upon that taste followeth a liking, then a desire, which moves him to commend it, and to accustom himself thereunto. 'Evil communications corrupt good manners,' 1 Cor. xv. 33. From words they proceed to deeds.

8. It suggests good effects and events to follow upon yielding to it, abusing that general principle of the apostle, 'All things work together for good,' Rom. viii. 28. Though God, through his unsearchable wisdom and almighty power, may bring good out of evil, yet is not sin the true and proper cause of good. To like purpose doth it pervert this apostolical cordial, 'Where sin abounded, grace did much more abound,' Rom. v. 20.

9. It much presseth the common practice of most men, charging such as yield not with singularity, and thereby deceives many.

10. It insisteth much upon moderation, and allegeth that a man may be 'righteous overmuch,' and to cast himself into many unnecessary dangers, Eccles. vii. 16.

11. It much inculcateth the power of repentance, that, supposing the worst that can be said of such and such a sin, it may be redressed by repentance, pressing Nathan's answer to David, 2 Sam. xii. 13; and the effect that followed upon that repentance of Manasseh, 2 Chron. xxxiii. 13; of Peter, Mat. xxvi. 75, and many others.

To conclude, herein appears the deceitfulness of sin, that there is scarce any sin committed for which he that committeth it hath not some defence to patronise it. As all manner of heretics and idolaters, so impious, profane, rebellious, unmerciful, intemperate, riotous, seditious, ambitious, and injurious persons have their apologies.

Sec. 149. *Of remedies against the deceitfulness of sin.*

Many of the means prescribed for perseverance, Sec. 70, may be applied against the deceitfulness of sin. But besides them, it is meet to set down other particulars parallel to the particular deceits of sin, which are such as follow. For this end pray, as Eph. i. 17, and Philip. i. 9, 10.

1. Thoroughly try matters, as it is said of the angel of the church of Ephesus, 'Thou hast tried them which say they are apostles, and are not, and hast found them liars,' Rev. ii. 2. By a due and thorough trial, false shows and pretences will be discovered.

2. Prize the uncertain advantages which sin maketh show of, with the certain damages that will follow upon yielding to sin. Thus will the fair proffers of sin be rejected. Moses 'esteemed the reproach of Christ greater riches than the treasure of Egypt; for he had respect unto the recompence of reward,' Heb. xi. 26. 'What is a man profited if he shall gain the whole world, and lose his own soul?' Mat. xviii. 26.

3. Be always watchful, so sin cannot seize upon thee unawares. This rule is for this end prescribed, 1 Thes. v. 3, 6.

4. Give no entertainment to sin at all, lest it so bewitch thee as thou canst not cast it off. Do as Joseph did in this kind, Gen. xxxix. 8, &c.

5. Seek not to satisfy thine humour. There is great danger therein. Thereby may we soon fall into great distempers. Solomon, to this purpose, gives this advice, 'Put a knife to thy throat, if thou be a man given to appetite,' Prov. xxiii. 2. And Christ thus, 'Take heed to yourselves, lest at any time your hearts be overcharged with surfeiting,' &c., Luke xxi. 34.

6. After some repulses prepare for more assaults. Satan three several times tempted Christ, and that three several ways: and when he departed from him it was but for a season, Luke iv. 13.

7. Avoid the least degree of sin; for sin is of a growing nature. Stinking weeds grow faster than sweet flowers. Men use to clip a proverb, in saying, 'A little hurts not.' The full proverb is this: '*Modicum non nocet, si non sumatur,*' 'A little hurts not, if it be not taken,' If the devil get in a claw, he will soon make way for his whole paw, yea, for head, body and all.

8. Judge not matters by events. Good things may have bad events; and evil things may have good events. It is not of the nature of evil that good followeth thereupon, but the almighty, over-ruling providence of God. A skilful apothecary can so temper poison with other ingredients, as to make a cordial thereof. Will it thereupon be safe for any man to drink poison?

9. 'Follow not a multitude to do evil,' Exod. xxiii. 2. Multitude is so far from justifying or extenuating sin, as it aggravateth the same; as many faggots make the fire to be the greater. A prophet hereby aggravateth the cause of Israel's captivity, that 'all Israel transgressed,' Dan. ix. 11. And herein the sin of the Sodomites is aggravated, that 'both old and young, even all the people from every quarter,' conspired therein, Gen. xix. 4.

10. Be well instructed in those things which concern God and his glory, and in the things that are

truly righteous, that in them thou mayest manifest thy holy zeal, and not be cooled with a pretence of undue moderation. In those things fear not the blame of being 'righteous overmuch.' A man may indeed be righteous overmuch in matters that have no warrant from God's word; but are either frothy apprehensions of his own brain, or vain inventions of other men. In that which is truly and properly righteous, one cannot be 'righteous overmuch.'

11. Take heed of yielding to sin upon presuming to repent. Repentance is not in thine own power: it is a special gift of God, Acts xi. 18, 2 Tim. ii. 25. It is not therefore safe in provoking God to presume of that which he only can give.

12. Be well instructed and exercised in God's word. By this thou mayest be made perfect, and thoroughly furnished to answer all vain apologies for sin. By the law of God David was made 'wiser than his enemies,' Ps. cxix. 98.

Sec. 150. *Of the resolutions and observations of* Heb. iii. 13.

Ver. 13. *But exhort one another daily, while it is called To-day, lest any of you be hardened through the deceitfulness of sin.*

The sum of this verse is, a direction to keep ourselves and others from backsliding.

Herein we may distinguish the inference and the substance.

The inference is in this causal particle γὰρ, *for.*

The substance lays down,
1. A duty.
2. The danger of neglecting that duty.

In the duty is laid forth,
1. The act to be performed, παρακαλεῖτε, *exhort.*
2. The persons, both agent and patient, ἑαυτούς, *one another.*
3. The time.

This is set out two ways:
1. By the extent, καθ' ἑκάστην ἡμέραν, *daily.*
2. By the restraint, ἄχρις οὗ τὸ σήμερον καλεῖται, *while it is called To-day.*

About the danger, observe,
1. The manner of expressing it, by caution, *lest.*
2. The matter whereof it consisteth.

Herein we may observe,
1. The kind of danger, hardness, σκληρυνθῇ, *be hardened.*
2. The persons that may fall into it, τις ἐξ ὑμῶν, *any of you.*
3. The cause of falling into it.

This is,
1. Generally set down to be ἁμαρτία, *sin.*
2. Particularly exemplified by this epithet, ἀπάτη, *deceitfulness.*

Observations.

I. *Directions must be added to dissuasions.* This I gather from the inference. In the former verse was a dissuasion; in this verse is added a direction. See Sec. 142.

II. *Christians have need to be incited to duty.* Why else should this duty of mutual exhortation be so pressed, as it is here? See Sec. 143.

III. *Christians must quicken themselves in quickening others.*

IV. *Christians must stir up others to that which they see meet for themselves.* These two arise out of this word *one another.* See Sec. 144.

V. *Private mutual incitations are special means of stability.* This word *one another*, intends private as well as public persons. And that which is required is for the establishing of one another. See Sec. 145.

VI. *Mutual duties must continually be performed.* So much is intended under this word *daily.* See Sec. 145.

VII. *There is a season of doing good.* This word *to-day* implieth a season. See Sec. 146.

VIII. *The opportunity of doing good must be taken.* This phrase, *while it is called To-day*, sets out the opportunity when the duty is to be done. See Sec. 146.

IX. *There is danger in omitting this season.* This particle *lest* intendeth a danger. See Sec. 147.

X. *Danger must be prevented in all sorts.* This phrase, *lest any of you*, is indefinite, and compriseth all of all sorts under it. See Sec. 147.

XI. *Man's heart neglected will soon wax cold.* This is the danger intended under this word *lest*, and expressed in this word *hardened.* See Sec. 147.

XII. *Sin causeth hardness of heart.* Thus much is here expressed. See Sec. 148.

XIII. *Sin is deceitful.* This epithet added to sin shews it to be so. See Sec. 148.

XIV. *Sin prevails the more by the deceivableness thereof.* This phrase, *through the deceitfulness of sin*, gives proof hereof. See Sec. 148.

Sec. 151. *Of being made partakers of Christ.*

Ver. 14. *For we are made partakers of Christ, if we hold the beginning of our confidence stedfast unto the end.*

This verse hath reference to the two former verses, and is added as a motive to enforce both the dissuasion from apostasy, ver. 12, and also the direction for preventing hardness of heart.

The first particle γὰρ, *for*, shews that it is inferred as a reason.

The force of the motive lieth in that privilege that belongeth to those that embrace the gospel. The privilege is, that they are made partakers of Christ.

The argument may be thus framed:

They who are made partakers of Christ must not depart from God, nor suffer themselves to be hardened.

But ye that profess the gospel are made partakers of Christ.

Therefore ye must not depart, &c.

Of this word μέτοχοι, *partakers*, see ver. 1, Sec. 17. Of this title *Christ*, see ver. 6, Sec. 54.

To be made partakers of Christ intends two mysteries:

One is a spiritual union betwixt Christ and believers, whereby they are made one body, 1 Cor. xii. 12: Christ the head, believers the members thereof.

The other is a right to that heavenly inheritance which properly belongeth to Christ as the only begotten Son of God, and whereunto believers in Christ are adopted, being made joint-heirs with Christ, Rom. viii. 17.

In both these respects believers are made partakers of Christ. Both these may stand together, severed they cannot be; for all that are united unto him as members to a head, shall partake of his glory: and none shall partake of his glory but his members.

I take the former mystery to be most principally here intended. For he saith 'partakers *of* Christ,' not 'partakers *together with* Christ,' as the Gentiles are said to be partakers, together with the Jews, of God's promise in Christ, Eph. iii. 6. The other mystery followeth upon this.

This phrase, 'are made partakers of Christ,' having reference to believers, sheweth that the faithful have a right to Christ; he appertaineth to them; he is theirs. In this respect he is said to be in them, Col. i. 27, John xvii. 23; to live in them, Gal. ii. 20; to dwell in their hearts, Eph. iii. 17; to be one with them, John xvii. 21, 22. This mystical union the Holy Ghost setteth out by many resemblances, as head and members, Eph. v. 30; husband and wife, 2 Cor. xi. 1, 2; vine and branches, John xv. 5; foundation and edifice, Eph. ii. 20 21; house and inhabitants, ver. 6; yea, we are said to put on Christ as a garment, Rom. xiii. 14.

Of this mystical union, the privileges, comforts, and duties thence arising, see *Domest. Dut.* on Eph. v. 30, treat. i. secs. 70, 71, &c.

The word γεγόναμεν, translated *made*, implieth that there was a time when they were not partakers of Christ. They were not so born. It was a privilege conferred on them, John i. 12. Thus it is said, they were made partakers of the Holy Ghost, Heb. vi. 4, μετόχους γενηθέντας, &c. This privilege, to be partakers of Christ, is one of those gifts which 'came down from the Father of lights,' James i. 17. It is supernatural; for all men by nature are 'without Christ,' Eph. ii. 12. This much amplifieth the privilege, and enforceth the duties inferred thereupon.

Sec. 152. *Of the meaning of the Greek word translated 'confidence.'*

These words, 'If we hold the beginning,' &c., are an evidence of our being partakers of Christ. That evidence is perseverance in the faith of Christ.

To hold the beginning of our confidence, is to persevere in that faith, wherein we have been formerly instructed, and whereof we have made profession.

The word ὑπόστασις, here translated *confidence*, is not the same, παῤῥησία, which was so translated, ver. 6, Sec. 61. The one and the other Greek word may intend one and the same grace, but in different respects.

That παῤῥησία sets out confidence, as it makes one freely and boldly profess the true faith; this ὑπόστασις, as it supporteth one's spirit. For the Greek word here used, according to the notation and proper use of it, signifieth *substance;* so it is translated, Heb. xi. 1, or *subsistence*. Thus it is applied to the second person in sacred Trinity, and translated *person*, Heb. i. 3, Sec. 21. There see the notation and derivation of the Greek word used in this text.

It here signifieth some special grace, that gives a subsistence or being to one, or which sustaineth or supporteth him.

Our former English translators, following Beza, thus expound the word by a periphrasis, 'Wherewith we are upholden,' *quo sustentamur*. In the same sense do most interpreters here explain it.

If due consideration be had about the grace which doth thus uphold us, it will be found to be faith. For thereby we lay hold on Christ, and are upheld by him.

Our last English translators turn it 'confidence,' which is an high degree of faith, and implieth a settled assurance. In this sense is this very word used, and so translated, 2 Cor. xi. 17, ὑπόστασις τῆς καυχήσεως, confidence of boasting.

And to like purpose is the same phrase used, though a little otherwise translated, 2 Cor. ix. 4.

Whether we take faith or confidence, for the grace here meant, the difference is not great, for both intend a resting on Christ; only this latter, namely, confidence, implieth some greater assurance. Where the like matter is set out, the apostle expressly mentioneth faith; thus, 'If you continue in the faith grounded and settled,' &c., Col. i. 23.

Many, both ancient and modern expositors,[1] take faith to be the grace here meant.

Two reasons may be given why the apostle setteth out faith under that Greek word which signifieth substance or subsistence.

One is to shew, that faith giveth a kind of substance, or being to things to come, which actually are not; for 'faith is the substance of things hoped for,' Heb. xi. 1. But things hoped for are not actually, while they are hoped for, but only expected to be. No man hopes for that which he actually enjoyeth. 'Hope, that is seen, is no hope,' Rom. viii. 24. But faith

[1] Ambr. de Vocat. Gent. l. 2. Chrys. Theophyl. Theodoret. Œcumen. Calv. Beza, Pareus, Scult. Œcolamp. Gryn. Nahum. Diodat. aliique.

gives a kind of present being to that which is hoped for. Thus, Abraham saw Christ's day, John viii. 56. Hereof see more on Heb. xi. 1.

The other reason is to declare, that it is faith which upholds us in all difficulties, and in our greatest weaknesses. By faith 'out of weakness, believers were made strong,' Heb. xi. 34. Hereupon it is said, that 'He who believeth shall not be confounded,' 1 Peter ii. 6. 'Believe in the Lord, so shall you be established,' said Jehoshaphat to his people, 2 Chron. xx. 20.

This is of force to stir up such as have not faith, to get it; and such as have it, to nourish it. Of both these, see *The Whole Armour of God*, treat. ii. part 6. Of faith, on Eph. vi. 16, sec. 17, &c., and sec. 64, &c.

Sec. 163. *Of faith making us partakers of Christ.*

Faith being the grace here intended, it appears that by faith we are made partakers of Christ: 'Christ dwelleth in our hearts by faith,' Eph. iii. 7. 'And we live by the faith of the Son of God,' Gal. ii. 20. For faith is that instrument which God by his Spirit worketh in us to lay hold on Christ, to be united unto him, and so to be made partakers of him.

God in his wisdom doth use this instrument of faith to that purpose, upon two especial grounds.

1. Because faith of all graces makes most to God's honour. Hereof see *The Whole Armour of God*, treat. ii. part 6, on Eph. vi. 16. Of faith, sec. 7.

2. Because faith doth most strip man of all conceit in himself. For faith is a hand which a man stretcheth out to another to receive what is needful for him. Hereby he shews, that he cannot find it in himself; but that which he looks for, is in him to whom he stretcheth his hand to receive it.

Against the foresaid doctrine, it may be objected, that 'Hereby we know that we dwell in Christ, and Christ in us, because he hath given us of his Spirit,' 1 John iv. 13. Hereupon another apostle saith, 'If any man have not the Spirit of Christ, he is none of his,' Rom. viii. 9. By these, and other like texts of Scripture, it appears that we are made partakers of Christ by his Spirit.

Ans. It is true that we are united to Christ by his Spirit, but that hindereth not our union also by faith. Both may stand together. For there is a double bond of our spiritual union with Christ: one on Christ's part, which is the Spirit; the other on our part, which is faith. Christ, by his Spirit, layeth hold on us, and we by faith lay hold on Christ.

If Christ be worth the having, and that it be a privilege to be made partakers of Christ, how blind are they that see it not! What sots are they that regard it not! Then labour to get, preserve, and well use faith, which is the means God hath appointed to that end. Hereof see *The Whole Armour of God*, in the places before quoted.

Sec. 154. *Of faith's increase.*

The Greek word translated *beginning*, may be taken either for a foundation whereupon an edifice is built; or for the first breeding or being of a thing.

In the former sense it is used, Heb. vi. 1, and translated *principle*. But in the margin the true sense of the Greek word is thus expressed, *the beginning*.

That the word *beginning* doth there signify foundation, is evident by this phrase following, 'Not laying again the foundation,' &c. *Beginning* and *foundation* are there put for one and the same thing.

In the latter sense, as it signifieth the first being of a thing, it is most frequently used, as, 'The beginning of the gospel,' Mark i. 1. By the gospel he means the preaching thereof. Now, because John was the first minister thereof, John's preaching of it is called the beginning of the gospel. So the first miracle that Christ wrought, is called, 'the beginning of miracles,' John ii. 11.

In the former sense, the apostle takes it for grant, that there had been a foundation of faith laid among them. Why else should he call upon them to hold it fast? This is it which is called, 'The form of sound words,' 2 Tim. i. 13, and a 'foundation,' Heb. vi. 1. On that place there will be a more just occasion to speak of this point.

In this place, as *beginning* signifieth the first being of a thing, it sheweth, that where it is begun, it must be preserved and increased. The apostle having testified to the Colossians, that he 'heard of their faith in Christ,' addeth, that he 'ceased not to pray that they might increase, and be strengthened therein,' Col. i. 4, 9–11.

Grace is not perfect at the first, 1 Cor. xiii. 9. By growth it attains to perfection.

Besides, growth in faith is an evidence of the truth of faith.

This is a point needful to be pressed in these declining days. Christ may well say to England, as he did to Ephesus, 'Thou hast left thy first love,' Rev. ii. 4. Where there is a stay in grace, there will be a decay. We have need to 'stir up the gift of God that is in us,' 2 Tim. i. 6. We that are made partakers of Christ, ought to 'grow up into him in all things,' Eph. iv. 15. Hereof see *The Whole Armour of God*, on Eph. vi. 16, treat. ii. part 6. Of faith, sec. 64, &c.

Sec. 155. *Of perseverance an evidence of our right to Christ.*

These words, *if we hold stedfast unto the end*, are the same that were used before, verse 6, and in the same sense.

Of this particle, ἐάν περ, *if*, see Sec. 60.

Of the emphasis of these words, μέχρι τέλους βεβαίαν κατάσχωμεν, 'hold fast to the end,' see Sec. 68.

This inference being here set down as a *proviso*,

sheweth, that it is perseverance in faith which giveth sure evidence that we are made partakers of Christ. Hereof see ver. 6, sec. 68.

Sec 156. *Of the resolution and observations of* Heb. iii. 14.

Ver. 14. *For we are made partakers of Christ, if we hold the beginning of our confidence stedfast to the end.*

The sum of this verse is, an evidence of our right to Christ.

Herein we are to observe,
1. The inference in this causal particle, *for*.
2. The substance. Wherein is set down,
1. A privilege.
2. An evidence thereof.

In setting down the privilege, two points are expressed:
1. The kind of privilege, *partakers of Christ*.
2. The ground thereof, in this verb, *we are made*.

About the evidence we may observe,
1. The manner of expressing it, by way of supposition, in this particle, *if*.
2. The matter.

Wherein is declared, 1, an act; 2, the subject.
The act is,
1. Propounded, in this word *hold*.
2. Amplified, and that two ways:
(1.) By the extent, in this epithet, *stedfast*.
(2.) By the continuance thereof, *unto the end*.
The subject points at,
1. The *beginning*.
2. The grace itself, *confidence*, or faith.

Doctrines.

I. *Men may be partakers of Christ*. This is here plainly expressed, and taken for grant. See Sec. 151.

II. *To be partakers of Christ is a supernatural gift*. This phrase, *we are made*, implieth as much See Sec. 151.

III. *Our right in Christ must make us faithful to him*; so faithful as we never depart from him, nor be hardened against him. The causal particle *for* intends thus much. See Sec. 151.

IV. *Faith upholds them that have it*. In this respect faith is here styled *substance*, or that which supports. See Sec. 152.

V. *Faith makes men partakers of Christ*. In that continuance in faith is here set down as an evidence of our union with Christ, it follows that by faith that union is wrought. See Sec. 153.

VI. *Faith begun must be nourished*. The prefixing of this word *beginning*, before confidence or faith, clears this doctrine. See Sec. 154.

VII. *They who are in Christ must look to their standing*. This conditional particle *if* hints so much. See Sec. 154.

VIII. *Perseverance in faith gives evidence of our true right to Christ*. The inference of the condition of perseverance upon the privilege of being partakers of Christ, proves this doctrine. See Sec. 154.

IX. *Perseverance must be without intermission*. This epithet *stedfast* demonstrates as much. See ver. 6, Sec. 68.

X. *True perseverance holds out till death*. For this is that end which is comprised under this phrase, *unto the end*. See ver. 6, Sec. 68.

Sec. 157. *Of this phrase, ' while it is said, To-day.*

Ver. 15. *Whiles it is said, To-day, if ye will hear his voice, harden not your hearts, as in the provocation.*

The apostle doth here begin to expound some passages of the foresaid testimony, taken out of Ps. xcv. 7, &c.

The first point expounded is the time intended by the psalmist, in this word *to-day*.

The apostle by this phrase, *whiles it is said, To-day*, sheweth that a continued time is meant.

The Greek phrase, ἐν τῷ λέγεσθαι, may word for word be thus translated, ' In this to be said to-day.' This is an apparent Hebraism. For the Hebrews do comprise the gerunds under the infinitive mood; and by prefixing a preposition, set out the time of doing a thing. This phrase, באמר, *in dicendo, in saying*, is thus translated, Ps. xlii. 3, ' while they say.' The Greek Septuagint do translate it in the very same words that are used by the apostle in this text, ἐν τῷ λέγεσθαι.

The phrase therefore is fitly translated by our English, and it doth well express the emphasis of the Hebraism, and the meaning of the apostle, which is to demonstrate, that so long as the opportunity of hearkening to the voice of Christ continueth, Christians must take that opportunity, and by no means harden their hearts against it. Hereof see more, Sec. 146.

Thus this verse fitly dependeth on the latter part of the former, as a further reason to stir us up to ' hold the beginning of our confidence,' or faith. The reason is taken from God's continuing to call upon us to hearken unto his voice, and not to harden our hearts.

The argument may be thus framed,
While it is said, ' To-day, if ye will hear his voice, harden not your hearts,' &c.; we ought to hold fast the beginning, &c.
But still it is said, ' To-day, if ye will hear,' &c.
Therefore still we ought to hold the beginning, &c.

Sec. 158. *Of extending Scripture instructions to future ages.*

The apostle here repeateth the very words of the psalmist, and applieth them to Christians.[1] The point itself, of taking the opportunity of hearkening to Christ's voice, is a very remarkable point, and of great concernment. So as repetitions of matters of moment are lawful and useful; and that whether they be re-

[1] See Chap. ix. 28, Sec. 138, and Chap. x. 8, Sec. 22.

peated in the same words, and same sense; or in the same sense, and different words. See more hereof in *The Saints' Sacrifice*, on Ps. cxvi.16, secs. 98, 107–109.

There is the more weight in repeating this point, because it is repeated in the very terms of sacred Scripture. Hereof see before, Sec. 74.

Of this expression of the time, *to-day*, see Sec. 76.
Of hearing Christ's voice, see Secs. 77, 78.
Of the heart, and hardening it, see Secs. 79, 80, &c.
Of this note of resemblance, *as*, see Sec. 89.
Of this title *provocation*, see Sec. 90.
Of the several observations gathered out of the several words of this verse, see ver. 7, 8, Sec. 120.

By repeating the very words of the psalmist, and applying them to Christians, the apostle giveth us to understand, that Scripture instructions are of perpetual use. As they were of use in the prophet's time, so also in the apostle's, so still in ours, so will they be in future ages till the world's end. They are as the lamps which continually gave light in the tabernacle, and were never put out, so long as it stood, Exod. xxvii. 20. So long as the church remaineth, these lamps ought to shine, yea, they will shine in it. The prophet is commanded to write his prophecy 'before the people in a table,' and to 'note it in a book, that it might be for the time to come, for ever and ever,' Isa. xxx. 8. An apostle saith that 'the prophets did minister unto us the things that are now reported,' 1 Peter i. 12.

God's truth is an everlasting truth, it 'endureth to all generations,' Ps. c. 5, 'even for ever,' Ps. cxvii. 2. God's truth is as himself, and his will as his nature: 'He changeth not,' Mal. iii. 6.

This justifieth such collections, inferences, and applications which preachers use to make of scriptures to their auditors; as where they find any general duty commanded, there to press it upon their people, as a duty whereunto their people are bound. We have the warrant of Christ and his apostles for this. When Christ was tempted to presumption, Mat. iv. 6, he knew that this precept of Moses, 'Ye shall not tempt the Lord,' Deut. vi. 16, belonged to him. So when he was tempted to fall down to the devil, and worship him, he pressed this injunction long before delivered by Moses, 'Thou shalt worship the Lord thy God, and him only shalt thou serve,' Mat. iv. 9, 10. In this respect, he reproved the Jews of his time for transgressing the commandments of God, given in their fathers' time, Mat. xv. 6. See more hereof, ver. 8, Secs. 89, 90, and Chap. xiii. 5, Sec. 68.

Sec. 159. *Of the resolution and observations of* Heb. iii. 15.

Ver. 15. *Whiles it is said, To-day, if ye will hear his voice, harden not your hearts, as in the provocation.*

The sum of this verse is, a direction for holding fast to Christ.

Two special points are observable herein:

1. The time when the duty is to be performed.
2. The means how it may be performed.

About the time we may observe,
1. The fitness of it, *to-day*.
2. The continuance thereof, *whiles it is said*.

In setting down the means, there is noted,
1. The manner of propounding the same, in this conditional particle, *if*.
2. The matter whereof it consisteth, which is set down both affirmatively, and also negatively.

In the affirmative there is expressed,
1. An act, *hear*.
2. An object, *his voice*.

The negative is propounded and aggravated.

In the proposition there is set down,
1. An act forbidden, *harden not*.
2. The object whereupon that act useth to be exercised, *your hearts*.

The aggravation is manifested by a resemblance to a former time.

In this aggravation is set down,
1. The note of resemblance, *as*.
2. A description of the time and place intended, *in the provocation*.

Doctrines.

I. *The opportunity of grace is to be taken.* This word, *to-day*, signifieth a season or opportunity. See Sec. 76.

II. *Improvement is to be made of the season so long as it lasteth.* This phrase, *whiles it is said*, implies a continuance. See Secs. 146, 147.

III. *God's word is man's rule.* This is *his voice* which we must hear. See. Sec. 78.

IV. *God's word is the most principal object of hearing.* It is here set down to be so. See Sec. 77.

V. *Hearing the gospel is a sovereign antidote against the poison of an hard heart.* This conditional clause, *If ye will hear*, presupposeth thus much. See Sec. 77.

VI. *A man's heart may be hardened.* This is here taken for grant. See Sec. 80.

VII. *A man may harden his own heart.* He speaks to men themselves not to do it. See Sec. 85.

VIII. *Hardness of heart is an hindrance to profitable hearing.* Therefore we are warned not to harden, if we would hear. See Sec. 77.

IX. *Sins of former ages are to be observed.* This is the end of this title, *provocation*. See Sec. 90.

X. *Sins of former ages are to be avoided.* This note of resemblance, *as*, hath reference to a former time. See Sec. 89.

XI. *The same points may be repeated.* For here the apostle repeateth what before he had delivered in the same words. See Sec. 158.

Sec. 160. *Of blaming some and not all, where some only are guilty.*

Verse 16. *For some, when they had heard, did provoke: howbeit not all that came out of Egypt by Moses.*

Here the apostle begins to shew what kind of persons sinned, and were punished. These are indefinitely hinted in this verse, and more clearly exemplified in the verses following.

He maketh mention of the persons, to give a more full evidence of the necessity of Christian watchfulness against hardness of heart, even because they whose hearts were hardened, provoked God to their own ruin.

This causal particle, γὰρ, *for*, demonstrateth so much, for it imports a reason of that which goeth before, as if he had more plainly said, Do not ye who now hear Christ's word, harden your hearts, because they who of old were hardened provoked God.

This pronoun, τινὲς, *some*, is a word of limitation, for it exempteth some, namely, such as were not guilty; therefore the apostle, by way of explanation, to make his mind the more clear, addeth this phrase, ' Howbeit not all.'

The apostle would not lay the blame on all, where he knew that not all, but only some, were guilty.

This is in this exemplification the more observable, because almost all at some time or other provoked God. For of all the six hundred thousand men, that came out of Egypt, Exod. xii. 37, there were but two that provoked not God to cut them off in the wilderness, Num. xiv. 29, 30.

Indeed, besides those two men, Joshua and Caleb, many that were under twenty year old, when they came out of Egypt, were not destroyed in the wilderness, for a great army went out of the wilderness into Canaan; therefore the apostle might well say, ' some, not all,' so as none are to be blamed but those that are guilty. All are not to be involved in the blame that lieth upon some. Such a limitation doth the apostle use, where he reckoneth up particular crimes of the Israelites in the wilderness; thus, some of them were idolaters, some of them committed fornication, some of them tempted Christ, some of them murmured, 1 Cor. x. 7–10.

To condemn all, where some only are guilty, is to condemn the just, which is as much before God, as to justify the wicked, Prov. xvii. 15.

This is too common a fault among many, who use to condemn all professors of hypocrisy, because some are hypocrites, and all ministers of pride, and all magistrates of injustice, and all lawyers of unconscionableness in maintaining unjust suits, and all physicians of unmercifulness, and all citizens of covetousness, and all tradesmen of deceitfulness, and all women of lightness, and all servants of unfaithfulness. See more hereof in *The Saints' Sacrifice*, on Ps. cxvi. 11, sec. 74.

General censures are for the most part unjust censures, yet too, too common.

This moderation of the apostle, in charging some only, affords a good lesson to ministers, magistrates, parents, masters, and others, not to censure or condemn a of the same place, state, calling, office, condition, degree, country, sex, or other community, for the fault of some.

Sec. 161. *Of God's putting difference betwixt different persons.*

This negative clause, πάντες, *not all*, being inferred upon the affirmative with this conjunction of opposition, ἀλλὰ, *but*, further shews that God, in mixed multitudes, can put difference betwixt persons that differ.

Though the persons comprised under the restrictive particle, τινὲς, *some*, before mentioned, were a very great multitude, and these comprised under this negative, *not all*, were very few in comparison, yet God, who took notice of that multitude, did also take special notice of these few. In such a case as this it is said, that ' They that feared the Lord spake often one to another: and the Lord hearkened, and heard it; and a book of remembrance was written before him for them that feared the Lord, and thought upon his name. And they shall be mine, saith the Lord, in the day that I make up my jewels,' Mal. iii. 16, 17. When the Lord sent a destroyer through the midst of Jerusalem, he commanded to ' set a mark upon the foreheads of the men that sighed,' &c., Ezek. ix. 4. An apostle giveth three instances hereof, which are as famous as ever the world afforded. One is of the difference that God put betwixt the angels that stood, and them that fell. The other is of the difference he put betwixt Noah's family and the old world. The third is of a like difference betwixt Lot and the people of Sodom and Gomorrah. Hereupon this conclusion is inferred, ' The Lord knoweth how to deliver the godly out of temptations, and to reserve the unjust unto the day of judgment to be punished,' 2 Peter ii. 4, &c.

' The eyes of the Lord are in every place, beholding the evil and the good,' Prov. xv. 3. As he hath an all-seeing eye, so also he hath a perfect discerning Spirit, ' whose fan is in his hand, and he will thoroughly purge his floor,' &c., Mat. iii. 12.

This is a great comfort and encouragement to such as are forced to complain, as David did: Ps. cxx. 5, ' Woe is me, that I sojourn in Meshech, that I dwell in the tents of Kedar!' And as another prophet, ' Woe is me, for I dwell in the midst of a people of unclean lips,' Isa. vi. 5. Though we live among such, God will not wrap us in the number of such, especially if we remain upright, as Noah did, Gen vi. 9; and righteous, as Lot did, 2 Peter ii. 8. Such are as precious stones; though they be in a heap of rubbish, God can and will find them out. God will not cast away the precious with the vile. God sees those whom man cannot see. When Elijah thought there had been none left but himself, the Lord discerned that there were ' seven thousand in Israel, which had not bowed their knee to Baal,' 1 Kings xix. 18.

Sec. 162. *Of professors provoking God while they hear his word.*

The sin of those *some* before mentioned is thus expressed, ' Some, when they had heard, did provoke.'

Of the derivation and emphatical signification of the word *provoke*, see ver. 8, Sec. 90.

This Greek verb, παρεπίκρανάν, is here only in this text of the New Testament used, but in the Old Testament by the Greek LXX more frequently, especially in the Psalms; as Ps. lxxviii. 17, 40, 56, and cvi. 7, 33, 43; so Jer. xliv. 8; and in sundry other places.

In the New Testament there are other Greek words which signify the same thing, carry as great emphasis, and translated *provoke*; as in this phrase, 'Do we provoke (παραζηλόω, *ad fervorem excito*) the Lord to jealousy,' 1 Cor. x. 22. Love 'is not provoked,' παροξύνω, *exacerbo*, 1 Cor. xiii. 5. 'Provoke not your children,' παροργίζω, *ad iram provoco*, Eph. vi. 4.

The word used in my text doth greatly aggravate the obstinacy of those who profess themselves to be God's people; they do, as much as in them lieth, embitter the Spirit of God, and vex him: 'They rebelled, and vexed his Holy Spirit,' Isa. lxiii. 10; hence is it that he is said to be grieved, ver. 10, sec. 103. What else can be expected but that God should vex them, as is threatened, Ps. ii. 5, and accomplished, 2 Chron. xv. 6. It is not safe to provoke the Almighty, and to cause him to turn his fatherly affection into the disposition of a judge.

This sin of theirs is yet further aggravated by their contempt of the means which God afforded to reclaim them, which was his word; for this act *hear* hath reference to 'the voice of God,' mentioned ver. 7.

The Greek word ἀκούσαντες is a participle of the present tense, and may be thus translated, 'Hearing, they provoked;' that is, while God was speaking, and they hearing, they still provoked.

They heard God directing them the right way, and inciting them to walk in that way, Deut. xxx. 15, 16.

They heard God admonishing them to take heed lest they should wander out of that way, Deut. viii. 11, 12.

They heard God promising blessings to them that obeyed him, and threatening curses against them that disobeyed, Deut. xxviii. 1, 2, 15, &c., yet 'they provoked.' God's word nothing at all wrought upon them.

Such was the disposition of the old world, 1 Pet. iii. 19, 20, of Sodom and Gomorrah, 2 Pet. ii. 8, of the Israelites in the time of the judges, Judges ii. 17, of the kings, 2 Kings xvii. 13, 14, and after their captivity, Ezra ix. 10; yea, in and after Christ's time, even till they came to be Lo-ammi, no people of God, Acts vii. 51, 1 Thes. ii. 15, 16.

The god of this world had blinded their eyes, 2 Cor. iv. 4, and hardened their hearts, as he did Judas his heart, John xiii. 27.

Hereby they shewed that they were not of God, John viii. 47, 1 John iv. 6. It is said of the sons of Eli, that 'they hearkened not unto the voice of their father, because the Lord would slay them,' 1 Sam. ii. 25.

God's word is the means which God hath sanctified to reclaim sinners. The case of those who hearken not thereto is very desperate. Oh take heed of sinning under the means which God affords to reclaim from sin.

Sec. 163. *Of Israel's coming out of Egypt.*

This phrase, *came out of Egypt*, is here added by way of description, or designation of that mixed multitude whereof many provoked God, others provoked him not.

The description is taken from a wonderful deliverance which God gave them; for Egypt was to the persons here meant a place of bondage. So it is said to be in the preface to the Decalogue, Exod. xx. 2.

Of the notation of this word *Egypt*, of the bondage of the Israelites therein, of their wonderful deliverance thereout, I have distinctly treated in a sermon on Isa. xiii. 3, entitled *Mercy's Memorial*.

This deliverance was one of the most marvellous and memorable that ever God wrought for his people. Sundry circumstances do much amplify the same; as the place whence and whither they came, and the manner of bringing them from the one place to the other.

1. The place whence they came was a place of a most miserable bondage, where 'their lives were made bitter unto them,' Exod. i. 14, and where 'their cry came up unto God,' Exod. iii. 9.

2. The place whither they were brought was a place of great freedom, and where God extraordinarily provided for them. See ver. 8, Sec. 92.

3. The manner of bringing them from one place to the other was with mighty power, Deut. ix. 29, and with great tenderness. See Chap. viii. 9, Sec. 55.

Besides, this word, ἐξελθόντες, 'came out,' implieth a free and a full deliverance, for it is a compound word.

The simple verb *came* implieth a voluntary act. They were not hauled or drawn, but they came willingly, cheerfully, joyfully; for upon their coming out of the Red Sea 'they sang praises to God,' Ps. cvi. 12, Exod. xv. 1, &c. It is indeed said that 'the Egyptians were urgent upon the people that they might send them out of the land in haste,' Exod. xii. 33; but that was not by reason of any unwillingness in the people to go as soon as they could, but rather by reason of that great fear wherein the Egyptians were, lest they should be all consumed if the Israelites tarried any longer.

The preposition ἐκ vel ἐξ, with which the verb is compounded, translated *out*, implieth a full deliverance. They were brought clean out of that land, and clean out of their bondage, and clean from their oppressors, even through the Red Sea into another land.

The more to manifest this full deliverance, the preposition *out* is twice used, both in composition, and also simply by itself, ἐξελθόντες ἐξ. The latter, which is the simple preposition, is here translated *of*, they 'came out of Egypt.'

All these circumstances—as, 1. The place whence they came. 2. The place whither they were brought. 3. The means used to bring them out, 'Mighty wonders.' 4. Their manner of coming out, voluntarily. 5. Their full deliverance, 'They came out'—all these circumstances, as they do much amplify the deliverance, so they do exceedingly aggravate the sin of those that were delivered.

They do also confirm two points before observed concerning God's wonderful and gracious deliverance of the Israelites out of Egypt.

One is, that extraordinary works work nothing at all upon the incredulous. See ver. 9, Sec. 99.

The other is, that no kindness works upon the obstinate. See ver. 8, Sec. 92. See also Chap. viii. 9, Sec. 57.

Sec. 164. *Of Moses his bringing Israel out of Egypt.*
The foresaid great deliverance is here by name attributed to Moses, in this phrase, *by Moses.*

Of Moses, see ver. 2, Sec. 37.

This preposition διά, *by*, is sometimes attributed to the principal author, sometimes to ministers.[1]

To the principal author, as to God, 1 Cor. i. 9, Father, Gal. i. 1, Son, John i. 3, Holy Ghost, Rom. v. 5.

To ministers, as to angels, Heb. ii. 2, and to men, as here to Moses.

It was indeed the Lord that brought them out of Egypt, Exod. xx. 2, yet it is here ascribed to Moses. Not only the people of Israel, but also God himself, doth ascribe this great work to Moses, and in that respect calleth the children of Israel the people of Moses, Exod. xxxii. 1, 7, and xxxiv. 10.

But herein Moses is to be considered as God's minister, whom God used under himself to bring this work to pass. For,

1. Moses brought them the first tidings of God's purpose to deliver them, Exod. iv. 28-30.

2. Moses went as a messenger from God to Pharaoh, to charge him to let the people go, Exod. v. 1.

3. Moses was God's instrument in bringing the plagues on Egypt, whereby Pharaoh was forced to let Israel go out of his land, Exod. vii. 20.

4. Moses, as their guide and captain, directed them when and how to go out, Exod. xiv. 13, Ps. lxxvii. 20.

5. Moses was used as a means, by striking the Red Sea, to divide the waters, and make a path for the Israelites to go through on dry land, Exod. xiv. 16, 21.

6. Moses was the means, by striking the sea again, to overwhelm the Egyptians, and so to destroy them all, Exod. xiv. 27.

Thus God's work is attributed to man. In this respect Moses is styled a deliverer, Acts vii. 35; so Othniel and Ehud, Judges iii. 9, 15, yea, all that God

[1] See Chap. ii. 9, Sec. 74, and Chap. vi. 12, Sec. 84.

used as instruments to work public deliverances for his people, are styled saviours, Neh. ix. 27; and Jonathan is said to 'work great deliverance in Israel,' 1 Sam. xiv. 45, and Mordecai to 'seek the wealth of his people,' Esther x. 3.

God doth herein and hereby honour their calling and service whom he is pleased to use as his ministers.

Should not people, then, respect and honour them whom God so honoureth as to ascribe unto them his own works? Shall men dare to despise them whom God doth so respect as to style them gods, and children of the Most High? Ps. lxxxii. 6.

The like dignity is ascribed to ministers of the word, who are styled fathers, 1 Cor. iv. 15, and are said to beget people to God, Philem. 10, yea, to save people, 1 Tim. iv. 16, and to be co-workers with God, 2 Cor. vi. 1.

This should make us conscionable in using men's ministry for attaining that good which God is pleased to effect thereby.

Sec. 165. *Of the resolution and observations of* Heb. iii. 16.

Ver. 16. *For some, when they had heard, did provoke: howbeit not all that came out of Egypt by Moses.*

The sum of this verse is, the notice which God taketh of different persons.

The parts are two:

1. An aggravation of the sin of them that sinned.
2. An exemption of others that sinned not.

The aggravation is manifested two ways.

1. By the effect that followed thereon, *they provoked.*
2. By the means which God afforded to reclaim them.

The means are of two sorts.

1. God's word which they heard.
2. His mighty work. This is described,
 1. By the place whence they were brought, *Egypt.*
 2. By the manner of delivering them, *they came out.*
 3. By the minister whom God used.

The exemption is, 1, intimated, *some*; 2, expressed, *not all.*

Doctrines.

I. *Professors' obstinacy provokes God.* Such were the persons, such the sin here mentioned. See Sec. 162.

II. *Neglect of God's word heard aggravates sin.* To this end this act, *they heard*, is here set down. See Sec. 162.

III. *Extraordinary works of God work not on incredulous.* This deliverance out of Egypt was extraordinary, yet it wrought not. See Secs. 163, 99.

IV. *Kindness works not on the obstinate.* This deliverance was a great act of kindness, yet it wrought not. See Sec. 92.

V. *God ascribes his own work to his ministers.* See Sec. 164.

VI. *All are not to be blamed for the fault of some.* See Sec. 160.

VII. *God can put difference betwixt different persons.* See Sec. 161.

Sec. 166. *Of propounding and resolving points interrogatory.*

Verse 17. *But with whom was he grieved forty years? Was it not with them that had sinned, whose carcases fell in the wilderness?*

The exemplification of the persons that sinned, and were punished in the wilderness, is laid down in this and the next verse.

That it might the better appear who they were that were exempted, the apostle here makes inquiry after those who grieved God, and thereupon were punished.

The particle of opposition, δὲ, *but,* intimateth that the questions in this verse propounded tend to that purpose: as if he had said, Seeing all of them provoked not God, who were they that provoked him?

By thus propounding the matter interrogatively, he gives them occasion more seriously to consider it. For a question propounded, makes them who hear it to think with themselves what fit resolution may be given thereto. For this end, these and such like phrases use to be set before questions, 'How think you?' 'What think you?' 'Do you think?' 'Tell me, how think you? If a man have an hundred sheep, and one of them be gone astray, doth he not leave?' &c., Mat. xviii. 12; 'What think you? a certain man had two sons,' &c., Mat. xxi. 28; 'Do you think that the Scripture saith in vain?' &c., James iv. 5; 'Tell me, which of them will love him most?' Luke vii. 42.

The apostle was desirous that they might clearly and fully understand the point in hand, and that they might well heed it, and therefore thus propounds it interrogatively. Parables, paraphrases, analyses, or resolutions of Scripture, and all manner of expositions tend to the same end.

That which the apostle expressed in the former verse under this word παρεπίκραναν, *provoked,* he here sets down under this metaphor, προσώχθισε, *grieved.* The former had reference to the people that sinned; they provoked God. This latter hath reference to God, and is an effect or consequence following thereupon. By their provoking God, God was grieved. Of grieving God, see verse 10, Sec. 103.

God's continuing to be grieved is expressed in these words 'forty years.' This circumstance of time was set down before in reference to the people's continuing in sin. See verse 10, Sec. 102.

Here it is applied to the continuance of God's grieving at them, and therein amplifies his patience in bearing with them so long. Hereof see verse 9, Secs. 100, 101.

The answer to the foresaid question is returned by another question, thus, 'Was it not with them that had sinned?' This manner of answering one question with another is very elegant and emphatical. It shews two points.

The first is conclusive, and implieth that the matter questioned is so clear and evident that no question need be made thereof: as where the apostle having made this question, 'Is God righteous, who taketh vengeance?' thus answereth it, 'Then how shall God judge the world?' Rom. iii. 5, 6. And to this question, 'Shall we sin, because we are under grace?' he giveth this answer, 'Know ye not that to whom ye yield yourselves servants to obey, his servants ye are? Rom. vi. 15, 16.

The other point is exclusive, and implieth, that God was grieved with none, and punished none, but such as sinned, Gen. xviii. 23, &c., Ezek. xviii. 4, &c., Ezek. ix. 4, Rev. vii. 2. For the Lord is a just and righteous God, Gen. xviii. 25.

Hereof see more in *The Plaster for the Plague,* on Num. xvi. 45, Secs. 12–15.

Sec. 167. *Of sin grieving God.*

The latter question, wherein the answer to the former consisteth, is set down negatively, thus, 'Was it not with them?' &c. This implieth a sure, certain, and unquestionable affirmation, and determination of a point: as where it is said, 'Have we not all one Father? Hath not one God created us?' Mal. ii. 10. This Christ maketh most clear: for after he had propounded this negative question, 'Shall not God avenge his own elect?' &c., he thus addeth, 'I tell you that he will avenge them speedily,' Luke xviii. 7, 8. This latter express conclusion, demonstrateth the infallible certainty of the former question.

In that this negative question infers that they that had sinned grieved God, it is most certain that it was the sin of the Israelites whereby God was so much grieved.

It was shewed, Sec. 148, that the Greek word ἁμαρτήσασι, here translated *sinned,* by an Hebrew notation signifieth to embitter and provoke. Sinners, therefore, must needs grieve God. It is said, that 'it grieved God at the heart' for the sins of the old world, Gen. vi. 6. And of the Son of God it is said, that 'he was grieved for the hardness of people's hearts,' Mark iii. 5.

Obj. It is also said, that 'the soul of the Lord was grieved for the misery of Israel,' Judges x. 16. If he be grieved at people's misery, then not at their sins only.

Ans. 1. Sin was the cause of their misery. So as in grieving at their misery, God also grieved at their sin; yea, sin also might be mixed with their misery.

2. There is a double kind of grief, one through indignation; the other through compassion. With the former God properly grieves at sin; with the latter at misery.

God cannot but be much grieved at sin, because it is directly contrary to his mind and will, to his purity and holiness, to his power and sovereignty, and to other his divine excellencies.

This ought to be as a bridle and curb to hold us in, and restrain us from sin. Who would grieve the divine majesty? especially so as to stir up the fire of his indignation. 'Who would set the briers and thorns against me in battle?' saith the Lord, 'I would go through them, I would burn them together,' Isa. xxvii. 4. Will any be so foolish as, being like briars and thorns, fit fuel for fire, to dare to blow up the fire of God's indignation?

Sec. 168. *Of the vengeance that followed upon grieving God.*

Another effect of their sin is set out in these words, 'whose carcases fell in the wilderness.'

This, as it was the fruit of their sin, so it was a just recompence of their grieving God. By their sin they grieved God; and God, being grieved, destroyed them.

The Greek word τὰ κῶλα, translated *carcases*, properly signifieth members of the body; but by a synecdoche it is put for the body, which is constituted of members. So this word is used in other Greek authors. It is nowhere else in the New Testament. The apostle hath taken it from the LXX. For they do oft translate the Hebrew word פגר, *cadaver*, which signifieth a carcase, or dead body, by his word; as where David saith, 'I will give the carcases of the host of the Philistines,' 1 Sam. xvii. 46. Three times is this word used in one chapter, Num. xiv. 29, 32, 33. Yea, this whole phrase is there thus used, 'Your carcases shall fall in this wilderness.' So as the apostle may seem to have taken it from thence.

Our English word *carcase* betokeneth a dead body: for they did not fall as living bodies, so as they might rise up again; but they were slain.

The verb ἔπεσε, *fall*, implieth a sudden and extraordinary kind of death. It is used to set out the fall of the walls of Jericho, Heb. xi. 30, and the fall of the house that was built on the sand, Mat. vii. 27; and of the blind man falling into a ditch, Mat. xv. 14; and to Ananias and Sapphira their sudden falling down dead, Acts v. 5, 10; and to Eutychus his falling down dead, Acts xx. 9; and to those 'three and twenty thousand which fell in one day in the wilderness,' 1 Cor. x. 8; and to the fall of Babylon, Rev. xiv. 8.

We do not read of any one that died a natural death (as we speak) in the wilderness all the time that the Israelites were there. Both Moses and Aaron died while they were in health, and might, according to the course of nature, have lived longer. Even their death was extraordinary, and a judgment on them, 'they fell;' and so did all the rest that died in the wilderness, 'they all fell.'

Mention is made of the wilderness, wherein the foresaid judgment was executed, to give a more clear evidence of the kind of judgment.

The wilderness was but a passage into the promised land. The reason of their long abode there, was their murmuring against God, Num. xiv. 33. To die in the wilderness was to come short of the promise made to their fathers. In this very respect, to die there was reckoned as a judgment to Aaron, Num. xx. 24, and to Moses, Deut. xxxii. 50, 51.

Of the wilderness, see ver. 8, Secs. 92, 93.

This issue of those sinners that grieved God, giveth evidence, that they who by their sins grieve God, do therein sin against their own souls; they pull vengeance upon themselves; so did the old world. Through their sin 'it grieved God at his heart that he had made man;' and thereupon he said, 'I will destroy man,' Gen. vi. 6, 7. 'God was displeased at Onan's sin, and slew him,' Gen. xxxviii. 10. 'When Ephraim offended in Baal, he died,' Hosea. xiii. 1. Read through the book of God, and you shall ever find some judgment following upon offending, grieving, or vexing the Lord.

His justice, power, prudence, truth, and other like attributes, stir him up thus to maintain the glory of them. Otherwise his wrath, his grief, and other like passions (to speak of God, ἀνθρωποπαθῶς, after the manner of man) would be little regarded, nay, altogether regarded.

This cannot but much work upon those that well heed it, and make them very wary in taking heed how they grieve God. If zeal of God's glory do not move them, yet let them have pity upon their own souls, that they bring not ruin to themselves.

Oh, what terror must this needs bring to obstinate sinners, who persist in grieving God! Where shall they appear? Where shall they stand? If the wrath of a mortal king be as the roaring of a lion: and if he that provoketh him to anger sinneth against his own soul, Prov. xix. 12, and xii. 1, what is the wrath of the almighty God! And how doth he sin against his own soul, that provoketh the wrath of the Lord!

Sec. 169. *Of the resolution and observations of* Heb. iii. 17.

Ver. 17. *But with whom was he grieved forty years? Was it not with them that had sinned, whose carcases fell in the wilderness?*

The sum of this verse is, the issue of them who grieve God.

Herein we may observe two points:

1. The manner of propounding the thing, interrogatively; and that by question upon question.

2. The matter. Whereabout we have,

1. A thing taken for grant.
2. A consequence following thereupon.

The thing taken for grant is,

1. Generally propounded, *God was grieved*.
2. In special amplified by the time, how long, *forty years*.

The consequence is a judgment that followed thereupon.

In it are set down,

1. The persons that were punished, *they that had sinned.*
2. The kind of judgment. This was an extraordinary death, *their carcases fell.*
3. The place where, *in the wilderness.*

Doctrines.

I. *Discussing of points by interrogations is emphatical.* The apostle's manner of handling his matter so, gives proof hereunto. See Sec. 166.

II. *God may be grieved.* This is here taken for grant. See ver. 10, Sec. 103.

III. *The Lord is a God of longsuffering.* To continue to be grieved forty years implieth much patience. See ver. 9, Sec. 101.

IV. *Sin grieveth God.* It is here said, that he was grieved with them that sinned. See Sec. 167.

V. *Sore vengeance follows upon grieving God.* The judgment whereunto the apostle hath reference, proveth as much. See Sec. 168.

VI. *God can suddenly destroy men.* So much is intended under this phrase, 'whose carcases fell.' See Sec. 168.

VII. *By sin men deprive themselves of blessings promised.* All that fell in the wilderness deprived themselves of the promised Canaan. See ver. 11, Sec. 118.

Sec. 170. *Of the meaning of* Heb. iii. 18.

Ver. 18. *And to whom sware he that they should not enter into his rest, but to them that believed not?*

The apostle having in the former verse set down in general, that sin was the cause of the people's destruction, in this verse he declareth what kind of sin in special it was : namely, unbelief; and withal he proceeds in his inquiry after the persons that did further provoke God, even to swear vengeance.

The apostle goeth on after the same emphatical manner that he did in the former verse, dialogue-wise. See Sec. 166.

The vengeance which God sware is thus expressed, 'that they should not enter into his rest.'

This is a great judgment. For to men that have long travelled, and been much troubled, rest is very comfortable and acceptable.

But what rest can be comparable to God's ? For it is *his* rest that is here spoken of. How can any more be deprived of it than by not entering into it ?

All these, and that as an aggravation of the punishment of the Israelites, have been before handled.

Of God's swearing vengeance, see ver. 11, Sec. 114.

Of the rest here meant, see ver. 11, Sec. 116 ; of God's rest, see Sec. 117.

Of not entering into that rest, see Sec. 116.

Of Israel's forfeiture thereof, see Sec. 118.

The sin here set down to be the cause of God's swearing the foresaid vengeance is unbelief.

In the Greek there are two conjunctions, which are comprised under this English particle *but.* Those two are εἰ μή, *si non, nisi, if not.* The sentence may thus be translated, ' to whom sware he,' *if not,* or *except,* or *unless* to such and such ?

Our English *but* doth sufficiently express the emphasis of both the Greek particles ; and it implieth, that these, and these alone, and none else, were the persons here meant.

This, then, gives us to understand, that all the sinners in the wilderness, which there perished, were guilty of the sin here mentioned, which is unbelief.

There were other apparent sins for which many of them were punished. Of these the apostle reckoneth up five kinds : as, 1, lust; 2, idolatry ; 3, fornication; 4, tempting Christ ; 5, murmuring, 1 Cor. x. 6, &c. Yet unbelief was the bitter root out of which all of them sprouted, and that sour leven with which they were all infected and tainted. See ver. 12, Sec. 128 ; see chap. xi. 31, Sec. 185.

Sec. 171. *Of the nature of unbelief.*

The Greek verb ἀπειθήσασι, translated *believed not,* is but one word, yet a compounded word. The simple verb πείθειν, signifieth to *persuade.*

The preposition ἀπὸ, added to it, is privative, and imports a negative : so as the foresaid verb πείθειν, joined to this preposition, sets out a not yielding, or refusing to be persuaded.

This refusal, in reference to the mind of him that refuseth, most properly intendeth unbelief; but in reference to the will it intendeth disobedience, or rebellion. In the New Testament it is for the most part taken in the former sense, for not believing ; yet sometimes also it is taken in the latter sense, for disobeying, and so translated, ' do not obey,' ἀπειθῶν, Rom. ii. 8 ; ' a disobedient people,' Rom. x. 21 ; ' disobedient,' 2 Peter ii. 7, 8. The Greek fathers do also use this word, sometimes in the one, sometimes in the other sense.

But other authors do take it for the most part in the former sense, namely, to disobey.

I see no cause in this place to alter our last English translation, but to interpret it as they do, namely thus, ' to them that believed not.' This is most agreeable to the apostle's scope, who earnestly exhorteth to take heed of unbelief, ver. 12. There the word doth properly and without all question signify unbelief. It is the same word that is used in the last verse of this chapter, wherein the same thing is set down that here in this verse is.

The word here used being thus taken for such as believed not, sheweth, that unbelief made the Israelites so to provoke God as to swear vengeance against them.

The fore-mentioned notation of the word (namely, *a not yielding to persuasion*), addeth much to the aggravation of the sin of unbelief. For persuasions use to be for a man's good; such are all God's persuasions. They who do not believe, do thereby imply, that they who persuade them intend not their good. Now their good being intended, what disgrace do they put upon him that persuades them! and what wrong do they to their own souls!

To those that are styled 'unbelieving Jews,' ἀπειθοῦντες, and 'Jews which believed not,' Acts xiv. 2, and xvii. 5, the apostle thus saith, 'Ye put from you the word of God, and judge yourselves unworthy of everlasting life,' Acts xiii. 46. Did not these do great wrong to their own souls?

This, this is it that exceedingly provokes God, and makes him thus complain, 'What could have been done more?' Isa. v. 4. And thus, 'O Ephraim, what shall I do unto thee? O Judah, what shall I do unto thee?' Hosea vi. 4. And Christ thus, 'O Jerusalem, Jerusalem, how often would I have gathered thy children together, even as a hen gathereth her chickens under her wing, and ye would not,' Mat. xxiii. 37. Is not God herein despised? No marvel, therefore, that God is so provoked by unbelief, as he is forced to swear vengeance. This turneth kindness into fury.

Read and observe the memorable judgments registered in Scripture, and you shall find that unbelief was a cause of them all. This was the cause of the first judgment inflicted on man, Gen. iii. 4, 5, &c. This was the cause of the general deluge, 1 Peter iii. 19, 20. So of other judgments.

Of unbelief, see more, ver. 12, Sec. 128, &c. See also Chap. iv. 1, Sec. 11.

Sec. 172. *Of the resolution and instructions of* Heb. iii. 18.

Ver. 18. *And to whom sware he that they should not enter into his rest, but to them that believed not?*

The sum of this verse is the damage of unbelief.

Here (as in the former verse) observe two points:
1. The manner of setting down his mind, interrogatively.
2. The matter; which containeth two things,
1. The principal sin, which is *unbelief*.
2. A fearful effect following thereon.

The effect was, an irreversible judgment.

Hereof are two parts:
1. An exclusion from rest; amplified by the kind of rest, which is God's rest: *they shall not enter into his rest.*

The ratification thereof: which is by God's oath, *he sware.*

Doctrines.

I. *God may be provoked to swear vengeance.* This is here taken for grant, see ver. 11, sec. 114.

II. *Unbelief is an high provoking sin.* This was it made God sware. See ver. 11, sec. 128.

III. *Unbelief is the root of every provoking sin.* This is inferred from this particle *but;* God swore against none except such as believed not. See Sec. 170.

IV. *There is a rest for God's people.* This is presupposed under this word rest. See ver. 11, Sec. 116.

V. *The rest of God's people is God's rest.* It is here, in reference to God, called his rest. See ver. 11, Sec. 117.

VI. *God's people may be deprived of their promised rest.* For that which they shall not enter into, they are deprived of. See ver. 11, Sec. 118.

Sec. 173. *Of the meaning of* Heb. iii. 19.

Ver. 19. *So we see that they could not enter in because of unbelief.*

The main point which is to be observed out of David's testimony before mentioned, ver. 7, &c., and out of the apostle's explication thereof, is here set down as a conclusion, thus, 'So we see,' &c.

The Greek particle translated *so,* is the ordinary copulative conjunction *and.* It might fitly have been here retained, as joining the issue of God's oath with the oath itself. Thus, 'God sware they should not enter, &c., *and* we see, that they could not enter in.' As if he had said, We find by the event, that what God did swear is accomplished.

This conclusion is here set down as a transition betwixt the two chapters. For it concludeth the accomplishment of that which went before; and it layeth down the ground of the admonition in the beginning of the next chapter. Of this phrase, *we see,* see Chap. ii. 9, Sec. 72.

This word here implieth an experimental proof, or a proof verified by experience, as that which we see with our eyes. In this sense, saith the apostle, 'I see another law in my members,' Rom. vii. 23. And again, 'Ye see your calling,' &c., 1 Cor. i. 26.

That which was so evident was, that they could not enter in. The same word is here used that was in the verse before this, and in the same sense.

The rest whereinto they could not enter is here understood, and may be repeated, ἀπὸ κοινοῦ, out of the former verse.

This causal conjunction *because,* is in Greek a preposition, διὰ, which may be translated *through.* But it signifieth the cause of a thing, and therefore is well for sense translated *because of.* Of the Greek preposition, see Chap. ii. 9, Sec. 74, and ver. 10, Sec. 89.

The word translated *unbelief,* is the same that was used, ver. 12. Hereof see Sec. 128.

Sec. 174. *Of the sure execution of divine vengeance.*

This conclusion, 'So we see that they could not enter,' &c., giveth evidence, that what God threatened was accordingly accomplished. So was it then: so was it ever before and after. Take for instance the first threatening that ever was made, which was this,

'In the day thou eatest thereof, thou shalt surely die,' Gen. ii. 17. So soon as ever man had eaten thereof, his body was made mortal, and he in the clutches of death, and guilty of eternal damnation. I might add hereunto all the judgments that ever God threatened, even from the first; and I might say of them all, as here it is said, 'So we see,' that thus and thus it fell out, even as God had threatened. 'The curse is poured upon us, and the oath that is written in the law of Moses,' saith a prophet, Dan. ix. 11. 'My words and my statutes which I commanded my servants the prophets, did they not take hold of your fathers?' Zech. i. 6.

Truth is manifested in every word of God, as well threatenings as promises; and by the execution of his threatenings, he is known to be a God of truth, as well as by accomplishment of promises.

Besides, 'The Lord is known by the judgment which he executeth,' Ps. ix. 16. His power, his justice, his hatred of evil, his jealousy, his truth, his providence, and other his divine attributes, are manifested evidently in and by his judgments.

Obj. Though many of God's judgments threatened have answerably been executed, yet not all. For God said to Hezekiah, 'Thou shalt die, and not live,' 2 Kings xx. 1; yet Hezekiah did not then die, but recovered of that disease. And God by his prophet Jonah said, 'That Nineveh should be overthrown within forty days; yet God repented of the evil, and he did it not,' Jonah iii. 4, 10.

Ans. 1. Concerning Hezekiah, the word of the Lord was not uttered in reference to the event, as if indeed he should then die; but in reference to the nature of the disease, which had so far seized upon Hezekiah, as in the ordinary course of nature it was impossible for him to recover, and so to live. His recovery was extraordinary, and even miraculous, as if he had been raised from death.

2. Concerning the threatening against Nineveh, it was but in part revealed. The whole was this, That Nineveh should be destroyed, except they repented. Such a threatening is in whole denounced against Abimelech, thus: 'Restore the man his wife, and thou shalt live: and if thou restore her not, know thou, that thou shalt surely die,' Gen. xx. 7. Now, in that Nineveh repented, the intent of the threatening was accomplished, though Nineveh were not destroyed.

The certainty of the execution of God's threatenings, should make us take heed of slighting them, lest he make us such examples of suffering vengeance, as others shall have cause to say, *So we see*, that they could not escape.

Thus saith the Lord of Zedekiah, 'Seeing he despised the oath, he shall not escape,' Ezek. xvii. 18. And thus saith Christ to the Jews, 'Ye generation of vipers, how can ye escape the damnation of hell?'

Sec. 175. *Of the resolution and observations of* Heb. iii. 18.

Ver. 18. *So we see that they could not enter in because of unbelief.*

The sum of this verse is, the certainty of divine vengeance.

The parts are two,

1. A description of the vengeance.
2. A declaration of the certainty thereof.

The vengeance is described,

1. By the cause thereof, *unbelief.*
2. By the effect following thereupon, *they could not enter in.*

The certainty is set out by an experimental proof, *So we see.*

Doctrines.

I. *Unbelief is the cause of divine vengeance.* It is here clearly expressed so to be. See Sec. 171.

II. *Promises are made void by unbelief.* So was the promise of entering into Canaan. See ver. 11, Sec. 118.

III. *Experience gives proof of the execution of God's threatenings.* This phrase, *So we see*, intends as much. See Sec. 174.

Hebrews 4

Sec. 1. *Of the analysis of* Heb. iv.

It was shewed in the first section of the third chapter, that the apostle having declared Christ to be a faithful prophet, advised those to whom he wrote to take heed of hardening their hearts against Christ's voice. The more thoroughly to enforce his advice, he setteth down the very words of David, which, for the better application thereof to Christians, he expoundeth.

Two points he expounded in the former chapter, namely, the time which David intended under this word *to-day;* and the persons that hardened their heart, and were punished.

The third point which in that testimony he expoundeth, is the *rest* that David meant. This he insisteth upon from the beginning of this chapter to verse 14; and in the three last verses of this chapter he entereth upon the priesthood of Christ.

Thus there are two parts of this chapter:
One concerneth the prophetical office of Christ;
The other his priestly function.

That which the apostle presseth in this chapter is the use to be made of Christ's prophetical office, which is participation of the rest that Christ by the gospel hath made known. For this end he giveth,

1. An admonition, to take heed of missing that rest, ver. 1, &c.

2. An exhortation to do our best for enjoying it, ver. 11, &c.

In the admonition,
1. The general is laid down, ver. 1.
2. The particular rest here intended is demonstrated.

The general is further amplified,
1. By the cause of missing the rest, which is unbelief, ver. 2.
2. By the event, which is twofold:

One event is of those that believed not, 'they entered not into the rest,' ver. 2.

The other of those that believed, 'they entered into it,' ver. 3.

In demonstrating the rest here intended,
1. He removes two kinds of rest that cannot be intended.
2. He infers that there remains another rest.

The first rest removed is God's rest after he had finished the creation, ver. 4. His argument is, that David speaks of a rest long after that, and different from that, ver. 5; therefore the rest of God cannot be meant by David.

The other rest removed is Israel's settling in Canaan.

He proves that this cannot be meant, by two arguments:

The first is taken from the event, which was, that they to whom the promise was made entered not; 'but some must enter,' ver. 6.

Upon removing those two rests he inferreth this conclusion, 'therefore there is another rest remaining,' ver. 9.

The second is taken from the time. That rest of Israel in Canaan was given by Joshua; but the psalmist speaketh of a rest in his own time, and in succeeding ages, vers. 7, 8.

The exhortation to press us on to do our best for attaining to this rest is laid down, ver. 11, and enforced by two motives.

The first motive is taken from the danger of not observing the exhortation, ver. 11.

The other is taken from the efficacy of the word. This is,
1. Propounded, ver. 12.
2. Confirmed by the piercing sight of God, whose word it is, ver. 13.

Hitherto of Christ's prophetical office; his priestly function followeth.

In the three last verses of this chapter there is a perfect transition betwixt those two functions of Christ, so as it hath a double reference.

1. To that which goeth before; so it is a ground of encouragement to observe the foresaid exhortation to enter into the rest, because we have an high priest entered before us and for us, ver. 14.
2. To that which followeth, in the fifth and other chapters, which treat of Christ's priesthood. So it layeth down two points:

1. The sum and substance of that which is after more distinctly and fully declared of Christ's priesthood, ver. 15.
2. The special use we are to make thereof, ver. 16.

Sec. 2. *Of godly jealousy over professors.*

Ver. 1. *Let us therefore fear, lest, a promise [being] left us of entering into his rest, any of you should seem to come short of it.*

This particle of inference, οὖν, *therefore*, leadeth us to a consideration of what went before. In the last verse of the former chapter, the apostle laid down a conclusion concerning the judgment that befell those that believed not. Thence he here inferreth an admonition to take heed of incurring the same danger, and depriving ourselves of the rest that is prepared for us.

He gave a like admonition before, chap. iii. 12, and he doth afterwards oft inculcate the like, as chaps. vi. 4, 11, and x. 23, &c., and xii. 15, 25, 28.

Hereby it appears that he was 'jealous over them with godly jealousy,' as 2 Cor. xi. 2. Certainly some had revolted, so much is implied Heb. x. 25; he was therefore the more jealous over the rest.

Herein he shewed himself like the good and chief Shepherd, who, when 'many of his disciples went back, and walked no more with him, said unto the twelve, Will ye also go away?' John vi. 66, 67.

A worthy pattern this is for all ministers, who are set as shepherds over the Lord's flock, 1 Peter v. 2.

This inference, οὖν, *therefore*, &c., upon the sin and judgment mentioned immediately before (chap. iii. 19), sheweth that judgments on sinners before us must make us the more fearful of such sins. See more hereof Chap. iii. 8, Sec. 89.

Sec. 3. *Of preachers preaching to themselves.*

The apostle, to mollify his jealousy, so sets it down as he includes himself in the number of those over whom he was so jealous. For he useth a verb of the plural number, φοβηθῶμεν, which compriseth all to whom he intendeth this epistle, and the first person, *us*, whereby he includes himself also, so as in admonishing others he admonisheth himself; and what he saw meet to be done for his own establishment, he did for the establishment of others. Of joining ourselves with others, and others with ourselves, in means of edification, see Chap. ii. 5, Sec 4, and Chap. iii. 13, Sec. 144.

He that thus joins himself with others in the same admonition, 'let us fear,' being an apostle, giveth evidence that the best of professors, yea, and ministers, have need of means of establishment as well as others. Christ prayed for Peter, that his faith might not fail, Luke xxii. 32. This apostle saith of himself, 'I keep under my body, and bring it into subjection,' &c., 1 Cor. ix. 27. 'Take heed unto yourselves,' &c., saith the apostle to the elders of Ephesus, Acts xx. 28. For,

1. The best are 'men of like passions with others,' Acts xiv. 15.
2. Great have been the slips of eminent men; as of Moses, Num. xx. 12; David, 2 Sam. xi. 4; Peter and Barnabas, Gal. ii. 12, 13.
3. The best are subject to the sorest temptations, Zech. iii. 1, Luke xxii. 31.
4. The falls of ministers and other eminent professors are most dangerous: they draw many after them, Gal. ii. 13, 2 Peter ii. 1, 2.

Preachers therefore have need to preach to themselves; and they that have charge of others, to take [care] of themselves; and the best and strongest to look to their standing, 1 Cor. x. 12.

Sec. 5. *Of fear lest we fall.*
The word whereby the apostle expresseth his jealousy is *fear*, φοβηθᾶμεν, 'let us fear.' This is a word of an ambiguous signification. Sometimes we are enjoined to fear, as Rom. xi. 20; and sometimes we are forbidden to fear, Luke xii. 32.

Fear is one of the disliking affections; and it is good or evil, according to the object on which it is placed, and according to the ordering of it thereon.

Of the general nature of fear, see Chap. xiii. 6, Sec. 84.

Here it is taken for a disliking affection placed on the right object, which is evil to be shunned, according to the notation of the Greek word, whereof see Chap. ii. 15, Sec. 149.

It here implieth two things:
1. A supposition of such an evil as may fall out.
2. A care to prevent that evil, and to keep it from falling out.

These two may be exemplified in Jacob, who thus saith of his brother Esau, 'I fear him, lest he will come and smite me,' &c. Thus he supposeth that an evil will fall out: hereupon he prayeth that God would deliver him, and withal useth means to prevent that evil, Gen. xxxii. 11, &c.

Thus upon supposal that we may fall, we ought to do what we can to prevent it.

In this sense is this word fear oft used, as Ps. ii. 11, Mal. ii. 5, Philip. ii. 12, Heb. xii. 28. Hence it is, that the man is pronounced happy 'that feareth alway,' Prov. xxviii. 14.

Man's natural proneness to fall, and the many temptations whereunto he is subject, together with the deceitfulness of sin, the subtilty and sedulity of Satan, and God's justice in leaving men to themselves, are strong enforcements of this duty of fear. Of all these, see Chap. iii. 12, Sec. 122.

Obj. We are in many places dehorted from fear, as Gen. xv. 1, and xxvi. 24, 2 Tim. i. 7, 1 John iv. 18.

Ans. We must distinguish in this case. There is a fear of the Creator, and of the creature. Both these are good and bad.

The good fear of the Creator, is such a reverent awe of the divine majesty, as maketh us very careful in all things to please him, and fearful of offending him. In this respect we are very suspicious and jealous over ourselves in regard of acts past, lest therein we have offended him, as Job said of his children, 'It may be that my sons have sinned,' Job i. 5; or in regard of the future, lest we should offend.

The evil fear of the Creator is a servile, distrustful affection and disposition, whereby we apprehend him to be so terrible a judge, as we shall never please him; and in that respect tremble at the very thought of God, of the day of judgment, and of hell fire. Thus the devils are said to tremble, James ii. 19. This is the spirit of bondage, and a slavish fear.

Of good and evil fear of man, see Chap. xiii. 6, Secs. 85, 86.

The fear here meant is that good fear of God, which makes us fearful of offending him, and thereupon very jealous over ourselves.

About this fear it becomes us thoroughly to examine ourselves, and upon finding any evidence thereof in our souls, to nourish and cherish the same, and to take heed both of such presumption as Peter fell into, Mat. xxvi. 33, 35; and also of such security as is implied to be in him who is resembled to an house swept and garnished, and thereby fitted for the devil, Luke xi. 25, 26.

The Greek word μήποτε, which implieth a danger and damage that may follow upon want of the foresaid fear, is thus translated *lest*. It is compounded of two conjunctions, whereof one, μή, intendeth a caution; the other, ποτέ, a continuance therein. Hereupon this very word is thus translated, 'lest at any time,' chap ii. 1.

In this extent it compriseth a perpetual jealousy.

This particle *lest*, intendeth jealousy, caution and circumspection.

This phrase, *at any time*, implieth continuance therein. Of both these, see Chap. iii. ver. 12, Secs. 122, 123, 124, 125.

Sec. 6. *Of promises of rest.*
In setting down the danger to be feared, the apostle takes it for grant that we have a promise of entering into God's rest, in this phrase, 'lest, a promise being left us of entering into his rest.'

The noun ἐπαγγελία, translated *promise*, is a compound. The simple verb ἀγγέλλειν, whence it is derived, signifieth *to declare,* or to bring tidings of a thing. Thence the word ἄγγελος, angel, which signifieth a *messenger*, is derived. The verb compounded ἐπαγγέλλομαι signifieth *to promise*, which is to declare one's mind beforehand, Acts vii. 5. A promise then is, a declaration beforehand of some good intended; yea, such a declaration as binds the promiser to perform what he hath declared; so as he who is faithful will answerably do it, 1 Thess. v. 24.

There are sundry promises of rest in sacred Scripture: some typical, prefiguring the rest here intended; others plainly expressing it, in the inchoation or consummation of it.

Promises of typical rest were these:
1. The Sabbath, Deut. v. 14.
2. The passover (Exod. xii. 16), and sundry other feasts.
3. Every seventh year, Lev. xxv. 4.
4. Every fiftieth year, called the jubilee, Lev. xxv. 10.
5. The land of Canaan, Deut. iii. 20.
6. Freedom from enemies, 1 Chron. xxii. 9.

The true rest, in regard of the inchoation, and beginning thereof, is,
1. Peace with God, Rom. v. 1; Philip. iv. 7. This Christ calleth 'his peace,' John xiv. 27, and xvi. 33.
2. Quiet of mind, Exod. xxxiii. 14; Mat. xi. 28, 29.
3. Joy in the Holy Ghost, Rom. xiv. 17.
4. Communion with Christ, Eph. ii. 5, 6.
5. Rest in the grave, as in a bed, Isa. lvii. 2.

The true rest, in the consummation and perfection thereof, shall be enjoyed in heaven, 2 Thess. i. 7.

The gospel promises of the true rest, both in the beginning and also in the full accomplishment thereof, are here specially intended: as peace with God, quiet of mind, rest in the grave, and fruition of heavenly glory. This last is the most principal, and promised under sundry other titles: as 'immortal inheritance,' 1 Pet. i. 4; 'kingdom,' Luke xii. 32; 'crown of glory,' 1 Pet. v. 4.

1. God in his unsearchable wisdom seeth it meet to set a long date before he give his children full fruition of the things which he hath determined for their good. Seventy years were set for the return of the Jews out of the Babylonish captivity, Jer. xxv. 11, 12; four hundred years for the settling of Abraham's seed in Canaan, Gen. xv. 13; four thousand years almost for the Redeemer of mankind to be actually exhibited. Six thousand years are going apace for the last coming of the great Judge, foretold by Enoch, Jude 14.

2. In like wisdom God oft brings his children to many trials. Instance the case of Israel in Egypt and in Babylon.

In these respects the Lord, to uphold the faith of them to whom those good things are intended, maketh promises of them beforehand.

The expectation of the rest of Canaan, promised to Abraham and his seed, supported the spirits of the believing Israelites in Egypt, and in the wilderness. Much more will the heavenly rest promised uphold the hearts of believing Christians. 'These things,' saith Christ to his disciples, 'I have spoken unto you, that ye might have peace,' &c. Upon the promise of this rest, the apostle makes this conclusion, 'Comfort one another,' 1 Thes. iv. 18.

That we may be the better established by these promises, we ought to set this rest before us, and much to meditate thereon, as Moses did, Heb. xi. 26, and Christ, Heb. xii. 2. Of applying promises, see *The Whole Armour of God*, treat. ii. part vi., on Eph. vi. 16. Of faith, Sec. 71.

Sec. 7. *Of forsaking a promise.*

The phrase καταλειπομένης ἐπαγγελίας, 'a promise being left us,' is somewhat ambiguous. The pronoun *us*, which causeth the ambiguity, is not in the Greek text. Our English seemeth to take the word *left* for *given*, as if it had been said, 'lest, a promise being given us.' If the pronoun had been expressed, it might have carried some such sense. This verb with a pronoun is thus translated, κατέλιπον ἐμαυτῷ, 'I have reserved to myself,' &c, Rom. xi. 4; and without a pronoun, thus, οὐ κατέλιπον τέκνα, 'they left no children,' Luke xx. 31.

The verb here used, καταλείπειν, properly signifieth to forsake, and so it is turned by these translators, Heb. xi. 27, 2 Peter ii. 15. Our former English translators thus rendered it in this place, 'by forsaking the promise.' The simple verb λείπω, *desum*, signifieth to *want*, or to be wanting, or to lack, Luke xviii. 22, Titus i. 5, and iii. 13.

The verb here used is of the passive voice, and it may be thus translated, 'the promise being left,' or forsaken. To leave or forsake a promise, is to neglect the course which is appointed for obtaining the thing promised. Thus the house of Eli left the promise made to them: whereupon the Lord saith, 'I said indeed that thy house, and the house of thy father, should walk before me for ever. But now the Lord saith, Be it far from me,' 1 Sam. ii. 30. In like manner Jeroboam forsook a promise: for proof hereof, compare 1 Kings xi. 38 with 1 Kings xiv. 9, 10.

Of unbelievers depriving themselves of the benefit of God's promises, see Chap. iii. 11, Sec. 118.

That which our last translators express under this phrase, 'a promise being left us,' is included in the word promise. For the very making of a promise to any, is a leaving it with them. In this sense it doth on the one side amplify God's goodness in leaving with them a precious promise of rest; and on the other side it doth aggravate their folly in losing the benefit of such a promise left them.

Sec. 8. *Of leaving the promise of rest.*

The thing promised is thus expressed, *entering into his rest*.

Of the notation of the Greek noun κατάπαυσις, translated *rest*, and of the emphasis of the verb εἰσελθεῖν, translated *enter into*, see Chap. iii. 11, Sec. 116.

The rest here meant, is that truth and substance which was typified by Canaan, namely, heaven itself, chap. ix. 24. This is the rest which remaineth to us, ver. 9; and this is it whereabout the apostle would have us jealous over ourselves, and fear lest we leave and forsake the promise of it. This is the rest which God will recompense to his servants that are here troubled, 2 Thes. i. 7. Hereby 'they who die in the Lord rest from their labours,' Rev. xiv. 13.

To shew that we ought not to leave the promise of this rest, we are exhorted to 'lay hold on eternal life,'

1 Tim. vi. 12; to 'strive to enter in at the strait gate,' Luke xiii. 24; to 'work out our salvation,' Philip. ii. 12. And this is to 'labour to enter into that rest,' Heb. iv. 11.

This metaphor *rest*, whereby our future happiness in heaven is set out, is a sufficient motive to enforce that duty.

Here in this world we are subject to hard travail, sore labour, manifold troubles, great dangers, fierce assaults, violent temptations, grievous sins, and many mischiefs, from all which we have rest in heaven. For then 'shall all tears be wiped away,' Rev. xxi. 4. In this respect they are pronounced blessed who attain to this rest, Rev. xiv. 13. This doth much aggravate their folly, who any way leave the promise of entering into this rest, by refusing to walk in that way, and to observe that course which is in God's word prescribed for attaining to this rest.

If the Israelites manifested egregious folly, and a wilful disposition, by depriving themselves of the rest promised in Canaan, what do they who leave the promise of entering into this rest?

This very rest is enough to make a wise man do and endure any thing, which may at length bring him thereunto.

The hireling cheerfully doth his work, the husbandman readily taketh pains, the soldier courageously adventureth his life, the mariner resolutely passeth over the seas, and others in their places take much pains, and endure much hardness, knowing that they shall have a rest: at least hoping for it. Should we Christians fail in our task, and leave the promise of entering into this rest?

This rest is a freedom from all outward molestations, from persecution, from grief and care of mind, from sickness, from pain, from all losses, and other crosses, yea, and from sin itself. Should we then leave the promise of entering thereinto?

Sec. 9. *Of heaven, styled God's rest.*

To amplify the rest here intended, the apostle, in reference to God, styleth it αὐτοῦ, '*his* rest.'

It was shewed before (Chap. iii. 11, Sec. 117), in what respects Canaan was called God's rest.

Much more fitly may this rest be so called, and that in these respects:

1. The rest of heaven was prepared by God from the foundation of the world, Mat. xxv. 34.
2. It was purchased by the precious blood of the Son of God, Heb. ix. 12.
3. We are conducted thereunto by the Spirit of God, Gal. v. 5, 25.
4. It is made known and promised to us by the word of God, Mat. xiii. 19.
5. Heaven is the habitation and resting-place of God, Mat. v. 34, and vi. 9.
6. There all believers shall rest with God, Father, Son, and Holy Ghost, and have their everlasting communion with him, John xvii. 21, 24; Heb. xii. 22, &c.
7. It is a most excellent rest. For things excellent are said to be of God, Ps. lxxxvii. 3.

This adds an edge to the foresaid duties of striving and labouring to enter into this rest. Who would not enter into the rest of God?

This also doth yet further aggravate the sin of those that leave the promise of this rest, in that it is God's rest.

Sec. 10. *Of jealousy over ourselves and others.*

The persons liable to the damage of leaving the foresaid promise, are set out in these words, τις ἐξ ὑμῶν, *any of you.*

The adjective τις, *any*, is an extensive word. It sheweth that the duty required must be performed to others, and that of what rank or degree soever. For all of all sorts are subject to this damage of coming short.

The pronoun following with the preposition, ἐξ ὑμῶν, *of you*, are words inclusive. They include men themselves; so as Christians must be jealous over others and themselves too, over themselves and others too. They must fear lest themselves, or any among them, come short.

Of circumspection over ourselves, and also over others, see Chap. iii. 12, Secs. 123, 124.

Sec. 11. *Of the damage of coming short of the promise.*

The damage like to follow upon leaving the promise of rest is comprised under this verb, ὑστερηκέναι, *come short.* The verb is derived from a root, ὕστερον, which signifieth *afterwards*, and that many times when it is too late, as the foolish virgins, the door being shut, 'afterwards came,' Mat. xxv. 11. Answerably this verb, ὑστερεῖσθαι, signifieth to come after, or behind, or short: 'Ye come behind in no gift,' saith the apostle; 1 Cor. i. 7; that is, ye come not behind them that have attained such and such gifts, but ye also have your part and portion therein.

It is sometimes taken to want or lack a thing, as, What lack I yet? ὑστερῶ, Mat. xix. 20. And 'he began to be in want,' ὑστερεῖσθαι, Luke xv. 14.

It is likewise taken to fail of a thing, as, 'lest any man fail,' ὑστερῶν, Heb. xii. 15.

Men want, lack, fail, or come short of a thing two ways.

1. When that which they had is exhausted and clean gone. Thus it is said, when the wine which was prepared for a wedding feast was all drunk up, 'they wanted wine,' John ii. 3.
2. When men have not attained to that which is set before them. Thus it is said of all unregenerate persons, 'They come short of the glory of God,' Rom. iii. 23.

The word used by the apostle is taken from runners in a race, who, if they be idle, secure, careless, heavy, lazy, come behind or short of the prize, and fail of obtaining it. So secure Christians, that fear not lest they leave the promise of entering into God's rest, will assuredly come short of it, and fail of the benefit thereof. Such, among others, are unbelievers. These shall never enter into God's rest.

This demonstrateth the wrong that unbelievers, and all careless, idle, and secure professors do to themselves. They come short of the glorious prize that is set before them, and so bring shame, disgrace, and irreparable damage to themselves. For lazy runners are shouted at, and that in scorn and derision, by all the spectators, and judged most unworthy of any approbation or remuneration. Their doom is expressly set down, Luke xiii. 27, 28, Mat. xxv. 11, 12, 28–30. Of the damage of unbelief, see more, Chap. iii. 12, Sec. 129, and ver. 18, Sec. 171.

Sec. 12. *Of not coming short of the goal.*

This metaphor of *coming short* having reference to runners in a race, doth afford good direction and great encouragement for doing our best to enter into God's rest.

Particular rules of direction are these and such like.
1. 'Be temperate in all things,' 1 Cor. ix. 25.
2. 'Lay aside every weight, and the sin which doth so easily beset us,' Heb. xii. 1.
3. 'Run the way of God's commandments,' Ps. cxix. 32; this is 'the race that is set before us,' Heb. xii. 1.
4. Make speed, and be not lazy, Ps. cxix. 60. The metaphor of running implies thus much.
5. Strive to outstrip others. We must 'seek that we may excel to the edifying of the church,' 1 Cor. xiv. 12.
6. Have an eye to that which is before, and look not back to what is behind, Philip. iii. 13.
7. Give not over till thou come to the goal, Rev. ii. 10. If thou givest over, thou mayest come short of the prize.

Encouragements are such as these:
1. A faithful endeavour will be accepted, 2 Cor. viii. 12, Philip. iii. 13.
2. Not one only (as in races among men), but all that do their best endeavour, shall partake of the prize. The apostle, speaking hereof, saith, 'The righteous Judge will give a crown, not to me only, but to them also that love his appearing,' 2 Tim. iv. 8. For 'whosoever shall call upon the name of the Lord shall be saved,' Rom. x. 13.
3. God, who seeth all, and beareth a like respect to all that run well, is the rewarder, Eph. vi. 8.
4. The crown that is given is incorruptible, 1 Cor. ix. 25.

Sec. 13. *Of this word 'seem.'*

There is further in this admonition a word inserted worthy our due consideration. It is this, δοκῇ 'should seem.' There are sundry respects in which it may be brought in, as,
1. To mitigate the sharpness of his admonition; in that he doth not positively conclude that he took them for apostates, but only implieth that they may seem to be in hazard of that case. It intends as much as the insinuation[1] doth, whereby he seems to call back or correct that, which might be so taken, as if he had surmised that they would prove apostates, Heb. vi. 7.
2. To stir up their fear the more, even against such coldness and dulness as might hazard the prize set before them. To such a purpose he saith, 'I am jealous over you with godly jealousy,' 2 Cor. xi. 2.
3. To manifest the extent of a Christian's watchfulness, which must be against a seeming, or appearing to be an apostate. We may not think it enough that we do not utterly fall away; but that we do not seem so to do, and that we do not give occasion to other Christians to think that we are fallen, or like to fall. The apostle to this purpose giveth this advice, 'Abstain from all appearance of evil,' 1 Thes. v. 22.
4. To demonstrate the condition of hypocrites, who seem to be what they are not: 'They think they stand,' 1 Cor. x. 12. 'That shall be taken from them which they seem to have,' Luke viii. 18. This an apostle doth thus clear, 'They went out from us, but they were not of us: for if they had been of us, they would no doubt have continued with us: but they went out, that they might be made manifest that they were not all of us,' 1 John ii. 19.
5. To aggravate the fault of backsliders. Through want of the foresaid Christian fear, they seem, or appear, or give evidence that they will come short of the prize. For to seem is oft put for an evidence. James, Cephas, and John seemed to be pillars, Gal. ii. 9, that is, they evidently appeared to be so.

Of the word here used, see more Chap. x. 29, Sec. 108.

Sec. 14. *Of the resolution and observations of* Heb. iv. 1.

1. *Let us therefore fear, lest, a promise being left us, of entering into his rest, any of you should seem to come short of it.*

The sum of this text is a caveat against backsliding.

Two points are hereabout to be observed:
1. The inference, *therefore.*
2. The substance.

Of the substance there are two parts:
1. An admonition.
2. An incitation to observe it.

(1.) The matter of the admonition is in this word, *fear.*

(2.) The manner is manifested in the first person, and plural number, *let us.*

In laying down the incitation, the apostle demonstrateth,
1. The ground.
2. The damage of backsliding.

[1] ἐπανόρθωσις.

The ground is expressed in this phrase, *a promise being left*. Here observe,
1. Their deficiency, *left*, &c.
2. The subject thereof, which was a *promise*.

Their deficiency is set out,
1. By the thing promised, *rest*.
2. By the kind of rest, *his*, namely God's.
3. By the fruition they might have had thereof, *entering into*.

2. The damage is,
1. Generally implied in this particle of supposition, *lest*.
2. Particularly exemplified,

In the exemplification are set down,
1. The kind of damage, *come short*.
2. The persons who incur that damage, *any of you*.
3. The time, *at any time*.
4. The extent of avoiding it, in this word *seem*.

Doctrines.

I. *We must be warned by others' harms.* For this end the apostle infers this admonition on judgments executed upon the Israelites, *therefore*. See Chap. iii. 8, Sec. 89.

II. *Admonishers of others' must admonish themselves.* The apostle in using the plural number admonisheth others, and using the first person he admonisheth himself, *let us*. See Sec. 3.

III. *Christians must be fearful of falling away.* This is it whereabout we are enjoined to fear. See Sec. 5.

IV. *There is a rest for God's people.* This is here taken for grant under this word *rest*. See Sec. 6.

V. *The rest prepared for saints is God's rest.* This relative *his* hath reference to God. See Sec. 9.

VI. *The good intended to God's people is promised to them.* This also is here taken for grant under this word, *a promise*. See Sec. 6.

VII. *It is dangerous to leave a promise.* This is here laid down as the ground of missing the promise. See Sec. 8.

VIII. *We must be circumspect.* This word of caution, *lest*, intends as much. See Sec. 5.

IX. *Our circumspection must be over ourselves and others impartially.* See Sec. 10.

X. *Apostates fail of the prize.* This metaphor, *come short*, intends this. See Sec. 11.

XI. *We must so run that we may obtain.* We are here forewarned not to *come short*. See Sec. 12.

XII. *Appearance of backsliding is to be avoided*, We may not *seem* to come short. See Sec. 13.

Sec. 15. *Of the inference of the second verse on the first.*

Verse 2. *For unto us was the gospel preached, as well as unto them: but the word preached did not profit them, not being mixed with faith in them that heard it.*

The apostle presseth his former admonition of fearing the like judgment that was inflicted on the Israelites, by the like means of stedfastness afforded to us that was afforded to them. The argument may be thus framed:

They who have like privileges, may expect the like judgments that were inflicted on them that perverted the privileges;

But we Christians have the same privileges that the Israelites had;

Therefore we Christians may expect the like judgments, if we pervert the privileges.

The particular privilege wherein the apostle exemplifieth his argument, is the gospel preached. It was preached to the Israelites, and it is preached to the Christians.

That this common privilege is here brought in as a reason to enforce the former admonition, is evident by the two first particles, καὶ γὰρ, *for, also ;* or *for, even*. It becomes us therefore well to use that privilege and means of salvation, which God still affordeth to us, as he had afforded to the Israelites, lest by our failing therein we provoke God to deal with us as he hath dealt with others on the like ground.

See more hereof on Chap. iii. 11, Sec. 113.

Sec. 16. *Of the blessing of the gospel.*

This phrase, *the gospel was preached*, is the interpretation of one Greek word, εὐηγγελισμένοι, which may be thus translated, *gospelised*, or *evangelised ;* the persons being added thereto, thus, ἐσμὴν, *we are evangelised*. This is a Greekism used again, ver. 6, and Mat. xi. 5.

Our English hath fully and fitly interpreted the Greekism, thus, 'unto us was the gospel preached.'

The verb is a compound. The simple verb ἀγγέλλειν signifieth to declare ; as to bring a message, tidings, or news. The adverb, ἔυ, with which it is compounded, signifieth *well ;* in composition *good*, as εὐαγγελίζεσθαι, to declare a good message, to bring good tidings. Of the notation and sense of this word, see *The Whole Armour of God*, on Eph. vi. 15, treat. ii. part v. sec. 4. See also Chap. vi. Sec. 35, and Chap. xiii. 9, Sec. 117.

This relative, *us*,—' unto us '—hath reference to the church, in and since Christ's time. For we are here set down in opposition to them that lived under the law.

The compound verb intendeth two things:

1. That the gospel is the ground of faith. It was for this end made known to the Israelites and Christians. Of the gospel working faith, see *The Whole Armour of God* on Eph. vi. 16. Of faith, treat. ii., part vi., secs. 19, 21.

2. That preaching the gospel is the most usual and powerful means to work faith, see Chap. ii. 3, Sec. 23.

The force of the foresaid reason intends a third point.

3. That where the gospel is preached, faith, obedience, and perseverance in our Christian course; this is it which the apostle presseth to restrain us

from the sins whereinto the Israelites fell, and to keep them from backsliding; and by consequence to make them faithful in their holy profession.

This motive did the forerunner of Christ, and Christ himself, use for that end, in these words, 'Repent, for the kingdom of heaven is at hand,' Mat. iii. 2, and iv. 17. So did Christ's apostles after him, Acts ii. 38, 39, and xvii. 30.

By preaching the gospel, offer is made of remission of sins, of reconciliation with God, and of eternal salvation.

Good reason therefore that repentance, faith, and new obedience are to be yielded. To refuse to yield to the gospel, is to reject the counsel of God against one's self, Luke vii. 30.

Just cause we have well to observe, what by the gospel is required and expected. In what age of the world, in what nation, in what city and place, hath the gospel been more plentifully, perspicuously and powerfully preached than among us?

Sec. 17. *Of the gospel preached before Christ's time, as well as since.*

The former argument the apostle yet further enforceth, by comparing the estate of Christians with the estate of the Israelites, in this phrase, *as well as unto them.* This intends thus much, that the gospel was preached to Christians, as well as to the Israelites.

The apostle layeth it down as a case unquestionable, that the gospel was preached to the Israelites, even under the law (for these are they who are comprised under these words, κἀκεῖνοι, ' as unto them'). This was before proved, Chap. ii. 3, Sec. 20.

The gospel only, and the preaching of it, is 'the power of God to salvation,' Rom. i. 16. They who, since Adam's fall, had not the gospel, had no ordinary way to be saved.

This gives us information of sundry remarkable points: as,

1. Of the antiquity of the gospel.
2. Of the constancy of God in saving man the same way.
3. Of the necessity of Jesus Christ, who is the very substance of the gospel.
4. Of the unity of the catholic church, which hath ever been the same, consisting of such as have believed the gospel.
5. Of the identity of the old and new covenant. I do not mean the old covenant of works made with Adam, in his innocency, but that which was confirmed to Abraham by circumcision, and to the Israelites by sacrifices, and other legal rites. For the gospel was comprised under that covenant.

This privilege concerning the gospel preached to the Jews, is here set down by way of comparison, in this word, καθάπερ, *as well.* It hath reference to Christians, who are not therein inferior to the Israelites.

There are many privileges wherein we go before them; as the actual exhibition of Christ, the clear revelation of the mysteries of godliness, the powerful operation of God's Spirit, the truth and substance of their types and shadows, the accomplishment of their prophecies and promises.[1] They did indeed 'eat spiritual meat, and drink spiritual drink, which was Christ;' but it was the same that we eat and drink, 1 Cor. x. 3, 4. We have a like figure to that which Noah had, 1 Peter iii. 20.

Should we now come behind them in any gift or grace? Can we think to go more scot-free than they did? Or to escape if we so slight the gospel, as they did? Well mark the inference which the apostle makes upon a like ground, 1 Cor. x. 6, &c.

Where like privileges and benefits are bestowed, there evidences are given of like grace and favour. Therefore like faith, like obedience, like patience, like thankfulness, like faithfulness, is expected.

Sec. 18. *Of the word of hearing.*

By this particle of opposition, ἀλλὰ, *but,* the apostle intends an unsuitable carriage in the Israelites to God's gracious dealing with them. God afforded them his gospel, but they gave not that respect to it which was meet. They believed it not; so as the most gracious message, and powerful means of working grace, nought wrought on the incredulous. Of people sinning under the gospel, see Chap. iii. 16, Sec. 162.

The word here intended is the gospel before mentioned. It is in Greek styled ὁ λόγος τῆς ἀκοῆς, *sermo auditionis,* 'the word of hearing,' after the Hebrew manner, for 'the word heard.'

The word spoken is as no word if it be not heard. Our former English translators thus turn it, 'the word that they heard.' It was a word which they did hear, or might, or should have heard.

The apostle thus styles it in two especial respects:

1. To demonstrate the necessity of hearing the word. The word, if we would receive any benefit thereby, must be heard. For the word spoken or preached can do no good to him that hears it not; no more than the light to him that seeth it not. The apostle saith of a word spoken in a strange language, that it cannot profit him who understands it not, 1 Cor. xiv. 9. Much less can any good be received by the word if it be not heard. It is as a necessary requisite required to hear, Gen. xlix. 2, Deut. v. 1, Acts ii. 22, Rev. ii. 7. Hearing is that proper sense, whereby words spoken may enter into the soul. Hereby we are informed that,

(1.) Deafness is a great calamity.

(2.) It is a wretched disposition to refuse to come where the sound of the word may be heard.

(3.) To sleep at church while the word is preaching is a great evil. They that are asleep cannot hear the word.

---

[1] Of the better things which Christians enjoy, see my sermon on Ezek. xxxvi. 11, entitled, *The Progress of God's Providence.*

(4.) A preacher's weak and low voice is a great discommodity.

(5.) Shoutings, or any other loud noises, or loud sounds near the place where the word is preached, or other divine service performed, are very inconvenient. The word cannot be in these cases a 'word of hearing.'

2. To take away vain pretences and excuses from such as grumble at judgments inflicted on such as profit not by the word.

The blame hereby appears to be in themselves, because it is 'a word of hearing. For if it be demanded, (as Rom. x. 18,) 'Have they not heard?' this phrase gives a ready answer; the word afforded unto them is 'a word of hearing.' It was heard, or might have been heard. It was not concealed, as the conference betwixt king Zedekiah and the prophet Jeremiah was, Jer. xxxviii. 27. It was not softly whispered in the ground, as the word of them that had familiar spirits was, Isa. viii. 19. It was not uttered in a strange language, which could not be understood by the hearers, 1 Cor. xiv. 2. But it was a word of hearing.

This doth not only take away all excuse from non-proficients, but it doth also much aggravate their sin. It is said of the Israelites, that the word of hearing profited them not, no, though it were heard by them. For these last words, 'in them that heard it,' take it for grant that the Israelites heard the word; so as the word heard may be without profit. Thus it is in most hearers. This Christ doth exemplify and evidence in the parable of the seed; wherein is shewed that of four sorts of hearers, only one sort proves profitable, Mat. xiii. 23. In that parable, sundry reasons are rendered of hearers' non-proficiency. It is therefore necessary to 'take heed how we hear,' Luke viii. 18. Hereof see more Chap. iii. 7, Sec. 77.

The word ὠφέλησε, translated *profited*, compriseth under it all manner of good, Mat. xv. 5. But a negative added thereunto implieth no good at all, Gal. v. 2. Such is the extent of the negative in this place: and of the privative compound ἀνωφελές, translated *unprofitableness*, Chap. vii. 8, Sec. 85.

Sec. 19. *Of faith making the word profitable.*

The apostle declareth an especial reason of hearers' non-proficiency, in these words, 'not being mixed with faith in them that heard it.' Our last English translators in their margin, note another reading, namely, this, 'because they were not united by faith to them that heard it.' Sundry Greek copies and fathers[1] so set down this text. Thus it carrieth this sense, the greatest part of Israel were not of the mind whereof Joshua, Caleb, and others, who believed God's promise of bringing them into Canaan, were; and thereupon reaped no benefit by the promise. Though there be a difference in the words betwixt this and the other reading, yet both agree in the same sense, which is this, that want of faith makes the word unprofitable; it makes even the gospel itself (which is 'the power of God unto salvation, to every one that believeth,' Rom. i. 16) altogether fruitless to such as believe not.

The Greek verb συγκεκραμμένος, thus translated, 'being mixed with,' is a compound. The simple verb κεραννύω, *vel* κεράννυμι, *infundo*, signifieth to pour in, or to fill, Rev. xviii. 5. Thence is derived a noun, κρατὴρ, that signifieth a chalice, or great cup whereinto they use to pour wine. The preposition σύν, wherewith the verb is here compounded, signifieth *with*; so as this compound implieth a pouring in of one thing with another, which is a mixing of them together. This word is translated tempered together, συνεκέρασε, 1· Cor. xii. 24.

The word is very pertinent to the point in hand. It is a metaphor taken from a potion, which, according to the ingredients put into it, is medicinable or mortal. The word preached is the potion, which, if it be mixed with faith, is sweet and wholesome; but, mixed with infidelity, is bitter and deadly. The word was so delivered to the Israelites, as they heard it. So much is here expressly set down, 'in them which heard it,' yet it was fruitless.

Thus we see that the gospel heard, if not believed, remains fruitless; as the brazen serpent was of no use to them that looked not upon it, Num. xxi. 8. 'He that believeth shall be saved; but he that believeth not shall be damned,' Mark xvi. 16. Therefore this act of believing is still applied to the word, where the power of it is set forth, Acts xv. 7, Rom. i. 16, Eph. i. 13.

The word doth only offer grace; it is faith that receiveth it. As to have meat set before one, or to have a potion or any other medicine prepared and offered, doth no good, if the meat be not eaten, the potion drunk, and the medicine applied; so the word preached and heard doth no good, except it be believed. Faith is the hand, mouth, and stomach of the soul, whereby we receive, eat, and digest all manner of spiritual food.

We are hereby taught how to hear, namely, so as we believe God's word, and all things contained therein, to be a truth, and thereupon to give due credence thereunto; yea, also, to believe it as a truth that concerns us in particular, and thereupon to apply it to ourselves. Thus will every part of God's word be useful and profitable unto us. The precepts thereof will direct us, the admonitions make us wary, the consolations cheer us, and the threatenings terrify us.

This mixing of faith with hearing the word shews that there is a mutual relation betwixt the word and faith. The word, as a mother, breeds and brings forth faith; faith, as a loving daughter, nourisheth and cherisheth the word, and makes it more fruitful. Without the word there can be no faith, Rom. x. 14, 17; without faith the word can have no power.

---

[1] Chrysost. Theophylact. Œcum. aliique in loc. Complut. '*Non profuit sermo auditus illis, non contemperatus fidei eorum qui obedierunt.*'—Aug. Error in Ps. lxxvii.

If we desire faith, we must be diligent in hearing the word. If we would have the word profitable, we must believe it. As hearing distinguisheth professors from profane, so believing distinguisheth the upright from hypocrites.

Sec. 20. *Of the resolution and observations of* Heb. iv. 2.

Ver. 2. *For unto us was the gospel preached, as well as unto them: but the word preached did not profit them, not being mixed with faith in them that heard it.*

The sum of this verse is, a motive against treading in the steps of the incredulous Israelites.

The causal conjunction *for*, sheweth that this is inferred upon the former verse, as a motive.

Of this motive there are two parts:
1. A like privilege afforded to Christians as to Israelites.
2. The ground of failing of the benefit of that privilege.

In the former,
1. The privilege is simply propounded.
2. Comparatively applied.

In the simple proposition there is,
1. The kind of privilege, *the gospel preached*.
2. The persons to whom that privilege was afforded, *to us*.

The comparative application implies a likeness betwixt Christians and Israelites in the same privilege, *as well as unto them*.

In setting down the ground of failing of the benefit of that privilege, two points are manifested:
1. The failing in general.
2. The particular cause thereof.

In the general,
1. There is a repetition of the privilege in this phrase, *word of hearing*.
2. An expression of the failing, *profited not*.

The cause of this failing is,
1. Propounded, in this phrase, *not being mixed with faith*.
2. Amplified by the persons, *in them that heard it*.

Doctrines.

I. *Abuse of like privilege causeth like judgment.* This is the main intendment of the apostle's reason, under this particle *for*. See Sec. 15.

II. *The gospel is an especial privilege.* To this end, mention is here made of it. See Sec. 16.

III. *The gospel is made powerful by preaching.* The word *evangelised* imports as much. See Sec. 16.

IV. *The gospel was preached to the Israelites before Christ.* This relative, *to them*, hath reference to those Israelites. See Sec. 17.

V. *Christians are partakers of the best privileges that the Jews had.* This note of similitude, *as well*, giveth evidence hereof. See Sec. 17.

VI. *The gospel is to be hearkened unto.* It is a word of hearing. See Sec. 18.

VII. *Faith makes the word profitable.* For the word which was not mixed with faith was unprofitable. See Sec. 19.

VIII. *Hearing without believing is in vain.* They who heard, because they believed not, received no profit. See Sec. 19.

Sec. 21. *Of the difference between believers and unbelievers.*

Ver. 3. *For we which have believed do enter into rest,* &c.

This causal conjunction $\gamma\grave{\alpha}\rho$, *for*, implieth, that this clause is added as a reason to confirm that which went before. The reason is drawn from the force of contraries. For logicians affirm, and experience confirms, that of contraries there be contrary consequences, *contrariorum contraria sunt consequentia*. Now faith and unbelief are contraries, therefore their consequences are contrary. Unbelievers cannot enter into God's rest, for believers enter thereinto. This is the privilege of believers.

Add to these words an exclusive particle, *only*, which must be understood, and the argument will be the more evident, thus: Believers only enter into God's rest; therefore unbelievers cannot enter thereinto.

Hereby it appears that there is as great a difference betwixt believers and unbelievers, as can be betwixt men, even as great as betwixt heirs of heaven and heirs of hell. For here heaven is made the portion of believers; but hell is the portion of unbelievers, Rev. xxi. 8.

What fellowship now and communion may there be betwixt them? Read, for this purpose, 2 Cor. vi. 14, 15.

Sec. 22. *Of Christians judging themselves and others.*

As the apostle, in case of Christian jealousy, joined himself with others in this phrase, $\varphi o\beta\eta\vartheta\tilde{\omega}\mu\varepsilon\nu$, *Let us fear*, ver. 1, so here he doth the like in the case of Christian assurance, using the first person in reference to himself, and the plural number in reference to others, thus, $\varepsilon i\sigma\varepsilon\rho\chi \acute{o}\mu\varepsilon\vartheta\alpha$, *we do enter*; what in judgment of certainty he knew of himself, in judgment of charity he professeth of others. Hence I infer two conclusions:

1. That a true believer may know that he doth believe; or, that he hath a true faith. See hereof *The Whole Armour of God*, on Eph. vi. 16, treat. ii. part v. Of faith, Sec. 86.

2. That what we know of ourselves we ought to judge of others who profess what we do. So did the apostle in these words, 'Knowing, brethren beloved, your election of God,' 1 Thes. i. 4.

And again, 'God hath from the beginning chosen you to salvation,' 2 Thes. ii. 13. Thus another apostle calls those to whom he wrote, 'a chosen generation,' 1 Pet. ii. 9. To these Hebrews saith this apostle, 'Beloved, we are persuaded of you, the things that accompany salvation,' Heb. vi. 9.

The rule of judging others is charity. But 'charity believeth all things, hopeth all things,' 1 Cor. xiii. 7. It believeth and hopeth the best that may be believed and hoped of another.

How contrary to the apostolical practice is the practice of most men, who are very rash and unjust censurers of others! Like to the pharisee, Luke xviii. 9, &c.

Sec. 23. *Of faith's giving right to God's promise.*

The qualification of such as reap the benefit of God's promise is thus set down, *which have believed.* To believe is to yield such credence to the truth of God's promise, as to rest on him for participation of the thing promised. Of faith, see *The Whole Armour of God* on Eph. vi. 16, treat. ii. part v. sec. 14, &c.

The word here used by the apostle is expressed in the time past, οἱ πιστεύσαντες, *which have believed*, to shew that we can have no assurance of the thing promised till we do believe the promise: 'After that ye believed, you were sealed with the Holy Spirit of promise,' Eph. i. 13. 'I know whom I have believed,' saith the apostle, and thereupon maketh this inference, 'and I am persuaded that he is able to keep that which I have committed unto him against that day,' 2 Tim. i. 12. This Christ manifested by the condition which he required of those whom he cured, thus, 'If thou canst believe, all things are possible,' &c., Mark ix. 23.

It is faith that settleth the right thereof upon us. 'As many as received Christ, to them gave he power to become the sons of God, even to them that believe on his name,' John i. 12.

This gives us just occasion to 'examine ourselves, whether we be in the faith,' 2 Cor. xiii. 5. Hereof see *The Whole Armour of God,* on Eph. vi. 16, treat. ii. part. v. Of faith, sec. 40, &c.

Of the persons to whom this rest belongeth, see Sec. 57.

Sec. 24. *Of future good things set down in the present tense.*

The thing promised is expressed in these words, εἰσερχόμεθα, *we do enter into rest.* Of the rest here intended, and of entering into it, see Secs. 6, 8, 9.

This is here set down in the present tense, *we do enter*, in a double respect:

1. In regard of the certainty of the thing. It is as sure as a thing in present possession. The prophets did use to set out future things, which were sure and certain, in the present tense, as Isa. lxii. 11, Zech. ix. 9. As for the point in hand, assurance is attributed to faith as a special property thereof, Heb. x. 22. He that said, 'I know that my Redeemer liveth: and though after my skin worms destroy this body, yet in my flesh shall I see God,' &c., Job xix. 25, 26, was sure of enjoying this rest. So he who said, 'I know whom I have believed, and I am persuaded that he is able to keep that which I have committed unto him against that day,' 2 Tim. i. 12. And again, 'I am persuaded that neither death,' &c., Rom. viii. 38. For true believers are 'fully persuaded that what God hath promised, he is able also to perform,' Rom. iv. 21. It therefore becomes all that would be accounted true believers, to get this evidence of the truth of their faith.

2. In regard of the beginning of that rest, which is here actually enjoyed. Of the beginning of heavenly rest here on earth enjoyed, see Sec. 6. The beginning of that rest is like that olive-leaf which the dove brought to Noah in the ark, which shewed that the earth was sending forth her fruit, Gen. viii. 11; and like the cluster of grapes, and the pomegranates, and the figs, which the searchers of the land of Canaan brought, and gave evidence of the fertility of that land, Num. xiii. 23; and like the first fruits that gave hope of a future harvest, 2 Kings iv. 40. Even so the beginning of rest here enjoyed, gives evidence of a full, perfect, and glorious rest to come.

These first-fruits the Lord here bestoweth on us to strengthen our faith in the full possession of that rest which is to come; to keep us from doubting, and to uphold us against the difficulties which we are like to meet withal, and against the obstacles that lie in the way to that rest.

Behold here the good care of God over man. He hath prepared a rest for him; but he seeth it meet to reserve it for time to come, and to bring men through many troubles thereunto; and thereupon gives grounds of assurance thereof beforehand.

Sec. 25. *Of God's speaking by prophets.*

Verse 3. *As he said, As I have sworn in my wrath, if they shall enter into my rest, &c.*

These words, *as he said,* &c., may have a double reference.

One immediate, to the words next before. So they are a proof of them, by the rule of contraries. Such a proof was noted before in this verse, Sec. 21.

The force of the argument resteth on that ruled case, which the apostle taketh for grant, ver. 6, namely, that 'some must enter' into that rest which God hath promised. Hereupon this argument may be made.

If some must enter, then believers or unbelievers;

But not unbelievers: for God by oath hath protested against them;

Therefore believers shall enter.

The other reference is more remote, to the latter part of the former verse. If the first clause of this verse be included in a parenthesis, the reference of this unto the former verse will appear to be the more fit. For it sheweth that unbelievers reap no benefit by the word of promise, because God hath sworn that such shall not enter into his rest.

This relative *he*, in this clause, 'as he said,' hath reference to God. It was the Lord that said and swore, that they should not enter into his rest.

That which he said was in and by David, ver. 7, and that in Ps. xcv. 11. It was God that spake in and by the prophets, as was noted Chap. i. 1, Sec. 11. The Holy Ghost spake what the prophets spake.

Yea, though that which is here quoted were the written word, yet he sets it out as uttered by word of mouth, thus, *he said*. See Chap. iii. 7, Sec. 74.

Sec. 26. *Of the certainty of judgment sworn by God.*

This particle of resemblance, *as*, hath on the one side reference to the sin and punishment of the Israelites; and on the other side to God's swearing that they should be so punished. As God had sworn, so it fell out. God's oath cannot be made frustrate, but shall assuredly be effected. No argument is more sure. Though an oath be in logic reckoned among inartificial arguments, which seem to be of small force, yet God's word, especially confirmed by his oath, is the surest of all arguments. Logicians count the surest demonstrations to be taken from the proper cause of a thing. But natural causes may fail, witness the fiery furnace into which God's three faithful servants were cast, yet 'upon their bodies the fire had no power, nor was a hair of their head singed, neither were their coats changed, nor the smell of fire had passed on them,' Dan. iii. 27. The sun stood still in Joshua his time, Josh. x. 13, and went backward in Hezekiah's time, 2 Kings xx. 11, and was darkened at the death of Christ, Luke xxiii. 45. The waters in the midst of the Red Sea rose up as a wall, and the bottom was a dry path, Exod. xiv. 22. Iron did swim in the water, 2 Kings vi. 6. In many other things hath the course of nature been altered.

The Lord God is above nature. Though he have tied his creatures to the course thereof, yet is not he bound thereto; but by his oath he binds himself, and is not free to alter it. Read Isa. liv. 9, 10. Hereupon it is said concerning God's oath, that he 'will not repent,' Ps. cx. 1. This is one of those 'immutable things, in which it is impossible for God to lie,' Heb. vi. 18.

God's oath doth manifest his peremptory resolution, which is, as his nature, unchangeable, Mal. iii. 6, more firm than 'the law of the Medes and Persians, which altereth not,' Dan. vi. 8.

God never rashly swears, but always 'in truth, in udgment, and in righteousness;' for that rule which he prescribes to us, Jer. iv. 2, he observes himself.

Take heed of provoking God to swear. They are in a fearful case against whom the Lord sweareth vengeance.

We ought the rather to take heed of this high provocation of his wrath, because he is not suddenly brought to it, but by degrees. For,

1. He declares his will, what he would have us to do.
2. He promiseth rewards to them that do it.
3. He makes known beforehand the issue of neglecting it.
4. He threateneth vengeance.
5. When no other course will serve, he sweareth vengeance. Woe to those against whom he swears.

Of God's swearing, and that in wrath; and of the form of God's oath; and of God's rest, and of not entering into it (which are points here expressly set down), see Chap. iii. 11, Secs. 113, 114, 115, 116, 117, 118.

Sec. 27. *Of choosing the best rest.*

Ver. 3. *Although the works were finished from the foundation of the world.*

In this latter part of the verse, and in the five verses following, the apostle doth by degrees lead these Hebrews to a consideration of an higher and better rest than ever was enjoyed in this world. There were two famous rests much insisted on in the Old Testament, as special pledges of God's favour: the Sabbath and the land of Canaan: the former styled 'a Sabbath of rest to the Lord,' Exod. xxxv. 2, and frequently styled 'the Sabbath of the Lord,' Exod. xx. 10; the latter styled 'the rest which the Lord gave them,' Deut. xii. 9, Josh. i. 15.

Of these the Hebrews might say, We have always enjoyed the Lord's Sabbath; and our predecessors have long inhabited Canaan. Why then do you speak so much about entering into God's rest?

To root out this conceit, the apostle is the more large and distinct in removing these two, and proving that neither of them could be meant by David, nor is intended by himself.

The rest intended by him is a matter of so great consequence, as he would not have them mistake the mark thereabouts.

He begins with the Sabbath, which is the first rest mentioned in Scripture.

The word of connection, or rather distinction, is a kind of compound. The first particle is the usual copulative, καὶ, *and*; the other, τοι, joined to it makes it a discretive conjunction, καὶ τοι, and is here fitly translated *although*. Hereby he sheweth that, albeit there is mention made of a rest in the beginning of the world, yet there is another rest to be entered into.

The rest of the Sabbath was a resemblance of the heavenly rest. The rest of Canaan was a type thereof. That therefore they might not be drawn by a resemblance and type from the thing itself and the truth (as the dog having flesh in his mouth and seeing the shadow of it in a clear running water, snapped at the shadow and lost the true flesh), he endeavoureth to draw them from resting upon those two rests. It is a dangerous thing to be drawn from truths by shadows. This is to pervert the helps which God doth afford unto us.

Sec. 28. *Of God's works, and his finishing them.*

Under this indefinite word τῶν ἔργων, *the works*, all the creatures which God made within the compass of the first six days are comprised.

The Greek noun ἔργον properly signifieth a thing done with pains and labour.

The verb ἐργαζομαι, which is of the same notation, signifieth to work or to labour, as 1 Cor. iv. 12, John xvi. 27. This is attributed to God by way of resemblance, after the manner of man. When a man hath effected a thing, and made that which was not before, we call it his work. Now, man can do nothing without some working or labouring about it. But God needs no such thing. What God willed to be, was so and so, as he willed it. Thus much is intended under this phrase, 'God said, Let there be,' &c., Gen. i. 3. By God's *saying* is meant the manifestation of his will. In this sense the centurion, who believed Christ to be God, said, 'Speak the word only, and my servant shall be healed,' Mat. viii. 8. Do but only declare thy will to heal my servant, and he shall be healed.

Of those works it is here said, that God finished them (γενηθέντων). The Greek word γίνομαι vel γίγνομαι *sum, fio*, translated *finished*, in general signifieth *to be* or *to be made*. But because a thing cannot properly be said to be, or to be made, till it be fully finished, and till all things appertaining thereto be accomplished, the word here in this place is fitly translated *finished;* the rather because it is attributed unto God, of whose works it is expressly said that, יכלו, they were finished, Gen. ii. 1.

God is said to finish his works in two especial respects.

1. In regard of the number of them. There was so full a number every where, that there was no need of adding any more thereto.

Obj. It is said after God's rest on the seventh day, that God planted a garden in Eden; and that he 'made out of the ground to grow every tree that is pleasant to the sight and good for food;' and it is also said that 'God made a woman,' Gen. ii. 8, 9, 22.

Ans. Though these be mentioned in the history after the mention of the Sabbath, yet they were all made within the six days. Eden and the trees therein were made on the fourth day, Gen. i. 12, and the woman on the sixth day; for then he made them 'male and female,' Gen. i. 27. All the creatures that were made are comprised in the first chapter of Genesis; in the second chapter he sets down the distinct manner of making many things. Mention is there made of the manner of making man himself, ver. 7, who notwithstanding is expressly said to be created on the sixth day, Gen. i. 27.

Here by the way take notice of the absurd doctrine of popish transubstantiation, whereby papists imagine such a creature to be made as God never made: a body that cannot be seen or felt; an human body in the form of bread; and blood which likewise cannot be seen nor felt, but appears in the show of wine. To omit other absurdities, this seemeth to add a strange new creature to the creatures which God made in the six days, as if he had not then finished all.

2. In regard of the perfection of every particular creature, God is said to finish his works. Nothing needed to be added to any, neither did any thing need to be altered to make it better. 'I know,' saith the wise man, 'that whatsoever God doth, it shall be for ever: nothing can be put to it, nor anything taken from it,' Eccles. iii. 14. In this respect it is said of every creature which God made, 'It was very good,' Gen. i. 36.

Such was God's wisdom as he saw what shape, stature, proportion, and property was fit for every thing.

Such was his power, as he was able to effect whatsoever in wisdom he saw meet.

Such was his goodness, as he would answerably create and order every thing.

Learn to admire every work of God, and to adore and reverence the Lord himself that made them.

Rest content in what he doth; submit to him in all his works. Seek not to alter them, Mat. v. 36, and vi. 27, and x. 30.

Learn of God to finish what belongeth unto thee before thou leave thy work of thyself. It was Christ's meat 'to do the will of him that sent him, and to finish his work,' John iv. 34. Yea, he layeth a necessity upon himself in this respect, saying, 'I must work the works of him that sent me while it is day.' We cannot finish our work till our day be ended. Therefore, 'whatsoever thine hand findeth to do, do it with thy might,' &c., Eccles. ix. 10.

Sec. 29. *Of this phrase, 'from the foundation of the world.'*

The time of God's finishing his works is thus expressed, 'from the foundation of the world.' There was before mention made of the foundation of the earth, Chap. i. 10, sec. 131. But there another Greek word, ἐθεμελίωσας, was used, which implied the stability of the earth. This word also may intimate a stability. The word καταβολή is a compound. The simple verb βάλλειν signifieth *to cast;* the compound καταβάλλειν, *to cast* or *lay down*. A foundation useth to be laid down in the earth. It is the lowest part of an edifice, whereupon all the rest of the structure lieth. The Latins use to express it by these two words, *jactum fundamentum*, a foundation laid.

The other noun, κόσμος, translated *world*, signifies in Greek, order, ornament, adorning. So it is translated, 1 Pet. iii. 3, ὧν κόσμος, 'whose adorning,' &c.

From this root there is a verb, κοσμεῖν,[1] derived which signifieth *to adorn*, as women adorned themselves, &c., 1 Tim. ii. 9, and *to garnish*, Mat. xii. 44.

Fitly doth this notation appertain to the world, as here it is taken, namely, for the universe, or whole fabric of all creatures, which were made by God in a most comely order and beauty; for 'God made every thing beautiful in his time,' Eccles. iii. 11. This was before shewed, Sec. 28.

This universe or world is here said to have a foundation, and that in two especial respects:

1. To intimate the stability of it. It was not like a building without a foundation; as that house was, which was built on the sand, and soon fell, Luke vi. 49. See Chap. i. ver. 10, sec. 131.

2. To demonstrate the beginning of it. For a foundation useth to be first laid. Thus it is used Heb. vi. 1.

In this latter sense, this phrase, *the foundation of the world*, is oft used. When mention is made of things eternal, a preposition, πρὸ, that signifieth *before*, is set before it. As of God's love to his Son, 'Thou lovedst me,' saith Christ to his Father, πρὸ καταβολῆς κόσμου, 'before the foundation of the world,' John xvii. 24. And of election, 'God hath chosen us before the foundation of the world, Eph. i. 4 ; 1 Pet. i. 20.

When the point is of things about the beginning of the world, this proposition ἀπὸ, *from*, is used. Christ is said to be 'a Lamb slain (ἀπὸ καταβολῆς) from the foundation of the world,' Rev. xiii. 8.

In this phrase, *from the foundation of the world*, doth the force of the apostle's argument especially lie. The rest of the Sabbath was upon the beginning of the world. Therefore it cannot be that rest which is to come.

Things of different times, whereof one is of time past, the other of time to come, cannot be the same. The paradise wherein Adam in his innocency was, cannot be the same which Christ has promised to him that overcometh, Rev. ii. 7. The calling of the Jews out of the Babylonish captivity cannot be that which is promised of calling them to embrace the gospel, Rom. xi. 26. David, that died many hundred years before the exhibition of Christ, cannot be that David which is promised to be a prince among Christians, Ezek. xxxiv. 24, and xxxvii. 24, 25.

Sec. 30. *Of the interpretation of the former part of Heb. iv. 4.*

Ver. 4. *For he spake in a certain place of the seventh day on this wise, And God did rest the seventh day from all his works.*

Both the particle of connection (which is a causal conjunction, γὰρ, *for*) and the very matter of this verse, do evidently demonstrate, that it is brought in as a proof of that which went before : namely, that God finished his works. This is proved by God's resting. A wise man that undertakes a work, will not rest, or clean give over his work, till it be finished. If any do otherwise, he gives occasion to men to mock him, Luke xiv. 29, 30. We cannot therefore think that God, who is wisdom itself, would rest till he had finished what he intended. Of man's imitating God herein, see the latter end of Sec. 28.

The kind of proof is drawn from a divine testimony, which is thus intimated, *He spake*.

1. He names not the author, but indefinitely saith *he*. This having reference to the sacred Scripture, out of which the words which he quoteth are taken, must needs be meant, if we consider the principal author, of the Holy Ghost, whom he expressed, chap. iii. ver. 7, or if we consider the penman, of Moses, who wrote the book out of which this testimony was taken. Now, these Hebrews well knew that God was the author of the whole Scripture, and that Moses wrote as he was moved by the Holy Ghost. Therefore, the apostle thought it sufficient thus to intimate the principal or ministerial author, εἴρηκε, 'he spake.'

2. He expresseth nor book, nor chapter, but only saith, που, '*in a certain place*.' Of this manner of quoting a text, and of the Greek particle thus translated, *in a certain place*, see Chap. ii. 6, Sec. 52.

Though the main scope of the apostle was to demonstrate a rest to be observed in the beginning of the world, yet because the very distinct day of rest was very remarkable in producing the testimony, he expressly premiseth, that the testimony is περὶ τῆς ἑβδόμης, '*of the seventh day*.'

The seventh day here mentioned was the last day of the first week that ever was.

It may be that from this instance of God's observing the first seventh day, the number of seven was in succeeding ages so highly esteemed, as it was accounted a number of perfection.

As at first, seven days made up a week, Gen. ii. 2, so sundry feasts consisted of seven days, Lev. xxiii. 3, 6, 15, 34. The year of rest was the seventh year, and the year of jubilee was the seven times seventh year, Lev. xxv. 4, 8. The time of a woman's uncleanness was seven days, Lev. xii. 2. A leper was to be cleansed on the seventh day, Lev. xiv. 9. Seven days was the time of consecrating a priest, Exod. xxix. 35; and the altar, Exod. xxix. 37. Seven days was the time for preparing a sacrifice, Lev. xxii. 27; and for keeping the Lord's watch, Lev. viii. 35. Blood of expiation was to be sprinkled seven times, Lev. xvi. 14; and also oil of consecration, Lev. viii. 11. Naaman was to wash himself seven times, 2 Kings v. 10. There were wont to be seven days of fasting, 1 Sam. xxxi. 13. And of feasting, 2 Chron. vii. 9; seven bullocks and seven rams used to be offered up to make an atonement. God commanded Job's friends so to do, Job xlii. 8; Balaam had learned as much, Num. xxiii. 1. Sundry other

---

[1] Κόσμος λέγεται ἡ τῶν ὅλων τάξις καὶ διακόσμησις ὑπὸ Θεοῦ τε καὶ διὰ Θεὸν φυλαττομένη.—*Arist. de Mund.*, cap. 2.

sevens are mentioned, both in the Old and New Testament, especially in the book of the Revelation. So as the number of seven had in it a mystery above other numbers.

That the proof might be the more clearly and fully discerned, the apostle makes profession of setting it down in the very words of the author thereof, as is implied by this phrase, οὕτω, *on this wise.* This is the interpretation of one Greek adverb, which word for word in English signifieth *so.* Of quoting Scripture in the very words thereof, see Chap. iii. 7, Sec. 74.

Sec. 31. *Of the rest of the Sabbath.*

The testimony itself, out of which the apostle draweth his argument, is thus expressed, 'And God did rest,' &c.

Two reasons may be given why the apostle retains this copulative conjunction, καί, *and.*

One is, because in Hebrew the verb ישבת, *rest,* is of the future tense, but a copulative joined to it gives it the force of the preterperfect tense, and makes it signify the time past.

The other is because the force of the argument lieth in the connection of this testimony with that which was set down in the third verse, namely, that God 'finished his works from the foundations of the world, and rested.' He did not rest till he had finished his works; but so soon as he had finished them, he rested. He finished his works from the foundation of the world, *and* from the foundation of the world he rested. Thus we see how useful it may be to retain seeming circumstantial particles of Scripture.

There are two distinct verbs used in Hebrew, both which are translated to rest.

One, נוח *quievit,* signifieth to be quiet and free from trouble. Thus it is applied to the ark, which after long tossing and driving hither and thither upon the waters, is said to rest upon the mountains, ותנח, Gen. viii. 4. The noun מנוחה, *quies,* used Ps. xcv. 11, and translated rest, is derived from this verb. Hereof see Chap. iii. 11, Sec. 116.

The other, שבת, *cessavit,* signifieth to cease from doing a thing, or to leave off. It is attributed to manna, which ceased (וישבת) to fall, as at other times it had done forty years together, Joshua v. 12. According to the Hebrew notation, we may here thus translate it, God did Sabbatize. The word שבת σάββατον, *Sabbathum, Sabbath,* is derived from this verb, and retained not only in Greek and Latin, but also in other languages among Christians.

The notation of this word sheweth in what respect God is said to rest; namely, by ceasing to create more creatures than he had done, which was his work in the other six days. These words following, 'he rested from all his works,' demonstrate as much.

1. By this kind of rest, it appears that this answer of Christ, 'My Father worketh hitherto,' John v. 17, doth not contradict that which is here said of God's rest; because the rest here is from creating new kinds of creatures: but the working whereof Christ speaks, is about God's doing good to the creatures, and it concerns God's providence, which never ceaseth; but every moment, day and night, on Sabbaths and other days, puts forth itself in preserving, sustaining, succouring, ordering, and governing his creatures.

2. This rest of God is set before us as a pattern, Exod. xx. 10, 11. We may therefore learn thereby wherein the rest of the Sabbath consisteth; not in idleness, or doing nothing at all, but in forbearing the ordinary works of the six days, the works of our worldly calling. Of the works which may and ought to be done on the Sabbath, see my treatise entitled, *The Sabbath's Sanctification,* quest. 5, &c.

3. This rest of God gives us a view of that kind of rest which we shall enjoy in heaven, namely, a ceasing from the works of this world, before we enter into heaven, for that rest is styled, σαββατισμός, *a keeping of a Sabbath.*

The seventh day mentioned in this testimony, is the same whereof mention is made, Gen. ii. 3, namely, a seventh after the six days which God spent in creating the world, and all things therein. So much is expressed, Exod. xx. 11; yea, in the first chapter of Genesis, it is expressly declared what particular creatures God made in every of the six days.

We are not to think that there was any such need of God's taking up so much time as he did in creating the world, as if he could not have done it in a shorter time. If it had been his pleasure, when he said, 'Let there be light,' to have said also at that time, 'Let there be a firmament,' 'Let there be waters and dry land,' 'Let the earth bring forth all manner of plants,' 'Let there be sun, moon, and stars, let there be fowl and fish, let there be beasts, all creeping things upon the earth, and let there be man,' they had all been so soon as there was light, even in the first day; yea, he could have made all in one moment.

Two reasons may be given of God's taking up six days in making the world.

One, that by a due consideration of every day's work, we might the better discern the difference of every creature, one from another; and the dependence of one upon another. For the creatures first made were for the use of such as followed after them.

The other, that God might be a pattern to children of men throughout all ages, how to spend their time, namely, by working six days in every week, and resting the seventh.

Of that objection, which, from this seventh day wherein God rested, is made against Christians keeping the Sabbath the next day, which is the first day of the week, see the fore-mentioned *Sabbath's Sanctification,* quest. 43, &c.

In the last place, this clause is added, *from all his works*, because he had finished them. Hereof see Sec. 28.

This general particle *all* compriseth under it the several works of God, of what kind or sort soever they were, whether above or below, great or mean, not any at all excepted.

This is to be noted against them who pretend this or that kind of works for violation of the Sabbath.

Some think that if the works be great and weighty, as carrying in of the harvest, when opportunity serveth upon the Sabbath day, which otherwise, they say, may be spoiled, the law of God is express against this excuse, Exod. xxxiv. 21.

Others think that they may do small matters, as if God took no notice of them. Let such consider the end of him that gathered sticks upon the Sabbath, Num. xv. 32.

Both these and all others that do any kind of works that ought not to be done on the Sabbath, swerve from this pattern of God, who rested from all his works.

Sec. 32. *Of the resolution of* Heb. iv. 3, 4.

3. *For we which have believed do enter into rest; as he said, As I have sworn in my wrath, if they shall enter into my rest: although the works were finished from the foundation of the world.*

4. *For he spake in a certain place of the seventh day on this wise, And God did rest the seventh day from all his works.*

The sum of these two verses is a difference betwixt two rests.

The one is a rest to be enjoyed in heaven.

The other is the rest of the Sabbath.

The former is, first, propounded; secondly, proved.

In the point propounded, are set down,

1. The persons whom it concerns.
2. The point itself concerned.

About the persons we have,

1. The manner of expressing them, in the first person, and plural number, and time past, *we that have*.
2. The grace whereby they are fitted for rest, *believed*.

In the point concerned is expressed,

1. The act in the time present, *do enter*.
2. The subject of that act, *into rest*.

The proof is,

1. Generally intimated in this phrase, *as he said*.
2. Particularly exemplified.

In the exemplification God himself is brought in speaking and confirming the point in hand, thus, *as I have*, &c.

Of God's speech there are two parts:

1. The argument that he useth.
2. The matter confirmed.

The argument is his oath, *sworn*, amplified by the kind of oath, *in wrath*, and by the manner of propounding it, in this particle *if*.

The matter confirmed is a heavy judgment, which was a failing of that which was prepared for them.

The thing prepared was *rest*, amplified by the author of it, *my rest*, saith God.

Their failing thereof is thus expressed, *if they shall enter;* or they shall not enter.

The other kind of rest was the rest of the Sabbath. In setting down this,

1. There is a note of distinction betwixt the two rests, *although*.
2. A declaration of the ground of this latter rest.

That ground is, 1, propounded; 2, proved.

In the proposition we have,

1. The kind of ground, which was God's finishing his works.
2. The time when, *from the foundation of the world*.

The proof is, 1, generally intimated; 2, particularly exemplified.

In the general there are four points to be considered:

1. The author thereof, *he said*.
2. The place where, *in a certain place*.
3. The subject whereabout, *the seventh day*.
4. The manner how, *on this wise*.

In the exemplification there are four observable points:

1. The person, God, *he*.
2. His act, *did rest*.
3. The time, *the seventh day*.
4. The object from what he rested, *from his works*.

This is amplified by the note of generality, *all*.

Sec. 33. *Of doctrines raised out of* Heb. iv. 3, 4.

I. *Unbelievers are excluded from the privilege of believers.* The inference of this verse upon the former, in this causal particle *for*, demonstrates thus much. See Sec. 21.

II. *True believers may know they have faith.* He was a true believer that said, We which have believed. See Sec. 22.

III. *Professors must judge of others as they do of themselves.* This apostle doth put others in the same rank with himself, by using the plural number. See Sec. 22.

IV. *Faith gives assurance of the thing promised.* For thus saith a believer, 'We do enter.' See Sec. 23.

V. *Future things promised are as sure as if they were present.* The rest concerning which he saith in the present, *we do enter*, was then to come. See Sec. 24.

VI. *Beginnings of heavenly rest are here enjoyed.* It is of the time of this life that he here saith, *we do enter*. See Sec. 24.

VII. *Rest is prepared for believers.* This is here set down as a granted case. See Sec. 24.

VIII. *God spake by his prophets.* This relative *he* hath reference to God, yet they were the words of David. See Sec. 25.

IX. *The word written is as a sermon preached.* That whereof this is spoken, *he said,* was the written word. See Sec. 25.

X. *That which unbelievers miss of, believers attain to.* This is the force of the apostle's argument implied in this conjunction *as.* God said that unbelievers should not enter into his rest; thence the apostle infers that believers do enter thereinto. See Sec. 25.

XI. *God's oath is an infallible argument.* Unbelievers shall not enter into rest, as God hath sworn, or because God hath sworn they should not enter. See Sec. 26.

Of doctrines gathered from God's oath, the form and matter thereof, see Chap. iii. 11, Sec. 120.

XII. *Things of the same name may be of different kinds.* This discretive conjunction *although* intends as much. Heaven and the Sabbath are both a rest, yet different rests. See Sec. 27.

XIII. *The creatures are God's work.* They are here so called. See Sec. 28.

XIV. *God in six days made up the full number of creatures.* In this sense it is here said that he finished them. See Sec. 28.

XV. *God perfected his creatures.* The word *finished* implieth thus much also. See Sec. 28.

XVI. *The world is a comely fabric.* The notation of the Greek word translated *world* intends as much. See Sec. 29.

XVII. *The world hath a foundation.* This is here taken for grant, by attributing a foundation to the world. See Sec. 29.

XVIII. *God's works were perfected at the very first.* This is the intendment of this preposition *from.* See Sec. 29.

XIX. *God left not off to work till he had finished his works.* The inference of God's resting upon finishing his works, by this causal conjunction *for,* proves this point. See Sec. 30.

XX. *A divine testimony is a sound argument.* This phrase, *for he said,* sheweth that the apostle useth this testimony to prove the point in hand. See Sec. 30.

XXI. *Scriptures may be quoted without naming the place.* So doth the apostle here. See Sec. 30.

XXII. *Seven is a number of perfection.* God rested on that day. See Sec. 30.

XXIII. *The very words of Scripture are to be expressed.* This phrase, *on this wise,* intends thus much. See Sec. 30.

XXIV. *God rested not till he had finished his works.* This copulative *and* intends so much.

XXV. *The last day of the week was the day of God's rest.* This was the seventh day here mentioned. See Sec. 31.

XXVI. *God made no new creatures after the first six days.* For in the seventh he rested from *all* his works. See Sec. 31.

XXVII. *The same word may have different senses.* The Sabbath, the land of Canaan, and celestial glory, are all called *rest,* but the apostle here proveth that they are different things. See Secs. 27, 31.

Sec. 34. *Of the meaning of* Heb. iv. 5.

Verse 5. *And in this place again, If they shall enter into my rest.*

This verse, like a perfect transition, may look two ways, to that which went before, and to that which followeth.

In the former reference it implieth that the foresaid rest of the Sabbath cannot be the rest whereinto Christians are to enter, because at another time he spake of this rest.

In the latter reference, namely to that which followeth, it lays down the ground of another rest than the land of Canaan.

The copulative conjunction, καί, *and,* hath reference to the first verb of the former verse, εἴρηκε, which is thus translated, *he spake.* To make up the sense, that verb must be repeated in this verse, thus, ἀπὸ κοίνου, ' And he spake in this place again.'

It was one and the same Spirit, even the Holy Ghost, that testified of the one and the other rest. So as both testimonies are of divine authority, and neither of them to be denied, but by distinction of rests to be reconciled.

By this phrase, ἐν τούτῳ, *in this place,* the apostle intends Ps. xcv. 11. He calls it *this place* because he had quoted it before, and expounded it, and applied it to the point in hand. It was the text whereupon he was then, in his epistle, commenting. As a preacher, having read and expounded a text of Scripture, so oft as he hath occasion in his sermon to speak of any point in or about that text, may say, *in this place,* so the apostle here in this his epistle of that text.

This adverb, πάλιν, *again,* is to be taken of another time than that which was mentioned in the former verse. Sometimes, indeed, it is used to join divers proofs of one and the same thing, as chap. i. 5, 6; but here to set forth distinct times for proof of different things. Thus in the beginning of the world there was mention made of a rest, which was the rest of the Sabbath day; but now again, above three thousand years after that, mention is made of another rest. That therefore cannot be this.

This phrase, *If they shall enter into my rest,* is here alleged, because therein mention is made of rest. The other part of the sentence, about God's oath, was not to the present purpose of the apostle; and therefore it was not here set down, though it would have made up the full sentence. It was twice before expressed, ver. 3, and chap iii. 11.

It is usual with the penmen of the New Testament to quote so much only of a parcel of Scripture as makes to the point in hand, though it make not up an entire sentence, as Mat. iv. 15; Rom. iv. 18; Gal. iii. 16.

The rest here mentioned is so set down, as it plainly appears to be a rest to come, so as it cannot be that rest which was at the beginning of the world.

Thus the first rest is removed, and this point proved, that another rest than the rest of the Sabbath is to be endeavoured after.

These words, *If they shall enter*, have the form of a strong negation. See Chap. iii. 11, Sec. 115. They there imply that the persons of whom they are spoken should not enter into the promised rest of Canaan.

From thence the apostle makes an inference in the next verse, that there must needs be another rest to come than that of Canaan.

Of this rest, of this epithet *my*, in reference to God, and of entering into it, see Chap. iii. 11, Secs. 116, 117, 118.

Sec. 35. *Of the resolution and observations of* Heb. iv. 5.

The sum of this verse is a transition about the removal of two rests from being the eternal rest proper to believers.

Hereof are two parts:
One wherein the rest of the Sabbath is removed.
This point is,
1. Intimated, by mentioning another rest to be entered into.
2. It is proved, and that two ways:
(1.) Implicitly, under this copulative *and*, which presupposeth the divine testimony, thus expressed, *he spake*, ver. 4.
(2.) Expressly, by two circumstances, one of the place, the other of the time.

The other part of this transition is, wherein the rest of Canaan is removed, and that by excluding them to whom it was promised, in these words, *If they shall enter*.

Doctrines.

I. *The Lord distinctly expresseth his mind concerning different things.* He spake so and so of the Sabbath, *and he spake* (for this word is to be repeated) so and so of another rest.

II. *Due observation of different texts will bring great light to doubtful points.* In the former verse the apostle notes out one text under this phrase, *in a certain place*; here in this verse, another under this phrase, *in this place*, and thereby clears the matter questioned. Several texts may have several circumstances to enlighten them.

III. *A right distinction of times may reconcile seeming differences.* This particle *again* intends a different time from the former, and thereupon a different matter.

IV. *Exclusion of some makes way for others.*

Privatio unius est inductio alterius. Unbelievers being excluded, believers gain assurance of admittance. The privation of one form is the induction of another.

Of other doctrines arising out of these words, *If any shall enter into my rest*, see Chap. iii. 11, Sec. 120.

Sec. 36. *Of the apostle's scope in the 6th verse.*

Verse 6. *Seeing therefore it remaineth that some must enter therein, and they to whom it was first preached entered not in because of unbelief.*

The two first words of this verse, ἐπεί, *seeing*, οὖν, *therefore*, are both relative conjunctions, and imply an inference upon that which went before.

In the former verse, God's protestation against unbelievers is set down, that they should not enter into his rest. The inference which the apostle makes thereupon is, that there is a rest for believers to enter into. The argument may be thus framed:

If the land of Canaan were not entered into by them to whom it was promised, there must needs be another rest, for those to whom a rest is promised, to enter into it;

But the land of Canaan was not entered into by those to whom it was promised;

Therefore there must needs be another rest.

The proposition is in this verse.
The assumption in the former.
The conclusion in the ninth verse.

The main force of this argument resteth in the truth of God's promise. So true and faithful is God in his promise, as they to whom it is expressly made, shall assuredly partake thereof.

This verse seems to conclude abruptly without full sense. But if the ninth verse be added as a conclusion thereunto, it will make up the sense. The apostle, in the two verses following, produceth another argument to prove the same point, therefore to hasten on that argument he puts the conclusion to the end of it.

Sec. 37. *Of the accomplishments of God's promise in some.*

This verb, ἀπολείπεται, *it remaineth*, is in Greek a compound. The simple λείπειν, linquere, signifieth *to leave;* the preposition signifieth *from;* the compound verb implieth a reservation of one thing upon the rejection of another, ver. 9. Where nothing is reserved, this word is joined with a negative. It is said of such as ' sin wilfully,' &c., ' there remaineth no more sacrifice for sin,' Heb. x. 26. This translation of the word *it remaineth* is here very fit.

The persons failing of the rest promised to them, it remaineth that other persons and another rest be inquired after. That which remains is, that some enter; for a promise of God cannot be utterly made void. Though many reap no good thereby, yet others shall be made partakers of the benefit of it. Most in the world refused to enter into the ark, yet Noah and his family had the benefit of it, Gen. vii. 7. Sodom and Gomorrah, and the cities about them, regarded not God's word to save themselves, yet Lot and his two daughters did, Gen. xix. 30. Though so many perished in the wilderness, yet Caleb and Joshua entered into Canaan, Num. xiv. 30.

If none should believe, but all be deprived of the promise by unbelief, God's promise and faith might seem to be without effect, and altogether in vain.

Learn hereby to take heed of questioning God's truth by reason of the unbelief of some : ' What if some do not believe ? shall their unbelief make the faith of God without effect ? God forbid,' Rom. iii. 3. The Lord knows that some will believe, and make a right use of his promise : ' He knoweth them that are his,' 2 Tim. ii. 19. For their sakes especially he makes his promise.

Be not discouraged that many are deprived of the promise. Believers will say, ' God is our refuge,' &c.; ' therefore will we not fear, though the earth be removed,' &c., Ps. xlvi. 1, 2. God can and will discern his, though men see them not, Rom. xi. 4. Let us therefore be of Joshua his resolution, Josh. xxiv. 15.

Sec. 38. *Of the meaning of these words, ' to whom it was first preached.'*

In joining the two parts of this sixth verse together, the relative conjunction is to be repeated thus, *And seeing they to whom*, &c.

This phrase, οἱ εὐαγγελισθέντες, to whom it was preached, is the interpretation of that word, ἐυηγγελισμένοι, which, ver. 2, was thus translated, *the gospel was preached*. Word for word, it may be here thus turned, *who were evangelised*. See Sec. 15. The word hath its notation from evangel, or gospel, and thereupon the word gospel might have been inserted thus, ' They to whom the gospel was preached,' as ver. 2 ; so as the Israelites under the law had the gospel preached unto them. See Sec. 17.

The word πρότερον, translated *first*, doth not necessarily imply that they to whom it is here applied were the first that ever heard the gospel. The gospel was preached to Abraham, Gen. xii. 2, 3, before the Israelites here meant ; and to Noah, Gen. vi. 14, &c., before Abraham ; and to Adam, Gen. iii. 15, before Noah. The word is of the comparative degree, and oft translated *before*, as John vi. 62, and vii. 51, and ix. 8 ; 2 Cor. i. 15 ; 1 Tim. i. 13. It is sufficient for the point in hand, that they who are intended in this text hear the gospel preached before them who are exhorted to give better heed thereto. See Sec. 41.

Sec. 39. *Of the blessing of faith resting on believers only, and vengeance on unbelievers only.*

The apostle, by mentioning again the forfeiture of rest upon other men's participation thereof, thus, Some must enter therein, and these entered not, sheweth, on the one side, that the benefit which believers received by the gospel brought no advantage to the unbeliever ; and that, on the other side, the forfeiture which unbelievers made of the benefit of the gospel brought no damage to believers. Of believers it is here said, They enter in ; of unbelievers, They enter not. The like may be exemplified in the stability of some angels, and falling away of others ; in the preservation of Noah, and destruction of the old world ; in the exemption of Israel from all plagues in Goshen, Exod. viii. 22, and the many plagues that fell upon the Egyptians ; in the receiving of the wise virgins into glory, and refusing the foolish ; and in the blessed sentence pronounced to the righteous, and woful doom against the unrighteous, Mat. xxv. 12, 41.

It cannot be denied but that the blessing that is conferred upon believers is a great aggravation of the judgment on unbelievers. In this respect unbelievers receive great prejudice from believers, but through their own default. On the other side, vengeance on unbelievers is a great amplification of the mercy shewed to believers. Contraries do set out each other.

Were it possible for unbelievers duly and thoroughly to consider the blessings which believers enjoy (whereof they deprive themselves by their unbelief), it could not but work upon them, and make them more fully to discern their folly.

Sec. 40. *Of unbelief's hindering the power of the gospel.*

From the notation of the verb εὐαγγελισθέντες, preached, which includeth the gospel, we may infer that unbelief takes away the power of the gospel ; but this not simply in regard of the gospel itself, for the gospel is ' the power of God unto salvation,' Rom. i. 16, but in regard of the influence of the power thereof to them. It is with the power of Christ's word as it was with the power of his works : ' He did not many works in his own country, because of their unbelief,' Mat. xiii. 58. Christ's power was not abated or weakened, but the benefit thereof was restrained from unbelievers ; it did not manifest itself to their good.

Unbelief is as a high strong dam against a flowing stream ; it may hinder the flowing of water into those places where the dam is set, but it doth not dry up or diminish the water ; that will find a current another way. See ver. 2, Sec. 19.

If the benefit of the gospel be duly weighed, this will be found to be a great aggravation of unbelief. See Chap. iii. 12, Secs. 128, 129.

Of the notation of the Greek word ἀπείθειαν, here translated *unbelief*, see Chap. iii. 18, Sec. 171.

Sec. 41. *Of the privilege of having the gospel before others, and abuse thereof.*

It is not without cause that the apostle adds this circumstance of time, πρότερον, *first*, or *before*. It was a kind of preferment to have the gospel before others ;

but that preferment was not regarded by them to whom it was afforded; they believed not, which was the greatest dishonour that could be done to the gospel. In all ages, many whom God in sundry privileges hath preferred before others have slighted God's favour. God made Saul the first king of Israel, but he did not walk worthy of that privilege, 1 Sam. xv. 17. Hezekiah was the first and only man that was expressly certified how long he should live; but 'he rendered not again, according to the benefit done unto him,' 2 Chron. xxxii. 25. The Jews, in the primitive time of the church, had the gospel first preached to them, but they put it far from them, Acts xiii. 46.

This ariseth partly from the blindness of their minds, which maketh them uncapable of discerning favours: 'She did not know,' saith the Lord to the church of the Jews, Hosea ii. 8, 'that I gave her corn, wine, and oil,' &c. Herein the prophet makes her more brutish than the most brutish creatures, the ox and the ass, Isa. i. 3. Partly from an evil disposition, an ungracious and ungrateful mind, 'they know not, neither will they understand,' Ps. lxxxii. 5.

This made the servant of the Lord thus to upbraid the people of God, 'Do you thus requite the Lord, O foolish people and unwise?' &c., Deut. xxxii. 6.

We of this nation have cause to take notice of the circumstance of time, and to lay it to heart; for by the divine providence the gospel was first preached to this kingdom. Some free states in Germany, Geneva, and other like places, had the gospel in this later spring thereof before us; but no kingdom universally professed it before England.

If we look so far backward as to John Wickliff's time, we may conclude, that the Lord caused the light of the gospel to pierce through the thick cloud of popery here in England before any other nation.

They who have had this honour, to be made partakers of the gospel before others, must consider what is here said of these Jews, to whom this privilege was vouchsafed: 'They entered not in;' so as men may make void their privileges. So much is threatened to Israel in these words, 'Thou shalt be the tail,' Deut. xxviii. 44; and in these, 'I will take away the hedge thereof, and it shall be eaten up,' Isa. v. 5; and in these, 'Ye are not my people, and I will not be your God,' Hosea i. 9; and in these, 'The kingdom of God shall be taken from you,' Mat. xxi. 43; 'I will remove thy candlestick out of his place,' Rev. ii. 5.

So much also hath been actually accomplished on the Jews, who had the gospel preached to them before the Gentiles, and on those churches of the Gentiles, who had the gospel first preached to them by the apostles. For where is Corinth? where Galatia? where Philippi? where Colosse? where Thessalonica? where Ephesus? and the other golden candlesticks to which Christ himself directed several epistles? Rev. ii. and iii. Is not the candlestick removed from all, and every of them? Yea, where is Rome? Is it not the very seat of antichrist? Oh let us, who in these western parts have had the gospel preached to us before many others, take heed, lest in us be accomplished that which Christ thus threatened, 'The first shall be last,' Mat. xx. 16.

Sec. 42. *Of the resolution and observations out of* Heb. iv. 6.

Ver. 6. *Seeing therefore it remaineth that some must enter therein, and they to whom it was first preached entered not in because of unbelief.*

The sum of this verse, a difference between believers and unbelievers. Hereabouts are two points:

1. An inference, in two relative conjunctions, *seeing, therefore.*
2. The substance.

Hereof are two parts:
1. The privilege of believers.
2. The damage of unbelievers.
1. In the former is noted,
 1. An indefinite expression of the persons, *some.*
 2. A declaration of their privilege, which is to enter into rest.
2. In the latter is noted:
 1. The persons.
 2. Their damage.
 3. The cause thereof.
1. The persons are described by the favour vouchsafed unto them, *to them it was preached,* and amplified by the time, *first.*
2. Their damage was, that *they entered not into the rest.*
3. The cause thereof is thus expressed, *because of unbelief.*

Doctrines.

I. *There is a rest to be entered into.* These two relatives, *seeing, therefore,* together with this concluding verb, *it remaineth,* intend thus much. See Sec. 36.

II. *Some may obtain what others miss.* This is expressed under this indefinite particle, *some.* See Sec. 37.

III. *What God hath promised shall be effected.* God promised rest, and the apostle here saith, *Some shall enter into it.* See Sec. 37.

IV. *The Israelites under the law had the gospel preached.* This is implied under the Greek word thus translated, *They to whom it was preached.* See Sec. 38.

V. *It is a privilege to have the gospel before others.* This is here set down as a privilege under this word *first.* See Secs. 38, 41.

VI. *Believers escape the damage of unbelievers.* Believers enter into that rest which unbelievers do not enter into. See Sec. 39.

VII. *Unbelievers partake not of the privilege of believers.* For unbelievers do not enter into the rest, which believers do. See Sec. 39.

VIII. *Unbelief makes void God's promises.* Namely to themselves, in that they believe them not.

Sec. 42. *Of the meaning of these words, 'Again, he limiteth a certain day.'*

Ver. 7. *Again, he limiteth a certain day, saying in David, To-day, after so long a time; as it is said, To-day, if ye will hear his voice, harden not your hearts.*

The apostle doth by this adverb πάλιν, *again*, add another argument to prove that there is another rest than the land of Canaan to be sought after.

Of adding proof to proof for confirmation of the same point, see Chap. i. 6, Sec. 77.

The argument which here the apostle useth, is taken from the time, which was pressed for seeking after the intended rest. It is thus expressed, ' He limiteth a certain day.'

The relative *he*, necessarily understood, though not distinctly expressed in the Greek, hath reference to the Holy Ghost, expressly mentioned, chap. iii. 7, where this testimony is first set down.

Thus the ground of the apostle's argument appears to be of divine authority.

The word translated ὁρίζει, *limiteth*, signifieth to bound, or to set limits to a thing. The noun ὅρος, *limes*, whence it is derived, signifieth a *limit* or *bound*, beyond which that which is limited or bounded doth not reach.

The like word in the plural number, ὅρια, is translated *coasts*, Mat. ii. 16, and *borders*, Mat. iv. 13. The verb here used, ὁρίζειν, *definire*, signifieth to *ordain*, Acts xvii. 31, and to *determine*, Acts xi. 29. It is oft used to set out the eternal and unchangeable decree of God, as Luke xxii. 22, Acts ii. 23, and x. 42. Now God's decree setteth bounds and limits to everything.

Here the word is fitly translated *limiteth*, for it is a set season that is comprised under that which is here said to be limited. This season here called, τινὰ ἡμέραν, *a certain day.* It is thus indefinitely set down *certain*, in relation to man, who knoweth not the uttermost extent thereof. For who knoweth how long the light of the gospel shall be continued to him? or how long he shall live? or how long the world shall last? These are the special periods which may be accounted the limits of the day here attended.

Sec. 43. *Of seasons limited by God.*

Though the limits of this day be unknown to man, and thereupon it be styled *a certain day*, yet God ' hath determined the times before appointed,' Acts xvii. 26. And in this respect, the *certain day* is said to be *limited.* God limits to man the seasons. He appoints when they shall begin, and how long they shall continue.

That which is said of a season to everything, and of a time to every purpose, is meant of the divine providence so ordering it. For it is said of God,

' He hath made everything beautiful in his time,' Eccles. iii. 1, 11.

Here mention is made of a limited day, and in other places of an hour, which is likewise limited, and that for doing or permitting anything to be done. Christ put off the manifestation of his power in supplying wine at a marriage-feast, John ii. 4, and his going to the feast at Jerusalem, John vii. 6, ' because his hour was not then come.' The Jews were not permitted to lay hold on Christ, ' till his hour was come,' John vii. 30, and viii. 20; but when the hour was come, then were they permitted to do what they would, John xii. 23, 27, Luke xxii. 53.

1. The Lord is the most high, supreme sovereign over all; and in that respect he hath an absolute power to appoint times and seasons, and to order matters to be done, when he seeth meet, Acts i. 7. This kind of power hath every governor within the circuit of his jurisdiction; much more the Lord of the whole world.

2. The understanding of this high sovereign is infinite, Ps. cxlvii. 5. He best knows which are the fittest times and seasons.

Hereby we are taught to ascribe the glory of all seasons for attaining any good thing to the Lord; to be thankful unto him for the same; to use them to that end for which he affords them; and to take heed that we let not slip that season which he limiteth for any purpose. No man can prorogue a season beyond the Lord's limits. See more hereof, Chap. iii. 7, Sec. 76, and ver. 13, Sec. 146.

Sec. 44. *Of David's penning the Psalms.*

The apostle, to prove that God limiteth times, hath recourse again to the text which he quoted, and inculcated again and again, Chap. iii. 7, 13, 15. So as he urgeth no other thing than what God of old had done, in and by his servant David.

This phrase, ἐν Δαβὶδ λέγων, *saying in David*, is tropical; for David is here put for the psalm which he penned; the author for his work,[1] as Rom. ix. 25. Or the preposition *in* is put for *by*, as Chap. i. 1, in the latter end of Sec. 11, ἐν τοῖς προφήταις, by the prophets.

Which way soever we take it, it confirmeth the divine authority of this proof (as was noted Sec. 42), yea, and of the whole book of Psalms, whereof David was the penman.

For it is thus written, ' David himself saith in the book of Psalms,' Luke xx. 42. And where testimonies are cited out of the Psalms, David is brought in as a witness, thus, ' How then doth David in spirit call him Lord?' Mat. xxii. 43, &c.'; and 'David speaketh concerning him,' &c., Acts ii. 25; and ' David describeth the blessedness of the man,' &c., Rom. iv. 6.

To make it the more clear, that what David penned was of divine authority, it is thus written, ' David

[1] μετωνυμία *efficientis.*

himself said by the Holy Ghost,' Mark xiii. 36, and 'the Holy Ghost by the mouth of David spake,' &c., Acts i. 16, and xiii. 35.

From the mention of David in reference to the psalm, we may probably conclude, that David was the penman of the whole book of Psalms, especially from this phrase, 'David himself saith in the book of Psalms,' Luke xx. 42.

Some exceptions are made against this conclusion, but such as may readily be answered.

Obj. 1. Sundry psalms have not the title of David prefixed before them; they have no title at all, as the first, second, and others.

Ans. If they have no title, why should they not be ascribed to David rather than to any other, considering that the book of Psalms is indefinitely attributed to him (as we heard out of the fore-mentioned place, Luke xx. 42), which is the title prefixed before all the Psalms, ספר תהלים, *liber psalmorum*, as comprising them all under it?

Besides, such testimonies as are taken out of psalms that have no title, are applied to David, as Acts iv. 25, and this testimony that is here taken out of Ps. xcv. 7.

Obj. 2. Some titles are ascribed to other authors, as Ps. lxxii. and cxxvii. to Solomon.

Ans. The Hebrew servile ל, *lamed*, is variously taken and translated; as sometimes *of*, Ps. iii. 1, לדוד מזמור, *psalmus Davidis*, a psalm of David. Then it signifieth the author. Thus it is used in most titles, especially when they are applied to David. Other times it is translated *for*, as Ps. lxxii. 1, and cxxvii.

In these it implieth, that the psalm was penned *for* Solomon's use, or for his instruction. It may also be thus translated, *concerning Solomon*. That the 72d psalm was penned by David is evident by the close thereof, in these words, 'The prayers of David the son of Jesse are ended.'

Obj. 3. Some titles attribute the psalm to this and that Levite, as Ps. lxxxviii. to Heman, and lxxxix. to Ethan; yea, twelve psalms to Asaph, and eleven to the sons of Korah.

Ans. All these were very skilful, not only in singing, but also in setting tunes to psalms. They were music-masters. Therefore David, having penned the psalms, committed them to the foresaid Levites, to be fitly tuned. As all those Levites were very skilful in music, so many of them were endued with an extraordinary spirit. Asaph was a seer, 2 Chron. xxix.; so also was Heman, 1 Chron. xxv. 5; and with these two was Ethan, as a chief singer and master of music, joined, 1 Chron. xv. 17, 19. The sons of Korah also were men of eminent parts, especially in music. Wisely therefore did David make choice of these men to tune and sing his psalms in public. It will not follow that any of them were inditers of any of the psalms, because their name is set in the title of some of them.

Obj. 4. The ninetieth psalm carrieth this title, 'A prayer of Moses the man of God.'

Ans. It is said to be the prayer of Moses, in regard of the substance and general matter of it; but, as a psalm, it was penned by David. He brought it into that form. David, as a prophet, knew that Moses had uttered such a prayer in the substance of it; therefore he prefixeth that title before it.

Obj. 5. The 137th Psalm doth set down the disposition and carriage of the Israelites in the Babylonish captivity, which was six hundred and forty years after David's time; and the 126th psalm sets out their return from that captivity.

Ans. To grant these to be so, yet might David pen those psalms. For by a prophetical spirit, he might foresee what would fall out, and answerably pen psalms fit thereunto. Moses did the like, Deut. xxix. 22, &c., and xxxi. 21, 22, &c. A man of God expressly set down distinct acts of Josiah three hundred and thirty years before they fell out, 1 Kings xiii. 2. Isaiah did the like of Cyrus, Isa. xliv. 28 and xlv. 1, which was about two hundred years beforehand.

Sec. 45. *Of seeking while the time of finding remaineth.*

That which the apostle would have especially to be observed in the testimony of David, is this word, *to-day.*

It is here indefinitely taken for a continued present time, as was shewed, Chap. iii. 7, Sec. 76, and verse 13, Sec. 146. For on that word resteth the force of this argument, whereby he proveth that Canaan cannot be the rest which David inciteth them to seek after.

To make this meaning the more clear, he addeth this clause, μετὰ τοσοῦτον χρόνον, 'after so long a time.' This hath reference to that time wherein the unbelieving Israelites perished in the wilderness, and entered not into Canaan, but their children entered, Num. xiv. 30, 31. Betwixt that and David's time, there passed more than four hundred and fifty years, Acts xiii. 20. Well therefore might the apostle use this indefinite phrase, 'after so long a time.'

The apostle's argument may thus be framed:

That rest whereinto men are invited to enter four hundred and fifty years after a rest possessed, is another rest than that which is possessed;

But the rest intended by David, is a rest whereinto he inviteth men to enter four hundred and fifty years after Canaan was possessed.

Therefore Canaan is not that rest whereinto David inviteth men to enter.

This continuance of *to-day*, after so long a time, and stirring up people to make the right use thereof, sheweth, that so long as the date of a promise lasteth, the fruit of that promise may be expected. Where the psalmist layeth down the ground of his hope in God, and of his seeking of mercy, he thus expresseth that ground, 'Is his mercy clean gone for ever? doth his promise fail for evermore?' Ps. lxxvii. 8. These interrogatives are strong negatives; as if he said, I am sure that his mercy is not clean gone, and that his promise doth not fail; therefore I hope for mercy, therefore I depend upon his promise. On this ground it is that the prophet exhorteth to 'seek the Lord while he may be found,' Isa. lv. 6, and that the apostle exhorteth to seek grace 'in the accepted time, and day of salvation,' 2 Cor. vi. 1, 2.

While the date of God's promise lasteth, God's truth stands engaged for the performance of his word; so as we may well expect the fruit of it if we seek it aright. Yet is the time for us to apply this point to ourselves; *to-day* is yet continued among us. As God in David, so still in his ministers, he 'limiteth a certain day, saying, To-day.'

Though it hath long continued, yet is not the date hereof clean past. Many in their times have made the right use of *to-day*, and are entered into rest; others have let it slip, and deprived themselves of rest.

For us who yet live, who yet live under the gospel, it remaineth either to make sure that rest to our souls, or to make irrecoverable forfeiture thereof. Be not therefore so foolish as to continue to provoke God's patience and long-sufferance till the date of it be past: 'Despisest thou the riches of God's goodness, and forbearance, and long-suffering, not knowing that the goodness of God leadeth thee to repentance? But after thy hardness, and impenitent heart, treasurest up unto thyself wrath against the day of wrath,' Rom. ii. 4, 5.

Sec. 46. *Of Scripture proofs inculcated*.

Because this is a matter of great concernment, to seek grace in the day of grace, the apostle further proves it by the express word of Scripture; first generally implied in this phrase, *as it is said;* then particularly expressed in these words, 'To-day if you will hear,' &c.

That general, *as it is said*, sheweth that Scripture-proof is a sound proof; well may we rest on this, *as it is said*, if that which is said be said in sacred Scripture, as here it is. Of Scripture proofs, see Chap. i. 5, Sec. 65.

The particular exemplification by the very words of Scripture further sheweth, that scriptures are to be alleged in their own words. See Chap. iii. 7, Sec. 74.

This is the fourth time that the point here set down (in these words, 'To-day, if ye will hear his voice, harden not your hearts') hath been inculcated, namely, Chap. iii. 7, 13, 15, and here. For it is a matter of moment; and matters of moment may be inculcated again and again.

Of repeating the same point, see Chap. iii. 15, Sec. 158.

Of the meaning of these words, 'To-day, if ye will hear,' &c., see Chap. iii. 7, Sec. 76, &c.

Sec. 47. *Of Jesus or Joshua, who settled Israel in Canaan.*

Ver. 8. *For if Jesus had given them rest, then would he not afterward have spoken of another day.*

This verse depends on the former, as a confirmation of the argument there pressed. This causal conjunction γὰρ, *for*, implieth as much. The confirmation consisteth in removing an objection, which is this: though some of the Israelites which were in the wilderness entered not into Canaan, yet others did; for Joshua settled their children, who were a great multitude, in Canaan, so as they entered into rest.

To take away this, the apostle proveth that there is another rest besides that. He doth not simply deny Canaan to be a rest, but he denies it to be the only rest; the rest so to be rested in as no other to be sought after.

By *Jesus*, here mentioned, is meant *Joshua;* for so doth his name sound in Hebrew. Of the notation of this Greek name *Jesus*, and of the Hebrew name *Joshua*, see Chap. ii. 9, Sec. 73. Of Joshua, see *The Church's Conquest*, on Exod. xvii. 9, sec. 9.

This Joshua was the first that was chosen general to fight against Israel's enemies anon after they came out of Egypt, Exod. xvii. 9. He being an especial minister of Moses, was in the mount with him when the people committed their great idolatry about the golden calf, Exod. xxiv. 13, and xxxii. 17. He was one of them that was sent to spy out the land of Canaan, who, together with Caleb, brought good tidings about the land; whereas the other spies brought an evil report of the land which they had searched. He and Caleb, believing that God would make good his promise, did what they could to encourage the people, who were thinking to return into Egypt. Whereupon, of the six hundred thousand men that came out of Egypt, only he and Caleb entered into Canaan, Num. xiv. 6, &c. He had not only the honour to enter in himself, but also to be a guide, a captain, a general, and chief governor; to lead in all the rest that entered, to vanquish their enemies, and to settle them in that promised land, Num. xxvii. 18, &c.; Deut. xxxi. 7, 14; Joshua i. 1, 2, &c.

Joshua was herein an especial type of Christ, who vanquisheth all our spiritual enemies, and settleth all his redeemed from bondage of Satan in the heavenly Canaan. It pleased God to raise up such temporal saviours to his people, to nourish their hope in that true Saviour the Lord Jesus, who should save them from all their spiritual enemies, Luke i. 68, 69.

Joshua gave them rest in Canaan, not Moses, the law-giver, to shew that the law cannot bring us to heaven; that work is reserved for Jesus.

Sec. 48. *Of Joshua's giving rest, and God's work attributed to man.*

This phrase, κατέπαυσε, *had given rest*, is the interpretation of one compound verb. (Of the simple verb and the compound noun, see Chap. iii. 11, Sec. 116). It is here used transitively. It doth not here signify only to rest, as it did ver. 4, but to give rest to others; for this relative αὐτοὺς, *them*, depends on it. It is in this respect like the Hebrew's third conjugation, which they call *hiphil* (הפעיל).[1]

The rest which is here implied to be given by Joshua was the land of Canaan; which was called *rest* in reference to the troubles of Israel in Egypt, and to their travels in the wilderness, on the one side; and on the other side, in reference to Israel's enjoying Canaan for a perpetual inheritance.

Joshua is said to give them that rest under God, as God's minister, whom God used to settle his people therein.

It was God that properly gave them that rest, Deut. iii. 20, and xxv. 19; Joshua xxii. 4, and xxiii. 1; yet Joshua is said to give them rest in these respects:

1. Joshua was appointed by God to be the chief governor over his people after Moses his death, at that time when they should enter into Canaan, Num. xxvii. 18, &c.; Deut. xxxi. 14.

2. God promised Joshua that he should settle his people in Canaan, Joshua i. 3, &c.

3. Joshua was their guide to lead them out of the wilderness to Canaan, and that through Jordan, Joshua iii. 8.

4. Joshua was the general in all the battles against the Canaanites, so as he had the chief hand in destroying them, Joshua xi. 18.

5. When the men of Ai once had the better over Israel, and put them to flight, Joshua by his prayer so prevailed with God, as the Lord was pleased to direct them how to regain their loss, and destroy those enemies, Joshua vii. 6, &c.

6. When they wanted time to destroy a numerous multitude of enemies, Joshua prayed, and the sun, moon, and whole host of heaven, stood still about a whole day, Joshua x. 12, &c.

7. Joshua at length so far destroyed all the inhabitants of the land of Canaan, as there was room enough for the Israelites to place their habitation there, Joshua xxi. 43.

8. Joshua by lot divided that land among the Israelites, and gave to every tribe their inheritance, Joshua xiv. 1.

9. When Joshua died, he left Israel in peace and rest, and that in their several inheritances, Joshua xxiv. 28.

All these were ministerial acts, done by warrant from God, and by the assistance of God himself. Hereby was Joshua much advanced above other men; but nothing at all was derogated from God.

This act of giving rest to Israel being ascribed to Joshua, manifested God's respect to man, in attributing his own divine work to man. The like he did to Moses, where he bid him divide the sea, Exod. xiv. 16, and where he said that Moses brought Israel out of Egypt, Exod. xxxii. 7. Thus the mighty work of God in the first conversion of sinners is ascribed unto men; in which respect Paul saith of himself, that he begat them through the gospel, 1 Cor. iv. 15; Philem. 10.

This God doth to honour man's nature, in making men co-workers with himself, 2 Cor. vi. 1, and to magnify his own power; for his strength is made perfect in weakness, 2 Cor. xii. 9.

This also he doth to move other men to submit themselves to them, whom he placeth over them, and whom he useth for their good.

To distrust the effecting of a matter, because God useth weak men as his ministers for bringing it to pass, is to oppose our shallow conceit to the unsearchable wisdom of God.

It becomes us to use such means as God is pleased to appoint: and in using of them to look unto him for good success and blessing.

There are two extremes whereinto men are prone to fall in this case.

The one is too much diffidence by reason of the seeming meanness of the means: as Christ's countrymen despised him and believed not, by reason of the meanness of his birth and education, Mark vi. 3.

The other is too much confidence in the means, giving the honour of God himself thereunto, as the Lycaonians, who accounted the apostles to be gods, Acts xiv. 11.

Sec. 49. *Of not resting on blessings below as the highest to be expected.*

This consequence,—'then would he not afterward,' &c.,—is here inferred, to prove that Joshua did not settle God's people in that rest which David intended. It is such a proof as was before noted, Sec. 45.

The force of the proof resteth on these two words, *after, another*. The argument may be thus framed:

If there had been no other rest for God's people to enter into than that wherein Joshua settled the Israelites, David would not after that settling have spoken of another time to enter into a rest;

But David after that settling spake of another day to enter into a rest;

Therefore there is another rest to enter into.

By this argument the apostle would draw the Hebrews from resting upon that typical rest which their fathers had long enjoyed. He plainly sheweth that the type is not the truth itself. Joshua was a type of Jesus, and Canaan was a type of heaven; but nor Joshua was Jesus himself, nor Canaan heaven itself. The ark was not it which saved those that were in it from eternal destruction (though it were a type thereof, 1 Peter iii. 21). For cursed

---

[1] Quæ in *Kal* sunt neutra in *Hiphil* sunt transitiva. Quæ in *Kal* sunt transitiva in *Hiphil* sunt vis [Qu. 'bis'?—ED.] transitiva; gemina ferè actio significatur.

Ham was in it. The cloud in the wilderness (Exod. xiii. 21) preserved not all that were under it from the scorching fire of God's wrath; for many of them were consumed in the wilderness. All that passed through the Red Sea, and thereby were saved from the Egyptian bondage, were not baptized in the blood of Christ, and thereby saved from the slavery of sin and Satan. All that did eat of manna, and drink of the water out of the rock, did not eat the flesh of Christ, and drink his blood, though all these were types and sacraments thereof. The many sacrifices under the law did not take away sin, Heb. x. 4, yet were the types of that sacrifice that did indeed take away sin.

Such external types, figures, and shadows were afforded to God's people under the law, in regard of their weakness, to raise up their minds and hearts to higher and greater matters; and to be as looking-glasses to shew unto them Christ Jesus, and such things as concerned their eternal salvation. They were not so given as to make God's people to rest in them, and not to seek after further truths.

We are taught hereby to take heed that we be not deceived in mistaking the mark, and placing happiness in that wherein it doth not consist. Peter mistook the brightness and glory that appeared at Christ's transfiguration, for the glory of heaven; and in that respect said, 'It is good to be here,' Mat. xvii. 4. There is great danger therein; for there is no proportion betwixt earthly and heavenly things. We were better to be without the best things here below, than so to doat and rest upon them, as to neglect the things above.

To apply this to our times: let us consider what resemblances, what first-fruits, what pledges, what evidences God now, under the gospel, giveth to us of our heavenly rest and glory. Such are,—

1. That portion of goods, those delights, that health, long life, and like blessings which here he bestows upon his saints.
2. That fellowship and communion which saints have one with another.
3. The peace and prosperity of churches.
4. Assemblies of saints for performing holy duties.
5. Liberty of Sabbaths and ordinances.
6. Comfort of soul, peace of conscience, joy in the Holy Ghost.

Though these, and other like things, be blessings of God, which we may enjoy, and for which we ought to be thankful, yet are they not wholly to be rested in.

For if true happiness consisted in these, then would not the Holy Ghost speak of an heavenly happiness, eternal glory, and everlasting life to be hereafter enjoyed.

Sec. 50. *Of truths couched under types.*

The *other day* here mentioned is that which hath been four times before insisted upon. See Sec. 45.

From this *other day*, which David mentioneth, a question may be moved, whether there were not a day, in Joshua's time, and before his time also, to enter into the rest that David afterward calls upon people to enter into. If there were a day before, why doth the apostle so much urge these words, *afterwards*, and *another*, after David's time?

Ans. The main scope of David, and of the apostle here (for both were of the same mind, and aimed at the same scope), their scope was to shew that Joshua's time was not the only day wherein rest was to be found; nor that rest which Joshua gave in Canaan, the only rest to be sought after.

The day for seeking the rest here intended began when God made this threatening against Satan, but promise to man, 'It shall bruise thy head,' Gen. iii. 15. This is a promise of conquest over Satan, and deliverance from his tyranny, and of the rest here intended following thereupon.

This day was also in Moses and Joshua's time; and this rest was typified to them under sundry legal rites and types, and under the land of Canaan.

Spiritual and celestial things were comprised under their external and legal types.

Their circumcision was, 'the putting off the body of the sins of the flesh,' Col. ii. 11. 'They were all baptized in the cloud, and in the sea.' In eating manna, 'they did eat the same spiritual meat' that we do, 'and did all drink the same spiritual drink: for they drank of that spiritual rock, which was Christ,' 1 Cor. x. 2, 3, 4. Their passover did typify Christ, 1 Cor. v. 7. So did all their sacrifices, Heb. ix. 9, 10, 11. The blood of sprinkling set out the blood of Christ, which cleanseth from all sin, Heb. ix. 13, 14. 1 John i. 7. The legal priesthood was a type of Christ's priesthood, Heb. iv. 14. The tabernacle set forth heaven, Heb. viii. 2. The Son of man was lift up before them in the brazen serpent, John iii. 14, 15. Not to insist on other particulars, in general it is said, that the tabernacle, and the things therein, was 'a figure,' namely, of spiritual things, Heb. ix. 9, and 'the law had a shadow of good things to come,' Heb. x. 1. Of particular rites it is said, 'They are a shadow of things to come: but the body is Christ,' Col. ii. 17.

Spiritual and celestial truths and substances were comprised under external and legal types, for these ends.

1. To shew that God, being a Spirit, delighteth in things spiritual, John iv. 24. In the time wherein legal services were of use, they were detested by God in three cases.

(1.) When they were performed in hypocrisy and show only. In this respect God thus upbraideth the Israelites: 'This people draw near me with their mouth, and with their lips do honour me, but have removed their heart far from me,' Isa. xxix. 13.

(2.) When they made them a cloak to cover over impiety and iniquity. In this respect saith God,

'Your new moons, and your appointed feasts, my soul hateth.' The reason thereof is thus rendered, 'Your hands are full of blood,' Isa. i. 14, 15. The like is noted, Jer. vii. 9, 11; Mat. xxiii. 14.

(3.) When people rested only on the external performance of legal rites, and expected to be accepted for those outward performances, not regarding the inward truth and substance. In this respect it is thus said to God, 'Sacrifice and offering thou didst not desire,' Ps. xl. 6, &c., and God himself saith, 'I will not reprove thee for thy sacrifices,' &c., Ps. l. 8, &c.

2. To demonstrate the ground of saints' faith: which was not the external rites that they performed, but the internal truth which they believed. 'By faith Abel offered unto God a more excellent sacrifice than Cain,' Heb. xi. 4. His faith had an eye upon Christ the truth; not simply upon the sacrifice that was offered. Abraham 'saw Christ's day,' John viii. 56. Moses 'esteemed the reproach of Christ great riches,' Heb. xi. 26, so as he suffered reproach for Christ.

Of other ends why the legal rites had their spiritual truths, see Sec. 49.

We may from hence infer, that the believing Jews did not rest in the performance of outward rites, nor in the possession of Canaan, nor in external blessings, but had their eye upon higher, spiritual and heavenly matters.

We may from hence gather, that it is pains worth the taking, to search after the spiritual, evangelical, and celestial truths that were comprised under their external and legal rites. By this means may we in many respects come to discern sundry particular benefits arising out of those truths, which it may be we should not so readily discern in a single, simple consideration of the truths themselves.

For finding out the truth of types, observe these rules:
1. Be well acquainted with the prophets, who were expounders of the law. A prophet will tell you, that circumcision intended the 'taking away of the foreskin of the heart,' Jer. iv. 4. Another will tell you, that sacrifices set out the offering of Christ, Ps. xl. 6.

2. Observe what applications in the New Testament are made of the legal rites unto their several truths. For the penmen of the New Testament were guided by the same Spirit that Moses was; and knew what was the intendment of his rites. Thereby we may know, that the rite of not breaking a bone of the paschal lamb, Exod. xii. 46, did prefigure the kind of Christ's death, and the not breaking of his bones, John xix. 36. Other types, applied to their truths in the New Testament, are set down before in this Section.

3. By just consequence may sundry truths be found out. For example, from this ground, that the high priest prefigured Christ, we may by consequence infer, that the high priest appearing before God for the people, and bearing their names in his breastplate, did prefigure Christ's appearing before God for us, and presenting us by name unto God, Exod. xxviii. 29. Thus may the high priest's robes and ornaments be applied to Christ.

4. A perpetual equity will lead us to find out the truth of a type; as the equity of this, that prayer shall ever be made unto God in the name of Christ, shews that the daily offering up of incense did typify as much, Mal. i. 11.

5. A fit analogy and resemblance of a type with the truth: as Israel's bondage under Pharaoh, with our spiritual bondage under sin; their deliverance by the Red Sea, with our redemption by the blood of Christ; the clouds sheltering them from the parching heat of the sun, with Christ's preserving us from the wrath of God. So in other things.

Sec. 51. *Of the resolution of* Heb. iv. 7, 8.

Ver. 7. *Again, he limiteth a certain day, saying in David, To-day, after so long a time: as it is said, To-day, if ye will hear his voice, harden not your hearts.*

8. *For if Jesus had given them rest, then would he not afterwards have spoken of another day.*

The sum of these two verses is this: Canaan is not the rest to be rested in. This is, 1, proved, ver. 7; 2, confirmed, ver. 8.

In the proof is set down,
1. An inference on that which went before, in this adverb *Again*.
2. The substance of the proof: which is, 1, propounded; 2, exemplified.

In the proposition there is,
1. An intimation of God's prerogative.
2. A manifestation thereof.

God's prerogative is set out,
1. By his act, *he limiteth*.
2. By the object thereof, *a certain day*.

The manifestation of God's prerogative is by a divine testimony.

In setting down the testimony is noted,
1. The penman of it; or the place of Scripture, *saying in David*.
2. The matter of it. That is,
(1.) Simply considered, in this word, *to-day*.
(2.) Relatively extended, in this phrase, *after so long a time*.

The exemplification of the point is,
1. Generally implied in this phrase, *as it is said*.
2. Particularly expressed, in these words of Scripture: *To-day, if ye will hear his voice, harden not your hearts.*

Of the particular branches of this scripture, see Chap. iii. ver. 7, Sec. 76, &c.

The confirmation of the former proof is in the 8 h verse. In it one thing is granted; another is inferred.

The thing granted is, that Joshua gave Israel a rest.

The point inferred is, that that rest was not a rest to be rested in.

In the thing granted we may distinguish the persons and the point. The persons are,

1. The donor, *Joshua*: and the donees, in this relative, *them*, under whom are comprised the then living Israelites.

2. The point, gift, or thing given, which was *rest*.

In setting down the inference, observe,

1. The manner, by way of supposition, *if, then*.

2. The matter, which contains a proof of the point, that Joshua did not give them the rest to be rested in.

The proof is double:

1. It is taken from this circumstance of time, *afterward*.

2. From the difference of time, when Joshua gave Israel rest, and David inviteth to enter into a rest. This latter is *another day*.

Sec. 52. *Of instructions raised out of* Heb. iv. 7, 8.

I. *Proof may be added to proof for confirmation of the same point.* This is implied under this adverb, *again*. See Sec. 42.

II. *God setteth seasons.* This is the intent of this word, *he limiteth*. See Sec. 43.

III. *Times are not known to man.* This word *certain* is not certain or sure, but indefinite. See Sec 42.

IV. *God spake by David.* This phrase, *saying in David*, hath reference to God. See Sec. 44.

V. *David was the penman of the book of Psalms.* That book is by a metonymy called *David*. See Sec. 44.

VI. *That whereunto we are invited to enter into long after, must needs be another rest than that which was possessed long before.* This is the apostle's argument. It is couched in this phrase, *after so long a time.* See Sec. 45.

VII. *There is hope of entering while the day continues.* This is the main end of pressing this word *to-day*. See Sec. 45.

VIII. *Scripture proofs may be inculcated.* Four times hath this proof, 'To-day, if ye will hear,' &c., been insisted upon. See Sec. 46.

Of sundry observations gathered out of these words, *To-day, if ye will hear,* &c., see Chap. iii. Sec. 120.

IX. *Joshua was Israel's governor.*

X. *Canaan was a place of rest to Israel.*

XI. *Joshua settled Israel in Canaan.*

XII. *God's work is ascribed to man.*

These four last doctrines are taken for grant, and made the ground for the inference following. See Sec. 47, 48.

XIII. *Canaan was not the rest to be rested in.* This is the main point which the apostle here proves. See Sec. 49.

XIV. *Scripture circumstances are observable.* The principal force of the apostle's argument resteth upon a circumstance of time. Because David, after Joshua had settled Israel in Canaan, speaketh of another day, therefore Joshua's rest was not a rest to be rested in. In another place the apostle draws an argument from this word *seed*, in the singular number, to prove that Christ was promised to Abraham, Gal. iii. 16.

XV. *The whole Scripture is given by inspiration of God,* 2 Tim. iii. 16. We may not therefore think the least tittle therein to be in vain.

It becomes us, in this respect, to be the more observant, not only of the general intendment and main scope of a place of Scripture, but also of the manner of setting it down, and of other circumstances appertaining thereunto.

Sec. 53. *Of setting down the conclusion of a discourse.*

Ver. 9. *There remaineth therefore a rest to the people of God.*

This verse sets down the conclusion of the apostle's discourse concerning the rest of the Sabbath, and of the land of Canaan, both which he had proved, by sundry arguments, not to be the rest intended by David. Thereupon he inferreth this conclusion, *there remaineth a rest*: that is, there is another kind of rest for God's people to rest in.

This concluding particle ἄρα, *therefore*, doth demonstrate this to be a conclusion. So it is used, Rom. viii. 1, Gal. iii. 7.

This conjunction is sometimes used by way of interrogation, as 'Shall he find faith?' Luke xviii. 8; so Acts viii. 30. Sometimes for confirmation of a point, and translated *no doubt*, and *truly;* as 'no doubt the kingdom of God is among you,' and 'truly ye bear witness,' Luke xi. 20, 48. Sometimes by way of addubitation or supposition, and translated *perhaps*, Acts viii. 22; *haply*, Acts xvii. 27. But most frequently it is used by way of inference, and translated *then*, as 'then are ye bastards,' Heb. xii. 8. This is in a manner all one, as here in my text, *therefore*.

An express setting down of a conclusion is an especial means of making one's mind and meaning clear. It shews what is the main intendment, and what is especially to be observed.

It is like a white in the butt, or a mark to such as shoot at rovers, to direct the archer in drawing his bow and shooting out his arrow; or rather, like to the lantern in the admiral ship, which directeth all the ships in the navy.

Thus the demonstration of the main conclusion gives great light to the whole discourse.

Sec. 54. *Of the rest to be laboured after.*

That which is here inferred is, that there is a rest. The Greek word σαββατισμός, here translated *rest*, is nowhere else used throughout the New Testament, nor in any other Greek author, except in some of the Greek fathers, who have taken it from this place.

The notation of it is taken from an Hebrew word which signifieth rest, and soundeth Sabbath. See Sec. 31. Hereupon the last translators have thus turned it in the margin, 'keeping a Sabbath;' so as the rest here intended is not simply a lying, sitting, or standing still, without doing anything at all, but a ceasing from such things as are done here in this world. These are called 'our own works' in the next verse. Of the heavenly rest here intended, see Secs. 6, 8, 9.

This word doth fitly set forth the rest that is to come: for as God, who rested on the Sabbath from creating new creatures, yet did other works of providence; and as God's people here on earth, who cease from the works of their calling on Sabbath days, yet do sundry works of piety and mercy, which are proper to the Sabbath; so in heaven the glorified saints, who rest from the works of this world, do many celestial works, which are proper to that place and time.

These works are excellent and glorious in their kind. The saints there have sufficient ability to perform them according to the mind of their Lord, and withal there is in them a ready willingness and forwardness to put out their ability, and that to the utmost, in those works.

Sec. 55. *Of rest in heaven from troubles on earth.*

That which under the word σαββατισμὸς, here translated *rest*, the apostle doth in special give us to understand, is, that there shall be a freedom from everything that is toilsome and grievous in this world. The wise man in Ecclesiastes declareth how full of outward molestations and inward vexations this world is, and that as long as men abide therein. Besides the many expressions that he hath of the vanity of the things of this world (sometimes, in way of aggravation, doubling the word, and adding this note of generality *all* unto it, thus, 'Vanity of vanity, vanity of vanities, all is vanity,' Eccles. i. 2, and xii. 8); and besides the labours, travails, and troubles that he there mentioneth ten several times, he useth this clause, ' Vexation of spirit.' But in the rest here mentioned, ' they rest from their labours,' Rev. xiv. 13 ; and ' all tears shall be wiped away from their eyes,' Rev. xxi. 4 ; under labours, all molestations of body are comprised; and under tears, all vexations of spirit.

Labours and troubles are not the things whereunto God hath ordained man, as unto his ultimate end. Man by sin hath pulled them upon himself. Sin was the cause of this doom upon the woman, ' I will greatly multiply thy sorrow,' &c ; and of this upon the man, ' In sorrow shalt thou eat,' &c., Gen. iii. 16, 17. From sin proceeded all manner of evils, even evils of punishment.

Obj. The Lord himself saith, ' I create evil,' Isa. xlv. 7. Hereupon a prophet maketh this inference, ' Shall there be evil in a city, and the Lord hath not done it?' Amos iii. 6.

Ans. By *evil* in those and other like places the just punishment of sin is intended. That God is said to create, and do in these respects ;—

1. God ordained that sin should be punished.

2. God by his providence ordereth the punishments which are inflicted on sin: and that for the kind, measure, and continuance thereof.

3. The ministers and means whereby sinners are punished, are appointed and sent by God.

On these grounds we may conclude, that God's people shall for the present be sufficiently supported in their afflictions; and at length be fully freed from all, 1 Cor. x. 13.

Upon expectation of the foresaid freedom and rest, it is just and equal both diligently to work the work of our Lord and Master, all the working time of this our pilgrimage ; and also patiently to endure whatsoever the Lord shall be pleased to lay upon us. Christ hath made himself a worthy pattern herein: ' I must' (saith he) ' work the works of him that sent me, while it is day,' John ix. 4. And ' Though he were a Son, yet learned he obedience by the things which he suffered,' Heb. v. 8. There being a freedom and rest to come, Christ had an eye thereto, Heb. xii. 2. So had Moses, Heb. xi. 26.

When we are pinched or grieved with any work, travail, trouble or affliction, let us call to mind and meditate on this freedom and rest. Mariners pass over many boisterous and dangerous seas, in hope of attaining to a quiet haven. Labourers toil all the day, in hope of rest at night. So others in other cases. Expectation of freedom, rest and recompence, upholds their spirits; yet they may fail of their expectation. But they for whom this rest is prepared shall not fail thereof. What then should we not do, what should we not endure, in hope of this rest? The rather, because hope thereof is certain and sure.

If the joy, honour, and glory which will accompany this rest were duly weighed, it would much more stir us up to this duty.

Sec. 56. *Of rest to come.*

Of the foresaid rest, it is here said that ἀπολείπεται, it *remaineth*. The same word is here used that was used before, ver. 6, Sec. 37, but in a different sense. There it was used impersonally: here it is governed by a nominative case, which is rest.

The verb is of the passive voice, and may word for word be thus translated, *a rest is left.* But in our English the active interpretation best expresseth the apostle's meaning: which is, that the rest here intended is reserved for us hereafter ; it is not here to be expected while we live in this world. ' He shall enter into peace,' Isa. lvii. 2. This rest shall be, ' when the Lord Jesus shall be revealed from heaven,' 2 Thes. i. 17. ' They that die in the Lord shall rest from their labours,' Rev. xiv. 13.

1. This world is not a fit place, nor this life a fit time, to enjoy such a rest as is reserved in heaven.

2. Rest here would glue our hearts too much to this world, and make us say, ' It is good to be here,' Mat. xvii. 4. It would slack our longing desire after Christ

in heaven. Death would be more irksome, and heaven the less welcome.

3. There would be no proof or trial of our spiritual armour, and of the several graces of God bestowed on us.

4. God's providence, prudence, power, mercy, and other like properties, could not be so well discerned, if here we enjoyed that rest.

This rest being to come, and reserved for us, it will be our wisdom, while here we live, to prepare for trouble, and to address ourselves to labour: as the soldiers in the field, and as the labourers in the day-time.

Yet withal to have our eye upon this rest to come; that thereby we may be the more encouraged and incited to hold out to the end, waiting for this rest that is to come.

Sec. 57. *Of God's people, to whom rest is reserved.*

The persons to whom the celestial rest is reserved, are styled 'the people of God.' The Greek noun λάος, translated *people*, may have a notation from the verb λάυειν, *frui*, that signifieth to *enjoy*: for people are such as enjoy society and communion one with another.

As this word hath reference to God, it implieth such as are God's confederates, such as are in league and covenant with him. For by virtue of the new covenant, God thus saith to his confederates, 'I will be their God, and they shall be my people,' Jer. xxxi. 33.

This people of God are such as God hath 'chosen to salvation,' 2 Thes. ii. 13; whom Christ 'hath redeemed to God by his blood,' Rev. v. 9, and whom the Holy Ghost hath sanctified, Rom. xv. 16. This is their right, and thus they are fitted to this rest.

By virtue of this relation betwixt God and them, God takes them to be in special manner 'a peculiar people to himself,' Deut. xiv. 2, 1 Pet. ii. 9, and they take the Lord in special manner to be their God, Josh. xxiv. 24.

Both these are to the life thus expressed, in relation to God and Israel, 'Thou hast avouched the Lord to be thy God, and the Lord hath avouched thee to be his peculiar people,' Deut. xxvi. 17, 18. Hereupon saith the Lord to them, 'I will say, It is my people; and they shall say, The Lord is my God,' Zech. xiii. 9.

The former implies a great dignity, in that God vouchsafeth to take us to be his peculiar people. The latter a bounden duty, whereby we tie ourselves to carry ourselves to God as becomes his peculiar people, who have taken him for our Lord.

This description of the persons is set down by way of restraint: and shews, that the rest here spoken of is only for them. None but God's people shall partake thereof. In this respect it is said of Jesus, 'He shall save his people from their sins,' Mat. i. 21. And he is 'the Saviour of the body,' Eph. v. 23. Of a righteous man it is said, 'He shall enter into peace,' Isa. lvii. 2. These are they that 'die in the Lord, and thereupon 'rest from their labours.' Such are they of whom this apostle thus saith, 'We which have believed do enter into rest,' ver. 3.

This is further manifest by the contrary end of such as are of a contrary disposition. 'To them who by patient continuance in well-doing seek for glory, &c., eternal life shall be given; but unto them who obey unrighteousness, shall be indignation and wrath,' Rom. ii. 7, 8. The like is noted, 2 Thes. i. 9; Mat. xxv. 41; Luke xvi. 23.

The ground of that rest which the former sort of people have, is God's free grace and rich mercy, together with the merit of Christ, Luke xii. 32, 1 Pet. i. 3, 19.

The ground of the contrary end that others attain unto, is their just desert, Rom. vi. 23.

None can justly rest upon attaining this rest, till he have some assurance that he is of the number of God's people: justified by faith (for we which have believed do enter into rest, ver. 3), and sanctified by the Spirit; for the unrighteous shall not inherit the kingdom of God, 1 Cor. vi. 9.

Excellent and glorious is this rest; but not fit for every one. There is a qualification required for such as enter thereinto. It becomes God's people to take God for their Lord, and accordingly to yield all holy obedience unto him. If through infidelity and impenitency God be provoked to say to any, '*Lo-ammi*, ye are not my people, Hos. i. 9, what can be expected, but that God should swear that they shall not enter into his rest, as he did to the Israelites? Ps. xcv. 11.

Sec. 58. *Of the inference of the* 10th *verse upon the* 9th.

Ver. 10. *For he that is entered into his rest, he also hath ceased from his own works, as God did from his.*

In this verse the apostle expressly and distinctly declareth, what that excellent rest is, whereof he hath spoken so much before, in this and the former chapter.

He purposely describeth it to shew what that is which 'remaineth for God's people;' and by this description he proveth that it yet *remaineth*, and is not here on earth possessed. The causal particle γὰρ, *for*, whereby this verse is inferred upon the former, sheweth that it is inferred as a proof of reason.

The reason is taken from the different estate of God's church here in this world, and in the world to come. This world is full of labour, travail, and trouble (as was shewed Sec. 55); but in the world to come there is a freedom from all these. Therefore the rest here spoken of is not to be found in this world, but is reserved for the world to come.

The argument is grounded upon an undeniable principle, oft inculcated by the apostle: namely, that there is a rest into which God's people shall enter.

The argument may be thus framed.

There is a rest to be entered into here or hereafter;
But not here; therefore hereafter.
Thus it *remaineth*.

The description of the rest in this verse proveth, that it cannot be entered into in this world. Whence another argument may thus be framed:

He that is entered into his rest hath ceased from his own works;
But no man in this world ceaseth from his own works;
Therefore no man in this world entereth into his rest.

Of the meaning of the word κατάπαυσις, here translated *rest*, and of this phrase, εἰσελθών εἰς, *enter into*, see Chap. iii. 11, Sec. 116.

This relative, αὐτοῦ, *his*, is not reciprocal, as if it had reference to him that entereth; but it hath reference to another, namely, to God; and it is taken in the same sense that it is taken verse 1. There is a like word, αὐτοῦ, consisting of the very same letters, but different spirits, used in this verse, which is reciprocal, and for distinction's sake translated *his own*. In what respect the heavenly rest here intended is called *God's rest*, see ver. 1, sec. 9.

Some apply this phrase of entering into his rest unto Christ, and to his resurrection and ascension; and thence infer a conformity of the members to their head. But no mention being heretofore made of Christ in the apostle's discourse about rest, it is not probable that he would have reference to Christ, without naming him.

Others apply it to a spiritual rest. But that rest is only a beginning of a rest. It cannot be the full rest here intended. It is therefore most proper and pertinent to the point in hand to refer it to our heavenly rest, which is to come.

Sec. 59. *Of the works which are here called his own works.*

For finding out the meaning of this phrase, ἔργα αὐτοῦ, *his own works*, we must consider the difference betwixt saints on earth and in heaven. For the rest here spoken of is proper to saints, who are God's people.

Man here on earth may be considered in that entire estate wherein God at first made him; and also in that corrupt estate whereinto he fell.

In his entire estate there were these kind of works:

1. Such as tended to the preservation of his body, as to eat, drink, and sleep. God gave man the fruits of the earth for meat, Gen. i. 29. And Adam slept, Gen. ii. 21. In heaven our bodies shall need no such means of preservation.

2. Such as were of use for increase of mankind. For thus saith God, 'Be fruitful and multiply,' Gen. 28. To this head may be referred all works, which by virtue of relations, as betwixt husband and wife, parents and children, and other superiors and inferiors, should have been performed. 'In heaven they neither marry, nor are given in marriage, but are as the angels,' Mat. xxii. 30.

3. Such as man used partly for obtaining things needful for his body, and partly for trial of his obedience, as diligence in his place and calling. For God put man into the garden of Eden, to dress it, and to keep it, Gen. ii. 15. In heaven there shall be no such labour.

In the corrupt estate whereinto man fell, we may consider sin itself, and the punishments thereof.

Here on earth we commit innumerable sins, but in heaven we are freed from all. Glorified saints are not only fully justified, but also perfectly sanctified. The church there is holy, and without blemish, Eph. v. 27.

The punishments of our sins are natural, or accidental.

Natural, are all manner of infirmities, whether of mind or body, or both.

Of mind, as anger, fear, care, grief, and such like.
Of body, all kind of labour, toil, wearisomeness, with the like.

Accidental, are all manner of miseries, calamities, crosses, losses, pains, torments, and finally death itself. Of these there shall be none in heaven, Rev. xiv. 13, and xxi. 4.

These, and other works like unto them, are said to be our works, in these respects:

1. We do them in, by, and of ourselves.
2. They come originally from ourselves.
3. They are most agreeable to our nature, mind, and will.

None of the fore-mentioned works are done in heaven. They therefore that enter into God's rest are truly and properly said to cease from them, and in that respect to rest. See Sec. 55.

The verb, κατέπαυσε, translated *cease*, is the very same that is used of God's forbearing to create any new creatures on the seventh day, and translated *rested*, ver. 4. From that verb the noun, κατάπαυσις, which is oft translated *rest*, is derived. So as to cease or rest, is to leave off doing such things as one did before. This is that σαββατισμός, *rest*, or keeping of a Sabbath, mentioned ver. 9, sec. 54.

This is a point of singular comfort; and sufficient to support us in all our toils, travails, troubles, cares, fears, griefs, sins, and effects thereof. There is a rest wherein we shall cease from them all.

By this kind of rest a vast difference betwixt earth and heaven is manifested, the ultimate end of God's people is demonstrated, and our likeness to God is consummated. In this rest, God is all in all.

Sec. 60. *Of saints ceasing from their own works, as God from his.*

The apostle, to express his mind more fully about

ceasing from one's own work, giveth instance of God's ceasing from his. Hereof he made mention before, ver. 4. There we shewed what works of God were meant, and how God ceased from them. See Sec. 31.

This note of resemblance, ὥσπερ, *as*, sheweth, that this instance of God is produced as an illustration of the point. Hereabout three things are observable:

1. That the works from which God ceased were his own. The Greek word ἴδια, translated *his own*, is emphatical. Indeed, many times it is indefinitely translated *his*, as here, and Mat. xxii. 5. Most usually this reciprocal particle, *own*, is added, as 'his own servants,' Mat. xxv. 14; 'his own clothes,' Mark v. 20. Sometimes this restrictive adjective *proper* is added, as 'their proper tongue,' Acts i. 19. 'His proper gift,' 1 Cor. vii. 7. It is attributable to the one, only-begotten, proper Son of God, and thus translated, 'his own Son,' Rom. viii. 32. The works which God created were the works from which he ceased, and these were his own proper works.

2. That God ceased from all his works. Hereof see Sec. 31 in the end.

3. That God utterly ceased from those his works. He never returned to the work of creation again.

In all these respects shall the people of God cease from their works:

1. They shall cease from their own proper works, even from their sins, which are most properly their own; and from all the effects which they have produced.

2. They shall cease from all manner of works, which here on earth they did and endured.

3. They shall utterly cease from all such works, as cumbered them here on earth, so as never to be encumbered with them again.

Thus God's people cease from their own works, as God did from his.

Besides, as God in ceasing from some works, namely, works of creation, yet continued to do other works, namely, works of providence, so God's people, though they cease from their works here on earth, shall have other kind of works which are fit for the place where they shall be, therein to exercise themselves. See Sec. 54.

Yet further, as God ceased not till the seventh day (for he continued to work all the six days, Exod. xx. 11), so saints shall not cease from all their works here on earth. Their days on earth are working days, wherein they do works of necessity, which tend to the preservation of their body: works of duty to God and man, and works of corruption. A full ceasing from all these works is not here to be expected. We are enjoined to do the works of our calling, Eccles. ix. 10, John ix. 4; and those works also needful for nature, Eccles. v. 18. Nature itself moveth us thereunto, Eph. v. 29, and while we live sin will retain some life in us, though it may be restrained and kept down, Rom. vii. 18, &c.

Sin remaining, the fruits also thereof must needs remain, as travail, trouble, losses, and all manner of crosses. The best of men are subject hereunto.

Surely they come short of the mark, who place the rest here spoken of in mortification of sin, and living to God, in peace of conscience, joy in the holy Ghost, and such like works of the Spirit. I will not deny that these are first fruits, seals, and evidences thereof. But the full fruition of this rest cannot be on earth.

Sec. 61. *Of the resolution and observations of* Heb. iv. 9, 10.

Ver. 9. *There remaineth therefore a rest to the people of God.*

10. *For he that is entered into his rest, he also hath ceased from his own works, as God did from his.*

The sum of these two verses is in two words, *saints, rest.*

Here is in particular to be considered,

1. The inference, in this word *therefore.*
2. The substance, which is,
1. Propounded, verse 9.
2. Exemplified, verse 10.

Rest propounded is set out,

1. By an intimation of the time when it is to be enjoyed, in this word *there remaineth.*
2. A restriction of the persons for whom it is reserved, *the people of God.*

The exemplification is set forth by a resemblance.

Of the resemblance there are two parts:

1. A proposition.
2. A reddition or application.

In the proposition there is,

1. A description of the person.
2. An exposition of the point.

The person is described,

1. By his act, *he is entered.*
2. By the subject whereinto he entered.

That subject is set out,

1. By the kind, *rest.*
2. By the author *his.*

In the exposition there is,

1. A cessation, or leaving off, *he also hath ceased.*
2. The matter left off, *his own works.*

Of the reddition there are two parts:

1. The person to whom the resemblance is made, *as God.*
2. The point wherein the resemblance consisteth, *did from his.*

Doctrines.

I. *The conclusion of a discourse is to be set down.* This verse is the conclusion of the apostle's discourse of rest. And the note of a conclusion, *therefore*, is expressed. See Sec. 53.

II. *There is a rest.* This is here taken for grant. See Sec. 6.

III. *That full rest is to come.* This word, *there remaineth*, intends as much. See Sec. 56.

IV. *The rest to come is as a Sabbath.* The word used by the apostle intends as much. See Sec. 55.

V. *The full rest to come is proper to God's people.* It remaineth to them. See Sec. 57.

VI. *Points of concernment are to be made clear.* For this end is this tenth verse inferred as a reason upon the former. See Sec. 58.

VII. *The rest prepared for saints is God's.* In reference to God it is styled *his.* See Sec. 9.

VIII. *Some shall enter into God's rest.* This is set down as a granted case, in these words, *he that is entered.* See Sec. 39.

IX. *Men on earth have works of their own.* See Sec. 59.

X. *God's rest on the Sabbath was a resemblance of saints' rest in heaven.* This note of resemblance, *as,* declares as much. Sec. 60.

XI. *Saints in heaven cease from their works on earth.* So much is here directly expressed. See Sec. 59.

XII. *God rested from all his works.* See Sec. 31.

XIII. *While saints are here, they cease not from their own works,* as God ceased not in the six days. See Sec. 60.

Sec. 62. *Of being like to God.*

Ver. 11. *Let us labour therefore to enter into that rest, lest any man fall after the same example of unbelief.*

This verse layeth down an especial use to be made of all that the apostle hath delivered about the rest before mentioned.

One use was before noted, verse 1, which was an admonition to fear, lest we come short of that rest.

The other use is an exhortation to do our best for attaining thereunto. This relative conjunction οὖν, *therefore,* imports as much. The Greek word here used is the very same that was used ver. 1, Sec. 2.

It may have either a remote or an immediate inference.

The remote reference is to all that hath formerly been delivered of the reality of that rest, that there is indeed such a rest, verse 9. Of the certainty of it, Sec. 24; and of the excellency of it, that it is God's rest, verse 1, Sec. 9.; and that it brings a freedom from all labour and trouble, verse 10, Secs. 59, 60. There being such a rest, we ought *therefore* to endeavour after it. See Sec. 63.

The immediate reference is to the last clause of the former verse, wherein God's pattern is set before us, in this phrase, 'As God did from his.' God having spent six days in creating all things, rested the seventh day from all his works. Let us *therefore,* having done our work here, labour to enter into his rest.

Thus God's practice is a pattern to us. It is set down in the law as a pattern for us to work in the six days, and rest on the seventh, Exod. xx. 11. Here it is propounded as a motive to stir us up to endeavour after a rest, that we may be like God, and rest from all our own works, as he did from his. God rested from his own works, *therefore* let us labour to enter into that rest, where we shall cease from our own works.

By this it appears, that saints should be such as God is. God at first 'made man after his own image,' Gen. i. 27, and we are exhorted to be 'renewed after God's image,' Ephes. iv. 23, 24, Col. iii. 10. In general, we are incited to be followers of God, Ephes. v. 1. In particular, to be 'holy as he is holy,' Levit. xix. 2, 1 Pet. i. 15, 16; to do good, as God doth, Mat. v. 45; to be kind and merciful, as he is, Luke vi. 35, 36; to love as God doth, 1 John iv. 11; to forgive one another as God doth, Eph. iv. 32; yea, to be perfect as he is, Mat. v. 28.

1. God's pattern is the most perfect that can be set before us; we may be sure not to err, if we hold close to it.

2. It is the best and most honourable pattern we can have.

3. It is the safest; for who can blame us for imitating God?

Obj. God's pattern is too high for any creature to set before him.

Ans. For clearing this point we must distinguish betwixt the things of God. There are incommunicable and communicable excellencies in God.

Some things are incommunicable by simple impossibility, others by a singular prerogative.

Of the former sort are such as these: eternity without beginning, infiniteness, omnipotency, all-sufficiency, ubiquity, omniscience, and such like; so these acts, to create, redeem, work miracles, search the heart, and such like.

The things which God reserveth to himself as singular prerogatives are these:

1. To forgive sins, Mark ii. 7.

2. To judge men's final estate, Rom. xiv. 10, 11.

3. To take revenge, Deut. xxxii. 35, Rom. xii. 19.

All these, and other things registered in Scripture, are for our learning, Rom. xv. 4. 2 Tim. iii. 16; but some things are matters of faith to be believed, and some things patterns for our imitation.

To know what things of God are patterns to us, we must compare God's practices with his precepts. What in God's word is enjoined to us to do, if God himself do the like, we may, we ought therein to imitate him. Such are the virtues and graces beforementioned.

Behold here the tender respect of God towards us children of men. He hath power to command and exact of us whatsoever he will; but, as a father, he goeth before us, and shews that he requires no more of us than what himself doth.

Who can now think that to be any way unseemly for him which seems not unseemly to God? In this case thus saith Christ, 'Ye call me Master and Lord, and ye say well: for so I am. If I then, your Lord and Master, have washed your feet, ye also ought to wash one another's feet,' John xiii. 14.

This is a great aggravation of their pride who scorn purity, meekness, mercifulness, holiness, and other like excellencies, as God in his own example commendeth unto us.

Of imitating Christ, see Chap. xiii. 13, Sec. 132. Of imitating saints, see Chap. xiii. 7, Sec. 101.

Sec. 63. *Of endeavouring after rest in heaven.*

The Greek verb σπουδάσωμεν, thus translated, *let us labour*, is derived from another verb, σπεύδω, *festino*, that signifieth *to make haste*. It intendeth an endeavour on man's part, and so it is translated, σπουδάσω, 2 Pet. i. 15, Eph. iv. 3, 1 Thes. ii. 17, but such an endeavour as makes a man forward to a thing, and is accompanied with study, labour, and diligence; answerably it is translated, as ἐσπούδασα, ' I *was forward* to do,' Gal. ii. 10; ' *study* to shew thyself approved,' 2 Tim. ii. 15; ' *give diligence*,' 2 Pet. i. 10.

This word then compriseth under it two duties:
1. That men endeavour after the foresaid rest.
2. That they be forward and diligent in their endeavour.

The general, concerning man's endeavour to attain to heaven, where this rest is enjoyed, is much pressed in Scripture, and that in these and such like phrases: ' Lay hold on eternal life,' 1 Tim. vi. 12; ' Strive to enter in at the strait gate,' Luke xiii. 24; ' Work out your salvation,' Philip. ii. 12. The apostle makes himself a worthy pattern in this case, where he saith, ' I press towards the mark,' Philip. iii. 14, &c.

Hereby that life, reason, grace, and ability which God anyway giveth is manifested; and God would have it to be so. When Christ put life into the ruler's daughter that was dead, he said unto her, ' Maid, arise,' Luke viii. 54; and to Lazarus he said, ' Lazarus, come forth,' John xi. 43.

Obj. Natural men are dead in sin, Eph. ii. 1.

Ans. Man may be considered in a double estate: 1, natural; 2, spiritual.

In his natural estate, so much is to be done as by a natural man may be.

That this may be the better conceived, I will exemplify a natural man's power in five branches.

1. In natural acts; as to move, go, stand, sit, eat, drink, see, hear, smell, taste, touch.
2. In civil acts about human affairs; as in arts, sciences, trades, sundry other callings, professions, and offices: likewise in governing kingdoms, cities, corporations, universities, colleges, schools, and families. Cain's posterity was skilful in such things, Gen. iv. 20, 21. The Sidonians were skilful about timber, 1 Kings v. 6. Saul, that was but a natural man, had a spirit given him fit for government, 1 Sam. x. 9.
3. In moral virtues; as justice, temperance, mercy, liberality, &c. In reference to these the apostle saith that ' the Gentiles do by nature the things contained in the law,' Rom. ii. 14.
4. In ecclesiastical matters, which tend to the external worship of God; as to go to church, hear the word, pray, fast, partake of the sacraments, read, search, and study the Scriptures, preach and confer about holy matters. Judas (whom Christ styled a devil, John vi. 70) went far herein.
5. In spiritual matters, by resisting the Spirit, and the motions thereof: ' Ye do always resist the Holy Ghost,' saith Stephen to such Jews as were uncircumcised in heart, Acts vii. 51.

According to the aforesaid power in men, they ought to go as far as they can; as to go to church, to attend upon the word, to forbear wicked acts and company. Though none of those gifts be supernatural, none simply preparatory to grace, yet if a natural man improve the abilities which he hath to his best advantage, God will not leave him, but give him more and better grace.

As for spiritual men, who are quickened, they must stir up the gift of God which is in them, 2 Tim. i. 6.

By this it is manifest that the proper cause of man's destruction is of himself, Hosea xiii. 9. None that perish do what they can to be saved.

Behold here the deceitfulness of most men's minds, and their folly about the salvation of their souls. They are careful to use all means about the preservation of their bodies, but put off all care for their souls, according to this cursed proverb, ' I will take care for my body, let God take care for my soul.' God will take care for men's souls in his own way and course.

Let us be exhorted to put out our ability in the things of eternal life, and both to learn what on our parts is to be performed, and also to put in practice what we shall be instructed in hereabouts.

The apostle setteth down his exhortation in the first person of the plural number thus, σπουδάσωμεν, ' Let us labour,' whereby he involveth himself among others, and incites, with others, himself to duty. Hereof see Chap. ii. 1, Sec. 4.

Sec. 64. *Of diligence in man's endeavour for attaining to rest.*

The extent of man's endeavour, that it should be with diligence, is implied in these words, *study*, *strive*, and *labour*, mentioned in the beginning of the former section, and more expressly in these phrases, ' Give all diligence,' 2 Pet. i. 5, 10, ' Let us run with patience,' Heb. xii. 1. David professeth as much in this phrase, ' I will run the way of thy commandments,' Ps. cxix. 32; and the church in this, ' We will run after thee,' Cant. i. 3; and the apostle in this, ' I press toward the mark,' Philip. iii. 14.

1. The excellency of the object set before us should quicken us up hereunto, for there is nothing that we can endeavour after to be compared unto this rest;

not the glory, honour, wealth, profits, or pleasures of this world. It is noted of Moses, that, in comparison of this recompence, he lightly esteemed the honours, profits, and pleasures of Egypt, Heb. xi. 24–26.

2. The necessity of attaining this rest requireth our best diligence. A man were better not be, or, having a being, to be as the brute beast, whose soul perisheth with his body, than, having an immortal soul, to miss of this rest. Hereof there is an absolute necessity.

3. The difficulty of attaining hereunto exacteth pains and labour. That which Christ saith of a rich man may in general be applied to every man: 'How hardly shall they enter into the kingdom of heaven,' Mark x. 23; 'The righteous are scarcely saved,' that is, not without much difficulty, 1 Pet. iv. 18. A Christian's course is resembled to a battle, 2 Tim. iv. 7; a race, Heb. xii. 1; a journey, Gen. xlvii. 5; a work, John iv. 34; all which are difficult tasks, and that in regard of our own weakness and manifest impediments. Diligence must be used in difficult matters.

Let us therefore put out our best strength, as the apostle did, Philip. iii. 13, 14. It is said, that 'in the days of John the Baptist, the kingdom of heaven suffered violence, and that the violent took it by force,' Mat. xi. 12. Those phrases set out men's forwardness and earnestness in seeking to enter into the kingdom of heaven. Assuredly where the word works kindly, it will inflame a man with an holy zeal after this rest. The Spirit that accompanieth the word is a Spirit of fervour, and will not suffer a man to rest till he have assurance of this rest. This, therefore, is a matter of trial.

Sec. 65. *Of the excellency of saints' rest in heaven.*

The preposition, εἰς, translated *into*, is doubled; for, first, it is compounded with the verb, εἰσελθεῖν, *enter*, then joined with the noun, εἰς κατάπαυσιν. This shews that perseverance must be added to our diligent endeavour. To labour to enter into a place, is to hold out and persevere in the use of means till we attain unto it, and have possession thereof. See Chap. iii. 11, Sec. 116.

Of perseverance, see Chap. iii. 6, Sec. 68, &c.

This article ἐκείνην, *that*, hath reference to the rest mentioned ver. 9, and described ver. 10.

That rest is the full rest, which bringeth freedom from all labour and trouble whereunto we are subject in this world; a rest to be hereafter enjoyed in heaven. See Secs. 55, 56.

This he pointeth at to quicken up their endeavours the more, and the rather to stir them up to hold out till they have attained this rest.

The more excellent the prize is that is set before us, the more care must be taken and pains used for attaining it, and the more constant we must be therein. The greatness of the reward moved Moses to 'esteem the rebuke of Christ greater riches than the treasures of Egypt,' Heb. xi. 26. It was inexpressible and unconceivable joy that moved Christ to 'endure the cross and despise the shame,' Heb. xii. 2. Therefore the apostle puts the Hebrews in mind of 'a better and an enduring substance in heaven,' when they suffered the spoiling of their goods, Heb. x. 35; yea, he sets out to the life the unparalleled disparity betwixt the afflictions here endured, and the glory hereafter to be enjoyed, 2 Cor. iv. 17.

Commendable in this respect is their pains, who endeavour to illustrate the glory of saints reserved for them in heaven. Treatises thereabouts are worth the reading.

It will be our wisdom frequently to meditate, and seriously to ponder thereon.

Sec. 66. *Of circumspection against falling away, like others, through unbelief.*

To enforce the foresaid exhortation, the apostle addeth the danger and damage that is like to follow upon neglect thereof.

Of this word ἵνα μὴ, *lest*, which importeth a damage, see Chap. iii. 13, Sec. 147. It is a word of caution, and implieth circumspection about preventing apostasy. Hereof see Chap. iii. 12, Sec. 122.

These two words, *any man*, are in Greek comprised under one small particle, τις, which extendeth the foresaid circumspection to others, as well as to one's self. See Chap. iii. 12, Secs. 123, 124.

The verb πέσῃ (πίπτω, *cado*), translated *fall*, doth oft set out a great and utter fall. See Chap. iii. 17, Sec. 168.

Metaphorically, this word is applied to falling from grace. It is used to set forth the Jews' universal apostasy, Rom. xi. 22, and here to professors departing from the Christian faith.

Thus this caution presupposeth that professors may fall away, and prove apostates. See Chap. iii. 12, Sec. 131.

The Greek noun ὑπόδειγμα, translated *example*, is a compound. The simple verb δεικνύω, *vel* δείκνυμι, *ostendo*, signifieth to shew or declare, as where the apostle saith, 'I shew you a more excellent way,' 1 Cor. xii. 31. A simple noun, δεῖγμα, thence ariseth, which signifieth *example*, Jude 7.

The noun here used is compounded of that simple noun, and a preposition ὑπό, *sub*, which signifieth *under*, so as it declareth such an example as is for another's use, which we call a pattern.

The compound verb ὑποδείκνυμι, signifieth to *shew beforehand*, or *forewarn*, Luke xii. 5. A pattern or example doth beforehand shew what one should do or not do. It is applied to types, that foreshewed truths to come, Heb. viii. 5.

It is used for a good pattern, John iii. 15, James v. 10, and also for an ill pattern, as here and 2 Peter ii. 6.

This relative phrase, ἐν τῷ αὐτῷ, *after the same*, hath reference to the Israelites who perished in the wilderness, chap. iii. 17, 18. Thereby he would have Christians so warned, as they fall not into the same sin, and cause the like judgment to fall upon them. See Chap. iii. 8, Secs. 89, 90, 95.

Their particular sin is here said to be unbelief. Of the Greek word ἀπειθεία, so translated, see Chap. iii. 18, Sec. 171.

By this it appeareth, that unbelief especially keeps men from the celestial rest. See Chap. iii. 12, Secs. 128, 129, and ver. 18, Sec. 171.

Sec. 67. *Of the resolution and observations of* Heb. iv. 11.

Ver. 11. *Let us labour therefore to enter into that rest, lest any man fall after the same example of unbelief.*

The sum of this text is, man's endeavour after rest. Herein consider,
1. The inference, *therefore*.
2. The substance.

Of the substance there are two parts:
1. An Exhortation.
2. A Prevention.

In the exhortation, observe both the manner and the matter.

The manner is in the first person and plural number, *let us*.

The matter consisteth of an act, and the end thereof.

The act intendeth an endeavour and diligence therein, *labour*.

The end compriseth another act, *enter;* and the subject-place, *into that rest*.

The prevention is,
1. Generally intimated.
2. Particularly exemplified.

In the intimation observe,
1. A caution, in this particle *lest*.
2. The persons, *any man*.
3. The kind of danger, *fall*.

In the exemplifications are hinted,
1. The persons, in this phrase, *after the same example*.
2. The cause, *unbelief*.

Doctrines.

I. *Saints must be like God.* The immediate inference of this particle of reference, *therefore*, intends as much. See Sec. 62.

II. *Rest is set before saints.* This is taken for grant, in that he exhorts us to enter into it. See Sec. 6.

III. *Men must endeavour after rest.* See Sec. 63.

IV. *To our endeavours diligence must be added.* These two last doctrines arise out of this word *labour*. See Sec. 64.

V. *Diligence must be followed with perseverance.* We must labour till we enter into rest. See Sec. 65.

VI. *The more excellent the prize is, the greater must our endeavour be after it.* This relative particle *that*, points at an especial rest, and thereby he quickens us up to labour after it. See Sec. 65.

VII. *Caution is requisite for Christians.* This is the intendment of this particle *lest*. See Sec. 66.

VIII. *Circumspection must be extended to others.* This word *any man* hath such an extent. See Sec. 66.

IX. *Professors may fall away.* This caution, *lest any fall*, implies as much. See Sec. 66.

X. *What befalls some may befall others.* This is intended under this phrase, *after the same example*. See Sec. 66.

XI. *Others' harms must make us wary.* This is the intendment of hinting God's judgments on the Israelites. See Sec. 66.

XII. *Unbelief is the cause of apostacy.* Upon this ground he here maketh mention of the Israelites' unbelief. See Sec. 66.

Sec. 68. *Of the inference of the* 12*th and* 13*th verses on that which went before*.

Ver. 12. *For the word of God is quick, and powerful, and sharper than any two-edged sword, piercing even to the dividing asunder of soul and spirit, and of the joints and marrow, and is a discerner of the thoughts and intents of the heart.*

Ver. 13. *Neither is there any creature that is not manifest in his sight: but all things are naked and opened unto the eyes of him with whom we have to do.*

These two verses are a close of Christ's prophetical function; and, as the first particle, γὰρ, *for*, importeth, they lay down a reason of that which was formerly delivered. The reason is taken from the efficacy of the word, whereby Christ exerciseth his prophetical office, ver. 12, and from the piercing Spirit of Christ, ver. 13.

It may be extended to the apostle's whole discourse about the use that we are to make out of that office of Christ; thus, we must hearken to Christ's office, and not harden our hearts, but take heed of departing from the living God; we must hold the beginning of our confidence, and labour to enter into the rest of the Lord, because the word of God is quick, and because we have to do with an all-seeing eye.

This reason also may have a more immediate reference to the last clause of the former verse, where the example of the Israelites falling in the wilderness is set down as a warning to Christians, lest they fall after the same example. This admonition is enforced by the efficacious virtue of the gospel, which will discover unbelievers.

Both these inferences do evidently demonstrate, that God's word shall not return void, Isa. lv. 11. In this respect the apostle thus saith of the gospel: 'We are unto God a sweet savour of Christ, in them that are saved, and in them that perish. To the one we are a savour of death unto death; and to the other the savour of life unto life,' 2 Cor. ii. 15, 16.

If we give heed to God's word, we shall find the

comfort and benefit of it; but if we turn from it, and believe it not, we shall feel the vengeance of it, we shall not escape. This, therefore, is on the one side a matter of singular comfort, and on the other side of horrible terror.

Sec. 69. *Of this phrase, 'the word of God.'*

Some[1] refer that which is comprised under this phrase, ὁ λόγος τοῦ Θεοῦ, *the word of God,* to *the Son of God*. It cannot be denied but that the Son of God is set forth under this title, 'the Word,' ὁ λόγος. I find five particular instances hereof: three in John i. 1, a fourth, John i. 14, the fifth, 1 John v. 7. I find him once called, ὁ λόγος τῆς ζωῆς, 'the Word of life,' 1 John i. 1; and once also, ὁ λόγος τοῦ Θεοῦ, 'the Word of God,' Rev. xix. 13. All these titles were used by one and the same author, which was the apostle John. In no other place of the New Testament do I find it given to the Son of God.

Most usually is this title *word of God* put for God's manifesting his will by voice, or writing in sacred Scripture. Thus it is oft used in this epistle, and styled, as here, 'the word of God,' chap. xiii. 7; ὁ τῆς ἀρχῆς τοῦ Χριστοῦ λόγος, 'the word of the beginning,' or doctrine 'of Christ,' chap. vi. 1; ὁ λόγος τῆς ἀκοῆς, 'the word preached,' or 'word of hearing,' chap. iv. 2; λόγος δικαιοσύνης, 'the word of righteousness,' chap. v. 13; ὁ λόγος παρακλήσεως, 'the word of exhortation,' or 'consolation,' chap. xiii. 22.

The several metaphors whereby the power of the word here intended is set out, may most fitly be applied to God's word preached, which the apostle doth thus manifest in another metaphor: 'The weapons of our warfare are not carnal, but mighty through God, to the pulling down of strongholds,' &c., 2 Cor. x 6. By this word have God's people in all ages been called to enter into that rest, whereof the apostle hath spoken so much before.

On these and other like grounds, we may so take *the word* in this place.

The foresaid word is said to be ὁ λόγος τοῦ Θεοῦ, 'the word of God,' in sundry respects.

1. In regard of the *author* of it, which is God: 'All Scripture is given by inspiration of God,' 2 Tim. iii. 16.

2. In regard of the *matter* of it, which is God's will. By the word God's will is revealed unto us, both concerning the good which he hath determined for us, Eph. i. 9, and also concerning the duty which he requireth of us, 2 Tim. iii. 16, 17.

3. In regard of the *end*, which is in general the glory of God; and, in particular, the manifestation of 'the manifold wisdom of God,' Eph. iii. 10.

4. In regard of the *efficacy* of it. For it is 'the power of God unto salvation,' Rom. i. 16.

All the life, virtue, and power appropriated to the

[1] Ambros. de Fide lib. iv. cap. iii.; Theophyl. in loc; Lyran. Cajet. Jun. Heins.

word, ariseth from this, that it is the word of God. Wheresoever mention is made of any power or efficacy of the word, it is there expressly, or by necessary consequence, applied to the word of God. No creature hath ability to put such life and virtue into his word, as is here spoken of. For, *nihil dat quod non habet*, no creature hath it in itself, therefore it cannot convey or give it.

Such ministers as desire to work upon people by their word, either by quickening or wounding, by comforting or beating down, must be sure that they preach the word of God. Not a man's own word, nor the word of other men, can do it. What was the reason that there was such an alteration wrought in people's hearts by the ministry of John, of Christ, of the apostles, and not by the ministry of the Scribes and Pharisees? John, Christ and his apostles, preached the word of God. The Scribes and Pharisees preached the tradition of their elders. This was the reason of the power of the preaching of Luther, and other reformers of our religion, more than of friars; they preached God's word; these, popish legends. Among us, the more purely God's word is preached, the more deeply it pierceth, the more kindly it worketh. Such sermons as are stuffed with human histories, and philosophical discourses, may tickle the ear, but work not upon the heart and soul. The apostle rendereth this reason of the efficacy of God's word on the Thessalonians, they received it, 'not as the word of man; but as it was in truth, the word of God,' 1 Thess. ii. 13.

Sec. 70. *Of God's word being quick and powerful.*

The first epithet given to the foresaid word of God, is thus translated, *quick*. The Greek word ζῶν properly signifieth *living*; so doth the English word *quick*. In which sense it is opposed to dead, as 'quick and dead,' Acts ii. 42. Thus the verb to quicken signifieth to give life, or to make to live, according to the notation of the Greek compound, ζωοποιεῖν, *vivificare*. Thus it intends a perpetual continuance of the vigour of the word, 1 Pet. i. 25. Though ministers be mortal, yet the word ever liveth, Zech. i. 5, 6. The participle of the present tense, *living*, intimateth a perpetuity.

This epithet *quick* implieth also a stirring virtue; such a virtue as makes another thing to stir. To express this emphasis, our former English translateth it *lively*. Thus do our last English translators translate this Greek word in other places, as Acts vii. 38, 1 Pet. i. 3, and ii. 5.

That is said to be quick or lively, which is active, nimble, and forward in putting out that vigour or virtue which it hath: as quick-silver, quick-sands, quick-sighted, quick-spirited. On the other side, things that have lost their vigour are said to be dead, as dead ware.

Two especial reasons may be given of this epithet attributed to the word:

One, to shew that it is not a dead seed, but living

and quick, which being sown in man's heart, either groweth and sprouteth forth therein, or else gnaweth and eateth up the soul and heart of man. It is in this respect called, 'not mortal seed, but immortal,' 1 Pet. i. 23; and it is styled ' the word of life,' Philip. ii. 16.

The other reason is, to shew the effect of the word. It putteth life and sense into such as are dead in sin. It either begets men unto God, and so puts into them the life of grace, whereby they are brought to the life of glory, James i. 18, John v. 25, or else it putteth so much life into their seared conscience, as they shall sensibly feel the wrath and vengeance of God against them for their contempt; as Judas did, when he laid violent hands upon himself, Mat. xxvii. 4, 5, Acts i. 17, 18.

To express this latter effect more to the full, the apostle addeth this other epithet, *powerful*. The Greek word ἐνεργής, so translated, is a compound, which implieth a working virtue.

The simple noun ἔργον signifieth *work*. The proposition ἐν, *in*.

The compound, ἐνεργής, a thing in work, operative, effectual. It is opposed to that which is idle, or unuseful, ἀεργὸς, *contracte* ἀργὸς, Mat. xx. 3, 6.

The word here used in this text is translated *effectual*, 1 Cor. xvi. 9, Philem. 6.

As the former epithet *quick* implied that the word of God was not a dead letter, so this, that it is not an idle or vain word, without fruit, but effectual, and performeth that whereunto it is appointed: whether it be to fasten[1] or harden, to raise up or cast down, to justify or condemn, to comfort or terrify. It is like a fire, to soften wax and to harden clay.

On the one side, it is said to quicken, Ps. cxix. 50, to beget, James i. 18, to convert souls, Ps. xix. 7, and to save souls, James. i. 21.

On the other side, it is said to be like ' an hammer that breaketh the rock in pieces,' Jer. xxiii. 29. It is also said to ' cast down imaginations, and every high thing that exalteth itself against the knowledge of God,' 2 Cor. x. 5.

The foresaid word of God is quick and powerful, because it is the word of him that hath life in himself, John v. 26, and hath power to work as it pleaseth him or others. See Sec. 69.

Obj. It doth not work on all, or some, for many hear it, and are nothing moved thereby.

Ans. 1. Either it entereth not into such, but is like the seed that was sown in the pathway, Mat. xiii. 4, 19, or it is choked, when it enters with some worldly lusts or cares, as the word that was sown amongst thorns, Mat. xiii. 7, 22.

2. It is sufficient for proof of the point, that it works upon some; for thereby it appears, that there is life and power in the word, because it works on any at all. If there were no life or power, it could not work on any.

[1] Qu. 'soften'?—ED.

3. Though it put not spiritual life into the soul of some men, yet it may pierce through the brawn of men's hard hearts to the quick. It may rub off the skin, and make them sensible of smart; it may make them tremble, as Felix did, Acts xxiv. 25, or fret and rage, as the Jews did, Acts vii. 54.

4. Though here in this world it work nothing at all, yet it may work thoroughly upon them at the day of judgment, Rev. vi. 15, 16.

Use 1. This is a strong inducement to us ministers, to be diligent and faithful in preaching this word, which is so quick and powerful. We may be sure that our labour shall not be in vain in the Lord. The apostle gave thanks unto God, in this respect, 2 Cor. ii. 14, 15.

2. This is a forcible incitation to people to attend upon the ministry of this word. ' Hear, and your souls shall live,' Isa. lv. 3. Is life to be desired ? Then use the means whereby it may be attained. When Christ had told the woman of Samaria, that he could give her living water to drink, such water as should make her never thirst again, she replies, ' Sir, give me this water,' John iv. 10, 14, 15. Behold, the word of God is such water. Attend upon it, to get life and to preserve life. ' As new born babes, desire the sincere milk of the word, that ye may grow thereby,' 1 Pet. ii. 2.

3. As we come ourselves, so let us bring others to the word. The foresaid woman of Samaria, discerning Christ to be he that was promised, went into the city, and saith unto the men, ' Is not this the Christ ?' John iv. 28, 29. Though they whom thou seekest to bring be yet dead in their sins, yet bring them, for this word hath a quickening virtue.

4. Ye that come unto the word, take heed how ye hear, Luke viii. 18. For it is impossible that this word should be preached in vain. It is quick and powerful. It will soften or harden. You cannot make it altogether fruitless. Every sermon that you hear, will either bring you nearer to heaven, or put you off further from it.

5. What thanks are we to give unto God for this evidence of his goodness to us, in vouchsafing a means so quick and powerful. We especially are bound in this case to praise God, on whom it worketh kindly, in convincing our judgment, in persuading our hearts, in subduing our corruptions, in altering our disposition, making lambs of lions, Isa. xi. 6.

Sec. 71. *Of the word's resemblance to a two-edged sword.*

What the apostle had simply set down concerning the efficacy of the word of God, he proceedeth to amplify comparatively. His comparison is taken from a sword.

A good sword useth to be made of hard steel, which of all metals may be made the sharpest, whereby it pierceth the more speedily; and being long and thin, the more deeply.

The Greek noun μάχαιρα, *gladius*, is derived, from a verb, μάχομαι, *pugno*, that signifieth to *fight*, James iv. 2. For a sword is the most usual instrument wherewith men fight. By it they may defend themselves, and annoy their enemies. For both these ends did Peter draw his sword, John xviii. 10.

Every soldier therefore hath his sword, beside the other warlike instruments which he useth; and most gentlemen use to put on their sword when they go abroad, and that for defence and offence, as occasion is offered. There is no other instrument more fit for both those uses.

Magistrates also use to have a sword carried before them, as a sign of that authority and power which they have to punish malefactors, to keep their people in awe, and to preserve peace. Hereunto the apostle alludes in this phrase, 'He beareth not the sword in vain,' Rom. xiii. 4. By the sword he means especially power of punishing, and that with the sword, even to death.

The sword is a mortal weapon; any limb, even the head itself, may be cut off thereby; or the body and the heart soon thrust through.

In all ages more have been slain by the sword than by any other instrument, therefore in Hebrew the same word חרב, *gladius*, *desolatio*, that is used for a *sword*, signifieth all *destruction*. This phrase, to 'slay with the sword,' is frequent in Scripture, 1 Kings xix. 10; Heb. xi. 37.

Fitly, therefore, is the word of God resembled to a sword. Nothing more destroyeth errors, heresies, blasphemies, all manner of corruptions and enormities, than the word of God.

To add emphasis to this metaphor, the apostle styleth it, ' a two-edged sword;' in Greek δίστομος, ' a two-mouthed sword.' In Hebrew, mouth is attributed to a sword, פי חרב, which we in English call the edge, because, as a mouth, especially of a ravenous beast or fish, devoureth that which entereth into it, so a sword destroyeth such as are struck therewith.

The other two learned languages, Greek and Latin, imitate the Hebrew herein, στόμα μαχαίρας, Luke xxi. 24, *os gladii*.

In reference to this metaphor, a sword is said to devour, אכל חרב, *gladius edit seu devorat*, 2 Sam. ii. 26, and xi. 25.

Now there are some swords which have two edges, or edges on both sides, and these are called חרב פיפיות, δίστομος μάχαιρα, two-mouthed or two-edged swords; they devour or cut on both sides, Ps. cxlix. 6; Rev. i. 16.

It appears that the two-edged swords used of all swords to be the sharpest, for this epithet *sharp* is frequently attributed to a two-edged sword, Rev. i. 16, and ii. 12.

The positive, τόμος, of the comparative, τομώτερος, translated *sharper*, is derived from a verb, τέμνω, *seco*, that signifieth to *cut*; so as it implieth such a sharpness as cutteth and pierceth.

The comparative is here used to shew that the thing compared, which is the word of God, far exceedeth in the sharpness and piercing power which it hath, the two-edged sword whereunto it is here resembled. And because some swords are sharper than others, he inserteth this particle, πᾶσαν, *any* or *every*, whereby he implieth that there never was, nor can be, any two-edged sword so sharp as the word.

There is included in this comparison a gradation of four steps.

1. The word is *sharp*.
2. It is *sharper* than a sword.
3. It is sharper than a *two-edged sword*.
4. It is sharper than *any* two-edged sword.

This resemblance of the word to a sword, and this manner of expressing it, ' sharper than any two-edged sword,' is added in sundry respects.

1. In general, for illustration of the point, resemblances being taken from things sensible, with which we are well acquainted, the virtue and efficacy whereof we well know, doth much illustrate and clearly set out the spiritual mystery that is resembled thereunto. To this end tend our sacraments.

2. In particular, for demonstration of the manifold uses of the word, which are such as these:

(1.) As a two-edged sword, so the word hath two sides or two parts, the law and the gospel: the law is one edge, to slay the impenitent sinner; the gospel another, to slay sin in the believer.

(2.) As a two-edged sword cuts which way soever it be turned, so the word of God. The word works in the godly and the ungodly. The promises and the threatenings thereof do all work, apply it to the mind or heart, to opinion, affection or action, to civil or ecclesiastical matters.

(3.) As with a two-edged sword a man may defend and offend, so with the word. Verity and virtue may be maintained and defended, and error and every enormity may be refelled and repelled. See *The Whole Armour of God*, treat. 2. part 8. Of the word of God, Secs. 4, 5, 11.

From this metaphor learn these lessons:

1. Take heed of opposing against the word, or hindering ministers from preaching it. It is the ensign of Christ's regiment, it is the sword that is carried before him. Will a magistrate endure such as strike down the sword that is borne before him, and thrust the sword-bearer out of his place? Woe to them that have any hand in opposing or interrupting the government of Christ!

2. Slight not God's word, as if it were a blunt thing, which could neither cut nor pierce. 'It is sharper than any two-edged sword.' The sword of Elisha, which was God's word in his mouth, slew those that escaped the sword of Hazael and Jehu, who were both mighty princes, 1 Kings xix. 17. 'I have hewed them by the prophets; I have slain them by the words of my mouth,' saith the Lord, Hosea vi. 5. It was in re-

ference to the word of God, that the Lord said thus to his prophet, 'See, I have this day set thee over the nations, and over the kingdoms, to root out, and to pull down, and to destroy,' &c., Jer. i. 10. It was in reference to God's word that it is said of Christ, 'He shall smite the earth with the rod of his mouth, and with the breath of his lips shall he slay the wicked,' Isa. xi. 4. Well therefore might the apostle say, that it is 'sharper than any two-edged sword.' It is not safe for children, such as we are in spiritual matters, to dally with such a sharp two-edged weapon as the word is. Slighting God's word hath been the cause of severe judgments, 1 Sam. ii. 25; 2 Kings xvii. 14; 2 Chron. xxxvi. 16.

3. Apply God's word to thy sins. It is a sword whereby thou mayest cut them down. As ministers in their ministry must do this to others, so every one to himself. Against profaneness, apply Heb. xii. 16; against hypocrisy, Mat. xxiv. 51; against swearing, Jer. xxiii. 10; against unmercifulness, James ii. 13; against whoremongers and adulterers, Heb. xiii. 4; against liars, Rev. xxi. 8. So in other cases.

4. Let all evil doers fear. This sword of the word, of all other swords, shall not be borne in vain, Rom. xiii. 4. This sword pricked the Jews in their heart, Acts ii. 32. This made Felix tremble, Acts xxiv. 25. This struck Ananias and Sapphira stark dead, Acts v. 5. Though these were extraordinary judgments, and do not ordinarily fall out, yet assuredly the souls of evil doers are ordinarily struck dead therewith.

5. Make use of both edges of the word, because it is a two-edged sword. Make use of the law and of the gospel for slaying thy corruptions.

6. Have this sword always in a readiness, as gentlemen use to have their swords. Have the word of God in readiness to defend thyself against all manner of assaults, and also to repel and drive away thy spiritual enemies.

7. Let them who are in authority lift up this sword of the word of God in all places where they have authority, for suppressing evil doers, and encouraging them that do well, Rom. xiii. 4.

Sec. 72. *Of the word a spiritual sword.*

The apostle, to make good what he had said of the sharpness of the word, namely, that it is 'sharper than any two-edged sword,' setteth down an induction of sundry powerful effects, which are such as cannot be effected by any material sword. No material sword can 'pierce to the dividing asunder of soul and spirit,' &c., but the word can so far pierce, therefore no material sword is so sharp as the word.

If we well observe the kinds of effects produced, we shall find them all to be spiritual. Thence we may infer, that the word is a spiritual sword. It is in this respect styled, 'the sword of the Spirit,' Eph. vi. 17. Such is the whole armour of God described, Eph. vi. 14, &c.

For man consisteth of a soul which is spiritual, as well as of a body. Though a material sword may be useful for the body, yet the soul, singly considered in and by itself, hath no need of it.

Besides, we have spiritual enemies, whom a material sword can no way annoy; and we are subject to spiritual assaults, which cannot be repelled by corporal weapons. In these respects we have great need and use of a spiritual sword, such an one as the word is.

Hereby we have an evidence of the wise and good providence of God, who affordeth means answerable for our need every way, corporal means for our bodies, spiritual means for our souls. And as in wisdom he suffereth spiritual enemies to assault us with spiritual temptations, so he furnisheth us with a weapon to resist those enemies, and withstand those temptations.

It is therefore a point of egregious folly to account this sword a needless weapon, or to be careless in the use of it.

But it will be our wisdom well to use it, for our soul's safety, against all spiritual enemies and assaults.

Sec. 73. *Of the words dividing soul and spirit, joints and marrow.*

The first particular instance of the piercing power of the word is, that it 'divideth asunder,' διϊκνούμενος, soul and spirit.

The simple verb ίκνούμαι, *venio*, whence the Greek participle, being a compound, here translated *piercing*, signifieth *to come*. But the preposition διά, *per*, with with which it is compounded, adds emphasis. For the compound διϊκνούμαι signifieth to *come to*, or *into*. Our English word *pierce* doth fully express as much. Our former English thus translates it, *entereth through*.

How far the word pierceth is demonstrated in this phrase, 'to the dividing asunder of soul and spirit.'

Of the Greek word translated *dividing asunder*, see Chap. ii. 4, Sec. 35.

The things here said to be divided are soul and spirit. Each of these words are oft put for the whole soul of man, specially when they are singly set and joined with the body by way of distinction, as 1 Cor. vi. 20, Mat. x. 28. But here both soul and spirit are put for particular distinct faculties.

The soul, as distinguished from the spirit, is put for the will and affections, which are accounted inferior faculties.

The spirit is put for the understanding or mind, which is accounted the highest faculty, commanding and guiding the rest.

Thus are they distinguished, 1 Thes. v. 23, Luke i. 36, 37.

The soul and spirit are as nearly and firmly knit together as any parts of the body can be; yet the word can divide them asunder, and that not only by distinguishing the one from the other, but also by discovering the several desires and delights, or dislikings and loathings, of the soul; and likewise of the castings, plottings, and contrivements of the spirit; and all these both in good and evil things.

Some apply these words, *soul, spirit,* to the natural and regenerate parts of man, to corruption and grace, which in Scripture are commonly called 'flesh and spirit,' Gal. v. 17. In this sense none can be here meant but such as are regenerate, because none else have the spirit in that sense. But the power of the word, as here intended, is much manifested on those that are not regenerate.

These words following, *joints and marrow,* are metaphorical, taken from the body, and applied to the soul. The Greek noun ἁρμῶν, translated *joints,* is derived from a verb, ἄρω, *apto, inde* ἁρμάζω, that signifieth to fit or prepare. 'I have espoused,' or fitted and prepared you, saith the apostle, 2 Cor. xi. 2. Joints are so fitted for that hollow place where they lie, as they are as close, and can as hardly be pierced or severed, as the entire bone. The substance of joints is bony, they are very bones, so as a sword that easily cutteth asunder the thin skin and soft flesh may stick at the bony joint, and not cut it asunder.

By these joints are meant resolute purposes of the mind, obstinate resolutions of the will, hard hearts, seared consciences, stubborn affections and passions. Though a sharp two-edged sword can hardly cut asunder hard bony joints, yet can God's word easily cut asunder the aforesaid joints of the soul. It can alter resolved purposes, change obstinate wills, beat down hard hearts, rouse up seared consciences, and subdue violent passions, though they cleave so close to the soul as they may seem to be a part thereof.

How did God's word pierce the joints of the soul of Ahab, 1 Kings xx. 43, and xxi. 27; and of the princes of Judah, Jer. xxxvi. 16; and of Pilate, John xix. 12. So in another kind it pierced the joints of the soul of Eli, 1 Sam. iii. 18; and of David, 2 Sam. xii. 13; and of Hezekiah, 2 Kings xx. 19; and of the king and people of Nineveh, Jonah iii. 5, 6; and of the Jews, who were converted at Peter's first sermon, Acts ii. 37.

The other metaphor of μυελῶν, *marrow,* doth yet further amplify the sharpness and efficacy of the word. Marrow is the inward pith of bones, so as an hard bone must be pierced or broken before the marrow within it can be touched.

The marrow doth here set out the inward thoughts, imaginations, desires, and lusts of the soul. The bones in which the marrow lieth, imply as much as the foresaid joints did. So as there is nothing so secret in a man, nothing held so fast and close in him, with the strongest resolution and greatest obstinacy, but the word can meet with it, as Christ's word met with Saul, Acts ix. 5.

The phrase of *dividing asunder,* applied to all the foresaid particulars, is taken from anatomists, who will open the corpse, and sever one inward part from another, and dissect every part, and lay open the sinews,
arteries, and every sprig. Thus they discern and discover what corruption, what malady, what redundancy of blood, or humour, or distemper is in any of them. So doth the word, as is shewed in the next section.

Sec. 74. *Of the word a discerner of thoughts and intents of the heart.*

This last phrase, *and is a discerner,* &c., is added to explain the former metaphors.

The Greek word κριτικὸς, translated *a discerner,* is very emphatical; so emphatical, as they who interpret the *word of God* to be the Son of God, press the emphasis of this word in this place to be such, as can agree to none but to God himself. To this I answer, that it is God himself who speaketh in the word here meant; see Sec. 69. So as the power thereof is divine, and experience sheweth, that God useth ordinarily to manifest this kind of power here expressed in discerning thoughts by the ministry of his word.

As for the original word here used by the apostle, it is derived from a verb, κρίνειν, that signifieth *to discern,* or *to judge,* John vii. 24. Thence a noun κριτής, that signifieth a *judge;* whence κριτικὸς, the word of my text, which is not elsewhere used in the New Testament. It signifieth one that is skilful, expert and forward in espying, discerning, and censuring matters.

We in English, according to the notation of the Greek word, call such an one a *critic.*

There were two ancient grammarians, Aristarchus and Aristophanes, who used thoroughly to search the books of such poets as had written before their days, and to pass their censure upon them concerning such verses as were genuine or spurious; and these were thereupon called κριτικοί, *critics.*

The apostle doth not use the verb *discerneth,* which noteth an effect, or an act, but the noun *a discerner,* which implieth a kind of property and excellency in the act of discerning, so as nothing can so narrowly and thoroughly search and discern as the word of God.

The subject whereon the word is here said to exercise his critical faculty, are thoughts and intents of the heart. The noun ἐνθυμήσεων, translated *thoughts,* is a compound. The simple noun, θυμὸς, *mens,* signifieth the *mind.* It also signifieth *wrath,* θυμὸς, *ira,* Eph. iv. 31, which is a commotion of the mind. In this sense, that word is frequently used in the New Testament.

The former, which is the most proper signification of the word, namely, *the mind,* is most pertinent to our purpose.

The preposition ἐν, with which the word of my text is compounded, signifieth *in.* The compound verb ἐνθυμέομαι, *animo concipio,* signifieth to *conceive in the mind,* Mat. i. 20, Acts x. 19. Thence the word in my text, ἐνθυμήσεων, which signifieth *a conception of the mind.*

Thus Christ expoundeth it, Mat. ix. 4. It implieth an inward motion of the mind, which cannot simply be discerned but by the divine Spirit which accompanieth the ministry of the word

The other word ἐννοιῶν, translated *intents*, intends as much as the former. It is such a compound as that was; for the Greek word νόος, νοῦς, *mens*, signifieth the *mind*, Rom. vii. 23, 25. The compound verb ἐννοέω, *mente concipio*, signifieth as the former, to *conceive in the mind*, or *to think with one's self*.

The noun here used, ἔννοια, signifieth a notion or understanding of a thing, yea, the very purpose of the mind; and in that respect it is here in the plural number fitly translated *intents*.

It is in the singular number translated *mind*, 1 Peter iv. 1; but by reason of this word *heart* added thereunto, the inward motions or intents of the mind must needs be here meant.

Of the heart, and the various acceptions thereof, see Chap. iii. 7, Sec. 79.

The heart is here put for the whole soul.

Mention is here made of the heart, because in Scripture the heart is said to be most inscrutable or unsearchable, Jer. xvii. 9. It is one of God's incommunicable properties to be a 'searcher of the heart,' 1 Kings viii. 39; Acts i. 24.

Beside, the heart is accounted to be the seat of the affections; and 'the intents of the heart' may comprise the likings and dislikings of the whole soul; so as the word can discern the innermost motions of will, mind, and affection. That which is here attributed to the word, is somewhat answerable to that which is said of God himself, 'God saw that every imagination of the thoughts of man's heart was only evil continually,' Gen. vi. 5.

Behold what emphasis every word carrieth. Here is an exact critic, that can dive into the innermost motions of the mind, purposes of the will, and desires of the heart.

This piercing and discerning power of the word was manifested in the ministry of John the Baptist, whereby Jerusalem and all Judea, and 'all the regions round about Jordan,' were moved to be 'baptized of him in Jordan, confessing their sins,' Mat. iii. 5, 6.

And the people, publicans, and soldiers, inquired what they should do, Luke iii. 10, &c.

At the word of Christ, 'They which heard it, being convicted in their own conscience, went out one by one,' John viii. 9. And at the word of Peter, the Jews which heard him, were 'pricked in their hearts,' Acts ii. 37.

And at Paul's word, 'many came and confessed, and shewed their deeds,' Acts xix. 18, 19. And Felix trembled, Acts xxiv. 23. It is indefinitely said, that when ministers prophesy, 'If there come in one that believeth not, or one unlearned, he is convinced of all, he is judged of all; and thus are the secrets of his heart made manifest, and so falling down on his face, he will worship God, and report that God is in you of a truth,' 1 Cor. xiii. 24, 25.

The variety and multiplicity of phrases and metaphors here used, sheweth, that nothing can be kept so close, or held so fast in the soul of man, but the word of God can find it out, and cast it out. Such dissemblers as conceal their disposition from ministers of the word, cannot conceal it from the word itself, Ezek. xiv. 4, and xxxiii. 31.

Sec. 75. *Of God's knowledge of every creature.*

Ver. 13. *Neither is there any creature that is not manifest in his sight: but all things are naked and opened unto the eyes of him with whom we have to do.*

This verse may be taken either as a reason of the fore-named power and efficacy of the word; which reason may be drawn from the nature of him whose word it is, namely, God; who, being himself a searcher of the heart, and a discerner of all things, though never so close and secret, is pleased to exercise that power in and by the ministry of his word.

Or, to distinguish this verse from the former, it may contain another distinct argument to press the main point in hand, which is, to hear Christ's voice, and not to harden our hearts, because our very heart, and the thoughts thereof, are all manifest before God.

Neither of these do thwart the other, but both may stand very well together; for they both intend the same thing, namely, that we ought to hearken to Christ's voice, because as God he is a searcher of hearts, and exerciseth that discerning power in and by his word.

The apostle here setteth down the piercing sight of God with such emphasis as he did the piercing power of the word of God.

The copulative particle καί, in the Greek, intends some correspondency betwixt God and his word.

The Greek word κτίσις, translated *creature*, is derived from a verb, κτίζω, that signifies to *create* or *make*, 1 Tim. iv. 3, 4. It is variously used.

For it is taken,

1. For the creation, Mark x. 6, Rom. i. 20.
2. For every thing that hath a being from God, Rom. viii. 39.
3. For the fabric of the visible world, Rom. viii. 19, &c.
4. For an earthly structure made with man's hands, Heb. ix. 11.
5. For reasonable creatures, which are the chiefest of God's creatures here in this world, Mark xvi. 15.
6. For a magistrate, who in regard of his office bears the image of God, 1 Peter ii. 13.
7. For a true saint, who is born again, and renewed after the image of God. In this sense it hath this epithet *new* annexed to it; as 'a new creature,' 2 Cor. v. 17, Gal. vi. 15.

Here it is especially taken in the fifth distinction;

for reasonable creatures on earth, of what sex, age, condition or disposition soever they be.

I will not deny but that this word *creature* may here be indefinitely and generally taken for every creature in heaven, earth, sea, or hell, visible or invisible, reasonable or unreasonable, living or without life. For he that made them all, and deputed to every one their several places and natures, cannot be ignorant of any of them. They must needs all of them without exception be manifest in his sight.

Yet questionless the reasonable creature is here especially meant. For,

1. Man, the lord of other creatures, is by an excellency God's creature.
2. Other creatures were made for man; but man for God, and his glory especially.
3. Man hath understanding above other creatures to conceive himself to be God's creature, the work of his hands, and accordingly to respect God as his Creator.

To shew that there is not any one man excepted, he useth this indefinite phrase, 'There is not a creature.' To make the emphasis more conspicuous, our English inserts this particle *any*. He that excepteth not any one includeth every one, good or evil, upright or hypocrite, great or mean, learned or unlearned, wise or foolish.

Sec. 76. *Of all things manifest in God's sight.*

This phrase, *that is not manifest*, is the interpretation of one Greek word, ἀφανὴς, which is a privative compound, and hath the force of a negative.

The simple verb φαίνω, *appareo, luceo*, as used in the New Testament, signifieth to *appear*, Mat. xiii. 26, and to *shine forth*, John i. 5, and v. 35.

The compound verb ἀφανίζω, ἀφανίζομαι, *obscuro, evanesco*, from whence the adjective here used is derived, is directly opposite to the simple verb, as in these words, 'a vapour that appeareth,' φαινομένη, 'vanisheth away,' ἀφανιζομένη, James iv. 14; so Mat. vi. 16. Of a compound noun derived from the same verb, see Chap. iii. 13, Sec. 80.

The negative conjunction οὐκ, annexed to this privative compound, adds emphasis. It is more than if he had said, every creature is manifest.

Two negatives in Greek make a strong affirmative. Sometimes to make the affirmative the stronger, the negative is doubled and trebled. See Chap. xiii. 5, Sec. 71.

This phrase implieth an impossibility of concealing anything from God.

According to the notation of the Greek word, it implieth a clear and bright manifestation of every creature.

This relative *his*,—'in his sight,'—may have reference to God, whose word the foresaid powerful word is said to be, in this phrase, 'the word of God.' Or it may have reference to Christ, of whose prophetical function he here treateth, and whose voice he advised us to hear, Chap. iii. 7, Sec. 78.

Betwixt these there is no difference; for Christ is God, and the voice of Christ is the word of God.

The phrase ἐνώπιον, *coram, in sight*, is in Greek an adverb, and properly signifieth *before*, and so it is turned, Luke i. 6. It is also turned *in the presence*, Luke i. 19. It is derived from a noun ὤψ, ὀπὸς, *vultus*, that signifieth *sight*. It is applied to men and angels, Luke xii. 9. To God it is applied by way of resemblance after the manner of man. So is this phrase in the next clause, ὀφθαλμοῖς, 'unto the eyes.' See Chap. i. 10, Sec. 132. It sets out God's perfect knowledge of all men, whether good or evil, Prov. xv. 3. Concerning the good it is said, 'The eyes of the Lord are over the righteous,' 1 Peter iii. 10; and 'He knoweth the way of the righteous,' Ps. i. 6. Concerning the evil it is also said: 'The eyes of the Lord are upon the sinful kingdom,' Amos ix. 8, and 'God saw that the wickedness of man was great,' &c., Gen. vi. 5.

This in general must needs be so, because he is himself everywhere present, Jer. xxiii. 23, and nothing can hinder his sight, Ps. cxxxix. 7, and Job xxii. 13, 14. As the sun is above all, and shineth everywhere, so much more God.

Besides, God made all things, and he governeth all things, and therefore it is requisite he should have a sight of all. And this the rather, because his glory is the end of all, Prov. xvi. 4, Rom. xi. 36. By his sight of all he can direct and turn them all to his glory.

In particular, God seeth all for the righteous' sake, to uphold, to encourage, and to take occasion of rewarding them; and for the wicked's sake, to curb, restrain, and punish them.

This is a great encouragement unto the righteous to hold on in their righteous courses; for though men may be ignorant thereof, as Potiphar was of Joseph's faithfulness, Gen. xxxix. 19, 20; or forget it, as Pharaoh's butler forgot Joseph's kindness, Gen. xl. 23; or wittingly wink at it, as Nabal did at David's goodness, 1 Sam. xxv. 10; or misconceive it, as Saul did David's faithfulness, 1 Sam. xxii. 8; or envy it, as John's disciples did at the power of Christ's ministry, John iii. 26; or hate them for it, as the Pharisees hated Christ, John xv. 24; yet God cannot be ignorant, will not forget, nor wink at, nor misinterpret, any good thing. So as this is sufficient to encourage the righteous, yea, and to comfort them in all their distresses, Exod. iii. 7.

On the other side, this is matter of great terror to the wicked, in that he that seeth all their wickedness will not suffer them to go scot-free: 'God shall bring every work into judgment, with every secret thing,' &c., Ezek. xii. 14.

Sec. 77. *Of all things naked and opened unto God.*

To set out God's omniscience the more to the full,

the apostle addeth this clause: 'But all things are naked and opened,' &c.

This clause is brought in with a particle of opposition, δὲ, *but*. The opposition is betwixt the different kinds of propositions, the one negative, the other affirmative: that implied, that nothing can be hid from God; this, that all things are seen by him. Nothing can be hid, but all things are seen. Thus this opposition implies that the latter is a reason of the former. There is nothing not manifest to God, because all things are open before him.

Those things are said to be γυμνὰ, *naked*, which have nothing to cover them. Thus our first parents were naked in paradise, Gen. ii. 25. Where Christ saith, 'I was naked, and ye clothed me,' Mat. xxv. 36, he sheweth that they are naked who are not clothed or covered.

Of a naked body, all the beauty, comeliness, and due proportion of the whole and every part is easily discerned, and every spot, sore, and defect, will soon be discovered.

Now, because a thing naked may outwardly appear fair, comely, and every way perfect, yet have many corruptions and defects in it, the apostle addeth another metaphor, whereby he sheweth that God can also discern all things within. That other metaphor is in this word τετραχηλισμένα, *opened*.

The Greek participle is derived from a noun, τράχηλος, *collum*, that signifieth *a neck*. The verb among other senses is used of such beasts as, being excoriated or flayed, were cut down from the neck to the rump,[1] all along the back-bone. By this means the beast was so opened as every part within it, yea, and the soundness or unsoundness of every part, might be seen. Heathen magicians used to look into the inward parts of beasts slain for sacrifices, and narrowly to observe the colour, shape, posture, defects, and other like circumstances, answerably to order their definitions for good or bad success. Hereunto the prophet alludeth in this phrase, 'He looked in the liver,' Ezek. xxi. 21.

From that custom arose this metaphor of laying a thing open, so as every secret therein might be discovered.

Thus are all things opened to God's eyes, so as nothing can be concealed from him: not without, for all things are naked; not within, for all things are opened, τοῖς ὀφθαλμοῖς αὐτοῦ, 'to his eyes.'

This metaphor of *eyes* attributed to God is used as this phrase, *in his sight*, was used, Sec. 76.

These metaphors, *naked*, *opened*, give evidence that men are every way known to God. As the former part of this verse shewed that all persons are known to God, so this that every way they are known to him. Without, all things are naked; within, all things are opened.

As 'God saw that the wickedness of man was great in the earth,' so he saw that 'every imagination of the thoughts of his heart was only evil continually,' Gen. vi. 5. The psalmist sets out this omniscience of God to the life, Ps. cxxxix. 1, 2, &c. Christ, by his divine Spirit, discerned Nathanael to be 'an Israelite indeed, in whom was no guile,' John iv. 47; and the ruler of the synagogue to be an hypocrite, Luke xiii. 15.

1. God was declared to be 'the searcher of hearts,' Sec. 74.

2. God, being the creator of all within and without, must needs understand them all, and that throughout, Ps. xciv. 9, &c.

This is a point of singular comfort to the upright; it upholds them against such false imputations as Job's friends laid to his charge.

On this ground, that God knoweth all things without and within, true saints can appeal to God in such cases as they are falsely charged withal, Ps. xxvi. 1, 2, and cxxxix. 23, 24.

In extremities this omniscience of God moveth true saints to plead their integrity before him, Isa. xxxviii. 3.

On the other side, this cannot but much affright the consciences of hypocrites, who, though they may with fair outward pretences soothe and deceive men, who can but judge according to outward appearance, yet they cannot deceive him ' to whose eyes all things are naked and opened.'

This affords a seasonable admonition to all of all sorts, narrowly to look to themselves; at all times, in all places, in all things, every way, in their outward conversation, and in their inward disposition, even because all things are naked and opened unto God.

Sec. 78. *Of God's seeing sin in such as are justified.*

This text, that doth so fully set out the omniscience of God, is fitly pressed against those who hold and teach that God can see no sin in justified persons. That they may more fully express their mind therein, they set it out by these two comparisons: the first of an hat put upon an hour-glass; the second, of a bottle of ink poured into a sea of water. They thus apply these comparisons: as a man cannot see the glass that is covered with an hat, nor the blackness of the ink in a sea of water, so God cannot see sin in the justified. To this I answer, that resemblances from man to God do not hold, because of the infinite disparity betwixt them.

To discover the vanity of the aforesaid assertion, I propound these queries:

1. Whether there be any sin at all in the justified, while here they live, or no? The Scriptures expressly saith that 'there is no man that sinneth not,' 1 Kings viii. 46; that 'in many things we offend all,' James iii. 2; that 'if we say that we have no sin, we deceive ourselves, and the truth is not in us,' John i. 8. Surely under these indefinite phrases, even the justified must needs be comprised. If sin be in them, the

---

[1] τραχηλίζειν, significat, διὰ τῆς ῥάχεως σχίζειν, per spinam dorsi findere.—*Varinus.*

foresaid description of God's omniscience plainly demonstrates that God sees it.

2. Do men see sin in others that are regenerate? This cannot be denied, for Nathan saw sin in David, 2 Sam. xii. 7, and Paul in Peter, Gal. ii. 11. Can it be imagined that man should see that which God cannot?

3. Can justified persons discern sin in themselves? If not, why do they complain thereof? as David, Ps. xxxviii. 4, and li. 1, &c.; yea, and the apostle Paul also, Rom. vii. 24. Surely God must needs see more in man than himself can.

How should God punish sin in justified persons (as in Moses, Num. xxvii. 14, in David, 2 Sam. xii. 10, &c., and in Solomon, 2 Sam. vii. 14) if he can see no sin in them? Or how should God order and dispose their sin to good (as he doth Rom. viii. 28) if he see no sin in them? The punishment here spoken of, is not to be taken for the vindictive judgment of a judge, simply for the crime committed, but for the corrective chastisement of a father, for the amendment of the offender, 2 Sam. vii. 14, Heb. xii. 10.

Many of their grounds whereupon they settle this opinion, that God seeth no sin in the justified, are raised from mistakes of sacred Scripture; so as I may say to them, as Christ said to the Sadducees, 'Ye do err, not knowing the scriptures, nor the power of God,' Mat. xxii. 29.

The first scripture which they mistake is this part of Balaam's prophecy, 'He hath not beheld iniquity in Jacob, neither hath he seen perverseness in Israel,' Num. xxiii. 21.

To take these words according to this translation, many judicious expositors[1] do thus interpret them: 'God hath not beheld iniquity in Jacob utterly to destroy them: or to give them over to their enemies.' Others[2] thus: 'He seeth not iniquity in Jacob, in that he imputeth it not to him.'

The true meaning of this scripture will be best found out by a due observance of the main scope thereof; which was this, to shew that God would suffer no attempts to prevail against his people:

1. In this case, not to behold, נבט, or, not to see, ראה, Esther viii. 6, is not to endure to see such and such a thing to be done. When a father seeth his child wronged, he may say, I will not see my child to be thus abused; that is, I will not suffer him so to be handled, I will rescue my child, and revenge the wrong-doer. Thus God may be said, not to see that which he doth not like, and that which he will not suffer. Our English expoundeth this phrase, *seeth not*, applied to God, thus, *approveth not*, Lam. iii. 36.

2. The words, און, translated *iniquity*, and עמל, *perverseness*, do most properly and usually signify wrong and grievance.

[1] Pelican annot. on Tindall transl. of Bible, Piscat. in loc.
[2] Hier. and Aug. in Ps. 31. Vatab. Calvin, Piscat.

The former, translated *iniquity*, signifieth unequal dealing, Ps. xciv. 23.

The latter, translated *perverseness*, signifieth also mischief, Ps. vi. 16.

Both these words in Balaam's prophecy imply evil in the enemies of Israel, rather than in Israel themselves, or in the people of God; so are both these words taken, Hab. i. 3.

3. By Jacob and Israel are meant the whole body of the people that were then in the wilderness, whereof many were not truly justified. For in the verse before he saith, 'God brought them out of Egypt.'

4. The preposition ב, translated *in*, signifieth also *to*, or *against*, as verse 23. So as the words may be thus translated, according to their true sense and meaning, 'God endureth not to behold wrong done against Jacob, nor to see grievance against Israel.' In this sense, what can be picked out to justify that gross error, that God seeth no sin in justified persons?

A second ground that they raise out of Scripture for the foresaid error, is taken from sundry metaphors, such as 'God blotteth out transgressions,' and 'putteth them away as a cloud,' and 'casteth them behind his back, and into the bottom of the sea,' &c. Of these, and other like metaphors, how they intend a full discharge of sin, see *A Guide to go to God, or, An Explanation of the Lord's Prayer*, 5th petition, sec. 130. To apply metaphorical phrases simply, and that beyond the intent of the Holy Ghost who useth them, is to pervert the Scripture.

A third ground is taken from the Holy Ghost's expression of the church's beauty in these and such like phrases: 'Thou art all fair, my love, there is no spot in thee,' Cant. iv. 7; and Christ 'gave himself for his church, that he might present it to himself a glorious church, not having spot or wrinkle, or any such thing; but that it should be holy, and without blemish,' Ephes. v. 25, 26.

Ans. These and such like places are meant partly of the robe of Christ's righteousness, wherewith justified persons are clothed while here they live; and partly of that glory wherewith the church shall be decked in the world to come. But from thence to infer, that there is no sin in justified persons while here they live, or that God can see no sin in them, is a false inference.

Sec. 79. *Of this phrase, 'with whom we have to do.'*

The last clause of the 13th verse, which is this, *with whom we have to do*, is ambiguous.

The word λόγος, translated *to do*, is the very same that was used ver. 12, and translated, *the word*.

It is derived from a verb λέγειν, that signifieth *to say*, or *to speak*, Mat. iii. 9. Answerably this word signifieth *word* or *speech* which is uttered.

In this sense the meaning is this, *of whom we speak*.

In this sense the Greek preposition πρὸς, which

properly signifieth *to*, must be put for *of*. The preposition περί, which properly signifieth *of*, is used in a like phrase, thus, 'Of whom we have many things to say,' Heb. v. 11.

The foresaid word doth also signify a matter, a thing, or case, as where Christ saith, 'I will ask you one thing,' λόγον ἕνα, Mat. xxi. 24; and where he saith, 'saving for the cause,' παρεκτὸς λόγου, Mat. v. 32. The Hebrews do also use דבר, *word*, for thing or matter, as Exod. xviii. 26, Esther ix. 31. In reference to this signification, it is here translated, 'with whom we have to do.'

This same word λόγος signifieth also an account. In this sense it is frequently used, and that both in taking an account, as Mat. xviii. 23, and xxv. 19, and also in giving an account, as Luke xvi. 2, Rom. xiv. 12. In this last signification of an account, the preposition πρὸς, *to*, is properly used, and it may be thus translated, 'to whom we are to give an account.'

None of these senses are impertinent.

Our former English translators mention the two former interpretations; one in the margin thus, 'concerning whom we speak;' the other in the text thus, 'with whom we have to do.'

The former of these giveth proof that Christ is the searcher of hearts; for Christ is he concerning whom the apostle especially speaketh. Thus all the points which were before in general delivered, of God's power and property in this respect, are in particular to be applied to Christ; yea, by just and necessary consequence, it also from thence followeth that Christ is true God. Hereof see Chap. i. 8, Sec. 107.

The latter giveth evidence that it is the Lord with whom we have especially to do in all things. Thus much is implied under this charge which God giveth to Abraham, 'Walk before me,' Gen. xvii. 1; so did Enoch, Gen. v. 24; Noah, Gen. vi. 9; Abraham and Isaac, Gen. xlviii. 15; and Joseph, Gen. xxxix. 9.

Under this interpretation may well be comprised that which was noted of giving an account to God. For they who have to do with God must give an account to him; and in giving an account to God they have to do with him. See Chap. ii. 13, Sec. 129.

God is the supreme sovereign over all; he hath appointed to every one his work. He is that Judge to whom all are to give an account.

On this ground we ought in all things to have an eye to him; in matters of his worship, and in our affairs with men, magistrates, subjects, masters, servants, all of all sorts apply this, Col. iii. 23, and iv. 1.

Sec. 80. *Of the resolution of* Heb. iv. 12, 13.

Ver. 12. *For the word of God is quick and powerful, and sharper than any two-edged sword, piercing even to the dividing asunder of soul and spirit, and of the joints and marrow, and is a discerner of the thoughts and intents of the heart.*

13. *Neither is there any creature that is not manifest in his sight; but all things are naked and opened unto the eyes of him with whom we have to do.*

The sum of these two verses is, the efficacy of God's word.

About it we may observe,
1. The point itself, ver. 12.
2. A proof thereof, ver. 13.

In laying down the point, the apostle expresseth,
1. The inference, in this causal particle *for*.
2. The substance: and that is declared, 1, simply; 2, comparatively.

In the simple consideration there is set down,
1. The thing described, *the word of God*.
2. The description thereof by two epithets: 1, *quick*; 2, *powerful*.

The comparison is taken from *a two-edged sword*.
In the comparison, the word is,
1. Generally said to be *sharper* than *any sword*.
2. It is particularly demonstrated, wherein it is sharper.

The particulars are set down, 1, metaphorically; 2, plainly.

The metaphor declares two virtues of the word:
1. A piercing virtue.
2. A dividing virtue.

The latter virtue is illustrated by the things divided, which are two couple:
1. Soul and spirit.
2. Joints and marrow.

The particular effect of the word plainly expressed is,
1. Propounded, in this word, *discerner*.
2. Amplified by the subject wherein that virtue is exercised. This is double:

1, Thought; 2, Intents of the heart.

The proof of the foresaid power of the word is taken from the omiscience of him whose word it is.

Hereabout there is,
1. A description of the point.
2. A declaration of the person.

The point itself is demonstrated two ways,
1, Negatively; 2, Affirmatively.

The negative noteth out,
1. The persons seen.
2. The manner of seeing them.

The persons seen are set out two ways:
1. By an indefinite title, *creature*.
2. By a negative extent, *not any*, that is, every one.

The manner of seeing them is set forth three ways:
1. By a double negative, *neither*, *not*, which maketh a strong affirmative.
2. By a clear manifestation, in this word *manifest*.
3. By an assured evidence, in this phrase, *in his sight*.

The affirmative part of the description implieth two points:
1. The general matter, *all things*.
2. The kind of discovering them: and that in two metaphors:

The first respecteth things outward, they are *naked*.

The second things inward, they are *opened*.

The foresaid metaphors are amplified by their evidence, thus, *in God's eyes*.

The person whose omniscience is thus laid out, is demonstrated by that reference which we have to him, in this phrase, *with whom we have to do*.

Sec. 81. *Of observations raised out of* Heb. iv. 12, 13.

1. *God hath vouchsafed his word to us.* This title, *the word of God*, takes this for grant. See Sec. 69.

II. *God's word shall not be in vain.* This ariseth from the inference. See Sec. 68.

III. *God's word is a living word.* It is *quick*. See Sec. 70.

IV. *God's word is a word of power.* It is *powerful*. See Sec. 70.

V. *God's word is sharp.* This is implied under this comparative degree, *sharper*. See Sec. 71.

VI. *God's word is as a two-edged sword.* Hereunto it is resembled. See Sec. 71.

VII. *God's word is sharper than the sharpest instrument.* A two-edged sword is the sharpest of instruments; but the word is sharper than it. See Sec. 71.

VIII. *God's word is a spiritual sword.* Spiritual effects are here attributed to it. See Sec. 72.

IX. *God's word divideth the closest and firmest things.* Such are *soul* and *spirit*. See Sec. 73.

X. *God's word pierceth the hardest things.* Such are the joints. See Sec. 73.

XI. *God's word pierceth to the innermost things.* Such is the marrow. See Sec. 73.

XII. *God's word is an exact censor.* It is a *critic*. See Sec. 74.

XIII. *God's word reacheth to men's thoughts.* This is here plainly expressed. See Sec. 74.

XIV. *God's word discovereth intents and purposes.* This also is here expressed. See Sec 74.

XV. *God's word searcheth the very heart.* For this end mention is here made of the *heart*. See Sec. 74.

XVI. *God's word is powerful as God himself.* This is gathered from the inference of this 13th verse. See Sec. 75.

XVII. *All of all sorts are known to God.* This negative, *not any*, intends as much. See Sec. 75.

XVIII. *God fully knows all.* This negative, *not manifest*, importeth so much. See Sec. 74.

XIX. *Both things and persons are under God's cognisance.* The distinction betwixt *creatures* and *things* implieth this point. See Sec. 77.

XX. *All outward things are clearly discovered to God.* They are as *naked*. See Sec. 77.

XXI. *God discerneth the innermost things.* This metaphor implied under this word *opened*, intendeth as much. See Sec. 77.

XXII. *God seeth sin in all.* Sin is comprised under this general, *all things*. See Sec. 78.

XXIII. *We have to do with God in all things.*

XXIV. *We must give an account to God.* These two last doctrines are implied in this phrase, *with whom we have to do*. See Sec. 79.

Sec. 82. *Of the inference of the* 14*th verse.*

Verse 14. *Seeing then that we have a great high priest, that is passed into the heavens, Jesus, the Son of God, let us hold fast our profession.*

This and the two next verses do so expressly speak of Christ's priesthood, as some expositors [1] think it fit to begin the fifth chapter with them. But I see no great cause to alter the ordinary division of these chapters. For those three last verses are as a perfect transition, which looketh backward and forward.

1. They look backward, to that which had been said of Christ's sitting on high, being the Son of God, chap. i. 3, 5, and to Christ Jesus his being 'the high priest of our profession,' chap. ii. 17, and iii. 1. In reference to these and other like passages, the apostle maketh this inference, 'Seeing then that we have a great high priest,' &c.

2. They look forward as the sum of that which the apostle delivereth in the chapters following, concerning Christ's priesthood.

The note of reference, οὖν, is this ordinary illative conjunction *therefore*, which we here translate *then*, and it implieth a consequence. The consequence here intended may be that which is here comprised under this phrase, 'Let us hold fast our profession.'

In looking backward it may imply a general, particular, and immediate reference.

1. The general reference is to all that hath been before spoken concerning the priesthood, exaltation, and sonship of Jesus, all which are here hinted as a motive to 'hold fast our profession.'

2. The particular reference is to that main point which the apostle presseth in this and the former chapter about 'entering into God's rest.' For if the question be asked, What hope we poor sinners may have of entering thereinto? the apostle here maketh answer, That Christ our great high priest being passed into heaven, we also in and by him have hope to enter.

3. The immediate reference is to that which he had delivered of the power of God's word, and piercing sight of God himself, vers. 12, 13. We shall be assuredly found out if we fall from our profession, it becomes us therefore to hold it fast.

All and every of these references teach us to improve to our best advantage the means which God affordeth to us. God hath given us his own Son, whose throne is in the heaven, who is 'the apostle and high priest of our profession,' who hath prepared an everlasting rest for us, whose word is exceeding powerful, and who himself is a searcher of hearts; *therefore* we ought to persevere in the faith of Christ, and hold fast our profession.

[1] Luther, Calvin.

Thus will it not repent the Lord that he hath given us his Son to be our king, priest, and prophet; and with him his powerful word. Thus shall we find and feel the sweet comforts and refreshments that flow from Christ, and partake of all his benefits. Thus shall we see just cause to bless the Lord for those great gifts bestowed on us.

Sec. 83. *Of having a great high priest.*

Most of the particulars here laid down about Christ's priesthood have been before handled, as, that Christ is a *priest,* an *high priest,* and *a great high priest.* Of these see Chap. ii. 17, Secs. 172, 173, &c.

We are said to *have* (ἔχοντες) this priest in sundry repects.

1. In that God the Father gave him to us by promise, Gen. iii. 15.

2. In that Christ is actually exhibited, being come down from heaven, having assumed our nature (in which respect he is 'taken from among men'), and in our nature done and endured whatsoever as a priest he was to do and endure.

3. In that, by the ministry of the gospel, he is offered and tendered unto us, Gal. iii. 1.

4. In that we profess to believe in him, and thereby take him for our priest, if at least we do indeed believe as we profess. For to *believe* in Christ is to *receive* him, John i. 12.

Thus we see that this word *having* carrieth emphasis; and is much more than if he had said, 'Seeing there is,' &c. This implieth a right to him, and a kind of possession of him.

This is a great privilege thus to *have* such a priest, such an high priest, so great an high priest. All men have not this priest.

How should we esteem him! How careful should we be to use him as our priest! See Chap. ii. 17, Sec. 175.

Oh let not that be verified in us, which the wise man thus hinteth of a fool, 'Wherefore is there a price in the hand of a fool to get wisdom, seeing he hath no heart to it?' Prov. xvii. 16.

Sec. 84. *Of Christ being in heaven as our priest.*

The place where Christ continueth to exercise his priesthood, is here said to be τοὺς οὐρανοὺς, *the heavens.* The plural number, *heavens,* is used to set out the height and excellency of the place. See Chap. i. 3, Sec. 35.

1. This is a strong argument against the ubiquity of Christ's body. For that which is contained in the heavens, is not everywhere present. I may in this case say, as the angels did to them that sought Christ in the grave when he was risen, Luke xxiv. 5, Why seek ye him that is in heaven among them that are on earth? Long may they so seek him, but while he abideth in heaven they shall not find him on earth. The like may be pressed against transubstantiation.

2. This sheweth the pre-eminency of Christ's priesthood above all others' priesthood. Others exercised their priesthood in places made with hands; but 'Christ is not entered into holy places made with hands, but into heaven itself, now to appear in the presence of God for us,' Heb. ix. 24.

3. This ministereth matter of great consolation to us, against whom heaven was shut by reason of our sins, but now it is opened by Christ; so as we may now well labour to enter into the celestial rest, as we were exhorted, ver. 11. For the way is made open, and places are there prepared for us, John xiv. 2. This is a strong inducement to stir us up to do as the people did in the days of John the Baptist, when 'the kingdom of heaven suffered violence, and the violent took it by force,' Mat. xi. 12.

4. This may stir us up to 'seek those things that are above, where Christ sitteth on the right hand of God;' and to 'set our affections on things above, not on things on the earth,' Col. iii. 1, 2.

5. This teacheth us in prayer to look up unto heaven, where Christ our high priest is. For this end Christ putteth us in mind of God's being in heaven, where he teacheth us thus to pray, 'Our Father which art in heaven,' Mat. vi. 9.

6. This assureth us that Christ is where his Father is, presenting himself as our high priest for us continually before his Father.

7. This giveth evidence that we also that believe in Christ shall have an habitation in heaven. For saith Christ to such, 'I go to prepare a place for you: and if I go and prepare a place for you, I will come again and receive you unto myself, that where I am, there ye may be also,' John xiv. 2, 3.

Sec. 85. *Of Christ's 'passing' into heaven, and our communion with him.*

Christ is said to have *passed* into the heavens. The Greek word διεληλυθότα, translated *passed,* is a compound. The simple verb ἔρχομαι signifieth *to come.* The preposition διὰ signifieth *through.* This compound signifieth to pass through, notwithstanding any difficulties that may seem to hinder. Thus it is said that an angel and Peter '*passed* the first and second ward,' Acts xii. 10.

Our Lord Christ having assumed our nature, passed through the Virgin's womb; and being born, in his infancy, childhood, and man-age, passed through many difficulties, as temptations, afflictions, persecutions, death itself, and the grave; yea, after his resurrection he passed through the three regions of the air, and the several orbs of the starry heavens, and so entered into the highest heavens.

Thus we see that nothing could hinder him from that place where he intended to appear as our priest for us before his Father.

On this ground we may be confident that we also who believe in Christ shall pass through all impediments and obstacles, to be in that rest where he is. As the head himself passed through all, so will he cause his members to pass through all, that they may be where he is.

The conjunction of these two points (1, that we have Christ for our priest; 2, that he is passed into the heavens) do prove, that Christ's bodily absence hinders not our communion with him, nor our participation of the benefit of his priesthood. We have him for our priest though he be passed into the heavens. Expressly is this again set down, Heb. viii. 1.

1. Though in body he be absent, yet in his divine Spirit he is ever with us, according to his promise, Mat. xxviii. 20.

2. Faith hath a virtue to pierce into heaven, where Christ is. It seeth him who is invisible, Heb. xi. 27; John xx. 29.

Singular comfort doth this minister to us on earth, that so great a distance as is betwixt heaven and earth cannot hinder our communion with Christ. We may by faith have recourse to him as if he were on earth; and though he were on earth, yet access to him would be to little purpose without faith, Mat. xiii. 58.

Sec. 86. *Of Christ a priest, both God and man, and of our duty thereupon.*

To shew distinctly who this priest was, he expresseth his name, *Jesus*. This name was his proper name, given to him upon his incarnation. Of it, see Chap. ii. 9, Sec. 73; Chap. iii. 1, Sec. 29.

By this title the apostle declareth Christ to be man, whereby he was fit to do all works of service and suffering that were to be done and endured by a priest. He declareth himself hereby to be a Saviour. See Chap. ii. 9, Sec. 73.

Because the priesthood which Christ undertook required matters of divine dignity and authority, the apostle addeth that special relation which Christ had to God, in this phrase, 'the Son of God.' Of this relation, see Chap. i. 2, Sec. 15.

By this it appeareth that our priest was both God and man, able and fit for that function. Hereby is Christ distinguished from Aaron, and from all other priests. Hereof see more, Chap. ii. 17, Sec. 172.

The duty required by virtue of Christ's priesthood is thus expressed, 'Let us hold fast our profession.'

Of the manner of the apostle's expressing his mind in the plural number and first person, whereby with others he incites himself, see ver. 1, Sec. 3.

By *profession* is here meant the true faith professed. Of the word ὁμολογία, here translated *profession*, see Chap. iii. 1, Sec. 27.

The verb κρατῶμεν, translated *hold fast*, signifieth to hold a thing so fast as not to let it go again. Thus it is used of holding Christ when they had apprehended him, Mat. xxvi. 48; and of Herod's holding John when he bound him in prison, Mark vi. 17. It is also used of the Jews holding the traditions of their elders, which they would by no means let go, Mark vii. 3, 4, 8. It is applied to retaining of sin in obstinate persons, which shall not be forgiven, John xx. 23; here it implieth perseverance. In this sense is this verb used three times by Christ, namely, in his epistle to Pergamos, Rev. ii. 13; to Thyatira, Rev. ii. 25; and to Philadelphia, Rev. iii. 11.

Of perseverance in the faith, see Chap. iii. 6, Sec. 68.

The inference of this duty upon the description of Christ our priest sheweth, that the ground of our perseverance resteth on Christ's priesthood. For this end doth the apostle exhort us to 'consider the High Priest of our profession,' chap. iii. 1.

The sacrifice which Christ as our priest once offered up, the intercession which he continually maketh, and the benefits which flow from his priesthood (whereof see Chap. ii. 17, Sec. 174), are both means and helps to perseverance.

It becomes us, even in this respect, to be well informed in this mystery of Christ's priesthood, much to meditate thereon, and well to place our confidence on it.

Sec. 87. *Of the inference of ver. 15.*

Ver. 15. *For we have not an high priest which cannot be touched with the feeling of our infirmities; but was in all points tempted like as we are, yet without sin.*

This verse is added to remove a scruple which might arise from the excellency of that priest, who is described in the former verse. For a poor sinner, upon a deep apprehension of his own unworthiness, vileness, and cursedness, might thus reason: True it is that Christ is a priest, but so great an high priest, sitting on a glorious throne in heaven, the very Son of God, as I, poor, weak, cursed sinner, who am subject to many infirmities and corruptions, dare not go to him for mediation.

To remove that scruple, the apostle here sheweth, that albeit he were so great and glorious a priest, yet he was withal 'touched with a feeling of our infirmities,' and 'tempted as we are;' so as we have good cause to believe that he will be merciful unto us, and ready to receive and relieve us. (Hereof see Chap. ii. 17, Sec. 176).

Thus this causal conjunction γὰρ, *for*, is here fitly added, in that it pointeth at a reason why we should hold fast the profession of our faith in Christ; because he is not only the Son of God, a great high priest in heaven (which was one reason), but also because he was 'touched with the feeling of our infirmities,' and 'tempted as we are,' which is another reason.

We may well hence infer, that it is necessary to be

instructed in Christ's humiliation, temptations, passions, and infirmities, as well as in his divine majesty, dignity, authority, and power. The sacred Scripture doth distinctly, perspicuously, and fully declare both. Where it speaks of the one, it frequently speaks of the other.

Christ's humiliation, infirmities, and sufferings, are the means whereby we have access to Christ; they are the ground of our encouragement to fly unto him. His divine dignity and power are means of strengthening our faith, and making us wholly to rely upon him. Were it not for the former, we durst not approach unto him; were it not for the latter, we could not with confidence rest upon him.

Sec. 88. *Of Christ's fellow-feeling.*

In setting down the infirmities of Christ, the apostle useth two negatives; thus, 'We have not an high priest which cannot be touched,' &c. This he doth to convince us the more of the truth of the point. Two negatives in Greek make a strong affirmative (as was shewed ver. 13, Sec. 76). It is more than if he had said, 'We have a high priest that can be touched,' &c. These two negatives intend an improbability, if not an impossibility, of the point; yea, they imply that it cannot be otherwise thought but that Christ should be so touched: of it we may not make any doubt or question.

The word δυνάμενον, here translated *can*, is in this case turned *able*, δύναται which implieth a fitness and readiness to a thing. See Chap. ii. 18, Sec. 183.

This phrase, *touched with a feeling*, is the interpretation of one Greek word, συμπαθῆσαι, which is a compound. The simple verb πάσχειν, *pati*, signifieth *to suffer*; the preposition σὺν, *with*. The compound συμπαθεῖν, to *suffer with*, or to be mutually affected with others' sufferings; even so as if those sufferings touched one's self, and he himself felt the weight or pain of them.

This word is used to set out the compassion which these Hebrews had of the apostle in his bonds, and it is thus translated, 'Ye had compassion of me in my bonds,' Heb. x. 34. They so tendered him, or were so affected towards him in his bonds, as they would have been toward themselves in the like case; according to that direction which is given Heb. xiii. 3. A participle derived from this verb συμπαθεῖς, is thus translated, *having compassion one of another*, 1 Peter iii. 8. This word, to *sympathise*, is drawn from that Greek word. Our English phrase, 'touched with a feeling,' implieth that Christ is so affected with our miseries as if he himself lay under them, and felt them as much as we.

To set forth the compassion of the high priest under the law, there is another compound, μετριοπαθεῖν, derived from the same simple verb, which signifieth to *have compassion with measure*, that is, to have so much compassion as is sufficient. Herein he was a type of Christ, who hath indeed as much compassion as is requisite. In this respect Christ is said to be 'a merciful high priest, in that he was made like to us.' See Chap. ii. 17, Sec. 176.

Sec. 89. *Of the infirmities whereof Christ hath a fellow-feeling.*

The particulars whereof Christ is here said to have a feeling are comprised under this word ἀσθενείαις, *infirmities*. The Greek word is a privative compound. The simple noun, σθένος, signifieth *strength*. Thence a verb, σθενεῖν, which signifieth to *strengthen*, 1 Peter v. 10. The privative compound, ἀσθενεῖν, hath a contrary signification, which is to *be sick or weak*, James v. 14, Rom. xiv. 2. So this noun signifieth *sickness*, John xi. 4, or any other *weakness* and infirmity, 2 Cor. xii. 9, 10.

The plural number, ἀσθενείαις, *infirmities*, is here used, because they were very many. They are said to be ἡμῶν, *our* infirmities, because they were such as we have in their kind, and because they were undertaken for our sakes. In this respect he is afterwards in this verse said to be 'tempted like as we are.'

We have infirmities of soul, and of the several faculties thereof; and of the body, and several parts thereof, both inward and outward; yea, all the temptations and afflictions from others whereunto we are subject, may be comprised under infirmities. Of all these had Christ a feeling.

That which is here taken for grant, that Christ was 'touched with a feeling of our infirmities,' may be taken two ways.

1. In reference to those infirmities wherewith he was in his own person afflicted. These were such as we are subject unto, as is shewed before. He was herein made like to us. See Chap. ii. 17, Sec. 169.

2. In reference to those infirmities wherewith we are afflicted. Christ being our head, he had a fellow-feeling of them. It is oft noted in the history of the Gospel, that he was 'moved with compassion.' See Chap. ii. 17, Sec. 176.

As an evidence of Christ's fellow-feeling of our infirmities, he wept, John xi. 35, Luke xix. 41; he groaned and mourned, Mark iii. 5; he invited such as were heavy laden to come unto him, Mat. xi. 28; he preached to the poor, Mat. xi. 5; he comforted the afflicted, Mat. ix. 2; and absolved the penitent sinner, Luke vii. 47, 48.

Because we are most affected with outward evidences, it is expressly noted that he fed the hungry, cleansed the lepers, healed the sick, eased the pained, gave sight, hearing, and speech to such as wanted them, restored limbs, raised the dead, and dispossessed devils.

To shew that he had this fellow-feeling, not on earth only, but that he retaineth it even still in heaven, he hath not only in general said concerning his people, 'He that toucheth you toucheth the apple of mine eye,' Zech. ii. 8 ; but also in particular, when his church was persecuted, he said to the persecutor, ' Saul, Saul, why persecutest thou me ?' Acts ix. 5. In this respect the apostle calleth the afflictions of the church, ' the remnant of the afflictions of Christ,' Col. i. 24, namely, such as Christ, through his compassion and fellow-feeling, suffereth in his mystical body.

Obj. It cannot stand with Christ's heavenly glory to have a fellow-feeling of miseries.

Ans. This fellow-feeling ariseth, not from any passion or proper suffering in soul or body, but from the mystical union which is betwixt him and his members. He accepts kindnesses done to them as done to himself, and accounts wrongs done to them as done to himself, Mat. xxv. 40, &c.

Christ is thus touched with the feeling of our infirmities, that we might be the better persuaded to seek to him for succour in all our needs. See Chap. ii. 17, Sec. 176 in the end.

This doth much commend Christ's tender-heartedness to us. He doth every way respect both our weakness and our wretchedness.

It becomes us oft to meditate hereon for strengthening our faith. It is a great encouragement for us to go unto him, especially if we consider how he was touched in his own person, and by reason of his union with us. Let us hereupon lay open our sores and griefs before him. The more we are afflicted, the more he will pity us.

Sec. 90. *Of Christ being tempted as we are.*

To prove that Christ was ' touched with the feeling of our infirmities,' the apostle sheweth how far he was tempted. This he bringeth in by a particle of opposition, δέ, *but*, which here importeth a reason of the aforesaid fellow-feeling, which was because he was tempted.

To make this reason the more clear, the apostle thus expresseth the extent of Christ's temptations, κατὰ πάντα, *in all points*, or according to all things, even all things wherein it was needful and useful for him to be tempted.

How Christ was tempted, and how many ways, see Chap. ii. 18, Sec. 182.

It is further added, *like as we are*, or word for word, καθ' ὁμοιότητα, *after the similitude;* so is this very phrase translated, Heb. vii. 15. Here the phrase is used after the Hebrew manner, for the adverb *similiter, like*, namely, like to us. Not unfitly therefore, for sense, is it here translated *like as we.* Christ was tempted as we are tempted, in that he assumed the nature of our infirmities, and thereby made himself subject to the infirmities of our nature. Thus was he made like us, and that in all things, as is shewed Chap. ii. 17, Sec. 68, 69.

This the apostle doth here thus distinctly set down, to assure us that Christ hath compassion on us, and will succour and support us in all our infirmities and distresses. See Chap. ii. 18, Sec. 186.

Sec. 91. *Of Christ's being without sin.*

To prevent a cavil against the foresaid truth, that Christ was ' in all things tempted as we are,' the apostle addeth this exception or limitation, yet χωρὶς ἁμαρτίας, *without sin.* Though Christ might be tempted to sin, yet could no sin seize upon him. See Chap. ix. 14, Sec. 80.

The purity of Christ is set out negatively, thus, *without sin*, to demonstrate the point more clearly and fully. For such as are just and holy, Mark vi. 20, righteous and blameless, Luke i. 6, may have sin in them ; for the regeneration of men is not perfect in this world, but to be without sin is to be perfectly pure, for sin only polluteth and defileth a man. Christ, then, is here set forth to be light, in whom is no darkness ; to be perfectly pure. There was no corruption within him, no speck or spot without him. This was prefigured by the quality of the sacrifices, which, under the law, were to be offered up as a type of him.

In general, every sacrifice was to be ' without blemish,' Lev. i. 10.

In particular, the paschal lamb, which was an especial type of Christ, was to be without blemish, Exod. xii. 5 ; and the red cow, which was a like special type, was to be ' without spot, and without blemish,' Num. xix. 2. The perfection of Christ's purity is more fully set forth under the legal sacrifice by these inhibitions, that they might not be blind, nor lame, nor sick, Mal. i. 8. That which was blind wanted a member ; that which was lame was defective in what it had ; that which was sick was inwardly infected. By these negatives is implied that the sacrifice should be sound within, and full in all the parts, and perfect in those which it had. Thus it set forth the inward sincerity of Christ, the outward integrity of all parts of obedience, and the perfection of everything that he did. In reference to the sacrifice under the law, Christ is styled ' a lamb without blemish, and without spot,' 1 Peter ii. 19.

As legal sacrifices, so priests also did set out the integrity of Christ ; for they were to have no blemish, Lev. xxi. 17, 18 ; and the high priest was to carry this title, ' Holiness to the Lord,' Exod. xxviii. 36.

The prophets also foretold as much, and that both negatively, thus, ' He had done no violence, neither was any deceit in his mouth,' Isa. liii. 9 ; and affirmatively, thus, ' The Spirit of the Lord shall rest upon him, the Spirit of wisdom,' &c., Isa. xi. 2, &c.

In these respects he is styled 'just,' Zech. ix. 9 ; the ' branch of righteousness,' Jer. xxxiii. 15 ; ' the Lord our righteousness,' Jer. xxxiii. 16 ; ' the holy of holiest,' Dan. ix. 24.

In the New Testament this is more plentifully and distinctly set forth in his conception, birth, and whole course of life, and thereupon called 'that holy thing,' Luke i. 35, and the 'just one,' Acts xxii. 14.

Obj. Sin is natural, John iii. 6, Ps. li. 5, Job xiv. 4.

Ans. 1. Sin is not essentially natural; it is only an accident.

2. It is an inseparable accident to such as come from man by man in the ordinary course of nature; yet not so but that God can sever this accident, and not destroy the nature.

3. Though Christ came *from* man, yet he came not *by* man. He was conceived by the Holy Ghost, Mat. i. 20.

Obj. 2. Christ was in the loins of Adam, and thereupon guilty of Adam's sin.

Ans. 1. The proposition may be denied if Adam be considered as a public person representing others, and receiving or losing for them. For Christ was himself another public person and root, as is evident by these phrases, 'the first Adam,' 'the last Adam;' 'the first man,' 'the second man,' 1 Cor. xv. 45, 47. In this respect Adam is styled the *figure* of Christ, Rom. v. 14. As Adam was a head and a root, so was Christ. If Adam had not fallen, Christ had not been born.

2. The consequence may also be denied; if the proposition be meant of that common matter from whence all men came; for though the matter of Christ's body were from Adam, yet it was not by natural generation, but by a supernatural operation of the Holy Ghost.

As there was no original sin in Christ, so nor actual. Not inward, for 'he knew no sin,' 2 Cor. v. 21. Not outward, for not in speech: 'no guile was found in his mouth,' 1 Peter ii. 22. Nor in deed, for he challenged his adversaries if they could impeach him of any blame. And when the devil himself sifted him, he found nothing in him, John xiv. 30; for he loved the Lord with all his heart, &c., and his neighbour as himself, and therein fulfilled the whole law, and so transgressed no part thereof.

As for Christ, it was sufficient that he took man's nature. He needed not to take his corruption.

This which the apostle here cites as a prerogative of Christ, discovers the dotage of papists about the conception of the virgin Mary without original sin. She was conceived by natural propagation, and so had sin conveyed into her. Had she had no original sin, she could have had no actual sin. If no actual sin, why was she reproved by Christ? Luke ii. 49, John ii. 4. If she had had no sin, she had needed no Saviour nor offering for sin, yet she acknowledged Christ her Saviour, Luke i. 47, and carried a pair of turtle doves for her offering, Luke ii. 24.

Christ was pure without sin upon these grounds:

1. That his human nature might be fit to be united to the divine nature.

2. That he might be a sufficient Saviour of others. 'For such an high priest became us, who is holy,' set apart by God for that function; 'harmless,' without actual sin, having never done harm nor wrong to God or man; 'undefiled,' free from original corruption; 'separate from sinners,' exempt from the common guilt of Adam's sin under which all men lie, Heb. vii. 26.

3. That 'we might be made the righteousness of God in him,' 2 Cor. v. 21, which he could not have been if he had not been without sin.

4. That we might be saved, and yet the law not frustrate, Rom. viii. 3, and x. 4.

5. That Satan might have nothing to object against him.

6. That death, grave, and devil might lose their power by seizing on him that was without sin.

1. The foresaid purity of Christ, to be without sin, puts a difference betwixt Christ and other priests, who 'offered for themselves, and for the errors of the people,' Heb. ix. 7; but Christ, 'being without sin,' offered not for himself.

2. It hence appeareth that no other man could have been a sufficient priest; for 'there is none righteous, no, not one.' 'All have sinned,' Rom. iii. 10, 23.

3. This affordeth much comfort to us against our manifold sins; for when we appear before God, he beholds us in our surety. God's eye is especially cast upon him who is 'without sin.'

4. This may be a good incitement unto us to cleanse ourselves from all sin, as far as possibly we can, that we may be like unto him. 'Every man that hath hope in Christ purifieth himself, even as he is pure,' 1 John iii. 3. Christ was free from original corruption. We must labour to subdue it in us, Eph. iv. 20–22. Christ knew no sin within him. We ought to be so circumspect over our inward disposition as in truth to say, 'I know nothing by myself,' 1 Cor. iv. 4. There was no guile found in Christ's mouth. We ought to 'put away lying, and speak every man truth with his neighbour,' Eph. iv. 25. Christ did not evil. We ought to 'abhor that which is evil, and to cleave to that which is good,' Rom. xii. 9.

Sec. 92. *Of the inference of the 16th verse.*

Ver. 16. *Let us therefore come boldly unto the throne of grace, that we may obtain mercy, and find grace to help in time of need.*

In this verse is laid down a second use of Christ's priesthood. The former was to 'hold fast our profession,' ver. 14. This is to 'approach to the throne of grace.' Both of them are brought in with this usual particle of reference, *therefore.*

This latter is inferred both upon the dignity and also upon the infirmities of Christ; the former especially upon his dignity. This shews Christ's readiness; that his ableness to help. Where these two concur, will and power, no question need be made of any needful succour. Well did the leper which came to Christ thus join them together, 'Lord, if thou wilt, thou canst make me clean,' Mat. viii. 2. Both these must be known, believed, and called to mind, when we go to God.

From this inference it may be inferred that without such a priest as Christ is, there is no access to God. If we must *therefore* go to God because we have such a priest, it followeth that without such a priest we cannot go to God. See Chap. ii. 17, Sec. 179.

The compound verb προσερχώμεθα, translated *come unto*, ariseth from the same simple verb, ἔρχομαι, that that other word, διεληλυθότα, did, which is translated *passed into*, ver. 14, Sec. 85.

It in general implieth an act on our part, which testifieth our endeavour after that which we desire. Hereof see ver. 11, Sec. 63.

Sec. 93. *Of boldness in going to God.*

The manner of going to God is thus expressed, *boldly*: word for word, μετὰ παῤῥησίας, *with boldness*, or confidence. Of this word, see Chap. iii. ver. 6, Sec. 61.

It is here opposed to distrustfulness and fearfulness. According to the notation of the original word, it implieth a free uttering of a man's whole mind, and craving whatsoever may and ought to be asked of God.

This is indeed a great privilege, but yet no other than what we may through Christ, our great high priest, lay claim unto, and in all our wants freely and warrantably use.

The main point is implied under these phrases, 'ask, seek, knock,' Mat. vii. 7; 'open thy mouth wide,' Ps. lxxxi. 10; especially under these qualifications, 'draw near in full assurance of faith,' Heb. x. 22; 'ask in faith, nothing wavering,' James i. 6. These phrases import such cheerfulness and confidence as may remove fear and dread of wrath and vengeance, and make us without staggering rest upon God's gracious accepting our persons and granting our desires. For Christ our priest hath done to the full whatsoever is requisite to satisfy justice, pacify wrath, procure favour, and obtain acceptance; on which grounds we may well go to God with an holy boldness and confidence. See more hereof, Chap. iii. 6, Sec. 61 in the end.

Sec. 94. *Of the throne of grace.*

The place whither we are exhorted to come is said to be a 'throne of grace.' A *throne* is a chair of state, or seat of majesty. See Chap. i. 8, Sec. 106. This is here metonymically applied to God, to set out his glorious majesty.

It is styled a throne *of grace*, because God's gracious and free favour doth there accompany his glorious majesty. Majesty and mercy do there meet together. This was under the law typified by the ark. At each end thereof was an angel, to set out God's glorious majesty. The cover of it is styled a 'mercy-seat,' Exodus xxv. 17, 18.

Of grace put for God's favour, see Chap. ii. 9, Sec. 78.

The place of our approaching to God being a throne of grace, it becomes us in approaching to him duly to consider his majesty and mercy, his greatness and goodness, and for this end to meditate on his glorious attributes and great works, which set forth his glory and majesty, and also to call to mind his promises, which declare his grace and mercy. See *The Guide to go to God*, or *Explanation of the Lord's Prayer*, on the preface, secs. 4, 6.

Sec. 95. *Of good to ourselves gotten by going to the throne of grace.*

To encourage us to go to the throne of grace, and that with boldness, the apostle addeth the end of approaching thereunto, which is in general our own good, 'that we may obtain,' &c. So as advantage to ourselves may be expected from our access to God; we may be sure not to lose our labour. 'If we ask, we shall receive; if seek, find; if knock, it shall be opened unto us,' Mat. vii. 7. 'Open thy mouth wide,' saith the Lord, 'and I will fill it,' Ps. lxxxi. 10. 'Thou, Lord, hast not forsaken them that seek thee,' Ps. ix. 10.

Obj. 1. 'They shall call upon me, but I will not hear; they shall seek me early, but they shall not find me,' Prov. i. 28.

Ans. That is spoken to despisers of God, who only in their extremities, to serve their own turn, call on God.

Obj. 2. Though Moses and Samuel stood before God, he would not hear them, Jer. xv. 1.

Ans. Though he would not hear them for a rebellious people, yet he would hear them for themselves.

Obj. 3. God heard not Paul praying for himself, 2 Cor. xii. 8.

Ans. Though God did not at the present grant the particular thing desired, which was to remove the temptation, yet he granted grace sufficient for him to withstand the temptation, which was equivalent.

Obj. 4. Christ prayed that the cup might pass from him, Mat. xxvi. 39, but it did not pass.

Ans. 1. He did not simply pray to have it clean pass away, but with submission to his Father's will.

2. 'He was heard in that he feared,' Heb. v. 7. He was supported and enabled to pass through all that was laid upon him.

To conclude. Saints well know what God hath absolutely promised, answerably they frame their petitions, as Daniel ix. 2, 3, &c.

Other things they pray for with submission to the will of God, 2 Sam. xv. 26; Mark i. 40; Mat. xxvi. 39.

God's granting the warrantable desires of his servants is a strong motive to 'go boldly to the throne of grace.' Many beggars are importunate suitors to men, yet oft in vain; so petitioners to kings, parliaments, judges, and other great ones. Believers may be sure to obtain their desire of God, therefore they may and must go to the throne of grace in faith, Mark xi. 24; James i. 6. We lose much for want of faith.

Sec. 96. *Of mercy and grace, receiving and finding.*

The benefits to be expected from our approach to the throne of grace are set down under these two words, *mercy, grace.* They are here metonymically put for all the effects of mercy and grace, even for whatsoever God in mercy and grace seeth meet to bestow on them that come to him; for mercy and grace are the cause of all.

Mercy (ἔλεος) hath particular reference to man's misery and wretchedness, so it implieth pity and compassion. See Chap. ii. 17, Sec. 176.

Grace (χάρις) hath reference to man's unworthiness, so as it implieth the free will of God; that what God doth he doth for his own sake, of his own gracious good pleasure, without any desert on man's part. For God's grace and man's works are diametrically opposed one to another, Rom. xi. 5. Of God's grace see Chap. ii. 9, Sec. 78.

As mercy and grace in general intend the same thing (namely, the fountain of all good and the free manner of conferring the same), so these two words *obtain, find,* imply the same thing, which is to be made partakers of such and such blessings.

The former Greek word, λαμβάνειν, signifieth to *take* or *receive,* Heb. v. 4, and vii. 5. It hath reference to *offering* or *giving* a thing, Mat. xx. 8, 9, and xxv. 15, 16. See Chap. vii. 5, Sec. 37.

The other word, εὑρίσκειν, *find,* hath reference to *seeking,* as Mat. vii. 7, 8. To be found without seeking is counted extraordinary, Isa. lxv. 1, or accidental and casual, as Acts v. 10.

The former presupposeth an offer or gift on God's part, whereupon we may be bold to take and receive.

The other implieth an act on our part, whereupon we may be sure to find, Luke xi. 9, 10.

The Greek word is also translated to *obtain,* Chap. ix. 12.

Sec. 97. *Of mercy and grace the ground of all good.*

The foresaid description of the benefit obtained by going to the throne of grace (in these words, to 'obtain mercy and find grace') shews that mercy and grace are the ground of all that good which we can expect from God. Therefore the apostles use to join them together in their salutations, wherein they desire all good for those to whom they write, thus: 'Grace and mercy from God,' &c., 1 Tim. i. 2; 2 Tim. i. 2; Titus i. 4; 2 John 3. All saints in all ages have acknowledged and pleaded this in their addresses to God, Num. xiv. 18, 19; Ps. li. 1; Daniel ix. 18.

There is nothing out of God which can move him to any thing. It must therefore be his grace and mercy that moves him to do good to man; the rather because man is in himself most miserable through sin, and in that respect a fit object of mercy; and withal most unworthy of the least good, so as free grace must needs come in to do him good. There is nothing in man to deserve, or any way procure, good from God.

Great is the pride of our adversaries the papists, who too too audaciously plead their own merits before God. Adam in his innocency could merit nothing of God, all that he could do was but duty. Should the glorious angels conceive any merit in what they did, they would stain their glorious works, and make themselves devils thereby. See *The Whole Armour of God,* treat. ii. part iv. of righteousness, sec. 7, on Eph. vi. 14.

Great also is the folly of those that trust to the supererogatory works of others, as if any man were able to do more than he is bound to do, or more than the law requires. This is an higher degree of presumption than the former.

No marvel that neither the one nor the other receive any fruit of mercy and grace. For by the conceit of merit and supererogation, mercy and grace are made null to them.

Considering mercy and grace are the ground of all hope, let us take due notice thereof; and as we cast one eye on our wretchedness and unworthiness, so let us cast another eye on God's mercy and grace, that by our wretchedness we be not discouraged from approaching to the throne of grace.

This brought the publican thither, who said, 'God be merciful to me a sinner,' Luke xviii. 13.

Of God's grace, see more, Chap. ii. 9, Sec. 78.

Sec. 98. *Of God's readiness to afford succour.*

A particular blessing arising from God's mercy and grace is thus expressed, 'to help in time of need.' The word βοήθεια, translated *help,* is a noun; for perspicuity's sake it may be thus translated, *for help,* (εἰς βοήθειαν.)

Of the emphasis of the Greek word translated *help,* see Chap. ii. 18, Sec. 184.

This word implieth a readiness in God to afford succour. God, according to the notation of the Greek word, is ready to run at the cry of his children to succour them.

He is said to 'ride upon the heavens for their help,' Deut. xxxiii. 26. God himself renders this reason of succouring his people in Egypt, 'I have heard their cry,' Exod. iii. 7. In this respect God is resembled to parents, Ps. ciii. 13, Isa. lxvi. 13, who use to run when they hear their child cry. Yea, God in pity and compassion is preferred before earthly parents, Ps. xxvii. 10, Isa. xlix. 15.

This is a point of admirable comfort to us that are subject to many miseries, and oft forced to cry bitterly. God hath an ear to hear our cries, and an heart to pity us. When Hagar's child cried, and Hagar could not help it, God heard the voice of the lad, and afforded help, Gen. xxi. 16, &c. This is sufficient to keep us from fainting in our distresses.

This also may be a motive to stir us up to cry and call to God in all our distresses. Children in their need will cry to their parents, yet it may be their parents hear them not; or if they hear them, are not able to help them, as Hagar could not help her child, Gen. xxi. 16. But God always hears, even our inward cries, Exod. xiv. 15.

Sec. 99. *Of God's doing good in season.*

This phrase, *in time of need*, is the interpretation of one Greek word, εὔκαιρον, which signifieth *seasonable*. It is translated *convenient*, Mark vi. 21. The substantive, εὐκαιρία, is translated *opportunity*, Mat. xxvi. 16. The adverb εὐκαίρως, *conveniently*, Mark. xiv. 11; and *in season*, 2 Tim. iv. 2.

The word is compounded of a noun, καιρός, that signifieth *season*, and an adverb that in composition signifieth *good*: so as this compound signifieth a *good season*.

The Grecians have two words that in general signify time. But one (χρόνος) useth to be indefinitely put for any kind of time, as Mat. xxv. 19. The other (καιρός) determinately for a season or fit time. It is translated *season*, Mark xii. 2; *due season*, Mat. xxiv. 45; *opportunity*, Gal. vi. 10, Heb. xi. 15. This interpretation, *in due time*, doth give the full sense of the word.

As the Grecians have two words to distinguish time and season, which are both set down together, Acts i. 7, so the Hebrews also have two distinct words: one, עת, *tempus*, for *time* indefinitely, Ps. xxxiv. 1; the other, מועד, *tempus statutum, opportunitas*, for *a set time* or *season*, Gen. i. 14, Hab. ii. 2.

The word here used by the apostle (signifying in the simple use thereof, *a season*, or fit time; and in the composition, *a good season*), gives us to understand, that God affords help in the best time, even the fittest season that can be. All things that God doth, he ordereth in due time and season, especially the succour that he affordeth unto his children. 'He giveth rain in his due season,' Deut. xi. 14. 'He giveth to all their meat in due season,' Ps. cxlv. 15. His saints reap that crop which he giveth 'in due season,' Gal. vi. 9. 'To every thing there is a season,' Eccles. iii. 1.

1. God herein doth much manifest his wisdom. For as in wisdom he made all things, Ps. civ. 24, so most wisely doth he dispose the same.

2. Hereby good things are clearly manifested to be of God; for 'in the mount the Lord shall be seen,' Gen. xxii. 14; that is, in the time of greatest need, and fittest season. To this purpose saith the Lord, 'In an acceptable time have I heard thee, and in a day of salvation have I helped thee,' Isa. xlix. 8.

3. Then will help do most good, when it is afforded in season.

This is a great inducement to wait for a season. God, who is the Lord of times and seasons, Acts i. 7, better knoweth which is the fittest season for succour than we can. Indeed, God oft seemeth long to put off help; but that is to afford help in the fittest season. Ignorance hereof makes many impatient.

Had the Israelites known the season of their deliverance through the Red Sea, they would not have murmured as they did, Exod. xiv. 11, &c. Nor would the king of Israel have blasphemed as he did, 2 Kings vi. 33, if he had understood the season of his deliverance. Men not knowing this, imagine that God hears them not, or regards them not, and hereby they deprive themselves of that good which otherwise they might have. So did Saul, 1 Sam. xiii. 8, 9. God himself is so punctual in observing his season, as he will not suffer it to be prevented or over-slipped. He therefore that believeth will not make haste, Isa. xxviii. 16.

Sec. 100. *Of the resolution of* Heb. iv. 14, 15, 16.

Ver. 14. *Seeing then that we have a great high priest, that is passed into the heavens, Jesus the Son of God, let us hold fast our profession.*

15. *For we have not an high priest which cannot be touched with the feeling of our infirmities; but was in all points tempted like as we are, yet without sin.*

16. *Let us therefore come boldly unto the throne of grace that we may obtain mercy, and find grace to help in time of need.*

The sum of these three verses is a transition from Christ's prophetical to his priestly function.

Hereabout we may observe,

1. The inference of Christ's priesthood on his prophetical office.

2. The substance of his priesthood.

Of the substance there are two parts,

1. A description of the person.

2. A declaration of the duties arising thereupon.

In the description are set down,

1. The function.

2. The person that executeth it.

In setting down the function three points are expressed.

1. The kind of function, *priest*.

2. The excellency of it, *high*.

3. The right which we have to it, in this phrase, *seeing we have*.

The person is illustrated,

1. By his dignity, ver. 14.

2. By his infirmities, ver. 15.

His dignity is manifested,

1. By the place where he is, *he is passed into the heavens*.

2. By his title, *Jesus*.

3. By his relation to God, *the Son of God*.

Upon this dignity of Christ the first duty is inferred. The duty is set out,

1. By an act, *let us hold fast*.

2. By the subject matter thereof, *our profession*.

Christ's infirmities are hinted two ways: 1, negatively; 2, affirmatively.

The negative is doubled to make the stronger affirmative.

The first branch of the negative again expresseth,
1. The kind of function, *priest*.
2. The excellency thereof, *high*.

The second branch sets down,
1. Christ's compassion, *touched with a feeling of*.
2. The object thereof, *our infirmities*.

The affirmative declareth,
1. The evidence of Christ's infirmities.
2. The limitation thereof.

The evidence is,
1. Propounded, in this word, *tempted*.
2. Amplified: 1, by the extent, *in all points*; 2, by the manner, *like as we are*.

The limitation is in this phrase, *yet without sin*.

The other duty arising from Christ's priesthood is set out,
1. By the kind thereof.
2. By the end thereof.

The kind of duty is set out,
1. By an act, *let us come*.
2. By the place, *throne of grace*.
3. By the manner, *boldly*.

The end is, 1, generally propounded; 2, particularly exemplified.

In the general is implied,
1. The ground of all goodness, in two words, *mercy, grace*.
2. The participation thereof in two other words, *obtain, find*.

The exemplification points at the benefit of mercy and grace.

This is set out,
1. By the kind of benefit, *help*.
2. By the seasonableness of it, *in time of need*.

Sec. 101. *Of observations raised out of* Heb. iv. 14–16.

I. *Means of grace are to be improved.* This ariseth from the inference, *then*, ver. 14. See Sec. 82.

II. *Christ is a priest.*

III. *Christ is an high priest.*

IV. *Christ is a great high priest.* These three doctrines are expressed in the text. See Sec. 83.

V. *We have a right to the great high priest.* This phrase, 'seeing that we have,' intends our right. See Sec. 83.

VI. *Heaven is the place where Christ exerciseth his priesthood.* The mention of heaven about this point declares as much. See Sec. 84.

VII. *Nothing could hinder Christ from entering into heaven.* The emphasis of the word translated *passed into* proves this point. See Sec. 85.

VIII. *Saints on earth have communion with Christ in heaven.* This is gathered from the conjunction of this act of ours, *we have*, with Christ's being in heaven. See Sec. 85.

IX. *Our priest is a Saviour.* The title *Jesus* signifieth a Saviour. See Sec. 86.

X. *Our priest is true God.* He is in a proper sense the Son of God. See Sec. 86.

XI. *Professors of the true faith must persevere therein.* This is to 'hold fast our profession.' See Sec. 86.

XII. *Christ's priesthood is the ground of our perseverance.* The inference of the duty upon Christ's priesthood proves this point. See Sec. 86.

XIII. *Christ was subject to infirmities.* This is here taken for grant. See Sec. 89.

XIV. *Christ had a fellow-feeling of our infirmities.* This is here set down with much emphasis by doubling the negative. See Sec. 88.

XV. *Christ's fellow-feeling of our infirmities should make us rather hold fast our profession.* This is here brought in as a reason thereof. See Sec. 87.

XVI. *Christ was tempted.* This is here plainly expressed. See Sec. 90.

XVII. *Christ was subject to all sorts of temptations.* This phrase, *in all points*, cleareth this point. See Sec. 90.

XVIII. *Christ was subject to such temptations as we are.* This phrase, *like as we*, declares as much. See Sec. 90.

XIX. *Christ was perfectly pure.* He was *without sin*. See Sec. 91.

XX. *Without such a priest as Christ, there is no access to God.* The inference of this duty of going to God on the description of Christ's priesthood implies this doctrine. See Sec. 92.

XXI. *In Christ we may and must go unto God.* This is the main duty here required. See Sec. 92.

XXII. *Believers may with confidence go to God.* This word *boldly* intends as much. See Sec. 93.

XXIII. *God, to whom we go, is a King of majesty.* He sits on a *throne*. See Sec. 94.

XXIV. *God's majesty is mixed with mercy.* His throne is a *throne of grace*. See Sec. 94.

XXV. *The benefit of going to God redounds to us.* This phrase, *that we may obtain*, imports our benefit. See Sec. 95.

XXVI. *Mercy moves God to succour us in our misery.* The object of mercy is misery. See Sec. 96.

XXVII. *The good which God affordeth is of his own good pleasure.* This word *grace* sets out God's good pleasure. See Sec. 96.

XXVIII. *God's mercy and grace are the ground of all our help.* They are here set down so to be. See Sec. 97.

XXIX. *God is ready to help.* This is gathered from the notation of the Greek word translated *help*. See Sec. 98.

XXX. *God's help is most seasonable.* The Greek word translated, *in time of need*, signifieth *seasonable*. See Sec. 99.

Hebrews 5

Sec. 1. *Of the analysis of* Heb. v.

That which the apostle had in general delivered about Christ's priesthood in the three last verses in the former chapter, he here beginneth to exemplify. This he doth very copiously from the beginning of this chapter to the 22d verse of the 10th chapter.

The main scope of this and the next chapter is to prepare the Hebrews to a diligent heeding of that which he intended to deliver about Christ's priesthood. For this end,

1. He layeth down the sum of that function, from the first to the eleventh verse.

2. He taxeth their non-proficiency in Christ's school from ver. 11 to the end.

In laying down the foresaid sum,

1, He propounds; 2, he proves the point.

He propounds it in a description of a priest, verses 1, 2.

He proves it two ways:

1. By an exemplification of the several branches of the description in legal priests.

2. By an application of the said branches to Christ himself.

Six points in the description are exemplified.

1. That a high priest is *taken from among men*.
2. That he is *ordained*.
3. That he is *for men*.
4. That he is *for men in things appertaining to God*.
5. That he is *to offer gifts*, &c.
6. That he must be one that *can have compassion*, &c.

In the exemplification these six points are proved, though not in that order:

1. He shews that the legal priests might be compassionate, in that they themselves were *compassed with infirmities*, ver. 2.
2. That they *offered* sacrifices, ver. 3.
3. That they offered them *for the people*, ver. 3.
4. That they were ordained, ver. 4.
5. That they were *in things pertaining to God*. This is implied by their offering for sins, ver. 4; for none can forgive sins but God only.
6. The mention of Aaron, ver. 4, sheweth that a legal priest was taken from among men, *so was Aaron*.

In the application of these points to Christ is shewed,

1. That Christ was *called*, vers. 5, 6.
2. That he was a true man, taken from among men. The mentioning of *the days of his flesh*, ver. 7, intimates as much.
3. That he was for man, even such as obey him, ver. 9.
4. That he had compassion. This is implied under his *crying and tears*, ver. 7.
5. That he offered is evident by his prayers and supplications, which were as incense offered. The mention of his death, ver. 7, implieth the sacrifice of himself, together with the things which he suffered, ver. 8.

6. That he was in things pertaining to God is clear, for he offered up prayers *to him that was able to save him from death*, and this was God his Father.

In this application, as the apostle makes a resemblance betwixt Christ and other priests, so in every of the branches he sheweth that Christ was much more excellent than they.

1. Christ was called after a more excellent order of priesthood, namely, *the order of Melchisedec*, vers. 6, 10, and that by an oath, Chap. vii. 21.

2. Christ was not only a true man, but also true God, even *the Son of God*, ver. 8. He was God-man, both natures united in one person.

3. He was *for men*, to obtain salvation for them, which no other priest could do.

4. Christ manifested more compassion than ever any priest, in that he himself suffered for us, ver. 8, and made strong cries with tears, ver. 7.

5. The sacrifice which Christ offered, being his own body, was more excellent than any sacrifice under the law, ver. 9.

6. He was in things pertaining to God after a more excellent manner, in that he became thereby *the author of eternal salvation*, ver. 9.

The apostle's taxation of the Hebrews' non-proficiency is,

1. Generally hinted, *seeing ye are dull of hearing*, ver. 11.

2. Particularly amplified, by two resemblances.

One taken from catechists, who were to be instructed in the first rudiments, ver. 12.

The other from babes, which must be fed with milk, ver. 12.

These resemblances are,

1. Propounded, ver. 12.
2. Amplified.

The amplification is by manifesting a difference betwixt babes and strong men.

Babes are *unskilful in the word of righteousness*, ver. 13.

Strong men *have their senses exercised to discern both good and evil*, ver. 14.

Sec. 2. *Of a priest being taken from among men.*

Ver. 1. *For every high priest taken from among men is ordained for men in things pertaining to God, that he may offer both gifts and sacrifices for sins.*

The description of an high priest is here set down, to demonstrate the truth of that which in the latter end of the former chapter was delivered concerning Christ's being an high priest. It is therefore inferred by this causal particle *for;* as if the apostle had said, I may well avouch that Christ is our high priest, *for* all the essential pains[1] of an high priest belong to him, so as Christ to the full underwent whatsoever was meet to be undergone by an high priest; for he came to save to the uttermost, Heb. vii. 25, and to leave nothing that he undertook to be finished by another.

Of a priest, and of an high priest, see Chap. ii. 17, Sec. 172.

The first branch in the description of an high priest is, that he is 'taken from among men;' that is, he being a man himself, of the same nature that others are, is taken out of the society of men, not out of the society of angels or of other spirits.

Or, according to the proper signification of the Greek preposition, it may be thus translated, ἐξ ἀνθρώπων, *out of man,* that is, out of the stock where others are, being of the same nature with others. In this sense all are said to be ἐξ ἑνὸς, *of one,* and to be 'partakers of flesh and blood,' Chap. ii. 11, Sec. 164, and ver. 14, Sec. 189.

The former English phrase, *from among men,* may intend as much. Thus it is said of the paschal lamb or kid, 'Ye shall take it out from the sheep, or from the goats,' Exod. xii. 5.

To shew that this holds true of all sorts of priests, —extraordinary, as Melchisedec; ordinary, as Aaron and his posterity; typical, as the legal priests; and the only true priest, Jesus Christ,—the apostle premiseth this general particle πᾶς, *every.* Hence it appeareth that no person can be a fit priest for men but a son of man, out of the same nature and mould, of the same fellowship and society. When God first ordained priests, he thus said, 'Take Aaron and his sons from among the children of Israel,' Exodus xxviii. 1.

1. Priests are in special manner for men. They stand betwixt God and men, and therefore it is requisite that they be men. For this end Christ himself was made man, chap. ii. 17.

2. It becomes priests to have compassion on their brethren; therefore they must be of the stock of mankind. For this end also was Christ of man, 'that he might be a merciful high priest,' chap. ii. 17.

1. This may well be pressed against those heretics that deny the human nature of Christ, or deny that he took that nature from the virgin Mary, but say he brought it from heaven. If so, then were he no true priest. Of these heretics, see Chap. ii. 14, Sec. 140. The like may be pressed against those who make angels mediators, and in that respect priests; for it belongs to the office of a priest to be a mediator betwixt God and man. This qualification of a priest, to be 'from among men,' cuts off all such spirits from that office; neither is there any clause of Scripture that makes for them in this case.

2. This instructs us in the great respect of God to man, and that two ways:

[1] Qu. 'points'?—ED.

(1.) In that he so beheld man's weakness as to afford unto him such a priest as he might endure. If Christ, only as God, had been our mediator, the brightness of his glory would have confounded us. The appearance of angels oft affrighted sons of men, though they appeared in man's shape. Instance the case of Gideon and Manoah, Judges vi. 22, and xiii. 22. The like is noted of Zacharias, Luke i. 12.

(2.) In that God did overlook our unworthiness. For though we had sinned, and thereby our nature was odious in his sight, and a fit object for his wrath, yet he made this very nature a means of mediation and reconciliation: 1, typically, in the legal priests; then truly in his own Son, a Son of man, Jesus Christ.

3. This is a matter of great comfort and encouragement to us children of men; for we may well infer, that he who hath ordained a priest from among men, will assuredly accept of us in that priest, and will not reject our persons or prayers. As Manoah's wife said to her husband, 'If the Lord were pleased to kill us, he would not have accepted a burnt-offering,' Judges xiii. 23, so we may say, If the Lord would condemn us all, he would not take a priest from among us to be for us in things pertaining to God.

Sec. 3. *Of priests being ordained.*

The second branch of the description of a priest is, that he is ordained.

Of the diverse acceptions of the Greek word καθίσταται, translated *ordained,* see Chap. ii. 7, Sec. 61. Here it may be taken actively (the verb being taken in the middle voice). Thus he may be said to order things which pertain to God. Our English takes it passively. Both acceptions may in general intend the same thing.

In the passive signification it implieth that priests must be ordained or appointed; they must be set apart to their function; they must have a call and warrant. Thus is this word used by Christ, where he said, 'Who made' or appointed 'me a judge?' Luke xii. 14. He would not take upon him that office whereunto he was not deputed. This word is also thus used of Pharaoh: 'He made' or appointed 'Joseph governor over Egypt,' Acts vii. 10. It is applied to ordaining elders, Titus i. 5; yea, and to making priests, Heb. vii. 28, so as they only are true priests who are lawfully called thereto. Of priests, this is expressly proved, ver. 4. Of the calling or ordaining of other ministers, see Chap. iii. 2, Secs. 34, 35.

Sec. 4. *Of the high priest's being for men.*

The third branch of the description of an high priest is, that he is *for men;* for their use, for their good.

The phrase translated *for* is used in a double sense:

1. It being joined with an accusative case, sig-

nifieth *above*; as, 'The disciple is not ὑπὲρ τὸν διδάσκαλον, *above his master*, nor the servant *above* his lord,' Mat. x. 24.

2. Joined with a genitive case, it importeth the end or good of a thing; as where Christ saith of his body given, and of his blood shed, ὑπὲρ ὑμῶν, *for you*, Luke xxii. 19, 20. So here, God appointed an high priest for the good of men. This may be exemplified in all the parts of his function. The gifts, sacrifices, incense, and all manner of oblations which he offered, were for the good of the people; so was his entering into the holy place, and carrying their names before the mercy-seat, together with other sacred duties.

The grounds hereof were man's need, and God's tender respect to man.

1. This sheweth, that they who sought the priesthood for their own advancement and advantage, clean perverted the end thereof; as they did against whom the prophets much cried out, and they who, in Christ's and in his apostles' time, thrust themselves into that function, though they were not of the posterity of Aaron. Likewise they who abused the priesthood for their own emolument, as the sons of Eli, 1 Sam. ii. 13; and Eliashib, Neh. xiii. 4, &c.

This may be applied to false prophets, false ministers of the gospel, and to such prophets and ministers as do all for filthy lucre's sake.

2. This warranteth us to apply what Christ did as an high priest to ourselves; for he was an high priest for men, even for their salvation.

3. This sheweth, that who have charge over others must seek their spiritual good. See Chap. vii. 27, Sec. 114.

Sec. 5. *Of an high priest's performing things pertaining to God.*

The fourth branch of an high priest's description is, that he be *in things pertaining to God*; word for word, τὰ πρὸς τὸν Θεὸν, *things that are to God*. Thus, by virtue of his office, he was a mediator betwixt God and man. This he was in a double respect:

1. In those things wherein people had to do with God.

2. In those things wherein God had to do with the people.

In the former, he represented the people.

In the latter, he stood in God's room.

As representing the people, he bare their names upon his breast, and approached to the mercy-seat; he offered all manner of sacrifices, and made intercession.

In God's room he heard and judged causes; he declared who were clean and unclean, and blessed the people.

All these, and other like points of mediation betwixt God and man, the legal priests did, as types of Jesus Christ the true priest.

1. This gives intimation of the wretched and woful estate of man by nature, who by himself can have no communion with God, nor do things pertaining to God.

2. This gives us evidence of the absolute necessity of a priest, and of the great mercy of God to man in affording his Son to be that priest.

Sec. 6. *Of priests offering to God.*

The fifth branch of an high priest's description is, ἵνα προσφέρῃ, *that he may offer*, &c. This is added as the end of all the former branches. Something, therefore, must be offered to God by those that have access to him. This is somewhat more expressly set down in this phrase, 'Every high priest is ordained to offer gifts and sacrifices,' Heb. viii. 3.

This property of a priest's offering concerns that which is declared, Sec. 3, of the calling of him that is for others in things pertaining to God. Uzziah, though a king, was struck with leprosy, for presuming to offer incense without a calling, 2 Chron. xxvi. 16. A great part of Uzziah's sin consisted in this, that he meddled with that which was without his calling, 2 Chron. xiii. 9, 10.

A special part of the priest's function was to offer.

The Greek word προσφέρειν, *afferre et offerre*, translated *offer*, is a compound, and properly signifieth *to bring to;* and it is so translated, Mark x. 13, Luke xii. 11.

There is another compound ἀναφέρειν, *sustollere*, and signifieth to *offer up*, Heb. vii. 27, and ix. 28, and xiii. 15, James ii. 21, 1 Peter ii. 5.

Gifts and sacrifices under the law were brought to God, and dedicated to him, in which respect this compound word is here fitly used. And the gifts which were brought and offered to God are called προσφοραί, *offerings*, Chap. x. 5, Sec. 16.

It is frequently translated *offer*. For offering presupposeth a bringing to one.

As for the gifts and sacrifices here intended, they were brought to God.

It is said of the princes of Israel, that they 'brought their offering before the Lord,' Num. vii. 3, and of the captains that overcame the Midianites, that 'they brought an oblation for the Lord, Num. xxxi. 50. These and other like gifts the priest offered unto the Lord.

Quest. Doth God stand in need of anything that man can give?

Ans. That which Elihu said of man's righteousness, Job xxxvii. 7; and Eliphaz of the fruit or profit thereof, Job xxii. 3, may much more be applied to the gifts and sacrifices which were offered to God. 'What givest thou to him? or what receiveth he of thine hand? Is it any pleasure to the Almighty? or is it gain to him' that thou dost this and that?

Of the Lord it is said, 'Sacrifice and offering thou didst not desire,' Ps. xl. 6. Yea, the Lord himself saith, 'I will take no bullock out of thy house,' &c.,

Ps. l. 9. But for the men's sake did the Lord accept gifts and sacrifices offered to him, and that on these grounds.

1. To shew that he acknowledged them for his people, and in testimony thereof accepted presents from them.
2. To gain proof of their obedience, faith, and thankfulness.
3. To prefigure the acceptable gifts and sacrifices, which our great high priest offereth to him.

Of giving to God, see *The Saints' Sacrifice* on Ps. cxvi. 17, Sec. 113.

1. This prerogative of priests *to bring to God,* sheweth one main difference betwixt priests and prophets. Priests bring from man to God, prophets bring from God to man. They bring instructions, directions, admonitions, consolations, promises, threatenings, and other like things. Herein also lieth a difference betwixt Christ's priestly and prophetical function. As priest he offered up prayers and supplications, yea, and his own body unto God. As prophet, he 'spake to the world those things which he had heard of his Father,' John viii. 26.
2. The priest's offering what was brought to God, Lev. ii. 2, and v. 8, was a type of Christ's offering whatsoever is acceptable to God. Wherefore, 'Whatsoever ye do, in word or deed, do all in the name of the Lord Jesus,' Col. iii. 17. Especially our spiritual sacrifices of prayers and praises must by him be offered to God. Hereof see *The Whole Armour of God,* on Eph. vi. 18, treat. 3 part 1, secs. 8, 62.

Sec. 7. *Of gifts and sacrifices.*

The things which priests offered are distinguished into two kinds, *gifts, sacrifices.*

Gifts, δῶρα, *dona,* according to the notation of the word,[1] signifieth such things as are given.

Gifts, being distinguished from *sacrifices,* are by some applied to peace-offerings, which were brought to God in way of thankfulness for peace and reconciliation with God; such were the offerings mentioned, Lev. iii.

Others apply them to such oblations as were of things without life. For the Greek word θυσία, translated *sacrifice,* is derived from a verb, θύειν, that signifieth to *kill or slay,* John x. 10, Luke xv. 23. Now, because beasts and fowls offered to God were slain, the verb is used to set out the slaying of a sacrifice, and translated *to sacrifice,* 1 Cor. v. 7, and x. 20, and *to do sacrifice,* Acts xiv. 23, 28, and the word of my text is frequently applied to such sacrifices. Only once mention is made of 'a living sacrifice,' Rom. xii. 1, but metonymically and purposely to distinguish the same from a legal sacrifice that was slain. The verb to *offer up,* applied to such sacrifices, implieth a slaying of them. So much is intended, chap. xi. 17.

[1] δωρέω, act. et δωρέομαι, med. dono, Marc. xv. 45.

The two words being thus distinguished, *gifts* are put for oblations without life and sense, and *sacrifices* for such creatures as were slain.

Under *gifts* may be comprised all those meat-offerings which are prescribed, Lev. chap. ii., and oil, frankincense, and salt mingled therewith; and firstfruits, tithes, and other free-will offerings. All things whatsoever were offered to God by the priest are comprised under these two words, *gifts, sacrifices.* Of the distinct kinds of sacrifices, see *The Saints' Sacrifice* on Ps. cxvi. 17, Sec. 111.

The priests' offering of gifts carrieth a perpetual equity, namely, that gifts be offered by such as are counted priests, as all saints are, Rev. i. 6, and v. 10, and xx. 6.

That they should be priests was of old foretold, Isa. lxvi. 21. They are styled an 'holy priesthood,' a 'royal priesthood,' and that for this very end, to offer up spiritual sacrifices, and to shew forth the praises of God, 1 Peter ii. 5, 9.

The offering of sacrifice gave a visible evidence of the desert of sin, which was death, Rom. vi. 23. For the sacrifice was slain instead of him that brought it; therefore, he was to lay his hand on it, Lev. i. 4, whereby he testified his own guiltiness, and that he deserved to be dealt withal, as the sacrifice was. He also testified his faith in God's preparing that sacrifice, as an atonement for him.

This was a type of Christ, who offered up himself for us, and made reconciliation betwixt God and us.

Sec. 8. *Of sin the end of sacrifices.*

The foresaid end, both of the type and truth, in offering sacrifice, is confirmed by this phrase, *for sins.*

The preposition ὑπέρ here used, and translated *for,* is the very same that was used Sec. 4. In general it here intends the end of a thing; but not, as there, the good of it, unless metonymically the effect be put for the efficient, sins for sinners; as where God saith, 'I will be merciful to their sins,' Heb. viii. 12, that is, to them that have sinned, in pardoning their sins. Thus saith the publican, 'God be merciful to me a sinner,' Luke xviii. 13.

The sacrifice may be said to be for sinners, even for their good, in that it was a means of removing the guilt and punishment thereof.

But this particle *for,* being indefinitely taken for an end, sins may here properly be understood, and sacrifices offered to obtain pardon of sins. Hereupon it is said concerning such an one as had a sacrifice offered up for his sin, 'It shall be forgiven him,' Lev. iv. 35.

If any will extend this end, *for sins,* to offering up of *gifts* also, the end must further be taken in reference to sin pardoned; for which mercy gifts, in testimony of thankfulness, were brought to God, as they who, to testify their thankfulness for God's bringing them out of their bondage into the promised land, brought gifts to be offered to the Lord, Deut. xxvi. 10.

But I take the former sense, of sacrifice offered for pardon of sin, to be most proper to this place.

Hereby is intended that sin is pardonable. All sacrifices for sin, all legal purgings for uncleanness, all prayers for pardon, all promises of pardon, all absolution of sinners, do prove as much.

1. This gives evidence of God's free grace and rich mercy to man, Exod. xxxiv. 7, Isa. xliii. 25.

2. This affords matter of admiration, in that none is like unto God herein, Micah vii. 18.

3. This is a ground of singular comfort, as Christ said to a poor distressed man, 'Son, be of good cheer, thy sins be forgiven thee,' Mat. ix. 2. Assurance of the pardon of sin is the most sovereign ground of comfort that can be.

4. This affords manifold directions, as,

(1.) To be well instructed in the grounds of pardon.
(2.) To consider the need we have thereof.
(3.) To apply it aright unto ourselves.
(4.) To rest thereupon.
(5.) To be watchful against sin for the future, John v. 14, and viii. 11.

See more hereof in my treatise *Of the Sin against the Holy Ghost*, Secs. 5, 6.

Sec. 9. *Of compassion in such as have to do with others in the things of God.*

Ver. 2. *Who can have compassion on the ignorant, and on them that are out of the way; for that he himself also is compassed with infirmities.*

The sixth branch of the description of an high priest is, that he *can have compassion*.

Of the notation of the Greek word μετριοπαθεῖν, translated *have compassion*, and of the Greek word δυνάμενος, translated *can*, how it signifieth a fitness and readiness to do a thing, see Chap. iv. ver. 15, Sec. 88.

From adding this property of an high priest, to have compassion, to the former, about his dealing for men with God, may be inferred that they who are to deal for men, especially about God, must be full of compassion. This the apostle implieth under sundry properties belonging to a servant of the Lord, who must be for men to God, 2 Tim. ii. 24.

1. He 'must not strive.' It is want of compassion that makes men strive or be contentious.

2. He must be 'gentle unto all men.' Gentleness and meekness arise from compassion.

3. He must be 'apt to teach.' None more fit and meet to teach others than men of compassion.

4. He must be 'patient,' ἀνεξίκακος, one ready to bear with the evils and weaknesses of others.

Such an one was Moses, who is said to be 'a man very meek above all the men which were upon the face of the earth,' Num. xii. 2. This language of the apostle Paul, 'My little children, of whom I travail in birth again,' Gal. iv. 19, sheweth him to be a man full of compassion.

All men are subject to many weaknesses and imperfections; yea, in many there is much perverseness, especially about the ways of God. They are as children, prone to provoke them that seek their good, so blind as they cannot discern their own good. If, therefore, they who have to do with them be not, as parents use to be to their children, full of compassion, they will soon cease to seek their good. There is no such means of overcoming evil with goodness as bowels of compassion.

Cruel and hard-hearted men are unfit to be ministers, who are to be for men in things pertaining to God. Ministers oft meet with cases which require much pity and great patience. If they be ready to fret and fume, and in scorn put away such as propound their cases to them, they may send away poor souls comfortless.

Let ministers therefore 'put on bowels of mercy, kindness, humbleness of mind, meekness, long-suffering,' Col. iii. 12. They are as priests for men in things pertaining to God.

That they may do this, let them consider that they with whom they have to do are their own flesh, Isa. lviii. 7; and that 'no man ever yet hated his own flesh, but nourisheth and cherisheth it,' Eph. v. 29. Let them also consider how our Lord pronounceth the merciful to be blessed, and promiseth that 'they shall obtain mercy,' Mat. v. 7.

Sec. 10. *Of ignorance.*

The persons on whom compassion is especially to be had are here specified to be of two sorts: 1, Such as are *ignorant*, τοῖς ἀγνοοῦσι. 2. Such as are *out of the way*.

Of the distinct kinds of ignorance, and of the dangers thereof, and duties thence arising, see Chap. iii. 10, Secs. 111, 112.

In that the ignorant are here brought in, as an instance of such sinners as were to have sacrifices offered up for their sins, the apostle giveth us to understand that ignorance is a sin. It is expressly said, that 'if any soul sin through ignorance, he shall bring a sin-offering,' Num. xv. 27, 28.

1. Ignorance is a transgression of the law of God, for it is contrary to that knowledge which the law requireth; but every transgression is sin, 1 John iii. 4.

2. Ignorance is a defect of that image of God after which God at first created man, for knowledge was a part of that image, Col. iii. 10.

3. Ignorance is an especial branch of that natural corruption which seized upon the principal part of man, namely, his understanding.

4. Ignorance is the cause of many other sins, Gal. iv. 8, 1 Tim. i. 13; therefore it must needs be a sin itself.

5. Judgments are denounced against ignorance as against a sin, Hosea iv. 6, 2 Thes. i. 8.

6. Ignorance is a punishment of other sins, Isa. vi. 10, John xii. 40.

Though ignorance be a sin, yet ignorant persons are here brought in as a fit object of compassion. Christ renders this ground of his praying for the Jews that had a hand in crucifying him, Luke xxiii. 34. And Peter allegeth it as a ground of his tendering mercy unto them, Acts iii. 17.

Ignorance is a spiritual blindness, so as they see not the dangerous course wherein they walk, and in that respect are the more to be pitied.

Sec. 11. *Of having compassion on all sorts of sinners.*

The other sort of persons on whom compassion is to be shewed are thus set out, on *them that are out of the way*, which is the interpretation of one Greek word, πλανωμένοις, which signifieth *to err*, and is so translated Chap. iii. 10.

Some here take it for erring in the will, which implieth wilfulness, which is an aggravation of sin, as was shewed Chap. iii. 10, Secs. 107, 108. Thus it implieth that compassion is to be had not only on the ignorant, but also on the wilful, provided that they be not such as are intended Heb. x. 26.

It will be the safest to take the word *erring*, or *being out of the way*, indefinitely, as if he had said, on the ignorant and on other sinners. God's law is styled a way. To transgress that law is to wander out of the way wherein we should walk, and to err. Thus it sheweth the extent of compassion to all sorts of sinners, ignorant and others; for thus saith the Lord, 'When a man or woman shall commit any sin that men commit, &c., they shall confess their sin,' &c., Num. v. 6.

Every sin is a spiritual malady, and makes a man miserable. Therefore, as Christ had compassion on blind, deaf, dumb, lame, sick, and others affected with any malady or misery, so ought the priest under the law to have compassion on all sorts of sinners. So also should we Christians, whom Christ hath made priests, Rev. i. 6.

This will be an evidence that the compassion we shew is not on by-respects, but for compassion and pity's sake; in tender love to our brother, which will make it to be the more acceptable, and manifest us to be the children of God herein.

Sec. 12. *Of high priests subject to infirmities.*

The reason of the priest's compassion is thus expressed, 'For that he himself also is compassed with infirmity.'

Of the Greek word ἀσθένεια, translated *infirmity*. See Chap. iv. 15, Sec. 89.

The singular number, *infirmity*, is here to be taken indefinitely. An indefinite expression is equivalent to a general, as, 'The wages of *sin* is death,' Rom. vi. 23; that is, of *every sin*. The high priest was subject to every infirmity, not any one excepted, whether natural or personal, whether inward in soul, as disturbed passions, and other the like; or outward in body, as sickness, lameness, and other maladies, whether oppressions and wrongs from men, or afflictions and crosses from God, or whatsoever else may be grievous to man, not sin itself excepted.

The word περίκειται, translated *compassed about*, implieth a necessary subjection to the foresaid infirmities, so as there is no avoiding of them.

I find the Greek word applied to a millstone hung about one's neck, Mark ix. 42, Luke xvii. 2; and to a chain wherewith one is bound, Acts xxviii. 20.

There is no avoiding these. It is also applied to a thick cloud that compasseth one about, Heb. xii. 1.

Here it implieth, that the high priest was at all times, and in all places, as it were, so hampered with infirmities, as he could not be clean freed from them; yea, and that everywhere arose occasions of more and more infirmities.

These words, *he himself also*, carries emphasis. They are to be taken in opposition to other men, on whom he was to have compassion by reason of their infirmities; as if it had been said, not only other men to whom compassion was to be shewed, were subject to infirmities, but even he also, who was to shew compassion.

The infirmity here intended being especially meant of sin, sheweth plainly that the high priest himself was subject, as to other human infirmities, so also to sin. Aaron, one of the best high priests that were, gave many evidences hereof; as his murmuring against Moses, Lev. xii. 1; his rebelling against God's word at the water of Meribah, Num. xx. 21; his making the molten calf, Exod. xxxii. 4: so Eli, who restrained not his son's vileness, 1 Sam. iii. 13; and Abiathar, who conspired with Adonijah, 1 Kings i. 7.

High priests were sons of Adam, their office did not alter their nature, they still continued weak and frail men, subject to the same temptations and passions that others are.

This the Lord suffered, that they might the better know in what need they themselves stood of a sacrifice, of others' prayers, of God's mercy, and of a Saviour; and this the rather, that they should not be too much puffed up with their function. This was further an occasion of making them careful in using means for redressing of sin, and establishing them in grace; and to make them also more ready to bear with others' infirmity, tenderly to deal with them, to comfort them, and to hope the best of them.

That which is here said of high priests may be applied to ministers of the word, even to extraordinary ministers.

Moses manifested his infirmity, Num. xx. 12; so did Peter, Gal. ii. 11.

People therefore had need to pray for their ministers.

But especially they must learn to distinguish betwixt a minister's office and person, and not despise the ministerial function by reason of the minister's infirmities.

Sec. 13. *Of experience of infirmities making fit to succour others.*

This phrase, *for that*, are the interpretation of one Greek particle, ἐπεί, which implieth a reason of a thing, and here sheweth, that sense and experience of infirmity makes one more fit and ready to succour others. This is a reason why Christ made himself subject to human infirmities. Hereof see Chap. ii. 18, Sec. 183, 186.

Sec. 14. *Of the meaning of* Heb. v. 3.

Ver. 3. *And by reason hereof he ought, as for the people, so also for himself, to offer for sins.*

In this verse is set down a consequence following upon the legal priest's infirmity, which is, that he offered for his own sins, as well as for others'.

This phrase, *and by reason hereof*, is in the Greek thus expressed, καὶ διὰ ταύτην, *and for this*. The particle *this* hath reference to the last word of the former verse, ἀσθένειαν; which being repeated, may thus make up the sense, *and for this infirmity*. Or else the word which signifieth cause, αἰτία, may be added, thus, *and for this cause*. Our English hath to the full expressed the sense of the phrase.

This verb ὀφείλει, *he ought*, implieth a necessity of the consequence.

The necessity is double:
1. *Necessitate præcepti*, in regard of God's command, Lev. iv. 3.
2. *Necessitate medii*, in regard of the means sanctified to obtain pardon. For by offering sacrifice, faith in the blood of Christ was testified, which was the only means of taking away sin.

The word of necessity here used, sheweth, that we ought to use the means which make for our own good.

This is to be done as we tender God's honour, and our own happiness.

God's honour is set out, in subjecting ourselves to his ordinance.

Our happiness may be promoted by using the means which make thereto.

This clause, *as for the people*, takes it for grant, that the priest was to offer for the people's sins. For he had said before, that the high priest was 'ordained for men;' namely, for other men than himself, and that he offered for sins, even the sins of others. See ver. 1, Secs. 4 and 8.

By *people* are here meant such as professed the Lord to be their God. See Chap. iv. 9, Sec. 57.

This particle *as* is premised to shew, that he who is a means of others' good, must also take care of his own. Therefore this reddition or application is added, *so also for himself.*

This is again thus testified, 'He offered for himself, and for the errors of the people,' Heb. ix. 7.
1. He hath need of the same means for himself as for others.
2. He may reap good thereby as well as others.

3. There was no other to offer for the high priest but himself. For there was but one high priest at a time.

This may be a good direction for us ministers, to preach to ourselves, to pray for ourselves, to apply to ourselves what we deliver to others. It was Paul's direction to the ministers at Ephesus, to 'take heed unto themselves, and to all the flock,' Acts xx. 28. So also to Timothy, to 'take heed unto himself,' &c.; and he renders this reason, 'Thou shalt both save thyself, and them that hear thee.' He well observed this direction in himself. For thus he saith, 'I keep under my body, and bring it into subjection; lest that by any means, when I have preached to others, I myself should be a castaway,' 1 Cor. ix. 27.

The verb *offer* compriseth sacrifice under it. See ver. 1, Sec. 6.

This last phrase, to *offer for sins*, hath reference to the priest, as well as to the people; and it declareth that the high priest was subject to sin. Sin is comprised under the word *infirmity*, ver. 2, Sec. 12.

This having reference to the high priest under the law, implieth two things, from which Christ the true high priest was exempt.

One was, that he was without sin. Hereof see Chap. iv. 15, Sec. 91.

The other is, that Christ offered not for himself, as the high priest under the law did: 'He needed not daily, as those high priests, to offer up sacrifice, first for himself,' &c., Heb. vii. 27. What Christ did in offering sacrifice, he did for others, who needed it. He himself needed none. Though in many other things he was like the high priest under the law, yet in these two he had a prerogative above them.

Sec. 15. *Of the resolution of* Heb. v. 1–3.

Ver. 1. *For every high priest, taken from among men, is ordained for men in things pertaining to God, that he may offer both gifts and sacrifices for sins,*

Ver. 2. *Who can have compassion on the ignorant, and on them that are out of the way; for that he himself also is compassed with infirmities.*

Ver. 3. *And by reason hereof he ought, as for the people, so also for himself, to offer for sins.*

The sum of these three verses is, a description of an high priest.

Two points are herein observable:
1. The connection of this description with that which was before delivered of Christ's priesthood. The connection is by this causal particle *for*.
2. The parts of the description, which are six.
(1.) The stock whence he is taken. Hereabout is set out,
[1.] A difference of priests, whereof one is an *high priest*.
[2.] A common condition, in this indefinite particle, *every*.
[3.] The kind of stock, *men*.

[4.] His rise from the same, *he is taken from among.*
(2.) His calling, in this word, *is ordained.*
(3.) A general end, *for men,* namely for their good.
(4.) The subject of his function, *things pertaining to God.*
(5) A special end, *to offer,* &c. In setting down this observe,
[1.] The priest's act, to offer.
[2.] The matter thereof.
This is of two sorts,
First, Gifts.
Secondly, Sacrifices.
[3.] The end thereof, *for sins.*
(6.) His qualification. About this is declared,
[1.] The point itself, ver. 2.
[2.] The consequence following, ver. 3.
In setting down the point is manifested,
First, The kind of qualification.
Secondly, The ground thereof.
The kind is propounded in this phrase, *who can have compassion.*
2. Amplified by a double object.
(1.) Them that are *ignorant.*
(2.) Them that are *out of the way.*
The ground of his compassion is his own condition. Herein observe,
1. The emphatical expression of the person, *for that he himself also.*
2. The ground itself, *infirmity.*
3. His subjection thereto, *is compassed with.*
2. The consequence is set out,
1. In general, *for by reason hereof.*
2. In particular, and that,
1. By an act, *to offer,* amplified by the necessity, *he ought.*
2. By the end thereof, *for sins.*
3. By the persons, whose sins they were. These are of two sorts.
1. The people's.
2. His own, *for himself.*
These are amplified by the manner of joining them together, by these particles of comparison, *as, so, also.*

Sec. 16. *Of observations out of* Heb. v. 1–3.
I. *Christ is a true priest.* For the essentials of a priest belong to him. See Sec. 2.
II. *There were divers kinds of priests.* For one was an high priest.
III. *All high priests are of the same mould.* This particle *every* includes all. See Sec. 2.
IV. *High priests were of man's stock.* For they were taken from among men. See Sec. 2.
V. *High priests were appointed to their function.* For they were ordained. See Sec. 3.
VI. *The high priests' function was for man's good.* This is the sense of this phrase, *for men.* See Sec. 4.
VII. *When men have to do with God, they have one to be for them.* See Sec. 5.

VIII. *High priests offer to God.* This is expressly set down. See Sec. 6.
IX. *Gifts may be tendered to God.* This is implied under the mention of gifts. See Sec. 7.
X. *Beasts under the law were slain for men.* These were the sacrifices here mentioned. See Sec. 7.
XI. *Sacrifices were offered for pardon of sin.* This is the meaning of this phrase, *for sins.* See Sec. 8.
XII. *Ministers must be men of compassion.* For priests were ministers, and it is said of them, *they can have compassion.* See Sec. 8.
XIII. *Ignorant persons are to be pitied.* Such are here set down as the object of the priest's compassion. See Sec. 9.
XIV. *Ignorance is a sin.* Sacrifice was to be offered for their sin. See Sec. 10.
XV. *Compassion is to be shewed to all sorts of sinners.* Under this phrase, *them that are out of the way,* all sorts are comprised. See Sec. 11.
XVI. *High priests were subject to all manner of infirmities.* He was *compassed about with infirmity.*
XVII. *Experience of infirmities is a means to make one compassionate.* The inference in this phrase, *for that,* intendeth this point. See Sec. 13.
XVIII. *Means afforded for our good must be used.* This phrase of inference, 'and by reason hereof he ought,' hinteth so much. See Sec. 14.
XIX. *Priests offered sacrifice for others.* This title, God's people, is a note of distinction from priests. See Sec. 14.
XX. *Priests offered sacrifices also for themselves.* This is expressly set down. See Sec. 14.
XXI. *High priests had sins.* For this end they offered sacrifices for themselves. See Sec. 14.

Sec. 17. *Of the meaning of these words, 'no man taketh to himself.'*
Ver. 4. *And no man taketh this honour unto himself, but he that is called of God, as was Aaron.*
The apostle in this verse gives an exemplification of the second branch of the description of an high priest, which is, that he was *ordained.* See Sec. 3.
The exemplification is set down in general terms, thus, *no man,* &c. But it is reduced to a particular instance of *Aaron.*
This general extent of the person, ὀυ τις, *not any,* or *no man,* is to be restrained to men of conscience, who will do nothing but that for which they have good warrant. For Korah sought the priesthood, Num. xvi. 10, though he were not called thereto by God. And sundry others usurped it, Luke iii. 2; Acts xxiii. 5.
That which is here spoken *de facto,* of fact, in this word, λαμβάνει, *taketh,* is intended *de jure,* of right, as if he had said, No man ought to take, or no man hath right to take.
This word, ἑαυτῷ, *to himself,* is also to be extended to a right, as due to himself, and intendeth two things.

1. Taking a thing upon one's own head without gift from another, or without any good warrant, 2 Tim. iv. 3.

2. Taking it to one's advantage, Luke xii. 21. But advantage to one's self is no good plea for an unlawful thing. As we may do no unjust or unwarrantable act for another, so neither for ourselves, Rom. xiv. 7. The righteous law is a rule for ourselves, as well as for others.

Sec. 18. *Of the honour of the high priest's function.*

The high priesthood is here styled an *honour*. For the relative τὴν, *this*, hath reference thereunto.

Of the Greek word τιμὴν, translated *honour*, see Chap ii. 10, Sec. 60.

It here declareth, that the high priest's function was an honourable function, which is thus manifested.

1. The solemn manner of inaugurating, or setting them apart thereto, Exod. xxix. 1.

2. His glorious apparel, Exod. xxviii.

3. The great retinue that attended him; as all sorts of Levites, together with sundry inferior priests, Num. iii. 9, and viii. 19.

4. The liberal provision made for him out of the meat-offerings, sacrifices, first-fruits, tenths, and other oblations, Levit. ii. 3, and v. 13, and vii. 6, Deut. viii. 3.

5. The difficult cases that were referred to him.

6. The obedience that was to be yielded to him.

7. The punishment to be inflicted on such as rebelled against him, Deut. xvii. 8–10, &c.

8. The sacred services which they performed, as to be for men in things pertaining to God; to offer up what was brought to God, ver. 1, and to do other particulars set down, Chap. ii. 11, Sec. 173.

9. In such honourable esteem were high priests, as kings thought them fit matches for their daughters, 2 Chron. xxii. 11.

10. The most principal honour intended under this word *honour* was, that the high priest by virtue of his calling, was a kind of mediator betwixt God and man. For he declared the answer of the Lord to man, and offered up sacrifices to God for man.

Hereby it appeareth, that it is an honourable employment to deal between God and man.

Hence it followeth, that the ministerial function is an honourable function; for ministers of the word are by virtue of their office for God to men, and for men to God.

Sec. 19. *Of the honour of the ministerial function.*

There are many considerations which prove the calling of ministers of the word to be honourable; as their master, their place, their work, their end, their reward.

1. Their Master is the great Lord of heaven and of earth. If it be an honour to be an especial minister of a mortal king, what is it to be the minister of such a Lord?

2. Their place is to be in the room of God, even in his stead, ambassadors for him, 2 Cor. v. 20.

3. Their work is to declare God's counsel, Acts xx. 17.

4. Their end is to perfect the saints, Eph. iv. 12.

5. Their reward is greater than of others, Dan. xii. 3.

Thus hath the Lord honoured this function, that it might be the better respected, and prove more profitable. Ministers, in regard of their persons, are as other men, of like passions with them, and subject to manifold infirmities, which would cause disrespect were it not for the honour of their function.

1. This honour should move ministers to carry themselves worthy thereof; answerably thereto, Eph. iv. 1. The apostle intendeth thus much under this exhortation: 'Let no man despise thy youth,' that is, give no just occasion to any to despise thee; 'but be thou an example,' &c., 1 Tim. iv. 12. Ministers are styled *angels*, that they should be as ready as angels to do God's will. They are *stewards*, and must be faithful, *elders* and grave, *rulers* and just. Thus shall they honour their Master, credit their place, make themselves respected, and their pains regarded.

2. The foresaid honour should move people to respect their ministers; officers of kings use to be respected. This is the rather to be done, because honour done to ministers is done to God himself, and to his Son Christ, John xiii. 20. The Galatians 'received Paul as an angel of God, even as Christ Jesus,' Gal. iv. 14.

3. On the other side, they who despise ministers, despise those whom God hath honoured, yea, and God himself, 1 Sam. viii. 7, Mal. iii. 8.

4. This is a great encouragement to ministers against that ordinary contempt which is cast upon them, even for their calling's sake. No calling ordinarily more contemptible; but we ought not to regard the censure of men in those things which God accounteth honourable.

Sec. 20. *Of God's calling high priests.*

The high priesthood is expressed under this word *honour*, as a reason why no man should 'take it to himself;' yet lest any should thence infer, that whosoever undertook it, presumed upon more than was meet, the apostle addeth this limitation, 'but he that is called.' This conjunction of opposition, ἀλλὰ, *but*, implieth that that may be done by one which may not be done by another.

To be *called*, καλούμενος, in this place signifieth as much as *ordained*, Sec. 3, and *appointed*, Chap. iii. 2, Sec. 22.

This passive, ὁ καλούμενος, 'he that is called,' hath reference to another that calleth him, and it is opposed to the former phrase, of 'taking to himself.' Thus it confirms the second part of the priest's description, that he must be ordained, ver. 1, Sec. 3. It was the brand of Jeroboam's false priests, that whosover would, he consecrated him, and he became one of the priests of the high places, 1 Kings xiii. 33.

That it might be distinctly known who was the first founder of the high priest's function, he is here expressly set down, namely God.

It was God that first said, 'Take Aaron from among the children of Israel, that he may minister unto me in the priest's office,' Exod. xxviii. 1. So as this function was of divine institution, none had power to call and appropriate any to appear for men before God, as the high priest did, but God himself. For this was a point of divine favour and grace.

As the high priest, so all other priests were of divine institution, Exod. xxviii. 1; and as priests, so other ministers of God, who are for men in things pertaining to God, must be called of God. See Chap. iii. 2, Secs. 34, 35.

Sec. 21. *Of Aaron's calling and name.*

The apostle gives a particular instance of an high priest's divine institution in Aaron, and that upon these grounds:

1. Aaron was the first national high priest that was ordained for the whole church in his time. Heads of families were before his time priests for distinct families.

2. All lawful legal priests descended from Aaron, and had that warrant to be priests, that by lineal descent they came from him, Exod. xxix. 9.

3. His calling to the priesthood by God himself is expressly set down, Exod. xxviii. 1.

4. His calling was ratified by a memorable miracle, Num. xvii. 8, 10.

5. They who opposed his calling were punished with a terrible judgment, Num. xvi. 10, 16, 17, 35.

6. This is one special reason why Aaron is called 'The saint of the Lord,' Ps. cvi. 16, because he was first chosen of God, and was anointed by God's appointment to be the first high priest, and the stock of all other priests.

This note of comparison, $\kappa\alpha\theta\acute{\alpha}\pi\varepsilon\rho$, *as*, implieth in general, that others must enter upon their function as Aaron did.

There is a copulative conjunction, $\kappa\alpha\acute{\iota}$, added in the Greek, which implieth some emphasis, and might be thus translated, *even as Aaron.*

This particular instance produced by the apostle as a proof of a general case, giveth evidence, that warrantable rules about some particular cases and persons may be applied to others of like kind, Rom. iv. 23, 24. See Chap. xiii. 5, Sec. 68.

Concerning this name, אהרן, *Aaron* or *Aharon*, it may be derived from a verb, הורו, *doce me*, that in the third active signifieth to teach, Ps. xxvii. 11.

Thus it implieth a teacher, and by a prophetical spirit it might be given him in reference to his calling, by virtue whereof he was to instruct people.

Or Aharon may be derived from a noun, הר, *mons*, that signifieth a *mountain;* and thus also be given him by a like spirit in reference to his priesthood, whereby he was lift up as a mountain above his brethren.

Abraham was the great-grandfather of Levi, and Levi the great-grandfather of Aaron: so as Aaron was the sixth degree from Abraham.

Sec. 22. *Of the resolution of* Heb. v. 4, *and of observations thence arising.*

The sum of this verse is, the high priest's calling. This is,

1. Generally propounded.
2. Particularly exemplified.

Of the general there are two parts:

1. The dignity of the function, in this phrase, *this honour.*

2. The authority which he had for the execution thereof.

The authority is set out two ways: 1, negatively; 2, affirmatively.

In the negative observe,

1. The manner of setting it down, in this general phrase, *no man.*

2. The matter, in this phrase, *taketh to himself.*

In the affirmative observe,

1. The kind of warrant, *called.*
2. The author thereof, *God.*

The exemplification is set out,

1. By a note of comparison, *as.*
2. By the first person that was called, *Aaron.*

Observations.

I. *The high priesthood was an honourable function.* This title *honour*, is put upon it. See Sec. 18.

II. *No man might intrude himself into the high priest's function.* This is the meaning of this phrase, *no man taketh to himself.* See Sec. 17.

III. *He that was called might take that honour on him.* This is implied under this particle of opposition, *but.* See Sec. 20.

IV. *God was the ordainer of the high priest's function.* He is here so expressed to be. See Sec. 20.

These four doctrines may be applied to ministers of the gospel. See Sec. 20.

V. *Particular cases approved in Scripture are directions for other like cases.* So was the particular case of Aaron about entering on the high priesthood. See Sec. 21.

Sec 23. *Of Christ doing what was warrantable.*

Ver. 5. *So also Christ glorified not himself to be made an high priest; but he that said unto him, Thou art my Son, to-day have I begotten thee.*

Here the apostle begins to apply to Christ what he had in general delivered about an high priest.

These two conjunctions, $o\ddot{v}\tau\omega$, $\kappa\alpha\acute{\iota}$, *so, also,* being joined together, are notes of a reddition, or latter part of a comparison, which is the application thereof.

This application may have reference either to the general proposition; thus, as no man taketh this honour unto himself, so also nor Christ: or to the particular instance of Aaron; thus, as Aaron took not to himself that honour, so nor Christ. Both tend to the same end. Christ would not take liberty to himself to do that which was unlawful, or unmeet for others to do. He made himself an example in all manner of good and warrantable matters; but would not be a pattern to bolster up any in an undue course. Thus his pattern is a guide, John xiii. 15.

Sec. 24. *Of Christ's not glorifying himself.*

Because the apostle had before declared the high priesthood to be τιμή, an *honour*, he here sheweth, that to attain thereunto, is to be glorified.

Glory, δόξα, implieth excellency (as was shewed Chap. i. 3, Sec. 19, and Chap. ii. 7, Sec. 6).

To glorify, δοξάζειν, according to the notation of the word, is to make glorious; and so it is translated, 2 Cor. iii. 10.

This is done two ways:

1. By ascribing to one that glory or excellency which is his own, most due to him. Thus creatures may glorify their Creator, Rev. xv. 4.

2. By conferring glory upon one, even such glory as he had not before. Thus the Creator glorifieth creatures, Acts iii. 13, Rom. viii. 30.

These words following, *to be made an high priest*, give evidence that the latter kind of glorifying is here meant; namely, a conferring of that glory upon Christ, which he had not before.

The high priesthood was an honour; for Christ to have taken that to himself, had been to glorify himself by conferring glory and honour upon himself.

This negative, that 'Christ glorified not himself,' giveth proof that Christ arrogated no honour to himself. 'I seek not my own glory,' saith he, John viii. 50. This Christ proveth by many arguments, John v. 31, &c.

Christ would not arrogate honour to himself, but rather wait upon the Father to confer upon him what honour he saw meet, that our faith might be the more strengthened in those things which Christ did on our behalf; and also that he might make himself an example unto us.

Let therefore 'the same mind be in us that was in Christ Jesus,' Philip. ii. 5. Let us not thrust ourselves into any place, before we are called; nor arrogate any honour to ourselves, that belongeth not unto us. We are by nature too prone hereunto. Let magistrates, ministers, and all of all sorts so carry themselves, as it may be truly said of them, They glorified not themselves.

The particular instance whereby this general negative, that 'Christ glorified not himself,' is evidenced, is the high priesthood; for that was an honour, and Christ, by having that conferred on him, was indeed glorified. So much is intended under this particle of opposition, ἀλλά, *but;* as if it had been said, Though Christ glorified not himself by assuming the priesthood to himself, yet he was glorified thereby, by his Father's conferring it upon him.

To make the apostle's meaning more clear, take all these words, 'He that said unto him, Thou art my Son, to-day have I begotten thee,' as a description of the Father; and repeat, ἀπό κοίνου, the word ἐδόξασε, *glorified* (which must needs be here understood), then the sense will appear to be this, 'Christ glorified not himself to be made an high priest, but his Father glorified him, in ordaining him to be the high priest.'

This verb γενηθῆναι, *to be made*, is inserted to confirm that which was before noted, ver. i, Sec. 3, about ordaining an high priest. For to be made an high priest is to be deputed or appointed and set apart to that function. In this sense is this word *made* frequently used, as Heb. vii. 16, 21, 22.

Sec. 25. *Of* Ps. ii. 7 *applied to Christ's priesthood.*

These words, 'He that said unto him, Thou art my Son, to-day have I begotten thee,' are taken out of Ps. ii. 7, and most fitly applied to God the Father in reference to his begotten Son, as we have shewed, Chap. i. 5, Sec. 48, &c., where the whole text is expounded.

The apostle doth here again allege it, to prove that the Father ordained Christ to be the high priest for his church.

Obj. In this testimony there is no mention of a priesthood.

Ans. 1. This testimony is an express description of the Father, and it being inserted upon the question of Christ's priesthood, it implieth that the Father made him high priest.

2. This word *begotten* may be extended to conferring dignity, or an honourable function upon one, as well as communicating essence.

3. It being taken for grant that Christ was an high priest, for the Father to acknowledge him to be his Son, ratifieth that function, and implieth that it was his Father's pleasure that he should be the high priest. Thus Christ being come a prophet into the world, his Father ratified that function by this testimony, 'This is my beloved Son, in whom I am well pleased,' and thereupon he inferreth this duty, 'Hear him,' Mat. xvii. 5.

4. The psalmist, immediately after this testimony, expresseth a branch of Christ's priesthood, in these words, 'Ask of me,' &c., Ps. ii. 8. Now in quoting a text it is not unusual to express only a part of it, because the remainder may be found in the place out of which it is quoted.

5. It was the purpose of the apostle to set out the dignity of the office, as well as the office itself. That this

was his purpose is evident by these two words, *honour, glorified,* applied thereunto. Now that God the Father should glorify his begotten Son by making him an high priest, much amplifieth the dignity of that function.

Thus is this testimony a most pertinent testimony. It is a testimony taken out of sacred Scripture, and in that respect the more sound, as was shewed Chap. i. 5, Sec. 46.

Of quoting the very words of Scripture, see Chap. iii. 7, Sec. 74.

Of quoting neither book nor verse, see Chap. ii. 6, Sec. 50.

Sec. 26. *Of Christ being glorified by his priesthood.*

Quest. How could the begotten Son of God, who is true God, equal to the Father, be glorified by being made an high priest?

Ans. 1. Distinguish between the Son of God singly considered in his divine nature, or as the second Person in the sacred Trinity; and united to the human nature, and thereby made also the Son of man. In this latter respect was he glorified.

2. Distinguish between honour conferred on one by such and such an undertaking, and the honour arising from undertaking such a thing. Though such a function can simply confer no honour on Christ, yet in the managing of it, he might bring much honour to himself and to his Father, who appointed him thereunto, as glory of mercy, justice, truth, wisdom, power, and other like attributes. Thus was Christ, and his Father by him, glorified in the lowest degree of his humiliation, even in his kind of death.

Such undertakings as bring glory to God, do glorify the undertakers. Therefore Christ exhorteth his to 'let their light so shine before men, that they may see their good works, and glorify their Father which is in heaven,' Mat. v. 16. No man can in a right way glorify God; but he shall therein glorify himself, and that,

1. In regard of the work itself. For everything is so much the more glorious, by how much the more God is glorified thereby.

2. In regard of the fruit and reward that will follow thereupon. For he that can and will perform what he hath said, hath said, 'Them that honour me I will honour,' 1 Sam. ii. 30.

This is the right way to be glorified. Walk in this way, whosoever thou art that wouldst be glorified.

Sec. 27. *Of God's begotten Son our high priest.*

A main point intended in the foresaid testimony is, that God the Father ordained his begotten Son to be an high priest.

In this respect is he said to be 'called of God an high priest,' verse 10. As he was 'appointed' a prophet, Chap. iii. 2, so an high priest.

In this respect he is said to be *sent,* John iii. 34, and *anointed,* Luke iv. 18.

There was an absolute necessity that this Son of God should be our priest, in two respects:

1. In that none was able to do the work that was to be done for us by our priest, but the Son of God. Of those works, see Chap. ii. 17.

2. In that none was worthy to appear before God for us but his own Son, and none fit but he for the honour of the true priesthood.

This doth much commend the love of God, who gave his begotten Son to be our priest, John iii. 16.

It doth also minister great ground of boldness unto us to approach the throne of grace, having the begotten Son of God to be our priest. We can make no question of his sufficiency to the whole work, which he is able to do to the very utmost; nor can we make any doubt of God's accepting him. He is the *begotten* Son of God, and *beloved*; in him 'the Father is well pleased,' Mat. iii. 17.

Sec. 28. *Of the coherence and meaning of the sixth verse.*

Ver. 6. *As he saith also in another place, Thou art a priest for ever after the order of Melchisedec.*

Because the former testimony was somewhat obscure, the apostle addeth this other, which is more perspicuous, and less subject to exception. For both the priesthood itself, and also God's deputing Christ thereunto, are here expressly set down.

These two conjunctions καθὼς, καὶ, *as, also,* give proof that the following testimony tends in general to the same purpose that the former did, so as more than one divine testimony may be produced to prove one and the same thing, as hath been shewed, Chap. i. 5, Sec. 67.

This verb λέγει, *he saith,* may admit a treble reference.

1. To David, who was the penman of this testimony.

2. To the Holy Ghost, who inspired David.

3. To God the Father, who is brought in conferring what is here affirmed upon his Son.

Neither of these cross the other, but all of them may stand together.

I take the last to be most principally intended, because the Father, who in the former testimony said to his Son, 'Thou art my Son, this day have I begotten thee,' saith also, 'Thou art a priest for ever,' &c. Thus will these two testimonies more fitly cohere.

This latter testimony is said to be ἐν ἑτέρῳ, *in another place.* Though the word *place* be not in the Greek, yet it is well supplied. For it is in another *psalm,* namely, Ps. cx. 4.

That psalm is a prophecy of Christ, as hath been proved, Chap. i. 13, Sec. 148. In this respect the proof is the more proper.

In this testimony Christ's priesthood is thus expressly asserted, 'Thou art a priest.' Of Christ's priesthood, see Chap. ii. 17, Secs. 172, 173.

God's deputing Christ to that function is here also declared. For it is the Lord that saith to him, 'Thou art a priest.' Of God's appointing Christ to be priest, see ver. 4, Sec. 20, 24.

Sec. 29. *Of the everlastingness of Christ's priesthood.*

The everlasting continuance of Christ's priesthood is plainly set down in this phrase, εἰς τὸν αἰῶνα, *for ever.*

Of the notation of the Greek word translated ever, see Chap. i. 8, Sec. 108. Many points there delivered about the everlastingness of Christ's kingdom may be applied to the everlastingness of Christ's priesthood.

It is here evident by this testimony that Christ is an everlasting priest, he ever remaineth to exercise this function himself. This point is oft pressed by this apostle, as Chap. vii. 17, 21, 24, 25, 28.

There were two parts of Christ's priesthood. One was to offer sacrifice, that is, he *gave*, Chap. vii. 27; the other to make intercession. This doth he continue for ever, and for this end ever remaineth a priest, Chap. vii. 25.

It is necessary that the church ever have a priest, and that such a priest as Christ is, as was shewed, Sec. 27.

If Christ should cease to be our priest, who should succeed him? No mere creature can go forward with that work which he hath begun.

The everlastingness of Christ's priesthood discovereth the vanity and folly of papists about their priests, whom they account true, real, sacrificing priests. What need other priests, Christ being 'a priest for ever'? Either Christ's execution of his priesthood is insufficient (which to hold is blasphemy), or their priests are altogether in vain.

This continuance of Christ's priesthood hath been the ground of the church's address to the throne of grace ever since the ascension of Christ into heaven, and so will be as long as the world continueth. For ever will this our priest be for us in things pertaining to God. So long as he continueth our king to govern us, so long will he continue our priest to intercede for us.

We may with as much confidence still apply the sacrifice of Christ as if his blood were still trickling down. His blood still speaks, Heb. xii. 24, and ever will, while there is any sin of any of God's elect to be expiated.

Sec. 30. *Of the order of Melchisedec.*

The word τάξις, translated *order*, signifieth a due and seemly disposition. It is derived from a verb, τάττω, that signifieth to *appoint* or set in order. It is applied to the setting of commanders or officers of war in their places, Luke vii. 8, yea, and to God's ordaining unto eternal life, Acts xiii. 48. The noun in my text is used to set out a decent ordering of church affairs, 1 Cor. xiv. 40, and a comely carriage of Christians, Col. ii. 5. It here implieth that the priesthood is a distinct kind of office, ordained and ordered by him that hath power to do it. It is in a like sense applied to Aaron's priesthood, Heb. vii. 11.

Hereby we are given to understand that the priesthood here mentioned, and the priesthood of Aaron, are two distinct kinds.

The apostle doth here bring in this priesthood as distinct from Aaron's, because there were many things in Christ which were not agreeable to the order of Aaron. As,

1. Christ was a king; but a king might not be of Aaron's order.

2. He was 'of the tribe of Judah, of which tribe no man gave attendance at the altar,' Heb vii. 13.

3. He neither had predecessor nor successor, Heb. vii. 24, but priests after Aaron's order had both.

Other differences are observed by this apostle, Chap. vii.

If, therefore, from such differences any should infer that Christ could not be a priest, the apostle sheweth that there was another order of priesthood.

Besides there were such infirmities and defects in the order of Aaron as were not agreeable to Christ's excellency, so as there must of necessity be another order of priesthood.

The infirmities and defects of Aaron's priesthood were these:

1. That the priests should offer for their own sins, ver. 3.

2. That they should offer beasts and birds, Lev. i. 2, 14.

3. That they should oft offer the same kind of sacrifices.

4. That they should offer such sacrifices as could not make perfect, Heb. x. 1.

There are but two kinds of typical priesthoods mentioned in Scripture, which are these: one, 'after the order of Melchisedec;' the other, 'after the order of Aaron.' Of these two the former was many ways the more excellent. Herein, therefore, is Christ said to be 'after the order of Melchisedec.'

Whatsoever was essentially belonging to a priest in Aaron, that was in the truth accomplished by Christ; and wherein there was any pre-eminent excellency in Melchisedec's priesthood above Aaron's, therein was Christ 'after the order of Melchisedec.' All these excellencies were really and properly accomplished in Christ.

The history of Melchisedec is set down, Gen. xiv. 18–20.

This apostle hath so distinctly and fully observed and applied to Christ everything that is expressed, or by just consequence may be inferred from that priesthood, in the seventh chapter of this epistle, as I suppose it meet to refer the explication of this mystery to that place.

In general this may be observed, that Christ was the most excellent priest that ever was. Melchisedec was more excellent than Aaron, Heb. vii. 4, yet was Melchisedec but a type of Christ. Therefore Christ the true priest must needs be more excellent than Melchisedec himself.

Sundry excellencies of Christ's priesthood, as the dignity of his person, his many great undertakings, and the glorious fruits and benefits flowing from thence, have been expressly noted, Chap. ii. 17, Secs. 173, 174.

If the Jews had Aaron's priesthood in high account, and Abraham the father of the Jews gave tithes of all to Melchisedec, and accounted himself blessed, being blessed of Melchisedec, how should we esteem Jesus Christ and his priesthood, and rest in his blessing!

Sec. 31. *Of the resolution of* Heb. v. 5, 6.

Ver. 5. *So also Christ glorified not himself to be made an high priest; but he that said unto him, Thou art my Son, to-day have I begotten thee.*

6. *As he saith also in another place, Thou art a priest for ever after the order of Melchisedec.*

The sum of these two verses is Christ's call to his priesthood.

Hereabout observe,

1. The connection of Christ's call with the call of other priests, *So also*.

2. The expression of Christ's calling.

This is done two ways:

1, Negatively; 2, Affirmatively.

In the negative,

1. Three things are taken for grant:

(1.) Christ's office, he was a *priest*.

(2.) His warrant, he was *made*.

(3.) The glorious effect thereof, in this word *glorified*.

2. One thing is expressly denied, namely an undue usurpation, in these words, *not himself*.

The affirmative is,

1. Implied, in this junction of opposition, *but*.

2. Confirmed, by two testimonies.

In the former testimony one thing is expressed, another understood.

That which is expressed is a description of the persons, which are of two sorts:

1. The ordainer; 2, the ordained.

Both these are,

1. Generally hinted in this phrase, *he that said to him*. This relative, *he*, pointeth at the ordainer; this correlative, *him*, at the ordained.

2. They are both distinctly expressed.

The ordainer is expressed in these pronouns of the first person, *my, I*; and in this act of paternity, *begotten*; amplified by the time, *to-day*.

The ordained is expressed in these pronouns of the second person, *thou, thee*; and in this correlative, *Son*.

The point understood is, that God glorified his Son in making him a priest.

In the other testimony we may observe,

1. The connection of it with the former.

2. The expression of the main point.

In the connection there is,

1. An agreement betwixt the two testimonies, in this phrase, *as he saith also*.

2. A difference betwixt them, in this phrase, *in another place*.

In the expression of the main point is set down,

1. The person deputed, *Thou art*.

2. The function whereunto he is deputed. This is,

1. Propounded, in this word, *a priest*.

2. Illustrated two ways:

(1.) By the kind of priesthood, *after the order of Melchisedec*.

(2.) By the continuance thereof, *for ever*.

Sec. 32. *Of observations out of* Heb. v. 5, 6.

I. *Christ took no unlawful liberty to himself.* As no other man took to himself to be an high priest, so also Christ did not. See Sec. 23.

II. *Christ usurped not the high priesthood.* Therein he glorified not himself. See Sec. 24.

III. *Christ was an high priest.* This is here taken for grant. See Sec. 24.

IV. *An high priest was instituted.* This is the meaning of this word *made*. See Sec. 24.

V. *Christ was ordained an high priest.* The conjunction *but* intends as much.

VI. *God gave his begotten Son to be our priest.* This is the intendment of this testimony. See Sec. 27.

VII. *The Son of God was glorified by his priesthood.* The inference of this testimony upon glorifying one by a priesthood proves as much. This will more evidently appear if the verb understood be expressed, which is this, *glorified him*. See Sec. 26.

(Other observations arising out of the letter of this testimony have been noted, Chap. i. 5, Sec. 65.)

VIII. *Many testimonies may be produced for proof of the same point.* These words, *as also in another place*, give proof hereof.

IX. *God spake in the Scripture.* This word, *he saith*, hath reference to God.

X. *Christ is a priest.* This is taken for grant in this testimony also.

XI. *God gave assurance to Christ that he was a priest.* For God expressly saith to him, *Thou art a priest*.

(Of the four last observations, see Sec. 28.)

XII. *Christ's priesthood is everlasting.* It is *for ever*. See Sec. 29.

XIII. *Christ's priesthood is after the most excellent order.* So was the order of Melchisedec. See Sec. 30.

Sec. 33. *Of this phrase, 'in the days of his flesh.'*

Ver. 7. *Who in the days of his flesh, when he had*

offered up prayers and supplications, with strong crying and tears, unto him that was able to save him from death, and was heard in that he feared.

The apostle having proved that Christ was called to be a priest, proceedeth to shew that the order of things which make up a priest belonged to him. He begins with this, that Christ was true man, *taken from among men.* This he gives us to understand by making mention of his flesh. Of the divers acceptions of *flesh*, and how it sets out the whole human nature, and that in reference to Christ, see Chap. ii. 14, Secs. 137, 139.

Christ's human nature is frequently set out by *flesh;* as in these phrases, 'The Word was made flesh,' John i. 14; 'God was manifest in the flesh,' 1 Tim. iv. 16.

Here by *days of flesh* the time wherein Christ lived on earth is set out. Where David saith, I will call upon God *in my days,* we thus translate it, 'as long as I live,' Ps. cxvi. 2.

The word *days* are used to shew the brevity of Christ's life. To this purpose saith Job, 'Are not man's days like the days of an hireling?' chap. vii. 1. In this respect the psalmist saith, 'Teach us to number our days,' Ps. xc. 12; that is, well to understand and consider the shortness of our time.

The word *flesh* is used to shew the infirmity of our nature. In this respect saith the psalmist, 'God remembered that they were but flesh,' Ps. lxxviii. 39; and another prophet, 'All flesh is grass,' Isa. xl. 6.

From this phrase, *in the days of his flesh,* some doubts arise.

Quest. 1. Did Christ after this life clean cast off his flesh?

Ans. No; after death he raised up his flesh, in which respect it is said, 'My flesh shall rest in hope,' Acts ii. 26. The angels that stood by while many witnesses saw Christ in his flesh ascend into heaven, said, 'This same Jesus, which is taken up from you into heaven, shall so come in like manner as ye have seen him go into heaven,' Acts i. 11.

Quest. 2. Why, then, is the time of Christ's life on earth styled the *days of his flesh?*

Ans. 1. In opposition to the time before his incarnation, to shew that then, when he took flesh, he properly and actually began to execute his priestly function.

2. In opposition to his glorified estate. Then his human nature was freed from all human infirmities; for *flesh* is here taken for his human nature compassed with all manner of infirmities, as 2 Cor. v. 16. This phrase therefore setteth out the time of Christ's humiliation.

Quest. 3. Did Christ cease to be a priest after this life?—

Ans. No; it was shewed (Sec. 29) that Christ remaineth a priest for ever. That part of Christ's priesthood which is restrained to the days of his flesh, is that which consisted in service and suffering, Luke xxiv. 26. As for his intercession, which he maketh at God's right hand, it is far different from the supplications which he made on earth.

The principal point intended under this phrase, *in the days of his flesh,* is, that Christ, as a true man, and a man subject to human infirmities, became a priest for us. Hereof see more, Chap. ii. 17, Sec. 166, &c.

This further shews that the days of our flesh, even the time of this life, is the time for us to do what works of service are to be done by us. It was David's commendation, that he 'served his own generation by the will of God,' Acts xiii. 36. This is he that said, 'I will call upon God as long as I live,' Ps. cxvi. 2.

This also is a matter of singular comfort to the members of Christ, whose deprecations against evils, whose crying and tears, are bounded within the days of their flesh, as Christ's were within the days of his flesh. For after those days 'they shall hunger no more, nor thirst any more,' &c.; 'but God shall wipe away all tears from their eyes,' Rev. vii. 16, 17.

Herein lieth a main difference betwixt Christ's members and others. In the days of this flesh 'all things come alike to all,' Eccles. ix. 2. But after these days then shall the wicked weep and gnash their teeth, Mat. xxii. 13. If the damned in hell had but so many years for their howling and crying, as saints have days, yea, minutes on earth, it might be some stay and ground of hope unto them; but they can have no such hope. We have cause patiently to endure what the Lord shall lay upon us in the days of our flesh, because no misery shall lie upon us any longer. Death is our last enemy; the pangs of death our last pangs.

Sec. 34. *Of Christ's frequent praying.*

The act here applied to Christ, as he is our priest, is thus expressed, *when he had offered up.* This is the interpretation of one Greek word, προσενέγκας (*participium aoristi primi*), which, in reference to things offered unto God, is proper to a priest. Hereof see Ver. 1, Sec. 6.

The word is a participle of the time past, to shew the efficacy of that which Christ did; for it hath reference to God's hearing Christ. Christ having offered up prayers to God, God heard him.

The word δεήσεις, translated *prayers,* is derived from a verb δέομαι, *egeo,* that signifieth *to need,* Acts xvii. 25, and also *to crave,* δέομαι, *oro;* for we use to crave the things which we need. This noun is oft indefinitely used for any kind of prayer, Philip. i. 4. Sometimes it is distinguished from προσευχή, *petition for good things,* and then it is put for *deprecation,* or prayer for removing evil, as Acts i. 14, Eph. vi. 18, 1 Tim. ii. 1. Our English, when it is thus distinguished, translates it *supplication.*

That which in general is here intended is, that prayer was the means which Christ used for help in time of need. He herein verified the foresaid double signification of the Greek word, which was to *need* and to *ask*.

The Holy Ghost takes special notice of Christ's frequent use of this duty in the days of his flesh, when he was compassed about with many infirmities, and stood in need of many things.

When Christ was first baptized he prayed, Luke iii. 21. Early in the morning, before he went out to preach, he prayed, Mark i. 35. He prayed all night, before he chose and sent forth his apostles, Luke vi. 12. After he had fed his hearers with his word in their souls, and with bread and fish in their bodies, and had sent them away, he went to a mountain to pray, Mark vi. 46. He prayed a little before he gave his disciples the power of binding and loosing, Luke ix. 18. He prayed when he prescribed a form of prayer, Luke xi. 1. At the raising of Lazarus he prayed, John xi. 41. When he first began to be troubled in his soul, he prayed, John xii. 27, 28. A solemn prayer of his is recorded, John xvii. In his great agony he prayed again and again, Mat. xxvi. 39, 42, 44. On the cross he prayed for his persecutors, Luke xxiii. 34, and for himself, Luke xxiii. 46. On sundry other occasions it is said, that he lift up his eyes and looked unto heaven, Mat. xiv. 19, John xvii. 1, which was an outward evidence of the prayer of his heart.

This Christ did: 1. In acknowledgment of his Father to be the fountain of all blessing.

2. To shew his prudent care and conscience in using warrantable means for obtaining what he desired, Mat. vii. 7.

3. To obtain a blessing upon what he had, 1 Tim. iv. 5.

4. To shew himself a worshipper of God, Ps. xcv. 6.

5. To shew himself to be of the number of God's people, who 'call upon God,' Ps. xcix. 6, Acts ix. 14, 1 Cor. i. 2, 2 Tim. ii. 22. Others 'call not upon God,' Ps. xiv. 4, Jer. x. 25.

6. To give evidence of the spirit of grace and supplication in him, Zech. xii. 10.

7. To make himself an example to us, John xiii. 15.

Of this duty of prayer, see *The Whole Armour of God*, treat. iii. part i. on Eph. vi. 18, sec. 4, &c.

Sec. 35. *Of Christ's supplication.*

The Greek word ἱκετηρίας, translated *supplications*, is nowhere else to be found in the New Testament, but in other authors it is oft used. It is derived from a verb ἵκω, *venio*, that signifieth *to come*. Thence a noun, ἱκέτης, *supplex*, which signifieth one that asketh a thing on his bended knee, or prostrate on the ground: we may call him a suppliant. Hence the word in my text.

This word in other authors signifieth such things as suppliants did bring in their hands: as a branch of an olive-tree wrapped about with wool.[1] Metonymically it is put for the supplication that was made by such an one, and in that respect is here fitly translated supplications, and especially intendeth such prayers as are made by such as kneel or lie prostrate on the ground. This may here have respect to Christ's manner of prayer, who 'kneeled down and prayed,' Luke xxii. 41, and 'fell on his face and prayed,' Mat. xxvi. 39.

By this pattern of Christ we are taught to tender our prayers to God with all humility, in the most submissive manner that we can. Hereof see more in *The Whole Armour of God*, treat. iii. part i. Of prayer, on Eph. vi. 18, sec. 9, &c.

Sec. 36. *Of the gifts Christ offered up.*

The foresaid prayers and supplications were some of those gifts which Christ as our priest offered up: they were in special as the incense under the law. As his body was the sacrifice, so these the gifts. These were offered up for himself, to enable him to go through the work; and for us, that we might be delivered and saved thereby.

Nothing could be more pleasing to God, nothing more honourable to him, nothing more effectual for our good.

Hereby we are taught what gifts we may offer unto God. These are the 'calves of the lips,' which the church promiseth to render, Hosea xiv. 2. This is that 'incense' which in every place shall be offered to God, Mal. i. 11.

Sec. 37. *Of the meaning of these words, 'with strong crying and tears.'*

The manner of offering the foresaid gifts, is with emphasis thus set forth, *with strong crying and tears*.

The verb κράζω, *clamo*, whence the Greek noun κραυγή, translated *crying*, is derived, useth to be applied to such as are in great distress; as to blind men, Mat. ix. 27; to men affrighted and in danger, Mat. xiv. 26, 30; to a woman in travail, Rev. xii. 2; to lamenters of great desolations, Rev. xviii. 18, 19; to such as seek others' destruction; and to such as seek pardon for others' sins, Acts vii. 57, 60.

There is also another verb, κραυγάζω, derived from this noun, that carrieth a greater emphasis, and is attributed to the woman who cried after Jesus for her child grievously vexed with a devil, Mat. xv. 22; to them that would have Christ crucified, John xviii. 40, and xix. 6, 15; and to them that would have Paul destroyed, Acts xxii. 23; yea, it is used to set out Christ's cry at the raising of Lazarus, John xi. 43.

This noun, κραυγή, is applied to that cry which was raised about the dissension betwixt Pharisees and Sadducees, Acts xxiii. 9; to the angel that called for

---

[1] ἱκετηρία, dicitur ramus oleæ lana obvolutus, quem supplex manu ferebat.

divine vengeance, Rev. xiv. 18 ; and to the cry that shall be at Christ's coming to judgment, Mat. xxv. 6.

Thus the word itself intendeth vehemency and ardency.

Whether we take crying for extension of voice (for so much is noted of Christ on the cross, Mat. xxvii. 46, and it may be that he did so in his agony in the garden, Mat. xxvi. 39), or to the inward extension, earnestness, and vehemency of his spirit, as Exod. xiv. 15, Ps. cxix. 145, Lam. ii. 18, it implieth one and the same thing, namely, ardency in prayer. Christ manifested his ardency both ways: by voice, Mat. xxvii. 46 ; in spirit, Luke xxii. 44.

To shew further that it was more than ordinary ardency, this epithet ἰσχυρᾶς, *strong*, is added thereunto.

This epithet is derived from a noun, ἰσχύς, *robur*, that signifieth *power*; thence a verb, ἰσχύω, *possum*, that signifieth *to be able*. It useth to be applied to such things as are extraordinarily strong, as a strong man, Mat. xii. 29 ; a strong wind, Mat. xiv. 30 ; a strong or mighty famine, Luke xv. 14 ; a strong or mighty city, Rev. xviii. 10 ; a strong or mighty thunder, Rev. xix. 6 ; a strong angel, Rev. v. 2 ; and to the strong Lord, Rev. xviii. 8.

Strong crying then implieth an extraordinary great crying.

This is yet further illustrated by adding *tears* thereunto, καὶ δακρύων ; for tears are signs of earnest prayer. Of this see *The Whole Armour of God*, treat. iii. part ii. Of prayer, on Eph. vi. 18, Sec. 97. Tears are an effect of inward anguish, Jer. xxxi. 15. They are attributed to the anguish of hell, Mat. viii. 12.

Sec. 38. *Of Christ's grievous agony.*

In these words, *with strong crying and tears*, the apostle hath an especial relation to Christ's agony, partly in the garden, and partly on the cross.

Christ's tears are not mentioned in his agony. Yet on other occasions they are mentioned : for he wept at Lazarus's grave, John xi. 35 ; and he wept over Jerusalem, Luke xix. 41.

As for Christ's agony, it may be well supposed that he also then shed tears ; for it is not credible, that he which wept at the sore sight of Jerusalem's calamity, had dry eyes in his own bitter agony. Can we think that his sweat should be ' as it were great drops of blood,' Luke xxii. 44, and that no tears should gush out of his eyes ? It doth not follow that he shed no tears because no mention is made thereof. ' Many other things did Jesus which are not written,' John xx. 30.

That which the apostle here saith of Christ's strong crying and tears, gives evidence of the great anguish that Christ endured. Christ had not a childish, womanish, faint spirit. Never any so manfully endured so much as Christ did.

If other circumstances be compared with these, it will appear that never such effects of anguish were manifested in any other.

To omit his falling to the ground, and grovelling thereon, his falling down to prayer, and rising up again and again, his bloody sweat, the matter of his prayer (' If it be possible, let this cup pass,' ' Why hast thou forsaken me ?') and the descent of an angel to strengthen him : all which do shew, that never any man's agony was like to his.

Besides these evidences, the Scripture saith, that at the time of his agony he began to be *sorrowful*, λυπεῖσθαι ; *to be sore troubled*, ἐκθαμβεῖσθαι ; and to be *very heavy*, ἀδημονεῖν ; and that in his agony his soul was exceeding sorrowful, περίλυπος, even unto the death, Mat. xxvi. 30, 39, Mark xiv. 33, 34 ; and troubled, τετάρακται, John xii. 27. Hence it appears that Christ's anguish was very great.

The cause hereof was our sin, and the just desert of it ; for he became our surety, and took upon him our debt. In this respect it is said that he was 'made sin for us,' 2 Cor. v. 21 ; and that he hath 'borne our griefs, and carried our sorrows,' Isa. liii. 3, &c. ; yea, it is said that he was ' made a curse for us,' Gal. iii. 13.

In this case, two things caused his foresaid agony.

1. The weight of the burden that lay upon him.
2. The weakness of his human nature.

1. The weight must needs be great, for it was the punishment of all the sins of all the elect. Sin being committed against God hath a kind of infinite heinousness, and the punishment must be proportionable. The punishment is God's wrath, and thereupon infinite. The reprobate, because they are not able to stand under it themselves, nor have any to bear it for them, lie eternally under it.

Obj. Christ was the Son of God's love, and never provoked his wrath, how then could it lie upon him ?

Ans. 1. To speak properly, God was never angry with his Son, nor did his wrath lie upon him, but rather the effects thereof. God was as well pleased with the person of his Son, even then when he was in his greatest agony, and said, ' Why hast thou forsaken me ?' as he was at his baptism and transfiguration, when he said, ' This is my beloved Son in whom I am well pleased.'

2. We must distinguish betwixt the person and undertaking of Christ. Though Christ in his person was the beloved Son of God, yet by his undertaking to be a surety, he stood in the room of sinners ; and though he himself never provoked God's wrath, yet they whose surety he was had provoked it, and for their sakes he endured the heavy burden thereof.

Obj. 2. The effects of God's wrath for sin is to be cast into hell, to lie in darkness, to be tormented with fire, and all this everlastingly.

Ans. The place, the distinct kind of torments, and other like circumstances, are but accidents belonging to the punishment of sin. God can in any place make the creature feel the fierceness of his wrath. As for darkness, fire, worm, and other like expressions of hell torments, they are but metaphors to aggravate hell's torment in our apprehensions. Concerning the eternity of hell's torment, it is because the damned are not able to bear it in time, and they have none to deliver them; but Christ, being supported by his divine power, was able at once to bear the burden of sin's punishment, and then to cast it from him. Besides, it could not stand with the dignity of his person for ever to lie under that burden, nor with the end for which he undertook that burden, which was to deliver them who were subject to bondage, Heb. ii. 15, and to free them from the curse, Gal. iii. 13.

2. As the burden which Christ undertook was very weighty, so the human nature which he assumed was very weak, in all things like ours, even in infirmities that were not sinful, chap. ii. 17, and iv. 15. His disability in bearing his cross gives instance of his weakness; for though at first the cross was laid upon himself, John xix. 17, yet, before he came to the place of execution, they were forced to lay it upon another, Luke xxiii. 26.

Quest. If such were the weight of the burden, and such his weakness, how was it that he was not overwhelmed therewith?

Ans. He was supported by his divine nature, which, though it somewhat withdrew assistance for a while, that he might feel the burden, yet it suffered him not to sink under the same, nor to be overwhelmed therewith.

Some, supposing it to be incongruous that the Son of God's love should lie under God's wrath, produce other reasons of the greatness of Christ's agony. As,

1. The apprehension of the terrible majesty of God, shewing himself a judge against sinners.

Ans. If there were no feeling of any effects of wrath coming from so terrible a judge, his terror might affright and astonish one, but would not make him cry, and weep, and pray, as Christ did.

2. The foresight of the Jews' rejection and dispersion, and of the persecution of the church; yea, also, that so excellent a person as his was should be so trodden under foot as a worm, and one so innocent as Christ was, be so evilly entreated, and Satan by his ministers so much prevail.

Ans. These and other like things were long before known by Christ. How then was it that they should then at the time of his death work upon him so much as they did, and not before?

3. His bodily pains, which they aggravate two ways: 1, by the kinds thereof; 2, by Christ's extraordinary sensibleness of them. For the kinds, they mention his scourging, the plaiting of a crown of thorns upon his head, and the nailing of his hands and feet unto the cross. His more than ordinary sensibleness they make to arise from a perfect mixture of humours and qualities in his body, so as a small prick on his flesh was more painful than a deep wound in another's.

And further they say, that his sense was not dulled by continual languishing, but that at the very instant of his death he retained the full vigour of his sense; for he 'cried with a loud voice, and gave up the ghost,' Mark xv. 37.

Ans. 1. True it is, that Christ's bodily torments were very great, and greater than by many they are taken to be; and it may be granted, that he retained the full vigour of all his senses to the last moment of his life. But yet I take it to be without question, that many martyrs have endured more sharp bodily torments, and that longer together than Christ did, and also in full vigour of sense, yet have they without such cryings as Christ made, endured all. Besides we never read that Christ twitched at his bodily pains. They, therefore, cannot be the reason of his great agony. Christ was cast into his agony before he felt any pains. It remains, therefore, that the burden and punishment of sin was it that made Christ to make such strong cries, and shed such tears, as are here noted, and that especially in his soul.

1. There is a conceit that many have, that the least drop of Christ's blood, even the prick of a needle in any part of his body, had been sufficient to redeem many worlds, by reason of the dignity of his person. But that which is noted in Scripture of the extreme agony of Christ, sheweth that this is but a mere conceit. Philosophers say, that nature doth nothing in vain. Much more may we Christians truly say, that Christ the God of nature, in that which he undertook for man's redemption, would do nothing in vain, nor more than was needful. Satisfaction was to be made to divine justice, which the prick of a needle could not do.

2. The great agony whereunto Christ was brought doth much amplify the incomprehensible love of God, Father and Son, to us sinners.

3. It doth also much aggravate that woful plight whereunto man by sin was brought. If such loud crying and tears were forced from our Surety by undertaking to free us, What should we ourselves have been brought to? Even 'unto outer darkness, where shall be weeping and gnashing of teeth,' and 'everlasting fire,' Mat. xxv. 30, 41. There can no like instance be given to aggravate the horrid and heavy burden of sin, as this of Christ's agony. Indeed, sin pressed the evil angels from the highest heaven to the lowest hell; it forced Adam out of paradise. It swept away the old world with a general deluge; it destroyed Sodom and other cities, and their inhabitants, with fire and brimstone; it brought sundry fearful judgments upon other people in every age of the world; it maketh the very life of many to be so grievous unto them, as to lay violent hands on themselves; it causeth merciless and remediless torments in hell. Yet this particular instance of the agony of him that was the Son of God, even true God, upon his undertaking to expiate sin, far surpasseth all other instances.

Quest. If such be the burden of sin, How is it that many wicked ones do so lightly carry it?

Ans. Two reasons may be given hereof:

1. Their spiritual senselessness and deadness. If a church lie upon a dead man, he feels nothing.

2. Sin is as the proper element wherein unregenerate persons lie and live. Now creatures feel no burden in their proper element, as fishes in a river.

4. Christ's crying and tears, as being our Surety for sin, should make us cry and weep for our sins. Shall we make light of that which forced our Surety to make such strong cries as he did? We have cause every one of us to say, 'Oh that my head were waters, and mine eyes a fountain of tears, that I might weep day and night for my sins,' Jer. ix. 1.

Sec. 39. *Of praying in distress.*

The foresaid agony of Christ put Christ upon praying. For his prayers and supplications were 'with ($\mu\epsilon\tau\grave{\alpha}$) strong crying and tears.' 'He being in an agony prayed more earnestly,' Luke xxii. 44. This prayer, 'My God, my God, why hast thou forsaken me?' Mat. xxvii. 46, was in the extremity of his agony.

1. Christ ever apprehended God to be his Father, even when he felt the greatest effects of his wrath, John xii. 27; Mat. xxvi. 39, and xxvii. 46.

2. Christ knew no better means of supportance and deliverance than prayer. Therefore as he prayed himself, so he called upon his disciples to 'watch and pray,' Mat. xxvi. 41.

1. Judge hereby what spirit is in them, who in their dangers and distresses cry aloud, and weep, and wail much, but offer up no prayers and supplications to God, Hosea vii. 14.

Others murmur against God, as the Israelites did ofttimes in the wilderness, Exod. xiv. 10, &c.

Others blaspheme God, 2 Kings vi. 33, Rev. xvi. 11.

2. Labour to be of the same mind that Christ was. Let distresses drive thee to God. Let the greatness of the distress enlarge thy heart, and open thy mouth in prayer to God. This hath been the mind of such in all ages as have been guided by the Spirit of Christ, Exod. xiv. 15; Ps. cxxx. 1; Jonah ii. 1.

Thus shalt thou find comfort and succour in thy distress.

The strong crying and tears of Christ here mentioned, were signs of an extraordinary distress, and they were also effects of extraordinary prayer; so as extraordinary need requireth extraordinary prayer. Of extraordinary prayer, see *The Whole Armour of God*, treat. iii. part 2. Of prayer, on Eph. vi. 18, Sec. 95, &c.

Sec. 40. *Of God's power a prop of faith in prayer.*

He to whom Christ offered up his prayers, is thus set out, 'Unto him that was able to save him from death.' This is a description of God, and giveth evidence that prayer is to be made to God, and to God alone. Hereof see *The Whole Armour of God*, treat. iii., part 1, on Eph. vi. 18, Secs. 5, 6.

God is here described by his power in this phrase, 'that was able,' $\pi\rho\grave{o}\varsigma\ \tau\grave{o}\nu\ \delta\upsilon\nu\acute{a}\mu\epsilon\nu o\nu$. Of God's power, see *The Guide to go to God*, or *An Explanation of the Lord's Prayer*, sec. 210, &c.

The power of God is here mentioned, to shew, that Christ's mind was on it in his great extremity, and that his faith was thereby supported in his prayer to God.

Hereby we are given to understand, that God's almighty power is to be known and believed by such as call on him.

It is said, that 'he that cometh to God must believe that he is, and that he is a rewarder of them that seek him,' Heb. xi. 6. I may in like manner say, he that cometh unto God must believe that God is able to help him. This is thus expressly affirmed of Christ, 'Abba, Father, all things are possible to thee,' Mark xiv. 36. So Asa, 'Lord, it is nothing with thee to help,' 2 Chron. xiv. 11. So the leper, 'Lord, if thou wilt thou canst make me clean,' Mat. viii. 2.

1. This is a strong encouragement to go to God. Who will go to such as they think cannot help them? This was thus upbraided to Amaziah: 'Why hast thou sought after the gods of the people, which could not deliver their own people out of thine hand?' 2 Chron. xxv. 15.

2. Meditation on God's power is a strong prop to faith in God's promise, Rom. iv. 21, Heb. xi. 19.

This is a sure ground of patience, and of subjection to God's will, Dan. iii. 17, Mark xiv. 36. He that knoweth that God is able to do what he desireth, will conclude, that if his desire be not granted, it is the best for him.

4. That we may be moved in our need with boldness and confidence to go to God, and be supported in our distresses, and willingly subject to what God doth, and patiently expect the issue which he will give, let us among other excellencies of God acquaint ourselves with his power. Hereof see *The Whole Armour of God*, treat. ii. part 6. Of faith, on Eph. vi. 16, sec. 26.

Sec. 41. *Of God's power over death.*

The particular object whereabout God's power is here said to be manifested, was death, that God was 'able to save him from death.' This is a great evidence of God's almighty power. Nothing is so powerful as death. No creature can save from it, Eccles. viii. 8, Ps. xlix. 7. This therefore is proper unto God.

God alone hath the power of death, Ps. ix. 13, and lxviii. 20; Hosea xiii. 14. On this ground have saints in danger of death called upon God, Isa. xxxviii. 3, John ii. 1.

Death itself is God's servant and minister. As it

was at first appointed by God, so God still holds his dominion over it.

Obj. The devil is said to have the power of death. Hereof see Chap. ii. 14, Sec. 143.

This is a great comfort in sickness, in imprisonment, against oppressions, treasons, invasions, and other dangers. When the people spake of stoning David, 'He encouraged himself in the Lord his God,' 1 Sam. xxx. 6. When Hezekiah had received the sentence of death, he was bold on this ground to call upon God to be preserved, Isa. xxxviii. 3.

This power of God over death is a good encouragement even in death itself. For God in death is able to save us from death, and to translate us unto life.

Sec. 42. *Of God's saving Christ from death.*

The exemplification of God's power over death, is here set down in this word σώζειν, *save*, which is used sometimes for temporary preservation, Mat. viii. 25, and sometimes for eternal salvation, Acts iv. 12. It is likewise put for a total freedom from all fear and danger, Heb. vii. 25, or for a supportance in danger. In which respect, the apostle being in great danger, said, 'The Lord will preserve (or save σώσει), me unto his heavenly kingdom,' 2 Tim. iv. 18. In this latter sense of supportance may the word be here taken. For by saving from death, we may not think that Christ desired a mere immunity, and freedom from death, so as he should not taste thereof, but rather a supporting and upholding him in death, that he should not be swallowed up thereof, or overcome thereby. For he apprehended death as the punishment of sin, the curse of the law, and the effect of God's wrath.

Thus it might seem dreadful and horrible unto him, and Christ as a weak man be so affrighted therewith, as to fear that he should not be able to stand under that insupportable burden.

By this he sheweth, that God is able to preserve those who are subject to death, from being swallowed up in death.

The children of Israel were under sore bondage in Egypt, yet God preserved them, and exceedingly multiplied them in that bondage. They went into the Red Sea, but passed safe through the Red Sea. God suffered Jonah to be swallowed up by a whale, but yet preserved him in the fish's belly, Jonah ii. 1. He suffered his three servants to be cast into a fiery furnace, yet preserved them in that furnace, Daniel iii. 25, and Daniel to be cast into the lions' den, but there kept him safe, Daniel vi. 22. Many such evidences doth the Scripture afford. Yea, all ages have afforded examples of God's powerful providence in this kind. To this end tends that promise, 'When thou passest through the waters, I will be with thee; and through the rivers, they shall not overflow thee: when thou walkest through the fire, thou shalt not be burnt; neither shall the flame kindle upon thee,' Isa. xliii. 2.

Such an absolute power hath God over death, as he can say to it, 'Hitherto shalt thou come, and no further; and here shall thy proud waves be stayed,' Job xxxviii. 11.

This ministereth much comfort and hope in death. In this respect we may, after an holy manner, insult over death, and say, 'O death, where is thy sting?' 1 Cor. xv. 55. Though death may arrest us, yet we need not fear that judgment and execution shall be got against us. To this may be applied that ancient prophecy, 'The sucking child shall play upon the hole of the asp, and the weaned child shall put his hand on the cockatrice's den,' Isa. xi. 8. Christ was saved from death, not as a private man, but as a public person, and as an head to save all his members from death, Heb. ii. 15.

The mention of death in this place gives us to understand, that Christ was offered up to death, though he prayed to be saved from death. As therefore his prayers and supplications were the gifts that as a priest he offered up, so the putting of his body to death was the sacrifice. Of Christ's death, see Chap. ii. 9, Secs. 80, 83.

Sec. 43 *Of God's hearing Christ.*

The issue of Christ's intercession as a priest, is thus expressed, *and was heard*. If we well observe the whole sentence in this verse, we shall find this copulative *and* to be a redundancy, or else the sentence must be extended unto the next verse.

The issue here set down sheweth, that the prayers Christ offered up to his Father, were accepted of him. They were not made in vain, but effectual and available.

The Greek word εἰσακουσθείς, translated *heard*, is a compound, and signifieth not only hearing, but also granting the request that is heard, Luke i. 13, Acts x. 31.

God's sending of an angel to strengthen him when he was in his prayer, is an evidence of God's hearing him, Luke xxii. 42, 43. When Christ at his baptism prayed, 'the heavens was opened, and the Holy Ghost descended, and a voice from heaven, which said, Thou art my beloved Son, in thee I am well-pleased,' Luke iii. 21, 22. When Christ in his agony thus prayed, 'Father, glorify thy name, there came a voice from heaven, saying, I have both glorified it, and will glorify it again,' John xii. 28. When Christ raised Lazarus, he thus said, 'Father, I thank thee that thou hast heard me, and I know that thou hearest me always,' John xi. 41, 42.

Such-like grounds as these may be produced for God's hearing Christ.

1. The dignity of Christ's person, and near relation betwixt him and the Father, Heb. i. 5.

2. The affection which the Father bare him; he was 'his beloved Son in whom he was well pleased,' Mat. iii. 17.

3. The matter of his prayer, which was according to the will of the Father: 'Not as I will, but as thou wilt,' saith Christ to his Father, Mat. xxvi. 39. 'If we ask anything according to his will, he heareth us,' 1 John v. 14.

4. The end of Christ's prayer, which was God's glory, 'Father, glorify thy name,' John xii. 28.

1. This respect of God to his Son in hearing his prayer, is a strong prop to our faith in the intercession of Christ. Whom can we better use to present our prayers to God, than he who is always heard?

2. This ratifieth God's approbation of Christ's priesthood. For the prayers which he offered up were a part of his priestly function. If God's hearing the prayer of Elijah did assure the people that he was a prophet sent of God, 1 Kings xviii. 36, much more doth God's hearing Christ shew that Christ is a priest ordained of God.

3. This may be an incitation unto us, when we are in any distress, and have cause to fear, in faith to offer up prayers unto God. As Christ's pattern is a motive to pray, so God's hearing him is a ground of faith; especially if our prayers be made through the mediation of Christ. He that heard Christ's prayer will hear those that pray in Christ's name.

Sec. 44. *Of the fear from which Christ was delivered.*

The Greek noun εὐλάβεια, translated *fear*, is compounded of a verb, λαμβάνειν, that signifieth to *take*; and an adverb, εὖ, that signifieth *well*; so as, according to the notation of the word, it implieth *well to take*, or apprehend a thing.[1] Thence followeth a wary circumspection, and an holy fear. They who are circumspect and wary about the things which concern God's worship, are expressed under this word εὐλαβὴς, which our English translates *devout*, Luke ii. 25; Acts ii. 5, and viii. 2. It is used to set forth natural fear, thus: 'The chief captain, εὐλαβηθείς, *fearing* lest Paul should have been pulled in pieces,' Acts xxiii. 10.

By reason of the diverse acceptations of the word, some translate it *piety*, or reverence, and some *fear*. Our last translators have noted both; the latter in the text, the former in the margin.

They who take it for piety or reverence, make this clause to be a cause why God heard him, which was that piety which was in Jesus, and reverence which he bare to his Father; and thus translate it, *for his piety*, or for his religion, or for his reverence. This interpretation may well stand with the general scope of the apostle, and with the analogy of faith; but it doth not well agree with the preposition ἀπό, which properly signifieth *from*.

The other acception of the word, which signifieth *fear*, will very well stand with the foresaid preposition; and word for word may be thus translated: 'He was heard from his fear;' that is, he was so heard as he was delivered from that which he feared.

This substantive is only twice used in the New Testament, and that in this epistle; once here, and again Heb. xii. 28, where it is translated 'godly fear.' A participle, εὐλαβηθείς, derived from the same root, is used Heb. xi. 7, and thus translated, 'moved with fear.'

Other authors do put this word for *fear*, and that where they speak of a natural fear. Thus may it be here taken, and imply that fear which possessed Christ in the depth of his agony, which was one of his sinless infirmities.

Christ, upon the present sense and feeling of that heavy burden, might in that instant fear lest he should be left alone, and pressed above his strength. Herein he was heard, in that he was not forsaken, nor overpressed, but enabled to bear the burden, and to free himself from it. Thus was Paul heard, when 'there was given to him a thorn in the flesh, the messenger of Satan to buffet him;' and he prayed, and received this answer, 'My grace is sufficient for thee,' 2 Cor. xii. 7-9.

This plainly sheweth that Christ was subject to fear. Christ's fear may be reckoned among the other infirmities whereunto in his human nature he was subject; so as natural fear is not simply in itself a sin.

Of the general nature of this passion of fear, see Chap. xiii. 6, Secs. 84, 85.

This effect of fear doth much amplify Christ's agony; it shews it to be exceeding great. For it was no small matter that could make Christ, who was of a most undaunted spirit, and of all the most courageous that ever was, to fear. Of the extremity of Christ's agony, see Sec. 38.

Sec. 45. *Of faith and fear standing together.*

The earnest prayer of Christ, together with the fruit thereof, which was God's hearing of him, is an evidence of his faith. In that his fear is here added, it plainly appeareth that faith and fear may stand together. Moses retained his faith when he said, 'I exceedingly fear and quake,' Heb. xii. 21.

Though these be distinct and different, yet are they not contrary but helpful one to another; as sight and hearing, which are distinct senses. Fear makes faith to look up unto God; faith supports and makes us rest upon God.

Let not us sever those things that may stand together, but in all our fears let us believe and pray; so shall we be heard in the things we fear. If faith be severed from fear, an infirmity will be made a vice, and that which is natural be made diabolical; but mixed with faith, it will be sanctified, and made very useful.

As a means hereunto, consider,

1. That God hath his hand in all things that may cause thee to fear, John xix. 11.

---

[1] πράγματα ἰυλαμβάνειν, *res bene capessere*, i.e. *caute, circumspecte*. ἰυλαβίομαι, *caveo*; *religio mihi est*; *religiose caveo*.

2. God remains thy Father in thy greatest fears, Mat. xxvi. 39.

3. God in wisdom ordereth thy estate, Mat. x. 29.

4. God can deliver thee from thy fears, Jer. xxxii. 27.

5. God is faithful, and will never fail thee, Heb. xiii. 6.

How faith may stand with fear, though it be somewhat a sinful fear, see *The Saints' Sacrifice*, on Ps. cxvi. 11, sec. 75.

The preposition ἀπὸ, *from*, set before Christ's fear, sheweth that God delivered him from his fear. He did not leave him therein, nor forsake him. Hereupon saints may rest upon this, not to be forsaken. See Chap. xiii. 6, Sec. 73.

Sec. 46. *Of the most excellent and dearest Son of God suffering.*

Ver. 8. *Though he were a Son, yet learned he obedience by the things which he suffered.*

This verse is added to satisfy a doubt which might be raised from the dignity of Christ, and from the relation betwixt the Father and him; for he is here styled *a Son*, υἱὸς, in reference to God the Father.

To express this relation the more clearly, the vulgar Latin setteth down the correlative thus, *filius Dei, Son of God*. But there is an emphasis in this indefinite expression *Son*, as was shewed Chap. i. 2, Sec. 15.

The doubt is this: Christ is the Son of God, far more excellent than the most excellent of creatures; he is the beloved Son of God: how, then, was it that he should be brought to such an agony as is mentioned in the former verse?

Ans. God would have it so, that his Son might experimentally know how far he ought to subject himself to his Father, namely, not only by doing what his Father required, but also by enduring what his Father was pleased to lay on him, and therein to make himself a pattern to others. This is the main scope of this verse.

This conjunction, καίπερ, *though*, is the note of an argument, that is called *diversum, diverse*, which sheweth a difference from another thing, not simply in the nature of the thing, but in some special respect; as where God saith of the Israelites, 'They brake my covenant, *although* I was a husband unto them,' Jer. xxxi. 32. To keep covenant with an husband well agree; but in them who kept not covenant with God, their husband, they did disagree. Thus to be a son, and to be free from suffering, may stand well together; but in Christ they were diverse, for he was a Son, yet not freed from suffering. Of the kinds of argument, see Chap. vi. 9, Sec. 59.

This title *Son*, in reference to God, properly belongeth to Christ, as hath been shewed Chap. i. 2, Sec. 15. It sets out the dignity and excellency of Christ above the most excellent of creatures, as hath been proved Chap. i. 4, Secs. 39, 41.

Here it is taken for Christ's person, consisting of two natures, God and man. As man, he suffered; as God, he was able to endure the utmost that was inflicted upon him.

From this instance we may well infer, that neither excellency in one's self, nor dearness unto God, exempteth any in this world from suffering.

Can any be thought to be more excellent than the Son of God, whom God hath set at his right hand, and made King of kings and Lord of lords? Or can any be thought dearer to God than his dear Son? styled, υἱὸς τῆς ἀγάπης αὐτοῦ, 'the Son of his love,' Col. i. 13; 'the beloved,' Eph. i. 6; 'his beloved Son, in whom he is well pleased,' Mat. iii. 17; 'his elect, in whom his soul delighteth,' Isa. xlii. 1.

If this Son be not exempted from suffering, who can look to be exempted? Many instances, in all ages, of such as have been highly advanced by God, and greatly beloved of him, might be produced to demonstrate, that neither excellency in place or parts, nor interest in God's favour, have exempted them from sufferings.

1. As for dignity and excellency, it makes no difference before God. God is the supreme Lord over all, and in reference to him all are fellow-servants, so as the greatest can plead no more immunity at God's hand than the meanest.

2. As for interest in God's favour, God can and will turn the sufferings of his children to his own glory and their good. Nothing ever made more to God's glory than Christ's sufferings, and nothing more made to Christ's advancement than they, Philip. ii. 8, 9.

1. Let them who have excellency above others in this world apply this to themselves, and be willing to put their necks under God's yoke, and contentedly bear what God shall lay upon them.

2. Let them who think they have interest in God's favour not so rely thereupon as to count themselves free from all correction. God is not like a foolish cockering mother; he knows that corrections are needful and useful for his children. They who take themselves to be beloved of God may rather look for trial of their obedience this way, Heb. xii. 6–8.

3. This is a matter of great consolation to such as are thus tried. Herein they are dealt withal as God useth to deal with his dearest. Herein also they are made conformable to Christ their head.

4. Let others take heed of censuring such as are brought to suffer. This was the error of Job's friends. God's best and dearest children may be thus miscensured.

Sec. 47. *Of experimental learning.*

It is said of the Son of God that, ἔμαθε, he 'learned obedience.'

A thing is learned two ways:

1. By attaining to the knowledge of that which we knew not before. In this sense saith Christ, 'Learn

what that meaneth, I will have mercy and not sacrifice,' Mat. ix. 13.

2. By an experimental evidence of what we knew before. In this sense saith the apostle, 'I have learned, in whatsoever state I am, therewith to be content,' Philip. iv. 11 ; that is, by experience I find that this is my best course. Thus it is said, 'They shall learn war no more,' Isa. ii. 4. They shall experimentally find no more war amongst them : 'I have learned by experience that the Lord hath blessed me for thy sake,' saith Laban to Jacob, Gen. xxx. 27. Thus we say in common speech, when by experience of paying another's debt we find how costly a thing it is to be a surety, 'I have learned what suretyship is.' Thus Christ learned what it was to be a surety for sinners.

In this particular case of Christ, that so excellent a person as the Son of God, so beloved of the Father, so pure, so harmless, should suffer so as he did, was a new lesson never heard before, first learned by him.

Yea, further, in his own example he so practised this lesson as he became an example to others, so to teach it others as they might learn it of him.

Christ had an experimental proof of sufferings. He had not only a general notion that the human nature which he assumed was subject to manifold sufferings, but he learned it to be so by experience in his own person ; he sensibly felt the smart, pain, weight, and grief thereof. Witness his great agony, set down Sec. 38.

Of the end and use of this experimental learning, see Chap. ii. 18, Secs. 183, 186.

Sec. 48. *Of Christ's obedience in suffering.*

The chief lesson which Christ by his suffering learned is here styled ὑπακοή, *obedience.* The Greek word is a compound. The simple verb, ἀκούω, from which it is derived, signifieth *to hear.* The preposition ὑπό, with which it is compounded, signifieth *under,* so as, according to the notation, it signifieth *subauscultare, to hearken under,* or to listen, as Rhoda did, Acts xii. 14, and Sarah, Gen. xviii. 10. Most usually it signifieth so to hearken to that which is required as to do and perform the same : this is to obey. Thus Abraham, being required of God to go to such a place, obeyed, for he went thither, Heb. xi. 8. In Latin, *dicto audiens,* he that hears what is spoken, is said to obey. This is the notation of the Greek word here translated obedience ; for obedience is a real demonstration of one's hearing that which is spoken to him, because a voice is attributed to God's rod, that is, to his chastisements ; and they who observe God's mind and meaning in correcting them are said to hear the rod, Micah vi. 9. Obedience is applied to enduring suffering.

Obedience therefore is manifested two ways :

1. By doing what is required, Rom. vi. 16.
2. By enduring what is laid upon one, Philip. ii. 8.

In this latter sense is the word here used ; for Christ by experience found that it became him willingly and patiently to bear what his Father was pleased to lay upon him.

Thus patience under a cross is a kind of obedience ; yea, it is a great degree of obedience, the highest and chiefest point of obedience: 'Unto you it is given, not only to believe on Christ, but also to suffer for his sake,' saith the apostle, Philip. i. 29. To believe is a great part of obedience, but to suffer is there made a greater.

Obj. We are oft brought to suffer, will we, nill we. There is a necessity of enduring. How then can this be counted obedience ?

Ans. Though the bearing of a burden be a matter of necessity, yet a patient and willing bearing is a point of obedience.

Herein lies a difference betwixt God's children and others. By their willing yielding they shew that they prefer the good pleasure of God before their own pleasure, yea, before their own ease, liberty, and life itself, if God call them to lose their life.

Let us not therefore think it sufficient that in peace, health, prosperity, we have yielded some active obedience to God's will for doing this or that, but let us also be ready to yield passive obedience. This is commanded Mat. xvi. 24, 2 Tim. ii. 3.

This hath been performed by God's servants, Heb. xi. 27. God hath commended it in them that have done it, Rev. ii. 3, and promised a great reward, Mat. v. 11. 12.

By this kind of obedience we shall shew that we serve God not simply for ourselves or our own advantage here in this world ; and hereby we shall answer that cavil of Satan, 'Doth he fear God for nought ?' Job i. 9.

If the things which Christ suffered be duly weighed, his obedience therein will more conspicuously be manifested. Hereof see Chap. ii. 9, Sec. 76.

Sec. 49. *Of the benefit of Christ's being perfected.*

Ver. 9. *And being made perfect, he became the author of eternal salvation unto all them that obey him.*

The blessed effects of Christ's suffering are here added, for further satisfaction of the doubt mentioned sec. 46 ; for here is shewed that glorious effects redounded to himself, and to such as believed on him. Therefore it is no wonder that so excellent a person and so dear to God as the Son was, should suffer as he did.

In reference to Christ himself it is here said that he was *made perfect,* namely, by his sufferings. This point is distinctly handled Chap. ii. 10, Sec. 97.

The manner of bringing in this effect, and inferring another effect concerning our salvation, by a participle, thus, 'Being made perfect, he became,' &c., sheweth that Christ, by his fulfilling all that was required for man's redemption, which is implied under this word *perfected,* wrought out our salvation. It was not only his incarnation, nor his living here on earth, nor his preaching and working miracles, but also his sufferings (even till it came to this, that he said, τετέλεσται, 'it is finished'), whereby he came to be 'the author of salvation.' We may not therefore sever Christ's active and passive obedience, nor think by this or that part of his active obedience, or by this or that part of his suffering, to be saved, but rest upon all that he did and endured, to the making of him perfect. For thus he comes to be the author of salvation.

Two things are comprised under the salvation here intended:
1. Final redemption from all misery.
2. Perfect fruition of all felicity.

This is the salvation which was prophesied of before Christ was exhibited, Isa. lxii. 11, Zech. ix. 9. This is it that was proclaimed upon his coming into the world, Luke i. 69, and ii. 30.

This was it that was confirmed by the apostles after Christ was taken out of the world, and by all faithful ministers age after age, Acts xxviii. 28, 2 Cor. vi. 2.

Man was implunged into such misery by sin, as, if this salvation had not been procured for him, it had been better for him never to have been. In this misery man was so far held as all creatures in the world could not help him; but Christ pitied him, and had compassion on him, as he had on the leper, Mark i. 41; and on the widow, Luke vii. 13, and thereupon saved him.

The necessity and benefit of Christ's priesthood is hereby demonstrated. By it that salvation is brought unto us, which, if we had been without, we had been worse than dogs, and in the case of devils. But by it we are brought into a better estate than that wherein Adam was created.

What matter of rejoicing doth this give unto us! Not only the mother of Jesus, Luke i. 47; and old Zacharias, Luke i. 68; and old Simeon, Luke ii. 28, &c.; and other sons of men that partake of the benefit of this redemption, much rejoiced and praised God for this salvation; but also the angels of heaven, Luke ii. 13, 14, praise God for the same, and that on man's behalf. How did the Israelites rejoice at that salvation which God gave them when they passed through the Red Sea! Exod. xv. 1, &c., and so upon other deliverances at other times. How much more ought we to be quickened up unto this holy and heavenly duty, to whom this great salvation belongeth!

Sec. 50. *Of the author of salvation.*

There is another effect of Christ's sufferings, whereby the scandal of his cross is taken away, thus expressed, 'He became the author of salvation.'

The Greek word αἴτιος, translated *author*, is not elsewhere to be found in the New Testament. Heathen philosophers attribute it to their gods,[1] whom they make the authors of all the good they have.

[1] Θεοὺς τῶν ἀγαθῶν ἡμῖν αἰτίους ὄντας.—*Isocrat. ad Phil.*

In such a sense as Christ is here called the author of salvation, he is styled the 'Captain of salvation,' Chap. ii. ver. 10, Sec. 95.

Christ is here called the author of salvation in a double respect:
1. In reference to his Father, of whom he purchased those whom he saveth, Acts xx. 28, Eph. i. 14.
2. In reference to Satan, whose slaves all mankind were. Him Christ overcame, and delivered them who were in bondage to him, and, having rescued them, made them 'heirs of salvation,' Heb. ii. 14, and i. 14.

1. Herein lieth an especial difference betwixt Christ, the true priest, and all other priests whatsoever. No priest that ever was before Christ was author of salvation. If any had been so, Christ needed not have been a priest.

2. This giveth us good ground to 'look unto Jesus,' Heb. xii. 2, because he is the author of salvation. We may safely rest and rely upon him for salvation. Incredulous persons, who refuse to rest upon Christ, and idolaters, who rest upon any other, deprive themselves of salvation, and deservedly perish.

3. Ascribe all glory for that hope of salvation which ye have unto Christ, as they who cried and said, 'Salvation to our God that sitteth on the throne, and unto the Lamb,' Rev. vii. 10. The equity hereof is thus set down: 'Of him, and through him, and to him are all things; to him be glory for ever,' Rom xi. 36.

Sec. 51. *Of 'eternal salvation.'*

Of the salvation here intended, see Chap. i. ver. 14, Sec. 159; and Chap. ii. ver. 10, Sec. 95.

The more to commend this salvation whereof Christ is the author, it is here said to be αἰώνιος, *eternal*. The Greek adjective is derived from that word αἰών (see Chap. i. ver. 8, Sec. 108), which is oft translated *ever*. Of eternity, see *The Guide to go to God*, or my *Explanation of the Lord's Prayer*, sec. 224.

Here it is taken for an everlasting continuance, without date or end. In this sense it is here said that salvation is eternal. This is that which is styled 'life eternal,' Mat. xxv. 46; and 'an inheritance incorruptible, that fadeth not away,' 1 Peter i. 4.

Thus is this salvation set forth, to manifest and magnify the greatness of his majesty, the riches of his mercy, and the worth of his sacrifice, that is the author thereof.

1. We have good ground hereupon to prefer this salvation before honour, ease, profit, pleasure, or anything else that this world can afford; for this world and all things therein are transitory. What shall it then profit a man to gain the whole world, which soon passeth away, and lose salvation, which is eternal? Consider how desirous men are of such inheritances of land and houses in this world, which have no date nor time of expiration; and yet expire they will, and must. There is no worldly inheritance so settled on

any but he must leave it, or it will leave him; but here is an everlasting inheritance, which shall never decay, never be taken away.

2. Well may we patiently endure whatsoever the Lord shall be pleased to lay on us, because 'our light affliction, which is but for a moment, worketh for us a far more exceeding and eternal weight of glory,' 2 Cor. iv. 17.

This made martyrs so patient and joyful in all their sufferings. See more of martyrs' sufferings, and of their joyful manner of suffering, in my sermon of *A Recovery from Apostasy*, on Luke xv. 31, Secs. 23, 25, 26.

Sec. 52. *Of obedience a sign of salvation.*

That it may be known to whom the foresaid salvation belongeth, the apostle addeth this description of them, 'to all them that obey him.' The participle, ὑπακούουσι, of the verb ὑπακούω, translated *obey*, is that from whence the noun ὑπακοή, *obedience*, is derived. Whereof see ver. 8, Sec. 48.

Hereby in this place is intended a doing of that which is required. He that requireth that which is to be done is comprised under this relative αὐτῷ, *him*, which hath reference to the Son, mentioned ver. 8. So that the obedience here set down is to that which Christ requireth, according to that which was noted of hearing Christ's voice, Chap. ii. ver. 7.

By this we may conceive that faith and other like graces are here comprised under this phrase *obey him*; for faith is much urged and pressed by Christ, John iii. 18, 36, and vi. 47. Therefore, he that believeth not is said to disobey, Chap. iii. ver. 18.

This qualification of the persons for whom salvation was purchased is here set down as a sign and mark, whereby they may have assurance in themselves, and may give evidence to others, that salvation belongeth unto them. For Christ hath set this mark upon his sheep, 'My sheep hear my voice, and I know them, and they follow me,' John x. 27.

Thus it appeareth that none can lay claim to salvation till they obey Christ.

This is a condition annexed to the participation of salvation; it is a way appointed for attaining thereunto.

1. This discovereth the folly of those who so rest upon what Christ hath done and endured for man's salvation, as they regard not Christ's voice, nor hearken to that which Christ requireth of them. Though the obedience here required be no cause of salvation, yet without it a man cannot attain to salvation.

2. Make this a trial of thy spiritual estate; and hereby examine thyself, that thou mayest know thy right to salvation. This sheweth that thou art a member of that body whereof Christ is the Saviour, Eph. v. 23.

3. As thou desirest to partake of this benefit of Christ's priesthood, so take him to be thy king; and let his will revealed in his word be thy rule and a law unto thee.

Sec. 53. *Of the extent of salvation, 'to all that obey.'*

As the foresaid point of obedience was a matter of restraint, excluding all that obeyed not from salvation, so this general particle, πᾶσι, *all*, is a note of extent, including all of all sorts, of what rank or degree soever they be, so as none at all that obey shall miss of salvation. He that observes the condition shall assuredly have the fruition of that which is promised. 'God rewardeth every man according to his works,' Ps. lxii. 12.

1. He that propoundeth the condition, bindeth himself to perform what is promised thereupon.

2. Christ is no respecter of persons, Acts x. 34. What he giveth to any one, he will give to every one that is guided by the same spirit.

All of all sorts, great and mean, rich and poor, male and female, or of what other rank or degree soever they be, that are in the number of those that obey, may on this ground lay hold on salvation, and rest assuredly to be made partakers thereof.

This may give a good direction to all that are in God's room over others, and have power to reward, that they do it impartially, and look to the work, not to the person.

Sec. 54. *Of Christ called a priest after the most excellent order.*

Ver. 10. *Called of God an high priest, after the order of Melchisedec.*

This verse is added as a conclusion of what the apostle had said concerning the acts and ends of Christ's priesthood; which were such as could agree to none of the priests under the law: so as he must needs be a priest after a more excellent order than the order of Aaron. This he had shewed before, verse 6, to be the order of Melchisedec, and thereupon concludeth that he is called of God an high priest after this order. The Greek word προσαγορευθείς, *cognominatus*, translated *called*, is a compound; here only used in the New Testament. It signifies a free, open acknowledging one; and as it were by name calling him.

This act is ascribed to God in this phrase, *called of God*, and implieth that God deputed Christ unto this excellent priesthood, as was noted before, Secs. 24, 27.

Of this phrase, *after the order of Melchisedec*, see ver. 6, Sec. 30.

Sec. 55. *Of the resolution of* Heb. v. 7–10.

Ver. 7. *Who in the days of his flesh, when he had offered up prayers and supplications, with strong crying and tears, unto him that was able to save him from death, and was heard in that he feared:*

8. *Though he were a Son, yet learned he obedience by the things which he suffered;*

9. *And being made perfect, he became the author of eternal salvation unto all them that obey him;*
10. *Called of God an high priest, after the order of Melchisedec.*

The sum of these four verses is, a proof of the excellency of Christ's priesthood.

Hereof are two parts:
1. A confirmation of the point, ver. 7–9.
2. A conclusion thereof, ver. 10.

The point in general was before declared, ver. 5, 6. It is here proved by an induction of particulars. The particulars may be brought to two heads.
1. The act of Christ's priesthood, ver. 7.
2. The ends thereof, ver. 8, 9.

The principal act is, 1, propounded; 2, illustrated. About the act four things are propounded.
1. The kind thereof, *he offered.*
2. The subject matter which he offered. Hereof are two branches:
1. *Prayers;* 2. *supplications.*
3. The manner of offering them up. Hereof are also two branches:
1. *With strong crying;* 2. *with tears.*
4. The person to whom he offered. This person was God, who is described,
(1.) By his ability to do what was desired, *to him that was able.*
(2.) By the extent of his power, in this phrase, *to save from death.*

The foresaid point is illustrated two ways:
1. By the time when it was done.
2. By the issue thereof.

The time is described two ways:
1. By the brevity of it, implied in this phrase, *in the days.*
2. By the infirmity of Christ's human nature, in this phrase, *of his flesh.*

The issue of Christ's prayers is set out,
1. By the kind thereof, *he was heard.*
2. By the subject whereabout he was heard, *in that he feared.*

The ends of Christ's executing his priesthood are here noted to be two: one in reference to his Father, ver. 8; the other in reference to his church, ver. 9.

In the former we may observe two points:
1. The manner of bringing it in, by these discretive particles, *though, yet.*
2. The matter whereof it consists. Hereof are two branches:
1. A lesson; 2. the means of learning it.

In the lesson are expressed,
1. The scholar, *a Son.*
2. The kind of learning, which was experience.
3. The lesson itself, *obedience.*

The means of learning the foresaid lesson were *sufferings.*

In declaring the other end, which hath reference to the church, there is noted,

1. The ground of it, Christ was *made perfect.*
2. The kind of it; this is,
1. Propounded.
2. Amplified.

In propounding the end is manifested,
1. The kind of it, *salvation.*
2. The continuance of it, *eternal.*

It is amplified,
1. By the efficient, in this phrase, *he became the author.*
2. By the persons to whose good it tended; these are manifested,
1. By a restraint, *them that obey him.*
2. By an extent of that restraint, in this general particle, *all.*

The conclusion is, that Christ is the most excellent priest.

Concerning this three points are expressed:
1. The author of his calling, *called of God.*
2. The kind of his function, *an high priest.*
3. The order after which he was a priest, *after the order of Melchisedec.*

Sec. 56. *Of observations raised out of* Heb. v. 7, 8, 9, 10.

I. *Christ's time on earth was but short.* Here it is set forth by *days.* See Sec. 33.

II. *Christ's human nature was a frail nature.* It was *flesh.* See Sec. 33.

III. *Christ's sufferings were only for the time of this life.* They were *in the days of his flesh.* See Sec 33.

IV. *Christ as our priest offered for us.* This is plainly expressed. See Sec. 34.

V. *The gifts which Christ offered up were prayers.* This also is plainly expressed. See Sec. 36.

VI. *Christ added supplications to prayers.* Of the difference betwixt prayers and supplications, see Sec. 35.

VII. *Christ's prayers were very ardent.* They were *strong cryings.* See Sec. 37.

VIII. *Christ's prayers were mixed with tears.* This is here expressed. See Sec. 37.

IX. *Christ's agony was very great.* The effects thereof here noted do demonstrate as much. See Sec. 38.

X. *In extraordinary distress, extraordinary prayer is to be made.* Christ's distress was extraordinary, so was his prayer. See Sec. 39.

XI. *Prayer is to be made to God alone.* Christ's pattern teacheth thus much. See Sec. 40.

XII. *They who call on God must believe that he is able to help.* For this end is God thus described, *who is able,* &c. See Sec. 40.

XIII. *God hath power over death.* For he *can save from death.* See Sec. 41.

XIV. *God can keep such as die from being swallowed up of death.* Thus was Christ saved from death. See Sec. 42.

XV. *Christ was offered up to death.* Thus much is intended by the mention of *death* in this place. See Sec. 42.

XVI. *Christ's prayers were heard.* This is expressly set down. See Sec. 43.

XVII. *Christ feared.* This is here taken for grant. See Sec. 44.

XVIII. *Christ was delivered from what he feared.* This is the meaning of this word, *he was heard.* See Sec. 44.

XIX. *Faith and fear may stand together.* Christ's prayer was an effect of faith, yet he feared. See Sec. 45.

XX. *Christ's sufferings are no matter of offence.* These discretive particles, *though, yet,* import as much. See Sec. 46.

XXI. *Christ was the Son of God.* This is here intended under this word, *a Son.* See Sec. 46.

XXII. *The best and dearest to God are subject to sufferings.* So was the Son of God. See Sec. 46.

XXIII. *Experience is a teacher.* This is the learning here intended. See Sec. 47.

XXIV. *Suffering is a kind of obedience.* This is the obedience here meant. See Sec. 48.

XXV. *Christ suffered much.* This is taken for grant, under this phrase, *by the things which he suffered.* See Sec. 48.

XXVI. *Christ was perfected by his sufferings.* This is here implied under this phrase, *being made perfect.* See Sec. 49.

XXVII. *What Christ suffered was for man's salvation.* Salvation is here laid down as the end of Christ's sufferings. See Sec. 49.

XXVIII. *Christ is the author of salvation.* These are the very words of the text. See Sec. 50.

XXIX. *Salvation purchased by Christ is eternal.* So is it here styled. See Sec. 51.

XXX. *True obedience is that which is yielded to Christ's word.* This relative *him* (*obey him*) hath reference to Christ and his word. See Sec. 52.

XXXI. *None but such as obey Christ can be saved.* Salvation is here appropriated to such. See Sec. 52.

XXXII. *All that obey Christ shall be saved.* The general particle *all* intends thus much. See Sec. 53.

XXXIII. *Christ was an high priest.*

XXXIV. *Christ was called of God to be an high priest.* These two last doctrines are in the words of them expressed.

XXXV. *Christ was an high priest after the most excellent order.* This was the order of Melchisedec. Of these three last doctrines, see Sec. 54.

Sec. 57. *Of the many profound mysteries of Christ's priesthood.*

Ver. 11. *Of whom we have many things to say, and hard to be uttered, seeing ye are dull of hearing.*

From this verse to the end of the sixth chapter, the apostle maketh a digression, which he doth of purpose to stir up the Hebrews more diligently to attend to that which he should further deliver about the excellency of Christ's priesthood.

This verse is a transition betwixt his former doctrine, and the following digression. It is a perfect transition, looking backward and forward. It looks backward to the former doctrine, by setting down the multitude and difficulty of mysteries concerning Melchisedec, in these two phrases, 'Many things hard to be uttered.' It looks backward to the digression in declaring their dulness; thus, 'Ye are dull of hearing.'

This relative *whom* (περὶ οὗ, of whom) hath reference to Melchisedec, the last word of the former verse; but so as it intends also Christ and his priesthood, which was ' after the order of Melchisedec.'

Of the Greek phrase, πολὺς ἡμῖν ὁ λόγος, thus translated, ' of whom we have many things to say,' see Chap. iv. 13, Sec. 79.

Thereby is implied that many mysteries were couched under that kind of priesthood; and the phrase following sheweth them to be very difficult.

This phrase, δυσερμήνευτος λέγειν, *hard to be uttered,* or hard by interpretation, to speak, or declare, manifesteth a difficulty,

The Greek word δυσερμήνευτος is a compound. The simple verb ἑρμηνεύω, signifieth to *intrepret,* and the particle δυς added thereto implieth a difficulty; as in this phrase, burdens grievous to be borne, or ' hard to be borne,' δυσβάστακτα, Luke. xi. 46; and this, ' hard to be understood,' δυσνόητα, 2 Pet. iii. 16.

Hereby we are given to understand, that the doctrine of Christ's priesthood contains many profound mysteries.

This is evident by sundry mysteries heretofore delivered on chap. ii. 17, 18, and on chap. iv. 15, 16, and on the beginning of this chapter; but especially by those which are set down in the 7th, and other chapters following.

Christ's priesthood is the main ground of our salvation. Most of the profoundest points of our Christian religion must be known for attaining the knowledge thereof: as the distinction between **Father** and **Son**, and betwixt the two natures of Christ, in both which he was our priest,—God, for works of authority and dignity; man, for works of service and suffering,— the union also of those two natures in one person, because the perfection of all those things which Christ as our priest did, consisted therein; yea, the several mysteries contained under the many rites of Aaron's priesthood, and the difference betwixt Aaron's and Melchisedec's priesthood, are to be known, as the apostle himself in the 7th chapter expressly sheweth.

1. This giveth evidence of the singular use and benefit of this epistle to the Hebrews. No part of Scripture doth more distinctly and fully lay forth the mysteries of Christ's priesthood than this. What wrong therefore do those to God's church, who im-

pugn the authority of this epistle! See Chap. i. Sec. 1, in the proem prefixed before this epistle.

2. It can be no wonder that so many heresies have been in all ages broached about the priesthood of Christ, in that it is a mystery so profound as it is. Most of the popish heresies, especially those that are most fundamental, are about Christ's priesthood. For of it there are two parts: the oblation of Christ's sacrifice, and his continual intercession, against which are most of their capital heresies; as the sacrifice of the mass, which they say is a true, real, propitiatory sacrifice for the quick and dead; their sacrificing priests, their doctrine of merit, of supererogation, of intercession of saints and angels; most of their errors about the sacraments, with many other.

3. Hereby we see how necessary it is to be well instructed in the priesthood of Christ.

4. This may stir up ministers, among other mysteries, to study and preach this mystery of Christ's priesthood; and this may also stir up people patiently and diligently to attend unto it.

Of the papists' cavil hence raised about the difficulty of the Scripture, see *The Whole Armour of God*, treat. ii. part 8, on Eph. vi. 16; of *God's word*, secs. 18, 19, &c.

Sec. 58. *Of men's dulness in hearing.*

The other part of the transition followeth in these words, *seeing ye are dull of hearing*, or slow in ears. The Greek word νωθροί, translated *dull*, properly signifieth slow, or slothful, and so it is translated, Heb. vi. 12. The Greek epithet νωθρός, vel νωθής, tardus, segnis, iners (στερησις τοῦ θεῖν, non potest currere), is attributed to an ass,[1] a slow beast; to an old man;[2] and to water,[3] running softly.

The other word, ἀκοαῖς (αἱ ἀκοαί, aures), translated *hearing*, doth signify ears, for it is of the plural number, and is translated ears, Mark vii. 35, Acts xvii. 20. They who are ready, willing, and forward to hearken to a thing are said to be ταχὺς, swift to hear, James v. 19. Contrarily, they who are negligent and careless are said to be slow in their ears, or slow in hearing. Hereby we see that their want of knowledge was through their own default, so as that dulness of understanding, which men by their own slothfulness bring upon themselves, makes the mysteries of the word to be more difficult than otherwise they would be. This is the reason that moved Christ to reprove his disciples for not understanding what he spake, Mat. xv. 16, and xvi. 9; Luke xxiv. 25; John iii. 10. So the apostles, 1 Cor. iii. 1, 2 Pet. iii. 16.

This affords matter of humiliation to all such as understand not the word, and the mysteries contained therein; for it sheweth that they have been slothful and careless about exercising themselves in God's word, and thereby they have made themselves dull in hearing, dull in conceiving.

[1] Homer.   [2] Lucian.   [3] Epigram.

Let them therefore lay the blame, not upon God's word, but upon themselves; for, take away dulness from men's understanding, and the Scriptures will appear to be much more easy than to many they appear to be.

Of the perspicuity of the Scripture, and of means to find out the sense and meaning thereof, see *The Whole Armour of God*, treat. ii. part 8, on Eph. vi. 17, secs. 3, 7, 18, 21.

This phrase, δυσερμήνευτος λέγειν, *hard to be uttered*, shews that hearers' dulness keeps ministers from a full and clear expressing of the mysteries of the word; they know not how to speak to their hearers, 1 Cor. iii. 1.

Hereby they are forced to pass over sundry mysteries, or to express them in such low terms as may seem more fit for dull capacities than for divine mysteries. This further aggravates that fault of dulness in hearing.

Sec. 59. *Of reproving upon just ground.*

Ver. 12. *For when for the time ye ought to be teachers, ye have need that one teach you again which be the first principles of the oracles of God, and are become such as have need of milk, and not of strong meat.*

In this verse the apostle gives a particular exemplification of that for which he had in general reproved them in the latter part of the former verse; namely, for their dulness in hearing.

This exemplification is brought in as a proof of his reproof. So much is manifest by this causal particle γὰρ, *for*; before which in Greek is set the copulative particle καί, γὰρ, which is not without emphasis, and may be thus translated, *for, even.*

The apostle's exemplification is set out in two metaphors: one is taken from catechists, who need to be instructed in the first principles of Christian religion, ver. 12; the other from children, who must have plain and easy matters delivered unto them, vers. 13, 14.

By this manner of proceeding, in shewing the ground of his reproof, we may observe that reproof must be upon good ground.

'If thy brother shall trespass, go and tell him his fault,' Mat. xviii. 15. This is to be done in private reproof: 'Them that sin rebuke before all,' 1 Tim. v. 24. This is to be done in public reproof. In the one and in the other there must be a *trespass*, a *sin*, for which the reproof is. Nicodemus took this for an undeniable principle, which he thus expresseth: 'Doth our law judge any man before it hear him, and know what he doth?' John vii. 51.

Hereby the reprover justifieth his deed, and sheweth that there was need thereof. Thus he maketh his reproof to pierce more deeply, and maketh the reproved see his fault, whereby he may be brought to confess and redress it; or at least his mouth will be stopped, that he shall not have to oppose against it.

To reprove upon light report or mere suspicion savoureth too rankly of that rashness which beseemeth not Christians in such a duty.

Sec. 60. *Of proficiency answerable to the means afforded.*

This phrase, διὰ τὸν χρόνον, *for the time*, implieth that these Hebrews had had the gospel many years preached unto them; thereby they were called unto the Christian church, and made scholars in Christ's school, and had Christ's ministers to be their instructors, and the holy Scriptures their books. This is here noted as an aggravation of their dulness, and implieth that our proficiency ought to be answerable to our continuance under the ministry of God's word. Christ thus blameth Philip for failing herein: 'Have I been so long time with you, and yet hast thou not known me, Philip?' John xiv. 9. Herein Moses aggravateth the sin of the Israelites in the wilderness, who had been there tutored forty years: 'Yet,' saith he, 'the Lord hath not given you an heart to perceive, and eyes to see, and ears to hear unto this day,' Deut. xxix. 4.

This also made Jeremiah to complain 'that three and twenty years together he had spoken to them the word of the Lord, but they had not hearkened,' Jer. xxv. 3.

The continuance of means of knowledge among us is a great aggravation of our people's ignorance; for who among us have not been born and brought up under the light of the gospel? Are there any now that were born before Queen Elizabeth's days? But from the beginning of her days till these our days hath the gospel been preached in this land, and I hope will continue to be preached to the world's end. The truth of God's word and mysteries of godliness have all this time been publicly preached and strongly maintained against papists and other adversaries. A shame, therefore, it is for people to be dull in hearing the mysteries of the word. See more hereof Sec. 63.

Of ignorance as it is a sin, see ver. 2, Sec. 10. Of the danger thereof, see Chap. iii. ver. 10, Sec. 112.

Sec. 61. *Of learners proving teachers.*

By the continuance of means which these Hebrews had enjoyed, the apostle here sheweth that they might have attained to such a measure of knowledge, as they might have been able to have instructed others.

The word διδάσκαλοι, translated *teachers*, is derived from a verb, διδάσκω, that signifieth *to teach*. It setteth forth such an one as hath been so taught, and thereupon hath so learned, as he is able and fit to teach others. Sometimes it is put for him that hath an office of teaching, Eph. iv. 11, 1 Cor. xii. 28; sometimes for him that hath ability to teach, Rom. ii. 20. So it is here taken; so as it will not follow that all who are able to instruct others should thereupon take upon them the ministerial function, without being called and set apart thereunto. All that have the office of teachers must have the ability of teachers, but all that have the ability need not have the office.

The word ὀφείλοντες, set before this, and translated *ye ought*, signifieth a bounden duty. Of the various acception of this word, see Chap. ii. 17, Sec. 166. Here it sheweth, that it became them, and it was their duty so to have improved the means of knowledge that was so long afforded unto them, as they might have been fit to have taught others. In this respect the apostle requires aged women to be teachers of good things, Titus ii. 4. Thus Aquila and Priscilla instructed Apollos, Acts xviii. 26.

By such proficiency, both God, his word, and ministers are much honoured; yea, thereby the church may be much increased, and they themselves made able to do much good to others, and to themselves.

What now may we judge of them, who do all they can to keep people from knowledge, and to nuzzle them up in ignorance. Hereof see *The Whole Armour of God*, treat. ii. part viii., on Eph. vi. 17, secs. 22–24. How such are made Satan's vassals, see *ibid.*, treat. i. part i., on Eph. vi. 12, sec. 24.

This may be a spur to such as think they have gone far, if they have attained to the knowledge of some fundamental principles. Are such fit to be teachers? Where is that fulness of knowledge, Col. i. 9, and abundance therein, 2 Cor. viii. 7, which is required of Christians?

If it be the duty of private Christians to be able to instruct others, how much more of ministers, governors of families, parents, and such as have charge over others? What a shame it is for such to be unable to be teachers.

It becomes us therefore to give the more earnest heed to the things we hear, Heb. ii. 1, so as we may the more profit thereby, and still more and more grow in knowledge, till we come to be able teachers.

Sec. 62. *Of instructing others according to their need.*

This phrase, χρείαν ἔχετε, *ye have need*, is brought in as a reason of the apostle's forbearing to handle deep points. They had need of other kind of instructions. So as people are to be instructed according to their need. 'Ye are not able to bear' such and such doctrines, 1 Cor. iii. 2; 'I have yet many things to say unto you, but you cannot bear them now,' saith Christ to his disciples, John xvi. 12. It is expressly said of him, that 'he spake the word unto them as they were able to bear it,' Mark iv. 33. This was the reason why Christ would not press upon his disciples that austere discipline of much fasting, while they were but novices. He declareth the equity hereof in two familiar comparisons: one taken from putting a piece of new cloth into an old garment; the other, from 'putting new wine into old bottles;' which he saith no man will do,' Mat. ix. 14, 15, &c. See more Sec. 66.

The Greek word χρεία, translated *need*, signifieth also *use*, Eph. iv. 29, Titus iii. 14. And experience teacheth, that things needful do prove useful.

It is therefore an especial point of wisdom in those who have a charge over others, carefully to observe of what they have need.

This conjunction, πάλιν, *again*, hath reference to their first entrance into Christ's school, and it intends as much as if he had thus said, As at the beginning, when ye first became hearers of the gospel, ye were ignorant of the mysteries thereof, and had need to be instructed in the first principles of Christian religion, so still ye remain ignorant; and notwithstanding the great means of knowledge afforded unto you, and the long time that you have enjoyed the same, ye are in such a case as you were in the beginning: so that it is needful that we begin all new again.

Hereby the apostle gives us to understand, that where need requires it, the same things are to be taught again, yea, and again. 'To write the same things to you, is for you safe,' saith the apostle, Philip. iii. 1. To this tends the prophet's ingemination, 'Precept must be upon precept, precept upon precept; line upon line, line upon line,' Isa. xxviii. 10.

Thus we deal with our friends about bodily food. If we observe that by reason of weakness they need to be fed with such sustenance as they used in their childhood, we will give them the same again. Physicians in deep consumptions use to advise well-grown persons to suck womens' breasts.

Should we not be as wise for people's souls as for their bodies?

Sec. 63. *Of the first principles of the oracles of God.*

That which these Hebrews had need to be taught again is thus expressed, 'The first principles of the oracles of God.'

The word στοιχεῖα, translated *principles*, is derived from a verb, στείχειν, that signifieth *to go*. This is the first evident demonstration of a child's strength, that he can feel his legs and go. The metaphor is transferred to arts, wherein the first things that are learned are called στοιχεῖα, *principles* or *elements*. All arts have their distinct principles, which they who desire to learn this or that art are first taught. So Christians have their principles, wherein they who desire knowledge of the Christian religion are instructed.

These are here said to be the first principles, or word for word, τὰ στοιχεῖα τῆς ἀρχῆς, 'the principles of the beginning;' such as at the beginning are first taught, and thereupon not unfitly turned 'first principles.'

More distinctly to shew what kind of principles he meaneth, he addeth this clause, τῶν λογίων τοῦ Θεοῦ, 'of the oracles of God.'

The word λόγια, translated *oracles*, is derived from another noun, λόγος, that signifieth *word* or *speech*. Heathen authors do put the word here used in the singular number, τὸ λόγιον, for a *divine answer, oraculum*. In English it is styled an oracle.

The apostle here, to shew distinctly what he means, adds this word, τοῦ Θεοῦ, *of God* ('oracles of God'). So as he means such principles as are made known by God in his word. Therefore the laws which Moses declared from God are styled oracles, Acts vii. 38; and the precepts committed to the Jews, Rom. iii. 2, and in general the whole word of God, 1 Peter iv. 11.

This is an aggravation of the fault of the Hebrews, in that they neglected not principles of human arts, but the very oracles of God himself.

In particular, these are called 'The principles of the doctrine of Christ,' Chap. vi. Sec. 3.

In this case to be ever learning, and never able to come to the knowledge of the truth, is a great shame, 2 Tim. iii. 7.

God himself is hereby much dishonoured, his word and ministers disgraced.

This nearly concerns such as have been ancient professors and hearers of God's word. The adversaries of our profession will be ready to open their mouths against such, so as the name of God may be blasphemed thereby, Rom. ii. 24.

Such also may soon be made a prey to every seducer, Eph. iv. 14.

Take heed therefore how you hear.

Sec. 64. *Of catechism.*

This phrase, 'Ye have need that one teach you again, which be the first principles,' &c., is a description of such as were to be instructed in the first principles of the Christian religion. Hereby it appeareth, that the primitive church, even in the apostles' days, had forms of catechisms, and a custom of catechising; as the Jews had the law for their catechism, and the abbreviation thereof, Mat. xxii. 37–39.

To *catechise*, κατηχίζειν, according to the notation of the Greek verb,[1] is to instruct, and that by word of mouth, or by sounding a thing in one's ears.

Among Christians, to catechise is to teach the first principles of Christian religion; and a catechism is a brief form of such principles. Such forms there were in the beginning of the primitive church. These and such like phrases import as much: 'a form of knowledge,' Rom. ii. 20; 'a form of doctrine,' Rom. vi. 17; 'a form of sound words,' 2 Tim. i. 13; 'the principles of the doctrine of Christ,' Heb. vi. 1; and this phrase in my text, 'the first principles of the oracles of God.' Thus was Theophilus, Luke i. 4, and Apollos catechised, Acts x. 25.

As in the apostle's time, so in succeeding ages, sundry churches had their distinct catechisms.

So frequent was the practice of catechising in ancient times, as they had ministers set apart for this

---

[1] ἦχος, *sonus*; κατηχεῖν, *insonare aliquid auribus alterius, vel instituere vivâ voce, vel initiare præceptis artis. Inde* κατηχίζειν, *rudimenta religionis docere.*

particular duty to catechise, called χατηχισται, catechisers, and all that were admitted to the church were from time to time catechised, and instructed in the principles of Christian religion, who, from the time of their entrance into the church, till they were judged fit to partake of the sacrament, were called κατηχητοι, κατηχουμενοι, catechised, or disciples of the catechisers.

Many of the ancient councils[1] have made sundry decrees for catechising. And many of the ancient fathers[2] have made treatises thereabouts.

Weighty reasons may be given for the necessity of catechising.

1. By catechising, a good and sure foundation is laid. Now, it is necessary that in all buildings a good foundation be laid, lest for want of it the building come to ruin, Mat. vii. 26, 27.

2. By catechising, people are by degrees made capable of deeper mysteries, as children by learning letters and syllables, and to spell them, are brought on to read distinctly. The most intelligent hearers are such as have been well instructed in the principles of religion.

3. By catechising, such as profess the faith are enabled to 'render a reason of the hope that is in them,' as is required, 1 Peter iii. 15. For a catechism well compiled, contains the sum and substance of all that a Christian is to believe.

4. By catechising, pastors may know their people's capacity and understanding, and this is requisite in two respects: 1, that he may know the better whom to admit to the Lord's table; 2, that he may the better discern how to order his preaching, both for matter and manner.

5. The fruits of catechising have ever been observed to be many and great. Thereby have families been made seminaries for the church. Catechising was one of the most effectual ordinary means of drawing pagans to embrace the Christian faith. The fruit which Julian the apostate observed to arise from instructing children in the principles of Christianity, made him put down all places that were used to that end. It hath ever been observed, that in this latter spring of the gospel, the use of catechising hath been an especial means of drawing people from the darkness of popery to the light of the gospel. For every reformed church hath her catechism, whereby multitudes have been so grounded in the true religion, as nothing could draw them from the same. Hereupon papists, by decree of their council at Trent,[3] were moved to compile a catechism of the principles of their religion.

If the question be demanded wherein the difference lieth betwixt catechising and preaching, I answer, in these particulars especially:

[1] Conci. Neocæs. Can. 6 and 7; Concil. Iber. 2 Concil. Bra. Can. 1; 4 Concil. Tolet. Can. 24.

[2] Clem. Alex Pædag.; Orig. περι αρχων; Cyril. Hieros. Myster; Aug. Enchir. et de Symbol. ad Catech.; Fulgent. de fide; Theodoret. Epitom. Lactant. Instit.

[3] Concil. Trident. Sess. ult. sub Pio iv. Decret. 19.

1. By catechising, a foundation is laid, Heb. vi. 1. By preaching, the building is farther reared up, beautified, and perfected.

2. By catechising, many and large points are contracted into brief sums, as in the ten commandments, creed, and Lord's prayer. By preaching, sundry points are amplified, enlarged, and sundry ways applied.

3. By catechising, weak and ignorant ones are fed, as with milk. By preaching, the strong are further nourished with strong meat. For in catechising the most necessary principles are plainly laid down; but in preaching all sorts of points, the difficult as well as easy, use to be handled; yea, and contrary errors refuted.

4. By catechising, a particular account is taken of the learners, which is not so done by preaching. For catechising is by question and answer, so as the catechised give an account of their proficiency; but preaching is only by a minister's declaring his mind.

5. Catechising is for such as are newly entered into the church, and that for a time, till they may be fitted for the sacrament. But preaching is for all of all sorts, so long as they live. For though a man had all knowledge, yet is preaching requisite to work upon their affections, and to bring to their mind and memory such things as they know. Preaching is profitable to all those uses that are mentioned, 2 Tim. iii. 16.

Hereby it is evident that catechising is to be used as well as preaching. In this respect,

1. They who are in authority to order church affairs, ought to make orders and laws for catechising, and be careful to see them put in execution.

2. Ministers who have the charge of souls committed unto them, must be conscionable in laying this foundation where they see just cause. Though they be learned, yet they need not be ashamed thereof. It is no shame to lay a foundation, but a great shame to build without a foundation.

3. Parents and governors of families are especially to be conscionable in catechising their families. This is intended, Deut. vi. 7, and commended by God himself in Abraham, Gen. xviii. 19. This would be a great help to the public ministry of the word. If in families milk were frequently and seasonably given, then might more strong meat be ministered unto them in public churches.

4. Such as are ignorant ought to suffer this foundation to be laid in their souls, and not think much to be catechised, that so they may better profit by the public ministry of the word.

Sec. 65. *Of grounding principles of religion on God's word.*

The addition of these words, *oracles of God*, giveth proof that the principles which are taught in catechisms ought to be grounded on God's word. Such were the principles in which these Hebrews were instructed. To this purpose this advice was given, 'If any man speak, let him speak as the oracles of God,' 1 Peter iv. 11. In this sense, catechistical points are styled ' the principles of the doctrine of Christ,' Heb. vi. 1.

These only are sound, 2 Tim. i. 13, or wholesome words, ' even the words of our Lord Jesus Christ, and the doctrine which is according to godliness,' 1 Tim. vi. 3.

1. This giveth a good direction to such as frame catechisms, that they be sure to have good warrant out of God's word for every principle that they set down. It will be useful in this respect, to quote the scriptures on which their principles are grounded in the margin.

2. This is a forcible motive to those that have such catechisms as may justly be styled, ' the first principles of the oracles of God,' conscionably to use them. Ministers, governors of families, parents, tutors, schoolmasters, and others that have the charge of souls, ought to be more conscionable in instructing such as are under them, because they are the oracles of God, wherein they do instruct them, and learners in that respect ought to be the more diligent in learning them.

Sec. 66. *Of instructing according to learners' ability.*

The apostle, the more to aggravate the fore-mentioned fault, setteth it out in a familiar comparison, taken from those that are fit to be fed with *milk* or *strong meat.*

Milk, γάλα, is a food of light digestion, fit for weak stomachs, such as children have.

Strong meat, στερεὰ τροφή, as bread, mutton, beef, and such like, is fit for strong stomachs, such as they have who are somewhat grown in years.

The foresaid first principles are resembled to milk, and deeper mysteries to strong meat.

By affirming that they had need of milk, he giveth them to understand that he could no otherwise account of them than of children.

He doth not simply say they had need, but γεγόνατε, ' ye are become such as have need.' Hereby he implieth that God had afforded them sufficient means to be as strong men, but they had made themselves to be as children. Thus this word is used James ii. 4, 11 ; yea, this very word is used in the verse before this text, but thus translated, *ye are*. It implieth that the fault was in themselves ; they brought upon themselves that unfitness to be fed with strong meat.

This negative, καὶ οὐ στερεᾶς τροφῆς, *and not of strong meat*, is to be taken comparatively, as if he had said, Ye have need of milk *rather* than of strong meat ; or else the word *need* must be taken for fit or meet, thus : Ye are such as milk, not strong meat, is fit for ; such as may be fit to have the principles of a catechism delivered to you, but not (or rather than) deep doctrines of divinity. That this is his meaning is clear by his own exposition of this phrase in the two next verses.

By this comparison, it appears that God's word is to be dispensed according to hearers' capacities. See Sec. 62.

The end of dispensing God's word is to edify, 1 Cor. xiv. 12, 26 ; but this is the readiest way to edify people. Children best thrive with milk, and grown men with strong meat. Wise schoolmasters will observe the capacities of their scholars, and answerably instruct them. Should not ministers much more ?

1. Contrary to this direction is an affectation of strong lines, as obscure preaching is called. Many so preach as none can understand them : it is well if they can understand themselves. Such were as good be silent; for as good never a whit as never the better. They think they shall be accounted deep scholars, but then it must be by such as know not what a scholar is.

2. They transgress the foresaid direction who put no difference betwixt auditors and places, but preach the same things in populous assemblies and country villages, that they do in universities or assemblies of divines, stuffing their sermons with unknown tongues, human testimonies, obscure comparisons, and curious school points, as if the doctrine of the sacred Scripture were too plain.

3. It will be the wisdom of ministers to distinguish betwixt persons and places, and carefully to observe what may be fitted for them with whom they have in present to do, especially for the meaner sort. It is better in this case to stoop too low than to soar too high. It is better to feed men with milk than to choke children with strong meat. ' Mind not high things, but condescend to men of low estate,' Rom. xii. 16. Note Paul's example in this case, 1 Cor. xiv. 18, 19.

Sec. 67. *Of blaming every one that deserveth blame.*

Ver. 13. *For every one that useth milk is unskilful in the word of righteousness ; for he is a babe.*

The apostle, to demonstrate the equity of his reproof, amplifieth his former comparison in this and the other verse following, and sheweth what a disgrace it is to stand always in need of milk, ver. 13, and what a benefit it is to be capable of strong meat, ver. 14.

The causal particle γὰρ, *for*, implieth a confirmation of that which went before, namely, that it is a shame to be so ignorant as to stand in need of learning the first principles of religion, in that he must needs be unskilful in the word of righteousness.

This point is set down in general terms thus : ' Every one that useth milk,' &c.

This general expression πᾶς, *every one*, compriseth all of all sorts, as magistrates, ministers, parents, other governors, and such as are under them ; and also statesmen, honourable, wealthy, aged persons, male and female professors and other sorts.

Of the meaning of the Greek word ὁ μετέχων, translated *useth*, see Chap. ii. 14, Sec. 139.

Here it is taken for the need wherein one standeth of milk, that is, of being instructed in the first principles. Now, no outward estate or condition can excuse such an one, or exempt him from blame, especially after long teaching. Read the prophets' reproofs of such, and you shall find that they spared none, nor princes, nor priests, nor prophets, nor people.

God is the master of all, all are his scholars; his instructions are given to all, all are bound to learn them; with whom is no respect of persons, to him king and beggar are alike.

How great is their folly who, to excuse themselves, put the blame on others! Poor and mean men will say, It is a shame for rich and great men to be ignorant. These again will lay the blame upon the meaner sort, as if they had more leisure to attend upon the means of knowledge. So others in other cases, one puts off to the other. Again, men of great place, much wealth, and many years, think they have a protection; and that, though they be ignorant, yet they ought not to be accounted or called babes.

For our parts, let us *every one* apply that which is here said by the apostle to ourselves, and, if we deserve the blame, lay it upon our own souls, that we may be humbled and moved to redress that wherein we have formerly failed.

Sec 68. *Of dulness from want of exercise in God's word.*

The disgrace and damage of the fore-named ignorant persons is thus expressed, *unskilful in the word of righteousness.*

The Greek word ἄπειρος, translated *unskilful*, is a compound. The simple noun πεῖρα, *conatus, experimentum*, signifieth endeavour or experience. The preposition (α) being privative, implieth want of experience.[1] He is as one that hath seldom heard, or at least little heeded, the word. He hath not exercised himself therein; he hath learned no skill thereby.

The apostle, by this phrase, pointeth at two points:

1. Dulness in hearing argueth want of exercise and experience in God's word.

2. Such dulness makes men unable to use God's word aright.

Concerning the former, exercise in any art and science maketh the mysteries of it easy and familiar to a man, as is evident by daily experience.

But among and above all other sciences, God's word hath an inward, quickening virtue, whereby it sharpeneth the wit of the most simple that exercise themselves therein, Prov. i. 4. It is therefore called quick and powerful, Heb. iv. 12. David thereby was 'made wiser than his enemies, than all his teachers, than the ancient,' Ps. cxix. 98-100.

Concerning the second point, that dulness in hearing makes men unable to use God's word aright. This also may be confirmed by experience, as the former; for he that is not his craft's master can do no good in that science which he doth profess.

Some do here object that many who read and hear much, still remain dull and uncapable of the mysteries of the word, being 'ever learning, and never able to come to the knowledge of the truth,' 2 Tim. iii. 7.

Ans. I may say of such as is said of many that pray, James iv. 3, 'They ask amiss.' They are like the grounds on which corn was sown, and yet brought forth no fruit; they either understand not the word, or suffer it not to take root in them, or, with the cares of this world, choke it, Mat. xiii. 19, &c.

1. This may be a matter of trial, whereby it may be known who have exercised themselves aright in the word, namely, they who understand the word, and are capable of the doctrines that are raised out of it; who can try the spirits, 1 John iv. 1; who can discern 'such as make divisions, contrary to wholesome doctrine,' Rom. xvi. 17; who are not 'as children carried about with every wind of doctrine,' Eph. v. 14; who are 'established with grace,' Heb. xiii. 9.

2. This manifesteth the great wrong that many do to themselves by slothfulness and dulness in hearing: they make that word which is in every respect profitable to be useless unto them; they can have no skill therein.

Sec. 69. *Of the word of righteousness.*

The word that is useless to dull hearers is styled *the word of righteousness.*[1] Hereby is meant the word of God, and that both as it is written and preached. This is it that is said to be 'righteous altogether,' Ps. xix. 9.

Thus it is in four especial respects:

1. In regard of the author thereof, who saith, 'All the words of my mouth are in righteousness,' Prov. vii. 8.

2. In regard to the matter contained therein, which is all manner of righteousness. It declareth all the parts of righteousness, and how a man may be made righteous.

3. In regard of the end for which it was written and given to men, which was to make them righteous. 'It is profitable for instruction in righteousness, that the man of God may be made perfect, thoroughly furnished unto all good works,' 2 Tim. iii. 16, 17.

4. In regard of the effect, it doth indeed make a man righteous; for it worketh faith, whereby he layeth hold on Christ's righteousness, Rom. x. 17, and also repentance, which maketh a man walk in the way of righteousness. The word is it whereby men come to be justified and sanctified, and to grow up in sanctification, till by degrees he come to be perfected, Eph. v. 26; James i. 18; John xvii. 17.

1. This much aggravateth their fault who do not

---

[1] ὁ μὴ ἔχων πεῖραν, *qui experientiam non habet; vel qui peritiam non habet.*

[1] Of righteousness, see Chap. i. 9, Sec. 114, and Chap. vi. 10, Sec. 61.

exercise themselves in this word, but are unskilful therein. It is the word of righteousness which they neglect.

2. How should this stir us up to give the more earnest heed to this word. What almost can more stir us up? Hereby we shall be directed to put on the breastplate of righteousness, Eph. vi. 14.

3. How do they pervert this word, who thereby pretend to justify error, falsehood, impiety, or iniquity?

Sec. 70. *Of children, wherein it is a grace or disgrace to be like them.*

The apostle, in following the metaphor of using milk, addeth this reason, *for he is a babe.* Babes must be fed with milk.

The Greek word, νήπιος, quasi νὴ εἴπειν, translated *babe*, according to the notation of it, signifieth one that cannot speak. To this purpose saith the prophet, 'I cannot speak, for I am a child,' Jer. i. 6.

An infant in Latin[1] hath also the same notation. He is not able to give an account of his faith.

This title *child* or *babe* is a word of disgrace to one grown in years. The apostle doth here use it for a further aggravation of the fore-mentioned fault of being dull in hearing.

Quest. How can that be a matter of reproach which is required of us; for we are commanded, ' as new-born babes to desire the sincere milk of the word,' 1 Peter ii. 2, and to be as children, Mat. xviii. 3.

Ans. The same thing in diverse respects may be diverse, and accordingly in one respect be praise-worthy, and in another respect blameworthy. Christ and righteous ones in courage are resembled to a lion, Rev. v. 5; Prov. xxviii. 1. Satan also and wicked ones in cruelty, 1 Peter, v. 8; Ps. x. 9. Christ in his sudden coming is resembled to a thief, Rev. xvi. 15, and false teachers in deceit, John x. 8. Christians in prudence are resembled to a serpent, Mat. x. 16, and wicked ones in venom or poison, Ps. lviii. 4. Man's regenerate part in softness is resembled to flesh, Ezek. xi. 19, and the unregenerate part in corruption, John iii. 6. The things of the kingdom of God in communicating their good savour are resembled to leaven, Mat. xiii. 33, and false doctrine in infecting, Mat. xvi. 6.

To apply this to the point in hand; there are sundry respects wherein it is commendable to be as a child or babe, and other respects wherein it is discommendable.

The former respects are these:

1. Simplicity, honesty, plainness, truth. These graces are implied to be in children, Isa. xi. 8. We have a proverb that Children will tell truth.

2. Humility and meekness. Herein doth Christ set forth children as a pattern, Mat. xviii. 4. So doth the psalmist, Ps. cxxxi. 2. By experience we see that a great man's child scorns not to play with the child of a mean man.

[1] Infans, qui fari non potest.

3. Freedom from rancour, malice, envy, and such like violent and evil passions, 1 Cor. xiv. 20.

4. Desire of milk, whereby they are nourished. A child is seldom quiet without the breast milk; that quickly quiets it. Herein we are exhorted to be like them, 1 Peter ii. 2.

5. Growing and increasing, 1 Peter. ii. 2. Childhood is a growing age. When men come to man-age, they use to stand at a stay.

6. Taking notice of their parents, and depending on them. Lambs, calves, and other young ones know their own dams, and will quickly find them out in a great flock or herd. The prophet sheweth that the ox and ass, the most brutish of brutes, know where they are fed, Isa. i. 3. 'Your heavenly Father knoweth that you have need of these and these things,' Mat. vi. 31. Will you not then depend on him?

7. Subjection to their parents' will, which is a law to children, 1 Peter i. 14, and seeking their parents' honour, Mal. i. 6. Christ hath made himself a pattern herein, Luke ii. 51.

8. Care to imitate their parents, and seeking to be like them, John viii. 39; Rom. iv. 12; 1 Peter i. 16, 17; Eph. v. 1; Mat. v. 48.

9. Retaining a childlike affection to their parents, and reverencing them, though they correct them, Heb. xii. 9.

10. Returning to them after they have offended them, Luke xv. 18. That affection which a child conceiveth to be in his parents towards him will be in him towards his parents.

The respects wherein it is discommendable and disgraceful to be as children are such as these.

1. Ignorance and want of capacity, 1 Cor. xiv. 20.

2. Vanity and delighting in toys, as painted pears, rattles, and such like: 'When I became a man, I put away childish things,' κατήργηκα τὰ τοῦ νηπίου, 1 Cor. xiii. 11.

3. Levity, inconstancy, Eph. iv. 14. We say of a child, that it is won with a nut, and lost with a shell.

4. Disability to manage weighty affairs, Eccles. x. 16, Isa. iii. 4. Jer. i. 6.

5. Non-proficiency and a small measure of knowledge, faith, and other graces. In this respect children are here opposed to men well-grown, and babes are counted carnal, and opposed to such as are spiritual. This last respect is here especially meant.

Sec. 71. *Of the disgrace of old babes.*

The apostle here useth this metaphor of babes in the worst part as a matter of disgrace, because after sufficient means to have made them strong men, they remained as babes; for they who, being long trained up under the gospel, grow not thereby in knowledge, may well be accounted babes, or young novices, or fresh men (as they say in schools), or nibs, or pages. The apostle calls them not only *babes*, but also *carnal*, 1 Cor. iii. 1.

It is not time and means which bringeth true honour, and makes men highly to be accounted of, but a good use of that time and means, and progress and proficiency answerable thereunto.

Without these, long standing and much means are but a reproach. In schools such an one is counted a dunce. As the bodies of men have their degrees of growth, so their spirits.

It is growth in knowledge and grace, and ripeness of understanding, that makes a Christian to be accounted strong and spiritual.

Among other motives to provoke every hearer to improve, to the best advantage that he can, the time and means which God doth afford to him, this is one, to avoid the reproach of an *old babe*.

These two epithets, *old* and *babe*, do not well agree. Oldness or antiquity is a matter of glory and dignity; the younger are to reverence them. But for old persons to be children or babes, doth not only take away their honour, but also bring a reproach upon them. A young babe is no disgrace, but an old babe is.

The philosopher[1] observed this to be a matter of infamy, and he puts no more difference betwixt a child in years than in understanding.

1. The babes of whom we speak may happily be deprived of such means as they shall never get again.
2. They may be made more uncapable of receiving benefit by such means.
3. Upon conceit, that it is a shame for them to be instructed in the first principles, they may reject those means.
4. Their ignorance may not be suspected, and thereupon means not afforded to them.

Thus we see what a disgrace and damage it is to be an old babe; yet what congregation is there wherein there be not many such?

Some lay the blame hereof upon their minister; and I cannot deny but that there may be a fault in some ministers, by not attending their flock as they should; yet that doth not wholly excuse the dull hearer, Ezek. iii. 18.

But the fault is not in every minister; witness the ministers whom God afforded to these Hebrews. Where there have been the best ministers, most painful, most faithful, yea, and prudent also in bringing forth both milk and strong meat, and that in due season, there have been old babes.

Sec. 72. Of men of full age, to whom strong meat belongeth.

Ver. 14. *But strong meat belongeth to them that are of full age, even those who by reason of use have their senses exercised to discern both good and evil.*

As the damage of non-proficiency in Christ's school was set down in the former verse, so here the advantage of good proficiency.

The conjunction of opposition δὲ, *but*, sheweth that

[1] Aristot. Ethic. Nicom., lib. i. cap. i.

a different, yea, and a contrary matter is here added; for contraries laid together do each of them appear more fully in their own colours. On this ground the wise man doth frequently oppose contraries, Prov. x. 1, 2, &c.

Strong meat is here opposed to milk, not as directly contrary thereunto, but differing in some circumstances; for the same matter may be milk and strong meat: *milk*, in the plain and easy manner of delivering it; *strong meat*, in collecting deep and profound mysteries out of it. As, to shew that there is a God, and but one God, yet distinguished into three persons, may be milk; but to shew how the persons are distinguished, by inward operations in relation to themselves, and by outward operations in reference to creatures, may prove strong meat. So to declare that Jesus Christ is both God and man, and our Saviour, may be milk; but distinctly to demonstrate what works are proper to each nature, and what are works of authority, what works of ministry, may be strong meat. They are not curious school-points, nor philosophical discourses, nor rhetorical affectations, which the apostle counteth strong meat; for such he protesteth against, 1 Cor. ii. 6; Col. ii. 8, but great and deep mysteries of the word, especially such as are not in direct terms expressed in the word; but such as by just and necessary consequence are drawn out of the same, whereof we have an instance, Heb. vii. 3.

The persons for whom strong meat is are said to be of full age, or as it is in the Greek, τελείων, *perfect*.

A person is said to be perfect two ways:

1. Simply; when he is so complete as nothing more, in that kind wherein he is said to be perfect, need to be added. Thus is the word used in this phrase, 'unto a perfect man,' Eph. iv. 13; and in this, 'that we may present every man perfect,' Col. i. 28.

2. Comparatively; in reference to such as have not attained to such a degree as they who are accounted perfect have.

Thus saith the apostle, 'We speak wisdom among them that are perfect,' 1 Cor. ii. 6; and, 'Let us, as many as be perfect, be thus minded,' Philip. iii. 15.

Here it is comparatively taken, in reference to babes; so as it implieth grown men, such as have well profited by the word, and attained to a great measure of knowledge and grace. When any are past childhood and youth, we say he is *adultus*, 'of age.' In this respect our English translateth the word *perfect* thus, *of full age*. Non-age and full age are opposites; yet he that is counted to be of full age may further grow both in years and stature. Therefore no absolute perfection can be here meant, nor such a state as should make men cease to learn; for whilst we live in this world, we know but in part, 1 Cor. xiii. 9. In this sense this very word is translated men, in opposition to children, thus: 'Be not children in understanding, but in understanding be τέλειοι, men.'

The right that these persons have to strong meat, is in our English thus expressed, *belongeth to them*, &c. In the Greek, this right is comprised under the genitive case, thus, τελείων ἔστι, *is of the perfect;* or, *is of them that are of full age.*

Thus Christ styleth the bread that belongeth to children 'children's bread,' or 'the bread of children,' τὸν ἄρτον τῶν τέκνων, Mat. xv. 26: that which is due to them, that whereunto they have a good right; and thus our English hath well expounded it in this phrase, *belongeth* to them.

Sec. 73. *Of ministers' ability to preach the deep mysteries of the word.*

In that 'strong meat belongeth to them that are of full age,' by just and necessary consequence it followeth, that ministers must be able to feed 'with strong meat. They must be able to preach the deeper mysteries of the gospel, as well as the easier principles; for that which belongeth to any must be given to him. The Lord sets it down as the part of a faithful steward to give the household τὸ σιτομέτριον, 'their portion of meat,' Luke xii. 42; that which in kind and quantity belongeth unto them. They who are not able themselves to understand deep mysteries, cannot reveal them to others. *Nihil dat quod non habet*, nothing gives that which it hath not.

That a minister must be able to declare deep mysteries, is evident by this qualification which the apostle requires of him, διδακτικός, 'apt to teach,' 1 Tim. iii. 2; and by this duty of ὀρθοτομεῖν τὸν λόγον, 'rightly dividing the word.' The apostle takes his metaphor from the priests, who divided the sacrifice, and laid every part in order, according to the prescript of the law.

1. The conceit which many have concerning the sufficiency of a minister, by this appears to be a plain deceit, namely, that it is enough to have knowledge of the principles of religion, if at least he have a free and ready speech, and a forward and zealous spirit; so as he can thunder out God's judgments against sinners, and pithily exhort to piety and virtue. I deny not but that these are needful and commendable; but this very text sheweth that they are not sufficient.

If it be said that they may be sufficient for country congregations,

I answer, that it is hard that there should be a congregation of Christians where no strong ones are. If no spiritual growth were required of Christians, but that they might always be babes, such might be sufficient ministers. But all ought to grow till they come to be strong and perfect. Will any account him a sufficient schoolmaster, to train up scholars for the university, who himself can only read? Are not ministers master-builders, and shall it be sufficient for them only to work some plain work, or to square out timber? Pharaoh would have 'men of activity to be rulers over his cattle,' Gen. xlvii. 6; and shall not choice men be feeders of the Lord's flock? It is recorded, as an aggravation of Jeroboam's sin, that priests were made of the lowest of the people, 1 Kings xiii. 33.

This then may be an aggravation of the sin of our times, that prentices, serving-men, tradesmen, and others like them, who have no learning, nor are able to give strong meat to them that are of full age, do notwithstanding usurp the ministerial function.

2. Parents and others that intend to have children, or others under them, to be ministers of the word, ought to take care about training them up in schools and universities where they may learn the deepest mysteries.

3. Such scholars as intend the ministry must endeavour to prepare themselves thereto by arts, tongues, diligent study, much reading, and other helps, whereby they may be enabled to give strong meat to such as are of full age, 2 Tim. ii. 15.

4. They that have the power of ordination must be careful that they ordain none but such, 1 Tim. v. 22.

Sec. 74. *Of delivering deep mysteries to fit auditors.*

That which is directly intended in these words, 'Strong meat belongeth to them that are of full age,' is this: Where there are fit auditors, deep mysteries may, and must be delivered. 'We speak wisdom among them that are perfect,' saith the apostle, 1 Cor. ii. 6. By wisdom he meaneth the mysteries of the gospel. That Paul did so, is evident by this phrase, 'In which' (namely, in Paul's epistles) 'are some things hard to be understood,' 2 Pet. iii. 16.

By this means may men grow more and more in knowledge, 'till they come unto a perfect man,' Eph. iv. 13. But so long as here we live we cannot attain to that perfection; therefore it is necessary that we have strong meat to bring us thereunto.

It will hereupon be a minister's wisdom to be thoroughly acquainted with his people, and to observe the assembly where he preacheth, that he may answerably order his matter. As there may be a fault in delivering too deep points to some, so also in delivering too plain points to others. There is a mean betwixt extremes. Because our assemblies are mixed with weak and strong, as occasion is offered, deep mysteries may be opened, and controversies touched, and objections answered; yet so conspicuously as the meanest may receive some profit.

Sec. 75. *Of the advantage of good proficients.*

That it might be the better known, who are of full age in Christ's family, the apostle describes them in these words, 'Even those who by reason of use,' &c.

That noun[1] which we translate *use*, the Latins translate *habitum*, and our English thence taketh this word *habit*. An *habit*, according to the Greek, Latin, and English notation, signifieth an inward qualification

---

[1] ἕξις ab ἔχω, habitus ab habeo.

which a man *hath*, or a ready ability, or able readiness in a man to do this or that. Of a scholar who is prompt and ready on any occasion to make verses, we say, he hath an habit of versifying. So in other things.

An habit is ordinarily gotten by diligent and frequent use of that whereof he hath the habit; thereupon not unfitly it is here translated *use*.

In natural matters, three things are requisite for attaining an habit:

1. A free inclination and disposition of a man's nature to a thing.
2. Good instruction and teaching, whereby nature is helped.
3. Much use and exercise, whereby life and vigour is added to the two former; namely, to nature and instruction.

Thus an habit is gotten by degrees.

In spiritual matters, which are things of the Spirit of God, and supernatural, there is no natural inclination or disposition, Gen. vi. 5, John iii. 6, Eph. ii. 1. By nature men favour the things of the flesh, and are wholly inclined thereto. All that disposition which is in any to spiritual matters, is infused into them by the Holy Spirit: 'They that are after the Spirit, savour the things of the Spirit,' Rom. viii. 5.

The fore-mentioned infusion is ordinarily by the use of means, public and private, as reading and hearing the word preached, partaking of the sacraments, holy conference, meditation, and prayer. Hereby grace is infused and increased; and by much exercise, through God's blessing, an holy habit is obtained.

This habit being obtained, maketh a man able readily to inform the judgment, resolve the conscience, and direct the practice of men.

This habit makes men more and more exercise the means; and as exercise causeth an habit, so an habit puts on men to exercise the more.

Hereupon the apostle addeth these following words, 'have their senses exercised.'

The Greek word $\alpha\dot{\iota}\sigma\theta\eta\tau\dot{\eta}\rho\iota\alpha$, translated *senses*, properly signifieth those organs or instruments, wherein and whereby the senses do exercise their several faculties,[1] as ears, eyes, &c. Here metonymically they are put for the senses themselves; yea, more principally and especially for the faculties of understanding, conceiving, judging, and discerning, as the words following do demonstrate.

This effect *exercised*, in Greek $\gamma\epsilon\gamma\upsilon\mu\nu\alpha\sigma\mu\acute{\epsilon}\nu\alpha$, is derived from a root $\gamma\upsilon\mu\nu\grave{o}\varsigma$, that signifieth *naked*. For among the Grecians they who strived to excel in bodily exercises and games, did use to strip themselves naked, that they might be the more free, ready, and nimble to do what they undertook.

In common use it is taken for a diligent exercising one's self to this or that. Hereby they attain to an ability to this or that.

That whereunto they are here said to be exercised,

[1] *Organa censoria.*

is thus expressed, *to discern*. The Greek word is a noun, $\pi\rho\grave{o}\varsigma\ \delta\iota\acute{\alpha}\kappa\rho\iota\sigma\iota\nu$, and implieth a judging, or putting difference betwixt things, as 1 Cor. xii. 10. This doth here set forth both the end which he who exerciseth himself aimeth at, and also the effect that followeth thereupon. For by exercise he is enabled to discern and put difference between things.

The general heads whereunto he referreth the things to be discerned are two, $\kappa\alpha\lambda o\tilde{u}\ \tau\epsilon\ \kappa\alpha\grave{\iota}\ \kappa\alpha\kappa o\tilde{u}$, *good and evil*. Under these all contraries of like kind are comprised, as true and false, lawful and unlawful, expedient and inexpedient; so as hereby is shewed the benefit of that habit and exercise before-mentioned. For thus men are made able to discern betwixt things that differ, and so to resolve themselves and others, as to choose the better, and leave the worse.

This description is noted as a reason, to shew why strong meat belongeth unto them that are of full rge, even because they can well use it, and they can well discern such false glosses, and undue consequences drawn from deep mysteries, as might deceive and seduce babes.

Thus it appears, that good exercising ourselves in God's word, works such an habit of knowledge and wisdom, as may make us able readily to judge betwixt things that differ. As a scholar exercised in versifying will readily distinguish betwixt a true and false verse, so logicians in syllogisms, so musicians in music, so jewellers in jewels.

Thus they who are well exercised in God's word will quickly, in matters of judgment, discern what is true or false; and in matters of conscience, what lawful or unlawful, meet or unmeet. This is it that the apostle prays for in the behalf of Christians, Rom. xvi. 17, Philip. i. 9, 10. This is it also whereunto they are exhorted, 1 Thess. v. 21, 1 John iv. 5.

1. There is a latent virtue in God's word, which worketh in and upon those as exercise themselves therein.
2. God's blessing doth accompany that divine exercise, and makes it effectual to the foresaid end.

Hereby we may gain assurance to ourselves, and give evidence to others, that we have been good proficients in Christ's school; and that we are not babes, but of full age.

Sec. 76. *Of the resolution of* Heb. v. 11–13.

Ver. 11. *Of whom we have many things to say, and hard to be uttered, seeing ye are dull of hearing.*

12. *For when for the time ye ought to be teachers, ye have need that one teach you again which be the first principles of the oracles of God; and are become such as have need of milk, and not of strong meat.*

13. *For every one that useth milk is unskilful in the word of righteousness; for he is a babe.*

14. *But strong meat belongeth to them that are of full age, even those who by reason of use have their senses exercised to discern both good and evil.*

The sum of these four last verses is, a taxation of non-proficients.

Hereabout two points are to be observed,
1. A transition from the main doctrine to a digression.
2. An intimation of their fault, for which they are taxed.

Of the transition there are two parts:
1. What he intended; 2, what hindered him from that which he intended.

That which he intended was to set out the excellency of Christ's priesthood, and that in two branches.
1. The multiplicity of mysteries couched therein, *of whom we have many things to say.*
2. The profundity of them, *and hard to be uttered.*

That which hindered him was their dulness in hearing.

The taxation of their non-proficiency is set down in two metaphors: one, of such as were to be catechised, ver. 12; the other, of children, ver. 13, 14.

In the first he declares, 1, what they might have been; 2, what they were.

The former sets out that measure of proficiency which they should have attained to, *they ought to be teachers;* and the ground thereof, which was their long continuance in Christ's school, in this phrase, *when for the time.*

Their present condition is, that they were as persons to be catechised.

This is aggravated by their need thereof, *ye have need;* and by their former instructions, implied in this word *again.*

Their former catechising is described:
1. By the groundwork thereof, *first principles.*
2. By the excellency of them, *oracles of God.*

The other metaphor taken from children is,
1, Propounded; 2, proved.

In the proposition is set down,
1. What they needed, *milk.* This is aggravated by their own default, in this phrase, *are become.*
2. Of what they were not capable, *strong meat.*

In the proof there is a difference betwixt non-proficiency and good proficiency.

Concerning the former, there is set down the damage of non-proficiency.

This is, 1, propounded; 2, confirmed.

In the proposition there is,
1. A description of the persons.
2. A declaration of the damage.

The persons are described,
1. By their generality, *every one.*
2. By their kind of nourishment, *that useth milk.*

The damage is propounded in this phrase, *is unskilful;* and aggravated by the subject-matter wherein he is unskilful, *the word of righteousness.*

The confirmation of their damage is by a disgraceful condition, *a babe.*

In setting down the advantage of good proficiency is manifested,
1, The privilege; 2, the reason thereof.

About the privilege is shewed,
1. What they are, *of full age.*
2. What belongeth to them, *strong meat.*

The reason is taken from their *habit,* and amplified by the effect following.

The effect is, 1, propounded, *they have their senses exercised.*
2. Amplified by the subject matter, wherein is expressed,
1. The end, *to discern.*
2. The object, *good and evil.*

Sec. 77. *Of observations collected out of Heb. v. 11–14.*

I. *It is useful to add uses to doctrine.* The apostle's digression consists of uses.

II. *Reproof is a warrantable use.* This is the first use which the apostle here maketh in this his digression. See Secs. 59, 67.

III. *Reproof must be on just ground.* Here the apostle laid down the ground of his reproof. See Sec. 59.

IV. *Hearers' dulness makes mysteries hard to be understood.* This made the mysteries about Melchisedec to be hard to these Hebrews. See Sec. 58.

V. *Proficiency must be answerable to means afforded.* Because these Hebrews profited not according to the time in which they enjoyed the gospel, they are blamed. See Sec. 60.

VI. *Learners by continuance may prove teachers.* This is plainly implied. See Sec. 61.

VII. *Instructions must be ordered according to hearers' need.* So doth the apostle here. See Sec. 62.

VIII. *The same things may be taught again.* This is implied under this phrase, *that one teach you again.* See Secs. 62, 66.

IX. *There are fundamental principles of religion.* These are here called *first principles.* See Sec. 63.

X. *Fundamental principles must be grounded on God's word.* They must be *oracles of God.* See Secs. 63, 65.

XI. *Catechising is needful.* This is to teach *first principles.* See Sec. 64.

XII. *Dulness of hearing ariseth from men's selves.* This phrase, *ye are become,* intendeth as much. See Sec. 66.

XIII. *Dulness in hearing argueth want of exercise in God's word.*

XIV. *Dulness in hearing makes men unfit to reap benefit by God's word.*

These two last doctrines arise out of the meaning of this word *unskilful.* See Sec. 68.

XV. *God's word is a word of righteousness.* So it is here expressly called. See Sec. 69.

XVI. *First principles are as milk.*

XVII. *Deep mysteries are as strong meat.* Both these resemblances are here used in this sense. See Secs. 66, 72.

XVIII. *It is a great disgrace to be an old babe.* This is here set down as a disgrace. See Sec. 71.

XIX. *Ministers must be able to instruct in deep mysteries.* This follows by consequence from that strong meat which is due to men of full age. See Sec. 73.

XX. *Deep mysteries are to be delivered to intelligent hearers.* Such mysteries do belong unto them. See Sec. 74.

XXI. *Good proficients are accounted men of full age.* So they are here called. See Sec. 75.

XXII. *Men of full age have a discerning gift.* They are here said to discern. See Sec. 75.

XXIII. *Things most to be discerned are good and evil.* These here are made the special object of discerning. See Sec. 75.

XXIV. *Exercise in God's word works an habit of discerning.* The word here translated *use* intends as much. See Sec. 75.

Hebrews 6

SEC. 1. *Of the analysis of* Heb. chap. vi.

In this chapter the apostle prosecuteth his digression, which he began chap. v. ver. 11.

The first part of his digression was reprehensory, in the four last verses of the fifth chapter.

The other part is exhortatory, throughout this whole chapter.

He exhorteth unto two Christian duties:

1. To *progress* in the Christian course, from the beginning to ver. 11.

2. To *perseverance* therein, from ver. 11 to the end.

His exhortation to progress is,

1. Briefly propounded, ver. 1; 2. Secondly, largely amplified.

In the amplification are set down,

1. The distinct heads of those first principles from which they must proceed, or wherein they must grow. These are six in number, ver. 1, 2.

2. A motive to enforce that progress.

Betwixt those heads and the motive there is a transition, ver. 3.

The motive is taken from the danger of not proceeding. This is first propounded, secondly illustrated.

The danger propounded is apostasy; which he sets out two ways.

1. By the steps whereon men ascend, before they fall, which are five, ver. 4, 5.

2. By the fearful downfall of apostates. This is,
1. Affirmed; 2. confirmed.

That which is affirmed is an impossibility of recovery, ver. 4, 6.

The confirmation is taken from an utter rejecting of the only means of recovery, ver. 6.

The illustration is set forth by a comparison of ground moistened with rain, ver. 6, 7.

Betwixt the fearful downfall of apostates, and the other part of the exhortation to perseverance, the apostle inserteth a sweet insinuation, whereby he testifieth,

1. His good persuasion of them, ver. 9.

2. The ground of that persuasion, ver. 10.

The second part of the apostle's exhortation is to perseverance.

This is, 1, propounded, ver. 11; 2, proved by sundry arguments.

1. By their own former practice, implied under this phrase, *the same diligence*, ver. 11.

2. By the pattern of such saints as were before them, ver. 12.

3. By the recompence of reward. This is,

1. Generally hinted in this phrase, *inherit the promises*, ver. 12.

2. Distinctly confirmed in Abraham's example, ver. 13.

The confirmation is by God's oath. About which the apostle noteth,

1. The object of it, God himself, ver. 13.

2. The form of it, ver. 14.

3. The issue of it, ver. 15.

4. The reason why God swore. This is set out two ways:

1. Comparatively, by men's confirming matters, ver. 16.

2. Simply, ver. 17, 18.

In the simple consideration, two reasons of God's oath are rendered: one in reference to God himself, which was to manifest his *immutable counsel*, ver. 17;

The other in reference to men: wherein two points are expressed:

1. The benefits arising from God's oath, *strong consolation*.

2. The persons that partake thereof, ver. 18.

The last argument which the apostle useth to incite them unto perseverance, is the certainty of their hope. This is,

1. Set out by a fit resemblance, namely, an *anchor*.
2. It is amplified by the place where that anchor is settled.

This place is described, 1, by a type, *the veil*, ver. 19; 2, by Christ's abode there.

For illustration of this last point, the apostle sets out Christ two ways:

1. In his entrance thither, as a *forerunner*.
2. In his abode there, as a *priest*. Thus he falleth upon the main point, from which he had digressed, namely, the *order* of Christ's priesthood, ver. 20.

Sec. 2. *Of adding exhortation to reproof.*

Ver. 1. *Therefore, leaving the principles of the doctrine of Christ, let us go on unto perfection; not laying again the foundation of repentance from dead works, and of faith towards God.*

The apostle here beginneth the second branch of his digression; which is in general an exhortation to the duties which they had neglected.

The first particle is a note of inference, Διο,[1] *therefore*; it hath reference to his former reproof, and sheweth that as faults be reproved, so remedies are to be prescribed.

This was usual with the prophets, as Isa. i. 16, with Christ himself, John vi. 27, and with the apostles, Gal. v. 1.

1. The end of reproof is reformation; even as the end of potions and pills is health, 2 Cor. ii. 7.
2. Thus it will appear that reproofs are not in malice to disgrace, but in love to amend; and that reprovers aim thereat.

This is a good direction for such as are in place to reprove. This also is a motive to such as are reproved, patiently to take reproof, and to endeavour to redress the faults reproved. Thus will reproof prove to be as good physic.

Sec. 3. *Of staying still upon the first principles.*

This word ἀφέντες, *leaving*, both in Greek and other languages, implieth two things:

1. Utterly to forsake a thing upon dislike. Thus those hypocrites that assayed to tempt Christ, but could not ensnare him, 'left him, and went their way,' Mat. xxii. 22. In this sense, saith Christ to his disciples, concerning blind leaders, ἄφετε, 'let them alone,' or leave them, Mat. xv. 14.
2. To go further off from a thing, without any dislike of it. In which sense, saith Christ, ἄφες, 'leave thy gift,' Mat. v. 24. He would not have him abide by his gift, while his brother remained offended with him; but rather go from his gift to his brother. Thus runners in a race leave the place where the race begins, and make speed to the goal where it ends.

[1] See Chap. x. 5, Sec. 13.

Thus grammar scholars leave their accidence. The meaning then of this phrase is, that they should not always stay, and abide in learning the first principles; but go on forward in learning more and more the doctrine of Christ. Thus the apostle expoundeth himself in these words following, 'let us go on.'

That which good Christians must so leave, is in our English styled 'The principles of the doctrine of Christ;' in Greek, τὸν τῆς ἀρχῆς τοῦ Χριστοῦ λόγον, 'the word of the beginning of Christ,' which intendeth the beginning of the doctrine of Christ; which is that word whereby we are at first brought to know Christ, and to believe in him. This is the very same which before he called 'the first principles of the oracles of God,' whereof see Chap. v. 12, Secs. 63, 65.

The main drift of the apostle's intendment lieth in this word *beginning*, or *principles*. For the word, or doctrine of Christ, generally taken, containeth all the mysteries of godliness, not the deepest excepted. In this extent Christ's word is to be left by none; no, not by the strongest.

It is a proud conceit for any to think that they are above or beyond the Scripture, which is the word of Christ. 'They are they,' saith Christ, 'which testify of me,' John v. 39. These are the things in which the apostle would have Timothy to continue, though he had 'known the holy Scriptures from a child,' 2 Tim. iii. 14, 15.

He terms it *the word of Christ*, because Christ was the subject matter thereof. For Christ is the object of a Christian's faith, and that which above all he most desires to be instructed in, 1 Cor. ii. 2.

But that which the apostle especially intendeth is, that Christians must not always be learning the first principles. That which he further mentioneth, of 'not laying again the foundation,' tendeth to the same purpose; for a wise builder will not always be spending his time, pains, and cost, upon the foundation only. If any should so do, all that behold him will mock him, saying, 'This man began to build, and was not able to finish,' Luke xiv. 28–30.

Such are those, who, being trained up in a religious family, or under a pious ministry, and taught the principles of religion, have no care to learn any more.

This incomparable privilege, that they live where the word and doctrine of Christ is taught, even the word of their salvation, doth much aggravate their carelessness. See more hereof, Chap. v. 12, Sec. 63, and ver. 13, Sec. 71.

This phrase, *principles of the doctrine of Christ*, gives us to understand that the church then had her catechism. See Chap. v. 12, Sec. 64.

Sec. 4. *Of going on in learning Christ.*

The word φερώμεθα, translated *let us go on*, is of the passive voice, thus, *let us be carried;* but it implieth a voluntary act, yet such an one as is performed with some earnestness and diligence. It is the word that is used of those that penned the Scriptures: 'They were moved (or carried) by the Holy Ghost,' 2 Pet. i. 21. They faithfully and diligently did what the Spirit moved them to do. In that a voluntary act on our part is here required, it is in our English not impertinently translated, 'let us go on.'

That whereunto we must proceed, is here said to be *perfection*, ἐπὶ τὴν τελειότητα. Perfection is taken simply, for that which is every way absolute, so as nothing need be added thereunto. In this sense, the apostle saith of charity, that it is 'the bond of perfection.' It being here thus taken, the *going on* here required implieth a faithful and constant endeavour after perfection. Thus Christ requireth us to be 'perfect, even as our Father which is in heaven is perfect,' Mat. v. 48.

Perfection is also taken comparatively, in reference to the first beginning of things. Thus in relation to the first principles, it implieth deeper mysteries; so as, going on to perfection, is a proceeding further and further in learning the deep mysteries concerning Christ. Hereof see more, Chap. v. 14, Sec. 72.

Both the foresaid acceptions tend to the same intent, namely, that there ought to be a continual progress in understanding the mysteries of godliness. Saints are in this respect resembled to growing cedars, Ps. xcii. 12; and to the increasing light of the sun, Prov. iv. 18; and to the increasing waters, that came out of the sanctuary, Ezek. xlvii. 3, &c.; and to the growing corn, Mark iv. 28; and mustard seed and leaven, Mat. xiii. 32, 33; and to the rising up of a building, Eph. ii. 21; yea, also, to runners in a race, 1 Cor. ix. 24.

Frequent are the exhortations of Scripture to this kind of proceeding, Philip. iii. 16; Eph. iv. 15; 1 Pet. ii. 2; 2 Pet. iii. 18. The metaphors also of walking and running, frequently used in Scripture, tend thereunto.

Of necessity there must be a going on, because that measure and degree which is appointed unto us, Eph. iv. 13, cannot be attained till death. Besides, the greater measure of grace that we here attain unto, the greater degree of glory we shall hereafter attain unto, Mat. xxv. 29.

This much concerns those who have well begun, to take heed that they stand not at a stay, but still go on. Herein lieth a main difference betwixt the upright and hypocrites. The former are never satisfied, but still desire more and more; the latter are contented with a mere show. Among good husbands, he is almost counted a prodigal who only keeps his own. Remember the doom of him that improved not his talent, Mat. xxv. 30. See more in *The Saint's Sacrifice*, on Ps. cxvi. 9, sec. 61.

Sec. 5. *Of endeavouring after perfection.*

The object whereat Christians should aim in their continual progress is perfection; which, whether it be taken simply for an absolute perfection, or comparatively, for an increase in measure, tends in general to the full scope, namely, that no stint must satisfy a Christian; he must not content himself with a mediocrity, but still proceed as far as possibly he can. We are hereupon exhorted to 'seek that we may excel,' 1 Cor. xiv. 12; to be 'rich in good works,' 1 Tim. vi. 18; to 'abound in the work of the Lord,' 1 Cor. xv. 58. Yea, more and more to 'abound in knowledge and in all judgment,' Philip. i. 9; to 'abound in hope,' Rom. xv. 13; and 'in faith, and in all diligence, and in love,' 2 Cor. viii. 7; and to be 'filled with the Spirit,' Eph. v. 18; and 'to be perfect,' 1 Cor. xiii. 11.

The patterns that are set before us, do prove as much, for the choicest worthies of God in all former ages are set before us as examples for us to follow, Heb. xi. We are commanded to 'take the prophets for an example,' who were endued with an extraordinary spirit, James v. 10; and an apostle requires us to follow him, 'as he followed Christ,' 1 Cor. xi. 1. And, as if the best patterns on earth were not sufficient, we are enjoined to pray, to 'do God's will on earth, as it is in heaven,' Mat. vi. 10; and, as if the patterns of all mere creatures were not sufficient, it is required that 'that mind be in us which was also in Christ Jesus,' Philip. ii. 9; yea, yet further, we are exhorted to be 'followers of God,' Eph. v. 1, and to be 'perfect as he is,' Mat. v. 48.

Such is the excellency, such the commodity, such the sweetness of Christian knowledge and grace, as a man ought never to be satisfied therewith.

How corrupt is the treasure of the men of this world, who account an earnest pursuance after those things to be more than needs? yea, not only needless, but madness, as Festus said to Paul, Acts xxvi. 24.

Let this add a spur to those who are most forward, still to press on further, and to do as the apostle professeth of himself, Philip. iii. 13, &c.

Of propounding a perfect pattern, and aiming at more than we can attain to, see *The Guide to go to God*, or my *Explanation of the Lord's Prayer*, on third petition, secs. 68, 69.

Sec. 6. *Of building upon a foundation well laid.*

This phrase, *not laying again the foundation*, is metaphorical. In effect it setteth down the same thing which was intended under this phrase, *leaving the principles*, Sec. 3. Only by this metaphor the point is more fully and plainly declared. For he resembleth principles to a foundation. If only a foundation be laid, and no more, no benefit will redound to the builder, but rather loss of labour: there is no fit house to dwell in. We can be no fit house, or temple, as is intended we should be, Heb. iii. 6; Eph. ii. 21; 1 Cor. iii. 16, if we stick only in principles.

What a θεμέλιον, *foundation*, in the proper signification of the word, is, hath been shewed, Chap. i. 10, Sec. 131.

A foundation is both the beginning of a greater building, Luke xiv. 29, 30, and also the groundwork, whereupon the rest of the building is erected, and whereby it is upheld, Eph. ii. 20, 21.

It is therefore needful that it be very solid and substantial, for it must last as long as the building, and it useth to be but once laid.

By the way, here note an undue cavil of the Rhemists against reading the Scriptures, and for traditions, raised out of this place, which is this: We see hereby that there was ever a necessary instruction and belief had by word of mouth and tradition, before men came to the Scriptures.

To grant there was such a kind of instruction, I deny that it was merely by tradition, without the word of God. I deny also that it was before men came to the Scriptures, for all sorts had liberty to read the Scriptures. As for the points which by word of mouth were taught them that were catechised, they were no other than the doctrine of the prophets and apostles, as also the higher and deeper mysteries were. For milk and strong meat may for matter be of the same doctrine, but the difference betwixt them is in the manner of delivering it. For that instruction which was brought into easy and familiar principles, and by word of mouth delivered to babes, was taken out of the Scripture, as the several heads following shew. See more hereof, Chap. v. 14, Sec. 75.

The participle καταβαλλόμενοι, laying, joined with this noun foundation, addeth further emphasis. It signifieth to cast, or lay down; and from thence is derived another Greek word, καταβολη, which also signifieth a foundation, as is shewed Chap. iv. 3, Sec. 29.

This conjunction πάλιν, again, giveth hint of a total apostasy, as if they were in danger to fall from all their former principles; so as a new foundation must be laid, or else there could be no further going on. This danger is more fully manifested ver. 6.

In this caution, not laying again the foundation, each word is observable.

1. For erecting a good edifice there must be θεμέλιον, a foundation; the first principles must be taught them who would be well instructed in the Christian faith. See Chap. v. 12, Sec. 64.

2. A foundation must be well laid, surely, and soundly. The notation of this word καταβαλλόμενοι, laying, intends as much. This Christ distinctly observeth, Luke vi. 48. This phrase, 'As a wise master builder, I have laid the foundation,' 1 Cor. iii. 10, sheweth that the apostle was very circumspect about laying the foundation. Now there is no such way to lay the foundation of religion soundly, as to ground it on God's word. See Chap. v. 12, Sec. 65.

3. Laying a foundation intendeth a further building; for a foundation is but the beginning of an edifice. The negative particle μὴ, not, imports thus much: for by forbidding to lay a foundation, he stirs them up to diligence in building up the house. So as more must be learned than the first principles, see Sec. 4.

4. The inserting this word again gives us to understand, that a foundation useth to be but once laid. A Christian once well instructed must not stand in need to be taught the first principles again. Such an one in disgrace is called a babe. See Chap. v. Sec. 71.

Sec. 7. *Of the six principles of the apostle's catechism.*

The manner of joining the particular principles following with this general word, foundation, sheweth that they are as so many stones of that foundation. They are joined with this note of the genitive case,[1] of. This phrase, 'The foundation of costly stones,' 1 Kings vii. 10, sheweth, that those stones made up the foundation.

The number of principles here set down is diversely taken by different expositors. I leave others to their own opinion. I suppose that the most proper distribution will be into six heads.

1. *Repentance* from dead works: which manifesteth the natural man's misery.

2. *Faith* towards God: which declareth the way of freeing man from misery, and bringing him to happiness.

3. The doctrine of *baptisms*: which pointeth at the outward means of working faith and repentance, and of revealing and sealing up unto us God's mercy, which are the word, and sacraments.

4. *Imposition* of hands: which hinteth the order and discipline of the church.

5. *Resurrection* from the dead; namely, of our bodies.

6. The eternal *judgment*: and that of all sorts, good and evil; the one to receive the sentence of everlasting life, the other the doom of eternal death.

These are the heads of that catechism which the church had in the apostle's time, and was to be learned of such as were to be admitted into the church.

Sec. 8. *Of repentance from dead works.*

The first of the foresaid principles is thus expressed, 'Repentance from dead works.' By dead works are meant all manner of sin; which are so styled in regard of their cause, condition, and consequence.

1. The cause of sin is privative, the want of that Spirit which is the life of the soul; as the want of life is the cause of putrefaction. Men that are without that Spirit are said to be dead in sin. They must needs be dead works which come from dead men, Eph. ii. 1.

2. The condition of sin is to be noisome and stinking in God's nostrils, as dead carrion, Ps. xxxviii. 5.

[1] Μετανοίας.

3. The consequence of sin is death, and that of body and soul, temporal and eternal, Rom. v. 12, and vi. 23.

Repentance implieth a turning from those works. The several notations of the word in all the three learned languages imply a turning. The Hebrew noun תשובה is derived from a verb, שוב, that signifies to *turn*, and is used Ezek. xxxiii. 11. The Greek word μετάνοια, according to the notation of it, signifies a change of the mind, or change of counsel, μεταμέλεια. So the Latin word also, *resipiscentia*.

Μετάνοια et μεταμέλεια componuntur ex prepositione μετά, quod significat *post*, Acts xv. 13.

Prior vox μετάνοια componitur ex μετά et νόος, *mens*, Titus i. 15, seu *intellectus*, Philip. iv. 7. Inde νοέω, *intelligo, considero*, Mat. xxiv. 15, μετανοέω, *post*, vel *iterum considero;* ut ii solent quos hujus vel illius facti pœnitet. Est igitur μετάνοια, *posterior cogitatio*, qualis fuit in prodigo, Luke xv. 17, μετανοέω et ἐπιστρέφω (converto, vel convertor) tanquam synonyma, conjunguntur, Acts iii. 19, and xxvi. 20.

Μεταμέλεια componitur ex μετά et μέλει, *cura est*. Est impersonale. Inde μεταμέλει *pœnitet*. Impersonale. Est enim pœnitentia posterior cura. Solemus nos pœnitere alicujus facti, cum animum id attentius expendentem cura et solicitudo subit.

Hinc μεταμελόμαι, *pœnitentia ducor*.

Μεταμέλεια exponitur apud alios authores *mutatio consilii*, sed nunquam legitur in novo testamento.

Alii componunt μεταμέλομαι, ex μετά et μελετάω, *meditor*, 1 Tim. iv. 15. Ita ut significet *iterum* vel *postea meditor*, ut senior filius, Mat. xxi. 29.

In general, repentance implieth a reformation of the whole man. It presupposeth knowledge, sense, sorrow, and acknowledgment of sin; but yet these make not up repentance, for they may all be where there is no true repentance. Judas had them all, yet was he not reformed. He retained a murderous mind, for he murdered himself.

Reformation makes a new man. A man turns from what he was, to what he was not. This the apostle thus expresseth, 'To turn them from darkness to light, and from the power of Satan unto God,' Acts xxvi. 18.

From this ground there are made two parts of repentance :

1. Mortification, whereby we die to sin. Sin is like the Egyptian darkness, which extinguished all lights; it is like thorns in the ground, which soak out all the life thereof. Sin therefore must be first mortified.

2. Vivification, which is a living in righteousness. If grace be not planted in the soul, it will be like the ground which will send forth weeds of itself.

The foresaid reformation is of the whole man. For the mind seeth a necessity thereof; the will pursueth it; the heart puts to an holy zeal, and the outward parts help to accomplish it.

Therefore repentance consisteth not simply in sin's leaving a man; for a prodigal, when he hath spent all, may cease to be prodigal; and an old adulterer, when his strength is ceased, may forbear his adulterous acts; but in these, and others like them, though the act be forborne, the inordinate desire may remain.

Nor doth repentance consist in leaving some sins only; so did Herod, Mark vi. 20. Nor in turning from one sin to another, as from profaneness to superstition; so did they whom the pharisees made proselytes, Mat. xxiii. 15.

Nor in a mere ceasing to do things unlawful; so may such as are idle on the Sabbath day.

The special principles that are comprised under this first head have reference either to the expression of dead works, or of repentance from them. They are such as these :

1. Man by nature is dead in sin, Eph. ii. 1, Titus i. 16, though he live a natural life, 1 Tim. v. 6.

2. All the acts of a natural man are dead works : his thoughts, words, and deeds, though they may seem never so fair, Gen. vi. 5, Titus i. 15, for they are acts of dead men.

3. The end of all a natural man doth is death, Rom. vi. 16.

4. There is a necessity of man's being freed; for there must be 'repentance from dead works.' He were better not be than not be freed. Repentance is necessary for freedom from dead works, Luke xiii. 3, 5; for this end knowledge, sense, sorrow, desire, resolution, and endeavour to forbear dead works, are requisite.

Under this first head is comprised whatsoever is meet to be taught in a catechism of the law, the rigour, and curse thereof; of sin, the kinds, and issue thereof; of death, and the several sorts of it; of all man's misery and impotency; of repentance, of the nature, necessity and benefit thereof; of means and motives to attain it, and signs to know it.

Sec. 9. *Of principles concerning God.*

The second principle is this, 'faith towards God.' By virtue of this principle they were instructed in two great points, one concerning *God*, the other concerning *faith*.

God is here to be considered essentially, in regard of his divine nature, or personally, in reference to the three distinct persons, Father, Son, Holy Ghost.

In the former respect they were taught what God is, what his divine properties, what his works.

In the latter respect they were taught the distinction betwixt the three persons, and that in regard of order, and kind of works, which are to beget, to be begotten, and to proceed, and also in their distinct manner of working, the Father by the Son and Holy Ghost; the Son from the Father by the Holy Ghost; the Holy Ghost, from the Father and the Son.

Concerning the Father, they were taught that he is the primary fountain of all good; that he sent his Son to save the world, John iii. 17 ; that he gave the Comforter, which is the Holy Ghost, John xiv. 16–26.

Concerning the Son, they were instructed in his two distinct natures, and the union of them in one person, which was ' God manifest in the flesh,' 1 Tim. iii. 16., and in his three offices, which were king, priest, and prophet.

A king, to gather, preserve, and protect his church. A priest, to make satisfaction for our sins by offering himself up a sacrifice ; and being risen from the dead, to make intercession for us, by entering into the most holy place, and there presenting himself to his Father for us.

A prophet, to make known his Father's will to us ; and to enlighten our understandings, so as we may conceive it.

Concerning the Holy Ghost, they were instructed that he was true God, a distinct person, and the Spirit of sanctification.

Sec. 10. *Of principles concerning faith.*

The reason why Christians were at first instructed in principles concerning God was, that they might believe on him. Therefore this principle is thus set down, ' faith towards God.'

The Greek preposition, ἐπὶ, translated *towards*, properly signifieth *to*, and it is oft used in the same sense that the preposition εἰς is, which we translate *on*, John i. 12. So is the preposition here used in this text oft translated by our English, as Acts ix. 42, and xxii. 19 ; Rom. iv. 5, 24.

Thus do most interpreters here translate it, *faith on God*. The faith then here meant is a justifying faith, about which they who are catechised might be instructed in these and such like principles :

God is to be believed on.

Faith in God is the means to free us out of our natural, miserable condition.

They might also be further instructed in the nature of faith, and in the distinct kinds thereof ; and how a justifying faith differeth from other kinds of faith ; and what are the grounds of faith, and what the fruits thereof ; how it is wrought, and how it worketh ; what are the signs and evidences thereof ; and concerning the benefits thereof, how thereby we have a right to the things of this world, yea, and a right to all that Christ did, and endured to purchase man's salvation, and thereupon a right to salvation itself.

Of faith, see more in *The Whole Armour of God*, treat. ii. part vi, on Eph. vi. 16, sec. 1, &c.

Sec. 11. *Of principles about God's word.*

Ver. 2. *Of the doctrine of baptisms, and of laying on of hands, and of resurrection of the dead, and of eternal judgment.*

This is the third principle, ' the doctrine of baptisms.' Some make these two distinct principles, comprising one under this word *doctrine*, the other under this word *baptisms*. Whether they be made two distinct principles, or only one, it is without question, that both the foresaid points of doctrine and baptisms are included, and were both taught, as repentance and dead works in the first principle, and God and faith in the second.

The Greek noun, διδαχή, translated *doctrine*, is derived from a verb, διδάσκω, that signifieth *to teach*. It pointeth at God's word in the holy Scriptures, whereby God instructeth us in his will. But more particularly the gospel may be here intended. For the gospel is the most proper means of working faith, Rom. i. 16, 17, and the gospel is in special manner the doctrine of baptism, that doctrine which first taught baptism, and whereof baptism is a seal.

About this *doctrine*, or word, they might be instructed in these particulars : that it is a doctrine of divine authority, even the word of God himself ; that it is the ground and rule of all things to be believed and practised about salvation ; that it instructeth us in all the ordinances of God, and declareth both what are divine ordinances, and also how they ought to be observed ; that it instructeth us in all manner of duties to be performed to God, or our neighbour ; that it is the only true light that can direct us in the way to salvation ; that it is the ordinary means to breed and increase grace ; that by preaching it is made most powerful ; that it containeth the covenant, whereof the sacraments are seals.

Of God's word, see more in *The Whole Armour of God*, treat. ii. part viii. on Eph. vi. 17, sec. 1, &c.

Sec. 12. *Of the reasons of* baptisms *in the plural number*.

Baptism is added to the foresaid *doctrine*, because the first preacher of the gospel did preach baptism ; and upon his preaching it people submitted themselves to that ordinance, Mark i. 4, 5 ; and because baptism is a seal of the gospel, and from time to time all that have embraced the gospel have been baptized.

The plural number, βαπτισμῶν, is here used, thus, *of baptisms*, whereabout sundry reasons are given, such as these :

1. To put a difference betwixt the baptism of John and the baptism of Christ ; for some affirm that they were two distinct baptisms, and that many that were baptized with John's baptism were rebaptized with the baptism of Christ, Acts xix. 5.

Ans. This is a great error ; John's baptism and Christ's were the same. For John preached the same doctrine that Christ and his apostles did, and with the same baptism confirmed it. Christ himself was baptized with John's baptism. He did thereupon confirm and sanctify that baptism, which ratification and sanctification that baptism which the Christian church now useth would want, if John's baptism were not the same with Christ's. Besides, the apostle acknowledgeth but one baptism, Eph. iv. 5. We cannot, therefore, imagine that there were two distinct and different baptisms taught in the apostles' time. As for that which is alleged about rebaptizing those which were before baptized by John, it is a manifest mistake of Scripture. For that baptism which is mentioned Acts xix. 5, was not a rebaptizing of those who were baptized before, but a declaration of the ground why they were at first baptized by John in the name of the Lord Jesus, namely, because John taught them that they should believe on Christ Jesus ; so as this phrase, 'when they heard this,' Acts xix. 5, hath reference to those who heard John preach, and not to those disciples with whom Paul then conferred.

It is again objected, that John professeth that he baptized with water, but Christ with the Holy Ghost, Mat. iii. 11.

Ans. John speaks of himself as a minister, who only could use the outward element ; and of Christ as of God, the author of baptism, who could also give the Holy Ghost. Peter, Paul, and other ministers of the gospel, may say as John did, ' We baptize with water,' for it is all that a mere man can do.

2. Others say, that the apostle hath respect in using this plural number, *baptisms*, to the legal washings which were among the Jews, and are called *baptisms*. For this word in the plural number is but three times more used throughout the new Testament, and in every one of them applied to legal washings, as Heb. ix. 10, Mark vii. 4.

Ans. All those legal washings were either abolished by the coming of the Messiah, or else they were but superstitious rites invented and used by men, so as it was not probable that the church then would instruct such as were to be her members therein.

3. Others suppose that the two parts of baptism, inward and outward, John iii. 5, are called baptisms.

Ans. This reason must warily be taken, for howsoever the inward and outward washing may be distinguished, and so respectively called baptisms, yet are they not to be severed ; they are but two parts of one and the same sacrament, and both of them indeed make but one baptism.

4. Others think that the apostle hath reference to a threefold baptism,[1] one of water, another of the Spirit, a third of blood, which they say martyrdom is. For this they allege 1 John v. 8, and compare together John iii. 5 and Mat. xx. 22 ; this is the reason ordinarily rendered by popish expositors. But they mistake the meaning of this word *blood*, mentioned 1 John v. 8 ; it is not the blood of martyrs, but the blood of Christ, which the apostle there meaneth.

5. Some of our best expositors are of opinion, that this plural number *baptisms* is here used in reference to the many persons which were baptized together, and to the several set times when baptism was administered, which reason is confirmed by that name, which in our ancient ecclesiastical authors is given

[1] Baptisma fluminis, flaminis et sanguinis.

to the days wherein baptism was solemnly administered, for they were called ' days of baptism.'

6. Baptism may here synecdochically be put for both sacraments ; and to shew that the Lord's Supper is included under the sacrament of baptism, the plural number, *baptisms*, is used.

Sec. 13. *Of principles about sacraments.*

We cannot imagine that the sacrament of the Lord's supper was clean left out of the catechism used in the primitive church. This therefore will be the fittest place to observe the principles about a sacrament in general, and in particular about baptism and the Lord's Supper. Wherefore about a sacrament there might be delivered such principles as these :

Christ instituted sacraments in his church. A sacrament was a seal of God's covenant. There were two parts of a sacrament, the outward sign and inward grace. A sacrament was of use to ratify God's promise, and to strengthen our faith.

It was of singular use in regard of our dulness to conceive, and backwardness to believe. The resemblance betwixt the sign and the thing signified was of use to help our understanding in the mysteries set out in a sacrament. There are only two sacraments of the new Testament : one, a sacrament of regeneration ; the other, a sacrament of spiritual nourishment.

Sec. 14. *Of principles about baptism.*

Baptism is a sacrament of regeneration. The outward sign in baptism is water. The inward thing, or substance thereof, is the blood of Christ. The pouring or sprinkling of water upon the party baptized setteth out the inward cleansing of the Holy Ghost. The form of baptism is, ' In the name of the Father, and of the Son, and of the Holy Ghost.' Baptism is to be administered by a minister of the word. They who profess the true faith are to be baptized. The children also of such are to be baptized. By baptism we are ingrafted into Christ's mystical body. Baptism setteth out both our dying to sin, and also our rising to righteousness. Baptism is but once to be administered. The force and efficacy of baptism lasteth as long as a man liveth.

Of baptism, see more in *Domestical Duties* on Eph. v. 26, treat. i. sec. 40, &c.

Sec. 15. *Of principles about the Lord's supper.*

The Lord's supper is a sacrament of spiritual nourishment. It is added to baptism, to shew the spiritual growth of such as are new born. There are two outward signs thereof, bread and wine. These set out the body and blood of Christ. The bread sheweth that Christ's body is spiritual nourishment ; the wine, that his blood is spiritual refreshing. These two elements shew, that Christ is sufficient nourishment. The bread and wine at the Lord's table differ from other bread and wine, in use only, not in substance. The form of that sacrament consisteth in the sacramental union betwixt the signs and things signified. A minister of the word must administer that sacrament. They who have been baptized, and are fit and worthy, may partake thereof. The minister is to bless the elements, to break the bread, to pour out the wine, and to give them to the people. The people are to take the elements, and to eat the one, and drink the other. The body of Christ is eaten, and his blood drunk, spiritually by faith. This sacrament is oft to be received, in regard of the weakness of our faith, and repentance, which need oft to be renewed, and that Christ might oft be remembered.

Sec. 16. *Of imposition of hands.*

The fourth principle is thus set down, ἐπιθέσεώς τε χειρῶν, ' of imposition of hands.' This hath been an ancient rite in the church of God: no other so long continued. Jacob, when he blessed the sons of Joseph, laid his hands upon them, Gen. xlviii. 14. Under the law it was usual to lay hands on the sacrifices that were offered up, Lev. iv. 15, xvi. 21, Num. viii. 12.

But because we have to do with the time of the gospel, and with a rite then used, we will pass over the times of the law, and shew about this rite of imposition of hands: 1, by what persons; 2, in what cases; 3, to what ends; 4, with what exercises, it was used.

1. They were public persons that used it, as Christ, Mark x. 16, Luke iv. 40; his apostles, Acts viii. 17; other public ministers and elders, 1 Tim. iv. 14, and v. 22.

2. It was used in extraordinary and ordinary cases. The extraordinary were spiritual or temporal. Spiritual extraordinary cases wherein imposition of hands was used, were the giving of extraordinary gifts, oft expressed under this title, the Holy Ghost, Acts viii. 17, 19, and xix. 6; extraordinary temporal cases were an extraordinary manner of restoring health, and other like miracles, Luke iv. 40, Mark vi. 5, Acts xxviii. 8. Ordinary cases wherein imposition of hands was used were,

(1.) Blessing children, Mark x. 16.

(2.) Setting men apart to a public function, as ministers of the word, 1 Tim. v. 22; and deacons, Acts vi. 6.

(3.) Deputing men to some special work, Acts xiii. 3.

(4.) Confirming such as had been instructed in the principles of religion.

This last particular is not expressly set down in Scripture, but gathered out of it by the ancient orthodox fathers; and with a joint consent acknowledged by most divines, not papists only, but protestants also. It hath indeed been much abused by papists, with their manifold superstitious additions, and vain opinions thereabout; which hath been, I suppose, one cause of protestants much neglecting it.

Imposition of hands for confirming him on whom hands were laid, was of old used in two cases.

1. When one of age, having been well instructed in the principles of Christian religion, was brought to the Church to be baptized.

2. When such as had been baptized in their infancy, and afterwards well instructed in the foresaid principles, were judged fit to be made partakers of the Lord's table.

Sec. 17. *Of laying on of hands at ordination.*

This rite of laying hands on them that were to be set apart to the ministry, is most expressly set down in God's word. For Timothy was set apart ' by laying on of the hands of the presbytery,' 1 Tim. iv. 14, and the apostle setteth out the act of ordination under this rite, when he saith, ' Lay hands suddenly on no man,' 1 Tim. v. 22.

Such as under the gospel are to be set apart for ordinary ministers, are pastors and teachers. Men's abilities to these functions are to be tried; and good testimony given of their orthodox judgment and pious conversation: and in a public assembly, on a day of fasting and prayer, they are, after some exhortation and direction concerning the ministerial function, and prayer made for God's blessing on them, they are to be set apart to the ministerial function, by this rite of imposition of hands.

This rite was used to shew that the blessing which they desired, and the ability which was given, or was further to be expected, was from above; and for obtaining thereof, prayer used to be joined with imposition of hands, Acts vi. 6, and xiii. 3, and xx. 8.

Of ordaining ministers, see more Chap. iii. 2, Sec. 35.

Sec. 18. *Of principles about prayer and thanksgiving.*

Because prayer was joined with imposition of hands, and lifting up of hands is a rite proper to prayer, and put for prayer, 1 Tim. ii. 8, I suppose this to be a fit place to bring in that head of our Christian religion, which was questionless one branch of that ancient catechism.

Principles about prayer may be such as these:

Prayer is a bounden duty. It is to be made only to God, and in the name of Jesus Christ. It is to proceed from the heart, and to be made with reverence, and in faith. It is a means of obtaining all needful blessings, All things that tend to God's glory, our own, or brother's good, whether temporal or spiritual, may be sought of God by prayer.

To this head also may thanksgiving be referred. Christians ought to be as conscionable in giving thanks as in making prayers. Hereby they shall testify their zeal of God's glory, as well as they testify their desire of their own good.

Thanks must be given to God, and that for all

things, and at all times, and in all places, publicly and privately, ever in the name and through the mediation of Jesus Christ.

Of prayer and thanksgiving, see more in *The Whole Armour of God*, treat iii. part i., on Eph. vi. 18, sec. 1, &c.

Sec. 19. *Of principles about death.*

The fifth principle is thus set down, 'and of the resurrection of the dead.' Of this principle there are two heads: one concerning *the dead;* the other concerning *their resurrection.*

About the dead, there might be these principles. No man ever yet remained alive on earth for ever. 'It is appointed unto men once to die,' Heb. ix. 27; only one exception is recorded, which was Enoch's, of whom it is said that 'God took him,' Gen. v. 24, which phrase the apostle thus expoundeth, 'Enoch was translated that he should not see death,' Heb. xi. 5. As for Elijah, who went up by a whirlwind into heaven, 2 Kings ii. 11, it is not expressly said that he died not; though in his body he were taken up from the earth, yet might his soul only be carried into heaven. Yet I will not deny, but that he also might be exempted from death. But if this be granted, there are only two that we read of exempted from this common condition; and one or two exceptions, especially they being extraordinary, do not infringe a general rule.[1] Death is only of the body, which the soul leaveth, and thereupon it remaineth dead; the soul itself is immortal, Eccles. xii. 7; man's body was not at first made mortal, for death came by sin, Rom. v. 12, yet by Christ is the sting of death pulled out, 1 Cor. xv. 55, and the nature of it is altered. For at first it was denounced as an entrance to hell, Gen. ii. 17, Luke xvi. 22, 23; by Christ it is made a sweet sleep, 1 Thess. iv. 13, and the entrance into heaven, 2 Cor. v. 1, Philip. i. 23; it is to believers, a putting off the rags of morality, 1 Cor. xv. 53, 54; it is a full abolition of sin, Rom. vi. 7, and they rest from all labours and troubles, Rev. xiv. 13.

Sec. 20. *Of principles about resurrection.*

The bodies of men are not like the bodies of beasts, which ever remain in the earth, but they shall be raised. Which the apostle proveth by many arguments, 1 Cor. xv. 12, &c. They shall be raised by the power of Christ's voice, John v. 29, and that at the last and great day, Mat. xiii. 49, all at once in a moment, 1 Cor. xv. 52, even the very same bodies that they had on earth, Job xix. 27; not the substance, but the quality only of the bodies shall be changed, 1 Cor. xv. 43, 44. Being raised, each body shall be united to his own soul, and that for ever, not to be separated again. As for men's souls, they never die; but immediately upon their separation from the body, they go to those places where, after the day of judgment, their bodies shall be with them, Luke xvi. 23. They that are living at the day of judgment shall be changed, 1 Cor. xv. 51, and suddenly caught up to judgment: only the dead shall first rise, and then the quick shall be taken up with them, 1 Thes. iv. 15, 17. Of Christ's resurrection, see Chap. xiii. 20, Sec. 164.

Sec. 21. *Of principles concerning the last judgment.*

The sixth and last principle is thus expressed, 'and of eternal judgment.'

This principle noteth out two points: 1, the matter itself, *judgment;* 2, the continuance thereof, *eternal.*

About the matter itself, these particulars following are observable:

There shall be a day of judgment. All men shall be judged. Jesus Christ in his human nature shall be the visible judge, Acts xvii. 31. He will judge all men according to their works, Mat. xvi. 27; every work shall be brought to judgment, whether it be open or secret, whether it be good or evil, Eccles. xii. 14; men shall give an account for every idle word, Mat. xii. 36. All shall not receive the same sentence: the righteous shall receive a blessed sentence of life; the wicked a fearful doom of condemnation, Mat. xxv. 34, &c. There is a set day for this judgment, Acts xvii. 31; but it is unknown to men and angels, that men might always watch, Mark xiii. 32, 33, but it shall not come till the number of God's elect shall be fulfilled, Rev. vi. 11.

The continuance of the day of judgment, under this word *eternal* (which is to be taken of the time following, that shall never have an end), hath respect to the reward of the righteous and of the wicked.

The righteous shall be taken with Christ into the highest heaven, where they shall enjoy such glory and happiness, as the tongue of man cannot express, nor heart of man conceive. It shall never be altered, but be everlasting, and therefore called 'eternal life,' Mat. xxv. 46.

The wicked shall be cast down into hell fire, prepared for the devil and his angels, where they shall be tormented in soul and body, which torment shall be endless and remediless, and therefore called eternal fire, Jude 7. Many more principles, especially such as may be counted strong meat, might have been reckoned up. But the principles intended by the apostle are such as may be comprised under the metaphor of milk. In that respect we have reckoned up no more. Yet these which are reckoned up do evidently demonstrate that the six principles named by the apostle are such as may comprise a complete catechism, even all the fundamentals of religion.

---

[1] This rule must not be extended to such as shall be living at the moment of Christ's coming to judgment; for in reference to them thus saith the apostle, 'We shall not all sleep,' 1 Cor. xv. 51; and again, 'We which are alive shall be caught up together in the clouds,' with them that are raised from the dead, 1 Thes. iv. 17.

Sec. 22. *Of the resolution of* Heb. vi. 1, 2.

Ver. 1. *Therefore, leaving the principles of the doctrine of Christ, let us go on unto perfection; not laying again the foundation of repentance from dead works, and of faith towards God,*

Ver. 2. *Of the doctrine of baptisms, and of laying on of hands, and of resurrection of the dead, and of eternal judgment.*

The sum of these two verses is an exhortation to progress in the Christian religion. Hereabout are two points:

1. An inference, *therefore*. 2. The substance.

The substance is set down two ways: 1. Negatively; 2. Affirmatively.

The negative declares *from* what we must proceed. The affirmative *to* what.

The negative is, 1, propounded; 2, repeated.

In the proposition there is,

1. An act required: *leaving.*
2. The object to be left. Herein is shewed,
1. The kind of object: *the principles of the doctrine.*
2. The author thereof: *Christ.*

The affirmative also noteth,

1. An act to be done: *let us go on.*
2. The mark to be aimed at: *unto perfection.*

In the repetition of the negative, another act is inhibited: *not laying again.* And another object is specified, and that is,

1. Generally set down in a metaphor: *the foundation.*
2. Particularly exemplified in six heads.

The first declares a duty, *of repentance;* and the subject thereof, *from dead works.*

The second manifesteth a grace, *of faith;* and the object thereof, *towards God.*

The third hinteth two special means of grace, *doctrine* and *baptisms.*

The fourth pointeth at an ancient rite, *laying on of hands.*

The fifth reveals a special privilege, *resurrection;* and the persons to be made partakers thereof, *the dead.*

The sixth declareth the last act of Christ as mediator, *judgment;* and the continuance or the issue thereof, *eternal.*

Sec. 23. *Of the doctrines raised out of* Heb. vi. 1, 2.

I. *To reproof, instruction must be added.* This chapter contains many instructions, which the apostle adds to his reproof, in the latter end of the former chapter. See Sec. 2.

II. *Christians must not always stick in first principles.* This is the meaning of this word *leaving.* See Sec. 3.

III. *The principles taught in Christ's church must be the doctrine of Christ.* This is here expressly set down. See Sec. 3.

IV. *Christians must daily grow in grace.* This is to go on. See Sec. 4.

V. *Perfection must be a Christian's aim.* This is it whereunto he must go on. See Sec. 5.

VI. *A foundation of religion must be laid.* This is implied under the metaphor of a foundation here used. See Sec. 6.

VII. *The foundation must be but once laid.* It is here forbidden to be laid again. See Sec. 6.

VIII. *The primitive church had a set catechism.* The distinct principles here set down import as much. See Sec. 7.

IX. *The natural man's works are all dead.* So here they are said to be. See Sec. 8.

X. *Repentance is necessary.* It is here set down as the first principle. See Sec. 8.

XI. *God is to be known.* For this end mention is here made of God. See Sec. 9.

XII. *Faith is a true grace.* It is therefore here expressly required. See Sec. 10.

XIII. *Faith is to be fixed on God.* This is the meaning of this phrase, *towards God.* See Sec. 10.

XIV. *God's word is the church's doctrine.* It is that wherein the members of the church are to be instructed. See Sec. 11.

XV. *Baptism is the church's privilege.* It is here reckoned among the privileges which belong to the church. See Sec. 14.

XVI. *There is an inward and outward baptism.* This may be one reason of using the plural number, *baptisms.* See Sec. 12.

XVII. *Baptism is common to many.* This may be another reason of the plural number. See Sec. 12.

XVIII. *Imposition of hands is an evangelical rite.* It is one of the principles of the Christian's catechism. See Sec. 16.

XIX. *Ministers may be set apart by imposition of hands.* Hereabout was this rite used in the apostle's time. See Sec. 17.

XX. *Our bodies are subject to death.* This is here taken for granted. See Sec. 19.

XXI. *Our dead bodies shall be raised.* The resurrection here mentioned is of our bodies. See Sec. 20.

XXII. *There shall be a general judgment.* This also is here taken for granted. See Sec. 21.

XXIII. *The sentence at the last judgment will be unalterable.* In this respect it is styled *eternal judgment.* See Sec. 21.

Sec. 24. *Of the sense of these words,* 'And this will we do.'

Heb. vi. 3, *And this will we do, if God permit.*

The apostle, to his exhortation made to the Hebrews, that they would 'go on to perfection,' by this copulative particle καὶ, *and,* addeth a promise of his own endeavour to do what in him lieth for helping them on in that progress.

The relative τοῦτο, *this,* hath reference to that

general point, which he intended about leaving principles, and going on to perfection.

Thereabout he maketh this promise, ποιήσομεν, *we will do*, namely, that which belonged to a minister, to help on people's going to perfection; which was not to lay the foundation again, but to open deeper mysteries, as he doth in the seventh and other chapters following.

In setting down the promise, he useth the plural number, *we* will do.

1. In reference to other ministers. For there were other ministers of this church besides the apostle himself, who were all of the same mind, as the apostle testifieth of himself and Titus thus : ' Walked we not in the same spirit ?' 2 Cor. xii. 18.

2. To set forth the disposition of other ministers in his own example, as where he saith, ' We, ambassadors for Christ, as though God did beseech you by us, we pray,' &c.

3. In relation to the endeavour of them to whom he wrote. For being persuaded that they would make progress according to that doctrine which should be delivered to them by him, he saith, ' This will we do.' I in doctrine, and you in proficiency, will go on to perfection. Thus he includes them with himself where he saith in the plural number and first person, φερώμεθα, ' let us go on,' ver. 1.

Thus it appears that it was not an ambitious, episcopal humour in which he here useth this plural number, as they who in their edicts thus begin, *We Gregory, We Pius*.

By expressing his mind in the future tense, he declareth his purpose beforehand, which is a lawful and useful course. Other faithful ministers in all ages have so done; yea, and Christ himself, especially about the time of his departure, as John xiv. 3, 13, 16, 18, 21, 23. All God's promises are such professions.

Such professions beforehand do much support the spirits of them to whom they are made, and make them expect the accomplishment of what is professed; yea, this is an holy tie and bond to him that maketh the profession, to be faithful in performing the same.

This may be a good pattern for such as intend good to others, freely to profess their intent beforehand, and that with a faithful resolution to perform what they profess.

Sec. 25. *Of the ministry of the word a means of going on to perfection.*

The foresaid apostolical promise is both a means to lead on people forward to perfection, and also a motive to stir up people to endeavour after it. That it is a means is evident, by this effect of making people *to grow*, attributed to the ministry of the word. In this respect saith an apostle, ' Desire the word, that you may grow thereby,' 1 Peter ii. 2; and, ' I commend you to the word, which is able to build you up,' Acts xx. 32.

God hath sanctified the ministry of the word, both for our spiritual birth and also for our spiritual growth, to begin and to perfect grace in us; in which respect ministers are styled *planters* and *waterers*, 1 Cor. iii. 6; *fathers* and *instructors*, 1 Cor. iv. 15.

Such ministers as, having well instructed their people in the first principles of religion, do there set down their staff, and go no further, though they may seem to have gone far, yet come far short of that which becomes a faithful minister. Should a parent that had well trained up his child in the childhood and youth thereof, then leave it, and take no care of fitting it unto some good calling, he would be counted both improvident and unnatural; much more ministers, that do not what they can to perfect their people. This was the end why Christ gave pastors and teachers, Eph. iv. 11–13.

Sec. 26. *Of ministers helping their people to attain perfection.*

As the apostle's promise was a means of drawing on his people to perfection, so it was a motive to incite them so to do. For a minister's pattern in doing his duty is a forcible inducement unto people for them to do their duty. Hereupon, saith the apostle, ' Brethren, be followers together of me,' &c., Philip. iii. 17.

Men are much moved by the example of their guides. A generous mind will count it a great disgrace to be a slothful hearer of a diligent preacher, and to remain ignorant under a well instructing minister.

This should stir up us ministers still to be going on in laying forth all the mysteries of godliness, that thereby we may draw on our people nearer and nearer to perfection.

This is the rather to be done because it is a singular help to people's progress, which ministers must endeavour every way they can. As they incite their people to perform duty, so they must direct them how to do it. Where the apostle exhorteth to ' covet earnestly the best gifts,' he further addeth, ' And yet shew I unto you a more excellent way,' 1 Cor. xii. 31. See Chap. iii. ver. 13, Sec. 142.

Thus there may be hope that a minister's labour shall not be in vain. Exhortation is of good use to work upon affection; but directory doctrine so worketh upon the understanding as a man's affection is thereby well ordered and directed.

They much fail in their ministerial function who are earnest in exhortation and reproof, but scanty in directing the people. They are like 'a foolish rider, who letteth go the reins of his bridle, and whips and spurs on his horse, so as the horse may carry him much further out of the way than he was before. Many cry out against ignorance and non-proficiency, and earnestly exhort to knowledge and good progress in grace; they complain that their people care not how they present themselves to the Lord's table; yet do not such ministers perform their duty in instructing their people, and building them up from one degree of grace to another.

For our parts, as we desire to be accounted faithful (as Moses was, Num. xii. 7), and would be 'pure from the blood of all men, let us not shun to declare unto our people all the counsel of God,' Acts xx. 26, 27, but upon the good foundation which we have laid, build gold, silver, and precious stones, 1 Cor. iii. 11, 12. This is the way to bring people to perfection.

Sec. 27. *Of subjecting our purposes to God's will.*

The apostle's foresaid promise is thus limited, 'if God permit.' The conditional particle, *if*, implieth such a limitation as makes him subject his purpose to the guiding providence of God: as if he had said, I fully purpose what I promise; but yet with this caution, if God suffer me to do what I intend; by which pattern we see that our purposes must be submitted to God's permittance. This is thus expressly commanded, 'Ye ought to say, If the Lord will,' James iv. 15; and this hath been the practice of God's saints. When David had a purpose to bring the ark of God into a settled place, he thus expresseth his purpose, 'If it be of the Lord our God,' 1 Chron. xiii. 2; and Saint Paul thus, 'I will return again unto you, if God will,' Acts xviii. 21; and again, 'I will come to you shortly, if the Lord will,' 1 Cor. iv. 19; and 'I trust to tarry a while with you, if the Lord will.'

This submission giveth evidence of that knowledge which we have of the over-ruling providence of God, of our faith therein, and respect thereto. For though there may be 'a preparation in the heart of man,' yet 'the answer of the tongue is from the Lord.' And though 'a man's heart deviseth his way,' yet 'the Lord directeth his steps,' Prov. xvi. 1, 9. So as a man's purposes and promises will be all in vain without this permission.

They are impious and blasphemous thoughts and speeches of men who think or say they will do this or that whether God will or no. An heathen poet[1] who noteth out this speech of Ajax, He that is nobody may, with the help of the gods, much prevail; but I am confident to get this done without them, withal observeth that divine vengeance followed him. How much more is that pope of Rome to be condemned,[2] who, being forbidden by his physician to eat of a dish which he liked exceeding well, but was hurtful to his health, blasphemously said, Bring me my dish in despite of God. Such speeches argue atheistical minds.

They go too far in this point of atheism who peremptorily promise, vow, and bind themselves to do such things as are against the mind and will of God, as those Jews who 'bound themselves under a curse to kill Paul,' Acts xxiii. 12.

It becomes us who are instructed in the over-ruling providence of God, to have always in our heart, and, as occasion is given, to manifest in our words, our submission of all our intents to the divine providence, that so we may rest content if at any time we be crossed in our intent. Well may we know what we would have fall out, but God doth best know what should fall out, and what is best so to do. Let us not, therefore, be too eager in pursuing our own purposes. This caution, being interposed, may keep us from breach of promise when matters fall out otherwise than we have promised.

Sec. 28. *Of the efficacy of man's ministry, depending on God's blessing.*

The Greek verb ἐπιτρέπῃ, which here setteth out God's permitting act, is a compound of a simple verb, τρέπω, *verto*, that signifieth to turn, and a preposition, ἐπί, that signifieth *unto*. He that permits a thing, to testify his permission, will turn to him and grant his desire.

The same simple verb joined with another preposition, ἀπό, that signifieth *from*, intendeth the contrary, namely, to turn from one, and that in dislike to what he desired. Thus is it used, 2 Tim. iii. 5.

The word of this text implieth God's approving of a thing, and such a permitting as he adds his helping hand thereunto. For God doth not barely suffer good things to be so and so done; but he hath his hand in ordering and disposing them, and thereby brings them to a good issue. Well therefore doth the apostle, in reference to the efficacy of his ministry, add this caution, 'If God permit;' for man's ministry is so far effectual, as God adds his blessing thereunto. 'I have planted,' saith the apostle, 'Apollos watered; but God gave the increase,' 1 Cor. iii. 6. In this respect also he saith, 'God hath made us able ministers of the New Testament,' 2 Cor. iii. 5. To this purpose may that in general be applied, both to the efficacy of man's ministry, and also to the profit of people's hearing, which a prophet thus expresseth, 'I am the Lord thy God, which teacheth thee to profit, which leadeth thee by the way that thou shouldst go,' Isa. xlviii. 17.

All means are voluntarily appointed by God, subordinate in his providence, and ordered thereby, as the lower wheels in a clock by the great one.

This is a great encouragement with diligence, good conscience, and in faith to use the means, which are warranted by God; and in the use of them to call on God, and to depend on him for a blessing.

Sec. 29. *Of the resolution and observations of* Heb. vi. 3.

Ver. 3. *And this will we do, if God permit.*

---

[1] Sophocl., in Ajac.

Θεοῖς μὲν κἄν ὁ μηδὲν ὢν ὁμοῦ,
Κράτος κατακτήσαιτ'· ἐγὼ δὲ καὶ δίχα
Κείνων πέποιθα τοῦτ' ἐπισπάσειν κλέος.

[2] Julius III., Balæi Chron. de Act. Pontif.

The sum of this verse is a minister's duty.

In it two points are observable:
1. The connection of this verse with the two former, by this copulative particle *and*.
2. A declaration of the duty itself. Hereabout is set down,
 1. The minister's intention; 2, the limitation thereof. In setting down the intention, the matter and manner are both observable.

The matter setteth out an act, *do*. And the object thereof, *this*.

The manner is manifested in two circumstances.
1. The plural number, *we*; 2, the time, future, *will*.

The limitation is, 1, generally propounded in this conditional particle, *if*.
2. Particularly expressed in this phrase, *God permit*.

Doctrines.

I. *Ministers must endeavour to effect what they exhort their people to.* This ariseth from the connection of this verse with the former, by this copulative *and*. See Sec. 24.

II. *Ministers must direct their people in what they incite them to.* By this word *do*, he intendeth his preaching or writing, which is a means to direct them. See Sec. 26.

III. *Ministers must lead on their people to perfection.* This relative *this* hath reference to that point. See Sec. 25.

IV. *Ministers must judge others in good things to be of their mind.*

The plural number *we* includeth other ministers. See Sec. 24.

V. *Good purposes may be beforehand professed.* This the apostle here doth by a word of the future tense, *we will do*. See Sec. 24.

VI. *Men's purposes must be submitted to God's providence.* This conditional particle *if*, as here used, intends as much. See Sec. 27.

VII. *God's blessing makes men's ministry effectual.* Thus much is intended under this phrase, *God permit*. See Sec. 28.

Sec. 30. *Of declaring beforehand the utmost danger.* Heb. vi. 4-6.

Ver. 4. *For it is impossible for those who were once enlightened, and have tasted of the heavenly gift, and were made partakers of the Holy Ghost,*

5. *And have tasted the good word of God, and the powers of the world to come,*

6. *If they shall fall away, to renew them again unto repentance; seeing they crucify to themselves the Son of God afresh, and put him to an open shame.*

In these three verses a strong reason is rendered to press the Hebrews on forward in their progress of religion. This causal particle *for* implieth as much.

It may have reference either to the apostle's promise, ver. 3, or to his exhortation, ver. 1. Both tend to the same end; for his promise is to help them on in that whereunto he exhorted them. Applied to his exhortation, it implieth thus much, be you careful to go on unto perfection, lest you fall into the fearful estates of apostates. Applied to his promise, it implieth that he would not fail to do his best endeavour to help them on to perfection, lest they should fall backward so far as to prove apostates.

The reason then is taken from the danger which they may fall into, who, having well begun, go not on forward till they come to perfection. That danger is set out in the estate of apostates, which is a most desperate estate.

The apostle's argument may be thus framed:

Whatsoever may bring professors unto apostasy is carefully to be avoided;

But negligence in going on unto perfection, may bring professors unto apostasy; therefore such negligence is to be avoided.

To enforce this argument the further, he describeth the woful estates of apostates, and that in such a manner, as the very hearing thereof may well work in men Belshazzar's passion, Dan. v. 6.

By this it is evident that the utmost danger, whereinto professors may fall, is to be laid before them. This did God, when he said to man, 'In the day that thou eatest of such a tree, thou shalt surely die,' Gen. ii. 17. So did Moses in those fearful curses that he denounced against God's people for their transgressions, Lev. xxvi. 16, Deut. xxviii. 15. This was usual with the prophets, Isa. v. 5, Hosea i. 9; with the forerunner of Christ, Mat. iii. 10; with Christ himself, Mat. xxiii. 85, Rev. xxv., and iii. 16; and with his apostles, Rom. xi. 21.

This may be an especial means to make men circumspect in avoiding all things which may bring us into that danger. Seafaring men, that are beforehand told of such and such quicksands, rocks, pirates, or other like dangers, will as warily as they can avoid them all. Of the great need wherein we do stand of circumspection in avoiding spiritual dangers, and particularly in doing all we can to prevent apostasy, see Chap. iii. 12, Sec. 122.

1. This is a good warrant, yea, and a motive also for ministers prudently to observe the danger whereunto people are subject, and plainly to declare as much unto them. 'Cry aloud, spare not,' &c., saith the Lord to a prophet in such a case, Isa. lviii. 1. If ministers in this case hold their peace, their people may fall into that danger, and the blood of people be required at the minister's hand, Ezek. iii. 18.

2. This should make people patient in hearing such kind of doctrine; and not think and say, as many use to do, Our preachers are more terrible than God; if God were not more merciful than they, we should all be damned. To remove this scandal, let these considerations be duly observed.

(1.) As prophets and apostles of old denounced such judgments as God's Spirit suggested to them, so we their successors denounce such as they have left recorded for all ages.

(2.) This is but an ancient cavil, which was made against God's own prophets. Of Jeremiah they said, 'he is mad,' Jer. xxix. 26; and of Paul, he was 'beside himself,' Acts xxvi. 24; yea, Jeremiah was further charged that he sought 'not the welfare of the people, but the hurt,' Jer. xxxviii. 4, and that 'the Lord had not sent him,' Jer. xliii. 2.

(3.) Such preachers as are counted *Boanerges*, sons of thunder, Mark iii. 17, may be most earnest with God for their people's good. Instance Moses, Exod. xxxii. 32. Who more grieved for the people's running on to destruction than Jeremiah? Jer. iv. 19, and ix. 1. Who more earnestly called upon God for them? Jer. xiv. 7, 8. Who more expostulated the people's case with God? Jer. xii. 1.

(4.) Ministers' declaration of danger beforehand may be a means of preventing the danger. Witness the case of Nineveh, Jonah iii. 10, and this is the end which good ministers do aim at. He that wisheth another's destruction will hold his peace, and not make known the danger whereunto he is subject.

Sec. 31. *Of five steps on which apostates may ascend towards salvation.*

In setting forth the danger whereunto professors are subject, the apostle sheweth how far such as fall may ascend upon the ladder to salvation; and withal how far they may fall from thence.

There are five steps, each higher than other, whereon he that falleth clean away may ascend.[1] Some refer those five steps to the fore-mentioned principles of the doctrine of Christ, as

1. Illumination, to 'repentance from dead works.' For till a man be enlightened, he cannot know his natural, miserable condition; but being enlightened, he well discerneth the same; so as he is brought to think of repentance from dead works.

2. The taste of the heavenly gift, to 'faith towards God.' For faith is an heavenly gift, and the means whereby we partake of such gifts as come from God, who is in heaven.

3. Participation of the Holy Ghost, to 'the doctrine of baptisms,' for they who having heard the word were baptized, had gifts of the Holy Ghost bestowed upon them, as a seal of God's accepting them, Acts ii. 38.

4. A taste of the good word of God, to 'the laying on of hands,' for they who having given evidence of their faith were baptized, were further by imposition of hands confirmed. Thus the gospel, which is here called the good word of God, was of use to build them up further, 1 Pet. ii. 2, Acts xx. 32.

[1] Junius in Paral.

5. A taste of 'the powers of the world to come,' to 'resurrection of the dead, and eternal judgment,' which are the two last principles, and they are the very beginning of that full happiness and glory, whereof here we have a taste.

By this comparing of these things together, some light is brought to a more full opening of them.

We will further proceed in handling the foresaid five steps distinctly by themselves.

Sec. 32. *Of the illumination of hypocrites.*

The first step is thus expressed, 'once enlightened.' The Greek word $\varphi\omega\tau\iota\sigma\theta\acute{\epsilon}\nu\tau\alpha\varsigma$, translated *enlightened*, is metaphorical. The noun $\varphi\tilde{\omega}\varsigma$, whence it is derived, signifieth *light*. The active verb, $\varphi\omega\tau\acute{\iota}\zeta\omega$, *to give light*, Luke xi. 36; metaphorically to give knowledge or understanding. Thus it is attributed to Christ, John i. 9. The passive, $\varphi\omega\tau\acute{\iota}\zeta o\mu\alpha\iota$, signifieth *to be endued with knowledge*, or understanding, Eph. i. 18. So it is here taken.

Illumination, then, is a work of the Holy Ghost, whereby man's mind is made capable of understanding the things of God, and able to discern divine mysteries. In one word, the grace or gift of a mind enlightened is knowledge: not such knowledge as heathen had, who by the heavens and other works of God, might somewhat conceive many invisible things of God, Rom. i. 20, Ps. xix. 1, but such as the word of God revealed concerning the mysteries of godliness. This is that knowledge whereof Christ speaketh, Luke xii. 47, and his apostle, 2 Pet. ii. 21.

This knowledge may make men acknowledge, profess, maintain, and instruct others in the mysteries of godliness, though they themselves be but hypocrites and reprobates. Judas did all these, for he was ordained an apostle, Luke vi. 13, 16, and therein so carried himself, as none of the other apostles could judge of him amiss, till Christ manifested his hypocrisy.

This kind of illumination is here said to be $\mathring{\alpha}\pi\alpha\xi$, *once*, in two especial respects:

1. Because there was a time when they were not enlightened, for they were 'once darkness,' Eph. v. 8. By nature men are blind in regard of spiritual matters, 2 Pet. i. 9, Rev. iii. 17. That desire which man had to know more than God would have him know, Gen. iii. 5, 7, brake his eye-strings, so as man is not now capable of understanding the things of God, 1 Cor. ii. 14.

Though the word be a bright light, yet to a natural man, it is but as the bright sun to a blind man. He must be enlightened before he can understand the mysteries of godliness.

2. Because, if after they are enlightened, they grow blind again, there is no recovery of their illumination. In such a sense 'the faith' is said to be 'once delivered unto the saints,' Jude 3. In, this sense also Christ is said to be 'once offered up.' And we are said 'once to die,' Heb. ix. 27, 28. Therefore, 'it had been

better for them not to have known the way of righteousness,' 2 Pet. ii. 21.

This gift of illumination is fitly set in the first place, because the Spirit first worketh this gift in a man. For it is the ground of all other spiritual gifts. Though it be not sufficient, yet is it of absolute necessity, a gift to be laboured after, 2 Pet. i. 5, Prov. iv. 5. Yea, we must seek to be 'filled with knowledge,' Col. i. 9, and to 'abound therein,' 2 Cor. viii. 7.

Quest. Wherein lieth the difference betwixt this knowledge, and the knowledge of them that are effectually called, which doth not thus vanish away?

Ans. 1. The knowledge of hypocrites is only a general knowledge of the word, and the mysteries thereof, that they are all true, but it is not an experimental knowledge of them in themselves. The power, wisdom, mercy, and other divine attributes of God are not experimentally known in themselves, nor the virtue of Christ's death, nor the misery of man, nor other like points. But this experimental knowledge is in those that are effectually called, Eph. i. 18, 19, Philip. iii. 8, Rom. vii. 24.

Ans. 2. It swimmeth only in the brain of hypocrites, it diveth not into their heart, to make them fear, and love God, and trust in him, to make them carry themselves according to that which they know of God's word, of God, and of themselves. But the knowledge of them who are effectually called doth so affect them, as it is accompanied with other saving graces. This knowledge is said to be life eternal, John xvii. 3.

Ans. 3. The knowledge which hypocrites have is as a wind that puffeth them up, 1 Cor. viii. 1; it makes them cast their eyes on their own parts, and to be too much conceited therein, John ix. 40, Rev. iii. 17; but the knowledge of them that are effectually called, maketh them abhor themselves, Job xlii. 6.

This, as it may be a trial of our knowledge, whether we may rest in it or no, so it may be an admonition unto such as know much, not to be proud thereof, in that it may be no other gift than that which an hypocrite and reprobate may have, and which may aggravate thy damnation, Luke xii. 47. Use all thy good means thou canst to get that eyesalve of the Spirit, whereunto Christ adviseth, Rev. iii. 18, which may sharpen thy eyesight, and make thee fully and distinctly know the word of salvation, and the mysteries thereof, to thy eternal happiness.

Sec. 33. *Of tasting the heavenly gift.*

The second step wheron hypocrites may ascend towards salvation is thus set down, *and have tasted of the heavenly gift.*

Of the meaning of this word *tasted*, see Chap. ii. 9, Sec. 79.

Tasting, *gustus*, is properly an effect of that sense which we call taste.

It is here metaphorically taken. Applied to the soul, it intendeth two things:

1. The beginning of true sound grace. For by taste, the sweetness and goodness of a thing is discerned, and an appetite after it provoked, yea, and much comfort received thereby, 1 Sam. xiv. 29. In this sense it is said, 'Oh taste and see that the Lord is good,' Ps. xxxiv. 8.

2. A shallow apprehension of the good and benefit of a thing; for by tasting only, and not eating, some sweet smack and relish may be in a man's mouth, but little or no nourishment received thereby. By this kind of taste the benefit of a thing is lost. A man may starve, though after this manner he taste the most nourishing meat that can be. In this sense this metaphor is here twice used: once in this verse, and again in the next verse.

In the former sense tasting is a preparation to eating, and it is opposed to an utter refusal and rejection of a thing, and implies a participation thereof.

In this sense Christ saith of those that refused to come, 'None of them shall taste of my supper,' Luke xiv. 24; that is, none of them shall any way partake thereof.

In the latter sense tasting is opposed to eating, and implieth no true and real participation of a thing; as they who, being at a feast, do only taste of that which is set before them, lose the benefit of that meat.

To follow this metaphor, Christ is set before all that are in the church as dainty, wholesome meat.

They who are effectually called, being as guests bidden to the table, do by a true justifying faith so eat, and digest this spiritual meat, as they are refreshed, nourished, strengthened, and preserved thereby unto everlasting life. But they who are only outwardly called, do only see, touch, and taste how comfortable and profitable a meat it is; yet in that they eat not thereof, the sweet taste in time vanisheth without any good, or benefit thereby.

By tasting faith is here meant. For faith is that gift whereby we do in any kind receive or apply Christ.

Of the nature of faith in general, and of the different kinds thereof, see *The Whole Armour of God*, treat. ii., part 6, on Eph. vi. 16, sec. 11, 12, &c.

Hypocritical and temporary faith is set out by tasting only, as opposed to eating; and this is the faith here meant. But justifying and saving faith is set forth by tasting, as it implieth participation of a thing. This cannot be here meant, because this kind of faith never falleth away.

The object of this faith is here styled, *the heavenly gift*. Hereby Christ himself is meant, together with all those blessings which, in him and with him, are received, Eph. i. 3.

Christ is called a gift, because he is given to us of God, John iii. 16, and iv. 10; so are all manner of spiritual graces, they are given of God. In this respect they are to be sought of God; and those means are to be used for partaking thereof which God hath appointed and sanctified. And the praise and glory of this gift is to be ascribed to God, by those that are made partakers thereof, Rom. xi. 35, 36.

This gift is called ἐπουράνιος, *heavenly;*—

1. In general, by reason of the excellency thereof, for excellent things are styled heavenly. See Chap. iii. 1, Sec. 15.

2. In a particular reference to the prime author, who is above in heaven, James i. 17, and to the kind of gift, which is sent down from heaven, Col. iii. 1, and worketh in us an heavenly disposition, Philip. iii. 20, Col. iii. 2; and also is a means to bring us to heaven, 2 Thes. ii. 12.

The description of the object of faith doth,

1. Aggravate the wretched disposition of apostates, who content themselves with a bare taste of such an heavenly gift.

2. It putteth us on more earnestly to seek after this gift, and not to rest till we find that we are truly and really made partakers thereof.

3. It should make us careful in proving our faith, whether it be a true justifying faith, or merely hypocritical and temporal.[1] Hereof see *The Whole Armour of God*, on Eph. vi. 16, sec. 12, 35, &c.

Sec. 34. *Of being made partakers of the Holy Ghost.*

The third step whereupon apostates are here said to ascend is in these words, 'And were made partakers of the Holy Ghost.'

Of the meaning of this word *partakers*, see Chap. iii. 1, Sec. 17.

Of this title *Holy Ghost*, see Chap. ii. 4, Sec. 35.

The Holy Ghost is here metonymically put for the gifts and operations of the Spirit of God, which he worketh in men. In this sense this title *Holy Ghost* is frequently used, as Acts viii. 15, and xix. 6. This is evident by joining of the gifts themselves to the Spirit; thus, 'The Spirit of wisdom, the Spirit of counsel, the Spirit of knowledge,' &c., Isa. xi. 2. So, 'The Spirit of faith,' 2 Cor. iv. 13.

They properly are said to be 'made partakers of the Holy Ghost,' in whom the sanctifying Spirit hath wrought special spiritual gifts, such as are above nature; even such as cannot be attained either by the instinct of nature, or by any help of man, without an especial work of the Holy Ghost. Such were those moral virtues which were wrought in him, of whom it is said, 'Jesus loved him,' Mark x. 20, 21. Such was that counsel wherewith Ahithophel was endued, 2 Sam. xvi. 23, and that ability which Saul had to govern the kingdom, 1 Sam. x. 9, and xi. 6, and that gift of prophecy and working of miracles that was bestowed on them whom Christ would not acknowledge, Mat. vii. 22, 23, and that obedience which Herod yielded to John's ministry, Mark vi. 20, and that rejoicing which the Jews had in that light which John held forth, John v. 35.

[1] That is, temporary.'—ED.

Quest. Can hypocrites and reprobates partake of the gifts of the sanctifying Spirit?

Ans. Yes, they may partake of such gifts as the sanctifying Spirit worketh, though not of his sanctifying gifts. They are said to be made partakers of the Holy Ghost, because that Spirit which sanctifieth others doth work these gifts in them; and because many of those gifts which are wrought in them prove in others to be sanctifying gifts; as knowledge, wisdom, faith, repentance, fear of God, temperance, and such like.

The difference betwixt that participation of the Holy Ghost, which they who are effectually called and they who are only formally called have, lieth in three things especially.

1. In the *kind* of them. For the former are altered, and renewed in their nature. In this sense saith David, 'Create in me a clean heart, O God; and renew a right spirit within me,' Ps. li. 10. The other are only restrained; as Saul and Ahithophel were.

This difference is herein discerned, in that they who are effectually called are wrought upon throughout, as David, who is said to have a perfect heart; but the other in some respects only, as Abijam, 1 Kings xv. 3, and Herod, Mark vi. 20.

2. In the *use* of them. Renewing gifts are for the good of the parties themselves, even their own salvation, Eph. ii. 8, 1 Peter i. 9. Restraining gifts are for the good of others; in which respect the apostle saith that they are 'given to profit withal,' 1 Cor. xii. 7; such was Ahithophel's prudence, 2 Sam. xvi. 23. These gifts are as the lantern in the admiral's ship, for the good of the whole navy.

3. In the *continuance* of them. Renewing gifts are permanent, they never decay, Rom. xi. 29.

The other are like the corn sown in stony ground, which endureth but for a while, Mat. xiii. 21. If they continue the whole time of a man's life, yet then they clean fall away. 'For when a wicked man dieth, his expectation shall perish,' Prov. xi. 7.

Quest. What difference is there betwixt the second and third step; namely, betwixt tasting the heavenly gift, and being made partakers of the Holy Ghost?

Ans. Though the second may be comprised under the third, for the taste of the heavenly gift is wrought by the Holy Ghost; yet by the latter, such effects as follow upon the former, and are extraordinary evidences of the work of God's Spirit in men, are meant. The effects are such as make a difference betwixt a diabolical and hypocritical faith. For the devil believes and trembles, James ii. 19; but many hypocrites who are outwardly called believe and rejoice, as the Jews did, John v. 35, and Herod, Mark vi. 20. This joy presupposeth comfort and contentment; and restraineth from many sins, and putteth upon the practice of many duties. Extraordinary evidences of God's Spirit are those gifts which the apostle reckoneth up, 1 Cor. xii. 8–10. These confirm the truth of

God's word to themselves and others. Thus they prove the more useful ; in which respect they who fall from them are the more inexcusable.

That which is here said of hypocrites being 'made partakers of the Holy Ghost,' should work care and diligence about trying and proving those gifts of the Spirit which we think we have, and not upon every work of the Spirit too rashly infer that we are certainly sanctified, and shall undoubtedly be saved.

Sec. 35. *Of tasting of the good word of God*, ver. 5.

The fourth step whereon hypocrites ascend towards salvation is thus expressed, 'And have tasted the good word of God.'

This metaphor, *taste*, is here used in the same sense wherein it was before, Sec. 33.

Of this phrase, *word of God*, see Chap. iv. 12, Sec. 69.

By *the good word of God*,[1] καλὸν, he meaneth the gospel, which, according to the Greek, and our English notation, also signifieth *a good word, a good speech*, or *good message* and tidings. Hereof see more Chap. iv. 2, Sec. 16.

The gospel brought the best tidings that ever was brought to any. The sum thereof is expressed John iii. 16.

The law also is called *good*, Rom. vii. 12; but a thing may be styled good two ways : 1, in the matter of it ; 2, in the effect that proceedeth from it.

The law, in regard of the matter of it, is most pure and perfect, no corruption, no falsehood therein ; and in this respect it is also styled holy and just, Rom. vii. 12.

The gospel is not only good in the matter of it, but also in the profit and benefit of it. The law to a sinner, in and by itself, brings no profit ; but the gospel doth, by making known a Saviour, and the means of attaining to salvation by him ; yea, further, the gospel is a word of power, enabling sinners to observe the condition which it requireth of them. In this respect it is styled 'the power of God unto salvation,' Rom. i. 16 ; for want of this power, the law is said to be a killing letter, a ministration of death, 1 Cor. iii. 6, 7, but the gospel the word of life.

To taste of the good word is not only to be enlightened in the truth thereof, which was comprised under the first step, Sec. 32, but also to have an apprehension and sense of the benefit of it, namely, of God's love to man, and of his gracious offer of Jesus Christ, and of pardon of sin and eternal salvation in and with Christ ; such a taste this may be as for the time to work a sweet smack, but yet to bring no true fruit nor lasting benefit to him that hath it.

This degree exceeds the other three in two especial respects :

1. In that it followeth after them, and pre-supposeth them to be first wrought in a man ; for upon enlightening and tasting of the heavenly gift, and partaking of the Holy Ghost, a man feels such sweetness in the means whereby those gifts were wrought as he doth exercise himself the more therein. He reads the word, and performs other duties of piety privately, and frequents the public ordinances of God, and that with some joy, in that he feels a smack of sweetness in them, Mark vi. 20, Mat. xiii. 20, John v. 35.

2. In that this good word is a means further to build up them who have been enlightened, and tasted of the heavenly gift, to build them up further in grace, and more and more to assure them of God's love, and of all those good and precious things which Christ by his blood hath purchased, Acts xx. 32.

The difference in tasting the good word of God betwixt the upright and hypocrites consisteth especially in this, that the upright do not only taste the sweetness of it, but also feel the power of it in their souls. There is such a difference between these as is betwixt the corn sown in the stony ground and in the good ground, Mat. xiii. 20, 23. Hypocrites only taste it. The upright eat it also, Ezek. iii. 3. David hid God's word in his heart, Ps. cxix. 11. The gospel came unto the Thessalonians ' not in word only, but also in power,' &c., 1 Thes. i. 5. The Romans ' obeyed from the heart that form of doctrine which was delivered to them,' Rom. vi. 17. This is that hearing and keeping of the word whereupon Christ pronounceth a man blessed.

This nearly concerns us who have any way tasted the sweetness of this good word of God, not to content ourselves with a mere taste, but so to eat it, so to believe it, so to conform ourselves thereby, as we may live thereby both here and hereafter, Isa. lv. 3.

Sec. 36. *Of tasting the powers of the world to come.*

The fifth and last step whereon hypocrites ascend toward salvation is in these words, *and the powers of the world to come.* The verb in the former clause, γευσαμένους, thus translated, *have tasted*, is here understood, and that in the same sense wherein it was there used.

Many expositors do here understand the militant church under the gospel to be meant by this phrase, *world to come*, as it was Chap. ii. 5, Sec. 41. But,

1. There is not the same Greek word here put for the world as was there. The word there used, οἰκουμένην, signifieth a place of habitation, and is frequently put for the earth. But the word here used, αἰὼν, signifieth a perpetual duration of time. Hereof see Chap. i. ver. 2, Sec. 18.

2. This text doth not so well bear the interpretation of the militant church as that ; here the triumphant church is meant. For this clause hath reference to the two last principles before mentioned, of the resurrection and eternal judgment. Besides, it

---

[1] Of the extent of this epithet *good*, see Chap. xiii. 9, Sec. 127.

is the highest step and degree that an hypocrite can attain unto.

3. The things which they intend who take the world to come, in this place, for the militant church, are gifts conferred on the church of the New Testament, which are comprised under the third step, namely, *partaking of the Holy Ghost*.

I take the state of the triumphant church in heaven to be here meant by *the world to come*, μέλλοντος αἰῶνος.

Thus is this phrase most properly and frequently used. Thus it is opposed to the world where here we live. For every one hath two worlds: one here present, the other to come. *The world to come* is indefinitely put for the future glorious estate of saints, though to the reprobate the world to come is a time and place of horror and torment, Luke xii. 36. Thus *resurrection* is indefinitely put for resurrection to life, because resurrection to condemnation is as no resurrection; for such as are raised thereto were better not be raised at all.

By the *powers* of this world to come, those excellent privileges whereof saints are made partakers in heaven are meant. These are, communion with God, Father, Son, and Holy Spirit; with glorious angels and glorified saints; the perfection and glory of their souls and bodies, and of all the powers and parts of them; immunity from all evil; fulness and satiety of all happiness; and these unchangeable, everlasting.

These privileges are called δυνάμεις, *powers*, ά δύναμαι, *possum*.

1. Because they are evident effects of God's mighty power.

2. Because they are ensigns and trophies of power, victory, and triumph over all our enemies.

3. Because no adverse power can ever prevail against them that are in that world to come. They are firmly established in Christ.

Hypocrites are said to taste of these powers, in that they have such an apprehension of that surpassing glory as to be enamoured and affected therewith; as he that said, 'Blessed is he that shall eat bread in the kingdom of God,' Luke xiv. 15. Balaam had a taste hereof, which moved him to say, 'Let me die the death of the righteous, and let my last end be like his,' Num. xxiii. 10. Though that glory and happiness be here concealed from our sight and sense, yet by faith, and that a temporary faith, it may be discerned and tasted. Thus they who are enlightened and have tasted of the heavenly gift, and have been made partakers of the Holy Ghost, and have tasted the good word of God, may also taste the powers of the world to come.

This step of an hypocrite's ascending towards heaven, is apparently higher than all the rest. The things themselves are the greatest privileges of saints, and a taste of them far surpasseth all the former tastes. Hereby an hypocrite's conceit may be, as it were, rapt out of his body, and out of this world into heaven; and he may be brought lightly to esteem all this world in comparison of the world to come.

It was the greatest prerogative that any had, who died in the wilderness, to see the land of Canaan, which was vouchsafed to Moses alone, Deut. xxxiv. 1. Even so, it is the greatest privilege of any that never enter into that glory, to have this taste of the powers of the world to come.

In this privilege there is a great difference betwixt the hypocrite and upright, in that the hypocrite contents himself with a bare apprehension of such excellencies, and a presumptuous conceit of some right that he may have thereunto; but he doth not thoroughly examine himself, whether he be fitly qualified for the same, nor is he careful to get true and sure evidences thereof, which the upright with the uttermost of his power endeavoureth to do. Briefly to sum all, these are the steps whereupon such as miss of salvation may ascend towards it:

1. Their mind may be supernaturally enlightened in the mysteries of the word.

2. They may have faith in those heavenly promises, which by the word of God are revealed.

3. They may have spiritual fruits of faith wrought in them by the Holy Ghost; as outward restraint from sin, practice of many good things, inward joy, &c.

4. A sweet apprehension of the gospel to be that good word of grace which bringeth salvation unto all men.

5. An inward sight and sense in spirit of that eternal glory and happiness which is provided for the saints.

Seeing that a hypocrite may go thus far, and yet come short of heaven, how diligent ought we to be in the trial of the truth of grace. We have before shewed in every branch differences betwixt the upright and hypocrite. In brief, the knowledge of the upright is experimental, their faith unfeigned, the work of the Holy Ghost renewing, the good word abideth ever in them, and they have assured evidence of their future happiness.

Sec. 37. *Of an hypocrite's fall*, ver. 6.

The apostle having declared in the two former verses how far an hypocrite may ascend on the ladder of salvation, in this sixth verse he declareth how far he may fall down. The main point is expressed in this phrase, *if they shall fall away*. In Greek thus, *and falling away*. For it depends on the former, thus, 'it is impossible, that person enlightened, &c.; and falling away,' &c.

The Greek particle, παραπεσόντας, is a compound, and here only used, and nowhere else throughout the New Testament. The simple verb, πίπτω, signifieth *to fall*. Of it see Chap. iii. 17, Sec. 168. The preposition παρά, with which it is compounded, signifieth *from.* The compound verb, παραπίπτω, *to fall from a thing*, or to fall clean away. The metaphor may be taken from an house that is fairly built above ground, but the foundation thereof not sound. The fall of such an house useth to be a total or universal fall, not of this or that part alone. Christ, speaking of the fall of such an house, saith, 'Great was the fall of it,' Mat. vii. 27.

This metaphor may also be taken from a man that, having ascended high on a ladder, falleth down to the bottom, and so bruiseth his body and breaketh his bones, as he is not able to rise up again. Thus the falling here spoken of, is not a falling away only from some particular graces and gifts received, nor from some measure of them, but a total and universal falling from them all, as in 'the angels which kept not their first estate, but left their own habitation,' Jude 6.

That the fall here spoken of may the better be discerned, I will here more distinctly shew how far such as profess the gospel (for the description before mentioned, vers. 4, 5, is of such) may fall.

Falling away may have respect to the measure or continuance of grace.

In regard of the measure, some fall away in part, some in whole.

In regard of continuance, some so fall as they recover themselves again, some so as they can never be recovered.

Both the degrees of the measure, namely, partial and total, have respect to the outward profession, and to the inward disposition of him that falleth away.

In profession he falleth away in part who denieth some of those principles of religion which formerly he professed, as Peter and Barnabas, Gal. ii. 12.

In disposition he falleth away in part, who, through his own weakness, carelessness, or temptations, decayeth in those graces which once he had, at least in the measure, power, and comfort of them. Hereof see Chap. iii. 12, Sec. 136.

In profession, he wholly falleth away who renounceth all his religion, even that whole faith which once he professed; as those Levites in the captivity, whom God afterwards, though they repented, would not admit to offer sacrifice before him, Ezek. xliv. 9, 10, and many Christians in the ten fiery persecutions, and many of our countrymen in Queen Mary's days.

They in disposition wholly fall away who do not only deny the faith, but also clean put away a good conscience, 1 Tim. i. 19, and iv. 1, 2. Hence followeth hatred of the truth, persecution against the preachers and professors thereof, and blasphemy against Christ himself. Such were many of the pharisees, Mark iii. 30; Hymeneus and Alexander, 1 Tim. i. 20, and Julian. These and such other fall away *toti, wholly,* in outward profession and inward disposition, in tongue and heart; and *a toto, from the whole,* even from all the articles of Christian religion; and *in totum, to the whole, or for ever,* even with a settled peremptory resolution never to return to the religion again.

They that fall away in these last respects are such as are here meant.

Seeing there are such degrees of falling away, let us take heed of proceeding from one degree to another. Let us carefully look both to our profession and disposition. If by our own weakness, or any temptation, we be brought any way to decay in grace, let us not renounce the faith. If by fear or other temptation we be brought to deny it, let us not put away a good conscience. If in part we be brought to do it, let us not still go on to add one degree to another, so as we should wholly fall from the whole for ever, which is a most fearful case.

The fore-mentioned degrees of falling away are to be noted, against the errors of Novatus.[1] He lived in the year of our Lord 253. He came from Africa to Rome. There fell an emulation betwixt him and Cornelius, bishop of Rome, that Cornelius had admitted into the church, upon their repentance, some that had fallen away in the seventh persecution under Decius. Hereupon Novatus published that none who had offered sacrifice to the heathen gods were to be admitted to repentance. He pressed this text to justify his error.

Some of the Latin fathers[2] and others, papists[3] and Lutherans,[4] have, upon a misinterpretation of this text, and other passages in this epistle, denied the canonical authority thereof.

Concerning the point in question, to deny this epistle to be canonical, because it avoucheth that 'it is impossible to renew again unto repentance' such as are there described, is, *nodum scindere, non solvere,* to cut, not to untie the knot.

That which the apostle here speaketh of is the 'sin unto death,' 1 John v. 16, which is the 'sin against the Holy Ghost;' but every outward denying of the faith for fear of persecution, is not the sin against the Holy Ghost. For Peter did as much, Mat. xxvi. 70, &c., yet, upon his repentance, was continued and confirmed in his apostleship, John xxi. 15, &c.

It is said of Novatus, that he was so puffed up against those that fell, as if there remained no hope of salvation for them.[5]

The Novatians affirm that not only sacrificing to idols, but also many other sins, are sins unto death.

---

[1] Novatus ab ecclesia Romana discessit, quòd Cornelius episcopus eos ad communionem admiserat, qui in persecutione ab imperatore Decio excitata diis sacrificaverant.—*Niceph. Histor. Eccles.*, lib. xi. cap. 14.
[2] Tertul., Cyprian, Lactant., Arnob.
[3] Cajetan. [4] Magdeburg.
[5] Contra lapsos inflatus, quasinulla illis reliqua esset salutis spes.—*Euseb. Histor. Eccles.*, lib. vi. cap. 43. Novatiani asserunt, non sacrificia deorum tantum, sed multa etiam alia, esse peccata ad mortem.—*Niceph. Hist. Eccles.*, lib. xiv. cap. 24. Pœnitentiam et benignitatem Dei e medio sustulerunt.—*Sozom. Hist. Eccles.*, lib. viii. cap. 1.

Thus they left no place for repentance, nor for the grace of God, especially to such as in times of persecution yielded to idolatry.

Hereby we see how dangerous it is to mistake and misapply the sense of sacred Scripture.

Sec. 38. *Of the impossibility of apostates' renovation.*

Of those who totally fall away, it is here said, that it is 'impossible to renew them.' This word ἀδύνατον, *impossible*, is a compound. The simple verb δύναμι, *possum*, whence it is derived, signifieth to be able; so as it intendeth δύναμις, *potentia*, a power, but the privative preposition ἀ taketh away all power.

A thing is said to be impossible two ways: 1, improperly; 2, properly. That improperly is said to be impossible, which can hardly be done. Thus doth Christ himself use the word. For where he had said, 'How hardly shall they that have riches enter into the kingdom of God?' he addeth, concerning the very same point, 'with men it is impossible,' Mark x. 23, 27.

A thing properly is said to be impossible, simply, or upon condition.

That is *simply* impossible which never was, is, or can be. Thus it is said, that 'it is impossible for God to lie,' ver. 18. See Sec. 141.

Upon supposition a thing is said to be impossible, either in regard of some present impediment, or of a perpetual impotency in nature.

It was a present impediment in that course which Christ had set down to work miracles amongst those that did believe, that Christ 'could do no mighty work' among his own kin, Mark vi. 4, 5, Mat. xiii. 58.

In regard of a perpetual impotency in nature, 'it is not possible that the blood of bulls and goats should take away sins,' Heb. x. 4.

Some take *impossible* in this text, in the first sense, for *hardly*.

Others for a present supposition, which may be taken away. But the reasons following do evidently demonstrate, that a permanent and perpetual impossibility is here meant; and that in regard of the course which God hath set down to bring men to repentance.

In this impossibility lieth a main difference betwixt the sin here meant and all other sins. For there are many sins, which in the event are not pardoned, yet are pardonable. In which respect Christ saith, in opposition to this sin, 'All sins shall be forgiven,' Mark iii. 28, that is, *may* be forgiven, or are pardonable.

Sec. 39. *Of renewing again.*

That which is here said to be impossible, is thus expressed, 'to renew them again unto repentance.'

The Greek word ἀνακαινίζειν, translated to *renew*, is a compound. The root, καινός, whence the simple verb is derived, signifieth *new*. Thence a verb, καινόω, καινίζω, *novo*, to *make new*. The preposition ἀνὰ, with which the verb is here compounded, signifieth *again*. The verb compounded herewith, ἀνακαινίζω, *renovo*, *to renew*. This hath reference to man's corrupt estate, into which he fell by Adam's first sin. Man's first estate was after God's image, Gen. i. 27. It was a new, fresh, flourishing, glorious estate. Man's corrupt estate is resembled to an old man, Eph. iv. 22, Rom. vi. 6. To have this old estate altered is to be, ἀνακαινούμενος, *renewed*, Col. iii. 10; and the grace itself is styled ἀνακαίνωσις, *renovatio*, *renewing*, Rom. xii. 2, Titus iii. 5.

The conjunction πάλιν, added hereunto, and translated *again*, hath reference to the falling away of those who were once before renewed, at least in appearance. And it intendeth a renewing again of him that had been before renewed. For it presupposeth a man to have cast off the old man, and to have purged out the old leaven; and so after a sort to have been made 'a new man,' 'a new lump;' so as 'having escaped the pollutions of the world, through the knowledge of the Lord and Saviour Jesus Christ, they are again entangled therein, and overcome, the latter end is worse with them than the beginning,' 2 Peter ii. 20. Such an one, if he be recovered, must have a second new birth, a second renovation; and this is it which the apostle saith is impossible.

That which is here said of the new lump, and new man, from which they fall, is to be understood of one so taken to be in the judgment of charity.

The word ἀνακαινίζειν, translated *to renew them*, is of the active voice. In this respect it is diversely applied.

Some refer it to apostates themselves; some to ministers; some to the word; some to God. I suppose that, without any contradiction, it may be referred to each and every of them; for,

1. It being applied to the apostates themselves, it implieth, that they cannot rise again, repent, and turn to God: in that they have deprived themselves of all that spiritual ability which was before wrought in them.

2. Applied to ministers, it implieth that they, though by virtue of their function and ministry they did formerly work upon these apostates, and still continue to work upon others, yet now to these their labour is altogether in vain; they can no more work upon them.

3. Applied to the word, it implieth that that which is a savour of life to others, is to such apostates a savour of death, and a killing letter.

4. Applied to God, it hath respect to his will, his determined purpose, and unchangeable truth, and so proves to be impossible. For as it is impossible that God should lie, so it is impossible that God should alter his determined purpose and resolution, ver. 18.

But to take away all dispute about this point, it may indefinitely, without respect to any particular person or means, be thus translated, 'it is impossible to renew them;' or it may be taken in sense passively, thus, 'it is impossible that they should be renewed again.' Thus some interpret it.

Sec. 40. *Of repentance the way to salvation.*

That whereunto apostates cannot be renewed again is here said to be μετάνοια, *repentance*. Of the notation of the Greek word translated *repentance*, and of the general nature thereof, see Sec. 8.

Some of the ancient fathers understand by this word *repentance*, that solemn form of repentance which was used in the primitive church, for admitting such into the church again, who for fear of persecution had denied the Christian faith, or otherwise had committed some foul and scandalous sin.

But surely that cannot be here intended; for,

1. We do not read of any such form in the apostles' time.
2. There is no impossibility of bringing men to such a form. The greatest apostate that ever was confessed his sin, and outwardly repented himself, Mat. xxvii. 3, 4, and probably might have been brought to such a form.
3. To bring sinners to a public form of repentance, doth not sufficiently express the emphasis of this phrase, to renew, εἰς, *unto*, repentance, or by repentance.
4. This phrase, 'whose end is to be burned,' ver. 8, will hardly admit such an interpretation.

Repentance, therefore, must here properly be taken for a change of the heart; or for such an alteration of mind and disposition as may produce a new life and conversation. It is impossible that the apostate before mentioned should have a new heart.

Mention is here made of repentance, because it is the only means of recovery, and the way to salvation, Luke xiii. 3, 5. So as the apostle here implieth, that it is impossible they should be saved, and that upon this ground, because they cannot repent. For repentance is necessary to salvation. This is the doctrine of the prophets, Isa. i. 16, 17, Jer. iii. 1, Ezek. xxxiii. 11; of the forerunner of Christ, Mat. iii. 7; of Christ himself, Mat. iv. 17; and of his apostles, Mark vi. 12, Acts ii. 38.

1. Repentance is necessary for justifying God's mercy; that it may appear that his free grace in pardoning sin giveth no occasion to continue in sin; but rather to break off sin. For by repentance sin is broken off.
2. Hereby the clamour of the law against the gospel is answered, in that they whose sins are pardoned do not continue in sin, but rather repent thereof; for Christ 'came to call sinners to repentance,' Mat. ix. 13.
3. The mouth of the damned is stopped, in that such sinners as are saved repented, which the damned did not, Luke xvi. 25.
4. By repentance men are made fit members for Christ, yea, and a fit spouse for him, Eph. v. 26. They are also fitted hereby for that place whereunto nothing that defileth can enter, Rev. xxi. 27.

1. This discovereth the vain hopes of them who, going on in sin, look for mercy. These are 'the ungodly men, who turn the grace of our God into lasciviousness,' Jude 4. 'The grace of God, that bringeth salvation, teacheth that, denying ungodliness and worldly lusts, we should live soberly, righteously, and godly,' &c., Titus ii. 11, 12.
2. This is a strong motive to such as have fallen away, and desire recovery, and to be freed from wrath, vengeance, and damnation, to repent; otherwise they cannot but perish, Luke xiii. 3, 5. Whensoever therefore thou goest to God for mercy, renew thy repentance, 1 Tim. ii. 8, Ps. xxvi. 6; otherwise thy prayer may be rejected, yea, and prove an abomination, Ps. lxvi. 18; John. ix. 31; Isa. i. 13, &c. Take heed lest continuance in sin harden thy heart, and make it impenitent, Rom. ii. 5.

We ought the rather to take the opportunities which God affordeth of repentance, because repentance is not in man's power. 'No man can come to Christ except the Father draw him,' John vi. 44. 'It is God which worketh in men, both to will and to do of his good pleasure,' Philip. ii. 13. Therefore saints have ever called upon God to turn them, Jer. xxxi. 18; Lam. v. 21; Ps. li. 10.

Men are wholly prone to evil by nature, as heavy things to fall downward.

It is therefore a very vain conceit to think that a man can repent when he will. Satan doth exceedingly beguile men herein. This makes many to lead all their life in sin, upon conceit that at their death they may repent. Hereof see more in *The Whole Armour of God*, treat. ii. part iv. of righteousness, on Eph. vi. 14, sec. 12.

Sec. 41. *Of apostates crucifying to themselves the Son of God afresh.*

The apostle having denounced a most fearful doom against apostates, in the latter part of the sixth verse, demonstrateth the equity thereof, in these words, *seeing they crucify to themselves the Son of God afresh*, &c.

These words, *seeing they crucify afresh*, are the interpretation of one Greek compound participle, ἀνασταυροῦντας, which word for word may thus be translated, *crucifying again*. Our English hath well set out the sense and emphasis of the word.

The root, σταυρός, from whence the simple verb is derived, signifieth *a cross*, Mat. xxvii. 32. Thence is derived a verb, σταυρόω, which signifieth *to crucify*, Mat. xxvii. 22. To crucify is properly to nail to a cross, or to hang upon a cross. This was the death whereunto Christ was put, Mat. xxvii. 35.

In reference hereunto the apostle here useth this

compound, *crucifying again*. For the adverb, ἀνά, with which it is compounded, signifieth *again*. This compound is here only used, and nowhere else in the New Testament. It implieth two things:

1. That the aforesaid apostates did so obstinately reject all the benefit of Christ's former death upon the cross, that if they should receive any benefit from Christ and his sacrifice, Christ must be crucified again.

2. That they made themselves like to the bitterest and deadliest enemies that ever Christ had, who were those Jews, whom nothing would satisfy but the death of Christ, even that ignominious, painful, and cursed death of the cross. For when the judge asked what he should do with Jesus, they answered, 'Let him be crucified,' Mat. xxvii. 22. Such is that hatred and malice of apostates, that they would, if they could, have him crucified again. Not unfitly therefore do our last English translators use this word *afresh*, for when the wounds of him that hath been healed are opened and bleed again, we use to say, *they bleed afresh*. This then implieth, that though Christ hath finished to the uttermost whatsoever was to be endured on earth, and is now in rest and glory in heaven, yet they would have all his sufferings afresh, all anew. They would have him suffer and endure as much as ever he did before.

To meet with an objection that might be made against this crucifying of Christ again, that it is a matter simply impossible for all the men in the world to do;—Christ being now settled a supreme sovereign in heaven, so as they may sooner pull the sun out of his sphere, than Christ from his throne;—the apostle addeth this restriction, ἑαυτοῖς, *to themselves*, which implieth two things:

1. That in their own imaginations and conceits they would do such a thing, they would do as much as in them lieth to crucify Christ again.

2. That they do so wholly, wilfully, and maliciously reject all the former sufferings of Christ, as to them themselves he must be crucified again. For they can have no benefit by his former sacrifice; though others may, yet not they.

The person whom they so disrespect and reject is here styled, τὸν υἱὸν τοῦ Θεοῦ, 'the Son of God.' Of this title *Son of God*, and of that excellency which belongs to Christ thereupon, see Chap. i. ver. 2, Sec. 15, and ver. 4. Sec. 41.

There is no other title whereby the excellency of Christ could more be set forth than this. It shews him to be not only true God, but also in such a respect God, as he might also become man, and be given for man. As Son of man he died, and shed his blood; as the Son of God, that blood which he shed was the blood of God, Acts xx. 28. To disrespect such a Son of man, as by his blood purchased their redemption, is more than monstrous ingratitude; but to do this against him that is also the Son of God, is the highest pitch of impiety that can be. These four degrees: 1, to *crucify*; 2, to crucify *again*; 3, to crucify again *to themselves*; 4, to do all this to the *Son of God;* do manifest a wonderful great aggravation of the sin of apostates, that they make the invaluable sacrifice of the Son of God, which hath been offered up, and the inestimable price, even the precious blood of God himself, which hath been paid for man's redemption, and is of sufficient worth to purchase a thousand worlds, to be of no worth to them. Another sacrifice must be offered up, and more blood shed, if such be redeemed. Is not this to 'tread under foot the blood of the covenant, and to account it an unholy thing'? Heb. x. 29.

Sec. 42. *Of apostates putting the Son of God to an open shame.*

Yet further to aggravate this sin of apostates, the apostle addeth another word, παραδειγματίζοντας, thus translated, *put to an open shame*. This is a compound word. The simple δείκνυμι, *ostendo*, signifieth to *shew*, Mat. iv. 7. Thence a noun, δεῖγμα, which signifieth a *spectacle*, or an *example*, Jude 7, and a verb, δειγματίζω, which signifieth to *make show of*, and thereupon to make an example. From thence ariseth the compound, παραδειγματίζω, here used, which for the most part is taken in the worst sense, namely, to make one an example of disgrace, to expose one to ignominy and open shame. It is used negatively of Joseph's mind to the Virgin Mary, he was not willing 'to make her a public example,' Mat. i. 19.

This compound verb is here fitly and fully thus translated, 'put him to an open shame.' This is an evidence of apostates' excessive envy, hatred, and malice against Christ; and it hath reference to their malicious handling of Christ at the time of his death.[1] For they sent men to apprehend him as a thief. When they had brought him to the high priest, they suborn false witness against him. The high priest's servants spit in his face, smite him with their hands and staves. They deliver him up to an heathen judge. They choose him rather to be put to death, than a notorious murderer. They all cry out to the judge to have him crucified. Soldiers, after he was whipped and condemned, in derision put a purple robe upon him, plait a crown of thorns upon his head, and put a reed for a sceptre into his hand. They lead him out to the common place of execution, making him to bear his own cross. They nail him to a cross, and so lift him up, and that betwixt two thieves, for the greater ignominy. They deride him so hanging upon the cross. They give him gall and vinegar to drink. These and sundry other ways did they, who first crucified Christ, put him to open shame.

In like manner do apostates deal with the Lord Jesus Christ. They blaspheme his name, they disgrace his gospel, they persecute his members, and that

[1] See more hereof Chap. xii. 2, Sec. 19.

in the sorest and rigourest manner that they can. If they could, they would pull Christ himself out of heaven, and handle him as shamefully as he was before handled; and all on mere malice, and that 'after they have been enlightened, tasted of the heavenly gift, been made partakers of the Holy Ghost, tasted of the good word of God, and of the powers of the world to come.' The fore-mentioned spiteful acts, after such mercies received, do manifestly demonstrate, that the sin here spoken of is the sin against the Holy Ghost; so as the apostle might well say, that it 'is impossible to renew them again unto repentance.' Of the nature of this sin, and of the reason why this above other sins shall never be pardoned, see my treatise of *The Sin against the Holy Ghost*, sec. 15, &c., and sec. 27, &c.

Sec. 43. *Of the resolution of* Heb. vi. 4–6.

Ver. 4. *For it is impossible for those who were once enlightened, and have tasted of the heavenly gift, and were made partakers of the Holy Ghost,*

5. *And have tasted the good word of God, and the powers of the world to come,*

6. *If they shall fall away, to renew them again unto repentance; seeing they crucify to themselves the Son of God afresh, and put him to an open shame.*

The main scope of these three verses is, to set out the state of apostates. In them observe,

1. The inference, in this causal particle *for*.
2. The substance, whereof are two parts:
1. The ascent; 2, the downfall of apostates.

Their ascent consisteth of five degrees.

1. Their *enlightening*, amplified by the time, *once*.
2. Their *taste of the heavenly gift*. In this is set down,
(1.) An act, *taste*; (2.) the object, *gift*, amplified by the excellency of it, *heavenly*.
3. Made *partakers of the Holy Ghost*. Here observe,
(1.) With what they are endowed, *the Holy Ghost*.
(2.) How they are endowed therewith, *made partakers*.
4. Have *tasted the good word of God*. Here again is expressed,
(1.) The former act, *have tasted*.
(2.) Another object. *The gospel*, styled the *word*, and amplified, 1, by the author, *God*; 2, by the quality, *good*.
5. The *powers of the world to come*. Here,
(1.) The act is understood.
2. The object is, 1, expressed, *powers*; 2, amplified by the place where they are, *world to come*.

Their downfall is, 1, propounded; 2, proved. In propounding it, there is,

1. A supposition, under which the kind of fall is comprised, *if they shall fall away*.
2. An inference, wherein is noted an impossibility of recovery. This is,

1. Generally expressed, *it is impossible*; 2, particularly exemplified in two branches.
1. The kind of recovery, to *renew*; 2, the means thereof, *unto repentance*.
2. The proof of the foresaid point is taken from two effects.

The first effect is described,

1. By the kind of act, *they crucify*.
2. By the reiteration thereof, *afresh*.
3. By the person crucified, *the Son of God*.
4. By their own damage, *to themselves*.

The second effect is thus set out, 'And put him to an open shame.'

Sec. 44. *Of observations gathered out of* Heb. vi. 4–6.

I. *The utmost danger is to be declared.* As the note of inference, *for*, so the general scope of these verses, afford this observation. See Sec. 30.

II. *Hypocrites may be enlightened.* This is here taken for granted. See Sec. 32.

III. *One can be but once enlightened.* This also is taken for granted. See Sec. 32.

IV. *God bestoweth gifts on hypocrites.* The word *gift* intends as much. See Sec. 33.

V. *Hypocrites may partake of heavenly gifts.* This epithet, *heavenly*, gives proof hereunto. See Sec. 33.

VI. *Hypocrites have but a smack of the gifts they have.* This metaphor *taste* implies as much. See Sec. 33.

VII. *The Holy Ghost is the worker of those gifts that any have.* He is therefore metonymically here put for the gifts themselves. See Sec. 34.

VIII. *Hypocrites may be made partakers of the Holy Ghost.* This is here expressly set down. See Sec. 34.

IX. *God's word is common to all of all sorts.* For hypocrites are here said to taste hereof. See Sec. 35.

X. *Hypocrites do but sip on God's word.* They do but *taste* it. See Sec. 35.

XI. *The gospel is a good word.* For by this phrase, *good word*, the gospel is meant. See Sec. 35.

XII. *There is a world yet to come.* This is here taken for granted. See Sec. 36.

XIII. *The things of the world to come may be here discerned.* This also is here taken for granted. See Sec. 36.

XIV. *The things of the world to come are as glorious trophies.* This is intended under this word *powers*. See Sec. 36.

XV. *Hypocrites may have a sweet apprehension of heavenly happiness.* They may *taste* the same. See Sec. 36.

XVI. *Hypocrites may totally fall away.* The emphasis of the Greek word translated *fall away* implies as much. See Sec. 37.

XVII. *The fall of apostates is irrecoverable.* This word *impossible* proves as much. See Sec. 38.

XVIII. *There is not a second renovation.* This particle *again* intends this point. See Sec. 39.

XIX. *Apostates are not capable of repentance.* They cannot be renewed thereunto. See Sec. 40.

XX. *Repentance is the way to recovery.* Thus much is intended by the mention of repentance about recovery. See Sec. 40.

XXI. *Apostates reject the Son of God.* This is plainly expressed. See Sec. 41.

XXII. *Apostates crucify afresh the Son of God.* This is in words expressed. See Sec. 41.

XXIII. *Apostates put the Son of God to open shame.* This is also in words expressed. See Sec. 42.

Sec. 45. *Of instructing by comparisons.* Heb. vi. 7, 8.

Ver. 7. *For the earth, which drinketh in the rain that cometh oft upon it, and bringeth forth herbs meet for them by whom it is dressed, receiveth blessing from God:*

8. *But that which beareth thorns and briers is rejected, and is nigh unto cursing; whose end is to be burned.*

These two verses are an amplification of the forementioned estate of apostates; and that by a comparison, whereby the equity of God's proceeding against them is demonstrated: in which respect this comparison is brought in as a confirmation of the point, and knit to the former verses with this causal particle, $\gamma \grave{a} \rho$, *for*.

The proof is from the less to the greater. If the senseless earth, $\gamma \widetilde{\eta}$, which after rain and tillage beareth thorns and briers, be rejected, cursed, and burned: much more shall reasonable men, who after illumination and other good gifts, crucify the Son of God, and put him to open shame, be rejected, not renewed again, but for ever accursed.

This argument is amplified by the contrary event of good and fertile ground. For as that earth receiveth blessing from God, so they who, having means of salvation afforded unto them, go on to perfection, shall be blessed of God.

Thus this comparison that is here set down by the apostle hath reference to those that well use the means of grace, to encourage them to hold on in so doing; and also to apostates, who pervert the means of grace, to keep men from apostasy.

This manner of the apostle's setting forth his mind under a comparison manifesteth his prudence, in laying before his people the equity of what he had delivered, and that so as they might the better discern the same, and be the more thoroughly convinced thereof. Thus might they be the more moved therewith, and the better edified thereby.

This is it which ministers ought especially to aim at. Seek, saith the apostle, 'Seek that ye may excel to the edifying of the church,' 1 Cor. xiv. 12. This will be best done by descending to the capacity of people, and by delivering the word after such a manner as it may best be conceived, relished, retained, and yielded unto.

For the foresaid end comparisons are a singular help. As they are warrantable, so they are profitable to edification. They have been much used by the prophets, and by Christ himself. Comparisons are of use,

1. To help understanding, and that by comparing things not so well known with such things as we are well acquainted withal.

2. To strengthen memory. For earthly things, from which comparisons use to be taken, are as coarse thread or wire, on which pearls use to be put, and thereby kept from scattering.

3. To work upon affection. For visible and sensible things do use most to work upon men, whether in matters pleasing and joyous, or displeasing and grievous.

Quest. How is it, then, that Christ taught people in parables, 'because they seeing, see not?' Mat. xiii. 13.

Ans. 1. When the understanding of hearers is closed, then they can reap no good by those means which are useful to others; as a blind man can reap no benefit by light.

Secondly, Christ opened not his parables to them as he did to his disciples, Mat. xiii. 18, &c. Parables are in this respect useful for instruction, because they may be applied to all sorts of cases. They have herein a fitness of teaching above true histories: it is not lawful to turn from the truth of an history upon any occasion. But in a parable there is no swerving from truth, because nothing is delivered for truth.

For well ordering comparisons, observe these rules:—

First, Take them from common, ordinary matters, well known and familiar to all of all sorts, especially to those for whose sakes the parables are used.

Secondly, Let not the matter of them be of matters impossible, no, nor improbable. So will they be taken to be untrue, and the use of them lost.

Thirdly, Let them be fitly applied, at least to the main point in hand; otherwise it cannot be well discerned what they aim at.

Fourthly, Let them be expounded when they are not conceived, or may be misapplied.

All those rules may be gathered out of Christ's parables, and his manner of using them; for,

First, They were taken from ordinary matters, such as every one knew, as from corn, mustard seed, leaven, and such other things, or else from familiar stories, Luke xv. 3, 8, 11.

Secondly, They were all carried with great likelihood of matters to be so as he set them out to be.

Thirdly, Christ, in all his parables, had an especial eye upon the main occasion for which he produced them, to make that most clear.

Fourthly, Christ was careful to expound his parables to his disciples: sometimes when they desired him to expound them, Mat. xv. 15, &c., and sometimes of his own motion, when he was not desired, Mark iv. 34.

Sec. 46. *Of the earth's drinking in the rain that oft cometh upon it.*

If the particular branches of the comparison be duly applied, the mind of the apostle will be better discerned.

I conceive that it may be thus fitly applied:

1. The *earth*, γῆ, may set out children of men. For the heart of man is as the ground, dry of itself, prone to bring forth all manner of sins, which are as weeds, briers, and thorns; but by good tillage, and sowing it with good seed, and rain seasonably falling upon it, it may be made fruitful.

Men's hearts, therefore, must be dealt withal as the ground is out of which men expect a good crop. If the ground be not ploughed, the seed may lie upon it as upon a path, and the fowls eat it. If it be not ploughed deep enough, it may be like the stony ground, in which that which quickly sprouteth up may quickly wither away. If briers and thorns be suffered to grow where the word is sown, the word may be choked, Mat. xiii. 19, &c.

2. By *dressing*, γεωργεῖται, the ground, the ministry of the word may be meant. For ministers are God's labourers and husbandmen, 1 Cor. iii. 9. By preaching the law, men's hearts are ploughed and harrowed; by preaching the gospel, they are as dunged and softened.

Ministers, by well observing the disposition of their people, and answerably ordering their ministry by instruction, refutation, exhortation, consolation, and correction, may well manure the heart of their people.

3. By *rain*, ὑετός, may be understood both the word of God, and also the operation of God's Spirit, without which all man's labour is in vain, 1 Cor. iii. 6; for man's heart is as the dry earth.

In the use of all means, ministers and people must look to God, pray to him, and depend on him. 'Behold, the husbandman waiteth for the precious fruit of the earth, and hath long patience for it, until he receive the early and latter rain,' James v. 7.

4. This metaphor of *drinking*, πιοῦσα, takes it for granted that the earth is a dry element, and philosophy teacheth us that dryness is the predominant quality in the earth. Wherefore, as a man or beast that is dry readily drinketh down beer or water, and is thereby refreshed and satisfied, so the earth. This metaphor here implieth a receiving and applying the means of grace, whereby they are refreshed, to men's selves. The metaphor further implieth a capacity in the earth to receive the rain, and to be bettered by it. Hard things receive not any rain into them, nor can they be mollified thereby. They, therefore, cannot be said to drink it.

God's word, as here understood by rain, is drunk in when it is applied to the soul by faith. Hereupon faith is oft set forth under drinking, John iv. 14, and vi. 53, 54, and vii. 37.

Let us therefore, who have the spiritual rain of God's word afforded unto us, be like the earth, and drink it in, and that by applying it to our own souls.

5. This phrase, *that cometh oft upon it*, πολλάκις ἐρχόμενον, setteth out the divine providence, which is ordered according to the need of creatures, and that in two respects:

(1.) In causing rain to come upon the earth; for the earth hath not rain in itself. God giveth rain from heaven, Acts xiv. 17. So doth God cause his word to come to us, and poureth his Spirit upon us.

(2.) In that rain cometh oft upon the earth. Though the earth be once thoroughly watered, yet it will soon be dry again; as Christ saith of men in reference to the ordinary water which they use, 'Whosoever drinketh of this water shall thirst again,' John iv. 13. Therefore God gives 'early and latter rain,' James v. 7, and that time after time. Thus doth he afford us his word frequently and plentifully. It is a sweet rain that cometh oft upon us. The earth doth not more need this oft coming of the rain than we the oft preaching of the word.

Let us not therefore lightly esteem this evidence of the divine providence by reason of the frequency thereof, as the Israelites did lightly esteem and even loathe manna that daily fell among them, Num. xi. 6, and xxi. 5. Let us rather well weigh our continual need of the word, and the great benefit that we may reap thereby, and in that respect be thankful for this plentiful provision.

Sec. 47. *Of God's blessing on bringing forth herbs meet for them, by whom the earth is dressed.*

6. *Bringing forth herbs* declareth the end of sending rain, and sheweth what is thereupon expected.

By herbs, βοτάνη,[1] are meant all manner of good fruit, whereunto briers and thorns are opposed. Thus here it is to be taken of those who, enjoying God's ordinances, do bring forth good fruit.

The verb τίκτουσα,[2] translated *bringeth forth*, is properly used of women's bringing forth children, Mat. i. 23, 25. Now the seed or root of herbs lieth in the earth, as a child in the womb of a woman, and when it sprouteth up, it is as it were brought out of the womb.

The Greek word translated *herb*, according to the notation of it, signifieth such a kind of herb as may be fed upon, which we call, from the Latin notation,[3] *pasture*. It implieth therefore such fruit as is pleasant and profitable.

---

[1] A verbo, Βόω, *pasco*; Βοσκή, *pabulum*.
[2] Thus lust is said to conceive and bring forth sin, James i. 15. The same word is there and here used.
[3] Pascuum, plur. pascua; pastura.

Hereupon it becomes us to 'prove what is the good, acceptable and perfect will of God,' Rom. xii. 2, that we may bring forth such fruit, and do such works as are intended under this metaphor *herbs*.

7. That we may be the better directed about that good fruit, the apostle thus describes the foresaid herbs 'meet for them by whom it is dressed.'

The verb γεωργεῖται, translated *dressed*, is a compound of two nouns, γῆ and ἔργον, which signify *earth* and *labour*.

The compound noun is translated 'an husbandman,' Mat. xxi. 33, 2 Tim. ii. 6, James v. 7. This title in English we give to such as till land.

The verb here compounded, γεωργεω, ἐργαζομαι γῆν γῆν, compriseth under it all that skill and pains which useth to be taken by such as till land.

By them that dress the earth, are here meant ministers of the word. So as fruit meet for them is such fruit as giveth proof of the minister's prudence, diligence, skill, and faithfulness, and so be fit for him.

The epithet εὔθετος, *meet*, is in Greek a compound. According to the composition, ἐυ, *bene*, θετος, *positus*, it signifieth *well set*, or *fit*, Luke ix. 62, and xiv. 35. Here it signifieth such fruit as is answerable to the means which hath been used to produce it, and that in the kind, quantity, and quality that is expected. Such fruit is expected of such as enjoy a faithful, painful, and powerful pastor. It is said of the husbandman, that he 'waiteth for the precious fruit of the earth,' James v. 7. So the Lord, where he affordeth means, looketh that fruit should be brought forth, Isa. v. 2, Luke xiii. 6. Such fruit is the end of tillage.

All ye to whom the Lord affords means, take notice of this end. To be bred and brought up where the word is preached, sacraments administered, name of God called upon, and other holy ordinances observed, is a great privilege. God, who affordeth this privilege, expects this duty, that fruit answerably be brought forth. Let us therefore, according to our duty, with the uttermost of our power, endeavour to satisfy the expectation of the Lord, that he may not repent of the goodness that he hath done unto us; as he repented his making of Saul king, 1 Sam. xv. 11.

8. The recompense of all is thus set out, *receiveth blessing from God*.

Blessing, according to the notation of the Greek word εὐλογία, yea, and of the Latin too, *benedictio*, signifieth a *speaking well*. It is translated *fair speech*, Rom. xvi. 18. Thus it is opposed to *cursing*, which is a foul speech, James iii. 10. Where it is attributed to us in reference to God, it can imply nothing but speaking well of him, Rev. v. 12, 13. For that is all the blessing that we can yield to God.

But where it is attributed to God in reference to us, it compriseth under it every good thing, that may make us happy, so as all that see it, or hear of it, may speak well of us, Eph. i. 3. See Sec. 102.

This blessing, a fruitful hearer of the word is said to *receive*, μεταλαμβάνει, in that he hath it not in himself, or of himself, he must receive it from another.

This act of receiving is set down in the present tense, to set out the certainty of it. He may be as sure of it as if he had it in his hand, and did actually enjoy it. To this purpose the prophets do usually set forth promises of things to come in the time present, Zech. ix. 9.

The time present may also be here used in regard of an actual and present possession of the blessing here promised. For that blessing may comprise under it both such gifts and graces, as God here in this world giveth, together with a continual increase of them, and also eternal glory in the world to come.

This blessing is here said to be from God: God blesseth with all blessing, Eph. i. 3, James i. 17. This God undertaketh to do.

1. That every one might have reward, for no creature can be too great to be rewarded of God, and the greatest that be need his reward, and he is able to reward the greatest. Yea, he can reward whole families, churches, and kingdoms. On the other side, God is so gracious, as he accounteth none too mean to be rewarded of him. 'He raiseth up the poor out of the dust, and lifteth up the beggar from the dunghill,' 1 Sam. ii. 8. When Dives and all his house scorned Lazarus, the Lord looked on him, and gave his angels charge over him, Luke xvi. 20.

2. That they might be sure of their reward. That which God taketh upon him to do, he will not fail to do: 'The Lord is faithful, and will do it,' 1 Thess. v. 24.

3. That the reward might be worth the having. God, in bestowing his rewards, respecteth what is meet for his excellency to give, and accordingly proportioneth his reward. As a king, when he would reward a faithful servant, contenteth not himself to give him a little money, but gives him high honours and dignities, great lordships, fair possessions, many immunities and privileges, gainful offices, and other like royal rewards. Pharaoh set Joseph over all the land of Egypt, Gen. xli. 41. Such a reward did Darius give to Daniel, Dan. vi. 2; and Ahasuerus to Mordecai, Esth. viii. 15. As God exceedeth these and all other monarchs in greatness, so will his reward be greater.

1. A great encouragement this is, for us to do our best in bringing forth fruit answerable to the means that God affordeth to us, 'knowing that our labour shall not be in vain in the Lord, 1 Cor. xv. 58. Men may be ignorant of the good fruit which we bring forth, as Joseph's master, Gen. xxxix. 19. Or forgetful, as Pharaoh's butler, Gen. xl. 23; or wittingly wink thereat, as Nabal, 1 Sam. xxv. 10; or misconstrue it, as Saul, 1 Sam. xxii. 7, 8; or envy at it, as Joshua, Num. xi. 29; or slander it, as the Pharisees, Mark iii. 22; or persecute for it, as the Jews did, John x. 32. Against these and all other like discouragements

our eyes must be lift up to the Lord, from whom we may be sure to receive blessing.

2. This directeth us whither to go for blessing, even to God, the author and fountain thereof. Be not like the Israelites, Jer. ii. 13, Isa. xxx. 1, &c. Observe the means which God hath sanctified for receiving blessing, and in a conscionable use of them depend on God for his blessing.

3. Return the praise and glory to God. This is, to bless him who blesseth thee, Eph. i. 3, Rom. xi. 36.

Sec. 48. *Of rejecting that which beareth thorns and briars.* Heb. vi. 8.

The apostle having declared the happy condition of such as well use the means of grace, addeth thereunto the woful plight of such as pervert those means. This particle of opposition, *but*, sheweth that these two verses set down contrary subjects.

In this verse the apostle followeth the former comparison. The principal subject mentioned in the beginning of the former verse, which is *earth*, must here be understood, thus, 'But the earth which, bearing thorns,' &c.

As in our English, so in the Greek, there are different words used in the former and this verse. For he doth not say as he did before, the earth which bringeth forth, τίκτουσα, but which beareth, ἐκφέρουσα. This latter word in Greek is a compound, and according to the composition, it signifieth to *carry out*, as men carry out a dead corpse, Acts v. 6, 9, 10. It implieth a thrusting out of that which it is not willing to retain.

The things so brought out are here said to be thorns and briers. These are not only unprofitable plants, but hurtful also, by reason of their prickles.

The notation of both Greek words imply a sharpness and prickliness.[1] They are oft joined together, as here, and Mat. vii. 16. So Isa. v. 6, and vii. 23–25.

Thorns were wreathed together, and plaited as a crown on Christ's head, to prick and gall him. With briers and thorns both, Gideon did tear the flesh of the princes of Succoth, Judges viii. 7. Both of them use to grow in the wilderness, Judges viii. 16, and grounds untilled, Isa. xxxii. 13.

Under these metaphors are here understood such sins as most grieve God's Spirit, and are most hurtful to men; as a renouncing of the Christian faith, blasphemy, oppression, persecution, and such other sins.

The land that after good tillage putteth forth such thorns and briers, is said to be *rejected*.

The Greek word ἀδόκιμος, translated *rejected*, is a compound. The simple δόκιμος signifieth that which upon experience and good proof is approved, Rom. xvi. 10; 2 Tim. ii. 15. The preposition with which it is compounded is privative, so as it setteth forth such a thing or person as can no way be approved, and thereupon to be utterly rejected. It is oft translated *reprobate*, 2 Cor. xiii. 5–7.

Hereby is evidently demonstrated, that they who despise the means of grace shall be utterly rejected of God; even as that land which, after much and long tillage, is so far from bringing forth a good crop, as it beareth thorns and briers. This name *Lo-ammi* is a title of rejection, Hosea i. 9; God's taking away the hedge of his vineyard, and breaking down the wall thereof, proves as much, Isa. v. 5. So doth his cutting down the fig-tree, Luke xiii. 7, and the putting of the axe to the root of the tree, Mat. iii. 10, and leaving Jerusalem desolate, Mat. xxiii. 38. All these threatenings are actually accomplished upon the Jews; and to shew that this case is not proper to the Jews only, the like is threatened to Christians, Rom. xi. 21. This may be exemplified in all the churches planted by the apostles. Where now is Ephesus? where Smyrna, and the other golden candlesticks of Asia? where Corinth? where Galatia, and the rest? Are they not all rejected? Where is Rome? Is it not a foul nest of unclean birds?

Common justice requires as much; whereupon parents, masters, all sorts of governors, use to do the like.

Besides, this makes much to the honour of God, lest otherwise he might seem to patronise such as are past hope.

Yea, further, this makes to the advantage of such as are faithful; for they are hereby admonished to be more careful in improving the means of grace afforded unto them, lest otherwise this great mischief should befall them.

Quest. How may men be said to be rejected?

Ans. 1. A nation is rejected when the gospel is taken away from them, and given to another nation, Mat. xxi. 43.

Ans. 2. A particular assembly is rejected when good pastors are taken away; and instead of them idle and idol shepherds are set over them, whereby they fall from that which before they seemed to have.

Ans. 3. Particular persons are rejected when they are given over to hardness of heart, as the Jews were, Isa. vi. 10. Thus they may stand as dead trees in an orchard, but at length they shall be cut down. All particular impenitent persons are utterly rejected by death.

Obj. So all may be rejected.

Ans. Not so; for such as bring forth good fruit are by death transplanted from the nursery of God's militant church to his glorious orchard of the triumphant church.

Take heed that you provoke not God to complain, and say, 'What could have been done more to my vineyard, that I have not done in it?' Isa. v. 4. God hath sent us many ministers time after time, and they have taken great pains in ploughing, digging, dunging

---

[1] Ἄκανθα, *Spira* (Ἀκή, *Cuspis*); Τριβολὸς, *Tribulus*; (Βολὶς, *Jaculum*).

and God hath sent down rain time after time : what then can be expected if, instead of herbs, we bear briers and thorns ?

Sec. 49. *Of being nigh unto cursing.*

To add the greater terror, the apostle thus aggravateth the fearful case of the fore-mentioned sinners in this phrase, *and is nigh unto cursing.*

The Greek word καταρα, translated *cursing,* is a compound. The simple noun, ἀρα, *diræ,* signifieth cursing, namely, such cursed speech as proceedeth out of the bitter spirit of corrupt man, Rom. iii. 14. It seemeth to be derived from an Hebrew root, ארר, *maledixit,* which signifieth to curse. The simple noun is but once used in the New Testament.

The preposition with which the word of my text is compounded adds a kind of aggravation. It is put for the curse of the law, Gal. iii. 10, 13 ; and the participle compounded with this preposition is applied to such as are devoted to hell fire, Mat. xxv. 41.

The word here signifieth that the curse which God will inflict is not only by word of mouth, but also in act and deed.

Yet by way of mitigation, this word ἐγγύς, *nigh,* is added. Where he spake of good ground, he absolutely said in the time present, ' It receiveth blessing ;' but here, as putting off revenge for a time, he saith, ' is nigh cursing.' This gives proof of God's patience, whereof see Chap. iii. 9, Sec. 101.

The connection of this cursing upon the fore-mentioned rejecting, is an evidence of God's curse following such as are rejected of him ; instance Saul, the nation of the Jews, and other churches before mentioned.

Such seem to be past hope. They have deprived themselves of blessing, and so made themselves liable to cursing.

This is a further aggravation.

Sec. 50. *Of apostates' end to be burned.*

The last clause of this verse, in these words, *whose end is to be burned,* is a further prosecution of the foresaid metaphor ; for of old men were wont to burn those fields which, after much and long tillage, would bring forth nothing but briers and thorns.[1]

That which the apostle here especially intendeth is, that such as are rejected of God and cursed shall assuredly be cast into hell fire. This is that unquenchable fire whereof the Baptist speaketh, Mat. iii. 12, and which Christ intendeth, Mat. ix. 43, &c.

This is thus made known, lest men should lightly esteem that which was before spoken of rejecting and cursing. When God is not seen in shewing mercy, he will shew himself the more terrible in his judgment.

Many think it is no great matter to be rejected and cursed. They will say, What if we be deprived of our ministers ? What if the gospel be taken away, so long as we enjoy peace and plenty ? But if the burning here intended were well known and believed, those forerunners thereof would not be so lightly esteemed.

The Greek noun καῦσις, translated *burning,* is not elsewhere used in the New Testament. It is here applied to the earth ; for this relative ἧς, *whose,* hath reference to the earth, ver. 7. Yet the verb καίω, *uro, uror,* from whence it is derived, is used to set out the burning of hell fire, Rev. xix 20, and xxi. 8, καιόμενος. And this word is here intended to set out, under this comparison, the torment of hell ; for there is no greater torment than that which cometh by burning.

The burning here meant is made the end of apostates ; for many are prone, upon present prosperity, to put off the fear of this burning. The apostle, therefore, puts them in mind of their latter end. Though God in his patience and long-suffering may bear with them some time, as he did with the fig-tree, Luke xiii. 7, yet burning, and that in hell, shall be their end. Their end is to burning, as the Greek phrase soundeth, τὸ τέλος εἰς καῦσιν. Burning is the goal whereunto at last they shall come. ' The end of the wicked shall be cut off,' Ps. xxxvii. 38. This is exemplified in sundry parables, Mat. iii. 10, and xiii. 42, 50.

' Fret not thyself, therefore, because of evil-doers,' Ps. xxxvii. 1, though they seem outwardly to prosper. Consider their end. Read to this purpose Ps. lxxiii.

Sec. 51. *Of the resolution of* Heb. Chap. vi. 7, 8.

Ver. 7. *For the earth, which drinketh in the rain that cometh oft upon it, and bringeth forth herbs meet for them by whom it is dressed, receiveth blessing from God:*

8. *But that which beareth thorns and briers is rejected, and is nigh unto cursing, whose end is to be burned.*

In these two verses, the difference between persevering and revolting professors is laid down, both of them in a comparison taken from the earth : one from good land, ver. 7 ; the other from bad, ver. 8. In setting down this comparison we may observe,

1. The occasion of bringing in this comparison, in this particle *for.*

2. The expression of the point itself. Hereof are two parts :

(1.) The state of persevering professors.

(2.) The state of apostates.

1. About the state of the former, four branches are expressed :

1. The condition of professors. They are as *earth.*

2. The means afforded for their growth, *rain.* This is amplified two ways :

(1.) By the *coming* of it upon the earth.

(2.) By the *frequency* of that coming, *oft.*

3. Their entertaining the means. This is manifested two ways :

---

[1] Steriles incendere profuit agros.—*Virgil. Georg.* lib. i.

1. They *drink it in.*
2. They bring forth fruit. This is amplified,
(1.) By the kind of fruit, *herbs.*
(2.) By the qualification thereof, *meet for them by whom,* &c.
4. The issue. This is set down,
1. By their act; they *receive.*
2. By the subject matter which they receive, amplified,
(1.) By the kind of it, *blessing.*
(2.) By the author of it, *from God.*
2. About the state of the latter, who are apostates, is set down,
1. The opposition betwixt them and such as persevere, in this particle *but.*
2. A declaration of their condition. This is set down,
1. By their effect, which is,
(1.) Generally propounded, *they bear.*
(2.) Particularly exemplified in two kinds of fruit, *thorns, briers.*
2. By the issue, and that in two branches:
1. They are *rejected.*
2. They are *nigh unto cursing.* Here observe,
(1.) The kind of judgment, *cursing.*
(2.) The limitation thereof, *nigh unto.*
3. Their *end,* which is, *to be burned.*

Sec. 52. *Observations raised out of* Heb. vi. 7, 8.

I. *Reasonable men may make God's dealings with senseless creatures a looking-glass to them.* They may thereby see what to expect from God. This ariseth from the inference of this comparison, as a proof of what he had before delivered. See Sec. 45.

II. *Comparisons are useful means of teaching.* This ariseth from the general matter of these two verses. See Sec. 45.

III. *Man's disposition is like the earth.* This is it that is here resembled to the earth. See Sec. 46.

IV. *God's word and Spirit are as rain.* They mollify men's hearts, and make them fruitful. See Sec. 46.

V. *A good heart receiveth God's word and Spirit into it, even as the earth receiveth the rain.* See Sec. 46.

VI. *The word and Spirit are given to man.* This word *cometh* intendeth as much. See Sec. 46.

VII. *Frequent preaching is needful.* Even as it is needful that rain oft come upon the earth. See Sec. 46.

VIII. *Fruit is expected of those who enjoy means.* This is here taken for granted. See Sec. 47.

IX. *Fruit must be wholesome and pleasant.* So is the *herb* here mentioned. See Sec. 47.

X. *Fruit must be answerable to the means afforded.* This is *meet fruit.* See Sec. 47.

XI. *Ministers are God's husbandmen.* These are they that dress his ground. See Sec. 47.

XII. *Fruit-bearers are blessed.* So they are expressly said to be. See Sec. 47.

XIII. *Blessing is received.* This also is plainly expressed. See Sec. 47.

XIV. *God is the author of blessing.* It is received from him. See Sec. 47.

XV. *The state of perseverers and revolters are contrary.* This is implied under this particle of opposition, *but.* See Sec. 48.

XVI. *Apostates thrust out their fruit.* The notation of this word *beareth* declareth as much. See Sec. 48.

XVII. *The fruit of apostates is very pernicious.* It is as thorns and briers. See Sec. 48.

XVIII. *Perverters of good means shall be rejected.* So much is here denounced. See Sec. 48.

XIX. *The rejected are accursed.* These two judgments are here knit together. See Sec. 49.

XX. *God oft forbears instantly to execute the deserved curse.* This word *nigh* implieth as much. See Sec. 49.

XXI. *Everlasting burning will be the end of apostates.* Their *end is to be burned.* See Sec. 50.

Sec. 53. *Of preventing a prejudicate opinion.* Heb. vi. 9, 10.

Ver. 9. *But, beloved, we are persuaded better things of you, and things that accompany salvation, though we thus speak.*

10. *For God is not unrighteous, to forget your work, and labour of love, which ye have shewed toward his name, in that ye have ministered to the saints, and do minister.*

It was a terrible doom that the apostle denounced in the former verses against backsliders. Now that these Hebrews might not thereby be induced to think that he judged them to be apostates, by a sweet insinuation, he plainly and expressly declareth his own good opinion of them, and entire affection toward them, that so he might make the better way to his exhortation following, ver. 11, &c.

The first particle, δὲ, *but,* as our English hath set it, gives evidence of the contrary, namely, that he had no such opinion of them; and it implieth a prevention of a prejudicate conceit, which they might have entertained thereabout. The apostle's meaning may thus be more fully expressed: 'You may haply think by that which I have delivered about the case of apostates, that I have reference to you therein, as if I judged you to be such. But know, that what I spake before, I spake indefinitely of that estate, whereinto professors of the gospel may fall. I did not say that you were fallen into such an estate; neither have I cause so to think, but rather the contrary. Believe me, I account you my beloved brethren, and I verily believe that your estate is far better than that whereof I spake; yea, that it is such an estate as will in the end bring you to eternal salvation.'

The apostle doth hereby give us to understand that conceits, which may alienate the hearts of hearers from their ministers, are as much as may be to be prevented. This doth the apostle much endeavour to do in the case of the Galatians. He had, in the beginning of his epistle, thundered out a dreadful curse against all that should preach any other gospel. He wondered that they should hearken to any such, and styled them foolish Galatians; asking them, 'who had bewitched them?' all which might exasperate them, and alienate their hearts from him. Therefore, to prevent that mischief, he doth thus sweetly insinuate himself into them, 'Brethren, I beseech you, be as I am, for I am as ye are,' &c., Gal. iv. 12, &c.

So long as a prejudicate opinion of a minister remains in his people's mind, his ministry cannot well relish, it cannot edify them. It is as choler in the stomach, which embittereth the most wholesome and pleasing food that can be put into it. This made Jeremiah's prophecy to be so little regarded as it was; for thus they say of him, This man seeketh not the welfare of this people, but the hurt, Jer. xxxviii. 4. So Ahab of Micaiah: 'He doth not prophesy good concerning me, but evil,' 1 Kings xxii. 8.

This course of the apostle, in seeking to root out such roots of bitterness before they spring up and trouble us, is an especial point of wisdom, and worthy to be endeavoured after.

Sec. 54. *Of sweet insinuations.*

The general and principal intendment of the apostle is, to insinuate himself into his people's heart, that they might retain a good opinion of him, as he did of them. The dependence of these verses upon the former, the main scope of them, this particle of opposition *but*, this loving title *beloved*, the good persuasion he had of them, and hope of their salvation, the testimony which he gives of their love to God and man, and the remembrance which he is confident God had thereof, do all prove as much; they are all evident demonstrations of his sweet disposition, and of his desire to preserve in them such an affection towards him, as he had towards them. See ver. 11, Sec. 76.

Of sweetening reproofs with mild insinuations, see Chap. iii. 12, Sec. 121.

Sec. 55. *Of ministers' loving respect to their people.*

This title ἀγαπητὸς, *beloved*, wherein and whereby the apostle expresseth his affection, is very observable. It is that whereby God the Father expresseth his entire affection to his only begotten Son, Mat. iii. 17, and xvii. 5, and xii. 18. It is translated 'beloved,' 1 Peter iv. 12; 'well-beloved,' Mark xii. 6; 'dear,' Eph. v. 1; 'dearly beloved,' Philip. iv. 1. This title is most frequently applied to a son, Mat. xvii. 5, 1 Cor. iv. 17; yet also to a brother, Eph. vi. 21; and to a fellow-servant, Col. i. 7.

Of the emphasis of this title, see Chap. iii. ver. 1, Sec. 17.

Here it sheweth that ministers must bear a loving respect to their people; even as a parent to his only child, or a husband to his wife, or a friend to his dearest friend; yea, and testify as much also, as the apostle here doth. Sundry like expressions are elsewhere used to give further proof hereof: as 'brethren,' 1 Cor. i. 10; 'my brethren,' Rom. xv. 14; 'my beloved brethren,' James i. 16; 'my brethren, dearly beloved and longed for,' Philip. iv. 1; 'children,' John xxi. 5; 'little children,' 'my little children,' 1 John ii. 12, and iii. 18; 'my little children, of whom I travail in birth again,' Gal. iv. 19. These and other like insinuations of love do give people to understand, that their ministers do what they do in love; that they instruct in love, that they exhort in love, that they reprove in love, that they denounce God's judgments in love; and thereupon will say, 'Let him smite me, it shall be a kindness; and let him reprove me, it shall be as an excellent oil, which shall not break my head,' Ps. cxli. 5. In this respect the caveat which the apostle giveth to fathers, Eph. vi. 4, 'provoke not to wrath;' and to husbands, Col. iii. 19, 'be not bitter;' is to be observed of all that have an occasion and calling to reprove others. Provocations are as scalding hot potions, which no patient can endure to drink down; and bitterness in reproof is like gall in the stomach, which it cannot retain, but will soon vomit it up. Indeed, all reproofs and denunciations of judgment seem hot and bitter; but testimonies of love cool the heat, and sweeten the bitterness of them. There must therefore be manifested good evidences of love, by those who desire to do good by denunciations of judgment, reprehension of vices, and other like sharp kinds of teaching.

Sec. 56. *Of judging the best of others.*

That the apostle might not seem to flatter those to whom he gave this title *beloved*, he plainly declares his opinion of them in these words, 'we are persuaded better things of you,' &c.

Of this manner of expressing his mind in the plural number thus, '*we are persuaded*,' see ver. 3, Sec. 24.

The Greek word πεπείσμεθα implieth such an opinion, as makes one confident that it is so, as he conceives it to be. Thus it is said, 'they be persuaded that John was a prophet,' Luke xx. 6. Matthew, speaking of the same thing, thus expresseth it, 'They held John as a prophet,' Mat. xxi. 26; and Mark thus, 'They counted John that he was a prophet indeed,' Mark xi. 32. By comparing these evangelists together, we see, that to hold, or to account a thing to be indeed so and so, is to be persuaded that it is so. Thus is this word frequently used, as Rom. xv. 14, 2 Tim. i. 5. It is translated 'to have confidence,' Gal. v. 10;

and to 'be confident,' Philip. i. 6; and to 'assure,' 1 John iii. 19. In this respect this word is joined with another that signifieth to know, as Rom. xiv. 14, Philip. i. 25.

This comparative, τὰ κρείττονα, *better*, which implieth the things that he was persuaded of, hath reference to the fore-mentioned case of apostates, as if he had thus expressed his mind, better than to be once enlightened, better than to have only tasted of the heavenly gift, better than to be made partakers of the common gifts of the Holy Ghost; better than to have only tasted the good word of God, and the powers of the world to come, and after all to fall clean away. We are persuaded that you are better principled than so; and that you have laid a better and surer foundation, which will never fail.

By this pattern we learn in general, to take heed of judging others over rashly; and particularly, of judging professors to be hypocrites, and such as will prove apostates. This is that judging which Christ expressly forbids, Mat. vii. 1; and therefore another evangelist adds this inhibition to us, 'condemn not,' Luke vi. 37.

Rash judging, especially in this kind, is first against Christ's prerogative, Rom. xiv. 10, 11. 2. Against the rule of charity, 1 Cor. xiii. 7. 3. It is a means to bring the like judgment upon ourselves, Mat. vii. 1, 2.

Yet notwithstanding it is too common in these our days thus to judge professors. Many put no difference betwixt a professor and an hypocrite; for they know no mean between profaneness and hyocrisy; if a man be not openly profane, he is then counted an hypocrite. Oh the subtilty of Satan! never had he any stratagem whereby he got greater advantage than this. There is hardly anything whereby true piety is sooner nipped in the head than by this. Many seem to be more profane than their conscience tells them they should be, to avoid this brand of hypocrisy. That we be no instruments of Satan in this kind, let us learn of our apostle to hope and think, to judge and speak the best of professors. It is necessary for ministers to shew some good hope of their people. If they have not some hope, what courage can they have to preach unto them? and if people conceive they have no hope, what comfort can they have to hear them?

Of the two it is better to have a good persuasion of those who inwardly are not sound (at least if we do not wittingly wink at the evil which is apparent and evident to all), than unjustly to censure and condemn the upright. In the latter, the rule of charity is expressly violated; but not so in the former.

Sec. 57. *Of salvation accompanying good works.*

What those better things are, the apostle doth thus express, *things that accompany salvation*. That these are the better things meant, is evident by this copulative conjunction *and*; for it joins this latter as an exposition of the former.

Of *salvation* see Chap. i. 14, Sec. 159.

The Greek word is of the genitive case, ἐχόμενα σωτηρίας, whereby is implied that the things here intended do, as it were, cleave to salvation;[1] salvation cannot be separated, nor taken away from them, it necessarily followeth upon them.

To express more distinctly what those things are, the apostle himself mentioneth those particulars: their work, their labour of love, their respect to God's name, that is, to his glory, their ministering to saints, and their continuance therein. To these may be added saving knowledge, justifying faith, patient hope, sound repentance, new obedience, humility, sincerity, constancy, and all other sanctifying graces, and perseverance in them.

This phrase, *such things as accompany salvation*, doth hereupon clearly demonstrate, that salvation is the recompence of good works. In this respect hope is styled 'the helmet of salvation,' Eph. vi. 17. Salvation is as an helmet upon the head of him that is possessed with hope, salvation is also said to be the 'end of our faith,' 1 Peter i. 9. More generally it is said that 'to them who continue in well-doing shall be eternal life,' Rom. ii. 7. And 'he that endureth to the end shall be saved,' Mat. x. 22. And 'he that soweth to the Spirit shall of the Spirit reap life everlasting,' Gal. vi. 8.

The special and only ground hereof is God's high account and good approbation of those things. Hereupon he promiseth salvation. Now 'faithful is he that hath promised,' Heb. x. 23; salvation therefore must needs follow upon such graces as have been before mentioned, and others like unto them.

Herein lieth a main difference betwixt common and renewing graces. They who are endued with the former may perish, Mat. vii. 22, 23. The other shall assuredly be saved, Rom. x. 9–11.

This is a strong motive to stir us up to use all good means, whereby we may attain unto those graces; and to give no rest to our souls till we have some assurance thereof; and in this assurance to rest quiet, in that salvation will be the end thereof. If salvation be worth the having, our endeavour after those graces will not be in vain. To enforce this motive, see the excellency of this salvation set out, Chap. i. 14, Sec. 159; and the eternity of it, Chap. v. ver. 9, Sec. 51.

Sec. 58. *Of one's persuasion of another's salvation.*

The copulative particle *and*, which joineth these two clauses, 'better things of you, *and* things that accompany salvation,' giveth proof that the apostle was persuaded of the one as well as of the other, namely, that the things that brought salvation, as well as of

---

[1] ἔχομαι cum genitivo significat *hærere alicui*, ut consequentia præcedentibus hærent.

the better things intended, so as Christians may be well persuaded of others' salvation. So was he who saith, 'I am confident of this very thing, that he which hath begun a good work in you will perform it unto the day of Jesus Christ,' Philip. i. 6. Who also saith of others, 'Christ shall confirm you unto the end,' &c., 1 Cor. i. 8. And of others thus, 'We are bound to give thanks alway to God for you, because God hath from the beginning chosen you to salvation,' 2 Thes. ii. 13.

Sanctifying graces are the work of the Spirit of Christ in men, which giveth evidence that they belong to Christ, who hath purchased salvation for them.

Object. 'What man knoweth the things of a man?' 1 Cor. ii. 11. 'The heart is deceitful above all things, who can know it?' Jer. xvii. 9. Many hypocrites have long carried a fair show, and thereby deceived many; instance Demas, 2 Tim. iv. 10.

Ans. There is a double persuasion: one of certainty, which a Christian may have of himself; the other of charity, which is all we can have of others; but evidences of others' truth may be such as may give good ground of a good persuasion.

The evidences we ought to take due notice of, that we may conceive the better hope of professors while they live, and receive the more comfort in their departure out of this world; for there is nothing that can give more sound comfort than persuasion of one's salvation.

Sec. 59. *Of threats and hope standing together.*

This conjunction, εἰ καὶ, *though,* in this clause, *though we thus speak,* is the note of such disagreeing matters as may agree together, but in some particular respects are diverse, as 2 Cor. iv. 16, and xi. 6. Of this kind of argument, see Chap. v. 8, Sec. 46.

To denounce judgments, and to suppose them against whom they are denounced to be liable to those judgments, may stand together, but in this apostle they were diverse, for he denounced a terrible judgment, yet did not think these Hebrews to be guilty thereof.

This clause, εἰ καὶ οὕτω λαλοῦμεν, *though we thus speak,* is therefore a kind of correction; and thereby we may see that denunciation of judgment doth not necessarily imply a guiltiness in those to whom the denunciation is manifested, much less an utter despair of them.

The apostle doth much aggravate God's severity about rejecting the Jews in writing to the Romans, and withal bids them take heed 'lest God spare not them;' yet thus he manifesteth his hope of them, 'I am persuaded of you, that you are full of goodness,' Rom. xi. 20, &c. and xv. 14.

Denunciations of judgment have especial respect to the future time, in regard of their use, namely, to prevent such things as cause such and such judgments. For dangers beforehand declared make men circumspect and watchful. If one tell a traveller that thieves in such and such places have robbed and killed other travellers, or tell mariners that pirates have in such places surprised other ships, it will make them the more wary in avoiding the like dangers.

People have on this ground just cause to bear with their ministers in like cases, and not to think that they account them as reprobates, and past all hope, because they take occasion to lay forth the severity of God before them. They may be better persuaded of them, though they speak such and such things. As ministers therefore are persuaded better things of their people, so must people be persuaded better things of their minister. Denunciations may be used with as tender pity, hearty affection, and true love, as the sweetest persuasions. But as physic is sometimes as needful for the body as food, so this kind of teaching is as needful and useful as that which is more mild and pleasing.

This mind of a minister is to be noted by two sorts of people.

1. By such as are of tender consciences. It cannot but much support them to believe that ministers in their threatening doctrines, are persuaded better things of them.

2. By men of heard hearts. For such to believe, that the desire and endeavours of their minister is to pull them out of the fire, cannot but somewhat work upon them.

Happy are they who rightly and wisely apply all to themselves.

Sec. 60. *Of God's perfect righteousness.*

Ver. 10. In the tenth verse is laid down the reason of that good persuasion which the apostle had of these Hebrews. The causal conjunction γὰρ, *for,* doth import as much. The reason is taken from God's righteousness or justice, which is set down negatively, thus, οὐκ ἄδικος, *not unrighteous.* Here are two negatives, one, οὐκ, a simple conjunction, the other a privative composition, *unrighteous.* These make the stronger affirmation. See Chap. iv. 13, Sec. 76.

This negative carrieth the greater emphasis, in that to do otherwise than is here noted of God, would be a part of injustice. But to conceive any matter of injustice in God is apparent blasphemy.

We may therefore from this negative expression of God's righteousness, 'God is not unrighteous,' infer that God is for certain most perfectly righteous. 'There is no unrighteousness in him.' The apostle, with a kind of indignation and detestation, removeth this blasphemous conceit; for where he had propounded this objection, 'Is God unrighteous?' and this, 'Is there unrighteousness with God?' he thus repelleth it, 'God forbid,' Rom. iii. 5, 6, and ix. 14. His answer implieth, that no such conceit should enter into a Christian's mind.

God's righteousness is his essence. He were not

God, if he were not perfectly righteous; neither could he judge the world, Rom. iii. 6, Gen. xviii. 25.

1. This should make us take heed of a thought to enter into our hearts, or of a word to slip out of our mouths against God's righteousness. If anything be done by God, whereof we cannot see the reason, we must lay our hand upon our mouth, and acknowledge that, notwithstanding, God is righteous therein. When Jeremiah stood amazed in such a case, he thus saith, 'Righteous art thou, O Lord, when I plead with thee,' Jer. xii. 1. God's will is the rule of righteousness. It is impossible that anything done by him should be unrighteous. It is therefore righteous, because it is done by him.

2. This should move us in all things that fall out, whether losses or any other crosses, to submit ourselves, as to that which is just and righteous. If the wicked flourish, if the godly be oppressed, acknowledge it to be just and righteous, in reference to God, by whose righteous providence all things are ordered. Such things as are unrighteously done by men, are righteously ordered by God, Acts ii. 23.

3. This should incite us to follow after righteousness, and therein to shew ourselves the children of God. 'The righteous Lord loveth righteousness,' both in himself, and in the children of men, Ps. xi. 7. Be righteous therefore in the whole course of thy life; righteous in all thy dealings with others. Thy righteousness will be an evidence that God's Spirit, the Spirit of righteousness, is in thee.

4. This cannot be but terror to unrighteous persons. 'The Lord trieth the righteous; but the wicked, and him that loveth violence, his soul hateth,' Ps. xi. 5.

Sec. 61. *Of the kinds of God's righteousness.*

The word ἄδικος, here translated *unrighteous*, is in other places translated *unjust*, as Mat. v. 45; Luke xvi. 11; 1 Cor. vi. 1. For righteousness and justice are ordinarily taken for the same thing.

The notation of the Greek word is taken from δίκη, *jus, right*, in that righteousness or justice consisteth in giving to every one that which is his right. The philosopher[1] taketh the notation from a word that signifieth two parts, or a dividing of things in two parts, whereby is intended the same thing, that there should be given to one that part which belongeth to him, and to the other that which of right he ought to have. See more hereof, Chap. i. 9, Sec. 114.

From this notation we may infer that righteousness or justice is an equal dealing. In reference to God, his righteousness is the integrity or equity of all his counsels, words, and actions.

This is manifested two ways.

1. Generally, in ordering all things most equally. In this respect Moses thus saith of him, 'His work is perfect; for all his ways are judgment: a God of truth, and without iniquity; just and right is he,' Deut. xxxii. 4. This may be called God's *disposing justice*, or righteousness.

2. Particularly, in giving reward or taking revenge; and this may be called *distributive justice*. Of both these it is thus said, ' God will render to every man according to his deeds,' Rom. ii. 6. This, the apostle saith, is ' a righteous thing with God,' 2 Thes. i. 6. This kind of righteousness is most agreeable to the foresaid notation.

That kind of God's righteousness which consisteth in giving reward, is here especially meant.

The ground and cause of God's giving reward, is not only grace and mercy, but also justice and righteousness; but that in reference to his promise, whereby he hath bound himself. For it is a point of justice or righteousness to keep one's word. Thus God's righteousness is his faithfulness. Therefore these two epithets, *faithful, just*, are joined together, as they are applied to God, 1 John i. 9.

This then is the intent of the apostle, that he may be well persuaded of these Hebrews in regard of their love to God and man, because God, who hath promised to recompense such, is faithful and righteous.

Sec. 62. *Of God's righteousness as it implies faithfulness.*

By the argument of the apostle, as righteousness is put for faithfulness, it is manifest that God's righteousness is a prop to man's faith and hope. Man may and must believe and expect a reward of every good thing from the righteousness of God; even because he is righteous, and will not fail to do what he hath promised. Herewith the apostle supporteth his own faith and hope, 2 Tim. iv. 8. And herewith he labours to support the faith and hope of those to whom he wrote, 2 Thes. i. 5, 7. On this ground saith the psalmist, 'Judge me, O Lord my God, according to thy righteousness,' Ps. xxxv. 24.

This righteousness of God assureth us of the continuance of his favour and mercy. What grace moved him to begin, righteousness will move him to continue and finish.

Of appealing to God's righteousness, see the *Saint's Sacrifice*, on Ps. cxvi. 5, sec. 28.

1. This informs us in the wonderful great condescension of God to man: even so low, as to bind himself to man, and that so far, as if he failed in what he had promised, he is willing to be accounted unrighteous. 'What is man, O Lord, thou shouldst be thus mindful of him?' God's grace, pity, mercy, truth, power, wisdom, and righteousness, are all props to our faith. The psalmist might well say, 'I will praise the Lord according to his righteousness,' Ps. vii. 17.

2. This doth much aggravate the sin of infidelity; which is not only against the grace and mercy of God, but also against his truth and righteousness. 'He that believeth not God, hath made him a liar,'

---

[1] Aristot. Ethic. lib. ii. cap. vii.

1 John v. 10. Infidelity doth, as much as in man lieth, make him that is not unrighteous to be unrighteous and unfaithful. Great dishonour is done unto God hereby, and great wrong to the unbeliever himself.

3. This teacheth us how to trust to God's mercy: even so as God may be just and righteous in shewing mercy. God's righteousness is manifested by performing his word, as he hath declared it. God's promise of rewarding men is made to such as are upright and faithful, as fear and obey him, as turn from sin, and persevere in grace. These are means, in reference to God's righteousness, of sharpening our prayers, and strengthening our faith: in which respect saints have pleaded them before God; as he that said, 'Remember now, O Lord, I beseech thee, how I have walked before thee in truth, and with a perfect heart, and have done that which is good in thy sight,' Isa. xxxviii. 3. On this ground the psalmist thus prayeth to God, 'In thy faithfulness answer me, and in thy righteousness,' Ps. cxliii. 1.

Sec. 63. *Of God's remembering good.*

The manifestation, evidence, or effect of God's being not unrighteous, is thus set out, ἐπιλαθέσθαι,[1] *to forget your work,* &c.

To *forget* is directly contrary to *remember.* He therefore that is not unrighteous to forget, is righteous to remember: his righteousness will move him to remember such and such persons or things.

These acts, *not to forget,* or *to remember,* are attributed to God metaphorically, by way of resemblance, after the manner of man. They imply that God is ever mindful of such and such persons, to support, to succour, and every way to do them good: and withal to recompense all the good they do. He that forgets not, doth ever remember. Hereupon the psalmist professeth, that 'the righteous shall be in everlasting remembrance,' Ps. cxii. 6. So faithful is God's remembrance of his saints, as a prophet herein prefers him before all parents, who use to be most mindful of their children, thus, 'Can a woman forget her sucking child? &c., yea, they may forget, yet will I not forget thee,' Isa. xlix. 15. On this ground doth the psalmist with much emphasis expostulate this case, 'Hath God forgotten to be gracious? hath he in anger shut up his tender mercy?' Ps. lxxvii. 9. These interrogations are strong negations: they imply that God neither doth, nor will, nor can forget. To assure us the more hereof, the Holy Ghost mentioneth certain books or rolls of remembrance written before God, wherein the righteous deeds of his servants are recorded. How this righteousness of God is a prop to man's faith, was shewed, Sec. 62.

1. This is a great inducement to labour after such things as God approveth. If once God like such a thing, he will never forget it; we may rest upon it,

[1] Of this compound verb, see Chap. xiii. 2, Sec. 12.

that what God hath in everlasting remembrance shall be abundantly recompensed. If a subject were sure that his prince would never forget what he doth for his sake, what would he not readily do? This is it, that saints have in all ages trusted to, and accordingly desired; namely, that God would remember them, Neh. v. 19, and xiii. 14, Ps. cvi. 4, Isa. xxxviii. 3. For well they knew, that upon God's remembrance, they might confidently expect an abundant recompence.

2. This may be an encouragement against man's ungrateful forgetfulness. Many are ready to forget all manner of kindness and goodness done to them, as Pharaoh's butler, Gen. xl. 23. Hereby it comes to pass that many repent of the good they have done, and wax weary in doing more. But if such would raise their eyes from man to God, and duly consider this evidence of his righteousness, certainly they would not, I am sure they need not, repent of any good thing they have done; for he that can most abundantly, and will most assuredly, recompense every good thing, nor can, nor will forget any. He is not unrighteous to forget them.

Sec. 64. *Of unrighteousness in forgetting kindness.*

In that this evidence is given of God's not being unjust, because he forgetteth not that which is good, it followeth that to forget a good work is a point of unrighteousness. Surely Ahasuerus by the light of nature discerned thus much, who, when by reading of the chronicles, he was put in mind of a great good thing that Mordecai had done for him, thus said, 'What honour and dignity hath been done to Mordecai for this?' Esther vi. 3. For hereby that which is due to a good deed is not rendered, which is apparent injustice and unrighteousness.

1. Hereby is discovered that palpable unrighteousness which is done by all sorts to God. How are his kindnesses forgotten? Moses and other prophets have much complained hereof. 'Of the rock that begat thee, thou art unmindful, and hast forgotten God that formed thee,' Deut. xxxii. 18. Israel is oft taxed for 'forgetting the Lord their God,' Judges iii. 7, 1 Sam. xii. 9, Ps. lxxviii. 11, Isa. xvii. 10. Who hath not cause to be humbled for this point of unrighteousness, and that both in regard of the people among whom he liveth, and also in regard of himself? Let this be the rather well noted, that we may hereafter be more righteous in this kind.

2. The unrighteousness of man to man is also hereby discovered. Both superiors and inferiors, in commonwealth, church, and state, are too prone to forget kindnesses done to them, and therein to prove unrighteous. If this were known to be a part of injustice and unrighteousness, it would assuredly be more amended than it is.

Sec. 65. *Of that work which God will not forget.*

The first particular which God is here said not to

forget, is thus expressed, τοῦ ἔργου ὑμῶν, *your work*. Some would have this to be joined to the next clause as a property of their love, as the next word, *labour*, is; as if he had thus said, *your working and laborious love*, but this cannot well stand in two respects.

1. Because the pronoun *your* is interposed; for if these two words, *work, labour*, were two epithets, this relative *your* should be referred to *love*, thus, ' the work and labour of your love.'

2. Because *labour* compriseth *work* under it; in which respect the word *work* would be to little purpose. I rather take these words, *your work*, to be a distinct clause by itself.

Quest. What kind of work may be here meant?

Ans. Most interpreters take *faith* to be the work here intended. Indeed, faith is a work; and this epithet may be given unto it, to set out the life and efficacy of it; but I do not find it simply styled a work; only this phrase, ' the work of faith,' is used, 1 Thes. i. 3, 2 Thes. i. 11, and this, ' This is the work of God, that ye believe on him whom he hath sent,' John vi. 29.

I will not deny but that faith, taken in a large sense, for a mother grace, accompanied with all her children, which are all manner of fruits of faith, may be here understood; for so it is all one, as the general work of grace, which I take to be here meant. Work, therefore, is here the same which the apostle in another place calleth ' a good work,' Philip. i. 6.

Obj. Thus it should rather be called, *the work of God*, than *your work*.

Ans. It may well be called both.

The work of God *originally*, because God is the author of it; but your work *instrumentally*, because men, assisted by God's Spirit, bring forth this fruit. Both these, God and man, are joined together in this work: ' God hath begun a good work in you,' Philip. i. 6. ' God worketh in you both to will and to do,' Philip. ii. 13.

This phrase, *your work*, generally taken, excludeth not faith, hope, repentance, or any other good grace, but compriseth all under it. Grace is expressed under this word *work*, to shew that it is operative and effectual; yea, also to shew, that it is a working grace which God forgets not. So as this is the point here especially intended, God will not forget the good work of grace. ' I know thy works,' saith Christ to the church at Ephesus, Rev. ii. 2. Well, mark such places of Scripture as mention God's approving remembrance of a grace, and you shall find the visible evidence thereof to be set down; as Neh. v. 19, Isa. xxxviii. 3.

1. Such a work is God's own work. ' Every good gift and every perfect gift is from above, and cometh down from the Father of lights,' James i. 17. So as God is the author and efficient cause of it.

2. In regard of the matter of it, it is agreeable to God's will. Where the apostle prayeth, that ' God would make them perfect in every good work,' he addeth this clause to set out the matter thereof, ' to do his will,' Heb. xiii. 21.

3. In regard of the form, it carrieth God's image. This is that ' new man, which after God is created in righteousness and true holiness,' Eph. iv. 24.

4. Thus it makes most to God's glory, which is the highest end of all; hereupon Christ gives this advice, ' Let your light so shine before men, that they may see your good works, and glorify your Father which is in heaven,' Mat. v. 16.

1. This sheweth the prerogative of grace, and the work thereof, above wealth, honour, beauty, or any other outward dignities, worldly desires, or excellent parts. God is not so taken with any of these, as to have them in continual remembrance, and not to forget them. ' Hath God eyes of flesh? or seeth he as man seeth?' Job x. 4. Grace, and the work thereof, is that which maketh a man most precious in God's eyes, and best remembered by him.

2. This should teach us to labour for this work, to nourish and cherish it, and to shew it forth; for this is it that will make us happy; for in God's remembrance doth our happiness consist. He will remember us, to give us more and more grace here in this world, Mat. xiii. 12, Philip. i. 6, and to give us eternal life in the world to come, Rom. ii. 7. Therefore ' be ye stedfast, unmoveable, always abounding in the work of the Lord, forasmuch as you know that your labour is not in vain in the Lord,' 1 Cor. xv. 58.

Sec. 66. *Of the Rhemists' collection about merit answered.*

The Rhemists, in their annotations on this place, thus vaingloriously insult against protestants: ' It is a world to see what wringing and writhing protestants make to shift themselves from the evidence of these words, which make it most clear to all that are not blind in pride and contention, that good works be meritorious, and the very cause of salvation, so far as God should be unjust, if he rendered not heaven for the same:' a blasphemous assertion against God, and slanderous against the professors of the true faith.

But distinctly to answer the several branches thereof:

1. Is it wringing, writhing, and shifting to deliver that which is not only the general tenant[1] of the word, but also the particular intent of this place; which the words do not only imply but also express? For wherein is God here said to be just? Is it not in remembering? What hath remembrance relation to? Hath it not relation to God's word and promise?

2. Consider how in the verses following the apostle labours to assure us of eternal life. Is there any title of merit in all his discourse to establish our faith? Doth he not set forth two immutable things, God's promise and oath?

[1] That is, ' tenor.'—ED.

3. Do we write this point of God's justice otherwise than the Holy Ghost hath taught us? Doth not an apostle link these two epithets, *faithful* and *just*, together; and that in forgiving sin? 1 John i. 9.

4. Our wringing and writhing is like to skilful musicians winding up the strings of their instrument to a congruous harmony.

5. Where they charge us with blindness through pride, let this very question decide the point, whether they or we are the prouder? They labour to find something in themselves to trust unto, to advance and puff up man; we do all we can to cast down man, and to advance God and his free grace.

6. For their position of merit, let the nature of merit be duly weighed, and any of mean capacity may perceive that it is not possible for any mere creature, much less for sinful man, to merit anything of God. See more hereof in *The Whole Armour of God*, treat. ii., part 4, of righteousness, on Eph. vi. 14, sec. 7. How good works may be necessary to salvation, though no cause thereof, is shewed in *The Saint's Sacrifice*, on Ps. cxvi. 9, sec. 59.

Sec. 67. *Of Christian love.*

The next thing that God is here said not to forget, is *labour of love*. *Love*, according to the notation of the Greek word ἀγάπη, signifieth a kind of complacency, a quieting or pleasing one's self in such a person or such a thing. The verb ἀγαπάω, whence it is derived, is compounded of an adverb, ἄγαν, *valde*, that signifieth *greatly*, and a simple verb, πάυομαι, *acquiesco*, which signifieth to rest. These joined signify *greatly to rest* in a thing. Men use to rest in what they love, and so much to rest therein, as they are loath to part with it.

Love is attributed to God and man. It is so eminently and transcendently in God, as he is said to be love, even love itself: 'God is love,' 1 John iv. 16.

Love is attributed to men in reference to God, and other men, as the object thereof: 'Thou shalt love the Lord.' 'Thou shalt love thy neighbour,' Mat. xxii. 37, 39.

In reference to other men, it is indefinitely taken without exception of any, Mat. v. 44.

Or determinately, and in a special respect to professors of the true faith; in which respect it is styled 'brotherly love,' 1 Thes. iv. 9.

This general word *love* is apparently distinguished from that particular *brotherly love*, both in name and thing, 2 Pet. i. 7. Yet that general is also put for this particular, as John xiii. 35. So here in this place; for it is exemplified by 'ministering to the saints,' which is a special fruit of brotherly love. It is therefore brotherly love which God cannot forget, but hath in perpetual remembrance. 'Thine alms,' saith an angel to Cornelius, 'are come up for a memorial before God,' Acts x. 4. By alms he meaneth such a ministering to saints as in this text is intended; and those were a fruit of such love as is here intended.

1. This love is the truest evidence that can be given of our love to God, 1 John iii. 17, and iv. 20. It is also a fruit of our faith in God, Gal. v. 6.

2. This love, of all other graces, maketh us most like to God, 1 John iv. 16, Mat. v. 45.

3. This love is a mother grace; it comprises all other graces under it, Gal. v. 14, Rom. xiii. 9.

4. This love seasoneth all things that we take in hand, 1 Cor. xvi. 14, and xiii. 2.

We have hereupon great and just cause to get this grace to be well rooted in our hearts, to nourish and cherish it, and on all occasions to shew forth the fruits of it. Hereof see more, Chap. xiii. 1, Sec. ii. &c.

Sec. 68. *Of labour of love.*

The aforesaid grace of love is much amplified by this epithet κόπος, *labor*, *labour*, which the apostle thus expresseth, 'labour of love.'

The Greek noun is derived from a verb, κόπτομαι, *premor laboribus*, which signifies to be pressed, namely, with pains. The verb κοπιάω, *laboro*, which in the New Testament is ordinarily translated *to labour*, and cometh from the same root, is frequently applied to such as take great pains; as to fishermen, and thus translated, 'we have toiled,' Luke v. 5; and to husbandmen, 2 Tim. ii. 6; and to such as labour in harvest, John iv. 38; and to travellers wearied in their journey, John iv. 6; and to handicraftsmen, Eph. iv. 28. All these shew that the word implieth a diligent and hard labour, so as it here intendeth, that love is industrious. It is not slothful or idle. It will make a man take any pains, endure any toil, be at any cost. Thus is this phrase, 'labour of love,' used 1 Thes. i. 3. And love is said to 'endure all things,' 1 Cor. xiii. 7. Love makes men strive to overcome evil with goodness; it makes men to bear much. It was love that moved Christ to travel till he was weary, and to forbear to refresh himself, John iv. 6, 32. It made him to watch all night in prayer, Luke vi. 12. It made him endure the greatest burden that could be laid upon any; witness his agony, Luke xxii. 44. It was love that moved the apostles to take the great pains they did. Of St Paul's pains, labours, travels, and sufferings, read 2 Cor. xi. 23, &c.

It was love that put him upon all, 2 Cor. xii. 15.

Love works upon the heart of men within; it moves the bowels; it puts life to their soul; it adds feet and wings to their body; it makes them readily run to do good to those whom they love. If they cannot run or go, yet it will make them creep, as we say in the proverb; it makes them willing, yea, and desirous to do what they can; it makes them spare nor pains nor cost; it will not suffer them easily to be hindered.

This is a matter of trial whether true love possess our souls or no. If all our love consist in pitiful affections and kind words, but fail in deeds (especially if pains be to be taken, and cost laid out thereabout), surely the love that we pretend is but a mere show of love. 'If a brother or sister be naked, and destitute of daily food, and one of you say unto them, Depart in peace, be ye warmed and filled; notwithstanding, ye give them not those things which are needful to the body, what doth it profit?' James ii. 15, 16, 1 John iii. 18. Nay, if pains or difficulties keep us from exercising love, surely love is not well rooted in our soul. Why do men take so much pains as they do for themselves? Surely love of themselves doth abound. It is abundance of love that makes parents so careful and diligent for the love[1] of their children as they are. The like may be said of diligent, faithful, and painful ministers, magistrates, servants, and all others; love abounds in them. On the other side, where magistrates, ministers, neighbours, or any others are kept from doing good by the pains and labour that is to be taken about that good, they do hereby declare, that they want true Christian love. Let us therefore, in what place, of what rank or degree soever we are, testify the truth of our love; let not pains, travail, cost, or any like thing hinder us from doing of good, which we might and ought to do. We here see that God will not forget labour of love; why should anything hinder us from that which God will not forget?

Sec. 69. *Of love to man for the Lord's sake.*

The love of the Hebrews is much commended in this phrase, 'which ye have shewed toward his name.

This relative, ἧς, *which*, hath apparent reference to ἀγάπης, *love*, the word immediately preceding; for they are both of the same gender, number, and person.

The other relative, αὐτοῦ, *his*, hath an as apparent reference to God, mentioned in the beginning of the verse. If the sentence here ended, the love before spoken of might be taken for their love of God; but because it is thus exemplified, ' in that ye have ministered to the saints,' their love must needs be applied to saints; and this clause, ' which ye have shewed towards his name,' be inserted as an amplification of their love of man.

By *the name of God* is indefinitely meant that whereby God doth make himself known unto us. Hereof see Chap. ii. 12, Sec. 112.

Here, as in sundry other places, it is put for God himself, or for his glory, as Ps. lxxvi. 1.

The verb ἐνεδείξασθε, translated *shewed*, is a compound. The simple verb δεικνύω, *vel* δείκνυμι, signifieth to shew and manifest a thing, as Mat. xvi. 21. The compound, ἐνδείκνυμι, carrieth emphasis, and implieth a clear and evident shewing of a thing. There are two nouns thence derived, ἔνδειγμα, which we interpret ' a manifest token,' 2 Thes. i. 5; and ἔνδειξις, ' an evident token,' Philip. i. 28, and ' a proof,' 2 Cor. viii. 24.

[1] Qu. 'good'?—ED.

Thus, by that love which they did bear to the saints, they evidently declared that they eyed God therein, and aimed at his glory, and the praise of his name.

This clause, ' which ye have shewed towards his name,' intendeth the end and manner of their loving the saints, namely, for the Lord's sake; because God commanded them so to do, because God approved them that so did, because God himself loved the saints, and because God accepted, as done to himself, what was done to the saints. Yea, hereby also is intended the effect and fruit that followed thereon, which was God's praise and glory. Thus the apostle, in a like case, thus expressly affirmeth, ' Which causeth through us thanksgiving to God.' For the administration of this service not only supplieth the want of the saints, but is abundant also by many thanksgivings unto God, 2 Cor. ix. 10, 11.

The general intendment of the apostle is this, that respect must be had to God in the duties of love which we perform to man. ' Do all to the glory of God,' 1 Cor. x. 31. ' Honour the Lord with thy substance,' Prov. iii. 9. The apostle, speaking of ministering to the saints, saith that it was administered 'to the glory of the Lord,' 2 Cor. viii. 9. He that, upon a work of mercy done to men, rendered this reason thereof, ' I fear God,' Gen. xlii. 18, had respect to God in what he did to men; so he that, in a like case, said, ' I thy servant fear the Lord from my youth,' 1 Kings xviii. 12. And he also who, forbearing to oppress subjects, as other governors had done, said, ' So did not I, because of the fear of God,' Neh. v. 15.

1. God is that high, supreme judge to whom we are to give an account of all things that we do, whether to God or man, whether they be works of piety, justice, or charity.

2. God's glory is the most high, supreme end, at which we ought to aim in all things, and whereunto all other ends ought to be subordinate. Whatsoever is not directed thereto, cannot be but odious and detestable before God.

3. It doth much amplify the comfort of doing good to men, when therein we shew respect towards the name of God.

(1.) Such works of mercy as are done to other ends do lose much of their glory, comfort, and reward. False ends, which many propound to themselves, are such as these:

[1.] Praise of men, Mat. vi. 2.

[2.] Advantage to them themselves who seem to shew mercy; as they who invite such to dinner or supper, as may bid them again, and a recompence be made them, Luke xiv. 12, Mat. v. 46.

[3.] Example of others, as they who otherwise would not shew the mercy that they do. They think it a disgrace to forbear that good which they see others do. Hereupon they ordinarily ask, What do such and such in this case? These and other like them may do good to others, but cannot expect to receive good to themselves, especially from the Lord.

(2.) Let our eye be on God in all the good we do to men, that it may be said thereof, 'which you have shewed toward God's name.' Set, therefore, God before thine eyes : do thou look to him, and believe that he looks on thee. Let his charge set thee on work : aim at his honour, rest upon his approbation and remuneration ; yea, in shewing mercy to saints, do it as to the members of Christ, and thus thou shalt do it to Christ himself ; then Christ will so accept it and reward it, Mat. xxv. 34, 35, &c. Who would not shew mercy to Christ ? who would not do good to him ?

(3.) In shewing mercy to man for the Lord's sake, even towards his name, resteth a main difference betwixt restraining and renewing grace, betwixt that love which a natural man sheweth, and a man regenerate. For renewing grace moveth a man regenerate to do the things that he doth to man ' toward the name of God.'

(4.) Respect to God in shewing mercy to man will take away all vain pretexts and excuses, such as these: He never did any good to me, nor can I expect hereafter any good from him ; the good I do may soon be forgotten ; I may want myself, and none do good to me. But if thou hast respect to God, thy conscience will tell thee that he hath done thee much good, and may do thee much more ; that he will never forget any kindness done for his sake ; that he will supply the wants of all that trust in him.

Sec. 70. *Of ministering to such as are in need.*

The particular instance of that love which God is here said not to forget, is thus set down, ' in that ye have ministered to the saints.' The effect itself is in this phrase, ' ye have ministered.' And the special object thereof in this word 'saints.'

The Greek word διακονήσαντες, translated *ministered*, is a compound. The simple, κονέω, *famulor*, signifieth to *serve*. The compound, διακονέω, *expedite, diligenter ministro*, implieth readiness and diligence therein. It is indefinitely used for any kind of service. It setteth out that service which angels performed to Christ, Mat. iv. 11, and which Martha did to him, Luke x. 40. It is oft applied to ecclesiastical performances, as to preaching the word, 2 Cor. iii. 3 ; but especially to shewing mercy to the poor, and ministering to their necessities, Rom. xv. 25. In this respect it is translated διακονείτωσαν, to use the office of a deacon, 1 Tim. iii. 10, 13. A noun, διακονία, that in general signifieth any kind of ministry or service, is thence derived, Luke x. 40. In special it setteth out the ministry of the word, Acts vi. 4. More particularly, distributing alms of the church, 2 Cor. ix. 1. Hereupon such persons as are deputed to that function are called διακονοι, *deacons*, 1 Tim. iii. 8, 12. Of this word, see more Chap. i. 14, Sec. 156.

Here it is taken in a particular respect for the relieving of such as are in need, whereby it appeareth that it is an especial fruit of love to succour such as are in need ; for it is here set down as a special instance and fruit of love. Christ sets it down as a fruit of love to 'give to him that asketh,' Mat. v. 42, meaning such as are in need. Where the apostle saith 'love is bountiful,' 1 Cor. xiii. 4, he meaneth in distributing to such as are in need.

Love is compounded of pity and mercy, which are so moved with misery as they cannot but afford succour.

This affords a good trial about the labour which we take, whether it be the labour of love or no. If it be simply for ourselves, and our own advantage, it may savour rank of self-love, but little of brotherly love. But if it be to do good to others, and to succour such as are in distress and need, then it may well be judged a fruit of love.

Behold, then, what love especially it is that God hath in remembrance, which his righteousness will not suffer him to forget, which argueth true love to be in our hearts, and giveth evidence that we [shew] it to the name of God. All these being here couched in my text, are a strong motive to stir us up herein to testify our labour of love.

Of distributing to such as are in need, see Chap. xiii. 16.

Sec. 71. *Of charity to saints.*

The particular object of the foresaid ministering are here said to be τοῖς ἁγίοις, *saints*. The Greek word is the same that was used, Chap. iii. ver. 1, Secs. 5, 6, and translated *holy*. There it was used as an adjective, here as a substantive ; but in both places the same persons are intended, namely, such as in the judgment of charity may be accounted holy ones; and that by reason of their profession of the true faith, and their answerable conversation.

Quest. Are saints the only object of charity ? Are they only to be ministered to in their necessity ?

Ans. No ; for the law saith, ' Thou shalt love thy neighbour ;' and our Lord by a parable demonstrateth, that any one that is in need is to be accounted our neighbour, Luke x. 27, 29, 30, &c. Yea, he expressly commandeth to 'give to every man that asketh,' Luke vi. 30 ; meaning every one whom we have cause to think to be in need. The apostle doth expressly clear this doubt in these words : ' Let us do good unto all men, especially unto them who are of the household of faith,' Gal. vi. 10 ; so as this object of charity, saints, is not to be taken here exclusively, but by way of eminency and preferment. So much doth this word μάλιστα, *especially*, Gal. vi. 10, intend. We are expressly enjoined to shew mercy to a stranger, Lev. xix. 34 ; yea, to enemies, to such as curse us and hate us, and to such as are evil and unjust, Mat. v. 44, 45.

1. The ground of charity is another's need, 1 John iii. 17.
2. All of all sorts are of our own flesh, Isa. lviii. 7.
3. God in this extent doth make himself a pattern to us, Mat. v. 45; yet notwithstanding, we may well infer from this particular instance of the apostle in this place, that saints are the most principal object of our love and mercy; they are especially, before and above others, with more readiness and cheerfulness to be ministered unto; for they are 'of the household of faith,' Gal. vi. 10. As here, so in other places, they are by a kind of excellency in this case named. The apostle saith, that he went to 'minister unto the saints,' Rom. xv. 25; and he was desired to take upon him 'the ministering to the saints,' 2 Cor. viii.
4. The psalmist professeth that his goodness extended to the saints, Ps. xvi. 2.

(1.) God is the most proper object of love, Mat. xxii. 37; and the nearer that any come to God, and are liker to him, the more they are to be preferred in love before others.

(2.) God himself doth prefer such; for he is said to be 'the Saviour of all men, especially of those that believe,' 1 Tim. iv. 10.

(3.) Saints are knit to us by the nearest bond that can be, which is the bond of the Spirit; in which respect we are said to be 'by one Spirit baptized into one body,' 1 Cor. xii. 13.

(4.) Christ is most properly ministered unto in saints, Mat. xxv. 40.

(5.) Charity to saints is best accepted, and shall be most rewarded; for 'he that shall receive a righteous man in the name of a righteous man, shall receive a righteous man's reward,' Mat. x. 41.

Quest. Are saints to be ministered unto before our kindred?

Ans. In the same degree saints are to be preferred; as if a man have divers children, and among them he observe some holy, some profane, he ought to prefer the holy; so a brother ought to prefer pious brethren and sisters before such as are impious. The opposition which the Holy Ghost maketh is not betwixt spiritual and carnal kindred; for kindred in the flesh may also be kindred in the Spirit, but betwixt such as are saints and non-saints. There is a double bond whereby we are tied to minister to our kindred: one general, which is the bond of charity and mercy, which is comprised under the sixth commandment; the other particular, which is a particular charge which God hath committed to us, comprised under the fifth commandment. Hereupon the apostle pronounceth him 'worse than an infidel that provideth not for his own,' 1 Tim. v. 8; and Christ condemneth such as, upon pretence of religion, neglect their parents, Mat. xv. 5, 6. If to the forementioned bonds this of an holy profession shall be added, it will make a treble bond to tie us to this duty, and 'a threefold cord is not quickly broken,' Eccles. iv. 12.

The order about using charity, so far as out of Scripture it may be gathered, is this:

1. Charity is to be shewed to a man's self; for this is the rule of love, 'Thou shalt love thy neighbour as thyself,' Mat. xxii. 39. In this respect the apostle saith, 'No man ever yet hated his own flesh; but nourisheth and cherisheth it.' Hereupon the apostle presseth husbands to love their wives, because 'he that loveth his wife loveth himself,' Eph. v. 28, 29.

2. It is to be shewed to his family. 'If any provide not for his own, and especially for those of his own house, he hath denied the faith,' &c., 1 Tim. v. 8.

3. To parents and progenitors out of the family. Children or nephews must 'learn first to shew piety at home, and to requite their parents,' 1 Tim. v. 4.

4. To other kindred, Acts vii. 14; Esther viii. 6.

5. To strangers, Deut. x. 19.

6. To enemies, Prov. xxv. 21.

Among these, if any be saints, charity is especially to be shewed to them. How greatly is their heart hardened whose bowels are closed against saints, especially in this respect that they are saints! The persecution of Saul (who was afterward Paul) is herein aggravated, that it was against 'the disciples of the Lord,' and against 'those that called on his name,' Acts ix. 1, 14. Yet too many, not only Turks, Jews, pagans, and papists, but also such as profess the faith, much wrong and oppress other professors, who it may be are more sincere than themselves in this respect, because their profession keeps them from revenge. Thus, Julian-like, they smite them on the right cheek, because Christ bids them in that case turn the other, Mat. v. 39. Many have these and such like scornful speeches in their mouths: Such professors cannot want; they have brothers and sisters enough; who can believe them? They are egregious dissemblers. Herein they shew themselves mere formal professors. Many that give thousands to outward pompous works, as alms-houses, hospitals, and the like, will deny all succour to saints. As those shew little love to the name of God, so God will shew as little love to them, and refuse to hear them when they call.

Let us for our parts have our bowels most moved in the necessities of saints, and be most forward to succour them. Thus may we have the greater assurance of God's love to us, and of our love to God, yea, and of our fellowship in the mystical body; for members of a body are most moved with the distress and need of fellow-members.

Of rules and motives to love of saints, see Chap. xiii. 1, Sec. 7, &c.

Sec. 72. *Of continuance in charity.*

The aforesaid charity towards saints is further enlarged by continuance therein, thus set down, *and do minister.* As in our English, so in the Greek, the former and latter word is the same for substance: διακονήσαντες, ministered; διακονοῦντες, minister. The difference only is in time. The former hath reference to the time past, shewing what they had done; the latter to the time present, shewing what they continued to do. This latter giveth proof that Christians must continue in doing good: 'Be not weary in well-doing,' Gal. vi. 9; 2 Thes. iii. 13. This phrase, 'Ye sent once and again unto my necessity,' Philip. iv. 16, intendeth continuance in charity; so doth this phrase, 'See that you abound in this grace,' 2 Cor. viii. 7. Abundance is manifested both in present bounty, and also in continuing, time after time, to do the same thing. This phrase, 'His righteousness endureth for ever,' Ps. cxii. 9, is by the apostle applied to mercifulness, 2 Cor. ix. 9, and extended to continuance therein.

This circumstance of continuance is requisite,

1. In regard of our brethren in need. They may long continue to be in want. He whose hunger is once satisfied may be hungry again, and he whose thirst is quenched may thirst again, John iv. 13; besides, others after them may stand in need of our charity: 'For you have the poor always with you,' Mat. xxvi. 11. But charity is not tied to once relieving of the same man, nor to relieving of one alone.

2. In regard of ourselves; for the reward is promised to such as continue in well-doing, Rom. ii. 7.

(1.) They certainly lose the glory and recompence of the good which they formerly have done, who know that there is need of continuing therein, and have both opportunity and ability, yet clean cease to do any more. Some who in their younger years, yea, and when their means was but small, have been very charitable, in their elder years, after that their wealth hath much increased, have grown hard-hearted and close-handed. There are too many who in this kind outlive their good days and their good deeds, yea, even such as have continued under the blessing of a powerful ministry, and under God's blessing on their outward affairs. Herein appears the corruption of nature, the deceitfulness of sin, and subtlety of Satan, that men should be made worse by the means and helps which God affordeth to make them better. What assurance can such have that they are plants of God? Of God's plants it is said, that they shall still bring forth fruit in old age, Ps. xcii. 14.

(2.) Let such as have begun well be exhorted to hold on; and as their means increase, let their charity increase. Let not former good deeds hinder latter. So long as God affordeth opportunity, improve the ability which God giveth thee in this kind, and let thy stock for the poor be increased according to the increase of the stock of thy wealth. God, by continuing occasion of charity, trieth the continuance of thy charity. Wilt thou, then, faint and shrink when God expecteth improvement? Of perseverance in well doing, see Chap. iii. 6, Sec. 68, &c.

Sec. 73. *Of the resolution of* Heb. vi. 9, 10.

Ver. 9. *But, beloved, we are persuaded better things of you, and things that accompany salvation, though we thus speak.*

10. *For God is not unrighteous to forget your work and labour of love, which ye have shewed toward his name, in that ye have ministered to the saints, and do minister.*

The sum of these two verses is a minister's insinuation into his people's heart. Hereabout observe,

1. The inference, in this particle *but*.
2. The substance, wherein is contained,
1. A friendly compellation, *beloved*.
2. A good opinion. Hereof are two parts:
1. The point itself, what he thought of them.
2. The proof, why he thought so of them as he did, ver. 10.

In propounding the point we may observe,

1. The manner of propounding it; 2, the matter of which it consisteth. The manner is manifested two ways:

1. By using the plural number *we are*, intimating a consent of others.

2. By his confident expressing of his opinion, in this word *persuaded*.

The matter is set down two ways:

1. By way of asseveration; 2, by way of correction.

The asseveration sets down the matter two ways:

1. Comparatively, *better things*.

2. Simply, in this phrase, *things that accompany salvation*. This sheweth the height of his good opinion of them.

The correction is in this phrase, *though we thus speak*.

The motive or reason of the apostle's foresaid opinion is taken from the fruits of their profession, amplified by God's remembrance of them.

The amplification is first set down.

In the reason, therefore, we may observe two effects: One on God's part, the other on man's.

In the former is expressed,

1. The kind of effect; 2, the ground thereof; both set down by their contraries.

The kind of effect, thus, *not forget;* the ground, thus, *not unrighteous*.

The effects on man's part are set down under two heads,

One general, *work;* the other particular, *love*.

Their love is first illustrated, secondly exemplified.

In the illustration is shewed,

1. The earnestness of their love, in this epithet, *labour*.
2. The end of it, which is commended,
1. By the excellency of it, *God's name*.
2. By the manifestation of it, *in that ye have shewed*.

The exemplification hath reference to the time present and past.

Here we are to observe, 1, their act, *ministering;* 2, their object, *saints*.

The different tenses (ye *have* ministered, and *do* minister), imply divers times.

The object, *saints*, is expressed in the former, understood in the latter.

Sec. 74. *Of observations raised out of* Heb. vi. 9, 10.

I. *Misconceits must be prevented.* This is the main end of the apostle's declaration of his opinion of these Hebrews. See Sec. 53.

II. *Ministers may insinuate themselves into their people's hearts.* This is the general scope of these two verses. See Sec. 54.

III. *Testifications of love are commendable.* Such an one was this title, *beloved*. Sec. Sec. 55.

IV. *The best things are to be judged of people.* So doth the apostle here. See Sec. 56.

V. *Salvation is the reward of good works.* These are such as accompany salvation. See Sec. 57.

VI. *Christians may be persuaded of others' salvation.* So was the apostle here. See Sec. 58.

VII. *Denunciation of judgment may stand with good hope.* This phrase of correction, *though we thus speak,* imports as much. See Sec. 59.

VIII. *They who judge according to the rules of charity may suppose others to be of their mind.* This is inferred out of the plural number, *we are persuaded.* See Sec. 59.

IX. *God is perfectly righteous.* These negatives, *not unrighteous*, intend as much. See Sec. 60.

X. *God's righteousness makes him remember his saints.* The conjunction of these two phrases, *not unrighteous, to forget*, proves as much. See Sec. 62.

XI. *God is ever mindful of his.* Not to forget is to be ever mindful. See Sec. 63.

XII. *God is especially mindful of the work of grace.* This is the work here mentioned. See Sec. 65.

XIII. *Love is the ground of mercy.* Thus it is here set down. See Sec. 67.

XIV. *Love is laborious;* for labour is here attributed to love. See Sec. 68.

XV. *Respect must be had to God's name in duties to man.* So did these Hebrews. See Sec. 69.

XVI. *Works of mercy are special evidences of love.* Ministering being a work of mercy, is here brought in as an evidence of their love. See Sec. 70.

XVII. *Charity is specially to be shewed to saints.* Such were they to whom these Hebrews ministered. See Sec. 71.

XVIII. *Christians must continue in well doing.* This is here expressly commended. See Sec. 72.

Sec. 75. *Of inciting those of whom we hope well.*

Ver. 11. *And we desire that every one of you do shew the same diligence, to the full assurance of hope unto the end.*

12. *That you be not slothful, but followers of them who through faith and patience inherit the promises.*

Here the apostle beginneth the second part of his exhortation, which is unto perseverance. The inference of this upon the former verses is observable. He had before testified his good opinion concerning their salvation; yet here he exhorteth them to use means for attaining thereunto.

Our English joineth these two with a copulative conjunction, *and*. The Greek doth it with a conjunction of opposition, δὲ, *but*, as if he had said, I conceive well of you, and of your former practice; but yet you must not thereupon wax secure, but use all means for attaining that salvation which I am persuaded is prepared for you.

Thus we see that assurance of the end is no sufficient cause to neglect means of attaining to the end. Election and vocation give assurance of salvation; yet the apostle exhorteth them who were called, and thereby had evidence of their election, to 'give diligence to make their calling and election sure,' 2 Pet. i. 10. Who could have greater assurance of salvation than Paul, Rom. viii. 38, 39, yet who more careful in using means for attaining thereto than he? 'I so run,' saith he, 'not as uncertainly: so fight I, not as one that beateth the air; but I keep under my body, and bring it into subjection,' &c., 1 Cor. ix. 26, 27. And again, 'I follow after, if that I may apprehend that for which also I am apprehended of Christ,' Philip. iii. 12. God, who hath promised the end, hath ordained the means for attaining thereto. He who is rightly assured of the end, as by faith he seeth the promise, and resteth on it, so he observeth the means which he that promised hath appointed for attaining of that promise, and thereupon is careful in using the same.

1. This discovereth the cavil of our adversaries against our doctrine about the certainty of salvation. Their cavil is, that it is a doctrine of presumption, liberty, and security. But they, making men's salvation to depend merely on conjectures, are no more able to judge of a true believer's assurance than a blind man of colours. It is their ignorance which makes them judge so perversely and preposterously, The assurance and certainty of salvation which we teach resteth not on man's strength and stability, but on the immutability of God's counsel and promise, on the efficacy of Christ's sacrifice and intercession, and on the continual assistance of God's Spirit. See more hereof Chap. iii. 12, Sec. 134.

Indeed, when we consider our own weakness and wearisomeness in holy duties, our mutability and inconstancy, together with the many violent temptations whereunto we are daily subject, we cannot deny but that there is great cause for us to fear.

Hence is it that there are sundry exhortations in Scripture on the one side to be confident, and on the other to fear.

When the Holy Ghost would shew what we are of ourselves, he useth such caveats as these: 'Let him that thinketh he standeth, take heed lest he fall.'

1 Cor. x. 12; 'Be not high-minded, but fear,' Rom. xi. 20; 'Work out your salvation with fear and trembling,' Philip. ii. 12. But when he would shew the unmoveable grounds of faith and perseverance, he useth such encouragements as these: 'Be ye of good cheer,' John xvi. 33; 'Fear not, little flock,' Luke xii. 32; 'Let us draw near with a true heart, in full assurance of faith,' Heb. x. 22. Yea, to shew that these are privileges not only to be endeavoured after, but such as may be and shall be attained, he expressly setteth down many promises of persevering, and obtaining the things promised, such as these: 'He that drinketh of this water shall never thirst again,' John iv. 14; 'He that believeth shall not be confounded,' 1 Pet. ii. 6; 'The gifts and calling of God are without repentance,' Rom. xi. 29; 'It is your Father's good pleasure to give you a kingdom,' Luke xii. 32.

Thus we see what good warrant we have to teach assurance of salvation to them that believe, and yet, withal, to press God's people to take heed, to fear, to use all means, to give all diligence, not to be presumptuous nor secure.

This is a good direction for ministers to continue to incite those of whom they are best persuaded to use all good means of growing and persevering; as it is a point of charity to hope the best, so of godly jealousy to fear the worst. In this respect, saith the apostle, 'I am jealous over you with godly jealousy,' 2 Cor. xi. 2.

Here, by the way, note how needful it is to have the word again and again preached, even to such as have knowledge, 2 Pet. i. 13.

Sec. 76. *Of mildness in teaching.*

The apostle sets down his exhortation by way of entreaty thus, Ἐπιθυμοῦμεν, *we desire*. The Greek word is a compound; the root whence it ariseth, θυμός, *animus*, signifieth the *mind*. To desire is an act of the mind. The composition of the word importeth such a desire as ariseth from the heart, and is earnest.

It is used to set out both an evil and a good desire, and that also earnest. When it setteth forth an evil desire, it is ordinarily translated 'to lust,' as Mat. v. 28; 1 Cor. x. 6; James iv. 2. In the better sense it is applied to the desire which righteous men had to see the day of Christ, Mat. xiii. 17; Luke xvii. 22; and to the desire which the angels had to look into the mysteries of the gospel, 1 Pet. i. 12; and to [that] which Christ had to eat the passover the last time with his disciples, Luke xxii. 15. All these were earnest desires. Yea, this word is used to set out the desire of such as are hungry to be filled, Luke xv. 16, and xvi. 21, and of such as are in anguish to die, Rev. ix. 6. These desires use to be very great and earnest; so was the apostle's in this place.

This compound word, then, setteth out two points: 1. The apostle's mild and gentle disposition; 2. His hearty and earnest desire.

The former is intended under the general force of the word *desire*. He wanted not authority to command duty, yet he rather entreated them thereto, as Philem. 8, 9.

People are with mildness to be induced to duty, 1 Pet. ii. 11; 2 John 5.

Thus will ministers' teaching be like his that said, 'My doctrine shall drop as the rain, my speech shall distil as the dew; as the small rain upon the tender herb, and as the showers upon the grass,' Deut. xxxii. 2. Such teaching will more mollify hard hearts, and better soak into them. See more hereof Chap. iii. 1, Sec. 4.

Sec. 77. *Of ministers' hearty desire of their people's edification.*

The hearty and earnest desire is implied under the nature and composition of the word. It is a desire of the heart, so as ministers must heartily and earnestly desire their people's edification and salvation: 'My heart's desire and prayer to God for Israel is, that they might be saved,' Rom. x. 1.

This will make ministers the more careful and diligent in using all means of doing spiritual good to their people. True, hearty, earnest desire, puts on men to do the utmost that they can.

Surely they are most unworthy of any charge over people who are destitute of such a desire for their good, which too many do manifest by their idleness and carelessness. They will do no more than needs must, and than law bindeth them unto.

If ministers did duly weigh the benefit that they may bring to their people, and the comfort thereby to themselves, their hearts would be enlarged with desire of doing all the good they could for their good.

They who, after they have taken all the pains they can for the spiritual good of their people, do, after all, earnestly call upon God for his blessing, and that not only publicly, but also privately and secretly, do manifest thereby such a desire of their people's good as is here intended by the apostle.

Sec. 78. *Of ministers' impartial respect to every one of their charge.*

This desire of the apostle is further amplified by the extent of it, thus expressed, ἕκαστον ὑμῶν, *every one of you*. Hereby he manifesteth an even and impartial respect which he did bear to them all. This impartial desire is thus further explained, 'I would to God that all that hear me this day were both almost and altogether such as I am,' Acts xxvi. 29; and again thus, 'I am debtor both to the Greeks and to the barbarians, both to the wise and to the unwise,' Rom. i. 14; and thus, 'We exhorted, and comforted, and charged every one of you, as a father doth his children,' 1 Thes. ii. 11. Here he sheweth that, as a father's heart is impartial to all his children, so was his to all that were under his charge; for, saith he, 'I ceased not to warn every one night and day.' Hereupon he maketh this inference, 'I am pure from the blood of all men,' Acts xx. 26, 31.

All Christians are as fellow members of one and the same mystical body: 1 Cor. xii. 12, 'There is neither Jew nor Greek, there is neither bond nor free, there is neither male nor female, for ye are all one in Christ Jesus,' Gal. iii. 28.

Contrary is their practice, who on by-respects dispense the ordinances of God, shewing more favour to great ones and rich ones than to the meaner and poorer sort. Gravely and severely is this unchristian practice censured by the apostle James, chap. ii. 1–3, &c.

Surely all that are faithful will be of this our apostle's mind. Moses's faithfulness is herein commended, that it was manifested 'in all the house of God,' Heb. iii. 2. Thus will men's ministry be the better accepted, and thus will they do the more good, and take away occasion of muttering and murmuring.

As ministers must bear an equal respect to every one, so every one, of what rank or degree soever, ought to subject themselves to their ministry, and use it for their own particular edification. Every one needs the benefit thereof. Every one may reap good thereby. Should not every one whose good a minister ought to endeavour, improve his minister's endeavour to his own good? The desire of the apostle is, that every one do so and so. See Chap. iii. 12, Sec. 123.

Sec. 79. *Of diligence about our own spiritual good, as well as about our brother's temporal good.*

That which the apostle desireth is, that they would *shew the same diligence*, &c. The verb ἐνδείκνυσθαι, translated *shew*, is the same that was used verse 10, and implieth an evident and clear manifestation of a thing. See Sec. 69.

It is not enough to have a purpose of doing a duty, or to do it in private, so as others can take no notice thereof, but we must shew that we do it, and give good proof thereof.

The noun σπουδὴν, here translated *diligence*, is derived from the same root that the verb σπουδάσωμεν, translated *labour*, chap. iv. 11, was. So as it intendeth both an endeavour, and also forwardness and earnestness therein, and is fitly interpreted diligence, which is to be used for attaining that which is endeavoured after. Hereof see chap. iv. 11, sec. 63–65.

This relative τὴν αὐτὴν, *the same*, hath reference to the 'labour of love' mentioned ver. 10, and intendeth two points;—

One general, that diligence in our Christian course be constant. Such diligence as we have formerly used must still be used, even the very same. We may not slacken, we may not cool, we may not wax more remiss therein. Hereof see Sec. 72, and Chap. iii. 6, Sec. 68, &c.

Thus this relative implieth a motive taken from their former diligence. For if they who have formerly been diligent grow negligent, their former diligence will be a witness against them, and an aggravation of their after negligence. Ephesus is checked for leaving her first love. This therefore is one motive to incite them to persevere: they had begun well.

The other point is more particular. That such labour and diligence as we shew in behalf of others' bodily need, we shew in behalf of our own souls' good, for assurance of hope tends to our spiritual good. In this respect the apostle commendeth such as had attained to, and given proof of the one and the other, namely, 'the work of faith,' which makes to our spiritual good, 'and labour of love,' 1 Thes. i. 3. And he makes this the end of the commandment, namely, charity and faith, 1 Tim. i. 5.

1. In both of them God is glorified. It was shewed, Sec. 69, how love in ministering to saints is shewed towards God's name. So by hope, faith, and other like graces which make to our salvation, God is glorified. Abraham, 'being strong in faith, gave glory to God,' Rom. iv. 20, and God accounted it a glory to be styled 'the hope of Israel,' Jer. xiv. 8, and xvii. 13.

(1.) By being diligent about the graces that make to our salvation, we manifest spiritual prudence about the good of our souls, as well as charity to the good of our neighbour's body, by diligence in ministering to them.

(2.) By our care about our soul's salvation, we manifest a Christian and heavenly disposition, which diligence about the temporal good of others doth not necessarily import. For heathen and other natural men may be very charitable to others about their temporal good.

They therefore exceedingly fail in Christian prudence, who are diligent in matters of charity for others' temporal good, but are careless and negligent about their own souls' eternal good. As they are justly taxed who make pretence of faith, and have not works of charity, James ii. 14, so they are more justly to be censured, who boast of their many good works to others, and have attained to no assurance of faith and hope in regard of their own salvation. Hereof popish and superstitious persons are very guilty.

Ministers may here learn a good lesson, namely, to press upon people diligence in both kinds of duties. Many are very earnest in stirring up people to works of charity and bounty, but neither instruct them in articles of faith, nor stir them up to diligence thereabout.

Let us learn to add grace to grace, and to 'give all diligence' therein, 2 Pet. i. 5–7. 'What God hath joined together, let no man put asunder,' Mat. xix. 6.

Sec. 80. *Of diligence in attaining assurance of hope.*

The especial matter whereabout the apostle would have them shew their diligence, is styled *full assurance of hope.* This phrase, *full assurance*, is the interpretation of one Greek word, πληροφορία, which is compounded of an adjective, πλήρης, that signifieth *full*, and a verb, φέρω, that signifieth *to bring,* The active verb, πληροφορέω, thence compounded, signifieth to *assure,* or make full proof, 2 Tim. iv. 5. The passive, πληροφορέομαι, to be fully persuaded or assured of a thing, Rom. iv. 21, and iv. 5. The noun πληροφορία, here used, is applied, as in this place to hope, so to faith, chap. x. 22 ; and to understanding, Col. ii. 2. It is opposed to wavering, doubting, and uncertainty.

By this it is evident that assurance is a property of hope. There are the same props to support hope as to support faith, which are God's promises and properties. They who deny assurance to hope contradict the Scripture, strip this grace of much joy and comfort, which it bringeth in afflictions, and take away the difference betwixt the hope of Christians and worldlings.

Quest. Is not then that true hope which wants assurance ?

Ans. Not the truth, but the perfection of hope consisteth in this assurance. That which the apostle saith of knowledge, 1 Cor. xiii. 9, may also be applied unto hope, and to other Christian graces : ' We hope in part.' So long as we remain in this flesh, the flesh remaineth in us, as well as the spirit.

From the flesh cometh doubting, wavering, and all manner of weakness, Mat. xxvi. 41. But as the spirit getteth strength, and prevaileth over the flesh, so will this doubting and wavering be more and more dispelled, and assurance more and more increased. Hereof see more in *The Whole Armour of God,* treat ii. part vi. ; of faith, on Eph. vi. 16, sec. 39.

Some take hope in this place to be put for faith. Indeed, these two graces do in many things so fitly agree, as not unfitly one may be put for the other. The matter is not great, whether the one or the other be here meant. In the exemplification of this point, both faith and hope are expressed : faith, ver. 12 ; hope, ver. 18. But because hope is here named by the apostle ; and that which is here spoken of it, may agree to hope as well as to faith, I take the literal expression to be the best and safest.

Of hope, what it is ; of assurance of hope ; of the agreement and disagreement betwixt it and faith, of the use and need of hope, see *The Whole Armour of God,* treat. ii. part vii. ; of hope, on Eph. vi. 17, secs. 3, 4, &c.

The apostle here gives us to understand, that Christians may by diligence attain unto assurance of hope.

God will bless his in a diligent and careful use of such means as he hath appointed for attaining such and such graces ; yea, and the measure of them.

This discovers the reason why many long continue wavering, and never get assurance. They take no pains, they use no diligence ; they think God should work in them this assurance, without any pains of their own.

Such may wish, as Balaam did, Num. xxiii. 10, for that which they shall never attain.

Let not us be wanting to ourselves. If we think assurance of hope worth the having, let us do to the utmost what God enableth us to do for attaining thereunto. Let us acquaint ourselves with the grounds of hope, God's promises and properties, and frequently and seriously meditate thereon. Let us conscionably attend God's ordinances, and earnestly pray that God would add his blessing to our endeavour. We are of ourselves backward, dull, and slow to believe and hope ; we are much prone to doubting. In these respects we ought to use the more diligence, and to quicken up our spirits unto this full assurance, and not cease till we have attained some evidence thereof.

This last phrase, *unto the end,* is in sense, and almost in words, the same that was used Chap. iii. 6. The difference is only in the prepositions, which are two distinct ones in letters, μέχρι and ἄχρι, but both signify one and the same thing.

It is hereby intended that perseverance must be added to diligence : perseverance, I say, as long as we live. For the word *end* hath reference to the time of our life. See more hereof Chap. iii. ver. 6, Sec. 68.

Sec. 81. *Of slothfulness about sanctifying graces,* ver. 12.

The apostle, to enforce his exhortation unto diligence, addeth an inference against the contrary vice, thus, ἵνα μὴ, *that ye be not slothful,* &c. By this inference it is implied that if they be not diligent, slothfulness will seize upon them ; which, if it do, they cannot attain to the fore-mentioned assurance.

The Greek word νωθροί, translated *slothful,* is the same that was interpreted *dull,* Chap. v. 11, Sec. 58. There is shewed the notation and emphasis of the word. In reference to the mind, it importeth dulness ; in reference to practice, it intendeth slothfulness : slothfulness, I say, in use of means whereby grace may grow and gather strength.

The word is properly used of such as are slow of pace, as an old man, or an ass. It is contrary to quickness.

Here it setteth out, not so much a natural imperfection as an acquired vice, which seized upon them by their carelessness. They had not exercised themselves in God's word, thereby to sharpen their wits, and make themselves more capable of the mysteries of godliness ; they had not acquainted themselves with the promises treasured up in the word, nor with the properties of him who made those promises, and thereupon became dull of hearing, and slow of believing.

Obj. The apostle commended their diligence in the former verse, and desireth them still to ' shew the same diligence.' Why, then, doth he here forewarn them of slothfulness?

Ans. 1. He that admonisheth one to do what he doth, commends him for so doing.[1]

Ans. 2. He commended their diligence in charity, but admonisheth them to take heed of slothfulness in matters of faith, hope, and other like graces. It appeareth that herein they were not so diligent, therefore he desireth that they be not slothful therein. For,

1. They who are forward in duties of love to man may be dull and slothful in knowledge, faith, hope, &c. Saul is thus commended, 'He clothed the daughters of Israel in scarlet, and put on ornaments of gold upon their apparel,' 2 Sam. i. 24. Yet was he slothful about sanctifying graces.

2. Duties of love to others are more outward, and in that respect more easy.

Obj. Love is a fruit of faith, Gal. v. 6.

Ans. Indeed, true Christian love is so; yet there may be many specious shows of such a love as sprouts not from faith. As Saul in his time was diligent in seeking and procuring the good of his people, yet slow in believing God's promises, and backward in relying and trusting on God's providence; so others in other ages, and in this our age also, many that have been abundant in works of charity have been of mean knowledge and weak faith, if they have had any faith at all. See more hereof Sec. 79.

Sec. 82. *Of avoiding vices contrary to duties required.*

The slothfulness here dissuaded is directly contrary to the fore-mentioned diligence, and mention is thereof made to shew that for the more prosperous flourishing of a virtue the contrary vice is to be avoided. This is oft noted by the Holy Ghost in general terms thus: 'Cease to do evil, learn to do well,' Isa. i. 16, 17; 'Put off the old man, put on the new man,' Eph. iv. 22, 24; 'Let us lay aside every weight, and let us run with patience the race which is set before us,' Heb. xii. 1. So in this particular, Prov. xii. 24, 27.

As virtue and grace is a fruit of the Spirit, so vice and sin of the flesh. 'Now these are contrary the one to the other,' Gal. v. 17. If the lusts of the flesh be nourished, and not rooted out as noisome weeds, they will hinder the growth of the sweet flowers. All contraries hinder each other, as darkness, light; moisture, dryness.

When, therefore, we set ourselves to practise any virtue, if we desire to be carried on therein to perfection, let us observe what is most contrary thereunto, to avoid the same. Physicians, chirurgeons, husbandmen, and other sorts of men who desire to have their work prosper, take this course, Jer. iii. 3, 4.

In particular, in all undertakings for growth in grace, shake off slothfulness; pretend not needless excuses of impossibility, of improbability, of difficulty, or of danger. 'The slothful man saith, There is a lion without, I shall be slain in the streets,' Prov. xxii. 13.

Sec. 83. *Of being quickened up to duties by precedents.*

As a further motive to enforce them unto the foresaid diligence, the apostle setteth before them the example of such as had well run the Christian race, and attained unto the end thereof, their eternal salvation. The particle by which he bringeth in this motive is a disjunctive conjunction, δὲ, *but*, set down by way of opposition unto slothfulness, implying that they who obtained the prize were not slothful. So as if we look to partake of the same blessing, we may not be slothful; for they in their times and places were diligent. Slothful persons hazard the crown. To have an eye upon such saints as have well finished their course before us, will be an especial means of avoiding slothfulness. To this very end doth the apostle set before these Hebrews a catalogue of the most faithful worthies that lived in former ages, Heb. xii. 1. The apostle expressly saith that 'salvation is come unto the Gentiles to provoke the Jews to jealousy,' Rom. xi. 11, namely, to be as forward in entertaining the gospel of Christ as the Gentiles were.

Precedents and examples do put a kind of life into men; yea, dumb creatures are hereby incited: a tired jade, seeing other horses to gallop before him, is soon put on to a gallop.

It will be therefore a good means for our quickening duly to observe the patterns of such as have been forward in the way of godliness. 'Mark them which walk so as you have us for an ensample,' saith the apostle, Philip. iii. 17. Till we behold others, we may soothe ourselves in our slothfulness, and think it to be a kind of diligence. But when we behold others' diligence, then shall we find our own supposed diligence to be but slothfulness. For quickening us up, patterns may be of more force than precepts.

Sec. 84. *Of the use of former patterns.*

This noun μιμηταί, *followers*, is derived from the same verb which is used Chap. xiii. 7, Sec. 100. The *following* here intended is a diligent endeavour to be like unto them, and in our time to do as they did. For he here speaks of such as had finished their course, and obtained the prize. Hereof see more in the place before quoted. The patterns and precedents here intended to be followed are set down in two respects:

1. As a motive to incite the living to follow those who attained heaven, for so may these followers attain thither also. This, then, is a second motive to perseverance. Of the first motive see Sec. 79.

Of the benefits of imitating saints, see Chap. xiii. 7, Sec. 104.

2. These patterns are as a direction to shew them

[1] Qui monet ut facias quod jam facis, ille monendo, Laudat, &c.—*Ovid. de Trist.*

the way to happiness. What better direction can there be to keep on in the right way than to follow such as have gone in that way before?

Sec. 85. *Of faith the means of enjoying God's promises.*

To direct them the better in imitating those that are here set before them, the apostle doth expressly set down two graces that are of singular use for obtaining eternal life, namely, faith and patience. These are set down with a preposition, διὰ, that implieth the means and way wherein and whereby the reward is obtained, which preposition is thus translated, *through*.

This preposition, as here used with the genitive case, doth set out in general the cause of a thing, and that both principal and instrumental, as hath been shewed, Chap. ii. 9, Sec. 74, and Chap. iii. 16, Sec. 164.

It also intends the means of effecting a thing, and then it useth to be translated *through*, as here, and 1 Cor. x. 1, Acts viii. 18, 1 Cor. iv. 15.

Here it implieth that the graces following are the means of obtaining the promises, for by faith we give such credence to the truth of the promises, and so apply them to ourselves as we account them our own, even as if we were in possession thereof. This is that receiving of the promises which is applied to Abraham, Heb. xi. 17. In this respect faith is said to be the evidence of things not seen, Heb. xi. 1.

Of faith giving right to God's promise, see Chap. iv. 3, Sec. 23.

That faith is needful for enjoying the benefit of God's promises is evident by this, that the reward promised is in Scripture attributed to faith: 'He that believeth hath everlasting life,' John iii. 36; 'Ye are saved through faith,' Eph. ii. 8. And to shew that faith is so necessary a means as the thing promised cannot be obtained without it, a *must* is put thereunto: 'He that cometh to God must believe that God is a rewarder,' &c., Heb. xi. 6. Yea, eternal life is denied to such as believe not: 'He that believeth not is condemned already, because he hath not believed,' &c.; and 'He that believeth not the Son shall not see life,' John iii. 18, 36. In this respect salvation is said to be the end of faith, 1 Peter i. 9.

Faith is that instrument which God sanctifieth to make us partakers of those invisible blessings which in and by his word are offered unto us. It is as an hand to receive spiritual and heavenly things.

Now as the offer of a thing makes it not our own unless it be received, so without faith the promises of God become void unto us: 'The word preached did not profit them, not being mixed with faith in them that heard it,' Heb. iv. 2.

Behold here the benefit and necessity of faith: the benefit, in that it brings the fruit of all God's promises unto us;

The necessity, in that promises are in vain to us without it.

The inheritance is purchased by the blood of Christ, but it is faith that settles a right upon us, and gives us as it were a possession of it. It gives a kind of being to things promised before the date be accomplished. This is it which makes us 'against hope to believe in hope,' Rom. iv. 18.

Of faith, of the nature of it, of the means of working, proving, prospering, and well using it, and of the benefit and power of it, see *The Whole Armour of God*, treat. ii. part vi.; of faith, on Eph. vi. 16, sec. 5, &c.

Sec. 86. *Of patience added to faith.*

To faith the apostle addeth patience, as another and a joint means for obtaining good things promised.

The Greek word translated *patience* is a compound, and that of an adjective, μακρὸς, that signifieth *long*, and a substantive, θυμὸς, *animus, iracundia*, that signifieth the *mind*, and the commotion thereof, Luke iv. 28. This compound then signifieth a long forbearing to be moved. The compound verb, μακροθυμεω, is translated to 'bear long,' Luke xviii. 7; to 'suffer long,' 1 Cor. xiii. 4, 2 Peter iii. 9; 'patiently to endure,' Heb. vi. 15; 'to have patience,' Mat. xviii. 26, 29; 'to be patient,' 1 Thes. v. 14, James v. 7, 8.

This compound noun is translated 'longsuffering,' Rom. ii. 4, 2 Cor. vi. 6, and 'patience' as here, and James v. 10.

There is another Greek word, ὑπομονη, ordinarily translated *patience*, which is often joined with this word in my text as setting forth the same thing, Col. i. 11, 2 Tim. iii. 10. That is compounded of a verb, μένω, *maneo*, that signifieth to *abide*, and a preposition, ὑπὸ, *sub*, which signifieth *under*. This notation doth fitly set out the nature of patience.

So also doth this word in my text; it implieth a long enduring with a meek mind, free from fretting and grudging; for patience is that grace whereby we quietly endure and hold out against everything that might hinder us or keep us from the fruition of that which God hath promised and faith believeth. In this respect it is resembled to shoes, or to soldier's greaves, Eph. vi. 15. A patient mind doth quietly and contentedly wait for the effecting of what it believeth. In this respect, as here, so in sundry other places, these two graces, faith and patience, are oft coupled together, as 2 Thes. i. 4, Rev. ii. 19, and xiii. 10. It is needful that patience be added to faith for two especial reasons:

1. For the trial of faith.
2. For the supporting of it.

1. Patience gives evidence and proof of the truth of faith: 'The trying of faith worketh patience,' James i. 3; hereupon 'he that believeth will not make haste,' Isa. xxviii. 16; the 'honest and good heart,' having 'heard the word, keeps it, and brings forth fruit with patience,' Luke viii. 15. Many hypocrites, making at first a fair flourish, but wanting patience, vanish to nothing, and waxing weary, they fall away.

2. Patience is needful for supporting faith in three especial respects.

(1.) In regard of the long date of many of God's promises.

(2.) In regard of the many troubles whereunto we are subject in this world.

(3.) In regard of our own weakness.

Of these three, and of the nature and ground of patience, and means whereby it is wrought, and necessity and use of it, see *The Whole Armour of God*, treat. ii. part v., on Eph. vi. 15, sec. 2, &c.

Sec. 87. *Of inheriting the promises.*

The reward that those saints which are set before these Hebrews obtained upon their faith and patience is thus expressed, *inherit the promises*. The word κληρονομούντων, translated *inherit*, is the same that was used Chap. i. 14, Secs. 160, 161, 162. This word sheweth both the right that believers have to salvation, and also the everlasting continuance thereof. See more hereof in the places quoted.

The word ἐπαγγελίας, translated *promises*, is the same that was used, Chap. iv. 1, Sec. 6. There see the notation thereof. The noun here used must be taken passively, for things promised, and in special for the inheritance promised, namely eternal life, which is called the promise of life, 2 Tim. i. 1, and ' promise of eternal inheritance,' Heb. ix. 15. Here, then, is a double trope; one a metonymy of the cause for the effect, for God's promise is the cause of that inheritance; the other a synecdoche, the plural number put for the singular; and this because many blessings are comprised under eternal life, and also because eternal life is many times and many ways promised. In which respect they may be counted many promises.

The apostle thus expresseth that recompence of reward to shew that God's promise is the ground and cause of eternal life, for God hath 'promised it to them that love him,' James ii. 5. Such are said to be ' heirs according to promise,' Gal. iii. 29, and ' children of promise,' Gal. iv. 28; and they who enjoy it are said to ' receive the promise,' Heb. x. 36.

1. God makes his promise to be the title of the heavenly inheritance, to manifest his free grace, good pleasure, and abundant mercy in bestowing it, Luke xii. 32; 1 Peter i. 3.

2. He doth it to strengthen our faith the more in that inheritance. For God's promise is one of those ' two immutable things, in which it was impossible for God to lie,' ver. 18.

3. To give proof that there is no ground of title in ourselves, nor title of birth, nor of desert, nor of purchase by ourselves.

1. On this ground we may with the more stedfast faith expect this inheritance. A surer ground cannot be had. God's promise, as it giveth evidence of his good pleasure, so it giveth assurance of his continuance thereof, and of that possession which we shall have of it. For by his promise, his truth, his righteousness, and faithfulness is engaged. ' Faithful is he that promised,' Heb. x. 23. On this ground the believer ' setteth to his seal that God is true,' John iii. 33. But on the contrary, ' he that believeth not God, hath made him a liar,' 1 John v. 10. It doth therefore much concern us well to acquaint ourselves with the promises of God. Hereof see *The Whole Armour of God*, treat. ii. part vi.; of faith on Eph. vi. 16, sec. 71, &c.

2. ' Having these promises, let us cleanse ourselves from all filthiness of the flesh and spirit, perfecting holiness in the fear of God,' 2 Cor. vii. 1.

3. God's binding himself to us by promise, giveth just occasion unto us, to make promises unto him of such duties as we owe to him, and he expecteth from us; that so we may not leave ourselves free to omit or intermit those duties, and having bound ourselves by promise, it becometh us to be faithful, as God is, in performing our promise. See *The Saint's Sacrifice* on Ps. cxvi. 9, sec. 64.

Sec. 88. *Of the reward of faith and patience.*

The issue of the inheritance promised is here set down as the reward of their faith and patience, and in that respect it is a third motive unto perseverance. Of the two former motives, see Sec. 84.

This motive is taken from the recompence of perseverance, which is that heavenly inheritance that God hath promised. This being annexed to faith and patience, giveth proof that those graces shall not lose their reward; hereupon the apostle saith of these graces, that they are ' a manifest token of the righteous judgment of God, that ye may be counted worthy of the kingdom of God,' 2 Thes. i. 4, 5.

God doth make high account of those graces, and in that respect will not suffer them to pass unrewarded.

Who would not, who should not, use the uttermost diligence that he can, for attaining faith and patience? What zealous followers should we be of them, who through faith and patience inherit the promises? That reward which is comprised under these promises is worth the having, but without these graces it cannot be had, yet through them it shall assuredly be obtained. In this respect, these and other like graces are said to ' accompany salvation.' Hereof see Sec. 57.

Sec. 89. *Of the resolution of* Heb. vi. 11, 12.

Ver. 11. *And we desire that every one of you do shew the same diligence, to the full assurance of hope unto the end:*

12. *That ye be not slothful, but followers of them who through faith and patience inherit the promises.*

The sum of these two verses is, an exhortation to perseverance. In setting down hereof observe,

1. The coherence, in this copulative particle *and*, or rather disjunctive *but*. See Sec. 75.

2. The substance; and therein, 1, the manner; 2, the matter.

The manner is by a word of entreaty, *we desire*.

The matter sets out, 1, the thing desired; 2, motives.

The thing desired, is to be as careful for our own spiritual good as for others' temporal good.

In setting out this point, four things are expressed:
1. The persons whom it concerns, *every one*.
2. The duty, which is set down,
    1. Affirmatively and positively, *diligence*. This is amplified by the extent of it, in this relative, *the same*, which also imports a motive. See Sec. 79.
3. The grace whereabout their diligence is to be exercised. This is,
    (1.) Expressly named, *hope*.
    (2.) Amplified by an especial property, *full assurance*.
4. Their continuance therein, *unto the end*.

The foresaid duty is enforced negatively, under the contrary vice forbidden, thus, *be not slothful*.

Another motive is taken from former patterns. In setting down this motive, three things are observable.
1. The opposition betwixt the fore-named vice and this pattern, implied in this particle *but*.
2. The expression of the duty thereupon required, in this word *followers*.
3. A description of the patterns. They are described,
    1. By two special graces, *faith and patience*.
    2. By the issue thereof, which is set out,
        (1.) By the kind of possession, *inherit*.
        (2.) By the ground thereof, *the promises*.

This issue, being set down as the recompence of their continuing in faith and patience, is a third motive unto perseverance.

Sec. 90. *Of observations raised out of* Heb. vi. 11, 12.

I. *Assurance of salvation takes not away the use of means.* This is gathered out of the inference. See Sec. 75.

II. *People are with mildness to be instructed.* To desire that which is a duty, is a mild kind of instruction. See Sec. 76.

III. *Ministers must earnestly desire their people's progress.* So did the apostle here. See Sec. 77.

IV. *Ministers must impartially seek the good of all their people.* This is the extent of this phrase, *every one*. See Sec. 78.

V. *Christians must be as diligent for their own souls, as they are for the bodies of others.* Thus much is implied under this relative, *the same*. See Sec. 79.

VI. *Diligence must be used for perseverance.* This is it for which diligence is here desired. See Sec. 79.

VII. *Good proof must be given of our diligence.* The verb *shew* intends as much. See Sec. 79.

VIII. *Hope is an especial grace to be sought for.* For this end it is here expressly mentioned. See Sec. 80.

IX. *Assurance is a property of hope.* See Sec. 80.

X. *Perseverance must be added to diligence.* For we must be diligent unto the end. See Sec. 80.

XI. *Slothfulness is unbeseeming Christians.* It is therefore here expressly forbidden. See Sec. 81.

XII. *Men diligent in love may be slothful in faith.* The inference of this verse upon the former intends as much. See Sec. 81.

XIII. *Vices contrary to duties are to be avoided.* This is here exemplified in slothfulness, which is contrary to diligence. See Sec. 82.

XIV. *Good patterns are for imitation.* We must be followers of such. See Sec. 83.

XV. *Good patterns are good invitations and directions.* For both these ends are they here propounded. See Sec. 84.

XVI. *Faith is an especial means of obtaining things promised.* For this end is faith here set down. See Sec. 85.

XVII. *Patience must be added to faith.* It is therefore here coupled with faith; *and patience*. See Sec. 86.

XVIII. *Heaven is saints' inheritance.* That is it which they are here said to inherit. See Sec. 87.

XIX. *God's promise is the ground of saints' inheritance.* That is therefore here called a promise. See Sec. 88.

XX. *Faith and patience shall be recompensed.* The inheritance promised is here set down as a recompence. See Sec. 88.

Sec. 91. *Of the coherence.* Heb. vi. 13–15.

Ver. 13. *For when God made promise to Abraham, because he could swear by no greater, he sware by himself,*

14. *Saying, Surely blessing I will bless thee, and multiplying I will multiply thee.*

15. *And so, after he had patiently endured, he obtained the promise.*

That which the apostle generally hinted about those patterns which he set before the Hebrews, namely, 'that through faith and patience they inherited the promises,' he here exemplifieth and confirmeth in Abraham's example, who also through faith and patience did inherit the promise. His faith was famous, and well known. For thus it is written of him, 'He believed in the Lord, and he counted it to him for righteousness,' Gen. xv. 6. His patience, and the recompence thereof, are thus expressed: 'After he had patiently endured, he obtained the promise,' ver. 15. To shew that the ground of his faith and patience rested on God's promise, the apostle setteth down both the ground itself, God's promise; and also the confirmation thereof, God's oath, ver. 13. Therefore this particular instance of Abraham is a pertinent proof of the general point, and fitly inferred thereupon, and that by this causal conjunction γὰρ, *for*.

The argument may be thus framed:

That benefit which Abraham the father of the faithful reaped through his faith and patience, other saints who are children of Abraham may expect; but Abraham, through faith and patience, inherited the promise; therefore other saints may expect through faith and patience to inherit the promise.

Sec. 92. *Of the dignity of Abraham's person.*

This example of Abraham is in particular mentioned, not because he alone obtained this reward of his faith and patience, for in the eleventh chapter there is a large catalogue of other like instances; and many millions more have on like grounds obtained the promise; but for two special reasons is his example produced.

One is, the dignity of his person.

The other is, the excellency of his faith. See Sec. 94.

Concerning his person:

1. He was among the Jews in highest account. They much gloried in him; they thought that his posterity, even according to the flesh, should never be cast off, Mat. iii. 9; they thought that, being Abraham's seed, they were the most free of all people, and did hold out this buckler, 'Abraham is our father,' against all threatenings, Job viii. 33, 39.

2. He is set forth to have the highest place in the kingdom of heaven, Mat. viii. 11. Yea, the place of deceased saints' rest is called 'Abraham's bosom,' Luke xvi. 22.

3. He was accounted and called 'the father of all them that believe,' Rom. iv. 11; and 'they which are of faith, the same are the children of Abraham,' Gal. iii. 7. He is in Scripture styled, 'a prince of God,' Gen. xxiii. 6; 'the friend of God,' James ii. 23; 'the father of circumcision,' Rom. iv. 12. In him were 'all families of the earth blessed,' Gen. xii. 3. And his faith is made a pattern to the Gentiles, Gal. iii. 7–9.

Sec. 93. *Of Abraham's names.*

4. Abraham's name shewed him to be a man of great note. His first name was אברם, *Abram*. That is a name in Hebrew, compounded of two nouns. The first, אב, *pater*, signifieth in Hebrew Chaldee, Syriac, and Arabic, *father*. The other, רם, *altus, excelsus*, signifieth high, excellent. Thence *Abram*, an high or excellent father. The name was questionless given to him at first by some special instinct and foresight of what he should be afterwards; or at least in desire or hope of some high excellency, whereunto he should be advanced.

The other name, אברהם, *Abraham*, hath the letter ה with a vowel in Hebrew added to it, in the beginning of the last syllable, whereby it consisteth of a syllable more. The former name, *Abram*, was of two syllables; this latter, *Abraham*, of three.

The letter *He* added to this latter name, is one of the letters of this sacred name יהוה, *Jehovah*, in which the letter *He* is twice expressed. Hence both Jewish and other expositors produce sundry mysteries, which I suppose to be over curious, and therefore pass over in this place.

Yet this we may affirm, that it was a great honour to Abraham to have any part of the Lord's name added to his. Thus it was an honour for הושע, *Oshea*, which signifieth a Saviour, to be called יהושע, *Jehoshua*, Num. xiii. 16, the first syllable being part of the foresaid proper name of the Lord *Jehovah*. This name *Jehoshua*, or as it is commonly called *Joshua*, as he was a type of Jesus, signifieth *The Lord a Saviour*.

In this name *Abraham*, there is not a tittle taken from the former name *Abram*, only there is an addition of dignity and honour, which God himself, who changed the name, thus expresseth, 'For a father of many nations have I made thee,' Gen. xvii. 5. *Ab* signifieth a father, the letter *R* is left in to retain that excellency which was in the former name, implied under this word *Ram*. *H* is the first letter, and *Ham* the first syllable, in *Hamon*, which signifieth a multitude. In Hebrew names, a letter is oft put for a word, as in *Joshua*, Num. xiv. 6; and *Samuel*, 1 Sam. i. 20.

The full meaning, then, of this name Abraham is, an excellent father of a multitude, אב, *pater ;* רם, *excelsus ;* הם, *multitudinis.*

The Lord, in rendering the reason of this name Abraham, addeth this word nations, Gen. xvii. 15, to shew the extent of that multitude, that not only the Israelites which came from Abraham after the flesh should be very numerous, nor yet that he should have other nations also sprout from him after the flesh, as the Ishmaelites, Gen. xvii. 20; and the other nations that descended from him by Keturah, Gen. xxv. 1, &c.; but that also all of all other nations that should be of the true faith, should be accounted to come from him, Rom. iv. 11, Gal. iii. 7, 29. Thus was his seed 'as the dust of the earth,' Gen. xiii. 15; 'as the stars of the heaven, and as the sand which is upon the sea shore,' Gen. xxii. 17. By this latter name was he ever called, after it was first given him. Indeed, he is called Abram twice after this, 1 Chron. i. 27, Nehem. ix. 7. But in both those places there is reference to the time before this name was given him, and withal in both those places there is express mention of changing that name *Abram* into *Abraham*.

By this name *Abraham*, God would support his servant's faith in that promise which he made unto him, when he bid him 'tell the stars, if he were able to number them,' and thereupon said, 'So shall thy seed be,' Gen. xv. 5. Thus we see how careful God is to establish the faith of his saints in the promises that he makes unto them. The like might be exemplified in sundry other names of persons, places, rites, types, and other like things.

This God did both by reason of the knowledge he had of our weakness, and also by reason of the great desire he had of our good, that we should not fail of the benefit of his promise. This made him add to his promise his oath, as we shall afterward see, ver. 17.

Sec. 94. *Of God's manifold promises to Abraham, and the excellency of his faith in resting on them.*

The excellency of Abraham's faith is clearly manifested by the kind of promises which he believed.

It is here said, that 'God made promise to Abraham.' This verb ἐπαγγειλάμενος, *made promise*, is such a compound as the noun ἐπαγγελία, *promise*, was, Sec. 87. It hath reference, as to the other promises which God made to Abraham, so in special to this, 'In blessing I will bless thee, and in multiplying I will multiply thy seed,' &c., Gen. xxii. 17, 18. For the words of that promise are here quoted, ver. 14. And to that promise was the oath in particular annexed, Gen. xxii. 16. The promises made to Abraham were very great; and many of them to man's reason seemed very improbable, if not impossible. For,

1. God called him from his kindred, and out of his own country; and promised him the possession of many nations, whereof 'he gave him none inheritance, no, not so much as to set his foot on,' Acts vii. 5.

2. He promised to bless him, and to make his name great, &c., Exod. xii. 2. This was a great promise in the kind of it.

3. He promised him seed as the stars, when he had no child, and had been many years childless, Gen. xv. 2, 5.

4. When his body was now dead, being about an hundred years old; and Sarah's womb dead, he promised to give him a son by Sarah, Rom. iv. 19.

5. After that son was given him, to whom the promise was appropriated, he was commanded to sacrifice him with his own hand; and upon that command he was ready to do it, and yet believed, Heb. xi. 19; see ver. 15.

In these and other like respects his faith is thus commended: 'Against hope he believed in hope;' 'he was not weak in faith;' 'he staggered not at the promise of God through unbelief;' 'he was strong in faith;' 'he was fully persuaded that what God had promised, he was able also to perform,' Rom. iv. 18–21.

In the 11th chapter of this epistle, ver. 8, &c., occasion will be given of setting forth Abraham's faith yet more largely.

Abraham's patience is expressly noted, ver. 15.

By this it appeareth how prudently and pertinently the apostle hath culled out Abraham's example, and set it in special before them. For if a father so believed, and had such patience, then must children endeavour to be like him. We are all children of Abraham, Gal. iii. 7, 29. Now, it is an honour for a child to be like his father. We ought then rather to be like him, because there are no such difficulties and obstacles opposed unto us. God's promises, and means of accomplishing them, do now sweetly concur. We live in times wherein we see the substance of all former promises accomplished, Rom iv. 24.

Sec. 95. *Of Christ comprised under the promises made to Abraham.*

The foresaid promises, and also Abraham's faith therein, were the greater, in that they held out Christ, and Abraham eyed Christ in them. For,

1. That general promise, that God would bless Abraham, did set out Christ; for all blessings come to children of men in Christ.

2. The promise of seed intended Christ, which the apostle proveth by the singular number, *seed*, spoken as of one, Gal. iii. 16.

3. The numerous increase, as the stars of heaven, dust of the earth, and sand of the sea, hath especial respect to the church, which is the body of Christ.

4. The extent of the blessing, *to all nations*, Gen. xii. 3, and xxii. 18, was in and by Christ accomplished.

5. The land of Canaan, which was promised, was a type of heaven, which was purchased by Christ, and where we shall have an eternal communion with Christ.

To Christ, therefore, Abraham had an eye in the promises which were made to him. In which respect Christ thus saith to the Jews, 'Your father Abraham rejoiced to see my day; and he saw it, and was glad,' John viii. 56.

Hereby we may learn what specially to behold in God's promises, namely, Jesus Christ, and in him God's favour, and all needful blessings that may bring us to an eternal communion with him. Thus shall our faith be more firmly stablished, and we made the more patient in expecting the issue and end of all, the salvation of our souls.

Sec. 96. *Of God's promise, the ground of faith and patience.*

The apostle, to give proof of Abraham's faith and patience, maketh mention of God's promise, to shew that God's promise is the only true ground of faith and patience. This made Caleb and Joshua constant in their faith and patience, forty years together in the wilderness, notwithstanding the many murmurings and rebellions of the other Israelites. This made David endure many years' persecution, from the time of his anointing to the time of his possessing the kingdom. This was the ground of the faith and patience of all martyrs, and other saints in all ages. The word which David intendeth, where he saith, 'Remember the word unto thy servant,' was a word of promise, whereof he thus further saith, 'upon which thou hast caused me to hope. This is my comfort in my affliction,' &c., Ps. cxix. 49, 50.

God's promise is as his very essence, which changeth not, Malachi iii. 6: 'Heaven and earth may pass away, but God's word shall not pass away,' Mark xiii. 31; for 'faithful is he which promiseth,' Heb. x. 23; and 'will also do it,' 1 Thes. v. 24.

For breeding and strengthening faith, for adding patience thereunto, and for making us without fainting to hold out, it will be needful and useful to acquaint ourselves with the promises of God, and with his truth in performing the same. Though God in his unsearchable wisdom may set a long date for the accomplishment of his promises, so as to us, who know not his time and season, he may seem to forget his promises, yet his justice, truth, faithfulness, and unchangeableness will not suffer him to make his promise utterly void. If a king or great man make a promise of this and that, we can wait for it; yet they are but men, and many ways subject to fail; for every man is a liar, but God most true, Rom. iii. 4. Let us not therefore by incredulity or impatiency make void to ourselves any promise of God, as the incredulous prince did, 2 Kings vii. 2, 20. Let us rather shew ourselves to be true children of Abraham, by such a faith as he had, and manifest the truth thereof by patience.

Sec. 97. *Of God's confirming his promise by oath.*

God that made the aforesaid promise to Abraham, did most solemnly confirm it by his oath. Thus it is here taken for granted, in that he sets down the bond whereby he bound himself, together with the reason thereof, in this manner, 'Because he could swear by no greater, he sware by himself.' Here therefore is to be considered,

1. This act of *swearing*, attributed to God.
2. The object by whom he swore, *himself.*
3. The reason hereof, *he could swear by no greater.*

Of the notation of the Hebrew word translated *swearing*, of the general nature of an oath, of this act attributed unto God, and of the bonds whereby God tieth himself in his oath, see Chap. iii. 11, Secs. 114, 115. Of the certainty or infallibility of God's oath, see Chap. iii. 3, Sec. 26.

God is oft said to swear in wrath, as we may see in the places whereunto reference is made. But here his swearing is in mercy, for confirmation of his promise made for the good of Abraham and his seed. Thus he confirmed the promise of Christ's priesthood, Ps. cx. 4; and of the everlasting continuance of David's kingdom, Ps. cxxxii. 11; and of the calling of the Gentiles, Isa. xlv. 23; and of the prosperity of the church, Isa. lxii. 8.

This manner of God's confirming his promise may not be imagined to arise from any variableness in God, but rather from his tender respect to man; partly to strengthen his faith the more, and partly to move him with patience to expect God's season for the accomplishment of his promise.

Obj. Abraham gave testimony of his faith; what need was there then that God should swear to him?

Ans. 1. Though in some things he testified a strong faith, Rom. iv. 18, &c., Heb. xi. 8, &c., yet he, being a man, was subject to human frailties. Instance his twice denial of Sarah to be his wife, and that for fear, Gen. xii. 12, and xx. 2. This phrase also, 'Lord God, whereby shall I know that I shall inherit it?' Gen. xv. 8, and his going in unto Hagar, Gen. xvi. 4, imply a kind of distrustfulness. We read the like of David, a man of great faith, as is evidenced by his setting upon a lion, and a bear, and a giant, 1 Sam. xvii. 36, and by his long bearing out Saul's persecution; yet afterwards he manifested great weakness, when he said in his heart, 'I shall now perish one day by the hand of Saul,' 1 Sam. xxvii. 1; and when in his haste he said, 'All men are liars,' Ps. cxvi. 11, which he especially intendeth of such prophets as told him he should be king.

Ans. 2. God's oath was needful for, and useful to, Isaac, who was newly delivered out of the very jaws of death, and then present when God confirmed his promise to Abraham by oath, Gen. xxii. 12, &c.; for the promise concerned Isaac as well as Abraham.

Ans. 3. That oath was needful to, and useful for, the seed of Abraham, generation after generation; for the promise concerned them all.

Sec. 98. *Of God's swearing by himself.*

The person by whom God swore is here expressly said to be *himself*: 'he sware by himself.' So much is expressly affirmed in the history: 'By myself have I sworn, saith the Lord,' Gen. xxii. 16. So Exod. xxxii. 13, Isa. xlv. 23, Jer. xxii. 5, Amos vi. 8.

Obj. In other places other things are mentioned whereby God sware: as his soul, Jer. li. 14; his name, Jer. xliv. 26; his right hand, Isa. lxii. 8; his strong arm, *ibid.*; his excellency, Amos viii. 7; his holiness, Ps. lxxxix. 35; his throne, Exod. xvii. 16.

Ans. Those seeming other things are no other than God himself; for there is nothing in God but God himself. Faculties, properties, parts of body, and other like things attributed unto God, are no other than his very essence. God is a simple, pure being, without mixture or composition. Properties, parts, and other like things are attributed to God merely by way of resemblance, for teaching's sake; to help us who are but of shallow capacities, and are brought to conceive divine mysteries the better by resemblances from such things. That there is nothing but a simple, pure being in God is evident by this title *Jehovah*, which implieth *all being*, and that by, from, and in himself. So doth this style, which God giveth to himself to be distinguished from all others, 'I am that I am,' Exod. iii. 14. In this respect sundry properties are applied to God not only in the concrete, thus, *wise, true, loving*, but also in the abstract, as *wisdom*, Prov. viii. 12, 14; *truth*, John xiv. 16; *love*, 1 John iv. 16; yea, those things which are qualities in man, being applied to God, are put for God himself, thus, 'the Wisdom of God said,' Luke xi. 49, that is, God himself; and thus, εἰ θέλει τὸ θέλημα τοῦ Θεοῦ, 'if the will of God will,' 1 Peter iii. 17, that is, if God will; we thus translate it, 'if the will of God be so.'

This, in general, may serve to satisfy that objection, which may more fully be satisfied if we distinctly consider the divers ways whereby God in swearing bindeth himself to make good his word. Of the bonds of an oath, and of a particular applying of them to God, see *The Church's Conquest*, on Exod. xvii. 16, Sec. 80.

Sec. 99. *Of God's having no greater to swear by than himself.*

The reason why God sweareth by himself is thus set down, 'because he could swear by no greater.' To set out the greatness of God above all others, this title, *a great God and a great King above all gods*, is by a kind of excellency ($\kappa\alpha\tau'$ $\dot{\varepsilon}\xi o\chi\eta\nu$) and propriety attributed to God, Ps. xcv. 3. There is scarce any other title more frequently attributed to God in Scripture than this, *Great*. The heathen by the light of nature discerned thus much, and thereupon gave this title to God, *Optimus Maximus*, the best, the greatest.

Everything but God, who is the creator of all, is a creature; but no creature can be greater than his creator; therefore everything else must needs be less than God. The apostle saith, 'Without all contradiction, the less is blessed of the better,' chap. vii. 7. Much more, without all contradiction, the less is created by the greater. It is impossible that the Creator should create a greater than himself. 'Who in heaven can be compared unto the Lord? who among the sons of the mighty can be likened unto the Lord?' Ps. lxxxix. 6. This being so, who can be imagined to be amongst creatures that God should take to be a witness and judge of that which he sweareth? What can there be out of God so fit and precious a pawn to bind himself by as that which is in God, even himself and his own excellencies? If, therefore, he sware, he must needs swear by himself.

That an inferior is not to be sworn by, but a greater, is laid down as a ruled case, ver. 16.

Sec. 100. *Of inferences upon God's swearing.*

God's swearing gives good evidence of his good respect to man, in that he condescends so low as by oath to bind himself to make his word good for our sakes. Herein he shews that he considers what is fit rather for our infirmity than his glorious majesty. Do magistrates, masters, parents, other superiors, ordinarily swear to make good their word to their inferiors? This useth to be exacted of inferiors, as Gen. xxiv. 3, but not so of superiors. The Romans nor exacted nor expected oaths of their magistrates, nor we in courts of justice of nobles. Yet God, who hath no greater than himself, binds himself to us his servants by oath. Thus he addeth seals to his covenant, Rom. iv. 11. Oh what matter of holy admiration doth this afford unto us! In this case we may say, 'What is man, that thou art mindful of him? and the Son of man, that thou visitest him?' Ps. viii. 4. What respect ought we to testify unto his majesty, who thus tendereth our infirmity! If this be not sufficient to make us cast off all diffidence, what can be sufficient? If now we believe not, God may well complain and say, 'What could have been done more, that I have not done?' Isa. v. 4.

What matter of humiliation doth this minister unto us, in regard of the proneness of our nature to distrustfulness! Most men make little more of God's promise, though confirmed by oath, than of man's. God's precious promises hardly make men to depend upon him, or to yield obedience to the means which are annexed to his promises for accomplishment of them. This sin, in regard of itself, and the cursed fruits thereof, is a most pestiferous sin. See more hereof in *The Whole Armour of God*, on Eph. vi. 16, treat. ii. part 6; of faith, sec. 34.

It becomes us, then, who bear any respect to God, to lay to heart this gracious condescension of God, and the means which he thus useth to strengthen our faith the more. That, therefore, our faith may be the more strengthened, let us oft meditate, as on God's promises, so on the bond whereby he binds himself to make them good for our good. This is next to that incomprehensible evidence of his love in giving his Son to us. Hereby he obligeth himself, his power, his truth, his holiness, his excellency, his name, his soul, and whatsoever is precious in him. He is content to be no more himself, or to retain anything whereof he makes account, if he fail in his promise to men. 'Oh the depth of the riches both of the wisdom and goodness of God!'

Should not this stir us up to bind ourselves by promise, by vow, by oath, by all warrantable means, to keep covenant with God. There was no need on God's part why he should bind himself by oath, yet he did so for our sakes. But there is great need on our part to bind ourselves to God. We are as prone to start from good purposes and promises as water heated to wax cold, and heavy things to fall downwards. Therefore we should, evening and morning, when we go to the house of God or to the Lord's table, on Sabbath days or fast days, solemnly bind ourselves to God. Promises, covenants, vows, oaths, and such like bonds, to tie us unto God, are as tutors to incite us unto duty, and to check us for neglect thereof. As, therefore, they are solemnly to be made, so oft to be renewed. This will make us more conscionable of duty, especially if it be done with a true purpose of performing what we tie ourselves unto, and in singleness of heart. See more hereof in *The Saints' Sacrifice*, on Ps. cxvi. 9, sec. 64; and on Ps. cxvi. 14, sec. 90, in the end of it, and 91.

Sec. 101. *Of this word, 'Surely.'*

Ver. 14. *Saying, Surely blessing I will bless thee, and multiplying I will multiply thee.*

In this verse the matter and form of God's promise is set down; whereby it is manifested to be an oath. The first word, *saying*, hath reference to God, and it implieth that the words of God himself are here produced.

The next word, *surely*, is in Greek used for the form of an oath.

The first particle ἦ, as here used with a circumflex, is a note of a strong asseveration: which itself alone signifieth *surely*, or truly.

The other particle, μὴν, joined thereto, addeth emphasis, as if we should say, *Certe quidem*, Surely in truth, see Chap. i. 6, Sec. 72. The LXX on Gen. xxii. 17 have used this word, to shew that that which followeth was the oath which God did swear. Other Greek authors[1] do also use it as a note of an oath.

Some, instead of the word used by the apostle, read *Amen*, which is a strong asseveration. Hereof see more in the *Guide to go to God*, or *Explanation of the Lord's Prayer*, Sec. 241. But I suppose the word used by the apostle to be the fittest for this place.

It is expressly said by God himself, 'I have sworn.' This clause, therefore, 'in blessing I will bless,' plainly demonstrates that this was God's oath, Gen. xxii. 16, 17.

Of God's confirming his promise by oath, see Sec. 97.

Sec. 102. *Of the blessing promised to Abraham.*

Two things doth God by oath promise to Abraham. One general, which is, *blessing*.

The other particular, which was, *multiplication of seed*.

Of the word translated *blessing*, see ver. 6, Sec. 47.

Here *blessing* compriseth under it every good and needful thing concerning body and soul, this life present, and the life to come; as health, wealth, honour, long life, with other temporal good things; and justification, sanctification, with other spiritual blessings; and the end of all, eternal salvation. All these make to man's happiness, and therefore are comprised under the word *blessing*.

Obj. Wicked men who are accursed enjoy the temporal blessings, and Christ himself saith, 'Woe unto you that are rich,' Luke vi. 24. How then do these tend to man's blessedness?

Ans. Wicked men pervert the use of temporal good things, and so make them to be a curse. But God bestoweth such grace on the children of Abraham, as they rightly use those temporal good things, and so they prove a blessing. See more hereof in *Domestical Duties*, treat. i. on Eph. vi. 3, secs. 101, 102, &c.

God said to Abraham, 'I am thy exceeding great reward,' Gen. xv. 1. Here he maketh it good, in this phrase, 'I will bless thee.' For God's reward is blessing; it makes a man blessed. So soon as God had made man, he blessed him, Gen. i. 28, and v. 2. After man's fall, all the good that God did and intended to man, is comprised under this word *blessed*; and that before, in, and after the time of the law; yea, in and after this world, Gen. ix. 1; Deut. xxviii. 3, &c.; Mat. v. 3, &c., and xxv. 34.

Blessedness is that *summum bonum*, that chief good, whereof the heathen had a glimpse, but could not find out wherein it consisted. It is that whereof Christ saith, 'One thing is needful,' Luke x. 42. He that is blessed in what he hath, needeth no more. He that hath abundance of such things as make not blessed, may be truly said to have nothing.

Indeed, there are many particulars to which blessedness is annexed. Christ giveth instance of eight together, which are commonly called the eight beatitudes, Mat. v. 3, &c. And the Scripture in other places gives instance of many hundreds more; but be they never so many, they all meet and determine in one chief good: as all the lines which proceed from a circumference meet and end in the centre, all rivers in the sea, all beams whereby the world is enlightened are from the sun, and in the sun. There are many members of one body, 1 Cor. xii. 12. The apostle reckoneth up many unities, Eph. iv. 4–6, which have reference to many hundreds and thousands, yea, and millions of particulars. There is one Lord, millions are servants to that Lord. There is one faith, but multitudes of believers that are of that faith. One baptism, but innumerable persons in all ages baptized. So there is one blessedness, yet many virtues, graces, duties, and means which concur to make up that blessedness.

But to make this point the more clear, blessedness is to be considered in the inchoation and progress thereof; or in the perfection and consummation of it.

In the inchoation and progress many means are used, many graces obtained, many duties performed. They that attain to blessedness must hear God's word, and keep it, must fear God, must be poor in spirit, must mourn, &c.

Blessedness is ascribed to all and every particular saving grace, in two respects especially.

1. Because no blessedness can be attained without all and every of them.

2. Because they who attain all and every of them shall assuredly be blessed.

Quest. What if a Christian attains some of them, though he have them not all?

Ans. Whosoever hath one sanctifying grace, hath every sanctifying grace. All sanctifying graces are as so many links of one chain, whereby we are brought to salvation. He that hath one hath all; he that hath not all, hath none at all.

He that hath any sanctifying grace is truly regenerate. Now regeneration consists of all the essential parts of a spiritual man, (which are all sanctifying

---

[1] Κατὰ παίδων ὤμνυες ἦ μὴν ἀπολωλέναι Φίλιππον.—*Demost.* Sic apud *Thucid. Xenoph. Platon.* aliosque veteres authores post ὀμόσαι addi solet ἦ μὴν: et jusjurandum indicat.

graces), as natural generation consisteth of all the essential parts of a natural man. Yea, though in natural generation there may be a defect and want of some parts, yet it never so falleth out in spiritual regeneration.

Fitly therefore is blessedness ascribed to every particular grace, because he that hath one hath also every one. He that is truly poor in spirit doth mourn, is meek, and so in the rest.

I will not deny but some graces may more conspicuously appear, and be in their kind greater and more eminent than others, as the stars in the heavens; yet in one degree or other, is every grace in every true saint, and that while here he lives on earth.

The perfection and consummation of blessedness consisteth in that incomprehensible and eternal glory, delight, and contentment which saints shall have in heaven, where they shall in a beatifical vision see God himself face to face, 1 Cor. xiii. 12, and where God will be all in all, 1 Cor. xv. 28.

1. God's magnificence is herein much commended, in that he maketh those blessed to whom he is pleased to manifest his favour, and whom he will reward.

Under blessedness, more is comprised than all the world can afford. All things without blessedness are nothing worth; blessedness is of itself invaluable. This is that treasure, and that pearl, for which he that knoweth the worth thereof will sell that he hath, and be no loser, Mat. xiii. 44–46.

2. Let him that would have his desire satisfied, seek after blessedness. Man can well desire no more than to be blessed. If he desire anything under it, or without it, his desire is a mean and base desire.

3. This should make us observe the means to which blessing is promised; and this should make us diligent in using those means. A man were better not be than not be blessed; but he that is blessed will have great and just cause to bless him that hath given him his being, and made him blessed.

4. This is a great aggravation of their wretched disposition, who being born and brought up under the light of the gospel, live, lie, and die in their natural, cursed condition.

The heathen could say that all things desire their good;[1] yet many men who live under the means whereby that good is revealed, will not learn how they may be blessed, much less walk in the way that leadeth to it. God for his part saith, 'Behold, I set before you a blessing and a curse,' Deut. xi. 26; but many wretched men regard not to 'choose the good part,' as Mary did, Luke x. 42. Oh more than monstrous ingratitude to God! Oh the irreparable damage that such bring to themselves!

Sec. 103. *Of God's abundant blessing.*

The foresaid blessing is further amplified by doubling the phrase, thus, *blessing I will bless.* This is an

[1] Αγαθοῦ παντα ἀφίεται.—*Arist. Ethic. Nicom.* lib. i. cap. i.

Hebraism, frequently used in the Old Testament; and it addeth much emphasis, for it setteth forth,

1. The certainty of a thing; as where the Lord saith, 'Seeing I have seen,' Exodus iii. 7. We thus interpret it, 'I have surely seen.'

2. Diligence and pains in a thing; as where the daughters of Reuel said to their father concerning Moses, 'drawing he drew us water,' Exodus ii. 19, that is, with great diligence and much pains he drew water for us.

3. Celerity and speed in doing a thing; as where David saith, It is better that 'escaping I should escape,' 1 Sam. xxvii. 1. We thus translate it, 'should speedily escape.'

4. Abundance in giving a thing; as in this, 'Blessing I will bless.' Our former English thus translated it in this place, ' I will abundantly bless thee.'

5. Success in doing a thing, or a thorough doing of it, or doing it to purpose; as where Saul saith to David, 'doing thou shalt do, and prevailing thou shalt prevail,' 1 Sam. xxvi. 25. We thus translate it, 'Thou shalt both do great things, and also shalt still prevail.'

6. Finishing and perfecting a thing; as where Solomon saith to God, 'Building I have built thee an house,' 1 Kings viii. 13. His meaning is, that he had perfectly finished it.

7. A wonderful increase of a thing; as in this phrase, 'Multiplying I will multiply.' Our former English thus translate it, 'I will multiply thee marvellously.'

8. Long continuance; as, 'waiting I have waited,' Ps. xl. 1, that is, I have long waited.

This phrase, 'blessing I will bless,' gives us to understand that blessings appertaining to Abraham and to his seed are abundant blessings. God is no way scanty to the sinful. He is exceeding bountiful to them every way. It is observable that the Hebrew useth this word *blessing* or *blessed* in the plural number,[1] which, to translate word for word, signifieth blessednesses. So much is intended under the first word of the first psalm.

More expressly doth the wise man thus set down the fore-mentioned point: 'A faithful man shall abound with blessings,' Prov. xxviii. 20. In this respect the psalmist saith, 'The Lord daily loadeth us with his blessings,' Ps. lxviii. 19; and the apostle thus, 'God hath blessed us with all spiritual blessings;' 'He hath abounded towards us,' &c., Eph. i. 3, 8. To this purpose it is said, 'Godliness is profitable unto all things, having promise of the life that now is, and of that which is to come,' 1 Tim. iv. 8.

God proportioneth his blessings according to his own greatness. He setteth forth his magnificence in blessing children of men.

Who would not depend upon such a Lord for blessing?

[1] אשרי, *beatitudines;* אשריך, *beatitudines tuæ,* Ps. cxxviii. 1, 2.

How ought we to enlarge our hearts and open our mouths in blessing God for so blessing us!

Sec. 104. *Of the extent of Abraham's blessing to all of his faith.*

In setting down this blessing, the persons blessing and blessed, the Giver and the receivers of the blessing are distinctly expressed under these two pronouns *I, thee*. The former hath reference to God, the latter to Abraham; for God saith to Abraham, 'I will bless thee.' God, then, is the author and giver of blessing. See ver. 6, Sec. 47.

Abraham is here to be considered as a public person, and the father of the faithful; so as what is here confirmed to Abraham, may be applied to all the faithful as truly and as effectually as if God had said it and sworn it to every one of them in particular. As Levi is said to pay tithes in Abraham, Heb. vii. 9, so all believers that have been since Abraham, and shall be to the end of the world, are blessed in Abraham: Gal. iii. 9, 'For it was not written for his sake alone, but for us also.' Rom. iv. 23.

All they that are of the faith of Abraham, and none but they, have a right to this blessing. For as there is an extent in this pronoun *thee* (which is to be extended to Abraham and his seed, Gen. xii. 3, and xxii. 17), so there is a restraint therein. They must be such as are of his faith, and in that respect accounted his children. 'For they are not all Israel which are of Israel; neither because they are the seed of Abraham, are they all children,' Rom. ix. 6, 7. 'But they which be of faith are blessed with faithful Abraham,' Gal. iii. 9.

Blessing, then, is proper only to the faithful. Read the Scripture thorough, and observe where you find any pronounced blessed; I dare boldly say, you shall find them in this sense to be of the seed of Abraham: namely, as they are of the faith of Abraham, and walk in the steps of Abraham, Ps. i. 1, and xxxii. 1, and cxix. 1, and cxii. 1, 2.

Christ is the fountain of all blessing; he is that blessed seed, Gal. iii. 16. Out of him there can be nothing but woe and curse. But all the faithful are comprised in his seed. They are members of that body, which is Christ, 1 Cor. xii. 12, and none but they. Of such saith the apostle, 'All are yours, and ye are Christ's,' 1 Cor. iii. 22, 23.

1. How should this stir us up to be of this seed; and to give no rest to our souls till we have some assurance thereof. It would be better never to have been of Adam, if we be not also of Abraham. *That* brought us into a cursed condition; *this* makes us blessed.

That we may be of this seed of Abraham, let us set Abraham before us, and consider how he believed, that we may be of the same faith, Gal. iii. 7. Let us also consider how he walked, that we may walk in such steps, Rom. iv. 12.

Quest. Is it possible that we may be such as Abraham was?

Ans. Yes; there are the same means and the same Spirit to make us so; and those means under the gospel are more perspicuous and powerful.

Besides, though we have not such faith in the quantity and measure, yet we may have it in the kind and quality, even so far as will make us blessed.

2. Let such as have assurance that they are of this seed content themselves in this, that they are thereupon blessed. They have no cause to envy any estate of others that are not of this seed. For what can a creature desire more than to be blessed? yea, what can the Creator give above that? This is the *summum bonum*, the chief good of all.

Sec. 105. *Of multiplication of seed, as a part of Abraham's blessing.*

One particular instance of the blessing promised to Abraham is thus expressed: *multiplying, I will multiply thee.*

The verb $\pi\lambda\eta\theta\acute{u}\nu\omega$, translated *multiply*, is derived from a noun, $\pi\lambda\tilde{\eta}\theta o\varsigma$, that signifieth a *multitude*, Acts iv. 32, which noun is derived from another verb, $\pi\lambda\acute{\eta}\theta\omega$, that signifieth *to fill*, Luke v. 7, for by multiplying a thing is made full.

Of the emphasis of doubling the word thus, 'multiplying I will multiply,' see Sec. 103.

The Hebrew, and the Greek LXX on Gen. xxii. 17, do add *thy seed* in this last clause, thus: 'I will multiply thy seed.' But the apostle, for brevity's sake, leaveth it out, and only repeateth this relative pronoun *thee*; for it is apparent that the multiplication here promised is, of Abraham's seed; a man cannot be multiplied but by his seed.

Quest. How can multiplication of seed be a part of that promise which Abraham is said to obtain (ver. 15), seeing in his lifetime he saw no great multiplication?

Ans. 1. Abraham saw the beginning and groundwork thereof; for he had seed of his own body, and that by Sarah his first wife, to whom the promise was made, as well as to himself, Gen. xvii. 16, and xviii. 10.

2. He lived to see seed of that seed; for Isaac had two sons of fifteen years old, whilst Abraham lived; which thus appeareth: Abraham lived one hundred and seventy five years, Gen. xxv. 7; Isaac was born when Abraham was an hundred years old, Gen. xxi. 5, Isaac was sixty years old when Esau and Jacob were born, Gen. xxv. 26; they therefore lived fifteen years in Abraham's time.

3. I might here further add that Ishmael his son had many children in his time, and that by Keturah he had six sons, Gen. xxv. 2, every of which might have many children in his days; but because the multiplication here mentioned is of the promised seed, I pass by this third answer: the two former are sufficient to satisfy the doubt.

But that which yet gives fuller satisfaction is the

vigour of his faith, whereby he saw the day of Christ, John viii. 56, and all that seed according to the flesh and spirit which was promised him. He was by faith as fully assured thereof, as if he had lived to the end of the world, and seen all with his bodily eyes.

Of the seed here especially intended, see Sec. 104.

The multiplication of seed here promised, being added to God's promise of blessing Abraham, giveth evidence, that multiplication of seed is a blessing. In this respect it is said, ' happy is the man that hath his quiver full of them,' Ps. cxxvii. 5. Blessing is thus exemplified : Ps. cxxvii. 5. ' Thy wife shall be as a fruitful vine, by the sides of the house : thy children like olive plants,' &c. ' Thou shall see thy children's children,' Ps. cxxviii. 3, 6. On this ground, the elders of Israel thus blessed Boaz : ' The Lord make the woman that is come into thine house like Rachel and like Leah, which two did build the house of Israel,' Ruth iv. 11.

Object. Multiplication of conception is set down as a curse, Gen. iii. 16.

Ans. 1. It is not simply the multiplication of seed that is there made a curse, but pain, and sorrow, and danger, which accompany the same. Hereupon this word *sorrow* is inserted thus : ' I will greatly multiply thy sorrow and thy conception. In sorrow thou shalt bring forth children.'

2. In Christ, that which was at first set down as a curse is made a blessing, 1 Tim. ii. 15.

Multiplication of seed is a means not only of increasing and continuing the world, but also of increasing and continuing the church in the world. And in this latter respect it is a blessing ; it is the multiplication of an holy seed, whereby Christ's kingdom is increased, and not Satan's.

This manifesteth the undue desires of many, who would have no children at all. To prevent children, some will not marry ; others, though they marry, wish that they may have no children, or if any, only one. Others that have many children wish them dead. Herein Christians use to be more faulty than the Jews were. What other reason can be rendered hereof, than covetousness, distrustfulness, discontentedness, and such like corruptions ? Let us, for our parts, shake off these corruptions, and depend upon God's providence for that seed which he shall be pleased to bestow upon us. See more hereof Chap. xi. 11, Sec. 54, and Chap. xiii. 5, Sec. 65.

Sec. 106. *Of God's multiplying seed.*

Concerning multiplication of seed, we ought the rather to depend on God's providence, because he saith, ' I multiply thee.' It is God that multiplieth seed. God, when he had made male and female, blessed them, and said unto them, ' Be fruitful, and multiply,' &c., Gen. i. 28. The like he said to Noah, after the flood, Gen. ix. 1. Therefore, children are said to be an ' heritage of the Lord,' &c., Ps. cxxvii.

3. God is said to ' open the womb,' Gen. xxix. 31, 33. He is also said to ' close the womb,' Gen. xx. 18. When Rachel said to her husband, ' Give me children,' Jacob thus answered, ' Am I in God's stead ?' &c., Gen. xxx. 2.

To give children is a kind of creation, which work is proper to the Creator.

1. Let such as desire seed, seek it of him who is able to give it, and multiply it. ' Isaac entreated the Lord for his wife, because she was barren : and the Lord was entreated of him, and Rebekah his wife conceived,' Gen. xxv. 21. The like is noted of Hannah, 1 Sam. i. 10. Many wives, that have no children, are ready to lay the blame upon their husbands, and many husbands upon their wives, and thus set one against another, and deprive themselves of that mutual comfort which they might have one in another. If they would consider that it is God who giveth increase of seed, such discontents would be much allayed.

2. Let such as have increase of seed, give the praise thereof to him who giveth it ; as Leah did, Gen. xxix. 35, and Hannah, 1 Sam. ii. 1, &c.

3. That which God giveth, is to be given to him again. To this purpose thus voweth Hannah, ' If thou wilt give unto thy handmaid a male child, then I will give him unto the Lord,' 1 Sam. i. 2. Children are given to the Lord when they are instructed in the will of God, and brought to fear God, and made his servants.

Sec. 107. *Of Abraham's numerous seed.*

This emphatical phrase, 'multiplying I will multipy,' sets out the exceeding great multitude of children that proceeded from Abraham, even his innumerable posterity, which is more expressly set down under these phrases, ' like the dust of the earth,' Gen. xiii. 16, ' like the stars in the heaven, and the sand which is upon the sea shore,' Gen. xxii. 17.

I suppose that there cannot be another instance given of so numerous a posterity, as Abraham had according to the flesh. But Abraham was a root of the church, and in that respect was this extent of God's promise especially verified.

This much commendeth the goodness of God, which is extended to so many ; and from hence we may infer, that they are not a few that shall be saved. For all Abraham's seed after the spirit shall partake of salvation. See more hereof Chap. ii. 10, Sec. 91, and Chap. ix. 28, Sec. 140.

We have just cause to take notice of this extent of the foresaid blessing ; for we among others partake of the benefit thereof. That promise hath been extended to us of this land, and that in these our days. Let our care be to shew ourselves true children of Abraham.

Sec. 108. *Of Abraham's patient enduring.*

Ver. 15. *And so, after he had patiently endured, he obtained the promise.*

These two particles, καὶ οὕτω, *and so*, imply a consequence following upon that which went before. The consequence hath reference to God's promise confirmed to Abraham by oath, which Abraham believing obtained the benefit thereof, which is here set down in this verse. That benefit is the consequence here intended.

This phrase, *after he had patiently endured*, is the interpretation of one Greek participle, μακροθυμήσας, which being of the first aorist, that setteth out the time past, may be thus also translated, *having patiently endured*. Both translations make to the same purpose, and shew that the reward of obtaining the promise followed upon his patient enduring.

Of the notation of the word translated *patiently endured*, see ver. 12, Sec. 86. It implieth two things, patience[1] and perseverance.[2] For it signifieth, long to endure with a meek and quiet mind. Thus it is applied to God himself, μακροθυμῶν, Luke xviii. 7, μακροθυμεῖ, 2 Peter iii. 9, and to a wise husbandman, James v. 7, under whose example the emphasis of the word is fitly set forth. For the husbandman waits for a crop from the seedtime to the harvest, and in that time he oft finds hard nipping frosts, blasting winds, scorching heats, yea, sometimes drought through want of rain, and sometimes floods through a great abundance of rain, yet he continueth to wait till the time of harvest, and, if he be not a covetous worldling, he waits with a quiet mind, still hoping for a good crop, for in that hope he soweth his seed.

This patient enduring hath reference both to a long date, which requireth enduring, and also to such difficulties as may fall out in that long time, which require patience.

That Abraham did long endure, and that with patience, is evident by the history of his life registered in sacred writ.

A child was one special thing comprised under the promise; for it he waited till he was an hundred year old. Was ever the like heard of any since the flood? Indeed, Shem was an hundred year old before he begat Arphaxad; but he was born, and lived a great part of his time before the flood. The other patriarchs that lived betwixt Shem and Abraham, had children before they were forty. Only Terah, the father of Abraham, was seventy years old before he had a child; but the thirty years which Abraham waited, after the seventieth year of his age, were much more than Terah's first seventy. It is said of Zacharias and Elizabeth his wife, that they were 'well stricken in years,' Luke i. 7, but their age was not comparable to Abraham's. He endured all his life long for the promised inheritance. That Abraham endured all that time patiently with a meek and quiet mind, is evident by that constant, cheerful, ready obedience, which he yielded to God upon all occasions; never gainsaying, or making question of any thing which

[1] Of patience, see ver. 12, Sec. 86.
[2] Of perseverance, see Chap. iii. ver. 6, Sec. 68, &c.

God said; never fretting, nor murmuring against any part of God's word. This may be exemplified in sundry particulars.

1. Upon God's command, 'he went out of his country, and from his kindred, and from his father's house,' Gen. xii. 1.
2. Upon God's appointment, he lived all his days in a strange country, Heb. xi. 9.
3. Famines and other difficulties did not move him to return to the place from whence God had called him; but other-where he provided for himself, Gen. xii. 10.
4. Because God would have him only there to sojourn, he was content to dwell in tents, Gen. xii. 8, and xviii. 1, Heb. xi. 9. He built no palace, castle, or house for himself.
5. In his ninety-ninth year, at God's command, he was circumcised, and all his house at that time, Gen. xvii. 23, 24. He feared not any such danger as befell the Shechemites upon a like occasion, Gen. xxxiv. 25, &c.
6. Upon God's command he cast Ishmael out of his house, though it were grievous to him, Gen. xxi. 12, 14.
7. Upon God's promise, 'against hope he believed in hope, that he might become the father of many nations,' Gen. xvii. 17, Rom. iv. 18.
8. Upon God's command, he was ready to sacrifice his only, his beloved son, the son of promise, Gen. xxii. 2, 10.
9. He purchased a burying-place for his wife, himself, and other patriarchs, in testimony of his faith that his posterity should enjoy that land, Gen. xxiii. 17, &c.
10. He would not suffer his son to be carried to the country, out of which God had called him, Gen. xxiv. 6.
11. He would not make affinity with those strangers, that were to be rooted out of that land, but sent to take a wife unto his son from among his kindred, Gen. xxiv. 3, &c.
12. He preferred the son of promise before all other his children, and sent them all away from Isaac, Gen. xxv. 6.

Of the difficulties which Abraham passed over, see ver. 13, Sec. 94.

Sec. 109. *Of the blessings which Abraham enjoyed.*

The main promise made to Abraham was to bless him, ver. 14, which compriseth under it all manner of good things, that any way tend to make man blessed. See ver. 14, Sec. 102.

Of this word *promise*, see ver. 12, Sec. 87.

It is here said, that he *obtained the promise*. The verb ἐπέτυχε, *obtained*, is in Greek a compound. The simple verb τυγχάνω signifieth as much, and is oft so translated, as Heb. xi. 35, Luke xx. 35. But the preposition ἐπὶ, *ad*, with which it is compounded, questionless addeth some emphasis. It may imply an obtaining to himself. He so obtained the promises, as he made them his own. He only and his seed did partake of the benefit thereof. Thus is this compound used, Heb. xi. 33, Rom. xi. 7. To exemplify this in some particulars, the good things promised, which Abraham obtained, may be drawn to three heads, temporal, spiritual, eternal.

Concerning temporal blessings,

1. He was honourable in the place of his abode. For the nations accounted him 'a prince of God' among them, Gen. xxiii. 16, that is, a great prince.

2. He was so mighty a man, as out of his own house he could raise an army, Gen. xiv. 14.

3. He was 'very rich in cattle, silver, and gold,' Gen. xiii. 2.

4. He was beloved of the nations thereabouts; instance the good entertainment which Pharaoh, king of Egypt, in a time of famine, Gen. xii. 16, and Abimelech, king of the Philistines, gave him, Gen. xx. 14. Instance also that courteous dealing which he found at the hand of the Hittites, Gen. xxiii. 6, &c.

5. He had an heir, a lovely and gracious son, a son of promise, Gen. xxi. 2, &c.

6. He saw his children's children; for Esau and Jacob lived some years in his time.

7. He lived many days, and those many days were good days, Gen. xxv. 8.

8. He was full of years, which phrase implieth, that he outlived not his good days. He was 'an old man and full of years, and died in a good old age,' Gen. xxv. 8.

9. He left a blessed memorial behind him, none ever a better. His memory yet as a laurel remaineth fresh and green in God's church. He is counted and called 'the father of the faithful,' Rom. iv. 11.

Concerning spiritual blessings, he was endued not only with those sanctifying graces, which were absolutely necessary to the salvation of his soul; but also with such as exceedingly adorned and beautified his profession, and made him a good parent, a good master, a good neighbour, and every way good. In regard of the eminency of those graces wherewith God endued him, he was called the friend of God, 2 Chron. xx. 7; Isa. xli. 8; James ii. 23.

Concerning eternal blessings, he had not only a part of that rich and glorious inheritance in heaven, which Christ by his blood hath purchased, but in some respects he may be accounted among men, the chiefest therein. See more hereof, Sec. 92.

Sec. 110. *Of waiting for God's promises.*

The points before noted of Abraham, are written not for his sake alone, but for us also, Rom. iv. 23, 24, even for our learning, Rom. xv. 4. So as from Abraham's example we may well infer these three points:

1. God's promises are to be waited for.

2. Waiting for God's promises must be with patience.

3. Fruition of the good things promised will be obtained by a patient waiting for them.

1. That God's promises are to be waited for, is manifest, not only by Abraham's approved example, but also by the example of other patriarchs. Jacob on his deathbed maketh this profession: 'I have waited for thy salvation, O Lord,' Gen. xlix. 18. 'I waited patiently for the Lord,' saith the psalmist, Ps. xl. 1. In the Hebrew, the word is doubled thus, קוה קויתי, *expectando expectavi*, 'waiting I have waited;' of the emphasis hereof, see ver. 14, Sec. 103. As this duty is commended by sundry approved examples, so it is expressly commanded: 'Wait on the Lord,' Ps. xxxvii. 34, Prov. xx. 22.

1. God in his wisdom oft setteth a long date for the accomplishment of his promises. All which time we must wait, lest we fail of obtaining the benefit of the promise.

2. God waiteth that he may be gracious to us, Isa. xxx. 18. Should not we then wait his good pleasure?

3. The time which God appointeth is the fittest season for effecting a thing. That time therefore is to be waited for. It is a great fault to prescribe a time to God; and if in that time God accomplish not his promise, to distrust the truth thereof, and thereupon either to faint, or to use indirect means, as Saul did, 1 Sam. xxviii. 7. It was an atheistical speech of a profane king to say, 'What should I wait for the Lord any longer?' 2 Kings vi. 33.

Sec. 111. *Of waiting with patience.*

It was shewed Sec. 108 that the word μακροθυμήσας, which the apostle useth, intendeth patience in waiting. This phrase, 'I was dumb, and opened not my mouth,' Ps. xxxix. 9, implieth the psalmist's meek and quiet spirit. 'It is good both to hope and to be silent,' Lam. iii. 26, that is, quietly to wait for the salvation of the Lord. For 'in rest and quietness shall you be saved,' Isa. xxx. 15. The psalmist giveth this reason thereof, 'because thou, Lord, didst it.' For such ought our respect to be to God, as we grudge not against anything that he doth, but contentedly and patiently expect the issue thereof, which will prove good to them that so wait.

Contrary hereunto is their perverse disposition who grudge and murmur at God's dealing with them, as when he stayeth longer than they looked for before he accomplish his promise, or when he bringeth them into any straits or distresses, or when some outward likelihoods appear against the promises which they have looked for. Examples of these and other like cases we have of the Israelites while they were in the wilderness, and of God's severe judgments on them for the same, whereupon the apostle giveth this admonition to Christians, 'Neither murmur ye, as some of them also murmured, and were destroyed of the destroyer,' 1 Cor. x. 10. Hereby they tempted God. See Chap. iii. 9, Sec. 96.

This discontented disposition argueth a light esteem of God, and a little faith in God's power, providence, wisdom, truth, mercy, and other divine properties. Though they may seem to wait, yet their waiting can be no way acceptable to God.

Sec. 112. *Of the benefit of patient waiting.*

The special benefit which they that patiently wait God's time for accomplishing his promise have is, that they shall obtain the good things promised. This in general was prayed ver. 12, Secs. 87, 88. It might further be confirmed by Caleb's and Joshua's and the other believing Israelites' entering into Canaan, and by David's possessing the kingdom of Israel, and by sundry other particular instances recorded in Scripture. It is said of old Simeon, that he 'waited for the consolation of Israel,' which was for the exhibition of the Messiah, and, according to his expectation, he saw him before he died, Luke ii. 25, &c. Especially is this verified in the heavenly inheritance, which all true believers that wait for it do enjoy. 'Wait on the Lord, and he shall save thee,' Prov. xx. 22.

The truth and faithfulness of him that maketh the promise giveth assurance hereof.

This is a strong motive to stir us up to shew ourselves to be children of Abraham, and that in a patient waiting for the accomplishment of such promises as God maketh to us. There are many great and precious promises made to Christians. They who, as Abraham, patiently wait, shall assuredly be made partakers of the good things promised. Acquaint yourselves, therefore, with these promises, and rest upon the accomplishment of them in due time.

Sec. 113. *Of the resolution of* Heb. vi. 13-15.

Ver. 13. *For when God made promise to Abraham, because he could swear by no greater, he sware by himself,*

14. *Saying, Surely blessing I will bless thee, and multiplying I will multiply thee.*

15. *And so, after he had patiently endured, he obtained the promise.*

The sum of these three verses is, the recompence of Abraham's faith.

Two things are here to be considered:
1. The occasion of producing this instance, in this causal particle *for.*
2. The exemplification of the point itself. Hereof are two parts:
1. The grounds of Abraham's faith.
2. The effect thereof, ver. 15.

The grounds are two: 1, God's promise; 2, God's oath.

In setting down the former, two things are expressed:
1. The persons. 2. The promise itself.

The persons are of two sorts:
1. He who maketh the promise, *God.*
2. He to whom the promise is made, *Abraham.*

The promise itself is,
1. Generally hinted in this phrase, *made promise.*
2. Particularly exemplified, ver. 14.

God's oath is, 1, generally affirmed thus, *he sware;* 2, particularly amplified by the object by whom he sware.

The object is, 1, propounded in this word, *himself.* 2. Proved by his superiority over all, thus expressed, *because he could swear by no other.*

In the exemplification of God's promise confirmed by oath is set down, ver. 14,
1. The note of the oath, *surely.*
2. The matter of the promise so confirmed. This is,
1. Propounded in two branches: one general, *blessing;* the other particular, *multiplying.*
2. Amplified by the measure of both, and that by doubling the words.

In setting down the effect or fruit of Abraham's faith, two points are noted, ver. 15:
1. The means used on Abraham's part.
2. The kind of effect.

The means noteth out two graces: 1, *enduring;* 2, *patience.*

In the effect is expressed,
1. An act, *obtained.* 2. The subject matter, *the promise.*

All these points are amplified by the order. First the means was used, then the reward was obtained.

Sec. 114. *Of observations raised out of* Heb. vi. 13-15.

I. *All believers may expect what Abraham obtained.* The connection of this example of Abraham with the former general exhortation, by this causal particle *for,* evidenceth as much. See Sec. 91.

II. *Abraham's example is an especial pattern.* It is therefore here produced. See Sec. 92.

III. *Fit names are of good use.* Abraham's faith was supported by his name. See Sec. 93.

IV. *God's promise is the ground of faith and patience.* For this end is mention here made of God's promise. See Sec. 96.

V. *God confirms his promise by oath.* He sware. See Sec. 97.

VI. *God sware by himself.* This is expressly set down. See Sec. 98.

VII. *None is greater than God.* This is taken for granted. See Sec. 99.

VIII. *An inferior must not be sworn by.* For this end God sware by himself. See Sec. 99.

IX. *God frameth his oath after the manner of man.* The Greek word translated *surely* was a word used in men's oaths. See Sec. 101.

X. *God's reward makes blessed.* It is therefore comprised under this word *blessing.* See Sec. 102.

XI. *God is the fountain of blessing.* It is God that saith, *I will bless.* See Sec. 104.

XII. *God blesseth abundantly.* The doubling of this phrase, *blessing I will bless,* intends as much. See Sec. 103.

XIII. *Blessing is proper to the faithful.* They are comprised under this pronoun *thee.* See Sec. 104.

XIV. *Children are a blessing.* For this end *multiplying* is added to blessing. See Sec. 105.

XV. *God gives children.* God saith, 'I will multiply.' See Sec. 106.

XVI. *Many children are a blessing.* This is intended under the doubling of this phrase, *multiplying I will multiply.* See Sec. 105.

XVII. *Abraham had an innumerable seed.* This doubled phrase, *multiplying I will multiply,* is applied to him. See Sec. 107.

XVIII. *Abraham long expected things promised.*

XIX. *Abraham's long expectation was with much patience.* These two last observations arise from the Greek compound word, thus translated, *patiently endured.* See Sec. 108.

XX. *Abraham enjoyed what he waited for.* This is expressly set down Sec. 109.

Of three general observations inferred from Abraham's pattern, see Secs. 110-112.

Sec. 115. *Of God's conforming himself to man.*

Ver. 16. *For men verily swear by the greater: and an oath of confirmation is to them an end of all strife.*

This verse is here inserted as a reason of that which went before. So much is evidenced by this causal particle γὰρ, *for.*

Now two things were before noted of God: one general, that *he sware;* the other particular, that he sware *by himself.* The reason of both these is here rendered.

The reason of the former is taken from the end of swearing, which is to work such credence in men's minds as may take away all doubt about the thing controverted, and end the strife.

The reason of the latter is taken from men's usual practice in swearing, which is to swear by the greatest.

The apostle begins with the particular, which is the person by whom men use to swear; because the latter, which is the general, will better agree with that which follows, about the end of God's swearing, vers. 17, 18.

The apostle here inserteth the ordinary note of asseveration, μὲν, *verily,* because experience verifieth the truth of what he affirms; and withal he gives us to understand that this is a considerable point. And surely it is very considerable that God should conform himself to man, as this causal particle *for,* and the force of the reason couched under it, doth intend. This is further manifested by those passions, affections, actions, parts, and other like things appertaining to man, which God assumeth to himself, and in Scripture are attributed to God.

This God doth to condescend to us, and to help our weakness, who cannot so well conceive heavenly mysteries unless they be set forth by earthly resemblances: 'If I have told you earthly things, and ye believe not, how shall ye believe if I tell you of heavenly things?' John iii. 12.

1. This doth much commend God's fatherly respect to us, and tender care over us.

2. This should stir us up to give the more heed hereunto, that we may be the better instructed hereby. Let our dealing one with another move us to have God's like dealing with us in higher account. If man's swearing be regarded, how much more should God's? As God is infinitely greater in majesty, power, truth, faithfulness, and other like excellencies, so ought we to give more credence to God's oath than to any man's.

Sec. 116. *Of man's swearing, and the lawfulness thereof.*

This phrase, *men swear,* implieth an usual custom, which is not disproved, but rather approved; and that two ways:

1. In that it is here brought in as a ratification of that which God did. God sware, because men use to do so.

2. In that God herein conforms himself to men; but the righteous God will not conform himself to any creature in any evil.

Obj. Hatred, anger, jealousy, revenge, with other like passions, are attributed to God.

Ans. These are not simply evil in themselves. Being placed on their right object, and well ordered, they are good; they are in that respect fruits and effects of justice.

By this act of swearing attributed to men, as here it is, it appears that it is lawful for men to swear: 'Thou shalt swear by the name of the Lord,' Deut. vi. 13. Express injunctions in sundry cases are given about this point; as Exod. xxii. 11; Num. v. 19; 1 Kings viii. 31. Saints, guided by God's Spirit, have both themselves solemnly sworn, Gen. xxi. 31; 1 Sam. xx. 42, and also caused others so to do, Gen. xxiv. 3, and xlvii. 31.

Obj. Those are instances of the Old Testament.

Ans. Approved examples about general moral duties, which belong to all ages, registered in the Old Testament, are good warrants for Christians living in the New Testament. Such things are written for our instruction, Rom. iv. 29, and xv. 4.

Besides, this prophecy, 'Every tongue shall swear unto the Lord,' is a prediction concerning the times of the gospel, Isa. xlv. 23. This phrase, 'I call God for a record upon my soul,' which the apostle useth, 2 Cor. i. 23, sets down the form of an oath. Angels are brought in swearing, Dan. xii. 7; Rev. x. 6; but a pattern taken from angels is for Christians as well as for Jews.

As for men's swearing, it is a branch of their respect to God and man:

1. To God, in that thereby his name is invocated, and he worshipped; yea, also in that sundry of his divine excellencies are acknowledged; as his omniscience, omnipresence, providence in ordering all things, sovereignty, power, justice, truth, &c.

2. To man, in that in sundry cases his innocency is cleared, suspicions are removed, truth is manifested, and controversies are ended.

These respects which an oath hath to God and man give good proof of the lawfulness of it.

Sec. 117. *Of swearing lawfully.*

That which in general is lawful must lawfully be used; it is therefore requisite to consider what things concur to the making up of a lawful oath. They are in special four:
1. The person that sweareth.
2. The matter that is sworn.
3. The manner of swearing.
4. The end of swearing.

1. Two things concur to make a man fit to swear:

(1.) That he be of understanding and discretion, well to know what he doth. On this ground babes, idiots, frenzy persons, are not fit to swear.

(2.) That they have power to make good what they swear. As they who are under the power of others might not make a vow of those things which they that were over them might null or make void, Num. xxx. 3, &c., so neither may such swear in like case.

2. Four things are requisite for the matter of an oath:

(1.) That that which is sworn be a truth; and that both logically, as the thing is indeed, and also morally, as he that sweareth conceiveth it to be. That which Paul thus by oath affirmed ('The things which I write unto you, behold, before God, I lie not,' Gal. i. 20), were logically true, and morally also.

(2.) That it be possible. To swear to do an impossible matter, is to bring a necessity of perjury. Well, therefore, did Abraham's servant interpose this caution: 'Peradventure, the woman will not be willing to follow me unto this land,' Gen. xxiv. 5.

(3.) That it be just and lawful. Righteousness is one of the requisites in an oath, Jer. iv. 2. To swear an unjust and unlawful thing is to impose a necessity of sinning, and that either by doing that which ought not to be done, or by not doing that which he hath sworn to do.

(4.) That it be weighty, and such a matter as no other way can be determined. This may be implied under this requisite of an oath, 'in judgment,' Jer. iv. 2. The highest judge is appealed to in an oath. But he must not be troubled in trifles; they must be great matters that should be brought to Moses, the highest judge among the Israelites, Exod. xviii. 22. Much more must they be great and weighty matters that are brought before the highest Judge of heaven and earth.

3. Two things especially are to be observed in the manner of swearing:

(1.) That it be done deliberately, and advisedly. This is also intended under this phrase, 'in judgment.'

(2.) That it be done piously, with hearts lift up unto him by whom we swear. These cautions are joined together: 'Thou shalt fear the Lord thy God, and serve him, and shalt swear by his name,' Deut. vi. 13. 'Be not rash with thy mouth, and let not thy heart be hasty to utter anything before God,' Eccles. v. 2. The apostle putteth a *Ecce* before his oath, 'Behold, before God I lie not,' Gal. i. 20.

4. There are two general ends of an oath: 1, God's glory; 2, man's good: and that in reference to others, or ourselves.

(1.) God's glory is aimed at, when, in respect to him and his divine attributes, we make him our Judge, and answerably order all things in the oath, as may set forth the glory of his excellencies. 'Whatsoever we do, we must do all to the glory of God,' 1 Cor. x. 31. Much more this great and weighty matter of an especial appeal to him.

(2.) Man's good is aimed at in reference to others, when we swear to clear his integrity, or to declare that which is his right. 'All things must be done with charity,' 1 Cor. xvi. 14. Much more this great and weighty matter.

The good which we ought to aim at in reference to ourselves is, that our innocency may be justified, 1 Kings viii. 32.

A special end of an oath is to put an end to controversies. Hereof see Sec. 121.

Sec. 118. *Of an oath, what it is.*

That the fore-named direction about swearing lawfully may be the better observed, it is requisite to know what an oath is; and what the several kinds thereof be.

An oath is a sacred attestation, whereby God is made a judge of what is attested.

This word *attestation* signifieth more than a bare affirming or denying of a thing. It is a kind of confirming of a thing by witness,[1] in that he by whom one swears is made a witness of that which is sworn, Rom. i. 9.

This epithet *sacred* is added, because therein the swearer hath to do with God, making his appeal to him, and calling upon him; for a right Christian oath must be made by God. See Sec. 120.

God is in an oath made a judge in two respects:

1. In regard of his omniscience, who knoweth all things, past, present, and to come; secret and open, yea, even the secret intentions of the heart.

---

[1] μαρτύρομαι, *attestor*, I call to witness, or, I affirm upon witness.

2. In regard to his omnipotency, in that he is able to take such vengeance as may make all creatures fear to provoke him.

Hence is it that an oath is counted so strong a bond, and that it putteth an end to differences, because it is supposed that no man dares make God a witness of any untruth, or provoke such a judge to execute vengeance. 'It is a fearful thing to fall into the hands of the living God, Heb. x. 31.

Sec. 119. *Of the several kinds of swearing,*

An oath may be distinguished according to the ground, matter, and manner of it.

1. The ground of an oath is either imposed, ὅρκος ἐπακτός, *juramentum delatum, ab alio impactum;* or free.

An oath may be imposed by such as have authority, or such as pretend damage.

By reason of his authority Abraham made his servant to swear, Gen. xxiv. 3, and Jacob his son, Gen. xlvii. 31. Thus might the high priest under the law impose an oath, Num. v. 19, and public judges, Exod. xxii. 8. This power public judges ever had and still have.

Upon pretence of damage one neighbour might require an oath of another, 1 Kings viii. 31, 32.

A free oath is that which one on his own pleasure taketh, to move others the more to believe what he saith. This may and must be done when the matter makes to the glory of God, 1 Kings xxii. 14, or our neighbour's special good, 1 Sam. xiv. 45, or our own suspected integrity, 1 Sam. xxvi. 10.

2. The matter of an oath is something past or present, or else something to come. The former end of an oath is called assertory, whereby something is affirmed or denied. Thus David by an oath affirmed that he was in danger of death, and the widow of Zarephath denied by oath that she had not a cake, &c., 1 Kings xvii. 12.

The latter kind of oath, which concerns things to come, is called promissory, as when king Zedekiah sware that he would not put Jeremiah to death, Jer. xxxviii. 16.

3. The manner of swearing hath respect to circumstances; as the persons betwixt whom the oath is made, the place where, the time when, the occasion why, with other the like. Thus an oath is public or private.

A public oath is many ways differenced, as when a nation or congregation swear to God, 2 Chron. xv. 14; or when one nation sweareth to another, as the Israelites did to the Gibeonites, Josh. ix. 15; or subjects to their governors, as the Gileadites to Jephthah, Judges xi. 10.

A private oath is betwixt particular persons, as that which was made between Jonathan and David, 1 Sam. xx. 42.

The evidences of all the fore-mentioned kinds of swearing, being approved in sacred Scripture, give proof that they are all warrantable.

Sec. 120. *Of swearing by God alone.*

The proper object of men's swearing is thus set down, κατὰ τοῦ μείζονος, *by the greater.* Hereby God is meant, God alone. For men that swear are here considered as creatures distinguished from their Creator. Now all creatures in reference to their Creator are fellow-servants; and in that respect none so great over another as meet to be sworn by. Besides, all other creatures were made for man. God gave man dominion over all creatures in the air, waters, and earth, Gen. i. 28. The heavens are made a covering for him; the sun, moon, and stars to give him light; yea, the angels have a charge given unto them to keep man in safety, Ps. xci. 11, and they are ministering spirits for him, Heb. i. 14. Now that for which other things are is counted the best.[1] There being then among creatures no greater than man by whom he may swear, he may swear only by the Creator.

As God, because he had no greater than himself, did swear by himself, so man, because he hath no greater than God, must, when he sweareth, swear by God. This exclusive particle *only*, which Christ addeth to serving of God, Mat. iv. 10, is to be applied to swearing by God. For both these are joined together, Deut. vi. 13. This phrase, 'unto me every tongue shall swear,' Isa. xlv. 23, is exclusive; it excludeth all but God; and this, 'he that sweareth in the earth, shall swear by the God of truth,' Isa. lxv. 16.

1. Divine properties are attributed to that by which men swear; as, omnipresence, omniscience, searching the heart, supreme sovereignty, power to revenge, and the like, which are proper to God alone. That which the Lord saith of the last of these, 'To me belongeth vengeance,' Deut. xxxii. 35, may be said of all the rest: to the Lord belongeth omnipresence, omniscience, &c., even to him alone.

2. Divine worship is given to him by whom men swear, for there is divine invocation comprised in an oath, which is a principal part of divine worship.

3. It is a great debasement for man to swear by any other than God, in that he maketh himself inferior to, and less and lower than that by which he sweareth.

4. It addeth much to God's honour, to have such a prerogative proper and peculiar to himself.

Sec. 121. *Of the inviolableness of an oath, whereby differences are ended.*

One special end of men's swearing is thus expressed, 'An oath for confirmation is to them an end of all strife.'

The principal end of an oath is εἰς βεβαίωσιν, *for confirmation;* the other words are as a consequence following thereupon, which is to end and determine matters in question, whereupon differences and controversies arise.

---

[1] Τὸ γὰρ οὗ ἕνεκα βέλτιστον.—*Arist. Phys.*, lib. ii. cap. iii.

The word βεβαίωσις, translated *confirmation*, is derived from that βέβαιος, which is translated *stedfast*, Chap. ii. 2, Sec. 11. It implieth such a confirmation as is not rashly to be gainsaid and contradicted, for it must put an end to contradictions.

The word ἀντιλογία, translated *strife*, properly signifieth *contradiction*. It is derived from a compound verb ἀντιλέγω, that signifieth *to speak against*, John xix. 12 ; or *contradict*, Acts xiii. 45 ; or *gainsay*, Rom. x. 21. Answerably this noun is translated *contradiction*, Heb. vii. 7, and xii. 3 ; and *gainsaying*, Jude 11

The noun πέρας, translated *end*, signifieth the utmost border or bound of a place. In the plural number, πέρατα, it is translated *utmost parts*, Mat. xii. 42 ; and *ends*, Rom. x. 18. A privative preposition, ἀ, joined with this word ἀπέραντος, signifieth *endless*, 1 Tim. i. 4.

By these notations of these words, this phrase appeareth to be very emphatical, and they shew that the use of an oath is fully to resolve matters in question, so as thereupon no gainsaying is to be made, in that there remains nothing to be further said in and about that point. This is the main end of an oath, to put an end to differences.

Many are of opinion that two ends are here intended. One in this phrase, *for confirmation* ; the other in this, *an end of all strife*.

The former, they refer to a promissory oath, the end whereof is,

First, To bind him that sweareth to make good his word.

Secondly, To persuade them for whose sake he sweareth to rest on his word.

Thus an oath is *for confirmation*.

The latter they refer to an assertory oath, which is,

1. To bind the swearer to utter the whole truth, and nothing but truth.

2. To persuade others, that that which is sworn is such a truth as they may well rest upon. Thus an oath proves to be ' an end of all strife.'

When no witnesses can be brought to prove a thing, nor sure evidence given, whereby the matter in question may appear to be true, nor undeniable reasons on either side given in matters of doubt, great controversy useth to be made thereabouts ; but an oath useth to end this controversy, and that because God, who knoweth the truth, who loveth truth, who hateth falsehood, who can and will revenge falsehoods, is made a witness and judge. And it is taken for granted, that no man will provoke God to take vengeance on him.

By this it appeareth that an oath is a most firm, and inviolable bond. Men living rest on it, as Abraham rested on his servant's fidelity, when his servant sware to him ; this was a promissory oath, Gen. xxiv. 9. So David rested upon Achish's favour, when he thus sware unto him, ' Surely, as the Lord liveth, thou hast been upright,' &c., 1 Sam. xxix. 6 ; this was an assertory oath. Yea, dying men also use to rest upon an oath, as Jacob did when Joseph sware to bury him as he desired, Gen. xlvii. 31.

The apostle inserteth this relative, αὐτοῖς, *to them*, in reference to *men* before mentioned, for they cannot know others' intents for things to come, nor the truth of their words concerning things past, but by proofs ; and an oath in sundry cases is the only proof and evidence that can be given. Men therefore use to rest therein, and so they ought to do. God knows the truth of men's words, either in asserting things past, or in promising things to come, so as in reference to God there is no need of an oath, neither is it properly to him an end of strife. But men need this kind of proof, and to them it is an end of strife.

This general πάσης, *all*, is added, because there are sundry cases concerning things past, present, and to come, public and private, as was shewed Sec. 119, wherein there is need of an oath to satisfy and settle men's minds about the truth of them, and in them all men must upon an oath rest satisfied, if at least there be no apparent reason to the contrary. 'An oath is an end of *all* strife.'

Sec. 122. *Of the error of anabaptists in condemning all swearing.*

There are sundry errors contrary to the fore-mentioned doctrine of an oath.

1. Anabaptists hold that it is unlawful for Christians to swear. The contrary doctrine, concerning the lawfulness of an oath, is sufficiently proved before, Sec. 116.

Anabaptists herein shew themselves disciples of the ancient Manichees, who denied the Old Testament to be God's word ; and that, among other reasons of theirs, because it justified the lawfulness of swearing.

The main ground that anabaptists pretend is taken from these words of Christ, ' Swear not at all, neither by heaven,' &c., Mat. v. 34. The like is set down James v. 12.

Ans. They raise their argument from a mistake of the true sense of these Scriptures, for they take that to be spoken simply, which is intended respectively.

That Christ did not simply forbid swearing, is evident by this which he saith before in his sermon, ' Think not that I am come to destroy the law or the prophets,' Mat. v. 17. Both law and prophets do approve swearing on just occasion, as was shewed Sec. 116. Christ's main scope in that part of his sermon, wherein he interpreteth many of the commandments of the moral law, is to clear that law from the false glosses of the pharisees. Now concerning this law of swearing, the pharisees taught two things.

1. That they might not forswear themselves, which if they did not, they thought that the third commandment was observed.

2. That they might swear by some creatures, as by heaven, earth, &c.

Against these two errors Christ directed his speech.

Against the first thus: To swear unduly is against the third commandment, which saith, 'Thou shalt not take the name of the Lord in vain,' Exod. xx. 7. So as they who did not rightly observe the rules of swearing, took God's name in vain, and brake the third commandment.

Against the second thus: God's glory is some way or other manifested in his creatures, for 'heaven is God's throne, earth his footstool,' and so in the rest. In which respect, to swear by creatures is to dishonour God.

Anabaptists urge this phrase, *not at all.* To this I answer, that the clause may have a double reference.

1. To vain swearing, which is the point that Christ there laboureth to suppress, so as in this sense he intends thus much: be not moved on any occasion to swear vainly and unduly.

2. To swearing by creatures, then it intends thus much, swear not at all, by heaven or earth, or any other creature.

Again, anabaptists press this phrase, 'Let your communication be, Yea, yea, Nay, nay,' Mat. v. 37.

In answer to this, I grant that these phrases, *Yea, yea, Nay, nay*, do imply a simple affimation or negation, without confirming it by oath; but withal I say, that this direction is about a man's ordinary and common communication, when there is no great or weighty cause to affirm or deny upon oath.

Lastly, they insist upon this phrase, 'Whatsoever is more than these cometh of evil.'

Two things are answered hereunto:

1. That the occasions that force men to swear, though the oath be duly and justly made, come of evil, namely, of the evil disposition of them who will not believe a truth spoken, unless it be confirmed by oath.

2. That to use asseverations and oaths in ordinary speech is of an evil disposition, or of the devil himself, who is that evil one.

As for that which is written, James v. 12, we are to hold that the disciple who useth his Master's own words, used them in his Master's sense. It appeared that the errors about swearing, which were frequent in Christ's time, continued also in that time wherein the apostle James wrote his epistle, and therefore in his Master's words and sense he laboured to suppress that evil custom.

Obj. To justify swearing is to give liberty to common swearing.

Ans. 1. Not so. Doth justifying true religion give liberty to superstition?

Ans. 2. Necessary truths must not be concealed, much less denied, because they may be perverted. Some men have such a spider-like disposition as they will suck poison out of the sweetest flowers.

Sec. 123. *Of undue swearing by creatures.*

A second error is swearing by creatures. This is not only practised by the vulgar sort of papists in their ordinary speech (who commonly swear by the rood, cross, mass, Virgin Mary, Peter, and sundry other saints), but it is also used in their public courts, and solemn oaths, thus, 'by God and the Virgin Mary,' 'by God and the holy gospel' yea, it is also justified by their divines.[1] The Rhemists, in their annotations on Mat. xxiii. 21, have this gloss: 'Swearing by creatures, as by the gospel, by saints, is all referred to the honour of God, whose gospel it is, whose saints they are.'

Ans. 1. Their manner of referring that which they do to the honour of God is without and against God's word, and this conceit hath been the occasion of most of their idolatry.

Ans. 2. God's honour is simply to be referred to himself, and not relatively in and through his creatures: 'I am the Lord,' saith he; 'that is my name, and my glory will I not give to another, neither my praise to graven images,' Isa. xlii. 8.

Ans. 3. That manner of referring honour to God draws men's minds from the Creator to the creature. They have in such an oath their minds so fixed on the creature by whom they swear, as they think not on God.

Herein papists do justify pagans, who swear by their false gods, as Laban did, Gen. xxxi. 53.

Scholars in their ordinary grammar schools, yea, and in universities too, and in other places where they write or speak Latin, do justify the practice of heathens herein by using the very words and phrases of the heathen, which were concise forms of their swearing by their idols, such as these, *Hercle, Mehercle, Pol, Ædepol, Dii immortales*, with the like.

Profane persons among us do herein exceed both papists and pagans. Scarce a creature can be thought on by which they do not swear. They swear by the heaven, by the sun, by the light, and by all the host of heaven. They swear by all things on earth that are for man's use, as bread, meat, drink, money, fire, and what not. They swear by the parts of man, as soul, heart, body, head, and other parts. They swear by the body of Christ himself, by his blood, by his wounds, by his cross, &c. They swear by graces and virtues, as faith, truth, honesty, with the like. They swear by mere toys. As the Gileadites and Ephraimites were distinguished by their manner of speech, Judges xii. 6, so many pagans, papists, profane and pious persons, be distinguished by their manner of speech. Pagans swear by false gods, papists by saints, profane persons by mute things, pious persons only by the true God, and that on just occasion, and in a due manner.

Sec. 124. *Of swearing things unlawful.*

A third error is either to swear, or to cause others to swear, that which is unlawful. Into this error do papists fall many ways.

[1] Douay divines in their annot. on Gen. xlii. 15.

1. They swear, and cause others to swear, that which oft proves to many impossible, as perpetual continency; for they who admit any into religious orders make them vow and swear perpetual continency;[1] and all that enter into such orders among them, do vow and swear as much. Now it is not in man's power to be perpetually continent. To many it is a matter of impossibility. Christ speaking of this point thus saith, 'He that is able to receive it, let him receive it,' Mat. xix. 12. Hereby he implieth that some are not able; it is not possible for them to be continent, at least in a single estate, without the benefit of marriage.

2. They take children that have parents living into religious orders, without and against their parents' consent;[2] which children being so taken in, they cause to swear obedience to these orders; yet such children are not in capacity to keep that oath. They are under the power of their parents, who have authority to make void their oath.

3. They make many to swear things uncertain, as in the case of regular obedience.[3] They who are placed under such and such superiors must swear to do what their superiors shall enjoin them; though when they take the oath they know not what they will enjoin. The rule of this blind obedience is that which Absalom gave to his servants in these words, 'have not I commanded you?' 2 Sam. xiii. 28. On this ground have many zealots attempted to commit treasons and murders, and received the reward of traitors and murderers.

To this head may be referred oaths of giving what others shall desire, though they know not what those others will desire. The head of John the Baptist was cut off by this means, Mat. xiv. 7-9.

4. They bring sundry of their profession to swear things apparently sinful, as they who bound themselves under a curse to kill Paul, Acts xxiii. 12. Many popish Hotspurs did swear to murder Queen Elizabeth, whom God preserved from all their plots.

Sec. 125. *Of equivocation upon oath.*

A fourth error is to swear deceitfully, which is commonly called equivocation. This is a most undue kind of swearing, whereof papists are in a high degree guilty. There is a kind of verbal equivocation, when a word or sentence may be diversely taken, which is a rhetorical figure, as when Christ said, 'Our friend Lazarus sleepeth'; and his disciples 'thought that he had spoken of taking rest in sleep,' John xi. 11, 13. But the equivocation which we speak of is a mental equivocation, and that is when a man sweareth a false thing, yet so as he reserveth something in his mind which, if it were uttered, would make the speech true; as if one guilty with others be upon oath demanded whether he ever saw such an one, answereth, I never saw him (though he have seen him often and well know him), reserving this clause in his mind, *in heaven,* which expressed maketh the answer true; but it is nothing to the mind of him that propoundeth the question, neither can any such matter be fetched out of the words, so as such an oath cometh nothing short of perjury. The end of an oath in determining controversies would thus be taken away.

Notwithstanding those enormous consequences of equivocation, papists use to equivocate, not only all their lifetime, but also upon their deathbeds. Francis Tresham, one of the conspirators in the gunpowder treason, a little before his death protested upon his salvation, that for sixteen years before that time he had not seen Henry Garnet, superior of the Jesuits in England, and yet both the said Henry Garnet himself and sundry others confessed that the said Garnet and Tresham had within two years' space been divers times together, and mutually conferred one with another. Garnet being then asked what he thought of Tresham's protestation, answered that he thought he made it by equivocation.

This kind of deceit papists have taken from Arius, an ancient heretic, who, being to be freed out of banishment if he would profess the Nicene faith, caused the articles of his own heretical faith to be written in a paper, and put them into his bosom; and in the presence of those who were to take his protestation, immediately after the articles of the Nicene faith were read unto him, laying his hand upon his bosom, protested that he would constantly hold that faith. His judges thought that he plainly meant the Nicene faith, but he himself meant his own faith that was in his bosom.

Of equivocation at large, see Chap. xi. 31, Sec. 189.

Sec. 126. *Of dispensing with oaths.*

A fifth error is to dispense with oaths. Popes of Rome usurp this power, as might be exemplified in many particulars; but I will insist only upon his dispensing with the solemn oath of subjects made to their lawful sovereign, or, to use their own words, absolving subjects from their oath. This is evidenced by that declaratory sentence (commonly called a *bull*) which Pope Pius the Fifth denounced against Queen Elizabeth.[1] In the very title thereof this clause is inserted, 'wherein also all subjects are declared to be absolved from the oath of allegiance.' In the body of the bull this, 'The peers, subjects, and people of the said kingdom, and all others, who have any way sworn to her, we declare to be for ever absolved from that oath,' &c. O antichristian presumption! This is he 'that opposeth, and exalteth himself above all that is called God,' 2 Thes. ii. 4. For oaths are

---

[1] Ubi usus adfuerit liberi arbitrii, licet votum continentiæ suscipere.—*Bellarm. de Monac.* lib. ii. cap. xxxv.

[2] Licet filiis, invitis parentibus, ingredi religionem.—*Bellarm. de Monac.* lib. ii. cap. xxxvi.

[3] Obedientia religiosa rectè vovetur.—*Bellarm. de Monac.* lib. ii. cap. xxi.

[1] Camdeni Annal. Anno Dom. 1570. An. R. Eliz. 12.

made to God; thereby men are bound to God. When Zedekiah had broken his oath made to the king of Babylon, the Lord said, 'Mine oath he hath despised,' Ezek. xvii. 19. Oaths are made in God's name; God is made a witness and judge in that case. Whosoever, therefore, dispenseth with an oath, or absolveth the swearer from it, maketh himself therein greater than God, and exalteth himself above God; which is a note of antichrist.

Sec. 127. *Of perjury.*

A sixth error is perjury. Perjury in general is a false swearing, or ratifying a lie with an oath.

Perjury may be distinguished according to the distinction of an oath set down, Sec. 119. It may have respect either to matters past or to come.

1. When a man swears that to be true which he knoweth or thinks to be false, he forsweareth himself.
2. When a man swears that to be false which he knoweth or believeth to be true, then also he forswears himself.
3. When a man by oath promises to do what he intends not, that is perjury.
4. When a man sweareth to do a thing, and at the time of swearing intends to do it, yet afterwards, though he might do it, yet doth it not, he forsweareth himself.

Perjury in every case is a most heinous sin, and that to God, our neighbour, and ourselves.

1. God's name is highly profaned thereby, and his majesty vilified; for he is made like the devil, a patron of a lie. In this respect he is provoked to execute extraordinary vengeance on perjured persons, as he did on Zedekiah, Ezek. xvii. 19. These two clauses, 'Ye shall not swear by my name falsely, neither shalt thou profane the name of thy God,' Lev. xix. 12, so joined together, give proof that to swear falsely is to profane God's name. Hereupon a false oath is put in the number of those things that God hateth, Zech. viii. 17. Surely there is no fear of God in false swearers; they seem to outface and to challenge the Most High against themselves.
2. Neighbours are exceedingly beguiled by such; they are made to believe a lie, and to expect that which will never fall out.
3. False swearers pull much mischief upon their own pates; they make themselves liable to his vengeance who is a consuming fire. He threateneth to be 'a swift witness' against such, Mal. iii. 5, and to 'cause his curse to remain in the midst of his house that sweareth falsely by his name, to consume it with the timber and stones thereof,' Zech. v. 4. There is no one sin that sets the conscience more on a rack, for the most part, than this, and none that ordinarily bringeth greater infamy upon a man.

Sec. 128. *Of common and rash swearing.*

A seventh error is ordinary and rash swearing, when men on every occasion, almost in every sentence that they utter, for every trifle, swear. This is a grievous sin, and a sin crying for vengeance. This is the sin against which in special Christ giveth this direction, 'Let your communication be Yea, yea; Nay, nay,' Mat. v. 37.

1. Hereby God's great name, which ought always to be reverenced and honoured, is frequently taken in vain.
2. Frequent swearing cannot be freed from forswearing.[1]
3. Rash swearing is herein aggravated, in that it hath not such temptations as other sins. Some sins are drawn on by preferment, others by reputation, others by delight, others by gain, others by other like temptations. But what preferment, what reputation, what gain, can be got by swearings, what delight can there be therein? Much swearing is a note of a profane disposition. Herein a difference is made betwixt a pious and impious person; the one 'feareth an oath,' the other 'sweareth,' namely, rashly and frequently, Eccles. ix. 2.
4. Sore judgments are threatened against this sin, Hos. iv. 2, 3. This phrase, 'Because of swearing the land mourneth,' Jer. xxiii. 10, implieth that severe judgments were executed on the land for this sin.

Even this one sin giveth unto us just cause of great humiliation; for the land is full of oaths. All sorts do too much accustom themselves thereunto; courtiers, citizens, countrymen, university men, high and low, rich and poor, magistrates and subjects, minister and people, masters and servants, male and female, parents and children; yea, little children, so soon as they can speak. A man cannot pass by shops or houses, but if he hear men speaking, he shall for the most part hear them swearing. Custom hath made it so familiar, as it is thought no sin. But Christians, 'be not deceived, God is not mocked,' Gal. vi. 7.

For avoiding it, keep not company with swearers; accustom not thyself thereto, reprove it in others.

Sec. 129. *Of the resolution and observations of* Heb. vi. 16.

Ver. 16. *For men verily swear by the greater; and an oath for confirmation is to them an end of all strife.*

The sum of this verse is, the end of an oath.

Hereof are two parts:
1. A description of an oath.
2. A declaration of the end thereof.

In the description we may observe,
1. The manner of setting it down in this note of asseveration, *verily.*
2. The matter, whereabout is expressed,
   1. The act itself, *swear.*
   2. The persons who swear, *men*, and by whom, *the greater.*

---

[1] Gravissimum peccatum est falsa jurare, quo citius cadit qui consuevit jurare.—*Aug. Epist.* 89.

In setting down the end, we may observe,
1. The kind of end, *for confirmation*.
2. A consequence following thereupon, which is, *an end of all strife*. This is amplified,
 1. By the persons to whom it is an end, *to them*, namely, to them betwixt whom there is controversy.
 2. By the extent thereof, in this general, *all*.

Doctrines.

I. *God in swearing conforms himself to men.* In the former verses, God's swearing was set down; here the reason of it is thus rendered, *For men swear*. See Sec. 115.

II. *Weighty truths may with an asseveration be set down;* so doth the apostle this truth thus, *Verily*. See Sec. 115.

III. *It is lawful for men to swear.* This is here taken for granted. See Sec. 116.

IV. *God only is to be sworn by.* God is comprised under this word, *the greater*. See Sec. 120.

V. *An oath confirms a truth.* It is here said to be *for confirmation*. See Sec. 121.

VI. *An oath is to determine controversies.* This phrase, *an end of all strife*, intendeth as much. See Sec. 121.

VII. *Men ought to rest in an oath.* For to them it is an end of strife. See Sec. 121.

VIII. *An oath is of use in all manner of differences.* It is an end of *all* strife. See Sec. 121.

Sec. 130. *Of God's willingness to do what he doth.*

Ver. 17. *Wherein God, willing more abundantly to shew unto the heirs of promise the immutability of his counsel, confirmed it by an oath.*

The application of the former comparison, taken from men's swearing, is in this and the next verse set down; and therein the reasons of God's swearing are expressly declared.

This relative, *wherein*, in grammatical construction, may have reference to the last word of the former verse, which in Greek is, ὅρκος, *an oath*. But I rather refer it to the whole sentence going before, or to the point in hand; as if he had said, 'In which matter,' or, 'in which case.' In which case, of confirming a matter by oath, 'God willing more abundantly,' &c. This then sheweth that God conformed himself to man's usual practice, for man's good.

The word βουλόμενος, translated *willing*, implieth an inclination and readiness of one's disposition unto a thing, so as he needs no other motive thereunto; it is that which he desireth to do. Covetous men are thus described; 'they that will be rich,' οἱ βουλόμενοι πλουτεῖν, or 'they that are willing to be rich,' 1 Tim. vi. 9, for it is the same word that is here used. A covetous man needeth no other motive than his own inward disposition to seek after riches. It is said of Pilate, that he was 'willing to content the people,' Mark xv. 15. It was his desire so to do.

Thus God was of himself ready and forward to do that which is here spoken of, and that of his own mere free grace; yea, he was desirous to do it. He was no way forced thereunto.

This then setteth down two points:
1. The *cause* of God's binding himself: his mere will and good pleasure. This is the ground of all the good he doth to man, Mat. xi. 26. See more hereof Chap. ii. 4, Sec. 37.
2. The *manner* of God's binding himself. God did it readily, cheerfully. This shewed that he was willing thereunto. He had in his eternal counsel decreed to do what he did, and yet would by oath bind himself thereunto; and this he was willing to do. He doth willingly what he hath bound himself to do.

This is a point worthy of all admiration, that God should of his own will willingly bind himself for our sake to accomplish his own determined counsel.

Should not we now rest with confidence on this good will and pleasure of God?

This ground and manner of God's doing what he doth, namely, willingly, should be a pattern unto us to do what we are bound unto willingly and cheerfully. The apostle, speaking of his duty in preaching the gospel, thus saith, ' Necessity is laid upon me; yea, woe is unto me if I preach not the gospel! But if I do this thing willingly, I have a reward,' 1 Cor. ix. 16, 17. God loveth such, 2 Cor. ix. 7, and accepteth what they are able to do, 2 Cor. viii. 12. This David pleaded before God, 1 Chron. xxix. 17, Ps. cxix. 108.

Sec. 131. *Of God's superabounding in means to make men believe.*

God's willingness to do good to man is exceedingly amplified in this word of the comparative degree, περισσότερον, *more abundantly*. Of a like word, see Chap. ii. 1, Sec. 5. Here it implieth more than was necessary; and it is fitly inserted to meet with a secret objection that might be made against God's binding himself by oath. For it might be said, God is the Lord God of truth; even truth itself. There is no fear, no possibility of his failing in any of his words or promises. Why then should he bind himself by oath? For satisfaction hereof, the apostle seemeth to grant that what God did in this case was *ex abundanti*, more than needed, namely, in regard of himself, his own excellency, and his own faithfulness; but yet he did that which was needful in regard of man, by reason of his weakness and dulness, his backwardness to believe, and proneness to doubt, in which respect God's word, promise, covenant, and oath, are all little enough. That God's binding of himself was for man's sake, is made evident in the next verse.

Hereby we see God's tender respect to man's weakness; see ver. 13, Sec. 100. It makes him do more than otherwise needed; it makes him respect our infirmity more than his own excellency. His promises and threatenings prove as much. The former are to allure us to duty; the latter to keep us from sin. Such is the supreme sovereignty of God, as it is enough for him to declare his mind to his creatures; to command what he would have, to forbid what he dislikes. To use any means for the one or other is *ex abundanti*, of his superabundant grace and goodness. What is it then to add his oath to promises and threatenings? The like may be said of God's adding seals to his covenants; such are the sacraments, Rom. iv. 11.

What other reason can be rendered hereof than the abundance of his grace and mercy?

1. This ministereth much matter of humiliation to us, who do in a manner provoke God to draw the line of his goodness to the uttermost extent thereof, and to make him exceed and abound; to make him do more than needs, if we were not so dull and slow in believing as we are.

2. This should move us to superabound in our high esteem of God, and in all thankfulness and obedience to him. In special it should move us with all stedfastness to believe that which God doth so abundantly confirm unto us. Let us not make God's surpassing and superabounding grace to be in vain. Let us not provoke him to say, 'What could have been done more that I have not done?' Isa. v. 4.

3. By this pattern of God we are taught to condescend to others' infirmity, and that in doing more than needs. One immutable thing is sufficient to settle a man's mind, yet God used two immutable things. Though we be conscious to our own integrity and truth which we utter, yet if others question it, and require further confirmation, let us not stand too much upon our own credit, but yield to their infirmity, and, if required, add an oath, provided it be made 'in truth, in righteousness, and in judgment,' Jer. iv. 2. It cannot be thought but that every word of God should be most true. It is impossible that he should lie, yet he useth two immutable things. But it may be thought that man may lie; that is not impossible, Rom. iii. 4. If God then use two immutable things, much more may man.

Sec. 132. *Of God's manifesting his goodness to men.*

The Greek word ἐπιδεῖξαι, translated *shew*, is a compound. The simple verb δεικνύειν, *ostendere*, signifieth also to *shew*. When God by a vision manifested to Peter that all sorts of creatures were clean, Peter thus expresseth the case, 'God hath shewed me,' &c., Acts x. 28. So it is used Heb. viii. 5.

But the compound carrieth an emphasis. It signifieth fully, clearly, evidently, to manifest and shew a thing. This word is used where it is said of Christ, 'He shewed them (ἐπέδειξε) his hands and his feet,' Luke xxiv. 40. And where Apollos his convincing of the Jews is thus expressed, 'shewing (ἐπιδεικνὺς) by the Scripture that Jesus was Christ,' Acts xviii. 28, that is, evidently demoustrating as much. Thus God's oath added to his promise, doth most fully, clearly, and evidently shew and demonstrate the truth of his promise, which is grounded on his counsel, and the immutability thereof. God's counsel is the most immutable thing that can be; but to men it would not have appeared so to be, unless God had clearly manifested as much by his oath.

God will have nothing wanting, on his part, that may help to support our faith. He makes matters tending thereunto clearer than the sun.

His desire is that his promises may attain the end for which they were made.

What now may we think of those who discern not that which is thus evidently and clearly shewed? We have too great cause to judge, that 'the God of this world hath blinded the minds of them which believe not, lest the light of the glorious gospel of Christ, who is the image of God, should shine unto them,' 2 Cor. iv. 4.

Sec. 133. *Of heirs of promise.*

The persons to whom God hath so shewed his superabundant goodness, are here styled *the heirs of promise.*

They are accounted *heirs*, who have such and such a thing by right of inheritance.

Of the word *inherit*, and of sundry instructions thence raised, see Chap. i. 14, Sec. 160.

Promise is here metonymically taken for the reward promised, as was shewed ver. 12, Sec. 87.

Abraham, Isaac, and Jacob, are styled 'heirs of promise,' in reference to the land of Canaan promised, as a type of the celestial Canaan, Heb. xi. 9. Here, in special, are meant the children of Abraham after the spirit: 'For the promise that Abraham should be the heir of the world, was not made to Abraham, or to his seed through the law, but through the righteousness of faith,' Rom. iv. 13. Hereupon it is said to believers, 'Ye are Abraham's seed, and heirs according to the promise,' Gal. iii. 29. All that are 'justified' are styled heirs, Titus iii. 7; and all that are 'led by the Spirit,' Rom. viii. 14, 17.

This dignity they have, because they are united to Christ, in which respect they are styled 'joint heirs with Christ,' Rom. viii. 17. By virtue of that union, they are adopted of God to be his children, Gal. iv. 5, and also regenerate, 1 Pet. i. 3.

This phrase, 'heirs of promise,' implieth an *extent* and a *restraint.*

An *extent* in relation to Abraham, to shew that God's oath rested not only in him, but extended itself to all his seed, according to that which the Lord saith, 'I will establish my covenant between me and thee, and thy seed after thee in their generations, for an everlasting covenant, to be a God unto thee, and to thy seed after thee,' Gen. xvii. 7.

It implieth also *a restraint*, in opposition to such as are incredulous and rebellious. They are not accounted heirs of promise, though after the flesh they descend from Abraham.

Hence may be inferred two general propositions:

1. The promise of blessing made to Abraham belongeth to all believers.

2. None but believers have a right to the promise made to Abraham.

Concerning the first, God in reference thereunto thus saith, 'In thy seed shall all the nations of the earth be blessed,' Gen. xxii. 18. Hereupon saith Peter, 'The promise is unto you, and to your children, and to all that are afar off, even as many as the Lord our God shall call,' Acts ii. 39. And Paul saith of God's imputing righteousness unto Abraham, 'It was not written for his sake alone, that it was imputed to him; but for us also,' &c., Rom. iv. 23, 24.

There are two especial grounds hereof.

One is the constant and unchangeable mind of him that makes the promise, he is always like himself, and sheweth like favour to them who are of like faith, of like disposition, and like conversation.

The other ground is the fountain and foundation of all God's promises, Jesus Christ, our head and our Redeemer. He properly is the true heir of all God's promises. 'All the promises of God in him are yea, and in him amen,' 2 Cor. i. 20; that is, they are all propounded, ratified, and accomplished in him. By reason hereof, all that believe in him are co-heirs with him.

1. Learn hereby how to take the promises of God's word, even as made to us; to stir us up to rely on God who made them, and to subject ourselves unto his word. The like power and benefit of God's promises resteth in this particular application of them. Admirable is the use of faith in this case. It will settle the soul of a believer on God's promises made in former times, as stedfastly as if in particular they had been directed to him by name.

2. This meets with an objection against the certainty of a particular man's faith. Many granting that the promises of God are sure in themselves, deny that thereupon they may be sure of the benefit of them, because they are not particularly directed to them by name. But if that promise which was made to Abraham were intended to all heirs of promise, they that are of the faith of Abraham have as good right thereto as if the promise had been directed to them by name.

Sec. 134. *Of the benefit of God's promise restrained to heirs of promise.*

The other general proposition inferred from this phrase, *heirs of promise*, is this, none but believers have a right to the promise made to Abraham. This the apostle cleareth, by excluding such as are not of the faith of Abraham, and are not his seed after the spirit, in these words, 'They are not all Israel which are of Israel; neither, because they are the seed of Abraham, are they all children,' &c. On this ground he thus concludeth, 'The children of the promise are counted for the seed,' Rom. ix. 6-8; and again thus, 'They which are of the faith, the same are the children of Abraham, and blessed with faithful Abraham,' Gal. iii. 7, 9.

They who believe not, despise the counsel of God, Luke vii. 32.

This is set forth to the full, Acts xiii. 45, 46.

1. This strips the Jews of all vain confidence in their external pedigree. Because they had Abraham to their Father, they imagined that the promises made to Abraham belonged unto them. John the Baptist expressly noteth this their vain confidence, Matt. iii. 9. So doth Christ, John viii. 33. 39.

In that they were not heirs of promise, their confidence was built upon a sandy foundation. The like may be said of hypocrites, of loose and carnal gospellers, of ignorant and profane persons, and of all who want that grace which shews them to be heirs of promise; namely, a true, justifying, sanctifying faith. They who look for benefit of the promise, must first prove themselves to be heirs of promise.

2. This doth highly commend the grace and favour of God, to those who are the heirs of promise. The more rare a grace is, the more rare it is; that is, the less common it is, and in that respect rare, the more admirable it is, and the more highly to be prized, and in that respect also rare. The consideration hereof should fill the hearts of those who have evidence that they are heirs of promise with an holy admiration, and move them to say as Judas did, 'Lord, how is it that thou wilt manifest thyself unto us, and not unto the world?' John xiv. 22; and thereupon to have our hearts the more enlarged unto greater thankfulness. On such a ground did Christ give thanks to his Father, Mat. xi. 25.

Sec. 135. *Of the immutability of God's counsel.*

That which the Lord was pleased clearly to manifest to the heirs of promise, is here said to be, *the immutability of his counsel.*

The Greek noun βούλη, translated *counsel*, is derived from a verb, βούλομαι, that signifieth *to will*. Hereof see Sec. 130. Answerably this noun is translated *will*, 'by the will of God,' Acts xiii. 36. For God's counsel is his will. That which God willeth is the best counsel that possibly can be. The will of God is the ground of his counsel. Well therefore is the epithet, τὸ ἀμετάθετον, *immutability*, here attributed unto it.

The word translated *immutability*, is a double compound. The simple root, τίθημι, signifieth *to put*, or *to set*, Mat. xiv. 3; Acts xiii. 47; the single compound μετατίθημι, *to remove*, or *translate*, Gal. i. 6, Heb. xi. 5. This double compound, having a privative preposition, *ἀ*, prefixed, signifieth *immutability*, that which cannot be altered. It is found only in this and the next verse. It is here so set down, as it carrieth the force of a substantive; answerably it is so translated, *immutability*.

The manifestation of the immutability of God's counsel is here brought in as one end of God's oath. God sware, that it might evidently appear, that what he had purposed, determined, and promised to Abraham and his seed, should assuredly be accomplished; there should be, there could be no alteration thereof. It was more firm than 'the law of the Medes and Persians, which altereth not,' Dan. vi. 12.

It is here taken for granted, that God's counsel is inviolable. His oath was to manifest as much. 'My counsel shall stand,' saith God by his prophet, Isa. xlvi. 10. To like purpose it is said, 'The counsel of the Lord, that shall stand,' Prov. xix. 21; Ps. xxxiii. 11.

The grounds of the immutability of God's counsel arise from God himself: even from the unchangeableness of his essence, the perfection of his wisdom, the infiniteness of his goodness, the absoluteness of his sovereignty, the omnipotency of his power.

1. God in his essence being unchangeable, Malachi iii. 6, his counsel also must needs be so. As darkness cannot come out of light, so nor changeable counsel from an immutable nature.

2. If God's counsel be changed, it must be to the better or worse. To the better it cannot be. For such is the perfection of God's wisdom, as at first he determined matters to the best. To the worse God will not suffer it to be. If he should, it must be because he discerneth not which is better or worse, or careth not which of them fall out, or is forced to suffer the worse to fall out: but none of these can be imagined to be in God.

(1.) That God should not be able to discern what is better or worse, cannot stand with the infiniteness of his wisdom and understanding. Such is the perfection of God's wisdom, as he is said, not only to *have* counsel and wisdom, but also, by an excellency (*κατ' ἐξοχὴν*) and property to *be* understanding, Prov. viii. 14.

(2.) That God should not care whether the better or worse fall out, cannot stand with the infiniteness of his goodness. Did the Lord at first so order all things, as when he took a view of them, he saw them all to be 'very good,' Gen. i. 31, and is that sceptre, whereby he still ordereth all things, a sceptre of righteousness, Ps. xlv. 6, and can it be thought that he should not care how things fall out?

(3.) That God should be oversway'd with a superior power, and forced to suffer the worse to fall out, cannot stand with the absoluteness of his sovereignty and omnipotency of his power. 'Our God is in the heavens, he hath done whatsoever he pleased,' Ps. cxv. 3.

Sec. 136. *Of objections against the immutability of God's counsel answered.*

Obj. God's counsel is free, therefore changeable.

Ans. I deny the consequence. Freedom and immutability may well stand together. Though freedom be opposed to constraint, yet not to constancy. Freedom hath relation to the cause; mutability or immutability to the event. God's counsel is most free in the cause; but in the event, immutable. If it be said, that that which is freely done may be ordered this way or that way, I deny also this consequence.

Besides, that which in the beginning might have been ordered this way, or that way, and therein the agent shew himself a free agent, being determined, remaineth no more free to be altered.

2. *Obj.* God is oft said to repent: and that sometimes of bestowing favours, Gen. vi. 6, 1 Sam. xv. 11. And sometimes of inflicting judgment, Ps. cvi. 45; Jer. xxvi. 3, 13, 19.

Ans. Repentance is not properly attributed to God, but merely by way of resemblance, *ἀνθρωποπάθως*, after the manner of man. When men see cause to alter that which is done, promised, or threatened, they are said to repent, because they find some reason to alter their former purpose and determination. But that which God altereth about anything formerly done, promised, or threatened, is according to his first purpose and determination; as when God said to Eli, 'Thy house, and the house of thy father, shall walk before me for ever,' his purpose was to cut off that house for their transgressions, 1 Sam. ii. 30. And when God said of Nineveh, 'Yet forty days, and Nineveh shall be overthrown,' his purpose was to spare Nineveh upon their repentance, Jonah iii. 4, &c. In those mutable sentences, God changed not his secret counsel, but his revealed word, *mutavit sententiam, non consilium*. God's purpose of casting off Eli's house, and sparing Nineveh, was immutable, and manifested by the event. The promise of shewing mercy to Eli's house, and the threatening of vengeance against Nineveh, was a means to accomplish that determined counsel of God: in that by the promise of mercy, the sins of Eli, and of his sons, were so aggravated, as they made themselves unworthy of that favour; and by the threatening of vengeance, Nineveh was brought to repentance.

3. *Obj.* Though the secret counsel of God be immutable, yet the alteration of God's revealed will argueth changeableness.

Ans. No such thing, but rather contrary; for those and such like promises and threatenings had their secret and concealed limitations, according to which they were to be performed. The limitation of the promise was, If they to whom it was made should walk in the ways of the Lord. Such a limitation was expressed in the promise to Jeroboam, 1 Kings xi. 38, which, because it was not observed, the promise was not performed, and yet God's truth therein, yea, and thereby accomplished. Put this into syllogistical form, and it will be the better discerned, thus:

If the house of Eli for ever remain upright, it shall for ever abide before me;

But it hath not remained upright, therefore it shall not abide before me.

So on the other side, the limitation of God's threatening against Nineveh was, *unless they repent.* Such a limitation is expressed in God's threatening against Abimelech, Gen. xx. 3, 7. Read a pregnant place to shew the limitation of God's promises and threatenings, Jer. xviii. 7, &c.

4. *Obj.* God's word hath been altered in plain, simple declarations, where no such limitation is intended. The word being neither promise nor threats, but a narration of an event; as where God said concerning Benhadad, 'Thou mayest certainly recover,' and yet he died, 2 Kings viii. 10, and concerning Hezekiah, 'Thou shalt die,' and yet he recovered, 2 Kings xx. 1.

Ans. God's word, in these and such like places, was uttered, not of the event, but of the natural and ordinary course of secondary causes. In regard hereof, Hezekiah could not have recovered, unless God had, against the course of these causes, restored his life. And Benhadad might have recovered, if Hazael had not treacherously, with a murderous hand, stifled him. God's word then rightly understood was true; but the event had reference to God's secret purpose; for the effecting hereof God's word, uttered in another sense, was an especial means. For God's declaration of Hezekiah's desperate disease made Hezekiah pray the more earnestly; and his declaration of Benhadad's possibility to recover moved Hazael to murder him.

5. *Obj.* Divine attributes have been altered. 'He took his mercy from Saul,' 2 Sam. iii. 13. 'His anger endureth but a moment,' Ps. xxx. 5.

Ans. In these and other like places the causes are put for the effects; mercy and anger for the effects that follow from them. The altering of those effects argued an alteration in men, that they continued not to be such as they were before; but constancy in God's dealing with them, according to their carriage towards him.

Sec. 137. *Of useful instructions arising from the immutability of God's counsel.*

1. The foresaid immutability of God's counsel putteth a difference betwixt the Creator and creatures. These are changeable, as in their nature, so in their counsels. It is said of the most stedfast of God's creatures, 'he charged his angels with folly,' Job iv. 18.

Obj. Good angels never altered their counsels, nor will glorified saints in heaven alter theirs.

Ans. That is not simply in the immutability of their counsel (instance the evil angels that fell, and Adam in his entire estate), but in the assisting grace of God. So as their immutability in regard of the event, is an evidence of God's immutability, for it cometh from God. See more hereof in *The Guide to go to God*, or *Explanation of the Lord's Prayer*, sec. 227.

2. This gives just matter of humiliation and cause of complaint in regard of that woe which Adam, through variableness, brought upon himself and his posterity; for man is now variable and inconstant in all his ways. Variableness in religion and piety is of all the most grievous. Prophets much complain hereof, Isa. i. 21, 22; Jer. ii. 11, 13; so the apostles, Gal. i. 6, and iii. 1; 2 Peter ii. 1, 21. Many in our days, who in their youth and former years shewed great zeal and forwardness, have since changed their counsel. This variableness is also blameworthy in reference to our dealing with men.

3. This is one special point wherein we ought to be followers of God, namely, immutability in our good counsels and purposes. We must be 'stedfast and unmoveable,' 1 Cor. xv. 58, and 'continue in the faith grounded and settled,' &c., Col. i. 23.

That our counsels may remain immutable, they must be surely and soundly grounded on a good foundation, which is God's revealed will. We may not be rash and over-sudden in our counsels. Wise statesmen will long consult upon that which they inviolably decree. *Diu deliberandum quod semel statuendum.* Wherein our unchangeableness must be manifested, see *The Guide to go to God*, sec. 228.

4. God's immutability is a good ground of submission to the manifestation thereof. It is impossible that God's counsel be altered. It is therefore in vain to struggle against it; but to yield unto it is to make a virtue of necessity.

5. This is a point of singular consolation to such as have evidence of God's eternal counsel concerning their salvation: they may be assured hereupon that they shall attain thereunto. Sanctifying graces do give unto us assured evidence of that good counsel of God, 1 Cor. i. 7–9, Philip. i. 6.

Of God's immutability in general, see *The Guide to go to God*, secs. 226–228.

Sec. 138. *Of God's oath a kind of suretyship.*

The means whereby God manifested the immutability of his counsel is thus set down, *confirmed it by an oath.* The particle *it* is not in the Greek.

The verb ἐμεσίτευσε, translated *confirmed*, is derived from an adjective, μέσος, that signifieth *middle*, as Mat. xviii. 2, 20. Thence a substantive, μεσίτης, that signifieth *a mediator*: one that standeth, as it were, in the midst betwixt two at variance. In this respect it is said that 'a mediator is not of one,' Gal. iii. 20. There must be different persons, and they also dissenting, where properly there needs a mediator. Thus this word is oft attributed to Christ, the mediator betwixt God and man, as 1 Tim. ii. 5; Heb. viii. 6, and ix. 15, and xii. 24. Hence the verb here used, μεσιτεύω, *interpono me*, is derived. It is interpreted by some *interposuit*,[1] he *interposed*; by others *fidejussit*,[2] he *undertook as a surety*; our former English thus, *he bound himself*.

This word implieth that the promise which God confirmed was that which he made in and through the mediation of Jesus Christ, and on that ground was God the more willing to bind himself by oath; for all the goodness that God shewed to man since his fall was in and through the mediation of Jesus Christ.

Of God's respect to man in binding himself by oath, see ver. 13, Sec. 97, &c.

Sec. 139. *Of God's condescending for man's sake.*

Ver. 18. *That by two immutable things, in which it was impossible for God to lie, we might have a strong consolation, &c.*

An especial end of God's willingness to bind himself by oath, and thereby to shew the immutability of his counsel, is to settle and quiet men's souls in his promise. This conjunction ἵνα, *that*, whereby this verse is inferred on the former, manifesteth as much. By this it appears that it is for man's sake, and for man's good, that God thus bindeth himself.

As this confirms God's tender respect to man (whereof see Sec. 131), so it should stir us up to the more thankfulness, and move us the rather to make the right use of that which God so aims at for our good, which is stedfastly to believe his word.

Of this word ἀμετάθετον, *immutable*, see Sec. 135.

The two things here said to be immutable are God's *promise* and God's *oath*. Both these are expressly set down, ver. 13. The other verses following that are an explanation and confirmation of God's promise and oath.

This word of number, δύων, *two*, is not here to be taken exclusively, as if there were no other things of God immutable (of other immutable things, see *The Guide to go to God*, sec. 227), but because those two are especially pertinent to the point in hand.

In that the apostle expressly mentioneth *two* immutable things, he plainly confirmeth that which he intended under this comparative, περισσότερον, 'more abundantly,' namely, that God did more than needed, as is shewed Sec. 131; for one would think that one immutable thing were sufficient to settle a man's mind. If God were well known, indeed it were sufficient. But God well knows us, and therefore, in tender respect of us and our weakness, he thinks not one sufficient, but adds another thereunto, and that a stronger, namely, his oath to his promise. This he doth for our sakes, as was shewed before. See more hereof, Sec. 131.

Sec. 140. *Of the immutability of God's oath and promise.*

The two things here intended shew that both God's

[1] Vulg. Lat.   [2] Beza.

oath and also his single promise are immutable. We heard before of the immutability of his counsel, Sec. 135. This phrase, 'the Lord hath sworn, and will not repent,' Ps. cx. 4, proveth the immutability of his oath. Not to repent is to remain immutable. To like purpose tendeth this phrase, 'the Lord hath sworn in truth: he will not turn from it,' Ps. cxxxii. 11; and this, 'I have sworn by myself, the word is gone out of my mouth in righteousness, and shall not return,' Isa. xlv. 23. Of God's single word it is thus said, 'God is not a man, that he should lie; neither the son of man, that he should repent: hath he said, and shall he not do it? or hath he spoken, and shall he not make it good?' Num. xxiii. 19, 20. 'My words shall not pass away,' saith Christ, Mark xiii. 31. In this respect it is said, 'Faithful is he that promised,' Heb. x. 23.

By just and necessary consequence, we may hence infer that whatsoever proceedeth from the mouth of God is unchangeable, and that upon the same grounds upon which his counsel was proved to be immutable, Sec. 135.

1. A strong motive this is to stir us up without wavering to believe; this is the end why God addeth one immutable thing to another.

This, therefore, is seriously and frequently to be meditated on. Nothing is of such force to remove all manner of doubts as this. There are many doubts which use to arise, partly from our own inward corruptions, and partly from Satan's injections. Sometimes doubts arise from the exceeding greatness of the things promised; sometimes from seeming difficulties; sometimes from oppositions, lets, and incumbrances; sometimes from our own unworthiness. But if God's word and oath be immutable, who can imagine that it shall not stand? Put these two immutable things into one scale, and all manner of doubts into the other, and you shall find that the former will infinitely weigh down the latter.

2. A good precedent this is to make us unchangeable in our promises and oaths. For this end we ought well to ponder what we promise and swear, Ps. cxix. 106.

Rashness in this kind oft causeth repentance, 1 Sam. xxv. 22, 33. See ver. 13, Sec. 100.

Sec. 141. *Of impossibility in reference to God.*

The immutability of the two foresaid things is amplified by the *impossibility* of altering them, which is thus expressed, 'In which it was impossible for God to lie.'

This relative, ἐν οἷς, *in which*, is of the plural number, and hath reference to the two intended things, God's promise and God's oath. These are the things which are impossible to be altered.

Of the derivation and divers acception of this word ἀδύνατον, *impossible*, see Sec. 38. It is here taken in the most proper, simple, and absolute sense that can be. Nothing can be more impossible than that which is here set down, namely, for God to lie.

Quest. Can omnipotency stand with impossibility in anything?

Ans. Yea, in such things as imply impotency; or which proceed from impotency, as lying doth. Omnipotency is a cause of such an impossibility.

Obj. The notation of this word *omnipotent*, or *almighty*, implieth an ability to anything.

Ans. 1. An infallible conclusion doth not necessarily follow from the notation of a word.

Ans. 2. The foresaid notation is but from part of the word, even from this general particle *all;* but the word *omnipotent*, or *almighty*, is a compound, and affordeth a double notation: one from the general particle *all*, the other from the word of *power* or *might*. Join both together, and the notation may well stand; for it sheweth that he that is omnipotent or almighty can do whatsoever requireth power for the effecting thereof. But those things which arise from impotency may not be brought within the compass of omnipotency. It may well be said of them, without impeachment of God's omnipotency, God cannot do them; it is impossible that he should do them.

Sundry of those things which God cannot do are distinctly noted in *The Guide to go to God*, sec. 210.

Sec. 142. *Of lying as it is impossible to God.*

The verb ψεύσασθαι, translated *to lie*, is of the passive voice, but is of a natural signification. It is derived from an active, ψεύδω, which signifieth *to deceive*, or to frustrate, fail, and disappoint; so as to lie is to utter a thing with a mind to deceive. The Latin word, according to the notation thereof, signifieth *to go*, or to speak, *against one's mind, mentiri est contra mentem ire.* To utter an untruth is not simply to lie, at least if a man be persuaded that that which he uttereth is a truth; but to utter a thing against conscience, and with a mind to deceive, is a plain lie. Thus Ananias and Sapphira lied, Acts v. 3, 4.

That which is so uttered is styled τὸ ψεῦδος, *a lie*, John viii. 44; τὸ ψεῦσμα, Rom. iii. 7; and he that uttereth it, ψεύδης, *a liar*, Rev. ii. 2; ψεύστης, John i. 44. The titles of such as deal falsely and deceitfully are compounded therewith; as ψευδάδελφος, *a false brother*, Gal. ii. 4; ψευδαπόστολος, *a false apostle*, 2 Cor. xi. 13; ψευδοδιδάσκαλος, *a false teacher*, 2 Peter ii. 1; ψευδολόγος, *a false speaker*, 1 Tim. iv. 2; ψευδομάρτυς, *a false witness*, Mat. xxvi. 60; ψευδοπροφήτης, *a false prophet*, Mat. vii. 15; ψευδό-χριστος, *a false Christ*, Mat. xxiv. 24; ψευδώνυμος, a thing *falsely called*, 1 Tim. vi. 20. That which is here intended to be impossible for God, is to fail in performing his promise, especially that which is confirmed by oath.

We shall not here need to speak of that which God confirmeth by oath; for it was shewed (Sec. 140) that God's oath is inviolable; and it will by necessary consequence follow, that if it be impossible that God should fail in any word at all, it would much more be impossible that he should fail in that which he confirmeth by oath.

For the general, that God cannot in any case lie, or fail of his word, is evident by an epithet attributed to him, ἀψευδής, which we thus translate, *that cannot lie*, Titus i. 2. It intends as much as this phrase, It is impossible for him to lie. The foresaid epithet is compounded with a privative preposition ἀ, that implieth an utter privation of such a thing, and that there is no inclination thereunto. As 'God is light, and in him is no darkness,' 1 John i. 5, so he is truth, and in him there can be no lie. 'The strength of Israel will not lie,' 1 Sam. xv. 29; herein is made a difference betwixt God and man: 'God is not a man, that he should lie,' Num. xxiii. 19; for God to lie were to deny himself; but 'God cannot deny himself,' 2 Tim. ii. 13.

God's truth is infinitely perfect; it admits 'no variableness, neither shadow of turning,' James i. 17. Yea, God's truth is essential to him, so as his essence may as soon be brought to nothing as his truth to a lie.

Sec. 143. *Of inferences from the impossibility of God to lie.*

1. The impossibility of God to lie is a great aggravation of the heinousness of unbelief; for 'he that believeth not God, hath made him a liar,' 1 John v. 10; which is in effect to make God no God. This is the rather to be noted, to stir up in us a diligent watchfulness against this sin, which many account no sin, but a mere infirmity. See more hereof ver. 13, Sec. 100.

2. This is a strong motive to believe. A greater cannot be given; for as there is no will, so neither power in God to lie. Men who are conscionable and faithful in keeping their word and promise are believed, yet being men, they are subject to lie, Rom. iii. 4. How much more should God be believed, who cannot possibly lie! If God cannot lie, what promise, what threatening of his, shall not be accomplished?

3. This should make ministers, who stand in God's room, and speak in God's name, to be sure of the truth of that which they deliver for God's word, else they make God a liar, for their word is taken for God's, Col. ii. 13. They are God's ambassadors. An ambassador's failing is counted his master's failing. Therefore the apostle useth this asseveration, 'I say the truth in Christ, I lie not, my conscience also bearing me witness in the Holy Ghost,' Rom. ix. 1. False prophets are branded for prophesying lies in God's name, Jer. xiv. 14. For preventing this, we must hold close to God's word.

4. Though we cannot attain to such an high pitch of truth, yet every one ought to endeavour to be like God herein, namely, in avoiding lying. Lying is a

sin unbeseeming any man, but most unbeseeming a professor of the true religion.

General arguments against lying are these:

1. Lying is condemned by those who were led by no other light than the light of nature; as philosophers, orators, poets. St Paul quoteth a verse out of Epimenides, whereby the Cretians were condemned for their frequent lying, Titus i. 12. To brand them the more for this vice, *to lie* was in a proverbial speech said Χρητίζειν, to *Cretize*, or play the Cretians.

2. Every man's conscience condemns lying. If one be not impudent, he will blush when he tells a lie; and infinite shifts are ordinarily made to cloak a lie, which shew that he is ashamed thereof, and that his conscience checketh him for it.

3. No man can endure to be accounted a liar. No word more provoketh rage than this, *Thou liest.* It is the cause of many duels.

4. Lying overthrows all society; 'for what man knoweth the things of a man?' 1 Cor. i. 11. A man's purposes must be made known, and speech is the best means thereof. If his speech be deceitful, how shall his mind be made known? If not, what commerce can there be with him and others?

5. A man taken tripping herein will be suspected in all his words and actions. He that is not true in his words can hardly be thought to deal honestly in his deeds.

Arguments against lying in professors of the Christian religion are these:

1. Lying is expressly forbidden in God's word, Lev. xix. 11; Eph. iv. 25; Col. iii. 9. Thus it is against the rule of Christians.

2. It is against knowledge and conscience; for a liar doth deceitfully utter for truth that which he knoweth to be false.

3. It is a filthy rag of the old man, and one of the most disgraceful; and therefore first set down in the particular exemplification of those filthy rags, Eph. iv. 22, 25.

4. It is most directly opposite to God, who is truth itself, and concerning whom we heard that it was impossible that he should lie.

5. Nothing makes men more like the devil; for 'he is a liar, and the father thereof,' John viii. 44. A lying spirit is a diabolical spirit. A liar carrieth the image of the devil, and doth the work of the devil, and therein shews himself a child of the devil.

6. As a lie is hateful to God, so it makes the practisers thereof abominable, Prov. vi. 16, 17, and xii. 22.

7. Lying causeth heavy vengeance. In general, it is said, 'The Lord will destroy them that speak lies,' Ps. v. 6; in particular, both temporal and eternal judgments are threatened against such: temporal, Hosea iv. 2, &c.; eternal, by excluding from heaven, Rev. xxi. 27, and by thrusting into hell, Rev. xxi. 8. Memorable was the judgment on Gehazi, 2 Kings v. 27; and on Ananias and Sapphira, Acts v. 5, 10.

Sec. 144. *Of comfort arising from faith in God's promise.*

The end of the two immutable things which God used is thus expressed, ἔχωμεν, 'that we might have,' &c. These words in general declare that it was for our good that God so far condescended, as was shewed, ver. 17, Sec. 131.

The particular good aimed at therein is in these words, ἰσχυρὰν παράκλησιν, *a strong consolation*.

Of the verb παρακαλέω, whence this noun *consolation* is derived, see Chap. iii. 13, Sec. 143.

Among other acceptions, the verb from whence this noun is derived signifieth *to comfort*, Col. iv. 8. Hereupon the Holy Ghost, who is the original cause of all true sound comfort, is styled Παράκλητος, *the Comforter*.

The word of my text, παράκλησις, is sometimes translated *exhortation*, Heb. xiii. 22; and sometimes *consolation*, Luke ii. 25. So it is here taken.

The consolation here meant, is such as ariseth from a true, sound, stedfast faith; so as God added to his promise his oath, that we might more stedfastly believe his promise, and in believing the same, receive comfort to our souls. Metonymically, the effect is put for the cause; comfort for faith, which worketh it.

Hence it is evident that credence given to God's promise bringeth great comfort to the soul. Hereupon, saith the psalmist, 'Remember thy word unto thy servant, upon which thou hast caused me to hope;' he means God's word of promise, and thence inferreth, 'This is my comfort in my affliction,' Ps. cxix. 49, 50. David himself gives a good evidence hereof; for when he was brought into the greatest strait that ever he was in, 'he encouraged himself in the Lord his God,' 1 Sam. xxx. 6, that is, calling to mind the promise that God made to him, his soul was quieted and comforted. Such is the comfort and confidence which ariseth from faith in God's promises, as it maketh true believers to 'cast their burden and care upon the Lord,' Ps. lv. 22, 1 Peter v. 7, and to 'lay themselves down in peace and sleep quietly,' Ps. iv. 8.

A believer is freed from all undue fears, doubts, surmises, and such like passions as most trouble and disquiet the soul, so as a man must needs be much comforted therein. That which the apostle saith of love, may fitly be applied to faith, 1 John iv. 18. There is no fear in faith, but perfect faith casteth out fear. Christ opposeth fear and faith where he saith, 'Why are ye fearful, O ye of little faith?' Mat. viii. 26. Comfort being the effect of faith in God's promises, should stir us up to labour for faith; and it should provoke us to yield all due credence to the promises of God, both in respect of God's honour, whose truth is sealed up thereby, John iii. 33, and also in respect of the peace and comfort of our own souls. Well weigh how sweet a thing true sound comfort is, yea, and how needful in regard of the many assaults, troubles, and vexations whereunto we are subject. They who are troubled in mind and disquieted in conscience, and thereupon want this comfort, have it in high account, and earnestly desire it; for the benefit of a good thing is commonly better discerned by the want than by the fruition of it. Behold here the only means to find comfort in all estates, namely, faith in God's promises; wherefore carefully use this means. All other means are but as shadows without substance, or as dew which is soon dried up with the sun. Wherefore 'believe in the Lord your God, so shall you be established; believe his prophets, so shall you prosper,' 2 Chron. xx. 20.

Sec. 145. *Of strong comfort.*

The fore-mentioned comfort is much illustrated by this epithet, ἰσχυρὰν, *strong*. Of the notation and emphasis of this epithet, see Chap. v. 7, Sec. 37. It is here opposed to that which is weak and wavering, and full of doubts and fears. Hereby then is shewed that God would have our comfort to be steady, like the shining of the sun in a fair bright day, and not in a cloudy, gloomy day, when it may for a while shine forth, and then presently be obscured. Paul's comfort was a strong and steady comfort; for he saith, 'Our consolation aboundeth by Christ,' 2 Cor. i. 5; and again, 'I am filled with comfort,' 2 Cor. vii. 4. In this respect he styleth it 'everlasting consolation,' 2 Thes. ii. 16.

Strong comfort doth much commend the means which God hath afforded for that purpose; and it is exceeding useful against the many fierce and strong temptations which will much impair our comfort unless it be strong. A foundation set on the sand will soon fail when the rain falls and the floods arise, and the winds blow and beat upon the house that is built on that foundation, Mat. vii. 26, 27. There will arise doubts and fears from the flesh; Satan also will add his storms and blusterings, and will do what lieth in him to bereave us of all comfort. It is therefore requisite that our comfort be strong and stedfast, and that we be as a well-rooted and a well-grounded oak, which stands steady against all storms.

1. Let us not be content either with seeming or small comforts, lest we be like those who dream that they eat, but when they awake, their soul is empty, &c., Isa. xxix. 8. Such are many who have been long trained up in Christ's school, and lived under the ministry of the word, by which God's promises have been tendered unto them, and the infallible truth of those promises demonstrated, and yet remain as weak and wavering, as full of doubts and fears as at the beginning. How can such be thought to be of the kingdom of God? The things of that kingdom, though they be small in their beginning, yet will grow to an admirable greatness, Mat. xiii. 31, &c.

2. For our parts, let us do our best for attaining that which God would have us attain to, and for which God affordeth us immutable things, namely, strong consolation. This may be attained by a diligent exercising ourselves in God's word publicly and privately, by a careful observing his promises, and by a due consideration of God's faithfulness and immutability.

Sec. 146. *Of flying for refuge to God's promise.*

The parties here specially intended for partaking of the fore-mentioned end of God's confirming his promise by oath are thus described, 'Who have fled for refuge to lay hold upon the hope set before us.'

This phrase, *fled for refuge*, is the interpretation of one Greek word, καταφυγόντες, which is a compound. The simple verb φεύγω signifieth *to fly*, Mat. ii. 13. This compound is only twice used in the New Testament, here and Acts xiv. 6. It carrieth emphasis, and that in a double respect.

1. As it intendeth safety, and is translated *fly for refuge*.
2. As it intendeth diligence and speed, and may be translated *fly with speed*.

In the former sense it sheweth, that they reap strong comfort from God's promise who make it their refuge. They who fled to the city of refuge, there rested quiet and secure, and feared not what their adversary could do against them, Num. xxxv. 12, 15. In this respect David oft styleth God his 'hiding place,' Ps. xxxii. 7, and cxix. 114.

This will be a means to root out all confidence in ourselves or other creatures, and rest on God alone and his word; for he that fled to the city of refuge there abode, and went not out of it, Num. xxxv. 25, 26.

1. This excludes all proud, self-conceited justiciaries from strong consolation.
2. This teacheth us to acquaint ourselves with our own guilt and emptiness, that thereby we may be moved to fly for refuge to God's word. Till we see *that*, we shall never do *this*.

Sec. 147. *Of diligence in attaining the hope set before us.*

As the foresaid compound, καταφυγόντες, implies diligence and speed, it is a metaphor taken from runners in a race, who use to put on with all the speed they can. This sense seems to be the more pertinent in this place, because the words following have reference thereunto. For,

1. *To lay hold*, κρατῆσαι, hath reference to a prize, for which runners in a race make the more speed.
2. *The hope*, ἐλπίδος, here mentioned is that prize.
3. This word *set before*, προκειμένης, useth to be spoken of runners in a race, before whom the prize is set, Heb. xii. 1.
4. There is mention made of a forerunner, πρόδρομος, ver. 20.

1. Our old English translation have reference hereunto; for thus they translate it, 'Which have fled to hold fast the hope laid before us.' In this sense do most expositors here take this word.

Thus the word implieth, that diligence must be used for attaining that which is hoped for; hereof see Chap. iv. 11, Sec. 64.

The Greek word κρατῆσαι, here translated *to lay hold upon*, is the same that is used, Chap. iv. 14, Sec. 86, and there translated *hold fast*. As there, so here, it implieth perseverance in our Christian course, till we have attained to the end thereof. Of perseverance, see Chap. iii. 6, Sec. 68.

Hope is here taken metonymically for the thing hoped for, as promise for the thing promised, ver. 12. Sec. 87. That which was hoped for is the very same as was promised, even eternal life. For this is the reward that is here said to be *set before us*.

Sec. 148. *Of heaven a believer's hope.*

That which before the apostle termed the promise, he here styleth the hope, to shew the mutual correspondency betwixt God's promise and man's hope. What God promiseth man hopeth for; and man cannot in faith hope for anything but that which God hath promised. See more hereof in *The Whole Armour of God*, treat. ii. part vii. sec. 3; of hope, on Eph. vi. 17.

If it be demanded what that hope is which is set before us, a ready answer may be gathered out of the two next verses, which shew that it is heaven itself, and the glory thereof, which is hoped for.

Heavenly glory is that which true believers hope for.* Hereupon their hope is styled, 'the hope of the glory of God,' Rom. v. 2, namely, that glory which with God they shall enjoy in heaven. It is also styled 'the hope of salvation,' 1 Thes. v. 8, and 'the hope of eternal life,' Titus iii. 7; it is in this respect called 'the hope which is laid up for us in heaven,' Col. i. 5; and 'that blessed hope,' Titus ii. 13, an hope that maketh us blessed; and the 'hope which shall be gladness,' Prov. x. 28.

1. Herein is manifested a main difference betwixt the hope of them that are regenerate, and them who remain in their natural estate. The utmost of the hope of these men is within the compass of this world. Hereupon their hope is said to perish, Prov. xi. 7. For the promises of things to come belong not to them.

Besides, they want the eyes of faith, whereby things invisible are seen, Heb. xi. 27; they walk by sense.

2. Herein further is manifested the ground of a believer's boldness. 'The righteous are bold as a lion,' Prov. xxviii. 1. He is bold in peace and trouble, in safety and danger, in life and death; and well may he be so, by reason of the hope that is set before him. Hereupon 'the righteous hath hope in his death,'

* See ver. 20, Sec. 157.

Prov. xiv. 32. This is that hope, whereof in a proverbial speech it is said, Were it not for hope the heart would break. This proverb holdeth most true in the hope that here we speak of, the hope of eternal life. 'If in this life only we have hope in Christ, we are of all men most miserable,' 1 Cor. xv. 19.

Sec. 149. *Of setting reward before us.*

This phrase, *set before*, is the interpretation of one Greek participle, προκειμένης; the root whereof, κεῖμαι, signifieth *to be set*, Philip. i. 17. The compound is only used in this epistle, and that three times, here and Chap. xii. 1, 2. It implieth a setting a thing before us, as for direction, Chap. xii. 1, to shew how we should attain it; so also for imitation, to stir us up to use our best endeavour for attaining it.

It is set before us by God himself in his word. We may therefore have our eye upon this hope, namely, upon that reward which is promised, and thereupon we may well hope for it. As God hath set it before us, so may we set it before ourselves, and thereby be encouraged to hold out in our Christian course. It is said of Christ, that 'for the joy which was set before him, he endured the cross,' Heb. xii. 2.

If Christ used this means to encourage him to endure the cross, much more may we by this means encourage ourselves to do and endure whatsoever God shall call us unto. Yea, I may add, that we must have our eye on that that is set before us. 'For he that cometh to God must believe that he is, and that he is a rewarder of them that diligently seek him,' Heb. xi. 6. Thus Abraham 'looked for an heavenly city,' and Moses 'had respect unto the recompence of the reward,' Heb. xi. 10, 26. With this doth the apostle thus persuade Christians to hold out under all their pressures, 'Our light affliction, which is but for a moment, worketh for us a far more exceeding and eternal weight of glory,' 2 Cor. iv. 17.

1. The weakness of our flesh needeth this support. The spirit may be willing, when the flesh is weak, Mat. xxvi. 41.

2. The difficulty of our task, for doing and suffering what we are bound unto, requires such an encouragement; because 'strait is the gate, and narrow is the way, which leadeth unto life,' Mat. vii. 14.

3. The imperfection of the sanctification of the best, while here they are in this world, needeth such an help. For 'we know in part,' 1 Cor. xiii. 9, and of all other graces we have but a part. If we were now as Adam in his innocency was, or glorified saints now are, we should need no such means.

4. Reward, especially the hope here spoken of, namely, of eternal life, is the end of our practice, Rom. vi. 22, and of our faith, 1 Pet. i. 9; therefore we may have our eye fixed on it.

5. God having promised that which we hoped for, we may well set it before us. For 'whatsoever good thing any man doth, the same shall he receive of the

Lord,' Eph. vi. 8; and in due season we shall reap, Gal. vi. 9.

6. None condemns this point of prudence in temporal things. Who condemns the husbandman for sowing bountifully, that he may reap bountifully? 2 Cor. ix. 6. It is by way of commendation said, 'The husbandman waiteth for the precious fruit of the earth,' James v. 7. 'He that striveth for a mastery, doth it to obtain a corruptible crown,' 1 Cor. ix. 25. All tradesmen, merchants, mariners, soldiers, and others, have that which they hope for in their eye.

1. *Obj.* It is a mercenary disposition, and the part of an hireling, to do duty for reward.

Ans. Not unless they do it wholly and only for reward; or at least, principally, according to this proverb, *No penny, no pater-noster.*

2. *Obj.* This argues self-love.

Ans. Indeed, the eyeing of such a reward argues a spiritual self-love; but this is very commendable, as is shewed in *Domest. Duties* on Eph. v. 29, treat. i. sec. 58.

Though this be lawful, yet it admitteth sundry cautions, such as these,

1. That the principal end we aim at in all our endeavours be God's will and his glory. We ought so far to aim at this mark, as if our salvation and God's glory should stand in opposition (which never can in a right course), we should with Moses wish to be blotted out of the book of life, Exod. xxxii. 32, and with Paul to be separated from Christ, rather than God's glory be dashed. Our aim, therefore, at our own happiness must be subordinate to God's glory.

2. That the particular thing which we aim at be such as proceedeth from God's love and favour, and bringeth us into communion with him.

3. That we aim at a reward, not as a due debt or matter of merit, but as that which God on his mere grace promiseth.

4. That the longer we be trained up in Christ's school, we do the more acquaint ourselves with the beauty and excellency of that which God requireth of us, and thereupon to yield unto it, for conscience sake, for the Lord's sake, for the love of goodness itself.

Sec. 150. *Of inferences upon doing and enduring for reward's sake.*

1. The foresaid doctrine of having an eye to the hope set before us, is the doctrine of all reformed churches, taught by their preachers in their pulpits, maintained by professors of divinity in their chairs, and published in the books that are printed about this point; and yet papists falsely charge us to deny that Christians should have any respect to reward. The Rhemists in their notes on Heb. xi. 26, thus, 'The protestants deny that we may or ought to do good, in respect or for reward in heaven.' And Bellarmine[1] chargeth Calvin to deny that we should do good in respect to reward. But in those places which he quoteth of Calvin, there is nothing to be found to that purpose.

2. It cannot be denied, but that there are some of this perverse opinion, to deny the truth of grace in them, who are either incited to good by hope of reward, or restrained from evil by fear of future revenge. But this conceit we utterly detest.

3. The foresaid doctrine giveth evidence of the great indulgency of God towards man, in affording such allurements to incite us unto our duty.

4. The said doctrine manifesteth the hardness of their hearts, who are no way wrought upon, but remain like the smith's anvil, which is softened neither with the beating of the hammer upon it, nor with any oil poured on it. They are like those that Christ complaineth of, who were wrought upon neither by piping nor dancing, Mat. x. 17.

5. Let this part of God's indulgency towards us quicken us up to use this help; and thereupon both to take notice of the hope that God hath set before us, and also seriously to meditate on the excellency thereof, and frequently to meditate thereon.

Sec. 151. *Of the resolution of* Heb. vi. 17, 18.

Ver. 17. *Wherein God, willing more abundantly to shew unto the heirs of promise the immutability of his counsel, confirmed it by an oath*:

18. *That by two immutable things, in which it was impossible for God to lie, we might have a strong consolation, who have fled for refuge to lay hold upon the hope set before us.*

The sum of these two verses is, a declaration of the ends of God's condescension to man.

Hereabout we are to observe the inference in this word *wherein,* and the substance in the words following.

The foresaid ends are two:

One in reference to God himself, ver. 17, the other in reference to man, ver. 18.

The former is, 1, propounded, in this phrase, *to shew the immutability of his counsel.*

2. It is illustrated by sundry circumstances.

In the point propounded we may observe,

1. God's act, thus expressed, *to shew.*

2. The object thereof, wherein is set down both the kind of object, *counsel,* and the stability of it, in this word *immutability.*

The circumstances of the illustration are four:

1. The manner of God's doing what he did, in this word *willing.*

2. The measure thereof, *more abundantly.*

3. The means whereby he did it, *his oath.* This is amplified by the validity of it, in this word *confirmed.*

4. The men to whom he did it, *heirs of promise.*

[1] Bellarm. de justificat. lib. v. cap. viii.

The other end, which hath reference to man, is,
1. Propounded; 2. amplified.
In the point propounded is set down,
1. The kind of benefit, *consolation*.
2. The quantity of it, *strong*.
3. The fruition of it, *might have*.
In the amplification is set down the means used on God's part, and the persons for whom. The means are set forth,
1. By their number, *two things*.
2. By their stability: which is, 1, expressed in this word *immutable*; 2, confirmed, in this phrase, *in which it was impossible for God to lie*.
The persons for whose sake God so far condescended are described,
1. By their act, *who have fled*.
2. By the end of that act, *to lay hold upon*.
3. By the prize, *the hope*.
4. By the ground thereof, *set before us*.

Sec. 152. *Of observations raised out of* Heb. vi. 17, 18.

I. *God conforms himself to man.* This I gather out of the inference from this word *wherein*. See Sec. 130.

II. *God willingly doth what he doth for man.* For it is here said, *God willing*. See Sec. 130.

III. *God doth more than needs for man's sake.* This phrase *more abundantly*, and this word *two things*, v. 18, intend as much. See Sec. 131, 139.

IV. *God clearly manifests his good will to man.* The word translated *to shew* signifieth a clear and full manifestation of a thing. See Sec. 132.

V. *All believers are God's heirs.*

VI. *None but believers are God's heirs.*

The extent and restraint of this word *heirs* prove these two last observations. See Secs. 133, 134.

VII. *God's promise is the ground of believers' inheritance.* For they are *heirs of promise*. See Sec. 133.

VIII. *God's counsel is immutable.* This is here taken for granted. See Sec. 135.

IX. *God's oath is a suretyship.* The word translated *confirmed* intendeth so much. See Sec. 138.

X. *God's promise is immutable.*

XI. *God's oath is immutable.* These are the *two things* that are here said to be immutable. See sec. 140.

XII. *Matters of impotency are impossible to God.* See Sec. 141.

XIII. *It is impossible for God to lie.* This is here expressly affirmed. See Sec. 141.

XIV. *Faith in God's promise worketh consolation.* For it is God's word believed whereby we come to have comfort. See Sec. 144.

XV. *God would have our consolation to be steady.* This is the meaning of this word *strong*. See Sec. 145.

XVI. *Believers make God their refuge.* They are here said to fly to his promise for refuge. See Sec. 146.

XVII. *Diligence must be used for obtaining life.* The verb translated *fled* implieth diligence. See Sec. 147.

XVIII. *God's promise is the ground of man's hope.* Hope is here put for that which God hath promised, and man believed. See Sec. 148.

XIX. *God hath set a prize before us.* This is here implied under this phrase, *set before us*. See Sec. 149.

XX. *We may aim at reward.* It is reward that is set before us: and it is here mentioned, to move us to have our eye upon it. See Sec. 149.

Sec. 153. *Of hope an anchor of the soul.* Heb. vi. 19, 20.

Ver. 19. *Which hope we have as an anchor of the soul, both sure and stedfast, and which entereth into that within the veil;*

20. *Whither the forerunner is for us entered, even Jesus, made an high priest for ever after the order of Melchisedec.*

In these two verses the apostle describeth hope, whereof he made mention in the former verse. Which description is here brought in for two principal ends. One, as a farther argument, to press the main point in hand, namely, perseverance without wavering. The other is a fit transition from his digression to the main matter in hand, concerning Christ's priesthood. See Sec. 161.

The apostle's argument is taken from that help and means which God affordeth to us for persevering, which is a safe and sure anchor.

Though hope in the former verse were taken metonymically for the thing hoped for (as was shewed Sec. 147), yet here it may properly be taken for that grace whereby we quietly wait for eternal life.

The word *hope* is not expressed in the Greek, but fitly supplied in our English; for the relative *which* hath reference thereunto.

Of the description of hope, and of sundry other points about that grace, see *The Whole Armour of God*, treat. ii. part. vii. sec. 3, &c.; of hope, on Eph. vi. 17.

The use of hope is excellently set forth under this metaphor of *an anchor*, which sheweth the nature and use of it; that is, to keep us steady against all temptations, that we be not tossed up and down, and carried this way and that way, or overwhelmed by them.

Saints are in this world as ships in the sea. A sea is oft very troublesome and dangerous, by reason of great waves raised by gusts and storms of wind. Thus the devil and his instruments bring saints into many troubles and dangers. Now, as an anchor is of great use to hold a ship fast in the midst of storms and tempests, so as it cannot be whirled up and down, this way and that way, nor cast upon rocks or sands, but kept steady in the place where the anchor is cast, so hope is of like use to the soul; it keeps it in the midst of all temptations and troubles settled and stedfast, so as they cannot remove it from the promise of God, whereon this anchor is cast, nor split it upon the rocks of presumption, or drive it into the sands of diffidence and despair.

Hope is here styled the 'anchor of the soul,' to distinguish it from iron anchors used for ships. By *the soul*, is here meant the spirit of a man, even the regenerate part.

Hope is a special means to keep the soul safe, and in that respect styled 'the hope of salvation,' 1 Thes. v. 8; and 'the helmet of salvation,' Eph. vi. 17. It is one part of that spiritual armour whereby the soul is fenced, and whereby it is kept safe from spiritual enemies and assaults. In this regard it is the more excellent in the kind of it, and more necessary for the use of it. Of spiritual armour, and spiritual enemies and assaults, which make much to the amplifying of this anchor of the soul, see *The Whole Armour of God*, treat. i. part ii. sec. 4, on Eph. vi. 11; and part iii. sec. 9, on Eph. vi. 12; and treat. ii. part viii. sec. 5, on Eph. vi. 17.

By this metaphor the apostle sheweth that hope is of special use to keep the soul safe in all troubles and trials. 'They that trust (or hope) in the Lord shall be as mount Zion, which cannot be removed, but abideth for ever,' Ps. cxxv. 1. Upon David's professing that he put his trust in God, he maketh this inference, 'I will not fear what flesh can do unto me,' Ps. lvi. 4. In this respect the apostle saith, that 'hope maketh not ashamed,' Rom. v. 5. It doth not disappoint him of that which he expecteth, so as he should be ashamed. In this respect there is another metaphor, whereunto the apostle resembleth hope, namely, an helmet; whereof see *The Whole Armour of God*, treat. ii. part vii. sec. 7.

Hope doth, as it were, fasten the man in whom it is to the promise of God, on whom it is fixed, and to heaven which he hopeth for; as by the anchor and cable a ship is fastened to the ground on which the anchor is cast. Now God's promise is a most firm ground, and heaven is so high, as nor Satan, nor any of his instruments, can come thither to loose it. Hope, therefore, must needs be of singular use to keep the soul safe.

1. This giveth proof both of the necessity and also of the benefit of hope. Of both these, see *The Whole Armour of God*, treat. ii. part vii. sec. 9.

2. This also may quicken us up to get and preserve this needful and useful grace. Hereof see *The Whole Armour of God*, treat. ii. part vii. sec. 13.

3. The resemblance of hope to an anchor affordeth a direction for well using of hope. Hereof also see *The Whole Armour of God*, treat. ii. part vii. sec. 16.

Sec. 154. *Of the certainty of hope.*

These two epithets, *sure and stedfast*, are so expressed as they may have reference either to the grace itself, which is hope, or to the metaphor, whereunto the grace is resembled; for they are all of the same case, gender, and number. In sense, both references tend to the same issue; for if it be referred to the metaphor, it implieth that hope is not only like an anchor, but also like a sure and stedfast anchor.

The first epithet, $\dot{\alpha}\sigma\varphi\alpha\lambda\tilde{\eta}$, translated *sure*, is a compound. The simple verb, $\sigma\varphi\dot{\alpha}\lambda\lambda\omega$, *labefacto*, *everto*, from whence it is derived, signifieth to weaken or overthrow. The verb is compounded with a privative preposition, and signifieth to make fast and sure, or to keep safe, Mat. xxvii. 64–66; Acts xvi. 28. Thence the adjective $\dot{\alpha}\sigma\varphi\alpha\lambda\dot{\eta}\varsigma$, here used, is derived, which signifieth *certain*, *sure*, *safe*; and a substantive, $\dot{\alpha}\sigma\varphi\dot{\alpha}\lambda\varepsilon\iota\alpha$, that signifieth *certainty*, or *sureness*, or *safety*, Luke i. 4, Acts v. 23; and an adverb, $\dot{\alpha}\sigma\varphi\alpha\lambda\tilde{\omega}\varsigma$, which signifieth *fast, surely, safely*, Acts xvi. 23, Mark xiv. 44.

This epithet applied to an anchor signifieth such an one as abideth fast and sure in the ground, and suffereth not the ship to be carried away, but keepeth it safe.

Of the other epithet, $\beta\varepsilon\beta\alpha\iota\alpha\nu$, translated *stedfast*, see Chap. ii. 2, Sec. 11, and Chap. iii. 6, Sec. 68.

These two epithets are joined together with a double copulative, $\tau\varepsilon$ $\varkappa\alpha\iota$, which our English thus expresseth, *both* sure *and* stedfast; to set out more fully and to the life the certainty of hope, according to that which Joseph said of Pharaoh's two dreams: 'It is because the thing is established by God,' Gen. xli. 32. This, then, giveth evident proof that a believer's hope is firm and stable. See ver. 11, Sec. 80.

The former of the foresaid epithets being sometimes used for *safe*, and joined with the other, that signifieth *stedfast*, giveth us further to understand that the spiritual safety of a Christian dependeth on the assurance of his hope, as the safety of a ship dependeth on the sureness of the anchor; for 'he that wavereth is like a wave of the sea, driven with the wind and tossed,' James i. 6. Hereupon the apostle exhorteth to be 'stedfast and unmoveable,' 1 Cor. xv. 58.

Satan will not cease to raise storms against us by himself and ministers; if therefore our anchor be not sure and stedfast, we shall be exposed to very great danger.

This should the more incite us to give all diligence to have our hope established. See ver. 11, Sec. 80.

Sec. 155. *Of entering into that within the veil.*

The object of hope, or ground whereon the anchor of the soul is cast, is thus described, *which entereth into that within the veil*. The Greek noun, $\varkappa\alpha\tau\alpha\pi\dot{\varepsilon}\tau\alpha\sigma\mu\alpha$, translated *veil*, is a compound. The simple verb, $\pi\varepsilon\tau\dot{\alpha}\nu\nu\nu\mu\iota$, signifieth *to open*. One compound, $\dot{\varepsilon}\varkappa\pi\varepsilon\tau\dot{\alpha}\nu\nu\nu\mu\iota$, signifieth to *stretch out*, Rom. x. 21; another, καταπετάννυμι, obtego, to cover. From thence is derived the word that signifieth *a veil*; for the use of a veil was to cover, Exodus xl. 21, or hide a thing.

The word τὸ ἐσώτερον, interius, translated *that within*, is of the comparative degree. The positive ἔσω, intus, signifieth *within*, and this comparative *inner*, Acts xvi. 24.

In this phrase the apostle alludeth to the tabernacle or temple, wherein the most holy place was severed from the other part of the temple by a veil, Exodus xxvi. 33; 2 Chron. iii. 14. That within the veil was the most holy place, which was a type of heaven. Hereof see more on Heb. ix. 13.

The hiding of the most holy place with a veil prefigured the invisibility of heaven to us on earth.

The comparative may be used either by way of distinction, and that betwixt this and the outward veil, whereby the holy place was divided from the court appertaining thereunto,—in reference hereunto, this inner veil is called 'the second veil,' Heb. ix. 3; or else the comparative may set out the inner part; for the noun *veil* is of the genitive case, τοῦ καταπετάσματος, as if it were thus translated, 'the inner part of the veil.' Thus it setteth out the most holy place, as was noted before.

Of the emphasis of this compound, εἰσερχομένην, *enter into*, see Chap. iii. 11, Sec. 116; and of doubling the preposition in the verb, and with the noun,[1] as if it were thus translated, *entereth in, into*, see Chap. iv. 11, Sec. 65.

Here it implieth the extent of a believer's hope, that it cannot rest till it have attained to heaven, and till it be well settled.

Herein lieth a difference betwixt the anchor of a ship, and this anchor of the soul. That is cast downwards to the bottom of the water where the ship is stayed; this is cast as high as heaven itself.

Sec. 156. *Of hope of things not seen*.

This part of the description of hope, that it 'entereth into that within,' sheweth that hope is of things not seen. This doth the apostle expressly prove, Rom. viii. 24. As faith, so hope is 'the evidence of things not seen,' Heb. xi. 1; by hope we 'look at the things which are not seen,' 2 Cor. iv. 18. 'God hath begotten us again unto a lively hope of an inheritance reserved in heaven,' 1 Pet. i. 3, 4.

This God hath so ordered to try our patience, faith, love, &c., 1 Pet. i. 7, 8.

1. Herein lieth a main difference betwixt a Christian's hope and sight. This latter is of things visible, the former of things invisible.

2. Herein lieth a main difference betwixt the hope of true Christians, and mere worldlings, whose hope is only on the things here below, which are visible.

3. This teacheth us to wait for the things which we hope for. For 'if we hope for that we see not,

[1] εἰσερχομένην εἰς τὸ ἐσώτερον.

then do we with patience wait for it,' Rom. viii. 25. It is very requisite that we wait with patience, lest otherwise we fail of the end of our hope.

Sec. 157. *Of hope of heaven*.

The mention of the *veil*, in this phrase, *that within the veil*, further sheweth that heaven is the object of a believer's hope. The apostle's description of the hope of God's calling doth evidently demonstrate thus much, Eph. i. 18; but more clearly doth another apostle thus set it out, 'God hath begotten us again unto a lively hope, to an inheritance incorruptible,' &c., 1 Pet. i. 3, 4. The apostle therefore joineth these two together, 'the blessed hope, and the glorious appearing of Christ,' Titus ii. 13. It is hereupon styled, 'hope of salvation,' 1 Thes. v. 8; 'an helmet of salvation,' Eph. vi. 17. The apostle takes this for granted, where he saith, 'If in this life only we have hope in Christ, we are of all men most miserable,' 1 Cor. xv. 19; and in this respect, saith the wise man, 'the righteous hath hope in his death,' Prov. xiv. 32. Heaven is the highest and chiefest of all God's promises, it is the end of them all. For the purchase hereof Christ came down from heaven.

1. Herein lieth another difference betwixt the hope of saints and worldlings. The hope of worldlings ariseth no further than the earth; the hope of saints ariseth as far as heaven.

2. Hereby proof may be made of the truth and excellency of a Christian's hope. If it be fixed on things below, it is base and false.

3. In all losses and crosses, let us have an eye to this object of our hope. So long as heaven abides, we need not be over careful. This makes believers think themselves happy, when the world accounts them miserable.

Sec. 158. *Of Christ's running in our race*.

Ver. 20. The first part of the twentieth verse is an explanation of the place where a believer's hope is fixed, in these words, 'whither the forerunner is for us entered.'

1. It is said to be a place entered into, εἰσῆλθε, and in that respect passable.

2. It is entered into by πρόδρομος, *a forerunner*. Thereupon we may be directed how to enter.

3. That forerunner is *Jesus* our Saviour; so as we may with the greater confidence follow him.

4. He did what he did for us. This adds much to the strengthening of our confidence.

The word translated *forerunner* is in this place only used.

As our English, so the Greek also is a noun compound. The simple verb[1] signifieth *to run*, Mat. xxviii. 8. The preposition πρὸ, *ante*, with which it is compounded, signifieth *before*, Luke xiv. 4. The verb

[1] Τρέχω, curro. praet. activ. δεδράμηκα; aor. ἔδραμον; praet. med. δίδρομα; inde δρόμος, cursus, 2 Tim. iv. 7.

thus compounded προέδραμε, præcurrit, is translated *outran*, John xx. 4. For he that outruns another, runs before him. The word may have reference to such as run in a race, and so outrun others, as they get first to the goal.

The Greek word πρόδρομος, here translated *forerunner*, is by other authors put, not only for such as in a race outrun others, but also for a *messenger* sent beforehand upon a business; or for a *scout* sent to descry an army; or for a *quartermaster*, who goeth beforehand to prepare quarters for soldiers; and for an *harbinger*, who is to prepare lodgings for a king's court in his progress; and for an *herald*, that declares such a personage to be coming; and for any that *prepareth the way* beforehand; and for a *guide* that goeth before to direct others. In sundry of these senses, John the Baptist was styled a forerunner. He was as an herald that declared Christ was coming; as an harbinger to make the way plain before Christ's coming; and as a guide to direct people in the way to Christ, Mat. iii. 1, &c.

But as this metaphor hath reference to heaven, whither the forerunner here mentioned entered, it is proper to Christ alone. For he is that only one who through his own merit opened heaven, and first entered into it, and made it passable for others after him to enter thereinto.

In general it may, from this metaphor, be inferred,
1. That Christ was a runner in the Christian race.
2. That he ran therein before others.

The first point is evident by the obedience which he performed, and sufferings which he endured in the days of his flesh.

1. Christ would run in the same race with others, to sanctify the same unto them. For this is one benefit of all Christ's undertakings, that the like thereby are sanctified unto us. Christ suffered himself to be assaulted by Satan, that he might sanctify like assaults to us, if it please God to bring us thereunto. In this respect Christ is said to be ὁ ἁγιάζων, 'he that sanctifieth,' and believers to be οἱ ἁγιαζόμενοι, 'they who are sanctified,' Heb. ii. 11.

2. Christ ran in the race wherein we run, to make it the more plain and easy for us. This is another benefit of Christ's undertakings. For Christ, as he met with blocks and incumbrances, removed them out of the way, which otherwise would have hindered us.

3. Christ did this to draw us on more readily and cheerfully to run our race. Company in a work or way, is a great means of encouragement; it puts life and vigour into such as are ready to faint; a tired jade with company will be drawn on.

This giveth an evidence of God's goodness to us, who hath provided such an excellent help for that whereunto he calls. He hath sent his Son from heaven, and set him in the same race, wherein we are to run. This is the rather to be thought on, because, without this help, it is not possible to hold out.

Sec. 159. *Of Christ's running before us.*

The second general point, that Christ ran in our race 'before us,' may be taken two ways.

1. In regard of the absolute perfection and surpassing excellency of all that he did, he far outstripped all; and thus by an excellency he is styled 'a forerunner.' This is one respect wherein he may be said to be 'anointed above his fellows.' See Chap. i. 9, Sec. 123.

2. In regard of his undertaking to be a guide and pattern for us to follow him; thus is he styled 'the Captain of our salvation.' See Chap. ii. 10, Sec. 95.

This much amplifieth the former point of Christ's being a runner in the Christian race. For if thereby the way were made more easy, and believers drawn on more cheerfully to run their race, much more by this, that Christ is a forerunner and a guide; such a forerunner as espieth all obstacles, and impediments that lie in the way, and will remove them before we come at them; yea, such a guide as can, and will direct us in the right way, for he is 'the way, the truth, and the life.' Therefore the apostle contenteth not himself with setting a cloud, that is, a thick multitude of others running in this race before us; but adds this forerunner, and bids us in special manner to look unto Jesus, Heb. xii. 1, 2.

Let us therefore look unto Jesus. The Israelites in the wilderness so looked unto the pillar or cloud that went before them, that 'when the cloud was taken up in the morning, then they journeyed. Whether it was by day, or by night, that the cloud was taken up, they journeyed; or whether it were two days, or a month, or a year, that the cloud tarried upon the tabernacle, they abode in their tents and journeyed not,' Num. ix. 21, 22. The Lord Jesus, our forerunner, was the truth and substance of that pillar. As then in the wilderness he went before his church, in that shadow and type, so much more brightly and visibly in the days of his flesh, when he 'fulfilled all righteousness,' Mat. iii. 15, and for righteousness' sake 'endured the cross and despised the shame,' Heb. xii. 2. The Lord Jesus is set before us, as the object of our faith, and a pattern for our imitation. We must therefore look unto him with the two eyes of our soul, understanding and faith; and follow him with both the feet of our soul, obedience and patience. The church undertakes thus much in this prayer and promise, 'Draw me, we will run after thee,' Cant. i. 3. The prayer gives evidence of her understanding and faith; the promise, of her obedience. We must look with the foresaid eyes to Jesus, that we may receive life, vigour, strength, and all needful ability: for 'of ourselves we are not sufficient to think anything as of ourselves,' 2 Cor. iii. 5. We must follow Christ that we may be both guided in the right way, and encouraged to go on therein. Thus Paul followed Christ himself, and exhorteth others to follow him as he followed Christ, 1 Cor. xi. 1. For this end we must,

1. Inquire what way Christ entered into heaven.
2. Consider what good reason we have, and how great equity there is, that we should follow him. For this end these three points are among others to be duly weighed:
1. The dignity of his person that is our forerunner.
2. The perfection of that course which he took. No such pattern was ever set before us. Every saint had his defects; but Christ did no sin, &c., 1 Pet. ii. 22.
3. The reward which followeth upon following him, 2 Tim. ii. 11, 12.

Sec. 160. *Of Christ's entering into heaven for us.*

It is said of the foresaid forerunner, that he entered thither where our hope is fixed. The word εἰσῆλθε, translated *entered*, is the same that was so translated in the former verse, Sec. 155. It sheweth that Christ attained the end of his race, at which he aimed. This was heaven itself, whereinto we also shall enter, if in our race we follow this our forerunner.

This act of Christ being premised, immediately before his priesthood, sheweth that heaven is the place where Christ continueth to exercise his priesthood.

1. That was prefigured by the most holy place, Heb. ix. 11.
2. There is the mercy-seat or throne of grace, whereon his Father sitteth, Heb. viii. 1.
3. That is the only place of true happiness.
4. That was shut against us by our sins; but Christ ' by his own blood entered in thither, having obtained eternal redemption for us,' Heb. ix. 12. See more hereof, Chap. iv. 14, Secs. 84, 85.

To move us the rather to apply this entering of Christ into heaven unto ourselves, the apostle here expressly saith that he did it *for us;* so as a main end of Christ's entering into heaven was for our good. As he came down from heaven for our good, so for the same end he entered into heaven again. Indeed, for us, and for our good, he did and endured all that he did and endured. See Chap. ii. Sec. 83.

In particular he entered into heaven for us,

1. To prepare places for us, John xiv. 2, and xii. 26.
2. To make continual intercession for us, Rom. viii. 34.
3. To make us partaker of his own glory, John xvii. 24, Rev. iii. 21, 2 Tim. ii. 12.

We are utterly unable of ourselves to enter into heaven, John iii. 13; therefore Christ ascended for us to open a passage for us, and to bring us thither.

1. This putteth a difference betwixt the ascension of Christ, and of others that ascend thither. Christ ascended by his own power, and for the good of others. But all others that enter into heaven, entered by virtue of Christ's entering thither, and for themselves. This phrase, 'God hath raised us up together, and made us sit together in heavenly places in Christ Jesus,' Eph. ii. 6., is very emphatical, and sheweth that we are not only in hope, but in deed entered into heaven in the person of Christ, and that by virtue of our near union with him.

2. This is a strong motive to believe in Christ. If Christ did all for us, is there not then good reason for us to apply what Christ did and suffered to ourselves? Meditate hereon for strengthening your faith. If we apply not to ourselves what Christ did, we do not only lose the benefit of all, but also we make void, as much as in us lieth, the main end of Christ's entering.

3. From the particular we may receive a general direction, to apply to ourselves, as Christ himself, so his offices, actions, natures, properties, value, and virtue of what he did and endured; for all was for us.

4. This ministereth singular comfort against all the troubles which in this world we are subject unto. 'Let not your hearts be troubled,' saith Christ; 'in my Father's house are many mansions, and I go to prepare a place for you,' John xiv. 1, 2. Thus Christ comforteth his disciples against troubles, upon this consideration, that he himself, as a forerunner, entered into heaven for their sakes, even to prepare places for them. On this ground we may support ourselves against trouble, because Christ in heaven prepareth a rest for us; and we have no cause to fret at the honours whereunto wicked men are advanced in this world, in that Christ prepares honour enough for us in heaven.

5. This sheweth the reason of the assurance of our hope, that is an anchor cast within the veil; namely, because Christ hath entered thither *for us,* that we should be made partakers of the happiness there enjoyed. For this cause doth the apostle here make mention of Christ's entering thither for us.

This assurance then ariseth not from ourselves: but from that order and means which God hath appointed and afforded to us.

That we might not be mistaken about the foresaid forerunner, and his entering into heaven for us, the apostle doth expressly name him, under this title *Jesus,* which signifieth a Saviour: and this amplifieth all the fore-mentioned points, that the forerunner is a Saviour, and he that[1] entered into heaven for us as a Saviour. Upon such a ground did this apostle thus set down Jesus by name, Chap. iv. 14. Sec. 86.

Of this name *Jesus,* See Chap. ii. 9, Sec. 73.

---

[1] Qu. 'that he'?—ED.

Sec. 161. *Of Christ a priest after the order of Melchisedec.*

The latter part of this verse (in these words, *made an highpriest for ever after the order of Melchisedec*) is a pertinent and perfect transition betwixt the apostle's digression, and his description of Christ's priesthood.

Of his digression, see Chap. v. 11, Sec. 57.

This transition eyeth both that which went before and that which followeth.

In reference to that which he had delivered about the forerunner's entering into heaven, he here sheweth what an one he was: even the only true highpriest, who is for us in things pertaining to God. Hereby the benefit of Christ's entering thither is much amplified.

In reference to that which followeth, this transition layeth down the sum of the apostle's large discourse about Christ's priesthood.

He doth here resume the very words at which he broke off his fore-mentioned discourse, Chap. v. 10, that thereby we might the better discern how he returns to his former matter, and proceeds therein.

This is the third time that this testimony of Christ's priesthood hath been alleged, namely, chap. vi. 6, and 10, and here. And it is twice more mentioned in the next chapter, verses 17 and 21; yea, twice more, hint thereof is given, chap. vii. 11, 15.

It is a testimony that setteth down sundry remarkable points about Christ's priesthood; as,

1. The warrant that Christ had to execute this function, in this word *made*; which by the apostle himself is thus explained, 'called of God,' Chap. v. 10, Sec. 54. Christ was deputed by God to this excellent function. That this word *made* implieth a deputation or ordination to a function, is shewed Chap. v. 5, Sec. 24, where this word *made* is used to the same purpose.

2. The kind of function, expressed in this word *priest*. That Christ was a true priest is proved Chap. ii. 17, Sec. 172.

3. The dignity of that function, in this word *high*; which declareth that Christ was the chiefest of priests, see Chap. ii. 17, Sec. 173.

4. The everlasting continuance of this function; for he is here said to be *a priest for ever*. See Chap. v. 6, Sec. 29.

5. The singular kind of priesthood; for this phrase, *after the order*, implieth a peculiar kind of function.

6. The eminency of Christ's priesthood; for the mention of this person, *Melchisedec*, sheweth that Christ's priesthood was of all the most eminent. He was such an one as never any like him. Of the two last points, see Chap. v. 6, Sec. 30.

Sec. 162. *Of the resolution of* Heb. vi. 19, 20.

The sum of these two verses is a description of Christian hope.

Of the description there are two parts:

One setteth out the use of hope.

The other, the qualities of it.

The use of hope is manifested in a metaphor, which is,

1. Propounded; 2, amplified.

The metaphor, as propounded, is in this word *anchor*.

It is amplified by the kind thereof, in this word *soul*, which sheweth it to be spiritual.

2. By the interest we have therein, in this word *we have*.

The qualities are, 1, expressed; 2, confirmed.

They are expressed in two epithets, *sure and stedfast*.

They are confirmed by the place whereon that anchor of the soul is settled.

That place is, 1, generally propounded; 2, particularly exemplified.

In the general there is noted,

1. An act, *which entereth*.

2. A type, whereby the place was prefigured, *that within the veil*.

The exemplification of the place is by Christ entering thereinto.

In this there is,

1. An expression of the act itself (*is entered*) illustrated by the end thereof, *for us*.

2. A description of the person who entered.

The person is described,

1. By his proper name, *Jesus*.

2. By his functions, which are two:

One a *forerunner*, the other *a priest*.

The latter function is set out,

1. By the warrant he had to exercise it, in this word *made*.

2. By the eminency of his office, *high priest*.

3. By the perpetuity of it, *for ever*.

4. By the distinct order of it, *after the order of Melchisedec*.

Sec. 163. *Of observations raised out* Heb. vi. 19, 20.

I. *Hope is an anchor.* See Sec. 153.

II. *Hope keeps safe.* This is gathered out of the meaning of the first epithet, translated *sure*. See Sec. 154.

III. *Hope is stedfast.* See Sec. 154.

IV. *Hope keeps the soul safe.* It is an anchor of the soul. See Sec. 153.

V. *Hope is settled in heaven.* Heaven is the place that is meant under this phrase, *that within*. See Sec. 155.

VI. *The most holy place was a type of heaven.* That within the veil was the most holy place, which typified heaven. See Sec. 155.

VII. *Heaven is invisible.* It is *within the veil*. See Sec. 155.

VIII. *Hope is of things not seen.* For that within the veil was not seen of the people. See Sec. 156.

IX. *Christ ran in the Christian race.* This is implied under this word *forerunner*. See Sec. 158.

X. *Christ is a forerunner.* This is plainly expressed. See Sec. 159.

XI. *Christ entered into heaven.* This phrase, *whither he entered*, intendeth as much. See. Sec. 160.

XII. *Christ ascended into heaven for us.* See Sec. 160.

XIII. *Christ is Jesus.* See Sec. 160.

Six other observations raised out of these words, 'made an high priest for ever, after the order of Melchisedec,' are distinctly set down, Sec. 161.

Hebrews 7

Sec. 1. *Of the resolution of* Heb. vii.

The apostle in this chapter returneth to that mysterious matter which he had interrupted, Chap. v. 11, which was concerning Christ's priesthood, after the order of Melchisedec.

The sum of this chapter is, the excellency of Christ's priesthood.

This is set out two ways:
1. By way of similitude.
2. By way of dissimilitude.

The similitude hath reference to the priesthood of Melchisedec, from the beginning to verse 11.

This dissimilitude to the priesthood of Aaron, from verse 11 to the end.

The apostle doth the rather induce these two orders, because there never were in the church any but these two orders of typical priests.

The Jews had the order of Aaron's priesthood in high account.

The apostle therefore proves the other order of Melchisedec, after which Christ was a priest, to be far the more excellent, that thereby he might draw the Hebrews from the legal ceremonies unto Christ and his gospel.

The excellency of Melchisedec's priesthood is demonstrated two ways:
1. Simply, ver. 1–3.
2. Comparatively, from ver. 4 to 11.

The simple demonstration is, 1, propounded; 2, illustrated.

It is propounded, 1, by an historical narration of sundry passages registered; 2, by a mystical explanation of some of them, and others.

Matters of history are four:
1. The name of the high priest here intended, *Melchisedec*.
2. His offices. These are two: 1, *a king*; 2, *a priest*.
3. His actions:

These are of two kinds: 1, royal, he *met Abraham*, returning from his victory; 2, priestly, he *blessed Abraham*.

4. His prerogative, which was to *receive tithes* of Abraham.

Matters of mystery are of things either revealed or unrevealed.

Two mysteries are gathered out of things revealed. One from his name *Melchisedec*, that he was a *king of righteousness*.

The other from the place of his government, *Salem*, that he was a *king of peace*.

Five mysteries are gathered from things concealed.
1. That he was *without father*.
2. That he was *without mother*.
3. That he was *without descent*.
4. That he had *no beginning of days*.
5. That he had *no end of life*.

The illustration is by a resemblance of Melchisedec to 'the Son of God,' ver. 3.

The comparative demonstration is from the excellency of Melchisedec above Abraham, out of whose loins Levi, Aaron, and all their posterity came.

This comparative excellency of Melchisedec is exemplified in three particulars.

1. That Abraham paid tithes to Melchisedec. This was an act of inferiority, and that in Abraham to Melchisedec. It is amplified by the relation betwixt Abraham and Aaron. Abraham was the great-grandfather of Levi, from whom Aaron descended, and whose posterity was deputed to the priesthood. Upon this account Levi and all his posterity were in the loins of Abraham, and in him paid tithes to Melchisedec.

The argument thus lieth:

That priesthood which received tithes of others is more excellent than that which paid tithes thereto;

But Melchisedec received in Abraham tithes of Levi, Aaron, and all their posterity;

Therefore Melchisedec's priesthood was the more excellent, ver. 4–6.

2. That Melchisedec blessed Abraham. This is an act of eminency and superiority; therefore Melchisedec was greater than Abraham, and by consequence greater than they who descended from Abraham, verses 6, 7.

3. That Melchisedec ever liveth, but all the Levitical priests died; therefore Melchisedec must needs be greater than Aaron and all the Levitical priests, ver. 8.

The extent of the first argument unto Levi and his posterity is asserted, verses 9, 10.

The dissimilitude betwixt Christ's priesthood and Aaron's is largely amplified in the remainder of this chapter.

The dissimilitude betwixt Christ's and the Levitical priesthood consists in this: that the Levitical priesthood was imperfect and insufficient, but Christ's every way perfect and all-sufficient; yea, the apostle distinctly noteth in every branch of the insufficiency of the Levitical priesthood, a sufficient and an abundant supply in and by Christ's priesthood.

This is exemplified in seven particulars.

1. The change of the Levitical priesthood. There was another order of priesthood to succeed the Levitical. Therefore the Levitical was imperfect. For that which is perfect needs not be altered, ver. 11.

The consequence is confirmed by this, that the change of the priesthood presupposeth the change of the law, ver. 12.

The proposition, that the Levitical priesthood was changed by a priesthood of another order, is hereby proved, that Christ, the other priest, was of another tribe (verses 13, 14), and that he was after the order of Melchisedec, ver. 15.

2. The weakness and unprofitableness of the Levitical priesthood, which is made up by the efficacy of Christ's priesthood, verses 16–19.

3. The manner of instituting the one and the other priesthood. The Levitical priesthood was instituted without an oath; but Christ's most solemnly by an oath, verses 20, 21.

Hence is inferred the excellency of the New Testament, ver. 22.

4. The mortality of the Levitical priests; but Christ ever remains, verses 23, 24.

Hence is inferred the fulness of that salvation which Christ hath wrought, ver. 25.

5. The sinfulness of the Levitical priests, which forced them to offer for themselves. But Christ was perfectly pure, ver. 26.

6. The reiteration of Levitical sacrifices. But Christ's was but once offered, ver. 27.

7. The nature of Levitical priests: they were but men. Christ was the Son, namely, of God, ver. 28.

Sec. 2. *Of Melchisedec, who he was.* Heb. vii. 1–3.

Ver. 1. *For this Melchisedec, king of Salem, priest of the most high God, who met Abraham returning from the slaughter of the kings, and blessed him;*

2. *To whom also Abraham gave a tenth part of all: first being, by interpretation, King of righteousness, and after that also, King of Salem, which is, King of peace:*

3. *Without father, without mother, without descent, having neither beginning of days, nor end of life; but, made like unto the Son of God, abideth a priest continually.*

The first particle (as our English hath it) is a causal conjunction, γὰρ, *for*, and implieth a reason of that which goeth before: which was, that Christ was 'an high priest after the order of Melchisedec.' The apostle here sheweth the reason why Christ was a priest after that order; even because Melchisedec was such an one as is here described.

The mystery concerning the order of Melchisedec, as it is a most excellent and useful mystery, so it is a very deep and difficult one; therefore the apostle doth largely and distinctly propound and expound it. For useful and hard mysteries are to be explained, otherwise the benefit of them will be lost.

The notation of this name *Melchisedec* is given by the apostle, ver. 2. Here therefore we will consider who is the person that is thus styled.

There ever hath been in the Christian church great difference about this point, and that by reason of the transcendent points here delivered by the apostle about him.

1. Some of old, not determining in particular who he was, have notwithstanding avouched him to be a person μειζότερον τοῦ Χριστοῦ,[1] greater than Christ, and that because he is said to be after the order of Melchisedec.

Ans. Though there may seem to be some modesty in this, that they determine not who he was, yet it is high presumption to assert him to be greater than Christ. Christ was true God. If greater than Christ, greater than God. Their own argument refuteth them; for Christ being high priest after the order of Melchisedec, Melchisedec was a type of Christ, and Christ the truth of that type; but the truth is greater than the type.

2. Others[2] hold that the Holy Ghost was this Melchisedec.

Ans. (1.) The Holy Ghost was never incarnate; but Melchisedec here mentioned was a true man, for he lived among men, and was a king of men.

(2.) The Holy Ghost cannot be said to be taken from among men, as every high priest is, Heb. v. 1. And it is necessary that he should be so, because he was to be as a middle person between God and man, 1 Tim. ii. 5.

(3.) The Holy Ghost was not a type of Christ; for a type must be visible, and a type is inferior to the truth.

3. Others[3] are of opinion that Melchisedec was an angel.

Ans. This cannot stand with the description of an high priest set down Chap. v. 1. An high priest must be taken from among men; neither can it stand with the history noted of Melchisedec, Gen. xiv. 18, &c.

4. There are that hold Melchisedec to be one of Ham's stock, because he was king of Salem, which was in Canaan. Many both ancient and latter divines are of this opinion.

Ans. Ham with his posterity were cursed, Gen. ix. 25; and it is not probable that any of that cursed generation should be of place and authority to bless Abraham, the father of the faithful.

As for their argument taken from Salem in Canaan, nothing hindereth but that one that was no Canaanite might live and reign there, at that time that is here intended, which was more than four hundred years before Joshua subdued the Canaanites.

---

[1] Epipha. Advers. Hær., lib. ii. her. 55.

[2] Ὁμὲν Ἱέραξ τοῦτον νομίζει Μελχισιδὲκ εἶναι τὸ Πνεῦμα τὸ ἅγιον.—*Epiph. loc. citat.* Melchisedechi tanta fuit excellentia ut a nonnullis dubitetur utrum homo an Angelus fuerit.—*Aug.* Quæst super, Gen. lib. i. cap. 70.

[3] Iren. Euseb. Calv. Musc. Merc. Jun. Perer.

5. The most common received opinion is, that Shem the son of Noah was this Melchisedec.

Our countryman, Mr Broughton, produceth two and twenty rabbis of the Jews to be of this opinion, and inferreth that it was the common opinion of the Jews.

Epiphanius reckoneth this among heresies, which he ascribeth to the Samaritans, and laboureth to disprove it by an argument, wherein he himself is much mistaken. For he affirmeth that Melchisedec[1] died eight and twenty or thirty years before Abraham rescued his brother Lot. But if the six hundred years which Shem lived be duly computed with the genealogy of Shem's posterity set down Gen. xi. 10, &c., it will be found that Shem lived about an hundred years in Isaac's time. That which deceived the foresaid, and other Greek fathers, was the false computation of the years of the patriarchs made by the LXX.

Some of the arguments to prove that this Melchisedec was Shem are these,

1. Shem lived an hundred years before the flood; and none born before that time was then living. So as his parentage might well then be unknown.

2. He was the most honourable then in the world, so as he might well be counted greater than Abraham.

3. Shem was a most righteous man, and in that respect the title Melchisedec might be given unto him. See Sec. 19.

4. God is styled 'the Lord God of Shem,' Gen ix. 26, so as he may fitly be called the ' priest of the most high God,' Gen. xiv. 18.

5. Shem was that stock from whence Christ according to the flesh descended, Luke iii. 36.

6. To Shem was the promise made, Gen. ix. 26, and in that respect, he the fittest to bless others.

7. Shem was the root of the church, even that root from whence Abraham and his posterity sprouted, so as he might well be accounted greater than Abraham, and fit to bless him.

8. All the following branches of the description of Melchisedec, may fitly be applied to Shem, as will appear in opening the particulars.

On these grounds I dare not gainsay this opinion.

6. There are that think it the safest to determine none at all to be this Melchisedec, but rather to speak and think of him as of one unknown, whose father, mother, kindred, age, and generation are not made known; and this the rather, because he is here so transcendently described.

This particular instance of Melchisedec giveth proof of profound mysteries to be couched in the sacred Scriptures, which require all the means that can be used for finding out the true and full sense of them. Of which means see *The Whole Armour of God*, treat. ii. part viii.; of God's word, on Eph. vi. 17, sec. 3.

Sec. 3. *Of monarchical government.*

The foresaid Melchisedec is here said to be *a king.*

[1] Qu. 'Shem'?—ED.

King is a title of sovereignty and superiority, as the notation of the word in all the three learned languages implieth.

The Hebrew word, מלך, *rex*, is derived from a verb[1] that signifeth to go, yea, and to go before. It hath the notation from another word בלך, *baculus*, that signifeth *a staff*. Now the use of a staff is to lean upon, or to defend one, or to drive away such as may be hurtful. A state is supported, provided for, and defended against enemies by a king, who is in that respect a stay and staff for it.

In Greek the notation of the word βασιλεὺς,[2] translated *king*, implieth that the stability of a state resteth on him.

In Latin, the word king, *rex à regendo*, is derived from a verb that signifeth to rule and reign.

In that this title, *king*, is given to Melchisedec, who was born an hundred years before the flood, who also was a righteous man, and took upon him nothing but that which was right, and belonged to him, it appears that monarchical government and kingly authority is both ancient and warrantable.

The choice which not only God's people, but also God himself, hath made of sundry kings, and the directions which he hath given unto them, how to manage their authority, and the promises which he hath made to them, and blessings which he hath bestowed on them, do all prove the lawfulness of this high function, for God would not call men unto unlawful callings. But most clear doth the apostle make this point, where he exhorteth Christians to be 'subject unto the higher powers;' and that on this ground, that 'there is no power but of God,' Rom. xiii. 1. Another apostle in this case of subjection nameth 'the king,' and that 'as supreme,' 1 Peter ii. 13.

The very heathen, by the light of nature, discerned the equity of this point. As most states in all ages have been after that manner governed, so their wise and learned philosophers have, upon discussing the point,[3] concluded a monarchical government to be the best kind of government.

Nature hath instilled thus much into sundry unreasonable creatures. The bees have a kind of king among them; so herds and flocks of great and small cattle. The cranes are said to follow one guide.[4]

By this kind of government will unity, peace, and order, which are the very nerves, whereby polities are fastened together, be better preserved. Where there are many of equal authority, especially if they have not one over them, to overrule them all, there cannot but be many distractions. *Quot homines tot sententiæ*; So many men, so many minds.

[1] הלך *inde* מלך *regnavit*. Regis est præire populo.
[2] Quasi βάσις τοῦ λαοῦ.
[3] Plat. de Repub. Dialog. 8. Arist. de Rep. lib. iii. cap. xiv. Plutar. Comment. An tract. sen. resp. sit.
[4] Rex unus apibus, Dux unus gregibus.—*Cypr. de Idol. vanit.* Grues unam sequuntur.—*Hier. ad Rustic.*

Besides, men's minds are raised up by a monarchical government to a due consideration of the eternal, unalterable, supreme monarch over all, the Lord God himself. For a monarchical government is a representation of the supreme sovereignty, which God the highest monarch hath over all.

Obj. Many eyes may see more than one can, *plus vident oculi quam oculus.* 'In the multitude of counsellors there is safety and stability,' Prov. xi. 14, and xv. 22.

Ans. True, it is so. In that respect wise monarchs have had their counsellors. Such were Ahithophel and Hushai to David and Absalom, 2 Sam. xv. 34, and xvii. 6; such were those old men that are said to stand before Solomon, and gave counsel to Reboboam his son, 1 Kings xii. 6; such were those seven counsellors that Artaxerxes had, Ezra vii. 14; such were those seven wise men, which are said to see the king's face, Esth. i. 14, that is, to have a free access into his presence, to advise with him about weighty affairs. Thus there were Ephori among the Lacedæmonians, for their kings to consult withal, and consuls and senators at Rome in the emperors' times.

1. This layeth a duty upon kings lawfully to use what is lawful in itself, lest they make that which is lawful in itself to be unlawful unto them. There are many directions in God's word given to this purpose, which as it is their duty, so it will be their wisdom well to observe.

2. This layeth a duty upon people, to be subject unto them in the Lord, Rom. xiii. 1–5, 1 Peter ii. 13. Herein they manifest subjection to God himself, whose image monarchs bear. Thus also they will bring much outward and inward peace to themselves, and avoid temporal and eternal vengeance.

Sec. 4. *Of Salem where Melchisedec reigned.*

The place where Melchisedec was king, is by the apostle styled Σαλήμ, *Salem*, which he taketh from Gen. xiv. 18. The apostle in the next verse expoundeth this word, and saith it signifieth *peace.*

The root in Hebrew, שׁלו, from whence this word is derived, signifieth *to be at peace*, Job xxii. 21, or to make peace, 1 Kings xxii. 44. And a noun, שׁלום, signifieth *peace* itself, Deut. xxiii. 6.

This Salem was in that place where afterwards Jerusalem was built. Jerusalem, ירושלם, is a noun compound. The first part is taken from that word which Abraham used to his son Isaac, who asked him where the lamb for a burnt offering was. Abraham answered, 'God (ראה) *will provide.'* *Jeru*, the first part of Jerusalem, is taken from that verb that is translated *provide*. *Salem* being added thereunto, maketh up *Jerusalem*, and signifieth, according to that composition, God will provide peace.

Jerusalem was called by this name *Salem* in David's time. For thus saith he, 'In Salem is God's tabernacle,' Ps. lxxvi. 2.

Salem might be called Jerusalem in memorial of God's providence in preserving Isaac from death, when his father was about to sacrifice him, Gen. xxii. 12, 14. This Salem was the place where Isaac should have been offered up, and where Solomon built his temple, 2 Chron. iii. 1; and where David offered up his sacrifice, whereby a great plague was stayed, 1 Sam. xxiv. 18. The Jews say that Abel and Noah here offered up their sacrifices. There was a city in Samaria near Shechem of this name, שׁלם, Gen. xxxiii. 18. But the former is here meant.

Questionless the people that lived under so righteous a king as Melchisedec was, who also was the priest of God, were in profession at least a church of God; so as we may not unfitly infer, that there may be a civil monarchical government in the church of God. Such were the kings of Israel, many of whom had care well to order the things of the church of God. This, as a lawful and beneficial thing, is promised to the Christian church, 'Kings shall be thy nursing fathers, and their queens thy nursing mothers,' Isa. xlix. 23. Great is the benefit that God's church hath in sundry ages reaped from this kind of civil government.

Christians therefore, among others, ought for conscience' sake, and for the Lord's sake, be subject unto them, Rom. xiii. 5, 1 Pet. ii. 13; and pray for them, 1 Tim. ii. 1, 2.

He is said to be king of Salem, for distinction's sake. There were then other kings besides him, Gen. xiv. 1, 2, but of other places. Though he was born almost an hundred years before the flood, and might be then the eldest man on the earth, yet he was content with that which God allotted to him. So ought all kings, and all others. Though God used monarchs to punish people, yet he punished them also for their ambitious humour, Isa. v. 10, &c., and xiv. 4, 5, &c.

Sec. 5. *Of Melchisedec a priest of God.*

Another function here attributed to Melchisedec is this, *a priest.* Of the notation and meaning of this word *priest*, see Chap. ii. 17, Sec. 172, and Chap. v. 1, Sec. 2.

He is here said to be a priest of God in sundry respects.

1. To shew that he was ordained of God. This apostle giveth an hint of his most solemn ordination, ver. 20, 21.

2. To shew that he made God the object of his service: his eye was upon God.

3. To distinguish him from heathenish priests, who were priests of idols.

4. To manifest the reason why Abraham had him in so high esteem, and did him such honour as he did. We cannot doubt but that Abraham knew him, and took him to be the priest of God.

Of this must all be sure that look for any acceptance from God, or respect from saints of God, that their calling be of God, that they may be truly said to be ministers of God.

Sec. 6. *Of God the most high.*

Both the penman of the history, whereunto this hath reference, Gen. xiv. 18, and also this apostle, having occasion to mention God, thus set him forth, *the most high God.*

The Hebrew word עליון, translated *most high*, is derived from a verb, עלה, that signifieth *to ascend on high*, Ps. lxviii. 18. The Greek word ὕψιστος, is of the superlative degree. The positive, ὕψος, *sublimitas*, signifieth *height*, Eph. iii. 18. This word in the singular number is attributed only to God in the New Testament. The Greek LXX do usually translate the foresaid Hebrew עליון, when it is attributed to God, with this Greek superlative ὕψιστος.

This noun is one of those ten names, which in Scripture are attributed unto God, to set forth his excellency unto us. Of those ten names, see *The Church's Conquest*, on Exod. xvii. 15, sec. 72.

This particular place is given to God in reference to his place and power.

1. In regard of his place, 'The Lord is exalted, for he dwelleth on high,' Isa. xxxiii. 5. In this respect, saith the psalmist, 'Who is like unto the Lord our God, who dwelleth on high,' Ps. cxiii. 5.

2. In regard of his power, dignity, and authority, he is higher than the highest, and above all kings. 'The Most High ruleth in the kingdom of men ;' and 'The most high God giveth majesty, glory, and honour,' Dan. iv. 32, and v. 18 ; 'The Lord is high above all nations, and his glory above the heavens,' Ps. cxiii. 4.

This title, here given to God, gives us to understand, that when we have occasion to speak or think of God, we do it with all reverence, and with an high esteem of him. So will dutiful subjects to their sovereign. Thus we use to speak of kings, *His Highness, His Excellency, His Majesty, His Excellent Majesty, His Most Excellent Majesty*. Should we not much more do it to him that is King of kings, to whom most properly highness, excellency, majesty, dignity, dominion, and all manner of glory and honour doth belong ?

It was usual with Christ, when he spake of God, thus to express him, 'your Father in heaven,' 'your heavenly Father,' Mat. v. 6, and vi. 32.

1. How far short do they come of this, who vainly, rashly, yea, many times profanely and blasphemously, use the name of God! This commination in the third commandment, 'The Lord will not hold him guiltless that taketh his name in vain,' is a fearful doom against such.

2. Wonderfully doth this amplify the condescension of God towards man. The Most High dwelleth in the lowest heart, Isa. lvii. 15.

3. This description of God affords singular comfort to the faithful ; their God is the Most High. He must therefore needs see them in all their cases, and be able to help them. To this purpose doth the psalmist thus press this title, 'He that dwelleth in the secret place of the Most High shall abide under the shadow of the Almighty,' Ps. xci. 1 ; and thereupon thus saith, 'I will cry unto God most high,' Ps. lvii. 2.

4. This cannot be but great terror to the wicked, in that their wickedness cannot be hid from the Most High, nor they have power to carry it out against him. 'The Lord most high is terrible,' Ps. xlvii. 2. It was a great aggravation of the sins of Israel, that they 'provoked the most high God. 'If therefore thou seest the oppression of the poor, &c., marvel not at the matter, for he that is higher than the highest regardeth,' Eccles. v. 7.

Sec. 7. *Of Melchisedec both king and priest.*

It is a surpassing excellency in Melchisedec, that he was both king and priest. The like is not noted in sacred Scripture of any mere man, namely, of any that rightly and lawfully held those two offices.

Some have intruded on them both. Among the heathen[1] very many; but none of those were priests of the most high God. Among the Jews, one king presumed to take upon him the priest's function ; but for that his presumption, he carried the stamp of God's indignation to his dying day, 2 Chron. xxvi. 16, &c. The like is noted of Jeroboam, 1 Kings xii. 33, and xiii. 1. But at that very time was a prophet sent to denounce a most heavy judgment against him and his posterity.

Melchisedec was herein a peculiar type of Christ, who was all in all to his church, both King, Priest, and Prophet.

By the way, take notice from hence of the arrogancy and presumption of the pope of Rome, who usurpeth those two offices of king and priest, which are called his two keys. Herein he sheweth himself to be plain antichrist. Arguments urged by them to this purpose are very ridiculous, as those words of Peter, 'Lord, behold here are two swords,' Luke xxii. 38 ; and this voice from heaven, 'Rise, Peter, kill and eat,' Acts x. 13.

We, in reference to Christ, may, in regard of the union of those two offices in his person, expect what good may be done by a king or a priest.

Sec. 8. *Of Melchisedec's royal entertaining Abraham's army.*

The first act here attributed to Melchisedec is a royal act. It is thus expressed, 'who met Abraham.' The Greek word συναντάω, *und occurro, occurro cum aliis*, translated *met*, is a compound. The simple, ἀντάω, *occurro*, signifieth to meet. The compound, to meet with, namely, with others. Thus Cornelius met Peter with many in his company, Acts x. 24, 25; and much people met Jesus, Luke ix. 37. This word

---

[1] Περὶ μὲν Αἰγυπτον οὐκ ἔξεστι βασιλεῖ χωρὶς ἱερατικῆς ἄρχειν —*Plat. Politis.*

is here fitly used; for Melchisedec did not come alone, but as a king, with great company and good provision. In the history whereunto this hath reference, it is thus set down, 'He brought forth bread and wine,' Gen. xiv. 18. Under this word *bread*, all needful and useful food is comprised. In this extent is the word *bread* frequently used in the Scripture, particularly in the Lord's prayer, Mat. vi. 11. See *The Explanation of the Lord's Prayer*, on the fourth petition, Sec. 81.

Under this word *wine*, is in general meant drink; but it further implieth a kind of choice and dainty refreshing: it was not water, which might have been sufficient for soldiers, but wine to cheer their spirits; for 'wine maketh glad the heart of man,' Ps. civ. 15. So as he brought forth not only that which was absolutely necessary to feed them, but also that which might cheer up their spirits: he made them a royal feast. Thus doth Josephus, a Jew, who wrote the history of the Jews, set down this point. He brought forth, saith he, great abundance of such things as the season afforded.[1]

This was a warrantable and a commendable act, and giveth proof that soldiers are to be succoured and rewarded. This must be taken of such soldiers as fight in a good cause. Joshua bountifully rewarded the Reubenites and others that assisted their brethren against the Canaanites, Joshua xxii. 8. It is said of Toi that he sent to salute David, and to bless him, because he had fought against Hadadezer, and withal he sent great presents, 2 Sam. viii. 10. God himself gave the rich land of Egypt to Nebuchadnezzar, 'because he had caused his army to serve a great service against Tyrus,' Ezek. xxix. 18, 19. On this ground it was a custom in Israel to meet such as returned with good success from the war 'with tabrets, with joy, and with instruments of music,' 1 Sam. xviii. 6, Judges xi. 34. Sore vengeance was executed on the men of Succoth and Penuel, because they refused to succour soldiers in such a case, Judges viii. 5, &c.

This kind of succour, as it argueth gratefulness for what hath been done, so it gives great encouragement for the future. Victory useth not to be easily gotten. Much hazard must be undergone, and great hardness endured for effecting it; no work like unto it.

Such as tarry at home perceive the fruit and benefit of soldiers' pains and danger; thereby their peace is maintained, and they preserved from much violence and oppression, which otherwise, through the fury of enemies, might fall upon them.

If encouragement is to be given to soldiers after the war is ended, much more while they are in war, that they may the better hold out, and not faint in their great undertakings.

As for those who deny to soldiers their due and just wages and allowance, they do the greatest injustice that can be. The apostle, as a ruled case, thus propounds this point, 'who goeth a warfare any time at his own charges?' 1 Cor. ix. 7. Who better deserve their wages than soldiers?

Commendable in this case is the charity of those who have built hospitals, or given revenues, or otherwise provided for such soldiers as have been maimed in war, and made thereby unable to provide for themselves.

Sec. 9. *Of kings slain in war.*

The time of Melchisedec's meeting Abraham is thus described, *returning from the slaughter*, &c. This hath reference to Abraham's arming soldiers, and pursuing those enemies that had sacked Sodom, and, among others of the city, had taken Lot and all that he had, Gen. xiv. 14, &c. Melchisedec's meeting Abraham, and royally entertaining him and his army after he had in a warlike manner set upon the enemies and slain them, testifieth his approbation of what Abraham had done, which is further confirmed by Melchisedec's blessing him for what he had done. This giveth a plain proof both of the lawfulness of war, and also of slaying enemies in war.

Of these two points, see *The Church's Conquest*, on Exod. xvii. 9, sec. 13, and on Exod. xvii. 13, sec. 60.

The parties here said to be slain are styled *kings*. There were four kings that joined together in that army which Abraham set upon, and by this text it appears that they were slain. To confirm the truth whereof, the history itself thus saith: Abraham 'divided himself against them, he and his servants by night, and smote them,' Gen. xiv. 15. The history in general saith, that the enemies were smitten, which includeth commanders, as well as common soldiers; and the apostle, who knew the full extent of that history, expressly mentioneth the kings themselves to be slain; so as the greatest that be among men have no privilege in war. Bullets, arrows, swords, and other warlike instruments, put no difference betwixt the greatest and the meanest. Not only Ahab, a wicked king of Israel, was in wars slain with an arrow, 1 Kings xxii. 34, but also Josiah king of Judah, one of the best kings that ever Judah had, 2 Chron. xxxv. 23. The flesh of kings, of captains, and mighty men, are in this respect said to be meat for the fowls of the air, Rev. xix. 18.

All that join in war are as members of the same body, and counted by the enemy common trespassers. The greater the commanders are, the more they are sought after by the enemy, and in that respect in greater danger; hereupon David's men would not suffer David himself to go with them in his own person, and that upon this reason, 'Thou art worth ten thousand of us,' 2 Sam. xviii. 3.

God also doth oft take occasion in this case to pun-

---

[1] Multam abundantiam rerum opportunarum exhibuit.— *Joseph. Antiq. Judaic.*, lib. i. cap. 18.

ish wicked kings, as Ahab, 1 Kings xxii. 28; or to punish people by taking away good kings, as Josiah, 2 Kings xxii. 29.

Kings therefore and other great ones have just cause, when they attempt war, to be sure that their cause be just and weighty, and to seek unto God for his protection and blessing, yea, and to commend their souls into his hands. As in other cases, so in war, 'unto God the Lord belong the issues from death,' Ps. lxviii. 20. See *The Church's Conquest*, on Exod. xvii. 16, sec. 86.

They who are here said to be slain, were those who had before gotten a great victory, and slain many on the other side, Gen. xiv. 10. So as this giveth proof that conquerers may soon be conquered. See *The Church's Conquests*, on Exod. xvii. 11, sec. 47.

Sec. 10. *Of succouring such as we are nearly related unto.*

The occasion Abraham took to wage the war whereunto this hath reference was, that his kinsman was taken by the enemies. For it is thus expressly said, 'When Abraham heard that his brother was taken captive, he armed his trained servants,' &c., Gen. xiv. 14. He that is styled his brother was Abraham's brother's son, Gen. xi. 27, and xiv. 12. It hereby is evident that distress of kindred is a just occasion to afford help unto them; and if their distress be captivity under an enemy (as Lot's was), it is a good ground to rescue them by force of arms. On this ground the Reubenites, Gadites, and half the tribe of Manasseh, who were settled in their own inheritance, were enjoined to help their brethren of the other tribes, against their common enemies; answerably they promised so to do, Num. xxxii. 20–25, and they performed their promise to the full, and were commended and rewarded for the same, Josh. xxii. 1, &c. On the other side, Reuben, Gilead, Dan, and Asher are reproved for failing to afford help to their brethren in their need, Judges v. 15–17.

This is one special end of those bonds of relation, whereby God hath knit us one to another.

This point is to be applied as God by his providence shall afford occasion.

This pattern of Abraham herein is the rather to be observed, because not long before this there was a strife between the herdsmen of Abraham's cattle and Lot's, Gen. xiii. 7. Besides, it was Lot's folly to dwell among the Sodomites.

Abraham would not suffer conceits of any such matters to hinder him from this work of charity; no, though there were danger in attempting the same against such potent enemies. That reason which the apostle useth, to stir up children or nephews to shew piety at home, and to requite their parents, may be applied to all that by any bond of relation are knit unto them, and that in all sorts of distresses. The reason is thus expressed, 'For that is good and acceptable before God,' 1 Tim. v. 4. Who would not be moved to a duty by so forcible a motive?

Sec. 11. *Of congratulating the success of neighbours of the same profession.*

The nearest relation that we read of betwixt Melchisedec and Abraham was neighbourhood or cohabitation. For Salem was not far from the place where Abraham sojourned. Abraham sojourned in the land of Canaan, and Salem was a place bordering near unto it. There might be also a spiritual relation to move Melchisedec to do the courtesy which he did to Abraham; for they both feared and worshipped the same God, and were of the same profession. This instance further sheweth, that neighbouring nations ought to congratulate one another's good success, especially if they be of the same religion.

Success against enemies of our neighbours may be a benefit to us that are their neighbours; for being common enemies, if they prevail against our neighbours, they may take occasion to annoy us. Enemies will not be content with one conquest. When they have subdued one neighbouring nation, they will be ready to set upon others; witness Nebuchadnezzar, Cyrus, Alexander, and other monarchs.

As occasion is offered, this pattern of Melchisedec is to be imitated, and that the rather because Melchisedec was a king of peace, ver. 2. Yet he congratulated him that was victorious over enemies.

Such victories are means of peace; for such enemies, if not subdued, will disturb the peace of all they can.

Besides, there ought to be a sympathy with such as are of the same profession and religion. They ought to 'rejoice with them that do rejoice,' Rom. xii. 15.

It is in these respects a point of wisdom to encourage such as God gives good success unto, especially against enemies of his church, and that in particular by congratulating that good success which God doth give them.

Sec. 12. *Of one man's blessing another.*

The next act attributed to Melchisedec in reference to Abraham is thus set down, *and blessed him.* Melchisedec blessed Abraham.

Of the notation of the Greek word εὐλογήσας, translated *blessed*, see Chap. vi. 6, Sec. 47.

The Hebrew root ברך signifieth sometimes to bow the knee, נברכה, *genuflectamus*, Ps. xcv. 6, 2 Chron. vi. 13; sometimes to wish well, or to pray for one, Ps. cxxix. 8. In this sense the Greek word used in this text is answerable unto it, and the LXX do ordinarily translate that Hebrew word with this Greek word. For when man is said to bless man, it is ordinarily intended of one man's wishing well to another, or praying for him. In the general, it may here be so taken; for in the history it is written to this effect, 'Melchisedec blessed Abram, and said, Blessed be Abram of the most high God,' Gen. xiv. 19.

The latter clause sheweth that Melchisedec prayed unto God to bless Abram, and in that respect is said to bless Abram.

It is also there noted that Melchisedec blessed God; 'Blessed be the most high God,' saith he.

Thus we see that this act of blessing is attributed to God and man. It is attributed to God in a double respect:

1. As he sanctifieth and setteth apart anything to an holy use. Thus God is said to 'bless the seventh day and sanctify it,' Gen. ii. 3.

2. As he conferreth some real actual good thing upon his creature. Thus God is said to bless man and woman, Gen. i. 28.

God's blessing man is in Greek and Latin set forth by words that signify to speak well, $εὐλογεῖν$, *benedicere*, to shew the power of God's word. It shall indeed be well to them to whom God wisheth or saith well. In the creation of God's works, it is on every day noted that 'God said, Let it be' so and so, and thereon it is inferred 'it was so,' Gen. i. 7, 9, &c. This is further manifest by the ratification of God's blessing, thus, 'I will bless thee, and thou shalt be a blessing,' Gen. xii. 2, and, 'Thou blessest, O Lord, and it shall be blessed for ever,' 1 Chron. xvii. 27. On this ground is the word oft doubled thus, 'In blessing I will bless thee,' Gen. xxii. 17; Ps. cxxxii. 15.

Of God's blessing his creatures, see more Chap. vi. 8, Sec. 47, and ver. 15, Sec. 102.

The act of blessing is here attributed to man.

Blessing attributed to man hath reference to the Creator and creatures. This Melchisedec blessed God, Gen. xiv. 20, as well as Abram.

God is blessed by man two ways.

1. By acknowledging and confessing God's excellencies, 1 Chron. xxix. 10, 11.

2. By thanking and praising God for the same, Ps. xxxiv. 1.

This is to be observed of such as think it an harsh speech to say that man blesseth God.

The creatures that are blessed by man are either other men or other kinds of creatures.

Other kinds of creatures are blessed by man two ways.

1. By way of supplication, by craving God's blessing upon them. Thus every creature is said to be 'sanctified, or blessed, by the word of God and prayer,' 1 Tim. iv. 5. God's word giveth warrant and direction for the right use of it, and prayer obtains a blessing thereupon. Thus it hath been of old, and still is, a commendable custom for saints to bless their meat. So did Samuel, 1 Sam. ix. 13, and Christ, Luke xxiv. 30: 'For man liveth not by bread only, but by every word that proceedeth out of the mouth of the Lord man liveth,' Deut. viii. 3. It is not the creature alone which can do us any good, but that blessing which God is pleased to give unto it.

2. By way of consecration, when a creature is by one sent of God, and standing in God's room, set apart in God's name to some religious use. In this respect the apostle thus saith of the sacramental cup, 'The cup of blessing which we bless,' 1 Cor. x. 16.

One man is blessed of another two ways.

1. By supplication, or gratulation. 2. By confirmation.

1. By supplication, when one prayeth for another, or desireth God to bless him. Thus any one may bless another. An inferior may bless a superior. Thus the workmen of Boaz blessed him, Ruth ii. 4. In this respect Christ adviseth to bless them that curse us, Mat. v. 44; so his apostle, Rom. xii. 14.

By gratulation, one man blesseth another by thanking him for a kindness, or by praising God for him, Job xxix. 11, and xxxi. 20.

2. By confirmation, when one in God's name assures another that God will bless him; thus is this an act of superiors. In this sense 'the less is blessed of the greater,' ver. 7. These must be such superiors as stand in God's room, and have an especial charge over them whom they bless.

Of these there are three sorts; governors of families, magistrates in commonwealths, ministers of God's word.

1. For governors of families, it is said that 'David returned to bless his household,' 2 Sam. vi. 20. Of these governors, parents have the most especial power to bless their children. Hereof see *Domest. Duties*, treat. v. sec. 9, and treat. vi. secs. 58, 59.

2. For governors in commonwealths, the highest therein have especially this prerogative. Joshua in his time blessed Caleb, Josh. xiv. 13; and he blessed the tribe of Reuben, Gad, and half-tribe of Manasseh, Josh. xxii. 6; so David blessed the people, 2 Sam. vi. 18; and Solomon, 1 Kings viii. 14.

3. For ministers of God's word, to them especially belongeth this solemn and public kind of blessing by way of confirmation, for they, in a most peculiar manner, stand in God's room: 'We are ambassadors for Christ, as though God did beseech you by us,' &c., 2 Cor. v. 20.

According to the different calling and function of ministers may their blessing be distinguished. Some ministers' calling is extraordinary, as the calling of prophets and apostles were; others ordinary.

The blessing of extraordinary ministers is more extraordinary in the kind, and infallible in the issue.

Their blessing extraordinary in the kind was by way of prediction. They foretold the future estate of those whom they blessed. In the issue it was infallible, in that the blessing that they foretold did so fall out in every circumstance, and failed not. Thus, Isaac 'blessed Jacob and Esau concerning things to come,' Heb. xi. 20, and accordingly they so fell out.

The blessing of ordinary ministers, though it be not so extraordinarily distinct and infallible a prediction of things to come, yet is it much more than a private prayer or desire; namely, a testimony, a pledge, and assurance of that which God will do. So as it is a kind of divine work, and a blessing rather of God than of man. The minister uttereth what he uttereth in God's name; or rather God uttereth it by his minister's mouth. In testimony hereof the minister useth to stand on high over the people, and to lift up his hand, to shew that he speaketh from him, who is above all. In this respect God having given a charge unto the priests under the law, to bless his people, addeth this ratification, and I will bless them, Num. vi. 27.

To apply what hath in general been said, to the blessing intended in my text; the blessing here spoken of was of one man's blessing another; and that man a public minister, and an extraordinary one. It was a most solemn blessing of confirmation; a part of his priestly function, wherein he shewed himself to be greater than Abraham, ver. 7.

Quest. What good thing was it that Melchisedec by this blessing ratified to Abraham?

Ans. 1. Because no particular is expressed, it may in general be extended to all those good things which God promised to Abraham, as the stock of the church, and the father of the faithful.

2. This apostle hinteth one main particular, where he saith of Melchisedec, in reference to Abraham, 'He blessed him that had the promises,' ver. 6. Now because the principal promise of all, under which all the rest may be comprised, was the blessed seed, questionless that blessing was here in special ratified and sealed up to Abraham.

Sec. 13. *Of saints' pious salutations.*

Melchisedec's foresaid blessing of Abraham, was in general a congratulation and salutation; and it sheweth how saints should carry themselves one towards another, when they first meet, even with wishing well one to another, and blessing one another. When Boaz came to see his reapers, he said, 'The Lord be with you,' and 'they answered him, The Lord bless thee,' Ruth ii. 4. This phrase, 'we have blessed you out of the house of the Lord,' Ps. cxviii. 26, implieth, that it was usual, especially for such as belonged to the house of the Lord, to bless those that came to them.

In that such holy wishes are denied to unworthy ones, it appears that it was very usual to bless those whom they deemed worthy. The denial hereof is thus expressed, 'Neither do they which go by say, The blessing of the Lord be upon you; we bless you in the name of the Lord,' Ps. cxxix. 8.

This kind of salutation is both a testification of mutual love, and also a means of preserving it.

1. Commendable in this respect is the common practice of Christians, who use to salute one another with these or such like speeches, 'God save you!' 'The Lord be with you!' Then especially are they most commendable, when they come from the heart.

2. What may be thought of the usual imprecations of many, when they meet one another? They are such as I am ashamed to name. Let them well weigh their doom thus expressed, 'As he loved cursing, so let it come unto him; as he delighted not in blessing, so let it be far from him,' &c., Ps. cix. 17, 18. See more hereof in *The Whole Armour of God*, on Eph. vi. 18, treat. iii. part ii. secs. 57, 58.

Sec. 14. *Of ministers blessing the people.*

Melchisedec being considered in general as a minister of God, giveth instance, that ministers of the word have power to bless God's people; to bless them, I say, not only with a mere desire and prayer, but also with a declaration of God's blessing them. Thus much is intended in this charge of Christ to his disciples, 'When ye come into an house, salute it,' Mat. x. 12. Hereby is meant the foresaid kind of blessing, as appears by this consequence, 'If the house be worthy, let your peace come upon it;' for this end did God prescribe an express form of blessing to the priests under the law, Num. vi. 23. The apostle useth a blessing, 2 Cor. xiii. 14, which the Christian church to this day observeth; so it doth Christ's blessing, Luke xi. 28.

Ministers stand in God's room, and are to people in his stead, and as his mouth, as was shewed before.

Such a ministerial blessing is of singular use, to strengthen the faith of God's people, and to settle their conscience. The calling and function of a minister maketh much hereunto.

As ministers are to be conscionable in performing their duty herein, so people must have this in high account; and not lightly esteem of it, as too many do. How usual is it for many to depart from the congregation before the minister's blessing be pronounced, and so go away without the grace of the Lord Jesus Christ!

Sec. 15. *Of Christ's blessing the faithful.*

As in other things, so in this act of blessing, Melchisedec was an especial type of Christ, and Abraham was there blessed as the father of the faithful; so as therein was prefigured an act of Christ towards the promised seed; which was, that Christ blesseth the faithful; such as are of the spiritual seed and faith of Abraham. A particular instance hereof is thus given, Christ 'lift up his hands, and blessed them,' Luke xiv. 50. And as a further evidence hereof, when Christ ascended 'he gave gifts unto men,' Eph. iv. 8.

Christ doth thus bless partly as God; thus he blessed Jacob, Gen. xxxii. 29; and partly as Mediator betwixt God and man. Thus God 'hath blessed us with all spiritual blessings in Christ,' Eph. i. 3.

1. No doubt but that this blessing wherewith Melchisedec blessed Abraham was a singular comfort unto him. Much more comfortable may the true blessing, which Christ conferreth on his church, be to the members thereof. They whom Christ blesseth are and ever shall be truly blessed.

2. This may be a great encouragement against the curses of idolaters and profane persons. They use to curse us, and to imprecate all evil against us, for Christ's sake, and for our profession's sake. We may in this case say, 'Surely there is no enchantment against Jacob, neither is there any divination against Israel,' Num. xxiii. 23. As God turned Balak's endeavour to curse into a blessing, so he will requite good for wicked men's cursing, 2 Sam. xvi. 12. It is further added in the history, that upon Abraham's victory, Melchisedec did not only bless Abraham himself, but also 'blessed the most high God,' which delivered his enemies into his hands, Gen. xiv. 20. Hereby he evidently sheweth that the praise of victory is to be given to God. See more hereof in *The Church's Conquest*, on Exod. xvii. 16, sec. 77.

Sec. 16. *Of Abraham's giving a tenth to Melchisedec.*
Ver. 2. It was an especial prerogative appertaining to Melchisedec, that Abraham gave a tenth part of all unto him. This relative, ψ, *to whom*, hath reference to Melchisedec.

The verb ἐμέρισε, translated *gave*, is derived from a noun, μερίς, that signifieth a *part* or *portion*, Acts viii. 21.

This verb, μερίζω, implieth a dividing or distributing that which is meet to be given to one. It is used where it is said, 'God hath dealt to every man the measure of faith,' Rom. xii. 3. See more in the emphasis of this word, Chap. ii. 4, Sec. 35.

Abraham saw it meet that Melchisedec should have a tenth of what he had.

Though the word *part* be not expressed in the Greek, yet it is here well supplied. The Greek word δεκάτη, translated *tenth*, when it is set alone, and hath not apparent reference to any particular thing, signifieth *a tenth part*. It is derived from that numeral noun, δέκα, which signifies *ten*.

This general phrase, ἀπὸ πάντων, *of all*, hath especial reference to the spoils that Abraham took in war; for so much is expressed, ver. 4. For God's people did use to give of that which they took in war unto the Lord, 1 Chron. xxvi. 27; and this was according to the commandments of the Lord, Num. xxxi. 28, &c.

This giving of a tenth the apostle here setteth down as an evidence of Abraham's respect to God's priest, and of his thankfulness to the king for that royal kindness and grace which he shewed him.

Principally and especially did Abraham give the tenth to Melchisedec, as he was a priest of God.

Two reasons moved Abraham to do this:
1. To shew that of Christ he held whatsoever he had; in testimony whereof he gives a part to him that was a type of Christ and stood in his room.
2. To shew how just and equal it is that they who communicate unto us spiritual blessings, should partake of our temporals.

These two reasons, resting upon a moral and perpetual equity, shew that in those general cases Abraham is a pattern to all sorts of saints in all ages, to do as he did, namely,

1. To testify their acknowledgment of all they have to come from Christ, and to testify that they hold all they have of Christ, by giving thereof to him. This is to 'honour the Lord with our substance, and with the first fruits of our increase,' Prov. iii. 9. Of offering gifts to God, see Chap. v. 1, Sec. 6.

2. To communicate of our temporals to such as make us partakers of their spirituals. See Sec. 18.

Sec. 17. *Of tenths, how far due to ministers of the word.*

About Abraham's giving a tenth to Melchisedec sundry questions are moved.

Quest. Have all ministers of the word the same right to tenths that Melchisedec had?

Ans. Not in every particular circumstance; for,

1. Melchisedec was an extraordinary type of Christ, and that both of his kingly and priestly function. By virtue of both those he received tithes. No other priest or ministers are such.

2. Melchisedec received tithes of Abraham in a mystery, to shew the pre-eminence of his priesthood, and withal the pre-eminence of Christ's priesthood above Levi's. This the apostle himself maketh manifest, ver. 4-6.

Yet there is a common and general equity in Melchisedec's receiving tithes, which may appertain to all sorts of God's ministers.

Quest. 2. Is the tenth part such an unalterable portion as to be due to all ministers at all times?

Ans. If that precise portion be not unalterable, yet that which is equivalent thereunto is, namely, that ministers be sufficiently and plentifully maintained.

There be some reasons rendered about the Levites receiving tenths which are proper to the Jews.

One is this, that the Jews, paying first fruits and tenths, did thereby testify their acknowledgment of God's bringing them out of the Egyptian bondage, and giving them Canaan as a settled inheritance, Deut. xxvi. 5, &c.

The other is this, a recompence for their having no inheritance proper to the tribe of Levi. Unto the tribe of Levi no inheritance was given, Joshua xiii. 14. But thus saith the Lord, 'I have given the children of Levi all the tenth in Israel for inheritance,' Num. xviii. 21.

Obj. Abraham paid tithes to Melchisedec before there was any distinction of tribes, Gen. xiv. 20.

And Jacob also, before that distinction of tribes, vowed to give the tenth unto God, Gen. xxviii. 22.

Ans. Neither of these carry the force of perpetual law.

The one was not constantly done, the other was not necessarily done. Abraham did not every year pay tithes, but only this once. Jacob's vow was a voluntary act of his own, and it was a vow made upon conditions, which no moral and inviolable precept will admit.

Quest. 3. Is the law of tenth utterly abolished?

Ans. In this case distinction must be made betwixt the ceremony and equity of a law.

1. That there should be altars, sacrifices, incense, &c., was a ceremony; but that there should be ordinances, wherein and whereby God should be worshipped, is a perpetual equity, Malachi i. 11.

2. That there should be sacrificing priests, and high priests, and other orders of Levites, was a ceremony; but that there should be ministers of the word, is a perpetual rule, Isa. lxvi. 21.

3. That in their fastings they put on sackcloth, and put ashes on their head, was a ceremony; but that there should be times of fasting, and therein men's souls afflicted, is a perpetual equity.

4. That women after child-bearing should be legally purified, was a ceremony; but that there should be public thanksgiving for their deliverance, is a perpetual equity.

Thus for the point in hand, though it be granted that the Levitical tenths were proper to the Jews, yet this is a general common equity, that they who labour in the word should live of the word; and that they should have sufficient maintenance from them for whom they do labour; that they should not be put otherwise to seek a maintenance, but rather live upon their labours, for whose spiritual good they watch.

Obj. Paul wrought for himself in another calling, Acts xviii. 3, and xx. 34.

Ans. The apostle himself implieth that he had power to forbear working, 1 Cor. ix. 6. That which he did, in the foresaid case, was extraordinary.

Quest. 4. Why are tenths under the gospel paid to ministers?

Ans. It is for the most part the fittest proportion, and that the very heathen did observe about their ministers. When God himself set down a particular and distinct portion for his ministers, he judged a tenth to be the most convenient. Hereupon good governors have in their commonwealths thought meet to establish such a portion. This general rule, 'Let him that is taught in the word communicate unto him that teacheth in all good things,' Gal. vi. 6, may be most fitly brought to the foresaid proportion of tenths. Where such a portion is established by law, people are bound in conscience to observe the same.

Obj. Establishment of a set maintenance maketh ministers negligent.

Ans. 1. It may make unconscionable ministers to be so; but not such as for the Lord's sake, and conscience' sake, perform their duty.

Ans. 2. Greater inconveniences may arise from not settling of any maintenance, but leaving it wholly to people's devotion; as,

1. If people be left at such liberty, they will be ready, upon all displeasures taken against their minister, to withdraw his maintenance; so as this may be a means to make ministers meal-mouthed, and to seek to please their people.

2. This kind of maintenance is accounted a mere benevolence; whereas in this case Christ and his apostles make it a matter of due debt; 'the workman is worthy of his meat,' Mat. x. 10, 1 Tim. v. 18. A minister's pains is a valuable consideration for the greatest allowance that people use to give. 'If we have sown unto you spiritual things, is it a great thing if we shall reap your carnal things?' 1 Cor. ix. 11.

3. This is an hindrance of the choice of good ministers; for many are ready to entertain ministers as they use to hire workmen, such as will come at the cheapest rate.

4. This may be a means of laying the heaviest burden upon the better sort. When a profaner sort withdraw, they that are of the better sort are forced to enlarge themselves the more.

5. From thence may follow undue emulation and ostentation, in seeking to be above others.

A set established maintenance is the nearest to God's order.

Sec. 18. *Of ministers' maintenance.*

This general point may well be inferred from Abraham's giving the tenth to Melchisedec, that God's ministers, who communicate unto us spiritual blessings, are to be made partakers of our temporal commodities. This is almost in these words set down by the apostle, 1 Cor. viii. 11, and again Gal. vi. 6. Our Lord Christ and his apostle witnesseth that a minister is ἄξιος, 'worthy,' hereof, Mat. x. 10, 1 Tim. v. 18. The apostle styleth the minister's allowance μισθὸς, 'wages,' for it is as due to him as wages is due to a servant, soldier, workman, or any other that taketh pains for our good. The apostle exemplifieth the equity of this by a soldier's living upon his warfare, by a vine-dresser's partaking of the fruit of it, by a shepherd's living upon the flock, by an ox's eating of the corn that he treadeth out, by a ploughman's, thresher's, reaper's, and other workmen's living upon their pains, yea, and of the Levites partaking of the sacrifices that they prepared, 1 Cor. ix. 7, &c.

1. Justice requires as much, and this is implied under these words *worthy*, *wages*, Luke x. 7. This, therefore, is one of those dues which the apostle would have Christians to render, Rom. xiii. 7, and that upon these and other like considerations.

(1.) Ministers use to spend the prime of their age in fitting themselves to this calling. They might otherwise have fitted themselves to another calling, whereupon they might have lived with greater plenty.

(2.) Their friends for the most part have been at great costs in training them up hereunto.

(3.) They are deprived of other means of maintenance by attending upon this calling.

(4.) The pains required to this calling useth to be very great, both while they are in fitting and preparing themselves thereto, and also when they come to exercise the same. Ministers are many times at their study while others are asleep, and have no other witness of their pains but their candle, which teacheth them to spend themselves in giving light to others.

(5.) The benefit received by their pains is invaluable; no calling affords greater; it concerneth the soul, the spiritual and eternal good thereof. If, therefore, recompence be given to men of other callings, much more to ministers of the word.

2. Gratefulness should move people to recompense their ministers, for good must be requited with good. This was one reason whereby Abraham was moved to give the tenth to Melchisedec. This is acceptable to God and man.

3. Wisdom should induce men hereunto, that ministers might thereby more diligently attend their calling, and be better enabled to go through the work of it, and so their people receive the more good from them. Daily wants whereby ministers are forced otherwise to provide for themselves and families, do make them more negligent in their calling. Men will well feed their beasts, that they may do the more and better work, 1 Cor. ix. 9.

4. That homage which they owe unto God should most of all stir up people to be liberal to their minister, for ministers stand to them in God's room, 2 Cor. v. 20. What is given to them as ministers of the word is given to God. The apostle therefore saith of that the Philippians sent him, 'I have received an odour of a sweet smell, a sacrifice acceptable and well pleasing to God,' Philip. iv. 18. In this respect God doth account himself robbed by such as withhold from his ministers their due, Mal. iii. 8, 9; for under the law first-fruits, tithes, and all manner of oblations, which were given to priests and Levites, were accounted to be given to the Lord.

People therefore ought, for the Lord's sake, John xiii. 20, for their soul's sake, Heb. xiii. 17, and for their own incomparable advantage, Mat. x. 41, to give to their ministers what is meet.

Many imagine that under the gospel there is no law to bind people to give anything to their minister, and that what in this kind they do is a mere benevolence and an arbitrary gratuity. But that which hath been before set down doth sufficiently manifest that people are bound by the strongest bonds that can be to maintain their ministers, namely, God's charge and invaluable benefits received. What law binds men to give such liberal fees as they ordinarily do to lawyers and physicians? Were they as sensible of their spiritual good as they are of their bodily welfare and temporal estate, they would be as liberal to their ministers as to others.

Sec. 19. *Of Melchisedec a king of righteousness.*

Sundry mysteries are by our apostle observed about the foresaid Melchisedec. The first is concerning his name. This, because it is the chiefest of all, and belonged unto him before he was king of Salem, the apostle bringeth it in in the first place with this particle of order, πρῶτον, *first*.

Of the adverb *truly*, mentioned in Greek, but not expressed in our English, see Ver. 5, Sec. 37.

This phrase ἑρμηνευόμενος, *being by interpretation*, implieth that his name did signify that which is here set down, and thereupon metonymically he is said to be 'by interpretation,' or being interpreted, as John i. 38, *King of righteousness*.

To interpret a word, ἑρμηνεύω, is to declare the meaning of that which otherwise would not be understood. Melchisedec was an Hebrew name. They to whom the apostle wrote understood Greek better than Hebrew; therefore he expounds the meaning of the Hebrew name in the Greek tongue, as we interpret the Greek in English.

Strange words are to be interpreted, so sentences also. It was usual with the penmen of the New Testament so to do, Mark xv. 20, 34. This is expressly commanded, 1 Cor. xiv. 27. For this end a peculiar gift of interpreting strange tongues was given to sundry particular persons in the primitive church, 1 Cor. xii. 10.

Strange words or sentences without interpretation are to no purpose; no profit can be reaped thereby. They are as musical instruments and trumpets sounded without any distinction, or like words spoken in the air, which soon vanish and come to nothing, 1 Cor. xiv. 7, &c. But on the other side, it much satisfieth one to have that which he cannot understand expounded and made clear, Gen. xl. 7, 8, and xli. 8; Dan. iv. 5, 6, and v. 29.

Great is that wrong which papists do to their people in and by their Latin liturgy. Latin is not a tongue which the common people do at this day in any part of the world understand. Yet among papists all their public prayers and other sacred ordinances, as reading the word or administering sacraments, are in Latin. It is a sore doom that the apostle denounceth against such in these words, 'Tongues (namely, strange tongues) are for a sign, not to them that believe, but to them that believe not,' 1 Cor. xiv. 22.

Too near to these do they come who fill their sermons with such words and sentences as their people cannot understand, and yet do not interpret them.

So do they also who affect strong lines; that is, such kind of phrases that their people understand not.

Seeing interpretation of strange tongues is necessary, surely it is requisite that ministers be expert in the learned tongues especially, that they may be able to interpret them. It is also requisite that they be well acquainted with the types, proverbs, prophecies, and other obscure passages in Scripture, that they may declare the meaning of them to the people, as the apostle here doth.

This name *Melchisedec*, מלכי־צדק, is a compound word, and containeth in it two Hebrew nouns. The former, מלך, *melec, rex,* a king. The title, *I*, in this word, מלכי, *rex meus, melchi,* may signify *my,* as if it were translated *my king,* Ps. v. 2, or else it may be enforced for composition's sake. The other word, צדק, *tsedec, justitia,* signifieth *righteousness,* Ps. xv. 2.

Of the Greek word δικαιοσύνη, translated *righteousness,* see Chap. i. 9, Sec. 114, and of the Hebrew and Greek word translated *king,* see ver. i. Sec. 3.

This name *Melchisedec* compriseth under it two things:
1. His function, he was a *king*.
2. His practice, he ruled in *righteousness*.

Whether this name was given him in his infancy, or after he was a king, is uncertain. If this Melchisedec were Shem (whereof see ver. i. Sec. 2), then Shem was his proper name given him in his infancy; so as it is most probable that it was given him after he was king, and manifested his righteousness in governing the people. On a like occasion Gideon was called *Jerubbaal,* Judges vi. 32; and Jacob was called *Israel,* Gen. xxxii. 28.

If this name were given him in his infancy, it was certainly by way of prophecy. The Spirit, foreseeing what his office should be, and what his practice would be, directed those that gave him his name, to give this name *Melchisedec*: as *Noah,* Gen. v. 29; and *Jacob,* Gen. xxv. 26; and *Solomon,* 2 Sam. xii. 24.

Of giving fit names to children, see *Domest. Duties,* treat, vi. sec. 20.

Whether this name were given in his infancy, or after he was king, both make to the same purpose. One implied a prediction of what should be, the other a ratification of what was.

In the name and meaning thereof, *Melchisedec* is to be considered two ways:
1. As a type.
2. As a pattern.

As a type he foreshewed two things.
1. That Christ was a true King.
2. That Christ reigned in righteousness.

Of both these, see Chap. i. 8, Secs. 111, 112, 113.

Sec. 20. *Of righteous kings.*

As Melchisedec was a pattern to future ages, his name importeth two other points:

1. Men may be kings. Hereof see ver. 5, Sec. 3.
2. Kings must rule in righteousness. They must so carry themselves as they may truly be called *Melchisedecs*. 'A king shall reign in righteousness,' Isa. xxxii. 1. Hereupon the psalmist thus prayeth, 'Give the king thy judgments, O God; and thy righteousness unto the king's son,' Ps. lxxii. 1. For this end, when David was near his death, he giveth his son, who was to be king after him, sundry directions for practice of righteousness, 1 Kings ii. 3, &c.

1. Kings do, after an especial manner, bear the image of God. They stand in his room, and reign for him; in which respect they are styled 'gods,' Ps. lxxxii. 6, and 'ministers of God,' Rom. xiii. 4. They 'judge for the Lord,' 2 Chron. xix. 6.

Now God is a righteous Lord, and loveth righteousness. See Chap. i. ver. 9, Secs. 114, 115.

2. Righteousness is the greatest ornament to a kingdom that can be. It is the very glory and beauty thereof. It makes it like unto heaven. Yea, it is the strength and stability of a kingdom. 'Righteousness exalteth a nation;' and 'the throne is established by righteousness,' Prov. xiv. 34, and xvi. 12. When the prophet had set down the everlasting unchangeableness of Christ's kingdom, he addeth this as a reason thereof, 'The sceptre of thy kingdom is a sceptre of righteousness,' Ps. xlv. 6.

3. Righteousness is an especial means to maintain peace. For all troubles, dissensions, tumults, insurrections, and wars, arise from unrighteousness, one way or other; from the agents or patients. Of the benefit of peace, see Sec. 22.

1. Kings in this especial point must shew themselves like to Melchisedec, and rule in righteousness. They shall thus gain a double benefit. One in regard of their persons, to themselves. The other in regard of their place, to their people.

2. People must pray for their kings, that they may be Melchisedecs. We have a pattern hereof, Ps. lxxii. 1, &c. This we may and must do with confidence, because 'the king's heart is in the hand of the Lord,' &c., Prov. xxi. 1. Pray that righteous laws may be made, and those righteously executed. Pray that the gospel, the rule of righteousness, may be established; that there may be righteous councillors, righteous magistrates. Thus will the eyes of the righteous Lord be upon it, to protect it, and to bless it with all needful blessings.

Sec. 21. *Of Christ a Prince of peace.*

A second mystery is taken from the place where Melchisedec reigned; which was *Salem,* and signifieth *peace,* as was shewed ver. 1, Sec. 4. In this also was Melchisedec both a type and a pattern.

As a type he prefigured Christ to be a King of peace. This is he who is styled the 'Prince of peace,' Isa. ix. 6, and said to be 'our peace,' Eph. ii. 14. As an evidence hereof, so soon as he was born, an heavenly host sang, 'On earth peace,' Luke ii. 14. The peace and unity of Christ's kingdom is eloquently and emphatically set out, Isa. ii. 4, and xi. 6, &c.

Two things there be which especially declare him to be a King of peace :

1. That peace which he made betwixt the Creator and creatures.

2. That which he made among creatures themselves.

God at first made all in perfect peace. There was a sweet harmony and consent. No discord, no dissension. Creatures by sin brought all out of frame. For,

1. God's wrath was incensed, and he made an enemy.

2. Good angels, holding close to their Lord, proved also enemies to such as rebelled against him, and became executioners of God's vengeance upon them.

3. There was variance in man himself. All the powers and parts of soul and body rising one against another; and conscience accusing and terrifying him.

4. Hatred, malice, and enmities were so betwixt man and man, as they became wolves, tigers, lions, yea, devils, one to another.

But Christ, being made King, made up all these breaches. For,

1. He satisfied God's justice, pacified his wrath, and reconciled man to God, Rom. iii. 25, and v. 8-10.

2. Christ took men, and made them members of his mystical body; and having so united them to himself, made angels to be at peace with them, Col. i. 20.

3. He communicateth his Spirit unto men, whereby all the powers of their souls, and parts of their body, are renewed and brought into a sweet harmony.

4. He brake down the partition wall betwixt Jew and Gentile, Eph. ii. 14, and made all one in himself, Gal. iii. 28, and so alters their disposition, as they may lovingly live together, Isa. xi. 6, &c.

Obj. Christ himself saith, that he 'came not to send peace, but a sword,' Mat. x. 34.

Ans. Three distinctions are here duly to be observed.

1. Betwixt peace and peace. There is a peace of the world, which is conspiracy of worldlings together in evil matters; and there is a peace of Christ, which is spiritual. The former Christ came not to send; the latter he gave to all his, John xiv. 27.

2. Betwixt persons and persons. Christ came not to make wicked ones at peace with his saints; but saints with saints.

We must distinguish betwixt the proper end of a thing, and a consequence following thereupon. Thus these words, 'I came not to send peace, but a sword,' Mat. x. 34, intend a consequence which followed upon Christ's coming into the world. For the gospel of Christ being a light, and professors thereof holding out this light, thereby is discovered the darkness and lewdness of the men of this world, which they can no way endure; but thereupon draw the sword, and raise all manner of persecution against those that hold out this light. By reason of this consequence, Christ is said not to come to send peace, but the sword.

The foresaid peace being proper to Christ's kingdom, serves as a matter of trial, to discover who are of the kingdom of Christ.

The subjects thereof are men of peace; and that,

1. As they are at peace with God, reconciled to him, and made subject to his will.

2. In that their consciences are pacified, and they cheerfully go on in their Christian course.

3. In that the several powers of their souls and parts of their bodies consent to do God's will.

4. In regard of their peaceable disposition; they pursue peace, and hurt none, Isa. xi. 9.

Peace being the property of Christ's kingdom, this is a strong attractive to draw men unto this kingdom, and move them there to abide. Who would not dwell in Salem, in a kingdom of peace? If the excellency and necessity of that peace which Christ bringeth were duly weighed, this would be found to be a very great privilege. All out of this kingdom are haters of God, and hated of him, θεοστυγεῖς, liable to God's wrath, vassals of Satan, heirs of hell; but all in and of this kingdom are lovers of God, and beloved of him, φιλόθεοι, his children, and heirs of glory.

Sec. 22. *Of righteousness and peace joined together.*

The conjunction of these two prerogatives, *King of righteousness*, and *King of Salem*, with conjunction upon conjunction, thus, *first*, πρῶτον μὲν, King of righteousness, *and after that also*, ἔπειτα καὶ, King of Salem, gives us to understand that a king of righteousness is also a king of peace. It is said of the king which judgeth with righteousness, that 'the mountains shall bring peace to the people by righteousness,' Ps. lxxii. 3. In this respect, 'righteousness and peace' are said to 'meet and kiss each other,' Ps. lxxxv. 10. After the Holy Ghost had set forth the righteousness of Christ, he addeth transcendent expressions of peace, Isa. xi. 4-6, &c.

This ariseth partly from their endeavour after peace, and partly from God's blessing upon their endeavour. Great are the benefits which peace brings to a kingdom. Therefore righteous kings seek it, and God gives it as a blessing to them.

Of the benefits of peace, see *The Church's Conquest*, sec. 96.

1. This may serve as a just taxation of those that delight in war, who are never well when they are out of war. They will therefore pick quarrels, thinking to get a name thereby, to live on spoils, to trample under and triumph over others. Such are no kings of righteousness. They are more fit to live in wildernesses among tigers, and other ravenous beasts, yea, in hell among devils, than among men.

2. Hereby kings and others may testify their righteous disposition, namely, by love of peace; hereunto we are much exhorted, Rom. xii. 18, Heb. xii. 14. Christ would have us not only keepers of peace, but also makers of peace, Mat. v. 9. Holiness and peace must go together, Heb. xii. 14. Neither must the unrighteousness of others make us break peace; nor must love of peace make us lose righteousness.

3. Pray that these two may ever go together; that Melchisedec may dwell in Salem. Pray that the wars begun may end in peace, and that that peace may be a peace of righteousness.

4. Be thankful to God for that peace that we have, so far as it meeteth with righteousness, and for the benefits that we enjoy thereby.

Sec. 23. *Of mysteries couched under histories.*

In the third verse there are four mysteries, taken from things concealed. They are all spoken of Melchisedec, as a type respectively, because they are not by the Holy Ghost expressed. For in those scriptures where mention is made of Melchisedec, there is not any mention made of his father, mother, descent, birth or death. But all those things are spoken of Christ the truth, simply and properly.

The Syriac, though it go from the words, and from the sense also, applied to Christ, yet in relation to Melchisedec giveth the right sense, thus,[1] whose father and mother are not written in the genealogies, nor the beginning of his days, nor end of his life.

A learned interpreter of the New Testament thus translates it,[2] who was of an unknown father, &c. This phrase, *without descent*, thus,[3] The original of whose stock cannot be declared.

Though these may shew the meaning of the words as applied to the type, yet they lose the emphasis of them, and obscure the mysteries contained in them.

Obj. There are many men mentioned in Scripture, whose father, mother, descent, birth, and death are not recorded in Scripture, as Obadiah, Habakkuk, Haggai, Malachi, and others.

Ans. The parentage, kindred, birth, and death of these, and sundry others, are passed over, because there was no great end of knowing them. But these were concealed in the history of this man, purposely to imply a mystery.

Quest. How may we know this?

Ans. Because the apostle, who was guided by the same Spirit that Moses and David were, hath observed as much. For the Spirit knoweth his own meaning. If one inspired by the Spirit of God had not revealed this mystery, all the private spirits of men that ever were could not have found it out, for it is a deep mystery, and as closely couched in the history as ever any was.

We may learn hereby diligently to compare the Old and New Testament together; thus may many profound mysteries be discovered. Thus thou shalt find the ark, 1 Peter iii. 21, the cloud, the Red Sea, the rock and manna, 1 Cor. x. 2, 3, to be such sacraments as ours. Thus thou shalt find the two children of Abraham, one born of a bond-woman, the other of a free-woman, to set forth children of the flesh, and of the spirit; and their two mothers, the two testaments, Gal. iv. 24, &c. Thus shalt thou find many legal rites and ceremonies applied to their proper truth and substance; and many dark and obscure prophecies clearly revealed and opened.

Sec. 24. *Of mysteries spoken of Melchisedec applied to Christ.*

The first three Greeks words, ἀπάτωρ, ἀμήτωρ, ἀγενεαλόγητος, translated, 'without father, without mother, without descent,' are here only used in the New Testament. They are all compound words, and that with the privative preposition, that implieth a plain negation of a thing,

1. This *without father* must needs be applied to the human nature of Christ. For as God, the second person in sacred Trinity, he is the Son of the first person, which is his Father, John v. 17. But as man he had no proper father, he was born of a pure virgin, Isa. vii. 14; Mat. i. 23; Luke i. 35. As for Joseph, the husband of his mother, it is said, that he was 'supposed' to be his father, Luke iii. 23, and that to hide this great mystery from such as were obstinately malicious.

2. This epithet, *without mother*, must needs have reference to Christ's divine nature; for we shewed before, that as man, he had a mother, he was born of the virgin Mary. The history of his birth is distinctly set down by the evangelists. But it is blasphemy to think that, as God, he should have a mother. The great Lord of heaven and earth is not like the gods of the heathen, who were imagined to have their wives, and some of them to be born of mothers.

Obj. The virgin Mary is styled Θεοτόκος, *Deipara*, the mother of God.

Ans. That is, by reason of the hypostatical union of his two natures, in which respect that which is proper to one nature is attributed to the other. Thus the 'Son of man' is said to be 'in heaven,' John iii. 13, because the divine nature, to which Christ's human nature was united, was in heaven. So God is said to purchase the church 'with his own blood,' Acts xx. 28, because the blood of that human nature, which was united to the divine, was shed to that end.

3. This epithet, *without descent*, or without pedigree, or without kindred, must also be meant of his divine nature, in reference whereunto he had no ancestors, no posterity. In reference to his human nature, both

---

[1] Cujus nec pater, nec mater scripti sunt in genealogiis, &c.—*Tremel. interpr.*

[2] Ignoti patris, ignotæ matris, &c.—*Sic Beza de' Erasmo.*

[3] ἀγενεαλόγητος. Cujus generis origo non possit reddi.—*Erasm. Annot. in loc.*

Matthew and Luke set down his distinct genealogy, Mat. i. 1, &c., Luke iii. 23, &c. In regard of his divine nature he was begotten of his Father, by an eternal, unalterable, unconceivable generation.

4. The last mystery consisteth of two branches: one, that he had no *beginning of days;* the other, *nor end of life.* These two set down a true proper eternity, without beginning and end. See hereof *The Explanation of the Lord's Prayer,* sec. 224.

This most properly and principally is to be taken of his divine nature. As God, he is 'Alpha and Omega,' Rev. i. 8.

Of Christ's eternity, see Chap. i. Secs. 129, 143, 145.

Christ, as man, had his beginning in the virgin's womb, after many hundred generations had passed in the world, even in the 3928th year of the world; and about thirty-four years after, there was an end of his mortal life in this world, for he was crucified, dead and buried. Indeed, he arose again from the dead, ascended into heaven, and there ever liveth and abideth in his human nature, so as in heaven he hath no end of life, but on earth he had. From the foresaid mysteries applied to Christ, we may infer these orthodox positions:

1. Christ is true God, without mother, &c.
2. This true God was not a made God, but eternal, without beginning. He had 'neither beginning of days nor end of life.'
3. Christ was true man, 'a son of man.'
4. This true God and true man is one person, even as the type Melchisedec was one. For the same person that, as God, was without mother, was also, as man, without father.
5. This person, God-man, is high-priest in both his natures; for Melchisedec, that high-priest, was in reference to Christ's human nature, without father; and in reference to his divine nature, without mother.

Most of their heresies which are mentioned, Chap. ii. 14, Sec. 140, are by these mysteries apparently refuted.

The foresaid mysteries, as in the truth and properties of them they belong unto Christ, who is our true high priest, are of singular use to strengthen our faith in and about his priesthood. For,

1. Knowledge of his manhood maketh us the more boldly and confidently to fly unto him, he being such an one as hath experience of our infirmities and necessities in himself.
2. Knowledge of his Godhead makes us more perfectly to rely upon him, and to trust unto him; for hereby we are assured that he is able to help.
3. Union of his two natures in one person strengtheneth our faith in his obedience, death, sacrifice, resurrection, and merit of all; for hereby we are assured that he is of infinite power, and that what he did and endured for us is of infinite value and worth.
4. His exercising of his priesthood in both natures, as he was God-man, maketh us with greater confidence to go to him, and to rest upon him, and to prefer him before all others, and to account him the only sufficient Mediator.

Sec. 25. *Of resemblances of Christ before his incarnation.*

Upon the fore-mentioned privileges the apostle maketh this inference, that Melchisedec was *made like unto the Son of God.* This inference the apostle bringeth in with this conjunction of opposition or discretion, δὲ, *but;* as if he had said, Though Melchisedec were a true man, yet in his singular prerogatives he was made like unto the Son of God. The word ἀφωμοιωμένος, translated *made like,* is here only used. It is a compound. The simple verb ὁμοιόω, signifieth *to liken* one thing to another, Mat. vii. 24. The preposition ἀπὸ, wherewith the verb here used is compounded, signifieth *to.* In this composition the word signifieth to represent the very form of another thing. Thus did Melchisedec, in the foresaid prerogatives, set out the very form and excellency of the Son of God. Jesus Christ is here meant by 'the Son of God.' See Chap. i. 2, Sec. 15.

Hereby we see that God of old gave visible types and resemblances of his Son, even before he was exhibited in the flesh.[1] Melchisedec was a mere true man, yet was he so set forth as he bare a resemblance of the Son of God. In other respects, Aaron and other priests, Moses and other prophets, David and other kings, were special types and resemblances of Christ. So were all the sacrifices, and especially the paschal lamb, 1 Cor. v. 7; so the ark, 1 Pet. iii. 21; so the Red Sea, the cloud, manna, and the rock, 1 Cor. x. 2, &c., and sundry other types.

God gave beforehand such resemblances of his Son for the good of his church in those ages; even to support their faith, and uphold their hope, till the fulness of time should come; that, when it was come, they might the more readily embrace and receive that truth, and more confidently rest upon it.

1. Herein the great and good care of God over his church is manifested; for though, in his unsearchable wisdom, he suffered many ages to pass before his Son was exhibited, yet he took such order for his church that was on earth before that fulness of time, as it should have means to partake of the benefit of those things which Christ should do and endure in that fulness of time. It is therefore said of those that lived many hundred years before that fulness of time was come, that 'they did all eat the same spiritual meat, and did all drink the same spiritual drink,' even the same that we do. For, by way of explanation, he addeth, 'They drank of that spiritual rock that followed them, and that rock was Christ,' 1 Cor. x. 3, 4. In this respect it is said of Abraham that he 'rejoiced

---

[1] See Chap. viii. 5, Sec. 13.

to see Christ's day; and that he saw it, and was glad,' John viii. 56.

The like care doth God shew over his church even now, now that the Son of God is taken into heaven; for we still enjoy his ministers, who are in his stead to us, 2 Cor. v. 20, and his sacraments; both the sacrament of regeneration and of spiritual nourishment; yea, also the benefit of his promise to be amongst us, Mat. xviii. 20, even to the end of the world, Mat. xxviii. 20. Wherefore as saints that lived before Christ was exhibited used priests, sacrifices, and other types of Christ before he was exhibited, so must we use his ministers, sacraments, and other ordinances now, after he is taken from us, as memorials of him.

Sec. 26. *Of Christ's everlasting priesthood prefigured in Melchisedec.*

The most especial and principal thing wherein Melchisedec was made like unto the Son of God was in this, that he *abideth a priest continually.*

In regard of the history concerning Melchisedec, this is to be taken, as the former points were, in the former part of this verse.

Melchisedec is said to 'abide a priest continually,' because the history which declareth him to be a priest maketh no mention either of the beginning of his priesthood or of the ending thereof. Thus was he said before to have 'neither beginning of days nor ending of life.'

There are two words that set forth the eternity of Christ's priesthood, in reference to the time future, which is beyond all determination or end, and in reference to the continuance thereof, without interruption or intermission.

The Greek word μένει, translated *abideth*, signifieth the continuance of a thing, Mat. xi. 23.

The other phrase, εἰς τὸ διηνεκές, translated *continually*, is another than that which is before translated *for ever*, εἰς τὸν αἰῶνα, Chap. v. 6. This word here used is a compound. The simple ἠνεκές, *protentum in longitudinem*, signifieth a long continuance. The preposition διά, wherewith this is compounded, signifieth *through*. Thus the word compounded with it, διηνεκές, *continua serie in perpetuum tendens*, signifieth a continuance *through perpetuity*, so as there is no intermission, no determination of the thing.

This applied to Christ the truth, whereof Melchisedec was a type, setteth out three points.

1. That Christ was a true priest. See Chap. ii. 17, Sec. 172.

2. That Christ's priesthood continueth for ever. See Chap. v. 6, Sec. 29.

3. That Christ continually executeth his priesthood without intermission.

In this respect, as a priest, he is said to 'continue ever,' and to 'have an unchangeable priesthood,' and 'ever to live to make intercession for us,' vers. 24, 25.

In regard of the continual efficacy of Christ's priesthood, it is said that 'he offered one sacrifice for sin for ever,' or continually, and to perfect continually, εἰς τὸ διηνεκές, them that are sanctified, Heb. x. 12, 14. Christ is in this respect as a spring that continually floweth forth.

There is in men a continual spring of corruption, which from time to time defileth them; so as they need continually to be cleansed. They also by their continual sins continually provoke God's wrath; so as they have need of a continual priest, to make continual atonement for them.

On this ground we have just cause on all occasions to look unto Jesus, to behold him our priest making continual intercession for us. A point this is of singular comfort.

Sec. 27. *Of the bread and wine which Melchisedec brought forth.*

Papists do here infer another mystery about the priesthood of Melchisedec, namely, that the bread and wine which he brought forth was the sacrifice proper to the order of his priesthood, and prefigured the body and blood of Christ, which they say is comprised in their mass under the show of bread and wine.[1]

Ans. If this were such a mystery, why did the apostle, in setting out so many mysteries as he did about Melchisedec, make no mention at all of this, which, as they say, is the greatest and most pertinent to Melchisedec's priesthood?

Bellarmine is forced in answer hereunto to say, that it was nothing to the apostle's purpose to make mention of it here.[2]

What! is it nothing to the purpose of him that sets down a special order of priesthood, to declare the special sacrifice that belongeth thereunto, and to give notice thereof to the Christian church?

It was too deep a mystery, saith Bellarmine, for the Hebrews.[3]

Ans. Was it deeper than those other mysteries which he mentioneth, ver. 2, and sundry others, in other parts of this epistle?

The truth is, that the thing itself, as they would have people to believe it, that the very body and blood of Christ, under the visible show of bread and wine, is offered up for a true, real, propitiatory sacrifice, is a mere mockage, apparently against Scripture, against reason, against sense.

1. The Scripture affirmeth that the body of Christ is in heaven, and there must continue until the times of restitution of all things, Acts iii. 21.

2. Reason tells us that a true body cannot be in divers places at once. But by their position the

---

[1] Bellarm. de Missa. lib. i, c. 6.
[2] Id ad propositum ejus non faciebat.
[3] Mysterium altius erat, quam ut ab illis capi tunc posset.

body of Christ must be in millions of places at the same time.

3. Sight, taste, smell, and feeling, tell men that that which they eat and drink at the sacrament is bread and wine: to say it is flesh and blood is against all those senses.

Papists press this phrase, 'he brought forth bread and wine,' as signifying an offering up of bread and wine.

Ans. 1. To *bring forth* doth not properly, nor necessarily in that place, import an offering up.

2. It was shewed (Sec. 8) that the bringing forth of bread and wine there, did declare a royal entertainment of Abraham and his army.

3. This was brought in the history, as an act of Melchisedec's kingly office, rather than of his priestly.

Papists reply that there was no need of refreshing Abraham's army, which had got great spoils.

Ans. 1. Though Abraham might not need such entertainment, yet Melchisedec might in good respect testify his bounty to Abraham.

2. Though there might be great spoils, yet they might want victuals.

3. Abraham might rather choose to have his army refreshed with Melchisedec's provision, than with the spoils that belonged to the king of Sodom, Gen. xiv. 23.

They further say, that if bread and wine were not Melchisedec's sacrifice, there is no mention of any sacrifice at all: whence it would follow that he should be a priest without sacrifice.

Ans. That would not follow. He might have sacrifices belonging to his priesthood, though they were not there mentioned; besides, though his order were another order than Aaron's, yet such sacrifices might belong to his priesthood as belonged to others' priesthood.

If bread and wine had been Melchisedec's offering, it had been most improper to bring them forth to Abraham; they should have been brought forth to God.

This improbable supposition of Melchisedec's offering up bread and wine, is too sandy a foundation for such a Babel as transubstantiation is to be built upon.

Sec. 28. *Of the resolution of* Heb. vii. 1–3.

Ver. 1. *For this Melchisedec, king of Salem, priest of the most high God, who met Abraham returning from the slaughter of the kings, and blessed him;*

2. *To whom also Abraham gave a tenth part of all: first being, by interpretation, King of righteousness, and after that also, King of Salem, which is King of peace:*

3. *Without father, without mother, without descent, having neither beginning of days nor end of life; but, made like unto the Son of God, abideth a priest continually.*

The sum of these three verses is, the excellency of Melchisedec's priesthood. Hereabout observe,

1. The inference, in this causal particle *for*. Ver. 1.

2. The substance: which is, 1, propounded; 2, illustrated, ver 3.

Of the substance propounded, there are two parts:

1. An historical narration of some passages.

2. A mystical application of others.

About the historical narration, there are two points. One concerns *Melchisedec*; the other, *Abraham*.

Three points concern Melchisedec:

1. His name.

2. His functions. These are two:

(1.) Kingly, amplified by the place, *King of Salem*.

(2.) Priestly, amplified by *the Lord*, whose priest he was.

This Lord is described,

(1.) By his nature, *God*.

(2.) By his sovereignty, *Most high*.

(3.) By his actions. These are of two sorts:

1. Regal: he met Abraham. Amplified by the victory which Abraham got.

This victory is described two ways:

(1.) By Abraham's return from the wars.

(2.) By the slaughter of the kings.

2. Priestly: he blessed him.

The act which concerned Abraham was an act of piety mixed with gratitude.

In setting it down are noted, 1. The person, Abraham.

2. His kind of act, *gave*.

3. The subject matter, *the tenth part*. This is amplified by the extent: *of all*.

The mystical application is of two sorts:

1. An interpretation of things expressed.

2. A manifestation of things concealed.

Two things are interpreted; 1. Melchisedec's name. 2. The city of his kingdom, Salem.

Five things concealed are in a mystery observed.

1. *Without father.* 2. *Without mother.* 3. *Without descent.* 4. *Without beginning* 5. *Without end.*

The illustration of the foresaid points is,

1. Generally expressed, *made like unto the Son of God*.

2. Particularly exemplified, *abideth a priest continually*.

Sec. 29. *Of observations raised out of* Heb. vii. 1–3.

I. *Deep mysteries must be explained.* This causal particle *for* sheweth the reason why the apostle doth unfold this mystery of Melchisedec, because he had implied that it was a deep mystery, Chap. v. 11. See Sec. 2.

II. *Melchisedec was an especial type of Christ*, This is the general sum of all.

III. *A king is a warrantable function.* It is warranted in the example of Melchisedec. See Sec. 3.

IV. *Kings have their special jurisdiction.* So was Salem to Melchisedec. See Sec. 4.

V. *True priests are priests of God.* Such an one was Melchisedec. See Sec. 5.

VI. *God is the Most High.* This is his title. See Sec. 6.

VII. *Melchisedec was both king and priest.* Both these functions are here expressly attributed to him. See Sec. 7.

VIII. *Kindred in distress are to be succoured.* Abraham succoured Lot his kinsman. See Sec. 10.

IX. *Neighbours ought to congratulate one another's victory.* So did Melchisedec, Abraham's neighbour. See Secs. 3, 11.

X. *Refreshing is to be afforded to soldiers.* So did Melchisedec to Abraham's soldiers. See Sec. 8.

XI. *Enemies in war may be slain.* The slaughter here mentioned is of such. See Sec. 9.

XII. *Kings in war are not free from slaughter.* Kings are here said to be slain. See Sec. 9.

XIII. *Pious salutations are commendable.* Melchisedec's blessing was in the general a salutation. See Sec. 13.

XIV. *Ministers have an especial power to bless people.* Melchisedec, as a minister of God, blessed Abraham. See Sec. 14.

XV. *Christ blesseth the faithful.* This is inferred from the type. See Sec. 15.

XVI. *Tenths were of old paid to God's ministers.* Abraham paid them to Melchisedec. See Secs. 16, 17.

XVII. *Ministers of the word must be maintained by people.* This is gathered from the general equity of tithes. See Sec. 18.

XVIII. *Strange tongues are to be interpreted.* This phrase, *by interpretation*, intendeth as much. See Sec. 19.

XIX. *Kings must be righteous.* This is the meaning of Melchisedec's name. See Secs. 19, 20.

XX. *Kings must be peaceable.* This is implied under this word *Salem.* See Sec. 22.

XXI. *Christ was a King of righteousness and peace.* He was the truth of both these. See Sec. 21.

XXII. *Matters concealed may be mysteries.* Here is an instance given of many particulars. See. Sec. 23.

XXIII. *Christ as man was without father.*

XXIV. *Christ as God was without mother and descent.*

XXV. *Christ was God eternal.* These were the truths of the things concealed. See Sec. 24.

XXVI. *There were resemblances of Christ before his incarnation.* Melchisedec is here said to be like him. See Sec. 25.

XXVII. *Christ was the Son of God.* Christ is here meant under that title. See Sec. 25.

XXVIII. *Christ is a perpetual priest.* He so *abideth continually.* See Sec. 26.

Sec. 30. *Of considering weighty points especially about Christ.*

Ver. 4. *Now consider how great this man was, unto whom even the patriarch Abraham gave the tenth of the spoils.*

The apostle having set forth Melchisedec's excellency in himself, proceedeth to amplify the same in reference to others; and first preferreth him before Abraham, from whom Levi, the head of all legal priests, descended.

Because Melchisedec was an especial type of Christ, and Abraham, the father of all the Jews, was counted by them the most excellent among them, the apostle adviseth to *consider* this argument of Melchisedec's excellency above Abraham's.

The word $\theta\varepsilon\omega\rho\varepsilon\tilde{\iota}\tau\varepsilon$, translated *consider*, doth properly belong to the bodily eyes, and is usually translated *to see*, $\theta\varepsilon\omega\rho\tilde{\eta}\sigma\alpha\iota$, Mat. xxviii. 1. It implieth a fast fixing of the eyes upon a thing, and is translated *beheld*, Mark xii. 41.

The word being applied to the mind, it signifieth a serious pondering of a matter, and is translated *perceive*, John xii. 19, or *consider*, as here.

It being here implied to the truth of the type, it implieth that we should with both the eyes of the soul, understanding, and faith, behold or consider Christ. So then, such points as set forth, in general, weighty matters, and, in particular, the excellencies of Christ, are seriously to be pondered. Hereof see more, Chap. iii. 1, Secs. 21–23.

Sec. 31. *Of the greatness of Melchisedec.*

The relative οὗτος, thus translated, *this man*, hath reference to Melchisedec.

It is sometimes used in scorn and derision. To manifest as much, our English useth to add this word *fellow*; thus, *this fellow*, Mat. xii. 24, Acts xviii. 13. And sometimes in honour, as where the penitent thief said of Christ, 'This man hath done nothing amiss,' Luke xxiii. 41. So here. The apostle, therefore, thus expresseth his excellency, $\pi\eta\lambda\iota\kappa\text{o}\varsigma$, *how great*. This is the interpretation of one Greek word, which is used interrogatively and indefinitely. It here implieth such an excellency as occasioneth much admiration.

I find this word only here and Gal. vi. 11. Another like word, $\dot{\eta}\lambda\iota\kappa\text{o}\varsigma$, of the same stem, differing only in one letter, is used in the same sense, Col. ii. 1, James iii. 5.

A correlative, $\tau\eta\lambda\iota\kappa\alpha\tilde{\upsilon}\tau\text{o}\varsigma$, derived from the same root, and translated *so great*, is used, Chap. ii. 3, Sec. 21. All of them carry a great emphasis, and imply a surpassing excellency.

Melchisedec is hereby implied to be the greatest among men.

I need not seek after more arguments than the apostle hath used in the former verses. He was especially the greatest, in that he was such a type of Christ, as none ever the like, before, or after him.

We may therefore well use this note of admiration, *how great!* If we may use it of the type, much more of the truth, Christ himself. See more hereof, Chap. ii. 17, Secs. 173, 174.

Take notice, by the way, of the blasphemous arrogancy of papists, who make their mass priests to be after the order of Melchisedec.

Thereby they would make them the greatest of men. They do much hereby infringe the apostle's argument, and pervert his main intent. If the prerogatives of a priest, after the order of Melchisedec (expressly set down, vers. 2, 3), be duly weighed, we shall find it a blasphemous institution to induct any mere man thereinto.

Sec. 32. *Of Abraham a patriarch.*

The argument whereby the apostle proves the greatness of Melchisedec, is Abraham's inferiority to him. The Jews counted Abraham the greatest among men. If therefore there were one greater than Abraham, how great must he needs be!

Of Abraham's excellency, see Chap. vi. 13, Secs. 91, 92.

As an amplification of Abraham's greatness, this title, *patriarch*, is attributed unto him.

Patriarch, πατριάρχης, is a noun compound. The first simple noun whereof it is compounded, πατήρ, signifieth *father;* and the other, ἀρχή, *principium, imperium,* beginning, or principality. Thus it implieth the first or chiefest father; or, the first and the chiefest of fathers, πατριάρχης, quasi, ἄρχων τῶν πατέρων, *princeps patrum.*

In the New Testament it is attributed, as to Abraham here, so to the twelve sons of Jacob, Acts vii. 8, 9; and to David, Acts iii. 29.

Abraham is called patriarch, because he was the first father of the stock of the Jews.

The twelve sons of Jacob were so styled, because they were the first heads and fathers of the twelve several tribes.

David had this title given him for excellency's sake, because he was a prime and principal father, or because he was the head and father of that stock whereof Christ as King should descend; or, some will have it, because the Sanhedrim, or senate of the Jews, were of his stock, and he the head thereof.

In the church of Christ under the gospel, which was a spiritual family, bishops were called by a Greek name παπαι, which signifieth *fathers,* and archbishops were called patriarchs, the chief of those fathers.

But when the number of bishops and archbishops increased, this high title patriarch was restrained to four chief archbishops: one at Rome, another at Jerusalem, the third at Antioch, the fourth at Alexandria.

In process of time, when the emperor had his seat at Constantinople, that city also had a patriarch.

All these continued with a kind of equal dignity, till the pride of Rome grew so great, as the bishop thereof would endure no mate, and thereupon had a new style, *papa universalis,* universal pope.

To return to the point in hand, this title *patriarch* doth much illustrate the dignity of Abraham, which much tendeth to the magnifying of Melchisedec's excellency, in that such a patriarch as Abraham was inferior to him.

Sec. 33. *Of Melchisedec's receiving tithes as a superior.*

The particular act whereby Abraham's inferiority to Melchisedec is demonstrated, is thus expressed, δεκάτην ἔδωκε, *gave the tenth.* This was before set down, ver. 2, Secs. 16, 17. Our English useth the same words in both places, but the Greek hath two distinct verbs. The former, ἐμέρισε, properly signifieth to *distribute,* as was shewed ver. 2, Sec. 16, which is a part of prudence. This other word ἔδωκε, signifieth *to give,* and that freely, cheerfully, which is a sign of love.

Both of them are applied to the same person, in the same act, and set out the prudence of his mind, and cheerfulness of his spirit, in what he did. Thus was his act the more commendable and acceptable.

Commendable through his prudence; acceptable through his cheerfulness, 'for God loveth a cheerful giver,' 2 Cor. ix. 7. Herein David shewed himself a son of Abraham, 1 Chron. xxix. 17. Let us all so do.

Of giving tithes, see ver. 2, Secs. 16, 17.

This act of Abraham's giving a tenth to Melchisedec implieth an inferiority in Abraham, that gave the tenth, and a superiority in Melchisedec, who received it, because the tenth was an holy tribute, due to God, and so it was paid by Abraham. His paying it to Melchisedec sheweth, that he gave it unto him as God's priest, standing in God's room, and in that respect greater than himself. A king's deputy is in that respect greater than those who are under the king.

Quest. 1. Was this the only end of tithes, to imply superiority in them that received them?

Ans. No; there were other reasons why Levites under the law received them: for the tribe of Levi, which had as great a right to a part of the land of Canaan as any other tribe, had none allotted them, upon this very ground, because they were to receive tenths of the people. Besides, they spent all their time and pains in and about those public services which by the people were due to God. As a recompence thereof, they received the tenth of the people. But these, and other like reasons, tended not in this place to the scope of the apostle; therefore he passeth them over, and insisteth only on this point of inferiority in giving, and superiority in taking tenths.

By the way, we may hereby learn to have an especial eye to what we have in hand, and to pass by other matters which might otherwise hinder us therein.

Quest. 2. Are all that receive tenths greater than they who give them?

Ans. 1. In this particular, as they who receive tithes receive them in God's stead, and as an homage due to God, they are greater than they of whom they receive them; yet not in outward estate and condition. Kings were not exempted from paying tenths; yet in their outward and civil state they were superior to priests, for Solomon a king put one high priest out of his place for misdemeanour, and set another in his room, 1 Kings ii. 35; and Hezekiah calleth priests and Levites his sons, which is a title of inferiority in them that are so styled.

It was an undue consequence of Pope Boniface to infer that popes are greater than kings, because kings pay tenths unto them.

This Boniface was the eighth of that name, who was that pope of Rome, of whom it was said, He entered as a fox, ruled as a wolf, and died as a dog.

The non-consequence grounded upon the text we have in hand, is manifest by these particulars.

1. The pope of Rome hath no right to take tenths of kings of other nations. It is a proud usurpation of the pope to demand it, and a slavish subjection in kings that yield it.

2. Receiving of tenths implieth no superiority in civil and secular affairs.

3. There is a vast difference betwixt Melchisedec and other ministers of God about receiving tithes. Abraham paid tenths to Melchisedec, as he was an extraordinary priest and type of Christ; and as a public testimony of that homage he owed to Christ, the great High Priest. But tenths are paid to other ministers for their maintenance.

4. The foresaid argument makes no more for the pope than for the meanest parson, or vicar of a parochial church.

5. By that argument an ordinary parson or vicar might be greater than the pope, for if the pope had land within the parsonage of the meanest parson, he must pay him tithes.

But to leave this point, the main scope of the apostle in setting forth the greatness of Melchisedec, is to commend unto us the greatness of him and his priesthood that was typified by Melchisedec and his priesthood; that is, the greatness of our Lord Jesus, who, without comparison, is the greatest priest that ever was. Hereof see Chap. ii. 17, Sec. 173.

Sec. 84. *Of giving the best to God.*

The subject matter, out of which Abraham is here said to pay the tenths, is thus expressed, *of the spoils*. The Greek word ἀκροθίνια, translated *spoils*, it is here only used in the New Testament. It is compounded of two nouns: the former, ἄκρον, signifieth the top or uppermost part of a thing; it being applied to the finger, is translated the *tip* thereof, Luke xvi. 24. It also signifieth the uttermost part of a thing, and applied to the earth it is translated *the uttermost part*, Mark xiii. 27.

The other word, θίς, *vel* θίν, *acervus*, signifieth *an heap*; so as to join them together, the Greek word here used being of the plural number, signifieth the tops, or uttermost parts of heaps. It is used to set forth first fruits, which were wont to be taken from the tops of such heaps of fruits as were taken from the earth and laid together. The tops of such heaps are commonly the best.

By heathen authors it is commonly taken for so much of the spoils as were dedicated to their gods. The apostle here useth the word as fit to his purpose; answerably most interpreters translate it *spoils*.

The tenth of spoils were given to God's priests, on these grounds:

1. That people might shew their willingness to give part of all they had to God's ministers, according to the equity of that rule which is prescribed by the apostle, Gal. vi. 6.

2. Upon a good persuasion, that people are blessed in their undertakings by the prayers of God's ministers.

3. In testimony of their acknowledgment of God's providence in giving them good success, whereby they obtained the spoils that they have.

The things which the other authors comprised under the Greek word here used were commonly the best, for the best things are to be given to God. 'Abel brought of the firstlings of his flock, and of the fat thereof unto the Lord,' Gen. iv. 4. The beast that had a blemish was not to be sacrificed to the Lord, Deut. xv. 21.

1. God is worthy of the best, for we have all from him.

2. That which is dedicated to God is best employed.

Herein is manifested the deceitfulness of their heart, and undue respect towards God, who seem to give something unto God, but of the worst that they have; and that in ministers' allowance, in setting apart some of their children to the ministry, in works of piety, of charity, and other like things.

Let us be otherwise minded, and as we desire to be accepted of God, give him the best we have, even our souls, our hearts, our strength, the best of our time, the towardest of our children, the best of our fruits, and the like in other things.

Sec. 35. *Of the resolution of* Heb. vii. 4, *and observations raised from thence.*

The sum of this verse is a proof of Melchisedec's greatness.

Here observe, 1. The manner of propounding it. 2. The matter.

The manner is in two branches,

1. By calling them to *consider* what he was.

2. By way of an indefinite interrogation, *how great this man was.* The matter sets out Abraham's inferiority to Melchisedec.

Of this there are two parts:

1. A description of his person.

2. Declaration of his act of inferiority.

The person is described,

1. By his name, *Abraham*.
2. By his dignity, *patriarch*.

His act is set out, 1. By the manner, *gave*, which implies readiness.

2. By the measure, *the tenth*.
3. By the subject matter, *spoils*.

Doctrines.

I. *Weighty matters must be well weighed.* Consider, saith the apostle. See Sec. 30.

II. *Melchisedec was super-excellently great.* This emphatical expression, *how great this man was*, implies as much. See Sec. 31.

III. *Tenths of old were paid.* Abraham paid them to Melchisedec. See ver. 2. Doct. 16.

IV. *What is given to God's ministers must be cheerfully given.* See Sec. 33.

V. *Abraham was a patriarch.* He is so expressly styled. See Sec. 32.

VI. *Just titles may be given to men.* Patriarch was Abraham's just title. See Sec. 32.

VII. *To receive tenth is an act of superiority.* Hereby Melchisedec is proved to be greater than Abraham. See Sec. 33.

VIII. *Victories are to be ascribed to God.* This did Abraham by giving of the spoils to God's priest. See Sec. 34.

IX. *The best is to be given unto God.* The Greek word translated *spoils* importeth as much. See Sec. 34.

Sec. 36. *Of the main scope of verses 5, 6, 7.*

Ver. 5. *And verily they that are of the sons of Levi, who receive the office of the priesthood, have a commandment to take tithes of the people according to the law, that is, of their brethren, though they come out of the loins of Abraham:*

6. *But he, whose descent is not counted from them, received tithes of Abraham, and blessed him that had the promises.*

7. *And, without all contradiction, the less is blessed of the better.*

In these three verses there is a confirmation of the former argument, whereby the greatness of Melchisedec above Abraham was proved. That argument was taken from Abraham's giving tithes to Melchisedec. See Sec. 33.

The confirmation of that argument is taken from that which in logic is called *à minori, the less*. In setting down this confirmation, there is a double difference of persons manifest.

1. A difference of the persons that received tithes.
2. A difference of the persons who gave tithes, or of whom tithes were received.

1. The persons that received tithes, being the sons of Levi, were of the same stock that the other Israelites who paid tithes were. But Melchisedec was not so.

2. The Levites received tithes of the children of Abraham. But Melchisedec received tithes of Abraham himself.

Two arguments out of the apostle's words may be gathered for confirmation of the former proof of Melchisedec's greatness, and thus framed:

Arg. 1. If among them that are brethren coming from the same stock, they who receive tithes, are in that respect the greater, then much more he whose descent is not counted among them of whom he received tithes;

But the Levites, who received tithes of their brethren, were in that respect greater than their brethren;

Therefore Melchisedec, whose descent is not from them of whom he received tithes, must needs be greater.

Arg. 2. He that receiveth tithes of the head and stock, is greater than they who receive tithes of the branches, that sprout out of that head and stock; but Melchisedec received tithes from Abraham, the father and stock of the Levites, who received tithes of the children of Abraham;

Therefore Melchisedec is greater than the Levites.

There are that make the first verse to contain an objection against the apostle's former argument, taken from Melchisedec's receiving tithes of Abraham, to be thereupon the greater, and an answer to be made to this objection in the sixth verse.

They make the objection to be this:

Object. The sons of Levi received tithes of the other Israelites, yet were not thereupon greater, for they were all brethren. Therefore Melchisedec's receiving tithes doth not argue him to be greater.

In answer to this objection, they say that the apostle granteth it to be true of the Levites, that their receiving tithes argued no superiority of them over the other Israelites, but that he denieth the consequence, namely, that thereupon it should follow, that Melchisedec's receiving tithes of Abraham did not argue him to be greater than Abraham, and that for two reasons here alleged: one, because Melchisedec was not counted to be of the same stock that Abraham was. But the Levites and other Israelites were all brethren of the same stock.

The other, because the Levites had a commandment to receive tithes; so as their brethren were bound by the law to pay them. But Abraham was bound by no such law. He gave tithes to Melchisedec voluntarily, in testimony of his reverence, subjection, and inferiority to Melchisedec, therefore Melchisedec's receiving of tithes may argue a superiority, though the Levites' receiving tithes do argue no such thing.

I take the apostle's confirmation of his former argument to be most especially here intended.

Sec. 37. *Of those sons of Levi that were priests.*

The Greek adverb $\mu \grave{\epsilon} \nu$, translated *verily*, is oft used merely in reference to the adversative conjunction $\delta \grave{\epsilon}$, translated *but*, which is used ver. 6, whereunto this hath reference. Sometimes it is a note of strong affirmation; so it is used Chap. iii. 5, Sec. 50, and Chap. vi. 16, Sec. 115. Other times it is used as a mere ornament of the Greek tongue, and is not translated in English, as Chap. i. 7, and in 2d and 8th verses of this chapter. So here it may be taken as a mere ornament. If it be further taken as a note of asseveration, it implieth, that the point here spoken of is the more thoroughly to be weighed, as a matter most certainly true.

This phrase, ἐκ τῶν υἱῶν Λευί, *they that are of the sons of Levi*, doth in general imply the posterity of Jacob's third son.

The notation of this name לוי, Λευί, Levi, is expressly given, Gen. xxix. 34. It appeareth that Jacob had taken more delight in Rachel's company than Leah's. But by this third son, God's blessing being manifested in making Leah fruitful, when her sister was barren, she was persuaded that her husband would now associate himself more with her, and thereupon, this son was named *Levi*. For the verb לוה, *mutuo accepit, accommodavit*, from whence this noun *Levi* hath his notation, in the passive, signifieth to be joined to one, Num. xviii. 2; Isa. lvi. 6. In desire, or hope, or foresight that her husband would be joined to her, and keep her company, this name Levi is given to her son.

Among the sons of Jacob, God chose Levi and his posterity to be his ministers in public, holy duties, and to attend the services of the tabernacle, in the room of all the rest of the children of Israel, Num. i. 50.

Of the sons of Levi, Aaron and his seed were chosen to serve in the priest's office. They, therefore, that were of Aaron's seed are here especially intended, as is evident by this clause, 'who receive the office of the priesthood.' So much was hinted in the first clause of this verse. He saith not in the nominative case, 'they that are the sons of Levi;' but in the genitive, and that with a preposition prefixed, 'they that are, ἐκ τῶν υἱῶν, of the sons of Levi.' This phrase, as it implieth such as descended from Levi, so a set and distinct number of them; some chosen out from among them. For all the children of Levi received not the priesthood, Num. xvi. 10, but only some of them, even Aaron and his posterity.

By ἱερατεία, *priesthood*, is here meant that office which belonged unto priests. It hath the same notation in Greek; whereof see Chap. ii. 17, Sec. 172. Of those general points which belong to a priest, see Chap. v. 1, Sec. 2, &c. This function is here brought in for honour's sake; for it implieth a dignity conferred upon those sons of Levi which are here meant. This function is expressly styled *an honour*. See Chap. v. 4, Sec. 18.

This verb, λαμβάνοντες,[1] *receive*, is relative, and hath reference to *giving*. It implieth that they had not this office of themselves, but that it was given them, namely, of God. For they only have a right to be

[1] See Chap. iv. 16, Sec. 96.

'for men in things pertaining to God' (as priests were), who are deputed thereunto by God. From hence it followeth that all true ministers must have their call from God, see Chap. iii. 2, Secs. 34, 35, and Chap. v. 4, Sec. 20.

Sec. 38. *Of the difference betwixt commandment and law.*

The manifestation of that honour and prerogative which the foresaid sons of Levi had, is in their power to receive tithes; thereupon it is added that they had a commandment to receive tithes.

That receiving tithes argued a superiority was shewed ver. 4, Sec. 33.

The ground of their receiving tithes is set down in this word, ἐντολή, *commandment*, and also in the other word following, νόμος, *law*.

Of the derivation of these two Greek words, see ver. 16, Sec. 80.

These are two of those ten words, which are used to set out the law or word of God; and are all of them set down in the 119th Psalm.

In that Psalm they are set down in this order:

1. דרך, *via*, *way*, ver. 1, whereby is meant that course which God hath set before us to walk in.

2. תורה, *lex*, *law*, ver. 1, whereby the will of God is made known unto us, and we enjoined to conform ourselves thereto.

3. עדות, *testimonium*, *testimony*, ver. 2, whereby testimony or witness is given of that which is good or evil.

4. פקדים, *precepta*, *precepts*, ver. 4. The Hebrew verb, פקד, *requisivit*, 1 Sam. xiv. 17, from whence the Hebrew noun translated *precepts* is derived, among other things, signifieth *to require*. The Rabbins say that those precepts especially which are written in man's heart, are intended under this word.

5. חקם, *statuta*, *statutes*, ver. 5. These do especially intend those ceremonial laws to which the Jews were bound.

6. מצוה, *mandatum*, *commandment*, ver. 6. Under this word such commandments as declared the power and authority of God over us, is declared.

7. משפטים, *judicia*, *judgments*, ver. 6. By these that mutual equity, or righteous dealing which should be betwixt man and man, is taught.

8. צדק, *justitia*, *righteousness*, or justice, ver. 7. By this what is due to every one is manifested.

9. דבר, *verbum*, *word*, ver. 9. There is also another noun, אמרה, *promissum*, which we translate *word*, ver. 11. These two last words are oft attributed to the whole law. The former signifieth the intent of the mind, expressed by words. The latter a promise expressed, and it is oft translated *promise*, Ps. lxxvii. 8.

The difference betwixt these two words, *commandment*, *law*, here used by the apostle, I take to be this, that *law* is here in general taken for a statute and rule that was set down unto them, that so much should be dedicated and given to the Lord; and *commandment*, for a particular warrant and direction to the sons of Levi, to receive such a part as by law was dedicated to God; as when a law or statute is made, that such subsidies shall be given to the king, the king thereupon gives command to such and such to receive the same.

Sec. 39. *Of God's ordering his precepts according to law.*

The inference of this phrase, κατὰ τὸν νόμον, *according to the law*, upon the commandment which was given, giveth evidence that God ordereth particular precepts according to his general law. If we compare the particular commandments which God from time to time gave to his people, we shall find them to be according to the law.

Obj. 1. The commandment given unto Abraham to sacrifice his son, Gen. xxii. 2, was not according to the law.

Ans. It was not a commandment of a thing simply and absolutely to be done, but a commandment of proof and trial. The event proveth as much.

Obj. 2. The commandment given to the Israelites to borrow of their neighbours jewels, raiment, and other things, thereby to spoil the Egyptians, was not according to law, Exod. iii. 22.

Ans. It was not against the law, which is that none defraud his neighbour of such goods as he hath a right unto.

2. The Israelites did not fraudulently take what they had of the Egyptians.

Concerning the right to that which the Israelites took, it appears to belong to the Israelites two ways:

(1.) By donation on God's part. For God is the most high supreme sovereign, and hath power to transfer what he will to whom he will.

(2.) By debt on the Egyptians' part. For Israel had long served the Egyptians, and done great work for them, yet were not satisfied for their pains.

Concerning the manner of the Israelites taking what they had of the Egyptians, they used no fraud therein. The word ושאלה, which our English thus translateth, *shall borrow*, doth properly signify *to ask*; so do the LXX, ἀιτήσει, the vulgar Latin, *postulabit*, and sundry other translators, turn it. Answerably the Egyptians gave to the Israelites what they asked; not simply to have the same restored, but to move them more speedily to depart, Exod. xii. 33. Besides, it appeareth that there was somewhat extraordinary in this case; for it is said, that 'the Lord gave the people favour in the sight of the Egyptians,' Exod. xii. 36.

To return to the main point, such is the immutability of God's justice, so perfect is the law of the Lord, so wisely is that law ordered, as the Lord will not suffer any particular precept to thwart and cross the same.

1. This giveth one evidence of the corruption of man's nature, which is so backward to, and averse from, that perfect law of God, and particular precepts of the word, which are all according to law. They who are truly renewed are otherwise minded, Ps. xix. 10, and cxix. 72, 103, 127.

2. This is a forcible motive to yield all holy obedience to the particular commandments which here and there are to be found in God's word; because they are all according to law, all grounded on common equity, and framed according to right; so as the benefit will redound to the practisers thereof.

3. God's prudence in ordering his commandments according to law, is a good pattern for such as are in God's stead, and have power to command others. Their rule must be God's law, and they ought to command nothing but what is according to that law. If God, who is the most supreme sovereign, and hath none higher than himself, orders his commandments according to law, how much more ought men so to do, who are to give an account of that which they enjoin to others. Indeed, God orders his commandments according to his own law, because there is no superior law, no law more just and equal. As he sware by himself, because he had no greater to swear by, chap. vi. 13, so he goeth by his own law, because there is none higher, none better.

If governors would order their commandments according to divine law, they might more boldly press them upon the people; yea, their people would more cheerfully yield unto them, and in case any should refuse to yield, they might with better conscience enforce them.

Sec. 40. *Of the law of paying tithes.*

The particular commandment here set down was *to take tithes of the people*. This phrase, *to take tithes of*, is the interpretation of one Greek word, ἀποδεκατοῦν, which we may answerably thus translate, *to tithe*. It is a compound verb. The simple verb is derived from that, δεκατη, which before was translated *tenth*, Sec. 16. It sometimes signifieth *to pay tithes*, as Luke xviii. 12; but here *to receive tithes*. So doth the simple verb signify both to receive and to pay tithes, ver. 6, 9. The circumstance therefore of the place must direct us in finding out the meaning of the word, of paying and receiving tenth. See ver. 2, Sec. 17.

By, λαὸν, *the people*, are here meant all the other tribes save the tribe of Levi, for none else were exempted from this tax. The children of Levi were for the people in things pertaining to God, and did for them what otherwise the people should have done themselves, and in recompence thereof the people paid them tithes.

The Greek phrase word for word thus soundeth, *to tithe the people* (ἀποδεκατοῦν τὸν λαὸν), which implieth both a duty on the people's part in paying tithe, and also a power or privilege on the Levites' part to receive tithe.

This was it which is here said to be according to the law; and that the judicial, ceremonial, and moral law.

1. By the judicial law the Levites had not their portion in Canaan for their inheritance, as other tribes had; therefore, in lieu thereof, by the said law, they had the tenth of the rest of the people.

2. The holy services which they performed to the Lord for the people were ceremonial. Therefore the recompence given was by a like law.

3. The general equity, that they who communicate unto us spiritual matters, should partake of our temporals; and that they who are set apart wholly to attend God's service, should live upon that service, is moral. See more hereof, ver. 2, Secs. 16, 17.

Sec. 41. *Of coming out of one's loins.*

The parties that paid tithes to the foresaid sons of Levi are thus described, *that is, of their brethren,* &c. Of the different acception of this title *brethren,* see Chap. xiii., Sec. 3. Here it is taken for all those that descended from Abraham, and in that respect were all of the same stock. So it is used Acts xiii. 26.

In this place it implieth a kind of equality among all the Israelites, of what tribe or what degree soever they were. The apostle's meaning is explained in these words, *though they came out of the loins of Abraham.*

The Greek word ὀσφύος, translated *loins,* is of the singular number. It is taken for that part of the back which useth to be girded,[1] Mat. iii. 4. The Hebrew word is of the dual number, חלצים, *lumbi,* because the loins are on both sides of the body. In Latin, English, and other languages, the word is of the plural number. In reference to the foresaid signification, the phrase of 'girding the loins' is frequent, and that for steadiness and strength, as soldiers use to gird their harness fast to their loins, Eph. vi. 14; or, for speed and expedition, as runners or travellers use to gird up their long-sided garments, Luke xii. 35.

This word *loins* is also taken for the inward and lower part of a man's belly, where his seed lieth.[2] In reference hereunto, the phrase of *coming out of the loins* is oft used, as Gen. iii. 11, so here.

By this phrase, they come out of the loins of Abraham, are meant, the very same whom before he called *the people* and *brethren.* It is here brought in to shew that they all came from the same stock, even Levites that received tithes, and the people their brethren that paid tithes.

The phrase of coming out of Abraham's loins is the rather mentioned, because Abraham, who paid tithes to Melchisedec, was the father of the Levites, who received tithes, as well as of those who paid tithes.

This discretive conjunction, καίπερ, *though,* implieth that that equality which was betwixt the tribe of Levi and other tribes was no hindrance to the Levites from receiving tithes, nor afforded any exemption to the other tribes from paying tithes. Though in the common stock, priests and others were equal, yet the priests in office were more excellent, and in this privilege of receiving tithes greater.

Thus we see, that equality in outward condition is no bar to superiority in office, nor hindrance to just rights appertaining thereunto. Moses and Aaron were uterine brothers, that came out of the same womb, yet Moses was so preferred in office before Aaron, as God himself said to Moses in reference to Aaron, 'Thou shalt be to him instead of God,' Exod. iv. 16. The Israelites were to choose a king from among their brethren, Deut. xvii. 15, yet being king, he had a superiority and dignity over his brethren. Men who were like unto others in their nature, are in regard of their functions styled 'gods and children of the Most High,' Ps. lxxxii, 6. The apostles were but of mean outward condition, yet in regard of their function, they were in a high degree advanced above others.

Excellency, dignity, superiority, and other like privileges, are not from nature, but from that order which God is pleased to set betwixt party and party.

They whom God advanceth, have in that respect an excellency, whatsoever their birth were: instance David, who though the youngest, yet was advanced above all his brethren.

Obj. The first-born had a dignity by their birth, Gen. iv, 7, and xlix. 3. So sons of kings and nobles have by their birth a dignity.

Ans. Even all these are from that order which God hath set amongst men.

On this ground we are to respect men according to that place and office wherein God setteth them. This may in particular be applied to ministers, whose function is not by birth. The Jews, looking upon Christ as a mere and mean man, born and brought up amongst them, did not discern either his excellent function or his eminent gifts, and thereupon despised him, Mat. xiii. 54, 55. From this evil disposition arose that proverb, 'A prophet is not without honour, save in his country, and in his own house,' Mat. xiii. 57. This was the pretended ground of Korah, Dathan, and Abiram's mutiny, Num. xvi. 3. Great damage doth hence arise, not only to ministers' persons, who are basely accounted of, but also to their function, which is too much disrespected. It hath been an old trick of Satan, thus to bring contempt upon ministers and ministry.

Sec. 42. *Of Melchisedec's priesthood greater than Levi.*

The main point, that Melchisedec exceeded Levi, is

---

[1] Ὀσφύς dicitur dorsi ea pars qua cingimur.—*H. Steph. Thesaur. Gr. ling.*

[2] Pars infimi ventris posterior et superior lumbos constituit.—*Casp. Bartol. Instit., Anatom.,* lib. i.

here proved in this sixth verse, and withal the consequence of the former argument, mentioned Sec. 36, is confirmed. The consequence was this. If the sons of Levi, in receiving tithes from their brethren, were therein counted greater than their brethren, then Melchisedec must needs be counted greater than they.

The confirmation of the consequence resteth on the person of whom Melchisedec received tithes, which was Abraham the father of Levi. For he that is greater than the father, must needs be greater than the son.

The former part of the sixth verse containeth a description of Melchisedec, in these words, ὁ μὴ γενεαλογούμενος ἐξ αὐτῶν, *he whose descent is not counted from them;* which are the interpretation of this mystery, ἀγενεαλόγητος, *without descent,* because his descent or pedigree was not reckoned up.

This phrase, *descent is counted,* is the interpretation of one Greek word, γενεαλογούμενος, which is a compound of a noun and a verb. The noun γενεά signifieth among other things *a progeny,* or *pedigree,* or *lineage.* The verb λέγειν signifieth to *utter,* or *declare,* or *reckon up;* so as to have one's descent counted is to have those from whom he cometh and who descend from him reckoned up and declared. But no such thing is done of Melchisedec; therefore it is said, ' his descent is not counted.'

This clause, ἐξ αὐτῶν, *from them,* is here added to shew a further difference betwixt Melchisedec and the Levites. Their descent was counted from Levi and from Abraham, but Melchisedec's from none such.

Or otherwise this phrase *from them* may indefinitely be taken, as if it had been said, ' from men;' for he was ' without descent,' as is noted Sec. 24.

This sheweth that the right which Melchisedec had to receive tithes was by no privilege of kindred, as being one of Abraham's progenitors or predecessors, but only in regard of his office, merely and simply because he was a priest of God, and in that respect hath a special prerogative, power, and dignity above Abraham. And if above Abraham, then much more above Levi, who descended from Abraham; and for this end it is again expressly mentioned that ' he received tithes from Abraham.'

The issue of all is, that Melchisedec's priesthood was greater than the priesthood of the Levites, and in that respect much more was Christ's priesthood greater, and thereupon the more to be admired, and with greater confidence to be rested upon. See ver. 4, Sec. 31, and ver. 11, Sec. 66.

Sec. 43. *Of Melchisedec's blessing Abraham.*

A second argument to prove the pre-eminence of Melchisedec's priesthood is taken from an act of superiority which Melchisedec performed in reference to Abraham, the father of Levi. This act was to bless.

The argument may be thus framed :
He that blesseth one is greater than he whom he blesseth ;
But Melchisedec blessed Abraham ; therefore Melchisedec was greater than Abraham.

The general proposition is cleared in the next verse. The assumption, which containeth the act itself, is here set down. Of the various acceptions of this word *blessed,* and of the particular intendment thereof in this place, see ver. 1, Secs. 12, 14, 15.

Sec. 44. *Of the privilege of having promises.*

The person blessed is not by name expressed, but thus described, τὸν ἔχοντα τὰς ἐπαγγελίας, *him that hath the promises.* This description doth so clearly belong to Abraham, as it may easily be known that he is meant thereby, for it hath reference to this phrase, ' God made promise to Abraham,' chap. vi. 13.

This participle, ἔχοντα, *had,* may have reference both to God, who made the promises, and so gave them to Abraham, and also to Abraham himself, who believed and enjoyed the benefit of the promises. In this respect he is said to have received the promises, chap. xi. 17, and to have obtained them, chap. vi. 15. Of this word *promise,* see Chap. iv. 1, Sec. 6, of promises.

This description of Abraham is set down for honour's sake ; for the apostle setteth forth Abraham's privileges, that thereby the privileges and dignities of Melchisedec might appear to be the greater.

Quest. Seeing the promises were such as appertained to the whole mystical body of Christ, why are they here appropriated to Abraham ?

Ans. God was pleased to choose Abraham as an head and father of his church, and that both of that peculiar visible church of the Jews, which for many ages was severed from the whole world, and also of that spiritual invisible church, the company of true believers, which should be to the end of the world, Rom. iv. 11.

Though this honour of having the promises be here in special applied to Abraham, yet it is not proper to him alone, but rather common to all that are of the same faith, who are styled ' heirs of promise,' chap. vi. 17.

It hereby appeareth that it is a great privilege to have a right to God's promises. Among other privileges belonging to the Jews this is one, that ' the promises pertain to them,' Rom. ix. 4. On the contrary side it is noted as a matter of infamy, to be ' aliens from the covenants of promise,' Eph. ii. 12.

God's promise is the ground of all our happiness. There is no other right whereby we may claim anything. Man by his fall utterly deprived himself of all the happiness wherein God made him. It is God's free promise that gives him any hope of other happiness, Gen. iii. 15. But they who have a right to God's promises have a right to all things that may make to their happiness. For what good thing is there whereof God hath not made promise?

Believers have much cause to rest hereupon, and to rejoice herein. Let Jews brag of their outward privileges: the promises made in Christ, whereof through infidelity they have deprived themselves, far exceed and excel all their privileges.

Let worldlings brag of their outward preferments, dignities, wealth, and other like things; if they have not a right to the promises, they have a right to nothing.

This should stir us up in general to walk worthy of the Lord, who hath made these promises, Col. i. 10, 1 Thes. ii. 12, and of the gospel, wherein and whereby they are tendered unto us, Philip. i. 27.

In particular, we ought hereupon to believe the promises made unto us; otherwise we deprive ourselves of the benefit of the promises, chap. iv. 1, 6.

2. It will be our wisdom to observe the conditions annexed to those promises.

3. It is just and equal that we moderate our care about the things of this world, and not seek great things for ourselves here, Jer. xlv. 5.

4. It becomes us to rest content in the state where God sets us. Having such promises as God hath made unto us, we have enough.

5. These promises should make us with patience expect the time appointed for the accomplishment of them.

Sec. 45. *Of the need that the best have of means to strengthen their faith.*

This phrase, *him that had the promises*, being inferred upon Melchisedec's blessing, giveth instance that the best faith needeth strengthening. Melchisedec's blessing was by way of ratification and confirmation of those promises which Abraham had. Now consider what a man Abraham was, and how great his faith was; yet this means of blessing was used to ratify the same. For this end God addeth promise to promise, and his oath also. See Chap. vi. 13, Sec. 97.

The ground hereof resteth not in ourselves; for,

1. As we know but in part, 1 Cor. xiii. 9, so we believe but in part. The best have cause to say, 'Lord, I believe, help thou my unbelief,' Mark ix. 24.

2. The flesh is in the best, which is weak when the spirit is ready, Mat. xxvi. 41.

3. The best are subject to many temptations: the better men are, the more will Satan seek to sift them, Luke xxii. 31.

How diligent should men hereupon be in observing what means God hath sanctified for strengthening their faith, and how conscionable in using the same.

Above all, let men take heed of too much confidence in themselves. God is thereby provoked to give men over to themselves, which if he do, Satan will soon take an advantage against them. Take instance hereof in Peter's example, Mat. xxvi. 69, &c.

Sec. 46. *Of undeniable principles.*

Ver. 7. The general proposition, noted Sec. 43, is here in the seventh verse expressly set down, namely, that he who blesseth is greater than he whom he blesseth.

So true and sure is this proposition, as the apostle premiseth this phrase of asseveration, *without all contradiction.*

The Greek noun ἀντιλογία, translated *contradiction*, is the same that was used Chap. vi. 16, sec. 121, and translated *strife*. The notation of the word was there declared.

This general particle, πάσης, *all*, addeth emphasis, and implieth, that none that is of understanding can or will deny the truth of the foresaid assertion.

This manner of asseveration, as it setteth forth the certainty of the thing itself, so a duty on our part, which is, to yield to the truth thereof, and not oppose against it.

From this particular instance may well be inferred this general observation;—

There are principles so infallibly true, as they admit no doubt or dispute thereabout. The apostle, about another and greater principle, useth a like asseveration, ὁμολογουμένως, *without controversy*, 1 Tim. iii. 16. To like purpose this phrase is used, 'This is a faithful saying, and worthy all acceptation.' 1 Tim. i. 15 and 4, 9.

1. Some principles are expressly set down in the word of truth; these are to be received without all contradiction. 'He that cometh unto God must believe that he is,' &c. Heb. xi. 6. A *must*, a necessity of believing it, is laid upon us. Such are all fundamental principles.

2. There are principles so agreeable to the light of nature, to reason itself, and common sense, as they admit no contradiction: such are these, a true body is circumscribed within a place, and it hath the essential properties of a body; a priest is greater than the sacrifice; works of merit must be answerable to the reward merited. They on whom we call must be able to hear us and help us.

1. The dotage of papists is hereby discovered, in that they maintain many heresies contradictory to express evidence of Scripture, and to principles of nature; as those before named, and sundry others. Therein they contradict those things which are *without all contradiction.*

2. It will be our wisdom carefully to observe such principles, and quietly to rest in them, neither stirring up needless controversies about them, nor suffering ourselves to be drawn from them. The philosopher thought not him worthy to be disputed withal that denied principles. If a man deny the fire to be hot, the best demonstration to prove it is, to put his finger or hand into the fire.

Sec. 47. *Of blessing as an act of pre-eminency.*

That principle which is here brought in, to be without all contradiction, is thus expressed, *The less is blessed of the better or greater.* Of the Greek word κρεῖττον, translated *better*, see Chap. i. 4, Sec. 39.

This comparative, τὸ ἔλαττον, *the less*, though it be of the neuter gender, yet it hath reference to Abraham, who is said to be blessed of Melchisedec, ver. 1. The neuter gender is used, because it is a general proposition, and may be extended to all sorts of things as well as persons.

The other comparative, *greater*, hath reference to Melchisedec, who blessed Abraham, ver. 1.

Of blessing in general, see Chap. vi.

That we may the better discern how the foresaid proposition is 'without all contradiction,' we must take notice of the kind of blessing that is here meant. For men may bless God, who is infinitely greater than all men, Judges v. 9, James iii. 9; and among men, the less in many cases bless the greater. As Solomon, a king, blessed his people, so the people blessed him, 1 Kings viii. 55, 56. Mean persons that are relieved, bless great ones that relieve them, Job xxxi. 20.

The blessing here meant is a blessing of ratification, whereby Melchisedec assureth Abraham of the full accomplishment of all those promises that God had made unto him. This Melchisedec did as a minister, and priest, and prophet of God: in all which functions he was greater than Abraham. Thus are all they who, by virtue of their calling, or relation to others, stand in God's room, and in God's name assure them of God's blessing to them, or at least call upon God for his blessing upon them. This is an authoritative kind of blessing, and argueth superiority in them who bless. Parents, governors of families, governors of commonwealths, and ministers of the word, have a power in this manner to bless. See more hereof, ver. 1, Sec. 12.

Object. Kings and other governors are ofttimes among them whom ordinary ministers bless. Are ministers thereupon greater than kings or other governors?

Ans. Though in their persons and civil government, kings and other governors are greater then ministers of the word, yet such ministers, in the execution of their office, are greater than the foresaid persons; for they stand in God's stead, and are God's mouth: they command in God's name, they exhort to do God's will. So they bless in God's name.

1. This doth much commend the ministerial function.
2. It should stir up men to have that calling in high account, and to believe God's word preached by them, 1 Thes. ii. 13.

The main point here proved is, that Melchisedec was greater than Abraham, and by consequence than Levi, and his priesthood greater than the priesthood of the Levites; and that thereupon Christ's priesthood, which is after the order of Melchisedec, is greater than the priesthood of the Levites; and answerably to be every way preferred.

Melchisedec, as a type, blessed Abraham the father of the faithful. Christ, as the truth, did not only bless little children, Mark x. 16, but also upon his ascension into heaven, 'he lifted up his hands and blessed' his apostles, Luke xxiv. 50, 51, and that in the room of all the faithful.

Sec. 48. *Of the resolution of* Heb. vii. 5–7.

Ver. 5. *And verily they that are of the sons of Levi, who receive the office of the priesthood, have a commandment to take tithes of the people, according to the law, that is, of their brethren, though they come out of the loins of Abraham:*

6. *But he, whose descent is not counted from them, received tithes of Abraham, and blessed him that had the promises.*

7. *And without all contradiction the less is blessed of the better.*

The sum of these three verses is a proof of Melchisedec's greatness above Abraham.

The parts are two:
1. A confirmation of a former argument.
2. Another argument.

The confirmation is taken from the difference betwixt Melchisedec and the Levites. Hereof are two branches:

One concerneth the Levites, the other Melchisedec.

In the former is set down,
1. A description of the persons; 2, a declaration of the difference.

The persons are described,
1. By their relation, *sons of Levi*, which is amplified by a select company, in this phrase, *of the sons*, namely, some of them.
2. By their function, which is set out,
   1. By the kind of it, *the office of the priesthood*.
   2. By their right to it, in this word *receive*.

The foresaid function is amplified by a privilege appertaining thereunto. Hereabout four points are observed:
1. The kind of privilege, *to take tithes*.
2. Their warrant for it, *they have a commandment*.
3. The rule, *according to law*.
4. The persons of whom they took tithes. These are,
   1. Generally expressed, *the people*.
   2. Particularly described: and that by a double relation:
      1. To themselves, in this word, *brethren*.
      2. To their common father. In setting him down, is noted,
         (1.) The kind of inference, in this particle *though*.
         (2.) The manner of coming from him, *they came out of his loins*.
         (3.) The name of their father, *Abraham*.

The other part of difference declareth two points:

1. Wherein Melchisedec agreed with Levi, *he received tithes*, ver. 6.

2. Wherein they differed. Hereof are two branches:

1. A description of Melchisedec, *he whose descent is not counted from them*.

2. The name of the person of whom he received tithes, *Abraham*.

The second argument whereby Melchisedec's greatness is proved, is an act of superiority on his part. Hereabout observe,

1. The substance of the argument; 2. an inference made thereupon.

In the substance we may observe,

1. The kind of act performed, *blessed*.

2. The person to whom it was performed, *him that had the promises*.

The inference is an excellency. In setting down whereof observe,

1. The manner of bringing it in, with this asseveration, *without all contradiction*.

2. The matter, which declareth the difference betwixt him that blessed and him that was blessed.

He that did bless was greater, the other less.

Sec. 49. *Of the doctrines raised out of* Heb. vii. 5–7.

I. *The excellency of Melchisedec's priesthood is a certain truth.* This note of asseveration, *verily*, proves as much. See Sec. 37.

II. *All Levi's sons had not the same dignity.* They were but some *of them*. See Sec. 37.

III. *The priesthood was a choice office.* So it is here brought in to be. See Sec. 37.

IV. *True priests were deputed to that office.* They received it. See Sec. 37.

V. *Tithes were due to priests.* They had a commandment to receive them. See Sec. 39.

VI. *God's command is a good warrant.* It was the Levites' warrant. See Sec. 39.

VII. *God's command was ordered according to law.* Hereof is given a particular instance. See Sec. 39.

VIII. *All sorts paid tithes.* Under this word *people* all sorts are comprised. See Sec 39.

IX. *An office may give a dignity over equals.* This phrase, *came out of the loins*, implieth an equality; yet priests had a dignity above others that came out of the same loins. See Sec. 41.

X. *Priests and others were brethren.* For priests received tithes of *their brethren*. See Sec. 41.

XI. *Melchisedec's pedigree was not counted from men*. This is here expressly affirmed. See Sec. 42.

XII. *Melchisedec received tithes of the father of Levi*, namely, of Abraham. See Sec. 42.

XIII. *There is an authoritative kind of blessing.* Such an one is here mentioned. See Sec. 43.

XIV. *Priests had a power to bless authoritatively.* So did Melchisedec. See Sec. 43.

XV. *The faith of the best needs strengthening.* Instance Abraham. See Sec. 45.

XVI. *It is a privilege to have a right to God's promises.* This is here noted as one of Abraham's privileges. See Sec. 44.

XVII. *There are unquestionable truths.* Even such as are *without all contradiction*. See Sec. 46.

XVIII. *To bless is an act of superiority.* In this was Melchisedec greater. See Sec. 47.

XIX. *To be blessed is an act of inferiority.* In this was Abraham less. See Sec. 47.

XX. *Christ is greater than all.* Christ was the truth of that which is here set down concerning Melchisedec's excellencies.

Sec. 50. *Of a likeness in unequals.*

Heb. vii. 8. *And here men that die receive tithes; but there he receiveth them, of whom it is witnessed that he liveth.*

In this verse the apostle produceth a third argument, to prove the excellency of Melchisedec's priesthood above the Levites. The argument is taken from the different condition of the priests. The Levites were mortal, Melchisedec not so.

The argument may be thus framed:

He that ever liveth, to execute his priesthood, is more excellent than they who are subject to death, and thereupon forced to leave their office to others;

But Melchisedec ever liveth, &c. And the Levites are subject to death, &c. Therefore Melchisedec is more excellent than they.

Of the adverb μὲν, *truly*, expressed in Greek, but not in English, see ver. 5, Sec. 37.

In setting down this argument, the apostle giveth an instance of a common privilege that belonged to the Levites as well as to Melchisedec, which was to receive tithes. How this was a privilege is shewed Sec. 33. Herein he giveth an evidence, that a common privilege in some things argueth not an equality in all. There may be a like resemblance in some particulars betwixt such things as are much different one from another. There is a like resemblance betwixt the sun and a candle in giving light; yet there is a great disparity betwixt these creatures. Man is said to be made in the image of God, and after his likeness, Gen. i. 26, 27. This implieth a resemblance betwixt God and man; which is further manifested by this title, *gods*, given to sons of men, Ps. lxxxii. 6. Yet, if any such imagine man to be equal to God, he neither knoweth God nor man aright.

1. Hereby sundry places of Scripture, which otherwise might seem very strange, are cleared; such as these, 'Walk in love, as Christ also hath loved us,' Eph. v. 2. 'Forgive one another, as God hath forgiven you,' Eph. iv. 32. 'Be perfect, even as your Father which is in heaven is perfect,' Mat. v. 48. 'Thy will be done in earth, as it is in heaven, Mat. vi. 10. 'Every man that hath hope in Christ puri-

fieth himself, even as he is pure,' 1 John iii. 3. All these and other like places are to be understood of such a resemblance as may stand with much inequality.

2. This discovereth the false inference which anabaptists do put upon sundry spiritual privileges which are common to all Christians; as, to be one in Christ, Gal. iii. 28; to be made free by Christ, Gal. v. 1; to have one father, one master, one teacher, and to be all brethren, Mat. xxiii. 8–10. From these and other like common privileges, they infer that all of all sorts, kings and subjects, masters and servants, and others differenced by other relations, are equal every way; and that the ordinary degrees of superiority and inferiority are against the warrant of God's word and common privilege of Christians. Herein they bewray much ignorance, being not able to discern betwixt those different respects, wherein things are equal and things differ. By this consequence the difference here noted betwixt Melchisedec and Levi would be taken away.

These two adverbs, ὧδε *here*, ἐκεῖ *there*, are fitly used in this place. For the apostle speaketh of the Levites as of his countrymen, dwelling where he did; but of Melchisedec as of a stranger, dwelling in a remote place.

2. He spake of the Levites as men of latter days, nearer his time; but of Melchisedec as of a man of ancient days, long before the Levites.

These two adverbs imply thus much: in this place, and in that place, everywhere; at this time, and at that time, at all times, priests of the Lord received tithes. This was not a prerogative proper to Melchisedec, but common also to the Levites. Prudently therefore is their due given to both parties.

Though the main drift of the apostle be to advance Melchisedec and his priesthood above the Levites and their priesthood, yet he denies not the Levites that prerogative which was due to them as well as to Melchisedec, which was to receive tithes.

This is [to] be noted against such wrangling sophisters and intemperate disputers, as, in their heat, through violence in opposing their adversaries, deny them that which is due unto them, and labour to debase them more than is meet; they will deny many truths, because they are averred by their adversaries.

Sec. 51. *Of ministers being mean men that die.*

Albeit there were a common privilege betwixt the Levites and Melchisedec, yet there was a great disparity in their persons; for of the Levites it is here said they were 'men that die,' but of Melchisedec 'he liveth.' So as there was as great a difference betwixt them as betwixt mortality and immortality.

There are two points observable in this phrase, *men that die*. The first is about this word ἄνθρωποι, *men*. The Greek word signifieth *ordinary, mean men*. It is the same that is used Chap. ii. 6, Sec. 54.

The other is in this word ἀποθνήσκοντες, *die*, meaning such as are subject unto death, and in their time shall die, and thereupon leave this world and all their employments therein; yea, so leave them as not to do anything about them any more; 'for there is no work, nor device, nor knowledge, nor wisdom in the grave,' Eccles. ix. 10.

The Greek verb translated *die* is a compound. The simple verb, θνήσκω, *mori*, signifieth to die, Mat. ii. 20. Thence an adjective, θνητός, *mortalis*, that signifieth *mortal*, 1 Cor. xv. 53, 54. The compound being with a preposition, ἀπὸ, *à vel ab*, that signifieth *from*, hath an emphasis, and implieth a departing from all that a man hath.

This mortality of the sons of Levi, who were priests, is in special here set down, to amplify the excellency of Melchisedec, who liveth; but withal it may be brought in as an evidence of the mutability of the legal priesthood, and that by a kind of resemblance betwixt the persons and their office; that, as the persons, who are priests, had their time, and after that were taken away, so their office, which was the priesthood, had an appointed time, after which it should be abrogated. This point of the mutability of the priesthood is expressly proved by the apostle, vers. 11, 12.

Of priests being subject to death, see ver. 23, Sec. 97.

That which is here said of the Levites is true of all ministers of the word, that they are but men, mean men, mortal men, that die. Hereupon this title, *son of man*, is given to a choice prophet, Ezekiel iii. 17; and choice apostles say thus of themselves, 'We also are men of like passions with you,' Acts xiv. 15. They said this when people so admired them as they supposed them to be gods, and would have sacrificed unto them.

God doth herein magnify his power, by enabling men, that are subject to death, to perform so great things as the ministerial function requireth to be performed.

1. This common condition of ministers to be men that die, should make them oft to look upon these black feet of theirs, that they do not too proudly strut out their gay peacock feathers; that they be not too conceited, either in any prerogatives belonging to their function, or in any abilities bestowed upon them for the execution thereof.

2. This is a forcible motive to raise up their eyes and hearts to God, for his divine assistance in their human weakness.

3. Herein ought people also to be helpful to their ministers, in calling on God for them. This is it which an apostle earnestly desired his people to do for him, Rom. xv. 30, Eph. vi. 19.

4. This also should move people to tender their ministers, as such as are men, and subject to human frailties, and thereupon bear with them.

5. Because ministers are mortal men that must die,

ministers themselves must be diligent in improving that time which God doth afford them, unto the best advantage that they can; and people must take the opportunity of their minister's life to reap the best good that they can while their ministers remain with them, even before they are taken away.

Sec. 52. *Of ministers' prerogatives notwithstanding their meanness.*

The inference of the prerogative of receiving tithes upon this their condition, that they were *men that die,* giveth instance that the common, frail, mortal, condition of ministers is no bar to the privileges and prerogatives of their function. This is verified not only in the ordinary privileges of ordinary men, but also in the extraordinary prerogatives that belonged to extraordinary ministers, as prophets and apostles; for these all were 'men that die.'

Sundry privileges that belong unto ministers may be gathered out of those titles that are given unto them in God's word. Some of those titles are given unto them in relation to God himself; as *angels,* Rev. i. 20; *ambassadors,* 2 Cor. v. 20; *revealers* of the gospel, Eph. vi. 19; *keepers of the keys of the kingdom of heaven,* Mat. xvi. 19; *remembrancers,* Isa. lxii. 6; *stewards,* 1 Cor. iv. 1.

Other titles have relation to people; as *fathers,* 1 Cor. iv. 15; *elders,* 1 Tim. v. 17; *rulers,* Heb. xiii. 7; *overseers,* Acts xx. 28; *pastors,* Eph. iv. 11; *teachers,* 1 Cor. xii. 28; *chariots and horsemen,* 2 Kings ii. 12.

Thus God honoureth them, lest by reason of their meanness they should be despised, and thereupon their ministry prove unprofitable.

Let people learn hereby to remove their eyes from the meanness of their ministers' persons, to the dignities of their office; and consider the place wherein God hath set them, and the work which he hath deputed unto them, and the end whereunto the ministry tends.

As the Israelites paid tithes to the priests, though they were men that die, so ought Christians to yield to their ministers whatsoever is their due, though they be such men.

Sec. 53. *Of Melchisedec's ever living.*

The other branch of the disparity betwixt Melchisedec and the sons of Levi, is in regard of Melchisedec's excellency, which is thus expressed, *of whom it is witnessed that he liveth.* The excellency itself consisteth in this, that he liveth. The other words are a proof hereof.

This phrase, ζῇ, *he liveth,* being of the time present, implieth a continual act, which ceaseth not. Many hundred, yea and thousand, years had passed betwixt that time wherein Melchisedec met Abraham, and that wherein the apostle wrote this epistle; yet he saith of him, *he liveth;* so as it implieth an everlasting life, which hath no end. This in reference to Melchisedec is to be taken mystically and typically.

Mystically, in that no mention in that history is made of his death.

Typically, in that he prefigured Christ, who doth indeed, and that properly, live for ever. It doth therefore set forth the everlastingness, as of Christ's person, so also of his priesthood. For Christ ever liveth to execute his priesthood in and by himself. Hereof see more, chap. v. 6, Sec. 29.

The proof of this great point is taken from a testimony: μαρτυρούμενος, *It is witnessed,* saith the apostle. Of the derivation of the Greek word, see Chap. iii. 6, Sec. 53.

This point is testified, first, negatively and implicitly, then affirmatively and expressly.

Negatively and implicitly the Holy Ghost witnesseth that Melchisedec liveth, in that he maketh no mention of his death, where he bringeth him forth as a priest, Gen. xiv. 18–20.

Affirmatively and expressly, where he saith, 'Thou art a priest for ever after the order of Melchisedec,' Ps. cx. 4.

Of the force of a testimony of Scripture, see Chap. i. 5, Sec. 46.

Of an implicit proof, see ver. 3, Sec. 23.

Of things spoken of Melchisedec and applied to Christ, see ver. 3, Sec. 24.

Sec. 54. *Of the resolution and observations of* Heb. vii. 8.

Ver. 8. *And here men that die receive tithes; but there he receiveth them of whom it is witnessed that he liveth.*

In this verse is a third proof of Melchisedec's excellency above the sons of Levi. Hereof are two parts: 1, an equality; 2, an inequality.

The equality was in *receiving tithes.*

Of the inequality there are two branches:
1. The mortality of the sons of Levi.
2. The immortality of Melchisedec. This is,
1. Implied, in this phrase, *he liveth.*
2. Proved, thus, *of whom it is witnessed.*

Doctrines.

I. *Argument may be added to argument to prove the same point.* This here is a third argument added to the two former.

II. *There may be a likeness betwixt unequals.* The sons of Levi and Melchisedec were much unequal; yet the like privilege of receiving tithes belonged to them both. See Sec. 50.

III. *Tithes have of old been paid.* Both Melchisedec and the Levites received them.

IV. *Ministers are mortal men.* Such were the Levites. See Sec. 51.

V. *A divine testimony is a sound proof.* This is the witness here intended.

VI. *Christ ever liveth.* Melchisedec, as he was a type of Christ, is said to live. See Sec. 53.

Sec. 55. *Of qualifying strange phrases.* Heb. vii. 9, 10.

Ver. 9. *And, as I may so say, Levi also, who receiveth tithes, paid tithes in Abraham.*

10. *For he was yet in the loins of his father, when Melchisedec met him.*

In these two verses the apostle maketh a particular application of that which he had delivered about Abraham's inferiority to Levi. This he doth by shewing, that what Abraham the father did, Levi also the son did. Thus he doth manifest, that what he had said of Abraham was not to vilify his person, but to draw the mind of the Hebrews from the priesthood of Levi to Christ's priesthood.

The foresaid point is brought in with a phrase of qualification, thus, ὡς ἔπος εἰπεῖν, *as I may so say.* In this mollifying clause there are two Greek words, that are of the same stem. One, expressed under this verb, εἰπεῖν, *say*; the other implied under this particle, ἔπος, *so.* This clause may be thus translated verbatim, *as to say the word,* that is, to use the phrase. Thus we see that a phrase or sentence which may seem strange is to be mollified. To this purpose tend these qualifications, 'I speak as a man,' Rom. iii. 5; 'I speak after the manner of men,' Rom. vi. 19; 'I speak this by permission,' 1 Cor. vii. 6.

This is a means to prevent misinterpretations, and to make that which is spoken to be more fairly and candidly taken.

Sec. 56. *Of Levi paying tithes in Abraham.*

Levi is here metonymically put for his sons, who are so set down ver. 5, Sec. 37. For Levi himself was no priest, nor did he receive tithes, but he was their great grandfather.

Two things are here spoken of Levi, one taken for granted, which was that he received tithes; the other expressed and proved, which was that he paid tithes.

The former was a prerogative and a sign of superiority. Of it, see ver. 2, Sec. 17, and ver. 4, Sec. 33.

The latter is a sign of inferiority. See ver. 4, Sec. 33.

Against this latter it might be objected that Levi was not then born when tenths were paid to Melchisedec. For Abraham met Melchisedec before Ishmael was born. Now he was born in the 86th year of Abraham, Gen. xvi. 16; Isaac was born 14 years after, in the 100th year of Abraham, Gen. xxi. 5; Jacob was born in the 60th year of Isaac, Gen. xxv. 26, which was 74 years after Ishmael's birth. Jacob was above 40 years old when he went to his uncle Laban, Gen. xxvi. 34. Thus there were 114 years betwixt Ishmael's birth and Jacob's going to Laban. How many years more there were betwixt Abraham's meeting Melchisedec and Ishmael's birth, and again betwixt Jacob's going to his uncle and the birth of Levi, is not expressly set down. This is certain, that Levi was born many more than 100 years betwixt Abraham's paying tenths to Melchisedec, and Levi's being in this world.[1] So as it may seem strange that Levi should pay tithes to Melchisedec.

To resolve this doubt, the apostle here expressly saith, that Levi paid tithes *in Abraham.*

From this answer ariseth another scruple, namely, that Christ was in Abraham as well as Levi, so as Christ himself should pay tithes by this reason, and therein be inferior to Melchisedec.

Ans. 1. In general it may be replied that Melchisedec was a type of Christ, and that that which is said of Melchisedec and his priesthood, is spoken of him as of a type, and that purposely to set forth the greatness and excellency of Christ and his priesthood. Wherefore to put Christ into the rank of those who are inferior to Melchisedec, is directly to cross the main scope of the apostle.

2. Christ consisted of two natures, divine and human. Though therefore he might be reckoned among the sons of Abraham in regard of his human nature, yet in regard of his person, which consisted of both natures, he was superior to Abraham, and greater than he. Thus David, whose son according to the flesh Christ was, calleth him Lord, in reference to his person, Mat. xx. 44.

3. Though Christ took flesh by ordinary descent from Abraham, yet came he not from Abraham by ordinary and natural generation. From his mother the Virgin Mary he received the substance and matter of his flesh, out of which it was raised and formed; yet, having no father, he came not by any natural act of generation. Though a mother afford matter for generation, yet the active force and virtue of generation cometh from the father. Hence is it that Christ was freed from the common contagion of original sin. For though he were of Adam, and so of Abraham, by reason of the substance of his flesh, yet he was not by Adam, or by Abraham. No son of their posterity was the procreant cause or begetter of him. Christ therefore cannot be said to do *in Abraham* those things which others of his posterity did.

Sec. 57. *Of children's being in their parents' condition.*

In that Levi paid tithes in Abraham, it appears that children are in the same common condition that their parents are. I say common condition, to exempt such particular privileges, as God by his providence may, and oft doth confer upon children above their parents. These privileges may be outward and inward.

Outward, in worldly dignities, as Saul and David were both advanced above their fathers, in that they were made kings.

Inward, in spiritual graces. Herein Hezekiah and

---

[1] This sentence is confused. The meaning evidently is, that many more than 100 years were betwixt Abraham's paying tithes to Melchisedec and Levi's being in the world. —Ed.

Josiah were much advanced above their fathers; so are all pious children that are born of impious fathers.

The inferiority of Abraham, and, in him, of Levi, here mentioned, was a common condition. None of their sons were exempted from it. Parents are themselves by nature unclean, so are all their children. 'Who can bring a clean thing out of an unclean?' Job xiv. 4. In this respect Bildad having said that 'man is a worm,' addeth, 'and the son of man is a worm,' Job xxv. 6. As man is, so is a son of man. In this respect this phrase is oft used, 'We are as all our fathers were,' 1 Chron. xxix. 15, Ps. xxxix. 12; and this, 'I am not better than my fathers,' 1 Kings xix. 4.

This the Lord so ordereth, 1. That the same laws, and ordinances, instructions and directions, exhortations and consolations, promises and threatenings might be of force and use to all of all ages.

2. That none might presume above others.

3. That none might be too much debased.

1. This gives a check to their pride, who, for some outward privilege, advance themselves above the common condition of man, as if they were gods and not men, from heaven and not from earth. Such were they who said, 'Let us break their bands asunder, and cast away their cords from us,' Ps. ii. 3; and such as said of Christ, 'We will not have this man to reign over us,' Luke xix. 14; Pharaoh was such an one, Exod. v. 2; and Nebuchadnezzar, Dan. iii. 15; and Haman, Esther iii. 2; and Tyrus, Ezek. xxviii. 2. Now mark the end of all these.

2. This puts us in mind to consider what our fathers have been, and to what they have been subject, and from thence to gather what we are subject unto; to what inferiority, infirmity, pains, diseases, distresses, and other calamities. A heathen man could say, I am a man, and find myself exempted from no human frailty.[1] We can better discern weakness and infirmities in others that have been before us, than in ourselves. We can speak much of our fathers' infirmities, imperfections, troubles, and mortalities; but self-love so blindeth our eyes as we cannot so well discern the same things in ourselves. The like may be applied to duties. In our fathers we may observe what duties we ourselves are bound unto.

Sec. 58. *Of the meaning of the tenth verse.*

Verse 10. In the tenth verse there is a confirmation and an explanation of Levi's paying tithes in Abraham. The causal conjunction γὰρ, *for*, sheweth that this verse is inferred as a confirmation of that which went before.

The argument is taken from that union that is betwixt a father and his posterity. They are all contained in him, and as one with him, so as what he doth they do.

The explanation is in this phrase, *he was in his father's loins.* By father is metonymically meant his

[1] Homo sum, humani nihil a me alienum sentio.

great-grandfather Abraham. In a third generation Levi descended from Abraham, in which respect he was in him. For that which cometh out of one must needs be first in him.

Of this word *loins*, and of coming out of one's loins, see ver. 5, Sec. 41.

This adverb of time, ἔτι, translated *yet*, signifieth for the most part a continuance of time, as Heb. xi. 4. 'Abel yet speaketh,' that is, he still continueth to speak.

It hath reference also to all distinctions of time, as to time present, thus, 'while he yet talked,' Mat. xii. 46, and to the time to come, John xiv. 30, and to the time past, Acts xxi. 28.

Here, without question, this particle hath reference to the time past, and for perspicuity's sake may be translated *then*. He was then in the loins of his father, when Melchisedec met him.

Of Melchisedec's meeting Abraham, see ver. 1, Sec. 8.

Sec. 59. *Of children's doing what their parents do, and that in their loins.*

Levi is said to do what Abraham did, because he was in Abraham's loins; so as parents bear in their bowels, and represent the persons of all that are to come from them. Not only Isaac, who was Abraham's immediate son, but also Jacob his son's son, yea, and Levi also, the son of his son's son, was (as the apostle here saith) in Abraham's loins, and paid tithe to Melchisedec. The like may be said of Aaron, who was the son of the son's son of Levi. For Kohath was Levi's son, Amram, Kohath's son, and Aaron, Amram's son, Exod. vi. 16, &c.

The like may be applied to all succeeding generations, which have been, and shall be to the end of the world.

God made this promise to Jacob, 'Kings shall come out of thy loins,' Gen. xxxv. 11. Yet there came not kings from Jacob's stock, not kings of Israel, which are especially meant in that promise, for the space of six hundred years after that. This is further manifested by these metaphors, wherein the extent of God's promise was manifested: 'Thy seed shall be as the dust of the earth,' Gen. xiii. 16, 'as the stars of heaven,' Gen. xv. 5, 'as the sand on the sea-shore,' Gen. xxii. 17. Hereby was meant the promised seed, out of which the church would sprout; yet Abraham himself had but one son of that seed, and that one son had but one other son, and that other many sons, the grandchild had but twelve sons; so as many generations, succeeding one after another, were comprised under the seed of Abraham.

God in his eternal counsel hath appointed that such and such shall by degrees come from such a stock; and thereupon he accounteth them to be in that very stock; and withal accounteth the things done by that stock to be done by all them, or by all that, time after time, shall sprout from thence.

Hereupon, as a corollary, and just consequence, it may be inferred, that children and children's children, generation after generation, stand accessory to the natural actions of parents. I say *natural*, because actions of grace are more properly the actions of God's Spirit than our own. 'For it is God (in that case), worketh in us, both to will and to do of his good pleasure,' Philip. ii. 13. All such graces are the 'fruit of the Spirit,' Gal. v. 22.

This action of Levi was an action of man's common condition.

In regard of God's accounting a man's posterity to be in his loins, the threatening against transgressors is thus enlarged, 'I will visit the iniquity of the fathers upon their children,' Exod. xxxiv. 7.

Obj. Promises also of reward, upon that grace that is in fathers, is extended unto their children, as well as threatening of revenge for sin, Exod. xx. 5, 6.

Ans. True, but upon a different ground. The promise of reward is of mere grace; but the threatening of vengeance is upon desert.

On the foresaid ground it may well be inferred, that all Adam's posterity did eat of the forbidden fruit in him. 'Wherefore by one man sin entered into the world, and death by sin; and so death passed upon all men, for that all have sinned,' namely in Adam. 'And by the offence of one, judgment came on all men to condemnation,' Rom. v. 12, 18. Herein this proverb is verified, 'The fathers have eaten sour grapes, and the children's teeth are set on edge,' Ezek. xviii. 2.

Obj. The Jews are blamed for using that proverb.

Ans. 1. They are blamed for putting sin off from themselves, as if they had been punished only for their fathers' sins; as they themselves, in their own persons, guiltless.

2. The foresaid proverb holdeth not in such as are true penitents; neither their own, nor their fathers' sins shall be laid to their charge.

A double instruction hence ariseth; one concerning children or posterity, the other concerning parents or progenitors.

The former, concerning children, is to instruct them how far they ought to ascend in examining their spiritual estate, and in making their confession of sin to God, even to their father and father's fathers, till they come to Adam. A due consideration hereof will be an especial means to humble our souls the more. For when we shall well weigh how to the numberless number of our own most heinous actual transgressions the sins of our forefathers lie upon our neck, it cannot but deeply humble us, especially if we well understand the heinousness of Adam's first sin, which, if well considered in all the circumstances thereof, will be found the greatest sin that ever was committed. As Levi in Abraham's loins, by giving tithes, testified an homage to Melchisedec, so we in Adam's loins, by eating the forbidden fruit, testified our homage to Satan.

The latter instruction concerning parents, is that they be the more wary and watchful of their actions, even for their children and posterity's sake. Because they are counted to do those things which themselves do. That damage which by our laws extendeth to the children and posterity of felons and traitors, restraineth many that have respect to their posterity from those transgressions. See more hereof in *Domest. Dut.* treat. vi. secs. 6, 7.

Sec. 60. *Of the resolution and observations of* Heb. vii. 9, 10.

Ver. 9. *And, as I may so say, Levi also, who receiveth tithes, paid tithes in Abraham.*

10. *For he was yet in the loins of his father when Melchisedec met him.*

The sum of these two verses is, Levi's paying tithes to Abraham. This is, 1, propounded, ver. 9; 2, proved, ver. 10.

In the proposition two points are observable:

1. The manner of bringing it in, thus, *As I may so say.*

2. The matter. This consisteth of two acts:

1. An act of superiority, which was to *receive tithes.*

2. An act of inferiority. Herein is laid down,

1. The kind of act, he *paid tithes.*

2. The manner of doing it, *in Abraham.*

In the proof are two points:

1. The union betwixt parents and children. A son is *in the loins of his father.*

2. The extent of this union unto succeeding generations. This is implied under this phrase, *when Melchisedec met him.*

Doctrines.

I. *Strange phrases must be mollified.* This phrase, *as I may so say*, is a mollifying phrase. See Sec. 55.

II. *Priests received tithes.* This is here taken for granted. See Sec. 56.

III. *Children in their parents do things before they are born.* Levi paid tithes in Abraham before he was born. See Secs. 56, 57.

IV. *Difficult and doubtful points are to be explained and confirmed.* This is the main scope of the tenth verse. See Sec. 58.

V. *Children are in their parents' loins.* An instance hereof is given in Levi. See Sec. 59.

VI. *Relations of children to parents continue generation after generation.* This description of the time of Levi's being in Abraham's loins, even when Melchisedec met him, proves this point. See Sec. 56.

Sec. 61. *Of the imperfection of the Levitical priesthood.*

Ver. 11. *If therefore perfection were by the Levitical priesthood (for under it the people received the law), what further need was there that another priest should rise after the order of Melchisedec, and not be called after the order of Aaron?*

Hitherto the apostle hath set forth the excellency of Christ's priesthood by way of similitude to Melchisedec's, who was a type of Christ: so as all the excellencies typically set out about Melchisedec were really and properly found in Christ, the truth.

Here further the apostle begins to declare the excellency of Christ's priesthood, by way of dissimilitude betwixt it and the Levitical priesthood; wherein he sheweth how far Christ's priesthood excelled Aaron's.

The Jews had Aaron's priesthood in high account; and so rested on that, as they little or nothing at all regarded Christ's. The apostle therefore endeavours to draw their mind from Aaron's priesthood to Christ's, which he proveth to be far the more excellent.

The foresaid dissimilitude is exemplified in seven particulars. See Sec. 1.

The first branch of dissimilitude is in the mutability of Aaron's priesthood, and the immutability of Christ's.

From the mutability of the former priesthood, the imperfection thereof is inferred, which is the first point laid down in this verse, and that by way of supposition, thus, *if therefore perfection*, &c.

The apostle here taketh it for granted, that perfection was not to be had by the Levitical priesthood. His argument may be thus framed:

If perfection were by the Levitical priesthood, there needed no other; but there needed another priesthood, therefore perfection was not by the Levitical.

Thus this conditional conjunction $\varepsilon\iota$, *if*, is the ground of a strong negation.

The illative conjunction $o\tilde{v}v$, *therefore*, hath reference to that which he had before produced out of Scripture concerning Melchisedec, who had another kind of priesthood than the sons of Levi; and concerning Christ, who was the truth typified by Melchisedec, and witnessed to be a priest after the order of Melchisedec. This, therefore, being so, perfection cannot be imagined to be by the Levitical priesthood.

Of the derivation of the Greek word $\tau\varepsilon\lambda\varepsilon\iota\omega\sigma\iota\varsigma$, translated *perfection*, see Chap. ii. ver. 10, Sec. 97.

Here it is taken in the largest latitude of perfection, namely, for such a fulness or absoluteness, as nothing needs be added thereto.

The Levitical priesthood was not so full and absolute; for the apostle here in this text implieth, that there was need of another priesthood.

The Levitical priesthood was that which the sons of Levi, namely, Aaron and his posterity, executed under the law.

The Greek word $\iota\varepsilon\rho\omega\sigma\acute{v}v\eta\varsigma$, translated *priesthood*, is not the very same that was used before, $\iota\varepsilon\rho\alpha\tau\varepsilon\acute{\iota}\alpha v$, ver. 5, $\iota\varepsilon\rho\acute{\alpha}\tau\varepsilon\upsilon\mu\alpha$, 1 Peter ii. 5, 9, but it is derived from the same root, and signifieth the same thing. See Sec. 37.

The main point here intended is, that the priesthood under the law was imperfect. This is proved in this chapter by many arguments which we shall note in their due place. Perfection here meant is a furnishing of men with all such graces as may make them eternally happy. It compriseth under it effectual vocation, justification, sanctification, yea, and glorification. That priesthood could not by true grace bring men to glory. In this respect it is said that the gifts and sacrifices which those priests offered up, 'could not make him that did the service perfect,' Heb. ix. 9. And that 'the law can never make the comers thereunto perfect,' Heb. x. 1.

Quest. Why then was this priesthood ordained?

Ans. It was ordained for a means to draw men on to Christ. In this respect the law is said to be 'our schoolmaster to bring us unto Christ,' Gal. iii. 24. See Sec. 68.

This point discovereth sundry dotages.

1. The dotage of the superstitious Jews, who lift up their eyes no higher than to this priesthood, whereon they rested and built their faith.[1] They would not be brought to subject themselves to any other. No, not when this was actually abrogated, and another more perfect actually established in the room of it. Herein they perverted the wisdom and goodness of God towards them, and the main end which he aimed at in appointing the Levitical priesthood, which was to lead them, as it were, by the hand to Christ, and to afford them some easy steps, in regard of their weakness, to ascend upon, and to see Christ the better thereby. The fulness of time when the Messiah was to be exhibited, was then to come. God therefore afforded means answerable to their condition, to support their faith and sustain their hope. But they made those means an occasion to withhold, or to withdraw them from Christ. Such an error this was, as the apostle saith of them that were seduced therewith, 'Christ shall profit you nothing,' Gal. v. 2. The Levitical priesthood and Christ's priesthood can no more stand together than Dagon and the ark of God.

2. The dotage of Christian Jews, or Jewish Christians, who conform themselves to the Jewish ceremonies.[2] If the forenamed error of them, who never made profession of Christ, be so heinous, as was before shewed, what may be thought of them who, being instructed in the Christian religion, and thereupon professing Christ, would induce a priesthood contrary to Christ's? For they who bring in Jewish ceremonies bring in the Jewish priesthood, under which the Jewish ceremonies were first established. Do not these cross the main scope of the apostle? Do they not advance the Levitical priesthood against Christ, and make Christ's priesthood imperfect?

3. The dotage of papists, who do directly establish another priesthood, which is neither Jewish nor Chris-

---
[1] See *The Progress of Divine Providence*, on Ezek. xxxvi. 11.
[2] See Chap. iv. 8, Sec. 49.

tian, nor after the order of Aaron, nor after the order of Melchisedec, a monstrous priesthood, such an one as never was heard of before. For,

1. Their priests are no such persons as Melchisedec was.
2. Their sacrifice, they say, is unbloody, and yet for sin; but 'without shedding of blood is no remission,' Heb. ix. 22.
3. They make their sacrifice to be for the sins of quick and dead; yet 'after death the judgment,' Heb. ix. 27.
4. They say that their sacrifice is the very flesh and blood of Christ; yet that which Melchisedec brought forth was true bread and wine.
5. The things that they say they offer, are indeed mere creatures, yet they call them their creator.
6. Their priests are not denied to be creatures, yet their sacrifice, they say, is their creator. Thus they make creatures greater then their creator; for the priest is greater than the sacrifice.
7. They pretend a priesthood after the order of Melchisedec, wherein there is nothing like to Melchisedec's.

But, to let other absurdities pass, if perfection be by Christ's priesthood, what further need was there that other priests should be established? Oh abominable religion, that obtrudes such an unheard of priesthood to the church!

Let us learn to use the priesthood of Christ, which succeeds the Levitical priesthood, and that whereby perfection may be had, so as to trust perfectly thereunto. If the Jews might conceive hope, and receive comfort by that Levitical priesthood, how much more hope, and more comfort, may we by the priesthood of Christ! Such is the dignity of this priest, being God and man; such the worth of his sacrifice, being the body of him that was God; so efficacious the sprinkling of his blood, his entering into the holy place, his intercession with God, as we may safely, securely, and confidently trust thereunto.

Let us do with our Priest, the Lord Jesus, as the Jews did with their priests. They brought all their sacrifices to them.

Let us first apply to ourselves Christ's sacrifice. This is a true Catholicon, a general remedy for every malady. Then let us offer up the sacrifice of a broken heart and contrite spirit, the offering of prayer and praise, and the oblation of new obedience to Christ.

Of yielding obedience to the gospel on such a ground, see Sec. 68 in the end thereof.

Sec. 62. *Of the meaning of these words, 'for under it the people received the law.'*

The apostle, before he bringeth in his proof of the imperfection of the Levitical priesthood, inserteth within a parenthesis, an especial privilege of that priesthood, which is thus set down, *for under it the people received the law.*

This causal conjunction, γὰρ, *for*, implieth a reason of that priesthood, why there was such a function, namely, that there might be a means of passing a law betwixt God and the people. Of this word λαὸς, *people*, see Sec. 40, and Chap. iv. 9, Sec. 57.

Here by people are meant the congregation, or nation of the children of Israel, for to them in special was the law given, Rom. ix. 4.

This phrase, *received the law*, is the interpretation of one Greek verb, νενομοθέτητο, which is a compound, and that of a verb, τίθημι, *pono*, that signifieth to *put*, Mat. xii. 18; to *make*, Heb. i. 13; and to *appoint*, Mat. xxiv. 51; and of a noun, νόμος, *lex*, that signifieth a *law*, ver. 5.

The verb active, νομοθετέω, *leges sancio*, signifieth *to make a law*, or *to appoint*, or *establish a law*.

The passive, νομοθετεῖσθαι, *lege sancitum esse*, signifieth *to be established by law*. This very word is used, chap. viii. 6, and translated *established*. The word *law*, included in the Greek compound, is not expressed in our English. The Latin, *sancitum*, there used by most interpreters, signifieth to establish by law. So much must be understood in our English.

The foresaid compound passive verb here used in my text, is joined with the noun *people*, to whom the law was given, λαὸς νενομοθέτητο, *populus legi subjectus fuit*. It cannot be word for word rendered in English. It is somewhat like to this phrase, ἀποδεκατοῦν τὸν λαὸν, *decimare populum*, to tithe the people, Sec. 40. And to this, Λευὶ δεδεκάτωται, *Levi decimatus est*, *Levi was tithed*. To come the nearest that we can to the original, it may be thus rendered, The people had a law made, or the people were subjected to the law.

Our English, which thus translates it, *the people received the law*, followeth the vulgar Latin, *legem accepit*, which hitteth the sense of the apostle.

By law, is here in special meant the ceremonial law, which was most proper to that priesthood, and which was most especially abrogated by Christ's priesthood.

This relative phrase, ἐπ' αὐτῇ, *under it*, hath reference to the Levitical priesthood.

The force of the reason lieth in the relation between a law and priesthood. There cannot pass a law of covenant between God and man without a priesthood. This is here taken for granted. Yea, further, he taketh it for granted, that the law and priesthood are answerable one to another; such as the law is, such is the priesthood.

Sec. 63. *Of the necessity of a priesthood to establish a law.*

An especial point intended by this clause, *for under it the people received the law*, is this;—

A priesthood is necessary for establishing ordinances betwixt God and man. The main end of a priest, is to be 'for men in things pertaining to God,' Heb. v. 1. In ordinances betwixt God and man, there is a kind of covenant, for which there must be a kind of mediator betwixt God and man.

There is no proportion betwixt God and man, whether we consider the greatness, the brightness, or holiness of God.

Obj. Before Aaron there was no priest.

Ans. The first-born were priests before the law. On this ground the Lord saith, 'I have taken the Levites from among the children of Israel instead of all the first-born.' And again he saith to Moses, 'Take the Levites instead of all the first-born,' Num. iii. 12, 45.

We may from hence infer, that there is a necessity of a priesthood in the church. This is as necessary as a covenant to pass betwixt God and man, as necessary as God's favour to be turned to man, and man's service accepted of God.

Our adversaries in the general grant a necessity of priesthood, and thereby think they have a great advantage against us. They much insult on this, that they have such priests as offer up an outward, real, propitiatory sacrifice.

But the truth is, that we have the substance, they but a shadow; we have the truth, they but a conceit of their own. We have that priesthood, which the apostle here so much commendeth, the priesthood which abolished Aaron's, and succeeded in the room thereof; a priesthood of God's own appointing, which is everlasting, and perfecteth all that trusteth thereunto. Our priest is both God and man, most holy, who offered himself up without spot, who actually entered into the true holy place, who there abideth ever before God the Father, who doth so fully effect all things belonging to a priest, as there needeth none to succeed him.

The popish pretended priesthood is indeed no priesthood. It was never ordained of God. It is of neither of those two orders, which only are mentioned in Scripture. Not of Aaron's, for they themselves will not say that they descend from him; nor of Melchisedec's, for in nothing they agree with him in his priesthood. Their priests are no whit better than the sons of Levi; for they are sons of men, sinful, mortal, yea, they are far worse than the Levites were, in their usurped power, and palpable idolatry.

Let them glory in their new non-priesthood, and in their devilish idolatry, but let us cleave to our ancient, true priest, and perfectly trust unto his priesthood, under which we the people of God receive all divine ordinances needful for, and useful to, the church.

Sec. 64. *Of the meaning of these words, 'What further need was there that another priest should rise?'*

The main force of the apostle's argument, whereby he proveth the imperfection of the Levitical priesthood, is thus interrogatively expressed, *What further need was there,* &c. This interrogation intendeth a strong negation. See Chap. i. 5, Sec. 46.

Of the word χρεία, translated *need*, see Chap. v. 12, Sec. 62.

An adjective ἀχρεῖος thence derived, and compounded with the privative preposition, signifieth *unprofitable*, Mat. xxv. 30. So as that whereof there is no need, especially if it hath been in use before, is unprofitable; so the Levitical priesthood.

The Greek adverb ἔτι, translated *further*, is the very same that was translated *yet*, Sec. 58. Here it hath reference to the time, wherein Christ the true priest, far more excellent every way than any of the sons of Levi, was exhibited. Hereby he granteth, that formerly the Levitical priesthood was needful and useful; but now affirmeth that there was no further use or need thereof.

The other priest whom here he intendeth, is Christ himself, who is expressly said to be 'after the order of Melchisedec.' Of that order, see Chap. v. 6, Sec. 30.

The verb ἀνίστασθαι, translated *rise*, is a compound; the simple verb ἵστημι, signifieth to *set* or *place*, Mat. iv. 5; the compound *to rise*, Mat. ix. 9, or *to raise*, Mat. xxii. 24. It is here used in the former sense, and fitly translated *rise*. It implieth a clear manifestation of a thing. Christ was ever. As God, he was from 'everlasting to everlasting,' Ps. xc. 2; as God-man, mediator, and priest, he was shadowed and typified in all the priests, that ever were from the beginning of the world; but being incarnate, he rose, as the sun, and by his rising dispelled the clouds and shadows of all the types and ceremonies.

Upon these premises, that Christ was a priest, and after another order than the sons of Levi, and raised up instead of them to perfect what they could not, the imperfection of the legal priesthood is evinced.

Sec. 65. *Of superfluous additions to perfection.*

From the apostle's argument that the Levitical priesthood was imperfect, because another was raised after it, it may be well inferred, that nothing need be added to that which is perfect. Hereby the wise man proveth the work of God to be perfect, because 'nothing can be put to it,' Eccles. iii. 14. The like may be said of the word of God; and thereupon the wise man giveth this advice, 'Add thou not unto his words,' Prov. xxx. 5, 6.

1. Whatsoever is added to that which is perfect, must needs be superfluous, because nothing is wanting or defective in that which is perfect.

2. An addition to that which is perfect is dishonourable, for it seemeth to impeach it of some imperfection.

Hereby is discovered the boldness, pride, and presumption of the Church of Rome, who, of her own idle brain, maketh many additions to things most absolute and perfect, as to God, Christ, the Holy Ghost, and holy ordinances.

1. To God, who is all-sufficient, they add many

idols to help them in their needs, as if God were not of himself able to help in all needs.

2. To Christ, who is in all that he undertaketh, willing and able to accomplish it, they add in all his offices coadjutors and helps. To his kingly office they add a viceroy, a head, a spouse of his church, as if he alone could not govern it; to his prophetical office they add a great prophet to coin new articles of faith, to turn those which Christ hath established this way, or that way, as the pope pleaseth; to his priesthood they add other priests to offer up, as they say, true, real, propitiatory sacrifices for the quick and dead; to his mediation and intercession they add the mediation and intercession of all the angels and saints in heaven; to his blood, the milk of the virgin Mary; to his wounds, the wounds of their Saint Francis; to his death, the death of martyrs, among whom they reckon many traitors and other notorious malefactors; to his merits, the merits of men's works.

3. To the Holy Ghost, who likewise is able to effect what he undertaketh (only in wisdom, in regard of man's weakness, he useth means, which means are but bare instruments), they add bishops and priests, to whom they give a divine power of breathing in an holy spirit, and to the sacraments of working grace by the very act done.

4. To the word of God, which is most perfect, they add canons of councils, decrees of popes, and sundry human traditions.

5. To the two sacraments, which Christ the wise king of his church hath thought sufficient, they add five others, namely, orders, penance, confirmation, matrimony, and extreme unction.

Against these, and all other like additions, may the apostle's argument be pressed. If God, Christ, the Holy Ghost, the word of God, and sacraments be perfect, then those additions are vain. But if there need such additions, then are not God, Christ, the Holy Ghost, the word of God, and sacraments perfect. Take notice hereby of the blasphemous positions of that whorish church.

2. Let us learn to testify our acknowledgment of God's, and Christ's, and the Spirit's all-sufficiency and perfection, by trusting wholly and only on them. The like is to be applied to Christ's offices, sacrifice, merits, word, and sacraments.

Sec. 66. *Of Christ's priesthood differing from Aaron's.*

The apostle sets down the difference betwixt the Levitical priesthood and Christ's both affirmatively, thus, *after the order of Melchisedec*, and negatively thus, *and not to be called after the order of Aaron*. This he doth purposely, to meet with an objection which might be made against his former arguments, namely, that a succession of one thing after another doth not necessarily imply an imperfection in the one, and perfection in the other. For Eleazar succeeded Aaron, and so other priests under the law one after another, yet the latter were not more perfect than the former.

Ans. The apostle doth not draw his argument simply from the succession of one priest to another, but of one priesthood, and that after another order.

These two orders of Melchisedec and Aaron are the only two orders of priesthood that ever were instituted in God's church. In this respect the numeration of orders here set down is full and perfect.

The former, after which Christ was, hath been proved to be far more excellent than the latter; see ver. 4, Sec. 31.

The latter, after which Christ was not, is styled the order of Aaron. Aaron was the first public legal priest; that priesthood was appropriated to him and his seed, and the laws concerning that priesthood were first given to him, and, in and under him, to his posterity. Fitly therefore is that priesthood said to be 'after the order of Aaron.'

This word $\lambda \acute{\varepsilon} \gamma \varepsilon \sigma \theta \alpha \iota$, *dici, called*, is not the same $\varkappa \alpha \lambda o \tilde{\upsilon} \mu \varepsilon \nu o \varsigma$, that was used, Chap. v. 4, Sec. 20, about God's deputing one to an office. It properly signifieth *to be said*, chap. iii. 15. For Christ is nowhere said to be a priest after the order of Aaron; but he is said to be after the order of Melchisedec, Ps. cx. 4. Of a negative argument, see Chap. i. 5, Sec. 46.

That then which is here to be especially observed, is, that Christ's priesthood is of another kind than Levi's was. The apostle proveth this by many arguments, namely, in that it was after another order, under another law, ver. 12; by a priest of another tribe, ver. 14; of greater efficacy, ver. 19; having a better sacrifice, chap. ix. 23; and a more glorious place, chap. ix. 24.

Aaron's priesthood was not sufficient actually and effectually to do the things which are to be done by that function. It could not cleanse from sin, it could not justify, it could not properly sanctify, it could not make perfect those which are under it, chap. x. 1, &c. Therefore that which doth these things must needs be of another kind.

This teacheth us to be of other minds and other manners, not to doat on outward rudiments; after another manner to come to Jesus and to use him than the Jews came to their priests and used them. We need not now go on pilgrimage to Jerusalem, but with the eye of faith look to heaven; we need not bring doves, sheep, goats, bulls, but spiritual sacrifices. Another priest requireth another kind of disposition and conversation. All things are now new; so must we be new creatures, 2 Cor. v. 17.

Sec. 67. *Of the meaning of the twelfth verse.*

Ver. 12. *For the priesthood being changed, there is made of necessity a change also of the law.*

The twelfth verse is inferred as a consequence upon the change of the Levitical priesthood. He proved in the former verse that that priesthood was changed by another, which was after another order, and substituted in the room of it. Hereupon he inferreth that the law also must needs be changed.

The causal conjunction, γὰρ, *for*, is here a note of a consequence. The consequence is inferred upon the privilege of a priesthood, which was inserted in the former verse within a parenthesis. The privilege was this : under the Levitical priesthood ' the people received the law.' Thence it followeth that upon the change of the priesthood the law also must be changed.

The noun ἱερωσύνης, translated *priesthood*, is the same that was used before, ver 11, Sec. 61.

Of this word μετατιθεμένης, *changed*, see Chap. vi. 18, Sec. 135. Here it implieth such a change as one priesthood is utterly abrogated and nulled, and another substituted in the room of it. This noun *change*, μετάθεσις, here signifieth in effect as much as the word ἀθέτησις, translated *disannulling*, doth, ver. 18. Both the words are compounded with the same simple verb τίθημι, but different prepositions. We may not therefore think that the apostle intends a translation of one and the same priesthood from one priest to another (though this word be sometimes used for translating the same thing from one place to another, chap. xi. 5, Acts vii. 16), but rather a taking of it clean away.

This phrase, ἐξ ἀνάγκης, *of necessity*, implieth that it could not be otherwise.

There is such a mutual dependence of the law and priesthood one upon another, as they cannot be separated. They are like Hippocrates's twins, they live together and die together.

By νόμου, *law*, some take the particular ordinances about the Levitical priesthood to be meant. But surely it here intendeth as much as it did in this clause, ' the people received the law,' ver. 11. Now the people did not receive such ordinances only as concerned the priesthood, but that whole law which concerned the whole polity of the Jews.

The apostle doth the rather take this occasion of demonstrating the abrogation of the law, to draw their mind and hearts from it, that they might more firmly and stedfastly be set and settled on that law, which is established by Christ's priesthood, and that is the gospel. This is the principal intendment of this epistle.

Sec. 68. *Of the abrogation of the ceremonial law.*

The apostle in these words, *the priesthood being changed*, taketh it for granted that the Levitical priesthood was abrogated ; for this he had proved in the former verse. The main point here intended is the abrogation of the law, upon which he layeth a necessity.

The Jews were under a threefold law, moral, ceremonial, and judicial.

The ceremonial law is here in particular intended, for that especially depended upon the Levitical priesthood.

The moral law concerns all the sons of Adam, but the two other concern the sons of Abraham.

The ceremonial law enjoins such services as were to be performed to God, and such ceremonies and rites as appertained thereunto ; and withal it directed priests and people in the use of them.

This is that law whereof the apostle thus speaks : ' There is verily a disannulling of the commandment,' ver. 18 ; this is that ' law of commandments,' which is said to be 'abolished' by Christ, Eph. ii. 15 ; this is that ' handwriting of ordinances' which is said to be ' blotted out,' Col. ii. 14.

Obj. This is it that is said to be ' a statute for ever,' Exod. xxviii. 43, and ' a covenant of salt for ever,' Num. xviii. 19.

Ans. 1. The Hebrew word עולם, translated *for ever*, is sometimes indefinitely put for a long season, the end whereof is not known to us, Eccles. xii. 5.

2. It is put for an unalterable stability so long as the date appointed continued. Thus, that which continued unalterable till the year of jubilee is said to be for ever, Exod. xxi. 6.

3. It is put for the continuance of one's life. Thus Samuel is devoted to ' abide before the Lord for ever,' 1 Sam. i. 22.

4. It is put for the whole time of the polity of the Jews. That which was to continue so long as that estate lasted is said to be for ever or everlasting, Gen. xvii. 8.

5. It is put for that which ended in the truth, the Lord Jesus, and so is said to be for ever, as Solomon's throne, 2 Sam. vii. 13.

In the first and two last respects before mentioned may the ceremonial law be said to continue for ever ; for it continued a long time, many hundred years, even so long as the polity of the Jews lasted, and it ended in Christ, the truth of all the legal ceremonies.

1. In this respect it could not properly continue for ever, but must vanish away, because it was the figure of a substance, the shadow of a body, and type of a truth, to come, Heb. x. 1. Now a figure and type ceaseth when the substance and truth is exhibited, and a shadow vanisheth away when the body is in place and present. Herein lieth a difference between shadows and types on the one side, and signs and sacraments on the other side : that the former are of things future, the latter of things exhibited and past. The former cannot retain their life and vigour together with the substance and truth ; the latter may retain their life and vigour together with the thing signified.

2. The ceremonial law was a wall of partition betwixt Jew and Gentile, whereby the Jews were so fenced as the Gentiles could not be mixed with them, as when beasts of one lord[1] are so fenced in a pasture as other beasts cannot come into their pasture. Therefore when Christ came to unite Jew and Gentile, and to make of them one, he is said to ' break down this

---

[1] Qu. ' herd ' ?—ED.

stop of partition wall,' Eph. ii. 14. If that law had not been abrogated, the Gentiles could not have been brought into Christ's fold, as of necessity they must be, John x. 16. Till the fulness of time, wherein the truth and substance of all the ceremonies and types was exhibited and accomplished, that law of ceremonies remained in force with the Jews upon these grounds :

1. The several branches thereof were part of God's outward worship.
2. Thereby they were kept from will-worship.
3. They were also thereby kept from conforming themselves to the Gentiles in their idolatrous services.
4. They being types and shadows of Christ to come, were as a looking-glass to shew unto them that image of Christ.
5. They being many, heavy, burdensome, painful, chargeable rites, they made the Jews the more to long after Christ. In this respect the apostle saith of this law that it was 'our schoolmaster to bring us unto Christ,' Gal. iii. 24. For,

It pointed out Christ under rudiments and ceremonies.

It forced men to seek help elsewhere, because it could not perfect those that came unto it.

1. This aggravateth those dotages which were noted, Sec. 61.
2. It informs us in God's goodness to us, who are reserved to that fulness of time wherein Christ hath been exhibited; for we are freed from that 'yoke which neither we nor our fathers are able to bear,' Acts xv. 10. This is a bondage worse than the Egyptian bondage. They that were freed from that bondage had many memorials of God's goodness to them therein, the more to quicken up their spirits to praise God for their deliverance, and to continue the memory thereof from generation to generation.
3. The change of the law is a strong motive to stir us up willingly and cheerfully to submit ourselves to this law whereinto that is translated; that is, to the law of the gospel, which is established under Christ's priesthood. This law requires not impossibilities, as to ascend into heaven, or to descend into the deep, Rom. x. 6, 7; but it requires faith and repentance, Mark i. 15. Faith, to give evidence to the free grace of God, who requireth of us but to receive what he graciously offereth; repentance, to demonstrate the purity of God, who, though he freely justify a sinner, yet he will not have have him continue in sin. Yea, this law of the gospel giveth power and ability to perform what it requireth. If this law, into which the other is translated, be thoroughly compared with that, we shall find just cause to acknowledge that this is 'an easy yoke, and a light burden,' Mat. xi. 30, but that a yoke and burden that none could bear, Acts xv. 10.

Sec. 69. *Of the judicial law of the Jews.*

Besides the ceremonial law, the Jews had a judicial law, proper and peculiar to that polity. This law concerned especially their civil estate. Many branches of that law appertained to the Jewish priesthood; as, the particular laws about the cities of refuge, whither such as slew any unawares fled, and there abode till the death of the high priest, Num. xxxv. 25. And laws about lepers, which the priest was to judge, Lev. xiv. 3. And sundry other cases which the priest was to judge of, Deut. xvii. 9. So also the laws of distinguishing tribes, Num. xxxvi. 7 ; of reserving inheritances to special tribes and families, of selling them to the next of kin, Ruth iv. 4 ; of raising seed to a brother that died without issue, Gen. xxxviii. 8, 9 ; of all manner of freedoms at the year of jubilee, Lev. xxv. 13, &c.

There were other branches of the judicial law which rested upon common equity, and were means of keeping the moral law: as putting to death idolaters and such as enticed others thereunto; and witches, and wilful murderers, and other notorious malefactors. So likewise laws against incest and incestuous marriages; laws of reverencing and obeying superiors and governors; and of dealing justly in borrowing, restoring, buying, selling, and all manner of contracts, Exod. xxii. 20; Deut. xiii. 9; Exod. xx. 18; Num. xxxv. 30; Lev. xx. 11, &c., xix. 32, 35.

The former sort were abolished together with the priesthood.

The latter remain as good directions to order even Christian polities accordingly.

1. By these kinds of laws the wisdom of God was manifested in observing what was fit for the particular kind and condition of people; and in giving them answerable laws, and yet not tying all nations and states thereunto.
2. That liberty which God affordeth to others to have laws most agreeable to their own country, so as they be not contrary to equity and piety, bindeth them more obediently to submit themselves to their own wholesome laws, and to keep peace, unity, and amity among themselves.

Sec. 70. *Of the moral law.*

The moral law is a general rule for all sorts of people. It was therefore given to Adam and his posterity; yea, it was engraven in man's heart, Rom. ii. 15. It is a perfect rule of all righteousness, whereby is declared what is due to God and man. It is an inviolable, unchangeable, and everlasting law; of perpetual use, never to be abrogated.

This is that law which Christ came ' not to destroy but to fulfil,' Mat. v. 17. This is the law which ' through faith we establish,' Rom. iii. 31. This is that law from which ' not one jot or one tittle shall pass till heaven and earth pass,' Mat. v. 18.

Yet because through man's corruption it is so far from bringing man to life (which was the primary and principal end thereof) as it beateth him down into a most woful and cursed estate, it is by Jesus Christ (who is the resurrection and life, John xi. 25), in sundry circumstances altered, or rather mollified.

It will be therefore requisite distinctly to declare, both wherein that alteration or qualification consisteth, and also wherein the moral law still remaineth of use to Christians.

It is mollified in these circumstances.

1. In regard of justification, Acts xiii. 39. The law was first given to justify the observers thereof; but now in regard of man's corruption, that is impossible, Rom. viii. 3, Gal. iii. 11. God therefore now hath appointed another means for that end, which is, Christ and faith in him, Acts xiii. 39, Rom. iii. 28.

2. In regard of the rigour thereof. The law accepteth no duty, but that which is every way absolute and perfect. Thus much is implied under this phrase, 'The man which doth these things, shall live by them,' Rom. x. 5. This therefore is the doom of the law, 'Cursed is every one that continueth not in all things which are written in the book of the law, to do them,' Gal. iii. 10. Yet there is a righteousness (though not framed according to this exact rule) which is accepted of God. This is the righteousness of faith, whereby laying hold on Christ's righteousness to be justified, 'we exercise ourselves to have always a conscience void of offence towards God and towards man,' Acts xxiv. 16. 'For if there be first a willing mind, it is accepted according to that a man hath, and not according to that he hath not,' 2 Cor. viii. 12.

3. In regard of an accidental power, which the law, through man's corruption, hath to increase sin, and to make it out of measure sinful, Rom. vii. 13. For the very forbidding of a sin by the law maketh the corrupt heart of man more eagerly pursue it; as a stubborn child will do a thing the more, because it is forbidden. Heathen, by the light of nature, discerned thus much, hereupon they had this proverb,

Nitimur in vetitum semper, cupimusque negata,

We are most prone to that which is forbidden, and desire things denied. There is a secret antipathy and contrary disposition in our corrupt nature to God's pure law; but by the Spirit of Christ that antipathy is taken away, and another disposition wrought in true believers, namely, a true desire, and faithful endeavour to avoid what the law forbiddeth, and to do that which it requireth. In this respect, saith the apostle, 'I delight in the law of God concerning the inward man,' Rom. vii. 22.

4. In regard of the curse of the law. For the law peremptorily denounceth a curse against every transgressor and transgression, Deut. xxvii. 26, Gal. iii. 10. The law admits no surety, nor accepts any repentance.

Thus, 'all men having sinned, come short of the glory of God,' Rom. iii. 23. Yet this curse doth not light on all; for 'Christ hath redeemed us from the curse of the law, being made a curse for us,' Gal. iii. 13. In this respect, 'there is no condemnation to them that are in Christ Jesus,' Rom. viii. 1.

Though the moral law be altered in the fore-mentioned respects, yet still it remains to be of use for instruction and direction.

1. For instruction, it demonstrateth these points following:

(1.) What God himself is, Exod. xx. 2.
(2.) What his holy will is, Ps. xl. 8.
(3.) What our duty is to God and man, Mat. xxii. 37–39.
(4.) What sin is, 1 John iii. 4, Rom. iii. 20.
(5.) What are the kinds of sin, James ii. 11, Rom. vii. 7.
(6.) What the pravity of our nature is, Rom. vii. 14.
(7.) What the sinfulness of our lives is, Rom. vii. 19.
(8.) God's approbation of obedience, Exod. xx. 6, 12.
(9.) God's detestation of transgressors, Exod. xx. 5, 7.
(10.) The fearful doom of sinners, Gal. iii. 10.
(11.) Man's disability to keep the law, Rom. viii. 3.
(12.) The necessity of another means of salvation, Rom. iii. 20, 21.

2. For direction. The law is of use to these points following.

(1.) To convince men of sin.
(2.) To humble them for the same.
(3.) To work an hatred of sin.
(4.) To restrain them from it.
(5.) To work self-denial.
(6.) To drive men to Christ.
(7.) To put them on to endeavour after as near a conformity to the law as they can.
(8.) To make them fearful of pulling upon their souls a more fearful doom than the curse of the law, which is by despising the gospel.
(9.) To make impenitents the more inexcusable.
(10.) To make believers more thankful for Christ's active and passive obedience, whereby as a surety he hath done for them what they could not; and endured that curse which they deserved, to free them from the same.

Sec. 71. *Of the resolution and observations of* Heb. vii. 11, 12.

Ver. 11. *If therefore perfection were by the Levitical priesthood (for under it the people received the law), what further need was there that another priest should rise after the order of Melchisedec, and not be called after the order of Aaron?*

12. *For the priesthood being changed, there is made of necessity a change also of the law.*

The sum of these two verses is a demonstration of the imperfection of the Levitical priesthood.

Thereof are two parts.

In the first, the point itself is laid down; in the second, a proof thereof.

The point itself is a priesthood. This is set out two ways.
1. By the kind of it. 2. By the privilege appertaining to it.

In setting down the kind of that priesthood, we are to observe,
1. The manner of setting it down, by way of supposition, in this particle *if*.
2. The matter whereof it consisteth. This hath two branches.
1. The persons exercising it, the sons of Levi, implied in this word *Levitical*.
2. The imperfection of it, implied in this supposition, *If perfection*, &c.

The privilege of a priesthood is a relation betwixt it and the law: *under it the law*, &c.

This is amplified, (1.) By the persons who received the law under it, *the people*.

(2.) By a consequence following upon it, ver. 12.

The proof of the point is from the need of another priesthood.

Here again we are to observe the manner and the matter.

The manner of expressing the proof is by an interrogation, *What need*, &c.

The matter is, (1.) Generally propounded in this phrase, *another priest*, &c.

(2.) Particularly exemplified.

The exemplification is in two orders.

The first order is asserted thus, *after the order of Melchisedec*.

The other order is removed thus, *not called after the order of Aaron*.

The consequence of the foresaid privilege of a priesthood, being a relation betwixt it and a law, is a change of the one with the other. Hereof are two parts.

One taken for granted. *The priesthood being changed.*

The other, an inference made upon that grant, *there is made a change*, &c.

This is amplified by the necessity of it, *of necessity*.

Doctrines.

I. *A conditional supposition may be the ground of a contrary conclusion.* This supposition, *if perfection*, &c., is a ground to prove the priesthood imperfect. See Sec. 61.

II. *There was a priesthood under the law.* This is here taken for granted. See Sec. 63.

III. *The priests under the law were sons of Levi.* This word *Levitical* sets out as much. See Sec. 61.

IV. *The priesthood under the law was imperfect.* This is implied under the consequence inferred upon this supposition, *If perfection*, &c. See Sec. 61.

V. *A priesthood was used for establishing a law.* This was the reason of this priesthood. See Sec. 63.

VI. *The law established by a priesthood is for people's use.* For *the people received it.* See Sec. 63.

VII. *An imperfect priesthood needs another.* This is here taken for granted. See Sec. 64.

VIII. *Nothing may be added to that which is perfect.* This by consequence followeth from the apostle's argument. See Sec. 65.

IX. *Christ came in the room of Levi.* This also is here taken for granted. See Sec. 64.

X. *Christ's priesthood is after the order of Melchisedec.* This is expressly affirmed. See Sec. 66.

XI. *Christ was not after the order of Aaron.* This also is expressly affirmed. See Sec. 66.

XII. *The legal priesthood is changed.* This is here presupposed. See Sec. 67.

XIII. *The law and priest depend each on other.* This is the force of the consequence here inferred. See Sec. 67.

XIV. *A law cannot stand without a priesthood.* This phrase, *of necessity*, intends as much. See Sec. 67.

Sec. 72. *Of the meaning of the 13th verse.*

Ver. 13. *For he of whom these things are spoken pertaineth to another tribe, of which no man gave attendance at the altar.*

14. *For it is evident that our Lord sprang out of Judah; of which tribe Moses spake nothing concerning priesthood.*

In these two verses the apostle giveth a proof of this main point, that Christ's priesthood was of another kind than the Levitical priesthood. His argument is drawn from the different tribes, whereof the one and the other priests were. The grounds of the argument resteth upon this, that God restrained the priesthood, under the law, to the tribe of Levi. None of any other tribe might be of that priesthood, Num. xviii. 1, &c. Christ therefore being of another tribe, was not a priest after that order. The first particle $\gamma \grave{\alpha} \varrho$, *for*, intendeth a reason.

These words, $\grave{\epsilon} \varphi'$ $\grave{o} \nu$ $\lambda \acute{\epsilon} \gamma \epsilon \tau \alpha \iota$, *He of whom these things are spoken*, are relative. They have reference to him that was the true priest, whom Melchisedec prefigured; and to whom all those excellent things, before mentioned of Melchisedec, as a type, most truly and properly appertained. This was Jesus Christ, who in the next verse is styled, 'our Lord.' This relative description of Christ, giveth good ground to apply that priesthood of Melchisedec, and other excellencies spoken of him thereabout, to Christ. See ver. 3, Secs. 25, 26, and ver. 4, Sec. 31.

Of the meaning of the Greek word $\mu \epsilon \tau \epsilon \acute{o} \chi \eta \kappa \epsilon \nu$, translated *pertaineth*, see chap. ii. 14, Sec. 139. Christ was pleased to associate himself among the people of God, and that so as to be of one of their tribes.

A *tribe*, $\varphi \upsilon \lambda \acute{\eta}$, was a company of people that descended from a distinct stock. Now Jacob or Israel having twelve sons, so many as descended from each of them were accounted to make so many tribes, and thereupon were called 'the twelve tribes of Israel,' Gen.

xlix. 28. This word *tribe* is also by way of resemblance, applied to other divisions, of people in other nations, and translated *kindred*, Rev. v. 9, but here it is taken in the first and proper sense.

This distributive pronoun, ἑτέρας, *another*, hath reference to the tribe of Levi, so as Christ was not of that tribe, yet of another. What that other tribe was, and why he was of that tribe, see ver. 14, Sec. 75.

This in general giveth evidence of a great condescension in Christ, who, being one of the glorious Trinity in heaven, vouchsafed to be of one of the twelve tribes of Israel on earth.

Of the tribe whereof Christ was, it is said, *no man gave attendance at the altar*.

An altar was that whereon sacrifices were offered up. The Hebrew word מזבח, *altare*, that signifieth an altar, is derived from a verb, זבו, *sacrificavit*, that signifieth to sacrifice. The Greek word here used, θυσιαστηρίῳ, is a compound of two nouns, whereof one signifieth a sacrifice, the other implieth a place to lay that sacrifice upon. Our English word *altar* is taken from the Latin *altare*, which signifieth a thing raised on high,[1] or so called because it used to be raised up and set in high places.

This phrase, *he gave attendance*, is the interpretation of one compound Greek word, προσέσχηκε, whereof see Chap. ii. 1, Sec. 6. There is shewed that it signifieth a serious heeding of a thing, or attending it, so as it is here fitly translated *gave attendance*; such are said, προσεδρεύειν, *assidere*,[2] to wait at the altar, 1 Cor. ix. 13.

The altar is here metonymically put for the priests offering sacrifices thereon, and the services about the altar are synecdochically put for all other services appertaining to that calling.

Where he saith, *no man gave attendance*, he speaks rather of right than of fact; for Uzziah, of the tribe of Judah, gave attendance at the altar of incense, 2 Chron. xxvi. 16, but without warrant, and against the law. He had no right so to do; he ought not to have done it.

In this last clause one thing is expressed, that none of another tribe gave attendance at the altar; another is implied, that the priests who were of the tribe of Levi did give attendance at the altar.

Sec. 73. *Of not intermeddling with things not appertaining to us, but attending our own business.*

From the foresaid point expressed, that none of another tribe gave attendance at the altar, we may well infer this general, that no man ought to meddle with that office which belongs not to him. When Christ was desired to decide a controversy betwixt brothers about their inheritance, he returned this answer, 'Man, who made me a judge, or a divider over you?' Luke xii. 13, 14. None could better have done it; but because it belonged not to him, he would not do it. 'Every fool will be meddling,' Prov. xx. 3. The apostle calls such 'busy bodies,' and saith that they 'walk disorderly,' 1 Thes. iv. 11. Another apostle gives Christians to understand that such meddling with other men's matters may cause suffering, but such suffering as a Christian can have no comfort in, and therefore adviseth that 'none suffer as a busy body,' 1 Pet. iv. 15. 'The wisdom of the prudent is to understand *his* way,' Prov. xiv. 8, and, 'The just man walketh in *his* integrity,' Prov. xx. 7. In these and other like places this relative *his* implieth that which in special appertaineth to him. Express in this case is this charge, '.Let every man abide in the same calling wherein he was called,' 1 Cor. vii. 20. This is the way to bring quietness to a man; thereupon saith the apostle, 'Study to be quiet, and to do your own business,' 1 Thes. iv. 11. Well weigh the direction which the Baptist giveth to those that inquired of him what they should do, and you shall find that it tends to this, to have an eye to the particular duties of their several callings, Luke iii. 10, &c.

See sundry grounds of the equity of this point in *The Whole Armour of God*, on Eph. vi. 14, treat. ii. part i. sec. 4.

Do they swerve from this ruled case who, being of other callings, give attendance at the pulpit? and such as, being ministers, give attendance at shops, farms, and other like places? so they who attend upon trades, wherein they were never trained up, nor have any skill? Many, Absalom-like, pretend to do great matters if they were in such and such places, 2 Sam. xv. 4, when they are most unfit so to do, and do the contrary. From that which is taken for granted, that they who are of the tribe of Levi gave attendance at the altar, it followeth that the duties which belong to our particular places must be carefully performed; we must be diligent and faithful therein. So were two of those servants whom the Lord entrusted with talents, Mat. xxv. 16, 17. So were other servants of God guided by his Spirit; and among others, Moses, and Christ himself, Chap. iii. 2.

Those two encouragements, which are of most force to quicken any hereunto, are both propounded in the parable of the talents—the Lord's gracious approbation and bountiful remuneration, Mat. xxv. 21.

It is observable that God frequently manifested some extraordinary evidence of his special favour to his servants while they were employed in their particular callings. The Lord first appeared unto Moses to make known unto him his purpose of advancing him to be a governor over his people, while he was keeping the sheep of his father-in-law, Exod. iii. 1, &c., for this was his particular calling. Thus Elisha was first called to be a prophet while he was ploughing, 1 Kings xix. 19. The good tidings that old Zacharias should have a son, was brought to him while he gave

---

[1] Altare ab adject. *altus:* quia altis locis excitari solebat.
[2] Προσεδρεύειν. Πρὸς τὸν ἴδιον. Proprio commodo invigilare.—*Arist. Polit.*

attendance at the altar, Luke i. 11. The first blessed tidings of our Saviour's birth was brought to shepherds while they were keeping their flocks, Luke ii. 8, &c. Many like instances might be given of God's approbation of men's diligence and faithfulness in their particular callings.

Of diligence in our undertakings, see Chap. iv. 11, Secs. 63, 64, and Chap. vi. 11, Sec. 79.

By way of resemblance I may further infer, that as they of the tribe of Judah had nothing to do with the ordinances proper to the tribe of Levi, so we Christians, with the altar and ordinances proper to the Jews; we are another people, and have another priesthood. We have the gospel and ordinances proper thereto; upon those we must give attendance. As they had an altar whereof we had no right to eat, so we have an altar whereof they have no right to eat, Heb. xiii. 10.

Sec. 74. *Of Christ our Lord.*

The fourth verse is added both as another argument to prove that Christ was not a priest after the order of Aaron (because he was of the tribe of Judah), and also as a confirmation of the former argument, that he was of another tribe; because he was of the tribe of *Judah*, which was another than the tribe of Levi. The causal conjunction, γάρ, shews that it is added as a reason.

The adjective πρόδηλον, translated *evident*, is a compound; properly, it signifieth *before-manifest*, or manifest beforehand. So it is translated 1 Tim. v. 24, 25; but here the preposition addeth emphasis. The simple noun, δῆλον, signifieth *manifest*, 1 Cor. xv. 27; sundry compounds, ἔκδηλος, 2 Tim. iii. 9, καταδηλόν, Heb. vii. 15, *very manifest*, which emphasis our English implieth under this word *evident*. Hereby he gives us to wit that it was most clear and unquestionable truth.

This title, *our Lord*, hath reference to Christ. *Lord* setteth out his supreme sovereignty, dignity, and dominion. Hereof see Chap. i. 10, Sec. 128.

This relative, *our*, hath special reference to the church, and to the several members thereof. So was the penman of this epistle, and they to whom he directed it.

Christ, then, is in special the Lord of the church. In this sense do the apostles use this correlative *our*, joined with *Lord*, in their salutations, Gal. i. 3, 2 Pet. i. 2; in their gratulations, Eph. i. 3, 1 Pet. i. 3; in their benedictions, Rom. xvi. 24, 2 Cor. xiii. 13; and on sundry other occasions. Yea, many times believers do appropriate this relation to themselves in the singular number; thus, *My Lord*, Ps. cx. 1, John xx. 28.

This being taken of Christ, as he is the mediator betwixt God and man, belongeth unto him sundry ways; as,

1. By God's ordination; for God himself saith of this his Son, ' I have set my King upon my holy hill of Zion,' Ps. ii. 6. And an apostle saith, ' God gave him to be the head over all things to the church,' Eph. i. 22.

2. By that redemption which Christ hath made of his church. He that redeemeth any out of bondage, is in that respect their lord, Exod. xx. 2. Therefore these two titles, *Lord, Redeemer*, are oft joined together, Isa. xliii. 14, and xliv. 24.

3. By a mutual compact and covenant betwixt Christ and his church, as it was of old betwixt God and Israel. God avouched Israel to be his peculiar people, and Israel avouched the Lord to be their God, Deut. xxvi. 17, 18. This was oft foretold by the prophets, Jer. xxxi. 33, Hosea ii. 23, Zech. xiii. 9. This the apostle testifieth to be accomplished in the Christian church, Heb. viii. 10. Christ in and by the gospel and sacraments offereth himself to be our Lord; and we take him so to be by subjecting ourselves to his ordinances.

4. By the laws and ordinances which Christ hath given to his church. It is the part of a lord to give laws, and he is their lord in special to whom he giveth his laws. But God's word, wherein his laws are contained, is in a peculiar manner given to his church, Ps. cxlvii. 19, 20. In this respect the church is styled 'the pillar and ground of truth,' 1 Tim. iii. 15.

5. By a special care which he taketh of his church. He doth good ' unto all men, especially unto them who are of the household of faith.' He is 'the Saviour of all men, specially of those that believe,' 1 Tim. iv. 10.

This special relation doth most of all bind those who profess themselves to be of the church, carefully to perform all duties which belong to Christ as a Lord, and with strong confidence to rest on him as their Lord, both for provision of all things needful, and for protection from all things hurtful.

Sec. 75. *Of God's performing promise.*

Of the fore-mentioned Lord, it is here said that *he sprang out of Judah.* The verb ἀνατέλλω, *exorior*, translated *sprang*, is for the most part in the New Testament used to set out the rising of the sun, as Mat. xiii. 6, James i. 11. A noun, ἀνατολή, *oriens*, thence derived, signifieth *the east*, whence the sun ariseth, Mat. ii. 2. Where a prophet resembleth Christ to the sun, and speaketh of the rising of the sun, Mal. iv. 1, the LXX render it with this word in my text ἀνατελεῖ ἥλιος. In reference hereunto it may be here thus translated, *our Lord rose*. Many expositors thus take it in this place. Others are of opinion that the apostle in using this word hath reference to that title, which in the Old Testament is oft given to Christ, and translated *branch*, Isa. iv. 2, Jer. xxiii. 5, Zech. vi. 12. The foresaid LXX do in all those places translate that Hebrew word צמח, *germen*, which signifieth a branch, by the Greek word ἀνατολή, which is derived from the verb here used. In this sense Judah is here resembled to a stock, and Christ to one of the branches that sprang out of that stock. In this sense our English translateth the verb ἀνατέταλκε, *sprang*. Hereby it is evidenced that Christ was a true man, a Son of man, man of man.

Judah is here metonymically put for the tribe of Judah.

Express mention is made of this tribe of Judah,

1. To make the argument more clear; for the tribe of Judah was another tribe than the tribe of Levi.

2. To shew that Christ was a royal Priest; for the royalty of a kingdom appertained to that tribe by virtue of Jacob's blessing, Gen. xlix. 10; and of God's promise made to David of that tribe, 2 Sam. vii. 16, Ps. lxxviii. 68, 70, &c.

3. To bring to their mind and memory the promise made to that tribe, and that under the fore-mentioned metaphor of a *branch*, Ps. lxxx. 15, Isa. xi. 1, Zech. iii. 8.

It is more than probable that the apostle had reference to that promise in using this phrase *sprang out of Judah*, and we may well from thence infer, that God is faithful in performing his promises. For this particular promise of Christ being a branch, brings to our mind that first promise made to man after his fall concerning the seed of the woman, Gen. iii. 15, which being accomplished, what question can be made of any other promise? That was the first and foundation of all other promises. 'All the promises of God in Christ are yea, and in him amen,' 2 Cor. i. 20; that is, they are all ratified and accomplished in Christ. God, in accomplishing his promises, is called *faithful*, Heb. x. 23; and *true*, Rom. iii. 4.

All promises made by God are made on good counsel, so as he will never repent thereof; they make much to the honour of his name, so as no doubt may be made of his accomplishing thereof.

1. Most heinous is the sin of infidelity, which questioneth a matter so infallible. See hereof Chap. vi. 13, Sec. 100, and ver. 18, Sec. 143.

2. It will be our wisdom to search after God's promises, and then for strengthening of our faith in them, seriously to consider the faithfulness of him who maketh the promises. If a man whom we judge faithful make us a promise, we rely much upon it, yet many things may intervene, which may make that man to fail; but nothing can make the faith of God to fail.

Sec. 76. *Of God's warrant for God's worship.*

The apostle's proof that they who were of the tribe of Judah, had nothing to do about Aaron's priesthood, is taken from Moses's silence thereabout, thus expressed, *of which tribe Moses spake nothing concerning the priesthood.*

The preposition translated *of*, especially as it is here joined with the accusative case, εἰς ἥν, most properly signifieth *to*. But the sense will hold the same, whether we translate it *of* or *to*.

Of Moses, see Chap. iii. 2, Sec. 37.

God used Moses to reveal and make known to his people in that time whatsoever he would have them to know, so as that which Moses did not speak and make known to them, was not taken to be the mind or will of God. The force then of the argument resteth on this, that by Moses speaking nothing about the priesthood to be of the tribe of Judah, it appeared that it was not the Lord's mind that any of the tribe of Judah should be of the priesthood.

Though this be a negative argument, yet it being concerning the worship of God, it is a sound concluding argument.

1. In that Moses spake nothing of it, it appears that God would not have it to be so. For whatsoever God would have to be done by his people at that time, he revealed to Moses, for him to make it known to them.

2. In that God declared nothing of his mind therein, it followeth that God would not have them that were of the tribe of Judah to be then his priests. God hath not left articles of faith, or parts of his divine worship, to man's invention and discretion. He then made known whatsoever he would have his church then believe and practise about his worship. What since that time, he would have his church to believe or practise thereabouts, since that time he hath by his prophets and apostles made known to his church, and caused to be registered in the sacred Scripture.

Thus we see that everything wherein and whereby God is worshipped, must have an express warrant from God's word. 'In vain they do worship God, teaching for doctrines the commandments of men,' Mat. xv. 9. It is the main scope of the second commandment to have our warrant from God to worship him.

1. No man can tell how God will be worshipped, or how therein they may please God.

2. Man's heart is very foolish, addicted to outward toys, as is evident by all manner of superstitions which are man's inventions.

1. I may use this apostolical argument against that mass of popish inventions wherein and whereby they worship God, and I may say, nor Moses, nor any other penman of Scripture, spake anything concerning such a kind of worshipping God. Therefore no good Christian is to join with them therein. What prophet or apostle ever spake anything of worshipping God before images, or in an unknown tongue, or in numeral prayers, or through the mediation of saints or angels, or by offering the sacrifice of the mass, or by adoring relics, or by crossing themselves, or by sprinkling of holy water, or by other sacraments than baptism and the Lord's supper, or by pilgrimages, or by going barefoot, or by wearing shirts of hair, or by forbearing flesh, or by vowing perpetual continency, voluntary poverty, regular obedience, or tying themselves to nunneries, friaries, abbeys, and such like places of retirement, or by making themselves hermits and anchorites, or by visiting the holy land, or doing other

like human inventions. These and thousands more, which they pretend to be matters of great devotion, and parts of God's worship, are nowhere spoken of in God's word, therefore no more acceptable to God than Uzziah's offering incense, 2 Chron. xxvi. 19.

2. Let us learn to search God's word concerning matters of his worship, and what we find prescribed therein, in faith perform, but let us take heed of all mere human inventions. A man can have no comfort in anything concerning God's worship, of which God's word speaketh nothing.

Sec. 77. *Of making points more and more clear.*

In the fifteenth verse there is another argument to prove that Christ's priesthood was not after the order of Aaron's.

The former argument was taken from the different tribes whereof Christ and Aaron were. See Sec. 72.

This, from the different order of Christ's and Aaron's priesthood.

This first clause, *and it is yet far more evident,* sheweth that another argument is here produced. Of the former argument, he said, *It is evident,* ver. 1. Of this, *it is yet far more evident.*

Of the Greek adjective translated *evident,* see ver. 14, Sec. 74.

Of this emphatical comparison, *far more,* see Chap. ii. 1, Sec. 5, and Chap. vi. 17, Sec. 131. The word intendeth an extension of the point to which it is applied. It is interpreted according to the matter in hand, as, *more earnest,* Chap. ii. 1; *more abundantly,* Chap. vi. 17; *far more,* in this text.

Of this adverb *yet,* see ver. 10, Sec. 58, and ver. 11, Sec. 64. Here it hath reference to a former evidence, and it implieth that the point in hand had by the former argument been made clear, and that by this argument so much more evidence was added as made it more clear.

This heaping up of these emphatical words, *evident, far more evident, yet far more evident,* do demonstrate that weighty points are to be made more and more clear. Argument is to be added to argument, and the latter argument more clear than the former. Thus did this apostle in setting out the deity of Christ, see Chap. i. 5, Sec. 63, and ver. 6, Sec. 77. The like he doth about the vigour of faith, Heb. xi. 1, 2, &c.

This is useful both in regard of men's understanding and judgment, and also in regard of their heart and affection.

1. Many proofs, the latter being clearer, are of the more force to enlighten men's minds, and convince their judgments of the truth and equity of a point. They are as many lights brought into a room, which, by their number, make everything seem more clearly. By one argument men may be brought to say, *it is evident,* but by many, *it is far more evident.*

2. The heart and affection is much more easily wrought upon, when the judgment is more clearly enlightened and thoroughly convinced. The understanding is a guide to the other faculties of the soul. The light thereof discovers all starting-holes; but if the judgment be not well informed and thoroughly convinced of the truth and equity of that which is delivered, the most pithy exhortations and powerful persuasions will be but as water poured upon a stone. Some that have been vehement and earnest in their exhortations, persuasions, yea, and denunciations of judgments, extending their voice, clapping their hands, beating the desk with their fist, stamping with their feet, and sweating in their whole body, have yet little moved their auditory. One reason may be want of convincing their judgments. When this is once done the heart will soon be wrought upon. While ministers are, in a doctrinal way, clearing the points they have in hand, and soundly proving the truth and equity of them, by argument upon argument, the hearts of hearers are oft wrought upon before the preacher cometh to his application. Then one word of exhortation or reprehension may more prevail than thousands without such a preparative.

Sec. 78. *Of the meaning of these words, 'For that after the similitude of Melchisedec there ariseth another priest.'*

The Greek conjunction εἰ, translated *for that,* is conditional. Most usually and properly it signifieth, and is translated, *if.* But it is also used as a causal conjunction, and made the ground or cause of that which is said or done, as where it is said, 'If we this day be examined,' Acts iv. 9, the meaning is, because we are examined. So here, *for that,* or *because.* Where the apostle speaketh of Christ's priesthood in reference to Melchisedec, six times he useth this word τάξιν, *order,* four times before this place, namely, Chap. v. 6, 10, Chap. vi. 20, and ver. 11 of this chapter; and twice afterwards, namely, ver. 17, 21. But here he useth the word ὁμοιότητα, *similitude,* or likeness.

Of the derivation of the Greek word, see Chap. iv. 15, Sec. 90.

These two words, *order* and *similitude,* explain each other.

The former sheweth that the priesthood whereof he speaketh is a warranted priesthood, appointed, and set every way most decently.

The latter sheweth that all the excellencies spoken of Melchisedec appertain to Christ; see ver. 3, Sec. 24.

As Christ was after the order of Melchisedec, so in all the excellencies of Melchisedec he was like him; yea, he was the truth and substance of them all. This likeness of Christ to Melchisedec was as the likeness of a body to the shadow. Christ was not only like Melchisedec in surpassing excellencies, but also he was a true priest, after that very order.

Of the Greek verb ἀνίσταται, *exoritur*, translated *ariseth*, see ver. 11, Sec. 64.

The present tense, *ariseth*, here used, implieth a present and continual being of Christ's priesthood, after the abolishing of the Levitical priesthood; for under this phrase, ἱερεὺς ἕτερος, *another priest*, the Lord Jesus is intended.

This adjective *another*, is used by way of distinction from Aaron. So much is plainly expressed in the latter end of the eleventh verse, thus, 'that another priest should rise after the order of Melchisedec, and not be called after the order of Aaron.' Christ in person was another than Melchisedec; yet in office he was after his order. But he was another than Aaron in person, in order, in office, in efficacy, and sundry other ways.

That Christ's priesthood was of another kind than Aaron's, is shewed, ver. 11, Sec. 66.

That Christ was like Melchisedec in all his excellencies is manifested, Chap. v. 6, Sec. 30, Chap. vii. 3, Sec. 24.

Sec. 79. *Of the resolution and observation of* Heb. vii. 13–15.

Ver. 13. *For he of whom these things are spoken pertaineth to another tribe, of which no man gave attendance at the altar.*

14. *For it is evident that our Lord sprang out of Judah; of which tribe Moses spake nothing concerning the priesthood.*

15. *And it is yet far more evident: for that after the similitude of Melchisedec there ariseth another priest.*

In these three verses it is proved that Christ's priesthood was not after the order of Aaron. The proofs are two.

The first proof is taken from the distinction of tribes. This is,

1. Propounded, ver. 13; 2, confirmed, ver. 14.

In the proposition there is,

1. A description of Christ by a reference to things before mentioned, thus, *he of whom these things are spoken.*

2. An expression of the argument, wherein we have,

1. The kind of proof, *he pertaineth to another tribe.*

2. The ground thereof. Here,

1. One thing is expressed, *of which no man gave attendance*, &c.

2. Another is implied, that they of the tribe of Levi gave attendance at the altar.

In the confirmation two points are to be observed:

1. The manner of bringing it in, *it is evident.*

2. The matter whereof it consisteth. Hereof are two parts:

1. An exemplification of the tribe whence Christ sprang. Here are distinctly noted:

1. The stock, *Judah*; 2, the branch, *our Lord*; 3, his manner of coming from thence, *he sprang.*

2. A manifestation of the reason why they of Judah attended not at the altar.

The reason is taken from Moses's silence thereabouts, he *spake nothing* about that matter.

The second proof is taken from distinction of orders.

Here note, 1. The manner of bringing in the proof. *It is yet far more evident.*

2. The matter of the proof; which is,

1. Generally expressed, *there ariseth another priest.*

2. Particularly exemplified, *after the similitude of Melchisedec.*

Doctrines.

I. *The excellencies spoken of Melchisedec belong to Christ.* The things before spoken were excellencies of Melchisedec. But here it is said concerning Christ, he of whom these things are spoken. See Sec. 72.

II. *Christ was of one of the tribes of Israel.* This is here taken for granted. See Sec. 72.

III. *None ought to intermeddle with others' function.* They who are of another tribe, might not meddle with the function that belonged to Levi. See Sec. 73.

IV. *Our own calling is to be attended upon.* This phrase, *gave attendance*, implies as much. See Sec. 73.

V. *Proofs must be clear.* This I gather from the apostle's premising this phrase, *it is evident.* See Sec. 74.

VI. *Christ is a Lord.* This very title is here given to him. See Sec. 74.

VII. *Christ is in special the Lord of the church.* This is implied under this relative, *our.* See Sec. 74.

VIII. *Christ was man of man.* As a branch he *sprang* out of a human stock. See Sec. 75.

IX. *Christ was of the tribe of Judah.* This is plainly expressed. See Sec. 75.

X. *What about God's worship is not revealed from God, ought not to be done thereabout.* Because Moses spake nothing of the tribe of Judah concerning the priesthood, therefore none of Judah was to meddle with those duties of God's worship. See Sec. 76.

XI. *Weighty points must be made more and more clear.* Thus much is intended under this phrase, *and it is here far more evident.* See Sec. 77.

XII. *Christ is another priest than Aaron was.* This relative, *another*, is spoken of Christ as distinguished from Aaron. See Sec. 78.

XIII. *Christ is like to Melchisedec.* He is here said to be after his *similitude*. See Sec. 78.

Sec. 80. *Of the meaning of these words, 'Who is made not after the law of a carnal commandment,'* Heb. vii. 16.

Ver. 16. *Who is made not after the law of a carnal commandment, but after the power of an endless life.*

The first proof of the imperfection of the Levitical priesthood was taken from the mutability thereof. See ver. 11, Sec. 61. A second proof is taken from the weakness of that priesthood, which was supplied by the powerful efficacy of Christ's priesthood. These two points are handled, vers. 16–19.

This relative phrase, ὃς γέγονε, *who is made*, hath reference to Jesus Christ, that other priest mentioned in the end of the former verse.

He is said to be made, in that he was appointed and deputed to his function. See Chap. v. 5, Sec. 14, in the end.

The more to commend Christ's priesthood, the apostle removeth from it such things as appertained to the Levitical priesthood, but were far before this other priesthood, therefore he saith negatively, *not after the law*, &c.

The noun νόμον, translated *law*, is derived from a verb, νέμω, *distribuo*, that signifieth *to give*, or *to distribute*, or *to govern*, for a law sheweth what is one's own, or what belongs to him. And by it men are governed.

The other noun, ἐντολη, translated *commandment*, cometh from a verb, ἐντέλλομαι, *mando*, that signifieth to *command*, John xv. 14, and it implieth a declaration of his will, who hath power and authority to command.

See a distinction betwixt *law* and *commandment*, ver. 5, Sec. 38.

Law is a more general and comprehensive word than commandment.

It is indefinitely used for all, or any, of those things which were by God given in charge to his people.

Commandment is here restrained to such ordinances as concerned the Levitical priesthood. It is metonymically put for the things commanded or enjoined thereabouts. Though those things were many, and delivered at sundry times, yet the singular number, *commandment*, is used to shew:

1. That they were in general all of one kind.
2. That they were all alike *carnal*.
3. That they all lived and died together.

This epithet, σαρκικὸς, *carnal*, is derived from a noun, σάρξ, *caro*, that signifieth *flesh*, 1 Pet. i. 24. It is therefore translated *fleshly*, 1 Pet. ii. 11.

In the New Testament it is applied three several ways.

1. By way of commendation. Thus it signifieth that which is soft and pliable, as 'fleshly tables of the heart,' 2 Cor. iii. 3. There is a little difference in the Greek word, σαρκίναις, translated *fleshly*, but it cometh from the same root the other doth.
2. By way of detestation, and that in four respects, as when it sets out,
(1.) Man's natural corruption, Rom. vii. 14.
(2.) A childish disposition, 1 Cor. iii. 3.
(3.) A politic and crafty intention, 2 Cor. i. 12.
(4.) A puffing humour, making men rest on weak means, 2 Cor. x. 4.
3. By way of diminution. Thus the goods of this world, in opposition to spiritual gifts and graces, are called *carnal*, Rom. xv. 27, 1 Cor. ix. 11.

Carnal things are much inferior to spiritual.

Thus this epithet *carnal* is here used. For as the goods of this world are not in themselves evil, but, compared with spiritual graces, very mean, small or no account to be put upon them, so the legal commandment about Aaron's priesthood was not evil in itself, but compared to the spiritual excellencies of Christ's priesthood, very mean, of no esteem, no way to come into competition with them.

Thus is the foresaid commandment called *carnal*, by way of diminution.

In the New Testament, *carnal* is oft opposed to *spiritual*, Rom. vii. 14, and xv. 27, and 1 Cor. iii. 1. If therefore we take a view of the transcendent excellency of that which is spiritual, we shall the better discern the diminution of this epithet *carnal*.

That which is spiritual is,
1. Internal, in the spirit and soul of man.
2. Divine, wrought by the Spirit of God.
3. Heavenly, coming from above.
4. Firm and stable, that cannot be removed.
5. Durable and perpetual, that never vanisheth.

In opposition hereunto things styled carnal are,
1. External, concerning the outward man.
2. Human, wrought by man.
3. Earthy, of things here below.
4. Alterable, which may be changed.
5. Momentary, which lasteth but for a time.

In all these respects was the foresaid commandment carnal.

Sec. 81. *Of the ceremonial law as a carnal commandment.*

The foresaid epithet given to the commandment whereby the Levitical priesthood was established, sheweth plainly, that the Jews' religion was but a carnal religion, consisting of outward, earthy, alterable, momentary matters, made with men's hands. The meanness thereof is further manifest by other epithets, as,

1. That it was *flesh*, Gal. iii. 3. *Flesh* implieth a greater diminution than *carnal*. It sheweth that it consisted of a putrefying matter.
2. The Jews then are said to be *in bondage under elements*, Gal. iv. 3. Those ordinances are styled *elements*, in that they were the horn-book (as we speak), or A B C, in comparison of the deep mysteries which are revealed and learned by the gospel. Under them men are said to be *in bondage*, in that they were as children, or schoolboys, kept under a mean and strait discipline.
3. Those elements are called *weak and beggarly* Gal. iv. 9, in that they had nothing in them that could make them thrive in grace, and be rich in God.
4. They are styled *shadows*, Col. ii. 17, which of themselves have no substance, but carry only a show and appearance of a body.

Take a view of the particulars comprised under the foresaid commandment, and you shall find it to be such a commandment as hath been set forth. Some of the particulars are these;—

The tabernacle, made of linen, stuffs, skins, and boards; the ark mercy-seat, cherubims, table and candlestick, made of gold; the incense and oil made of spices, and shew-bread made of flour, the altars and lavers made of brass; the high-priest's robes, and other priests' garments; were not these, and the other like to these, external, earthy, alterable? Their sacrifices, were they not of beasts and birds? See ver. 11, Sec. 61.

Obj. Excellent ends of the ceremonial law are set down, ver. 12, Sec. 68. How then can this commandment be carnal?

Ans. It may be considered two ways: 1, simply; 2, comparatively.

The simple consideration admits also a distinction. For,

1. The ceremonial law being instituted by God, as the outward part of his worship, and prescribing types of Christ the truth, may be accounted spiritual and divine; and thus it was had in high account amongst saints, till all things typified thereby were accomplished in Christ.

2. That law consisting of external matters specified before, those external things, separated from Christ, the divine and spiritual truth, was but carnal. In this respect the Lord saith, 'I will take no bullock out of thy house,' &c., Ps. l. 9; and to the Lord it is said, 'Sacrifice and offering thou didst not desire,' &c., Ps. xl. 6.

Comparatively, and that in opposition to the gospel, it was indeed a carnal commandment, especially as it was used for justification and salvation, through the observing of it, whether joined with Christ or excluding Christ.

Sec. 82. *Of men's carnal disposition in worshipping God.*

That which hath been said of the carnal commandment, discovereth the carnal disposition of sons of men. As most Jews, before and after Christ, doated upon the ceremonial law as it was carnal, so the Gentiles in all ages had a kind of worship, but merely carnal, in external, earthly ordinances. Yea, many Gentiles, converted by the gospel to the Christian faith, much doated upon carnal ordinances, Gal. iii. 1, &c. Cast your eyes throughout the world, and take notice of the worship of several nations, and you shall find it to be a carnal worship.

Papists exceed herein. Their religion is merely carnal. It consisteth in outward rites: as in erecting curious images and manifold altars, in arraying priests with glorious copes, in pompous processions, in melodious music, in abundance of tapers, in sprinkling water, in magical crossings, in numeral prayers, in mimical gestures, and a thousand others.

These are carnal in their kind and use.

1. In their kind. They are outward, and mere inventions of man.

2. In their use. They are all in an unknown tongue; yet their whole service consisteth herein. Fitly is that church resembled to a woman upon a scarlet-coloured beast, arrayed in purple, &c., Rev. xvii. 3. This is that glorious religion which is so much admired and followed in the world.

If the extent of this epithet *carnal* be duly weighed, many professors of the true reformed religion will be found to be of carnal dispositions, in that they content themselves with a carnal serving of God, and observing Christian ordinances carnally. For howsoever the ordinances that we use, as assembling together to worship God, prayers, thanksgiving, reading, expounding and preaching the word and hearing the same, administering and partaking of the sacraments, be ordinances warranted by the gospel, and so spiritual and excellent in their kind as never better to be expected while the world stands; yet as men content themselves with a mere outward performing of them they are made carnal, and prove to be but 'bodily exercises which profit little,' 1 Tim. iv. 8.

Sec. 83. *Of the meaning of these words, 'But after the power of an endless life.'*

This clause, *but after the power of an endless life*, is added in opposition to that which was said of the *carnal commandment*, as is evident by this conjunction of opposition, ἀλλά, *but*.

This last clause is spoken of Christ's priesthood; that is it which was 'after the power of an endless life.'

He calleth the word whereby Christ was made priest δύναμις, *power*, in that Christ's priesthood had a virtue, efficacy, and power, to effect, and that to the full, all the things for which it was ordained: as to cleanse from sin, to reconcile to God, to justify our persons, to sanctify us throughout, and eternally to save us.

These ends of Christ's priesthood are comprised under this word ζωῆς, *life*, so as that which the apostle saith of the gospel, Rom. i. 16, may be here fitly applied to Christ's priesthood, 'It is the power of God unto salvation;' it is a divine power; a power that can and will effect what it undertaketh.

The Greek epithet ἀκαταλύτου, translated *endless*, is a double compound. The simple verb, λυω, *solvo*, signifieth to *loose*, John i. 27. The first compound καταλύω, *destruo*, signifieth *to destroy*, Acts vi. 14. This double compound ἀκαταλύτου being with a privative preposition, ἀ, signifieth that which cannot be dissolved or destroyed, but ever remaineth the same; and in that respect is fitly translated *endless*.

This epithet is here used in distinction from or opposition to our body, which is thus described, 'our earthly house of this tabernacle,' whereof it is said that it may be 'dissolved,' 2 Cor. v. 1.

Here are three distinct points, wherein the excellency of Christ's priesthood is commended, and whereby a supply is made of those things which the Levitical priesthood could not do.

1. That it was a priesthood of power. In which respect it is said of this priest, 'He is able to save them to the uttermost that come unto God by him,' ver. 25. Thus may we safely and securely rest upon him.
2. Christ's priesthood brings to life. His power tends to this, even to save, ver. 25.
3. The life which Christ brings men unto is indissolvable. In this respect it is styled 'an inheritance incorruptible (ἄφθαρτον) and that fadeth not away (ἀμάραντον), 1 Peter i. 4, and a crown of glory that fadeth not away,' ἀμαράντινον 1 Peter v. 4. The latter epithet thus translated, *that fadeth not away*, is the name of a flower called *amarantus*, which is said to continue fresh and flourishing winter and summer. The word *amarantus*, according to the Greek notation, signifieth that which fadeth not.[1] A crown or garland made of such flowers was counted a not fading crown or garland.

The foresaid benefit and effect of Christ's priesthood is a strong motive to make us patiently endure the changes and alterations of this life. They are but for a time. After a little enduring, we shall come to a settled and immutable estate. 'Our light affliction, which is but for a moment, worketh for us a far more exceeding and eternal weight of glory,' 2 Cor. iv. 17.

This also is a great encouragement against death itself. Sooner or later 'our earthly house of this tabernacle shall be dissolved;' but then we have a building that cannot be dissolved, 2 Cor. v. 1.

Sec. 84. *Of the meaning of the 17th verse.*

Ver. 17. *For he testifieth, Thou art a priest for ever, after the order of Melchisedec.*

This verse is added as a proof of that everlasting power, virtue, and efficacy of Christ's priesthood, which is asserted in the latter part of the former verse.

To make the proof to be the more heeded, the apostle premiseth the ground of his proof, which is a divine testimony. He sets it down indefinitely thus, μαρτυρεῖ, *he testifieth*, meaning the Holy Ghost; for the testimony is expressly set down in sacred Scripture, concerning which the apostle useth this phrase, *the Holy Ghost saith*, chap. iii. 7.

The confirmation, being taken out of sacred Scripture, is demonstrated to be a very sound one, Chap. i. 5, Sec. 46.

Of the manner of quoting it, without naming author, book, chapter, and verse, and of the emphasis of this word *testifieth*, see Chap. ii. 6, Secs. 50, 51.

The apostle's argument, to prove the perpetual efficacy of Christ's priesthood, is taken from the kind of priesthood after which Christ was.

Herein two branches make much to the proof of the point:

One is the excellency of Christ's priesthood, which was *after the order of Melchisedec*, and thereupon consisted not of such carnal things as Aaron's priesthood did. See ver. 4, Sec. 31, and ver. 11, Sec. 66.

The other is the perpetuity of Christ's priesthood, expressed in this phrase *for ever*. By this means it hath a power to make us partakers of an endless life. See ver. 3, Sec. 26.

Of a further opening of this description of Christ's priesthood, see Chap. v. 6, Sec. 28, &c.

Sec. 85. *Of the meaning of the 18th verse.*

Ver. 18. *For there is verily a disannulling of the commandment going before, for the weakness and unprofitableness thereof.*

This verse is inferred as a consequence following upon the establishing of Christ's priesthood. This causal conjunction, γὰρ, *for*, doth sometimes point at a consequence, as ver. 12, Sec. 67.

The consequence is a disannulling of the former carnal commandment, for two opposite laws cannot stand together, Gal. v. 2–4.

To add the more force to this consequence, he inserteth this adverb of asseveration, μὲν, *verily*. See ver. 5, Sec. 37.

That which before, ver. 12, Sec. 67, was termed μετάθεσις, *a change*, is here styled ἀθέτησις, *a disannulling*. Disannulling implieth a plain abrogation and clean taking away of a thing.

How far the commandment here intended is disannulled, see ver. 12, Sec. 68.

This phrase, προαγούσης, *going before*, is the interpretation of one compound particle, and properly translated according to the true meaning thereof.

The commandment concerning the Levitical priesthood is here said to *go before* in reference to Christ's priesthood.

The Levitical priesthood was a type of Christ's; therefore the commandment concerning that must needs, even in time, go before this, for this succeeded that, to accomplish what that could not.

Weakness and unprofitableness imply two reasons of disannulling the foresaid commandment.

Of the derivation of the Greek word τὸ ἀσθενὲς, translated *weakness*, see Chap. iv. 15, Sec. 89. The word there used is a substantive, and this an adjective, but both from the same root; and this adjective, being of the neuter gender, is as a substantive.

---

[1] Ἀμάραντος, flos est qui non marcescit.—*Plin.* Ἀμαράντινοι στέφανοι, coronæ quæ fiunt ex amaranto. Amarantum coronis solebant adhibere.

Ut quum contexunt amarantis alba puellæ
Lillia.—*Tibull.* lib. iii. El. 4.

The weakness here spoken of consisted in this, that that law was utterly unable by itself, and by strict observance of the rites thereof, to do that which was needful to be done, namely, to make the observers perfect.

This word is translated *impotent*, and applied to him that was born a cripple, Acts iv. 9. It is also translated, according to the composition of it, *without strength*, and applied to a natural man's condition, Rom. v. 6. In this respect the ordinances of this law are called *weak elements*, Gal. iv. 9.

The other word ἀνωφελές, translated *unprofitable*, is also a compound, and an adjective used as a substantive.

The simple verb ὠφελέω, signifieth *to profit*, Rom. ii. 25; from thence an adjective ὠφέλιμος, signifying *profitable*, 1 Tim. iv. 8.

This compound with a privative preposition, ἀ, hath the force of a negative. So it is used, Titus iii. 9. It implieth that though a man be zealous of the law, and take much pains, and be at great cost thereabouts, yet he shall get nothing thereby, but lose all his pains and costs: all will be in vain. Therefore these two epithets are joined together, ἀνωφελεῖς καὶ μάταιοι, *unprofitable and vain*, Titus iii. 9. The apostle found this true by experience; for after he had set forth his zeal about the law, and declared how blameless he was, touching the righteousness which is in the law, he addeth, 'What things were gain to me, those I counted loss and dung,' Philip. iii. 6–8.

The negative is frequently used of such things as are here called unprofitable. Thus, 'meats which have not profited them which have been occupied therein,' Heb. xiii. 9; 'bodily exercise' (that is, external performances of duties of piety) 'profiteth little,' 1 Tim. iv. 8; 'the flesh profiteth nothing,' John vi. 63; that is, an external apprehension and observation of things spiritually meant.

These two epithets, *weakness* and *unprofitableness*, do much aggravate the folly of those who doat on carnal ordinances, which cannot be but weak and unprofitable; and when men have spent themselves thereupon, if they look ' on the labour that they have laboured to do, they will behold all to be vanity and vexation of spirit,' as the wise man complaineth of the works that he had wrought, Eccles. ii. 11.

These fools are set down in their ranks, Sec. 82.

Sec. 86. *Of the meaning of these words, 'for the law made nothing perfect.'*

Ver. 19. *For the law made nothing perfect, but the bringing in of a better hope did; by the which we draw nigh unto God.*

In this verse an evidence is given of the weakness and unprofitableness of the Levitical law, which is this, that οὐδὲν ἐτελείωσεν, *it made nothing perfect*. What is meant by perfection hath been shewed, ver. 11, Sec. 61. If we put the apostle's argument into a syllogistical form, the point intended by the apostle will appear to be most clear, thus:

That law which makes nothing perfect is weak and unprofitable;

But the law of the Levitical priesthood makes nothing perfect; therefore it is weak and unprofitable.

The force of the argument lieth in this, that it is the end of a law to make those to whom it belongeth perfect. Now that law which cannot effect that which is the main end thereof, must needs be weak and unprofitable.

To *make perfect*, so as is here intended, namely, to work and accomplish all those graces that may bring men to glory, is above the power of any external thing done by man. To work such perfection of grace as may bring to perfect glory is a divine work, and cannot be effected but by a divine power, even the power of God himself.

He here useth a word of the neuter gender, οὐδὲν, *nothing*, as being most fit to set forth an universality; but he intendeth thereby men's persons, as if he had said *no man*. Thus the neuter gender is used to set out persons, Job vi. 37–40. ' All (πᾶν) that the Father giveth me,' and ' every one (πᾶς) which seeth the Son.'

Upon that which hath been said of the weakness and unprofitableness of the law of the Levitical priesthood, and upon the foresaid ground hereof, the position of papists about sacraments conferring grace, *ex opere operato*, by the work done, appeareth to be false and heretical. The sacraments which the Jews had, are comprised under that law. In regard of the external work, What have the sacraments of the New Testament more than the sacraments of the Old? They are all institutions and ordinances of God, and external parts of his worship, and appointed in general to the same ends; namely, to keep men in obedience, to strengthen their faith, and testify their repentance. They all have the same spiritual object and thing signified. The Jews in their sacraments ' did eat the same spiritual meat, and drink the same spiritual drink,' 1 Cor. x. 3, 4. The difference was in the manner of setting out Christ, the thing signified. They were types of Christ to come, and set him out more obscurely; ours are memorials of Christ exhibited, and set him out more clearly. In that power which they give to sacraments, they make them plain idols, for they attribute to them that which is proper to God. To make perfect is to regenerate, justify, and sanctify men; but all these are the work of God, John i. 13; Isa. lii. 11; Rom. i. 4.

Sec. 87. *Of Christ's bringing in a better hope.*

To shew that though the law could not make perfect, yet God left not his church without all hope of being made perfect, the apostle declareth a means that can do it. This he bringeth in by the conjunction of opposition, δὲ, *but*; and that to amplify the power of this means, which could do that that the law could not.

The means is thus set down, *the bringing in of a better hope.*

The Greek word ἐπεισαγωγή, translated *bringing in,* is a double compound. The simple verb, ἄγω, *duco,* signifieth *to bring,* Mat. xxi. 2. The simple compound εἰσάγω, *induco, to bring in,* Luke xiv. 21. The double compound ἐπεισάγω, *superinduco, to superinduce,* or *to bring in upon another.* There is a double emphasis in this word, *bringing in.*

1. In that the abstract or substantive is used. He doth not say, 'it doth bring in a better hope,' or, 'is the bringer in thereof,' but, 'the bringing in,' which implieth that Christ's priesthood doth this, and that nothing but Christ's priesthood can do it.

This work is appropriated to this office.

2. In that a double compound word is used. The Grecians use this double compound for such things as are brought in from another place, over and above that which is at home, or in their own country; as wines, oranges, spices, and other such commodities, as are not in our own countries, but brought to us out of other countries.

This word then implieth that Christ is such a bringer of a better hope, as cometh from another order and kind of priesthood than Levi's.

Fitly is this word here used, to shew that the powerful means here spoken of is brought upon the disannulling of the former, to effect that which the former could not. This emphatical word is found only in this place of the New Testament.

That which is here said to be so brought in, is styled, κρείττων ἐλπίς, *a better hope.*

Hope is here metonymically put for the cause of that hope, which was the priesthood of Christ. This he styleth *hope* in a double respect.

1. In reference to the time wherein David made known the excellency of this priesthood. Then it was to come, and hoped for.

2. In reference to that perfection which is, and shall be, effected by Christ's priesthood. This is to us, while here we live, to come, and hoped for. For heaven, where all things are made perfect, is the hope of believers. See Chap. vi. 18, Sec. 148.

Of *hope,* see Chap. iii. 6, Sec. 62.

Under this phrase, *the bringing in of hope,* Christ's priesthood is comprised, for that is the ground of hope. The law proving bankrupt, man's hope was gone. As when a supposed able man, having undertaken to do some great work, as to erect a college or hospital, faileth in his estate, or ability to accomplish that work, men's hope of having it effected faileth. But Christ's priesthood being established in the room of the Levitical priesthood, another and surer ground of hope is given. Thus is Christ's priesthood ' the bringing in of a better hope.'

The foresaid hope is called *better* in two respects.

One in regard of the *matter,* or things hoped for. By the Levitical priesthood nothing could be hoped for but legal purifications, outward privileges, and earthly inheritances. Such blessings as are promised, Lev. xxvi. 4, &c., Deut. xxviii. 1, &c. But by Christ's priesthood all manner of spiritual graces here, and eternal glory hereafter, are hoped for.

The other in regard of the *manner* of revealing the spiritual and heavenly things hoped for, namely, more immediately, more perspicuously, more efficaciously than under the law.

It cannot be denied, but that all true saints, even under the law, had the hope of the spiritual and eternal things here intended. For 'Jesus Christ is the same yesterday, and to day, and for ever,' Heb. xiii. 8; and that both in regard of God's promise, which is as sure as the performance itself, and also in regard of the efficacy of all that Christ did and endured for man's redemption, which was as effectual to purge Adam's sins as it shall be to purge the sins of the last man that shall be purged.

Under the law Christ was the bringing in of a better hope, because the promise which was made of him, made them to hope for better things than the law could afford unto them.

Thus Abraham, and all the holy patriarchs, prophets, and saints under the law, 'looked for a city whose builder and maker is God;' they 'desired a better country, that is, an heavenly,' Heb. xi. 10–16. This better hope was grounded on Christ, who was promised unto them, and confirmed in the legal rites. But now under the gospel, Christ hath actually performed all things that were promised and foretold under the law; and by the revelation of Christ in the gospel, the whole counsel of God is most clearly and perspicuously opened. So as now 'we all with open face behold, as in a glass, the glory of the Lord,' 2 Cor. iii. 18. As the hope which we have by Christ's priesthood is better, so the covenant and testament ratified thereby, and promises depending thereon, and sacrifices appertaining thereto, all better, ver. 22, chap. viii. 6, and ix. 23; Hereupon Christ's blood is said to 'speak better things,' chap. xii. 24; and God is said to have 'provided some better things for us,' chap. xi. 40.

The principal point here intended is, that by Christ's priesthood is effected to the full, what could not be effected by the Levitical priesthood. Oft doth the apostle observe this point; for where he noteth a defect in that priesthood, he sheweth a supply in this, as here in this text, and vers. 16, 23, 24, 27, 28, and chap. ix. 9, &c. This was long observed before by David, Ps. xl. 6–8.

This gives a demonstration both of the excellency, and also of the necessity, of Christ's priesthood.

The excellency thereof appears in this, that it doth that which no other priesthood before it could do.

The necessity is this, that that which must needs be done to bring man to happiness, was done thereby to the full.

Sec. 88. *Of the privilege of Christ's priesthood, whereby we draw near to God.*

An effect and proof of the foresaid bringing in of a better hope, is added as an especial privilege of Christ's priesthood.

This relative, δἰ ἧς, *by the which*, may have reference to this word, ἐπεισαγωγὴ, *the bringing in*, or to the word, ἐλπίδος, *hope*. They are all of the same gender, number, and person.

The former reference sheweth that Christ's priesthood is the ground of our access to God.

The latter, that our hope, resting thereupon, puts us on to draw nigh to God.

Both references tend to the same end. For Christ's priesthood is the ground of our drawing nigh to God, because we hope thereon; and our hope makes us go to God, because it is fixed on Christ's priesthood. To say that we are justified in the blood of Christ, and to say we are justified by faith in the blood of Christ, intends one and the same thing.

This verb, ἐγγίζομεν, *to draw nigh*, is in Greek derived from an adverb, ἐγγὺς, *prope*, that signifieth *nigh*, or *near*, Mat. xxiv. 32, 33.

It is applied to times, Mat. xxi. 34; to things, Luke xxi. 20, 28; and to persons, Luke xxii. 47. It is opposed to *far off*, Mat. xv. 8. Hence this usual phrase, *far and near*, Esther ix. 20.

Among persons it is applied to God in reference to men, and to men in reference to God, James iv. 8. God draweth nigh to us by giving unto us evidences of his favour, especially when he heareth our prayers. We draw nigh to God by hearty prayer and praise, by attending upon his word, by partaking of his sacraments, by a due observation of his sacred ordinances, by holy meditation, and by all manner of pious devotion.

In our drawing nigh to God, and God's drawing nigh to us, consisteth our communion with God, which is an high privilege and a great prerogative, especially if we duly consider the infinite distance betwixt God and man; and that both in regard of God's surpassing majesty, and excellency, and our meanness and baseness; and also in regard of his infinite holiness, and our vile sinfulness.

This privilege we have by virtue of Christ's priesthood. Christ doth not only appear before God as our priest for us, but also 'maketh us priests unto God,' Rev. i. 6, that we ourselves may draw nigh to God. It was not so under the law. Only the high priest might go into the most holy place, and draw nigh to the mercy-seat; yet that not at all times, Lev. xvi. 2, but once a year, Heb. ix 7. As for the people, they stood without, Luke i. 10. It is Christ that, by his priesthood, hath procured this liberty for us to draw nigh to God.

Let us therefore go boldly to the throne of grace. See Chap. iv. 16, Secs. 62, 63.

Sec. 89. *Of the resolution of* Heb. vii. 16–19.

Ver. 16. *Who is made, not after the law of a carnal commandment, but after the power of an endless life.*

17. *For he testifieth, Thou art a priest for ever, after the order of Melchisedec.*

18. *For there is verily a disannulling of the commandment going before, for the weakness and unprofitableness thereof.*

19. *For the law made nothing perfect, but the bringing in of a better hope did; by the which we draw nigh unto God.*

In these four verses the pre-eminence of Christ's priesthood above the Levitical priesthood is proved.

Hereof are two parts:

1. The insufficiency of the Levitical priesthood.
2. The all-sufficiency of Christ's priesthood.

These two are so opposed, as wherein the insufficiency of the former is manifested, the sufficiency of the latter is demonstrated; and that to shew, that by this latter a supply is made of whatsoever is wanting in the former.

The insufficiency of the Levitical priesthood is proved by three arguments; and the all-sufficiency of Christ's by as many.

The first argument to prove the former point is taken from the law after which it was made. It was a *law of a carnal commandment*.

The latter point is proved,

1. Generally, by denying it to be after that law, *not after*, &c.
2. By affirming another law, which is styled *the power*. This is both illustrated and confirmed.

The illustration is taken from the end of it, *life*, and amplified by the continuance of it, *endless*.

The confirmation is from a divine testimony, ver. 17. This is, 1. Generally hinted thus, *for he testifieth*.

2. Particularly exemplified. *Thou art a priest*, &c. Hereof see Chap. v. 6, Sec. 31.

The second argument to prove the insufficiency of the Levitical priesthood is taken from the abrogation of it. This is,

1. Expressed thus, *There is verily a disannulling of the commandment*.
2. Confirmed by two epithets; which are,

(1.) Expressed in these words, *weakness* and *unprofitableness*.

(2.) Confirmed by failing in the main end thereof, which was to make perfect, *the law made nothing perfect*.

Another argument to prove the sufficiency of Christ's priesthood is taken from the ability thereof to do what the other priesthood could not.

This is,

1. Generally intimated in this particle of opposition, *but*.
2. Particularly expressed; and that two ways,

(1.) By a description of Christ's priesthood.

(2.) By a declaration of a privilege thereof.

Christ's priesthood is described,

1. By substituting it in the room of the other priesthood, implied under this word, *bringing in;* and amplified by the object thereof, *a better hope.*

The privilege is access to God, *by the which we draw near to God.*

Sec. 90. *Of observations raised out of* Heb. vii. 16–19.

I. *Christ was ordained a priest.* This is comprised under this phrase, *who is made.* See Sec. 80.

II. *Christ was not such a priest as the Levitical priests were.* This is the intent of this negative, *not after the law.* See Sec. 80.

III. *The Levitical priesthood had a law for it.* This is taken for granted in this phrase, *after the law.* See Sec. 80.

IV. *The ordinances about the Levitical priesthood were carnal.* The commandment, which is here said to be carnal, comprised those ordinances under it. See Sec. 81.

V. *Christ's priesthood was with power.* This phrase, *after the power,* being meant of Christ's priesthood, intendeth as much. See Sec. 83.

VI. *The end of Christ's priesthood was life;* even to bring men to life. It is therefore styled, *the power of life.* See Sec. 83.

VII. *The life which Christ brings is everlasting.* This epithet, *endless,* intends so much. See Sec. 83.

VIII. *A divine testimony is a sufficient proof.* See Sec. 84.

IX. *Christ is a priest after the most excellent order;* even *after the order of Melchisedec.* See Sec. 84.

[Of other doctrines arising out of this testimony. See Chap. v. 6, Sec. 32.]

X. *The law about the Levitical priesthood is abrogated.* This is here affirmed with a note of asseveration. *For there is verily,* &c: See Sec. 85.

XI. *The ceremonial law was weak.*

XII. *The ceremonial law was unprofitable.*

These two are expressly affirmed to be so. See Sec. 85.

XIII. *No perfection can be attained by the law.* This is expressly affirmed. See Sec. 86.

XIV. *Christ's priesthood succeeded in the room of the Levitical priesthood.* The emphasis of this word, *the bringing in,* imports thus much. See Sec. 87.

XV. *Christ's priesthood is the ground of hope.* Therefore it is said to be *the bringing in of hope.* See Sec. 87.

XVI. *Hope of Christians is better than the hope of the Jews was.* This comparative, *better,* intends as much. See. Sec. 87.

XVII. *We may draw nigh to God.* This is here taken for granted. See Sec. 88.

XVIII. *Christ's priesthood is the means of our drawing nigh to God.* This phrase, *by the which,* hath reference to Christ's priesthood. See Sec. 88.

Sec. 91. *Of the meaning of* ver. 21.

Ver. 20. *And inasmuch as not without an oath he was made priest:*

21. (*For those priests were made without an oath; but this with an oath, by him that said unto him,* The Lord sware, and will not repent, Thou art a priest for ever, after the order of Melchisedec:)

22. *By so much was Jesus made a surety of a better testament.*

A third argument to prove the excellency of Christ's priesthood above the Levitical, see Sec. 1, is taken from the different manner of instituting the one and the other. Christ's institution was more solemn than the Levites'. Theirs without an oath, Christ's with an oath.

The argument may be thus framed.

That priesthood which is established by an oath is more excellent than that which is without an oath;

But Christ's priesthood is with an oath, and theirs without, therefore, &c.

The proposition is implied by the inference of the 22d verse on the 20th, for the 21st verse is included in a parenthesis.

Both parts of the assumption are expressly set down in verse 21.

The copulative conjunction καὶ, *and,* joineth arguments, and sheweth that this is another argument to prove the point in hand.

This relative phrase, καθ' ὅσον, *inasmuch,* hath reference to the first clause of the 22d verse, which is a correlative; and both may be thus joined together, *inasmuch, by so much.* ' Inasmuch as not without an oath, by so much is Jesus,' &c.

These two negatives, οὐ, *not,* χωρὶς, *without,* intend a strong affirmation. See Chap. iv. 13, Sec. 76.

It is here taken for granted that Christ was most solemnly instituted a priest, even by an oath, the oath of God himself; which is the greatest and most solemn manner of institution that can be.

God's oath importeth two things.

1. An infallible certainty of that which he sweareth. See Chap. vi. 18, Sec. 140.

2. A solemn authority and dignity conferred upon that which he instituted by oath.

Great and weighty matters of much concernment use to be established by oath. Hereby it appeareth, that Christ's priesthood is a matter of great moment, and of much concernment. This will appear the more evident, if we consider the person who was priest, the ends why he undertook the function, and the benefits which accrue from thence.

1. The person was the greatest that could be, ver. 28, Chap. i. 3, therefore he is fitly called, 'a great High Priest,' Chap. iv. 14.

2. The ends of Christ's priesthood were very weighty, and that in reference to God and man.

To God, for manifestation of his perfect justice, infinite mercy, almighty power, unsearchable wisdom, and other divine attributes, which never were, nor ever can be so manifested, as in and by Christ's priesthood.

To man, that God's wrath might be averted, his favour procured, man's sin purged, he freed from all evil, and brought to eternal happiness.

3. The benefits of Christ's priesthood are answerable to the foresaid ends. For what Christ aimed at, he effected to the full; and all for man's good.

1. That little which hath been noted, and that much more which might be observed about Christ's priesthood, much aggravateth all those errors, which are about that function of Christ. Such are most of the controversies betwixt us and papists. God speaks to his Son as God and man; yet papists say, that Christ is a priest only in his human nature. God saith to his Son in the singular number, speaking to him alone, 'Thou art a priest,' yet they make many priests. God made him a priest after the order of Melchisedec, who was without father and mother, &c.; yet they make ordinary sons of men to be after that order. God makes his son a priest for ever; yet they substitute others in his room. God gave him to offer up but one sacrifice, and that but once; they every day offer up many sacrifices in their mass. God gave him to offer up himself; but they offer up bread and wine upon pretence that it is the body and blood of Christ. Christ's sacrifice was a bloody sacrifice; they style theirs an unbloody sacrifice.

2. The weightiness of Christ's priesthood should stir us up the more to search into that mystery, that we may be the better acquainted therewith, and receive the greater benefit thereby.

These last words, *he was made priest*, are not in the original; yet fitly added by our translators, to make up the sense, which is better understood in the Greek than in our English.

Sec. 92. *Of the meaning of* ver. 21.

The apostle, before he concludes the main point, setteth down, within a parenthesis, a proof of the argument; and that it may appear, that his main drift is to advance Christ his priesthood above the Levitical, he premiseth this, that 'those priests were made without an oath,' οἱ μὲν χωρὶς ὀρκωμοσίας, so as they were not instituted after so solemn a manner as Christ was.

Obj. He bringeth no proof for it.

Ans. By alleging an express testimony for the affirmative, concerning the manner of instituting Christ's priesthood, he implieth that there was no such matter concerning the Levitical priesthood; and thereupon he might well conclude that they were ordained without an oath. If we thoroughly search all those scriptures where mention is made of instituting priests, we shall find no hint of any oath.

The first institution of those priests is set down, Exod. xxviii. 1, &c. The manner of consecrating them, Exod. xxix. 1, &c. The confirmation of the high priest's office to Phinehas, and his seed for ever, Num. xxv. 13. Yet in none of those places is any mention of an oath.

Obj. This is but a negative argument.

Ans. In such things as the Holy Ghost hath set down every particular that is requisite to be known, a negative argument holdeth good. See Chap. i. 5, Sec. 46.

That which was taken for granted in the 20th verse, is here expressed, in these words, ὁ δὲ μετὰ ὀρκωμοσίας, *but this with an oath*; and it is confirmed in the words following.

The confirmation is taken from a divine testimony. This testimony is,

1. In general hinted, thus, διὰ τοῦ λέγοντος, *by him that said to him*.

2. Particularly expressed, in the words following.

In the general, this relative *him* is twice used.

The first in this phrase, διὰ τοῦ, *by him*, hath reference to God the Father. The other in this phrase, πρὸς αὐτόν, *to him*, to God the Son. 'The Lord said to my Lord,' saith David, Ps. cx. 1. See Chap. v. 6, Sec. 28.

The particular testimony is in these words, *The Lord sware*, &c.

Of God's swearing, see Chap. vi. 13, Sec. 97.

How God doth add dignity and authority to that which by oath he instituteth, see ver. 20, Sec. 91.

It is further said of God, οὐ μεταμεληθήσεται, *he will not repent*. To repent, in Greek and Latin, doth signify, to change one's mind and counsel. That God doth not, that God will not repent, see Chap. vi. 18, Secs. 133, 136.

God is here said not to repent, to confirm the everlastingness of Christ's priesthood.

He addeth this clause, εἰς τὸν αἰῶνα, *for ever*, because God will never repent his establishing his Son to be a priest.

The gifts which God will continue in his saints are styled, 'gifts without repentance,' ἀμεταμέλητα, Rom. xi. 29. Repentance itself, which is true and sound, is styled 'repentance not to be repented of,' μετάνοιαν ἀμεταμέλητον, 2 Cor. vii. 10. This clause, therefore, *and will not repent*, being added to God's swearing, giveth proof that God's oath is immutable and inviolable. See Chap. vi. 18, Sec. 140.

Of this testimony, 'thou art a priest for ever after the order of Melchisedec,' see Chap. v. 6, Secs. 28–30.

Sec. 93. *Of Christ as surety.*

Ver. 22. *By so much was Jesus made surety of a better Testament.*

In this verse the main point is concluded, namely, that Christ's priesthood is more excellent than the Levitical. It is laid down comparatively, thus, κατὰ τοσοῦτον, *by so much was Jesus*, &c. This phrase, *by so much*, hath reference to the 20th verse, and sheweth that *by how much* that which is established with an oath is better than that which is established without an oath, *so much* more excellent is Christ's priesthood than the Levitical.

Because that which followeth concerning Christ's suretyship tendeth much to our salvation, the apostle useth this title, *Jesus*, which signifieth a *saviour*. Hereof see Chap. ii. 9, Sec. 73.

Whom he hath hitherto styled *priest*, he here calleth *surety*; for a priest is for men in things pertaining to God; he stands betwixt a creditor and debtor, which is the part of a surety.

The Greek word ἔγγυος, translated *surety*, is but this once used in the New Testament; but in other Greek authors it is frequently used for one that undertaketh for another. The root out of which this word sprouteth, in general signifieth a part of man's body, and in particular, the hand (τὸ γυῖον, *membrum, manus*). For sureties were wont to strike hands with the party to whom they bound themselves. Hereunto the wise man alludeth, where he saith, 'If thou be surety for thy friend, if thou hast stricken thy hand,' Prov. vi. 1.

Others take the notation from a noun, γύη, *sive* γῆ, *terra*, that signifieth earth, which is firm and fast fixed; for a surety is fast bound and tied. Hereupon saith a wise man to a surety, 'Thou art snared, thou art taken,' Prov. vi. 2.

This office, a surety, being applied to Christ, sheweth that he hath so far engaged himself for us, as he neither can nor will start from his engagement; earth may sooner be removed than he not perform his engagement. He hath undertaken for all that can be required of us, or desired by us. There is another word, μεσίτης, applied to Christ, and translated *mediator*, chap. viii. 6, which in general intendeth as much. But this word is the more emphatical.

As *mediator*, Christ standeth betwixt God and man, to make intercession to God for man, and to declare God's will to man.

As *surety*, he engageth himself for man to God, and for God to man.

For man to God, Jesus undertaketh for what can be required of man.

For God to man, he undertaketh for what can be desired of God.

We ought therefore in this respect duly to consider both what may be required of man, and what may be desired by man.

Two things are required of man.

1. A perfect fulfilling of all righteousness according to the tenor of the law.
2. Full satisfaction for every transgression.

1. That Christ might fulfil all righteousness, he was 'made under the law,' Gal. iv. 4, by a voluntary subjection of himself thereunto; and being under the law he fulfilled all righteousness, Mat. iii. 15. That this he did for us, is evident by this phrase, 'By the obedience of one shall many be made righteous,' Rom. v. 19; and by this, 'we are made the righteousness of God in him,' 2 Cor. v. 21.

2. That Jesus might make full satisfaction for all our sins, 'he was made a curse for us, whereby he hath redeemed us from the curse of the law,' Gal. iii. 13. All his sufferings were for us.

All that can be desired of God by man, is mercy and truth. Mercy in regard of our misery, truth in reference to God's promises.

That which moved Christ to engage himself as a surety for us was his respect to God and man.

To God, for the honour of his name. Nor the mercy, nor the truth, nor the justice of God had been so conspicuously manifested if Jesus had not been our surety.

2. To man, and that to help us in our succourless and desperate estate. No creature would, or if any would, could it discharge that debt wherein man stood obliged to the justice of God.

1. This is an evidence of the endless love of Christ. We count it a great evidence of love for a friend to be surety for us, when we intend no damage to him thereupon. If a friend be surety for that which he knoweth the principal debtor is not able to pay, and thereupon proposeth to pay it himself, this is an extraordinary evidence of love. What is it then if he engage his person and life for his friend? 'Skin for skin, yea, all that a man hath will he give for his life,' Job ii. 4. If a friend, to free a captive, or one condemned to death, do put himself into the state and condition of him whom he freeth, that would be an evidence of love beyond all comparison. But if the dignity of Christ's person and our unworthiness, if the greatness of the debt and kind of payment, and if the benefit which we reap thereby, be duly weighed, we shall find these evidences of love to come as much behind the love of Christ as the light of a candle cometh short of the light of the sun.

2. Christ's suretyship is a prop to our faith. It is as sure a ground of confidence as can be. By virtue hereof, we have a right to appeal to God's justice; for this surety hath made full satisfaction, and to exact a debt which is fully satisfied, is a point of injustice.

Quest. Why then do saints appeal from the throne of justice to the seat of mercy?

Ans. In regard of themselves, and their manifold pollutions and imperfections. In this respect they cannot abide the trial of God's justice. But in confidence of that full satisfaction which Christ hath made, they dare and do appeal to God's justice. This is an especial means to settle troubled consciences. A debtor that hath a surety that is able and willing to pay his debt, yea, who hath fully paid it, fears not his creditor.

Sec. 94. *Of the better covenant or testament.*

The subject whereabout Christ's suretyship is exercised, is here styled διαθήκης, *testament*. Indeed the Greek word so translated is oft put for a testament, as Mat. xxvi. 28; Gal. iii. 15; Heb. ix. 16, 17.

The derivation of the word doth also imply as much; for it is derived from a verb, διατίθεμαι, *testor, testamento statuo*, that signifieth among other acceptions, to *dispose of a thing by will*. But that Greek verb doth also signify to make a covenant,[1] and from that signification, the Greek noun here used may be translated *a covenant*; and so it is most usually taken in the New Testament, Luke i. 72; Acts iii. 25, vii. 8; Rom. xi. 27; Heb. viii. 6.

There is another Greek word, συνθήκη, *pactum, fœdus*, which, by other authors, is used for a covenant, but not in the New Testament.

The Hebrew word, ברית, *fœdus* (a ברה *elegit.*, 1 Sam. xvii. 8),[2] doth properly signify a covenant, as is evident by the notation thereof. The LXX (whose phrase and style the penmen of the New Testament do much follow), do translate that Hebrew word which properly signifieth a covenant, with the Greek word that is here used in this text.

In this place the word *covenant* seems to be the more proper; for the office of a surety hath a more fit relation to a covenant than to a testament. Yet I will not deny, but that which is *a covenant* in matter, and in the manner of making it, may in regard of the confirmation thereof by death, be *a testament*. Thus that which in the Old Testament was a *covenant*, by the death of Christ, may in the New Testament be styled a *testament*.

Quest. Wherein lieth the difference betwixt a covenant and a testament?

Ans. 1. A covenant is an agreement between two, at least. A testament is the declaration of the will of one.

2. The two, or more, between whom a covenant passeth, must be all living. A testament receiveth force by the death of him that made it.

3. A covenant is ratified by the mutual consent of all that make it, on every side. A testament is ratified by the will only of him that made it.

4. A covenant useth to be made on conditions on both sides. A testament is made upon the mere favour and grace of the testator.

---

[1] Διατίθεσθαι διαθήκην, pacisci fœdus, Acts iii. 25.

[2] In fœderibus sanciendis solent esse selectæ personæ, conditiones, aliæque circumstantiæ. ברה *edit*, 2 Sam. xiii. 6, 10. In fœderibus paciscendis solebant epulari, Gen. xxvi. 30, et xxxi. 46, ברית transposita litera a בתר *divisit*. Nam fœdera olim fiebant dividendis sacrificiis, Gen. xv. 10; Jer. xxxiv. 18, 19. Livius Hist., Dec. 1, lib. 1, de more feriendi fœderis. 'Si populus Rom. defexit dolo malo, tu Jupiter sic ferito, ut ego hunc porcum feriam. Id ubi dixit, sacerdos, porcum saxo silice percussit.' ברית sæpe jungitur cum ברת percussit. Nam fœdere ineundo solebant complodere manus; seu jungere dextras, Job xvii. 3. ברה ברית et sæpe junguntur, Exod. xxxiv. 10, 12, 15, 27, et ברית intelligetur cum ברה exprimitur, 1 Sam. xx. 16, 1 Kings viii. 9.

The covenant or testament here mentioned is called better, in reference to the covenant that was made under the Levitical priesthood; not in the matter, but rather in the form and manner of delivering it; not in the substance, but rather in certain accidents or circumstances; which are these:

1. A more clear manifestation thereof by the gospel, Eph. iii. 5.

2. A most sure ratification of it by the death of Christ, Heb. ix. 15.

3. A more mighty operation by the work of God's Holy Spirit, accompanying the ministry of the gospel, 2 Cor. iii. 6.

Sec. 95. *Of the resolution and observations of* Heb. vii. 20–22.

Ver. 20. *And inasmuch as not without an oath he was made priest:*

21. (*For those priests were made without an oath; but this with an oath by him that said unto him, The Lord sware, and will not repent, Thou art a priest for ever, after the order of Melchisedec.*)

22. *By so much was Jesus made a surety of a better testament.*

These three verses contain a proof the solemnity of Christ's priesthood above the Levitical priesthood.

Hereof are two parts: 1, the kind of solemnity; 2, the kind of proof.

The solemnity is set down two ways: 1, simply; 2, comparatively.

The simple consideration sheweth how Christ was instituted.

Therein observe, 1, the substance; 2, the consequence, ver. 22.

In the substance is noted, 1, the manner of expressing the point.

2. The matter whereof it consisteth.

The manner is set out, 1, by a relative expression, thus, *in as much, by so much*.

2. By a double negative, *not without*.

The comparative consideration manifesteth a difference betwixt the institution of the Levitical priesthood and Christ's, that *without*, this *with* an oath.

The proof is by a divine testimony, which is,

1. Intimated, in this phrase, *by him that said unto him.*

2. Expressed. In the expression there is,

1. The kind of proof; 2, the thing proved.

The kind of proof is, 1, propounded in this phrase, *the Lord sware.*

2. Amplified by the inviolableness thereof, thus, *and will not repent.*

The thing proved is the excellency of Christ's priesthood. Herein,

1. The person deputed, *thou art*.

2. The function whereunto he is deputed. This is,

1. Propounded, in this word *priest*.

2. Illustrated, and that two ways:

(1.) By the kind of priesthood, *after the order of Melchisedec.*
(2.) By the continuance thereof, *for ever.*
The consequence is, 1, hinted in this phrase, *by so much was.*
2. Expresed herein, (1.) the person, *Jesus*; (2.) the office.
The office is set out, 1, by the kind of it, *surety.*
2. By the subject whereabout it is exercised.
The subject is, 1, simply propounded in this word *testament.*
2. Comparatively amplified in this word *better.*

Doctrines.

I. *Christ was solemnly ordained a priest.* This is implied in this relative connection, *inasmuch as.* See Sec. 91.

II. *The solemnity whereby Christ was instituted a priest was an oath.* This is also plainly expressed. See Sec. 91.

III. *The Levitical priesthood was instituted a priest without an oath.* This is also plainly expressed. See Sec. 92.

IV. *The Levitical priesthood was not with such solemnity ordained as Christ's.* That without an oath, this with an oath.

V. *A divine testimony is a sound proof.* Such a proof is here produced. See Sec. 92.

VI. *God in weighty matters sweareth.* A particular instance is here given. See Sec. 92.

VII. *God repenteth not of that which he sweareth.* So much is here expressed. See Sec. 92.

[Of other doctrines concerning this testimony, see Chap. v. 6, Sec. 32.]

VIII. *Christ is a Saviour.* He is *Jesus.* See Sec. 93.

IX. *Our Saviour is our surety.* For Jesus is a surety. See Sec. 93.

X. *Jesus is a surety of the covenant betwixt God and man.* This is the testament here mentioned. See Sec. 94.

XI. *The covenant made with Christians is better than that which was made with the Jews.* The comparison in this word *better* is betwixt Christians and Jews. See Sec. 94.

Sec. 96. *Of the meaning of the 23d verse.* Heb. vii. 23, 24.

Ver. 23. *And they truly were many priests, because they were not suffered to continue by reason of death.*

24. *But this man, because he continueth ever, hath an unchangeable priesthood.*

In these two verses there is a fourth argument to prove the excellency of Christ's priesthood above the Levitical. See Sec. 1.

The argument is taken from the different condition of the one and other persons. Christ ever endureth. They did not so.

The argument may be thus framed :

He that ever remaineth, to execute his office himself, is more excellent than they who are forced by death to leave their office to others;

But Christ ever remaineth, &c. And the Levites were forced by death to leave their office to others; therefore Christ was more excellent.

The copulative particle καί, *and*, whereby these verses are knit to the former, sheweth that these verses contain in general the same matter that the former did.

Of the adverb μὲν, translated *truly*, see ver. 5, Sec. 37.

This numeral adjective πλείονες, *many*, may imply many priests *together;* because one was not able to perform all the offices appertaining to the priesthood. Or it may be taken of many *successively*, one after another, because one could not ever remain in that office; but as one died, another must come in his room.

Both these were points of infirmity, and in both Christ excelled the Levitical priests; for he alone did all that his priesthood required. No creature afforded any assistance or help unto him. And he ever liveth, so as he needeth no successor. The circumstances of the text do plainly demonstrate, that the latter is here especially intended; for the apostle himself rendereth this reason why ' they were many priests, because they were not suffered to continue,' &c.

This phrase *they were not suffered*, is the interpretation of one Greek word κωλύεσθαι, which signifieth to *hinder*, Luke xi. 52; or *forbid*, Mark ix. 38. So here they are forbidden by death, or hindered; death, as an injurious lord, forbids men always to abide here, and hinders them in their work.

The verb παραμένειν, translated *to continue*, is a compound. The simple verb signifieth to remain. This compound hath an emphasis, which the Latin expresseth with a like composition, *permaneo;* but our English, with these words, *abide*, 1 Cor. xvi. 16; *continue*, James i. 25. Death suffers them not to abide or continue on earth for ever, no nor very long. See Sec. 97.

Sec. 97. *Of priests subject to death.*

By the foresaid explanation of the verse, it is evident that priests under the law were subject to death. There needs no proof of the point. Experience hath confirmed the truth thereof. For where now are any of them ? Are they not all dead ?

1. They were sons of Adam, and therefore subject to that doom which was denounced against him, Gen. iii. 19.

2. Sin was in them. They brought it into the world, and retained it while they lived in the world, Rom. v. 12, 1 Kings viii. 46.

Of applying this to ministers, see ver. 8, Sec. 51.

Priests under the law had a great privilege, yet it exempted them not from death, neither doth any outward privilege: 'Do the prophets live for ever?' Zech. i. 5. Where are the patriarchs? Where kings, where other great ones? It is appointed unto men,' none excepted, 'once to die,' Heb. ix. 27.

Should outward privileges exempt men from death, they would puff them up too much. Hezekiah having assurance of fifteen years' continuance on earth, rendered not again, according to the benefit done unto him, for his heart was lifted up, 2 Kings xx. 6, 2 Chron. xxxii. 25.

This may be a good warning to such as are advanced above others, whether kings, nobles, rich, magistrates, masters, or others.

Though those priests were as other men, subject to death, besides other infirmities, yet that was no impediment to that function whereunto God had called them, so long as God was pleased to preserve them on earth. Though they were taken from among men, and so as other men, yet they were for men in things pertaining to God, Heb. v. 1. The like may be said of prophets, ministers, magistrates, and other sorts.

God who appointeth them their place, giveth them power to do their work. When God made Saul king, he gave him 'another heart,' 1 Sam. v. 9. When, by God's appointment, there were seventy elders chosen to assist Moses, the Lord gave 'the spirit of Moses' unto them, Num. xi. 25. God maketh 'able ministers of the New Testament,' 2 Cor. iii. 6.

This is a great encouragement to those who are deputed according to God's word to any function.

It also warneth others more to consider the special function of men than their common condition.

That which is here noted of the power of death, that it 'suffers not men to continue,' shews that there is no hope of ever abiding here. He that well knew this said, 'Here have we no continuing city,' Heb. xiii. 14.

This is for the comfort of believers, but for terror to the impenitent.

Believers have a better place provided for them, where they shall ever be.

Impenitents shall have another place, where they shall receive the just desert of their sins, even easeless and endless torments.

This clause, they were *many priests*, is a consequence following upon the foresaid mortality of priests, and sheweth that among men it is needful that a succession of ministers be nourished for continuing God's service. To this end governors of families succeeded one another, as Isaac succeeded Abraham. Afterwards sons of priests succeeded one another, as Eleazer succeeded Aaron. There were after that schools and colleges of prophets to train up the younger to succeed the elder, as they should be taken away, 1 Sam. xix. 20, 2 Kings ii. 3, 5, and vi. 2, and xxii. 14. These were as nurseries. Commendable in this respect is their care, who have erected schools and colleges, which ought to be continued and prayed for.

Sec. 98. *Of Christ's enduring ever.*

It was a deficiency and imperfection which was before noted of the mortality of the legal priests, therefore the apostle setteth out Christ in a contrary condition, as appears by this conjunction of opposition δὲ, *but*, which is frequently so used in the Proverbs.

The Greek particle ὁ, here translated *this man*, is not the same that was so translated ver. 4, Sec. 31. It is here a single article, which signifieth *he*.

The continuance of Christ, here intended and expressed under this word μένει, *endureth*, is not to be taken as that continuance which was denied to the priests in the former verse, namely, here on earth; for Christ did not here ever endure; but of a continuance where he may exercise his priestly function, and that is in heaven.

The other priests' functions was to be exercised on earth.

Of the phrase εἰς τὸν αἰῶνα, translated *ever*, see Chap. v. 6, Sec. 29. That which is here said of Christ *enduring ever*, is applied to him, as he was man, and mediator betwixt God and man, and priest for men in things appertaining to God. Thus is 'Jesus Christ the same yesterday, and to-day, and for ever,' Heb. xiii. 8.

'The son abideth for ever,' John viii. 35. So clear was this point that the adversaries of Christ could say, 'We have heard out of the law that Christ abideth for ever,' John xii. 34.

His human nature being united hypostatically to the divine nature, it was not possible that he should be holden of death, Acts ii. 24.

Obj. Christ did die, Mat. xxvii. 50.

Ans. 1. It was no forced death, but that whereunto he voluntarily subjected himself, John x. 18; for, when it pleased him, he took up his life again, John ii. 19, Rom. i. 4.

2. He continued under the power of death but three days.

3. Christ's death was a part of the execution of his priestly function, so as it caused no intermission of his office.

4. Christ being raised from the dead, dieth no more: 'Death hath no more dominion over him,' Rom. vi. 9. This is he that saith of himself, 'I am he that liveth, and was dead'; and behold I am alive for evermore,' Rev. i. 18. This is the enduring ever, whereof the apostle here speaketh.

1. Great ground of confidence hence ariseth. It was the ground of Job's confidence, that his Redeemer lived, Job xix. 25. By reason of the mystical and spiritual union that is betwixt Christ and his believers, they may rest upon it, that so long as the head liveth, the members shall not be utterly destroyed. 'Because I live, ye shall live also,' saith Christ, John xiv. 19; 'God hath given unto us eternal life, and this life is in his Son,' 1 John v. 11; 'Your life is hid with Christ in God,' Col. iii. 3.

2. The apostle layeth down this as a special point, wherein we should be like unto Christ, Rom. vi. 11. For this end we must labour to feel the life of Christ in us, Gal. ii. 20. And we must nourish the spirit of Christ in us, Rom. viii. 11.

3. This is a forcible motive to draw us to Christ, and to make us hold close unto him, and never depart from him. Christ being the living God, is to be trusted in, 1 Tim. iv. 10, and vi. 17. Peter and the rest of the disciples would not depart from Christ, because he had 'the words of eternal life,' and was 'the Son of the living God,' John vi. 68, 69. We cannot go from him, but to death and damnation.

4. On this ground we need not fear man, for 'his breath is in his nostrils,' Isa. ii. 22. Hezekiah was encouraged against the railings of a potent enemy, because he reproached the living God, Isa. xxxvii. 17.

Sec. 99. *Of the unchangeableness of Christ's priesthood.*

An especial consequence that followeth upon Christ's abiding ever is thus expressed, *he hath an unchangeable priesthood.*

Of the Greek word ἱερωσύνη, translated *priesthood*, see ver. 11, Sec. 61.

The adjective ἀπαράβατον, translated *unchangeable*, is here only used in the New Testament. It is a double compound. The simple verb, βαινω, *vado*, whence it is derived, signifieth *to go*. The first compound, παραβαίνω, *transgredior, to go* or *pass over*. This compound is in the New Testament used metaphorically to *transgress* a law, Mat. xv. 2, 3, 2 John 9. This double compound is with a privative preposition, ἀ. It signifieth that which cannot pass away and perish, in which respect some translate it *everlasting*; our last English translators, *unchangeable*. It signifieth also that which *cannot pass from one to another*. This our last English translators have noted in the margin thus, 'which passeth not from one to another.' This I take to be here especially intended. Though both be true, yet the latter is most proper and pertinent. It giveth proof that the priesthood of Christ is inseparably annexed to his own person. It cannot pass from him, nor be transferred upon another. As the meaning of the word, so the force of the apostle's argument declares as much. For herein lieth a main difference betwixt the Levitical priesthood and Christ's, that that passeth from party to party, but this not so. The type doth excellently clear this; for Melchisedec had no predecessor, no successor. Hence it is that Christ's sacrifice was but one, and but once offered up, ver. 27.

1. There is no need that Christ's priesthood should pass from himself, because he is sufficient of himself to do all things required thereby.

Three things make Christ sufficient priest of himself:
(1.) His almighty power.
(2.) The perpetual vigour of his sacrifice, Heb. ix. 28.
(3.) His continual abode at God's right hand, Heb. x. 12.

2. There is none able to go on in it if he should pass it over, and that in three respects:
(1.) The impotency of creatures in so great a work.
(2.) Their unworthiness to have any hand in such a work.
(3.) Their mortality.

This is an unanswerable argument against popish priests, who, they say, succeed Christ. In this and the former verse, there are four arguments against that heretical position.

1. The difference betwixt Christ, who is only one, able to do all of himself, and them, who are many.
2. Their mortality.
3. Christ's eternity.
4. The inseparableness of Christ's priesthood from himself.

This one heresy is enough to make us separate from the Church of Rome, and have no communion with her.

Learn we, as to stick close to Christ our only priest, so to rest us wholly and only upon his priesthood, which passeth not away from him.

Sec. 100. *Of the resolution and observations of Heb.* vii. 23, 24.

Ver. 23. *And they truly were many priests, because they were not suffered to continue by reason of death.*

24. *But this man, because he endureth ever, hath an unchangeable priesthood.*

The sum of these two verses is a difference between Christ and the Levitical priests. The difference is especially about the continuance of the one and of the other.

There are two parts:
1. The mutability of the Levitical priesthood, ver. 23.
2. The stability of Christ's priesthood, ver. 24.

There is to be considered in both, 1, the substance; 2, a consequence.

In the substance of the former is set down,
1. The point itself, *they continued not.*
2. The reason thereof, *by reason of death.*
The consequence thereof is implied in this word *many*.

In the substance of the latter is set down,
1. The point itself, *he endureth.*
2. The extent thereof, *for ever.*

The consequence hereof is, that he *hath an unchangeable priesthood.*

Doctrines.

I. *The Levitical priesthood did not always continue.* This is expressed. See Sec. 97.

II. *Death is an imperious lord.* This phrase, *suffered not*, implieth as much. See Sec. 96.

III. *Death hinders a perpetual abode on earth.* It suffers not to continue. See Sec. 97.

IV. *God's service on earth is continued by succession.* This is intended under the noun of multitude, *many.* See Sec. 97.

V. *Christ still exerciseth his priesthood.* In this respect he is said to endure. See Sec. 98.

VI. *There is no end of Christ's priesthood.* As priest he endureth ever. See Sec. 98.

VII. *Christ's priesthood cannot be passed over to another.* Thus it is *unchangeable.* See Sec. 99.

Sec. 101. *Of the meaning of these words, 'Wherefore he is able also to save.'*

Ver. 25. *Wherefore he is able also to save them to the uttermost that come unto God by him, seeing he ever liveth to make intercession for them.*

In this verse an inference is made upon Christ's everlasting priesthood. This is evident by the first illative conjunction ὅθεν, *wherefore.* Hereof see Chap. ii. 17, Sec. 166.

The reference may in general be extended to all that hath been before said of the excellency of Christ's priesthood. Because he is the Son of God, and entered into heaven, made a great high priest for ever after the order of Melchisedec, arising and remaining after Levi, making all things perfect, being instituted by the solemn and sacred oath of God, and endureth ever, he is able to save, &c.

But in that the apostle in the latter part of this verse expressly mentioneth his ever living to make intercession, a more particular and special reference is here intended, namely, to the verse immediately going before; thus, Christ ever endureth and hath an unchangeable priesthood, therefore he is able to save, &c.

This copulative particle, translated *also,* implieth that Christ ever endureth not only for his own honour, but *also* for our good.

The verb δύναται, translated *able,* doth most properly imply power and ability to do a thing; but withal it compriseth under it a fitness and readiness to do a thing. See Chap. ii. 18, Sec. 183.

Here it may intend both, especially in relation to the foresaid general inference.

Of the various acception of this word, σώζειν, *save,* see Chap. v. 7, Sec. 42. Here it is taken in the largest extent, for preservation from all misery, and for settling in all happiness. This salvation is the end and benefit of Christ's priesthood. He was priest, and he continueth priest, to save man. Of the salvation whereunto we are brought by Christ, see Chap. v. 9, Sec. 50.

The copulative particle καὶ, commonly translated *and,* in this place hath an especial emphasis, and is not unfitly translated *also.* It pointeth at one main end of Christ's being such a priest as he was, even to save, &c.

Sec. 102. *Of Christ's power to save.*

This word *able* is here inserted by the apostle to shew that Christ can and will accomplish that salvation which he aimed at. There is in this respect a title, σωτὴρ, given unto him, and translated, *saviour,* which is proper to such a Saviour as is here spoken of. The heathen did appropriate that title both to their chief god,[1] and also to other gods[2] that had preserved them. The Roman orator did upbraid it to Verres,[3] that he applied that title to himself, and caused it to be set over a city gate. Most truly and properly is it attributed to Christ; and thereupon his name *Jesus* was given unto him, see Chap. ii. 9, Sec. 73. In this respect this metaphor, κέρας σωτηρίας, *cornu salutis, horn of salvation,* is also attributed to him, Luke i. 69. By *horn,* power is meant; therefore it is reckoned up among other like metaphors, as, 'castle,' 'rock,' 'fortress,' 'shield,' Ps. xviii. 1.

The metaphor is taken from horned beasts, whose chiefest strength is in their horns; thereby they defend themselves, and seek to annoy those that they are afraid of. In reference hereunto Zedekiah the false prophet made him horns of iron; and said to Ahab, 'With these shalt thou push the Syrians, until thou have consumed them,' 2 Kings xxii. 11.

By this metaphor the power of monarchs is set forth, Dan. vii. 7, 8, and viii. 3, 4.

1. Christ is of almighty power, and by his power he hath overcome all the enemies that any way hinder our salvation.

2. Christ is of infinite dignity in his person, and what he did and endured for man is accompanied with an infinite merit; thus is he fit to enter into the place of glory and salvation for us.

Good ground have we hereupon to trust unto Christ. The Philistines much trusted in their champion Goliath, 1 Sam. xvii. 4, &c.; yet was he but a man, and as a man was overthrown. Our Lord Christ is another kind of champion, who cannot be overcome.

Hereof we are to take notice in regard of the power of those enemies which seek to hinder our salvation, who, though they may seem terrible, especially the devil, 1 Peter v. 8, yet he and all the rest are but weakness in comparison of Christ's power, Heb. ii. 14.

This also may support us against our own weakness. We are as water spilt on the ground, not able to stand of ourselves; we must therefore do as Jehoshaphat did, 2 Chron. xx. 12.

Sec. 103. *Of Christ's saving to the uttermost.*

The foresaid power of Christ in saving is much amplified by this phrase, εἰς τὸ παντελὲς, *to the uttermost,* for it setteth forth the full perfection thereof.

The Greek adjective, παντελὲς, translated *uttermost,*

---

[1] Διὸς σωτηρος. Jovis Servatoris.—*Athen. lib.* 7.
[2] Θεοῖς σωτῆρσι. Diis servatoribus.—*Lucian.*
[3] Verrem non solum patronum istius insulæ, sed etiam σωτῆρα, inscriptum vidi Syracusis. Hoc quantum est? ita magnum ut Latino uno verbo exprimi non possit. Is est nimirum σωτὴρ, qui salutem dedit.—*Cic. in Ver.*

is compounded of two nouns, whereof one, παν, signifieth *all*, and the other, τέλος, *end;* so as it implieth that which is brought to a full end, nothing need more to be done thereabouts. Our English word, *uttermost*, signifieth as much as can be done. There is nothing beyond the uttermost. There is nothing beyond his power in the work of salvation, that is able to save to the uttermost. Nothing needeth to be added as an help to him; whatsoever is requisite thereunto is in him. Thus the salvation which Christ giveth is full and perfect; in this respect Christ is called, τό σωτήριον, *salvation* itself, Luke ii. 30.

If we duly weigh the misery from which we are saved, and the felicity wherein we are estated by Christ, we may well discern that he saveth to the uttermost.

He saveth from sin, Mat. i. 21. Sin is the cause of all misery. They who are saved from it, are saved from all manner of evil.

There is nothing hurtful to a man, but what is caused or poisoned by sin. Before sin there was no misery, and he that is altogether freed from sin, is freed from all manner of misery.

Christ saves from the contagion, guilt, punishment, power, and remainder of sin. Of the felicity wherein Christ settleth those who are saved, see Chap. i. 14, Sec. 159.

1. Hereby is discovered the vanity of the supposed church's treasure, wherein papists make their foolish people to trust, as man's satisfaction, intercession of angels and saints, merits of men, priests, oblations, the church's indulgencies, popes' pardons, and such like trash.

2. This fulness of salvation wrought by Christ, giveth us further ground to trust wholly and only on Christ, and utterly to reject all other grounds of salvation.

Sec. 104. *Of salvation appropriated to those that come to God.*

Great is the benefit which is brought to the sons of men by Christ's priesthood, even full and perfect salvation; but it is here limited and restrained to such as endeavour to obtain it. This endeavour is expressed under this phrase of ' coming unto God.' And the parties that partake of the foresaid benefit are thus expressed, τοὺς προσερχομένους τῷ Θεῷ, *they that come unto God.*

This in general giveth proof that man's endeavour must be used for attaining salvation. See Chap. iv. 11, Sec. 63.

The limitation of the salvation which Christ bringeth to such persons, is not to be taken in reference to the power of Christ, as if that were restrained thereby, but to the fruit and benefit of that which Christ hath done, whereof none can partake but such as come to God.

Of this word *coming*, as here used, see Chap. iv. 16, Sec. 92. The phrase is metaphorical, transferred from the body to the soul. The foot of the soul whereby we go to God is faith, that hath a power to carry up our soul to heaven, where God sitteth on a throne of grace; so as to go or come to God, and to come to the throne of grace, do both intend one and the same thing.

The point here intended is this, that they only partake of salvation, that by faith in Christ seek it of God, and rest on God for it. This is frequently set forth under the metaphor of coming or going, as Isa. lv. 1, Mat. xi. 28, Heb. iv. 16 and x. 22, Rev. xxii. 17.

This act of coming doth not imply any matter of merit. For what merit is there in a beggar's coming to one for alms and craving it?

This duty is enjoined to raise up in us a desire of salvation, and an expectation thereof, together with a good esteem thereof.

1. Hereby we see that the benefit of redemption is not universal. All shall not be saved.

2. This cannot be but a matter of great terror to all such as on any ground refuse to come to God. Note the issue of all those that refused to come to the king's supper, Luke xiv. 24. It skilleth not whether their refusal be upon despising the offer or upon despair. If they come not to God, they cannot be saved.

3. This should stir us up to go to God by prayer, by frequenting all his ordinances, and by oft raising our hearts unto him. Salvation is worth the seeking.

4. This is a matter of great comfort to such as have their hearts bent to go to God : ' Him that cometh to me, I will in no wise cast out,' saith Christ, John vi. 37.

In that salvation is thus appropriated to them that come to God, by just consequence it followeth, that they who come to God shall be saved.

Sec. 105. *Of Christ the means to bring us to God.*

The means or way here prescribed to come unto God is, δι' αὐτοῦ, *by Christ;* for by Christ only is access made to God, Eph. iii. 12. Hereupon this inference is made upon Christ's being our priest, ' let us therefore come boldly,' Heb. iv. 16, and ' let us draw near,' chap. x. 22. In this respect he is styled ' the mediator betwixt God and man,' 1 Tim. ii. 5 ; and ' the way,' John xiv. 6, wherein we may go to God, even ' a new and living way,' Heb. x. 20 ; and ' the door,' John x. 9, whereby we may have entrance unto God.

Of the grounds and reasons hereof, see *The Whole Armour of God,* treat. iii. part. ii. ; of prayer, sec. 62.

1. Hereby is discovered the folly of those, who either presume to come to God by themselves alone, without Jesus Christ their mediator, as Jews, Turks, and all manner of pagans ; or use other mediators, as papists do ; none of these can have any access unto God, for ' there is one mediator between God and

men, the man Christ Jesus,' 1 Tim. ii. 5. The word *one* is there meant exclusively, as if he had said, *only one*, or *one alone*.

2. Hereby let us learn in all our addresses to God to have our eye upon Christ, and our faith fast fixed on him; so may we be sure of a gracious admittance to God. Do all therefore in his name. In his name pray, John xvi. 23; and give thanks, Eph. v. 20; and all other things, Col. iii. 17.

Sec. 106. *Of Christ's intercession.*

The ground of that power or opportunity which Christ hath to save such as come to God is thus expressed, *seeing he ever liveth*, &c.

This phrase, πάντοτε ζῶν, *he ever liveth*, intends as much as this, μένει εἰς τὸν αἰῶνα, *he endureth ever*. Both this and that hath reference to Christ's priesthood. See ver. 24, Sec. 98.

This latter phrase, *he ever liveth*, addeth some light to the former, in that it sheweth that he doth not only endure, as a lifeless and senseless thing may do; (witness sun and moon, Ps. lxxii. 5; and the earth, Ps. lxxviii. 69); but as one living to take notice of his church, generation after generation, and to do for it what he seeth needful and meet to be done.

The adverb πάντοτε, here translated *ever*, is not the same that was used before, ver. 24, Sec. 98, but it intendeth as much, and it implieth not only an enduring without end, but also without intermission, 1 Thes. iv. 17.

Upon Christ thus living for ever, this particular end, to make intercession, is inferred.

The verb ἐντυγχάνειν, translated *intercession*, is a compound. The simple verb τυγχάνω,[1] signifieth to *have*, or to *enjoy*, Acts xxiv. 2, or to *obtain*, Heb. xi. 35. This compound signifieth to call upon one. It is a juridical word, and importeth a calling upon a judge to be heard in this or that, against another, Acts xxv. 24, Rom. xi. 2; or for another, Rom. viii. 34. So here Christ maketh intercession for them. The metaphor is taken from attorneys or advocates, who appear for men in courts of justice; or from councillors who plead their clients' cause, answer the adversary, supplicate the judge, and procure sentence to pass on their clients' side; thus is Christ styled our παράκλητος, *advocate*, 1 John ii. 1.

This act of making intercession may also be taken for kings' favourites, who are much in the king's presence, and ever ready to make request to the king for their friend.

Though this be thus attributed to Christ, yet we may not think that in heaven Christ prostrateth himself before his Father, or maketh actual prayers. That was a part of his humiliation, which he did in the days of his flesh, Heb. v. 7. But it implieth a presenting of himself a sacrifice, a surety, and one that hath made satisfaction for all our sins, together with manifesting of his will and desire that such and such should partake of the virtue and benefit of his sacrifice. So as Christ's intercession consisteth rather in the perpetual vigour of his sacrifice, and continual application thereof, than in any actual supplication.[1]

This is to be noted, to meet with an objection against the all-sufficiency of Christ's sacrifice, which is this:

Obj. If it be requisite to add intercession unto Christ's oblation, then was not that obligation[2] perfect and all-sufficient.

Ans. This intercession is not any addition of new merit, but only an application of the same. This application is not by reason of any defect in the sacrifice, but by reason of the need of the church, whose members do arise one after another, and that in time, so as his body shall not be full till the end of the world, and then will there be no more need of this intercession.

The intendment of this phrase applied to Christ, *to make intercession*, is to shew that Christ, being God's favourite, and our advocate, continually appeareth before God to make application of that sacrifice, which once he offered up for our sins.

That he is God's favourite, is evident by this testimony which God from heaven gave of him, 'This is my beloved Son, in whom I am well pleased,' Mat. iii. 17. He is expressly called 'an advocate with the Father,' 1 John ii. 1. It is expressly said, that he 'entered into heaven, now to appear in the presence of God for us,' Heb. ix. 24.

This Christ doth, 1, to present unto his Father himself the price of our redemption.

2. To make application of his sacrifice to his church time after time, according to the need of the several members thereof.

3. To make our persons, prayers, services, and all good things acceptable to God.

1. This sheweth that the church needeth no other sacrifice, nor yet a reiteration of that sacrifice. The reason which papists forge for their supposed unbloody sacrifice, is directly against this intercession of Christ, for if Christ still remain our priest in heaven, and as our priest still makes intercession for us, what need is there of any other priest, or any other sacrifice?

2. We may in faith and with boldness at all times approach to the throne of grace, in that we have an advocate, who also is God's favourite, there, always present; an advocate that is able to make our cause good. He himself hath done and endured whatsoever is requisite to make our cause good. He is a favourite to whom God will hearken. Though we be unworthy, and have much incensed God's wrath, yet there is

---

[1] De hoc verbo, vide Chap. viii. 8, Sec. 23.

[1] Filius in hoc interpellare Deum dicitur, dum semper Patri hominem quem suscepit quasi nostrum pignus ostendit et offert, ut verus pontifex et æternus —*Hier. Comment. in Rom.* viii. [2] Qu. 'oblation'?—ED.

hope, so as we need not despair, 1 John ii. 1. On this ground the apostle with an holy insultation saith, 'Who is he that condemneth? It is Christ that died, yea rather, that is risen again, who is even at the right hand of God, who maketh continual intercession for us.' When thou art troubled with horror of sin, when thou art in any distress, when thou art going out of this world, lift up the eyes of thy soul to Christ thy advocate at the throne of grace making intercession for thee, and in faith commend thy case and soul to him.

3. This is a good ground of assurance of God's constant favour to us, and of our persevering unto the end, and it is the more sure, because it is not in ourselves, but in Christ.

4. This is a further ground of presenting our persons, prayers, and all our services to God in the name of Christ. See Sec. 105.

This relative, *for them*, hath reference to the persons described in the former part of this verse; it intendeth such a limitation as excludeth all others. So as Christ doth not make intercession for all, John xvii. 19. See Chap. ii. 9, Sec. 81.

Sec. 107. *Of the resolution and observations of Heb. vii. 25.*

Ver. 25. *Wherefore he is able also to save them to the uttermost that come unto God by him, seeing he ever liveth to make intercession for them.*

The sum of this verse is, the all-sufficiency of Christ's priesthood. In setting down hereof, observe,

1. The inference, in this word *wherefore*; 2, the substance. In it,

1. An effect; 2, the means of accomplishing it.

The effect is set out,

1. By the kind of it, *to save*.
2. By the ground of it, *he is able*.
3. By the extent, *to the uttermost*.
4. By the persons that are saved. These are described,

1. By their act, *them that come*.
2. By the object to whom, *unto God*.
3. By the mediator, *by Christ*.

The means of accomplishing the foresaid effect is, 1, Propounded; 2, amplified.

In the point propounded there is, 1, an act, *he liveth*; 2, a continuance therein, *for ever*.

In the amplification of it we have, 1, the end, to *make intercession*; 2, the persons for whom, *for them*.

Doctrines.

I. *Christ's excellencies made him an all-sufficient priest.* The general reference of this verse to all that went before intends thus much. See Sec. 101.

II. *Salvation is the end of Christ's priesthood.* He was such a priest as is before described, *to save*. See Sec. 101.

III. *Christ was able and meet to accomplish what he undertook.* This is exemplified in this particular of saving. See Sec. 102.

IV. *The salvation which Christ bringeth is full and perfect.* It is *to the uttermost*. See Sec. 103.

V. *Men must endeavour to be saved.* They must come. See Sec. 104.

VI. *Salvation belongs to those that come to God.* This is here taken for granted. See Sec. 104.

VII. *Christ is the means to bring us to God.* Christ is understood under this relative *him*. See Sec. 105.

VIII. *Christ still liveth as our priest.* So much is intended under this phrase, *he ever liveth*. See Sec. 106.

IX. *Christ maketh intercession.* This is plainly expressed. See Sec. 106.

X. *Christ maketh intercession for such as he intends to save.* This relative, *for them*, hath reference to such. See Sec. 106.

Sec. 108. *Of Christ, such an high priest as became us.*

Ver. 26. *For such an high priest became us, who is holy, harmless, undefiled, separate from sinners, and made higher than the heavens.*

27. *Who needeth not daily, as those high priests, to offer up sacrifice, first for his own sins, and then for the people's: for this did he once, when he offered up himself.*

In these two verses, a fifth argument is laid down to prove the excellency of Christ's priesthood above the Levitical. See Sec. 1. The argument is taken from the difference of the persons that executed the one and the other. Christ was perfectly pure, ver. 26, but the Levitical priest polluted, ver. 27.

Of Christ's being a priest, and an high priest, see Chap. ii. 17, Secs. 172, 173.

The apostle, to make the force of his argument more evident, premiseth a necessity of such an high priest as Christ was, in this phrase, ἔπρεπεν ἡμῖν, *it became us*.

Of the various acception of this word *became*, see Chap. ii. 10, Sec. 86.

It signifieth both a decency or glory, and also a necessity.

In the former respect it hath reference to God, whose glory is much set forth thereby.

In the latter respect it hath reference to man, who could not have been saved without such a priest as is here set forth. Well, therefore, might he say, τοιοῦτος, *such an high priest*. He is such an one as never the like was, or can be. Christ being the truth of that which was prefigured in Melchisedec, and being so far preferred before Aaron as he is in this chapter, this relative *such*, and that in the largest extent, may well be applied to him.

How God's glory is set out by Christ's priesthood, wherein he humbled himself to death, was shewed Chap. ii. 10, Sec. 87.

In reference to Christ himself, that there was a meetness, a necessity, for Christ to be like man, is shewed Chap. ii. 27, Sec. 166.

But here, in reference to man, a meetness, a necessity of Christ's excellency above all men is set forth, and that in purity and dignity. Therefore

'Such a priest became us,' because there was no other way to effect that which he did for us, nor other means to free us out of our misery. We were every way unholy. Our actual sins are many, Isa. lix. 12; we are by nature impure, Ps. li. 5; we are guilty of Adam's sin, Rom. v. 12; by sin we implunged ourselves into such a gulf of misery, and made ourselves such vassals of Satan, and such vessels of God's wrath, as none but such an one as was so pure as Christ was, and so high as Christ was, could deliver us. No man so pure, no angel so high, higher than the heavens.

Thus it appeareth that Christ was the fittest high priest and Saviour that could have been given for man, Acts iv. 12.

1. From hence the bottomless depth of man's misery may be inferred, that no other high priest could be fit for him but the Son of God made son of man; so pure, so high as he was.

2. Herein appears the wonderful great and good respect of God to man, that would do for him what best became man, though it were to give his Son.

3. This giveth proof of the wisdom of God, whereby he ordereth things so as best become himself, Chap. ii. 10, Sec. 86; yea, also, which may be fittest for man, and best become him.

4. This teacheth us in all things to aim at that which becomes us: 'Whatsoever things are true, or honest, or just, or pure, or lovely, or of good report, think on those things,' Philip. iv. 8. This was the argument which Christ pressed upon the Baptist, Mat. iii. 15. Ministers must 'speak the things which become sound doctrine,' Titus ii. 1; women must 'adorn themselves as becometh such as profess godliness,' 1 Tim. ii. 10; all saints must 'walk worthy of their holy calling,' Eph. iv. 1; this is it that becomes them.

5. As God did that which becomes us, so we must do that which becomes him, and in this respect 'do all things to the glory of God,' 1 Cor. x. 31.

Sec. 109. *Of Christ being holy, harmless, undefiled, separate from sinners.*

The purity of Christ, as he is our priest, is set out in four distinct branches.

The first is this, ὅσιος, *holy*. This implieth one that is dedicated and consecrated to God. Herein the apostle hath reference to the condition of the high priests under the law, who were counted and called *holy*. Aaron had this style, 'the holy one of the Lord,' Ps. cvi. 16. As his person, so his apparel was counted holy, Exod. xxviii. 2. So the place where he exercised his ministry was the holy place, Exod. xxviii. 29, and the place whereinto the high priest went once a year 'the holy of holies,' Heb. ix. 3. All appertaining to him was accounted holy, therefore there was engraven on the breast-plate, when he went before the Lord, 'Holiness to the Lord,' Exod. xxviii. 36. All these shewed that in his office he was sanctified and consecrated to God. So was Christ, but in a far more excellent manner. The legal priests were holy in an outward and legal manner; so they might be holy priests, yet unholy men. Christ was inwardly, truly, properly, every way holy. This is evident by the other parts following concerning Christ's purity, to which points, parts, and degrees of holiness none of those priests ever attained.

The second is ἄκακος, *harmless*. This is a privative compound. The simple noun, κάκος, signifieth an hurtful or mischievous person. He that wronged his fellow-servant hath this title given unto him, and it is translated *evil*, Mat. xxiv. 28. The wrongs which Saul did to the church are comprised under this word κακὰ, Acts ix. 13.

This compound signifieth one that doth no wrong. In Latin, it is fitly translated *innocent*,[1] one that doth no wrong. Every sin is a wrong to God or man. This, therefore, sheweth that Christ was free from all actual sin within and without. He never did any wrong or harm to God or man in thought, word, or deed, and in that respect this epithet *harmless*, or *innocent*, is attributed to him. He never committed any offence outwardly either in speech (for 'no guile was found in his mouth,' 2 Pet. ii. 22) nor in deed. In this respect he challenged his adversaries, John viii. 46. When the devil came to sift him, he 'found nothing in him,' John xiv. 30. Neither did he inwardly commit any sin, for 'he knew no sin,' 2 Cor. v. 21. Had there been any in him, he must needs have known it. As privatively he did no offence, so positively he performed all duty; for he fulfilled the law to the full. He loved God 'with all his heart, with all his soul, with all his mind, and with all his strength, and his neighbour as himself,' Luke x. 27. In reference to God he saith, 'I have finished the work which thou gavest me to do,' John xvii. 4; and in reference to man thus, 'Greater love hath no man than this, that a man lay down his life for his friends,' John xv. 13, and so did Christ.

The third is ἀμίαντος, *undefiled*. This word also is a compound. The simple verb μιαίνω, *polluo*, signifieth *to pollute*, chap. xii. 15. This compound is fitly translated *undefiled*, Heb. xiii. 4. Here it hath reference to original corruption, whereby man's nature is polluted throughout, in every power of soul and part of body. But in Christ there is no speck of corruption. He is holy and fully free from this, even as from all actual sin. Hereupon the angel that brought the first news of his conception thus styleth him,

[1] *Innocens.— Vulg. Lat.*

'That holy thing which shall be born,' &c., Luke i. 35. See more hereof, Chap. iv. 15, Sec. 91.

The fourth is κεχωρισμένος ἀπὸ τῶν ἁμαρτωλῶν, *separate from sinners*. The verb χωρίζω, whence this word is derived, signifieth *to remove*, or separate from a place, Acts xviii. 1, 2 ; from a person, Philip. v. 15, 1 Cor. vii. 10, 11, 15 ; and from an estate or condition, Rom. viii. 35, 39.

Under the word *sinners*, all sorts of men, even all that come from Adam, are comprised. This then hath reference to the guilt of Adam's sin, whereunto all his posterity stood obliged, even all men as they came out of his loins, for he as a public person bore them all in his loins, Rom. v. 18.

Obj. Christ also came from Adam. See the answer hereunto, Chap. iv. 15, Sec. 91. There is further shewed how Christ as our high priest is perfectly pure.

Sec. 110. *Of Christ made higher than the heavens.*

The dignity of Christ as our high priest is thus set out, 'made higher than the heavens.'

This word γενόμενος, *made*, having reference to Christ's exaltation, intends his advancement thereunto, as if it had been thus expressed, *exalted higher*, &c. That word is used to shew, that the exaltation here mentioned is to be understood of Christ, as he was man, and mediator betwixt God and man, for he is exalted partly in regard of his human nature, and partly in regard of his office.

This adjective ὑψηλότερος, *higher*, is the comparative of that positive ὑψηλός, which is translated *high*, Chap. i. 3, Sec. 15.

The word *heavens* may here be taken properly, and so imply, that Christ is advanced above all the visible heavens, even the starry sky. Or it may be taken metonymically, for the inhabitants of the highest heaven, which are glorified saints and glorious angels.

Obj. God himself is said to be in heaven, but Christ is not advanced above him.

Ans. God is not properly in heaven as contained therein, but because his glory is there most manifested. See *The Guide to go to God*, or *Explanation of the Lord's Prayer*, preface, sec. 16.

The point principally here intended is this, Christ our priest is advanced above all creatures. Thus is he said to ' ascend up far above all heavens,' Eph. iv. 10, ' far above all principalities,' &c., Eph. i. 21.

Of this exaltation of Christ, see Chap. i. 3, Secs. 34, 35, and ver. 13, Sec. 149, and Chap. iv. 14, Secs. 84, 85.

Sec. 111. *Of Christ not offering for himself.*

In the 27th verse, the other part of the difference between Christ and the Levitical priests is set down. It is concerning the sinfulness of those priests, which is proved by an act of theirs. They offered up sacrifice for their sins, therefore they were sinners.

To shew that this effect is here mentioned, purposely to magnify Christ above them, the apostle thus bringeth it in, ' who needeth not,' &c.

This relative ὅς, *who*, hath reference to Christ, described in the former verse. For that which is here said can be applied to none else.

This word ἔχει ἀνάγκην, *needeth*, though it be the same in our English, which was used chap. v. 12, yet in Greek there are two distinct words in this and that place. That word χρεία implieth a need through deficiency ; this a necessity. This is that word which is used, ver. 12, and translated *necessity*.

It is here negatively spoken of Christ, ὅς οὐκ ἔχει ἀνάγκην, *who needeth not*, in reference to the legal priests, on whom there lay a necessity of offering up sacrifices for their sins.

This negative giveth us to understand, that Christ died not for himself. He needed no sacrifice for himself. When mention is made of the end of Christ's sacrifice, we shall find it to be for others, Isa. liii. 4, 5, Eph. v. 25.

The two points before noted of Christ, his perfect purity and high dignity, demonstrate as much.

1. This is an evident argument against Christ's meriting for himself. 'See Chap. ii. 9, Sec. 74.

2. This much amplifieth Christ's love to us, that though there were no need of his offering up a sacrifice for himself, yet he would do it for us.

3. This is a good pattern to us, to do good to others, though there should be no need therein for ourselves.

From the force of this negative argument, that Christ offered up no sacrifice for himself, we may well infer, that things which need not are not to be done. God is ' not to be worshipped with men's hands ; because he needeth not any such thing,' Acts xvii. 25. Christ would not wash Peter's hands and head, because ' he that is washed needeth not save to wash his feet,' John xiii. 9, 10. In the city that had no need of the sun or moon, they shined not, Rev. xxi. 23.

That which needs not is superfluous, and all superfluity is at least in vain.

How vain are popish images, and all their superstitious ceremonies ! How vain are their multitudes of mediators ! How vain are their sacrificing priests and bloody sacrifices ! How vain are prayers for the dead, and a thousand like things, which they do even in God's worship, whereof there is no need !

It becomes us duly to weigh in all our weighty enterprises, especially in those wherein we have to do with God, what need we have of them, and answerably to do them, or forbear them.

Sec. 112. *Of daily sacrifices.*

Of the Greek phrase καθ' ἡμέραν, translated *daily*, see Chap. iii. 13, Sec. 145. It is here set down as another difference between Christ's sacrifice and the sacrifices of the legal priests. *They* were offered up day after day, *this* only once. For Christ at once did to the full what was to be done by his sacrifice. But they did not so by theirs.

Herein is couched a sixth argument to prove the excellency of Christ's priesthood above the Levitical; see Sec. 1. It is taken from the oft offering up of their sacrifices, which argueth imperfection. But Christ's perfect sacrifice was once only offered up.

This word *daily* intends two points.

1. An *insufficiency* in those sacrifices. For oft renewing and reiterating a thing, implies an imperfection thereof. 'Would they not have ceased to be offered,' if they had made perfect? Heb. x. 2.

By this our Lord proves that ordinary water could not thoroughly quench thirst for ever, because whosoever drinketh thereof shall thirst again, John iv. 13.

There is no need of reiterating that which is perfect and maketh perfect; and if there be no need thereof, it must needs be superfluous and vain. See Sec. 111.

The blasphemous doctrine of the mass is hereby discovered, for papists say that therein they offer up that very sacrifice which Christ himself offered upon the cross. They offer it up daily, thereby they make it imperfect. They can never be able to answer this argument.

This further sheweth, that our ordinances are not simply to be rested in, as in things that can make us perfect. They are in themselves but as 'bodily exercises which profit little,' 1 Tim. iv. 8. That which the Baptist said, is true of all the ministers of the gospel, 'they baptize but with water,' Mat. iii. 11. Men may eat and drink sacramental bread and wine, and yet 'eat and drink damnation to themselves,' 1 Cor. xi. 29. The gospel preached may prove 'a savour of death,' 2 Cor. ii. 16. In the use therefore of outward ordinances, Christ must be beheld, and faith fixed on him; so may they be called helps to spiritual grace and heavenly blessings. Thus might the sacrifices and other prescribed rites be under the law.

2. A *duty*, which is frequently to observe such warrantable means and sanctified helps as cannot at first do all that for which they are enjoined. On this ground we must 'exhort one another daily.' See more hereof, Chap. iii. 13, Sec. 145.

By oft use of such helps, supply may be made of that defect and imperfection which is in them through our weakness. By long putting in water into a vessel drop by drop, it may be filled, though it have but a small vent.

It will be our wisdom to observe what means God hath sanctified for our spiritual edification, and to be frequent and constant in the use of them. Ministers must 'preach the word,' and be 'instant in season and out of season,' 2 Tim. iv. 2. People must 'search the Scriptures daily,' Acts xvii. 11. So they must 'pray without ceasing,' 1 Thes. v. 17. They must also frequent the public ministry of the word and the Lord's table. Nature and reason teach men daily to eat, drink, and sleep, because once doing of these things cannot be sufficient. Let God's word and true religion teach us to be as wise for our souls.

Sec 113. *Of cleansing one's self first.*

They who did that which Christ needed not, are thus expressed, *as those high priests.*

The particle, ὥσπερ, *as*, being inferred on a negative, implieth a dissimilitude; the dissimilitude is betwixt Christ and the legal high priests. For this relative pronoun, οἱ ἀρχιερεῖς, *those*, hath reference to the priests of whom he had before spoken, vers. 11, 20, 23.

An especial work of those priests was *to offer up sacrifice.*

Of priests, and of their offering sacrifice, see Chap. v. 1, Secs. 6, 7.

A double end of the legal priest's sacrifices is here set down:

One was for his own sins; the other for the sins of the people.

That sacrifices were for sins is proved, Chap. v. 1, Sec. 8.

That priests offered sacrifices for their own sins, is also proved, Chap. v. 3, Sec. 14.

This adverb of order, πρότερον, *first*, is remarkable; for it implieth, that they who use means of cleansing others, must first seek to cleanse themselves. 'First cast out the beam out of thine own eye,' Mat. vii. 5; 'Physician, heal thyself,' Luke iv. 23. The apostle 'kept under his own body, and brought it into subjection: lest that by any means, when he had preached to others, he himself should be a castaway,' 1 Cor. ix. 27.

By this course of a man's first cleansing himself, the means which he useth for others will be the more powerful and effectual, and that in three respects:

1. God's blessing doth usually most accompany such a course.

2. The mind and disposition of those whose cleansing is endeavoured, will more readily be made subject to the means used in such a manner of proceeding.

3. The conscience of those who use the means will be more cheerful in performing that duty. A self-condemning conscience is a great hindrance to such duties.

This is a good direction to ministers, who pray for and preach to others, to pray for and preach to themselves. Though in regard of their calling they teach, yet in regard of their persons they must learn what they teach others, and apply all to themselves. The like may be said of parents, masters, and other governors. All that by virtue of their general or particular calling seek to instruct and inform others, must consider what in this case is said, 'Thou which teachest another, teachest thou not thyself?' Rom. ii. 21.

Of the word ἀναφέρειν, ἀνενέγκας, here twice used, and translated, according to the composition of it, *offered up*, see Chap. v. 1, Sec. 6.

Sec. 114. *Of cleansing others also.*

The other end of a priest's offering sacrifice, was for the people's sins. Hereof see Chap. v. 3, sec. 14.

This correlative adverb, ἔπειτα, *then*, is also observable. It gives us to understand, that it is not sufficient for them who have charge over others, to cleanse themselves, unless also they seek to cleanse others. Though they must first cleanse themselves, yet withal they must seek to cleanse others. So did Jacob, Gen. xxxv. 2; Joshua, chap. xxiv. 15; Hezekiah, 2 Chron. xxix. 2, &c.; Josiah, 2 Chron. xxxiv. 31, 32; Ezra, chap. x. 5. This charge did David give to the chief of the Levites: 'Sanctify yourselves, ye and your brethren,' 1 Chron. xv. 12; and Christ to Peter, 'When thou art converted, strengthen thy brethren,' Luke xxii. 32.

Thus men ought to do, in regard of God, those others, and themselves.

1. It is an evidence of an holy zeal of God's glory, to bring others with ourselves to God.
2. It is a fruit of brotherly love, to promote the spiritual good of others as of our own.
3. We shall by this means give up our account to God with joy and not with grief.

Let all those who are conscionable in observing the former duty of cleansing themselves, know that if their care and endeavour be only for themselves, they come very short of performing what they should, and may lose the glory and comfort thereof.

Sec. 115. *Of Christ offering up himself once.*

The latter part of this verse containeth a reason why Christ needed not to offer his sacrifice daily. *For this did he once.* The causal particle γὰρ, *for*, sheweth that this clause is added as a reason.

The relative pronoun τοῦτο, *this*, hath reference to that which goeth before. That reference may either be general, to the act of offering, which he did once, or else particular, to the first clause of this verse; and then these words of order, 'first for his own sins, and then for the people's,' be included in a parenthesis. Or it may have reference to this clause immediately before, *for the people's*. If it should have reference to the order of priest's offering sacrifice, 'first for his own sins, and then for the people's,' it would contradict the description of Christ's purity, ver 26.

The adverb ἐφάπαξ, *once*, is here used exclusively. It excludeth all iterations, as if he had said, once for all, once and but once, never again.

There is a little difference in the Greek betwixt this word, and that (ἅπαξ) which is translated *once*, Chap. vi. 4, Sec. 32; and that by prefixing a preposition, ἐπί, before this adverb here. But both words are used in the same sense, and applied to the same thing, as Heb. ix. 28, and x. 10.

In this very sense is Christ's sacrifice or offering said to be *one* (μία θυσία, μία προσφορὰ), namely, exclusively; only one, but one, and no more, Heb. x. 12, 14.

That this adverb *once* is thus to be taken exclusively, is evident, in that where the apostle said, 'Christ died once,' it is also said, 'Christ being raised from the dead, dieth no more,' Rom. vi. 9, 10. So as to die once, is to die but once and no more. In the very same sense it is said, 'It is appointed unto men once to die,' Heb. ix. 27. Now we know by experience, that men use to die but once and no more.

It was a full and absolute perfection of Christ's sacrifice, and of his offering up thereof, that caused that sacrifice to be but one, and that offering to be but once.

A wonder it is that papists should be so blinded as they are in this case; for hereby it is evident, that the sacrifice of the mass, which they *daily* offer up, is both erroneous and blasphemous: *erroneous*, in that it expressly contradicteth the Scripture; *blasphemous*, in that it maketh Christ's sacrifice, offered by himself, to be imperfect. I would demand of them whether the sacrifice of the mass be the very same that Christ offered upon the cross or no. If they should say *no*, then they make that imperfect, by adding another unto it. Thus the sacrifice of the New Testament would not be one, and in that respect not perfect. If they say *yea*, that it is the very same, then Christ's offering up his sacrifice was not sufficient, in that it is offered up more than once; yet four several times doth the apostle apply this exclusive adverb, *once*, to Christ's offering, namely, in this verse, Chap. ix. 26, 28, and x. 10.

All the show of answer that they can make is, by a foolish and false distinction of a bloody and unbloody sacrifice. That sacrifice, say they, which Christ himself offered up upon the cross was a bloody sacrifice, and that was but once offered up; but that which is offered up in the mass is unbloody, and this is daily offered up.

Ans. 1. This distinction is without ground of Scripture. There is no hint of any such distinction there.

2. It taketh away all the pretended virtue and efficacy of that sacrifice. They hold that their sacrifice is a true, real, propitiatory sacrifice for the sins of the quick and dead; but an unbloody sacrifice cannot be so, for 'without shedding of blood is no remission,' Heb. ix. 22. This phrase, 'without shedding,' answers their conceit of transubstantiating wine into blood, for by shedding of blood is meant slaughter, or taking away of life.

3. Those terms, *bloody and unbloody*, being contradictory, cannot be attributed to the very same thing, as they say the body of Christ crucified and the bread transubstantiated are the very same body (*idem numero*).

4. According to their own position their sacrifice is not unbloody, for they say the wine is transubstantiated into blood. To this they rejoin that that blood is not shed.

And if not shed, then no sacrifice. But is not the wine poured out of the chalice when it is drunk, and may not some of it fall out of the cup, or from the mouth or beard of him that drinketh it?

They much press this, that the ancient fathers[1] call the eucharist an unbloody sacrifice.

Ans. 1. They call it a sacrifice metonymically and sacramentally, because it is a memorial of the sacrifice of Christ,[2] and unbloody to distinguish it from Christ's sacrifice on the cross. There blood was shed, here is no blood at all.

2. They called it an unbloody sacrifice in reference to the praises then offered to God,[3] which they called sacrifices without body[4] as well as without blood, and an unbloody service.[5]

That which is implied in this word *once*, namely, the perfection of Christ's sacrifice, should make us perfectly, yea, wholly and only, trust thereunto. As it is perfect in itself, so must we account of it as of that which can make us perfect. This will be manifested by our stedfast relying upon it, without doubting or wavering, and without trusting to anything else. Blessed be the gospel, that hath revealed the perfection of this sacrifice, and blessed are they that trust unto it.

This is the rather to be done by reason of the kind of sacrifice which is thus expressed, ' he offered up (ἑαυτὸν) himself.' Hereof see Chap. i. 3, Sec. 29. See also *Domest. Duties*, treat. i. sec. 29.

This intimation of time, *when*, hath reference to Christ's death upon the cross. I grant that this particle *when* is not expressed in the Greek, yet it is implied in the participle, which may thus be translated, *having offered up*. If, then, that which is comprised under the word once was accomplished, how shall he be offered up again in the mass?

Sec. 116. *Of the resolution and observations of* Heb. vii. 26, 27.

Ver. 26. *For such an high priest became us, who is holy, harmless, undefiled, separate from sinners, and made higher than the heavens.*

27. *Who needeth not daily, as those high priests, to offer up sacrifices, first for his own sins, and then for the people's; for this did he once when he offered up himself.*

The sum of these two verses is the excellency of Christ above other priests. Hereof are two parts:

1. A description of Christ, ver. 26.
2. A declaration of the difference betwixt Christ and other priests.

In the description there is set down,

1. The person described; 2, the substance of the description.

The person is set out by his office, *high priest*.

In the substance we may observe two points:

1. The purity of Christ; 2, his dignity.

The purity of Christ is, 1, set down in four properties;

2. Amplified by the ground thereof.

Among the foresaid properties, one in general hath respect to his function, which is *holy*. The other three are a qualification of his person, namely, *harmless, undefiled, and separate from sinners*.

About the ground of these is noted,

1. The kind of ground, *became*;
2. The persons whom it concerneth, *us*.

The dignity of Christ is, 1, set out by the place, *heavens*;

2. Amplified by a comparative expression, *higher than*.

The difference betwixt Christ and other priests is,

1. Propounded; 2, proved.

The point propounded is a dissimilitude, wherein is,

1. Intimated an agreement betwixt them;
2. Is expressed a difference.

The agreement is in offering sacrifice.

The difference is in three points:

1. In time: they offered *daily*, Christ *once*.
2. In the extent of the end: they for their own sins and others, Christ only for others. The extent of their offering is amplified by the order, *first* for their own sins, *then* for the people's.
3. In the kind of sacrifice: Christ offered up himself, they offered up other sacrifices.

Doctrines.

I. *Christ was an high priest.* He is so styled. See Sec. 108.

II. *Christ was such a priest as was every way fit.* This relative, *such*, in this place implieth as much. See Sec. 108.

III. *God ordered matters so as our need required.* Even so as *became us*. See Sec. 108.

IV. *Christ by his function was an holy one.* In this respect he is here styled *holy*. See Sec. 109.

V. *Christ never committed any actual sin.* He was *harmless*. See Sec. 109.

VI. *Christ was without original sin.* He was *undefiled*. See Sec. 109.

VII. *Christ was not guilty of Adam's sin.* In this sense he is said to be *separate from sinners*. See Sec. 109.

VIII. *Christ was perfectly pure.* This general is gathered out of all the fore-mentioned particulars. See Sec. 109.

IX. *Christ as our priest is above all creatures.* This phrase, *higher than the heavens*, intendeth as much. See Sec. 110.

---

[1] Cyril. ad Reg.; Euseb. de Demonst. lib. i.
[2] Ut earum, quæ pro nobis suscepta sunt, perpessionem recordaremur.—*Theo. in cap. viii. ad Hebr.*
[3] ἀναιμάκτους θυσίας καὶ δοξολογίας.—*Cyril ad Reg.*
[4] θυσίας ἀσωμάτους.—*Euseb. de Demonst.*, lib. i.
[5] ἀναίμακτον λατρείαν.—*Cyril. Hieros. Myst. Catechis.* 5.

X. *Christ as mediator is advanced to that high dignity which he hath.* The word *made*, as here used, implieth as much. See Sec. 110.

XI. *Christ needed not the things which other priests did.* Thus much is expressed in this phrase, *needed not*. See Sec. 111.

XII. *Priests offered up sacrifices.* This is taken for granted. See Sec. 113.

XIII. *Legal priests oft offered up their sacrifices*, even daily. See Sec. 112.

XIV. *What cannot at once be effected must by daily performance be helped on.* This is the reason why the priests daily offered. See Sec. 112.

XV. *Legal priests offered sacrifices for their own sins.* This is plainly expressed. See Sec. 113.

XVI. *They who are in place to cleanse others must first be cleansed themselves.* This adverb of order, *first*, demonstrateth as much. See Sec. 113.

XVII. *Priests offered sacrifice for others also.* This is plainly expressed. See Sec. 114.

XVIII. *They who have charge over others must seek their cleansing.* This correlative conjunction, *then*, intends so much. See Sec. 114.

XIX. *Christ only once offered up his sacrifice.* This adverb *once* is exclusive. See Sec. 115.

XX. *Christ offered up himself.* This is clearly expressed. See Sec. 115.

Sec. 117. *Of the meaning of* Heb. vii. 28.

Ver. 28. *For the law maketh men high priests which have infirmity; but the word of the oath, which was since the law, maketh the Son, who is consecrated for evermore.*

The causal conjunction γὰρ, *for*, sheweth that this verse contains a reason of that which went before. It giveth a reason of both parts of the former dissimilitude, namely,

1. That the Levitical priests offered oft, and Christ but once, and that only for others, because he is the Son of God.

This verse doth withal set down a seventh argument (see Sec. 1), to prove the excellency of Christ's priesthood above the Levitical. The argument is taken from the different nature of the one and of the other priest. They were mere men, Christ was the Son of God.

This being taken for granted, which is an undeniable principle, that the more excellent the priest is the more excellent his priesthood is, the argument thus lieth.

The Son of God, perfected for evermore, hath a more excellent priesthood than men which have infirmity; but Christ is the Son, &c., and legal priests men, &c.; therefore Christ's priesthood is more excellent than theirs.

Against this argument there lie sundry exceptions.

Except. 1. Christ was a true man.

Ans. He was not a mere man. He was more than a man. He was God-man. And in his priesthood he must be so considered.

Except. 2. Christ was subject to infirmities as well as other men, chap. ii. 17, 18.

Ans. He was not subject to sinful infirmities, chap. iv. 15. But these are the infirmities which are here principally intended. For such infirmities were sacrifices offered up.

This last argument is so framed, as it compriseth under it the sum of the former arguments whereby Christ's priesthood was proved to be more excellent than the Levitical.

1. Christ's priesthood succeeded that, ver. 11. For the word that makes Christ priest is *since the law*.

2. They were made priests by a carnal law, ver. 16. This is the *law* here intended.

3. They were made priests without an oath, ver. 21. The *word of oath* whereby Christ was ordained is here expressed.

4. They died, ver. 23. Christ is *consecrated for evermore.*

5. They were sinful, ver. 27. Here they are said *to have infirmity.* But Christ is perfected.[1]

6. They offered for themselves, and that oft, ver. 27; but Christ only for others, and that but once. Thus much is implied under this phrase, *consecrated for evermore.*

By the law, ὁ νόμος, here mentioned is meant the law of ceremonies, which is called 'the law of a carnal commandment.' See ver. 16, Secs. 80, 81.

The verb καθίστησι, translated *maketh*, implieth an ordination or institution to such and such a function. See Chap. v. 1, Sec 3.

The noun ἀνθρώπους, translated *men*, is here used in the same sense that it was Chap. v. 1, Sec. 2.

What, ἀρχιερεῖς, an high priest is, hath been shewed, Chap. ii. 17, Sec. 172.

The noun ἀσθένεια, translated *infirmity*, is used in the same sense that it was Chap. v. 2, Sec. 12.

By ὁ λόγος ὁρκωμοσίας, *the word of oath*, is meant that expression of God's oath, whereof see vers. 20, 21, Secs. 91, 92.

The word of oath is here said to be μετὰ τὸν νόμον, *since*, or *after the law*, namely, the law of ordaining priests before mentioned.

For clearing this point sundry doubts are to be resolved.

1. The law is said to be four hundred and thirty years after the covenant that was confirmed in Christ, Gal. iii. 17. How then is this word of oath *since the law?*

Ans. The covenant there said to be confirmed in Christ hath respect to a particular promise of Christ himself, even of his person to descend from Abraham. But this word of oath is a confirmation of a special office.

2. The law doth not so follow and succeed the fore-

---

[1] Qu. 'perfect'?—Ed.

named covenant as Christ's priesthood did the Levitical. The law was added to shew what need there was for the covenant to be confirmed in Christ, and to drive us to Christ, Gal. iii. 19, 24. But Christ's priesthood came in the room of the Levitical, and thrust it clean out.

Doubt 2. The law that came after the foresaid covenant had no excellency thereupon above the covenant. How then doth the establishing of Christ's priesthood after the Levitical give an excellency to that above this?

Ans. It is not simply the coming after, but the coming in the room of it, to supply that which the former could not effect, which argueth the excellency of Christ's priesthood. That therefore the church might with confidence expect that to be perfected which could not be by the Levitical priesthood and law thereof, the word of oath was since the law.

Doubt 3. Christ was 'a Lamb slain from the beginning of the world,' Rev. xiii. 8.

Ans. That is spoken in reference,

1. To God's purpose in giving his Son, which was from everlasting.
2. To the promise made in the beginning of the world, Gen. iii. 15.
3. To the efficacy of Christ's sacrifice, which was, as Christ himself, ever the same, Heb. xiii. 8.
4. To the vigour of faith; for Abel's faith eyed Christ and his sacrifice as steadily as believers that lived since Christ was actually sacrificed, Heb. xi. 4.

But this is spoken of a solemn manifestation and confirmation of Christ's priesthood. Therefore this phrase, 'which was since the law,' as here used, confirmeth that which was delivered concerning the imperfection of the Levitical priesthood, that needed another to come after it, ver. 11, Sec. 64, and the excellency of Christ, which came in the room of the former, and perfected that which the former could not, ver. 19, Sec. 87.

This title, υἱὸν, *Son*, is here set down by an excellency; such a Son as none like him, who alone deserveth this title properly, as it hath reference to God the Father, so as the Son of God is here meant. Of this Son of God, see Chap. i. 2, Sec. 15. Of God's Son made high priest, see Chap. v. 5, Sec. 27.

This verb *maketh* is not here expressed in the Greek, but necessarily to be understood; for this latter clause hath reference to the first clause of this verse, and dependeth upon καθίστησι, the verb there used, and is fitly here supplied by our English.

Of the divers acceptions of the Greek verb τετελειωμένον, translated *consecrated*, see Chap. ii. 10, Sec. 97.

According to the notation of the word is implied such a solemn setting apart of the Son of God to his priestly function, as he was every way made perfect thereunto, and also makes all that come to him and rest upon him perfect. Our English, therefore, in the margin have thus expressed this sense, Greek, *perfected*.

Herein Christ far excelleth the legal priests, who were neither perfect themselves nor could make others perfect, ver. 11, Sec. 61, Chap. x. 1.

The phrase, εἰς τὸν αἰῶνα, translated *evermore*, is the same that was used, Chap. v. 6, Sec. 29; and that to set out the everlastingness of Christ's priesthood. Thus we see how this verse is a recapitulation of the most material points before set down concerning the excellency of Christ's priesthood above the Levitical. For this is the main scope of it, and here it is fitly brought in as the conclusion of all.

Sec. 118. *Of the resolution and observations of* Heb. vii. 28.

The general sum of this verse, as of sundry others before it, is a proof of the excellency of Christ's priesthood above the Levitical. Hereof are two parts:

1. The meanness of the Levitical priesthood.
2. The greatness of Christ's.

The former is set out,

1. By the ground or warrant which they had, *the law*.
2. By the kind of persons who were priests, *men*. This is amplified by their condition, *which have infirmity*.

The latter is set out,

1. By the ground or warrant which he had, *the word of oath*.
2. By the time, or order, when he was confirmed, *since the law*.
3. By the dignity of his person, *Son*.
4. By the manner of institution, *consecrated*.
5. By the continuance of his priesthood, *for evermore*.

Doctrines.

I. *There were high priests under the law.* This is here taken for granted. See Chap. ii. 17, Sec. 173.

II. *The ceremonial law was the Levitical priest's warrant.* That law *made* them. See ver. 16, Sec. 80.

III. *The legal high priests were subject to infirmity.* This is plainly expressed. See Chap. v. 2, Sec. 12.

IV. *The warrant of Christ's priesthood was the word of oath.* That made him priest. See ver. 20, Sec. 91.

V. *Christ's priesthood succeeded the legal.* This is intended under this phrase, *since the law*. See ver. 19, Sec. 87.

VI. *The Son of God is our high priest.* He is comprised under this title, *Son*. See Chap. v. 5, Sec. 27.

VII. *Christ was solemnly instituted into his priesthood.* This word *consecrated*, having reference to God's oath, importeth thus much. See ver. 20, Sec. 91.

VIII. *Christ's is a perfect, perfecting priesthood.* The notation of the Greek word translated *consecrated*, proveth this extent. See Chap. ii. 10, Sec. 97.

IX. *Christ's is an everlasting priesthood.* See Chap. v. 6, Sec. 29.

Puritan Classic Reprints

Solid Ground Christian Books is delighted to announce that we are beginning a new series of *Puritan Reprint*, we are convinced are needed at this time in history. Below we are listing the titles we have in print and those we are hoping to reprint in 2006.

THE REDEEMER'S TEARS WEPT OVER LOST SOULS
A Puritan View of Our Lord's Weeping Over Jerusalem
by John Howe

Although written in 1684 ands in the style of the day, this classic volume will be of interest to all who recognize the imperative of winning souls for Christ. Here is a fine biblical exposition of Luke 19:41,42 (Jesus weeping over Jerusalem), with appropriate application that is as suitable today as when Howe wrote it. The first part portrays the Savior as He looked down upon Jerusalem - a stirring scene filled with divine pathos. Then follows a series of explanations and admonitions, all breathing a compassionate anxiety to win the lost for Christ.

HEAVEN UPON EARTH: *Jesus, The Best Friend in the Worst Times*
by James Janeway

"This book is as precious as the finest gold. Its author, James Janeway, stirs the hearts of his readers, not to rest in a cold, speculative knowledge of God, but to seek that experimental knowledge of Him which enflames hearts, transforms lives, and affords unspeakable happiness throughout eternity. There is no friend in all the world like Jesus Christ, our blessed Saviour! So take this book, read it prayerfully, and discover for yourselves the intimacy of His blessed presence and company. Here is pure heart religion, needed more than anything else in these barren and lifeless times. James Janeway will help us to understand what John Holland, another Puritan, meant, when on his death-bed, he called out, 'Oh, speak it when I am gone, and preach it at my funeral - that God dealeth familiarly with men.'"
- **Malcolm H. Watts,** Minister of Emmanuel Church, Salisbury, England

A BODY OF DIVINITY: *Being the Sum and Substance of the Christian Religion*
By Archbishop James Ussher

"Though he is best known for his biblical chronology, I believe that Ussher's Body of Divinity is his most valuable legacy. This volume, long overdue to be reprinted."
- **Dr. Joel Beeke,** Puritan Reformed Theological Seminary, Grand Rapids, MI

THE COMPLETE WORKS OF THOMAS MANTON (in 16 volumes)

This is our largest and most challenging project ever attempted. We plan to take the entire 22 volumes and re-typeset them and rearrange them into 16 hardcover volumes. We agree with **J.C. Ryle** who said, "If any recommendation of mine can help them in bringing out the writings of this admirable Puritan in a new form, I give it cheerfully and with all my heart."

Call us Toll Free at 1-877-666-9469
Send us an e-mail at sgcb@charter.net
Visit us on line at solid-ground-books.com

More Solid Ground Titles

In addition to the book in your hand, Solid Ground is honored to offer other uncovered treasure, many for the first time in more than a century:

NOTES ON GALATIANS by J. Gresham Machen
EXPOSITION OF THE BAPTIST CATECHISM by Benjamin Beddome
PAUL THE PREACHER: *Sermons from Acts* by John Eadie
THE COMMUNICANT'S COMPANION by Matthew Henry
THE CHILD AT HOME by John S.C. Abbott
THE LIFE OF JESUS CHRIST FOR THE YOUNG by Richard Newton
THE KING'S HIGHWAY: *10 Commandments for the Young* by Richard Newton
HEROES OF THE REFORMATION by Richard Newton
FEED MY LAMBS: *Lectures to Children on Vital Subjects* by John Todd
LET THE CANNON BLAZE AWAY by Joseph P. Thompson
THE STILL HOUR: *Communion with God in Prayer* by Austin Phelps
COLLECTED WORKS of James Henley Thornwell (4 vols.)
CALVINISM IN HISTORY *by Nathaniel S. McFetridge*
OPENING SCRIPTURE: *Hermeneutical Manual by Patrick Fairbairn*
THE ASSURANCE OF FAITH *by Louis Berkhof*
THE PASTOR IN THE SICK ROOM *by John D. Wells*
THE BUNYAN OF BROOKLYN: Life & Sermons of I.S. Spencer
THE NATIONAL PREACHER: Sermons from 2nd Great Awakening
**FIRST THINGS: F*irst Lessons God Taught Mankind* Gardiner Spring
BIBLICAL & THEOLOGICAL STUDIES *by 1912 Faculty of Princeton*
THE POWER OF GOD UNTO SALVATION *by B.B. Warfield*
THE LORD OF GLORY *by B.B. Warfield*
A GENTLEMAN & A SCHOLAR: *Memoir of J.P. Boyce by J. Broadus*
SERMONS TO THE NATURAL MAN *by W.G.T. Shedd*
SERMONS TO THE SPIRITUAL MAN *by W.G.T. Shedd*
HOMILETICS AND PASTORAL THEOLOGY *by W.G.T. Shedd*
A PASTOR'S SKETCHES 1 & 2 *by Ichabod S. Spencer*
THE PREACHER AND HIS MODELS *by James Stalker*
IMAGO CHRISTI: *The Example of Jesus Christ by James Stalker*
LECTURES ON THE HISTORY OF PREACHING *by J. A. Broadus*
THE SHORTER CATECHISM ILLUSTRATED *by John Whitecross*
THE CHURCH MEMBER'S GUIDE *by John Angell James*
THE SUNDAY SCHOOL TEACHER'S GUIDE *by John A. James*
CHRIST IN SONG: *Hymns of Immanuel from All Ages by Philip Schaff*
DEVOTIONAL LIFE OF THE S.S. TEACHER *by J.R. Miller*

Call us Toll Free at 1-877-666-9469
Send us an e-mail at sgcb@charter.net
Visit us on line at solid-ground-books.com
Uncovering Buried Treasure to the Glory of God

www.ingramcontent.com/pod-product-compliance
Lightning Source LLC
Chambersburg PA
CBHW080403300426
44113CB00015B/2390